Welcome ~~to~~ MyOBLab™

To start using MyOBLab you will need a valid email address, that you check on a regular basis, and the access code that is printed beneath the scratch-off panel below.

Your Access code is:

C D
on Return
at back.

Register for MyOBLab

To access MyOBLab, you must complete an easy, one-time registration process.

1. Go to www.pearsoned.com.au/MyOBLab and click the register button for students.
2. Follow the on-screen instructions to enter your student access code, your instructor supplied course ID, contact information, and create a login code and password.

If you need help during the online registration click help.

After you have registered you are ready to log in to MyOBLab anytime

Logging in to MyOBLab

You can log in to MyOBLab anytime after you register, by using the login name and password you created during registration

1. Go to www.pearsoned.com.au/myoblab and click the login button for students
2. Enter the login name and password you created during registration
3. Select the book

Begin exploring MyOBLab

  Need help?

Visit http://247.global.pearsoned.c

D1330732

MyOBLab™

Save time and improve your grades with Pearson's MyOBLab

MyOBLab is your online study tool designed to complement Robbins *Organisational Behaviour 5e* and enhance your learning experience. The lab will test your knowledge, help design your study plan and give you the learning tools you need to improve your grades.

MyOBLab's interactive **3-step approach** is engaging, simple to use and will ensure you have mastered the text's concepts for your exams.

> ### Step 1: Pre-test
> **Have you mastered the topics in the chapter?**
> Complete the objective-specific *pre-test* and find out. If you pass the test, move ahead in your study. If not, you will be directed to the tools you need to learn the topic in your automatically designed *Study Plan*.

> ### Step 2: Study Plan
> **Have you got a study plan?**
> Based on your *pre-test* results, MyOBLab will create a *study plan* to suit your personal learning needs. As part of your *study plan* you will be directed to online learning materials designed to help you master the topic. Materials will include engaging tools such as e-text, interactive diagrams, flash cards, PowerPoints and videos.

> ### Step 3: Post-test
> **Are you ready for your exam?**
> Once you have have worked through the online learning materials, test your new knowledge by completing the relevant *post-test*. You are ready for success!

MyOBLab™

Save your time > Improve your results
www.pearsoned.com.au/MyOBLab

ORGANISATIONAL BEHAVIOUR

FIFTH EDITION

AUTHOR DEDICATIONS

ORGANISATIONAL BEHAVIOUR

STEPHEN P. ROBBINS • TIMOTHY A. JUDGE
BRUCE MILLETT • TERRY WATERS-MARSH

PEARSON
Education
Australia

FIFTH EDITION

Pearson Education Australia
Unit 4, Level 3
14 Aquatic Drive
Frenchs Forest NSW 2086

www.pearsoned.com.au

Senior Acquisitions Editor: Frances Eden
Senior Project Editor: Rebecca Pomponio
Project Editor: Katie Millar
Development Editor: Roisin Fitzgerald
Editorial Coordinator: Jo Davis
Copy Editor: Robyn Flemming
Proofreader: Robyn Flemming
Copyright and Pictures Editor: Brett Steel
Cover and internal design by Peta Nugent
Cover photograph from Photolibrary
Typeset by Midland Typesetters, Australia

Printed in China (GCC)

4 5 12 11 10

National Library of Australia
Cataloguing-in-Publication Data

     Organisational behaviour.

     5th ed.
     Includes index.
     ISBN 9780733977664 (pbk).

     1. Organizational behavior. I. Robbins, Stephen P.

     302.35

An imprint of Pearson Education Australia (a division of Pearson Australia Group Pty Ltd)

OVERVIEW

CONTENTS

PART 4 THE ORGANISATION · 539

PREFACE

ORGANISATIONAL BEHAVIOUR (OB) is focused on understanding the behaviour of people at work. Managers worldwide fully appreciate the significance of OB and how, as a field of study, it assists them in dealing with issues of job performance and job satisfaction. Since almost all of us are interested in human behaviour and expect to work at least part of our adult lives, OB has the potential to be a very interesting and relevant subject.

This book grew out of the need for a comprehensive introductory textbook about organisational behaviour in Australia and the Asia-Pacific region. Students, lecturers and tutors of OB told us they wanted a textbook using local examples from Australasian workplaces, yet still covering all the central aspects of OB theory which have developed over the past 100 years. The first, second, third and fourth editions of the text were released in 1994, 1998, 2001 and 2004, respectively. The text has become one of the top local management texts, and we hope that the publication of the fifth edition of *Organisational Behaviour* will constitute another milestone in the teaching of OB in the Asia-Pacific region.

Stephen Robbins first published an OB text in the United States in 1979, and since that time the Robbins book has been read by more than a million students and used by students at more than a thousand colleges and universities worldwide. If there is such a thing as a 'global textbook', the current edition and adaptations have probably earned that label. It is the number-one selling organisational behaviour textbook in Australia, Hong Kong, Singapore, Thailand, the Philippines, Taiwan, South Korea, Malaysia, Indonesia, the United States, Canada, Mexico, Central America, South America, India, China, Sweden, Finland, Denmark and Greece. There are also translations available in German, Chinese, Japanese, Korean, Thai, Spanish, Portuguese and Indonesian; and this adaptation provides students with country-specific examples and content in the Asia-Pacific, including Australia, New Zealand, Fiji, Singapore and Malaysia.

THE FOUNDATIONAL FEATURES OF THE BOOK

Although the field of OB has changed significantly in the last 25 years and, with it, the contents of this textbook, a number of features have been retained from past editions. It is these features, in fact, that we think largely explain this book's success. They include the conversational writing style, the cutting-edge content, the extensive use of current examples, the three-level integrative model, the 'point/counterpoint' dialogues, integration of globalisation, diversity and ethics, the 'Myth or Science?' boxes, the end-of-chapter pedagogy, and the comprehensive supplement package. Let's elaborate on each of these points.

Writing style. This book is most often singled out for the writing style. Reviewers and users regularly tell us that it's 'conversational', 'interesting', 'student-friendly' and 'very clear and understandable'. We believe the fifth edition maintains that tradition.

Cutting-edge content. This book was the first OB textbook to have chapters on power and politics, conflict, organisational culture and motivation. Most recently, it is the first OB textbook to have a chapter devoted to emotions and moods. The book continues to provide cutting-edge content that is often missing in other OB books.

Examples. Our teaching experience tells us that students may not remember a concept, but they will remember an example. Moreover, a good example goes a long way in helping students to better understand a concept. So, as with the previous editions of this book, you will find this revision packed full of recent real-world examples drawn from a variety of organisations—business and not-for-profit, large and small, and local and international. The 'OB in Practice' boxes also provide insights into people and organisations and how they grapple managing issues in OB.

The three-level model of analysis. Since its first edition, this book has presented OB at three levels of analysis. It begins with individual behaviour and then moves to group behaviour. Finally, it adds the organisation system to capture the full complexity of organisational behaviour. Students seem to find this approach logical and straightforward.

'Point/Counterpoint' dialogues. These focused arguments allow students to see two sides of an OB controversy and to stimulate their critical thinking. Lecturers and tutors say they find these dialogues to be excellent devices for stimulating class discussion and getting students to think critically about OB issues in the workplace.

Integration of globalisation, diversity and ethics. The topics of globalisation and cross-cultural differences, workforce diversity and ethics are discussed throughout this book. Rather than being presented in stand-alone chapters, they have been woven into the context of relevant issues. We have found that this integrative approach makes these issues more fully part of OB and reinforces their importance.

'Myth or Science?' boxes. This feature presents a commonly accepted 'fact' about human behaviour, followed by confirming or disproving research evidence. Some examples include 'You Can't Teach an Old Dog New Tricks', 'Happy Workers are Productive Workers' and 'It's First Impressions That Count'. These boxes provide repeated evidence that common sense can often lead you astray in the attempt to understand human behav-

iour, and that behavioural research offers a means for testing the validity of commonsense notions. These boxes are meant to help you to see how the field of OB, built on a large body of research evidence, can provide valuable insights towards understanding and explaining human behaviour at work.

Pedagogy. This edition continues the tradition of providing the most complete assortment of in-text pedagogy available in any OB book. Features include new cases, *Ethical Dilemma* situations, *Questions for Critical Thinking* and the integration of the *Self-Assessment Library* (SAL) within the chapter. See the visual preface on pages xx–xxiii for a complete list and description of the pedagogical features.

Supplement package. This text provides the most comprehensive teaching and learning support package available, including local videos, and a new-generation online learning and assessment experience. It is described in detail in the latter part of this preface.

WHAT'S NEW IN THE 5TH EDITION?

Users of the previous edition will find quite a few differences in content and structure:

CONTENT

- New discussion on deviant workplace behaviour (Chapter 1)
- Revised discussion on general intelligence (Chapter 2)
- New discussion on effective, normative and continuance commitment (Chapter 3)
- Expanded material on Hofstede (Chapter 4)
- Discussion of values moved to Chapter 4, now titled 'Personality and Values'
- Condensed MBO coverage moved to Chapter 6 to bring it closer to the discussion on goal setting theory, and the job characteristics model coverage moved to Chapter 7
- New material on justice theory and equity (Chapter 6)
- A completely new chapter on emotions and moods, reflecting current research (Chapter 8)
- Updated critique of the path–goal model (Chapter 12)

- Restructured 'Contemporary Issues in Leadership' chapter (Chapter 13)
- Increased coverage of transformational leadership (Chapter 13)
- Updated material on sexual harassment based on recent research (Chapter 14)
- Revised and updated spirituality and organisational culture section (Chapter 17)
- Extensive development of the human resource management chapter, now titled 'Organisational Performance Systems' (Chapter 18)
- Stress management moved to the 'Organisational Performance Systems' chapter (Chapter 18)
- The final chapter is now devoted to organisational change and development (Chapter 19)

PEDAGOGY

- Each chapter has two *OB in Practice* boxes in order to provide students with current examples of how managers are dealing with a range of OB issues.

- The *Self-Assessment Library* (SAL) is now integrated within the chapter so that students take the test right after they have learned a concept. SAL allows students to assess their knowledge, beliefs, feelings and actions in regard to a wide range of personal skills, abilities and interests.

- *Ethical Dilemma* situations provide important ethical discussion, debate and reflection.
- End-of-chapter *Experiential Exercises* give students the opportunity to apply the concepts discussed in the chapter.
- All cases have been updated and are of short, medium and extended length. Refer to the Case Matrix on pages xxiv–xxvii.

SUPPLEMENTS

We have developed supplementary material that is designed to complement the textbook.

INSTRUCTOR'S RESOURCE MANUAL
Instructor's Manual
Each chapter of the manual includes expanded outlines of the topics in each chapter, teaching tips to accompany the boxed text and exercises, and answers to all question material.

PowerPoint Slides
Over 250 full-colour slides have been developed to highlight the key concepts of the text.

AUSTRALIAN DVD AND VIDEO
DVD: The *Fusion Documentary Series* is a new supplement and has been specially developed to support our *Management* and *Organisational Behaviour* texts. These real-life case studies are fast-paced and engaging for today's students, fusing theory and practice. Numerous companies offer their experience in areas such as: motivating employees; leadership; organisational culture; innovation/change; and emotions and moods.

Video: The supplementary video comprises six segments and covers the topics of: teams; communication; leadership; conflict; organisational culture; and human resources. Each segment features five managers from a variety of organisation types. The managers provide a practical point of view of these important OB topics. A theoretical perspective is provided by Emma Bowyer of UTS, who introduces the segments and acted as content consultant.

ONLINE LEARNING ENVIRONMENT

Pearson is committed to providing its customers with market-leading assessment and learning capabilities. **MyOBLab** offers more than online content: it offers a complete online course experience for students and lecturers. Features include:
- An online course management system with chapter and objective-specific, pre-loaded content. The content is customisable and the management system easy to use!
- Next-generation assessment technology and *Gradebook*, which offers advanced report creation capability.
- Chapter and objective-specific diagnostic tests for students that create a personalised study plan to suit their own study needs.
- Media-rich study-plan resources, including links to the online text for efficient use of time.
- Help where and when students need it.
<www.pearsoned.com.au/MyOBLab>

PRENTICE HALL'S SELF-ASSESSMENT LIBRARY (SAL)

SELF
ASSESSMENT
LIBRARY

A hallmark of the Robbins series, SAL is a unique learning tool that allows students to assess their knowledge, beliefs, feelings and actions in regard to a wide range of personal skills, abilities and interests. Now tightly integrated into the text, the 51 behavioural questionnaires help students to better understand their interpersonal and behavioural skills as they relate to the theoretical concepts presented in each chapter.

HIGHLIGHTS
- **51 research-based self-assessments:** Our entire collection

of 51 instruments, 10 of which are new to this edition, are from sources such as *Journal of Social Behavior and Personality, Harvard Business Review, Organizational Behavior: Experiences and Cases, Journal of Experimental Education, Journal of Applied Measurement* and more.

- **Work-life and career focus:** All self-assessments are focused to help individuals better manage their work-lives or careers. Organised in three parts—*What About Me? Working with Others* and *Life in Organisations*—these instruments offer you one source from which to learn more about yourself.
- **Choice of formats:** The Self-Assessment Library is available in your choice of format: CD-ROM or online. It is integrated into the online resources for use within the course management system, MyOBLab.
- **Save feature:** Students can take the self-assessment an unlimited number of times, and save and print their scores for class discussion.
- **Scoring key:** The scoring key to the self-assessments has been edited by Steve Robbins to allow students to quickly make sense of the results of their score.
- **Instructor manual:** An instructor manual guides instructors in interpreting self-assessments and helps facilitate better classroom discussion.

TABLE OF CONTENTS

ACKNOWLEDGMENTS

Textbooks are a team project and many people have contributed to our team. A number of colleagues have been kind enough to make suggestions for improvement and to review all or parts of this text. This is a better book because of insights and suggestions provided by:

Bruce Acutt, Central Queensland University
Kevin Fagg, Central Queensland University
Gordon Ray, retired
Lee Di Milia
Anneke Fitzgerald, University of Western Sydney
Matt Ngui, University of Wollongong
Sugumar Mariappanadar, Australian Catholic University
Jim Winter, Curtin University
Melanie Bryant, Monash University
Lorraine Carey, University of Canberra
Paul Nesbit, Macquarie University
Louise Brown, Charles Sturt University
Lisa Hewerdine, University of Adelaide
Syed Uddin, University of Ballarat
Karin Garrety, University of Wollongong
Sandra Kiffin-Petersen, University of Western Australia

Also, many thanks to those colleagues who contributed new, valuable case studies:

Kim Southey, School of Business, University of Southern Queensland
The 'High School Casual' (closing case Chapter 1)

Dr Angela Martin, School of Management, University of Tasmania
Tasmania Fire Service (opening case Chapter 2)

Glyn Jones, Waikato University, New Zealand
Plumbing Company and Motivation (opening case Chapter 3)
Decision Time for Ella (opening case Chapter 5)
Managing Performance at PBL (Part 2 integrative case)

Dr Glenice Wood, School of Business, University of Ballarat
Dr Jackie Fairley (opening case Chapter 4)
Kylie Kwong (opening case Chapter 6)

Trust: The Foundation of Leadership in Politics? (Part 3 integrative case)

Kerrie Unsworth, Queensland University of Technology
What Motivates Matt? (closing case Chapter 6)

Professor Neal Ashkanasy and Marissa Edwards, UQ Business School, University of Queensland
Diagnosing Queensland Health (Part 2 integrative case)

Bernadette Lynch, School of Management and Organisational Behaviour, University of Southern Queensland
Flight Centre (opening case Chapter 7)
Abu Graihb: Who is to Blame? (Part 4 integrative case)

Maree Boyle, University of Queensland
The Merger of Synergis and Abacus (Part 3 integrative case)

Dr Christine Ho, School of Commerce, University of Adelaide
Workplace Divorce (Part 4 integrative case)
Tania Major, ATSIC (Part 2 integrative case)

We also acknowledge the contribution of Ron Cacioppe as an author on the first three editions of this text.

Regardless of how good the manuscript is, it is only a tall pile of paper until our friends at Pearson Education Australia swing into action. Pearson's crack team of editors, production personnel, designers, marketing specialists, artists and sales representatives turn that pile of paper into a bound textbook and see to it that it gets into faculty and students' hands. Our special thanks on this go to Frances Eden, Roisin Fitzgerald, Rebecca Pomponio, Joanna Davis and Katie Millar for their support and encouragement. We would also like to thank Robyn Flemming for her excellent work with the manuscript.

Finally, we want to acknowledge with gratitude the hundreds of academics teaching and researching in the OB discipline in Australia and New Zealand. These people demonstrate amazing commitment and dedication, often in the face of severe resource cutbacks and constraints, to teaching and research in OB in their respective countries. They are not afraid to take risks, to experiment and to share their successes and failures with others in the discipline. They are the true pioneers in the quest to define, refine and communicate the unique aspects of Australian and New Zealand OB for the benefit of our two societies.

One last point. We are always looking for suggestions on how to improve later editions of this book. If you have some ideas and would like to share them with us, drop us a line care of: Bruce Millett, Faculty of Business, University of Southern Queensland, Darling Heights Post Office, Toowoomba, Queensland, 4350, Australia (or email to millett@usq.edu.au). We look forward to hearing from you.

Bruce Millett
Toowoomba, Queensland

Terry Waters-Marsh
Rockhampton, Queensland

VISUAL PREFACE

Chapter Learning Objectives To make your learning more efficient, each chapter opens with a list of learning objectives that describe what you should be able to do after studying the chapter. These objectives are designed to focus your attention on the major issues within each chapter.

Chapter Opening Story Each chapter opens with a case example about an individual or an organisation, which relates to the particular content in that chapter. The featured individuals, or organisations, come from a broad and varied spectrum and each example is selected specifically to help you link OB concepts to OB practice.

OB in Practice These boxes look at current issues in OB and put forward the differing points of view that surround the issue.

'Myth or science?' boxes present a commonly accepted 'fact' about human behaviour, followed by confirming or disproving research evidence. They help you see how the field of OB, built on a large body of research evidence can provide valuable insights towards understanding and explaining human behaviour at work.

The **Learning Objective** is repeated in the margin where the relevant text appears in the chapter.

Key Terms These terms are highlighted in bold print when they first appear and are defined at the time in the adjoining margin. These same terms are also grouped together at the end of the book in the Glossary.

Self-assessment library (SAL) How does the theory link to you? SAL offers 51 online self-assessments, allowing you to assess your knowledge, beliefs, feelings and actions in regard to a range of skills, abilities and interests. SAL is now integrated within the chapter so that you take the test right after you have learned the concept.

As you might imagine, sleep quality affects mood. Undergraduates and adult workers who are sleep-deprived report greater feelings of fatigue, anger and hostility.[52] One of the reasons why less sleep, or poor sleep quality, puts people in a bad mood is because it impairs decision making and makes it difficult to control emotions.[53] A recent study suggests that poor sleep the previous night also impairs people's job satisfaction the next day, mostly because they feel fatigued, irritable and less alert.[54]

'SHARING GOOD NEWS AFFECTS OUR MOODS'

When good things happen to you, do you immediately call a friend or a fellow employee to share the joy? If this isn't your style, you might reconsider. A study shows that those who sought out others when good things happened to them were consistently happier than those who didn't share their good news. Additionally, this 'capitalising' effect held irrespective of the events themselves, meaning that if two people both had positive things happen to them, the happier person would be the one who shared the good news. The study ruled out alternative explanations for this finding. For example, personality didn't play a role, given that the results weren't due to high levels of extroversion in the study's participants.

People's responses to an individual's good news are also important. Only when others reacted with genuine enthusiasm (as opposed to indifference or feigned happiness) did sharing make people happier. So, happiness isn't just the result of sharing joy; rather, it is also a result of sharing good news with the right people.

But how does capitalising on positive events affect an individual's job satisfaction? Sharing news about a promotion, a new appointment or a completed sale contributed to positive moods at work and satisfaction with one's work. Again, the type of response mattered—that is, employees were happiest when they shared positive events with others who were truly happy for them.

EXERCISE

You often hear that people should exercise to improve their mood. But does 'sweat therapy' really work? It appears so. Research consistently shows that exercise enhances people's positive mood.[55] It appears that the therapeutic effects of exercise are strongest for those who are depressed. Although the effects of exercise on moods are consistent, they are not terribly strong. So, exercise may help put you in a better mood, but don't expect miracles.

AGE

Do you think that young people experience more extreme, positive emotions (so-called youthful exuberance) than older people do? If you answered 'yes', you were wrong. One study of people aged 18 to 94 years revealed that negative emotions seem to occur less as people get older. Periods of highly positive moods lasted longer for older individuals and bad moods faded more quickly.[56] The study implies that emotional experience tends to improve with age, so that as we get older, we experience fewer negative emotions.

GENDER

The common belief is that women are more in touch with their feelings than men are—that they react more emotionally and are better able to read emotions in others. Is there any truth to these assumptions?

The evidence does confirm differences between men and women when it comes to emotional reactions and the ability to read others. In contrasting the genders, women show

---

The Smith Family's Learning for Life program has provided financial and personal assistance to around 46 000 children and young people throughout Australia.

WHAT IS ORGANISATIONAL CULTURE?

A number of years back, an executive was asked what he thought *organisational culture* meant. He gave essentially the same answer that a US Supreme Court Justice once gave in attempting to define pornography: 'I can't define it, but I know it when I see it.' This executive's approach to defining organisational culture isn't acceptable for our purposes. We need a basic definition to provide a point of departure for our quest to better understand the phenomenon. In this section, we propose a specific definition and review several peripheral issues that revolve around this definition.

A DEFINITION

There seems to be wide agreement that **organisational culture** refers to a system of shared meaning held by members that distinguishes the organisation from other organisations.[5] This system of shared meaning is, on closer examination, a set of key characteristics that the organisation values. The research suggests that there are seven primary characteristics that, in aggregate, capture the essence of an organisation's culture.[6]

1. *Innovation and risk taking*: the degree to which employees are encouraged to be innovative and take risks.
2. *Attention to detail*: the degree to which employees are expected to exhibit precision, analysis and attention to detail.
3. *Outcome orientation*: the degree to which management focuses on results or outcomes rather than on the techniques and processes used to achieve those outcomes.
4. *People orientation*: the degree to which management decisions take into consideration the effect of outcomes on people within the organisation.
5. *Team orientation*: the degree to which work activities are organised around teams rather than individuals.
6. *Aggressiveness*: the degree to which people are aggressive and competitive rather than easygoing.
7. *Stability*: the degree to which organisational activities emphasise maintaining the status quo in contrast to growth.

organisational culture |
A system of shared meaning held by members that distinguishes the organisation from other organisations.

---

skills, making it difficult to get a definition of EI. One researcher may study self-discipline. Another may study empathy. Another may look at self-awareness. As one reviewer noted, 'The concept of EI has now become so broad and the components so variegated that … it is no longer even an intelligible concept.'[104]

EI CAN'T BE MEASURED

Many critics have raised questions about measuring EI. Because EI is a form of intelligence, for instance, there must be right and wrong answers about it on tests, they argue. Some tests do have right and wrong answers, although the validity of some of the questions on these measures is questionable. For example, one measure asks you to associate particular feelings with specific colours, as if purple always makes us feel cool, not warm. Other measures are self-reported, meaning there is no right or wrong answer. For example, an EI test question might ask you to respond to the statement, 'I'm good at "reading" other people.' In general, the measures of EI are diverse, and researchers haven't subjected them to as much rigorous study as they have measures of personality and general intelligence.[105]

THE VALIDITY OF EI IS SUSPECT

Some critics argue that because EI is so closely related to intelligence and personality, once you control for these factors, EI has nothing unique to offer. There is some foundation to this argument. EI appears to be highly correlated with measures of personality, especially emotional stability.[106] But there hasn't been enough research on whether EI adds insight beyond measures of personality and general intelligence in predicting job performance. Still, EI is very popular among consulting firms and in the popular press. For example, one company's promotional materials for an EI measure claimed, 'EI accounts for more than 85 percent of star performance in top leaders.'[107] To say the least, it is hard to validate this statement with the research literature.

Whatever your view of EI, one thing's for sure: the concept is here to stay. Now that you know more about emotional intelligence, do you think you are a good judge of people? Do you think you can determine what makes someone tick? Check out the Self-Assessment feature to determine your EI.

WHAT'S MY EMOTIONAL INTELLIGENCE SCORE?

In the Self-Assessment Library (available on CD and online), take assessment I.E.1 (What's My Emotional Intelligence Score?) and answer the following questions.
1. How did you score relative to your classmates?
2. Did your score surprise you? Why or why not?
3. What might you do to improve your ability to read others' emotions?

OB APPLICATIONS OF EMOTIONS AND MOODS

We conclude our discussion of emotions and moods by considering their specific application to OB. In this section, we assess how an understanding of emotions and moods

Summary and Implications for Managers Each chapter concludes with a concise summary of the key themes in the chapter in bullet point form.

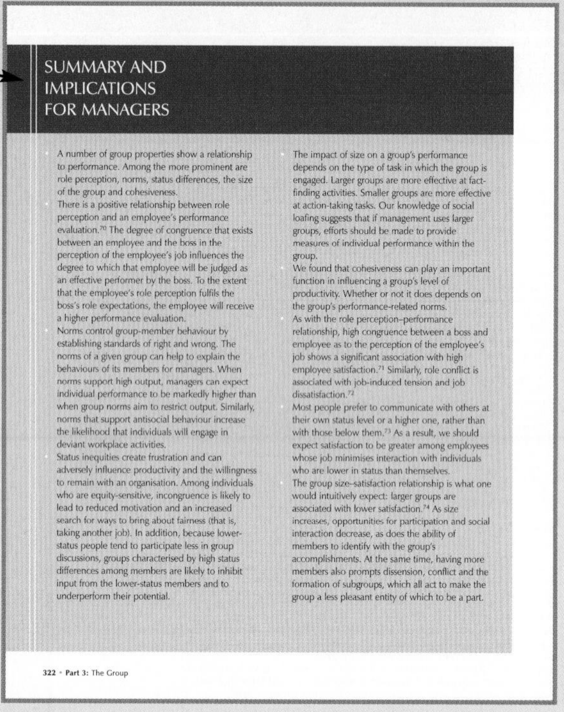

SUMMARY AND IMPLICATIONS FOR MANAGERS

- A number of group properties show a relationship to performance. Among the more prominent are role perception, norms, status differences, the size of the group and cohesiveness.
- There is a positive relationship between role perception and an employee's performance evaluation.[70] The degree of congruence that exists between an employee and the boss in the perception of the employee's job influences the degree to which that employee will be judged as an effective performer by the boss. To the extent that the employee's role perception fulfils the boss's role expectations, the employee will receive a higher performance evaluation.
- Norms control group-member behaviour by establishing standards of right and wrong. The norms of a given group can help to explain the behaviours of its members for managers. When norms support high output, managers can expect individual performance to be markedly higher than when group norms aim to restrict output. Similarly, norms that support antisocial behaviour increase the likelihood that individuals will engage in deviant workplace activities.
- Status inequities create frustration and can adversely influence productivity and the willingness to remain with an organisation. Among individuals who are equity-sensitive, incongruence is likely to lead to reduced motivation and an increased search for ways to bring about fairness (that is, taking another job). In addition, because lower-status people tend to participate less in group discussions, groups characterised by high status differences among members are likely to inhibit input from the lower-status members and to underperform their potential.
- The impact of size on a group's performance depends on the type of task in which the group is engaged. Larger groups are more effective at fact-finding activities. Smaller groups are more effective at action-taking tasks. Our knowledge of social loafing suggests that if management uses larger groups, efforts should be made to provide measures of individual performance within the group.
- We found that cohesiveness can play an important function in influencing a group's level of productivity. Whether or not it does depends on the group's performance-related norms.
- As with the role perception–performance relationship, high congruence between a boss and employee as to the perception of the employee's job shows a significant association with high employee satisfaction.[71] Similarly, role conflict is associated with job-induced tension and job dissatisfaction.[72]
- Most people prefer to communicate with others at their own status level or a higher one, rather than with those below them.[73] As a result, we should expect satisfaction to be greater among employees whose job minimises interaction with individuals who are lower in status than themselves.
- The group size–satisfaction relationship is what one would intuitively expect: larger groups are associated with lower satisfaction.[74] As size increases, opportunities for participation and social interaction decrease, as does the ability of members to identify with the group's accomplishments. At the same time, having more members also prompts dissension, conflict and the formation of subgroups, which all act to make the group a less pleasant entity of which to be a part.

322 • **Part 3:** The Group

Point/Counterpoint dialogues These focused arguments allow you to see two sides of an OB controversy. These dialogues help to stimulate class discussion and encourage you to think critically about OB issues in the workplace.

POINT / COUNTERPOINT

All Jobs Should Be Designed around Groups

• POINT

Groups, not individuals, are the ideal building blocks for an organisation. There are at least six reasons for designing all jobs around groups.

1. Small groups are good for people. They can satisfy social needs and provide support for employees in times of stress and crisis.
2. Groups are good problem-finding tools. They are better than individuals in promoting creativity and innovation.
3. In a wide variety of decision situations, groups make better decisions than individuals do.
4. Groups are very effective tools for implementation. Groups gain commitment from their members so that group decisions are likely to be carried out willingly and more successfully.
5. Groups can control and discipline individual members in ways that are often extremely difficult through impersonal, quasi-legal disciplinary systems. Group norms are powerful control devices.
6. Groups are a means by which large organisations can fend off many of the negative effects of increased size. Groups help to prevent communication lines from growing too long, the hierarchy from growing too steep and the individual from getting lost in the crowd.

Given the above argument for the value of group-based job design, what would an organisation look like that was truly designed around group functions? This might best be considered by merely taking the things that organisations do with individuals and applying them to groups. Instead of hiring individuals, they would hire groups. Similarly, they would train groups rather than individuals, pay groups rather than individuals, promote groups rather than individuals, fire groups rather than individuals, and so on.

The rapid growth of team-based organisations over the past decade suggests that we may well be on our way towards the day when almost all jobs are designed around groups.

• COUNTERPOINT

Designing jobs around groups is consistent with an ideology that says that communal and socialistic approaches are the best way to organise our society. This might have worked well in the former Soviet Union or Eastern European countries, but capitalistic countries such as Australia, New Zealand, the United States, Canada and the United Kingdom value the individual. Designing jobs around groups is inconsistent with the economic values of these countries. Moreover, as capitalism and entrepreneurship have spread throughout Eastern Europe, we should expect to see less emphasis on groups and more on the individual in workplaces throughout the world. Cultural and economic values have shaped employee attitudes towards groups.

Capitalism was built on the ethic of the individual. Individualistic cultures such as Australia, New Zealand, Canada and the United States strongly value individual achievement. They praise competition. Even in team sports, they want to identify individuals for recognition. People from these countries enjoy being part of a group in which they can maintain a strong individual identity. They don't enjoy sublimating their identity to that of the group.

The Western industrial worker likes a clear link between his or her individual effort and a visible outcome. The United States, for example, has had a considerably larger proportion of high achievers than exists in most of the world. America breeds achievers, and achievers seek personal responsibility. They would be frustrated in job situations in which their contribution is commingled and homogenised with the contributions of others.

Western workers want to be hired, evaluated and rewarded on their individual achievements. They believe in an authority and status hierarchy. They accept a system in which there are bosses and subordinates. They aren't likely to accept a group's decision on such issues as their job assignments and wage increases. It is harder yet to imagine that they would be comfortable in a system in which the sole basis for their promotion or termination would be the performance of their group.

SOURCE: Points in this argument are based on H. J. Leavitt, 'Suppose We Took Groups Seriously', in E. L. Cass and F. G. Zimmer (eds), *Man and Work in Society* (New York: Van Nostrand Reinhold, 1975), pp. 67–77.

Chapter 9: Foundations of Group Behaviour • **323**

A **Case Study** at the end of every chapter gives you the opportunity to apply the knowledge gained in the chapter to hypothetical situations that could be encountered in organisations.

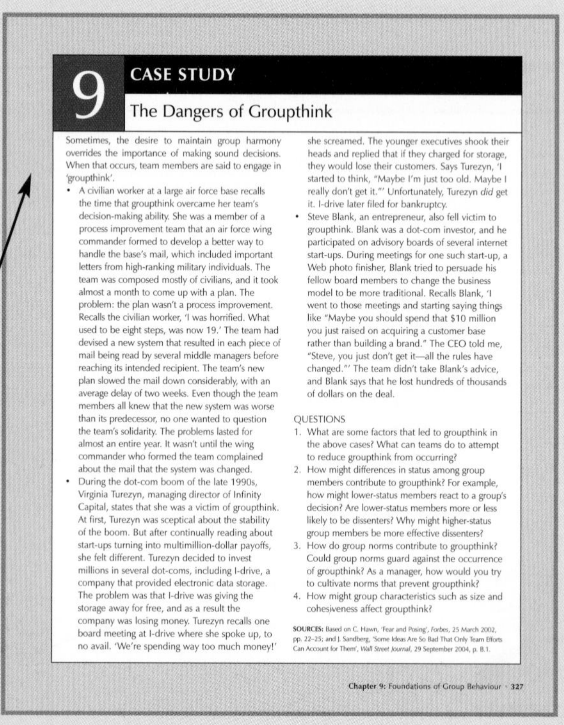

9 CASE STUDY

The Dangers of Groupthink

Sometimes, the desire to maintain group harmony overrides the importance of making sound decisions. When that occurs, team members are said to engage in 'groupthink'.

- A civilian worker at a large air force base recalls the time that groupthink overcame her team's decision-making ability. She was a member of a process improvement team that an air force wing commander formed to develop a better way to handle the base's mail, which included important letters from high-ranking military individuals. The team was composed mostly of civilians, and it took almost a month to come up with a plan. The problem: the plan wasn't a process improvement. Recalls the civilian worker, 'I was horrified. What used to be eight steps, was now 19.' The team had devised a new system that resulted in each piece of mail being read by several middle managers before reaching its intended recipient. The team's new plan slowed the mail down considerably, with an average delay of two weeks. Even though the team members all knew that the new system was worse than its predecessor, no one wanted to question the team's solidarity. The problems lasted for almost an entire year. It wasn't until the wing commander who formed the team complained about the mail that the system was changed.
- During the dot-com boom of the late 1990s, Virginia Turezyn, managing director of Infinity Capital, states that she was a victim of groupthink. At first, Turezyn was sceptical about the stability of the boom. But after continually reading about start-ups turning into multimillion-dollar payoffs, she felt different. Turezyn decided to invest millions in several dot-coms, including I-drive, a company that provided electronic data storage. The problem was that I-drive was giving the storage away for free, and as a result the company was losing money. Turezyn recalls one board meeting at I-drive where she spoke up, to no avail. 'We're spending way too much money!' she screamed. The younger executives shook their heads and replied that if they charged for storage, they would lose their customers. Says Turezyn, 'I started to think, "Maybe I'm just too old. Maybe I really don't get it."' Unfortunately, Turezyn *did* get it. I-drive later filed for bankruptcy.
- Steve Blank, an entrepreneur, also fell victim to groupthink. Blank was a dot-com investor, and he participated on advisory boards of several internet start-ups. During meetings for one such start-up, a Web photo finisher, Blank tried to persuade his fellow board members to change the business model to be more traditional. Recalls Blank, 'I went to those meetings and starting saying things like "Maybe you should spend that $10 million you just raised on acquiring a customer base rather than building a brand." The CEO told me, "Steve, you just don't get it—all the rules have changed."' The team didn't take Blank's advice, and Blank says that he lost hundreds of thousands of dollars on the deal.

QUESTIONS

1. What are some factors that led to groupthink in the above cases? What can teams do to attempt to reduce groupthink from occurring?
2. How might differences in status among group members contribute to groupthink? For example, how might lower-status members react to a group's decision? Are lower-status members more or less likely to be dissenters? Why might higher-status group members be more effective dissenters?
3. How do group norms contribute to groupthink? Could group norms guard against the occurrence of groupthink? As a manager, how would you try to cultivate norms that prevent groupthink?
4. How might group characteristics such as size and cohesiveness affect groupthink?

SOURCES: Based on C. Hawn, 'Fear and Posing', *Forbes*, 25 March 2002, pp. 22–25; and J. Sandberg, 'Some Ideas Are So Bad That Only Team Efforts Can Account for Them', *Wall Street Journal*, 29 September 2004, p. B.1.

Chapter 9: Foundations of Group Behaviour • **327**

Ethical Dilemma Box Based on real business scenarios and situations that have posed an ethical dilemma, you are asked how you would have responded in the same situation.

Integrative Cases appearing at the end of most parts.

ETHICAL DILEMMA

Are Workplace Romances Unethical?

A large percentage of married individuals first met in the workplace. A 2005 survey revealed that 58 per cent of all employees have been in an office romance. Given the amount of time people spend at work, this isn't terribly surprising. Yet, office romances pose sensitive ethical issues for organisations and employees. What rights and responsibilities do organisations have to regulate the romantic lives of their employees?

Take the case of former General Electric (GE) CEO Jack Welch and journalist Suzy Wetlaufer. The two met while Wetlaufer was interviewing Welch for a *Harvard Business Review* article, and Welch was still married. Once their relationship was out in the open, some accused Wetlaufer of being unethical for refusing to disclose the relationship while working on the article. She eventually left the *Harvard Business Review*. Others accused Welch of letting his personal life get in the way of the interests of GE and its shareholders. Some even blamed the scandal for a drop in GE stock.

Welch and Wetlaufer didn't even work for the same company. What about when two people work together in the same work unit? For example, Soomay, an account executive at a Sydney advertising firm, started dating Kevin, one of her account supervisors. Their innocent banter turned into going out for drinks, and then dinner, and soon they were dating. Kevin and Soomay's bosses were in-house competitors. The problem: sometimes in meetings Kevin would make it seem that Soomay and he were in agreement on important issues even when they weren't. In response,

Soomay's boss began to isolate her from key projects. Soomay broke up with Kevin, who then tried to have her fired. Soomay said, 'I remember times when I would be there all night photocopying hundreds of pages of my work to show that [Kevin's] allegations [of her incompetence] were unfounded. It was just embarrassing because it became a question of my professional judgment.'

These examples show that while workplace romances are personal matters, it is hard to keep them out of the political complexities of organisational life.

QUESTIONS

1. Do you think organisations should have policies governing workplace romances? What would such policies stipulate?
2. Do you think romantic relationships would distract two employees from performing their jobs? Why or why not?
3. Is it ever appropriate for a supervisor to romantically pursue a subordinate under his or her supervision? Why or why not?
4. Some companies openly try to recruit couples. Do you think this is a good idea? How would you feel working in a department with a 'couple'?

SOURCES: 'Cupid in the Cubicle, Says New Vault Survey', Vault, Inc. (<www.vault.com>); S. Shellenbarger, 'The Nasty Downside of Office Romances', *The Wall Street Journal*, 2005 (<www.wsj.com>); and J. Amber, 'Office Romance' (<www.yourjournlife.com>).

A — INTEGRATIVE CASE STUDY

Tania Major: A woman of substance

DR GLENICE WOOD
SCHOOL OF MANAGEMENT, UNIVERSITY OF BALLARAT

Tania Major, at 22, is the youngest person to be elected to the board of the Aboriginal and Torres Strait Islander Commission (ATSIC), and she believes she is ready for the challenge. She is a graduate in criminology from Sydney University, and has been mentored by Noel Pearson, a lawyer and entrepreneur, since she was aged 12. This mentoring involved her being sponsored throughout her secondary and tertiary education.

As a mentor, Noel would have conveyed some of his passion about his belief that passive welfare dependency is the primary cause of Aboriginal squalor and poverty, along with alcohol and drug abuse. Tania agrees with this philosophy, and considers that Aboriginal people are their own worst enemies. She is concerned that Aboriginal communities become ghettos, and believes her own home town, Kowanyama (*Place of Many Waters*), near the west coast of Cape York, has this potential problem.

Tania is passionate in her belief that violence, drug and alcohol abuse, rife in most remote Aboriginal communities, combine to create a seriously destructive force for Aboriginal people. In many of these communities, Aboriginal women have been forced to organise night patrols in an attempt to reduce the effects of alcohol and substance abuse. Some communities have also set up women's shelters to deal with the spiralling cases of violence to women and children. Tania has described this as a 'stifling blanket of shame and silence', which she believes has to be lifted in order for it to be addressed.

Tania's view is that education and health are pivotal in turning around the disastrous experience for young people growing up in these communities. She has personal experience in the very low levels of literacy and numeracy which she had acquired before going to school in Brisbane, and this made her feel as if she had missed out on her primary education. The problem

appears to be that the curriculum in the communities is pitched at a very low level, and this resulted in her receiving 'straight As' in Kowanyama but Cs or Ds in Brisbane. She believes this is caused by new teachers just out of training being sent to remote communities; they lacked commitment, didn't care, and believed that white children were smarter than Aboriginal pupils. These teachers didn't remain. Therefore, there is an enormous gap between what Aboriginal communities receive in their primary education and what is delivered to other children in cities. Tania believes that the outcome of the education offered in remote communities reinforces a lack of self-esteem and low expectations in young people, when its aim should be to deliver self-confidence and drive. This then motivates students to take up significant roles in the community with the belief that they can make a difference, rather than seeing their lives as hopeless.

Tania further believes there is a relationship between poor-quality education and poor health. 'People whose self-esteem and pride have been decimated by a substandard education system and a social system that creates an addiction to passive welfare have little reason to live healthy lives'. In Tania's view, the health of indigenous people is getting worse, not better, and the cause of this is that health services on offer are confined to the clinic, rather than being seen as a holistic relationship between physical, mental and spiritual health. Health care needs to be taken out of the clinic and put into the 'lives and homes of community people'.

Life under these circumstances isn't easy for young Aboriginal people, especially women. Tania paints a grim picture of what it is like growing up in an Aboriginal community today. In her home town, she was one of 15 in a class. Of this group, she is the only one who completed her secondary education, the only girl who didn't become pregnant at 15, and the only person who went on to university. Seven of the boys in her class have been incarcerated for murder, rape or

QUESTIONS FOR CRITICAL THINKING

1. In your opinion—and drawing from the arguments in the chapter—are there core or fundamental emotions that everyone experiences? If so, what are they?
2. What has research shown on the relationship between emotions and rational thinking? Do these findings surprise you? Why or why not?
3. Do emotions and moods matter in explaining behaviour in organisations? How so?
4. What, if anything, can managers do to manage their employees' emotions? Are there ethical implications in any of these actions? If so, what are they?
5. Give some examples of situations in which the overt expression of emotions might enhance job performance.
6. From an emotional labour perspective, how does dealing with an abusive customer lead to stress and burnout?
7. If you were a recruiter for a customer-service call centre, what personality types would you prefer to hire, and why? In other words, what individual differences are likely to affect whether an employee can handle customer abuse on a day-to-day basis?
8. Emotional intelligence is one's ability to detect and to manage emotional cues and information. How might emotional intelligence play a role in responding to abusive customers? What facets of emotional intelligence might employees possess who are able to handle abusive customers?
9. What steps should companies take to ensure that their employees are not the victims of customer abuse? Should companies allow a certain degree of abuse if that abuse results in satisfied customers and perhaps greater profit? What are the ethical implications of this?

EXPERIENTIAL EXERCISE

Who Can Catch a Liar?

Earlier in the chapter we discussed how people determine emotions from facial expressions. There has been research on whether people can tell whether someone is lying based on facial expression. Let's see who is good at catching liars.

Split up into teams, and follow these instructions:

1. Randomly choose someone to be the team organiser. Have this person write down on a piece of paper 'T' for truth and 'L' for lie. If there are, say, six people in the group (other than the organiser), then three people will get a slip with a 'T' and three a slip with an 'L'. It is important that all team members keep what's on their slip of paper a secret.
2. Each team member needs to come up with a true or false statement depending on whether he or she holds a 'T' or an 'L' slip. Try not to make the statement so outrageous that no one would believe it (for example, 'I have flown to the moon').
3. The organiser will have each member make his or her statement. Group members should then examine the person making the statement closely to try to determine whether he or she is telling the truth or lying. Once each person has made his or her statement, the organiser will ask for a vote and record the tallies.
4. Each person should now indicate whether the statement was the truth or a lie.
5. How good was your group at catching the 'liars'? Were some people good liars? What did you look for to determine if someone was lying?

Questions for Critical Thinking offer you the opportunity to develop this important skill.

Experiential Exercises encourage group work and classroom interaction while improving communication, knowledge and critical thinking skills.

CASE MATRIX

PART	CHAPTER	CASE TYPE	CASE DETAILS	COMPANY
1	1. What is Organisational Behaviour?	Opening case	Narelle Anderson, CEO	CBD Enviro Services
		OB in Practice	The Great Talent Race	Fujitsu Australia
		OB in Practice	Culture, Ethics and Productivity at NAB	NAB
		End chapter case	The 'High School Casual'	Hypothetical
2	2. Foundations of Individual Behaviour	Opening case	Tasmania Fire Service	Tasmania Fire Service
		OB in Practice	The Benefits of Cultural Intelligence	Hypothetical
		OB in Practice	Don't Forget the Impact of Siblings!	N/A
		End chapter case	Professional Sports: Rewarding and Punishing the Same Behaviour?	NRL Chief, David Yallop
	3. Attitudes and Job Satisfaction	Opening case	Plumbing Company and Employees' Motivation	Snow Bros Ltd
		OB in Practice	Chinese Employees and Organisational Commitment	
		OB in Practice	Job Satisfaction (Australian Academics) Hits Record Lows	Universities
		End chapter case	Long Hours, Hundreds of Emails and No Sleep: Does this Sound Like a Satisfying Job?	Westpac, Goldman Sachs, Capital Alliance Partners, MTV
	4. Personality and Values	Opening case	Dr Jackie Fairley	Starpharma Holdings Ltd
		OB in Practice	A Global Personality	N/A
		OB in Practice	Rising Stars or Falling Nuclear Bombs?	N/A
		End chapter case	The Rise and Fall of Carly Fiorina	Hewlett-Packard
	5. Perception and Individual Decision Making	Opening case	Decision Time for Ella	Hypothetical
		OB in Practice	Google and the Winner's Curse	Google
		End chapter case	Whistle-blowers: Saints or Sinners?	Enron, Bundaberg Base Hospital
	6. Motivation Concepts	Opening case	Kylie Kwong	Billie Kwong
		OB in Practice	Goal Setting for Success	Australian Institute for Fitness
		OB in Practice	What Motivates Gen Y?	Minter Ellison, Westpac
		End chapter case	What Motivates Matt?	Hypothetical

PART	CHAPTER	CASE TYPE	CASE DETAILS	COMPANY
	7. Motivation: From Concepts to Applications	Opening case	Flight Centre	Flight Centre
		OB in Practice	The Rise and Fall of Share Options	AMP, Westpac, Microsoft
		OB in Practice	Cultural Differences in Job Characteristics and Job Satisfaction	N/A
		End chapter case	Motivation for Change	RSPCA Victoria
	8. Emotions and Moods	Opening case	Toni Powell	*Heart of Gold* Film Festival
		OB in Practice	Emotional Recognition: Universal or Culture-specific?	N/A
		OB in Practice	Workplace Grief Costs Everyone	N/A
		End chapter case	The Upside of Anger	Hypothetical
		Integrative case	Tania Major, ATSIC	ATSIC
		Integrative case	Diagnosing Queensland Health	Queensland Health
		Integrative case	Managing Performance at PBL	Hypothetical
3	9. Foundations of Group Behaviour	Opening case	Team-based Structure	HeiTech Padu Berhad, Malaysia
		OB in Practice	A Team Culture at Hilton	Hilton Hotel, Kuching
		OB in Practice	Learning From the Experience of Team Management	Coffey International, TASKey
		End chapter case	The Dangers of Groupthink	N/A
	10. Understanding Work Teams	Opening case	Integral Systems Pty Ltd: Virtual Teams	Integral Systems Pty Ltd
		OB in Practice	Developing Capabilities in Virtual Teaming	Siemens, IBM, Goldman Sachs
		OB in Practice	The Team Approach at Wotif.com	Wotif.com
		End chapter case	Team-building Retreats	Adventure Out Australia
	11. Communication	Opening case	The Meeting Dilemma	AMP Financial Services, Microsoft
		OB in Practice	The Danger of Communicating Emotions via Email	Allens Arthur Robinson
		OB in Practice	Lost in Translation?	BHP Billiton, Siemens
		End chapter case	Bruce Swanepoel Has Communication Problems	Hypothetical

PART	CHAPTER	CASE TYPE	CASE DETAILS	COMPANY
	12. Basic Approaches to Leadership	Opening case	Leadership Abilities	Wesfarmers
		OB in Practice	The Traits of Successful Women Entrepreneurs	Pow Wow Events, Joanne Mercer Footwear, Intimo Lingerie, Nad's Natural Hair Removal Gel
		OB in Practice	Leadership Success: The Eye of the Beholder	*BRW* Survey, Macquarie Bank
		End chapter case	Switching from Colleague to Boss	Georges Group, IBM, AXB
	13. Contemporary Issues in Leadership	Opening case	Effective Leadership of Naomi Milgram and Penny Maclagan	Computershare, Sussan Group
		OB in Practice	Team Leadership at Adsteam Marine	Adsteam Marine
		OB in Practice	The Challenge of Leadership Development	DDI, AGL
		End chapter case	Generation Gap: Mentors and Protégés	N/A
	14. Power and Politics	Opening case	Diversity in Senior Management Ranks: Elizabeth Proust	
		OB in Practice	Influence Tactics in China	N/A
		OB in Practice	Power and Influence in Australia	Right Management Consultants, Kraft Foods
		End chapter case	The Politics of Backstabbing	Hypothetical
	15. Conflict and Negotiation	Opening case	Bob Atkinson: Queensland Commissioner of Police	Queensland Commissioner of Police
		OB in Practice	Constructive Conflict and the Performance Appraisal	HCL Technologies
		OB in Practice	Negotiating across Cultures	Aviation Compliance Solutions
		End chapter case	Managing the Team Spirit	Hypothetical
		Integrative case	Trust: The Foundation of Leadership in Politics?	Peter Costello
		Integrative case	The Merger of of Synergis and Abacus	Synergis, Abacus
4	**16. Foundations of Organisation Structure**	Opening case	Structuring University Work: Universities versus Private Sector	N/A
		OB in Practice	Letting Go of the Desk at Westpac	Westpac
		OB in Practice	Structuring in Accountability, Teamwork and Talent	Woods Bagot
		End chapter case	No Bosses at W. L. Gore & Associates	W. L. Gore & Associates

PART	CHAPTER	CASE TYPE	CASE DETAILS	COMPANY
	17. Organisational Culture	Opening case	Culture Change at AXA Asia Pacific	AXA Australia
		Cultural	Transformation at ANZ	ANZ
		OB in Practice	All Smiles at the Ritz	Ritz-Carlton, Shanghai
		End chapter case	A Culture Clash	Salingers, Yuppy
	18. Organisational Performance Systems	Opening case	Performance and Talent Go Hand in Hand	N/A
		OB in Practice	Managing the Performance Review	EMA Consulting, Dale Carnegie Training
		OB in Practice	The Rise and Rise of Talent Management	N/A
		End chapter case	A Unique Training Program at UPS	United Parcel Services Inc.
	19. Organisational Change and Development	Opening case	NAB's Turnaround Strategy	NAB
		OB in Practice	Change Management and Mergers	Upstream Technology and Print Solutions
		OB in Practice	Leadership and Learning at Fremantle Ports	Fremantle Ports
		End chapter case	Innovating Innovation	Procter & Gamble
		Integrative case	Abu Ghraib: Who is to Blame?	Abu Ghraib Prison, Iraq
		Integrative case	Workplace Divorce	Hypothetical

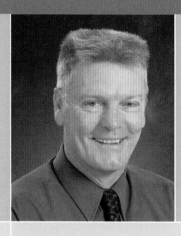

BRUCE MILLETT

Education
Ph.D, Griffith University

Professional Experience
- **Academic Position:** Associate Dean (Learning and Teaching), Faculty of Business, University of Southern Queensland.
- **Research:** Research interests have focussed on how organisations develop their strategic capability through leadership, organisational change and innovation, performance management, organisational learning and leadership.
- **Books Published:** Apart from 5 editions of *Organisational Behaviour*, Bruce has also co-authored books of readings in organisational behaviour as well as human resource management.

TERRY WATERS-MARSH

Education
Master of Business (Management), Queensland University of Technology

Professional Experience
- **Academic Positions:** Senior Lecturer, Central Queensland University, Queensland University of Technology.
- **Research:** Research interests have focused on leadership, training, group learning, conflict, power and politics in organisations, and change management.
- **Professional Affiliations:** Member of the Australia–New Zealand Academy of Management, Academy of Management, Society of Human Resources Management.
- **Other Interests:** Keen genealogist and family historian, church responsibilities and family interests.

STEPHEN P. ROBBINS

Education

Ph.D, University of Arizona

Professional Experience

- **Academic Positions:** Professor, San Diego State University, Southern Illinois University at Edwardsville, University of Baltimore, Concordia University in Montreal and University of Nebraska at Omaha.
- **Research:** Research interests have focused on conflict, power and politics in organisations, behavioural decision making, and the development of effective interpersonal skills.
- **Books Published:** World's best-selling author of textbooks in both management and organisational behaviour. His books are used at more than a thousand US colleges and universities, have been translated into 16 languages and have adapted editions for Canada, Australia, South Africa and India. These include:
  - *Essentials of Organizational Behavior*, 8th ed. (Prentice Hall, 2005)
  - *Management*, 8th ed., with Mary Coulter (Prentice Hall, 2005)
  - *Human Resource Management*, 8th ed., with David DeCenzo (Wiley, 2005)
  - *Prentice Hall's Self-Assessment Library 3.0* (Prentice Hall, 2005)
  - *Fundamentals of Management*, 5th ed., with David DeCenzo (Prentice Hall, 2006)
  - *Supervision Today!*, 4th ed., with David DeCenzo (Prentice Hall, 2004)
  - *Training in Interpersonal Skills*, 3rd ed., with Phillip Hunsaker (Prentice Hall, 2003)
  - *Managing Today!*, 2nd ed. (Prentice Hall, 2000)
  - *Organization Theory*, 3rd ed. (Prentice Hall, 1990)
  - *The Truth About Managing People ... And Nothing But the Truth* (Financial Times/Prentice Hall, 2002)
  - *Decide and Conquer: Make Winning Decisions and Take Control of Your Life* (Financial Times/Prentice Hall, 2003).

Other Interests

In his 'other life', Dr Robbins actively participates in masters' track competition. Since turning 50 in 1993, he has won 14 national championships, nine world titles and set numerous US and world age-group records in the 60, 100, 200 and 400 metres.

TIMOTHY A. JUDGE

Education

Ph.D, University of Illinois at
Urbana-Champaign

Professional Experience

- **Academic Positions:** Matherly-McKethan Eminent Scholar in Management, Warrington College of Business Administration, University of Florida, Stanley M. Howe Professor in Leadership, Henry B. Tippie College of Business, University of Iowa, Associate Professor (with tenure), Department of Human Resource Studies, School of Industrial and Labor Relations, Cornell University, Lecturer, Charles University, Czech Republic, and Comenius University, Slovakia, Instructor, Industrial/Organizational Psychology, Department of Psychology, University of Illinois at Urbana-Champaign.
- **Research:** Dr Judge's primary research interests are in (1) personality, moods and emotions; (2) job attitudes; (3) leadership and influence behaviours; and (4) careers

(person–organisation fit, career success). Dr Judge has published more than 90 articles in these and other major topics in journals such as *Journal of Organizational Behavior, Personnel Psychology, Academy of Management Journal, Journal of Applied Psychology, European Journal of Personality, European Journal of Work* and *Organizational Psychology*.

- **Fellowship:** Dr Judge is a fellow of the American Psychological Association and the Society for Industrial and Organizational Psychology.
- **Awards:** In 1995 Dr Judge received the Ernest J. McCormick Award for Distinguished Early Career Contributions from the Society for Industrial and Organizational Psychology and in 2001 he received the Larry L. Cummings Award for mid-career contributions from the Organizational Behavior Division of the Academy of Management.
- **Books Published:** H. G. Heneman III and T. A. Judge, *Staffing Organizations*, 4th ed. (Madison, WI: Mendota House/Irwin, 2003).

PART 1

INTRODUCTION

1

WHAT IS ORGANISATIONAL BEHAVIOUR?

LEARNING OBJECTIVES

AFTER STUDYING THIS CHAPTER, YOU SHOULD BE ABLE TO:

1. DESCRIBE WHAT MANAGERS DO

2. DEFINE ORGANISATIONAL BEHAVIOUR (OB)

3. EXPLAIN THE VALUE OF THE SYSTEMATIC STUDY OF OB

4. IDENTIFY THE CONTRIBUTIONS MADE BY THE MAIN BEHAVIOURAL SCIENCE DISCIPLINES TO OB

5. EXPLAIN THE NEED FOR A CONTINGENCY APPROACH TO THE STUDY OF OB

6. LIST THE MAIN CHALLENGES AND OPPORTUNITIES FOR MANAGERS TO USE OB CONCEPTS

7. IDENTIFY THE THREE LEVELS OF ANALYSIS IN THIS BOOK'S OB MODEL

8. DESCRIBE WHY MANAGERS REQUIRE A KNOWLEDGE OF OB

Narelle Anderson runs CBD Enviro Services, a waste management company operating in a male-dominated and highly competitive industry. That doesn't worry Anderson. She appreciates that running a successful business is about having the essential management and leadership knowledge and skills, rather than being male or female.

WASTE MANAGEMENT isn't about finding the cheapest way to pick up rubbish for delivery to a landfill. For Sydney-based CBD Enviro Services it's all about cooperatively developing with its clients an approach that integrates environmental and sustainable waste management and recycling solutions.

Sounds like an attractive place to work? Well, it's a tough industry and you don't often see a young woman running the business in a male-dominated and highly contested landscape. Not that it stopped Narelle Anderson taking over CBD Enviro Services in 2000, giving up her job as accounts manager at Andersen Consulting in favour of helping a friend who owned CBD Enviro at the time. As Anderson points out, she started on the Monday, then the owner went overseas the following Monday and she found herself running the business. At that stage the company had been running for ten years and consisted of one person in the office, one truck, four subcontractors and plenty of problems. By Anderson's reckoning, the founder had lost his passion, staff morale was low and there was a complete lack of systems.

In the first months the drivers met regularly to discuss how to get rid of Anderson, but by the time the owner returned six months later she had achieved some significant results. He offered to sell her the business. The operation wasn't sexy, and Anderson didn't have any great passion for the garbage industry. But she bought the company despite her competitors dismissing her as the secretary who bought the boss's business. By 2006, CBD Enviro's revenue had risen by 35 per cent to about $3 million, and Anderson is forecasting a further 70 per cent growth—to about $5 million—in the near future.

Being young and female meant that few employees and competitors took her seriously—until, of course, she won her first big contract: helping one of Sydney's biggest office buildings to design and meet a landfill-reduction target.

Anderson insists that gender is irrelevant when it comes to business, pointing out that her company isn't successful because she happens to own some skirts. For her, it's about getting the right staff, understanding the marketplace and listening to customers. You have to get your hands dirty, because staff resent doing tasks that managers snub. You have to reward staff for hard work. And you have to keep up to date with new technology. Good people and new technology provide potential competitive advantages.[1]

If you don't fail, then you can't be trying. The successful innovators are the organisations that accept that failure happens.
David Gann

NARELLE ANDERSON HAS LEARNED what most managers learn very quickly: a large part of the success in any management job is developing good interpersonal, or people, skills. Managers need to be technically competent in their area of expertise, but technical knowledge isn't enough. Successful managers, entrepreneurs and employees also need interpersonal skills in order to work with others.[2]

Although practising managers have long understood the importance of interpersonal skills to managerial effectiveness, business schools were slower to get the message. Until the late 1980s, business school curricula focused almost singularly on the technical aspects of management, emphasising courses in economics, accounting, finance and quantitative techniques. Course work in human behaviour and people skills received minimal attention relative to the technical aspects of management. Over the past decade and a half, however, business faculties have come to realise the importance of an understanding of human behaviour in determining a manager's effectiveness, and required courses on people skills have been widely added to the curriculum.

Recognition of the importance of developing managers' interpersonal skills is closely tied to the need for organisations to get and keep high-performing employees. This becomes particularly crucial in a tight labour market.[3] Companies with reputations as a good place to work—such as Virgin Blue Airlines, Singapore Airlines, Bunnings, Mounties, Cisco Systems and Officeworks—have a big advantage. A national study of the workforce in the United States found that wages and salary benefits aren't the reason people like their jobs or stay with an employer. Far more important is the quality of the employees' jobs and the supportiveness of their work environments.[4] In Australia, a Morgan and Banks survey found that Australian workers rate their general experience of job satisfaction ahead of remuneration levels.[5] Like their American counterparts, they too look for a supportive and satisfying work environment. A recent survey of 148 large businesses in Asia and Australasia claimed that lack of recognition and opportunities for development are the main reasons employees leave their jobs.[6] So, having managers with good interpersonal skills is likely to make the workplace more pleasant, which, in turn, makes it easier to hire and keep qualified people.

We have come to understand that technical skills are necessary, but insufficient, for succeeding in management. In today's increasingly competitive and demanding workplace, managers can't succeed on their technical skills alone. They also have to have good people skills. This book has been written to help managers, potential managers and professionals develop those people skills.

managers | Individuals who achieve goals through other people.

organisation | A consciously coordinated social unit, composed of two or more people, that functions on a relatively continuous basis to achieve a common goal or set of goals.

WHAT MANAGERS DO

Let's begin by briefly defining the terms *manager* and the place where managers work—the *organisation*. Then let's look at the manager's job; specifically, what do managers do?

Managers get things done through other people. They make decisions, allocate resources and direct the activities of others to attain goals. Managers do their work in an organisation. An **organisation** is a consciously coordinated social unit, composed of two or more people, that functions on a relatively continuous basis to achieve a common goal or set of goals. On the basis of this definition, manufacturing and service firms are organisations, and so are schools, hospitals, churches, military units, retail stores, police departments, and local, state and Commonwealth government agencies. The people who oversee the activities of others and who are responsible for attaining goals in these organisations are managers (although they are sometimes called *administrators*, especially in not-for-profit organisations).

MANAGEMENT FUNCTIONS

In the early part of the 20th century, a French industrialist by the name of Henri Fayol wrote that all managers perform five management functions: they plan, organise, command, coordinate and control.[7] Today, we have condensed these to four: planning, organising, leading and controlling.

- *Planning*: define goals, establish strategies, and develop plans to implement the strategies and achieve the goals.
- *Organising*: determine the tasks, who does them, how they are done, and responsibilities for decisions and follow-up.
- *Leading*: motivate employees, direct the activities of others, select the most effective communication channels, or resolve conflicts among group members.
- *Controlling*: monitor and compare performance with goals, and address performance shortfalls.

Since organisations exist to achieve goals, someone has to define those goals and the means by which they can be achieved. Management is that someone. The **planning** function encompasses defining an organisation's goals, establishing an overall strategy for achieving those goals, and developing a comprehensive hierarchy of plans to integrate and coordinate activities.

Managers are also responsible for designing an organisation's structure. We call this function **organising**. It includes the determination of what tasks are to be done, who is to do them, how the tasks are to be grouped, who reports to whom, and where decisions are to be made. Every organisation contains people, and it is management's job to direct and coordinate those people. This is the **leading** function. When managers motivate employees, direct the activities of others, select the most effective communication channels or resolve conflicts among members, they are engaging in leading.

The final function managers perform is **controlling**. To ensure that things are going as they should, management must monitor the organisation's performance. Actual performance must be compared with the previously set goals. If there are any significant deviations, it's management's job to get the organisation back on track. This monitoring, comparing and potential correcting is what is meant by the controlling function.

So, using the functional approach, the answer to the question, 'What do managers do?' is that they plan, organise, lead and control.

MANAGEMENT ROLES

In the late 1960s, a graduate student at Massachusetts Institute of Technology (MIT) in the United States, Henry Mintzberg, undertook a careful study of five executives to determine what these managers did on their jobs. On the basis of his observations of these managers, Mintzberg concluded that managers perform ten different, highly interrelated roles, or sets of behaviours attributable to their jobs.[8] As shown in Table 1.1, these ten roles can be grouped as being primarily concerned with interpersonal relationships, the transfer of information and decision making.

planning | A process that includes defining goals, establishing strategy, and developing plans to coordinate activities.

----

organising | Determining what tasks are to be done, who is to do them, how the tasks are to be grouped, who reports to whom, and where decisions are to be made.

----

leading | A function that includes motivating employees, directing others, selecting the most effective communication channels and resolving conflicts.

----

controlling | Monitoring activities to ensure they are being accomplished as planned and correcting any significant deviations.

Role	Description	Examples
Interpersonal		
Figurehead	Symbolic head; required to perform a number of routine duties of a legal or social nature	Ceremonies, status requests, solicitations
Leader	Responsible for the motivation and direction of employees	Virtually all managerial activities involving employees
Liaison	Maintains a network of outside contacts who provide favours and information	Acknowledgment of mail, external board work
Informational		
Monitor	Receives wide variety of information; serves as nerve centre of internal and external information of the organisation	Handling all mail and contacts categorised as concerned primarily with receiving information
Disseminator	Transmits information received from outsiders or from other employees to members of the organisation	Forwarding mail into organisation for informational purposes; verbal contacts involving information flow to employees, such as review sessions
Spokesperson	Transmits information to outsiders on organisation's plans, policies, actions and results; serves as expert on organisation's industry	Board meetings; handling contacts involving transmission of information to outsiders
Decisional		
Entrepreneur	Searches organisation and its environment for opportunities and initiates projects to bring about change	Strategy and review sessions involving initiation or design of improvement projects
Disturbance handler	Responsible for corrective action when organisation faces important, unexpected disturbances	Strategy and review sessions involving disturbances and crises
Resource allocator	Making or approving significant organisational decisions	Scheduling; requests for authorisation; budgeting; the programming of employees' work
Negotiator	Responsible for representing the organisation at major negotiations	Contract negotiation

SOURCE: Adapted from H. Mintzberg, *The Nature of Managerial Work*. Copyright © Reprinted by permission of Pearson Education, Inc., Upper Saddle River, NJ.

INTERPERSONAL ROLES

All managers are required to perform duties that are ceremonial and symbolic in nature. When the chancellor of a university hands out diplomas at graduation, or a factory supervisor gives a group of high school students a tour of the factory, he or she is acting in a *figurehead* role. All managers also have a *leadership* role. This role includes hiring, training, motivating and disciplining employees. The third role within the interpersonal grouping is the *liaison* role. Mintzberg described this activity as contacting outsiders who provide the manager with information. These may be individuals or groups inside or outside the organisation. The sales manager who obtains information from the company's quality-control manager has an internal liaison relationship. When that sales manager has contacts with other sales executives through a marketing trade association, he or she has an outside liaison relationship.

INFORMATIONAL ROLES

All managers, to some degree, collect information from organisations and institutions outside their own. Typically, they get information by reading newspapers and magazines and talking with other people to learn of changes in the public's tastes, what competitors may be planning, and the like. Mintzberg called this the *monitor* role. Managers also act as a conduit to transmit information to organisational members. This is the *disseminator* role. In addition, managers perform a *spokesperson* role when they represent the organisation to outsiders.

DECISIONAL ROLES

Finally, Mintzberg identified four roles that revolve around the making of choices. In the *entrepreneur* role, managers initiate and oversee new projects that will improve their organisation's performance. As *disturbance handlers*, managers take corrective action in response to unforeseen problems. As *resource allocators*, managers are responsible for allocating human, physical and monetary resources. Last, managers perform a *negotiator* role, in which they discuss issues and bargain with other units to gain advantages for their own unit.

MANAGEMENT SKILLS

Looking at what managers do from a different perspective is to look at the skills or competencies they need to achieve their goals. Robert Katz has identified three essential management skills: technical, human and conceptual.[9]

TECHNICAL SKILLS

Technical skills encompass the ability to apply specialised knowledge or expertise. When you think of the skills held by professionals such as civil engineers or oral surgeons, you typically focus on their technical skills. Through extensive formal education, they have learned the special knowledge and practices of their field. Of course, professionals don't have a monopoly on technical skills, and not all technical skills have to be learned in TAFE or technical colleges or formal training programs. All jobs require some specialised expertise, and many people develop their technical skills on the job.

technical skills | The ability to apply specialised knowledge or expertise.

HUMAN SKILLS

The ability to work with, understand and motivate other people, both individually and in groups, describes **human skills**. Many people are technically proficient but

human skills | The ability to work with, understand and motivate other people, both individually and in groups.

interpersonally incompetent. They might be poor listeners, unable to understand the needs of others, or have difficulty managing conflicts. Since managers get things done through other people, they must have good human skills in order to communicate, motivate and delegate.

CONCEPTUAL SKILLS

conceptual skills | The mental ability to analyse and diagnose complex situations.

Managers must have the mental ability to analyse and diagnose complex situations. These tasks require **conceptual skills**. Decision making, for example, requires managers to recognise problems, identify alternatives that can correct them, evaluate those alternatives and select the best one. Managers can be technically and interpersonally competent, yet still fail because of an inability to rationally process and interpret information.

EFFECTIVE VERSUS SUCCESSFUL MANAGERIAL ACTIVITIES

Fred Luthans and his associates looked at the issue of what managers do from a somewhat different perspective.[10] They asked the question: 'Do managers who climb the promotions ladder most quickly in an organisation do the same activities and with the same emphasis as managers who do the best job?' You would tend to think that the managers who were the most effective in their jobs would also be the ones who were promoted fastest. But that's not what appears to happen.

Luthans and his associates studied more than 450 managers. What they found was that these managers all engaged in four managerial activities:

1. *Traditional management*: decision making, planning and controlling.
2. *Communication*: exchanging routine information and processing paperwork.
3. *Human resource management*: motivating, disciplining, managing conflict, staffing and training.
4. *Networking*: socialising, politicking and interacting with outsiders.

The 'average' manager in the study spent 32 per cent of their time in traditional management activities, 29 per cent communicating, 20 per cent in human resource management activities and 19 per cent networking. However, the amount of time and effort that different managers spent on those four activities varied a great deal. Specifically, as shown in Figure 1.1, managers who were *successful* (defined in terms of the speed of promotion within their organisation) had a very different emphasis than managers who were *effective* (defined in terms of the quantity and quality of their performance and the satisfaction and commitment of their employees). Among successful managers, networking made the largest relative contribution to success, and human resource management activities made the smallest relative contribution. Among effective managers, communication made the largest relative contribution and networking the smallest. A recent study of Australian managers further confirms the importance of networking in relation to success.[11] Australian managers who actively networked received more promotions and enjoyed other rewards associated with career success.

This research adds important insights to our knowledge of what managers do. On average, managers spend approximately 20–30 per cent of their time on each of the four activities: traditional management, communication, human resource management and networking. However, successful managers don't give the same emphasis to each of those activities as do effective managers. In fact, their emphases are almost the opposite. This finding challenges the historical assumption that promotions are based on performance, vividly illustrating the importance that social and political skills play in getting ahead in organisations.

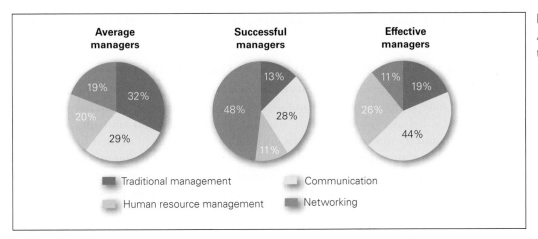

SOURCE: Based on F. Luthans, R. M. Hodgetts and S. A. Rosenkrantz, *Real Managers* (Cambridge, MA: Ballinger, 1988).

A REVIEW OF THE MANAGER'S JOB

One common thread runs through the functions, roles, skills and activities approaches to management: each recognises the paramount importance of managing people. Regardless of whether it is called 'the leading function', 'interpersonal roles', 'human skills' or 'human resource management, communication and networking activities', it is clear that managers need to develop their people skills if they are going to be effective and successful.

ENTER ORGANISATIONAL BEHAVIOUR

LEARNING OBJECTIVE **2**

Define organisational behaviour (OB)

We have made the case for the importance of people skills. But neither this book, nor the discipline on which it is based, is called *People Skills*. The term that is widely used to describe the discipline is *organisational behaviour*.

Organisational behaviour (often abbreviated as **OB**) is a field of study that investigates the impact that individuals, groups and structure have on behaviour within organisations for the purpose of applying such knowledge towards improving an organisation's effectiveness. That's a lot of words, so let's break down this definition.

Organisational behaviour is a field of study. This statement means that it is a distinct area of expertise with a common body of knowledge. What does it study? It studies three determinants of behaviour in organisations: individuals, groups and structure. In addition, OB applies the knowledge gained about individuals, groups and the effect of structure on behaviour in order to make organisations work more effectively.

To sum up our definition, OB is concerned with the study of what people do in an organisation and how that behaviour affects the performance of the organisation. And because OB is concerned specifically with employment-related situations, you shouldn't be surprised to find that it emphasises behaviour as related to concerns such as jobs, work, absenteeism, employment turnover, productivity, human performance and management.

There is increasing agreement as to the components or topics that constitute the subject area of OB. Although there is still considerable debate as to the relative importance of each, there appears to be general agreement that OB includes the core topics of motivation, leader behaviour and power, interpersonal communication, group structure and processes, learning, attitude development and perception, emotions, change

organisational behaviour (OB) | A field of study that investigates the impact that individuals, groups and structure have on behaviour within organisations, for the purpose of applying such knowledge towards improving an organisation's effectiveness.

processes, conflict, work design and work stress, which are topics that will be explored in later chapters throughout this text.[12]

COMPLEMENTING INTUITION WITH SYSTEMATIC STUDY

Each of us is a student of behaviour. Since almost our birth, we have watched the actions of others and have attempted to interpret what we see. Whether or not you have explicitly thought about it before, you have been 'reading' people almost all your life. You watch what others do and try to explain to yourself why they have engaged in their behaviour. In addition, you have attempted to predict what they might do under different sets of conditions. Unfortunately, your casual or commonsense approach to reading others can often lead to erroneous predictions. However, you can improve your predictive ability by supplementing your intuitive opinions with a more systematic approach.

The systematic approach used in this book will uncover important facts and relationships and will provide a base from which more accurate predictions of behaviour can be made. Underlying this systematic approach is the belief that behaviour isn't random. Rather, there are certain fundamental consistencies underlying the behaviour of all individuals that can be identified and then modified to reflect individual differences.

These fundamental consistencies are very important. Why? Because they allow predictability. When you get into your car, you make some definite and usually highly accurate predictions about how other people will behave. In Australia, for instance, you would predict that other drivers will stop at stop signs and red lights, drive on the left side of the road, pass on your right, and not cross the solid double line on mountain roads. Notice that your predictions about the behaviour of people behind the wheels of their cars are almost always correct. Obviously, the rules of driving make predictions about driving behaviour fairly easy.

What may be less obvious is that there are rules (written and unwritten) in almost every setting. We would argue that it is possible to predict behaviour (undoubtedly, not always with 100 per cent accuracy) in supermarkets, classrooms, doctors' surgeries, elevators, and in most structured situations. For instance, do you turn around and face the doors when you get into an elevator? Almost everyone does. But did you ever read that you are supposed to do this? Probably not! Just as we make predictions about the behaviour of motorists (based on the rules of the road), we can make predictions about the behaviour of people in elevators (where there are few written rules). In a class of 60 students, if you wanted to ask a question of the tutor, we predict that you would raise your hand. Why don't you clap, stand up, raise your leg, cough, or yell 'Hey, over here!'? The reason is that you have learned that raising your hand is appropriate behaviour in school. These examples support a major contention in this textbook: behaviour is generally predictable, and the systematic study of behaviour is a means to making reasonably accurate predictions.

systematic study | Looking at relationships, attempting to attribute causes and effects, and drawing conclusions based on scientific evidence.

When we use the phrase **systematic study**, we mean looking at relationships, attempting to attribute causes and effects, and basing our conclusions on scientific evidence—that is, on data gathered under controlled conditions and measured and interpreted in a reasonably rigorous manner. (See the appendix at the back of the book for a basic review of research methods used in studies of organisational behaviour.)

intuition | A feeling not necessarily supported by research.

Systematic study adds to **intuition**, or those 'gut feelings' about 'why I do what I do' and 'what makes others tick'. Of course, a systematic approach doesn't mean that the things you have come to believe in an unsystematic way are necessarily incorrect. Some of the conclusions we make in this text, based on reasonably substantive research findings, will only support what you always knew was true. But you will also be exposed to research

PRECONCEIVED NOTIONS VERSUS SUBSTANTIVE EVIDENCE

Assume you signed up to take an introductory course in calculus. On the first day of class your lecturer asks you to take out a piece of paper and answer the following question: 'Why is the sign of the second derivative negative when the first derivative is set equal to zero, if the function is concave from below?' It is unlikely you would be able to answer that question. Your reply to that lecturer would probably be something like, 'How am *I* supposed to know? That's why I'm taking this course!'

Now, change the scenario. You are in an introductory course in organisational behaviour. On the first day of class your lecturer asks you to write an answer to the following question: 'Why are employees not as motivated at work today as they were 30 years ago?'

You might feel a bit of reluctance, but we would guess you would begin writing. You would have no problem coming up with an explanation to this question of motivation.

These two scenarios are meant to demonstrate one of the challenges of teaching a course in OB. You enter an OB course with a lot of *preconceived notions* that you accept as *facts*. You think you already know a lot about human behaviour.[13]

Typically, that isn't true in calculus, physics, chemistry or even accounting. So, in contrast to many other disciplines, OB not only introduces you to a comprehensive set of concepts and theories; it also has to deal with a lot of commonly accepted 'facts' about human behaviour and organisations that you have acquired over the years. Some examples might include 'You can't teach an old dog new tricks'; 'happy workers are productive workers' and 'two heads are better than one'. But these 'facts' aren't necessarily true. So, one of the objectives of a course in organisational behaviour is to replace popularly held *notions*, often accepted without question, with science-based conclusions.

As you will see in this book, the field of OB is built on decades of research. This research provides a body of substantive evidence that is able to replace preconceived notions. Throughout this book, we have included boxes such as this one, entitled 'Myth or Science?'. They call your attention to some of the more popular of these notions or myths about organisational behaviour. We use the boxes to show how OB research has disproved them or, in some cases, shown them to be true. We hope that you will find these boxes interesting. But more importantly, they should help to remind you that the study of human behaviour at work is a science and that you need to be vigilant about 'seat of the pants' explanations of work-related behaviours.

evidence that runs counter to what you may have thought was common sense. One of the objectives of this text is to encourage you to enhance your intuitive views of behaviour with a systematic analysis, in the belief that such analysis will improve your accuracy in explaining and predicting behaviour.

CONTRIBUTING DISCIPLINES TO THE OB FIELD

LEARNING OBJECTIVE 4
Identify the contributions made by the main behavioural science disciplines to OB

Organisational behaviour is an applied behavioural science that is built on contributions from a number of behavioural disciplines. The predominant areas are psychology, sociology, social psychology, anthropology and political science. As we shall learn, psychology's contributions have been mainly at the individual or micro level of analysis, while the other four disciplines have contributed to our understanding of macro concepts such as group processes and organisation. Figure 1.2 is an overview of the main contributions to the study of organisational behaviour.

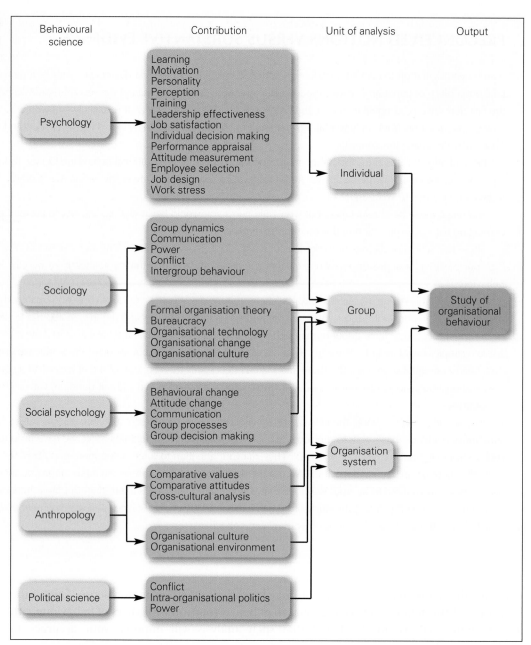

Behavioural science	Contribution	Unit of analysis	Output
Psychology	Learning Motivation Personality Perception Training Leadership effectiveness Job satisfaction Individual decision making Performance appraisal Attitude measurement Employee selection Job design Work stress	Individual	Study of organisational behaviour
Sociology	Group dynamics Communication Power Conflict Intergroup behaviour Formal organisation theory Bureaucracy Organisational technology Organisational change Organisational culture	Group	
Social psychology	Behavioural change Attitude change Communication Group processes Group decision making		
Anthropology	Comparative values Comparative attitudes Cross-cultural analysis Organisational culture Organisational environment	Organisation system	
Political science	Conflict Intra-organisational politics Power		

PSYCHOLOGY

psychology | The science that seeks to measure, explain and sometimes change the behaviour of humans and other animals.

Psychology is the science that seeks to measure, explain and sometimes change the behaviour of humans and other animals. Psychologists concern themselves with studying and attempting to understand individual behaviour. Those who have contributed and continue to add to the knowledge of OB are learning theorists, personality theorists, clinical psychologists and, most important, industrial and organisational psychologists.

Early industrial/organisational psychologists concerned themselves with the problems of fatigue, boredom and other factors relevant to working conditions that could impede efficient work performance. More recently, their contributions have been expanded to include learning, perception, personality, emotions, training, leadership effectiveness, needs and motivational forces, job satisfaction, decision-making processes, performance appraisals, attitude measurement, employee selection techniques, work design and job stress.

SOCIOLOGY

While psychologists focus their attention on the individual, sociologists study the social system in which individuals fill their roles; that is, **sociology** studies people in relation to their fellow human beings. Specifically, sociologists have made their greatest contribution to OB through their study of group behaviour in organisations, particularly formal and complex organisations. Some of the areas within OB that have received valuable input from sociologists are group dynamics, design of work teams, organisational culture, formal organisation theory and structure, organisational technology, communications, power and conflict.

sociology | The study of people in relation to their fellow human beings.

SOCIAL PSYCHOLOGY

Social psychology is an area within psychology, blending concepts from both psychology and sociology. It focuses on the influence of people on one another. One of the main areas receiving considerable investigation from social psychologists has been *change*—how to implement it and how to reduce barriers to its acceptance. In addition, we find social psychologists making significant contributions in the areas of measuring, understanding and changing attitudes; communication patterns; building trust; the ways in which group activities can satisfy individual needs; and group decision-making processes.

social psychology | An area within psychology that blends concepts from psychology and sociology and that focuses on the influence of people on one another.

ANTHROPOLOGY

Anthropology is the study of societies to learn about human beings and their activities. For example, anthropologists' work on cultures and environments has helped us to understand differences in fundamental values, attitudes and behaviour between people in different countries and within different organisations. Much of our current understanding of organisational culture, organisational environments and differences between national cultures is the result of the work of anthropologists or those using their methods.

anthropology | The study of societies to learn about human beings and their activities.

POLITICAL SCIENCE

Although frequently overlooked, the contributions of political scientists are significant to the understanding of behaviour in organisations. **Political science** studies the behaviour of individuals and groups within a political environment. Specific topics of concern here include the structuring of conflict, allocation of power, and how people manipulate power for individual self-interest.

political science | The study of the behaviour of individuals and groups within a political environment.

THERE ARE FEW ABSOLUTES IN OB

LEARNING OBJECTIVE **5**

Explain the need for a contingency approach to the study of OB

There are few, if any, simple and universal principles that explain organisational behaviour. There are laws in the physical sciences—chemistry, astronomy, physics—that are consistent and apply in a wide range of situations. They allow scientists to generalise about the pull of gravity or to be confident about sending astronauts into space to repair satellites. But as one noted behavioural researcher aptly concluded, 'God gave all the easy problems to the physicists.' Human beings are complex. Because they are not alike, our ability to make simple, accurate and sweeping generalisations is limited. Two people often act very differently in the same situation, and the same person's behaviour changes in different situations. For example, not everyone is motivated by money, and you behave differently at a sporting match on Sunday than you did at a party the night before.

That doesn't mean, of course, that we can't offer reasonably accurate explanations of human behaviour or make valid predictions. However, it does mean that OB concepts must reflect situational, or contingency, conditions. We can say that x leads to y, but only under conditions specified in z (the **contingency variables**). The science of OB was developed by using general concepts and then altering their application to the particular situation. So, for example, OB scholars would avoid stating that effective leaders should always seek the ideas of their followers before making a decision. Rather, we shall find that in some situations a participative style is clearly superior, but, in other situations, an autocratic decision-making style is more effective. In other words, the effectiveness of a particular leadership style is contingent on the situation in which it is used.

As you proceed through this book, you will encounter a wealth of research-based theories about how people behave in organisations. But don't expect to find a lot of straightforward cause-and-effect relationships. There aren't many! Organisational behaviour theories mirror the subject matter with which they deal. People are complex and complicated, and so too must be the theories developed to explain their actions.

contingency variables | Situational factors: variables that moderate the relationship between two or more other variables and improve the correlation.

LEARNING OBJECTIVE 6
List the main challenges and opportunities for managers to use OB concepts

CHALLENGES AND OPPORTUNITIES FOR OB

Understanding organisational behaviour has never been more important for managers. A quick look at a few of the dramatic changes now taking place in organisations supports this claim. For example, the typical employee is getting older; more and more women and members of minority groups are in the workplace; corporate downsizing and the heavy use of temporary employees are severing the bonds of loyalty that historically tied many employees to their employers; and global competition is requiring employees to become more flexible and to learn to cope with rapid change.

In short, there are a lot of challenges and opportunities today for managers to use OB concepts. In this section, we review some of the more critical issues confronting managers for which OB offers solutions—or at least some meaningful insights towards solutions.

RESPONDING TO GLOBALISATION

Organisations are no longer constrained by national borders. A British firm owns Burger King, and McDonald's sells hamburgers in 87 countries around the world. ExxonMobil, a so-called American company, receives almost 75 per cent of its revenues from sales outside the United States. New employees at Finland-based phone maker Nokia are increasingly being recruited from India, China and other developing countries—with non-Finns now outnumbering Finns at Nokia's renowned research centre in Helsinki. And all major automobile manufacturers now build cars outside their borders; for example, Honda builds cars in the United States; General Motors builds Daewoo vehicles in South Korea and Holdens in Australia; and both Mercedes and BMW build their cars in South Africa.

These examples illustrate that the world has become a global village. In the process, the manager's job is changing.

INCREASED FOREIGN ASSIGNMENTS

If you are a manager, you are increasingly likely to find yourself in a foreign assignment— transferred to your employer's operating division or subsidiary in another country. Once there, you will have to manage a workforce that is likely to be very different in needs, aspirations and attitudes from those you were used to back home.

WORKING WITH PEOPLE FROM DIFFERENT CULTURES

Even in your own country, you are going to find yourself working with bosses, peers and other employees who were born and raised in different cultures. What motivates you may not motivate them. Or your style of communication may be straightforward and open, but they may find this approach uncomfortable and threatening. To work effectively with people from different cultures, you need to understand how their culture, geography and religion have shaped them, and how to adapt your management style to their differences.

COPING WITH AN ANTI-CAPITALISM BACKLASH

Capitalism's focus on efficiency, growth and profits may be generally accepted in Australia, Singapore and Hong Kong, but these capitalistic values aren't nearly as popular in places such as France, the Middle East and the Scandinavian countries. For instance, because Finland's egalitarian values have created a 'soak the rich' mentality among politicians, traffic fines are based on the offender's income rather than the severity of the offence.[14] So when one of Finland's richest men (he is heir to a sausage fortune), who was making close to US$9 million a year, was ticketed for doing 80 kilometres an hour through a 40-kilometre zone in central Helsinki, the Finnish court hit him with a fine of US$217 000!

Managers at global companies such as McDonald's and Coca-Cola have come to realise that economic values aren't universally transferable. Management practices need to be modified to reflect the values of the different countries in which an organisation operates.

OVERSEEING MOVEMENT OF JOBS TO COUNTRIES WITH LOW-COST LABOUR

It is increasingly difficult for managers in advanced nations, where minimum wages are typically US$8 or more an hour, to compete against firms who rely on workers from China and other developing nations where labour is available for less than US$1 an hour. It's not by chance that a good portion of Australians and New Zealanders wear clothes made in China and work on computers whose microchips came from Taiwan. In a global economy, jobs tend to flow to places where lower costs provide business firms with a comparative advantage. Such practices, however, often come with strong criticism from unions, politicians, local community leaders, and others who see this exporting of jobs as undermining the job markets in developed countries. Managers must deal with the difficult task of balancing the interests of their organisation with their responsibilities to the communities in which they operate.

MANAGING PEOPLE WHEN THE THREAT OF TERRORISM IS HIGH

If you read the paper or watch the evening news, chances are you will find that acts of terrorism are among the top stories. But as you read such stories, do you think about the workplace? Probably not. So you might be surprised to learn that terrorism has had a profound effect on the business world. In fact, surveys suggest that fear of terrorism is the number one reason business travellers have cut back on their trips. But travel isn't the only concern. Increasingly, organisations need to find ways to deal with employee fears about security precautions (in many cities, you can't get into an office building without passing through several layers of airport-like security) and assignments abroad.[15] (How would you feel about an assignment in a country with substantial sentiments against people from your country?) An understanding of OB topics such as emotions, motivation, communication and leadership can help managers to deal more effectively with their employees' fears about terrorism.

MANAGING WORKFORCE DIVERSITY

One of the most important and broad-based challenges currently facing organisations is adapting to people who are different. The term we use for describing this challenge is *workforce diversity*. While globalisation focuses on differences between people *from* different countries, workforce diversity addresses differences among people *within* given countries.

workforce diversity | The concept that organisations are becoming more heterogeneous in terms of gender, race, ethnicity and inclusion of other diverse groups.

Workforce diversity means that organisations are becoming more heterogeneous in terms of gender, race and ethnicity—in other words, there are more differences than there are similarities among members of the organisation. But the term encompasses anyone who varies from the so-called norm. In addition to the more obvious groups—women, indigenous Australians, Asians—it also includes the physically or intellectually less-abled, gays and lesbians, and the elderly. Moreover, it is an increasingly important organisational issue in places such as Australia, New Zealand, Canada, South Africa, Japan, Malaysia, Singapore and Western Europe. Managers in Australia and Canada, for example, are having to adjust to large influxes of Asian employees. The 'new' South Africa is increasingly characterised by blacks holding important technical and managerial jobs, as well as the

---

OB IN PRACTICE

THE GREAT TALENT RACE

Labour shortages in Australia and elsewhere have made the issue of talent management a strategic issue. According to Melanie Laing, regional director of human resources for Unisys Asia-Pacific, 'There is a compelling business case for the creation and development of innovative talent management programs because companies that do this well will rise above their competitors.' She adds, 'A 25-year-old Generation Y employee hoping to quickly rise to a junior management position has very different needs in terms of talent management than an employee with 20 years' experience looking to move to a senior management role.'

Fujitsu Australia has a competitive advantage in acquiring and developing talented employees. Rod Vawdrey joined Fujitsu Australia as CEO in 2003. His objective was to revise the company's business model and then develop a suitable organisational model to support that model. The type of organisation he envisaged involved creating an environment in which people could thrive, and creating a performance culture that identifies 'the Fujitsu Way'.

Vawdrey believes that to achieve such a culture, his organisation needs to have a formal, disciplined talent management system that includes making sure there is clear career succession, and appraisal and feedback systems are in place. Getting the right people in the right jobs is a priority. Vawdrey believes that there is still a lot of recycled material in middle management in Australia—a 'permafrost', he calls it—that is stopping the real talent from coming through. He reinforces the old cliché: 'People are our only sustainable asset, and you attract people to the organisation because of how it is perceived in the market and how it treats its people.'

Fujitsu has now become an employer of choice through its emphasis on talent management and developing a culture where, as Rod Vawdrey points out, '...we treat our employees well ... we are an employer where you get rewarded for your effort and get recognised for your contribution; you get respected as a person and you get the opportunity to make a name for yourself.'

SOURCES: Craig Donaldson, 'Skill Shortages Drive Talent Management', *Human Resources*, 21 March 2006: <www.humanresourcesmagazine. com.au/articles/52/0C03DF52.asp?Type=59&Category=917>; and Richard Jones, 'Creating an Industrial-Strength Company', *Management Today*, September 2006: <www.aim.com.au/DisplayStory.asp?ID=601>.

problems posed by there being 11 official national languages. Women, long confined to low-paying temporary jobs in Japan, Malaysia and Singapore, are moving into managerial positions. And the European Union cooperative trade arrangement, which opened up borders throughout much of Europe, has increased workforce diversity in organisations that operate in countries such as Germany, Poland, Portugal, Italy and France.

EMBRACING DIVERSITY

We used to take a melting-pot approach to differences in organisations, assuming that people who were different would somehow automatically want to assimilate. But we now recognise that employees don't set aside their cultural values and lifestyle preferences when they come to work. The challenge for organisations, therefore, is to make themselves more accommodating to diverse groups of people by addressing their different lifestyles, family needs and work styles. The melting-pot assumption is being replaced by one that recognises and values differences.[16]

Haven't organisations always included members of diverse groups? Yes, but they were a small percentage of the workforce and were, for the most part, ignored by large organisations. Moreover, it was assumed that these minorities would seek to blend in and assimilate. For example, the bulk of the pre-1980s workforce in Australia were white, predominantly European Anglo-Saxon males working full-time to support a non-employed wife and school-aged children. Since then, the workforce demographics have changed considerably.

CHANGING DEMOGRAPHICS

In 2006, women held approximately 34 per cent of full-time employment positions in Australia. This represented a significant increase in participation since 1980. However, the difference in average weekly income for men and women in full-time employment hasn't changed significantly since 1983. In May 2006, the average for men was $1168 and $948 for women. The proportion of minorities in the workforce has also increased.

The ageing of the Australian workforce is becoming a significant management issue. Mature-age workers (those aged 45 years and over) currently make up almost a third of the labour force. The retention of older workers in the labour force is seen by the government as a potential solution to the problem of Australia's ageing population. This is in contrast to a decrease in the participation of older Australians over the past 30 years, particularly for men over 45 years of age. While the participation of women has risen substantially over the last 50 years, the participation of women at near retirement age is still much lower than that of men. In 2002, women aged 55–59 had a labour force participation rate of 51 per cent, compared with 72 per cent for men, while for those aged 60–64 the rates were 24 per cent and 47 per cent, respectively.[17]

IMPLICATIONS

Workforce diversity has important implications for management practice. Managers have to shift their philosophy from treating everyone alike, to recognising differences and responding to those differences in ways that ensure employee retention and greater productivity while, at the same time, not discriminating. This shift includes, for example, providing diversity training and revamping benefits programs to accommodate the different needs of different employees. Diversity, if positively managed, can increase creativity and innovation in organisations, as well as improve decision making by providing different perspectives on problems.[18] When diversity isn't managed properly, there is a potential for higher turnover, more difficult communication and more interpersonal conflicts.

IMPROVING QUALITY AND PRODUCTIVITY

A 2006 study found that the average unproductive time in Australian companies in the past three years was 32.2 per cent, while the average for the United Kingdom was 36.6 per cent.[19] These figures highlight the general push globally for improving quality and productivity by many firms such as General Electric, where the Six Sigma production technique has been introduced. This technique improves quality and productivity in the production process by removing any unwanted variations and defects. Australia's largest telecommunications company, Telstra, has adopted the Six Sigma program in a bid to cut $100 million from the company's operating costs. BHP Billiton has been using the program for several years to manage its production costs in the context of fluctuating commodity prices.[20]

In the 1990s, organisations around the world added capacity in response to increased demand. Companies built new facilities, expanded services and added staff. The result? Today, almost every industry suffers from excess supply. Retail suffers from too many malls and shopping centres. Automobile factories can build more cars than consumers can afford. The telecom industry is drowning in debt from building capacity that might take 50 years to absorb, and most cities now have far more restaurants than their communities can support.

Excess capacity translates into increased competition. And increased competition is forcing managers to reduce costs and, at the same time, improve their organisation's productivity and the quality of the products and services they offer. Management guru Tom Peters says, 'Almost all quality improvement comes via simplification of design, manufacturing, layout, processes, and procedures.' To achieve these ends, managers are implementing programs such as **quality management (QM)** and **process reengineering**— programs that require extensive employee involvement.

Today's managers understand that the success of any effort at improving quality and productivity must include their employees. These employees will not only be a major force in carrying out changes, but increasingly will actively participate in planning those changes. OB offers important insights into helping managers work through these changes.

quality management (QM) | The constant attainment of customer satisfaction through the continuous improvement of all organisational processes.

process reengineering | Reconsidering how work would be done and an organisation structured if it were starting over.

RESPONDING TO THE LABOUR SHORTAGE

Economic ups and downs are difficult to predict. The world economy in the late 1990s, for example, was generally quite robust and labour markets were tight. Most employers found it difficult to find skilled employees to fill vacancies. Then, in 2002/03, most developed countries suffered an economic recession, in part fuelled by the war on terrorism. Layoffs and retrenchments were widespread, and the supply of skilled employees became much more plentiful in the short term. Judging from history, the past shortages of skilled labour will reappear in the not too distant future and the whole cycle will repeat itself. In contrast, demographic trends are much more predictable. And we are facing one that has direct implications for OB: barring some unforeseeable economic or political calamity—such as the recession in 2002/03—there will be a labour shortage for at least another ten to 15 years.[21] This shortage of skilled labour is already affecting Australia and New Zealand, and is also likely to be just as prevalent in most of Europe due to a greying population—13 per cent of Australia's population is over 65 years of age—and a declining birth rate—less than 21 per cent of households have members aged under 15 years.

The skilled labour shortage is a function of two factors—birth rates and labour participation rates. From the late 1960s to the late 1980s, employers benefited from the large number of baby-boomers (those born between 1946 and 1965) entering the workforce. Specifically, there are millions of baby-boomers in the workforce. But there are many fewer Gen-Xers to replace them when they retire. Some baby-boomers have already retired early. The problem is becoming more severe as the major exodus of baby-boomers from the workplace has begun. Importantly, in spite of continued increases in immigration, new entrants to the workforce from foreign countries won't do much to correct the labour supply shortage.

The labour shortage problem is compounded by the fact that the latter part of the 20th century benefited from a huge increase in the number of women entering the workforce, which provided a new supply of talented and skilled employees. This source has now been tapped. Moreover, there is declining interest by older employees in staying in the labour force. In 1950, nearly 80 per cent of all 62-year-old men were still working. Today, only slightly more than half are still in the labour force. Improved pensions, expanded Social Security and health-care benefits, and a healthy share market have led many employees to retire early, especially those whose jobs were stressful or unchallenging. So, the combination of the smaller Generation X population, the already high participation rate of women in the workforce and early retirements will lead to a significantly smaller future labour pool from which employers can hire.

In times of labour shortage, good wages and benefits aren't going to be enough to get and keep skilled employees. Managers will need sophisticated recruitment and retention strategies. And OB can help managers to create these. In tight labour markets, managers who don't understand human behaviour and fail to treat their employees properly risk having no one to manage!

IMPROVING CUSTOMER SERVICE

Recently, one of the authors of this book purchased a DVD drive for his computer from Officeworks. A week later, while shopping at Officeworks for something else, he noticed that the price of the DVD drive was quite a bit cheaper than when he had purchased one a week earlier. Slightly disappointed, he later happened to mention the drop in price to the sales assistant at the checkout. Much to his surprise, the sales assistant immediately refunded the difference—and in the process won the author's continued business and a customer for life.

Today, the majority of employees in developed countries work in service jobs. In Australia, 73 per cent work in service industries, while in the United States it is almost 80 per cent. In the United Kingdom, Germany and Japan, the percentages are 69, 68 and 65, respectively. Examples of these service jobs include technical support representatives, call-centre operators, fast-food counter employees, sales clerks, teachers, waiters or waitresses, nurses, automobile repair technicians, consultants, credit representatives, financial planners and flight attendants. The common characteristic of these jobs is that they require substantial interaction with an organisation's customers. And since an organisation can't exist without customers—whether that organisation is Royal & SunAlliance, National Australia Bank, an electricity utility, a law firm, a museum, a school or a government agency—management needs to ensure that employees do what it takes to please its customers. OB can help in that task.

An analysis of a Qantas Airways' passenger survey confirms the role that employees play in satisfying customers. Passengers were asked to rate their 'essential needs' in air travel.

Almost every factor listed by passengers was directly influenced by the actions of Qantas's employees—from prompt baggage delivery, to courteous and efficient cabin crews, to assistance with connections, to quick and friendly airport check-ins. Is it any wonder that John Travolta decked his private jet out in Qantas colours and acts as their global ambassador?

Except for OB researchers' interest in customer satisfaction through improvements in quality, the field of OB has generally ignored the customer. Focusing on the customer was thought to be the concern of people who study and practise marketing. But OB can contribute to improving an organisation's performance by showing managers how employee attitudes and behaviours are associated with customer satisfaction.[22] Many an organisation has failed because its employees failed to please the customer. So, management needs to create a customer-responsive culture. And OB can provide considerable guidance in helping managers to create such cultures—cultures in which employees are friendly and courteous, accessible, knowledgeable, prompt in responding to customer needs, and willing to do what is necessary to please the customer.[23]

IMPROVING PEOPLE SKILLS

We opened this chapter by demonstrating how important people skills are to managerial effectiveness. We said, 'This book has been written to help managers, potential managers and professionals develop those people skills.'

As you proceed through this book, we will present relevant concepts and theories that can help you to explain and predict the behaviour of people at work. In addition, you will gain insights into specific people skills that you can use on the job. For example, you will learn ways to design motivating jobs, techniques for improving your listening skills, and how to create more effective teams.

EMPOWERING PEOPLE

If you pick up any popular business periodical nowadays, you will read about the reshaping of the relationship between managers and those they are supposedly responsible for managing. You will find managers being called coaches, advisers, sponsors or facilitators. In some organisations, employees are now called associates. And there is a blurring between the roles of managers and employees. Decision making is being pushed down to the operating level, where employees are being given the freedom to make choices about schedules and procedures and to solve work-related problems.[24] In the 1980s, managers were encouraged to get their employees to participate in work-related decisions. Now, managers are going considerably further by allowing employees full control of their work. An increasing number of organisations are using self-managed teams, in which employees operate largely without bosses.

empowering employees | Putting employees in charge of what they do.

What's going on? What's going on is that managers are **empowering employees**. They are putting employees in charge of what they do. And, in so doing, managers are having to learn how to give up control, and employees are having to learn how to take responsibility for their work and make appropriate decisions. In later chapters, we will show how empowerment is changing leadership styles, power relationships, the way work is designed and the way organisations are structured.

COPING WITH 'TEMPORARINESS'

Managing used to be characterised by long periods of stability, interrupted occasionally by short periods of change. Managing today would be more accurately described as long periods of ongoing change, interrupted occasionally by short periods of stability. The world that most managers and employees face today is one of permanent temporariness. The actual jobs that employees perform are in a permanent state of change, so employees need to update their knowledge and skills continually in order to perform new job requirements. For example, production employees at companies such as General Motors-Holden, Ford and Toyota in Australia now need to know how to operate computerised production equipment. This wasn't part of their job descriptions 20 years ago. Work groups are also increasingly in a state of change. In the past, employees were assigned to a specific work group, and that assignment was relatively permanent. There was a considerable amount of security in working with the same people day in and day out. That predictability has been replaced by temporary work groups, teams that include members from different departments and whose members change all the time, the use of online employees telecommuting from other locations or even other countries, and the increased use of employee rotation to fill constantly changing work assignments. Finally, organisations themselves are in a state of change. They continually reorganise their various divisions, sell off poor-performing businesses, downsize operations, subcontract non-critical services and operations to other organisations, and replace permanent employees with temporary employees.

Today's managers and employees must learn to cope with temporariness. They have to learn to live with flexibility, spontaneity and unpredictability. The study of OB can provide important insights into helping you better understand a work world of continual change, how to overcome resistance to change, and how best to create an organisational culture that thrives on change.

STIMULATING INNOVATION AND CHANGE

Whatever happened to HIH, Ansett Airlines, Olympia and OneTel? All these giants went bust. Why have other giants, such as AMP, Telstra, Optus, Austar and Lucent Technologies, implemented huge cost-cutting programs and eliminated thousands of jobs? The answer is simple—to avoid going bust.

Today's successful organisations must foster innovation and master the art of change or they will become candidates for extinction. Victory will go to the organisations that maintain their flexibility, continually improve their quality, and beat their competition to the marketplace with a constant stream of innovative products and services. Domino's single-handedly brought on the demise of thousands of small pizza parlours whose managers thought they could continue doing what they had been doing for years. Amazon.com is putting a lot of independent bookstores out of business in many countries, as it proves that books can be sold successfully from an internet website. Dell has become the world's largest seller of computers by continually reinventing itself and outsmarting its competition.

An organisation's employees can be the impetus for innovation and change, or they can be a major stumbling block. The challenge for managers is to stimulate their employees' creativity and tolerance for change. The field of OB provides a wealth of ideas and techniques to aid in realising these goals.

HELPING EMPLOYEES BALANCE WORK/LIFE CONFLICTS

The typical employee in the 1960s or 1970s showed up at the workplace from Monday to Friday and did his or her job in eight- or nine-hour chunks of time. The workplace and hours were clearly specified. That is no longer true for a large segment of today's workforce. Employees are increasingly complaining that the line between work and non-work time has become blurred, creating personal conflicts and stress.[25]

A number of forces have contributed to blurring the lines between employees' work life and personal life. First, the creation of global organisations means their world never sleeps. At any time and on any day, for example, thousands of Malaysian, Singapore and Qantas airline flight crews are working somewhere. The need to consult with colleagues or customers eight or ten time zones away means that many employees of global firms are 'on call' 24 hours a day. Second, communication technology allows employees to do their work at home, in their cars, or on the beach in Thailand or on the Gold Coast in Queensland. This lets many people in technical and professional jobs do their work any time and from any place. Indeed, one of the authors of this book teaches his OB students over the internet and has maintained contact with them even when he was in Asia, Europe and North America attending conferences. Third, organisations are asking employees to put in longer hours. Finally, fewer families have only a single breadwinner. Today's married employee is typically part of a dual-career couple. This makes it increasingly difficult for married employees to find the time to fulfil commitments to home, spouse, children, parents and friends.

Employees are increasingly recognising that work is squeezing out personal lives, and they are not happy about it. For example, recent studies suggest that employees want jobs that give them flexibility in their work schedules so that they can better manage work/life conflicts.[26] In addition, the next generation of employees is likely to show similar concerns.[27] A majority of TAFE and university students say that attaining a balance between personal life and work is a primary career goal. They want 'a life' as well as a job. Organisations that don't help their people achieve work/life balance will find it increasingly hard to attract and retain the most capable and motivated employees. The increasing need will be for family-friendly organisations.

As you will see in later chapters, the field of OB offers a number of suggestions to guide managers in designing workplaces and jobs that can help employees deal with work/life conflicts.

IMPROVING ETHICAL BEHAVIOUR

In an organisational world characterised by retrenchments, expectations of increasing employee productivity and tough global competition in the marketplace, it's not altogether surprising that many employees feel pressured to cut corners, break rules and engage in other forms of questionable practices.

ethical dilemmas | Situations in which individuals are required to define right and wrong conduct.

Members of organisations are increasingly finding themselves facing **ethical dilemmas**, situations in which they are required to define right and wrong conduct. For example, should they 'blow the whistle' if they uncover illegal activities taking place in their company? Should they follow orders with which they don't personally agree? Do they give an inflated performance evaluation to an employee whom they like, knowing that such an evaluation could save that employee's job? Do they allow themselves to 'play politics' in the organisation if it will help their career advancement?

What constitutes good ethical behaviour has never been clearly defined. And, in recent years, the line differentiating right from wrong has become even more blurred. Employees see people all around them engaging in unethical practices—Australian politicians are charged for padding their travel accounts; successful executives use insider information for personal financial gain; some university administrators 'look the other way' when full-fee paying international students struggle to meet the standards; and even a president of the

United States distorted the truth under oath and broke the law—but survived impeachment for doing so. They hear people, when caught, giving excuses such as 'everyone does it', or 'you have to seize every advantage nowadays' or 'I never thought I'd get caught'.

Managers and their organisations are responding to this problem from a number of directions.[28] They are writing and distributing codes of ethics to guide employees through ethical dilemmas. They are offering seminars, workshops and similar training programs to try to improve ethical behaviours. They are providing in-house advisers who can be contacted, in many cases anonymously, for assistance in dealing with ethical issues. And they are creating protection mechanisms for employees who reveal internal unethical practices.

Today's manager needs to create an ethically healthy climate for his or her employees, where they can do their work productively and confront a minimal degree of ambiguity regarding what constitutes right and wrong behaviours. In upcoming chapters, we will discuss the kinds of actions managers can take to create an ethically healthy climate and to help employees sort through ethically ambiguous situations. We will also present a number of exercises that will allow you to think through ethical issues and assess how you would handle them.

WORKING IN NETWORKED ORGANISATIONS

Computerisation, the internet, and the ability to link computers within organisations and between organisations have created a different workplace for many employees—a networked organisation. It allows people to communicate and work together even though they may be thousands of kilometres apart. It also allows people to become independent contractors, who can telecommute via computer to workplaces around the globe and change employers as the demand for their services changes. Software programmers, graphic designers, systems analysts, technical writers, photo researchers, book editors and medical transcribers are just a few examples of jobs that people can now perform from home or other non-office locations.

The manager's job is different in a networked organisation, especially when it comes to managing people. For instance, motivating and leading people and making collaborative decisions 'online' requires different techniques than those needed in dealing with individuals who are physically present in a single location.

As more and more employees do their jobs linked to others through networks, managers need to develop new skills. OB can provide valuable insights to help with honing those skills.

COMING ATTRACTIONS: DEVELOPING AN OB MODEL

We conclude this chapter by presenting a general model that defines the field of OB, stakes out its parameters, and identifies its primary dependent and independent variables. The end result will be a 'coming attraction' of the topics making up the remainder of this book.

AN OVERVIEW

A **model** is an abstraction of reality, a simplified representation of some real-world phenomenon. A mannequin in a retail store is a model. So, too, is the accountant's formula: Assets + Liabilities = Owners' Equity. Figure 1.3 presents the skeleton on which

model | An abstraction of reality. A simplified representation of some real-world phenomenon.

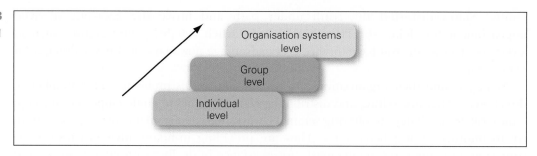

we will construct our OB model. It proposes that there are three levels of analysis in OB and that, as we move from the individual level to the organisation systems level, we add systematically to our understanding of behaviour in organisations. The three basic levels are analogous to building blocks; each level is constructed on the previous level. Group concepts grow out of the foundation laid in the individual section; we overlay structural constraints on the individual and group in order to arrive at organisational behaviour.

THE DEPENDENT VARIABLES

dependent variable | A response that is affected by an independent variable.

Dependent variables are the key factors that you want to explain or predict and that are affected by some other factor. What are the primary dependent variables in OB? Scholars have historically tended to emphasise productivity, absenteeism, turnover and job satisfaction. More recently, two additional variables—deviant workplace behaviour and organisational citizenship—have been added to this list. Let's briefly review each of these variables to ensure that we understand what they mean and why they have achieved their level of distinction.

PRODUCTIVITY

productivity | A performance measure that includes effectiveness and efficiency.

effectiveness | Achievement of goals.

efficiency | The ratio of effective output to the input required to achieve it.

An organisation is productive if it achieves its goals and does so by transferring inputs to outputs at the lowest cost. As such, **productivity** implies a concern for both **effectiveness** and **efficiency**.

A hospital, for example, is *effective* when it successfully meets the needs of its patients. It is *efficient* when it can do so at a low cost. If a hospital manages to achieve higher output from its present staff by reducing the average number of days a patient is confined to a bed or by increasing the number of staff–patient contacts per day, we say that the hospital has gained productive efficiency. A business firm is effective when it attains its sales or market share goals, but its productivity also depends on achieving those goals efficiently. Popular measures of organisational efficiency include return on investment, profit per dollar of sales and output per hour of labour.

We can also look at productivity from the perspective of the individual employee. Take the cases of Mike and Ted, who are both long-distance truck-drivers. If Mike is supposed to haul his fully loaded rig from Sydney to its destination in Perth in 75 hours or less, he is effective if he makes the trip within that time period. But measures of productivity must take into account the costs incurred in reaching the goal. That is where efficiency comes in. Let's assume that Mike made the Sydney to Perth run in 68 hours and averaged 5 kilometres per litre of fuel. Ted, on the other hand, made the trip in 68 hours also, but averaged 6.5 kilometres per litre. (Their rigs and loads are identical.) Both Mike and Ted were effective—they accomplished their goal—but Ted was more efficient than Mike because his rig consumed less fuel and, therefore, he achieved his goal at a lower cost.

Organisations in service industries need to include additionally 'attention to customer needs and requirements' in assessing their effectiveness. Why? Because in these types of businesses, there is a clear chain of cause-and-effect running from employee attitudes and behaviour to customer attitudes and behaviour to an organisation's revenues and profits. The US department store Sears, in fact, has carefully documented this chain.[29] The company's management found that a 5 per cent improvement in employee attitudes led to a 1.3 per cent increase in customer satisfaction, which in turn translated into a 0.5 per cent improvement in revenue growth. More specifically, Sears found that by training employees to improve the employee–customer interaction, it was able to improve customer satisfaction by 4 per cent over a 12-month period, which generated an estimated US$200 million in additional revenues.

In summary, one of OB's main concerns is productivity. We want to know what factors will influence the effectiveness and efficiency of individuals, of groups and of the overall organisation.

ABSENTEEISM

Australian Bureau of Statistics figures indicate that illness costs Australian businesses $37 billion per year. Furthermore, Health Services Australia research found that in any given week, 4 per cent of the Australian workforce is absent, costing Australian business $7 billion each year.[30]

At the job level, a one-day absence by a clerical employee can cost an employer several hundred dollars in reduced efficiency and increased supervisory workload. These figures indicate the importance to an organisation of keeping **absenteeism** low.

absenteeism | The failure to report to work.

It is obviously difficult for an organisation to operate smoothly and to attain its objectives if employees fail to report to do their jobs. The work flow is disrupted, and often important decisions must be delayed. In organisations that rely heavily on assembly-line production, absenteeism can be considerably more than a disruption; it can result in a drastic reduction in the quality of output, and, in some cases, it can bring about a complete shutdown of the production facility. But levels of absenteeism beyond the normal range in any organisation have a direct impact on that organisation's effectiveness and efficiency.

Are *all* absences bad? Probably not. Although most absences have a negative impact on the organisation, we can conceive of situations in which the organisation may benefit by an employee's voluntarily choosing not to come to work. For example, illness, fatigue or excess stress can significantly decrease an employee's productivity. In jobs in which an employee needs to be alert—surgeons and airline pilots are obvious examples—it may well be better for the organisation if the employee doesn't report to work rather than show up and perform poorly. The cost of an accident in such jobs could be prohibitive. Even in managerial jobs, where mistakes are less spectacular, performance may be improved when managers absent themselves from work rather than make a poor decision under stress. But these examples are clearly atypical. For the most part, we can assume that organisations benefit when employee absenteeism is low.

TURNOVER

Turnover is the voluntary and involuntary permanent withdrawal from an organisation. A high turnover rate results in increased recruiting, selection and training costs. What are those costs? They are higher than you might think. For example, in Australia the cost for a typical information-technology company to replace a programmer or systems analyst can

turnover | The voluntary and involuntary permanent withdrawal from an organisation.

be approximately $50 000; and the cost of a retail store to replace a lost sales clerk can be approximately $30 000. In addition, a high rate of turnover can disrupt the efficient running of an organisation when knowledgeable and experienced personnel leave and replacements must be found and prepared to assume positions of responsibility.

All organisations, of course, have some turnover. In fact, if the 'right' people are leaving the organisation—the marginal and submarginal employees—turnover can be positive. It may create the opportunity to replace an underperforming individual with someone who has higher skills or motivation, open up increased opportunities for promotions, and add new and fresh ideas to the organisation.[31] In today's changing world of work, reasonable levels of employee-initiated turnover facilitate organisational flexibility and employee independence, and they can lessen the need for management-initiated layoffs.

But turnover often involves the loss of people the organisation doesn't want to lose. For example, one study covering 900 employees who had resigned from their jobs found that 92 per cent earned performance ratings of 'satisfactory' or better from their superiors.[32] So, when turnover is excessive, or when it involves valuable performers, it can be a disruptive factor, hindering the organisation's effectiveness and, from a management perspective, indicating that there may be problems in the workplace.

DEVIANT WORKPLACE BEHAVIOUR

Given the cost of absenteeism and turnover to employers, more and more OB researchers are studying these behaviours as indicators or markers of deviant behaviour. Deviance can range from someone playing his music too loud, to violence. Managers need to understand this wide range of behaviours to address any form of employee dissatisfaction. If managers don't understand why an employee is acting up, the problem will never be solved.

deviant workplace behaviour | Antisocial actions by organisational members that intentionally violate established norms and that result in negative consequences for the organisation, its members, or both.

We can define **deviant workplace behaviour** (also called antisocial behaviour or workplace incivility) as voluntary behaviour that violates significant organisational norms and, in doing so, threatens the well-being of the organisation or its members. What are organisational norms in this context? They can be company policies that prohibit certain behaviours such as stealing. But they also can be unspoken rules that are widely shared, such as not playing loud music in one's workspace. Consider, for example, an employee who plays Powderfinger at work with the speakers amped up. Yes, he may be showing up at work, but he may not be getting his work done, and he could also be irritating co-workers or customers (unless they are Powderfinger fans themselves). But deviant workplace behaviours can be much more serious than an employee playing loud music. For example, an employee may insult a colleague, steal, gossip excessively, or engage in sabotage, all of which can wreak havoc on an organisation.

Managers want to understand the source of workplace deviance in order to avoid a chaotic work environment, and workplace deviance can also have a considerable financial impact. Although the annual costs are hard to quantify, estimates are that deviant behaviour costs employers dearly—for example, in the United States, from US$4.2 billion annually for violence to US$200 billion for theft to US$7.1 billion for corporate security against cyberattacks.[33]

Deviant workplace behaviour is an important concept because it is a response to dissatisfaction, and employees express this dissatisfaction in many ways. Controlling one behaviour may be ineffective unless one gets to the root cause. The sophisticated manager will deal with root causes of problems that may result in deviance, rather than solving one surface problem (excessive absenteeism) only to see another one crop up (increased theft or sabotage).

ORGANISATIONAL CITIZENSHIP BEHAVIOUR

Organisational citizenship behaviour (OCB) is discretionary behaviour that isn't part of an employee's formal job requirements, but that nevertheless promotes the effective functioning of the organisation.[34]

Successful organisations need employees who will do more than their usual job duties—who will provide performance that is *beyond* expectations. In today's dynamic workplace, where tasks are increasingly done in teams and where flexibility is critical, organisations need employees who will engage in 'good citizenship' behaviours such as making constructive statements about their work group and the organisation, helping others on their team, volunteering for extra job activities, avoiding unnecessary conflicts, showing care for organisational property, respecting the spirit as well as the letter of rules and regulations, and gracefully tolerating the occasional work-related impositions and nuisances.

Organisations want and need employees who will do those things that aren't in any job description. And the evidence indicates that the organisations that have such employees outperform those that don't.[35] As a result, OB is concerned with OCB as a dependent variable.

JOB SATISFACTION

The final dependent variable we will look at is **job satisfaction**, which we define simply, at this point, as an individual's general attitude towards his or her job. (We expand considerably on that definition in later chapters.) Unlike the previous five variables, job satisfaction represents an attitude, rather than a behaviour. Why, then, has it become a primary dependent variable? It has become so for two reasons: its demonstrated relationship to performance factors; and the value preferences held by many OB researchers.

The belief that satisfied employees are more productive than dissatisfied employees has been a basic tenet among managers for many years. Although much evidence questions that assumed causal relationship, it can be argued that advanced societies should be concerned not only with the quantity of life—that is, concerns such as higher productivity and material acquisitions—but also with its quality. Those researchers with strong humanistic values argue that satisfaction is a legitimate objective of an organisation. Not only is satisfaction negatively related to absenteeism and turnover, but also, they argue, organisations have a responsibility to provide employees with jobs that are challenging and intrinsically rewarding. Therefore, although job satisfaction represents an attitude rather than a behaviour, OB researchers typically consider it an important dependent variable.

THE INDEPENDENT VARIABLES

What are the main determinants of productivity, absenteeism, turnover, deviant workplace behaviour, OCB and job satisfaction? Our answer to that question brings us to the **independent variables**. Consistent with our belief that organisational behaviour can best be understood when viewed essentially as a set of increasingly complex building blocks, the base, or first level, of our model lies in understanding individual behaviour.

INDIVIDUAL-LEVEL VARIABLES

It has been said that 'managers, unlike parents, must work with used, not new, human beings—human beings whom others have gotten to first'.[36] When individuals enter an

organisational citizenship behaviour (OCB) | Discretionary behaviour that isn't part of an employee's formal job requirements, but that nevertheless promotes the effective functioning of the organisation.

job satisfaction | An individual's general attitude towards his or her job.

independent variable | The presumed cause of some change in the dependent variable.

CULTURE, ETHICS AND PRODUCTIVITY AT NAB

The National Australia Bank (NAB), Australia's biggest bank, sacked eight people, including four senior executives, after a damning report into its 2004 $360 million currency options scandal. The extent of the cultural breakdown at NAB was revealed by David Lewis who headed the investigation team into the scandal. His team found that there were issues in the systems and culture that allowed the dealers to conceal losses and record false trades.

Lewis's team interviewed a lot of people. The four traders who were at the centre of the scandal were young, highly motivated and very gung ho. One thing became clear to Lewis: the people involved didn't think they had done anything wrong. Lewis added that the investigation revealed widespread issues within NAB, despite a sophisticated system of controls, and most were connected with cultural and human elements, as opposed to system breakdowns. In particular, there was a culture in which risk management controls were negotiable rather than taken as checks and balances for risk-taking behaviour. However, despite the huge cultural breakdown at NAB, Lewis said, the bank's response has been impressive, and within the organisation the whole affair has been enormously cathartic. The bank has set about a program of corporate renewal that is unprecedented in Australian financial institutions. There is a greater sensitivity to organisational behaviour and to the relationships between culture, ethics and the drive for productivity and the need for cultural change.

Elizabeth Hunter, as head of NAB's people and culture section, is entrenched in the ambitious transformation program designed to redevelop and revitalise the bank. Hunter pointed to a number of issues that the program is attempting to tackle.

The organisation is too bureaucratic and cumbersome. It was inward-looking and not customer-focused. It had a weak compliance framework. And most significant, the investigation into the scandal highlighted major gaps in NAB's cultural framework. Hunter revealed that while the bank had a set of values, people weren't held accountable and values weren't reflected in the way people were assessed. Culture change programs were voluntary, and there was a lack of visible and consistent leadership in this area.

The 2005 employee opinion survey results strongly reinforced that staff are committed to NAB's customers, but it also highlighted a major challenge of getting staff to rebuild their connection with NAB. Hunter said, 'We recognise we have a way to go on our cultural journey. The thing we're most encouraged about is that our people are passionate about the customer and providing outstanding service—this is a great base on which to build the business and culture we need.' The NAB experience highlights for all managers the need to have a sound understanding of organisational behaviour in order to manage the intricacies of an organisation's culture.

Culture was found to be a significant factor in the currency options scandal at National Australia Bank (NAB). The investigation found that the bank's gung ho approach to risk management allowed dealers to conceal losses and record false trades.

SOURCES: Melinda Finch, 'NAB and the Art of Corporate Renewal', *Human Resources*, no. 104, 16 May 2006, pp. 10–11; Stuart Fagg, 'Inside NAB's Culture Nightmare', *Human Resources*, 6 September 2005; and Stephen Long, 'Eight Sacked over NAB Currency Trading Scandal', *The World Today*, 12 March 2004.

organisation, they are a bit like used cars. Each is different. Some are 'low-mileage'—they have been treated carefully and have had only limited exposure to the realities of the elements. Others are 'well worn', having been driven over some rough roads. This metaphor indicates that people enter organisations with certain characteristics that will influence their behaviour at work. The more obvious of these are personal or biographical characteristics such as age, gender and marital status; personality characteristics; an inherent emotional framework; values and attitudes; and basic ability levels. These characteristics are essentially intact when an individual enters the workforce, and, for the most part, there is little management can do to alter them. Yet, they have a very real impact on employee behaviour. Therefore, each of these factors—biographical characteristics, ability, values, attitudes, personality and emotions—will be discussed as independent variables in Part 2 of the text.

There are four other individual-level variables that have been shown to affect employee behaviour: perception, individual decision making, learning and motivation. Those topics will also be introduced and discussed in Part 2.

GROUP-LEVEL VARIABLES

The behaviour of people in groups is more than the sum total of all the individuals acting in their own way. The complexity of our model is increased when we acknowledge that people's behaviour when they are in groups is different from their behaviour when they are alone. Therefore, the next step in the development of an understanding of OB is the study of group behaviour.

In Part 3, Chapter 9 lays the foundation for an understanding of the dynamics of group behaviour. That chapter discusses how individuals in groups are influenced by the patterns of behaviour they are expected to exhibit, what the group considers to be acceptable standards of behaviour, and the degree to which group members are attracted to each other. Chapter 10 translates our understanding of groups to the design of effective work teams. Chapters 11 to 15 demonstrate how communication patterns, leadership, power and politics, and levels of conflict affect group behaviour.

ORGANISATION SYSTEMS-LEVEL VARIABLES

Organisational behaviour reaches its highest level of sophistication when we add formal structure to our previous knowledge of individual and group behaviour. Just as groups are more than the sum of their individual members, so are organisations more than the sum of their member groups. The design of the formal organisation, work processes and jobs; the internal culture; and the organisational performance systems (including training and development, staff evaluation and stress management) all have an impact on the dependent variables. These are discussed in detail in Part 4, Chapters 16 to 18.

TOWARDS A CONTINGENCY OB MODEL

Our final model is shown in Figure 1.4. It shows the six key dependent variables and a large number of independent variables, organised by level of analysis, that research indicates have varying effects on the former. As complicated as this model is, it still doesn't do justice to the complexity of the OB subject matter, but it should help to explain why the chapters in this book are arranged as they are and help you to explain and predict the behaviour of people at work.

For the most part, our model doesn't explicitly identify the vast number of contingency variables because of the tremendous complexity that would be involved in such a diagram.

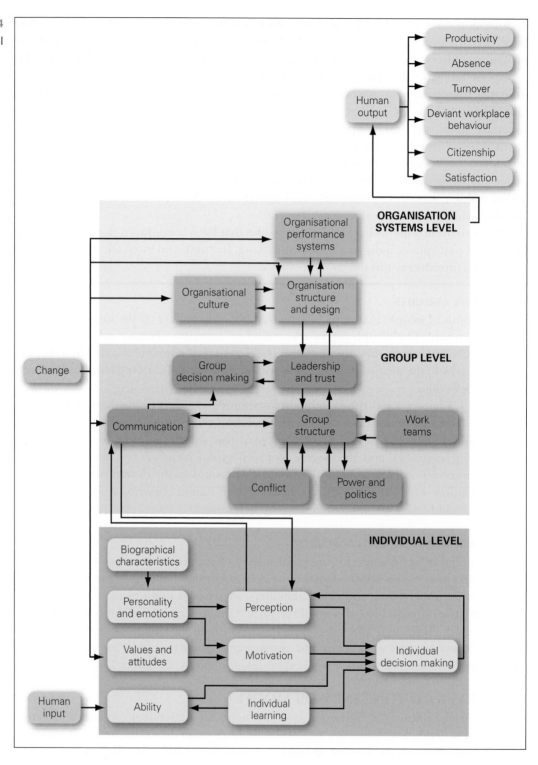

Rather, throughout this book we will introduce important contingency variables that will improve the explanatory linkage between the independent and dependent variables in our OB model.

Note that we have included the concept of change in Figure 1.4, acknowledging that the dynamics of behaviour is an individual, group and organisational issue. Specifically, in the final chapter, we will discuss the change process and ways to manage organisational change, and identify key change issues currently facing managers.

Also note that Figure 1.4 includes linkages between the three levels of analysis. For example, organisational structure is linked to leadership. This link is meant to convey that authority and leadership are related; management exerts its influence on group behaviour through leadership. Similarly, communication is the means by which individuals transmit information; thus, it is the link between individual and group behaviour.

- Managers need to develop their interpersonal or people skills if they are going to be effective in their jobs. Organisational behaviour (OB) is a field of study that investigates the impact that individuals, groups and structure have on behaviour within an organisation, and then applies that knowledge to make organisations work more effectively. Specifically, OB focuses on how to improve productivity, reduce absenteeism, turnover and deviant workplace behaviour, and increase employee citizenship and job satisfaction.

- We all hold generalisations about the behaviour of people. Some of our generalisations may provide valid insights into human behaviour, but many are erroneous. Organisational behaviour uses systematic study to improve predictions of behaviour that would be made from intuition alone. But, because people are different, we need to look at OB in a contingency framework, using situational variables to moderate cause-and-effect relationships.

- Organisational behaviour offers both challenges and opportunities for managers. It offers specific insights to improve a manager's people skills. It recognises differences and helps managers to see the value of workforce diversity and practices that may need to be changed when managing in different countries. It can improve quality and employee productivity by showing managers how to empower their people, design and implement change programs, and help employees balance work/life conflicts. It provides suggestions for helping managers meet chronic labour shortages. It can help managers to cope in a world of temporariness and to learn ways to stimulate innovation.

- Finally, OB can offer managers guidance in creating an ethically healthy work climate.

POINT / COUNTERPOINT

In Search of the Quick Fix

● POINT

Walk into your nearest major bookstore. You will undoubtedly find a large section of books dedicated to management and managing human behaviour. A close look at the titles will reveal that there is certainly no shortage of popular books on topics related to organisational behaviour. To illustrate the point, consider the following popular book titles that are currently available on the topic of leadership:

- *Catch! A Fishmonger's Guide to Greatness* (BerrettKoehler, 2003)
- *Leading with the Heart: Coach K's Successful Strategies for Basketball, Business, and Life* (Warner Business Books, 2001)
- *The Art of Leadership by Sun Tzu* (Premier, 2000)
- *Power Plays: Shakespeare's Lessons on Leadership and Management* (Simon & Schuster, 2000)
- *The Hod Carrier: Leadership Lessons Learned on a Ladder* (Kimbell, 2002)
- *Leadership Wisdom from the Monk Who Sold His Ferrari* (Hay House, 2003)
- *Tony Soprano on Management: Leadership Lessons Inspired by America's Favourite Mobster* (Berkeley, 2004)
- *If You Don't Make Waves You'll Drown: 10 Hard Charging Strategies for Leading in Politically Correct Times* (John Wiley & Sons, 2005)
- *Organizational Jazz: Extraordinary Performance through Extraordinary Leadership* (eContent Management, 2005)

Organisations are always looking for leaders; and managers and manager-wannabes are continually looking for ways to hone their leadership skills. Publishers respond to this demand by offering hundreds of titles that provide insights into the complex subject of leadership. Books like these can provide people with the secrets to leadership that others know about.

● COUNTERPOINT

Beware of the quick fix! We all want to find quick and simplistic solutions to our complex problems. But here's the bad news: on problems related to organisational behaviour, the quick and simple solutions are often wrong because they fail to consider the diversity among organisations, situations and individuals. As Einstein said, 'Everything should be made as simple as possible, but not simpler.'

When it comes to trying to understand people at work, there is no shortage of simplistic ideas and the books and consultants to promote them. And these books aren't just on leadership. Consider three recent bestsellers. *Who Moved My Cheese?* is a metaphor about two mice that is meant to convey the benefits of accepting change. *Fish!* tells how a fish market in Seattle made its jobs motivating. And *Whale Done!* proposes that managers can learn a lot about motivating people from techniques used by whale trainers at Sea World. Are the 'insights' from these books generalisable to people working in hundreds of different countries, in a thousand different organisations, and doing a million different jobs? It's very unlikely.

Popular books on organisational behaviour often have cute titles and are fun to read. But they can be dangerous. They make the job of managing people seem much simpler than it really is. They are also often based on the author's opinions, rather than substantive research.

Organisational behaviour is a complex subject. There are few, if any, simple statements about human behaviour that are generalisable to all people in all situations. Should you really try to apply leadership insights you got from a book on Sun Tzu, Shakespeare or jazz to managing software engineers in the 21st century?

The capitalistic system ensures that when a need exists, opportunistic individuals will surface to fill that need. When it comes to managing people at work, there is clearly a need for valid and reliable insights to guide managers and those aspiring to managerial positions. However, most of the offerings available at your local bookstore tend to be overly simplistic solutions. To the degree that people buy these books and enthusiastically expect them to provide them with the secrets to effective management, they do a disservice to themselves and those they are trying to manage.

QUESTIONS FOR REVIEW

MyOBLab Do you understand this chapter's content?
Find out at **www.pearsoned.com.au/MyOBLab**

1. How are OB concepts addressed in management functions, roles and skills?
2. Define *organisational behaviour*. Relate it to *management*.
3. What is an organisation? Is the family unit an organisation? Explain.
4. Identify and contrast the three general management roles.
5. What is a 'contingency approach' to OB?
6. Contrast the contributions of psychology and sociology to OB.
7. 'Behaviour is generally predictable, so there is no need to formally study OB.' Why is this statement wrong?
8. What are the three levels of analysis in our OB model? Are they related? If so, how?
9. If job satisfaction isn't a behaviour, why is it considered an important dependent variable?
10. What are effectiveness and efficiency, and how are they related to organisational behaviour?

QUESTIONS FOR CRITICAL THINKING

1. Contrast the research comparing effective managers with successful managers. What are the implications from the research for practising managers?
2. Why do you think the subject of OB might be criticised as being 'only common sense', when one would rarely hear such a criticism of a course in physics or statistics?
3. Millions of workers have lost their jobs due to downsizing. At the same time, many organisations are complaining that they cannot find qualified people to fill vacancies. How do you explain this apparent contradiction?
4. On a scale of 1 to 10 measuring the sophistication of a scientific discipline in predicting phenomena, mathematical physics would probably be a 10. Where do you think OB would fall on the scale? Why?
5. What do you think is the single most critical 'people' problem facing managers today? Give specific support for your position.

EXPERIENTIAL EXERCISE

Workforce Diversity

Purpose:
To learn about the different needs of a diverse workforce.

Time required:
Approximately 40 minutes.

Participants and roles:
Divide the class into six groups of approximately equal size. Each group is assigned one of the following roles:

- *Nell* is 28 years old. She is a divorced mother of three children, aged three, five and seven. She is the department head. She earns $65 000 a year on her job and receives another $4500 a year in child support from her ex-husband.
- *Enid* is a 72-year-old widow. She works 25 hours a week to supplement her $10 000 annual pension. Including her hourly wage of $10, she earns $22 000 a year.
- *John* is a 34-year-old Maori born in New Zealand who is now an Australian permanent resident. He is married and the father of two small children. John attends university at night and is within a year of earning his bachelor's degree. His salary is $35 000 a year. His wife is a solicitor and earns approximately $70 000 a year.
- *Lu* is a 26-year-old physically impaired male Asian Australian. He is single and has a master's degree in education. Lu is paralysed and confined to a wheelchair as a result of a car accident. He earns $40 000 a year.
- *Maria* is a single 22-year-old Samoan woman. Born and raised in Samoa, she came to Australia only three months ago. Maria's English needs considerable improvement. She earns $25 000 a year as a cleaner.
- *Mike* is a 16-year-old white male high school student who works ten hours a week after school and during holidays. He earns $10.20 an hour, or approximately $5600 a year.

The members of each group are to assume the character consistent with their assigned role.

Background:

Our six participants work for a company that has recently installed a flexible benefits program. Instead of the traditional 'one benefit package fits all', the company is allocating an additional 25 per cent of each employee's annual pay to be used for discretionary benefits. Those benefits and their annual cost are listed below.

- Supplementary health care for employee:
  Plan A (no deductible and pays 90 per cent)
  = $3000
  Plan B ($200 deductible and pays 80 per cent)
  = $2000
  Plan C ($1000 deductible and pays 70 per cent)
  = $500
- Supplementary health care for dependants (same deductibles and percentages as above):
  Plan A = $2000
  Plan B = $1500
  Plan C = $500
- Supplementary dental plan = $500
- Life insurance:
  Plan A ($25 000 coverage) = $500
  Plan B ($50 000 coverage) = $1000
  Plan C ($100 000 coverage) = $2000
  Plan D ($250 000 coverage) = $3000
- Mental health plan = $500
- Prepaid legal assistance = $300
- Leave = 2 per cent of annual pay for each week, up to six weeks a year
- Superannuation at retirement equal to approximately 50 per cent of final annual earnings = $1500
- Four-day work week during the summer months (available only to full-time employees) = 4 per cent of annual pay
- Day-care services (after company contribution) = $2000 for all of an employee's children, regardless of number
- Company-provided transportation to and from work = $750
- University fees reimbursement = $1000
- Language class fees reimbursement = $500

The task:

1. Each group has 15 minutes to develop a flexible benefits package that consumes 25 per cent (and no more!) of their character's pay.
2. After completing step 1, each group appoints a spokesperson who describes to the entire class the benefits package they have arrived at for their character.
3. The entire class then discusses the results. How did the needs, concerns and problems of each participant influence the group's decision? What do the results suggest for trying to motivate a diverse workforce?

Note: Special thanks to Professor Penny Wright (San Diego State University) for her suggestions during the development of this exercise.

ETHICAL DILEMMA

Lying in Business

Do you think it is ever OK to lie? If one was negotiating for the release of hostages, most people would probably agree that if lying would lead to their safe release, it's OK. What about in business, where the stakes are rarely life or death? Business executives such as Rodney Adler have gone to gaol for lying (making false statements about investments in HIH Insurance). Is misrepresentation or omitting factors OK as long as there is no outright lie?

Consider the negotiation process. A good negotiator never shows all his or her cards, right? And so omitting certain information is just part of the process. Well, it may surprise you to learn that the law will hold you liable for omitting information if the partial disclosure is misleading, or if one side has superior information not accessible to the other.

In one case (*Jordan v Duff and Phelps*), the company (Duff and Phelps) withheld information from an employee—Jordan—about the impending sale of the company. The problem: Jordan was leaving the organisation and therefore sold his shares in the company. Ten days later, those shares became worth much more once the sale of the company became public. Jordan sued his former employer on the argument that it should have disclosed this information. Duff and Phelps countered that it never lied to Jordan. The Court of Appeals in the United States argued that in such situations one party cannot take 'opportunistic advantage' of the other. In the eyes of the law, sometimes omitting relevant facts can be as bad as lying.

QUESTIONS

1. In a business context, is it ever OK to lie?
2. If you answered 'yes', what are those situations? Why is it OK to lie in these situations?
3. In business, is withholding information for one's advantage the same as lying? Why or why not?
4. In a business context, if someone has something to gain by lying, what percentage of the people, do you think, would lie?

SOURCES: Based on 'Brain Scans Detect More Activity in Those Who Lie', *Reuters*, 29 November 2004: <www.msnbc.msn.com/id/6609019>; P. Ekman and E. L. Rosenberg, *What the Facts Reveal: Basic and Applied Studies of Spontaneous Expression Using the Facial Action Coding System (CAPS)*, 2nd expanded ed. (New York: Oxford University Press, 2004; and Rodney Adler: <www.abc.net.au/sundayprofile/stories/s1345088.htm>.

CASE STUDY

1

The 'High School Casual'

The Australian retail industry provides approximately 15 per cent of all jobs in Australia and is a heavy user of casual employment, with about 45 per cent of retail jobs reportedly casual in nature. The food, personal and household retail sectors of the Australian market are dominated by Coles Myer Ltd and Woolworths Limited. Most Australians are familiar with the store brands owned by the two giants, such as Kmart, Target and Big W. Listed in the Fortune 500 Global Index, Coles Myer employs over 190 000 staff across 2600 stores. Woolworths follows with 145 000 staff employed in 1600 stores Australia-wide. Combined, these two companies account for 22 per cent of all people employed in retail trade.

Competing against such retail giants is an independent retail variety store, Waltons' Emporium. Waltons' Emporium employs 35 high school students as casual employees to work late night and weekend trading. Most of the casuals are hired from the age of 15, generally as a result of 'cold calling' at the store for casual work. The store's trainee manager selects the casual employee based on the young person's enthusiasm, presentation and the results of a simple numerical test. A number of the casuals retain their job throughout their high school years before attending university or launching into full-time work with another employer. However, it is not unusual for Waltons' Emporium casuals to resign from their position because of study pressures. In some cases, they resign to work for more appealing outlets such as music stores, trendy fashion stores or 'classier' department stores.

Working hours can vary, although the casuals generally anticipate Friday evening and all day Saturday. However, unexpectedly and without reason, a casual will be dropped from a shift for two or three weeks. The perception among the casuals is that this is a covert means of punishment, perhaps for being observed for talking too much, taking too long on a tea break, or an incorrectly balanced cash register. They are never quite sure of how the store management views their performance. They are not subject to any formal performance review because they are not seen by Waltons' management as a source of future full-time employees. For the casuals, work at the store reverts very quickly to a 'means to an end'; that is, to earn money for reasons such as saving for a car and/or supporting social activities.

Relations between the casual staff and full-time staff are not particularly affable at Waltons' Emporium. During the holiday period, the casual staff work additional daytime shifts. However, a number of the full-time staff find they are more of a hindrance than a help because they assume the casuals have a higher level of knowledge about the store operations than they have in reality. The high school casuals, in return, generally find the full-time staff to be disparaging and impatient.

During the first two weeks of employment, on-the-job training takes place on duties that specifically relate to customer service at the checkout, such as operating the scanner and balancing the register. Apart from this, training on aspects such as product lines, store layout, weekly catalogue specials and general customer service isn't provided to the casuals. What is available in this type of training is reserved for the full-time staff. The result is that when approached by customers seeking product information, the high school casual is often in the dark as to what advice he or she can give them. One or two supervisors are rostered to oversee the store operations during these times, but they too are often casual employees with limited knowledge in aspects beyond the customer checkout operations. Furthermore, some supervisors display demeanours that intimidate inexperienced junior employees, rendering them unapproachable. The result is that the high school casual, working on the shop floor, often gives poor service and assistance to duly unimpressed customers.

QUESTIONS

1. Organise the issues raised in the case into individual, group and organisational system-level issues.

2. Discuss store management's approach to the high school casuals in terms of management's planning, organising, leading and controlling functions.

3. What prediction would you make about the likely level of the high school casuals'

organisational citizenship and the likelihood of absenteeism and turnover?

SOURCES: Australian Bureau of Statistics, *Australian Labour Market Statistics, Retail Trade*, May 2006, Cat. No. 6105.0, Table 2.2; Cable News Network: <http://money.cnn.com/magazines/fortune/global500/2006/> (24 August 2006); Coles Myer Ltd: <www.colesmyer.com.au> (24 August 2006); Commonwealth of Australia, 'Industry Strategies Taskforce National Strategy for the Retail Industry' (2005): <www.workplace.gov.au> (24 August 2006); and Woolworths Limited: <www.woolworthslimited.com.au> (24 August 2006).

ENDNOTES

1. Kristen Le Mesurier, 'Rubbishing the Competition', *Business Review Weekly*, 31 August 2006, pp. 98–99; and Janine Perrett, 'Garbo Doesn't Want to be Alone', *Sydney Morning Herald*, 20 August 2004: <http://businessnetwork.smh.com.au/articles/2004/10/21/677.html> (31 August 2006).

2. See, for example, R. A. Baron and G. D. Markman, 'Beyond Social Capital: How Social Skills Can Enhance Entrepreneurs' Success', *Academy of Management Executive*, February 2000, pp. 106–16.

3. See, for instance, C. Penttila, 'Hiring Hardships', *Entrepreneur*, October 2002, pp. 34–35.

4. *The 2002 National Study of the Changing Workforce* (New York: Families and Work Institute, 2002).

5. Georgina Curry. 'Most Value Pleasure over Pay Rate—Survey', *The Canberra Times*, 8 April 2001.

6. 'Staff Seek Paths', *Courier-Mail*, 29 January 2002.

7. H. Fayol, *Industrial and General Administration* (Paris: Dunod, 1916).

8. H. Mintzberg, *The Nature of Managerial Work* (Upper Saddle River, NJ: Prentice Hall, 1973).

9. R. L. Katz, 'Skills of an Effective Administrator', *Harvard Business Review*, September–October 1974, pp. 90–102.

10. F. Luthans, 'Successful vs. Effective Real Managers', *Academy of Management Executive*, May 1988, pp. 127–32; and F. Luthans, R. M. Hodgetts and

S. A. Rosenkrantz, *Real Managers* (Cambridge, MA: Ballinger, 1988). See also F. Shipper and J. Davy, 'A Model and Investigation of Managerial Skills, Employees' Attitudes, and Managerial Performance', *Leadership Quarterly*, vol. 13, 2002, pp. 95–120.

11. P. H. Langford, 'Importance of Relationship Management for the Career Success of Australian Managers', *Australian Journal of Psychology*, December 2000, pp. 163–69.

12. See, for instance, J. E. Garcia and K. S. Keleman, 'What is Organizational Behavior Anyhow?', paper presented at the 16th Annual Organizational Behavior Teaching Conference, Columbia, Missouri, June 1989; and C. Heath and S. B. Sitkin, 'Big-B Versus Big-O: What is Organizational about Organizational Behavior?', *Journal of Organizational Behavior*, February 2001, pp. 43–58. For a review of what one eminent researcher believes *should* be included in organisational behaviour, based on survey data, see J. B. Miner, 'The Rated Importance, Scientific Validity, and Practical Usefulness of Organizational Behavior Theories: A Quantitative Review', *Academy of Management Learning & Education*, September 2003, pp. 250–68.

13. See F. D. Richard, C. F. Bond, Jr. and J. J. Stokes-Zoota, '"That is Completely Obvious . . . and Important": Lay Judgments of Social Psychological Findings', *Personality and Social*

Psychological Bulletin, April 2001, pp. 497–505; and L. A. Burke and J. E. Moore, 'A Perennial Dilemma in OB Education: Engaging the Traditional Student', *Academy of Management Learning & Education*, March 2003, pp. 37–52.

14. 'In Finland, Fine for Speeding Sets Record', *International Herald Tribune*, 11 February 2004, p. 2.

15. Chris Woodyard, 'War, Terrorism Scare off Business Travelers', *USA Today*, 25 March 2003.

16. O. C. Richard, 'Racial Diversity, Business Strategy, and Firm Performance: A Resource-Based View', *Academy of Management Journal*, April 2000, pp. 164–77.

17. Australian Bureau of Statistics: <www.ausstats.abs.gov.au/ausstats/subscriber.nsf/0/8383493CEB94F224CA2571290070FF86/$File/6106055001_2003.pdf>; and <www.abs.gov.au/AUSSTATS/abs@.nsf/DetailsPage/6302.0May%202006?OpenDocument> (31 August 2006).

18. See M. E. A. Jayne and R. L. Dipboye, 'Leveraging Diversity to Improve Business Performance: Research Findings and Recommendations for Organizations', *Human Resource Management*, Winter 2004, pp. 409–24; S. E. Jackson and A. Joshi, 'Research on Domestic and International Diversity in Organizations: A Merger that Works?', in N. Anderson et al. (eds), *Handbook of Industrial, Work & Organizational Psychology*, vol. 2 (Thousand Oaks, CA: Sage, 2001),

pp. 206–31; and L. Smith, 'The Business Case for Diversity', *Fortune*, 13 October 2003, pp. S8–S12.

19. '$171 Billion: The Cost of Poor Productivity', *Human Resources*, no. 109, 25 July 2006, p. 9: <www.human resourcesmagazine.com.au/articles/41/0C0 42E41.asp?Type=59&Category=917> (31 August 2006).

20. David James, 'The Quality Equation', *Business Review Weekly*, 2–8 October 2003, pp. 64–65.

21. This section is based on M. Bolch, 'The Coming Crunch', *Training*, April 2001, pp. 54–58; P. Nyhan, 'As Baby Boomers Retire, They'll Leave Big Gap in the Work Force, Chao Warns', *Seattle Post-Intelligencer*, 24 August 2001, p. C1; G. M. McEvoy and M. J. Blahna, 'Engagement or Disengagement? Older Workers and the Looming Labor Shortage', *Business Horizons*, September–October 2001, pp. 46–52; P. Francese, 'Looming Labor Shortages', *American Demographics*, November 2001, pp. 34–35; and D. Eisenberg, 'The Coming Job Boom', *Time*, 6 May 2002, pp. 40–44.

22. See, for instance, E. Naumann and D. W. Jackson, Jr., 'One More Time: How Do You Satisfy Customers?', *Business Horizons*, vol. 42, no. 3, 1999, pp. 71–76; W-C. Tsai, 'Determinants and Consequences of Employee Displayed Positive Emotions', *Journal of Management*, vol. 27, no. 4, 2001, pp. 497–512; S. D. Pugh, 'Service with a Smile: Emotional Contagion in the Service Encounter', *Academy of Management Journal*, October 2001, pp. 1018–27; M. K. Brady and J. J. Cronin, Jr., 'Customer Orientation: Effects on Customer Service Perceptions and Outcome Behaviors', *Journal of Service Research*, February 2001, pp. 241–51; and M. Workman and W. Bommer, 'Redesigning Computer Call Center Work: A Longitudinal Field Experiment', *Journal of Organizational Behavior*, May 2004, pp. 317–37.

23. See, for example, M. D. Hartline and O. C. Ferrell, 'The Management of Customer-Contact Service Employees: An Empirical Investigation', *Journal of Marketing*, October 1996, pp. 52–70; Naumann and Jackson, 'One More Time: How Do You Satisfy Customers?',

pp. 71–76; Tsai, 'Determinants and Consequences of Employee Displayed Positive Emotions'; and Pugh, 'Service with a Smile: Emotional Contagion in the Service Encounter'.

24. J. Flaherty, 'Suggestions Rise from the Floors of U.S. Factories', *New York Times*, 18 April 2001, p. C1; see also W. M. Greenfield, 'Decision Making and Employee Engagement', *Employment Relations Today*, Summer 2004, pp. 13–24.

25. See, for example, P. Cappelli, J. Constantine and C. Chadwick, 'It Pays to Value Family: Work and Family Tradeoffs Reconsidered', *Industrial Relations*, April 2000, pp. 175–98; M. A. Verespej, 'Balancing Act', *Industry Week*, 15 May 2000, pp. 81–85; and R. C. Barnett and D. T. Hall, 'How to Use Reduced Hours to Win the War for Talent', *Organizational Dynamics*, vol. 29, no. 3, 2001, pp. 192–210.

26. M. Conlin, '9 to 5 Isn't Working Anymore', *Business Week*, 20 September 1999, p. 94; and 'The New World of Work: Flexibility is the Watchword', *Business Week*, 10 January 2000, p. 36.

27. S. Shellenbarger, 'What Job Candidates Really Want to Know: Will I Have a Life?', *Wall Street Journal*, 17 November 1999, p. B1; and 'U.S. Employers Polish Image to Woo a Demanding New Generation', *Manpower Argus*, February 2000, p. 2.

28. See, for example, G. R. Weaver, L. K. Trevino and P. L. Cochran, 'Corporate Ethics Practices in the Mid-1990's: An Empirical Study of the Fortune 1000', *Journal of Business Ethics*, February 1999, pp. 283–94; and C. De Mesa Graziano, 'Promoting Ethical Conduct: A Review of Corporate Practices', *Strategic Investor Relations*, Fall 2002, pp. 29–35.

29. A. J. Rucci, S. P. Kirn and R. T. Quinn, 'The Employee–Customer–Profit Chain at Sears', *Harvard Business Review*, January–February 1998, pp. 83–97.

30. Anon, 'Healthy Workers More Productive', *Human Resources*, 29 November 2005: <www.humanresourcesmagazine.com.au/ articles/0F/0C038F0F.asp?Type= 59&Category=917>.

31. See, for example, D. R. Dalton and W. D. Todor, 'Functional Turnover: An Empirical Assessment', *Journal of Applied Psychology*, December 1981, pp. 716–21;

G. M. McEvoy and W. F. Cascio, 'Do Good or Poor Performers Leave? A Meta-Analysis of the Relationship between Performance and Turnover', *Academy of Management Journal*, December 1987, pp. 744–62; S. Lorge, 'When Turnover Isn't So Bad', *Sales & Marketing Management*, September 1999, p. 13; and M. C. Sturman and C. O. Trevor, 'The Implications of Linking the Dynamic Performance and Turnover Literatures', *Journal of Applied Psychology*, August 2001, pp. 684–96.

32. Cited in 'You Often Lose the Ones You Love', *Industry Week*, 21 November 1988, p. 5.

33. R. J. Bennett and S. L. Robinson, 'The Past, Present and Future of Workplace Deviance Research', in J. Greenberg (ed.), *Organizational Behavior: The State of the Science*, 2nd ed. (Hillsdale, NJ: Lawrence Erlbaum Associates, 1994); R. J. Bennett and S. L. Robinson, 'Development of a Measure of Workplace Deviance', *Journal of Applied Psychology*, vol. 85, no. 3, 2000, pp. 349–60; A. M. O'Leary-Kelly, M. K. Duffy and R. W. Griffin, 'Construct Confusion in the Study of Antisocial Work Behavior', *Research in Personnel and Human Resources Management*, vol. 18, 2000, pp. 275–303; and C. Porath, C. Pearson and D. L. Shapiro, 'Turning the Other Cheek or an Eye for an Eye: Targets' Responses to Incivility', Paper interactively presented at the annual meeting of the National Academy of Management, August 1999.

34. D. W. Organ, *Organizational Citizenship Behavior: The Good Soldier Syndrome* (Lexington, MA: Lexington Books, 1988), p. 4. See also J. A. LePine, A. Erez and D. E. Johnson, 'The Nature and Dimensionality of Organizational Citizenship Behavior: A Critical Review and Meta-Analysis', *Journal of Applied Psychology*, February 2002, pp. 52–65.

35. P. M. Podsakoff, S. B. MacKenzie, J. B. Paine and D. G. Bachrach, 'Organizational Citizenship Behaviors: A Critical Review of the Theoretical and Empirical Literature and Suggestions for Future Research', *Journal of Management*, vol. 26, no. 3, 2000, pp. 543–48.

36. H. J. Leavitt, *Managerial Psychology*, rev. ed. (Chicago: University of Chicago Press, 1964), p. 3.

PART 2

THE INDIVIDUAL

2

FOUNDATIONS OF INDIVIDUAL BEHAVIOUR

LEARNING OBJECTIVES

AFTER STUDYING THIS CHAPTER, YOU SHOULD BE ABLE TO:

1. IDENTIFY THE TWO MAIN TYPES OF ABILITY

2. DEFINE THE KEY BIOGRAPHICAL CHARACTERISTICS

3. DESCRIBE THE VARIOUS THEORIES OF LEARNING

4. OUTLINE THE PROCESS OF BEHAVIOUR SHAPING

5. IDENTIFY AND DISTINGUISH AMONG THE FOUR SCHEDULES
   OF REINFORCEMENT

What do your feelings about heights and dark, confined spaces say about your cognitive abilities to control those feelings?

DECIDING WHO WILL MAKE A GOOD FIREFIGHTER is an important task for the human resources office at the Tasmania Fire Service (TFS). The suitability of applicants for firefighter training positions is evaluated using a variety of procedures and tests. Some of these tests assess cognitive abilities, such as problem solving, and others examine psychological characteristics that relate to how likely the person is to cope with the stresses and demands of the job. A number of the tests relate to applicants' physical abilities, as firefighting obviously involves strenuous physical work. The work is often undertaken in adverse conditions while the firefighter is wearing heavy protective equipment. This places a heavy load on the cardiovascular, oxygen consumption and musculoskeletal systems of the body.

While height and weight requirements were once used as screening characteristics, tests of demonstrated physical abilities are now used to select potential trainees. The Physical Fitness Assessment involves undertaking the shuttle run (or beep test), which evaluates an applicant's aerobic fitness. This test requires participants to run between two cones that are placed 20 metres apart. Runners go back and forth between the cones, keeping up with electronic beeps that start off slow but become progressively faster. Each increase in speed is referred to as a level (level 1, level 2, and so on). Applicants are required to achieve level 9.6 to successfully complete the test, which takes approximately ten minutes. Further assessment of physical abilities involves a series of tasks that are simulations of actual tasks performed on the job. These tasks must be completed consecutively without a break. A total of five abilities are assessed: working at heights; working in an enclosed space; manual dexterity; balance and coordination; and physical endurance/strength. Applicants have to drag a 64-metre hose line full of water for 30 metres within 30 seconds to demonstrate the required level of muscular strength and endurance. They need to climb a ladder to a platform (approximately 15 metres high) and lean over it to read a sign below. Another task designed to simulate the critical task of rescuing an injured workmate from a fire scene involves dragging a 90-kilogram rescue mannequin around a marked course and back (a distance of 30 metres) within 60 seconds. Finally, the applicant's ability to operate in a confined area while wearing protective equipment and a breathing apparatus is assessed by having the applicant crawl through a darkened narrow space using a rope guideline for direction. Obviously, successful completion of all of these tasks is critical in being considered for a trainee firefighter position.

Too bad that all the people who really know how to run the country are busy driving taxi cabs and cutting hair.
George Burns

PHYSICAL ABILITIES AND COGNITIVE SKILLS are very high on the list for firefighting recruits. However, these are just some of the characteristics that people may need to bring with them when they join an organisation. In this chapter, we look at how individual differences in the form of ability (which includes intelligence) and biographical characteristics (such as age, gender, marital status, ethnicity and race, and seniority) affect employee performance and satisfaction. Then we show how people learn behaviours and what management can do to shape those behaviours.

People, of course, differ in many ways. Appearance-related differences—such as height, weight, skin, hair and eye colour—are the most obvious. Interestingly, there is evidence that appearance matters in the workplace. For example, tall people—because they are seen as more leader-like—actually earn higher performance evaluations as well as more money.[1] Evidence also suggests that physical attractiveness matters in OB. For example, applicants judged as physically attractive are more likely to get the job.[2] Throughout this chapter we look at how basic individual differences affect employee performance and satisfaction.

Now you may wonder: wouldn't personality be considered a basic individual difference, too? Yes, it would. Personality is so fundamental and important that we need to devote an entire chapter to it. So, keep this in mind as you read through the chapter that we will cover personality in detail in Chapter 4.

LEARNING OBJECTIVE 1

Identify the two main types of ability

MyOBLab

Do you know this material? Let MyOBLab tell you where you need help and devise a personal study plan for you
www.pearsoned.com.au/ MyOBLab

ABILITY

Contrary to what we were taught in school, we weren't all created equal. Most of us are to the left of the median on some normally distributed ability curve. For example, regardless of how motivated you are, it is unlikely that you can act as well as Russell Crowe, play cricket as well as Sir Donald Bradman, write as well as J. K. Rowling or swim as fast as Leisel Jones. Of course, just because we aren't all equal in abilities doesn't imply that some individuals are inherently inferior to others. What we are acknowledging is that everyone has strengths and weaknesses in terms of ability that make them relatively superior or inferior to others in performing certain tasks or activities.[3] From management's standpoint, the issue isn't whether people differ in terms of their abilities. They clearly do. The issue is knowing *how* people differ in abilities and using that knowledge to increase the likelihood that an employee will perform their job well.

What does 'ability' mean? As we will use the term, **ability** refers to an individual's capacity to perform the various tasks in a job. It is a current assessment of what one can do. An individual's overall abilities are essentially made up of two sets of factors: *intellectual* and *physical*.

ability | An individual's capacity to perform the various tasks in a job.

INTELLECTUAL ABILITIES

intellectual abilities | The capacity to do mental activities such as thinking, reasoning and problem solving.

Intellectual abilities are those needed to perform mental activities—for thinking, reasoning and problem solving. People in most societies place a high value on intelligence, and for good reason. Smart people generally earn more money and attain higher levels of education. Smart people are also more likely to emerge as leaders of groups. Intelligence quotient (IQ) tests, for example, are designed to ascertain one's general intellectual abilities. So, too, are university admission tests such as the uni TEST and STAT and graduate admission tests in business (GMAT), law (ALSET) and medicine (UMAT and GMAC), and English language proficiency (IELTS). These testing firms don't make the argument that their tests assess intelligence, but users know that they do.[4]

The seven most frequently cited dimensions making up intellectual abilities are number aptitude, verbal comprehension, perceptual speed, inductive reasoning, deductive reasoning, spatial visualisation and memory.[5] Table 2.1 describes these dimensions.

■ TABLE 2.1
Dimensions of intellectual ability

Dimension	Description	Job example
Number aptitude	Ability to do speedy and accurate arithmetic	Accountant: Calculating the GST on a set of items
Verbal comprehension	Ability to understand what is read or heard, and the relationship of words to each other	Factory manager: Following corporate policies
Perceptual speed	Ability to identify visual similarities and differences quickly and accurately	Fire investigator: Identifying clues to support a charge of arson
Inductive reasoning	Ability to identify a logical sequence in a problem and then solve the problem	Market researcher: Forecasting demand for a product in the next time period
Deductive reasoning	Ability to use logic and to assess the implications of an argument	Supervisor: Choosing between two different suggestions offered by employees
Spatial visualisation	Ability to imagine how an object would look if its position in space were changed	Interior decorator: Redecorating an office
Memory	Ability to retain and recall past experiences	Salesperson: Remembering the names of customers

Jobs differ in the demands they place on incumbents to use their intellectual abilities. The more complex a job is in terms of information-processing demands, the more general intelligence and verbal abilities will be necessary to perform the job successfully.[6] Of course, a high IQ isn't a requirement for all jobs. For jobs in which employee behaviour is highly routine and there are few or no opportunities to exercise discretion, a high IQ isn't as important to performing well. However, that doesn't mean that people with high IQs cannot have an impact on jobs that are traditionally less complex.

There is another key reason why intelligent people are better job performers: they are more creative. Smart people learn jobs more quickly, are more adaptable to changing circumstances, and are better at inventing solutions that improve performance.[7] In other words, intelligence is one of the better predictors of performance across all sorts of jobs.[8]

It might surprise you that the most widely used intelligence test in hiring decisions takes only 12 minutes. It is called the Wonderlic Personnel Test. There are different forms of the test, and each form has 50 questions. Here are a few example questions from the Wonderlic:

- When rope is selling at $0.10 a metre, how many metres can you buy for $0.60?
- Assume the first two statements are true. Is the final one:

1. true, 2. false, 3. not certain?
a. The boy plays football.
b. All football players wear jerseys.
c. The boy wears a jersey.

The Wonderlic is both a speed (almost no one has time to answer every question) and a power (questions get harder as you go along) test, so the average score is pretty low—usually about 21/50. And because it is able to provide valid information at a cheap price, more and more companies are using the Wonderlic in hiring decisions. For example, Subway, Macquarie University, Harcourt Assessment, Acer and many others use Wonderlic. Most companies that use the Wonderlic don't use it in place of other hiring tools such as application forms or the interview. Rather, they add the Wonderlic as another source of information—in this case, because of the Wonderlic's ability to provide valid data on applicants' intelligence levels.

Interestingly, while intelligence is a big help in performing a job well, it doesn't make people happier or more satisfied with their jobs. The correlation between intelligence and job satisfaction is about zero. Why? Research suggests that although intelligent people perform better and tend to have more interesting jobs, they also are more critical in evaluating their job conditions. Thus, smart people have it better, but they also expect more.[9]

In the past decade and a half, researchers have begun to expand the meaning of intelligence beyond mental abilities. Some researchers believe that intelligence can be better understood by breaking it down into four subparts: cognitive, social, emotional and cultural.[10] *Cognitive intelligence* encompasses the aptitudes that have long been tapped by traditional intelligence tests. *Social intelligence* is a person's ability to relate effectively to others. *Emotional intelligence* is the ability to identify, understand and manage emotions.

OB IN PRACTICE

THE BENEFITS OF CULTURAL INTELLIGENCE

Have you ever noticed that some individuals seem to have a knack for relating well to people from different cultures? Some researchers have labelled this skill 'cultural intelligence', which is an outsider's natural ability to interpret an individual's unfamiliar gestures and behaviours in the same way that others from the individual's culture would. Cultural intelligence is important because when conducting business with people from different cultures, misunderstandings can often occur, and as a result, cooperation and productivity may suffer.

Consider the following example. An American manager was meeting with his fellow design team engineers, two of whom were German. As ideas floated around the table, the manager's German colleagues quickly condemned them and remarked how poor the ideas were. The American thought the feedback was harsh and concluded that his German colleagues were rude. However, they were merely criticising the ideas, not the individual—a distinction that the American was unable to make, perhaps due to a lack of cultural intelligence. As a result, the American became wary of contributing potentially good ideas. Had the American been more culturally intelligent, he likely would have recognised the true motives behind his colleagues' remarks and thus may have been able to use those remarks to improve his ideas.

It is unclear whether the notion of cultural intelligence is separate from other forms of intelligence, such as emotional intelligence, and even whether cultural intelligence is different from cognitive ability. However, it is clear that the ability to interact well with individuals from different cultures is a key asset in today's global business environment.

SOURCE: Based on C. Earley and E. Mosakowski, 'Cultural Intelligence', *Harvard Business Review*, October 2004, pp. 139–46.

And *cultural intelligence* is awareness of cross-cultural differences and the ability to function successfully in cross-cultural situations. It is important to note that this line of inquiry—towards **multiple intelligences**—is in its infancy, and the claims made don't always match the scientific evidence. Furthermore, measuring intelligences other than cognitive intelligence hasn't proven to be easy.[11] Of course, there are many cases in which so-called smart people—those with high cognitive intelligence—don't necessarily adapt well to everyday life, work well with others, or succeed when placed in leadership roles.

multiple intelligences | Intelligence contains four subparts: cognitive, social, emotional and cultural.

PHYSICAL ABILITIES

To the same degree that intellectual abilities play a larger role in complex jobs with demanding information-processing requirements, specific **physical abilities** gain importance for successfully doing less-skilled and more-standardised jobs. For example, jobs in which success demands stamina, manual dexterity, leg strength or similar talents require management to identify an employee's physical capabilities.

physical ability | The capacity to do tasks demanding stamina, dexterity, strength and similar characteristics.

Research on the requirements needed in hundreds of jobs has identified nine basic abilities involved in the performance of physical tasks.[12] These are described in Table 2.2. Individuals differ in the extent to which they have each of these abilities. Not surprisingly, there is also little relationship among them: a high score on one is no assurance of a high score on others. High employee performance is likely to be achieved when management has ascertained the extent to which a job requires each of the nine abilities and then ensures that employees in that job have those abilities. This has been the approach taken in the recruitment of Tasmanian firefighters, discussed at the start of this chapter.

■ TABLE 2.2
Nine basic physical abilities

Strength factors	
1. *Dynamic strength*	Ability to exert muscular force repeatedly or continuously over time
2. *Trunk strength*	Ability to exert muscular strength using the trunk (particularly abdominal) muscles
3. *Static strength*	Ability to exert force against external objects
4. *Explosive strength*	Ability to expend a maximum of energy in one or a series of explosive acts
Flexibility factors	
5. *Extent flexibility*	Ability to move the trunk and back muscles as far as possible
6. *Dynamic flexibility*	Ability to make rapid, repeated flexing movements
Other factors	
7. *Body coordination*	Ability to coordinate the simultaneous actions of different parts of the body
8. *Balance*	Ability to maintain equilibrium despite forces pulling off balance
9. *Stamina*	Ability to continue maximum effort requiring prolonged effort over time

SOURCE: Adapted from *Human Resources* magazine, published by the Society for Human Resource Management, Alexandria, VA. Courtesy of *Human Resources*, 21 September 2005, <www.humanresourcesmagazine.com.au>.

THE ABILITY–JOB FIT

Our concern is with explaining and predicting the behaviour of people at work. We have demonstrated that jobs make differing demands on people and that people differ in their abilities. Therefore, employee performance is enhanced when there is a high ability–job fit.

The specific intellectual or physical abilities required for adequate job performance depend on the ability requirements of the job. So, for example, airline pilots need strong spatial-visualisation abilities; surf lifeguards need both strong spatial-visualisation abilities and body coordination; senior executives need verbal abilities; high-rise construction workers need balance; and journalists with weak reasoning abilities would likely have difficulty meeting minimum job-performance standards. Directing attention at only the employee's abilities or only the ability requirements of the job ignores the fact that employee performance depends on the interaction of the two.

What predictions can we make when the fit is poor? As alluded to previously, if employees lack the required abilities, they are likely to fail. If you are hired as a word processor and you can't meet the job's basic keyboard typing requirements, your performance is going to be poor irrespective of your positive attitude or your high level of motivation. When the ability–job fit is out of alignment because the employee has abilities that far exceed the requirements of the job, our predictions would be very different. Job performance is likely to be adequate, but there will be organisational inefficiencies and possible declines in employee satisfaction. Given that pay tends to reflect the highest skill level that employees possess, if an employee's abilities far exceed those necessary to do the job, management will be paying more than it needs to. Abilities significantly above those required can also reduce the employee's job satisfaction when the employee's desire to use his or her abilities is particularly strong and is frustrated by the limitations of the job.

LEARNING OBJECTIVE 2

Define the key biographical characteristics

BIOGRAPHICAL CHARACTERISTICS

As discussed in Chapter 1, this textbook is essentially concerned with finding and analysing the variables that have an impact on employee productivity, absence, turnover, deviance, citizenship and satisfaction. The list of those variables—as shown in Figure 1.4—is long and contains some complicated concepts. Many of the concepts—for instance, motivation, power, politics or organisational culture—are hard to assess. It might be valuable, then, to begin by looking at factors that are easy to define and easily available; data that can be obtained, for the most part, simply from information available in an employee's personnel file. What factors would these be? Obvious **biographical characteristics** would be an employee's age, gender, marital status, ethnicity and race, and length of service with an organisation. Fortunately, there is a sizeable amount of research that has specifically analysed many of these characteristics.

biographical characteristics | Personal characteristics—such as age, gender, marital status, ethnicity and race, and length of service—that are objective and easily obtained from personnel records.

AGE

The relationship between age and job performance is likely to be an issue of increasing importance during the next decade. Why? There are at least three reasons. First, there is a widespread belief that job performance declines with increasing age. Regardless of whether it is true or not, a lot of people believe it and act on it. Second, as noted in Chapter 1, is the reality that the workforce is ageing. The third reason is anti-discrimination legislation that, for all intents and purposes, outlaws mandatory retirement. Most Australians today no longer have to retire at the age of 65.

What is the perception of older employees? Evidence indicates that employers hold mixed feelings.[13] They see a number of positive qualities that older employees bring to their jobs: specifically, experience, judgment, a strong work ethic and commitment to quality. But older employees are also perceived as lacking flexibility and as being resistant to new technology. And in a time when organisations actively seek individuals who are adaptable and open to change, the negatives associated with age clearly hinder the initial hiring of older employees and increase the likelihood that they will be let go during cutbacks. Now let's take a look at the evidence. What effect does age actually have on turnover, absenteeism, productivity and satisfaction?

The older you get, the less likely you are to quit your job. That conclusion is based on studies of the age–turnover relationship.[14] Of course, this shouldn't be too surprising. As employees get older, they have fewer alternative job opportunities. In addition, older employees are less likely to resign than are younger employees because their long tenure tends to provide them with higher wage rates, longer paid holidays and more-attractive retirement benefits.

It is tempting to assume that age is also inversely related to absenteeism. After all, if older employees are less likely to quit, won't they also demonstrate higher stability by coming to work more regularly? Not necessarily. Most studies do show an inverse relationship, but close examination finds that the age–absence relationship is partially a function of whether the absence is avoidable or unavoidable.[15] In general, older employees have lower rates of avoidable absence than do younger employees. However, they have higher rates of unavoidable absence, probably due to the poorer health associated with ageing and the longer recovery period that older employees need when injured.

How does age affect productivity? There is a widespread belief that productivity declines with age. It is often assumed that an individual's skills—particularly speed, agility, strength and coordination—decay over time and that prolonged job boredom and lack of intellectual stimulation all contribute to reduced productivity. The evidence, however, contradicts that belief and those assumptions. For instance, during a three-year period, a large hardware chain staffed one of its stores solely with employees aged over 50 and compared its results with those of five stores with younger employees. The store staffed by the over-50 employees was significantly more productive (measured in terms of sales generated against labour costs) than two of the other stores and held its own with the other three.[16] Other reviews of the research find that age and job performance are unrelated.[17] Moreover, this finding seems to be true for almost all types of jobs, professional and non-professional. The natural conclusion is that the demands of most jobs, even those with heavy manual labour requirements, aren't extreme enough for any declines in physical skills attributable to age to have an impact on productivity; or, if there is some decay due to age, it is offset by gains due to experience.[18]

Com Care values the work ethic of older employees who staff its call centre. The youngest staff member is 44. Some employees work permanent part-time schedules of five hours a day, five days a week. Two older employees are sharing one full-time position—both are grandmothers who work alternate weeks and spend the other week babysitting their grandchildren. Com Care finds that older employees with flexible working arrangements are more reliable and productive than younger employees have been in the past.

Our final concern is the relationship between age and job satisfaction. On this issue, the evidence is mixed. Most studies indicate a positive association between age and satisfaction, at least up to age 60.[19] Other studies, however, have found a U-shaped relationship.[20] Several explanations could clear up these results, the most plausible being that these studies are intermixing professional and non-professional employees. When the two types are separated, satisfaction tends to continue to increase among professionals as they age, whereas it falls among non-professionals during middle age and then rises again in the later years.

GENDER

Few issues initiate more debates, misconceptions and unsupported opinions than whether women perform as well on jobs as men do. In this section, we review the research on that issue.

The evidence suggests that the best place to begin is with the recognition that there are few, if any, important differences between men and women that will affect their job performance. There are, for instance, no consistent male–female differences in problem-solving ability, analytical skills, competitive drive, motivation, sociability or learning ability.[21] Psychological studies have found that women are more willing to conform to authority and that men are more aggressive and more likely than women to have expectations of success, but these differences are minor. Given the significant changes that have taken place in the past 40 years in terms of increasing female participation rates in the workforce and the re-thinking of what constitutes male and female roles, you should operate on the assumption that there is no significant difference in job productivity between men and women.[22]

One issue that does seem to differ between genders, especially when the employee has preschool-age children, is preference for work schedules.[23] Working mothers are more likely to prefer part-time work, flexible work schedules, job sharing and telecommuting in order to accommodate their family responsibilities. As noted earlier, more older employees are being asked by their children to assist with child-care duties for the grandchildren, so that both parents can both work despite the rising costs of child care. This trend is placing more pressure on the grandparents to have flexible work arrangements as well.

But what about absence and turnover rates? Are women less stable employees than men? First, on the question of turnover, the evidence indicates no significant differences.[24] Women's quit rates are similar to those for men. The published research on absence, however, consistently indicates that women have higher rates of absenteeism than men do.[25] The most logical explanation for this finding is that the research was conducted in North America, and North American culture has historically placed greater home and family responsibilities on the woman than on the man. When a child is ill or someone needs to stay home to wait for the plumber, it has been the woman who has traditionally taken time off from work. However, this research is undoubtedly both time-bound and culturally bound.[26] The historical role of the woman in caring for children and as secondary breadwinner has definitely changed in the past generation, and a larger proportion of men nowadays are as interested in day care and the problems associated with child care in general as are women.

MARITAL STATUS

Research consistently indicates that married employees have fewer absences, undergo fewer job turnovers and are more satisfied with their jobs than are their unmarried fellow

DON'T FORGET THE IMPACT OF SIBLINGS!

The impact of genetics, parents and peers has long been studied to help explain why people are the way they are. However, one area that has only recently started to attract some serious research has been the impact of siblings on the way we develop. The preliminary findings are adding another dynamic piece to the puzzle.

One of the first findings is how important the impact of siblings is on social skill development. A major element of the sibling relationship is conflict—or, more importantly, how they resolve conflicts. Where young children have learned how to resolve conflicts with their siblings, their conflict resolution skills later in life tend to be superior to those who didn't learn these in their childhood. Importantly, siblings teach and learn negotiation skills in interacting with one another.

Being a parent's favourite will be quickly observed and capitalised upon by siblings. Knowing that one child is the favourite allows the siblings to exploit that fact to their benefit. The siblings will use the favourite to get benefits for all the siblings, a valuable skill when it comes to getting desired outcomes from superiors in organisations. Managers also have favourites among their employees (discussed in the leadership chapters), so being able to exploit this for the advantage of all is a social skill developed among siblings while still very young.

Siblings will also help to cement the gender differences we observe in organisations. Different sex siblings teach each other about the different perspectives of each, how to relate to those of the opposite gender and, importantly, how to negotiate and resolve cross-gender differences. They also tend to strengthen gender identity—boys will be more atypically boys and girls more atypically girls where there are different gender siblings. This is because each gender will be carving out their distinct gender niche rather than trying to be like their opposite gender siblings.

Where does this leave single child people (called 'singletons' in the research)? Are they disadvantaged by the lack of siblings? The preliminary research suggests that while their social skill development takes longer, in fact there is very little difference in adults from single-child families as compared with people who grew up with siblings. The main difference seems to be in time allocation. Whereas siblings spend a lot of time with siblings, even in their adult life, singletons channel their time into life-fulfilling activities and those activities that further their careers.

SOURCE: Adapted from J. Kluger, 'The New Science of Siblings', *Time*, 10 July 2006, pp. 44–53.

employees.[27] Marriage imposes increased responsibilities that may make a steady job more valuable and important. But the question of causation isn't certain. For instance, do married employees have higher job satisfaction because they can pick and choose their job more easily with the support of a working spouse than a single person who has to rely on their own efforts to earn a living? Further, it may well be that reliable and satisfied employees are more likely to be married for non-work-related reasons that less reliable and satisfied single employees lack. Another issue in this topic of marital status is the dynamic changes to marital status in the past two decades. Whereas two decades ago most cohabiting couples were married, today it is more than twice as likely that cohabiting couples aren't married.[28] This suggests that the role of marital status needs much more research to find causal factors often noted with marital status.

ETHNICITY AND RACE

Ethnicity and race are controversial issues. They can be so contentious that it is tempting to avoid these topics. A complete picture of individual differences in OB, however, would be incomplete without a discussion of ethnicity and race.

What does ethnicity and race mean? Before we can discuss how ethnicity and race matter in OB, first we have to reach some consensus about what ethnicity and race are, and that is not so easily done. Some scholars argue that it is not productive to discuss ethnicity and race for policy reasons (it is often a divisive issue), for political reasons (it often sets neighbour against neighbour), for biological reasons (a large percentage of us are a mixture of races), or for genetic and anthropological reasons (many anthropologists and evolutionary scientists reject the concept of distinct racial categories).

Ethnicity is perhaps the more difficult of the two terms to define. This is because it doesn't rely as much as race does on identifiable and obvious characteristics. **Ethnicity** refers to the notion of a group of people who believe they are unique on the basis of their speech, history, origins, culture or other unique characteristics. For instance, the residents of Norfolk Island, off the coast of Australia, see themselves as a distinct ethnic grouping.[29] This is despite the fact that they share common ancestry with both Great Britain and with Tahiti as Polynesians through inter-marriage and breeding. Known as the *Bounty* mutineers and their descendants, the original Norfolk settlers arrived from Pitcairn Island in June 1856. (Pitcairn Island was the island that Fletcher Christian and his men and their wahines fled to after the *Bounty* mutiny in 1789, but it proved too small to support more than about 100 people.) On Pitcairn and Norfolk islands today, most of the islanders have the surname 'Christian', 'Young', 'Adams', 'Quintal', 'McCoy', 'Buffett', 'Evans' or 'Nobbs', reflecting the small number of males who formed what is now an identifiably ethnic community.

Most people in the United States identify themselves according to a racial group. (However, in countries such as Japan, Brazil and Australia, people are less likely to define themselves according to distinct racial categories.) The US Department of Education, for instance, classifies individuals according to five racial categories: African American, Native American (American Indian/Alaskan Native), Asian/Pacific Islander, Hispanic and White. We'll define **race** as the biological heritage people use to identify themselves. This definition allows each individual to define his or her race. However, many people, such as the professional golfer Tiger Woods, refuse to place themselves into a single racial category, emphasising instead their multi-ethnic roots. In his one and only media statement on this issue, Woods stated, 'Yes, I am the product of two great cultures, one African-American and the other Asian. On my father's side, I am African-American. On my mother's side, I am Thai. Truthfully, I feel very fortunate, and equally proud, to be both African-American and Asian! The critical and fundamental point is that ethnic background and/or composition should not make a difference. It does not make a difference to me. The bottom line is that I am an American ... and proud of it!'[30] Indeed, many Hispanics refuse to see themselves as such and prefer to call themselves 'Latinos' instead.

Race has been studied quite a bit in OB, particularly as it relates to employment outcomes such as personnel selection decisions, performance evaluations, pay and workplace discrimination. Doing justice to all of this research isn't possible here, so let's summarise a few key points identified in the research.

First, in employment settings, there is a tendency for individuals to favour colleagues of their own race in performance evaluations, promotion decisions and pay raises.[31] Second, there are substantial racial differences in attitudes towards affirmative action (set quotas to ensure minority groups get a certain percentage of jobs at all levels of the organisation), with minority races approving such programs to a greater degree than the majority group.[32] Third, minority races generally fare worse than the majority in employment decisions. For example, minorities receive lower ratings in employment interviews, are paid less and are promoted less frequently.[33]

The main dilemma faced by employers who use mental ability tests for selection, promotion, training and similar personnel decisions is concern that they may have a

ethnicity | The grouping of people recognised as unique on the basis of their speech, history, origins, culture or other unique characteristics.

race | Biological heritage that distinguishes one group of people from another.

Singapore is a small island nation that has a wide diversity of cultures and ethnic groupings in its society. Despite the best efforts to create a common sense of community, it cannot be denied that certain ethnic groups, particularly the Malays, tend to have less access to education, training, employment and well-paid employment than do other ethnic groups in Singapore.

negative impact on racial and ethnic groups.[34] For instance, some minority groups score, on the average, as much as 1 standard deviation lower than the majority group on verbal, numerical and spatial ability tests, meaning that only 10 per cent of minority group members score above the average for the majority group. However, after reviewing the evidence, researchers have concluded that 'despite group differences in mean test performance, there is little convincing evidence that well-constructed tests are more predictive of educational, training, or occupational performance for members of the majority group than for members of minority groups'.[35] The issue of racial differences in cognitive ability tests continues to be hotly debated.[36]

SENIORITY

The last biographical characteristic we will look at is length of service, or seniority. With the exception of the issue of male–female differences, few issues are more subject to misconceptions and speculations than the impact of seniority on job performance.

Extensive reviews of the seniority–productivity relationship have been conducted.[37] If we define seniority as time on a particular job, we can say that the most recent evidence demonstrates a positive relationship between seniority and job productivity. So seniority, expressed as work experience, appears to be a good predictor of employee productivity.

The research relating seniority to absence is quite straightforward. Studies consistently demonstrate seniority to be negatively related to absenteeism.[38] In fact, in terms of both frequency of absence and total days lost at work, seniority is the single most important explanatory variable.[39]

Seniority is also a potent variable in explaining turnover. The longer a person is in a job, the less likely they are to quit.[40] Moreover, consistent with research that suggests that past behaviour is the best predictor of future behaviour,[41] evidence indicates that seniority on an employee's previous job is a powerful predictor of that employee's future turnover.[42] The evidence indicates that seniority and job satisfaction are positively related.[43] In fact, when age and seniority are treated separately, seniority appears to be a more consistent and stable predictor of job satisfaction than is chronological age.

LEARNING OBJECTIVE   3

Describe the various theories of learning

LEARNING

All complex behaviour is learned. If we want to explain and predict behaviour, we need to understand how people learn. In this section, we define learning, present three popular learning theories, and describe how managers can facilitate employee learning.

A DEFINITION OF LEARNING

What is learning? A psychologist's definition is considerably broader than the layperson's view that 'it's what we did when we went to school'. In actuality, each of us is continuously 'going to school'. Learning occurs all the time. Therefore, a generally accepted definition of **learning** is *any relatively permanent change in behaviour that occurs as a result of experience*.[44] Ironically, we can say that changes in behaviour indicate that learning has taken place and that learning is a change in behaviour.

The previous definition suggests that we can see changes taking place but not the learning itself. The concept is theoretical and, hence, not directly observable:

> You have seen people in the process of learning, you have seen people who behave in a particular way as a result of learning and some of you (in fact, I guess the majority of you) have 'learned' at some time in your life. In other words, we infer that learning has taken place if an individual behaves, reacts, responds as a result of experience in a manner different from the way he formerly behaved.[45]

Our definition has several components that deserve clarification. First, learning involves change. Change may be good or bad from an organisational point of view. People can learn unfavourable behaviours—to hold prejudices or to shirk their responsibilities, for example—as well as favourable behaviours. Second, the change must become ingrained. Immediate changes may be only reflexive or as a result of fatigue (or a sudden burst of energy) and thus may not represent learning. Third, some form of experience is necessary for learning. Experience may be acquired directly through observation or practice, or it may be acquired indirectly, as through reading. The crucial test still remains: does this experience result in a relatively permanent change in behaviour? If the answer is 'yes', we can say that learning has taken place.

THEORIES OF LEARNING

How do we learn? Three theories have been offered to explain the process by which we acquire patterns of behaviour. These theories are classical conditioning, operant conditioning and social learning.

CLASSICAL CONDITIONING

Classical conditioning grew out of experiments to teach dogs to salivate in response to the ringing of a bell, conducted in the early 1900s by Russian physiologist Ivan Pavlov.[46] A simple surgical procedure allowed Pavlov to measure accurately the amount of saliva secreted by a dog. When Pavlov presented the dog with a piece of meat, the dog exhibited a noticeable increase in salivation. When Pavlov withheld the presentation of meat and merely rang a bell, the dog didn't salivate. Then Pavlov proceeded to link the meat and the

learning | Any relatively permanent change in behaviour that occurs as a result of experience.

classical conditioning | A type of conditioning in which an individual responds to some stimulus that wouldn't ordinarily produce such a response.

ringing of the bell. After repeatedly hearing the bell before getting the food, the dog began to salivate as soon as the bell rang. After a while, the dog would salivate merely at the sound of the bell, even if no food was offered. In effect, the dog had learned to respond—that is, to salivate—to the bell. Let's review this experiment to introduce the key concepts in classical conditioning.

The meat was an *unconditioned stimulus*; it invariably caused the dog to react in a specific way. The reaction that took place whenever the unconditioned stimulus occurred was called the *unconditioned response* (or the noticeable increase in salivation, in this case). The bell was an artificial stimulus, or what we call the *conditioned stimulus*. Although it was originally neutral, after the bell was paired with the meat (an unconditioned stimulus), it eventually produced a response when presented alone. The last key concept is the *conditioned response*. This describes the behaviour of the dog; it salivated in reaction to the bell alone.

Using these concepts, we can summarise classical conditioning. Essentially, learning a conditioned response involves building a link between a conditioned stimulus and an unconditioned stimulus. When the stimuli, one compelling and the other one neutral, are paired, the neutral one becomes a conditioned stimulus and, hence, takes on the properties of the unconditioned stimulus.

Classical conditioning can be used to explain why Christmas carols often bring back pleasant memories of childhood; the songs are associated with the holiday spirit and evoke fond memories and warm feelings. In an organisational setting, we can also see classical conditioning operating. For example, at one manufacturing plant, every time the top executives from the head office were scheduled to make a visit, the plant management would clean up the administrative offices and wash the windows. This went on for years. Eventually, employees would turn on their best behaviour and look prim and proper whenever the windows were cleaned—even in those occasional instances when the cleaning wasn't paired with a visit from the top brass. People had learned to associate the cleaning of the windows with a visit from the head office.

Classical conditioning is passive. Something happens and we react in a specific way. It is elicited in response to a specific, identifiable event. As such, it can explain simple reflexive behaviours. But most behaviour—particularly the complex behaviour of individuals in organisations—is emitted rather than elicited. That is, it is voluntary rather than reflexive. For example, employees choose to arrive at work on time, ask their boss for help with problems, or 'goof off' when no one is watching. The learning of those behaviours is better understood by looking at operant conditioning.

OPERANT CONDITIONING

Operant conditioning argues that behaviour is a function of its consequences. People learn to behave to get something they want or to avoid something they don't want. Operant behaviour means voluntary or learned behaviour in contrast to reflexive or unlearned behaviour. The tendency to repeat such behaviour is influenced by the reinforcement or lack of reinforcement brought about by the consequences of the behaviour. Therefore, reinforcement strengthens a behaviour and increases the likelihood that it will be repeated.

What Pavlov did for classical conditioning, the Harvard psychologist B. F. Skinner did for operant conditioning.[47] Skinner argued that creating pleasing consequences to follow specific forms of behaviour would increase the frequency of that behaviour. He demonstrated that people will most likely engage in desired behaviours if they are positively reinforced for doing so; that rewards are most effective if they immediately follow the desired response; and that behaviour that isn't rewarded, or is punished, is less likely to be

operant conditioning |
A type of conditioning in which desired voluntary behaviour leads to a reward or prevents a punishment.

repeated. For example, we know a lecturer who places a mark by a student's name each time the student makes a contribution to class discussions. Operant conditioning would argue that this practice is motivating because it conditions a student to expect a reward (earning class credit) each time they demonstrate a specific behaviour (speaking up in class). The concept of operant conditioning was part of Skinner's broader concept of **behaviourism**, which argues that behaviour follows stimuli in a relatively unthinking manner. In Skinner's form of radical behaviourism, concepts such as feelings, thoughts and other states of mind are rejected as causes of behaviour. In short, people learn to associate stimulus and response, but their conscious awareness of this association is irrelevant.[48]

behaviourism | A theory which argues that behaviour follows stimuli in a relatively unthinking manner.

You see apparent illustrations of operant conditioning everywhere. For example, any situation in which it is either explicitly stated or implicitly suggested that reinforcements are contingent on some action on your part involves the use of operant learning. Your lecturer says that if you want a high grade in the course you must supply correct answers on the exam. A commissioned salesperson wanting to earn a sizeable income finds that doing so is contingent on generating high sales in their territory. Of course, the linkage can also work to teach the individual to engage in behaviours that work against the best interests of the organisation. Assume that your boss tells you that if you will work overtime during the next three-week busy season, you will be compensated for it at your next performance appraisal. However, when performance-appraisal time comes, you find that you are given no positive reinforcement for your overtime work. The next time your boss asks you to work overtime, what will you do? You will probably decline! Your behaviour can be explained by operant conditioning: if a behaviour fails to be positively reinforced, the probability that the behaviour will be repeated declines.

SOCIAL LEARNING

Individuals can also learn by observing what happens to other people and just by being told about something, as well as by direct experiences. So, for example, much of what we have learned comes from watching models—parents, teachers, peers, motion picture and television performers, bosses, and so forth. This view that we can learn through both observation and direct experience is called **social-learning theory**.[49]

social-learning theory | The view that people can learn through observation and direct experience.

Although social-learning theory is an extension of operant conditioning—that is, it assumes that behaviour is a function of consequences—it also acknowledges the existence of observational learning and the importance of perception in learning. People respond to how they perceive and define consequences, not to the objective consequences themselves.

The influence of models is central to the social-learning viewpoint. Four processes have been found to determine the influence that a model will have on an individual:

1. *Attentional processes.* People learn from a model only when they recognise and pay attention to its critical features. We tend to be most influenced by models that are attractive, repeatedly available, important to us, or similar to us in our estimation.
2. *Retention processes.* A model's influence will depend on how well the individual remembers the model's action after the model is no longer readily available.
3. *Motor reproduction processes.* After a person has seen a new behaviour by observing the model, the watching must be converted to doing. This process then demonstrates that the individual can perform the modelled activities.
4. *Reinforcement processes.* Individuals will be motivated to exhibit the modelled behaviour if positive incentives or rewards are provided. Behaviours that are positively reinforced will be given more attention, learned better and performed more often.

SHAPING: A MANAGERIAL TOOL

Because learning takes place on the job as well as before, managers will be concerned with how they can teach employees to behave in ways that most benefit the organisation. When we attempt to mould individuals by guiding their learning in graduated steps, we are **shaping behaviour**.

Consider the situation in which an employee's behaviour is significantly different from that sought by management. If management rewarded the individual only when he or she showed desirable responses, there might be very little reinforcement taking place. In such a case, shaping offers a logical approach towards achieving the desired behaviour.

We *shape* behaviour by systematically reinforcing each successive step that moves the individual closer to the desired response. If an employee who is always half an hour late for work is only 20 minutes late, we can reinforce that improvement. Reinforcement would increase as responses more closely approximated the desired behaviour.

shaping behaviour | Systematically reinforcing each successive step that moves an individual closer to the desired response.

'YOU CAN'T TEACH AN OLD DOG NEW TRICKS!'

This statement is false. It reflects the widely held stereotype that older employees have difficulties in adapting to new methods and techniques. Studies consistently demonstrate that older employees are perceived as being relatively inflexible, resistant to change, and less willing and able to be trained than their younger counterparts. But these perceptions are mostly wrong.

Evidence does indicate that older employees (typically defined as people aged 50 and over) are less confident of their learning abilities (perhaps due to acceptance of societal stereotypes). Moreover, older employees do seem to be somewhat less efficient in acquiring complex or demanding skills, and, on average, they are not as fast in terms of reaction time or in solving problems. That is, they may take longer to train. Finally, older employees receive less support from supervisors and fellow employees for engaging in learning and developmental activities. However, once trained, research indicates that older employees actually learn more than their younger counterparts, and they are better at transferring what they have learned to the job.

The ability to acquire the skills, knowledge, or behaviour necessary to perform a job at a given level—that is, trainability—has been the subject of much research. And the evidence indicates that there are differences between people in their trainability. A number of individual-difference factors (such as low ability and reduced motivation) have been found to impede learning and training outcomes. However, age hasn't been found to influence these outcomes. In fact, older employees actually benefit more from training. Still, the stereotypes persist.

SOURCES: T. Maurer, K. Wrenn and E. Weiss, 'Toward Understanding and Managing Stereotypical Beliefs about Older Workers' Ability and Desire for Learning and Development', *Research in Personnel and Human Resources Management*, vol. 22, 2003, pp. 253–85; T. J. Maurer, E. M. Weiss and F. G. Barbeite, 'A Model of Involvement in Work-Related Learning and Development Activity: The Effects of Individual, Situational, Motivational, and Age Variables', *Journal of Applied Psychology*, vol. 88, no. 4, 2003, pp. 707–24; J. A. Colquitt, J. A. LePine and R. A. Noe, 'Toward an Integrative Theory of Training Motivation: A Meta-Analytic Path Analysis of 20 Years of Research', *Journal of Applied Psychology*, vol. 85, no. 5, 2000, pp. 678–707; and K. A. Wrenn and T. J. Maurer, 'Beliefs about Older Workers' Learning and Development Behavior in Relation to Beliefs about Malleability of Skills, Age-Related Decline, and Control', *Journal of Applied Social Psychology*, vol. 34, no. 2, 2004, pp. 223–42.

MYTH OR SCIENCE?

METHODS OF SHAPING BEHAVIOUR

There are four ways in which to shape behaviour: through positive reinforcement, negative reinforcement, punishment and extinction.

Following a response with something pleasant is called *positive reinforcement*. This would describe, for instance, the boss who praises an employee for a job well done. Following a response by the termination or withdrawal of something unpleasant is called *negative reinforcement*. If your lecturer asks a question and you don't know the answer, looking

LEARNING OBJECTIVE 4
Outline the process of behaviour shaping

through your lecture notes is likely to preclude your being called on. This is a negative reinforcement because you have learned that looking busily through your notes prevents the lecturer from calling on you. *Punishment* is causing an unpleasant condition in an attempt to eliminate an undesirable behaviour. Giving an employee a two-day suspension from work without pay for showing up drunk is an example of punishment. Eliminating any reinforcement that is maintaining a behaviour is called *extinction*. When the behaviour isn't reinforced, it tends to be gradually extinguished. Lecturers who wish to discourage students from asking questions in class can eliminate this behaviour by ignoring those who raise their hands to ask questions. Hand-raising will become extinct when it is invariably met with an absence of reinforcement.

Both positive and negative reinforcement result in learning. They strengthen a response and increase the probability of repetition. In the preceding illustrations, praise strengthens and increases the behaviour of doing a good job because praise is desired. The behaviour of 'looking busy' is similarly strengthened and increased by its terminating the undesirable consequence of being called on by the teacher. However, both punishment and extinction weaken behaviour and tend to decrease its frequency. In shaping behaviour, the timing of reinforcements is critical. This is an issue we will consider in the next section.

Before we move on, check out the Self-Assessment feature on the CD supplied with this book where you can assess your disciplining skills. The Self-Assessment feature is a unique learning tool that allows you to assess your knowledge, beliefs, feelings and actions in regard to a wide range of personal skills, abilities and interests. You will find one of these in most chapters.

SELF-ASSESSMENT LIBRARY

HOW GOOD AM I AT DISCIPLINING OTHERS?

In the Self-Assessment Library (available on CD and online), take Self-Assessment 33 (How Good Am I at Disciplining Others?) and answer the following questions.

1. Are you surprised by your results?
2. Drawing from the material in the chapter, how might you improve your disciplining skills?

LEARNING OBJECTIVE **5**

Identify and distinguish among the four schedules of reinforcement

continuous reinforcement | Reinforcing a desired behaviour each time it is demonstrated.

SCHEDULES OF REINFORCEMENT

The two main types of reinforcement schedules are *continuous* and *intermittent*. A **continuous reinforcement** schedule reinforces the desired behaviour each and every time it is demonstrated. Take, for example, the case of someone who historically has had trouble arriving at work on time. Every time he or she isn't tardy their manager might compliment them on their desirable behaviour. In an intermittent schedule, on the other hand, not every instance of the desirable behaviour is reinforced, but reinforcement is given often enough to make the behaviour worth repeating. This latter schedule can be compared to the workings of poker machines, which people will continue to play even when they know that it is adjusted to give a considerable return to the club. The intermittent payoffs occur just often enough to reinforce the behaviour of slipping in coins and pressing the button. Evidence indicates that the intermittent, or varied, form of reinforcement tends to promote more resistance to extinction than does the continuous form.[50]

An **intermittent reinforcement** can be of a ratio or interval type. *Ratio schedules* depend on how many responses the subject makes. The individual is reinforced after giving a certain number of specific types of behaviour. *Interval schedules* depend on how much time has passed since the previous reinforcement. With interval schedules, the individual is reinforced on the first appropriate behaviour after a particular time has elapsed. A reinforcement can also be classified as fixed or variable.

When rewards are spaced at uniform time intervals, the reinforcement schedule is of the **fixed-interval** type. The critical variable is time, and it is held constant. This is the predominant schedule for most salaried employees. When you get your pay on a weekly, fortnightly, monthly or other predetermined time basis, you are rewarded on a fixed-interval reinforcement schedule.

If rewards are distributed in time so that reinforcements are unpredictable, the schedule is of the **variable-interval** type. When a lecturer advises her class that pop quizzes will be given during the term (the exact number of which is unknown to the students) and the quizzes will account for 20 per cent of the term grade, she is using a variable-interval schedule. Similarly, a series of randomly timed, unannounced visits to a company office by the corporate audit staff is an example of a variable-interval schedule.

In a **fixed-ratio** schedule, after a fixed or constant number of responses are given, a reward is initiated. For example, a piece-rate incentive plan is a fixed-ratio schedule; the employee receives a reward based on the number of work pieces generated. If the piece rate for a zipper installer in a dressmaking factory is $10 a dozen, the reinforcement (money, in this case) is fixed to the number of zippers sewn into garments. After every dozen is sewn in, the installer has earned another $10.

When the reward varies relative to the behaviour of the individual, he or she is said to be reinforced on a **variable-ratio** schedule. Salespeople on commission are on such a reinforcement schedule. On some occasions, they may make a sale after only two calls on a potential customer. On other occasions, they might need to make 20 or more calls to secure a sale. The reward, then, is variable in relation to the number of successful calls the salesperson makes. Table 2.3 summarises the schedules of reinforcement.

intermittent reinforcement | Reinforcing a desired behaviour often enough to make the behaviour worth repeating but not every time it is demonstrated.

fixed-interval schedule | Spacing rewards at uniform time intervals.

variable-interval schedule | Distributing rewards in time so that reinforcements are unpredictable.

fixed-ratio schedule | Initiating rewards after a fixed or constant number of responses.

variable-ratio schedule | Varying the reward relative to the behaviour of the individual.

■ TABLE 2.3
Schedules of reinforcement

Reinforcement schedule	Nature of reinforcement	Effect on behaviour	Example
Continuous	Reward given after each desired behaviour	Fast learning of new behaviour but rapid extinction	Compliments
Fixed-interval	Reward given at fixed time intervals	Average and irregular performance with rapid extinction	Weekly pay packets
Variable-interval	Reward given at variable times	Moderately high and stable performance with slow extinction	Pop quizzes
Fixed-ratio	Reward given at fixed amounts of output	High and stable performance attained quickly but also with rapid extinction	Piece-rate pay
Variable-ratio	Reward given at variable amounts of output	Very high performance with slow extinction	Commissioned sales

REINFORCEMENT SCHEDULES AND BEHAVIOUR

Continuous reinforcement schedules can lead to early supply to excess, and under this schedule behaviour tends to weaken rapidly when reinforcers are withheld. However, continuous reinforcers are appropriate for newly emitted, unstable or low-frequency responses. In contrast, intermittent reinforcers preclude early supply to excess because they don't follow every response. They are appropriate for stable or high-frequency responses.

In general, variable schedules tend to lead to higher performance than fixed schedules (see Figure 2.1). For example, as noted previously, most employees in organisations are paid on fixed-interval schedules. But such a schedule doesn't clearly link performance and rewards. The reward is given for time spent on the job, rather than for a specific response (performance). In contrast, variable-interval schedules generate high rates of response and more stable and consistent behaviour because of a high correlation between performance and reward and because of the uncertainty involved—the employee tends to be more alert because there is a surprise factor.

■ FIGURE 2.1

Intermittent schedules of reinforcement

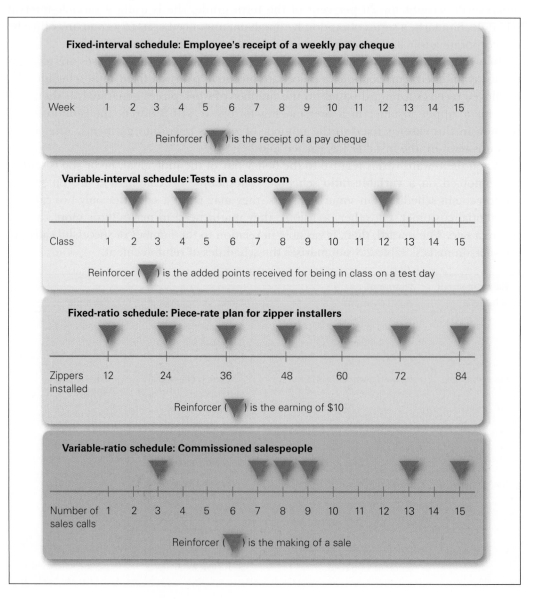

BEHAVIOUR MODIFICATION

There is a now-classic study that took place a number of years ago with freight packers at Emery Air Freight (now part of the global courier company FedEx).[51] Emery's management wanted packers to use freight containers for shipments whenever possible because of specific economic savings. When packers were asked about the percentage of shipments contained, the standard reply was 90 per cent. An analysis by Emery found, however, that the actual container utilisation rate was only 45 per cent. In order to encourage employees to use containers, management established a program of feedback and positive reinforcements. Each packer was instructed to keep a checklist of daily packings, both containerised and non-containerised. At the end of each day, the packer calculated the container utilisation rate. Almost unbelievably, container utilisation jumped to more than 90 per cent on the first day of the program and held at that level. Emery reported that this simple program of feedback and positive reinforcements saved the company $2 million over a three-year period.

This program at Emery Air Freight illustrates the use of behaviour modification, or what has become more popularly called **OB Mod**.[52] It represents the application of reinforcement concepts to individuals in the work setting. The typical OB Mod program follows a five-step problem-solving model: (1) identifying critical behaviours; (2) developing baseline data; (3) identifying behavioural consequences; (4) developing and implementing an intervention strategy; and (5) evaluating performance improvement.[53]

OB Mod | The application of reinforcement concepts to individuals in the work setting.

Everything an employee does on the job isn't equally important in terms of performance outcomes. The first step in OB Mod, therefore, is to identify the critical behaviours that make a significant impact on the employee's job performance. These are those 5 to 10 per cent of behaviours that may account for up to 70 to 80 per cent of each employee's performance. Freight packers using containers whenever possible at Emery Air Freight is an example of a critical behaviour.

The second step requires the manager to develop some baseline performance data. This is obtained by determining the number of times the identified behaviour is occurring under present conditions. In our freight-packing example at Emery, this would have revealed that 45 per cent of all shipments were containerised.

The third step is to perform a functional analysis to identify the behavioural contingencies or consequences of performance. This tells the manager the antecedent cues that emit the behaviour and the consequences that are currently maintaining it. At Emery Air Freight, social norms and the greater difficulty in packing containers were the antecedent cues. This encouraged the practice of packing items separately. Moreover, the consequences for continuing the behaviour, prior to the OB Mod intervention, were social acceptance and escaping more demanding work.

Once the functional analysis is complete, the manager is ready to develop and implement an intervention strategy to strengthen desirable performance behaviours and weaken undesirable behaviours. The appropriate strategy will entail changing some elements of the performance–reward linkage—structure, processes, technology, groups or the task—with the goal of making high-level performance more rewarding. In the Emery example, the work technology was altered to require the keeping of a checklist. The checklist plus the calculation, at the end of the day, of a container-utilisation rate acted to reinforce the desirable behaviour of using containers.

The final step in OB Mod is to evaluate performance improvement. In the Emery intervention, the immediate improvement in the container-utilisation rate demonstrated that behavioural change took place. That it rose to 90 per cent and held at that level further indicates that learning took place. That is, the employees underwent a relatively permanent change in behaviour.

OB Mod has been used by a number of organisations to improve employee productivity; to reduce errors, absenteeism, tardiness and accident rates; and to improve friendliness towards customers.[54] For instance, a clothing manufacturer saved $60 000 in one year from fewer absences. A packing firm improved productivity by 16 per cent, cut errors by 40 per cent, and reduced accidents by more than 43 per cent—resulting in savings of over $1 million. A bank successfully used OB Mod to increase the friendliness of its tellers, which led to a demonstrable improvement in customer satisfaction.

PROBLEMS WITH OB MOD AND REINFORCEMENT THEORY

Although the effectiveness of reinforcements in the form of rewards and punishments has a lot of support in the literature, that doesn't necessarily mean that Skinner was right or that OB Mod is the best way to reward people. What if the power of reinforcements isn't due to operant conditioning or behaviourism? One problem with behaviourism is research showing that thoughts and feelings immediately follow environmental stimuli, even those explicitly meant to shape behaviour. This is contrary to the assumptions of behaviourism and OB Mod, which assume that people's innermost thoughts and feelings in response to the environment are irrelevant.

Think about praise from a supervisor. For example, assume your course lecturer compliments you for asking a good question. A behaviourist would argue that this shapes our behaviour because we find the stimulus (the compliment) pleasant and therefore respond by attempting to ask other questions that will generate the same reward. However, imagine, for example, that you had to weigh the pleasant feelings produced by your lecturer's praise against the snickers of jealous classmates who whisper 'brown noser'. Your choice of what to do would likely be dictated by weighing the value of these stimuli, which may be a rather complex mental process involving thinking and feeling.

Also, is it really shaping if the compliment was given without an intention of moulding behaviour? Isn't it perhaps overly restrictive to view all stimuli as motivated to obtain a particular response? Is the only reason we tell someone we love them because we wish to obtain a reward or to mould their behaviour?

Because of these problems, among others, operant conditioning and behaviourism have been superseded by other approaches that emphasise cognitive processes.[55] There is no denying, though, the contribution of these theories to our understanding of human behaviour.

British Airways uses OB Mod to strengthen desirable performance behaviours. The airline installed Web-enabled employee performance software as an intervention strategy to monitor and analyse each employee's output in the areas of ticket sales, customer service and customer complaints. In tracking individual employees' productivity, the new technology identifies top performers and directly applies incentive bonuses into their pay cheques.

- Ability directly influences an employee's level of performance and satisfaction through the ability–job fit. Given that it is management's desire to get a compatible fit, what can be done to achieve this?
- An effective selection process will improve the fit. A job analysis will provide information about jobs currently being done and the abilities that individuals need to perform the jobs adequately. Applicants can then be tested, interviewed and evaluated on the degree to which they possess the necessary abilities.
- Promotion and transfer decisions affecting individuals already in the organisation's employ should reflect the abilities of candidates. As with new employees, care should be taken to assess critical abilities that incumbents will need in the job and to match those requirements with the organisation's human resources.
- The fit can be improved by fine-tuning the job to better match an incumbent's abilities. Often, modifications can be made in the job that, while not having a significant impact on the job's basic activities, better adapt it to the specific talents of a given employee. Examples would be to change some of the equipment used or to reorganise tasks within a group of employees.

- Biographical characteristics are readily observable to managers. However, just because they are observable doesn't mean they should be explicitly used in management decisions.
- Any observable change in behaviour is prima facie evidence that learning has taken place.
- We found that positive reinforcement is a powerful tool for modifying behaviour. By identifying and rewarding performance-enhancing behaviours, management increases the likelihood that they will be repeated. Our knowledge about learning further suggests that reinforcement is a more effective tool than punishment. Although punishment eliminates undesired behaviour more quickly than negative reinforcement does, punished behaviour tends to be only temporarily suppressed rather than permanently changed. And punishment may produce unpleasant side effects, such as lower morale and higher absenteeism or turnover. In addition, the recipients of punishment tend to become resentful of the punisher. Managers, therefore, are advised to use reinforcement rather than punishment.

All Human Behaviour is Learned

● POINT

Human beings are essentially blank slates that are shaped by their environment. B. F. Skinner, in fact, summarised his belief in the power of the environment to shape behaviour when he said, 'Give me a child at birth and I can make him into anything you want.'

We have numerous societal mechanisms that exist because of this belief in the power of learned behaviour. Let us identify some of them:

- *Role of parenting.* We place a great deal of importance on the role of mothers and fathers in the raising of children. We believe, for instance, that children raised without fathers will be hindered by their lack of a male role model. And parents who have continual run-ins with the law risk having government authorities take their children from them. The latter action is typically taken because society believes that irresponsible parents don't provide the proper learning environment for their children.

- *Importance of education.* Most advanced societies invest heavily in the education of their young. They typically provide ten or more years of free education. And in many countries, going on to university after finishing high school has become the norm rather than the exception. This investment in education is undertaken because it is seen as a way for young people to acquire knowledge and skills.

- *Job training.* Most individuals who don't go on to university will pursue job-training programs (apprenticeships or traineeships) to develop specific work-related skills. They will take courses to become proficient as auto mechanics, dental assistants, and the like. Similarly, people who seek to become skilled tradespeople will pursue apprenticeships as carpenters, electricians or pipe fitters. In addition, business firms invest billions of dollars each year in training and education to keep current employees' skills up to date.

- *Manipulating of rewards.* Complex compensation programs are designed by organisations to reward employees fairly for their work performance. But these programs are also designed with the intention to motivate employees. They are designed to encourage employees to engage in behaviours that management desires and to extinguish behaviours that management wants to discourage. Salary levels, for instance, typically reward employee loyalty, encourage the learning of new skills, and motivate individuals to assume greater responsibilities in the organisation.

These mechanisms all exist and flourish because organisations and society believe that people can learn and change their behaviour.

● COUNTERPOINT

Although people can learn and can be influenced by human behaviour, evolutionary and cognitive psychology tells us that human beings are basically hardwired at birth. We are born with ingrained traits, honed and adapted genetically over millions of years that shape and limit our behaviour.

All living creatures are 'designed' by specific combinations of genes. As a result of natural selection, genes that produce faulty design features are eliminated. Characteristics that help a species to survive tend to endure and get passed on to future generations. Many of the characteristics that helped early *homo sapiens* to survive live on today and influence the way we behave. Here are a few examples:

- *Emotions.* Stone Age people, at the mercy of wild predators and natural disasters, learned to trust their instincts. Those with the best instincts survived. Today, emotions remain the first screen to all information we receive. We know we are supposed to act rationally, but our emotions can never be fully suppressed.

- *Risk avoidance.* Ancient hunter-gatherers who survived weren't big risk takers. They were cautious. Today, when we are comfortable with the status quo, we typically see any change as risky and, thus, tend to resist it.

- *Stereotyping*. To prosper in a clan society, Early Man had to quickly 'size up' who he could trust and who he couldn't. Those who could do this quickly were more likely to survive. Today, like our ancestors, we naturally stereotype people based on very small pieces of evidence, mainly their looks and a few readily apparent behaviours.
- *Male competitiveness*. Males in early human societies frequently had to engage in games or battles in which there were clear winners and losers. Winners attained high status, were viewed by females as more attractive mates and therefore were more likely to reproduce. The ingrained male desire to do public battle and display virility and competence persists today.

Evolutionary psychology challenges the notion that people are free to change their behaviour if trained or motivated. It doesn't say that we can't engage in learning or exercise free will. What it *does* say is that nature predisposes us to act and interact in particular ways in particular circumstances. As a result, we find that people in organisational settings often behave in ways that don't appear to be beneficial to themselves or their employers.

SOURCES: Points in this argument are based on N. Nicholson, 'How Hardwired is Human Behavior?', *Harvard Business Review*, July–August 1998, pp. 135–47; and B. D. Pierce and R. White, 'The Evolution of Social Structure: Why Biology Matters', *Academy of Management Review*, October 1999, pp. 843–53.

QUESTIONS FOR REVIEW

MyOBLab Do you understand this chapter's content? Find out at www.pearsoned.com.au/MyOBLab

1. Assess the validity of using intelligence scores for selecting new employees.
2. Describe the specific steps you would take to ensure that an individual has the appropriate abilities to satisfactorily do a given job.
3. How do age, gender, marital status, ethnicity and race, and seniority affect performance at work?
4. Explain classical conditioning.
5. Contrast classical conditioning, operant conditioning and social learning.
6. How might employees actually learn unethical behaviours on their jobs?
7. Describe the four types of intermittent reinforcers.
8. What are the five steps in behaviour modification?
9. If you had to take disciplinary action against an employee, how, specifically, would you do it?
10. Describe the four processes in successful social learning.

QUESTIONS FOR CRITICAL THINKING

1. 'All organisations would benefit from hiring the smartest people they can get.' Do you agree or disagree with this statement? Support your answer.
2. What do you think is more likely to lead to success on a job—a good ability–job fit or personality–organisation fit? Explain.
3. What abilities do you think are especially important for success in senior-level management positions?
4. What have you learned about 'learning' that could help you to explain the behaviour of students in a classroom if: (a) The lecturer gives only one test—a final examination at the end of the course? (b) The lecturer gives four exams during the term, all of which are announced on the first day of class? (c) The student's grade is based on the results of numerous exams, none of which are announced by the lecturer ahead of time?

EXPERIENTIAL EXERCISE

Positive Reinforcement versus Punishment

Time required:
Approximately 20 minutes.

Participants (steps 1–4):

1. Two volunteers are selected to receive reinforcement or punishment from the class while performing a particular task. The volunteers leave the room.
2. The lecturer identifies an object for the student volunteers to locate when they return to the room. (The object should be unobstructed but clearly visible to the class. Examples that have worked well include a small triangular piece of paper that was left behind when a notice was torn off a classroom bulletin board, a smudge on the chalkboard, and a chip in the plaster of a classroom wall.)
3. The lecturer specifies the actions that will be in effect when the volunteers return to the room. For punishment, students should hiss or boo when the first volunteer is moving away from the object. For positive reinforcement, they should cheer and applaud when the second volunteer is getting closer to the object.
4. The lecturer should assign a student to keep a record of the time it takes each of the volunteers to locate the object.

Volunteer 1 (steps 5 and 6):

5. Volunteer 1 is brought back into the room and is told, 'Your task is to locate and touch a particular object in the room and the class has agreed to help you. You cannot use words or ask questions. Begin.'
6. Volunteer 1 continues to look for the object until it is found, while the class engages in the punishing behaviour.

Volunteer 2 (steps 7 and 8):

7. Volunteer 2 is brought back into the room and is told, 'Your task is to locate and touch a particular object in the room and the class has agreed to help you. You cannot use words or ask questions. Begin.'
8. Volunteer 2 continues to look for the object until it is found, while the class assists by giving positive reinforcement.

Class review (steps 9 and 10):

9. The timekeeper will present the results on how long it took each volunteer to find the object.
10. The class will discuss: What was the difference in behaviour of the two volunteers? What are the implications of this exercise to shaping behaviour in organisations?

SOURCE: Adapted from an exercise developed by Dr Larry K. Michaelson of the University of Oklahoma. Reproduced with permission.

ETHICAL DILEMMA

Is OB Mod a Form of Manipulation?

Two questions: Is OB Mod a form of manipulation? And if it is, is it unethical for managers to manipulate the behaviour of employees?

Critics of OB Mod say that it manipulates employees. These critics argue that when managers purposely select consequences to control employee behaviour, they rob employees of their individuality and freedom of choice. For instance, some companies reinforce safe working conditions through a game called Safety Bingo. Every day that the workplace has no accidents, employees can draw a number for their bingo card. The first employee to fill a bingo card wins a television set. This program, critics might argue, pressures employees to behave in ways they might not otherwise engage in. It makes these human beings little different from the seal at the circus who, every time it does its assigned trick, is given a fish by its trainer. Only instead of getting a fish, some employee walks off with a television or similar prize.

On the question regarding the ethics of manipulation, the answer typically surrounds what the term 'manipulation' means to you. Some people believe the term has a negative connotation. To manipulate is to be devious or conniving. Others, however, would argue that manipulation is merely the thoughtful effort to control outcomes. In fact, one can say that 'management is manipulation' because it is concerned with planned efforts to get people to do what management wants them to do.

What do you think?

CASE STUDY

Professional Sports: Rewarding and Punishing the Same Behaviour?

NRL chief David Yallop is feeling the heat, but not the kind an action-packed rugby league match brings. He has been faced with a mounting number of off-field incidents involving high-profile league players where violence and heavy drinking have occurred, sometimes involving violence towards women. Despite severe penalties from clubs and the NRL, these incidents continue to tarnish the reputation of rugby league as a family recreation and sport. On one hand, clubs invest heavily in honing their athletes' physical skills and teamwork skills involving a lot of team bonding, but when these same players need to unwind afterwards, those same attributes are causing problems. Alcohol and violence often go together, but when it involves high-profile NRL players, it creates many problems. It turns otherwise normal people into media villains and darkens the game's reputation. This often occurs when teammates, whom clubs encourage to bond together for superior performance on the field, get into serious trouble off the field.

But here is the problem: the same system that punishes those who become involved in off-field incidents may also reinforce such behaviour. Rugby league administrators appear to be genuinely interested in eliminating off-field incidents involving alcohol, but are quite happy to receive large amounts of advertising revenues for sponsorship of the game. And the current repercussions for players may not serve as a strong deterrent, judging from the frequency of incidents. A fine of between $10 000 and $50 000, or a four-match suspension, may be a relatively minor setback compared to the hundreds of thousands that can be earned for becoming an all-star player.

Take Tavita Latu, formerly a star player of the Cronulla Sharks club, as an example. In 2006, he became the first rugby league player to be summarily sacked in the wake of an off-field incident involving alcohol and claims of assault. Now his rugby league career is over, with David Yallop telling all the clubs that the NRL will never again license this player. No appeal was permitted, despite no criminal charges being heard in court at the time of the sacking. Despite his apology to the club, his teammates and rugby league's fans, this young star's career is over for good. Meanwhile, the NRL and many of the rugby league clubs continue to accept significant sponsorship from alcohol producers.

It appears that professional sports may be trying to have their cake and eat it too. As we have seen, behaviour that may lead individuals and teams to fame and fortune on the field may also be behaviour worthy of punishment off the field.

QUESTIONS

1. What type of reinforcement schedule does severe monetary fines and/or suspensions for alcohol-related behaviour represent? Is this type of schedule typically effective or ineffective?

2. What are some examples of behaviours in typical organisations that supervisors reward, but which may actually be detrimental to others or to the organisation as a whole? As a manager, what might you do to try and avoid this quandary?

3. If you were the chief executive officer of the NRL, what steps would you take to try to reduce the alcohol-related incidents off the field? Is punishment likely to be the most effective deterrent? Why or why not?

4. Is it ever OK to allow potentially unethical behaviours, which on the surface may benefit organisations, to persist? Why or why not?

SOURCE: Adapted from <www.nrl.com/News/MediaReleases/Media ReleaseArticle/tabid/79/NewsId/1294/Default.aspx> (14 June 2006).

ENDNOTES

1. T. A. Judge and D. M. Cable, 'The Effect of Physical Height on Workplace Success and Income: Preliminary Test of a Theoretical Model', *Journal of Applied Psychology*, vol. 89, no. 3, 2004, pp. 428–41.

2. M. Hosoda, E. F. Stone-Romero and G. Coats, 'The Effects of Physical Attractiveness on Job-Related Outcomes: A Meta-Analysis of Experimental Studies', *Personnel Psychology*, vol. 56, no. 2, 2003, pp. 431–62.

3. K. R. Murphy (ed.), *Individual Differences and Behavior in Organizations* (San Francisco: Jossey-Bass, 1996).

4. L. S. Gottfredson, 'The Challenge and Promise of Cognitive Career Assessment', *Journal of Career Assessment*, vol. 11, no. 2, 2003, pp. 115–35.

5. M. D. Dunnette, 'Aptitudes, Abilities, and Skills', in M. D. Dunnette (ed.), *Handbook of Industrial and Organizational Psychology* (Chicago: Rand McNally, 1976), pp. 478–83.

6. J. F. Salgado, N. Anderson, S. Moscoso, C. Bertua, F. de Fruyt and J. P. Rolland, 'A Meta-Analytic Study of General Mental Ability Validity for Different Occupations in the European Community', *Journal of Applied Psychology*, December 2003, pp. 1068–81; and F. L. Schmidt and J. E. Hunter, 'Select on Intelligence', in E. A. Locke (ed.), *Handbook of Principles of Organizational Behavior* (Malden, MA: Blackwell, 2004).

7. J. A. LePine, J. A. Colquitt and A. Erez, 'Adaptability to Changing Task Contexts: Effects of General Cognitive Ability, Conscientiousness, and Openness to Experience', *Personnel Psychology*, vol. 53, no. 3, 2000, pp. 563–93; J. A. Colquitt, J. A. LePine and R. A. Noe, 'Toward an Integrative Theory of Training Motivation: A Meta-Analytic Path Analysis of 20 Years of Research', *Journal of Applied Psychology*, vol. 85, no. 5, 2000, pp. 678–707; and J. A. Harris, 'Measured Intelligence, Achievement, Openness to Experience, and Creativity', *Personality and Individual Differences*, vol. 36, no. 4, 2004, pp. 913–29.

8. See, for instance, J. E. Hunter and R. F. Hunter, 'Validity and Utility of Alternative Predictors of Job Performance', *Psychological Bulletin*, January 1984, pp. 72–98; J. E. Hunter, 'Cognitive Ability, Cognitive Aptitudes, Job Knowledge, and Job Performance', *Journal of Vocational Behavior*, December 1986, pp. 340–62;

W. M. Coward and P. R. Sackett, 'Linearity of Ability–Performance Relationships: A Reconfirmation', *Journal of Applied Psychology*, June 1990, pp. 297–300; M. J. Ree, J. A. Earles and M. S. Teachout, 'Predicting Job Performance: Not Much More Than g', *Journal of Applied Psychology*, August 1994, pp. 518–24; F. L. Schmidt and J. E. Hunter, 'The Validity and Utility of Selection Methods in Personnel Psychology: Practical and Theoretical Implications of 85 Years of Research Findings', *Psychological Bulletin*, September 1998, pp. 262–74; and M. J. Ree, T. R. Carretta and J. R. Steindl, 'Cognitive Ability', in N. Anderson, D. S. Ones, H. K. Sinangil and C. Viswesvaran (eds), *Handbook of Industrial, Work & Organizational Psychology*, vol. 1 (Thousand Oaks, CA: Sage, 2001), pp. 219–32.

9. Y. Ganzach, 'Intelligence and Job Satisfaction', *Academy of Management Journal*, vol. 41, no. 5, 1998, pp. 526–39; and Y. Ganzach, 'Intelligence, Education, and Facets of Job Satisfaction', *Work and Occupations*, vol. 30, no. 1, 2003, pp. 97–122.

10. This section is based on R. E. Riggio, S. E. Murphy and F. J. Pirozzolo (eds), *Multiple Intelligences and Leadership* (Mahwah, NJ: Lawrence Erlbaum, 2002).

11. D. Lubinski Benbow and C. P. Benbow, 'An Opportunity for Empiricism', *PsycCRITIQUES*, 2004.

12. E. A. Fleishman, 'Evaluating Physical Abilities Required by Jobs', *Personnel Administrator*, June 1979, pp. 82–92.

13. 'Valuing Older Workers: A Study of Costs and Productivity', a report prepared for AARP by ICF Inc., 1995; W. C. K. Chiu, A. W. Chan, E. Snape and T. Redman, 'Age Stereotypes and Discriminatory Attitudes towards Older Workers: An East–West Comparison', *Human Relations*, May 2001, pp. 629–61; I. Glover, 'Ageism Without Frontiers', in I. Glover and M. Branine (eds), *Ageism in Work and Employment* (Aldershot, England: Ashgate, 2001), pp. 115–50; K. Greene, 'Older Workers Can Get a Raw Deal—Some Employers Can Admit to Promoting, Challenging Their Workers Less', *Wall Street Journal*, 10 April 2003, p. D2; and K. A. Wrenn and T. J. Maurer, 'Beliefs about Older Workers' Learning and Development Behavior in Relation to Beliefs about Malleability of Skills, Age-

Related Decline, and Control', *Journal of Applied Social Psychology*, vol. 34, no. 2, 2004, pp. 223–42.

14. S. R. Rhodes, 'Age-Related Differences in Work Attitudes and Behavior: A Review and Conceptual Analysis', *Psychological Bulletin*, March 1983, pp. 328–67; J. L. Cotton and J. M. Tuttle, 'Employee Turnover: A Meta-Analysis and Review with Implications for Research', *Academy of Management Review*, January 1986, pp. 55–70; and D. R. Davies, G. Matthews and C. S. K. Wong, 'Ageing and Work', in C. L. Cooper and I. T. Robertson (eds), *International Review of Industrial and Organizational Psychology*, vol. 6 (Chichester, England: Wiley, 1991), pp. 183–87.

15. Rhodes, 'Age-Related Differences in Work Attitudes and Behavior', pp. 347–49; R. D. Hackett, 'Age, Tenure, and Employee Absenteeism', *Human Relations*, July 1990, pp. 601–19; and Davies, Matthews and Wong, 'Ageing and Work', pp. 183–87.

16. Cited in K. Labich, 'The New Unemployed', *Fortune*, 8 March 1993, p. 43.

17. See G. M. McEvoy and W. F. Cascio, 'Cumulative Evidence of the Relationship between Employee Age and Job Performance', *Journal of Applied Psychology*, February 1989, pp. 11–17; and F. L. Schmidt and J. E. Hunter, 'The Validity and Utility of Selection Methods in Personnel Psychology: Practical and Theoretical Implications of 85 Years of Research Findings', *Psychological Bulletin*, September 1998, pp. 262–74.

18. See, for instance, F. J. Landy, et al., *Alternatives to Chronological Age in Determining Standards of Suitability for Public Safety Jobs* (University Park, PA: Center for Applied Behavioral Sciences, Pennsylvania State University, 1992).

19. A. L. Kalleberg and K. A. Loscocco, 'Ageing, Values, and Rewards: Explaining Age Differences in Job Satisfaction', *American Sociological Review*, February 1983, pp. 78–90; R. Lee and E. R. Wilbur, 'Age, Education, Job Tenure, Salary, Job Characteristics, and Job Satisfaction: A Multivariate Analysis', *Human Relations*, August 1985, pp. 781–91; and Davies, Matthews and Wong, 'Ageing and Work', pp. 176–83.

20. K. M. Kacmar and G. R. Ferris, 'Theoretical and Methodological Considerations in the Age–Job Satisfaction

Relationship', *Journal of Applied Psychology*, April 1989, pp. 201–7; G. Zeitz, 'Age and Work Satisfaction in a Government Agency: A Situational Perspective', *Human Relations*, May 1990, pp. 419–38; and W. A. Hochwarter, G. R. Ferris, P. L. Perrewe, L. A. Witt and C. Kiewitz, 'A Note on the Nonlinearity of the Age–Job Satisfaction Relationship', *Journal of Applied Social Psychology*, June 2001, pp. 1223–37.

21. See, for example, A. H. Eagly and L. L. Carli, 'Sex Researchers and Sex-Typed Communications as Determinants of Sex Differences in Influenceability: A Meta-Analysis of Social Influence Studies', *Psychological Bulletin*, August 1981, pp. 1–20; J. S. Hyde, 'How Large Are Cognitive Gender Differences?', *American Psychologist*, October 1981, pp. 892–901; P. Chance, 'Biology, Destiny, and All That', *Across the Board*, July–August 1988, pp. 19–23; E. M. Weiss, G. Kemmler, E. A. Deisenhammer, W. W. Fleischhacker and M. Delazer, 'Sex Differences in Cognitive Functions', *Personality and Individual Differences*, September 2003, pp. 863–75; and A. F. Jorm, K. J. Anstey, H. Christensen and B. Rodgers, 'Gender Differences in Cognitive Abilities: The Mediating Role of Health State and Health Habits', *Intelligence*, January 2004, pp. 7–23.

22. See, for example, M. M. Black and E. W. Holden, 'The Impact of Gender on Productivity and Satisfaction among Medical School Psychologists', *Journal of Clinical Psychology in Medical Settings*, March 1998, pp. 117–31.

23. See, for example, S. Shellenbarger, 'More Job Seekers Put Family Needs First', *Wall Street Journal*, 15 November 1991, p. B1.

24. R. W. Griffeth, P. W. Hom and S. Gaertner, 'A Meta-Analysis of Antecedents and Correlates of Employee Turnover: Update, Moderator Tests, and Research Implications for the Next Millennium', *Journal of Management*, vol. 26, no. 3, 2000, pp. 463–88.

25. See, for instance, K. D. Scott and E. L. McClellan, 'Gender Differences in Absenteeism', *Public Personnel Management*, Summer 1990, pp. 229–53; and A. VandenHeuvel and M. Wooden, 'Do Explanations of Absenteeism Differ for Men and Women?', *Human Relations*, November 1995, pp. 1309–29.

26. See, for instance, M. Tait, M. Y. Padgett and T. T. Baldwin, 'Job and Life Satisfaction: A Reevaluation of the Strength of the Relationship and Gender Effects as a Function of the Date of the Study', *Journal of Applied Psychology*, June 1989, pp. 502–07; and M. B. Grover, 'Daddy Stress', *Forbes*, 6 September 1999, pp. 202–08.

27. H. Mackay, *Reinventing Australia: The Mind and Mood of Australia in the 90s* (Sydney: Angus & Robertson, 1993); and H. Mackay, *Turning Point: Australians Choosing Their Future* (Sydney: Macmillan, 1999).

28. Mackay, *Turning Point*.

29. This section was based on <www.norfolk island.com.au/history_and_culture/>; <www.discovernorfolkisland.com/norfolk/ history.html>; and <www.norfolk.gov.nf/>.

30. See <www.rjgeib.com/heroes/tiger/ tiger.html>.

31. J. M. Sacco, C. R. Scheu, A. M. Ryan and N. Schmitt, 'An Investigation of Race and Sex Similarity Effects in Interviews: A Multilevel Approach to Relational Demography', *Journal of Applied Psychology*, vol. 88, no. 5, 2003, pp. 852–65; G. N. Powell and D. A. Butterfield, 'Exploring the Influence of Decision Makers' Race and Gender on Actual Promotions to Top Management', *Personnel Psychology*, vol. 55, no. 2, 2002, pp. 397–428; and M. K. Mount, M. R. Sytsma, J. F. Hazucha and K. E. Holt, 'Rater–Ratee Race Effects in Developmental Performance Ratings of Managers', *Personnel Psychology*, vol. 50, no. 1, 1997, pp. 51–69.

32. D. A. Kravitz and S. L. Klineberg, 'Reactions to Two Versions of Affirmative Action among Whites, Blacks, and Hispanics', *Journal of Applied Psychology*, vol. 85, no. 4, 2000, pp. 597–611.

33. G. F. Dreher and T. H. Cox, Jr, 'Labour Market Mobility and Cash Compensation: The Moderating Effects of Race and Gender', *Academy of Management Journal*, vol. 43, no. 5, 2000, pp. 890–900; A. I. Huffcutt and P. L. Roth, 'Racial Group Differences in Employment Interview Evaluations', *Journal of Applied Psychology*, vol. 83, no. 2, 1998, pp. 179–89; and J. M. Sacco, C. R. Scheu, A. M. Ryan and N. Schmitt, 'An Investigation of Race and Sex Similarity Effects in Interviews: A Multilevel Approach to Relational Demography', *Journal of Applied Psychology*, vol. 88, no. 5, 2003, pp. 852–65.

34. P. Bobko, P. L. Roth and D. Potosky, 'Derivation and Implications of a Meta-Analytic Matrix Incorporating Cognitive Ability, Alternative Predictors, and Job Performance', *Personnel Psychology*, Autumn 1999, pp. 561–89.

35. Ree, Carretta and Steindl, 'Cognitive Ability', p. 228.

36. See Rushton and Jenson, 'Thirty Years of Research on Race Differences in Cognitive Ability', *Psychology, Public Policy, and the Law*, vol. 11, no. 2, 2005, pp. 235–95; and R. E. Nisbett, 'Heredity, Environment, and Race Differences in IQ: A Commentary on Rushton and Jensen (2005)', *Psychology, Public Policy, and the Law*, vol. 11, no. 2, 2005, pp. 302–10.

37. M. E. Gordon and W. J. Fitzgibbons, 'Empirical Test of the Validity of Seniority as a Factor in Staffing Decisions', *Journal of Applied Psychology*, June 1982, pp. 311–19; M. E. Gordon and W. A. Johnson, 'Seniority: A Review of Its Legal and Scientific Standing', *Personnel Psychology*, Summer 1982, pp. 255–80; M. A. McDaniel, F. L. Schmidt and J. E. Hunter, 'Job Experience Correlates of Job Performance', *Journal of Applied Psychology*, May 1988, pp. 327–30; and M. A. Quinones, J. K. Ford and M. S. Teachout, 'The Relationship between Work Experience and Job Performance: A Conceptual and Meta-Analytic Review', *Personnel Psychology*, Winter 1995, pp. 887–910.

38. Garrison and Muchinsky, 'Attitudinal and Biographical Predictors of Incidental Absenteeism'; N. Nicholson, C. A. Brown and J. K. Chadwick-Jones, 'Absence from Work and Personal Characteristics', *Journal of Applied Psychology*, June 1977, pp. 319–27; R. T. Keller, 'Predicting Absenteeism from Prior Absenteeism, Attitudinal Factors, and Nonattitudinal Factors', *Journal of Applied Psychology*, August 1983, pp. 536–40; and I. R. Gellatly, 'Individual and Group Determinants of Employee Absenteeism: Test of a Causal Model', *Journal of Organizational Behavior*, September 1995, pp. 469–85.

39. P. O. Popp and J. A. Belohlav, 'Absenteeism in a Low Status Work Environment', *Academy of Management Journal*, September 1982, p. 681.

40. Griffeth, Hom and Gaertner, 'A Meta-Analysis of Antecedents and Correlates of Employee Turnover'.

41. R. D. Gatewood and H. S. Field, *Human Resource Selection* (Chicago: Dryden Press, 1987).

42. J. A. Breaugh and D. L. Dossett, 'The Effectiveness of Biodata for Predicting Turnover', Paper presented at the National Academy of Management Conference, New Orleans, August 1987.

43. A. G. Bedeian, G. R. Ferris and K. M. Kacmar, 'Age, Tenure, and Job Satisfaction: A Tale of Two Perspectives', *Journal of Vocational Behavior*, February 1992, pp. 33–48; and W. van Breukelen, R. van der Vlist and H. Steensma, 'Voluntary Employee Turnover: Combining Variables from the "Traditional" Turnover Literature with the Theory of Planned Behavior', *Journal of Organizational Behavior*, vol. 25, no. 7, 2004, pp. 893–914.

44. See, for instance, H. M. Weiss, 'Learning Theory and Industrial and Organizational Psychology', in M. D. Dunnette and L.M. Hough (eds; *Handbook of Industrial & Organizational Psychology*, 2nd ed., vol. 1 (Palo Alto, CA: Consulting Psychologists Press, 1990), pp. 172–73.

45. W. McGehee, 'Are We Using What We Know about Training? Learning Theory and Training', *Personnel Psychology*, Spring 1958, p. 2.

46. I. P. Pavlov, *The Work of the Digestive Glands*, trans. W. H. Thompson (London: Charles Griffin, 1902). See also the special issue of *American Psychologist* (September 1997, pp. 933–72) commemorating Pavlov's work.

47. B. F. Skinner, *Contingencies of Reinforcement* (East Norwalk, CT: Appleton-Century-Crofts, 1971).

48. J. A. Mills, *Control: A History of Behavioral Psychology* (New York: New York University Press, 2000).

49. A. Bandura, *Social Learning Theory* (Upper Saddle River, NJ: Prentice Hall, 1977).

50. F. Luthans and R. Kreitner, *Organizational Behavior Modification and Beyond*, 2nd ed. (Glenview, IL: Scott, Foresman, 1985); and A. D. Stajkovic and F. Luthans, 'A Meta-Analysis of the Effects of Organizational Behavior Modification on Task Performance, 1975–95', *Academy of Management Journal*, October 1997, pp. 1122–49.

51. 'At Emery Air Freight: Positive Reinforcement Boosts Performance', *Organizational Dynamics*, Winter 1973, pp. 41–50.

52. F. Luthans and R. Kreitner, *Organizational Behavior Modification and Beyond: An Operant and Social Learning Approach* (Glenview, IL: Scott, Foresman, 1985); Stajkovic and Luthans, 'A Meta-Analysis of the Effects of Organizational Behavior Modification on Task Performance, 1975–95'; and A. D. Stajkovic and F. Luthans, 'Behavioral Management and Task Performance in Organizations: Conceptual Background, Meta-Analysis, and Test of Alternative Models', *Personnel Psychology*, Spring 2003, pp. 155–92.

53. Stajkovic and Luthans, 'A Meta-Analysis of the Effects of Organizational Behavior Modification on Task Performance', p. 1123.

54. See, for instance, L. W. Frederiksen, *Handbook of Organizational Behavior Management* (New York: Wiley, 1982); B. Sulzer-Azarof, B. Loafman, R. J. Merante and A.C. Hlavacek, 'Improving Occupational Safety in a Large Industrial Plant: A Systematic Replication', *Journal of Organizational Behavior Management*, vol. 11, no. 1, 1990, pp. 99–120; J. C. Landau, 'The Impact of a Change in an Attendance Control System on Absenteeism and Tardiness', *Journal of Organizational Behavior Management*, vol. 13, no. 2, 1993, pp. 51–70; C. S. Brown and B. Sulzer-Azaroff, 'An Assessment of the Relationship between Customer Satisfaction and Service Friendliness', *Journal of Organizational Behavior Management*, vol. 14, no. 2, 1994, pp. 55–75; F. Luthans and A. D. Stajkovic, 'Reinforce for Performance: The Need to Go Beyond Pay and Even Rewards', *Academy of Management Executive*, May 1999, pp. 49–57; and A. D. Stajkovic and F. Luthans, 'Differential Effects of Incentive Motivators on Work Performance', *Academy of Management Journal*, vol. 44, no. 3, 2001, pp. 580–90.

55. E. A. Locke, 'Beyond Determinism and Materialism, or Isn't It Time We Took Consciousness Seriously?', *Journal of Behavior Therapy & Experimental Psychiatry*, vol. 26, no. 3, 1995, pp. 265–73.

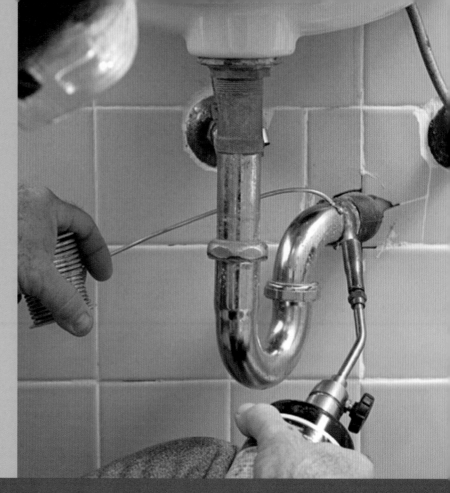

3

ATTITUDES AND JOB SATISFACTION

CHAPTER OUTLINE

ATTITUDES

JOB SATISFACTION

LEARNING OBJECTIVES

AFTER STUDYING THIS CHAPTER, YOU SHOULD BE ABLE TO:

1. CONTRAST THE THREE COMPONENTS OF AN ATTITUDE

2. IDENTIFY THE ROLE THAT CONSISTENCY PLAYS IN ATTITUDES

3. SUMMARISE THE RELATIONSHIP BETWEEN ATTITUDES AND BEHAVIOUR

4. DISCUSS SIMILARITIES AND DIFFERENCES BETWEEN JOB SATISFACTION AND THE OTHER JOB ATTITUDES DISCUSSED

5. SUMMARISE THE MAIN CAUSES OF JOB SATISFACTION

6. IDENTIFY FOUR EMPLOYEE RESPONSES TO DISSATISFACTION

Finding what makes people committed to their work is crucial to improving job satisfaction—
and job performance.

SNOW BROS LTD IS A PLUMBING AND DRAINAGE COMPANY founded in 1968 by Kevin and Maurice Snow. The firm started as a partnership but in 1971 incorporated as Snow Bros Ltd. In 1986, with 18 staff, it moved to its present premises. By 2002, the number of staff had grown to 55.

The company's functional structure reflects the original purpose of the business. Kevin was responsible for the plumbing side, while Maurice ran the drainage side.

In 1996, Kevin suffered a heart attack, which forced him to retire. Maurice assumed responsibility for both plumbing and drainage, but by 2000 he found that the pressures were too great. In 2002, he sold the company to another small plumbing firm, John Grant Ltd. John decided not to change the name because of the company's reputation around the town.

Within a year, John found that there were problems with the way the company was run. The most serious problem was finding and keeping good staff, with turnover in 2005 reaching 20 per cent. John talked with the supervisors and staff about what they wanted from their jobs, and three main issues surfaced:

1. Younger staff felt that there weren't enough incentives, apart for their wages, to commit to the company. They pointed out that Snow Bros paid the 'going rate', but no more, and had very little in the way of incentives to motivate them to stay or work harder.
2. Although most of the older staff, particularly the supervisors, had worked with the company for many years, they felt little sense of 'ownership' of it.
3. The apprentices, in particular, felt that they were at the bottom of a long, steep ladder and there didn't seem any scope to develop their career in the company. Hence, as soon as they qualified, they went looking for other positions.

John could see their point, since the company was in all respects still a traditional structure, with traditional ideas about how it should be managed. There were no incentives other than the weekly wage. He wasn't sure how the issue of 'ownership' could be tackled since he was, legally, the sole owner. He decided to talk with a manager friend, who had recently completed an MBA, about what ideas he might consider employing to tackle the 'people' issues John had uncovered.

I have long been of the opinion that if work were such a splendid thing the rich would have kept more of it for themselves.

Bruce Grocott

AS WE SEE IN THE CASE of Snow Bros, it is important that companies monitor employee attitudes. In this chapter, we look at attitudes, their link to behaviour, and how employees' satisfaction or dissatisfaction with their jobs impacts the workplace.

ATTITUDES

attitudes | Evaluative statements or judgments concerning objects, people or events.

Attitudes are evaluative statements—either favourable or unfavourable—concerning objects, people or events. They reflect how one feels about something. When I say, 'I like my job', I am expressing my attitude about work.

Attitudes are complex. If you ask people about their attitude towards soccer, John Howard or the organisation they work for, you may get a simple response, but the reasons underlying the response are probably complex. In order to fully understand attitudes, we need to consider their fundamental properties. In the material that follows, we will answer six questions about attitudes that will help you to understand them better:

1. What are the main components of attitudes?
2. How consistent are attitudes?
3. Does behaviour always follow from attitudes?
4. What are the main job attitudes?
5. How are employee attitudes measured?
6. What is the importance of attitudes to workplace diversity?

WHAT ARE THE MAIN COMPONENTS OF ATTITUDES?

Typically, researchers have assumed that attitudes have three components: cognition, affect and behaviour.[1] Let's look at each of these components.

The belief that 'discrimination is wrong' is an evaluative statement. Such an opinion is the **cognitive component of an attitude**. It sets the stage for the more critical part of an attitude—its **affective component**. Affect is the emotional or feeling segment of an attitude and is reflected in the statement, 'I don't like Jon because he discriminates against minorities.' Finally, and we will discuss this issue at considerable length later in this section, affect can lead to behavioural outcomes. The **behavioural component of an attitude** refers to an intention to behave in a certain way towards someone or something. So, to continue our example, I might choose to avoid Jon because of my feelings about him.

Viewing attitudes as made up of three components—cognition, affect and behaviour— is helpful in understanding their complexity and the potential relationship between attitudes and behaviour. Keep in mind that these components are closely related. In particular, in many ways, cognition and affect are inseparable. For example, imagine that you concluded that someone had just treated you unfairly. Aren't you likely to have feelings about that, occurring virtually instantaneously with the thought? Thus, cognition and affect are intertwined.

Figure 3.1 illustrates how the three components of an attitude are related. In this example, an employee didn't get a promotion she thought she deserved; a fellow employee got it instead. The employee's attitude towards her supervisor is illustrated as follows: cognition (the employee thought she deserved the promotion), affect (the employee

LEARNING OBJECTIVE 1

Contrast the three components of an attitude

MyOBLab

Do you know this material? Let MyOBLab tell you where you need help and devise a personal study plan for you www.pearsoned.com.au/ MyOBLab

cognitive component of an attitude | The opinion or belief segment of an attitude.

affective component of an attitude | The emotional or feeling segment of an attitude.

behavioural component of an attitude | An intention to behave in a certain way towards someone or something.

Cognition, affect and behaviour are closely related.

Cognitive = evaluation
My supervisor gave a promotion to a co-worker who deserved it less than me. My supervisor is unfair.

Affective = feeling
I dislike my supervisor!

Behavioural = action
I'm looking for other work; I've complained about my supervisor to anyone who would listen.

Negative attitude towards supervisor

strongly dislikes her supervisor) and behaviour (the employee is looking for another job). As we previously noted, although we often think that cognition causes affect, which then causes behaviour, in reality these components are often difficult to separate.

In organisations, attitudes are important because of their behavioural component. If employees believe, for example, that supervisors, auditors, bosses and time-and-motion engineers are all in conspiracy to make employees work harder for the same or less money, it makes sense to try to understand how these attitudes were formed, their relationship to actual job behaviour, and how they might be changed.

HOW CONSISTENT ARE ATTITUDES?

Did you ever notice how people change what they say so that it doesn't contradict what they do? Perhaps a friend of yours has consistently argued that the quality of Australian cars isn't up to that of the imported brands and that she would never own anything but a Japanese or German car. But her dad gives her a late-model Ford Monaro, and suddenly Australian cars aren't so bad. Or, when standing for election to Parliament, a new potential candidate believes that public service is a good chance to achieve social goals and plays a very important role. If she fails to get elected, however, she may say: 'I recognise that political office isn't all it's cracked up to be, anyway!'

Research has generally concluded that people seek consistency among their attitudes and between their attitudes and their behaviour.[2] This means that individuals seek to reconcile divergent attitudes, and to align their attitudes and behaviour so they appear rational and consistent. When there is an inconsistency, forces are initiated to return the individual to an equilibrium state in which attitudes and behaviour are again consistent. This can be done by altering either the attitudes or the behaviour, or by developing a rationalisation for the discrepancy.

Tobacco executives provide an example.[3] How, you might wonder, do these people cope with the ongoing barrage of data linking cigarette smoking and negative health outcomes? They can deny that any clear causation between smoking and cancer, for instance, has been established. They can brainwash themselves by continually articulating the benefits of

tobacco. They can acknowledge the negative consequences of smoking but rationalise that people are going to smoke and that tobacco companies merely promote freedom of choice. They can accept the research evidence and begin actively working to make more healthy cigarettes or at least reduce their availability to more vulnerable groups, such as teenagers. Or they can quit their job because the dissonance is too great.

Can we also assume from this consistency principle that an individual's behaviour can always be predicted if we know their attitude on a subject? If Mr Jones views the company's pay level as too low, will a substantial increase in his pay change his behaviour—that is, make him work harder? The answer to this question is, unfortunately, more complex than merely a 'yes' or 'no'.

cognitive dissonance |
Any incompatibility between two or more attitudes, or between behaviour and attitudes.

In the late 1950s, Leon Festinger proposed the theory of **cognitive dissonance**.[4] This theory sought to explain the linkage between attitudes and behaviour. 'Dissonance' means an inconsistency. *Cognitive dissonance* refers to any incompatibility that an individual might perceive between two or more attitudes, or between behaviour and attitudes. Festinger argued that any form of inconsistency is uncomfortable and that individuals will attempt to reduce the dissonance and, hence, the discomfort. Therefore, individuals will seek a stable state, in which there is a minimum of dissonance.

No individual, of course, can completely avoid dissonance. You know that cheating on your income tax is wrong, but you 'fudge' the numbers a bit every year and hope you are not audited. Or you tell your children to floss their teeth every day, but *you* don't. So, how do people cope? Festinger would propose that the desire to reduce dissonance would be determined by the *importance* of the elements creating the dissonance, the degree of *influence* the individual believes he or she has over the elements, and the *rewards* that may be involved in dissonance.

If the elements creating the dissonance are relatively unimportant, the pressure to correct this imbalance will be low. However, say that a corporate manager—Mrs Smith—believes strongly that no company should pollute the air or water. Unfortunately, Mrs

Smith, because of the requirements of her job, is placed in the position of having to make decisions that would trade off her company's profitability against her attitudes on pollution. She knows that dumping the company's partially treated sewage into the local river (which we shall assume is legal) is in the best economic interest of her firm. What will she do? Clearly, Mrs Smith is experiencing a high degree of cognitive dissonance. Because of the importance of the elements in this example, we cannot expect Mrs Smith to ignore the inconsistency. There are several paths she can follow to deal with her dilemma. She can change her behaviour (stop polluting the river). Or she can reduce dissonance by concluding that the dissonant behaviour isn't so important after all. ('I've got to make a living, and in my role as a corporate decision maker, I often have to place the good of my company above that of the environment or society.') A third alternative would be for Mrs Smith to change her attitude. ('There's nothing wrong with polluting the river.') Still another choice would be to seek out more consonant elements to outweigh the dissonant ones. ('The benefits to society from manufacturing our products more than offset the cost to society of the resulting water pollution.')

The degree of influence that individuals believe they have over the elements will have an impact on how they will react to the dissonance. If they perceive the dissonance to be due to something over which they have no control, they are less likely to be receptive to attitude change. If, for example, the dissonance-producing behaviour is required as a result of the boss's directive, the pressure to reduce dissonance would be less than if the behaviour was performed voluntarily. Though dissonance exists, it can be rationalised and justified.

Rewards also influence the degree to which individuals are motivated to reduce dissonance. High rewards accompanying high dissonance tend to reduce the tension inherent in the dissonance. The rewards act to reduce dissonance by increasing the consistency side of the individual's balance sheet.

These moderating factors suggest that even though individuals might experience dissonance, they won't necessarily move directly towards reducing it. If the issues underlying the dissonance are of minimal importance, if individuals perceive that the dissonance is externally imposed and is substantially uncontrollable by them, or if rewards are significant enough to offset the dissonance, the individual won't be under great tension to reduce the dissonance.

What are the organisational implications of the theory of cognitive dissonance? It can help to predict the propensity to engage in attitude and behavioural change. For example, if individuals are required by the demands of their job to say or do things that contradict their personal attitude, they will tend to modify their attitude in order to make it compatible with the cognition of what they have said or done. In addition, the greater the dissonance—after it has been moderated by importance, choice and reward factors—the greater the pressures to reduce it.

DOES BEHAVIOUR ALWAYS FOLLOW FROM ATTITUDES?

LEARNING OBJECTIVE 3
Summarise the relationship between attitudes and behaviour

We have maintained that attitudes affect behaviour. Early research on attitudes assumed that they were causally related to behaviour—that is, the attitudes that people hold determine what they do. Common sense, too, suggests a relationship. Isn't it logical that people watch television programs that they say they like, or that employees try to avoid assignments they find distasteful?

However, in the late 1960s this assumed relationship between attitudes and behaviour was challenged by a review of the research.[5] Based on an evaluation of a number of studies that investigated the attitudes–behaviour relationship, the reviewer concluded that attitudes were unrelated to behaviour or, at best, only slightly related.[6] More recent research has demonstrated that attitudes significantly predict future behaviour, and has confirmed Festinger's original belief that the relationship can be enhanced by taking moderating variables into account.[7]

MODERATING VARIABLES

The most powerful moderators of the attitudes–behaviour relationship have been found to be the *importance* of the attitude, its *specificity*, its *accessibility*, whether there exist social pressures, and whether a person has *direct experience* with the attitude.[8]

Important attitudes are ones that reflect fundamental values, self-interest, or identification with individuals or groups that a person values. Attitudes that individuals consider important tend to show a strong relationship to behaviour. The more specific the attitude and the more specific the behaviour, the stronger the link between the two. For instance, asking someone specifically about her intention to stay with the organisation for the next six months is likely to better predict turnover for that person than if you asked her how satisfied she was with her pay.

Attitudes that are easily remembered are more likely to predict behaviour than attitudes that aren't accessible in memory. Interestingly, you are more likely to remember attitudes that are frequently expressed. So the more you talk about your attitude on a subject, the more you are likely to remember it, and the more likely it is to shape your behaviour.

Discrepancies between attitudes and behaviour are more likely to occur when social pressures to behave in certain ways hold exceptional power. This tends to characterise behaviour in organisations. This may explain why an employee who holds strong anti-union attitudes attends union strike meetings, or why tobacco executives who aren't smokers themselves, and who tend to believe the research linking smoking and cancer, don't actively discourage others from smoking in their offices.

Finally, the attitude–behaviour relationship is likely to be much stronger if an attitude refers to something with which the individual has direct personal experience. Asking university students with no significant work experience how they would respond to working for an authoritarian supervisor is far less likely to predict actual behaviour than asking that same question of employees who have actually worked for such an individual.

Amcor is an Australian-based global packaging company with 240 plants in 42 countries. It places high importance on the attitude of taking personal responsibility within the company and the community. Amcor is a signature on the National Packaging Covenant aimed at educating and fostering greater sustainability of precious resources used in packaging by responsible packaging design and recycling. As part of this commitment, it sponsors the Australia-wide education of schoolchildren in recycling principles as well as being the sponsor of the National Community Value award category as part of the Young Australian Achievement awards.

SELF-PERCEPTION THEORY

Although most attitudes–behaviour studies yield positive results, researchers have achieved still higher correlations by pursuing another direction—looking at whether or not behaviour influences attitudes. This view, called

self-perception theory, has generated some encouraging findings. Let's briefly review the theory.[9]

When asked about an attitude towards some object, individuals often recall their behaviour relevant to that object and then infer their attitude from their past behaviour. So, if an employee was asked her feelings about being a training specialist at the Transport Department, she would likely think: 'I've had this same job with the Transport Department as a trainer for ten years. No one has forced me to stay on in this job. So I must like it!' Self-perception theory, therefore, argues that attitudes are used, after the fact, to make sense out of an action that has already occurred, rather than as devices that precede and guide action. And contrary to cognitive dissonance theory, attitudes are just casual verbal statements. When people are asked about their attitudes and they don't have strong convictions or feelings, self-perception theory says they tend to create plausible answers.

Self-perception theory has been well supported.[10] While the traditional attitude–behaviour relationship is generally positive, the behaviour–attitude relationship is just as strong. This is particularly true when attitudes are vague and ambiguous. When you have had few experiences regarding an attitude issue or have given little previous thought to it, you will tend to infer your attitudes from your behaviour. However, when your attitudes have been established for a while and are well defined, those attitudes are likely to guide your behaviour.

WHAT ARE THE MAIN JOB ATTITUDES?

A person can have thousands of attitudes, but OB focuses our attention on a very limited number of work-related attitudes. These work-related attitudes tap positive or negative evaluations that employees hold about aspects of their work environment. Most of the research in OB has been concerned with three attitudes: job satisfaction, job involvement and organisational commitment.[11] A few other attitudes are attracting attention from researchers, including perceived organisational support and employee engagement; we will also briefly discuss these.

JOB SATISFACTION

The term **job satisfaction** can be defined as a positive feeling about one's job resulting from an evaluation of its characteristics. A person with a high level of job satisfaction holds positive feelings about the job, while a person who is dissatisfied holds negative feelings about the job. When people speak of employee attitudes, more often than not they mean job satisfaction. In fact, the two are frequently used interchangeably. Because of the high importance OB researchers have given to job satisfaction, we will review this attitude in considerable detail later in this chapter.

JOB INVOLVEMENT

Although much less studied than job satisfaction, a related concept is job involvement.[12] **Job involvement** measures the degree to which people identify psychologically with their job and consider their perceived performance level important to self-worth.[13] Employees with a high level of job involvement strongly identify with and really care about the kind of work they do. A closely related concept is **psychological empowerment**, which is employees' belief in the degree to which they impact their work environment, their competence, the meaningfulness of their job, and the perceived autonomy in their work.[14] For example, one study of nursing managers in Singapore found that good leaders empower their employees by involving them in decisions, making them feel that their work is important, and giving them discretion to 'do their own thing'.[15]

---

self-perception theory | Attitudes are used after the fact to make sense out of an action that has already occurred.

LEARNING OBJECTIVE 4

Discuss similarities and differences between job satisfaction and the other job attitudes discussed

job satisfaction | A positive feeling about one's job resulting from an evaluation of its characteristics.

job involvement | The degree to which a person identifies with a job, actively participates in it and considers performance important to self-worth.

psychological empowerment | Employees' belief in the degree to which they impact their work environment, their competence, the meaningfulness of their job, and the perceived autonomy in their work.

High levels of job involvement and psychological empowerment are positively related to organisational citizenship and job performance.[16] In addition, high job involvement has been found to be related to fewer absences and lower resignation rates.[17]

ORGANISATIONAL COMMITMENT

The third job attitude we will discuss is **organisational commitment**, which is defined as a state in which an employee identifies with a particular organisation and its goals, and wishes to maintain membership in the organisation.[18] So, high job involvement means identifying with one's specific job, while high organisational commitment means identifying with one's employing organisation.

There are three separate dimensions to organisational commitment:[19]

1. **Affective commitment**—an emotional attachment to the organisation and a belief in its values. For example, a Purina employee may be affectively committed to the company because of its involvement with animals.

2. **Continuance commitment**—the perceived economic value of remaining with an organisation compared to leaving it. An employee may be committed to an employer because she is paid well and feels it would hurt her family if she were to quit.

3. **Normative commitment**—an obligation to remain with the organisation for moral or ethical reasons. For example, an employee who is spearheading a new initiative may remain with an employer because he feels it would 'leave the employer in the lurch' if he left.

There appears to be a positive relationship between organisational commitment and job productivity, but the relationship is modest.[20] And, as with job involvement, the research evidence demonstrates negative relationships between organisational commitment and both absenteeism and turnover.[21] In general, it seems that affective commitment is more strongly related to organisational outcomes such as performance and turnover than the other two commitment dimensions. One study found that affective commitment was a significant predictor of various outcomes (perception of task characteristics, career satisfaction, intent to leave) in 72 per cent of the cases, compared to only 36 per cent for normative commitment and 7 per cent for continuance commitment.[22] The weak results for continuance commitment make sense in that it really isn't a strong commitment at all. Rather than an allegiance (affective commitment) or an obligation (normative commitment) to an employer, a continuance commitment describes an employee who is 'tethered' to an employer simply because there isn't anything better available.

There is reason to believe that the concept of commitment may be less important to employers and employees than it once was. The unwritten loyalty contract that existed 30 years ago between employees and employers has been seriously damaged, and the notion of employees staying with a single organisation for most of their career has become increasingly obsolete. As such, 'measures of employee–firm attachment, such as commitment, are problematic for new employment relations'.[23] This suggests that *organisational commitment* is probably less important as a work-related attitude than it once was. In its place we might expect something akin to *occupational commitment* to become a more relevant variable because it better reflects today's fluid workforce.[24]

OTHER JOB ATTITUDES

Perceived organisational support is the degree to which employees believe the organisation values their contribution and cares about their well-being (for example, an employee believes that his organisation would accommodate him if he had a child-care

CHINESE EMPLOYEES AND ORGANISATIONAL COMMITMENT

Are employees from different cultures committed to their organisations in similar ways? A 2003 study explored this question and compared the organisational commitment of Chinese employees to the commitment of Canadian and South Korean workers. Although results revealed that the three types of commitment—normative, continuance and affective— are present in all three cultures, results also showed that there are some differences among the three countries in terms of the importance they place on each type of commitment.

Normative commitment, an obligation to remain with the organisation for moral or ethical reasons, was higher in the Chinese sample of employees than in the Canadian and South Korean sample. Affective commitment, an emotional attachment to the organisation and a belief in its values, was also stronger in China compared to Canada and South Korea. Chinese culture may explain why. The Chinese emphasise loyalty to one's group, and in this case, one's 'group' may be the organisation that one works for, so employees may feel a certain loyalty from the start and may become more emotionally attached as their time with the organisation grows. To the extent that the Chinese view their organisation as part of their group and become emotionally attached to that group, they will be more committed to their organisation. Perhaps as a result of this emphasis on loyalty, the normative commitment of Chinese employees strongly predicted intentions to maintain employment with the organisation.

Continuance commitment, the perceived economic value of remaining with an organisation compared to leaving it, was lower in the Chinese sample than in the Canadian and South Korean sample. One reason for the lower degree of continuance commitment is that Chinese workers value loyalty towards the group more than individual concerns.

It appears that although all three countries experience normative, continuance and affective commitment, the degree to which each form of commitment is important differs across countries.

SOURCE: Based on Y. Cheng and M. S. Stockdale, 'The Validity of the Three-Component Model of Organizational Commitment in a Chinese Context', *Journal of Vocational Behavior*, June 2003, pp. 465–89.

---

problem or would forgive an honest mistake on his part). Research shows that people perceive their organisation as supportive when rewards are deemed fair, when employees have a voice in decisions, and when their supervisors are seen as supportive.[25]

A very new concept is **employee engagement**, which can be defined as an individual's involvement with, satisfaction with, and enthusiasm for, the work they do. For example, one might ask employees about the availability of resources and the opportunities to learn new skills, whether they feel their work is important and meaningful, and whether their interactions with their fellow employees and supervisors were rewarding.[26] A recent study of nearly 8000 business units in 36 companies found that business units whose employees had high–average levels of engagement had higher levels of customer satisfaction, were more productive, had higher profits, and had lower levels of turnover and accidents.[27] Because the concept is so new, we don't know how engagement relates to other concepts such as job satisfaction, organisational commitment, job involvement or intrinsic motivation to do one's job well. Engagement may be broad enough that it captures the intersection of these variables. In other words, engagement may be what these attitudes have in common.

employee engagement | An individual's involvement with, satisfaction with, and enthusiasm for the work they do.

ARE THESE JOB ATTITUDES REALLY ALL THAT DISTINCT?

You might wonder whether these job attitudes are really distinct. After all, if people feel deeply involved in their job (high job involvement), isn't it probable that they like it (high job satisfaction)? Similarly, won't people who think their organisation is supportive (high perceived organisational support) also feel committed to it (strong organisational commitment)? Evidence suggests that these attitudes are highly related, perhaps to a troubling degree. For example, the correlation between perceived organisational support and affective commitment is very strong.[28] The problem is that a strong correlation means that the variables may be redundant (so, for example, if you know someone's affective commitment, you basically know her perceived organisational support). But why is this redundancy so troubling? Well, why have two steering wheels on a car when you only need one? Why have two concepts—going by different labels—when you only need one? This redundancy is inefficient and confusing. Although we OB researchers like proposing new attitudes, often we haven't been good at showing how each attitude compares and contrasts to the others. There is some measure of distinctiveness among these attitudes—they aren't exactly the same—but they overlap greatly. The overlap may exist for various reasons, including the employee's personality. Some people are predisposed to be positive or negative about almost everything. If someone tells you she loves her company, it may not mean a lot if she is positive about everything else in her life. Or the overlap may mean that some organisations are just all around better places to work than others. This may mean that if you as a manager know someone's level of job satisfaction, you know most of what you need to know about how the person sees the organisation.

HOW ARE EMPLOYEE ATTITUDES MEASURED?

As we have seen, knowledge of employee attitudes can be helpful to managers in attempting to predict employee behaviour. But how does management get information about employee attitudes? The most popular method, because of its ease of implementation and speed of results, is through the use of **attitude surveys**.[29]

attitude surveys | Eliciting responses from employees through questionnaires on how they feel about their jobs, work groups, supervisors and the organisation.

The typical attitude survey presents the employee with a set of statements or questions with a rating scale indicating the degree of agreement. Some examples might include: 'This organisation's wage rates are competitive with those of other organisations'; 'My job makes the best use of my abilities'; and 'I know what my boss expects of me.' Ideally, the items should be tailored to obtain the specific information that management desires. An individual's attitude score is achieved by summing up responses to the questionnaire items. These scores can then be averaged for work groups, teams, departments, divisions or the organisation as a whole.

Results from attitude surveys can frequently surprise management. Often they think everything is great, a view usually predicated on performance and output data and not on what the employees' attitudes are.[30] Further, because managers and executives tend to be older, they often have quite different perceptions than do younger employees who come from cohorts with quite different world-views. Another complicating factor is the reality that traditional attitude and satisfaction surveys are viewed sceptically or suspiciously by many employees concerned about confidentiality, leading to unusable or invalid results. One way to overcome this scepticism and suspicion is to employ an outside body to conduct and analyse the data so that 100 per cent confidentiality is assured. Publishing the full results also helps to reduce the concerns of many employees. Still, as senior management at both Roche Australia and OPSM found, the surveys will often identify more issues than the organisation can address at the same time. Management therefore needs to select two or three key issues and address those fully before moving on to other issues. In doing so, trust and commitment is built with all employees, but especially with the sceptical and suspicious employees, as they see progress in addressing issues in a non-threatening manner.

Using attitude surveys on a regular basis provides managers with valuable feedback on how employees perceive their working conditions. Policies and practices that management views as objective and fair may be seen as unfair and inequitable by employees in general or by certain groups of employees. If distorted perceptions lead to negative attitudes about the job and organisation, it is important for management to know about it. Why? Because, as we will elaborate on later in this book, employee behaviours are based on perceptions, not reality. The use of regular attitude surveys can alert management to potential problems and employees' intentions early so that action can be taken to prevent negative repercussions.[31]

WHAT IS THE IMPORTANCE OF ATTITUDES TO WORKPLACE DIVERSITY?

Managers are increasingly concerned with changing employee attitudes to reflect shifting perspectives on racial, gender and other diversity issues. A comment to a fellow employee of the opposite sex that 20 years ago might have been taken as a compliment—for

JOB SATISFACTION HITS RECORD LOWS

There is now longitudinal evidence produced by the Australian government that job satisfaction levels among academics in Australian universities are dropping significantly. It is hard to know for sure whether this downward trend will continue, but some recent evidence provides some intriguing suggestions. This decline is found among academics of all ages, but most notably among mid-career academics who make up the bulk of the workforce. This same group report increased stress and workloads at levels higher than for early- or late-career academics. Female academics generally find they have to put more time into their workloads than before, due to work stressors, but at the same time report slightly higher satisfaction levels. The question not researched was whether the increased satisfaction reported was warranted, or whether it was the academic's way of reducing cognitive dissonance. There are also variations in satisfaction between regional and capital city universities, as well as between newer and older 'sandstone' universities; satisfaction in the latter tends to be higher, and with fewer stressors, than in the regional and new universities.

What are the strongest areas of dissatisfaction? Probably the biggest area of dissatisfaction is the increased workloads caused by increasing use of computer technologies in teaching. While academics are having to come to grips with this increased teaching workload, the emphasis in the promotions and rewards systems is still on research, rather than on teaching. Indeed, 91 per cent of academics saw research being used exclusively for the determination or rewards and promotions, whereas their teaching commitment as a percentage of their workload is rising exponentially. Further creating low job satisfaction among academics is the lack of formal training or qualifications in teaching, courseware design and the new teaching technologies available to them. The report suggests that as many as 75 per cent of academics have no teaching training. The combination of increased workloads with little or no formal teacher training, and little or no ongoing staff development, was cited by many respondents as a major source of dissatisfaction.

Other indicators of falling job satisfaction for Australian academics were the decline in satisfaction with salary, which dropped to just 31 per cent, and with job security, which dropped to 43 per cent. All this information points to significant concerns for Australian universities, particularly as dissatisfied teachers are often not good at hiding their dissatisfaction from their students. Given that the most dissatisfied group were mid-career academics, who form the largest group of teaching staff, ignoring the problem will have dire consequences for the future.

SOURCE: Based on Department of Education, Science and Training, *Report on the Work Roles of Academics in Australian Universities*, 1999, accessed online at <www.dest.gov.au/archive/highered/eippubs/eip00_5/execsum.htm>.

OB IN PRACTICE

instance, a male telling a female colleague that he thinks her outfit is sexy—can today become a career-stopping episode. As such, organisations are investing in training to help reshape the attitudes of employees.

The majority of Australian state and federal departments and an increasing number of private employers now sponsor some sort of diversity training.[32] Some examples: All new employees at Cummins South Pacific start with a 40-minute online diversity training program and then receive regular diversity training, while supervisors and managers undergo a 12-module program to assist them to manage diversity effectively. The Bristol-Myers Squib pharmaceutical company starts with a mission statement that includes its commitment to foster a globally diverse workforce and backs that up with an ongoing and sustained leadership development program that all employees and managers must participate in every year, as well as bi-monthly leadership forums so that diversity remains at the forefront in people's minds. The Australian Taxation Office (ATO) uses the diversity of its own workforce to reach out to non-English-speaking members of the Australian community through videos, interviews, guest radio and TV appearances, and providing speakers for community groups. The ATO's goal is to help explain the Australian tax system and the obligations of all income-earners to pay taxes. Using staff members to deliver the message in the audience's own language, and with the correct cultural mannerisms, makes this goal more achievable.

What do these diversity programs look like and how do they address attitude change?[33] They almost all include a self-evaluation phase. People are pressed to examine themselves and to confront any ethnic and cultural stereotypes they might hold. They are also asked to share their values and what they respect and expect in return. Then participants typically take part in group discussions or panels with representatives from diverse groups. So, for instance, a Hmong man might describe his family's life in Southeast Asia and explain why they resettled in Melbourne; or a lesbian might describe how she discovered her sexual identity and the reaction of her friends and family when she no longer hid her sexual orientation.

Additional activities designed to change attitudes include arranging for people to do volunteer work in community or social service centres in order to meet face-to-face with individuals and groups from diverse backgrounds, and using exercises that let participants feel what it is like to be different. For example, when people participate in the exercise *Blue Eyes–Brown Eyes*, in which people are segregated and stereotyped according to their eye colour, participants see what it is like to be judged by something over which they have no control. Evidence suggests that this exercise reduces negative attitudes towards individuals who are different from the participants.[34]

JOB SATISFACTION

We have already discussed job satisfaction briefly—earlier in this chapter, as well as in a previous chapter. In this section, we want to dissect the concept more carefully. How do we measure job satisfaction? How satisfied are employees in their jobs? What causes an employee to have a high level of job satisfaction? How do dissatisfied and satisfied employees affect an organisation?

MEASURING JOB SATISFACTION

We have previously defined job satisfaction as a positive feeling about one's job resulting from an evaluation of its characteristics. This definition is clearly a very broad one.[35] Yet this is inherent in the concept. Remember, a person's job is more than just the obvious activities of shuffling papers, writing programming code, waiting on customers or driving a truck. Jobs require interaction with fellow employees and bosses, following organisational rules and policies, meeting performance standards, living with working conditions that are often less than ideal, and the like.[36] This means that an employee's assessment of how satisfied or dissatisfied he or she is with the job is a complex summation of a number of discrete job elements. How, then, do we measure the concept?

The two most widely used approaches are a single global rating and a summation score made up of a number of job facets. The single global rating method is nothing more than asking individuals to respond to one question, such as: 'All things considered, how satisfied are you with your job?' Respondents then reply by circling a number between 1 and 5 that corresponds to answers from 'highly satisfied' to 'highly dissatisfied'. The other approach—a summation of job facets—is more sophisticated. It identifies key elements in a job and asks for the employee's feelings about each. Typical factors that would be included are the nature of the work, supervision, present pay, promotion opportunities, and relations with fellow employees.[37] These factors are rated on a standardised scale and then added up to create an overall job satisfaction score.

Is one of the foregoing approaches superior to the other? Intuitively, it would seem that summing up responses to a number of job factors would achieve a more accurate evaluation of job satisfaction. The research, however, doesn't support this intuition.[38] This is one of those rare instances in which simplicity seems to work as well as complexity. Comparisons of one-question global ratings with the more lengthy summation-of-job-factors method indicate that the former is essentially as valid as the latter. The best explanation for this outcome is that the concept of job satisfaction is inherently so broad that the single question captures its essence. Another explanation may be that some important facets are left out of the summation of job facets. Both methods are helpful. For example, the single global rating method isn't very time consuming, which frees up managers so that they can address other workplace issues and problems. And the summation of job facets helps managers to zero in on where problems exist, making it easier to deal with unhappy employees and to solve problems more quickly and more accurately.

HOW SATISFIED ARE PEOPLE IN THEIR JOBS?

Are most people satisfied with their jobs? The answer seems to be a qualified 'yes' in most developed countries. Independent studies, conducted among workers in the United States over the past 30 years, generally indicate that the majority of workers are satisfied with their jobs.[39] Although the percentage range is wide, more people report that they are satisfied than not. Moreover, these results generally apply to other developed countries. For instance, comparable studies among workers in Canada, Mexico and Europe indicate more positive than negative results.[40]

Research shows that satisfaction levels vary a lot depending on which facet of job satisfaction you are talking about. As shown in Figure 3.2, people are on average satisfied with their jobs overall, with the work itself, and with their supervisors and fellow employees. However, they tend to be less satisfied with their pay and with promotion opportunities. It is not really clear why people dislike their pay and promotion possibilities more than other aspects of their jobs.[41] But what about you? Do you like your job? See the Self-Assessment Library feature below where you can determine your level of satisfaction with your current or past jobs.

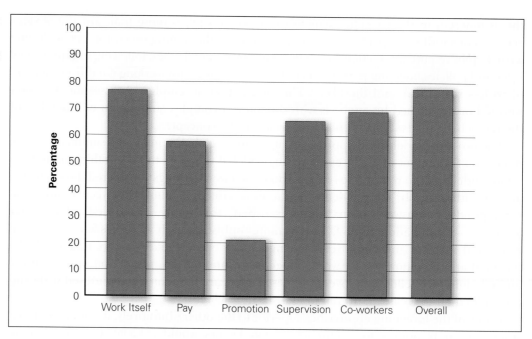

SELF-
ASSESSMENT
LIBRARY

HOW SATISFIED AM I WITH MY JOB?

In the Self-Assessment Library (available on CD and online), take Self-Assessment I.B.3 (How Satisfied Am I with My Job?) and answer the following questions.

1. How does your job satisfaction compare to others in your class who have taken the assessment?
2. Why do you think your satisfaction is higher or lower than average?

LEARNING OBJECTIVE 5

Summarise the main
causes of job
satisfaction

WHAT CAUSES JOB SATISFACTION?

Think about the best job you ever had. What made it so? Chances are you probably liked the work you did. In fact, of the major job-satisfaction facets (work itself, pay, advancement opportunities, supervision, fellow employees), enjoying the work itself is almost always the facet most strongly correlated with high levels of overall job satisfaction. Interesting jobs that provide training, variety, independence and control satisfy most employees.[42] In other words, most people prefer work that is challenging and stimulating over work that is predictable and routine.

You have probably noticed that pay comes up often when discussing job satisfaction. Let's explore this topic some more. There is an interesting relationship between salary and job satisfaction. For people who are poor (for example, living below the poverty line), or who live in poor countries, pay does correlate with job satisfaction and with overall happiness. But, once an individual reaches a level of comfortable living (in Australia, that occurs at about $60 000 a year, depending on the region and family size), the relationship virtually disappears. In other words, people who earn $80 000 are, on average, no happier with their jobs than those who earn close to $40 000. Jobs that are compensated handsomely have average job satisfaction levels no higher than those that are paid much

Instructions: Circle whether you are on average satisfied, neutral or dissatisfied with each item below.

The city in which you live	Satisfied	Neutral	Dissatisfied
The neighbours you have	Satisfied	Neutral	Dissatisfied
The high school you attended	Satisfied	Neutral	Dissatisfied
The climate where you live	Satisfied	Neutral	Dissatisfied
Movies being produced today	Satisfied	Neutral	Dissatisfied
The quality of food you buy	Satisfied	Neutral	Dissatisfied
Today's cars	Satisfied	Neutral	Dissatisfied
Local newspapers	Satisfied	Neutral	Dissatisfied
Your first name	Satisfied	Neutral	Dissatisfied
The people you know	Satisfied	Neutral	Dissatisfied
Telephone service	Satisfied	Neutral	Dissatisfied
A4-size paper	Satisfied	Neutral	Dissatisfied
Restaurant food	Satisfied	Neutral	Dissatisfied
Modern art	Satisfied	Neutral	Dissatisfied

SOURCE: T. A. Judge and C. L. Hulin, 'Job Satisfaction as a Reflection of Disposition: A Multiple-Source Causal Analysis', *Organizational Behavior and Human Decision Processes*, 1993, vol. 56, pp. 388–421. Copyright 1993, reprinted with permission of Elsevier.

less. To further illustrate this point, one researcher even found no significant difference when he compared the overall well-being of the richest people on the Forbes 400 list (similar to the BRW 100 list) with that of Maasai herdsmen in East Africa.[43]

Now, money *does* motivate people, as we will discover later. But what motivates us isn't necessarily the same as what makes us happy. A recent poll by the University of California, Los Angeles, and the American Council on Education found that first-year students rated becoming 'very well off financially' first on a list of 19 goals, ahead of helping others, raising a family or becoming proficient in an academic pursuit. Maybe your goal isn't to be happy. But if it is, money is probably not going to do much to get you there.[44]

Job satisfaction isn't just about job conditions. Personality also plays a role. For example, some people are predisposed to like almost anything, and others are unhappy even in the seemingly greatest jobs. Research has shown that people who have a negative personality (for example, those who tend to be grumpy, critical and negative) are usually less satisfied with their jobs. The Neutral Objects Satisfaction Questionnaire (see Figure 3.3) is a measure for understanding the link between personality and job satisfaction. For example, one study showed that nurses who were dissatisfied with the majority of the items on the list were also dissatisfied with their jobs. This isn't surprising—after all, if someone dislikes his first name, his telephone service and even A4-size paper, you would expect him to dislike most things in his life—including his job.

THE IMPACT OF DISSATISFIED AND SATISFIED EMPLOYEES ON THE WORKPLACE

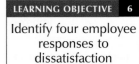

LEARNING OBJECTIVE 6

Identify four employee responses to dissatisfaction

There are consequences when employees like their jobs, and when they dislike their jobs. One theoretical framework—the exit–voice–loyalty–neglect framework—is helpful in understanding the consequences of dissatisfaction. Figure 3.4 illustrates the framework's four responses, which differ from one another along two dimensions: constructive/destructive and active/passive. The responses are defined as follows:[45]

'HAPPY WORKERS ARE PRODUCTIVE WORKERS'

This statement is generally true. The idea that 'happy workers are productive workers' developed in the 1930s and 1940s largely as a result of findings drawn by researchers conducting the Hawthorne studies at Western Electric. Based on those conclusions, managers worked to make their employees happier by focusing on working conditions and the work environment. Then, in the 1980s, an influential review of the research suggested that the relationship between job satisfaction and job performance wasn't particularly high. The authors of this review even went so far as to label the relationship as 'illusory'.

More recently, a review of more than 300 studies corrected some errors in this earlier review. It estimated that the correlation between job satisfaction and job performance is moderately strong. This conclusion also appears to be generalisable across international contexts. The correlation is higher for complex jobs that provide employees with more discretion to act on their attitudes.

It is important to recognise that the reverse causality might be true—productive workers are likely to be happy workers, or productivity leads to satisfaction. In other words, if you do a good job, you intrinsically feel good about it. In addition, your higher productivity should increase your recognition, your pay level, and your probabilities for promotion. Cumulatively, these rewards, in turn, increase your level of satisfaction with the job.

It is probably the case that both arguments are right: that satisfaction can lead to high levels of performance for some people, while for others, high performance may cause them to be satisfied.

SOURCES: M. T. Iaffaldano and M. Muchinsky, 'Job Satisfaction and Job Performance: A Meta-Analysis', *Psychological Bulletin*, March 1985, pp. 251–73; T. A. Judge, C. J. Thoresen, J. E. Bono and G. K. Patton, 'The Job Satisfaction–Job Performance Relationship: A Qualitative and Quantitative Review', *Psychological Bulletin*, May 2001, pp. 376–407; T. Judge, S. Parker, A. E. Colbert, D. Heller and R. Ilies, 'Job Satisfaction: A Cross-Cultural Review', in N. Anderson, D. S. Ones, H. K. Sinangil and C. Viswesvaran (eds), *Handbook of Industrial, Work, & Organizational Psychology*, vol. 2 (Thousand Oaks, CA: Sage, 2001, p. 41); C. N. Greene, 'The Satisfaction–Performance Controversy', *Business Horizons*, February 1972, pp. 31–41; E. E. Lawler III, *Motivation in Organizations* (Monterey, CA: Brooks/Cole, 1973); and M. M. Petty, G. W. McGee and J. W. Cavender, 'A Meta-Analysis of the Relationship between Individual Job Satisfaction and Individual Performance', *Academy of Management Review*, October 1984, pp. 712–21.

exit | Dissatisfaction expressed through behaviour directed towards leaving the organisation.

voice | Dissatisfaction expressed through active and constructive attempts to improve conditions.

loyalty | Dissatisfaction expressed by passively waiting for conditions to improve.

neglect | Dissatisfaction expressed through allowing conditions to worsen.

- **Exit**: Behaviour directed towards leaving the organisation, including looking for a new position as well as resigning.
- **Voice**: Actively and constructively attempting to improve conditions, including suggesting improvements, discussing problems with superiors, and some forms of union activity.
- **Loyalty**: Passively but optimistically waiting for conditions to improve, including speaking up for the organisation in the face of external criticism and trusting the organisation and its management to 'do the right thing'.
- **Neglect**: Passively allowing conditions to worsen, including chronic absenteeism or lateness, reduced effort and increased error rate.

Exit and neglect behaviours encompass our performance variables—productivity, absenteeism and turnover. But this model expands employee response to include voice and loyalty—constructive behaviours that allow individuals to tolerate unpleasant situations or to revive satisfactory working conditions. It helps us to understand certain situations, such as those that are sometimes found among employees working in highly unionised workplaces, for whom low job satisfaction is coupled with low turnover.[46] Union members often express their dissatisfaction through the grievance procedure or through formal enterprise bargaining negotiations. These voice mechanisms allow union members to continue working in their jobs while convincing themselves that they are acting to improve the situation.

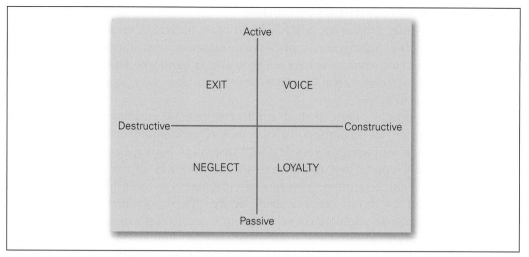

As helpful as this framework is in presenting the possible consequences of job dissatisfaction, it is quite general. We now discuss more specific outcomes of job satisfaction and dissatisfaction in the workplace.

JOB SATISFACTION AND JOB PERFORMANCE

As the 'Myth or Science?' box concludes, happy workers are more likely to be productive workers, although it is hard to tell which way the causality runs. Some researchers used to believe that the relationship between job satisfaction and job performance was a management myth, but a review of 300 studies suggested that the correlation is pretty strong.[47] As we move from the individual level to that of the organisation, we also find support for the satisfaction–performance relationship.[48] When satisfaction and productivity data are gathered for the organisation as a whole, we find that organisations with more satisfied employees tend to be more effective than organisations with fewer satisfied employees.

JOB SATISFACTION AND OCB

It seems logical to assume that job satisfaction should be a major determinant of an employee's organisational citizenship behaviour (OCB).[49] Satisfied employees would seem more likely to talk positively about the organisation, help others and go beyond the normal expectations in their job. Moreover, satisfied employees might be more prone to go beyond the call of duty because they want to reciprocate their positive experiences. Consistent with this thinking, early discussions of OCB assumed that it was closely linked with satisfaction.[50] More recent evidence, however, suggests that satisfaction influences OCB, but through perceptions of fairness.

There is a modest overall relationship between job satisfaction and OCB.[51] But satisfaction is unrelated to OCB when fairness is controlled for.[52] What does this mean? Basically, job satisfaction comes down to conceptions of fair outcomes, treatment and procedures.[53] If you don't feel that your supervisor, the organisation's procedures or pay policies are fair, your job satisfaction is likely to suffer significantly. However, when you perceive organisational processes and outcomes to be fair, trust is developed. And when you trust your employer, you are more willing to voluntarily engage in behaviours that go beyond your formal job requirements.

JOB SATISFACTION AND CUSTOMER SATISFACTION

As we noted previously, employees in service jobs often have high interaction levels with customers. Since the management of service organisations should be concerned with pleasing those customers, it is reasonable to ask: Is employee satisfaction related to positive customer outcomes? For frontline employees who have regular contact with customers, the answer is 'yes'.

The evidence indicates that satisfied employees increase customer satisfaction and loyalty.[54] Why? In service organisations, customer retention and defection are highly dependent on how frontline employees deal with customers. Satisfied employees are more likely to be friendly, upbeat and responsive—which customers appreciate. And because satisfied employees are less prone to turnover, customers are more likely to encounter familiar faces and to receive experienced service. These qualities build customer satisfaction and loyalty. In addition, the relationship seems to apply in reverse: dissatisfied customers can increase an employee's job dissatisfaction. Employees who have regular contact with customers report that rude, thoughtless or unreasonably demanding customers adversely affect the employees' job satisfaction.[55]

A number of companies are acting on this evidence. Service-oriented businesses such as Virgin Blue, Flight Centre, Marriott Hotels, Singapore Airlines and Westpac obsess about pleasing their customers. Towards that end, they also focus on building employee satisfaction—recognising that employee satisfaction will go a long way towards contributing to their goal of having happy customers. These firms seek to hire upbeat and friendly employees, they train employees in the importance of customer service, they reward customer service, they provide positive employee work climates, and they regularly track employee satisfaction through attitude surveys.

JOB SATISFACTION AND ABSENTEEISM

We find a consistent negative relationship between satisfaction and absenteeism, but the correlation is moderate to weak.[56] While it certainly makes sense that dissatisfied employees are more likely to miss work, other factors have an impact on the relationship and reduce the correlation coefficient. For example, organisations that provide liberal sick leave benefits are encouraging all their employees—including those who are highly satisfied—to take days off. Assuming that you have a reasonable number of varied interests, you can find work satisfying and yet still take time off work to enjoy a three-day weekend or tan yourself on a warm summer day if those days come free with no penalties.

An excellent illustration of how satisfaction directly leads to attendance, when there is a minimum impact from other factors, is a study done at Sears, Roebuck, a large American department store chain.[57] Satisfaction data were available on employees at Sears' two headquarters in Chicago and New York. In addition, it is important to note that Sears' policy wasn't to permit employees to be absent from work for avoidable reasons without penalty. The occurrence of a freak snowstorm in Chicago on 2 April created the opportunity to compare employee attendance at the Chicago office with attendance in New York, where the weather was fine. The interesting dimension in this study is that the snowstorm gave the Chicago employees a built-in excuse not to come to work. The storm crippled the city's transportation, and individuals knew they could miss work this day with no penalty. This natural experiment permitted the comparison of attendance records for satisfied and dissatisfied employees at two locations—one where you were expected to be at work (with normal pressures for attendance) and the other where you were free to choose with no penalty involved. If satisfaction leads to attendance, when there is an absence of outside factors, the more satisfied employees should have come to work in Chicago, while dissatisfied employees should have stayed home. The study found that on this particular day in April, absenteeism rates in New York were just as high for satisfied groups of workers as for dissatisfied groups. But in Chicago, the workers with high satisfaction scores had much higher attendance than did those with lower satisfaction levels. These findings are exactly what we would have expected if satisfaction is negatively correlated with absenteeism.

JOB SATISFACTION AND TURNOVER

Satisfaction is also negatively related to turnover, but the correlation is stronger than what we found for absenteeism.[58] Yet, again, other factors such as labour-market conditions, expectations about alternative job opportunities, and length of tenure with the organisation are important constraints on the actual decision to leave one's current job.[59]

Service organisations know that satisfied and loyal customers depend on how frontline employees deal with customers. Singapore Airlines has earned a reputation among world travellers for outstanding customer service. The airline's 'putting people first' philosophy applies to both its employees and customers. In recruiting flight attendants, the airline selects people who are warm, hospitable and happy to serve others. Through extensive training, Singapore moulds recruits into attendants focused on complete customer satisfaction.

Evidence indicates that an important moderator of the satisfaction–turnover relationship is the employee's level of performance.[60] Specifically, level of satisfaction is less important in predicting turnover for superior performers. Why? The organisation typically makes considerable efforts to keep these people. They get pay raises, praise, recognition, increased promotional opportunities, and so forth. Just the opposite tends to apply to poor performers. Few attempts are made by the organisation to retain them. There may even be subtle pressures to encourage them to quit. We would expect, therefore, that job satisfaction is more important in influencing poor performers to stay than superior performers. Regardless of level of satisfaction, the latter are more likely to remain with the organisation because the receipt of recognition, praise and other rewards gives them more reasons for staying.

JOB SATISFACTION AND WORKPLACE DEVIANCE

Job dissatisfaction predicts a lot of specific behaviours, including involvement with unions, substance abuse, surfing the internet, stealing at work, undue socialising, leaving early and tardiness. Researchers argue that these behaviours are indicators of a broader syndrome that we would term 'deviant behaviour in the workplace' (or 'employee withdrawal').[61] The key is that if employees don't like their work environment, they will respond somehow. It isn't always easy to forecast exactly how they will respond. One worker's response might be to quit. But another may respond by taking work time to surf the internet, taking stationery supplies from work to home for personal use, and so on. If employers want to control the undesirable consequences of job dissatisfaction, they had best attack the source of the problem—the dissatisfaction—rather than trying to control the different responses.

SUMMARY AND IMPLICATIONS FOR MANAGERS

- Managers should be interested in their employees' attitudes, because attitudes give warnings of potential problems and influence behaviour.
- Satisfied and committed employees, for instance, have lower rates of turnover, absenteeism and withdrawal behaviours.
- Satisfied employees also perform better on the job.
- Given that managers want to keep resignations and absences down—especially among their more productive employees—they will want to do the things that will generate positive job attitudes.
- The most important thing managers can do to raise employee satisfaction is to focus on the intrinsic parts of the job, such as making the work challenging and interesting.
- While paying employees poorly will likely not attract high-quality employees to the organisation, or keep high performers, managers should realise that high pay alone is unlikely to create a satisfying work environment.
- Managers should be aware that employees will try to reduce cognitive dissonance and that dissonance can be managed.
- If employees are required to engage in activities that appear inconsistent to them or that are at odds with their attitudes, the pressures to reduce the resulting dissonance are lessened when employees perceive that the dissonance is externally imposed and is beyond their control, or if the rewards are significant enough to offset the dissonance.

POINT / COUNTERPOINT

Managers Can Create Satisfied Employees

● POINT

A review of the evidence has identified four factors conducive to high levels of employee job satisfaction: mentally challenging work, equitable rewards, supportive working conditions and supportive colleagues. Importantly, each of these factors is controllable by management.

- *Mentally challenging work*. Generally, people prefer jobs that give them opportunities to use their skills and abilities and offer a variety of tasks, freedom and feedback on how well they are doing. These characteristics make work mentally challenging.
- *Equitable rewards*. Employees want pay systems that they perceive as being just, unambiguous, and in line with their expectations. When pay is seen as fair, based on job demands, individual skill level and community pay standards, satisfaction is likely to result.
- *Supportive working conditions*. Employees are concerned with their work environment for both personal comfort and facilitating doing a good job. Studies demonstrate that employees prefer physical surroundings that are not dangerous or uncomfortable. In addition, most employees prefer working relatively close to home, in clean and relatively modern facilities, and with adequate tools and equipment.
- *Supportive colleagues*. People get more out of work than merely money or tangible achievements. For most employees, work also fulfils the need for social interaction. Not surprisingly, therefore, having friendly and supportive colleagues leads to increased job satisfaction. The behaviour of one's boss is also a major determinant of satisfaction. Studies find that employee satisfaction is increased when the immediate supervisor is understanding and

friendly, offers praise for good performance, listens to employees' opinions and shows a personal interest in them.

● COUNTERPOINT

The notion that managers and organisations can control the level of employee job satisfaction is inherently attractive. It fits nicely with the view that managers directly influence organisational processes and outcomes. Unfortunately, there is a growing body of evidence that challenges the notion that managers control the factors that influence employee job satisfaction. The most recent findings indicate that employee job satisfaction is largely genetically determined.

Whether a person is happy or not is essentially determined by gene structure. Approximately 50–80 per cent of people's differences in happiness, or subjective well-being, has been found to be attributable to their genes. Identical twins, for example, tend to have very similar careers, have similar levels of job satisfaction, and change jobs at similar rates.

Analysis of satisfaction data for a selected sample of individuals conducted over a 50-year period found that individual results were consistently stable over time, even when these individuals changed employers and occupations. This and other research suggests that an individual's disposition towards life—positive or negative—is established by genetic makeup, holds over time, and carries over into a disposition towards work.

Given these findings, there is probably little that most managers can do to influence employee satisfaction. In spite of the fact that managers and organisations go to extensive lengths to try to improve employee job satisfaction through actions such as manipulating job characteristics, working conditions and rewards, people will inevitably return to their own 'set point'. A bonus may temporarily increase the satisfaction level of a negatively disposed worker, but it is unlikely to sustain it. Sooner or later, new areas of fault will be found with the job.

The only place where managers will have any significant influence will be through their control of the selection process. If managers want satisfied workers, they need to make sure their selection process screens out negative people who derive little satisfaction from their jobs, irrespective of its conditions.

SOURCES: Points in this argument are based on T. Judge, S. Parker, A. E. Colbert, D. Heller and R. Ilies, 'Job Satisfaction: A Cross-Cultural Review', in N. Anderson, D. S. Ones, H. K. Sinangil and C. Viswesvaran (eds), *Handbook of Industrial, Work, & Organizational Psychology*, vol. 2 (Thousand Oaks, CA: Sage, 2001); T. A. Judge and A. H. Church, 'Job Satisfaction: Research and Practice', in C. L. Cooper and E. A. Locke (eds), *Industrial and Organizational Psychology: Linking Theory with Practice* (Oxford, UK: Blackwell, 2000), pp. 166–98; L. Saari and T. A. Judge, 'Employee Attitudes and Job Satisfaction', *Human Resource Management*, vol. 43, no. 4, 2004, pp. 395–407; R. D. Arvey, B. McCall, T. J. Bouchard, Jr and P Taubman, 'Genetic Influences on Job Satisfaction and Work Values', *Personality and Individual Differences*, July 1994, pp. 21–33; D. Lykken and A. Tellegen, 'Happiness is a Stochastic Phenomenon', *Psychological Science*, May 1996, pp. 186–89; D. Lykken and M. Csikszentmihalyi, 'Happiness—Stuck With What You've Got?', *Psychologist*, September 2001, pp. 470–72; and 'Double Take', *UNH Magazine*, Spring 2000: <www.unhmagazine.unh.edu/sp00/twinssp00.html>.

QUESTIONS FOR REVIEW

1. Contrast the cognitive and affective components of an attitude.
2. What is cognitive dissonance and how is it related to attitudes?
3. What is self-perception theory? How does it increase our ability to predict behaviour?
4. What moderating factors can improve the statistical relationship between attitudes and behaviour?
5. How can managers get employees to more readily accept working with colleagues who are different from themselves?
6. What explains the recent declines in employee job satisfaction?
7. Do you think job satisfaction means the same thing in all countries? Why or why not?
8. Are happy workers productive workers?
9. Contrast exit, voice, loyalty and neglect as employee responses to job dissatisfaction.
10. What is the relationship between job satisfaction and absenteeism? Turnover? Which is the stronger relationship?

QUESTIONS FOR CRITICAL THINKING

1. 'Managers should do everything they can to enhance the job satisfaction of their employees.' Do you agree or disagree? Support your position.
2. Discuss the advantages and disadvantages of using regular attitude surveys to monitor employee job satisfaction.
3. 'It doesn't matter how employees say they feel about their employers. What really matters in terms of behaviour is whether they have better options out there.' Is there any evidence to support or refute this statement?
4. When employees are asked whether they would again choose the same work or whether they would want their children to follow in their footsteps, typically less than half answer in the affirmative. What, if anything, do you think this implies about employee job satisfaction?
5. George Loewenstein, an economist at Carnegie-Mellon University in the United States, recently said: 'I think it is possible to way overestimate the importance of happiness. Part of the meaning of life is to have highs and lows. A life that was constantly happy was not a good life.' Do you agree or disagree with Professor Loewenstein?

EXPERIENTIAL EXERCISE

Challenges in Negotiating with Chinese Executives

Purpose:
To demonstrate the exercise of power and negative reinforcement.

Time required:
Approximately 50–60 minutes.

Participant roles:
Team members developing strategy.

The task:
Form into teams of three to five members each. All your team's members work for a company in the western suburbs of Melbourne that manufactures porcelain bathroom fixtures such as sinks, toilets and bathtubs. Your company's senior management has decided to make a serious effort to expand sales of its fixtures into the Chinese market. To begin the process, your team has been chosen to make a ten-day trip to Beijing and Shanghai to meet with purchasing executives at half-a-dozen Chinese residential and commercial real estate construction developers.

Your team will be leaving for its trip in a week. You will have a translator in both cities, but your team wants to do whatever it can to make a good impression on the Chinese executives they will be meeting. Unfortunately, the members of your team have a relatively limited knowledge of Chinese culture. To help with the trip, one of your team members has found a brochure that summarises some of the unique characteristics of the Chinese and that might prove valuable in opening negotiations. The highlights of that brochure included:

- China is a group-oriented society and any negotiations must cover the interests of many different parties.
- Emphasis is placed on trust and mutual connections, especially extended family ones.
- The Chinese are interested in long-term benefits.
- The Chinese seem to have a compelling need to dwell on the subject of friendship.
- Initial business meetings are devoted to pleasantries, such as serving tea and engaging in chit-chat.

- So as not to lose face, Chinese prefer to negotiate through an intermediary.
- Chinese expect reciprocal invitations—if a banquet is given in the honour of your team, they expect you to give a banquet for their team.
- Chinese are sensitive about foreigners' comments on Chinese politics.
- Chinese are punctual and expect others will arrive promptly on time for each meeting.
- Chinese are well aware of Australians' reputation for abruptness and impatience. They will often take their time in decision making to gain an advantage in negotiations.
- Chinese don't like to be touched or slapped on the back, or even to shake hands. A slight bow and a brief shake of the hands are more appropriate.
- Chinese generally believe that foreign businesspeople will be highly qualified technically in their specific area of expertise.
- Chinese become rigid in posture whenever they feel their goals are being compromised.
- Very often, several visits are necessary to consummate any business transaction.
- Foreigners shouldn't focus on the individual Chinese person but rather on the group of individuals who are working to achieve a particular goal.
- Telephone calls, emails and fax machines are a vital part of Chinese business, but the Chinese think important business should be conducted face-to-face.
- In negotiations with Chinese, nothing should be considered final until it has been actually realised.

Your team has 30 minutes to rough out a strategy for meeting with the Chinese purchasing executives. Be as specific as possible. When finished, be prepared to present your strategy to the entire class.

SOURCE: This exercise is based on information in R. Harris and R. T. Moran, *Managing Cultural Differences*, 4th ed. (Houston, TX: Gulf Publishing, 1996), pp. 252–57.

ETHICAL DILEMMA

Are Americans Overworked?

Europeans pride themselves on their quality of life, and rightly so. In a recent worldwide analysis of quality of life, the United States ranked 13th. The 12 nations that finished ahead of the United States were all from Europe. Factors considered in the analysis were material well-being, health, political stability, divorce rates, job security, political freedom and gender equality, among other factors.

Many Europeans would credit their high quality of life to their nations' free health care, more generous unemployment benefits, and greater emphasis on leisure as opposed to work. Consider that most European nations mandate restricted work week hours and a month or more of vacation time, but Americans have among the fewest vacation days and longest average work week in the world. Juliet Schor, a Harvard economist who has written on the subject, argues that the United States 'is the world's standout workaholic nation', and that US employees are trapped in a 'squirrel cage' of overwork. Some argue that mandated leisure time would force companies to compete within their industry by raising productivity and product quality, rather than by requiring workers to put in more hours.

Many European nations also place limits on the hours employers can require employees to work. France, Germany and other nations limit the work week to 35 hours. Recently, after much debate, the French parliament voted to do away with the rule that set 35 hours as the maximum work week. The justification was that more flexible rules would allow French companies to compete more effectively so that, if business required it, they could pay employees for longer hours. Opponents of the new rules argue that it puts the decision of how much to work in the individual's hands. These people argue that it will inevitably detract from quality of life and give employers power to exploit workers. A French union leader said, 'They say it is the worker who will choose how much to work, but they are lying because it is always the employer who decides.'

QUESTIONS

1. Why do you think quality of life is lower in the United States compared to many European nations? Do you think quality of life in the United States would increase if the government required a minimum number of vacation days or limited work week hours?

2. Where do you think Australia would place in comparison with the countries named above? Why should Australia be ranked lower than America on quality of life if we have 35-hour work weeks and at least four weeks' annual leave each year?

3. Do you think the French parliament was right to eliminate the 35-hour work week limit? Do you think the quality of French life will suffer? How might it impact on the high unemployment rate in France if those who are employed are able to work longer hours?

4. Do you think employers have an obligation to watch out for the quality of life of their employees? Could that translate into protecting employees from being overworked?

5. Does it make a difference that the unemployment rate in Europe is roughly double that of the United States and that Europe's gross domestic product is about half that of the United States?

SOURCES: Juliet Schor, *The Overworked American: The Unexpected Decline of Leisure* (New York: Basic Books, 1992); C. S. Smith, 'Effort to Extend Workweek Advances in France', *New York Times*, 10 February 2005, p. A9; and 'The Economist Intelligence Unit's Quality-of-Life Index', *The Economist*, 2005: <www.economist.com/media/pdf/QUALITY_OF_LIFE.pdf>.

CASE STUDY

Long Hours, Hundreds of Emails and No Sleep: Does this Sound Like a Satisfying Job?

Although the 35-hour work week is now the exception rather than the norm, some individuals are taking things to the extreme.

- David Morgan is the CEO of Westpac bank in its Sydney headquarters. He openly admits that he works six days and five nights a week. An average work day starts at 6 am, he has meetings all day, and he returns home for dinner at 7 pm. After dinner, he will work at home for many more hours. He loves his job but admits that he is not setting a good example in an organisation that wants its employees to see the organisation as a family-friendly workplace and strives to encourage each employee to find a good work/life balance. Morgan recognises that he is a workaholic, but realistically, it isn't at all unusual to expect a CEO of one of Australia's largest corporations to work 90 to 100 hours a week.

- Irene Tse, 34, heads the government bond-trading division at Goldman Sachs. For ten years, she has seen the stock market go from all-time highs to recession levels. Such fluctuations can mean millions of dollars in either profits or losses. 'There are days when you can make a lot, and other days where you lose so much you're just stunned by what you've done,' says Tse. She also states that she hasn't slept completely through the night in years and frequently wakes up several times during the night to check the global market status. Her average work week? Eighty hours. 'I've done this for ten years, and I can count on the fingers of one hand the number of days in my career when I didn't want to come to work. Every day I wake up and I can't wait to get here.'

- Tony Kurtz, 33, is a managing director at Capital Alliance Partners and raises funds for real-estate investments. However, these aren't your average properties. He often travels to exotic locations such as Costa Rica and Hawaii, wooing prospective clients. He travels nearly 500 000 kilometres a year, often sleeping on planes and dealing with jet lag. Kurtz isn't the only one he knows with such a hectic work schedule. His girlfriend, Avery Baker, logs around 600 000 kilometres a year, working as a senior marketing executive for a clothing retailer. 'It's not easy to maintain a relationship like this', says Kurtz. But do Kurtz and Baker like their jobs? You bet.

- David Clark, 35, is the vice president of global marketing for MTV. His job often consists of travelling around the globe to promote the channel, as well as to keep up with the global music scene. If he isn't travelling (Clark typically logs over 300 000 kilometres a year), a typical day consists of waking at 6.30 am and immediately responding to numerous messages that have accumulated over the course of the night. He then goes to his office, where throughout the day he will respond to another 500 messages or so from clients around the world. If he is lucky, he gets to spend an hour a day with his son, but then it's back to work until he finally goes to bed around midnight. Says Clark, 'There are plenty of people who would love to have this job. They're knocking on the door all the time. So that's motivating.'

Many individuals would balk at the prospect of a 60-hour or more work week with constant travelling and little time for anything else. However, some individuals are exhilarated by such professions. According to the Australian Council of Trade Unions (ACTU), in 2002, about 31 per cent of all employees worked more than 48 hours per week, with 2.4 million employees working more than 45 hours per week. Figures for managers aren't available but are likely to be much higher, with 60-hour weeks the norm for most managers. But the demands of such jobs are clearly not for everyone. Many quit, with turnover levels at 55 per cent for consultants and 30 per cent for investment bankers. However, it is clear that such jobs, which are time consuming and often stressful, can be satisfying to some individuals.

QUESTIONS

1. Do you think that only certain individuals are attracted to these types of jobs, or is it the characteristics of the jobs themselves that are satisfying?
2. What are some characteristics of these jobs that might contribute to greater levels of job satisfaction?
3. Given that the five individuals we just read about tend to be satisfied with their jobs, how might this satisfaction relate to their job performance, citizenship behaviour and turnover?
4. Recall David Clark's statement, 'There are plenty of people who would love to have this job.' How might Clark's perceptions of having a job that many others desire contribute to his job satisfaction?

SOURCES: Based on L. Tischler, 'Extreme Jobs (and the People Who Love Them)', *Fast Company*, April 2005, pp. 55–60: <www.glo-jobs.com/article.php?article_no=87>; and ACTU, 'ACTU Reasonable Hours Test Case Affiliates Information Kit', accessed online at www.actu.asn.au/public/papers/affiliateskit/>.

ENDNOTES

1. S. J. Breckler, 'Empirical Validation of Affect, Behaviour, and Cognition as Distinct Components of Attitude', *Journal of Personality and Social Psychology*, May 1984, pp. 1191–205; and S. L. Crites, Jr, L. R. Fabrigar and R. E. Petty, 'Measuring the Affective and Cognitive Properties of Attitudes: Conceptual and Methodological Issues', *Personality and Social Psychology Bulletin*, December 1994, pp. 619–34.
2. See, for instance, I. R. Newby-Clark, I. McGregor and M. P. Zanna, 'Thinking and Caring about Cognitive Consistency: When and for Whom Does Attitudinal Ambivalence Feel Uncomfortable?', *Journal of Personality & Social Psychology*, February 2002, pp. 157–66; and D. J. Schleicher, J. D. Watt and G. J. Greguras, 'Reexamining the Job Satisfaction–Performance Relationship: The Complexity of Attitudes', *Journal of Applied Psychology*, vol. 89, no. 1, 2004, pp. 165–77.
3. See, for instance, M. Geyelin, 'Tobacco Executive Has Doubts about Health Risks of Cigarettes', *Wall Street Journal*, 3 March 1998, p. B10; and J. A. Byrne, 'Philip Morris: Inside America's Most Reviled Company', *US News & World Report*, 29 November 1999, pp. 176–92.
4. L. Festinger, *A Theory of Cognitive Dissonance* (Stanford, CA: Stanford University Press, 1957).
5. A. W. Wicker, 'Attitude versus Action: The Relationship of Verbal and Overt Behavioral Responses to Attitude Objects', *Journal of Social Issues*, Autumn 1969, pp. 41–78.
6. Ibid, p. 65.
7. See S. J. Kraus, 'Attitudes and the Prediction of Behavior: A Meta-Analysis of the Empirical Literature', *Personality and Social Psychology Bulletin*, January 1995, pp. 58–75; I. Ajzen, 'The Directive Influence of Attitudes on Behavior', in M. Gollwitzer and J. A. Bargh (eds), *The Psychology of Action: Linking Cognition and Motivation to Behavior* (New York: Guilford, 1996), pp. 385–403; S. Sutton, 'Predicting and Explaining Intentions and Behavior: How Well Are We Doing?', *Journal of Applied Social Psychology*, August 1998, pp. 1317–38; and I. Ajzen, 'Nature and Operation of Attitudes', in S. T. Fiske, D. L. Schacter and C. Zahn-Waxler (eds), *Annual Review of Psychology*, vol. 52 (Palo Alto, CA: Annual Reviews, Inc., 2001), pp. 27–58.
8. Ibid.
9. D. J. Bem, 'Self-Perception Theory', in L. Berkowitz (ed.), *Advances in Experimental Social Psychology*, vol. 6 (New York: Academic Press, 1972), pp. 1–62.
10. See C. A. Kiesler, R. E. Nisbett and M. Zanna, 'On Inferring One's Belief from One's Behavior', *Journal of Personality and Social Psychology*, April 1969, pp. 321–27; S. E. Taylor, 'On Inferring One's Attitudes from One's Behavior: Some Delimiting Conditions', *Journal of Personality and Social Psychology*, January 1975, pp. 126–31; and A. M. Tybout and C. A. Scott, 'Availability of Well-Defined Internal Knowledge and the Attitude Formation Process: Information Aggregation versus Self-Perception', *Journal of Personality and Social Psychology*, March 1983, pp. 474–91.
11. P. P. Brooke, Jr, D. W. Russell and J. L. Price, 'Discriminant Validation of Measures of Job Satisfaction, Job Involvement, and Organizational Commitment', *Journal of Applied Psychology*, May 1988, pp. 139–45; and R. T. Keller, 'Job Involvement and Organizational Commitment as Longitudinal Predictors of Job Performance: A Study of Scientists and Engineers', *Journal of Applied Psychology*, August 1997, pp. 539–45.
12. See, for example, S. Rabinowitz and D. T. Hall, 'Organizational Research in Job Involvement', *Psychological Bulletin*, March 1977, pp. 265–88; G. J. Blau, 'A Multiple Study Investigation of the Dimensionality of Job Involvement', *Journal of Vocational Behavior*, August 1985, pp. 19–36; N. A. Jans, 'Organizational Factors and Work Involvement', *Organizational Behavior and Human Decision Processes*, June 1985, pp. 382–96; and I. M. Paullay, G. M. Alliger and E. F. Stone-Romero, 'Construct Validation of Two Instruments Designed to Measure Job Involvement and Work

Centrality', *Journal of Applied Psychology*, vol. 79, no. 2, 1994, pp. 224–28.

13. Based on G. J. Blau and K. R. Boal, 'Conceptualizing How Job Involvement and Organizational Commitment Affect Turnover and Absenteeism', *Academy of Management Review*, April 1987, p. 290.

14. K. W. Thomas and B. A. Velthouse, 'Cognitive Elements of Empowerment: An "Interpretive" Model of Intrinsic Task Motivation', *Academy of Management Review*, vol. 15, no. 4, 1990, pp. 666–81; G. M. Spreitzer, 'Psychological Empowerment in the Workplace: Dimensions, Measurement, and Validation', *Academy of Management Journal*, vol. 38, no. 5, 1995, pp. 1442–65; G. Chen and R. J. Klimoski, 'The Impact of Expectations on Newcomer Performance in Teams as Mediated by Work Characteristics, Social Exchanges, and Empowerment', *Academy of Management Journal*, vol. 46, no. 5, 2003, pp. 591–607; R. C. Liden, S. J. Wayne and R. T. Sparrowe, 'An Examination of the Mediating Role of Psychological Empowerment on the Relations between the Job, Interpersonal Relationships, and Work Outcomes', *Journal of Applied Psychology*, vol. 85, no. 3, 2000, pp. 407–16; and S. E. Seibert, S. R. Silver and W. A. Randolph, 'Taking Empowerment to the Next Level: A Multiple-Level Model of Empowerment, Performance, and Satisfaction', *Academy of Management Journal*, vol. 47, no. 3, 2004, pp. 332–49.

15. B. J. Avolio, W. Zhu, W. Koh and P. Bhatia, 'Transformational Leadership and Organizational Commitment: Mediating Role of Psychological Empowerment and Moderating Role of Structural Distance', *Journal of Organizational Behavior*, vol. 25, no. 8, 2004, pp. 951–68.

16. J. M. Diefendorff, D. J. Brown, A. M. Kamin and R. G. Lord, 'Examining the Roles of Job Involvement and Work Centrality in Predicting Organizational Citizenship Behaviors and Job Performance', *Journal of Organizational Behavior*, February 2002, pp. 93–108.

17. G. J. Blau, 'Job Involvement and Organizational Commitment as Interactive Predictors of Tardiness and Absenteeism', *Journal of Management*, Winter 1986, pp. 577–84; K. Boal and R. Cidambi, 'Attitudinal Correlates of Turnover and Absenteeism: A Meta Analysis', Paper presented at the meeting of the American Psychological Association, Toronto, Canada, 1984; and M. R. Barrick, M. K. Mount and J. P. Strauss, 'Antecedents of Involuntary Turnover Due to a

Reduction in Force', *Personnel Psychology*, vol. 47, no. 3, 1994, pp. 515–35.

18. Blau and Boal, 'Conceptualizing', p. 290.

19. J. P. Meyer, N. J. Allen and C. A. Smith, 'Commitment to Organizations and Occupations: Extension and Test of a Three-Component Conceptualization', *Journal of Applied Psychology*, vol. 78, no. 4, 1993, pp. 538–51.

20. M. Riketta, 'Attitudinal Organizational Commitment and Job Performance: A Meta-Analysis', *Journal of Organizational Behavior*, March 2002, pp. 257–66.

21. See, for instance, W. Hom, R. Katerberg and C. L. Hulin, 'Comparative Examination of Three Approaches to the Prediction of Turnover', *Journal of Applied Psychology*, June 1979, pp. 280–90; H. Angle and J. Perry, 'Organizational Commitment: Individual and Organizational Influence', *Work and Occupations*, May 1983, pp. 123–46; J. L. Pierce and R. B. Dunham, 'Organizational Commitment: Pre-Employment Propensity and Initial Work Experiences', *Journal of Management*, Spring 1987, pp. 163–78; and T. Simons and Q. Roberson, 'Why Managers Should Care about Fairness: The Effects of Aggregate Justice Perceptions on Organizational Outcomes', *Journal of Applied Psychology*, vol. 88, no. 3, 2003, pp. 432–43.

22. R. B. Dunham, J. A. Grube and M. B. Castañeda, 'Organizational Commitment: The Utility of an Integrative Definition', *Journal of Applied Psychology*, vol. 79, no. 3, 1994, pp. 370–80.

23. D. M. Rousseau, 'Organizational Behavior in the New Organizational Era', in J. T. Spence, J. M. Darley and D. J. Foss (eds), *Annual Review of Psychology*, vol. 48 (Palo Alto, CA: Annual Reviews, 1997), p. 523.

24. Ibid; K. Lee, J. J. Carswell and N. J. Allen, 'A Meta-Analytic Review of Occupational Commitment: Relations with Person- and Work-Related Variables', *Journal of Applied Psychology*, October 2000, pp. 799–811; G. Blau, 'On Assessing the Construct Validity of Two Multidimensional Constructs: Occupational Commitment and Occupational Entrenchment', *Human Resource Management Review*, Fall 2001, pp. 279–98; and E. Snape and T. Redman, 'An Evaluation of a Three-Component Model of Occupational Commitment: Dimensionality and Consequences among United Kingdom Human Resource Management Specialists', *Journal of Applied Psychology*, vol. 88, no. 1, 2003, pp. 152–59.

25. L. Rhoades, R. Eisenberger and S. Armeli,

'Affective Commitment to the Organization: The Contribution of Perceived Organizational Support', *Journal of Applied Psychology*, vol. 86, no. 5, 2001, pp. 825–36.

26. D. R. May, R. L. Gilson and L. M. Harter, 'The Psychological Conditions of Meaningfulness, Safety and Availability and the Engagement of the Human Spirit at Work', *Journal of Occupational and Organizational Psychology*, vol. 77, no. 1, 2004, pp. 11–37.

27. J. K. Harter, F. L. Schmidt and T. L. Hayes, 'Business-Unit-Level Relationship between Employee Satisfaction, Employee Engagement, and Business Outcomes: A Meta-Analysis', *Journal of Applied Psychology*, vol. 87, no. 2, 2002, pp. 268–79.

28. L. Rhoades and R. Eisenberger, 'Perceived Organizational Support: A Review of the Literature', *Journal of Applied Psychology*, vol. 87, no. 4, 2002, pp. 698–714; R. L. Payne and D. Morrison, 'The Differential Effects of Negative Affectivity on Measures of Well-Being versus Job Satisfaction and Organizational Commitment', *Anxiety, Stress & Coping: An International Journal*, vol. 15, no. 3, 2002, pp. 231–44.

29. See, for example, L. Simpson, 'What's Going On in Your Company? If You Don't Ask, You'll Never Know', *Training*, June 2002, pp. 30–34.

30. J. Stack, 'Measuring Morale', *INC.*, January 1997, pp. 29–30.

31. This paragraph is based on Simpson, 'What's Going On in Your Company?'; K. Brown, 'Taking the Personnel Pulse: Employee Surveys', *Human Resources*, no. 81, 31 May 2005, pp. 16–17; and C. Donaldson, 'Taking the Pulse', *Human Resources*, no. 105, 30 May 2006, pp. 18–19.

32. See Society for Human Resource Management, 'Impact of Diversity on the Bottom Line': <www.fortune.com/sections> (31 August 2001), pp. 5–12; M. Bendick, Jr, M. L. Egan and S. M. Lofhjelm, 'Workforce Diversity Training: From Anti-Discrimination Compliance to Organizational Development', *Human Resource Planning*, vol. 24, no. 2, 2001, pp. 10–25; and S. T. Brathwaite, 'Denny's: A Diversity Success Story', *Franchising World*, July/August 2002, pp. 28–30.

33. This section is based on A. Rossett and T. Bickham, 'Diversity Training: Hope, Faith and Cynicism', *Training*, January 1994, pp. 40–46: <www.diversityaustralia. gov.au/>; for the union perspective, see

<www.actu.asn.au/public/news/10669706 25_5384.html>; and for the federal government view, see <www.psm.act.gov.au/edt/resources.html>.

34. T. L. Stewart, J. R. LaDuke, C. Bracht, B. A. M. Sweet and K. E. Gamarel, 'Do the "Eyes" Have It? A Program Evaluation of Jane Elliott's "Blue-Eyes/Brown-Eyes" Diversity Training Exercise', *Journal of Applied Social Psychology*, vol. 33, no. 9, 2003, pp. 1898–921.

35. For problems with the concept of job satisfaction, see R. Hodson, 'Workplace Behaviors', *Work and Occupations*, August 1991, pp. 271–90; and H. M. Weiss and R. Cropanzano, 'Affective Events Theory: A Theoretical Discussion of the Structure, Causes and Consequences of Affective Experiences at Work', in B. M. Staw and L. L. Cummings (eds), *Research in Organizational Behavior*, vol. 18 (Greenwich Press, CT: JAI Press, 1996), pp. 1–3.

36. The Wyatt Company's 1989 national *WorkAmerica* study identified 12 dimensions of satisfaction: work organisation, working conditions, communications, job performance and performance review, co-workers, supervision, company management, pay, benefits, career development and training, job content and satisfaction, and company image and change.

37. See E. Spector, *Job Satisfaction: Application, Assessment, Causes, and Consequences* (Thousand Oaks, CA: Sage, 1997), p. 3.

38. J. Wanous, A. E. Reichers and M. J. Hudy, 'Overall Job Satisfaction: How Good Are Single-Item Measures?', *Journal of Applied Psychology*, April 1997, pp. 247–52.

39. A. F. Chelte, J. Wright and C. Tausky, 'Did Job Satisfaction Really Drop During the 1970s?', *Monthly Labor Review*, November 1982, pp. 33–36; 'Job Satisfaction High in America, Says Conference Board Study', *Monthly Labor Review*, February 1985, p. 52; E. Graham, 'Work May Be a Rat Race, but It's Not a Daily Grind', *Wall Street Journal*, 19 September 1997, p. R1; and K. Bowman, 'Attitudes about Work, Chores, and Leisure in America', *AEI Opinion Studies*, released 25 August 2003.

40. L. Grant, 'Unhappy in Japan', *Fortune*, 13 January 1997, p. 142; 'Survey Finds Satisfied Workers in Canada', *Manpower Argus*, January 1997, p. 6; and T. Mudd, 'Europeans Generally Happy in the Workplace', *Industry Week*, 4 October 1999, pp. 11–12.

41. W. K. Balzer, J. A. Kihm, P. C. Smith, J. L. Irwin, P. D. Bachiochi, C. Robie,

E. F. Sinar and L. F. Parra, *Users' Manual for the Job Descriptive Index (JDI; 1997 Revision)* and *The Job in General Scales* (Bowling Green, OH: Bowling Green State University, 1997).

42. J. Barling, E. K. Kelloway and R. D. Iverson, 'High-Quality Work, Job Satisfaction, and Occupational Injuries', *Journal of Applied Psychology*, vol. 88, no. 2, 2003, pp. 276–83; F. W. Bond and D. Bunce, 'The Role of Acceptance and Job Control in Mental Health, Job Satisfaction, and Work Performance', *Journal of Applied Psychology*, vol. 88, no. 6, 2003, pp. 1057–67.

43. E. Diener, E. Sandvik, L. Seidlitz and M. Diener, 'The Relationship between Income and Subjective Well-Being: Relative or Absolute?', *Social Indicators Research*, vol. 28, 1993, pp. 195–223.

44. E. Diener and M. E. P. Seligman, 'Beyond Money: Toward an Economy of Well-Being', *Psychological Science in the Public Interest*, vol. 5, no. 1, 2004, pp. 1–31; A. Grant, 'Money=Happiness? That's Rich: Here's the Science Behind the Axiom', *The Sun Herald*, 8 January 2005: <www.sunherald.com/mld/thesunherald/news/world/10595331.htm>.

45. See D. Farrell, 'Exit, Voice, Loyalty, and Neglect as Responses to Job Dissatisfaction: A Multidimensional Scaling Study', *Academy of Management Journal*, December 1983, pp. 596–606; C. E. Rusbult, D. Farrell, G. Rogers and A. G. Mainous III, 'Impact of Exchange Variables on Exit, Voice, Loyalty, and Neglect: An Integrative Model of Responses to Declining Job Satisfaction', *Academy of Management Journal*, September 1988, pp. 599–627; M. J. Withey and W. H. Cooper, 'Predicting Exit, Voice, Loyalty, and Neglect', *Administrative Science Quarterly*, December 1989, pp. 521–39; J. Zhou and J. M. George, 'When Job Dissatisfaction Leads to Creativity: Encouraging the Expression of Voice', *Academy of Management Journal*, August 2001, pp. 682–96; J. B. Olson-Buchanan and W. R. Boswell, 'The Role of Employee Loyalty and Formality in Voicing Discontent', *Journal of Applied Psychology*, December 2002, pp. 1167–74; and A. Davis-Blake, J. P. Broschak and E. George, 'Happy Together? How Using Nonstandard Workers Affects Exit, Voice, and Loyalty among Standard Employees', *Academy of Management Journal*, vol. 46, no. 4, 2003, pp. 475–85.

46. R. B. Freeman, 'Job Satisfaction as an Economic Variable', *American Economic Review*, 8 January, pp. 135–41.

47. T. A. Judge, C. J. Thoresen, J. E. Bono and G. K. Patton, 'The Job Satisfaction–Job Performance Relationship: A Qualitative and Quantitative Review', *Psychological Bulletin*, May 2001, pp. 376–407.

48. C. Ostroff, 'The Relationship between Satisfaction, Attitudes, and Performance: An Organizational Level Analysis', *Journal of Applied Psychology*, December 1992, pp. 963–74; A. M. Ryan, M. J. Schmit and R. Johnson, 'Attitudes and Effectiveness: Examining Relations at an Organizational Level', *Personnel Psychology*, Winter 1996, pp. 853–82; and J. K. Harter, F. L. Schmidt and T. L. Hayes, 'Business-Unit Level Relationship between Employee Satisfaction, Employee Engagement, and Business Outcomes: A Meta-Analysis', *Journal of Applied Psychology*, April 2002, pp. 268–79.

49. Spector, *Job Satisfaction*, pp. 57–58.

50. See T. S. Bateman and D. W. Organ, 'Job Satisfaction and the Good Soldier: The Relationship between Affect and Employee "Citizenship"', *Academy of Management Journal*, December 1983, pp. 587–95; C. A. Smith, D. W. Organ and J. Near, 'Organizational Citizenship Behavior: Its Nature and Antecedents', *Journal of Applied Psychology*, October 1983, pp. 653–63; A. P. Brief, *Attitudes in and around Organizations* (Thousand Oaks, CA: Sage, 1998), pp. 44–45; and M. Podsakoff, S. B. MacKenzie, J. B. Paine and D. G. Bachrach, 'Organizational Citizenship Behaviors: A Critical Review of the Theoretical and Empirical Literature and Suggestions for Future Research', *Journal of Management*, vol. 26, no. 3, 2000, pp. 513–63.

51. D. W. Organ and K. Ryan, 'A Meta-Analytic Review of Attitudinal and Dispositional Predictors of Organizational Citizenship Behavior', *Personnel Psychology*, Winter 1995, p. 791; and J. A. LePine, A. Erez and D. E. Johnson, 'The Nature and Dimensionality of Organizational Citizenship Behavior: A Critical Review and Meta-Analysis', *Journal of Applied Psychology*, February 2002, pp. 52–65.

52. J. Fahr, P. M. Podsakoff and D. W. Organ, 'Accounting for Organizational Citizenship Behavior: Leader Fairness and Task Scope versus Satisfaction', *Journal of Management*, December 1990, pp. 705–22; R. H. Moorman, 'Relationship between Organization Justice and Organizational Citizenship Behaviors: Do Fairness Perceptions Influence Employee Citizenship?', *Journal of Applied*

Psychology, December 1991, pp. 845–55; and M. A. Konovsky and D. W. Organ, 'Dispositional and Contextual Determinants of Organizational Citizenship Behavior', *Journal of Organizational Behavior*, May 1996, pp. 253–66.

53. D. W. Organ, 'Personality and Organizational Citizenship Behavior', *Journal of Management*, Summer 1994, p. 466.

54. See, for instance, B. Schneider and D. E. Bowen, 'Employee and Customer Perceptions of Service in Banks: Replication and Extension', *Journal of Applied Psychology*, August 1985, pp. 423–33; W. W. Tornow and J. W. Wiley, 'Service Quality and Management Practices: A Look at Employee Attitudes, Customer Satisfaction, and Bottom-line Consequences', *Human Resource Planning*, vol. 4, no. 2, 1991, pp. 105–16; J. J. Weaver, 'Want Customer Satisfaction? Satisfy Your Employees First', *Human Resources*, February 1994, pp. 110–12; E. Naumann and D. W. Jackson, Jr, 'One More Time: How Do You Satisfy Customers?', *Business Horizons*, May–June 1999, pp. 71–76; D. J. Koys, 'The Effects of Employee Satisfaction, Organizational Citizenship Behavior, and Turnover on Organizational Effectiveness: A Unit-Level, Longitudinal Study', *Personnel Psychology*, Spring 2001, pp. 101–14; and J. Griffith, 'Do Satisfied Employees Satisfy Customers? Support-Services Staff Morale and Satisfaction among Public School Administrators, Students, and Parents', *Journal of Applied Social Psychology*, August 2001, pp. 1627–58.

55. M. J. Bitner, B. H. Booms and L. A. Mohr, 'Critical Service Encounters: The Employee's Viewpoint', *Journal of Marketing*, October 1994, pp. 95–106.

56. E. A. Locke, 'The Nature and Causes of Job Satisfaction', in M. D. Dunnette (ed.), *Handbook of Industrial and Organizational Psychology* (Chicago: Rand McNally, 1976), p. 1331; S. L. McShane, 'Job Satisfaction and Absenteeism: A Meta-Analytic Re-Examination', *Canadian Journal of Administrative Science*, June 1984, pp. 61–77; R. D. Hackett and R. M. Guion, 'A Reevaluation of the Absenteeism–Job Satisfaction Relationship', *Organizational Behavior and Human Decision Processes*, June 1985, p. 340–81; K. D. Scott and G. S. Taylor, 'An Examination of Conflicting Findings on the Relationship between Job Satisfaction and Absenteeism: A Meta-Analysis', *Academy of Management Journal*, September 1985, pp. 599–612; R. Steel and J. R. Rentsch, 'Influence of Cumulation Strategies on the Long-Range Prediction of Absenteeism', *Academy of Management Journal*, December 1995, pp. 1616–34; and G. Johns, 'The Psychology of Lateness, Absenteeism, and Turnover', in N. Anderson, D. S. Ones, H. K. Sinangil, C. Viswesvaran (eds), *Handbook of Industrial, Work and Organizational Psychology*, vol. 2. (Thousand Oaks, CA: Sage, 2001), p. 237.

57. F. J. Smith, 'Work Attitudes as Predictors of Attendance on a Specific Day', *Journal of Applied Psychology*, February 1977, pp. 16–19.

58. W. Hom and R. W. Griffeth, *Employee Turnover* (Cincinnati, OH: Southwestern, 1995); R. W. Griffeth, P. W. Hom and S. Gaertner, 'A Meta-Analysis of Antecedents and Correlates of Employee Turnover: Update, Moderator Tests, and Research Implications for the Next Millennium', *Journal of Management*, vol. 26, no. 3, 2000, p. 479; Johns, 'The Psychology of Lateness, Absenteeism, and Turnover', p. 237.

59. See, for example, C. L. Hulin, M. Roznowski and D. Hachiya, 'Alternative Opportunities and Withdrawal Decisions: Empirical and Theoretical Discrepancies and an Integration', *Psychological Bulletin*, July 1985, pp. 233–50; and J. M. Carsten and P. E. Spector, 'Unemployment, Job Satisfaction, and Employee Turnover: A Meta-Analytic Test of the Muchinsky Model', *Journal of Applied Psychology*, August 1987, pp. 374–81.

60. D. G. Spencer and R. M. Steers, 'Performance as a Moderator of the Job Satisfaction–Turnover Relationship', *Journal of Applied Psychology*, August 1981, pp. 511–14.

61. K. A. Hanisch, C. L. Hulin and M. Roznowski, 'The Importance of Individuals' Repertoires of Behaviors: The Scientific Appropriateness of Studying Multiple Behaviors and General Attitudes', *Journal of Organizational Behavior*, vol. 19, no. 5, 1998, pp. 463–80; C. L. Hulin, 'Adaptation, Persistence, and Commitment in Organizations', in Marvin D. Dunnette and Leaetta M. Hough (eds), *Handbook of Industrial and Organizational Psychology*, 2nd ed., vol. 2 (Palo Alto, CA: Consulting Psychologists Press, Inc., 1991), pp. 445–505.

4

PERSONALITY AND VALUES

LEARNING OBJECTIVES

AFTER STUDYING THIS CHAPTER, YOU SHOULD BE ABLE TO:

1. EXPLAIN THE FACTORS THAT DETERMINE AN INDIVIDUAL'S PERSONALITY

2. DESCRIBE THE MYERS-BRIGGS TYPE INDICATOR PERSONALITY FRAMEWORK

3. IDENTIFY THE KEY TRAITS IN THE BIG FIVE PERSONALITY MOD[EL]

4. EXPLAIN HOW THE MAJOR PERSONALITY ATTRIBUTES PREDIC[T] BEHAVIOUR AT WORK

5. CONTRAST TERMINAL AND INSTRUMENTAL VALUES

6. LIST THE DOMINANT VALUES IN TODAY'S WORKFORCE

7. IDENTIFY HOFSTEDE'S FIVE VALUE DIMENSIONS OF NATIONA[L] CULTURE

Jackie Fairley is unusual—a female CEO. But it is more than gender that determines who and what we are.

STARPHARMA HOLDINGS LIMITED is a world leader in the development of dendrimer nanotechnology (one million nanometers equal one millimetre) for pharmaceutical, life-science and other applications.[1] In July 2006, the company appointed Dr Jackie Fairley, a 43-year-old mother of two, to the role of chief executive officer (CEO).

Dr Fairley is well qualified for the role, holding first-class honours degrees in Science (pharmacology/pathology) and Veterinary Science, as well as an MBA from the prestigious Melbourne Business School. She brings to the role more than 16 years' experience in business development and senior management roles in the pharmaceutical and biotechnology industries, in companies that have generated revenues of over $20 million. She is also a member of the federal government's Pharmaceutical Industry Working Party and the Australian Biotechnology Advisory Council.

What is it about Jackie Fairley that makes her unique? A recent Australian report, 'Equal Opportunity for Women in the Workplace, 2006', has released figures that are 'desultory' in terms of the advancement of women into senior positions of management in Australia. In the top 200 Australian companies, there are only six female CEOs, and this figure will fall to four when two incumbents move into other areas in the near future. In addition, only 8.7 per cent of board positions are filled by women in these top companies (half of which have no women on the board). Most damning of all is the finding that 'the number of senior women had grown by just 0.7% between 2003–2005', and this more than two decades after Equal Employment Opportunity was legislated in this country (1986).

Dr Jackie Fairley believes that her field of science is more merit-based than other industry areas, with output in this field being more measurable through visible publications, conferences and grants. She is a firm believer in having the support of strong networks of role models who can assist in breaking down the myths of how to succeed. Although she has experienced sexism in the past, her view is that women can break through these barriers and achieve their aspirations: 'It can be done … Being CEO of a company requires sacrifice whether you are male or female or a parent. But it's harder for people with young kids.'

As you read through this chapter, consider what personality determinants would be most influential in forging the behaviour of Dr Jackie Fairley. In terms of personality traits, what do you think her dominant features would be in terms of the Big Five (extraversion, agreeableness, conscientiousness, emotional stability and openness to experience)? Where do you think she would fall in terms of her locus of control? What do you think her terminal and instrumental values would be?

I was a personality before I became a person—I am simple, complex, generous, selfish, unattractive, beautiful, lazy and driven.

Barbra Streisand

OUR PERSONALITY SHAPES OUR BEHAVIOUR. So if we want to better understand the behaviour of someone in an organisation, it helps if we know something about his or her personality. In the first half of this chapter, we review the research on personality and its relationship to behaviour. In the latter half, we look at how values shape many of our work-related behaviours.

PERSONALITY

Why are some people quiet and passive, while others are loud and aggressive? Are certain personality types better adapted for certain job types? Before we can answer these questions, we need to address a more basic one: What is personality?

WHAT IS PERSONALITY?

When we talk of personality, we don't mean that a person has charm, a positive attitude towards life, a smiling face, or is a finalist for the Brownlow medal for the 'best and fairest' in the Australian Football League. When psychologists talk of personality, they mean a dynamic concept describing the growth and development of a person's whole psychological system. Rather than looking at parts of the person, personality looks at some aggregate whole that is greater than the sum of the parts.

The most frequently used definition of personality was produced by Gordon Allport nearly 70 years ago. He defined personality as 'the dynamic organisation within the individual of those psychophysical systems that determine his unique adjustments to his environment'.[2] For our purposes, you should think of **personality** as the sum total of ways in which an individual reacts to and interacts with others. It is most often described in terms of measurable traits that a person exhibits.

personality | The sum total of ways in which an individual reacts and interacts with others.

PERSONALITY DETERMINANTS

An early debate in personality research centred on whether an individual's personality was the result of heredity or of environment. Was the personality predetermined at birth, or was it the result of the individual's interaction with his or her surroundings? Clearly, there is no simple answer to this question. Personality appears to be a result of both hereditary and environmental factors.

HEREDITY

Heredity refers to those factors that were determined at conception. Physical stature, facial attractiveness, gender, temperament, muscle composition and reflexes, energy level, and biological rhythms are characteristics that are generally considered to be either completely or substantially influenced by who your parents are—that is, by their biological, physiological, and inherent psychological makeup. The heredity approach argues that the ultimate explanation of an individual's personality is the molecular structure of the genes, located in the chromosomes.

Three different streams of research lend some credibility to the argument that heredity plays an important part in determining an individual's personality. The first looks at the genetic underpinnings of human behaviour and temperament among young children. The second addresses the study of twins who were separated at birth. The third examines the consistency in job satisfaction over time and across situations.

Studies of young children lend strong support to the power of heredity.[3] Evidence demonstrates that traits such as shyness, fear and aggression can be traced to inherited genetic characteristics. This finding suggests that some personality traits may be built into the same genetic code that affects factors such as height and hair colour.

Researchers have studied more than 100 sets of identical twins who were separated at birth and raised separately.[4] If heredity played little or no part in determining personality, you would expect to find few similarities between the separated twins. But the researchers found they had a lot in common. For almost every behavioural trait, a significant part of the variation between the twins turned out to be associated with genetic factors. For instance, one set of twins who had been separated for 39 years and raised 70 kilometres apart were found to drive the same model and colour car, chain-smoked the same brand of cigarette, owned dogs with the same name, and regularly holidayed within three blocks of each other in a beach community 2400 kilometres away. Researchers have found that genetics accounts for about 50 per cent of the personality differences and more than 30 per cent of the variation in occupational and leisure interests.

Interestingly, the twin studies have suggested that the parental environment doesn't add much to our personality development. In other words, the personalities of identical twins raised in different households are more similar to each other than the personalities of the separated twins are to those of the siblings they were actually raised with. Ironically, the most important contribution our parents may have made to our personalities is giving us their genes!

Further support for the importance of heredity can be found in studies of individual job satisfaction. Individual job satisfaction is found to be relatively stable over time. This result is consistent with what you would expect if satisfaction is determined by something inherent in the person rather than by external environmental factors. In fact, research has shown that identical twins reared apart have similar job satisfaction levels, even if their jobs are completely different.[5]

ENVIRONMENT

Among the factors that exert pressures on our personality formation are the culture in which we are raised; the norms among our family, friends and social groups; and other influences that we experience. These environmental factors play a role in shaping our personalities.

For example, culture establishes the norms, attitudes and values that are passed along from one generation to the next and create consistencies over time. An ideology that is intensely fostered in one culture may have only moderate influence in another. For instance, Australians have had the themes of industriousness, success, competition, independence, mateship and a strong work ethic constantly instilled in them through books, the school system, family and friends. Australians, as a result, tend to be ambitious and aggressive relative to individuals raised in cultures that have emphasised getting along with others, cooperation, and the priority of family over work and career.

There is another way that the environment is relevant to forming personality. An individual's personality, although generally stable and consistent, does change in different situations. Although we have not yet been able to develop a neat classification scheme for these situations, we know that some—for example, attending church or an employment interview—constrain many behaviours, and others—for example, a picnic in a public park—constrain relatively few.[6] In other words, the different demands of different situations call forth different aspects of one's personality. Therefore, we shouldn't look at personality patterns in isolation.[7]

Careful consideration of the arguments favouring either heredity or environment as the primary determinant of personality forces the conclusion that both are important. Heredity provides us with inborn traits and abilities, but our full potential will be determined by how well we adjust to the demands and requirements of the environment.

PERSONALITY TRAITS

The early work in the structure of personality revolved around attempts to identify and label enduring characteristics that describe an individual's behaviour. Popular characteristics include shy, aggressive, submissive, lazy, ambitious, loyal and timid. Those characteristics, when they are exhibited in a large number of situations, are called **personality traits**.[8] The more consistent the characteristic and the more frequently it occurs in diverse situations, the more important that trait is in describing the individual.

personality traits | Enduring characteristics that describe an individual's behaviour.

Why has so much attention been paid to personality traits? Researchers have long believed that these traits could help in employee selection, matching people to jobs, and guiding career development decisions. For instance, if certain personality types perform better on specific jobs, management could use personality tests to screen job candidates and improve employee job performance.

There were a number of early efforts to identify the primary traits that govern behaviour.[9] However, for the most part, these efforts resulted in long lists of traits that were difficult to generalise from and provided little practical guidance to organisational decision makers. Two exceptions are the Myers-Briggs Type Indicator and the Big Five Model. Over the past 20 years, these two approaches have become the dominant frameworks for identifying and classifying traits.

LEARNING OBJECTIVE   2

Describe the Myers-Briggs Type Indicator personality framework

THE MYERS-BRIGGS TYPE INDICATOR

The Myers-Briggs® Type Indicator (MBTI)[10] is the most widely used personality-assessment instrument in the world.[11] It is a 100-question personality test that asks people how they usually feel or act in particular situations. On the basis of the answers individuals give to the test, they are classified as extraverted (also known as 'extroverted') or introverted (E or I), sensing or intuitive (S or N), thinking or feeling (T or F), and judging or perceiving (J or P). These terms are defined as follows:

Myers-Briggs Type Indicator (MBTI) | A personality test that taps four characteristics and classifies people into one of 16 personality types.

- *Extraverted vs Introverted*: Extraverted individuals are outgoing, sociable and assertive. Introverts are quiet and shy.
- *Sensing vs Intuitive*: Sensing types are practical and prefer routine and order. They focus on details. Intuitives rely on unconscious processes and look at the 'big picture'.
- *Thinking vs Feeling*: Thinking types use reason and logic to handle problems. Feeling types rely on their personal values and emotions.
- *Judging vs Perceiving*: Judging types want control and prefer their world to be ordered and structured. Perceiving types are flexible and spontaneous.

These classifications are then combined into 16 personality types. To illustrate, let's take several examples. INTJs are visionaries. They usually have original minds and great drive for their own ideas and purposes. They are characterised as sceptical, critical, independent, determined and often stubborn. ESTJs are organisers. They are realistic, logical, analytical and decisive, and have a natural head for business or mechanics. They like to organise and run activities. The ENTP type is a conceptualiser. He or she is innovative, individualistic, versatile, and attracted to entrepreneurial ideas. This person tends to be resourceful in solving challenging problems but may neglect routine assignments. A book that profiled 13 contemporary businesspeople who created super-successful firms including Apple Computer, FedEx, Honda Motors, Microsoft and Sony found that all 13 were intuitive thinkers (NTs).[12] This result is particularly interesting because intuitive thinkers represent only about 5 per cent of the population.

Many tens of thousands of people a year take the MBTI in Australia and its use in some Asian countries is starting to rise as well. Organisations using the MBTI include hospitals, IT firms, banks, universities, emergency services (fire, police, paramedics), finance companies, call centres, local councils and even the Australian Defence Forces. Results from all the MBTI tests reveal that, in general, managers in education and HR managers, along with politicians, tend to have higher intuition scores, while managers in the armed forces, police and financial management tend to have lower scores in intuition.[13] One of the problems with the MBTI is that it forces a person to be categorised as either one type or another (that is, you are either introverted or extraverted). There is no in-between, though people can be both extraverted and introverted to some degree. The best we can say is that it can be a valuable tool for increasing self-awareness and for providing career guidance. But because MBTI results tend to be unrelated to job performance, it probably shouldn't be used as a selection test for choosing among job candidates.

THE BIG FIVE MODEL

The MBTI may lack strong supporting evidence, but that can't be said for the five-factor model of personality—more typically called the 'Big Five'. In recent years, an impressive body of research supports the theory that five basic dimensions underlie all others and encompass most of the significant variation in human personality.[14] The Big Five factors are:

- **Extraversion**: This dimension captures one's comfort level with relationships. Extraverts tend to be gregarious, assertive and sociable. Introverts tend to be reserved, timid and quiet.
- **Agreeableness**: This dimension refers to an individual's propensity to defer to others. Highly agreeable people are cooperative, warm and trusting. People who score low on agreeableness are cold, disagreeable and antagonistic.
- **Conscientiousness**: This dimension is a measure of reliability. A highly conscientious person is responsible, organised, dependable and persistent. Those who score low on this dimension are easily distracted, disorganised and unreliable.
- **Emotional stability** (often labelled by its converse, neuroticism): This dimension taps a person's ability to withstand stress. People with positive emotional stability tend to be calm, self-confident and secure. Those with high negative scores tend to be nervous, anxious, depressed and insecure.
- **Openness to experience**: The final dimension addresses one's range of interests and fascination with novelty. Extremely open people are creative, curious and artistically sensitive. Those at the other end of the openness category are conventional and find comfort in the familiar.

Before we discuss the Big Five factors in more detail, check out the Self-Assessment feature to see how you score on those factors.

In addition to providing a unifying personality framework, research on the Big Five also has found relationships between these personality dimensions and job performance.[15]

extraversion | A personality dimension describing someone who is sociable, gregarious and assertive.

agreeableness | A personality dimension that describes someone who is good-natured, cooperative and trusting.

Identify the key traits in the Big Five personality model

conscientiousness | A personality dimension that describes someone who is responsible, dependable, persistent and organised.

emotional stability | A personality dimension that characterises someone as calm, self-confident, secure (positive) versus nervous, depressed and insecure (negative).

openness to experience | A personality dimension that characterises someone in terms of imagination, sensitivity and curiosity.

WHAT'S MY BASIC PERSONALITY?

In the Self-Assessment Library (available on CD and online), take Self-Assessment I.A.1 (What's My Basic Personality?) and answer the following questions.

1. How did you score on each of the Big Five factors? Did your scores surprise you? Why or why not?
2. What was your highest score? Your lowest?
3. Do you think this set of scores does a good job of describing your basic personality? Why or why not?

A broad spectrum of occupations were looked at: professionals (including engineers, architects, accountants, lawyers), police, managers, salespeople, and semi-skilled and skilled employees. Job performance was defined in terms of performance ratings, training proficiency (performance during training programs), and personnel data such as salary level. The results showed that conscientiousness predicted job performance for all occupational groups. 'The preponderance of evidence shows that individuals who are dependable, reliable, careful, thorough, able to plan, organised, hardworking, persistent, and achievement-oriented tend to have higher job performance in most if not all occupations.'[16] In addition, employees who score higher in conscientiousness develop higher levels of job knowledge, probably because highly conscientious people exert greater levels of effort in their jobs. The higher levels of job knowledge then contribute to higher levels of job performance.[17] Consistent with these findings, evidence also finds a relatively strong and consistent relationship between conscientiousness and organisational citizenship behaviour (OCB).[18] This, however, seems to be the only Big Five personality dimension that predicts OCB.

For the other personality dimensions, predictability depended on both the performance criterion and the occupational group. For instance, extraversion predicted performance in managerial and sales positions. This finding makes sense because those occupations involve high social interaction. Similarly, openness to experience was found to be important in

Virgin owner and CEO Richard Branson scores high on the extraversion dimension of the Big Five Model. Described as gregarious and innovative (high openness to new experiences), he is always finding new frontiers, new challenges and new opportunities for his global aviation and media conglomerate. It was his idea for his company to be the first commercial airline to take customers into space! As CEO, Branson travels the world meeting with customers, employees, aircraft builders, scientists and investors.

predicting training proficiency, which, too, seems logical. What wasn't so clear was why positive emotional stability wasn't related to job performance. Intuitively, it would seem that people who are calm and secure would do better on almost all jobs than people who are nervous and depressed. The answer might be that some aspects of negative emotional stability—such as nervousness—might actually help job performance. Think about animals. A deer that wasn't easily startled by noises wouldn't last long near a major highway. Consider a share trader at Goldman Sachs JBWere, a stockbroking firm trading on the Australian Stock Exchange. If the broker fails to research all investments thoroughly and is never nervous about making the wrong transaction, he or she may fail to see the danger in, say, purchasing shares in a volatile young company. The other aspect of negative emotional stability—a depressive outlook—is bad for every job. Why? Because when you are depressed, it is difficult to motivate yourself, to make a decision or to take a risk. So, it may be that negative emotional stability has aspects that both help and hinder performance.[19]

Now that we have dealt with performance, you will be interested to know that the Big Five have other implications for work and for life. Let's look at these implications one at a time.

Compared to introverts, extraverts tend to be happier in their jobs and in their lives as a whole. They usually have more friends and spend more time in social situations than introverts. But they also appear to be more impulsive, as evidenced by the fact that extraverts are more likely to be absent from work and to engage in risky behaviour such as unprotected sex, excessive drinking, and other impulsive or sensation-seeking behaviour.[20]

You might expect agreeable people to be happier than disagreeable people, and they are, but only slightly. When people choose romantic partners, friends or organisational team members, agreeable individuals are usually their first choice. Agreeable children do better in school and as adults are less likely to get involved in drug taking or binge drinking.[21]

Interestingly, conscientious people live longer because they tend to take better care of themselves (eat better, exercise more) and engage in fewer risky behaviours (smoking, drinking/drugs, risky sexual or driving behaviour).[22] Still, there are downsides to conscientiousness. It appears that conscientious people, probably because they are so organised and structured, don't adapt as well to changing contexts. Conscientious people are generally performance-oriented. They have more trouble than less conscientious people learning complex skills early on, because their focus is on performing well rather than on learning. Finally, conscientious people are often less creative, especially artistically.[23]

People who score high on emotional stability are happier than those who score low on emotional stability. Of the Big Five, emotional stability is most strongly related to life satisfaction, job satisfaction, and low stress levels. High scores on emotional stability also are associated with fewer health complaints. One upside for low emotional stability: when in a bad mood, such people make faster and better decisions compared with emotionally stable people in bad moods.[24]

Finally, individuals who score high on openness to experience are more creative in science and in art, tend to be less religious, and are more likely to be politically liberal than those who score lower on openness to experience. Open people cope better with organisational change and are more adaptable in changing contexts.

MEASURING PERSONALITY

The most important reason why managers need to know how to measure personality is because research has shown that personality tests are useful in hiring decisions. Scores on personality tests help managers to forecast who is the best bet for a job.[25] And some managers want to know how people score on personality tests in order to better understand and more effectively manage the people who work for them.

There are three main ways personality is measured:

- self-report surveys;
- observer-ratings surveys; and
- projective measures (Rorschach Inkblot Test and Thematic Apperception Test).

Self-report surveys—which are completed by the individual—are the most common way to measure personality. One concern with self-report surveys, however, is that the individual might lie or practise impression management—that is, the person could 'fake good' on the test to create a good impression. This is especially a concern when the survey is the basis for employment. Another concern is accuracy—for instance, a perfectly good candidate could have just been in a bad mood when the survey was taken.

Observer-ratings surveys have been developed to provide an independent assessment of personality. Therefore, instead of an individual taking the survey—as in the case of self-report surveys—perhaps a fellow employee could do the rating (sometimes with the knowledge of the individual, sometimes not). Even though self-report surveys and observer-ratings surveys are strongly correlated, research suggests that observer-ratings surveys are a better predictor of success on the job.[26] However, it is important to realise that both self-report surveys and observer-ratings surveys can tell us something unique about an individual's behaviour in the workplace.

Some examples of projective measures are the Rorschach Inkblot Test and the Thematic Apperception Test (TAT). In the Rorschach Inkblot Test, the individual is supposed to state what inkblots seem to resemble. The TAT is a series of pictures (drawings or photos) on cards (see an example in Figure 4.1). The individual being tested writes a story about each picture. With both the Rorschach and the TAT, clinicians then score the responses. However, assessing responses has proven to be a challenge because one clinician often perceives the results differently from another. Therefore, it is no surprise that a

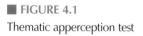
FIGURE 4.1
Thematic apperception test

SOURCE: <www.inkblottestwallpaper.com> (accessed 15 December 2006).

recent study suggested that projective measures aren't very effective. For this reason they are rarely used.[27]

MAJOR PERSONALITY ATTRIBUTES INFLUENCING OB

LEARNING OBJECTIVE   4

Explain how the major personality attributes predict behaviour at work

In this section, we want to evaluate more carefully specific personality attributes that have been found to be powerful predictors of behaviour in organisations. The first attribute is related to one's core self-evaluation. The others are Machiavellianism, narcissism, self-monitoring, propensity for risk taking, and the Type A and proactive personalities.

CORE SELF-EVALUATION

People differ in the degree to which they like or dislike themselves, and in whether they see themselves as capable and effective. This self-perspective is the concept of **core self-evaluation**. People who have positive core self-evaluations like themselves, and see themselves as effective, capable and in control of their environment. Those with negative core self-evaluations tend to dislike themselves, question their capabilities, and view themselves as powerless over their environment.[28]

core self-evaluation | Degree to which individuals like or dislike themselves, whether they see themselves as capable and effective, and whether they feel they are in control of their environment or powerless over their environment.

An individual's core self-evaluation is determined by two main elements: self-esteem and locus of control. **Self-esteem** is defined as individuals' degree of liking or disliking themselves, and the degree to which they think they are worthy or unworthy as a person.[29] It is easy to see why self-esteem is a reflection of core self-evaluation: people who have a positive view of themselves and their capabilities tend to like themselves and see themselves as valuable. People with low self-esteem, however, are more susceptible to external influences, suggesting that low-self-esteem individuals depend on the receipt of positive evaluations from others. As a result, people with low self-esteem are more likely to seek approval from others and are more prone to conform to the beliefs and behaviours of those they respect than are people who believe in themselves. Studies have shown that people with low self-esteem may benefit more from training programs because their self-concept is more influenced by such interventions.[30]

self-esteem | Individuals' degree of liking or disliking themselves and the degree to which they think they are worthy or unworthy as a person.

The second element that determines core self-evaluation is locus of control. **Locus of control** is the degree to which people believe that they are masters of their own fate. **Internals** are individuals who believe that they control what happens to them. **Externals** are individuals who believe that what happens to them is controlled by outside forces such as luck or chance.[31] Locus of control is an indicator of core self-evaluation because people who think that they lack control over their lives tend to lack confidence in themselves. For example, if you think your success at university is determined by the whim of your lecturers or by blind luck, you probably don't have a lot of confidence in your ability to get high marks. You would have an external locus of control, and most likely this would reflect a negative core self-evaluation.

locus of control | The degree to which people believe that they are masters of their own fate.

internals | Individuals who believe that they control what happens to them.

How is the concept of core self-evaluations related to job satisfaction? People with positive core self-evaluations see more challenge in their job, making it more satisfying to them. Individuals with positive core self-evaluations also tend to obtain more complex and challenging jobs. If you think about it, this makes sense. If I think I am no good and incapable of performing, why would I take on a complicated job? I would be sure to fail. People with positive core self-evaluations also perceive themselves as having control over their jobs, and also tend to attribute positive outcomes to their own actions.[32]

externals | Individuals who believe that what happens to them is controlled by outside forces such as luck or chance.

But what about job performance? People with positive core self-evaluations perform better because they set more ambitious goals, are more committed to their goals, and persist longer at attempting to reach these goals. For example, one study of life insurance

A positive core self-evaluation helps US Secretary of State Condoleezza Rice meet the daunting challenges and complexities of her job. Confident, skilled in diplomacy and possessing a relentless work ethic, Rice views the challenges of her job as an opportunity to shape American foreign policy and to take a global leadership role in spreading democracy and constructing a peaceful international climate. Rice works towards these goals by managing relationships with leaders of 191 countries, such as Sudanese Vice President Salva Kiir, shown here.

agents found that core self-evaluations were critical predictors of performance. In life insurance sales, 90 per cent of sales calls end in rejection, so one has to believe in oneself to persist. In fact, this study showed that the majority of the successful salespersons had positive core self-evaluations.[33]

You might wonder whether someone can be *too* positive. In other words, what happens when someone thinks he is capable, but he is actually incompetent? Surely, one can think of many situations in which an inflated view of oneself is bad. One study of top company CEOs, for example, showed that many CEOs are overconfident and that this self-perceived infallibility often causes them to make bad decisions.[34] Yes, one might be too confident, but very often we sell ourselves short and are less happy and effective than we could be because of it. If I decide I can't do something, for example, I won't try, and not doing it only reinforces my self-doubts.

MACHIAVELLIANISM

Kuzi is a young bank manager in Taiwan. He has had three promotions in the last four years. Kuzi makes no apologies for the aggressive tactics he has used to propel his career upward. 'I'm prepared to do whatever I have to do to get ahead', he says. Kuzi would properly be called Machiavellian. Nidhi led her Mumbai-based company last year in sales performance. She is assertive and persuasive, and she is effective at manipulating customers to buy her product line. Many of her colleagues, including her boss, also consider Nidhi as Machiavellian.

The personality characteristic of **Machiavellianism** (Mach) is named after Niccolo Machiavelli, who wrote in the 16th century on how to gain and use power. An individual high in Machiavellianism is pragmatic, maintains emotional distance, and believes that ends can justify means. 'If it works, use it' is consistent with a high-Mach perspective. A considerable amount of research has been directed towards relating high- and low-Mach personalities to certain behavioural outcomes.[35] High Machs manipulate more, win more, are persuaded less, and persuade others more than do low Machs.[36] Yet, these high-Mach outcomes are moderated by situational factors. It has been found that high Machs flourish (1) when they interact face-to-face with others rather than indirectly; (2) when the situation has a minimum number of rules and regulations, thus allowing latitude for improvisation; and (3) when emotional involvement with details irrelevant to winning distracts low Machs.[37]

Should we conclude that high Machs make good employees? That answer depends on the type of job and whether you consider ethical implications in evaluating performance. In jobs that require bargaining skills (such as labour negotiation) or that offer substantial rewards for winning (as in commissioned sales), high Machs will be productive. But if ends can't justify the means, if there are absolute standards of behaviour, or if the three situational factors noted in the preceding paragraph are not in evidence, our ability to predict a high Mach's performance will be severely curtailed.

Machiavellianism | Degree to which an individual is pragmatic, maintains emotional distance, and believes that ends can justify means.

NARCISSISM

Hans likes to be the centre of attention. He likes to look at himself in the mirror a lot. He has extravagant dreams and seems to consider himself a person of many talents. Hans is a narcissist. The term is from the Greek myth of Narcissus, the story of a man so vain and proud that he fell in love with his own image. In psychology, **narcissism** describes a person who has a grandiose sense of self-importance, requires excessive admiration, has a sense of entitlement and is arrogant.[38]

A study found that while narcissists thought they were *better* leaders than their colleagues, their supervisors actually rated them as *worse* leaders. For example, an Oracle executive described that company's CEO, Larry Ellison, as follows: 'The difference between God and Larry is that God does not believe he is Larry.'[39] Because narcissists often want to gain the admiration of others and receive affirmation of their superiority, they tend to 'talk down' (treating others as if they were inferior) to those who threaten them. Narcissists also tend to be selfish and exploitive, and they often carry the attitude that others exist for their benefit.[40] Studies indicate that narcissists are rated by their bosses as less effective at their jobs, particularly when it comes to helping other people.[41]

narcissism | The tendency to be arrogant, have a grandiose sense of self-importance, require excessive admiration and have a sense of entitlement.

SELF-MONITORING

Joyce is always in trouble at work. Though she is competent, hardworking and productive, her performance reviews tend to rate her no better than average and she seems to have made a career of irritating bosses. Joyce's problem is that she is politically inept. She is unable to adjust her behaviour to fit changing situations. As she puts it, 'I'm true to myself. I don't remake myself to please others.' We would be correct to describe Joyce as a low self-monitor.

Self-monitoring refers to an individual's ability to adjust his or her behaviour to external, situational factors.[42] Individuals high in self-monitoring show considerable

self-monitoring | A personality trait that measures an individual's ability to adjust his or her behaviour to external, situational factors.

adaptability in adjusting their behaviour to external situational factors. They are highly sensitive to external cues and can behave differently in different situations. High self-monitors are capable of presenting striking contradictions between their public persona and their private self. Low self-monitors, like Joyce, can't disguise themselves in that way. They tend to display their true dispositions and attitudes in every situation; hence, there is high behavioural consistency between who they are and what they do.

The evidence indicates that high self-monitors tend to pay closer attention to the behaviour of others and are more capable of conforming than are low self-monitors.[43] They also receive better performance ratings, are more likely to emerge as leaders, and show less commitment to their organisations.[44] In addition, high self-monitoring managers tend to be more mobile in their careers, receive more promotions (both internal and cross-organisational), and are more likely to occupy central positions in an organisation.[45] We might also hypothesise that high self-monitors will be more successful in managerial positions in which individuals are required to play multiple, and even contradicting, roles. The high self-monitor is capable of putting on different 'faces' for different audiences.

RISK TAKING

Gerry Harvey of Harvey Norman stands out for his willingness to take risks. He started with almost nothing, selling vacuum cleaners door-to-door in the 1960s. By the mid-1970s, he had made a fortune from his retail chain Norman Ross. Then, the economy slumped and the business floundered. Never fearful of taking chances, Gerry Harvey leveraged the few assets he had left and developed a unique approach to consumer product marketing in his new Harvey Norman stores. He hit it big again. In 2005, *Business Review Weekly* estimated his net worth at $3.2 billion.[46]

People differ in their willingness to take chances. This propensity to assume or avoid risk has been shown to have an impact on how long it takes managers to make a decision and how much information they require before making their choice. For instance, 79 managers worked on simulated personnel exercises that required them to make hiring decisions.[47] High risk-taking managers made more rapid decisions and used less information in making their choices than did the low risk-taking managers. Interestingly, the decision accuracy was the same for both groups.

Although previous studies have shown managers in large organisations to be more risk averse than growth-oriented entrepreneurs who actively manage small businesses, recent findings suggest that managers in large organisations may actually be more willing to take a risk than entrepreneurs.[48] For the work population as a whole, there are also differences in risk propensity.[49] As a result,

Gerry Harvey is willing to take chances. His risk-taking personality enables him to thrive in situations that others find perilous and stressful. Although his retail chain Norman Ross collapsed and disappeared, Gerry continues to build his net worth by developing new retail approaches and systems that competitors are hard pressed to try and match. Gerry is also passionate about the environment and is willing to take chances there, too, investing in new approaches to land and water management.

it makes sense to recognise these differences and even to consider aligning risk-taking propensity with specific job demands. For instance, a high risk-taking propensity may lead to more effective performance for a stock trader in a brokerage firm because that type of job demands rapid decision making. On the other hand, a willingness to take risks might prove a major obstacle to an accountant who performs auditing activities. The latter job might be better filled by someone with a low risk-taking propensity.

TYPE A PERSONALITY

Do you know people who are excessively competitive and always seem to be experiencing a sense of time urgency? If you do, it's a good bet that those people have a Type A personality. A person with a **Type A personality** is 'aggressively involved in a chronic, incessant struggle to achieve more and more in less and less time, and, if required to do so, against the opposing efforts of other things or other persons'.[50] In Western cultures such as Australia, such characteristics tend to be highly prized and positively associated with ambition and the successful acquisition of material goods. Type A's:

- are always moving, walking and eating rapidly;
- feel impatient with the rate at which most events take place;
- strive to think or do two or more things at once;
- cannot cope with leisure time; and
- are obsessed with numbers, measuring their success in terms of how many or how much of everything they acquire.

Type A personality | Aggressive involvement in a chronic, incessant struggle to achieve more and more in less and less time and, if necessary, against the opposing efforts of other things or other people.

The Type B personality is exactly the opposite. Type B's are 'rarely harried by the desire to obtain a wildly increasing number of things or participate in an endless growing series of events in an ever decreasing amount of time'.[51] Type B's:

- never suffer from a sense of time urgency with its accompanying impatience;
- feel no need to display or discuss either their achievements or accomplishments unless such exposure is demanded by the situation;
- play for fun and relaxation, rather than to exhibit their superiority at any cost; and
- can relax without guilt.

Type A's operate under moderate to high levels of stress. They subject themselves to more-or-less continuous time pressure, creating for themselves a life of deadlines. These characteristics result in some rather specific behavioural outcomes. For example, Type A's are fast workers, because they emphasise quantity over quality. In managerial positions, Type A's demonstrate their competitiveness by working long hours and, not infrequently, making poor decisions because they make them too quickly. Type A's are also rarely creative. Because of their concern with quantity and speed, they rely on past experiences when faced with problems. They won't allocate the time necessary to develop unique solutions to new problems. They rarely vary in their responses to specific challenges in their milieu; hence, their behaviour is easier to predict than that of Type B's.

Do Type A's differ from Type B's in their ability to get hired? The answer appears to be 'yes'.[52] Type A's do better in job interviews because they are more likely to be judged as having desirable traits such as high drive, competence, aggressiveness and success motivation.

PROACTIVE PERSONALITY

Did you ever notice that some people actively take the initiative to improve their current circumstances or create new ones, while others sit by passively reacting to situations? The former individuals have been described as having a **proactive personality**.[53] Proactives

proactive personality | People who identify opportunities, show initiative, take action, and persevere until meaningful change occurs.

identify opportunities, show initiative, take action, and persevere until meaningful change occurs. They create positive change in their environment, regardless or even in spite of constraints or obstacles.[54] Not surprisingly, proactives have many desirable behaviours that organisations covet. For instance, the evidence indicates that proactives are more likely to be seen as leaders and more likely to act as change agents within the organisation.[55] Other actions of proactives can be positive or negative, depending on the organisation and the situation. For example, proactives are more likely to challenge the status quo or voice their displeasure when situations aren't to their liking.[56] If an organisation requires people with entrepreneurial initiative, proactives make good candidates; however, these are people that are also more likely to leave an organisation to start their own business.[57] As individuals, proactives are more likely to achieve career success.[58] This is because they select, create and influence work situations in their favour. Proactives are more likely to seek out job and organisational information, develop contacts in high places, engage in career planning, and demonstrate persistence in the face of career obstacles.

PERSONALITY AND NATIONAL CULTURE

Do personality frameworks such as the Big Five Model transfer across cultures? Are dimensions such as locus of control and the Type A personality relevant in all cultures? Let's try to answer these questions.

The five personality factors identified in the Big Five Model appear in almost all cross-cultural studies.[59] This includes a wide variety of diverse cultures—such as China, Israel, Germany, Japan, Spain, Nigeria, Norway, Pakistan and the United States. Differences tend to surface by the emphasis on dimensions and whether countries are predominantly individualistic—meaning that people prefer to act as individuals rather than as members

MYTH OR SCIENCE?

'DEEP DOWN, PEOPLE ARE ALL ALIKE'

This statement is essentially false. Only in the broadest sense can we say that people are all alike. For instance, it is true that people all have values, attitudes, likes and dislikes, feelings, goals, and similar general attributes. But individual *differences* are far more illuminating.[60] People differ in intelligence, personality, abilities, ambition, motivations, emotional display, values, priorities, expectations, and the like. If we want to understand, explain or predict human behaviour accurately, we need to focus on individual differences. Your ability to predict behaviour will be severely limited if you constantly assume that all people are alike or that everyone is like you.

As an illustration, consider the task of selecting among job applicants. Managers regularly use information about a candidate's personality (in addition to experience, knowledge, skill level and intellectual abilities) to help make their hiring decisions. Recognising that jobs differ in terms of demands and requirements, managers interview and test applicants to (1) categorise them by specific traits, (2) assess job tasks in terms of the type of personality best suited for effectively completing those tasks, and (3) match applicants and job tasks to find an appropriate fit. So, by using an individual-difference variable—in this case, personality—managers improve the likelihood of identifying and hiring high-performing employees.

SOURCE: Based on P. L. Ackerman and L. G. Humphreys, 'Individual Differences Theory in Industrial and Organizational Psychology', in M. D. Dunnette and L. M. Hough (eds), *Handbook of Industrial & Organizational Psychology*, 2nd ed., vol. 1 (Palo Alto, CA: Consulting Psychologists, 1990), pp. 223–82.

A GLOBAL PERSONALITY

JOB IN PRACTICE

Determining which employees will succeed on overseas business assignments is often difficult for an organisation's managers because the same qualities that predict success in one culture may not do so in another. Researchers, however, are naming personality traits that can help managers to home in on which employees would be suited for foreign assignments.

Organisational psychologist Robert Hogan, for example, states that emotional maturity, remaining composed under pressure, and being comfortable with uncertainty are traits that breed success in most jobs, and these traits may be especially valuable for the overseas employee to possess. In addition, according to the Center for Global Assignments (CGA), successful global executives tend to be open-minded and imaginative, and they also enjoy talking and networking with others. Other traits that have been linked to overseas employment success include curiosity and risk tolerance.

Viewed from the perspective of the Big Five, characteristics such as open-mindedness and curiosity are similar to the Big Five trait *openness to experience*, while characteristics such as enjoying talking with others and networking resemble the Big Five trait *extraversion*. For the overseas employee, being more open and extraverted may be particularly helpful in breaching communication barriers and cultivating trust, which in turn promotes cooperation.

What is the ultimate upshot for organisations? When it comes to choosing employees for global assignments, personality can make a difference.

SOURCE: Based on J. E. Fernandez, 'The Making of a Global Executive', *Journal of Business Strategy*, vol. 24, no. 5, 2003, pp. 36–38.

---

of groups—or collectivistic—where there is a tight social framework in which people expect others in groups of which they are a part to look after them and protect them.

Chinese, for example, use the category of conscientiousness more often, and use the category of agreeableness less often, than do Americans. And the Big Five appear to predict a bit better in individualistic cultures than in collectivist ones.[61] But there is a surprisingly high amount of agreement, especially among individuals from developed countries. As a case in point, a comprehensive review of studies covering people from the 15-nation European Community found that conscientiousness was a valid predictor of performance across jobs and occupational groups.[62] This is exactly what US studies have found.

There are no common personality types for a given country. You can, for instance, find high and low risk takers in almost any culture. Yet, a country's culture influences the dominant personality characteristics of its population. We can see this by looking at locus of control and the Type A personality.

There is evidence that cultures differ in terms of people's relationship to their environment.[63] In some cultures, such as those in Australia, New Zealand and North America, people believe that they can dominate their environment. People in some other societies, such as Middle Eastern countries, believe that life is essentially preordained. Note the close parallel to internal and external locus of control.[64] We should expect, therefore, a larger proportion of internals in the Australian and New Zealand workforces than in the Saudi Arabian or Iranian workforce.

The prevalence of Type A personalities will be somewhat influenced by the culture in which a person grows up. There are Type A's in every country, but there will be more of them in capitalistic countries, where achievement and material success are highly valued.

For instance, it is estimated that about 50 per cent of the North American population is Type A.[65] This percentage shouldn't be too surprising. The United States and Canada both have a high emphasis on time management and efficiency, as does Australia. All three have cultures that stress accomplishments and acquisition of money and material goods. In cultures such as Sweden and France, where materialism is less revered, we would predict a smaller proportion of Type A personalities.

Having discussed personality traits—the enduring characteristics that describe a person's behaviour—we now turn to values. Although personality and values are related, they are not the same. Values are often very specific and describe belief systems rather than behavioural tendencies. Some beliefs or values don't say much about a person's personality, and we don't always act in ways consistent with our values.

VALUES

Is capital punishment right or wrong? If a person likes power, is that good or bad? The answers to these questions are value-laden. Some might argue, for example, that capital punishment is right because it is an appropriate retribution for crimes such as murder and treason. However, others might argue, just as strongly, that no government has the right to take anyone's life.

values | Basic convictions that a specific mode of conduct or end-state of existence is personally or socially preferable to an opposite or converse mode of conduct or end-state of existence.

Values represent basic convictions that 'a specific mode of conduct or end-state of existence is personally or socially preferable to an opposite or converse mode of conduct or end-state of existence'.[66] They contain a judgmental element in that they carry an individual's ideas as to what is right, good or desirable. Values have both content and intensity attributes. The content attribute says that a mode of conduct or end-state of existence is *important*. The intensity attribute specifies *how important* it is. When we rank an individual's values in terms of their intensity, we obtain that person's **value system**. All of us have a hierarchy of values that forms our value system. This system is identified by the relative importance we assign to values such as freedom, pleasure, self-respect, honesty, obedience and equality.

value system | A hierarchy based on a ranking of an individual's values in terms of their intensity.

Are values fluid and flexible? Generally speaking, no. Values tend to be relatively stable and enduring.[67] A significant portion of the values we hold is established in our early years—from parents, teachers, friends and others. As children, we are told that certain behaviours or outcomes are *always* desirable or *always* undesirable. There were few grey areas. You were told, for example, that you should be honest and responsible. You were never taught to be just a little bit honest or a little bit responsible. It is this absolute or 'black-or-white' learning of values that more or less ensures their stability and endurance. The process of questioning our values, of course, may result in a change. More often, our questioning merely acts to reinforce the values we hold.

IMPORTANCE OF VALUES

Values are important to the study of organisational behaviour because they lay the foundation for the understanding of people's attitudes and motivation, and because they influence our perceptions. Individuals enter an organisation with preconceived notions of what 'ought' and what 'ought not' to be. Of course, these notions aren't value free. On the contrary, they contain interpretations of right and wrong. Furthermore, they imply that certain behaviours or outcomes are preferred over others. As a result, values cloud objectivity and rationality.

Values generally influence attitudes and behaviour.[68] Suppose that you enter an organisation with the view that allocating pay on the basis of performance is right, while allocating pay on the basis of seniority is wrong. How are you going to react if you find that the organisation you have just joined rewards seniority and not performance? You are likely to be disappointed—and this can lead to job dissatisfaction and the decision not to exert a high level of effort since 'it's probably not going to lead to more money, anyway'. Would your attitudes and behaviour be different if your values aligned with the organisation's pay policies? Most likely.

TYPES OF VALUES

Can we classify values? The answer is: 'Yes'. In this section, we review two approaches to developing value typologies.

ROKEACH VALUE SURVEY

Milton Rokeach created the Rokeach Value Survey (RVS).[69] The RVS consists of two sets of values, with each set containing 18 individual value items. One set, called **terminal values**, refers to desirable end-states. These are the goals that a person would like to achieve during his or her lifetime. The other set, called **instrumental values**, refers to preferable modes of behaviour, or means of achieving the terminal values. Table 4.1 gives common examples for each of these sets.

Several studies confirm that the RVS values vary among groups.[70] People in the same occupations or categories (for example, corporate managers, union members, parents,

LEARNING OBJECTIVE 5

Contrast terminal and instrumental values

terminal values | Desirable end-states of existence; the goals that a person would like to achieve during his or her lifetime.

instrumental values | Preferable modes of behaviour or means of achieving one's terminal values.

■ TABLE 4.1

Terminal and instrumental values in the Rokeach Value Survey

Terminal values	Instrumental values
A comfortable life (a prosperous life)	Ambitious (hardworking, aspiring)
An exciting life (a stimulating, active life)	Broad-minded (open-minded)
A sense of accomplishment (lasting contribution)	Capable (competent, efficient)
A world at peace (free of war and conflict)	Cheerful (lighthearted, joyful)
A world of beauty (beauty of nature and the arts)	Clean (neat, tidy)
Equality (brotherhood, equal opportunity for all)	Courageous (standing up for your beliefs)
Family security (taking care of loved ones)	Forgiving (willing to pardon others)
Freedom (independence, free choice)	Helpful (working for the welfare of others)
Happiness (contentedness)	Honest (sincere, truthful)
Inner harmony (freedom from inner conflict)	Imaginative (daring, creative)
Mature love (sexual and spiritual intimacy)	Independent (self-reliant, self-sufficient)
National security (protection from attack)	Intellectual (intelligent, reflective)
Pleasure (an enjoyable, leisurely life)	Logical (consistent, rational)
Salvation (saved, eternal life)	Loving (affectionate, tender)
Self-respect (self-esteem)	Obedient (dutiful, respectful)
Social recognition (respect, admiration)	Polite (courteous, well-mannered)
True friendship (close companionship)	Responsible (dependable, reliable)
Wisdom (a mature understanding of life)	Self-controlled (restrained, self-disciplined)

EXECUTIVES		UNION MEMBERS		ACTIVISTS	
Terminal	Instrumental	Terminal	Instrumental	Terminal	Instrumental
1. Self-respect	1. Honest	1. Family security	1. Responsible	1. Equality	1. Honest
2. Family security	2. Responsible	2. Freedom	2. Honest	2. A world of peace	2. Helpful
3. Freedom	3. Capable	3. Happiness	3. Courageous	3. Family security	3. Courageous
4. A sense of accomplishment	4. Ambitious	4. Self-respect	4. Independent	4. Self-respect	4. Responsible
5. Happiness	5. Independent	5. Mature love	5. Capable	5. Freedom	5. Capable

SOURCE: Based on W. C. Frederick and J. Weber, 'The Values of Corporate Managers and Their Critics: An Empirical Description and Normative Implications', in W. C. Frederick and L. E. Preston (eds), *Business Ethics: Research Issues and Empirical Studies* (Greenwich, CT: JAI Press, 1990), pp. 123–44.

■ TABLE 4.2

Mean value ranking of executives, union members and activists (top five only)

students) tend to hold similar values. For instance, one study compared corporate executives, members of a steelworkers' union, and members of a community activist group. Although a good deal of overlap was found among the three groups,[71] there were also some very significant differences (see Table 4.2). The activists had value preferences that were quite different from those of the other two groups. They ranked 'equality' as their most important terminal value; executives and union members ranked this value 12th and 13th, respectively. Activists ranked 'helpful' as their second-highest instrumental value. The other two groups both ranked it 14th. These differences are important, because executives, union members and activists all have a vested interest in what corporations do. These differences make it difficult when these groups have to negotiate with each other and can create serious conflicts when they contend with each other over the organisation's economic and social policies.[72]

LEARNING OBJECTIVE 6

List the dominant values in today's workforce

CONTEMPORARY WORK COHORTS

We have integrated several recent analyses of work values into four groups that attempt to capture the unique values of different cohorts or generations in the workforce.[73] Table 4.3 proposes that employees can be segmented by the era in which they entered the workforce. Because most people start work between the ages of 18 and 23, the eras also correlate closely with the chronological age of employees.

Before going any further, let's acknowledge some limitations of this analysis. First, we make no assumption that this framework would apply universally across all cultures. Second, there is very little rigorous research on generational values, so we have to rely on an intuitive framework. Finally, these are imprecise categories. There is no law that someone born in 1985 can't have similar values to someone born in 1955. You may see your values better reflected in other generations than in your own. Despite these limitations, values do change over generations,[74] and there are some useful insights to be gained from analysing values this way.

Workers who grew up influenced by the Great Depression, the Second World War, the singing trio the Andrews Sisters, and the Berlin blockade entered the workforce through the 1950s and early 1960s believing in hard work, the status quo and authority figures. We call them *Veterans* (some use the label *Traditionalists*). Once hired, Veterans tended to be loyal to their employer and respectful of authority. They tend to be hardworking and practical. In terms of the terminal values on the RVS, these employees are likely to place the greatest importance on a comfortable life and family security.

TABLE 4.3

Dominant work values in today's workforce

Cohort	Entered the workforce	Approximate current age	Dominant work values
Veterans	1950s or early 1960s	65+	Hardworking, conservative, conforming; loyalty to the organisation
Boomers	1965–1985	Early 40s to mid-60s	Success, achievement, ambition, dislike of authority; loyalty to career
Xers	1985–2000	Late 20s to early 40s	Work/life balance, team-oriented, dislike of rules; loyalty to relationships
Nexters	2000 to present	Under 30	Confident, financial success, self-reliant but team-oriented; loyalty to both self and relationships

Boomers (*baby-boomers*) are a large cohort who were born after the Second World War when veterans returned to their families and times were good. Boomers entered the workforce from the mid-1960s through the mid-1980s. This cohort was influenced heavily by the civil rights movement, women's liberation, the Beatles, the Vietnam War and baby-boom competition. They brought with them a large measure of the 'hippie ethic' and distrust of authority. But they place a great deal of emphasis on achievement and material success. They work hard and want to enjoy the fruits of their labours. They are pragmatists who believe that ends can justify means. Boomers see the organisations that employ them merely as vehicles for their careers. Terminal values such as a sense of accomplishment and social recognition rank high with them.

Xers' (Generation X) lives have been shaped by globalisation, two-career parents, MTV, AIDS and computers. They value flexibility, life options and the achievement of job satisfaction. Family and relationships are very important to this cohort. Unlike Veterans, Xers are sceptical, particularly of authority. They also enjoy team-oriented work. Money is important as an indicator of career performance, but Xers are willing to trade off salary increases, titles, security and promotions for increased leisure time and expanded lifestyle options. In search of balance in their lives, Xers are less willing to make personal sacrifices for the sake of their employer than previous generations were. On the RVS, they rate high on true friendship, happiness and pleasure.

The most recent entrants to the workforce, Generation Y (also called *Neters*, *Millennials*, *Nexters* and *Generation Next*) grew up during prosperous times but find themselves entering a post-boom economy. Gone are the days of hiring bonuses and abundant jobs. Now they face insecurity about jobs and careers. Yet, they have high expectations and seek meaning in their work. Generation Y are at ease with diversity and are the first generation to take technology for granted. They have lived much of their lives with ATMs, DVDs, mobile phones, laptops and the internet. This generation tends to be money-oriented and desirous of the things that money can buy. They seek financial success. Like Xers, they enjoy teamwork but they are also highly self-reliant. They tend to emphasise terminal values such as freedom and a comfortable life.[75]

An understanding that individuals' values differ but tend to reflect the societal values of the period in which they grew up can be a valuable aid in explaining and predicting behaviour. Employees in their late sixties, for instance, are more likely to accept authority than their co-workers who are 10 or 15 years younger. And workers in their thirties are more likely than their parents to balk at having to work on weekends and more prone to leave a job in mid-career to pursue another that provides more leisure time.

VALUES, LOYALTY AND ETHICAL BEHAVIOUR

Has there been a decline in business ethics? Recent corporate scandals such as the Australian Wheat Board, HIH and OneTel—involving bribery, accounting manipulations, cover-ups and conflicts of interest—certainly suggest such a decline. But is this a recent phenomenon?

Although the issue is debatable, a lot of people think ethical standards began to erode in the late 1970s.[76] If there has been a decline in ethical standards, perhaps we should look to our work cohorts model (see Table 4.3) for a possible explanation. After all, managers consistently report that the actions of their bosses are the most important factor influencing ethical and unethical behaviour in their organisations.[77] Given this fact, the values of those in middle and upper management should have a significant bearing on the entire ethical climate within an organisation.

Through the mid-1970s, the managerial ranks were dominated by Veterans, whose loyalties were to their employers. When faced with ethical dilemmas, their decisions were made in terms of what was best for their organisation. Beginning in the mid- to late 1970s, Boomers began to rise into the upper levels of management. By the early 1990s, a large portion of middle and top management positions in business organisations was held by Boomers. The loyalty of Boomers is to their careers. Their focus is inward and their primary concern is with looking out for 'Number One'. Such self-centred values would be consistent with a decline in ethical standards. Could this help to explain the alleged decline in business ethics beginning in the late 1970s?

The potential good news in this analysis is that Xers are now in the process of moving into middle-management slots and soon will be rising into top management. Since their loyalty is to relationships, they are more likely to consider the ethical implications of their actions on others around them. The result? We might look forward to an uplifting of ethical standards in business over the next decade or two merely as a result of changing values within the managerial ranks.

VALUES ACROSS CULTURES

In Chapter 1, we described the new global village and said 'managers have to become capable of working with people from different cultures'. Because values differ across cultures, an understanding of these differences should be helpful in explaining and predicting the behaviour of employees from different countries.

HOFSTEDE'S FRAMEWORK FOR ASSESSING CULTURES

One of the most widely referenced approaches for analysing variations among cultures was developed in the late 1970s by Geert Hofstede, who surveyed more than 116 000 IBM employees in 40 countries about their work-related values.[78] He found that managers and employees vary on five value dimensions of national culture. They are listed and defined as follows:

- **Power distance**: The degree to which people in a country accept that power in institutions and organisations is distributed unequally. A high-power-distance rating means that large inequalities of power and wealth exist and are tolerated in the culture. Such cultures are more likely to follow a class or caste system that discourages upward mobility of its citizens. A low-power-distance ranking indicates the culture discourages differences between power and wealth. These societies stress equality and opportunity.
- **Individualism** versus **collectivism**: Individualism is the degree to which people prefer to act as individuals rather than as members of groups and believe in

power distance | A national culture attribute describing the extent to which a society accepts that power in institutions and organisations is distributed unequally.

individualism | A national culture attribute describing the degree to which people prefer to act as individuals rather than as members of groups.

collectivism | A national culture attribute that describes a tight social framework in which people expect others in groups of which they are a part to look after them and protect them.

individual rights above all else. Collectivism emphasises a tight social framework in which people expect others in groups of which they are a part to look after them and protect them.

- **Masculinity** versus **femininity**: The degree to which the culture favours traditional masculine roles such as achievement, power and control versus a culture that views men and women as equals. A high-masculinity rating indicates the culture has separate roles for men and women, with men dominating the society. A high-femininity rating means that the culture has little differentiation between male and female roles. To clarify, high femininity doesn't mean that the culture emphasises feminine roles; rather, it emphasises equality between men and women. In such cultures, women are treated as the equals of men in all aspects of the society.

- **Uncertainty avoidance**: The degree to which people in a country prefer structured over unstructured situations. In cultures that score high on uncertainty avoidance, people have an increased level of anxiety about uncertainty and ambiguity. Such cultures tend to emphasise laws, regulations and controls that are designed to reduce uncertainty. In cultures that score low on uncertainty avoidance, individuals are less dismayed by ambiguity and uncertainty and have a greater tolerance for a variety of opinions. Such cultures are less rule-oriented, take more risks, and accept change more readily.

- **Long-term** versus **short-term orientation**: This is the newest addition to Hofstede's typology. It focuses on the degree of a society's long-term devotion to traditional values. People in cultures with long-term orientations look to the future and value thrift, persistence and tradition. In a short-term orientation, people value the here-and-now; change is accepted more readily, and commitments don't represent impediments to change.

How do different countries score on Hofstede's dimensions? Table 4.4 shows the ratings for the countries for which data are available. For example, Malaysia has the largest index number in the power distance category. This means that power distance is higher in Malaysia than in any other country, which gives it its number-one rank. As you can see, the United States is the most individualistic nation of all, closely followed by Australia and Great Britain. Australia and the United States also tend to be short-term in their orientation and both are low in power distance. (People tend not to accept built-in class differences between people.) Australia and the United States are also relatively low on uncertainty avoidance, meaning that most Australians and Americans are relatively tolerant of uncertainty and ambiguity. Both Australia and the United States score relatively high on masculinity, meaning that most Australians and Americans emphasise traditional gender roles (at least relative to countries such as Denmark, Finland, Norway and Sweden).

Note that *individualistic* countries such as Australia, Canada, the United States and Great Britain tend to be low-power-distance countries and *collectivistic* countries such as India, Malaysia and Mexico tend to be high-power-distance countries. Also, you will notice regional differences. Western and Northern nations such as Canada and the Netherlands tend to be more individualistic. Poorer countries such as Mexico and the Philippines tend to be higher on power distance. South American nations tend to be higher on uncertainty avoidance, and Asian countries tend to have a long-term orientation.

Hofstede's culture dimensions have been enormously influential on OB researchers and managers. Nevertheless, his research has been criticised. First, although the data have since been updated, the original data are from 30 years ago and were based on a single company (IBM). Since these data were originally gathered, a lot has happened on the

masculinity | A national culture attribute describing the extent to which the culture favours traditional masculine work roles of achievement, power and control. Societal values are characterised by assertiveness and materialism.

femininity | A national culture attribute that has little differentiation between male and female roles, where women are treated as the equals of men in all aspects of the society.

uncertainty avoidance | A national culture attribute describing the extent to which a society feels threatened by uncertain and ambiguous situations and tries to avoid them.

long-term orientation | A national culture attribute that emphasises the future, thrift and persistence.

short-term orientation | A national culture attribute that emphasises the past and present, respect for tradition, and fulfilling social obligations.

Since entering the Chinese market in 1984, FedEx (one of the world's largest courier and delivery companies) has expanded its service to more than 220 Chinese cities. The success of FedEx in China, which has a long-term orientation as opposed to its short-term orientation in the United States, stems from the company's understanding of and respect for China's cultural traditions. Doing business in China requires a slow, persistent approach in creating and nurturing relationships built on trust and reliability.

world scene. Some of the most obvious include the fall of the Soviet Union, the transformation of Central and Eastern Europe, the end of apartheid in South Africa, the spread of Islam throughout the world, and the rise of China as a global power. Second, few researchers have read the details of Hofstede's methodology closely and therefore are unaware of the many decisions and judgment calls he had to make (for example, reducing the cultural values to just five). Some of the Hofstede results are unexpected. For example, Japan, which is often considered a highly collectivist nation, is considered only average on collectivism under Hofstede's dimensions.[79] Despite these concerns, Hofstede has been one of the most widely cited social scientists ever, and his framework has left a lasting mark on OB.

THE GLOBE FRAMEWORK FOR ASSESSING CULTURES

Begun in 1993, the Global Leadership and Organizational Behavior Effectiveness (GLOBE) research program is an ongoing cross-cultural investigation of leadership and national culture. Using data from 825 organisations in 62 countries, the GLOBE team identified nine dimensions on which national cultures differ.[80] (See Table 4.5 for examples of country ratings on each of the dimensions.)

- *Assertiveness*: The extent to which a society encourages people to be tough, confrontational, assertive and competitive versus modest and tender.
- *Future orientation*: The extent to which a society encourages and rewards future-oriented behaviours such as planning, investing in the future and delaying gratification. This is essentially equivalent to Hofstede's long-term/short-term orientation.
- *Gender differentiation*: The extent to which a society maximises gender role differences. This is equivalent to Hofstede's masculinity–femininity dimension.
- *Uncertainty avoidance*: As identified by Hofstede, the GLOBE team defined this term as a society's reliance on social norms and procedures to alleviate the unpredictability of future events.
- *Power distance*: As did Hofstede, the GLOBE team defined this as the degree to which members of a society expect power to be unequally shared.
- *Individualism/collectivism*: Again, this term was defined, as was Hofstede's, as the degree to which individuals are encouraged by societal institutions to be integrated into groups within organisations and society.
- *In-group collectivism*: In contrast to focusing on societal institutions, this dimension encompasses the extent to which members of a society take pride in membership in small groups, such as their family and circle of close friends, and the organisations in which they are employed.

TABLE 4.4 Hofstede's cultural values by nation

Country	Power distance Index	Rank	Individualism versus collectivism Index	Rank	Masculinity versus femininity Index	Rank	Uncertainty avoidance Index	Rank	Long- versus short-term orientation Index	Rank
Argentina	49	35–36	46	22–23	56	20–21	86	10–15		
Australia	36	41	90	2	61	16	51	37	31	22–24
Austria	11	53	55	18	79	2	70	24–25	31	22–24
Belgium	65	20	75	8	54	22	94	5–6	38	18
Brazil	69	14	38	26–27	49	27	76	21–22	65	6
Canada	39	39	80	4–5	52	24	48	41–42	23	30
Chile	63	24–25	23	38	28	46	86	10–15		
Colombia	67	17	13	49	64	11–12	80	20		
Costa Rica	35	42–44	15	46	21	48–49	86	10–15		
Denmark	18	51	74	9	16	50	23	51	46	10
Ecuador	78	8–9	8	52	63	13–14	67	28		
Finland	33	46	63	17	26	47	59	31–32	41	14
France	68	15–16	71	10–11	43	35–36	86	10–15	39	17
Germany	35	42–44	67	15	66	9–10	65	29	31	22–24
Great Britain	35	42–44	89	3	66	9–10	35	47–48	25	28–29
Greece	60	27–28	35	30	57	18–19	112	1		
Hong Kong	68	15–16	25	37	57	18–19	29	49–50	96	2
Indonesia	78	8–9	14	47–48	46	30–31	48	41–42		
India	77	10–11	48	21	56	20–21	40	45	61	7
Iran	58	29–30	41	24	43	35–36	59	31–32		
Italy	50	34	76	7	70	4–5	75	23	34	19
Japan	54	33	46	22–23	95	1	92	7	80	4
Korea (South)	60	27–28	18	43	39	41	85	16–17	75	5
Malaysia	104	1	26	36	50	25–26	36	46		
Mexico	81	5–6	30	32	69	6	82	18		
Netherlands	38	40	80	4–5	14	51	53	35	44	11–12
Norway	31	47–48	69	13	8	52	50	38	44	11–12
New Zealand	22	50	79	6	58	17	49	39–40	30	25–26
Pakistan	55	32	14	47–48	50	25–26	70	24–25	0	34
Peru	64	21–23	16	45	42	37–38	87	9		
Philippines	94	4	32	31	64	11–12	44	44	19	31–32
Portugal	63	24–25	27	33–35	31	45	104	2	30	25–26
South Africa	49	35–36	65	16	63	13–14	49	39–40		
Singapore	74	13	20	39–41	48	28	8	53	48	9
Spain	57	31	51	20	42	37–38	86	10–15	19	31–32
Sweden	31	47–48	71	10–11	5	53	29	49–50	33	20
Switzerland	34	45	68	14	70	4–5	58	33	40	15–16
Taiwan	58	29–30	17	44	45	32–33	69	26	87	3
Thailand	64	21–23	20	39–41	34	44	64	30	56	8
Turkey	66	18–19	37	28	45	32–33	85	16–17		
United States	40	38	91	1	62	15	46	43	29	27
Venezuela	81	5–6	12	50	73	3	76	21–22		
Regions:										
Arab countries	80	7	38	26–27	53	23	68	27		
East Africa	64	21–23	27	33–35	41	39	52	36	25	28–29
West Africa	77	10–11	20	39–41	46	30–31	54	34	16	33

SOURCE: Copyright © Geert Hofstede BV; hofstede@bovt.nl. Reproduced with permission.
Scores range from 0 = extremely low on dimension, to 100 = extremely high. NOTE: 1 = highest rank.

	TABLE 4.5
	GLOBE highlights

Dimension	Countries rating low	Countries rating moderate	Countries rating high
Assertiveness	Sweden New Zealand Switzerland	Egypt Ireland Philippines	Spain United States Greece
Future orientation	Russia Argentina Poland	Slovenia Egypt Ireland	Denmark Canada Netherlands
Gender differentiation	Sweden Denmark Slovenia	Italy Brazil Argentina	South Korea Egypt Morocco
Uncertainty avoidance	Russia Hungary Bolivia	Israel United States Mexico	Austria Denmark Germany
Power distance	Denmark Netherlands South Africa	England France Brazil	Russia Spain Thailand
Individualism/collectivism*	Denmark Singapore Japan	Hong Kong United States Egypt	Greece Hungary Germany
In-group collectivism	Denmark Sweden New Zealand	Japan Israel Qatar	Egypt China Morocco
Performance orientation	Russia Argentina Greece	Sweden Israel Spain	United States Taiwan New Zealand
Humane orientation	Germany Spain France	Hong Kong Sweden Taiwan	Indonesia Egypt Malaysia

*A low score is synonymous with collectivism.

SOURCE: M. Javidan and R. J. House, 'Cultural Acumen for the Global Manager: Lessons from Project GLOBE', *Organizational Dynamics*, Spring 2001, pp. 289–305. Copyright © 2001. Reproduced with permission from Elsevier.

- *Performance orientation*: This refers to the degree to which a society encourages and rewards group members for performance improvement and excellence.
- *Humane orientation*: This is defined as the degree to which a society encourages and rewards individuals for being fair, altruistic, generous, caring and kind to others.

A comparison of the GLOBE dimensions against those identified by Hofstede suggests that the former has extended Hofstede's work rather than replaced it. The GLOBE project confirms that Hofstede's five dimensions are still valid. However, it has added some additional dimensions and provides us with an updated measure of where countries rate on each dimension. As generations evolve and immigrants enter a nation, a country's cultural values can change. For instance, the GLOBE survey suggests that the United States has become somewhat less individualist over time. We can expect future cross-cultural studies of human behaviour and organisational practices to increasingly use the GLOBE dimensions to assess differences between countries.

IMPLICATIONS FOR OB

Twenty years ago, it would have been fair to say that *organisational behaviour* had a strong American bias. Most of the concepts had been developed by Americans using American subjects within domestic contexts. For instance, a comprehensive study published in the early 1980s covering more than 11 000 articles published in 24 management and organisational behaviour journals over a ten-year period found that approximately 80 per cent of the studies were done in the United States and had been conducted by Americans.[81] But times have changed.[82] Although the majority of published OB findings still focus on Americans, recent research has significantly expanded OB's domain to include European, South American, African and Asian subjects. Additionally, there has been a marked increase in cross-cultural research by teams of researchers from different countries.[83]

OB has become a global discipline and, as such, its concepts need to reflect the different cultural values of people in different countries. Fortunately, a wealth of research has been published in recent years, which allows us to specify where OB concepts are universally applicable across cultures and where they are not. In future chapters, we will regularly stop to consider the generalisability of OB findings and how they might need to be modified in different countries.

LINKING AN INDIVIDUAL'S PERSONALITY AND VALUES TO THE WORKPLACE

Thirty years ago, organisations were concerned only with personality because their primary focus was to match individuals to specific jobs. That concern still exists. But, in recent years, this interest has expanded to include how well the individual's personality *and* values match the *organisation*. Why? Because managers today are less interested in an applicant's ability to perform a *specific* job than with the *flexibility* to meet changing situations and commitment to the organisation.

We will now discuss person–job fit and person–organisation fit in more detail.

PERSON–JOB FIT

Matching the job requirements with personality characteristics is best articulated in John Holland's **personality–job fit theory**.[84] The theory is based on the notion of fit between an individual's personality characteristics and the job. Holland presents six personality types and proposes that satisfaction and the propensity to leave a position depend on the degree to which individuals successfully match their personalities to a job. Each one of the six personality types has a congruent occupation. Table 4.6 describes the six types and their personality characteristics, and gives examples of congruent occupations.

Holland has developed a *Vocational Preference Inventory* questionnaire that contains 160 occupational titles. Respondents indicate which of these occupations they like or dislike, and their answers are used to form personality profiles. Using this procedure, research strongly supports the hexagonal diagram shown in Figure 4.2.[85] This figure shows that the closer two fields or orientations are in the hexagon, the more compatible they are. Adjacent categories are quite similar, whereas those diagonally opposite are highly dissimilar.

What does all this mean? The theory argues that satisfaction is highest and turnover lowest when personality and occupation are in agreement. Social individuals should be in social jobs, conventional people in conventional jobs, and so forth. A realistic person in a realistic job is in a more congruent situation than is a realistic person in an investigative

personality–job fit theory | Identifies six personality types, and proposes that the fit between personality type and occupational environment determines satisfaction and turnover.

Type	Personality characteristics	Congruent occupations
Realistic: Prefers physical activities that require skill, strength and coordination	Shy, genuine, persistent, stable, conforming, practical	Mechanic, drill press operator, assembly-line worker, farmer
Investigative: Prefers activities that involve thinking, organising and understanding	Analytical, original, curious, independent	Biologist, economist, mathematician, news reporter
Social: Prefers activities that involve helping and developing others	Sociable, friendly, cooperative, understanding	Social worker, teacher, counsellor, clinical psychologist
Conventional: Prefers rule-regulated, orderly and unambiguous activities	Conforming, efficient, practical, unimaginative, inflexible	Accountant, corporate manager, bank teller, file clerk
Enterprising: Prefers verbal activities in which there are opportunities to influence others and attain power	Self-confident, ambitious, energetic, domineering	Lawyer, real estate agent, public relations specialist, small business manager
Artistic: Prefers ambiguous and unsystematic activities that allow creative expression	Imaginative, disorderly, idealistic, emotional, impractical	Painter, musician, writer, interior decorator

■ TABLE 4.6

Holland's typology of personality and congruent occupations

job. A realistic person in a social job is in the most incongruent situation possible. The key points of this model are that (1) there do appear to be intrinsic differences in personality among individuals, (2) there are different types of jobs, and (3) people in jobs congruent with their personality should be more satisfied and less likely to voluntarily resign than should people in incongruent jobs.

PERSON–ORGANISATION FIT

As previously noted, attention in recent years has expanded to include matching people to *organisations* as well as *jobs*. To the degree that an organisation faces a dynamic and changing environment and requires employees who are able to readily change tasks and move easily between teams, it is more important that employees' personalities fit with the overall organisation's culture than with the characteristics of any specific job.

The person–organisation fit essentially argues that people leave organisations that are not compatible with their personalities.[86] Using the Big Five terminology, for instance, we

■ FIGURE 4.2

Relationships among occupational personality types

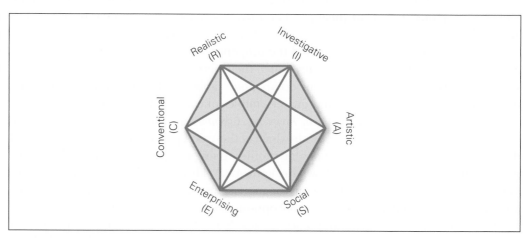

RISING STARS OR FALLING NUCLEAR BOMBS?

Every organisation is looking for those unique individuals who possess the right qualities, skills and abilities to lead, motivate and inspire those around them. But how does the organisation's leadership know when the possible new manager is a rising star who will meet these special requirements, or a 'nuclear bomb' waiting to explode? It is a fine line between persons who are independent, self-motivated, inspiring and honest leaders, and those who are self-centred, narcissistic and manipulative, and interested only in achieving their own personal goals by any means possible.

A recent study identified some key characteristics of these organisational 'bombs'. The first characteristic is the pursuit of both power and knowledge. These individuals will subtly amass power, often based on having complete knowledge of some key aspect of the organisational processes, and will then use this power and knowledge to achieve their personal goals. For instance, knowledge of the organisational budgeting processes will give holders both power and knowledge, chiefly because it gives them access to and control of resources, and knowledge of how to access those resources. Because there are never enough resources, those who know where they are and can control their allocation soon acquire power far beyond what is healthy for the organisation.

Lack of integrity is another characteristic of these organisational 'bombs'. They lie and play the 'blame game' well. Negative outcomes are always due to the efforts of others, but positive outcomes were always their idea or due to their personal efforts. Lying about other people, even about superiors, is a distinguishing feature of these organisational 'bombs'. Even when their lies and falsehoods are revealed, they will deny them. This characteristic is often coupled with their 'saviour' role, where they create a crisis and then 'solve' it, appearing as a hero in the process.

Finally, these 'bombs' are not innovators. They are usually conservative, and seek to perform their tasks in a conventional manner in order to conceal their true personal motives and the fact that they are rarely gifted or highly intelligent. What they excel at is doing simple tasks well, averting or solving crisis situations (often caused by them in the first place) and not attracting scrutiny of their activities from those in senior positions. Rising stars or falling nuclear bombs—it is often hard to tell, but failure to do so can be very costly for organisations!

SOURCES: This discussion was based on T. Domke and G. Lange, *Cain and Abel at Work: How to Overcome Office Politics and the People Who Stand Between You and Success* (New York: Broadway Books, 2001); and C. N. Sargent, 'Company Officer Development: Dangerous Minds', *FireRescue Magazine*, vol. 24, no. 2, 2006: <www.firerescue1.com/firerescue-magazine/24-2/17248/>.

could expect that people high on extraversion fit better with aggressive and team-oriented cultures, that people high on agreeableness match up better with a supportive organisational climate than one that focuses on aggressiveness, and that people high on openness to experience fit better into organisations that emphasise innovation rather than standardisation.[87] Following these guidelines at the time of hiring should lead to selecting new employees who fit better with the organisation's culture, which, in turn, should result in higher employee satisfaction and reduced turnover.

Research on person–organisation fit has also looked at people's values and whether they match the organisation's culture. The fit of employees' values with the culture of their organisation predicts job satisfaction, commitment to the organisation and low turnover.[88]

The Organisational Culture Profile (OCP) can help to assess whether or not an individual's values match those of the organisation (see Figure 4.3).[89] The OCP helps individuals to sort their characteristics in terms of importance, which indicates what a person values. The reason individuals sort characteristics—as opposed to just rating them on a scale such as 1 = *this characteristic doesn't matter to me* versus 10 = *this characteristic is extremely important to me*—is that all values are desirable. In other words, who would want to work in an unsupportive organisation, or one with a bad reputation? So, if people were using the rating scale, they might rate all the values as extremely important. The forced-choice nature of the OCP makes sense because it is only through having to make hard choices that one's true values become apparent. For example, Motorola emphasises

You will find 40 characteristics that describe people. Please consider each characteristic according to the question: **How well does this characteristic describe me?**

The boxes range from the **most characteristic** to **least characteristic**. Place each characteristic as it describes you in an appropriate box. Each box receives only one attribute. For example, only two items may be 'most characteristic' of you and your ideal organisation, while eight items must be 'neither characteristic nor uncharacteristic'. You can write the item number in the box rather than the words. It may be easiest to read through the entire list of characteristics looking for extremes first. Although this sorting may appear difficult, it goes quickly if you cross items off as you place them.

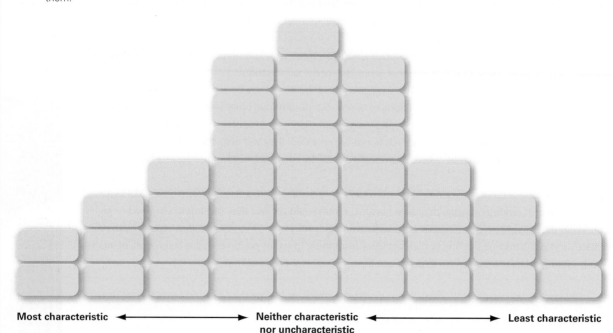

Most characteristic ⟷ Neither characteristic ⟷ Least characteristic
nor uncharacteristic

The characteristics are

1. Adaptability
2. Stability
3. Being reflective
4. Being innovative
5. Being quick to take advantage of opportunities
6. Taking individual responsibility
7. Risk taking
8. Opportunities for professional growth
9. Autonomy
10. Being rule-oriented
11. Being analytical
12. Paying attention to detail
13. Confronting conflict directly
14. Being team-oriented
15. Sharing information freely
16. Being people-oriented
17. Fairness
18. Not being constrained by many rules
19. Tolerance
20. Informality
21. Decisiveness
22. Being competitive
23. Being highly organised
24. Achievement orientation
25. Having a clear guiding philosophy
26. Being results-oriented
27. Having high performance expectations
28. Being aggressive
29. High pay for good performance
30. Security of employment
31. Offers praise for good performance
32. Being supportive
33. Being calm
34. Developing friends at work
35. Being socially responsible
36. Enthusiasm for the job
37. Working long hours
38. Having a good reputation
39. An emphasis on quality
40. Being distinctive/different from others

innovation, tolerance for diversity and teamwork. These values are assessed in the OCP. So, if these were at the high end of your pyramid, then you would probably be happy in this type of culture. But you might not be as happy in General Electric's culture, which emphasises achievement, performance, results and individual responsibility.

SUMMARY AND IMPLICATIONS FOR MANAGERS

- 'The outcome of those 80-plus years of research was that personality and job performance were not meaningfully related across traits or situations.'[90]
- However, the past 20 years have been more promising, largely due to the findings surrounding the Big Five. Seeking employees who score high on conscientiousness, for instance, is probably sound advice.
- Screening candidates for managerial and sales positions to identify those high in extraversion also should pay dividends.
- In terms of exerting effort at work, there is impressive evidence that people who score high on conscientiousness, extraversion and emotional stability are likely to be highly motivated employees.[91]
- Of course, situational factors need to be taken into consideration.[92] Factors such as job demands, the degree of required interaction with others, and the organisation's culture are examples of situational variables that moderate the personality–job performance relationship. So you need to evaluate the job, the work group, and the organisation to determine the optimum personality fit.

- Even though the MBTI has been widely criticised, it may have a place for use in training and development, as it can help employees to better understand themselves, it can provide aid to teams by helping members to better understand each other, and it can open up communication in work groups, thereby reducing conflicts.
- Values strongly influence a person's attitudes, behaviours and perceptions. So, knowledge of an individual's value system can provide insight into what 'makes the person tick'.
- Managers can use the Rokeach Value Survey to assess potential employees and determine if their values align with the dominant values of the organisation.
- Employees' performance and satisfaction are likely to be higher if their values fit well with the organisation.
- Management can strive during the selection of new employees to find job candidates who not only have the ability, experience and motivation to perform, but who also have a value system that is compatible with the organisation's value system.

POINT / COUNTERPOINT

Traits Are Powerful Predictors of Behaviour

● POINT

The essence of trait approaches in OB is that employees possess stable personality characteristics that significantly influence their attitudes towards, and behavioural reactions to, organisational settings. People with particular traits tend to be relatively consistent in their attitudes and behaviour over time and across situations.

Of course, trait theorists recognise that all traits are not equally powerful. They tend to put them into one of three categories. *Cardinal traits* are those so strong and generalised that they influence every act a person performs. *Primary traits* are generally consistent influences on behaviour, but they may not show up in all situations. Finally, *secondary traits* are attributes that don't form a vital part of the personality but come into play only in particular situations. For the most part, trait theories have focused on the power of primary traits to predict employee behaviour.

Trait theorists do a fairly good job of meeting the average person's face-validity test. Think of friends, relatives and acquaintances you have known for a number of years. Do they have traits that have remained essentially stable over time? Most of us would answer that question in the affirmative. If Cousin Anne was shy and nervous when we last saw her ten years ago, it would be unlikely to find her outgoing and relaxed now.

Managers seem to have a strong belief in the power of traits to predict behaviour. If managers believed that situations determined behaviour, they would hire people almost at random and structure the situation properly. But the employee selection process in most organisations places a great deal of emphasis on how applicants perform in interviews and on tests. Assume you are an interviewer and ask yourself: 'What am I looking for in job candidates?' If you answered with terms such as *conscientious*, *hardworking*, *persistent*, *confident* and *dependable*, you are a trait theorist.

● COUNTERPOINT

Few people would dispute that there are some stable attributes that affect reactions to the workplace. But trait theorists go beyond that generality and argue that individual behaviour consistencies are widespread and account for much of the differences in behaviour among people.

There are two important problems with using traits to explain a large proportion of behaviour in organisations. First, organisational settings are strong situations that have a large impact on employee behaviour. Second, individuals are highly adaptive and personality traits change in response to organisational situations.

It has been well known for some time that the effects of traits are likely to be strongest in relatively weak situations and weakest in relatively strong situations. Organisational settings tend to be strong situations because they have rules and other formal regulations that define acceptable behaviour and punish deviant behaviour; and they have informal norms that dictate appropriate behaviours. These formal and informal constraints minimise the effects of personality traits.

By arguing that employees possess stable traits that lead to cross-situational consistencies in behaviours, trait theorists are implying that individuals don't really adapt to different situations. But there is a growing body of evidence that supports the theory that an individual's traits are changed by the organisations in which that individual participates. If the individual's personality changes as a result of exposure to organisational settings, in what sense can that individual be said to have traits that persistently and consistently affect his or her reactions to those very settings? Moreover, people typically belong to multiple organisations that often include very different kinds of members. And they adapt to those different situations. Instead of being the prisoners of a rigid and stable personality framework, as trait theorists propose, people regularly adjust their behaviour to reflect the requirements of various situations.

SOURCES: Points in this argument are based on W. Fleeson, 'Moving Personality Beyond the Person–Situation Debate: The Challenge and the Opportunity of Within-Person Variability', *Current Directions in Psychological Science*, vol. 13, no. 2, 2004, pp. 83–87; R. T. Hogan and B. W. Roberts, 'Introduction: Personality and Industrial and Organizational Psychology', in R. T. Hogan and B. W. Roberts (eds), *Personality Psychology in the Workplace* (Washington, DC: American Psychological Association, 2001), pp. 3–16; and N. Schmitt, 'Beyond the Big Five: Increases in Understanding and Practical Utility', *Human Performance*, vol. 17, no. 3, 2004, pp. 347–57.

QUESTIONS FOR REVIEW

1. What is *personality*?
2. What is the Myers-Briggs Type Indicator (MBTI)?
3. Describe the factors in the Big Five Model. Which factor shows the greatest value in predicting behaviour and why?
4. What behavioural predictions might you make if you knew that an employee had (a) low core self-evaluation? (b) a low Mach score? (c) a Type A personality?
5. Do people from the same country have a common personality type? Explain.
6. Contrast the Veteran, Boomers, Xers and Nexters cohort value classifications with the terminal values identified in the Rokeach Value Survey.
7. What are the five value dimensions of national culture as defined by Hofstede? Based on your own national culture, if you were a manager working in Australia, do you think you would find it difficult to lead a team? What about in Japan? How would you create an effective team atmosphere in both countries?
8. What were the six personality types identified by Holland?
9. What is person–job fit, and how is it different from person–organisation fit?
10. Why might managers today pay more attention to the person–organisation fit than the person–job fit?

QUESTIONS FOR CRITICAL THINKING

1. 'Heredity determines personality.' (a) Build an argument to support this statement. (b) Build an argument against this statement.
2. 'The type of job an employee does moderates the relationship between personality and job productivity.' Do you agree or disagree with this statement? Discuss.
3. One day your boss comes in and he is nervous, edgy and argumentative. The next day he is calm and relaxed. Does this behaviour suggest that personality traits aren't consistent from day to day?
4. 'Thirty-five years ago, the young employees we hired were ambitious, conscientious, hardworking and honest. Today's young workers don't have the same values.' Do you agree or disagree with this manager's comments? Support your position.
5. Do you think there might be a positive and significant relationship between the possession of certain personal values and successful career progression in organisations such as Macquarie Bank, the ACTU and the Queensland Police Service? Discuss.

Is it Possible to Have a Team Personality?

Purpose:
To encourage critical thinking on the field of personality.

Time required:
Approximately 50–60 minutes.

Participant roles:
Team members brainstorming ideas (and perhaps developing a team personality in the process?).

The task:
It is an unusual organisation in today's world that doesn't use work teams. But not everyone is a good team player. This prompts the questions: What individual personality characteristics enhance a team's performance? And what characteristics might hinder team performance?

Break into groups of five or six. Based on the research presented in this chapter, each group should:

1. identify personality characteristics they think are associated with high-performance teams and justify their choices;
2. identify personality characteristics they think hinder high-performance teams and justify their choices;
3. resolve whether it is better to have teams composed of individuals with similar or dissimilar traits; and
4. discuss what role values play in the development of a team personality.

Each group should keep notes of the discussions and have one member present the team's conclusions to the whole class.

ETHICAL DILEMMA

Hiring Based on Genetic Data

The Human Genome Project (HGP) began in 1990. Its goal was to identify the approximately 35 000 genes in human DNA and to map out and sequence the 3 billion chemical base pairs that make up human DNA. As the director of the project said, HGP will allow us to read 'our own instruction book'.

The project was completed in 2003. And now that it's finished, we are faced with a number of ethical issues as to how the information it developed will be used. From an OB perspective, we should be concerned with how genetic information might be used by employers to screen job applicants and employees.

It is now possible for employers to identify predisposed and presymptomatic genetic conditions. People who are predisposed don't have a disease but have an increased likelihood of developing it. Presymptomatic genetic conditions means a person will develop a disease if they live long enough. For instance, there is a gene that predisposes an individual to diabetes and another that is presymptomatic of Huntington's disease.

There are laws in many countries that protect individuals against misuse of genetic data. For instance, the *Americans with Disabilities Act* protects individuals against genetic discrimination in the workplace. But this applies only to organisations with 15 or more employees. And the law doesn't restrict employers from using genetic testing if it is related to job performance. Other countries, such as Australia and most Asian countries, have no laws protecting employees from misuse of genetic information by employers.

Employers and insurance companies argue that genetic information is important to limit potential liability for health and life insurance. Critics respond that employees are entitled to their privacy.

Where it is legal, do you think it is ethical for employers to engage in genetic testing with the intent to screen for diseases or potential diseases? Is it permissible, for example, to use a blood test to perform genetic testing on employees without their consent? What about with their consent? Is your answer any different if the genetic information is reasonably related to specific job performance?

SOURCE: This dilemma is based on R. A. Curley, Jr and L. M. Caperna, 'The Brave New World is Here: Privacy Issues and the Human Genome Project', *Defense Counsel Journal*, January 2003, pp. 22–35.

The Rise and Fall of Carly Fiorina

For a long time, Carleton S. ('Carly') Fiorina was one of the best-known CEOs in the world. Brought in as Hewlett-Packard's (HP) CEO in 1999, Fiorina was instantly recognisable for her charisma, visibility and aggressiveness. Practically every OB book (including past editions of this one) featured her. She was even mentioned as a possible cabinet member of the Bush administration or a Senate candidate from California. Widely praised as a change agent and a visionary leader at Lucent Technologies—which she led before joining HP—Fiorina had a way of generating enthusiasm and excitement. Some called her a 'rock star' CEO.

However, under Fiorina's leadership, HP struggled as the world's second-largest computer company. Although revenue climbed steadily under her leadership, profits did not. Nor did the stock price—an investor who bought HP stock the day Fiorina was hired would have seen 55 per cent of the investment vanish by the time she was fired. Her acquisition of Compaq in 2002, which Walter Hewlett (son of the company's co-founder and one of HP's largest shareholders) was adamantly against, never paid off as promised.

As a result of these struggles, the HP board tried to find a way to limit Fiorina's powers and give more authority to other executives. A month before her firing, Fiorina was told point-blank by three board members that she had to change her style. She adamantly refused. A month later, when informed of the board's decision to fire her, Fiorina was 'stunned'.

After her firing, there was no shortage of experts to point out her failings. Some felt that Fiorina spent too much time on the road talking to groups and not enough time inside the company. Others felt she overpromised results. One HP executive stated, 'There were people inside HP who loved Carly because of her ability to architect a strategy, but then there were the people who thought that she was drawn to all the pomp and circumstance.' Another HP observer claimed after Fiorina was ousted, 'The stock is up a bit on the fact that nobody liked Carly's leadership all that much.' Others argued that HP employees never accepted Fiorina's attempts to change HP culture, or her high-profile ways. (She placed her portrait in HP headquarters next to the HP founders, and she frequently rubbed elbows with rock stars such as U2's the Edge, Gwen Stefani and Sheryl Crow.)

For someone who was praised for her energy and leadership, how could the tides have turned so dramatically against her? For now, the rock star CEO is without a band.

QUESTIONS

1. Why is it that the qualities that seemingly were a great asset to Fiorina and HP—energy, enthusiasm, charisma, vision, tenacity and aggressiveness— became liabilities? Does this case contradict the view that personality is important? Explain.

2. Some have argued that Fiorina failed because her personality was 'too big' and that she became more focused on herself than on the nuts-and-bolts of business. Can a person's personality be too strong? How so?

3. Some have argued that Fiorina's firing is an example of the double standard that being aggressive and forceful works for men but backfires for women. Do you think gender had anything to do with Fiorina's firing?

4. Fiorina had to complete a two-hour, 900-question personality test as part of the process to select her as CEO. Does this suggest that personality testing has little value?

SOURCE: Based on J. Markoff, 'When + Adds Up to Minus', *New York Times*, 10 February 2005, pp. C1, C7; and P. R. La Monica, 'Fiorina out, HP Stock Soars', CNN/Money: <www.money.cnn.com/2005/02/09/technology/hp_fiorina/> (10 February 2005).

ENDNOTES

1. This section is based on N. Ahmed, *The Age*, 2 September 2006, p. 5; Equal Opportunity for Women in the Workplace Agency, Australian Census of Women in Leadership, 2006: <www.eowa.gov.au>; K. Simpson, *The Age*, 2 September 2006, Business, p. 1; <www.foresight.org/Nanomedicine/>; <www.luxexecutive summit.com/Speakers/Speakers.php?spkr_id=jackie_fairley>; and <www.nsti.org/press/Prshow.html>.

2. G. W. Allport, *Personality: A Psychological Interpretation* (New York: Holt, Rinehart & Winston, 1937), p. 48. For a brief critique of current views on the meaning of personality, see R. T. Hogan and B. W. Roberts, 'Introduction: Personality and Industrial and Organizational Psychology', in B. W. Roberts and R. Hogan (eds), *Personality Psychology in the Workplace* (Washington, DC: American Psychological Association, 2001), pp. 11–12.

3. See, for instance, M. B. Stein, K. L. Jang and W. J. Livesley, 'Heritability of Social Anxiety-Related Concerns and Personality Characteristics: A Twin Study', *Journal of Nervous and Mental Disease*, April 2002, pp. 219–24; and S. Pinker, *The Blank Slate: The Modern Denial of Human Nature* (New York: Viking, 2002).

4. See R. D. Arvey and T. J. Bouchard, Jr, 'Genetics, Twins, and Organizational Behavior', in B. M. Staw and L. L. Cummings (eds), *Research in Organizational Behavior*, vol. 16 (Greenwich, CT: JAI Press, 1994), pp. 65–66; W. Wright, *Born That Way: Genes, Behavior, Personality* (New York: Knopf, 1998); T. J. Bouchard, Jr and J. C. Loehlin, 'Genes, Evolution, and Personality', *Behavior Genetics*, May 2001, pp. 243–73; and G. Lensvelt-Mulders and J. Hettema, 'Analysis of Genetic Influences on the Consistency and Variability of the Big Five across Different Stressful Situations', *European Journal of Personality*, September–October 2001, pp. 355–71.

5. R. Ilies and T. A. Judge, 'On the Heritability of Job Satisfaction: The Mediating Role of Personality', *Journal of Applied Psychology*, vol. 88, no. 4, 2003, pp. 750–59.

6. W. Mischel, 'The Interaction of Person and Situation', in D. Magnusson and N. S. Endler (eds), *Personality at the Crossroads: Current Issues in Interactional Psychology* (Hillsdale, NJ: Erlbaum, 1977), pp. 166–207.

7. R. C. Carson, 'Personality', in M. R. Rosenzweig and L. W. Porter (eds), *Annual Review of Psychology*, vol. 40 (Palo Alto, CA: Annual Reviews, 1989), pp. 228–29.

8. See A. H. Buss, 'Personality as Traits', *American Psychologist*, November 1989, pp. 1378–88; R. R. McCrae, 'Trait Psychology and the Revival of Personality and Culture Studies', *American Behavioral Scientist*, September 2000, pp. 10–31; and L. R. James and M. D. Mazerolle, *Personality in Work Organizations* (Thousand Oaks, CA: Sage, 2002).

9. See, for instance, G. W. Allport and H. S. Odbert, 'Trait Names, A Psycholexical Study', *Psychological Monographs*, no. 47, 1936; and R. B. Cattell, 'Personality Pinned Down', *Psychology Today*, July 1973, pp. 40–46.

10. See R. R. McCrae and T. Costa, Jr, 'Reinterpreting the Myers-Briggs Type Indicator from the Perspective of the Five Factor Model of Personality', *Journal of Personality*, March 1989, pp. 17–40; and N. L. Quenk, *Essentials of Myers-Briggs Type Indicator Assessment* (New York: Wiley, 2000).

11. 'Identifying How We Think: The Myers-Briggs Type Indicator and Herrmann Brain Dominance Instrument', *Harvard Business Review*, July–August 1997, pp. 114–15.

12. G. N. Landrum, *Profiles of Genius* (New York: Prometheus, 1993).

13. See, for instance, W. L. Gardner and M. L. Martinko, 'Using the Myers-Briggs Type Indicator to Study Managers: A Literature Review and Research Agenda', *Journal of Management*, vol. 22, no. 1, 1996, pp. 45–83; W. D. Mitchell, 'Cautions Regarding Aggregated Data Analyses in Type Research', *Journal of Psychological Type*, vol. 53, 2000, pp. 19–30; T. L. Bess and R. J. Harvey, 'Bimodal Score Distributions and the Myers-Briggs Type Indicator: Fact or Artifact?', *Journal of Personality Assessment*, February 2002, pp. 176–86; R. M. Capraro and M. M. Capraro, 'Myers-Briggs Type Indicator Score Reliability across Studies: A Meta-Analytic Reliability Generalization Study', *Educational & Psychological Measurement*, August 2002, pp. 590–602; and R. C. Arnau, B. A. Green, D. H. Rosen, D. H. Gleaves and J. G. Melancon, 'Are Jungian Preferences Really Categorical? An Empirical Investigation Using Taxometric Analysis', *Personality & Individual Differences*, January 2003, pp. 233–51.

14. See, for example, J. M. Digman, 'Personality Structure: Emergence of the Five-Factor Model', in M. R. Rosenzweig and L. W. Porter (eds), *Annual Review of Psychology*, vol. 41 (Palo Alto, CA: Annual Reviews, 1990), pp. 417–40; R. R. McCrae,

'Special Issue: The Five-Factor Model: Issues and Applications', *Journal of Personality*, June 1992; D. B. Smith, P. J. Hanges and M. W. Dickson, 'Personnel Selection and the Five-Factor Model: Reexamining the Effects of Applicant's Frame of Reference', *Journal of Applied Psychology*, April 2001, pp. 304–15; and T. A. Judge, D. Heller and M. K. Mount, 'Five-Factor Model of Personality and Job Satisfaction: A Meta-Analysis', *Journal of Applied Psychology*, June 2002, pp. 530–41.

15. See, for instance, M. R. Barrick and M. K. Mount, 'The Big Five Personality Dimensions and Job Performance: A Meta-Analysis', *Personnel Psychology*, Spring 1991, pp. 1–26; R. P Tett, D. N. Jackson and M. Rothstein, 'Personality Measures as Predictors of Job Performance: A Meta-Analytic Review', *Personnel Psychology*, Winter 1991, pp. 703–42; O. Behling, 'Employee Selection: Will Intelligence and Conscientiousness Do the Job?', *Academy of Management Executive*, February 1998, pp. 77–86; G. M. Hurtz and J. J. Donovan, 'Personality and Job Performance: The Big Five Revisited', *Journal of Applied Psychology*, December 2000, pp. 869–79; T. A. Judge and J. E. Bono, 'Relationship of Core Self-Evaluations Traits—Self-Esteem, Generalized Self-Efficacy, Locus of Control, and Emotional Stability—With Job Satisfaction and Job Performance: A Meta-Analysis', *Journal of Applied Psychology*, February 2001, pp. 80–92; J. Hogan and B. Holland, 'Using Theory to Evaluate Personality and Job-Performance Relations: A Socioanalytic Perspective', *Journal of Applied Psychology*, February 2003, pp. 100–12; and M. R. Barrick and M. K. Mount, 'Select on Conscientiousness and Emotional Stability', in E. A. Locke (ed.), *Handbook of Principles of Organizational Behavior* (Malden, MA: Blackwell, 2004), pp. 15–28.

16. M. K. Mount, M. R. Barrick and J. P. Strauss, 'Validity of Observer Ratings of the Big Five Personality Factors', *Journal of Applied Psychology*, April 1994, p. 272. Additionally confirmed by Hurtz and Donovan, 'Personality and Job Performance: The Big Five Revisited'; and M. R. Barrick, M. K. Mount and T. A. Judge, 'The FFM Personality Dimensions and Job Performance: Meta-Analysis of Meta-Analyses', *International Journal of Selection and Assessment*, vol. 9, 2001, pp. 9–30.

17. F. L. Schmidt and J. E. Hunter, 'The Validity and Utility of Selection Methods in

Personnel Psychology: Practical and Theoretical Implications of 85 Years of Research Findings', *Psychological Bulletin*, September 1998, p. 272.

18. D. W. Organ, 'Personality and Organizational Citizenship Behavior', *Journal of Management*, Summer 1994, pp. 465–78; D. W. Organ and K. Ryan, 'A Meta-Analytic Review of Attitudinal and Dispositional Predictors of Organizational Citizenship Behavior', *Personnel Psychology*, Winter 1995, pp. 775–802; M. A. Konovsky and D. W. Organ, 'Dispositional and Contextual Determinants of Organizational Citizenship Behavior', *Journal of Organizational Behavior*, May 1996, pp. 253–66; and P. M. Podsakoff, S. B. MacKenzie, J. B. Paine and D. G. Bachrach, 'Organizational Citizenship Behaviors: A Critical Review of the Theoretical and Empirical Literature and Suggestions for Future Research', *Journal of Management*, vol. 6, no. 3, 2000, pp. 513–63.

19. T. A. Judge, A. E. M. Van Vianen and I. E. De Pater, 'Emotional Stability, Core Self-Evaluations, and Job Outcomes: A Review of the Evidence and an Agenda for Future Research', *Human Performance*, vol. 17, 2004, pp. 325–46.

20. L. I. Spirling and R. Persaud, 'Extraversion as a Risk Factor', *Journal of the American Academy of Child & Adolescent Psychiatry*, vol. 42, no. 2, 2003, p. 130.

21. B. Laursen, L. Pulkkinen and R. Adams, 'The Antecedents and Correlates of Agreeableness in Adulthood', *Developmental Psychology*, vol. 38, no. 4, 2002, pp. 591–603.

22. T. Bogg and B. W. Roberts, 'Conscientiousness and Health-Related Behaviors: A Meta-Analysis of the Leading Behavioral Contributors to Mortality', *Psychological Bulletin*, vol. 130, no. 6, 2004, pp. 887–919.

23. S. Lee and H. J. Klein, 'Relationships between Conscientiousness, Self-Efficacy, Self-Deception, and Learning over Time', *Journal of Applied Psychology*, vol. 87, no. 6, 2002, pp. 1175–82; G. J. Feist, 'A Meta-Analysis of Personality in Scientific and Artistic Creativity', *Personality and Social Psychology Review*, vol. 2, no. 4, 1998, pp. 290–309.

24. M. Tamir and M. D. Robinson, 'Knowing Good from Bad: The Paradox of Neuroticism, Negative Affect, and Evaluative Processing', *Journal of Personality & Social Psychology*, vol. 87, no. 6, 2004, pp. 913–25.

25. K. I. van der Zee, J. N. Zaal and J. Piekstra, 'Validation of the Multicultural Personality Questionnaire in the Context of Personnel Selection', *European Journal of Personality*, 2003, pp. S77–S100.

26. T. A. Judge, C. A. Higgins, C. J. Thoresen and M. R. Barrick, 'The Big Five Personality Traits, General Mental Ability, and Career Success across the Life Span', *Personnel Psychology*, vol. 52, no. 3, 1999, pp. 621–52.

27. J. F. Kihlstrom, 'Implicit Methods in Social Psychology', in C. Sansone, C. C. Morf and A. Panter (eds), *Handbook of Methods in Social Psychology* (Thousand Oaks, CA: Sage, 2003).

28. T. A. Judge and J. E. Bono, 'A Rose by any Other Name … Are Self-Esteem, Generalized Self-Efficacy, Neuroticism, and Locus of Control Indicators of a Common Construct?', in B. W. Roberts and R. Hogan (eds), *Personality Psychology in the Workplace* (Washington, DC: American Psychological Association), pp. 93–118.

29. See J. Brockner, *Self-Esteem at Work* (Lexington, MA: Lexington Books, 1988); N. Branden, *Self-Esteem at Work* (San Francisco: Jossey-Bass, 1998); and T. J. Owens, S. Stryker and N. Goodman (eds), *Extending Self-Esteem Theory and Research: Sociological and Psychological Currents* (New York: Cambridge University Press, 2001).

30. P. A. Creed, T. D. Bloxsome and K. Johnston, 'Self-Esteem and Self-Efficacy Outcomes for Unemployed Individuals Attending Occupational Skills Training Programs', *Community, Work and Family*, vol. 4, no. 3, 2001, pp. 285–303.

31. J. B. Rotter, 'Generalized Expectancies for Internal versus External Control of Reinforcement', *Psychological Monographs*, vol. 80, no. 609, 1966.

32. T. A. Judge, J. E. Bono and E. A. Locke, 'Personality and Job Satisfaction: The Mediating Role of Job Characteristics', *Journal of Applied Psychology*, vol. 85, no. 2, 2000, pp. 237–49.

33. A. Erez and T. A. Judge, 'Relationship of Core Self-Evaluations to Goal Setting, Motivation, and Performance', *Journal of Applied Psychology*, vol. 86, no. 6, 2001, pp. 1270–79.

34. U. Malmendier and G. Tate, 'CEO Overconfidence and Corporate Investment', Research Paper #1799, Stanford Graduate School of Business: <http://gobi.stanford.edu/ResearchPapers/detail1.asp?Document_ID=2528> (June 2004).

35. R. G. Vleeming, 'Machiavellianism: A Preliminary Review', *Psychological Reports*, February 1979, pp. 295–310.

36. R. Christie and F. L. Geis, *Studies in Machiavellianism* (New York: Academic Press, 1970), p. 312; and N. V. Ramanaiah, A. Byravan and F. R. J. Detwiler, 'Revised Neo Personality Inventory Profiles of Machiavellian and Non-Machiavellian People', *Psychological Reports*, October 1994, pp. 937–38.

37. Christie and Geis, *Studies in Machiavellianism*.

38. R. P. Brown and V. Zeigler-Hall, 'Narcissism and the Non-Equivalence of Self-Esteem Measures: A Matter of Dominance?', *Journal of Research in Personality*, vol. 38, no. 6, December 2004, pp. 585–92.

39. M. Maccoby, 'Narcissistic Leaders: The Incredible Pros, the Inevitable Cons', *The Harvard Business Review*: <www.maccoby.com/Articles/NarLeaders.html> (January–February 2000).

40. W. K. Campbell and C. A. Foster, 'Narcissism and Commitment in Romantic Relationships: An Investment Model Analysis', *Personality and Social Psychology Bulletin*, vol. 28, no. 4, 2002, pp. 484–95.

41. T. A. Judge, J. A. LePine and B. L. Rich, 'Loving Yourself Abundantly: Relationship of the Narcissistic Personality to Self and Other Perceptions of Workplace Deviance, Leadership, and Task and Contextual Performance', *Journal of Applied Psychology*, in press.

42. See M. Snyder, *Public Appearances/Private Realities: The Psychology of Self-Monitoring* (New York: W. H. Freeman, 1987); and S. W. Gangestad and M. Snyder, 'Self-Monitoring: Appraisal and Reappraisal', *Psychological Bulletin*, July 2000, pp. 530–55.

43. Snyder, *Public Appearances/Private Realities*.

44. D. V. Day, D. J. Schleicher, A. L. Unckless and N. J. Hiller, 'Self-Monitoring Personality at Work: A Meta-Analytic Investigation of Construct Validity', *Journal of Applied Psychology*, April 2002, pp. 390–401.

45. M. Kilduff and D. V. Day, 'Do Chameleons Get Ahead? The Effects of Self-Monitoring on Managerial Careers', *Academy of Management Journal*, August 1994, pp. 1047–60; and A. Mehra, M. Kilduff and D. J. Brass, 'The Social Networks of High and Low Self-Monitors: Implications for Workplace Performance', *Administrative Science Quarterly*, March 2001, pp. 121–46.

46. <www.theage.com.au/articles/2003/10/18/1066364536966.html?from=storyrhs>.

47. R. N. Taylor and M. D. Dunnette, 'Influence of Dogmatism, Risk-Taking Propensity, and Intelligence on Decision-Making Strategies for a Sample of Industrial Managers', *Journal of Applied Psychology*, August 1974, pp. 420–23.

48. I. L. Janis and L. Mann, *Decision Making: A Psychological Analysis of Conflict, Choice, and Commitment* (New York: Free Press, 1977); W. H. Stewart, Jr and L. Roth, 'Risk Propensity Differences between Entrepreneurs and Managers: A Meta-Analytic Review', *Journal of Applied Psychology*, February 2001, pp. 145–53; J. B. Miner and N. S. Raju, 'Risk Propensity Differences between Managers and Entrepreneurs and between Low- and High-Growth Entrepreneurs: A Reply in a More Conservative Vein', *Journal of Applied Psychology*, vol. 89, no. 1, 2004, pp. 3–13; and W. H. Stewart, Jr and P. L. Roth, 'Data Quality Affects Meta-Analytic Conclusions: A Response to Miner and Raju (2004) Concerning Entrepreneurial Risk Propensity', *Journal of Applied Psychology*, vol. 89, no. 1, 2004, pp. 14–21.

49. N. Kogan and M. A. Wallach, 'Group Risk Taking as a Function of Members' Anxiety and Defensiveness', *Journal of Personality*, March 1967, pp. 50–63.

50. M. Friedman and R. H. Rosenman, *Type A Behavior and Your Heart* (New York: Alfred A. Knopf, 1974), p. 84.

51. Ibid, pp. 84–85.

52. K. W. Cook, C. A. Vance and E. Spector, 'The Relation of Candidate Personality with Selection-Interview Outcomes', *Journal of Applied Social Psychology*, vol. 30, 2000, pp. 867–85.

53. J. M. Crant, 'Proactive Behavior in Organizations', *Journal of Management*, vol. 26, no. 3, 2000, p. 436.

54. S. E. Seibert, M. L. Kraimer and J. M. Crant, 'What Do Proactive People Do? A Longitudinal Model Linking Proactive Personality and Career Success', *Personnel Psychology*, Winter 2001, p. 850.

55. T. S. Bateman and J. M. Crant, 'The Proactive Component of Organizational Behavior: A Measure and Correlates', *Journal of Organizational Behavior*, March 1993, pp. 103–18; A. L. Frohman, 'Igniting Organizational Change from Below: The Power of Personal Initiative', *Organizational Dynamics*, Winter 1997, pp. 39–53; and J. M. Crant and T. S. Bateman, 'Charismatic Leadership Viewed from Above: The Impact of Proactive Personality', *Journal of Organizational Behavior*, February 2000, pp. 63–75.

56. Crant, 'Proactive Behavior in Organizations'.

57. See, for instance, R. C. Becherer and J. G. Maurer, 'The Proactive Personality Disposition and Entrepreneurial Behavior among Small Company Presidents', *Journal of Small Business Management*, January 1999, pp. 28–36.

58. S. E. Seibert, J. M. Crant and M. L. Kraimer, 'Proactive Personality and Career Success', *Journal of Applied Psychology*, June 1999, pp. 416–27; Seibert, Kraimer and Crant, 'What Do Proactive People Do?'; and J. D. Kammeyer-Mueller and C. R. Wanberg, 'Unwrapping the Organizational Entry Process: Disentangling Multiple Antecedents and Their Pathways to Adjustment', *Journal of Applied Psychology*, vol. 88, no. 5, 2003, pp. 779–94.

59. P. L. Ackerman and L. G. Humphreys, 'Individual Differences Theory in Industrial and Organizational Psychology', in M. D. Dunnette and L. M. Hough (eds), *Handbook of Industrial & Organizational Psychology*, 2nd ed., vol. 1 (Palo Alto, CA: Consulting Psychologists, 1990), pp. 223–82.

60. See, for instance, J. E. Williams, J. L. Saiz, D. L. Formy-Duval, M. L. Munick, E. E. Fogle, A. Adom, A. Haque, F. Neto and J. Yu, 'Cross-Cultural Variation in the Importance of Psychological Characteristics: A Seven-Country Study', *International Journal of Psychology*, October 1995, pp. 529–50; R. R. McCrae and P. T. Costa, Jr, 'Personality Trait Structure as a Human Universal', *American Psychologist*, 1997, pp. 509–16; R. R. McCrae, 'Trait Psychology and the Revival of Personality-and-Culture Studies', *American Behavioral Scientist*, September 2000, pp. 10–31; S. V. Paunonen, M. Zeidner, H. A. Engvik, P. Oosterveld and R. Maliphant, 'The Nonverbal Assessment of Personality in Five Cultures', *Journal of Cross-Cultural Psychology*, March 2000, pp. 220–39; H. C. Triandis and E. M. Suh, 'Cultural Influences on Personality', in S. T. Fiske, D. L. Schacter and C. Zahn-Waxler (eds), *Annual Review of Psychology*, vol. 53 (Palo Alto, CA: Annual Reviews, 2002), pp. 133–60; R. R. McCrae and J. Allik, *The Five-Factor Model of Personality across Cultures* (New York: Kluwer Academic/Plenum, 2002); and R. R. McCrae, P. T. Costa, Jr, T. A. Martin, V. E. Oryol, A. A. Rukavishnikov, I. G. Senin, M. Hrebickova and T. Urbanek, 'Consensual Validation of Personality Traits across Cultures', *Journal of Research in Personality*, vol. 38, no. 2, 2004, pp. 179–201.

61. A. T. Church and M. S. Katigbak, 'Trait Psychology in the Philippines', *American Behavioral Scientist*, September 2000, pp. 73–94.

62. J. F. Salgado, 'The Five Factor Model of Personality and Job Performance in the European Community', *Journal of Applied Psychology*, February 1997, pp. 30–43.

63. F. Kluckhohn and F. L. Strodtbeck, *Variations in Value Orientations* (Evanston, IL: Row Peterson, 1961).

64. P. B. Smith, F. Trompenaars and S. Dugan, 'The Rotter Locus of Control Scale in 43 Countries: A Test of Cultural Relativity', *International Journal of Psychology*, June 1995, pp. 377–400.

65. Friedman and Rosenman, *Type A Behavior and Your Heart*, p. 86.

66. M. Rokeach, *The Nature of Human Values* (New York: Free Press, 1973), p. 5.

67. M. Rokeach and S. J. Ball-Rokeach, 'Stability and Change in American Value Priorities, 1968–1981', *American Psychologist*, vol. 44, no. 5, 1989, pp. 775–84; and B. M. Meglino and E. C. Ravlin, 'Individual Values in Organizations: Concepts, Controversies, and Research', *Journal of Management*, vol. 24, no. 3, 1998, p. 355.

68. See, for instance, Meglino and Ravlin, 'Individual Values in Organizations', pp. 351–89.

69. Rokeach, *The Nature of Human Values*, p. 6.

70. J. M. Munson and B. Z. Posner, 'The Factorial Validity of a Modified Rokeach Value Survey for Four Diverse Samples', *Educational and Psychological Measurement*, Winter 1980, pp. 1073–79; and W. C. Frederick and J. Weber, 'The Values of Corporate Managers and Their Critics: An Empirical Description and Normative Implications', in W. C. Frederick and L. E. Preston (eds), *Business Ethics: Research Issues and Empirical Studies* (Greenwich, CT: JAI Press, 1990), pp. 123–44.

71. Frederick and Weber, 'The Values of Corporate Managers and Their Critics'.

72. Ibid, p. 132.

73. See, for example, R. Zemke, C. Raines and B. Filipczak, *Generations at Work: Managing the Clash of Veterans, Boomers, Xers, and Nexters in Your Workplace* (New York: AMACOM, 1999); P. Paul, 'Global Generation Gap', *American Demographics*, March 2002, pp. 18–19; L. C. Lancaster and D. Stillman, *When Generations Collide* (San Francisco: Jossey-Bass, 2002); and N. Watson, 'Generation Wrecked', *Fortune*, 14 October 2002, pp. 183–90.

74. K. W. Smola and C. D. Sutton, 'Generational Differences: Revisiting Generational Work Values for the New Millennium', *Journal of Organizational Behavior*, vol. 23, 2002, pp. 363–82; K. Mellahi and C. Guermat, 'Does Age Matter? An Empirical Examination of the Effect of Age on Managerial Values and Practices in India', *Journal of World Business*, vol. 39, no. 2, 2004, pp. 199–215.

75. M. Dittman, 'Generational Differences at Work', *APA Monitor*, vol. 36, no. 6, pp. 65–55; S. L. Clausing, D. L. Kurtz, J. Prendeville and J. L. Walt, 'Generational Diversity—The Nexters', *AORN Journal*: <www.findarticles.com/p/articles/mi_m0FSL/is_3_78/ai_109352507> (September 2003).

76. R. E. Hattwick, Y. Kathawala, M. Monipullil and L. Wall, 'On the Alleged Decline in Business Ethics', *Journal of Behavioral Economics*, vol. 18, 1989, pp. 129–43.

77. B. Z. Posner and W. H. Schmidt, 'Values and the American Manager: An Update Updated', *California Management Review*, vol. 34, no. 3, 1992, p. 86.

78. G. Hofstede, *Culture's Consequences: International Differences in Work-Related Values* (Beverly Hills, CA: Sage, 1980); G. Hofstede, *Cultures and Organizations: Software of the Mind* (London: McGraw-Hill, 1991); G. Hofstede, 'Cultural Constraints in Management Theories', *Academy of Management Executive*, vol. 7, no. 1, 1993, pp. 81–94; G. Hofstede and M. F. Peterson, 'National Values and Organizational Practices', in N. M. Ashkanasy, C. M. Wilderom and M. F. Peterson (eds), *Handbook of Organizational Culture and Climate* (Thousand Oaks, CA: Sage, 2000), pp. 401–16; and G. Hofstede, *Culture's Consequences: Comparing Values, Behaviors, Institutions, and Organizations across Nations*, 2nd ed. (Thousand Oaks, CA: Sage, 2001). For criticism of this research, see B. McSweeney, 'Hofstede's Model of National Cultural Differences and Their Consequences: A Triumph of Faith—a Failure of Analysis', *Human Relations*, vol. 55, no. 1, 2002, pp. 89–118.

79. M. H. Bond, 'Reclaiming the Individual from Hofstede's Ecological Analysis—a 20-Year Odyssey: Comment on Oyserman et al. (2002)', *Psychological Bulletin*, vol. 128, no. 1, 2002, pp. 73–77; G. Hofstede, 'The Pitfalls of Cross-National Survey Research: A Reply to the Article by Spector et al. on the Psychometric Properties of the Hofstede Values Survey Module 1994', *Applied Psychology: An International Review*, vol. 51, no. 1, 2002, pp. 170–78; T. Fang, 'A Critique of Hofstede's Fifth National Culture Dimension', *International Journal of Cross-Cultural Management*, vol. 3, no. 3, 2003, pp. 347–68.

80. M. Javidan and R. J. House, 'Cultural Acumen for the Global Manager: Lessons from Project GLOBE', *Organizational Dynamics*, vol. 29, no. 4, 2001, pp. 289–305; and R. J. House, P. J. Hanges, M. Javidan and P. W. Dorfman (eds), *Leadership, Culture, and Organizations: The GLOBE Study of 62 Societies* (Thousand Oaks, CA: Sage, 2004).

81. N. J. Adler, 'Cross-Cultural Management Research: The Ostrich and the Trend', *Academy of Management Review*, vol. 8, no. 2, 1983, pp. 226–32.

82. See, for instance, S. Werner, 'Recent Developments in International Management Research: A Review of 20 Top Management Journals', *Journal of Management*, vol. 28, no. 3, 2002, pp. 277–305.

83. M. Easterby-Smith and D. Malina, 'Cross-Cultural Collaborative Research: Toward Reflexivity', *Academy of Management Journal*, vol. 42, no. 1, 1999, pp. 76–86; and R. House, M. Javidan and P. Dorfman (eds), 'Project GLOBE: An Introduction', *Leadership, Culture, and Organizations: The GLOBE Study of 62 Societies* (Thousand Oaks, CA: Sage, 2004).

84. J. L. Holland, *Making Vocational Choices: A Theory of Vocational Personalities and Work Environments* (Odessa, FL: Psychological Assessment Resources, 1997).

85. See, for example, A. R. Spokane, 'A Review of Research on Person–Environment Congruence in Holland's Theory of Careers', *Journal of Vocational Behavior*, June 1985, pp. 306–43; J. L. Holland and G. D. Gottfredson, 'Studies of the Hexagonal Model: An Evaluation (or, The Perils of Stalking the Perfect Hexagon)', *Journal of Vocational Behavior*, April 1992, pp. 158–70; T. J. Tracey and J. Rounds, 'Evaluating Holland's and Gati's Vocational-Interest Models: A Structural Meta-Analysis', *Psychological Bulletin*, March 1993, pp. 229–46; J. L. Holland, 'Exploring Careers with a Typology: What We Have Learned and Some New Directions', *American Psychologist*, April 1996, pp. 397–406; and S. X. Day and J. Rounds, 'Universality of Vocational Interest Structure among Racial and Ethnic Minorities', *American Psychologist*, July 1998, pp. 728–36.

86. See B. Schneider, 'The People Make the Place', *Personnel Psychology*, Autumn 1987, pp. 437–53; D. E. Bowen, G. E. Ledford, Jr and B. R. Nathan, 'Hiring for the Organization, Not the Job', *Academy of Management Executive*, November 1991, pp. 35–51; B. Schneider, H. W. Goldstein and D. B. Smith, 'The ASA Framework: An Update', *Personnel Psychology*, Winter 1995, pp. 747–73; A. L. Kristof, 'Person–Organization Fit: An Integrative Review of Its Conceptualizations, Measurement, and Implications', *Personnel Psychology*, Spring 1996, pp. 1–49; B. Schneider, D. B. Smith, S. Taylor and J. Fleenor, 'Personality and Organizations: A Test of the Homogeneity of Personality Hypothesis', *Journal of Applied Psychology*, June 1998, pp. 462–70; A. L. Kristof-Brown, K. J. Jansen and A. E. Colbert, 'A Policy-Capturing Study of the Simultaneous Effects of Fit with Jobs, Groups, and Organization', *Journal of Applied Psychology*, October 2002, pp. 985–93; and J. W. Westerman and L. A. Cyr, 'An Integrative Analysis of Person–Organization Fit Theories', *International Journal of Selection & Assessment*, vol. 12, no. 4, 2004, pp. 252–61.

87. Based on T. A. Judge and D. M. Cable, 'Applicant Personality, Organizational Culture, and Organization Attraction', *Personnel Psychology*, Summer 1997, pp. 359–94.

88. M. L. Verquer, T. A. Beehr and S. E. Wagner, 'A Meta-Analysis of Relations between Person–Organization Fit and Work Attitudes', *Journal of Vocational Behavior*, vol. 63, no. 3, 2003, pp. 473–89.

89. B. Adkins and D. Caldwell, 'Firm or Subgroup Culture: Where Does Fitting in Matter Most?', *Journal of Organizational Behavior*, vol. 25, no. 8, 2004, pp. 969–78; H. D. Cooper-Thomas, A. van Vianen and N. Anderson, 'Changes in Person–Organization Fit: The Impact of Socialization Tactics on Perceived and Actual P-O Fit', *European Journal of Work & Organizational Psychology*, vol. 13, no. 1, 2004, pp. 52–78; C. A. O'Reilly, J. Chatman and D. F. Caldwell, 'People and Organizational Culture: A Profile Comparison Approach to Assessing Person–Organization Fit', *Academy of Management Journal*, vol. 34, no. 3, 1991, pp. 487–516.

90. L. A. Witt, 'The Interactive Effects of Extraversion and Conscientiousness on Performance', *Journal of Management*, vol. 28, no. 6, 2002, p. 836.

91. T. A. Judge and R. Ilies, 'Relationship of Personality to Performance Motivation: A Meta-Analytic Review', *Journal of Applied Psychology*, August 2002, pp. 797–807.

92. R. P. Tett and D. D. Burnett, 'A Personality Trait-Based Interactionist Model of Job Performance', *Journal of Applied Psychology*, June 2003, pp. 500–17.

5

PERCEPTION AND INDIVIDUAL DECISION MAKING

CHAPTER OUTLINE

WHAT IS PERCEPTION?

FACTORS INFLUENCING PERCEPTION

PERSON PERCEPTION: MAKING JUDGMENTS ABOUT OTHERS

THE LINK BETWEEN PERCEPTION AND INDIVIDUAL DECISION MAKING

HOW SHOULD DECISIONS BE MADE?

HOW ARE DECISIONS ACTUALLY MADE IN ORGANISATIONS?

WHAT ABOUT ETHICS IN DECISION MAKING?

LEARNING OBJECTIVES

AFTER STUDYING THIS CHAPTER, YOU SHOULD BE ABLE TO:

1. EXPLAIN HOW TWO PEOPLE CAN SEE THE SAME THING AND INTERPRET IT DIFFERENTLY

2. LIST THE THREE DETERMINANTS OF ATTRIBUTION

3. DESCRIBE HOW SHORTCUTS CAN ASSIST IN OR DISTORT OUR JUDGMENT OF OTHERS

4. EXPLAIN HOW PERCEPTION AFFECTS THE DECISION-MAKING PROCESS

5. OUTLINE THE SIX STEPS IN THE RATIONAL DECISION-MAKING MODEL

6. DESCRIBE THE ACTIONS OF THE BOUNDED-RATIONAL DECISION MAKER

7. LIST AND EXPLAIN THE COMMON DECISION BIASES OR ERRORS

8. IDENTIFY THE CONDITIONS IN WHICH INDIVIDUALS ARE MOST LIKELY TO USE INTUITION IN DECISION MAKING

9. CONTRAST THE THREE ETHICAL DECISION CRITERIA

Making decisions isn't always straightforward or easy. It's no easier making decisions within organisations.

ELLA SPENT FOUR YEARS WORKING towards her Bachelor of Electronic Commerce degree and had set her sights on getting a first-class honours. While studying at university, she sought any opportunity to gain useful work experience. This included carrying out research for her lecturers, which led to co-authored conference papers and several part-time office jobs. Ella felt the key was to differentiate herself from the other graduates in the job market.

While looking for positions, Ella came across a graduate internship with one of the world's leading software companies. She thoroughly researched the company and applied for the position. As the candidate list dropped from 48 to six, and finally two, Ella felt optimistic. Within an hour of the final interview, she received a call offering her a marketing internship with the company. She jumped at the chance.

The decision, however, wasn't straightforward. Taking up the internship meant temporarily abandoning her honours study. This meant that at the end of the internship she wouldn't have completed the required submissions for her degree. Ella was concerned about whether she would ever complete her degree after experiencing the financial freedom of working. She also worried about the high level of specialisation that went with the internship, which she felt might narrow her future prospects, and wondered if she would be better to maintain a broader focus to develop her career path. On the other hand, given the competitive nature of the graduate market, such openings were few and far between.

One year later Ella was forced to make a decision: should she take up a permanent position with the company or return to university? She had enjoyed being a well-paid employee, and the prospect of becoming a penniless student again didn't appeal. But the honours qualification would help her leverage the year's full-time work experience and create wider options.

How should Ella weigh up the options? Should she return to her studies? And if so, would she later regret giving up the opportunity of building a career in a top company?

He who is not every day conquering some fear has not learned the secret of life.

Ralph Waldo Emerson

ELLA HAS SOME TOUGH DECISIONS to make. In organisations, decision making is a very important factor as good decision making will see the organisation prosper but poor decision making could cost it a lot and even lead to its demise altogether. In this chapter, we will look at decision making, how decisions should be made, and review how decisions are actually made in organisations. However, before we do so, we need to look at perception, as we need to explain how perceptions shape the judgments we make about others and the world around us. This is important, as our perceptions influence all the decisions we make. Then we will look briefly at ethical issues in decision making.

WHAT IS PERCEPTION?

perception | A process by which individuals organise and interpret their sensory impressions in order to give meaning to their environment.

Perception is a process by which individuals organise and interpret their sensory impressions in order to give meaning to their environment. However, what one perceives can be substantially different from objective reality. There need not be, but there is often, disagreement. For example, it is possible that all employees in a firm may view it as a great place to work—favourable working conditions, interesting job assignments, good pay, excellent benefits, an understanding and responsible management—but, as most of us know, it is very unusual to find such agreement.

Why is perception important in the study of OB? Simply because people's behaviour is based on their perception of what reality is, not on reality itself. The world as it is perceived is the world that is behaviourally important.

FACTORS INFLUENCING PERCEPTION

LEARNING OBJECTIVE 1
Explain how two people can see the same thing and interpret it differently

MyOBLab

Do you know this material? Let MyOBLab tell you where you need help and devise a personal study plan for you
www.pearsoned.com.au/MyOBLab

How do we explain that individuals may look at the same thing, yet perceive it differently? A number of factors operate to shape and sometimes distort perception. These factors can reside in the *perceiver*, in the object or *target* being perceived, or in the context of the *situation* in which the perception is made (see Figure 5.1).

When an individual looks at a target and attempts to interpret what he or she sees, that interpretation is heavily influenced by the personal characteristics of the individual perceiver. Personal characteristics that affect perception include a person's attitudes, personality, motives, interests, past experiences and expectations. For instance, if you expect police officers to be authoritative, young people to be lazy, or individuals holding public office to be unscrupulous, you are more likely to perceive them as such regardless of their actual traits.

Characteristics of the target being observed can affect what is perceived. Loud people are more likely to be noticed in a group than quiet ones. So, too, are extremely attractive or unattractive individuals. Because targets are not looked at in isolation, the relationship of a target to its background also influences perception, as does our tendency to group close things and similar things together. Members of any group that has clearly distinguishable characteristics are often perceived as alike in other totally unrelated characteristics.

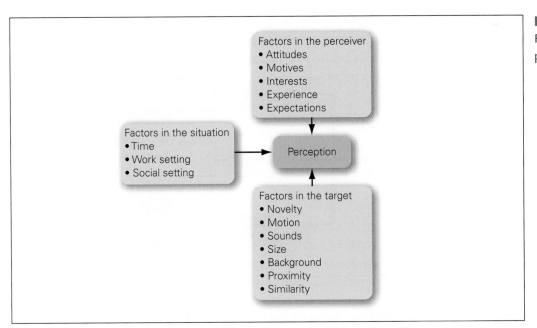

Factors in the perceiver
• Attitudes
• Motives
• Interests
• Experience
• Expectations

Factors in the situation
• Time
• Work setting
• Social setting

Perception

Factors in the target
• Novelty
• Motion
• Sounds
• Size
• Background
• Proximity
• Similarity

The context in which we see objects or events is also important. The time of day at which we see an object or event can influence our attention, as can location, light, temperature, or any number of situational factors. For example, at a nightclub on a Saturday night, you may not notice an attractive 22-year-old female 'dressed to the nines'. Yet, if that same woman, dressed in the same clothes, turned up for your Monday morning management tutorial she would certainly catch your attention (and that of the rest of the class!). Neither the perceiver nor the target changed between Saturday night and Monday morning, but the *situation* is different.

PERSON PERCEPTION: MAKING JUDGMENTS ABOUT OTHERS

Now we turn to the most relevant application of perception concepts to OB. This is the issue of *person perception*. By that, we mean the perceptions people form about each other.

ATTRIBUTION THEORY

Our perceptions of people differ from our perceptions of inanimate objects such as desks, machines or buildings, because we make inferences about the actions of people that we don't make about inanimate objects. Non-living objects are subject to the laws of nature, but they have no beliefs, motives or intentions. People do. The result is that when we observe people, we attempt to develop explanations of why they behave in certain ways. Our perception and judgment of a person's actions, therefore, will be significantly influenced by the assumptions we make about that person's internal state.

Attribution theory has been proposed to develop explanations of the ways in which we judge people differently, depending on what meaning we attribute to a given behaviour.[1] Basically, the theory suggests that when we observe an individual's behaviour, we attempt to determine whether it was internally or externally caused. That determination, however, depends largely on three factors: (1) distinctiveness, (2) consensus, and (3) consistency.

attribution theory | An attempt when individuals observe behaviour to determine whether it is internally or externally caused.

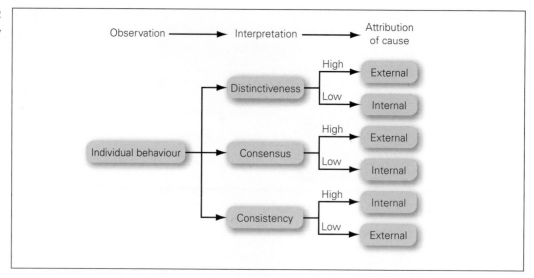

First, let's clarify the differences between internal and external causation and then we will elaborate on each of the three determining factors.

Internally caused behaviours are those that are believed to be under the personal control of the individual. *Externally* caused behaviour is seen as resulting from outside causes; that is, the person is seen as having been forced into the behaviour by the situation. For example, if one of your employees is late for work, you might attribute his lateness to his partying into the wee hours of the morning and then oversleeping. This would be an internal attribution. But if you attribute his arriving late to an automobile accident that tied up traffic on the road that this employee regularly uses, then you would be making an external attribution.

Now let's discuss each of the three determining factors. *Distinctiveness* refers to whether an individual displays different behaviours in different situations. Is the employee who arrives late today also the source of complaints by co-workers for being someone who regularly doesn't pull his weight? What we want to know is whether this behaviour is unusual. If it is, the observer is likely to give the behaviour an external attribution. If the action isn't unusual, it will probably be judged as internal.

If everyone who faces a similar situation responds in the same way, we can say the behaviour shows *consensus*. The behaviour of the employee discussed above would meet this criterion if all employees who took the same route to work were also late. From an attribution perspective, if consensus is high, you would be expected to give an external attribution to the employee's tardiness, whereas if other employees who took the same route made it to work on time, your conclusion as to causation would be internal.

Finally, an observer looks for *consistency* in a person's actions. Does the person respond the same way over time? Coming in ten minutes late for work isn't perceived in the same way for the employee for whom it is an unusual case (she hasn't been late for several months) as it is for the employee for whom it is part of a routine pattern (she is late two or three times a week). The more consistent the behaviour, the more the observer is inclined to attribute it to internal causes.

Figure 5.2 summarises the key elements in attribution theory. It would tell us, for instance, that if your employee—Kim Randolph—generally performs at about the same level on other related tasks as she does on her current task (low distinctiveness), if other employees frequently perform differently—better or worse—than Kim does on that current task (low consensus), and if Kim's performance on this current task is consistent over time (high consistency), you or anyone else who is judging Kim's work is likely to hold her primarily responsible for her task performance (internal attribution).

One of the more interesting findings from attribution theory is that there are errors or biases that distort attributions. For instance, there is substantial evidence that when we make judgments about the behaviour of other people, we have a tendency to underestimate the influence of external factors and overestimate the influence of internal or personal factors.[2] This is called the **fundamental attribution error** and can explain why a sales manager is prone to attribute the poor performance of her sales agents to laziness rather than to the innovative product line introduced by a competitor. There is also a tendency for individuals and organisations to attribute their own successes to internal factors such as ability or effort, while putting the blame for failure on external factors such as bad luck or unproductive co-workers. This is called the **self-serving bias**.[3] For example, when the Iraq War appeared to go well, the White House declared 'mission accomplished'. But when it became clear that there were no weapons of mass destruction and that the fighting was far from over, the White House rushed to blame intelligence failures.

Are these errors or biases that distort attributions universal across different cultures? The evidence is mixed, but most of it suggests that there are cultural differences.[4] For instance, a study of Korean managers found that, contrary to the self-serving bias, they tended to accept responsibility for group failure 'because I was not a capable leader', instead of attributing it to group members.[5] Attribution theory was developed largely based on experiments with Americans and Western Europeans. But the Korean study suggests caution in making attribution theory predictions in non-Western societies, especially in countries with strong collectivist traditions.

FREQUENTLY USED SHORTCUTS IN JUDGING OTHERS

We use a number of shortcuts when we judge others. Perceiving and interpreting what others do is burdensome. As a result, individuals develop techniques for making the task more manageable. These techniques are frequently valuable—they allow us to make accurate perceptions rapidly and provide valid data for making predictions. However, they are not foolproof. They can and do get us into trouble. An understanding of these shortcuts can be helpful in recognising when they can result in significant distortions.

SELECTIVE PERCEPTION

Any characteristic that makes a person, object or event stand out will increase the probability that it will be perceived. Why? Because it is impossible for us to assimilate everything we see—only certain stimuli can be taken in. This tendency explains why you are more likely to notice cars like your own or why some people may be reprimanded by their boss for doing something that, when done by another employee, goes unnoticed. Because we can't observe everything going on about us, we engage in **selective perception**. A classic example shows how vested interests can significantly influence which problems we see.

Dearborn and Simon performed a perceptual study in which 23 business executives read a comprehensive case describing the organisation and activities of a steel company.[6] Of the 23 executives, 6 were in sales, 5 in production, 4 in accounting, and 8 in miscellaneous functions. Each manager was asked to write down the most important problem he found in the case. Eighty-three per cent of the sales executives rated sales as important; only 29 per cent of the others did so. This, along with other results of the study,

fundamental attribution error | The tendency to underestimate the influence of external factors and to overestimate the influence of internal factors when making judgments about the behaviour of others.

self-serving bias | The tendency for individuals to attribute their own successes to internal factors while putting the blame for failures on external factors.

LEARNING OBJECTIVE 3

Describe how shortcuts can assist in or distort our judgment of others

selective perception | Selectively interpreting what one sees on the basis of one's interests, background, experience and attitudes.

led the researchers to conclude that the participants perceived aspects of a situation that were specifically related to the activities and goals of the unit to which they were attached. A group's perception of organisational activities is selectively altered to align with the vested interests they represent. In other words, when the stimuli are ambiguous, as in the steel company case, perception tends to be influenced more by an individual's base of interpretation (that is, attitudes, interests and background) than by the stimulus itself.

But how does selectivity work as a shortcut in judging other people? Because we cannot assimilate all that we observe, we take in bits and pieces. But those bits and pieces aren't chosen randomly; rather, they are selectively chosen according to our interests, background, experience and attitudes. Selective perception allows us to 'speed-read' others, but not without the risk of drawing an inaccurate picture. Because we see what we want to see, we can draw unwarranted conclusions from an ambiguous situation.

HALO EFFECT

halo effect | Drawing a general impression about an individual on the basis of a single characteristic.

When we draw a general impression about an individual on the basis of a single characteristic, such as intelligence, sociability or appearance, a **halo effect** is operating.[7] This phenomenon frequently occurs when students appraise their classroom instructor. Students may give prominence to a single trait such as enthusiasm and allow their entire evaluation to be tainted by how they judge the instructor on that one trait. Thus, an instructor may be quiet, assured, knowledgeable and highly qualified, but if his or her style lacks zeal, those students would probably give the instructor a low rating.

The reality of the halo effect was confirmed in a classic study in which subjects were given a list of traits such as intelligent, skilful, practical, industrious, determined and warm, and were asked to evaluate the person to whom those traits applied.[8] When those traits were used, the person was judged to be wise, humorous, popular and imaginative. When the same list was modified—cold was substituted for warm—a completely different set of perceptions was obtained. Clearly, the subjects were allowing a single trait to influence their overall impression of the person being judged.

The propensity for the halo effect to operate isn't random. Research suggests that it is likely to be most extreme when the traits to be perceived are ambiguous in behavioural terms, when they have moral overtones, and when the perceiver is judging traits with which he or she has had limited experience.[9]

CONTRAST EFFECTS

contrast effects | Evaluation of a person's characteristics is affected by comparisons with other people recently encountered who rank higher or lower on the same characteristics.

There is an old adage among entertainers who perform in variety shows: 'Never follow an act that has kids or animals in it.' Why? The common belief is that audiences love children and animals so much that you will look bad in comparison. This example demonstrates how **contrast effects** can distort perceptions. We don't evaluate a person in isolation. Our reaction to one person is influenced by other persons we have recently encountered.

An illustration of how contrast effects operate is an interview situation in which an interviewer sees a pool of job applicants. Distortions in any given candidate's evaluation can occur as a result of his or her place in the interview schedule. A candidate is likely to receive a more favourable evaluation if preceded by mediocre applicants and a less favourable evaluation if preceded by strong applicants.

PROJECTION

It is easy to judge others if we assume that they are similar to us. For instance, if you want challenge and responsibility in your job, you assume that others want the same. Or, you are honest and trustworthy, so you take it for granted that other people are equally honest and trustworthy. This tendency to attribute one's own characteristics to other people—which is called **projection**—can distort perceptions made about others.

People who engage in projection tend to perceive others according to what they themselves are like, rather than according to what the person being observed is really like. When managers engage in projection, they compromise their ability to respond to individual differences. They tend to see people as more homogeneous than they really are.

projection | Attributing one's own characteristics to other people.

STEREOTYPING

When we judge someone on the basis of our perception of the group to which he or she belongs, we are using the shortcut called **stereotyping**.[10] We rely on generalisations every day because they help us to make decisions quickly and as accurately as possible. It is a means of simplifying a complex world, and it permits us to maintain consistency. It is less difficult to deal with an unmanageable number of stimuli if we use stereotypes.

stereotyping | Judging someone on the basis of one's perception of the group to which that person belongs.

As an example, assume you are a sales manager looking to fill a sales position in your territory. You want to hire someone who is ambitious and hardworking and who can deal well with adversity. You have had success in the past by hiring individuals who participated in athletics during university. So you focus your search by looking for candidates with that background. In so doing, you have cut down considerably on your search time. Furthermore, to the extent that athletes are ambitious, hardworking and able to deal with adversity, the use of this stereotype can improve your decision making. The problem, of course, is when we inaccurately generalise or overgeneralise.[11] In other words, not all university athletes are ambitious, hardworking or good at dealing with adversity. In organisations, we frequently hear comments that represent stereotypes based on gender, age, race, ethnicity and even weight:[12] 'Women won't relocate for a promotion.' 'Men aren't interested in child care.' 'Older workers can't learn new skills.' 'Asian immigrants are hardworking and conscientious.' 'Overweight people lack discipline.' From a perceptual standpoint, if people expect to see these stereotypes, that is what they will perceive, whether or not they are accurate.

Obviously, one of the problems of stereotypes is that they are widespread and often useful, despite the fact that they may not contain a shred of truth when applied to a particular person or situation. So, we constantly have to check ourselves to make sure we are not unfairly or inaccurately applying a stereotype in our evaluations and decisions. Stereotypes are an example of the saying, 'The more useful, the more danger from misuse.'

SPECIFIC APPLICATIONS OF SHORTCUTS IN ORGANISATIONS

People in organisations are always judging each other. Managers must appraise their employees' performances. We evaluate how much effort our co-workers are putting into their jobs. When a new person joins a work team, he or she is immediately 'sized up' by the other team members. In many cases, these judgments have important consequences for the organisation. Let's briefly look at a few of the more obvious applications.

EMPLOYMENT INTERVIEW

A major input into who is hired and who is rejected in any organisation is the employment interview. It is fair to say that few people are hired without an interview. But the evidence indicates that interviewers make perceptual judgments that are often inaccurate.[13] In addition, agreement among interviewers is often poor; that is, different interviewers see different things in the same candidate and thus arrive at different conclusions about the applicant.

Interviewers generally draw early impressions that become very quickly entrenched. If negative information is exposed early in the interview, it tends to be more heavily weighted than if that same information comes out later.[14] Studies indicate that most interviewers' decisions change very little after the first four or five minutes of the interview. As a result, information elicited early in the interview carries greater weight than does information elicited later, and a 'good applicant' is probably characterised more by the absence of unfavourable characteristics than by the presence of favourable ones.

Importantly, who you think is a good candidate and who another thinks is one may differ markedly. Because interviews usually have so little consistent structure and interviewers vary in terms of what they are looking for in a candidate, judgments about the same candidate can vary widely. If the employment interview is an important input into the hiring decision—and it usually is—you should recognise that perceptual factors influence who is hired and, eventually, the quality of an organisation's labour force.

PERFORMANCE EXPECTATIONS

There is an impressive amount of evidence that demonstrates that people will attempt to validate their perceptions of reality, even when those perceptions are faulty.[15] This characteristic is particularly relevant when we consider performance expectations on the job.

The term **self-fulfilling prophecy**, or *Pygmalion effect*, has evolved to characterise the fact that an individual's behaviour is determined by other people's expectations. In other words, if a manager expects big things from his people, they are not likely to let him down. Similarly, if a manager expects people to perform minimally, they will tend to behave so as to meet those low expectations. The result then is that the expectations become reality.

An interesting illustration of the self-fulfilling prophecy is a study undertaken with 105 soldiers in the Israeli Defence Forces who were taking a 15-week combat command course.[16] The four course instructors were told that one-third of the specific incoming trainees had high potential, one-third had normal potential, and the potential of the rest was unknown. In reality, the trainees were randomly placed into those categories by the researchers. The results confirmed the existence of a self-fulfilling prophecy. The trainees whom instructors were told had high potential scored significantly higher on objective achievement tests, exhibited more positive attitudes, and held their leaders in higher regard than did the other two groups. The instructors of the supposedly high-potential trainees got better results from them because the instructors expected it.

ETHNIC PROFILING

Following the attacks on the World Trade Center towers in New York and the Pentagon in Washington, DC on 11 September 2001, thousands of Americans of Arab heritage were subjected to increased police and security forces attention. These people became far more likely to suffer full searches at airports than non-Arab-looking people. Many were reported to police for simply looking 'Arab', and those dressing in Muslim dress (particularly women wearing the *hijab*, a Muslim head scarf) were refused service in shops and restaurants. Countless Arab-looking men were arrested, questioned and later released simply because they looked like the terrorists who crashed the planes. The reason for this action? The US government and the wider population feared that these Arab-looking or Arab-descended Americans might hold pro-terrorist attitudes and conspire more attacks against the United States. Over time, it is hoped that most Americans will come to see this as a terrible mistake and make amends for their folly.[17]

The extra attention paid to Arab-looking persons is an example of **profiling**—a form of stereotyping in which a group of individuals is singled out—typically on the basis of race or ethnicity—for intensive inquiry, scrutinising or investigation. While most people look at such actions in shame and embarrassment, profiling continues throughout the United States and in other countries such as Australia. Indigenous Australian drivers continue to be stopped by police in some states merely because of the colour of their skin. Middle Easterners are closely scrutinised when they go through security at airports—indeed, a colleague of one of this book's authors was searched five times at American airports because he looked Arab, despite being of entirely Italian descent. In the United Kingdom, people from Ireland are often singled out as potential terrorists. And in Israel, every Palestinian is seen as a potential suicide bomber.

But we are interested in organisational behaviour. Since September 11, ethnic profiling has increased implications for OB, specifically as it relates to people of Arab ancestry. Fellow employees and managers may look at Arab colleagues through new eyes. They may question why Arab colleagues dress differently or engage in religious practices they don't understand. In fact, Arab Americans' complaints of workplace discrimination grew dramatically after the September 11 attacks; many of them argued that they felt under constant surveillance at work.[18] The result? This suspicious climate creates distrust and conflicts, undermines motivation, and potentially reduces job satisfaction for ethnic minorities. It is also likely to result in losing quality job candidates when profiling takes place during the employment screening process.

Since September 11, ethnic profiling has become the subject of much debate.[19] On one side, proponents argue that profiling people of Arab descent or appearance is necessary in order to prevent cases of terrorism. After all, a good percentage of the large-scale terrorist attacks that have taken place over the past 30 years have been carried out by Muslim terrorists.[20] On the other side, critics and fair-minded people argue that profiling is demeaning, discriminatory and an ineffective way to find potential terrorists, and that Muslims are law-abiding citizens. The debate is important and implies the need to balance the rights of individuals against the greater good of society. Organisations need to sensitise employees and managers to the damage that profiling can create. Diversity training programs, which we discuss in a later chapter, are increasingly being expanded to particularly address ethnic stereotyping and profiling.

profiling | A form of stereotyping in which a group of individuals is singled out—typically on the basis of race or ethnicity—for intensive inquiry, scrutinising or investigation.

PERFORMANCE EVALUATION

Although the impact of performance evaluations on behaviour will be discussed fully in a later chapter, it should be pointed out here that an employee's performance appraisal is very much dependent on the perceptual process.[21] An employee's future is closely tied to the appraisal—promotions, pay increases and continuation of employment are among the most obvious outcomes. The performance appraisal represents an assessment of an employee's work. Although the appraisal can be objective (for example, a salesperson is appraised on how many dollars of sales she generates in her territory), many jobs are evaluated in subjective terms. Subjective measures are easier to implement, they provide managers with greater discretion, and many jobs don't readily lend themselves to objective measures. Subjective measures are, by definition, judgmental. The evaluator forms a general impression of an employee's work. To the degree that managers use subjective measures in appraising employees, what the evaluator perceives to be good or bad employee characteristics or behaviours will significantly influence the outcome of the appraisal.

THE LINK BETWEEN PERCEPTION AND INDIVIDUAL DECISION MAKING

decisions | The choices made from among two or more alternatives.

Individuals in organisations make **decisions**. That is, they make choices from among two or more alternatives. Top managers, for instance, determine their organisation's goals, what products or services to offer, how best to finance operations, or where to locate a new manufacturing plant. Middle- and lower-level managers determine production schedules, select new employees, and decide how pay increases are to be allocated. Of course, making decisions isn't the sole province of managers. Non-managerial employees also make decisions that affect their jobs and the organisations for which they work. The more obvious of these decisions might include whether or not to come to work on any given day, how much effort to put forth once at work, and whether or not to comply with a request made by the boss. In addition, an increasing number of organisations in recent years have been empowering their non-managerial employees with job-related decision-making authority that historically was reserved for managers alone. Individual decision making, therefore, is an important part of organisational behaviour. But how individuals in organisations make decisions and the quality of their final choices are largely influenced by their perceptions.

problem | A discrepancy between some current state of affairs and some desired state.

Decision making occurs as a reaction to a **problem**.[22] That is, there is a discrepancy between some current state of affairs and some desired state, requiring the consideration of alternative courses of action. So, if your car breaks down and you rely on it to get to work, you have a problem that requires a decision on your part. Unfortunately, most problems don't come neatly packaged with a label 'problem' clearly displayed on them. One person's *problem* is another person's *satisfactory state of affairs*. One manager may view her division's 2 per cent decline in quarterly sales as a serious problem requiring immediate action on her part. In contrast, her counterpart in another division of the same company, who also had a 2 per cent sales decrease, may consider that percentage quite acceptable. So, the awareness that a problem exists and that a decision needs to be made is a perceptual issue.

Moreover, every decision requires the interpretation and evaluation of information. Data are typically received from multiple sources and they need to be screened, processed and interpreted. Which data, for instance, are relevant to the decision and which are not? The perceptions of the decision maker will answer that question. Alternatives will be developed, and the strengths and weaknesses of each will need to be evaluated. Again, because alternatives don't come with 'red flags' identifying them as such or with their strengths and weaknesses clearly marked, the individual decision maker's perceptual process will have a large bearing on the final outcome. Finally, throughout the entire decision process, perceptual distortions often surface that have the potential to bias analysis and conclusions.

Symantec CEO John Thompson made a decision in reaction to the problem of an explosion of internet viruses. Thompson said, 'About every 15 to 18 months, there is a new form of attack that makes old technologies less effective.' So he decided to acquire 13 companies that specialise in products such as personal firewalls, intrusion detection and early warning systems that protect everything from corporate intranets to consumer email inboxes.

HOW SHOULD DECISIONS BE MADE?

LEARNING OBJECTIVE 5

Outline the six steps in the rational decision-making model

Let's begin by describing, at least in theory, how individuals should behave in order to maximise or optimise a certain outcome. We call this the rational decision-making process.

THE RATIONAL DECISION-MAKING PROCESS

We often think that the best decision maker is **rational**. That is, he or she makes consistent, value-maximising choices within specified constraints.[23] These choices are made following a six-step **rational decision-making model**.[24] Moreover, specific assumptions underlie this model.

rational | Making consistent, value-maximising choices within specified constraints.

THE RATIONAL MODEL

The six steps in the rational decision-making model are listed in Figure 5.3. The model begins by *defining the problem*. As noted previously, a problem exists when there is a discrepancy between an existing and a desired state of affairs.[25] If you calculate your monthly expenses and find you are spending $100 more than you allocated in your budget, you have defined a problem. Many poor decisions can be traced to the decision maker overlooking a problem or defining the wrong problem.

rational decision-making model | A decision-making model that describes how individuals should behave in order to maximise some outcome.

Once a decision maker has defined the problem, he or she needs to *identify the decision criteria* that will be important in solving the problem. In this step, the decision maker determines what is relevant in making the decision. This step brings the decision maker's interests, values and similar personal preferences into the process. Identifying criteria is important because what one person thinks is relevant, another person may not. Also keep in mind that any factors not identified in this step are considered irrelevant to the decision maker.

The criteria identified are rarely all equal in importance. So, the third step requires the decision maker to *weight the previously identified criteria* in order to give them the correct priority in the decision.

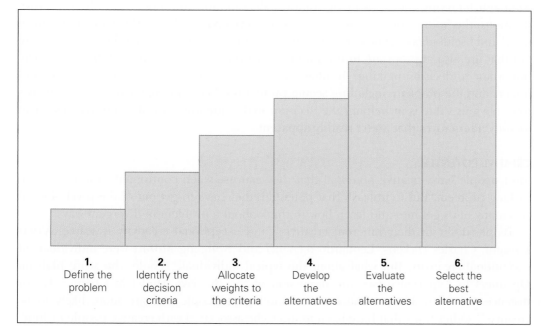

■ **FIGURE 5.3**
Steps in the rational decision-making model

| 1. Define the problem | 2. Identify the decision criteria | 3. Allocate weights to the criteria | 4. Develop the alternatives | 5. Evaluate the alternatives | 6. Select the best alternative |

The fourth step requires the decision maker to *generate possible alternatives* that could succeed in resolving the problem. No attempt is made in this step to appraise these alternatives, only to list them.

Once the alternatives have been generated, the decision maker must critically analyse and evaluate each one. This is done by *rating each alternative on each criterion*. The strengths and weaknesses of each alternative become evident as they are compared with the criteria and weights established in the second and third steps.

The final step in this model requires *calculating the optimal decision*. This is done by evaluating each alternative against the weighted criteria and selecting the alternative with the higher total score.

ASSUMPTIONS OF THE MODEL

The rational decision-making model we just described contains a number of assumptions.[26] Let's briefly outline them.

1. *Problem clarity*. The problem is clear and unambiguous. The decision maker is assumed to have complete information regarding the decision situation.
2. *Known options*. It is assumed the decision maker can identify all the relevant criteria and can list all the viable alternatives. Furthermore, the decision maker is aware of all the possible consequences of each alternative.
3. *Clear preferences*. Rationality assumes that the criteria and alternatives can be ranked and weighted to reflect their importance.
4. *Constant preferences*. It is assumed that the specific decision criteria are constant and that the weights assigned to them are stable over time.
5. *No time or cost constraints*. The rational decision maker can obtain full information about criteria and alternatives because it is assumed that there are no time or cost constraints.
6. *Maximum payoff*. The rational decision maker will choose the alternative that yields the highest perceived value.

IMPROVING CREATIVITY IN DECISION MAKING

Although following the steps of the rational decision-making model will often improve decisions, the rational decision maker also needs **creativity**—that is, the ability to produce novel and useful ideas.[27] These are ideas that are different from what has been done before but that are also appropriate to the problem or opportunity presented. Why is creativity important to decision making? It allows the decision maker to more fully appraise and understand the problem, including seeing problems others can't see. However, creativity's most obvious value is in helping the decision maker identify all viable alternatives, or to identify alternatives that aren't readily apparent.

creativity | The ability to produce novel and useful ideas.

CREATIVE POTENTIAL

Most people have creative potential that they can use when confronted with a decision-making problem. But to unleash that potential, they have to get out of the psychological ruts many of us get into and learn how to think about a problem in divergent ways.

People differ in their inherent creativity, and exceptional creativity is scarce. Albert Einstein, Charles Dickens, Leonardo da Vinci and Wolfgang Mozart were individuals of exceptional creativity. But what about the typical individual? People who score high on Openness to Experience (see the discussion of the Big Five Model in Chapter 4), for instance, are more likely to be creative. Intelligent people also are more likely to be creative.[28] Other traits that have been found to be associated with creative people include:

independence, self-confidence, risk taking, an internal locus of control, tolerance for ambiguity, and perseverance in the face of frustration.[29]

A study of the lifetime creativity of 461 men and women found that fewer than 1 per cent were exceptionally creative.[30] But 10 per cent were highly creative and about 60 per cent were somewhat creative. This suggests that most of us have creative potential; we just need to learn to unleash it. Assess your own level of creativity by taking the following self-assessment.

HOW CREATIVE AM I?

In the Self-Assessment Library (available on CD and online), take Self-Assessment I.A.5 (How Creative Am I?) and answer the following questions.

1. Did you score as high as you thought you would?
2. What are limitations to self-assessments like this?
3. If others [friends, classmates] rated you, would they rate you differently? Why or why not?
4. What could you do to increase your creativity?

SELF-ASSESSMENT LIBRARY

THREE-COMPONENT MODEL OF CREATIVITY

Given that most people have the capacity to be at least somewhat creative, what can individuals and organisations do to stimulate employee creativity? The best answer to this question lies in the **three-component model of creativity**.[31] Based on an extensive body of research, this model proposes that individual creativity essentially requires expertise, creative-thinking skills and intrinsic task motivation (see Figure 5.4). Studies confirm that the higher the level of each of these three components, the higher the creativity.

Expertise is the foundation for all creative work. Many of the Sydney trio Wolfmother's lyrics, for example, were based on their childhood experiences and dreams. Mr Movies, Bill Collins, has been presenting movies on Australian television for over 30 years but his encyclopaedic knowledge of movies wouldn't have the impact it does were it not for his

three-component model of creativity | The proposition that individual creativity requires expertise, creative-thinking skills and intrinsic task motivation.

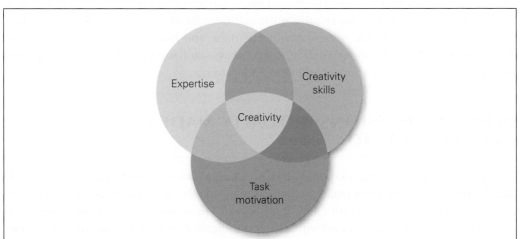

■ **FIGURE 5.4**
The three components of creativity

SOURCE: Copyright © 1997, by The Regents of the University of California. Reproduced from *The California Management Review*, vol. 40, no. 1. With permission of The Regents.

keen interest in and study of literature, music and the arts, all of which he brings to the fore in his presenting of movies. The potential for creativity is enhanced when individuals have abilities, knowledge, proficiencies and similar expertise in their field of endeavour. For example, you wouldn't expect someone with a minimal knowledge of programming to be very creative as a software engineer.

The second component is *creative-thinking skills*. This encompasses personality characteristics associated with creativity, the ability to use analogies, as well as the talent to see the familiar in a different light.

Research suggests that we are more creative when we are in good moods, so if we need to be creative we should do things that make us happy. Perhaps that is listening to music we enjoy, eating foods we like, watching funny movies, or socialising with others.[32] There is also evidence that suggests being around others who are creative can actually make us more inspired, especially if we are creatively 'stuck'.[33]

The effective use of analogies allows decision makers to apply an idea from one context to another. One of the most famous examples in which analogy resulted in a creative breakthrough was Alexander Graham Bell's observation that it might be possible to take concepts of how the ear operates and apply them to his 'talking box'. He noticed that the bones in the ear are operated by a delicate, thin membrane. He wondered why, then, a thicker and strong piece of membrane shouldn't be able to move a piece of steel. Out of that analogy, the telephone was conceived.

Some people have developed their creative skills because they are able to see problems in a new way. They are able to make the strange familiar and the familiar strange.[34] For instance, most of us think of hens laying eggs. But how many of us have considered that a hen is only an egg's way of making another egg?

The final component in the three-component model of creativity is *intrinsic task motivation*. This is the desire to work on something because it is interesting, involving, exciting, satisfying or personally challenging. This motivational component is what turns creativity *potential* into *actual* creative ideas. It determines the extent to which individuals fully engage their expertise and creative skills. So, creative people often love their work, to the point of seeming obsessed. Importantly, an individual's work environment can have a significant effect on intrinsic motivation. Work-environment stimulants that have been found to foster creativity include a culture that encourages the flow of ideas, fair and constructive judgment of ideas, and rewards and recognition for creative work; sufficient financial, material and information resources; freedom to decide what work is to be done and how to do it; a supervisor who communicates effectively, shows confidence in others, and supports the work group; and work-group members who support and trust each other.[35]

HOW ARE DECISIONS ACTUALLY MADE IN ORGANISATIONS?

Are decision makers in organisations rational? Do they carefully assess problems, identify all relevant criteria, use their creativity to identify all viable alternatives, and painstakingly evaluate every alternative to find an optimal choice? For novice decision makers with little experience, decision makers faced with simple problems that have few alternative courses of action, or when the cost of searching out and evaluating alternatives is low, the rational model provides a fairly accurate description of the decision process.[36] But such situations are the exception. Most decisions in the real world don't follow the rational model. For instance, people are usually content to find an acceptable or reasonable solution to their problem rather than an optimal one. As such, decision makers generally make limited use of their creativity. Choices tend to be confined to the neighbourhood of the problem symptom and to the neighbourhood of the current alternative. As one expert in decision making put it: 'Most significant decisions are made by judgment, rather than by a defined prescriptive model.'[37]

The following discusses a large body of evidence to provide you with a more accurate description of how most decisions in organisations are actually made.[38]

BOUNDED RATIONALITY

When you considered which university to attend, did you look at every viable alternative? Did you carefully identify all the criteria that were important in your decision? Did you evaluate each alternative against the criteria in order to find the optimal university? We expect you answered 'No' to these questions. Well, don't feel bad. Few people made their university choice this way. Instead of optimising, you probably satisficed.

When faced with a complex problem, most people respond by reducing the problem to a level at which it can be readily understood. This is because the limited information-processing capability of human beings makes it impossible to assimilate and understand all the information necessary to optimise.[39] So people *satisfice*; that is, they seek solutions that are satisfactory and sufficient.

Because the capacity of the human mind for formulating and solving complex problems is far too small to meet the requirements for full rationality, individuals operate within the confines of **bounded rationality**. They construct simplified models that extract the essential features from problems without capturing all their complexity.[40] Individuals can then behave rationally within the limits of the simple model.

How does bounded rationality work for the typical individual? Once a problem is identified, the search for criteria and alternatives begins. But the list of criteria is likely to be far from exhaustive. The decision maker will identify a limited list made up of the more conspicuous choices. These are the choices that are easy to find and that tend to be highly visible. In most cases, they will represent familiar criteria and previously tried-and-true solutions. Once this limited set of alternatives is identified, the decision maker will begin reviewing them. But the review won't be comprehensive—not all the alternatives will be carefully evaluated. Instead, the decision maker will begin with alternatives that differ only in a relatively small degree from the choice currently in effect. Following along familiar and well-worn paths, the decision maker proceeds to review alternatives only until he or she identifies an alternative that is 'good enough'—one that meets an acceptable level of performance. The first alternative that meets the 'good enough' criterion ends the search. So the final solution represents a satisficing choice, rather than an optimal one.

One of the more interesting aspects of bounded rationality is that the order in which alternatives are considered is critical in determining which alternative is selected. Remember, in the fully rational decision-making model, all alternatives are eventually listed in a hierarchy of preferred order. Because all alternatives are considered, the initial order in which they are evaluated isn't relevant or important.

Every potential solution would get a full and complete evaluation. But this isn't the case with bounded rationality. Assuming that a problem has more than one potential solution, the satisficing choice will be the first *acceptable* one the decision maker encounters. Because decision makers use simple and limited models, they typically begin by identifying

bounded rationality | Making decisions by constructing simplified models that extract the essential features from problems without capturing all their complexity.

Operating within the confines of bounded rationality, Rose Marie Bravo revitalised the British retailer Burberry Group PLC when she became CEO. Based on her retail experience as president of Saks in the United States, Bravo decided to capitalise on Burberry's quality heritage and trademark plaid design as the solution to the company's stagnant growth. She repositioned Burberry as a global luxury retailer by opening stores around the world, running a celebrity ad campaign with female supermodel Ben Grimes to redefine the brand's image as hip for the younger generation, and by using the plaid design on new lines of swimwear, footwear and children's clothing.

alternatives that are obvious, ones with which they are familiar, and those not too far from the status quo. The solutions that depart least from the status quo and meet the decision criteria are those most likely to be selected. A unique and creative alternative may present an optimising solution to the problem; however, it is unlikely to be chosen, because an acceptable solution will be identified well before the decision maker is required to search very far beyond the status quo.

COMMON BIASES AND ERRORS

LEARNING OBJECTIVE **7**

List and explain the common decision biases or errors

Decision makers engage in bounded rationality, but an accumulating body of research indicates that decision makers also allow systematic biases and errors to creep into their judgments.[41] These biases and errors are a result of attempts to shortcut the decision process. To minimise effort and avoid difficult trade-offs, people tend to rely too heavily on experience, impulses, gut feelings and convenient 'rules of thumb'. In many instances, these shortcuts are helpful. However, on the other hand they can lead to severe distortions from rationality. The following material highlights the most common distortions.

OVERCONFIDENCE BIAS

It has been said that 'no problem in judgment and decision making is more prevalent and more potentially catastrophic than overconfidence'.[42] When we are given factual questions and asked to judge the probability that our answers are correct, we tend to be far too optimistic. For instance, studies have found that, when people say they are 65 to 70 per cent confident that they are right, they were actually correct only about 50 per cent of the time.[43] And when they say they are 100 per cent sure, they tended to be 70 to 85 per cent correct.[44] Here is another interesting example. In one random-sample national poll, 90 per cent of respondents said they expected to go to heaven. But in another random-sample national poll, only 86 per cent thought the humanitarian Mother Theresa was in heaven. Talk about an **overconfidence bias**!

From an organisational standpoint, one of the more interesting findings related to overconfidence is that those individuals whose intellectual and interpersonal abilities are *weakest* are most likely to overestimate their performance and ability.[45] So, as managers and employees become more knowledgeable about an issue, the less likely they are to display overconfidence.[46] And overconfidence is most likely to surface when organisational members are considering issues or problems that are outside their area of expertise.[47]

overconfidence bias | The tendency to overestimate the probability that one's judgment in arriving at a decision is correct.

ANCHORING BIAS

The **anchoring bias** is a tendency to fixate on initial information. Once set, we then fail to adjust adequately for subsequent information.[48] The anchoring bias occurs because our mind appears to give a disproportionate amount of emphasis to the first information it receives. So, initial impressions, ideas, prices and estimates carry undue weight relative to information received later.[49]

Anchors are widely used by people in professions—such as advertising, management, politics, real estate and law—where persuasion skills are important. For instance, in a mock jury trial, one set of jurors was asked by the plaintiff's attorney to make an award in the range of $15 million to $50 million. Another set of jurors was asked for an award in the range of $50 million to $150 million. Consistent with the anchoring bias, the mock jury awards were $15 million in the first case and $50 million in the second condition.[50]

Consider the role of anchoring in negotiations and interviews. Any time a negotiation takes place, so does anchoring. As soon as someone states a number, your ability to objectively ignore that number has been compromised. For instance, when a prospective employer asks how much you were making in your prior job, your answer typically anchors the employer's offer. You may want to keep this in mind when you negotiate your salary, but remember to set the anchor only as high as you realistically can. (In other words, it probably won't work to ask for as much as James Packer makes.)

anchoring bias | A tendency to fixate on initial information, and to then fail to adjust adequately for subsequent information.

CONFIRMATION BIAS

The rational decision-making process assumes that we objectively gather information. But we don't. We *selectively* gather information. The **confirmation bias** represents a specific case of selective perception. We seek out information that reaffirms our past choices, and we discount information that contradicts past judgments.[51] We also tend to accept information at face value that confirms our preconceived views, while being critical and sceptical of information that challenges these views. Therefore, the information we gather is typically biased towards supporting views we already hold. This confirmation bias

confirmation bias | The tendency to seek out information that reaffirms past choices and to discount information that contradicts past judgments.

influences where we go to collect evidence because we tend to seek out places that are more likely to tell us what we want to hear. It also leads us to give too much weight to supporting information and too little to contradictory information.

AVAILABILITY BIAS

Many more people suffer from fear of flying than fear of driving in a car. The reason is that many people think flying is more dangerous. It isn't, of course. With apologies ahead of time for this graphic example, if flying on a commercial airline was as dangerous as driving, the equivalent of two 747s filled to capacity would have to crash every week, killing all aboard, to match the risk of being killed in a car accident. But the media gives a lot more attention to plane crashes, so we tend to overstate the risk of flying and understate the risk of driving.

availability bias | The tendency for people to base their judgments on information that is readily available to them.

This illustrates an example of the **availability bias**, which is the tendency for people to base their judgments on information that is readily available to them.[52] Events that evoke emotions, that are particularly vivid, or that have occurred more recently tend to be more available in our memory. As a result, we tend to be prone to overestimating unlikely events such as a plane crash. The availability bias can also explain why managers, when doing annual performance appraisals, tend to give more weight to recent behaviours of an employee than to behaviours of six or nine months before.

REPRESENTATIVE BIAS

representative bias | Assessing the likelihood of an occurrence by inappropriately considering the current situation as identical to ones in the past.

Many male Aboriginal and Tiwi Islander teenagers in Australia talk about the goal of playing football in the Australian Rules Football League (AFL).[53] In reality, these young people have a far better chance of becoming medical doctors than they do of playing in the AFL, but these kids are suffering from a **representative bias**. They tend to assess the likelihood of an occurrence by inappropriately considering the current situation as identical to past ones.[54] They hear about a young man from their community 20 years ago who went on to play professional Australian Rules football. Or they watch AFL games on television and think that indigenous players such as Michael Long or Nicky Winmar are like them.

We are all guilty of falling into the representative bias at times. Managers, for example, frequently predict the performance of a new product by relating it to a previous product's success. Or if three graduates from the same university were hired and turned out to be poor performers, managers may predict that a current job applicant from the same university won't be a good employee.

ESCALATION OF COMMITMENT

escalation of commitment | An increased commitment to a previous decision in spite of negative information.

Another distortion that creeps into decisions in practice is a tendency to escalate commitment when a decision stream represents a series of decisions.[55] **Escalation of commitment** refers to staying with a decision even when there is clear evidence that it is wrong. For example, consider a friend who has been dating his girlfriend for about four years. Although he admitted to you that things weren't going too well in the relationship, he said that he was still going to marry her. His justification: 'I have a lot invested in the relationship!'

It has been well documented that individuals escalate commitment to a failing course of action when they view themselves as responsible for the failure.[56] That is, they 'throw good money after bad' to demonstrate that their initial decision wasn't wrong and to avoid having to admit they made a mistake. Escalation of commitment is also congruent with

Research suggests that sports teams give more playing time to highly drafted players even if their recent performance is no better than lower-drafted players. This is an example of escalation of commitment. Dale Thomas of the Collingwood AFL Club, shown here trying to take a mark, was the number 2 pick in the 2005 AFL National Draft. Escalation of commitment predicts that Collingwood will play Thomas more, even if he is no better than a lower-draft pick, as a means of justifying their decision. As it turned out, Thomas fully rewarded Collingwood for picking him, playing a key role in 15 of the first 18 games of the 2006 season. (He was unable to play the rest of the season due to a broken clavicle received in week 18. There is always next season!)

evidence that people try to appear consistent in what they say and do. Increasing commitment to previous actions conveys consistency.

Escalation of commitment has obvious implications for managerial decisions. Many an organisation has suffered large losses because a manager was determined to prove his or her original decision was right by continuing to commit resources to what was a lost cause from the beginning. In addition, consistency is a characteristic often associated with effective leaders. So managers, in an effort to appear effective, may be motivated to be consistent, when switching to another course of action may be preferable. In actuality, effective managers are those who are able to differentiate between situations in which persistence will pay off and situations in which it won't.

RANDOMNESS ERROR

Human beings have a lot of difficulty dealing with chance. Most of us like to believe we have some control over our world and our destiny. Although we undoubtedly can control a good part of our future by rational decision making, the truth is that the world will always contain random events. Our tendency to believe we can predict the outcome of random events is the **randomness error**.

Consider share-price movements. In spite of the fact that short-term share-price changes are essentially random, a large proportion of investors—or their financial advisers—believe they can predict the direction in which stock prices will move. For instance, when a group of subjects was given share prices and trend information, these subjects were approximately 65 per cent certain they could predict the direction of stocks. In actuality, these individuals were correct only 49 per cent of the time—about what you would expect if they were just guessing or flipping a coin.[57]

Decision making becomes impaired when we try to create meaning out of random events. One of the most serious impairments caused by random events is when we turn

randomness error | The tendency of individuals to believe that they can predict the outcome of random events.

imaginary patterns into superstitions.[58] These can be completely contrived ('I never make important decisions on a Friday the 13th') or evolve from a certain pattern of behaviour that has been reinforced previously (Tiger Woods often wears a red shirt during the final round of a golf tournament because he won many junior golf tournaments while wearing red shirts). Although many of us engage in some superstitious behaviour, it can be debilitating when it affects daily judgments or biases major decisions. At the extreme, some decision makers become controlled by their superstitions—making it nearly impossible for them to change routines or objectively process new information.

WINNER'S CURSE

winner's curse |
A decision-making dictum that argues that the winning participants in an auction typically pay too much for the winning item.

The **winner's curse** is a decision-making dictum that argues that the winning participants in an auction typically pay too much for the winning item. The winner's curse occurs in competitive bidding. Some buyers will underestimate the value of an item and others will overestimate it, and the highest bidder (the winner) will be the one who overestimated the most. Therefore, unless the bidders dramatically undervalue, there is a good chance that the 'winner' paid too much for the item.

Imagine, for example, that all members of your class are bidding on a painting. Obviously, there will be variation in bids, and the person who places the highest bid will receive the painting (in return for the amount that he or she bid). Unless people grossly underestimated the value of the painting, it is likely that the highest bidder will have paid too much. Logic predicts that the winner's curse gets stronger as the number of bidders increases. This is because the more bidders there are, the more likely it is that some of them have greatly overestimated the good's value. So, beware of auctions in which an unexpectedly large number of bidders are involved—good advice if you are buying a home in an Australian capital city these days!

HINDSIGHT BIAS

hindsight bias |
The tendency for us to believe falsely that we would have accurately predicted the outcome of an event, after that outcome is actually known.

The **hindsight bias** is the tendency for us to believe falsely that we would have accurately predicted the outcome of an event, after that outcome is actually known.[59] When something happens and we have accurate feedback on the outcome, we seem to be pretty good at concluding that this outcome was relatively obvious. For instance, a lot more people seem to have been sure about the inevitability of who would win an election on the day after the poll than they were the day before.[60]

What explains the hindsight bias? We apparently aren't very good at recalling the way an uncertain event appeared to us before we find out the actual results of that event. However, we seem to be fairly well adept at reconstructing the past by overestimating what we knew beforehand based upon what we learned later. So, the hindsight bias seems to be a result of both selective memory and our ability to reconstruct earlier predictions.[61]

The hindsight bias reduces our ability to learn from the past. It permits us to think that we are better at making predictions than we really are and can result in our being more confident about the accuracy of future decisions than we have a right to be. If, for instance, your actual predictive accuracy is only 40 per cent, but you think it is 90 per cent, you are likely to become falsely overconfident and less vigilant in questioning your predictive skills.

intuitive decision making
| An unconscious process created out of distilled experience.

INTUITION

Intuitive decision making is an unconscious process created out of distilled experience.[62] It doesn't necessarily operate independently of rational analysis; rather, the two complement each other. And, importantly, intuition can be a powerful force in decision making. For instance, research on chess playing provides an excellent illustration of how intuition works.[63]

LEARNING OBJECTIVE 8

Identify the conditions in which individuals are most likely to use intuition in decision making

Novice chess players and grand masters were shown an actual, but unfamiliar, chess game with about 25 pieces on the board. After five or ten seconds, the pieces were removed and each was asked to reconstruct the pieces by position. On average, the grand master could put 23 or 24 pieces in their correct squares, while the novice was able to replace only 6. Then the exercise was changed. This time the pieces were placed randomly on the board. Again, the novice got only about 6 correct, but so did the grand master! The second exercise demonstrated that the grand master didn't have any better memory than the novice. What the grand master did have was the ability, based on the experience of having played thousands of chess games, to recognise patterns and clusters of pieces that occur on chessboards in the course of games. Studies further show that chess professionals can play 50 or more games simultaneously, in which decisions often must be made in only seconds,

GOOGLE AND THE WINNER'S CURSE

OB IN PRACTICE

One way the winner's curse is revealed is in initial public offering (IPO) pricing schemes. IPOs occur when a company decides to 'go public'—offer itself for sale to investors. In such a case, potential investors need to estimate what the market value of a company's stock will be lest they pay too much for the stock. Here is how the winner's curse operated with the pricing of Google.

Google auctioned off a portion of its stock, with the shares sold to those who paid the most per share. Google explicitly warned potential investors of the winner's curse in its Securities Exchange Commission (akin to the Australian Competition and Consumer Commission, or ACCC) registration statement. (The company warned: 'The auction process for our public offering may result in a phenomenon known as the "winner's curse", and, as a result, investors may experience significant losses.') Despite this warning, the winning investors paid more than ten times the estimated pre-IPO value for Google shares. (The estimated value of the Google shares was US$2.7 billion before the IPO, compared to the US$36 billion that was estimated to be paid for the shares.) The winner's curse is hardly confined to Google or other IPOs. Any time auctions or bidding is involved, for instance on eBay or in house auctions, the potential of the winner's curse is very real. So, how can the winner's curse be avoided?

Savvy bidders will avoid the winner's curse by bid shading, or placing a bid that is below what they believe the good is worth. This may make it less likely that the bidder will win the auction, but it also will protect them from overpaying in the cases where they do win. Savvy bidders know that they don't want to win if it means they will pay more than a good is worth. For example, assume that before the auction you think a share of Google is worth $100. But you figure that if you end up being a winner in the auction it means that most investors think Google is worth less than $100. (By the way, some investors paid more than US$200 for Google stock!) Because fear of the winner's curse can scare away potential bidders, auction sites need to put in place mechanisms that protect novice buyers from accidentally overpaying. Some ideas:

- Provide lots of information about the items for sale.
- Draw as many informed bidders to your auction site as possible.
- Share the risk. Bidders will pay more if the seller or auctioneer provides a warranty.

SOURCES: Based on J. D. Miller, 'Google's "Winner's Curse"', 4 May 2004; G. Anandalingam and Henry C. Lucas, 'Beware the Winner's Curse: Victories That Can Sink You and Your Company', November 2004; G. P. Zachary, 'Google's Dirty Little Secrets: Investors May Suffer from Winner's Curse', *Sunday*, 8 August 2004, p. E-3; and D. Marasco, 'The Winner's Curse', <http://economics.about.com/cs/baseballeconomics/a/winners_curse.htm>.

and exhibit only a moderately lower level of skill than when playing one game under tournament conditions, where decisions take half an hour or longer. The expert's experience allows him or her to recognise the pattern in a situation and to draw on previously learned information associated with that pattern to arrive at a decision choice quickly. The result is that the intuitive decision maker can decide rapidly based on what appears to be very limited information.

For most of the 20th century, researchers believed that the use of intuition by decision makers was irrational or ineffective. That is no longer the case.[64] There is growing recognition that rational analysis has been overemphasised and that, in certain instances, relying on intuition can improve decision making.

When are people most likely to use intuitive decision making? Eight conditions have been identified: (1) when a high level of uncertainty exists; (2) when there is little precedent to draw on; (3) when variables are less scientifically predictable; (4) when 'facts' are limited; (5) when facts don't clearly point the way; (6) when analytical data are of little use; (7) when there are several plausible alternative solutions from which to choose, with good arguments for each; and (8) when time is limited and there is pressure to come up with the right decision.[65]

Although intuitive decision making has gained respectability, don't expect people— especially in Western cultures in which rational analysis is the approved way of making decisions—to readily acknowledge that they are using it. People with strong intuitive abilities don't usually tell their colleagues how they reached their conclusions. And since rational analysis continues to be more socially desirable, intuitive ability is often disguised or hidden. As one top executive commented, 'Sometimes one must dress up a gut decision in "data clothes" to make it acceptable or palatable, but this fine-tuning is usually after the fact of the decision.'[66]

INDIVIDUAL DIFFERENCES

Decision making in practice is characterised by bounded rationality, common biases and errors, and the use of intuition. In addition, there are individual differences that create deviations from the rational model. In this section, we look at two individual-difference variables: personality and gender.

PERSONALITY

There hasn't been much research on personality and decision making. One possible reason is that most researchers who conduct decision-making research aren't trained to investigate personality. However, the studies that have been conducted suggest that personality does influence decision making. The research has considered *conscientiousness* (as you will recall, this is one of the Big Five traits we discussed in Chapter 4) and *self-esteem* (which we also considered in that chapter). Let's discuss each of these.

First, some research has shown that specific facets of conscientiousness—rather than the broad trait itself—affect escalation of commitment.[67] Interestingly, one study revealed that the two facets of conscientiousness—achievement-striving and dutifulness—actually had opposite effects on escalation of commitment. For example, achievement-striving people were more likely to escalate their commitment, whereas dutiful people were less likely to escalate. Why might this be the case? Generally, achievement-oriented people hate to fail, so they escalate their commitment hoping to forestall failure. Dutiful people, however, will be more inclined to do what they see as best for the organisation. Second, achievement-striving individuals appear to be more susceptible to the hindsight bias, perhaps because they have a greater need to justify the appropriateness of their actions.[68] Unfortunately, we don't have evidence on whether dutiful people are immune to the hindsight bias.

Finally, people with high self-esteem appear to be especially susceptible to the self-serving bias. Why? Because high self-esteem people are strongly motivated to maintain their self-esteem, so they use the self-serving bias to preserve it. That is, they blame others for their failures while taking credit for their successes.[69]

GENDER

Recent research on rumination offers insights into gender differences in decision making.[70] Overall, the evidence indicates that women analyse decisions more than men do.

Rumination refers to reflecting at length. In terms of decision making, it means overthinking about problems. And women, in general, are more likely than men to engage in rumination. Twenty years of study find that women spend much more time than men in analysing the past, present and future. They are more likely to overanalyse problems before making a decision and to rehash the decision once it has been made. On the positive side, this is likely to lead to more careful consideration of problems and choices. However, it can make problems harder to solve, increase regret over past decisions, and increase depression. On this last point, women are nearly twice as likely as men to develop depression.

Why women ruminate more than men isn't clear. Several theories have been suggested. One view is that parents encourage and reinforce the expression of sadness and anxiety more in girls than in boys. Another theory is that women, more than men, base their self-esteem and well-being on what others think of them. A third theory is that women are more empathetic and more affected by events in others' lives, so they have more to ruminate about.

This rumination tendency appears to be moderated by age. Gender differences surface early. By age 11, for instance, girls are ruminating more than boys. But this gender difference seems to lessen with age. Differences are largest during young adulthood and smallest after age 65, when both men and women ruminate the least.[71]

ORGANISATIONAL CONSTRAINTS

Organisations can constrain decision makers, creating deviations from the rational model. Managers, for instance, shape their decisions to reflect the organisation's performance evaluation and reward system, to comply with the organisation's formal regulations, and to meet organisationally imposed time constraints. Previous organisational decisions also act as precedents to constrain current decisions.

PERFORMANCE EVALUATION

Managers are strongly influenced in their decision making by the criteria on which they are evaluated. If a division manager believes that the manufacturing plants under his responsibility are operating best when he hears nothing negative, we shouldn't be surprised to find his plant managers spending a good part of their time ensuring that negative information doesn't reach the division boss. Similarly, if a faculty dean believes that an instructor should never fail more than 10 per cent of her students—to fail more reflects on the instructor's ability to teach—we should expect that instructors who want to receive favourable evaluations will decide not to fail too many students.

REWARD SYSTEMS

The organisation's reward system influences decision makers by suggesting to them what choices are preferable in terms of personal payoff. For example, if the organisation rewards risk aversion, managers are more likely to make conservative decisions. From the 1930s through the mid-1980s, General Motors (GM) consistently gave out promotions and bonuses to managers who kept a low profile, avoided controversy and were good team players. The result was that GM managers became very adept at dodging tough issues and passing controversial decisions on to committees.

FORMAL REGULATIONS

David Jackson, a shift manager at a McDonald's Family Restaurant in Sydney, describes constraints he faces on his job: 'I've got rules and regulations covering almost every decision I make—from how to make a burger to how often I need to clean the restrooms. My job doesn't come with much freedom of choice.' David's situation isn't unique. All but the smallest of organisations create rules, policies, procedures, and other formalised regulations in order to standardise the behaviour of their members. By programming decisions, organisations are able to get individuals to achieve high levels of performance without paying for the years of experience that would be necessary in the absence of regulations. And of course, in so doing, they limit the decision maker's choices.

SYSTEM-IMPOSED TIME CONSTRAINTS

Organisations impose deadlines on decisions. For instance, department budgets need to be completed by next Friday. Or the report on new-product development has to be ready for the executive committee to review by the first of the month. A host of decisions must be made quickly in order to stay ahead of the competition and keep customers satisfied. And almost all important decisions come with explicit deadlines. These conditions create time pressures on decision makers and often make it difficult, if not impossible, to gather all the information they might like to have before making a final choice.

HISTORICAL PRECEDENTS

Decisions aren't made in a vacuum. They have a context. In fact, individual decisions are more accurately characterised as points in a stream of decisions.

Decisions made in the past are ghosts that continually haunt current choices—that is, commitments that have already been made constrain current options. To use a social situation as an example, the decision you might make after meeting 'Mr or Ms Right' is more complicated if you are already married to someone else than if you are single. Prior commitments—in this case, having chosen to get married—constrain your options. Consider another example. Government budget decisions also offer an illustration of our point. It is common knowledge that the largest determining factor of the size of any given year's budget is last year's budget.[72] Choices made today, therefore, are largely a result of choices made over the years.

CULTURAL DIFFERENCES

The rational model makes no acknowledgment of cultural differences. But Indonesians, for instance, don't necessarily make decisions the same way that Australians do. Therefore, we need to recognise that the cultural background of the decision maker can have significant influence on the selection of problems, depth of analysis, the importance placed on logic and rationality, or whether organisational decisions should be made autocratically by an individual manager or collectively in groups.[73]

Cultures, for example, differ in terms of time orientation, the importance of rationality, their belief in the ability of people to solve problems, and their preference for collective decision making. Differences in time orientation help us to understand why managers in Egypt will make decisions at a much slower and more deliberate pace than their Australian counterparts. Whereas rationality is valued in individualistic cultures such as Australia, Canada and America, that is not true everywhere in the world. An Australian manager might make an important decision intuitively but knows that it is important to appear to proceed in a rational fashion. This is because rationality is highly valued in the West. In countries such as Iran and Syria, where rationality isn't deified, efforts to appear rational aren't necessary.

Some cultures emphasise solving problems, while others focus on accepting situations as they are. New Zealand and Australia fall into the former category; Thailand and Indonesia are examples of cultures that fall into the latter category. Because problem-solving managers believe they can and should change situations to their benefit, American managers might identify a problem long before their Thai or Indonesian counterparts would choose to recognise it as such.

Decision making by Chinese managers is much more group-oriented than in Australia. The Chinese value conformity and cooperation. So, before Chinese executives make an important decision, they collect a large amount of information, which is then used in consensus-forming group decisions.

WHAT ABOUT ETHICS IN DECISION MAKING?

No contemporary discussion of decision making would be complete without the inclusion of ethics, because ethical considerations should be an important criterion in organisational decision making. This is certainly more true today than at any time in the recent past, given the scandals at companies such as Enron, OneTel, NIH Insurance and the Australian Wheat Board. In this final section, we present three different ways to frame decisions ethically and look at how ethical standards vary across national cultures.

THREE ETHICAL DECISION CRITERIA

LEARNING OBJECTIVE 9
Contrast the three ethical decision criteria

An individual can use three different criteria in making ethical choices—utilitarianism, rights and justice.[74] The first, the *utilitarian* criterion, is when decisions are made solely on the basis of their outcomes or consequences. The goal of **utilitarianism** is to provide the greatest good for the greatest number. This view tends to dominate business decision making. It is consistent with goals such as efficiency, productivity and high profits. By maximising profits, for instance, a business executive can argue she is securing the greatest good for the greatest number—as she hands out dismissal notices to 15 per cent of her employees.

utilitarianism | Decisions made to provide the greatest good for the greatest number.

The second ethical criterion is to focus on *rights*. This calls on individuals to make decisions consistent with fundamental liberties and privileges as set forth in documents such as the US Bill of Rights. An emphasis on rights in decision making means respecting and protecting the basic rights of individuals, such as the right to privacy, to free speech and to due process. For instance, use of this criterion would protect **whistle-blowers**— individuals who report unethical or illegal practices by their employer to outsiders—from

whistle-blowers | Individuals who report unethical practices by their employer to outsiders.

retaliation and retribution when they reveal unethical practices by their organisation to the press or government agencies on the grounds of their right to free speech.

The third criterion is to focus on *justice*. This requires individuals to impose and enforce rules fairly and impartially so that there is an equitable distribution of benefits and costs. Union members typically favour this view. It justifies paying people the same wage for a given job, regardless of performance differences, and using seniority as the primary determination in making layoff decisions.

Each of these three criteria has advantages and liabilities. A focus on utilitarianism promotes efficiency and productivity, but it can result in ignoring the rights of some individuals, particularly those with minority representation in the organisation. The use of rights as a criterion protects individuals from injury and is consistent with freedom and privacy, but it can create an overly legalistic work environment that hinders productivity and efficiency. A focus on justice protects the interests of the underrepresented and less powerful, but it can encourage a sense of entitlement that reduces risk taking, innovation and productivity.

Decision makers, particularly in for-profit organisations, tend to feel safe and comfortable when they use utilitarianism. A lot of questionable actions can be justified when framed as being in the best interests of 'the organisation' and shareholders. But many critics of business decision makers argue that this perspective needs to change.[75] Increased concern in society about individual rights and social justice suggests the need for managers to develop ethical standards based on non-utilitarian criteria. This presents a solid challenge to today's managers, because making decisions using criteria such as individual rights and social justice involves far more ambiguities than using utilitarian

MYTH OR SCIENCE?

'ETHICAL PEOPLE DON'T DO UNETHICAL THINGS'

This statement is mostly true. People with high ethical standards are less likely to engage in unethical practices, even in organisations or situations in which there are strong pressures to conform. The essential issue that this statement addresses is whether ethical behaviour is more a function of the individual or the situational context. The evidence indicates that people with high ethical principles will follow them in spite of what others do or the dictates of organisational norms. But when an individual's ethical and moral development aren't of the highest level, he or she is more likely to be influenced by strong cultures. This is true even when those strong cultures encourage questionable practices.

Because ethical people essentially avoid unethical practices, managers should be encouraged to screen job candidates (through testing and background investigations) to determine their ethical standards. By seeking out people with integrity and strong ethical principles, the organisation increases the likelihood that employees will act ethically. Of course, unethical practices can be further minimised by providing individuals with a supportive work climate. This would include clear job descriptions, a written code of ethics, positive management role models, the evaluating and rewarding of means as well as ends, and a culture that encourages individuals to openly challenge questionable practices.

SOURCES: L. Kohlberg, 'Stage and Sequence: The Cognitive-Developmental Approach to Socialization', in D. A. Goslin (ed.), *Handbook of Socialization Theory and Research* (Chicago: Rand McNally, 1969), pp. 347–480; B. Victor and J. B. Cullen, 'The Organizational Bases of Ethical Work Climates', *Administrative Science Quarterly*, March 1988, pp. 101–25; J. C. Wimbush, 'The Effect of Cognitive Moral Development and Supervisory Influence on Subordinates' Ethical Behavior', *Journal of Business Ethics*, February 1999, pp. 383–95; and D. K. Peterson, 'Deviant Workplace Behavior and the Organization's Ethical Climate', *Journal of Business and Psychology*, Fall 2002, pp. 47–61.

criteria such as effects on efficiency and profits. This helps to explain why managers are increasingly criticised for their actions. Raising prices, selling products with questionable effects on consumer health, closing down inefficient plants, laying off large numbers of employees, moving production overseas to cut costs, and similar decisions can be justified in utilitarian terms. But that may no longer be the single criterion by which good decisions should be judged.

ETHICS AND NATIONAL CULTURE

What is seen as an ethical decision in China may not be seen as such in Canada. The reason is that there are no global ethical standards.[76] Contrasts between Asia and the West provide an illustration.[77] Because bribery is commonplace in countries such as China, an Australian working in China might face the dilemma: Should I pay a bribe to secure business if it is an accepted part of the country's culture? Or how about this for a shock? A manager of a large multinational company operating in China caught an employee stealing. Following company policy, she fired him and turned the employee over to the local authorities. Later, she was horrified to learn that the employee had been summarily executed by firing squad![78]

Although ethical standards may seem ambiguous in the West, criteria defining right and wrong are actually much clearer in the West than in Asia. Few issues are black and white there; most are grey. The need for global organisations to establish ethical principles for decision makers in countries such as India and China, and modifying them to reflect cultural norms, may be critical if high standards are to be upheld and consistent practices achieved.

SUMMARY AND IMPLICATIONS FOR MANAGERS

- It is the individual's perception of a situation, rather than the actual reality, that becomes the basis for that individual's behaviour.
- Whether or not a manager successfully plans and organises the work of employees and actually helps them to structure their work more efficiently and effectively is far less important than how employees perceive the manager's efforts.
- Therefore, to be able to influence productivity, it is necessary to assess how workers perceive their jobs.
- Absenteeism, turnover and job satisfaction are also reactions to the individual's perceptions.
- Managers must spend time understanding how each individual interprets reality and, when there is a significant difference between what is seen and what exists, try to eliminate the distortions. Failure to deal with the differences when individuals perceive the job in negative terms will result in increased absenteeism and turnover and lower job satisfaction.
- Individuals think and reason before they act, making an understanding of how people make decisions helpful for explaining and predicting their behaviour.
- Under some decision situations, people follow the rational decision-making model, but for most people, and most non-routine decisions, this is probably more the exception than the rule.
- Few important decisions are simple or unambiguous enough for the rational model's assumptions to apply, so we find individuals looking for solutions that satisfice rather than optimise, injecting biases and prejudices into the decision process, and relying on intuition.
- Five suggestions are given for how managers can improve their decision making:
  1. Analyse the situation, adjusting your decision-making approach to the national culture you are operating in and to the criteria your organisation evaluates and rewards.
  2. Be aware of biases and then try to minimise their impact using strategies suggested in Figure 5.5.
  3. Combine rational analysis with intuition.
  4. Try to enhance your creativity. Overtly look for novel solutions to problems, attempt to see problems in new ways, and use analogies.
  5. Remove work and organisational barriers that might impede creativity.

◼ FIGURE 5.5 Towards reducing biases and errors

Focus on goals. Without goals, you can't be rational, you don't know what information you need, you don't know which information is relevant and which is irrelevant, you'll find it difficult to choose between alternatives, and you're far more likely to experience regret over the choices you make. Clear goals make decision making easier and help you to eliminate options that are inconsistent with your interests.

Look for information that disconfirms your beliefs. One of the most effective means for counteracting overconfidence and the confirmation and hindsight biases is to actively look for information that contradicts your beliefs and assumptions. When we overtly consider various ways we could be wrong, we challenge our tendencies to think we're smarter than we actually are.

Don't try to create meaning out of random events. The educated mind has been trained to look for cause-and-effect relationships. When something happens, we ask why. And when we can't find reasons, we often invent them. You have to accept that there are events in life that are outside your control. Ask yourself if patterns can be meaningfully explained or whether they are merely coincidence. Don't attempt to create meaning out of coincidence.

Increase your options. No matter how many options you've identified, your final choice can be no better than the best of the option set you've selected. This argues for increasing your decision alternatives and for using creativity in developing a wide range of diverse choices. The more alternatives you can generate, and the more diverse those alternatives, the greater your chance of finding an outstanding one.

SOURCE: S. P. Robbins, *Decide & Conquer: Making Winning Decisions and Taking Control of Your Life* (Upper Saddle River, NJ: Financial Times/Prentice Hall, 2004), pp. 164–68.

POINT / COUNTERPOINT

When in Doubt, Do!

● POINT

Life is full of decisions and choices. The real question is not 'To be, or not to be?', but rather 'To do, or not to do?'. For example, should I confront my lecturer about my assignment grade? Should I buy a new car? Should I accept a new job? Should I choose this major? Very often, we are unsure of our decision. In such cases, it is almost always better to choose action over inaction. In life, people more often regret inaction than action. Take the following simple example:

Act	State	
	Rain	Shine
Carry umbrella	Dry (except your feet!)	Inconvenience
Don't carry umbrella	Miserable drenching	Bliss unalloyed

Say you carry an umbrella and it doesn't rain, or you don't carry an umbrella and it does rain. In which situation are you worse off? Would you rather experience the mild inconvenience of the extra weight of the umbrella or get drenched? Chances are you will regret inaction more than action. Research shows that once a decision has been made, inaction is regretted more than action. Although we often regret actions in their immediate aftermath, over time regrets over actions decline markedly, whereas regrets over missed opportunities increase. For example, you finally decide to take that trip to Europe. You had an amazing time, but a few weeks after you get back, your credit card bill arrives—and it isn't pretty. Unfortunately, you have to work overtime and miss a few dinners out with friends to pay off the bills. A few months down the road, however, you decide to reminisce by looking through your photos from the trip, and sure enough you can't imagine never having gone. So, when in doubt, just do!

● COUNTERPOINT

It is just silly to think that when in doubt, you should always act. Mistakes will undoubtedly be made when following such simple advice. For instance, you are out of work, but you still decide to purchase your dream car—a BMW that is fully loaded with all the bells and whistles (extra options). Not the smartest idea. So, why is the motto 'Just do it' dangerous? Because there are two types of regrets that people can have: hot regret, in which the individual kicks him- or herself for having caused something bad, and wistful regret, in which he or she fantasises about how things might have turned out. The danger is that actions are more likely to lead to anguish or hot regret, and inaction is more likely to lead to wistful regret. So, the bottom line is that we can't apply simple credos such as 'Just do it' to important decisions.

SOURCES: Points in this argument are based on T. Gilovich, V. H. Medvec and D. Kahneman, 'Varieties of Regret: A Debate and Partial Resolution', *Psychological Review*, vol. 105, 1998, pp. 602–05; see also M. Tsiros and V. Mittal, 'Regret: A Model of Its Antecedents and Consequences in Consumer Decision Making', *Journal of Consumer Research*, March 2000, pp. 401–17.

QUESTIONS FOR REVIEW

1. Define *perception*.
2. What is attribution theory? What are its implications for explaining organisational behaviour?
3. How are our perceptions of our own actions different from our perceptions of the actions of others?
4. How does selectivity affect perception? Give an example of how selectivity can create perceptual distortion.
5. What is the rational decision-making model? Under what conditions is it applicable?
6. What is the anchoring bias? How does it distort decision making?
7. What is the availability bias? How does it distort decision making?
8. What role does intuition play in effective decision making? Is it likely to be most effective?
9. Describe organisational factors that might constrain decision makers.
10. Are unethical decisions more a function of the individual decision maker or the decision maker's work environment? Explain.

QUESTIONS FOR CRITICAL THINKING

1. How might the differences in the experiences of students and lecturers affect their perceptions of students' written work?
2. An employee does an unsatisfactory job on an assigned project. Explain the attribution process that this person's manager will use to form judgments about this employee's job performance.
3. 'For the most part, individual decision making in organisations is an irrational process.' Do you agree or disagree? Discuss.
4. What factors do you think differentiate good decision makers from poor ones? Relate your answer to the six-step rational model.
5. Have you ever increased your commitment to a failed course of action? If so, analyse the follow-up decision to increase your commitment and explain why you behaved as you did.

EXPERIENTIAL EXERCISE

Biases in Decision Making

Step 1:

Answer each of the following problems.

1. The following ten companies were ranked by *Business Review Weekly* magazine to be among the 100 largest Australian-based firms according to sales volume for 2006:

   Group A: Harvey Norman, Westfield Holdings, BHP-Billiton, Woolworths, Lion Nathan

   Group B: Cochlear, Affinity Health, NAB, Telstra, Coles Myer

   Which group of five organisations listed (A or B) had the larger total sales volume? By what percentage (10 per cent, 50 per cent, 100 per cent, or …?) do you think the higher group's sales exceeded the lower group's?

2. The best student in an introductory MBA class this past semester at Griffith University writes poetry and is rather shy and small in stature. What was the student's undergraduate major: Chinese studies or psychology?

3. Which of the following causes more deaths in Australia each year?
   (a) Bowel cancer
   (b) Motor vehicle accidents.

4. Which would you choose?
   (a) A guaranteed payment of $240
   (b) A 25 per cent chance of winning $1000 and a 75 per cent chance of winning nothing.

5. Which would you choose?
   (a) A sure loss of $750
   (b) A 75 per cent chance of losing $1000 and a 25 per cent chance of losing nothing.

6. Which would you choose?
   (a) A sure loss of $3000
   (b) An 80 per cent chance of losing $4000 and a 20 per cent chance of losing nothing.

Step 2:

Break into groups of three to five members. Compare your answers. Explain why you chose the answers that you did.

Step 3:

Your lecturer will give you the correct answers to each problem. Now discuss the accuracy of your decisions, the biases evident in the decisions you reached, and how you might improve your decision making to make it more accurate.

SOURCE: These problems are based on examples provided in M. H. Bazerman, *Judgment in Managerial Decision Making*, 3rd ed. (New York: John Wiley & Sons, 1994).

ETHICAL DILEMMA

Five Ethical Decisions: What Would You Do?

Consider the following ethical decisions. How would you respond to each of the following situations?

1. Assume you are a middle manager in a company with about 1000 employees. You are negotiating a contract with a potentially very large customer whose representative has hinted that you could almost certainly be assured of getting his business if you gave him and his wife an all-expenses-paid cruise around the South Pacific. You know the representative's employer wouldn't approve of such a 'payoff', but you have the discretion to authorise such an expenditure. What would you do?

2. You have an autographed CD by Wolfmother. You have put the CD up for sale on eBay. So far, the highest bid is $44.50. You have a friend who has offered you $75 for the CD, commenting to you that he could get $125 for the CD on eBay in a year's time. Given the current eBay bid, and having followed similar events, you know this is highly unlikely. Should you tell your friend that you have listed your CD on eBay?

3. Assume you work for a company and often have to travel on company business. Your company policy on reimbursement for meals while travelling on company business is that you will be repaid for your out-of-pocket costs, not to exceed $180 a day. You don't need receipts for these expenses—the company will take your word. When travelling, you tend to eat at fast food places and rarely spend in excess of $30 a day. Most of your colleagues put in reimbursement requests in the range of $155 to $160 a day regardless of what their actual expenses

are. How much would you request for your meal reimbursements?

4. You work for a company that manufactures, markets and distributes various products, including nutritional supplements, to health food and nutrition stores. One of the company's best-selling products is a herbal supplement called Rosalife. The company advertises that Rosalife 'achieves all the gains of estrogen hormone replacement therapy without any of the side effects'. One day a research assistant stops by your office with some troubling information. She tells you that while researching another product, she came across a recent study that suggests that Rosalife doesn't offer the benefits the company claims it does. You show this study to your supervisor, who says: 'We're not responsible for validating non-government-controlled products and nobody's hurt anyway.' Indeed, you know this isn't the case. What is your ethical responsibility?

5. Assume you are the manager at a gaming company, and you are responsible for hiring a group to outsource the production of a highly anticipated new game. Because your company is a giant in the industry, there are numerous companies trying to get the tender. As the primary contact, one of the outsourcers offers you some kickbacks (financial inducements) if you give it the tender, but ultimately it is up to your bosses to decide on the company. So, you don't mention the incentive, but push upper management to give the company that offered you the kickback the tender. In this case, is withholding the truth as bad as lying? Why or why not?

Whistle-blowers: Saints or Sinners?

Corporate whistle-blowers—individuals who report company wrongdoings—are often lauded for their courage and integrity. For example, one world-famous whistle-blower, former Enron executive Sherron Watkins, was named by *Time* magazine as one of 2002's Persons of the Year. Her evidence helped American prosecutors bring the senior executives of Enron to account, with several being convicted and given very long gaol sentences. Given that whistle-blowers face unemployment and, often-times, expensive litigation from their company, many people don't come forward to report illegal activity. In Australia, there is virtually no legal protection for whistle-blowers, making the act even more dangerous for those tempted to come forward. With legal costs and settlements often exceeding millions of dollars, whistle-blowers can easily be bankrupted or silenced with the threat of litigation.

Take the example of nurse Toni Hoffman. In 2005, Hoffman appeared on the ABC program *Australian Story* where she recounted her efforts to address the official cover-up of Dr Jayant Patel's alleged malpractice that allegedly cost up to 80 patients their lives at the Bundaberg Base Hospital in Queensland. For several years Hoffman and some of her nursing colleagues tried in vain to get the hospital administration and the state government Health Department to investigate her claims. Rather than be concerned with patient care and public welfare, bureaucrats ignored and threatened Hoffman for raising her concerns. The Ethical Standards Branch actually threatened all hospital staff with gaol terms if they took their claims outside of the hospital. It seems that meeting department goals and financial targets (which Dr Patel assisted greatly in achieving) was more important than investigating the rants and raves of 'just a nurse'. The management even awarded Dr Patel an 'Employee of the Month' award!

Frustrated by official inaction and driven by her professional commitment to patient well-being, Hoffman finally went outside the chain of command and gave her information to an opposition party politician. This politician raised the claims in Parliament under privilege, but initially the state government's reaction was to close ranks behind the hospital and deny the reports. It would have died there if it were not for a journalist who followed up the claims and investigated Dr Patel's past. In just a few moments the journalist discovered that the doctor had a long history of medical malpractice causing deaths in a Portland, Oregon hospital and that his licence to practise medicine in the United States had been revoked! The resulting exposure of these facts added enough pressure to force the state government to set up a Royal Commission to investigate the matter.

Some of the facts the Royal Commission uncovered about how management tried to 'hide' the problem shocked the public. For instance, despite the allegations that his medical malpractice was possibly responsible for up to 80 deaths, Patel was given a free air ticket by the hospital management and urged to leave Australia before the Police could interview him. Several managers even tried to close the Royal Commission down, forcing the state government to appoint a new commissioner to replace the original commissioner, Mr Tony Morris. It also came out that several nurses had been sexually harassed by Patel, but again management had ignored the complaints and awarded Patel the 'Employee of the Month' award.

Being a whistle-blower took a high personal toll on Toni Hoffman. Isolated publicly and marginalised at work, she doubted her own abilities as a professional nurse. Often she would be castigated by critics who would ask why she waited so long before coming forward; others tried to assert that her complaints were frivolous, petty and personally motivated. Because her complaints to senior management weren't taken seriously, her confidence in the public health system was also severely undermined. Seeing Patel given the opportunity to flee Australia, and at taxpayer expense, was particularly heart-wrenching. Yet, despite Hoffman's experience (and eventual vindication by the Royal Commission), there is still no effective legislative protection for whistle-blowers in Queensland (or the rest of Australia, for that matter).

QUESTIONS

1. Do you believe that whistle-blowing is good for organisations, its members or the wider community?
2. How might the self-fulfilling prophecy affect a whistle-blower's search for incriminating evidence against a company?
3. When frivolous legal actions by individuals or organisations are laid against whistle-blowers,

how might these cases affect future whistle-blowers who have a valid legal claim against their company? Would they be more or less likely to come forward? How might their claims be evaluated? What should companies and the government do to protect whistle-blowers?
4. Do you believe that employees of a company have an ethical obligation to attempt to report wrongdoing to members of the company itself first, or should they go straight to the authorities when they suspect illegal activity? What are some advantages and disadvantages of both actions?

SOURCES: Based on N. Weinberg, 'The Dark Side of Whistle-blowing', *Forbes*, 14 March 2005, pp. 90–95; <www.abc.net.au/widebay/stories/s1399124.htm>; ABC Television Productions, *Australian Story*, aired on ABC TV on 25 June 2005; <www.tonykevin.com/BundabergHospital.html>; and <www.mja.com.au/public/issues/181_01_050704/fau10254_fm.html>.

ENDNOTES

1. H. H. Kelley, 'Attribution in Social Interaction', in E. Jones et al. (eds), *Attribution: Perceiving the Causes of Behavior* (Morristown, NJ: General Learning Press, 1972).
2. See L. Ross, 'The Intuitive Psychologist and His Shortcomings', in L. Berkowitz (ed.), *Advances in Experimental Social Psychology*, vol. 10 (Orlando, FL: Academic Press, 1977), pp. 174–220; and A. G. Miller and T. Lawson, 'The Effect of an Informational Option on the Fundamental Attribution Error', *Personality and Social Psychology Bulletin*, June 1989, pp. 194–204.
3. See, for instance, G. Johns, 'A Multi-Level Theory of Self-Serving Behavior in and by Organizations', in R. I. Sutton and B. M. Staw (eds), *Research in Organizational Behavior*, vol. 21 (Stamford, CT: JAI Press, 1999), pp. 1–38; N. Epley and D. Dunning, 'Feeling "Holier Than Thou": Are Self-Serving Assessments Produced by Errors in Self- or Social Prediction?', *Journal of Personality and Social Psychology*, December 2000, pp. 861–75; and M. Goerke, J. Moller, S. Schulz-Hardt, U. Napiersky and D. Frey, '"It's Not My Fault—But Only I Can Change It": Counterfactual and Prefactual Thoughts of

Managers', *Journal of Applied Psychology*, April 2004, pp. 279–92.
4. See, for instance, G. R. Semin, 'A Gloss on Attribution Theory', *British Journal of Social and Clinical Psychology*, November 1980, pp. 291–30; M. W. Morris and K. Peng, 'Culture and Cause: American and Chinese Attributions for Social and Physical Events', *Journal of Personality and Social Psychology*, December 1994, pp. 949–71; and D. S. Krull, M. H-M. Loy, J. Lin, C-F. Wang, S. Chen and X. Zhao, 'The Fundamental Fundamental Attribution Error: Correspondence Bias in Individualistic and Collectivist Cultures', *Personality & Social Psychology Bulletin*, October 1999, pp. 1208–19.
5. S. Nam, 'Cultural and Managerial Attributions for Group Performance', unpublished doctoral dissertation, University of Oregon. Cited in R. M. Steers, S. J. Bischoff and L. H. Higgins, 'Cross-Cultural Management Research', *Journal of Management Inquiry*, December 1992, pp. 325–26.
6. D. C. Dearborn and H. A. Simon, 'Selective Perception: A Note on the Departmental Identification of Executives', *Sociometry*, June 1958, pp. 140–44. Some of the conclusions in this classic study

have recently been challenged in J. Walsh, 'Selectivity and Selective Perception: An Investigation of Managers' Belief Structures and Information Processing', *Academy of Management Journal*, December 1988, pp. 873–96; M. J. Waller, G. Huber and W. H. Glick, 'Functional Background as a Determinant of Executives' Selective Perception', *Academy of Management Journal*, August 1995, pp. 943–74; and J. M. Beyer, P. Chattopadhyay, E. George, W. H. Glick, D. T. Ogilvie and D. Pugliese, 'The Selective Perception of Managers Revisited', *Academy of Management Journal*, June 1997, pp. 716–37.
7. See K. R. Murphy and R. L. Anhalt, 'Is Halo a Property of the Rater, the Ratees, or the Specific Behaviors Observed?', *Journal of Applied Psychology*, June 1992, pp. 494–500; K. R. Murphy, R. A. Jako and R. L. Anhalt, 'Nature and Consequences of Halo Error: A Critical Analysis', *Journal of Applied Psychology*, April 1993, pp. 218–25; A. L. Solomonson and C. E. Lance, 'Examination of the Relationship between True Halo and Halo Error in Performance Ratings', *Journal of Applied Psychology*, October 1997, pp. 665–74; and C. E. Naquin and R. O. Tynan, 'The Team Halo Effect: Why

Teams are Not Blamed for their Failures', *Journal of Applied Psychology*, April 2003, pp. 332–40.

8. S. E. Asch, 'Forming Impressions of Personality', *Journal of Abnormal and Social Psychology*, July 1946, pp. 258–90.

9. J. S. Bruner and R. Tagiuri, 'The Perception of People', in E. Lindzey (ed.), *Handbook of Social Psychology* (Reading, MA: Addison-Wesley, 1954), p. 641.

10. J. L. Hilton and W. von Hippel, 'Stereotypes', in J. T. Spence, J. M. Darley and D. J. Foss (eds), *Annual Review of Psychology*, vol. 47 (Palo Alto, CA: Annual Reviews Inc., 1996), pp. 237–71.

11. See, for example, C. M. Judd and B. Park, 'Definition and Assessment of Accuracy in Social Stereotypes', *Psychological Review*, January 1993, pp. 109–28.

12. See, for example, G. N. Powell, 'The Good Manager: Business Students' Stereotypes of Japanese Managers versus Stereotypes of American Managers', *Group & Organizational Management*, March 1992, pp. 44–56; W. C. K. Chiu, A. W. Chan, E. Snape and T. Redman, 'Age Stereotypes and Discriminatory Attitudes towards Older Workers: An East–West Comparison', *Human Relations*, May 2001, pp. 629–61; C. Ostroff and L. E. Atwater, 'Does Whom You Work With Matter? Effects of Referent Group Gender and Age Composition on Managers' Compensation', *Journal of Applied Psychology*, August 2003, pp. 725–40; and M. E. Heilman, A. S. Wallen, D. Fuchs and M. M. Tamkins, 'Penalties for Success: Reactions to Women Who Succeed at Male Gender-Typed Tasks', *Journal of Applied Psychology*, June 2004, pp. 416–27.

13. H. G. Heneman III and T. A. Judge, *Staffing Organizations* (Middleton, WI: Mendota House, 2006).

14. See, for example, E. C. Webster, *Decision Making in the Employment Interview* (Montreal: McGill University, Industrial Relations Center, 1964).

15. See, for example, D. Eden, *Pygmalion in Management* (Lexington, MA: Lexington, 1990); D. Eden, 'Leadership and Expectations: Pygmalion Effects and Other Self-Fulfilling Prophecies', *Leadership Quarterly*, Winter 1992, pp. 271–305; D. B. McNatt, 'Ancient Pygmalion Joins Contemporary Management: A Meta-Analysis of the Result', *Journal of Applied Psychology*, April 2000, pp. 314–22; O. B. Davidson and D. Eden, 'Remedial Self-Fulfilling Prophecy: Two Field Experiments to Prevent Golem Effects among Disadvantaged Women', *Journal*

of Applied Psychology, June 2000, pp. 386–98; D. Eden, 'Self-Fulfilling Prophecies in Organizations', in J. Greenberg (ed.), *Organizational Behavior: The State of the Science*, 2nd ed. (Mahwah, NJ: Erlbaum, 2003), pp. 91–122; and D. B. McNatt and T. A. Judge, 'Boundary Conditions of the Galatea Effect: A Field Experiment and Constructive Replication', *Academy of Management Journal*, August 2004, pp. 550–65.

16. D. Eden and A. B. Shani, 'Pygmalion Goes to Boot Camp: Expectancy, Leadership, and Trainee Performance', *Journal of Applied Psychology*, April 1982, pp. 194–99.

17. Based on C. Murphy, 'Muslim U.S. Workers Hope to Break Image: Start of Ramadan Offers Chance to Reach Out in Faith', *Washington Post*, 6 November 2002, p. B3; J. Curiel, 'Muslims Find Bay Area Leans toward Tolerance: But Even Here, Many Experience 9/11 Backlash', *San Francisco Chronicle*, 22 May 2004, p. A-1; 'Muslim Woman Sues Goodwill for Alleged Workplace Discrimination', *The New Standard*, 24 November 2004: <http://newstandardnews.net/content/?action=show_item&itemid=1255>; T. Chris, 'Muslim Woman Sues Disney for Discrimination', September 2004: <http://talkleft.com/new_archives/006595>.

18. See W. J. Haddad, 'Impact of the September 11th Attacks on the Freedoms of Arabs and Muslims', Arab-American Bar Association of Illinois: <www.arabbar.org/art-sept11impact.asp>.

19. See, for example, J. Wilgoren, 'Struggling to be Both Arab and American', *New York Times*, 4 November 2001, p. B1; J. Q. Wilson and H. R. Higgins, 'Profiles in Courage', *Wall Street Journal*, 10 January 2002, p. A12; and P. R. Sullivan, 'Profiling', *America*, 18 March 2002, pp. 12–14.

20. See <http://search.localcolourart.com/search/encyclopedia/List_of_terrorist_incidents/>.

21. See, for example, R. D. Bretz, Jr, G. T. Milkovich and W. Read, 'The Current State of Performance Appraisal Research and Practice: Concerns, Directions, and Implications', *Journal of Management*, June 1992, pp. 323–24; and S. E. DeVoe and S. S. Iyengar, 'Managers' Theories of Subordinates: A Cross-Cultural Examination of Manager Perceptions of Motivation and Appraisal of Performance', *Organizational Behavior and Human*

Decision Processes, January 2004, pp. 47–61.

22. R. Sanders, *The Executive Decision-Making Process: Identifying Problems and Assessing Outcomes* (Westport, CT: Quorum, 1999).

23. See H. A. Simon, 'Rationality in Psychology and Economics', *Journal of Business*, October 1986, pp. 209–24; and E. Shafir and R. A. LeBoeuf, 'Rationality', in S. T. Fiske, D. L. Schacter and C. Zahn-Waxler (eds), *Annual Review of Psychology*, vol. 53 (Palo Alto, CA: Annual Reviews, 2002), pp. 491–517.

24. For a review of the rational model, see E. F. Harrison, *The Managerial Decision-Making Process*, 5th ed. (Boston: Houghton Mifflin, 1999), pp. 75–102.

25. W. Pounds, 'The Process of Problem Finding', *Industrial Management Review*, Fall 1969, pp. 1–19.

26. J. G. March, *A Primer on Decision Making* (New York: Free Press, 1994), pp. 2–7; and D. Hardman and C. Harries, 'How Rational Are We?', *Psychologist*, February 2002, pp. 76–79.

27. T. M. Amabile, 'A Model of Creativity and Innovation in Organizations', in B. M. Staw and L. L. Cummings (eds), *Research in Organizational Behavior*, vol. 10 (Greenwich, CT: JAI Press, 1988), p. 126; and T. M. Amabile, 'Motivating Creativity in Organizations', *California Management Review*, Fall 1997, p. 40; and J. E. Perry-Smith and C. E. Shalley, 'The Social Side of Creativity: A Static and Dynamic Social Network Perspective', *Academy of Management Review*, January 2003, pp. 89–106.

28. Gregory J. Feist and Frank X. Barron, 'Predicting Creativity from Early to Late Adulthood: Intellect, Potential, and Personality', *Journal of Research in Personality*, vol. 37, no. 2, April 2003, pp. 62–88.

29. R. W. Woodman, J. E. Sawyer and R. W. Griffin, 'Toward a Theory of Organizational Creativity', *Academy of Management Review*, April 1993, p. 298; and J. M. George and J. Zhou, 'When Openness to Experience and Conscientiousness are Related to Creative Behavior: An Interactional Approach', *Journal of Applied Psychology*, June 2001, pp. 513–24.

30. Cited in C. G. Morris, *Psychology: An Introduction*, 9th ed. (Upper Saddle River, NJ: Prentice Hall, 1996), p. 344.

31. This section is based on Amabile, 'Motivating Creativity in Organizations', pp. 42–52.

32. A. M. Isen, 'Positive Affect', in T. Dalgleish

and M. J. Power (eds), *Handbook of Cognition and Emotion* (New York: John Wiley & Sons Ltd, 1999), pp. 521–39.

33. J. Zhou, 'When the Presence of Creative Coworkers is Related to Creativity: Role of Supervisor Close Monitoring, Developmental Feedback, and Creative Personality', *Journal of Applied Psychology*, vol. 88, no. 3, June 2003, pp. 413–22.

34. W. J. J. Gordon, *Synectics* (New York: Harper & Row, 1961).

35. See T. M. Amabile, *KEYS: Assessing the Climate for Creativity* (Greensboro, NC: Center for Creative Leadership, 1995); N. Madjar, G. R. Oldham and M. G. Pratt, 'There's No Place Like Home? The Contributions of Work and Nonwork Creativity Support to Employees' Creative Performance', *Academy of Management Journal*, August 2002, pp. 757–67; and C. E. Shalley, J. Zhou and G. R. Oldham, 'The Effects of Personal and Contextual Characteristics on Creativity: Where Should We Go from Here?', *Journal of Management*, November 2004, pp. 933–58.

36. D. L. Rados, 'Selection and Evaluation of Alternatives in Repetitive Decision Making', *Administrative Science Quarterly*, June 1972, pp. 196–206; and G. Klein, *Sources of Power: How People Make Decisions* (Cambridge, MA: MIT Press, 1998).

37. M. Bazerman, *Judgment in Managerial Decision Making*, 3rd ed. (New York: John Wiley & Sons, 1994), p. 5.

38. See, for instance, L. R. Beach, *The Psychology of Decision Making* (Thousand Oaks, CA: Sage, 1997).

39. D. Kahneman, 'Maps of Bounded Rationality: Psychology for Behavioral Economics', *The American Economic Review*, vol. 93, no. 5, 2003, pp. 1449–75.

40. See H. A. Simon, *Administrative Behavior*, 4th ed. (New York: Free Press, 1997); and M. Augier, 'Simon Says: Bounded Rationality Matters', *Journal of Management Inquiry*, September 2001, pp. 268–75.

41. S. P. Robbins, *Decide & Conquer: Making Winning Decisions and Taking Control of Your Life* (Upper Saddle River, NJ: Financial Times/Prentice Hall, 2004), p. 13.

42. S. Plous, *The Psychology of Judgment and Decision Making* (New York: McGraw-Hill, 1993), p. 217.

43. S. Lichtenstein and B. Fischhoff, 'Do Those Who Know More Also Know More about How Much They Know?', *Organizational Behavior and Human Performance*, December 1977, pp. 159–83.

44. B. Fischhoff, P. Slovic and S. Lichtenstein, 'Knowing with Certainty: The Appropriateness of Extreme Confidence', *Journal of Experimental Psychology: Human Perception and Performance*, November 1977, pp. 552–64.

45. J. Kruger and D. Dunning, 'Unskilled and Unaware of It: How Difficulties in Recognizing One's Own Incompetence Lead to Inflated Self-Assessments', *Journal of Personality and Social Psychology*, November 1999, pp. 1121–34.

46. Fischhoff, Slovic and Lichtenstein, 'Know with Certainty: The Appropriateness of Extreme Confidence'.

47. Kruger and Dunning, 'Unskilled and Unaware of It: How Difficulties in Recognizing One's Own Incompetence Lead to Inflated Self-Assessments'.

48. See, for instance, A. Tversky and D. Kahneman, 'Judgment under Uncertainty: Heuristics and Biases', *Science*, September 1974, pp. 1124–31.

49. J. S. Hammond, R. L. Keeney and H. Raiffa, *Smart Choices* (Boston: HBS Press, 1999), p. 191.

50. R. Hastie, D. A. Schkade and J. W. Payne, 'Juror Judgments in Civil Cases: Effects of Plaintiff's Requests and Plaintiff's Identity on Punitive Damage Awards', *Law and Human Behavior*, August 1999, pp. 445–70.

51. See R. S. Nickerson, 'Confirmation Bias: A Ubiquitous Phenomenon in Many Guises', *Review of General Psychology*, June 1998, pp. 175–220; and E. Jonas, S. Schultz-Hardt, D. Frey and N. Thelen, 'Confirmation Bias in Sequential Information Search after Preliminary Decisions', *Journal of Personality and Social Psychology*, April 2001, pp. 557–71.

52. See A. Tversky and D. Kahneman, 'Availability: A Heuristic for Judging Frequency and Probability', in D. Kahneman, P. Slovic and A. Tversky (eds), *Judgment under Uncertainty: Heuristics and Biases* (Cambridge: Cambridge University Press, 1982), pp. 163–78; and B. J. Bushman and G. L. Wells, 'Narrative Impressions of Literature: The Availability Bias and the Corrective Properties of Meta-Analytic Approaches', *Personality and Social Psychology Bulletin*, September 2001, pp. 1123–30.

53. Anon, 'Influence of Aboriginal Players', accessed at <http://afl.com.au/default.asp?pg=aflinfosheets&spg=display&articleid=240718>; M. Hutton, 'Black Youths All but Ignore Tennis, Golf and Swimming as They Eye NBA', *The Post-Tribune*, 18 February 2002: <www.post-trib.com/news/race10.html>.

54. See Tversky and Kahneman, 'Judgment under Uncertainty: Heuristics and Biases'.

55. See B. M. Staw, 'The Escalation of Commitment to a Course of Action', *Academy of Management Review*, October 1981, pp. 577–87; C. R. Greer and G. K. Stephens, 'Escalation of Commitment: A Comparison of Differences between Mexican and U.S. Decision-Makers', *Journal of Management*, vol. 27, no. 1, 2001, pp. 51–78; H. Moon, 'Looking Forward and Looking Back: Integrating Completion and Sunk-Cost Effects within an Escalation-of-Commitment Progress Decision', *Journal of Applied Psychology*, February 2001, pp. 104–13; and A. Zardkoohi, 'Do Real Options Lead to Escalation of Commitment? Comment', *Academy of Management Review*, January 2004, pp. 111–19.

56. B. M. Staw, 'Knee-Deep in the Big Muddy: A Study of Escalating Commitment to a Chosen Course of Action', *Organizational Behavior and Human Performance*, vol. 16, 1976, pp. 27–44.

57. B. Fischhoff and P. Slovic, 'A Little Learning . . . Confidence in Multicue Judgment Tasks', in R. Nicherson (ed.), *Attention and Performance*, vol. 8 (Mahwah, NJ: Erlbaum, 1980).

58. See, for instance, A. James and A. Wells, 'Death Beliefs, Superstitious Beliefs and Health Anxiety', *British Journal of Clinical Psychology*, March 2002, pp. 43–53.

59. R. L. Guilbault, F. B. Bryant, J. H. Brockway and E. J. Posavac, 'A Meta-Analysis of Research on Hindsight Bias', *Basic and Applied Social Psychology*, September 2004, pp. 103–17; and L. Werth, F. Strack and J. Foerster, 'Certainty and Uncertainty: The Two Faces of the Hindsight Bias', *Organizational Behavior and Human Decision Processes*, March 2002, pp. 323–41.

60. J. M. Bonds-Raacke, L. S. Fryer, S. D. Nicks and R. T. Durr, 'Hindsight Biases Demonstrated in the Prediction of a Sporting Event', *Journal of Social Psychology*, June 2001, pp. 349–52.

61. See, for instance, E. Erdfelder and A. Buckner, 'Decomposing the Hindsight Bias: A Multinomial Processing Tree Model for Separating Recollection and Reconstruction in Hindsight', *Journal of Experimental Psychology: Learning, Memory, and Cognition*, March 1998, pp. 387–414.

62. See O. Behling and N. L. Eckel, 'Making

Sense out of Intuition', *Academy of Management Executive*, February 1991, pp. 46–54; and T. Gilovich, D. Griffin and D. Kahneman, *Heuristics and Biases: The Psychology of Intuitive Judgment* (New York: Cambridge University Press, 2002).

63. As described in H. A. Simon, 'Making Management Decisions: The Role of Intuition and Emotion', *Academy of Management Executive*, February 1987, pp. 59–60.

64. See, for instance, L. A. Burke and M. K. Miller, 'Taking the Mystery out of Intuitive Decision Making', *Academy of Management Executive*, November 1999, pp. 91–99; N. Khatri and H. A. Ng, 'The Role of Intuition in Strategic Decision Making', *Human Relations*, January 2000, pp. 57–86; J. A. Andersen, 'Intuition in Managers: Are Intuitive Managers More Effective?', *Journal of Managerial Psychology*, vol. 15, no. 1–2, pp. 46–67; D. Myers, *Intuition: Its Powers and Perils* (New Haven, CT: Yale University Press, 2002); and L. Simpson, 'Basic Instincts', *Training*, January 2003, pp. 56–59.

65. See, for instance, W. H. Agor (ed.), *Intuition in Organizations* (Newbury Park, CA: Sage Publications, 1989); L. A. Burke and M. K. Miller, 'Taking the Mystery out of Intuitive Decision Making', *Academy of Management Executive*, November 1999, pp. 91–99; Khatri and Ng, 'The Role of Intuition in Strategic Decision Making'; Andersen, 'Intuition in Managers: Are

Intuitive Managers More Effective?'; Myers, *Intuition: Its Powers and Perils*; and L. Simpson, 'Basic Instincts', *Training*, January 2003, pp. 56–59.

66. Agor, *Intuition in Organizations*, p. 15.

67. H. Moon, J. R. Hollenbeck, S. E. Humphrey and B. Maue, 'The Tripartite Model of Neuroticism and the Suppression of Depression and Anxiety within an Escalation of Commitment Dilemma', *Journal of Personality*, vol. 71, 2003, pp. 347–68; H. Moon, 'The Two Faces of Conscientiousness: Duty and Achievement Striving in Escalation of Commitment Dilemmas', *Journal of Applied Psychology*, vol. 86, 2001, pp. 535–40.

68. J. Musch, 'Personality Differences in Hindsight Bias', *Memory*, vol. 11, 2003, pp. 473–89.

69. W. K. Campbell and C. Sedikides, 'Self-Threat Magnifies the Self-Serving Bias: A Meta-Analytic Integration', *Review of General Psychology*, vol. 3, 1999, pp. 23–43.

70. This section is based on S. Nolen-Hoeksema, J. Larson and C. Grayson, 'Explaining the Gender Difference in Depressive Symptoms', *Journal of Personality & Social Psychology*, November 1999, pp. 1061–72; S. Nolen-Hoeksema and S. Jackson, 'Mediators of the Gender Difference in Rumination', *Psychology of Women Quarterly*, March 2001, pp. 37–47; S. Nolen-Hoeksema, 'Gender Differences in Depression', *Current*

Directions in Psychological Science, October 2001, pp. 173–76; and S. Nolen-Hoeksema, *Women Who Think Too Much* (New York: Henry Holt, 2003).

71. M. Elias, 'Thinking It Over, and Over, and Over', *USA Today*, 6 February 2003, p. 10D.

72. A. Wildavsky, *The Politics of the Budgetary Process* (Boston: Little, Brown, 1964).

73. N. J. Adler, *International Dimensions of Organizational Behavior*, 4th ed. (Cincinnati, OH: Southwestern, 2002), pp. 182–89.

74. G. F. Cavanagh, D. J. Moberg and M. Valasquez, 'The Ethics of Organizational Politics', *Academy of Management Journal*, June 1981, pp. 363–74.

75. See, for example, T. Machan (ed.), *Commerce and Morality* (Totowa, NJ: Rowman and Littlefield, 1988).

76. T. Jackson, 'Cultural Values and Management Ethics: A 10-Nation Study', *Human Relations*, October 2001, pp. 1267–302; see also J. B. Cullen, K. P. Parboteeah and M. Hoegl, 'Cross-National Differences in Managers' Willingness to Justify Ethically Suspect Behaviors: A Test of Institutional Anomie Theory', *Academy of Management Journal*, June 2004, pp. 411–21.

77. W. Chow Hou, 'To Bribe or Not to Bribe?', *Asia, Inc.*, October 1996, p. 104.

78. P. Digh, 'Shades of Gray in the Global Marketplace', *Human Resources*, April 1997, p. 91.

6

MOTIVATION CONCEPTS

LEARNING OBJECTIVES

AFTER STUDYING THIS CHAPTER, YOU SHOULD BE ABLE TO:

1. OUTLINE THE MOTIVATION PROCESS

2. DESCRIBE MASLOW'S NEEDS HIERARCHY

3. DIFFERENTIATE MOTIVATORS FROM HYGIENE FACTORS

4. LIST THE CHARACTERISTICS THAT HIGH ACHIEVERS PREFER IN A JOB

5. SUMMARISE THE TYPES OF GOALS THAT INCREASE PERFORMANCE

6. DISCUSS WAYS SELF-EFFICACY CAN BE INCREASED

7. STATE THE IMPACT OF UNDER-REWARDING EMPLOYEES

8. CLARIFY THE KEY RELATIONSHIPS IN EXPECTANCY THEORY

9. EXPLAIN HOW THE CONTEMPORARY THEORIES OF MOTIVATION COMPLEMENT EACH OTHER

Kylie Kwong displays high motivation in her career as celebrity chef, restaurateur and author.

'**I KNOW WHERE I'VE COME FROM** and I guess it gives you a confidence to go out into the world and do what you love to do and follow your dreams.' Celebrity chef, restaurateur and author Kylie Kwong attributes much of her success to her sense of connection with her extended family and her Chinese cultural heritage.

Cooking and family have always been integral to Kylie's life. Kylie had no formal training in cooking but acquired much of her passion for good food from her mother, in particular. 'For we Cantonese people, the most important thing about cooking and food is the quality of the produce. It is number one—the freshness. Ever since we were little, my mother has drummed that into us. It's like the food, the actual ingredient itself, has vitality—an inner life force, you might call it. So, of course, when you're cooking with it with the same vibrancy, you can't help but taste that food as you're eating it.'

However, it wasn't until she was 26 that Kylie moved into cooking as a profession, having first tried her hand at graphic art. 'Even though I did enjoy those few years in advertising, what I didn't enjoy was the structure and the rigidity of graphic art—millimetres and everything. I'm not a measured person.' In other words, graphic art didn't give Kylie sufficient scope for her creative urge.

Within a decade of moving into cooking professionally, Kylie had opened her highly successful Sydney restaurant Billie Kwong and had gone global with her first TV series and its accompanying book, *Kylie Kwong: Heart and Soul*.

Kylie Kwong's story is about the experience of real motivation towards one's work, primarily through the experience of meaningful work. In this chapter we dispel the myth that people are either born motivated or they are not. We also dispel the myth that the opposite of being motivated is being lazy. We present motivation as something that can be engineered into the workplace through good management practice. Perhaps through her own intuitive processes, Kylie Kwong guided herself to a career that gave her an opportunity to be both productive and satisfied in her work. In this chapter, we consider how managers can build work contexts that routinely get the best out of their people.[1]

Set me anything to do as a task, and it is inconceivable the desire I have to do something else.

George Bernard Shaw

MOTIVATION IS ONE of the most frequently researched topics in OB.[2] One reason for its popularity is revealed in a recent Gallup Poll, which found that 20 per cent of Australian workers were 'actively disengaged' at work and only 18 per cent considered themselves to be engaged with their job.[3] Clearly, such low motivation suggests a problem, as it is likely to be costing industry, and the economy, billions of dollars. The good news is that all this research provides us with considerable insights into how to improve motivation.

In this chapter, we will review the basics of motivation, assess a number of motivation theories, and provide an integrative model that shows how the best of these theories fit together.

DEFINING MOTIVATION

What is motivation? Maybe the place to begin is to say what motivation *isn't*. Many people incorrectly view motivation as a personal trait—that is, some have it and others don't. In practice, inexperienced managers often label employees who seem to lack motivation as lazy. Such a label assumes that an individual is always lazy or lacking in motivation. Our knowledge of motivation tells us that this just isn't true. Think about Kylie Kwong. She is *highly* motivated, just not motivated in the same direction as you and me. The question, then, isn't usually whether someone is motivated, but *what* are they motivated by?

What we know is that motivation is the result of the interaction of the individual and the situation. Certainly, individuals differ in their basic motivational drive. But the same student who finds it difficult to read a textbook for more than 20 minutes may devour a *Harry Potter* book in one day. For this student, the change in motivation is driven by the situation. So, as we analyse the concept of motivation, keep in mind that the level of motivation varies both between individuals and within individuals at different times.

We define **motivation** as the processes that account for an individual's intensity, direction and persistence of effort towards attaining a goal.[4] While general motivation is concerned with effort towards attaining *any* goal, we will narrow the focus to *organisational* goals in order to reflect our singular interest in work-related behaviour.

The three key elements in our definition are intensity, direction and persistence. *Intensity* is concerned with how hard a person tries. This is the element most of us focus on when we talk about motivation. However, high intensity is unlikely to lead to favourable job-performance outcomes unless the effort is channelled in a *direction* that benefits the organisation. Therefore, we have to consider the quality of effort as well as its intensity. Effort that is directed towards, and is consistent with, the organisation's goals is the kind of effort that we should be seeking. Finally, motivation has a *persistence* dimension. This is a measure of how long a person can maintain effort. Motivated individuals stay with a task long enough to achieve their goal.

motivation | The processes that account for an individual's intensity, direction and persistence of effort towards attaining a goal.

EARLY THEORIES OF MOTIVATION

The 1950s were a fruitful period in the development of motivation concepts. Three specific theories were formulated during this period, which, although heavily attacked and now questionable in terms of validity, are probably still the best-known explanations for employee motivation. These are the hierarchy of needs theory, Theories X and Y, and the two-factor theory. As you will see later in this chapter, we have since developed more valid explanations of motivation, but you should know these early theories for at least two reasons: (1) they represent a foundation from which contemporary theories have grown, and (2) practising managers still regularly use these theories and their terminology in explaining employee motivation.

HIERARCHY OF NEEDS THEORY

It is probably safe to say that the most well-known theory of motivation is Abraham Maslow's **hierarchy of needs**.[5] He hypothesised that within every human being there exists a hierarchy of five needs. These needs are:

1. *Physiological*: Includes hunger, thirst, shelter, sex and other bodily needs.
2. *Safety*: Includes security and protection from physical and emotional harm.
3. *Social*: Includes affection, belongingness, acceptance and friendship.
4. *Esteem*: Includes internal esteem factors such as self-respect, autonomy and achievement; and external esteem factors such as status, recognition and attention.
5. *Self-actualisation*: The drive to become what one is capable of becoming; includes growth, achieving one's potential and self-fulfilment.

As each of these needs becomes substantially satisfied, the next need becomes dominant. In terms of Figure 6.1, the individual moves up the steps of the hierarchy. From the standpoint of motivation, the theory would say that although no need is ever fully gratified, a substantially satisfied need no longer motivates. So, if you want to motivate someone, according to Maslow, you need to understand what level of the hierarchy that person is currently on and focus on satisfying the needs at or above that level.

Maslow separated the five needs into higher and lower orders. Physiological and safety needs were described as **lower-order needs** and social, esteem and self-actualisation as **higher-order needs**. The differentiation between the two orders was made on the premise that higher-order needs are satisfied internally (within the person), whereas lower-order

LEARNING OBJECTIVE 2

Describe Maslow's needs hierarchy

hierarchy of needs theory | A hierarchy of five needs—physiological, safety, social, esteem and self-actualisation—exists such that as each need is substantially satisfied, the next need becomes dominant.

self-actualisation | The drive to become what one is capable of becoming.

lower-order needs | Needs that are satisfied externally; physiological and safety needs.

higher-order needs | Needs that are satisfied internally; social, esteem and self-actualisation needs.

■ **FIGURE 6.1**
Maslow's hierarchy of needs

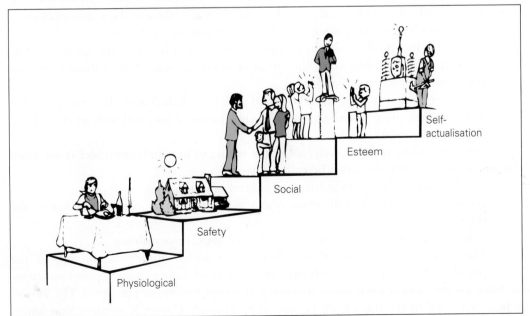

needs are predominantly satisfied externally (by things such as pay, union contracts and tenure).

Maslow's needs theory has received wide recognition, particularly among practising managers. This can be attributed to the theory's intuitive logic and ease of understanding. Unfortunately, however, research doesn't validate the theory. Maslow provided no empirical substantiation, and several studies that sought to validate the theory found no support for it.[6]

ERG theory | A theory that posits three groups of core needs: existence, relatedness and growth.

Clayton Alderfer attempted to rework Maslow's needs hierarchy to align it more closely with empirical research. His revised needs hierarchy is labelled **ERG theory**.[7] Alderfer argued that there are three groups of core needs—existence (similar to Maslow's physiological and safety needs), relatedness (similar to Maslow's social and status needs), and growth (similar to Maslow's esteem needs and self-actualisation).

Unlike Maslow's theory, ERG doesn't assume that there exists a rigid hierarchy in which a lower need must be substantially gratified before one can move on. For example, ERG argues that a person can be working on growth needs even though existence or relatedness needs are unsatisfied. An individual could also be focusing on all three need categories simultaneously. Moreover, Alderfer believed that frustration in satisfying a higher-order need might lead to regression to a lower need. Despite these differences, empirical research hasn't been any more supportive of ERG theory than of the needs hierarchy.[8]

Old theories, especially ones that are intuitively logical, apparently die hard. Although the needs hierarchy theory and its terminology have remained popular with practising managers, there is little evidence that need structures are organised along the dimensions proposed by Maslow or Alderfer, that unsatisfied needs motivate, or that a satisfied need activates movement to a new need level.[9]

THEORY X AND THEORY Y

Theory X | The assumption that employees dislike work, are lazy, dislike responsibility and must be coerced to perform.

Douglas McGregor proposed two distinct views of human beings: one basically negative, labelled **Theory X**, and the other basically positive, labelled **Theory Y**.[10] After viewing the way in which managers dealt with employees, McGregor concluded that managers' views of the nature of human beings are based on a certain grouping of assumptions and that they tend to mould their behaviour towards employees according to these assumptions.

Under Theory X, the four assumptions held by managers are:
1. Employees inherently dislike work and, whenever possible, will attempt to avoid it.
2. Since employees dislike work, they must be coerced, controlled or threatened with punishment to achieve goals.
3. Employees will avoid responsibilities and seek formal direction whenever possible.
4. Most workers place security above all other factors associated with work and will display little ambition.

Theory Y | The assumption that employees like work, are creative, seek responsibility and can exercise self-direction.

In contrast to these negative views about the nature of human beings, McGregor listed the four positive assumptions that he called Theory Y:
1. Employees can view work as being as natural as rest or play.
2. People will exercise self-direction and self-control if they are committed to the objectives.
3. The average person can learn to accept, even seek, responsibility.
4. The ability to make innovative decisions is widely dispersed throughout the population and isn't necessarily the sole province of those in management positions.

What are the motivational implications if you accept McGregor's analysis? The answer is best expressed in the framework presented by Maslow. Theory X assumes that lower-

'PEOPLE ARE INHERENTLY LAZY'

This statement is false on two levels. *All* people are not inherently lazy, and 'laziness' is more a function of the situation than an inherent individual characteristic. If this statement is meant to imply that *all* people are inherently lazy, the evidence strongly indicates the contrary. Many people today suffer from the opposite affliction—they are overly busy, overworked and suffer from overexertion. Whether externally motivated or internally driven, a good portion of the labour force is anything *but* lazy.

Managers frequently draw the conclusion that people are lazy from watching some of their employees, who may be lazy at work. But these same employees are often quite industrious in one or more activities *off* the job. People have different sets of needs. Unfortunately for employers, work often ranks low in its ability to satisfy individual needs. So, the same employee who shirks responsibility on the job may work obsessively on reconditioning an antique car, maintaining an award-winning garden, perfecting bowling skills, or selling Amway products on weekends. Very few people are perpetually lazy. They merely differ in terms of the activities they most enjoy doing. And because work isn't important to everyone, they may appear lazy.

SOURCES: See, for example, E. E. Lawler III, *Motivation in Work Organizations* (Belmont, CA: Brooks/Cole, 1973); B. Weiner, *Human Motivation* (New York: Holt, Rinehart and Winston, 1980); K. W. Thomas, *Intrinsic Motivation at Work* (San Francisco: Berrett-Koehler, 2000); and K. A. Kovach, 'What Motivates Employees? Workers and Supervisors Give Different Answers', *Business Horizons*, September–October 1987, p. 61. This research was updated in 1995 and reported in a paper by K. A. Kovach, 'Employee Motivation: Addressing a Crucial Factor in Your Organization's Performance' (Fairfax, VA: George Mason University).

order needs dominate individuals, while Theory Y assumes that higher-order needs dominate individuals. McGregor himself held to the belief that Theory Y assumptions were more valid than Theory X assumptions. Therefore, he proposed such ideas as participative decision making, responsible and challenging jobs, and good group relations as approaches that would maximise an employee's job motivation.

Unfortunately, there is no evidence to confirm that either set of assumptions is valid or that accepting Theory Y assumptions and altering one's actions accordingly will lead to more motivated workers. OB theories need to have empirical support for us to accept them. Similar to the hierarchy of needs theories, such empirical support is lacking for Theory X and Theory Y.

TWO-FACTOR THEORY

The **two-factor theory**—also called *motivation-hygiene theory*—was proposed by psychologist Frederick Herzberg.[11] In the belief that an individual's relation to work is basic and that one's attitude towards work can very well determine success or failure, Herzberg investigated the question, 'What do people want from their jobs?' He asked people to describe, in detail, situations in which they felt exceptionally *good* or *bad* about their jobs. These responses were then tabulated and categorised.

From the categorised responses, Herzberg concluded that the replies people gave when they felt good about their jobs were significantly different from those given when they felt bad. As seen in Figure 6.2, certain characteristics tend to be consistently related to job satisfaction and others to job dissatisfaction. Intrinsic factors, such as advancement, recognition, responsibility and achievement, seem to be related to job satisfaction. Respondents who felt good about their work tended to attribute these factors to themselves. However, dissatisfied respondents tended to cite extrinsic factors, such as supervision, pay, company policies and working conditions.

LEARNING OBJECTIVE 3

Differentiate motivators from hygiene factors

two-factor theory |
A theory that relates intrinsic factors to job satisfaction, while associating extrinsic factors with dissatisfaction.

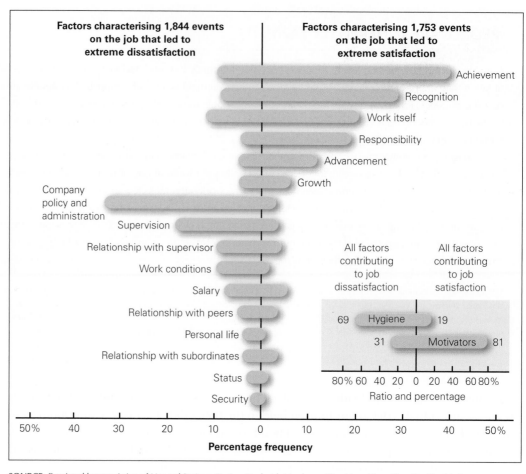

The data suggest, said Herzberg, that the opposite of satisfaction isn't dissatisfaction, as was traditionally believed. Removing dissatisfying characteristics from a job doesn't necessarily make the job satisfying. As illustrated in Figure 6.2, Herzberg proposed that his findings indicated the existence of a dual continuum: the opposite of 'Satisfaction' is 'No Satisfaction', and the opposite of 'Dissatisfaction' is 'No Dissatisfaction'.

According to Herzberg, the factors leading to job satisfaction are separate and distinct from those that lead to job dissatisfaction. Therefore, managers who seek to eliminate factors that can create job dissatisfaction may bring about peace but not necessarily motivation. They will be placating their workforce, rather than motivating them. As a result, conditions surrounding the job, such as quality of supervision, pay, company policies, physical working conditions, relations with others, and job security, were characterised by Herzberg as **hygiene factors**. When they are adequate, people won't be dissatisfied; neither will they be satisfied. If we want to motivate people on their jobs, Herzberg suggested emphasising factors associated with the work itself or outcomes directly derived from it, such as promotional opportunities, opportunities for personal growth, recognition, responsibility and achievement. These are the characteristics that people find intrinsically rewarding.

hygiene factors |
Factors—such as company
policy and administration,
supervision and salary—
that, when adequate in a
job, placate workers.
When these factors are
adequate, people won't be
dissatisfied.

Google's Sydney office is jam-packed with positive hygiene factors. Employees who work in the offices not only enjoy a fantastic view out over Darling Harbour, but they also get free lunches and free drinks and snacks, massage is available on-site, and there is a pool table that overlooks the Sydney city sky-line.

The two-factor theory hasn't been well supported in the literature, and it has many detractors.[12] The criticisms of the theory include the following:

1. The procedure that Herzberg used is limited by its methodology. When things are going well, people tend to take credit themselves. Contrarily, they blame failure on the extrinsic environment.

2. The reliability of Herzberg's methodology is questioned. Raters have to make interpretations, so they may contaminate the findings by interpreting one response in one manner while treating a similar response differently.

3. No overall measure of satisfaction was utilised. A person may dislike part of a job yet still think the job is acceptable overall.

4. The theory is inconsistent with previous research. The two-factor theory ignores situational variables.

5. Herzberg assumed a relationship between satisfaction and productivity, but the research methodology he used looked only at satisfaction, not at productivity. To make such research relevant, one must assume a strong relationship between satisfaction and productivity.

Regardless of criticisms, Herzberg's theory has been widely read and few managers are unfamiliar with his recommendations.

It is important to realise that even though we may intuitively *like* a theory, that doesn't mean that we should accept it. Many managers find need theories intuitively appealing— but remember, at one time the world seemed intuitively flat. Sometimes science backs up intuition, and sometimes it doesn't. In the case of the two-factor theory—like the need hierarchy—it didn't.

CONTEMPORARY THEORIES OF MOTIVATION

The previous theories are well known but, unfortunately, haven't held up well under close examination. However, all is not lost. There are a number of contemporary theories that have one thing in common—each has a reasonable degree of valid supporting documentation. Of course, this doesn't mean that the theories we are about to introduce are unquestionably right. We call them 'contemporary theories' not because they necessarily were developed recently, but because they represent the current state of thinking in explaining employee motivation.

McCLELLAND'S THEORY OF NEEDS

You have one beanbag and there are five targets set up in front of you. Each one is progressively further away and, hence, more difficult to hit. Target A is a cinch. It sits almost within arm's reach of you. If you hit it, you get $2. Target B is a bit further out, but about 80 per cent of the people who try can hit it. It pays $4. Target C pays $8, and about half the people who try can hit it. Very few people can hit Target D, but the payoff is $16 if you do. Finally, Target E pays $32, but it is almost impossible to achieve. Which target would you try for? If you selected C, you are likely to be a high achiever. Why? Read on.

McClelland's theory of needs | A theory stating that achievement, power and affiliation are three important needs that help to explain motivation.

need for achievement | The drive to excel, to achieve in relation to a set of standards, to strive to succeed.

need for power | The need to make others behave in a way that they wouldn't have behaved otherwise.

need for affiliation | The desire for friendly and close interpersonal relationships.

McClelland's theory of needs was developed by David McClelland and his associates.[13] The theory focuses on three needs: achievement, power and affiliation. They are defined as follows:

- **Need for achievement**: The drive to excel, to achieve in relation to a set of standards, to strive to succeed.
- **Need for power**: The need to make others behave in a way that they wouldn't have behaved otherwise.
- **Need for affiliation**: The desire for friendly and close interpersonal relationships.

Some people have a compelling drive to succeed. They are striving for personal achievement, rather than for the rewards of success per se. They have a desire to do something better or more efficiently than it has been done before. This drive is the achievement need (*nAch*). From research into the achievement need, McClelland found that high achievers differentiate themselves from others by their desire to do things better.[14] They seek situations in which they can attain personal responsibility for finding solutions to problems, in which they can receive rapid feedback on their performance so they can determine easily whether they are improving or not, and in which they can set moderately challenging goals. High achievers aren't gamblers; they dislike succeeding by chance. They prefer the challenge of working at a problem and accepting the personal responsibility for success or failure, rather than leaving the outcome to chance or the actions of others. Importantly, they avoid what they perceive to be very easy or very difficult tasks. They prefer tasks of intermediate difficulty.

High achievers perform best when they perceive their probability of success as being 0.5—that is, when they estimate that they have a 50:50 chance of success. They dislike gambling with high odds because they get no achievement satisfaction from happenstance success. Similarly, they dislike low odds (high probability of success) because then there is

Graeme Samuel is the Chairman of the Australian Competition and Consumer Commission (ACCC). His professional career has spanned the law, investment banking and, since the early 1990s, a number of roles in the public service covering diverse interests including sport, the arts, health, business affairs and competition policy. His broad range of experience has allowed him to apply strategic thinking to a variety of corporate and public service environments, enabling those organisations to respond to the myriad challenges presented in a fast-moving business sector.

no challenge to their skills. They like to set goals that require stretching themselves a little.

The need for power ($nPow$) is the desire to have impact, to be influential and to control others. Individuals high in nPow enjoy being 'in charge', strive for influence over others, prefer to be placed into competitive and status-oriented situations, and tend to be more concerned with prestige and gaining influence over others than with effective performance.

The third need isolated by McClelland is affiliation ($nAff$). This need has received the least attention from researchers. Individuals with a high affiliation motive strive for friendship, prefer cooperative situations rather than competitive ones, and desire relationships that involve a high degree of mutual understanding.

Relying on an extensive amount of research, some reasonably well-supported predictions can be made based on the relationship between achievement need and job performance. Although less research has been done on power and affiliation needs, there are consistent findings here, too.

First, as shown in Figure 6.3, individuals with a high need to achieve prefer job situations with personal responsibility, feedback and an intermediate degree of risk. When these characteristics are prevalent, high achievers will be strongly motivated. The evidence consistently demonstrates, for instance, that high achievers are successful in entrepreneurial activities such as running their own businesses and managing a self-contained unit within a large organisation.[15] Furthermore, evidence from Australia shows that not only are many female entrepreneurs high in nAch,[16] but that middle managers with higher nAch also had higher salaries.[17]

Second, a high need to achieve doesn't necessarily lead to being a good manager, especially in large organisations. People with a high achievement need are interested in how well they do personally and not in influencing others to do well. High-nAch salespeople don't necessarily make good sales managers, and the good general manager in a large organisation doesn't typically have a high need to achieve.[18]

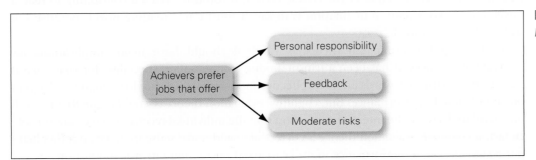

■ FIGURE 6.3

Matching achievers and jobs

Third, the needs for affiliation and power tend to be closely related to managerial success. The best managers are high in their need for power and low in their need for affiliation.[19] In fact, a high power motive may be a requirement for managerial effectiveness.[20] Of course, what the cause is and what the effect is are arguable. It has been suggested that a high power need may occur simply as a function of one's level in a hierarchical organisation.[21] The latter argument proposes that the higher the level an individual rises to in the organisation, the greater is the incumbent's power motive. As a result, powerful positions would be the stimulus to a high power motive.

Finally, employees have been successfully trained to stimulate their achievement need. Trainers have been effective in teaching individuals to think in terms of accomplishments, winning, and success, and then helping them to learn how to *act* in a high-achievement way by preferring situations in which they have personal responsibility, feedback and moderate risks. So, if the job calls for a high achiever, management can select a person with a high nAch or develop its own candidate through achievement training.[22]

COGNITIVE EVALUATION THEORY

cognitive evaluation theory | A theory stating that allocating extrinsic rewards for behaviour that had been previously intrinsically rewarding tends to decrease the overall level of motivation.

The legend of the struggling artist, or the penniless writer, who loses their talent after becoming successful may have support from the research.[23] It is called **cognitive evaluation theory** and it proposes that the introduction of extrinsic rewards, such as pay, for work effort that was previously intrinsically rewarding due to the pleasure associated with the content of the work itself tends to decrease overall motivation.[24] Cognitive evaluation theory has been extensively researched, and a large number of studies have been supportive.[25] As we will show, the major implications for this theory relate to the way in which people are paid in organisations, such as reinforcement theory.

Historically, motivation theorists generally assumed that intrinsic motivators such as achievement, responsibility and competence were independent of extrinsic motivators such as high pay, promotions, good supervisor relations and pleasant working conditions. But cognitive evaluation theory suggests otherwise. It argues that when extrinsic rewards are used by organisations as payoffs for superior performance, the intrinsic rewards, which are derived from individuals doing what they like, are reduced. In other words, when extrinsic rewards are given to someone for performing an interesting task, it causes intrinsic interest in the task itself to decline.

Why would such an outcome occur? The popular explanation is that the individual experiences a loss of control over his or her own behaviour so that the previous intrinsic motivation diminishes. Furthermore, the elimination of extrinsic rewards can produce a shift—from an external to an internal explanation—in an individual's perception of causation of why he or she works on a task. If you are reading a novel a week because your English literature lecturer requires you to, you can attribute your reading behaviour to an external source. However, after the course is over, if you find yourself continuing to read a novel a week, your natural inclination is to say, 'I must enjoy reading novels because I'm still reading one a week.'

If the cognitive evaluation theory is valid, it should have major implications for managerial practices. It has been a truism among compensation specialists for years that if pay or other extrinsic rewards are to be effective motivators, they should be made contingent on an individual's performance. But, cognitive evaluation theorists would argue that this will only tend to decrease the internal satisfaction that the individual receives from doing the job. In fact, if cognitive evaluation theory is correct, it would make sense to make an individual's pay *non-contingent* on performance in order to avoid decreasing intrinsic motivation.

We noted earlier that the cognitive evaluation theory has been supported in a number of studies. Yet it has also been met with attacks, specifically on the methodology used in these studies[26] and in the interpretation of the findings.[27] But where does this theory stand today? Can we say that when organisations use extrinsic motivators such as pay and promotions and verbal rewards to stimulate workers' performance, they do so at the expense of reducing intrinsic interest and motivation in the work being done? The answer is not a simple 'Yes' or 'No'.

Extrinsic rewards that are verbal (receiving praise from a supervisor or co-worker) or tangible (money) can actually have different effects on people's intrinsic motivation. That is, verbal rewards increase intrinsic motivation, while tangible rewards undermine it. When people are told they will receive a tangible reward, they come to count on it and focus more on the reward than on the task.[28] Verbal rewards, however, seem to keep people focused on the task and encourage them to do it better.

A more recent outgrowth of the cognitive evaluation theory is **self-concordance**, which considers the degree to which people's reasons for pursuing goals are consistent with their interests and core values. For example, if individuals pursue goals because of an intrinsic interest, they are more likely to attain their goals and are happy even if they don't attain them. Why? Because the process of striving towards them is fun. In contrast, people who pursue goals for extrinsic reasons (money, status or other benefits) are less likely to attain their goals and are less happy even when they do achieve them. Why? Because the goals are less meaningful to them.[29] OB research suggests that people who pursue work goals for intrinsic reasons are more satisfied with their jobs, feel like they fit into their organisations better and may perform better.[30]

What does all of this mean? It means: choose your job carefully. Make sure that you are choosing to do something for reasons other than extrinsic rewards. For organisations, managers need to provide intrinsic rewards in addition to extrinsic incentives. In other words, make the work interesting, provide recognition, and support employee growth and development. Employees who feel that what they do is within their control and a result of free choice are likely to be more motivated by their work and committed to their employers.[31]

self-concordance | The degree to which a person's reasons for pursuing a goal are consistent with their interests and core values.

GOAL-SETTING THEORY

Gene Broadwater, coach of the Hamilton High School cross-country team, gave his squad these last words before they approached the line for the league championship race: 'Each one of you is physically ready. Now, get out there and do your best. No one can ever ask more of you than that.'

You have heard this phrase a number of times yourself: 'Just do your best. That's all anyone can ask for.' But what does 'do your best' mean? Do we ever know if we have achieved that vague goal? Would the cross-country runners have recorded faster times if Broadwater had given each member of the team a specific goal to shoot for? Might you have done better in your high school English class if your parents had said, 'You should strive for 85 per cent or higher on all your work in English', rather than telling you to 'do your best'? The research on **goal-setting theory** addresses these issues, and the findings, as you will see, are impressive in terms of the effect that goal specificity, challenge and feedback have on performance.

In the late 1960s, Edwin Locke proposed that intentions to work towards a goal are a major source of work motivation.[32] That is, goals tell an employee what needs to be done and how much effort will need to be expended.[33] The evidence strongly supports the value of goals. More to the point, we can say that specific goals increase performance; that

LEARNING OBJECTIVE 5
Summarise the types of goals that increase performance

goal-setting theory | The theory that specific and difficult goals, with feedback, lead to higher performance.

difficult goals, when accepted, result in higher performance than do easy goals; and that feedback leads to higher performance than does non-feedback.[34]

Specific goals produce a higher level of output than does the generalised goal of 'do your best'. Why? The specificity of the goal itself seems to act as an internal stimulus. For instance, when a truck driver commits to making seven round-trip hauls between Adelaide and Melbourne each week, this intention gives him a specific objective to try to attain. We can say that, all things being equal, the driver with a specific goal will outperform a counterpart operating with no goals or the generalised goal of 'do your best'.

If factors such as acceptance of the goals are held constant, we can also state that the more difficult the goal, the higher the level of performance. Of course, it is logical to assume that easier goals are more likely to be accepted. But once a hard task is accepted, the employee can be expected to exert a high level of effort to try to achieve it.

But why are people more motivated by difficult goals?[35] First, difficult goals direct our attention to the task at hand and away from irrelevant distractions. Challenging goals get our attention and thus tend to help us focus. Second, difficult goals energise us because we have to work harder to attain them. For example, think of your study habits. Do you study as hard for an easy exam as you do for a difficult one? Probably not. Third, when goals are difficult, people persist in trying to attain them. Finally, difficult goals lead us to discover strategies that help us to perform the job or task more effectively. If we have to struggle for a way to solve a difficult problem, we often think of a better way to go about it.

People will do better when they get feedback on how well they are progressing towards their goals because feedback helps to identify discrepancies between what they have done and what they want to do; that is, feedback acts to guide behaviour. But all feedback isn't equally potent. Self-generated feedback—for which employees are able to monitor their own progress—has been shown to be a more powerful motivator than externally generated feedback.[36]

If employees have the opportunity to participate in the setting of their own goals, will they try harder? The evidence is mixed regarding the superiority of participative over assigned goals.[37] In some cases, participatively set goals elicited superior performance, while in other cases, individuals performed best when assigned goals by their boss. But a

OB IN PRACTICE

GOAL SETTING FOR SUCCESS

Two millionaire entrepreneurs in the fitness industry have shown just how important goal setting can be to success. Kerry McEvoy and his wife and business partner Rowena Szeszeran-McEvoy founded the Australian Institute for Fitness (AIF) and, more recently, the National College of Business, and now have an estimated personal wealth of $20 million. Moreover, they love their jobs. McEvoy says: 'The rewards—in particular, watching our staff and students grow—make me feel like I haven't worked at all. The more value you add to people's lives, the more return you get spiritually. The money follows.'

One of the keys to their success has been the use of goal setting. At the age of 31, and without any money in the bank, Kerry McEvoy set himself a goal to be financially independent by age 45—he reached that self-set goal in five years. His commitment to the goal, its specificity and difficulty, and the feedback of seeing the money coming in would have all contributed to increasing his motivation. Now he uses goal setting when teaching fitness instructors, and the response from fitness employers has been fantastic—they are knocking the door down to employ AIF instructors.

SOURCE: Kristen Le Mesurier, 'Fit and Happy', *Business Review Weekly*, 15 September 2005.

major advantage of participation may be in increasing acceptance of the goal itself as a desirable one towards which to work.[38] As we will note shortly, commitment is important. If participation isn't used, then the purpose and importance of the goal needs to be explained clearly by the individual assigning the goal.[39]

Are there any contingencies in goal-setting theory, or can we take it as a universal truth that difficult and specific goals will *always* lead to higher performance? In addition to feedback, three other factors have been found to influence the goals–performance relationship. These are goal commitment, task characteristics and national culture. Goal-setting theory presupposes that an individual is committed to the goal; that is, an individual is determined not to lower or abandon the goal. Behaviourally, this means that an individual (a) believes he or she can achieve the goal and (b) wants to achieve it.[40] Goal commitment is most likely to occur when goals are made public, when the individual has an internal locus of control (see Chapter 4), and when the goals are self-set rather than assigned.[41] Research indicates that goal-setting theory doesn't work equally well on all tasks. The evidence suggests that goals seem to have a more substantial effect on performance when tasks are simple rather than complex, well-learned rather than novel, and independent rather than interdependent.[42] On interdependent tasks, group goals are preferable.

Finally, goal-setting theory is culture-bound. First, the types of goals that are important will differ across cultures. Recent research comparing the goals of people in Australia and in Sri Lanka found that Australians' goals were much more individualistic. Sri Lankans also had some important individual goals, but in general, their goals were much more oriented towards the family and the group.[43] Second, goal-setting theory is well adapted to countries such as Australia and the United States because its key components align reasonably well with our cultures. It assumes that employees will be reasonably independent (not too high a score on power distance), that managers and employees will seek challenging goals (low in uncertainty avoidance), and that performance is considered important by both (high in achievement). So, don't expect goal setting to necessarily lead to higher employee performance in countries such as Portugal or Chile, where the opposite conditions exist.

Our overall conclusion is that intentions—as articulated in terms of difficult and specific goals—are a potent motivating force. The motivating power of goal-setting theory has been demonstrated on over 100 tasks involving more than 40 000 participants in many different kinds of industries—from timber, to insurance, to automobiles. Basically, setting specific, challenging goals for employees is the best thing managers can do to improve performance.

When it comes to your courses, what goals do you set for yourself? Do you want to prove yourself to your lecturer? Are you thinking about furthering your education? See the following Self-Assessment feature, and you can find out what drives you to study.

Goal setting has been used successfully in a wide variety of settings and can help not only businesses, but also the environment. For instance, the recent construction of a sports stadium in Melbourne used goal setting to reduce waste of construction materials. Each fortnight, performance measures of waste and recycling were calculated and fed back to managers and employees. The goal-setting intervention led to an overall improvement in the efficiency of using timber and construction materials, and to a reduction in the volume of waste being disposed of as landfill.

MBO PROGRAMS: PUTTING GOAL-SETTING THEORY INTO PRACTICE

Goal-setting theory has an impressive base of research support. But as a manager, how do you make goal setting operational? One answer to that question is: install a management by objectives (MBO) program. MTW Corporation, a provider of software services mainly for insurance companies and state governments in the United States, has an MBO-type program.[44] Management attributes this program with helping the company to average a 50 per cent-a-year growth rate for five years in a row and cutting employee turnover to one-fifth of the industry norm.

management by objectives (MBO) | A program that encompasses specific goals, participatively set, for an explicit time period, with feedback on goal progress.

Management by objectives emphasises participatively set goals that are tangible, verifiable and measurable. MBO's appeal undoubtedly lies in its emphasis on converting overall organisational objectives into specific objectives for organisational units and individual members. MBO operationalises the concept of objectives by devising a process by which objectives cascade down through the organisation. As depicted in Figure 6.4, the organisation's overall objectives are translated into specific objectives for each succeeding level (that is, divisional, departmental, individual) in the organisation. But because lower-unit managers jointly participate in setting their own goals, MBO works from the 'bottom up' as well as from the 'top down'. The result is a hierarchy that links objectives at one level to those at the next level. And for the individual employee, MBO provides specific personal performance objectives.

There are four ingredients common to MBO programs. These are goal specificity, participation in decision making (including participation in the setting of goals or

■ FIGURE 6.4
Cascading of objectives

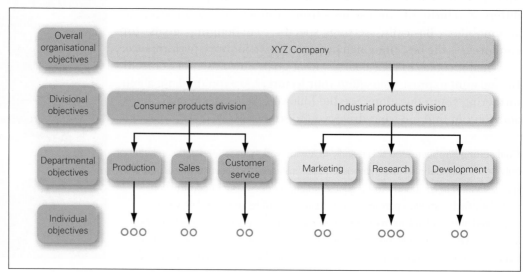

192 • Part 2: The Individual

objectives), an explicit time period, and performance feedback.[45] Many of the elements in MBO programs match goal-setting theory's propositions. For example, having an explicit time period in which to accomplish objectives matches goal-setting theory's emphasis on goal specificity. Similarly, we noted earlier that feedback about goal progress is a critical element of goal-setting theory. The only area of possible disagreement between MBO and goal-setting theory relates to the issue of participation—MBO strongly advocates it, while goal-setting theory demonstrates that managers assigning goals is usually just as effective.

You will find MBO programs in many business, health-care, educational, government and non-profit organisations.[46] MBO's popularity shouldn't be construed to mean that it always works. There are a number of documented cases in which MBO has been implemented but failed to meet management's expectations.[47] When MBO doesn't work, the culprits tend to be factors such as unrealistic expectations regarding results, lack of commitment by top management, and an inability or unwillingness by management to allocate rewards based on goal accomplishment. Failures can also arise out of cultural incompatibilities. For instance, Fujitsu recently scrapped its MBO-type program because management found it didn't fit well with the Japanese culture's emphasis on minimising risk and emphasising long-term goals.

SELF-EFFICACY THEORY

LEARNING OBJECTIVE 6
Discuss ways self-efficacy can be increased

Self-efficacy (also known as 'social cognitive theory' or 'social learning theory') refers to an individual's belief that he or she is capable of performing a task.[48] The higher your self-efficacy, the more confidence you have in your ability to succeed in a task. So, in difficult situations, we find that people with low self-efficacy are more likely to lessen their effort or give up altogether, while those with high self-efficacy will try harder to master the challenge.[49] In addition, individuals high in self-efficacy seem to respond to negative feedback with increased effort and motivation, while those low in self-efficacy are likely to lessen their effort when given negative feedback.[50] Indeed, recent research on triathletes competing in the Australian Ironman Competition found that self-efficacy was significantly related to the athletes' performance.[51] So, how can managers help their employees achieve high levels of self-efficacy? By bringing together goal-setting theory and self-efficacy theory.

self-efficacy | The individual's belief that he or she is capable of performing a task.

Goal-setting theory and self-efficacy theory don't compete with one another; rather, they complement each other. Figure 6.5 shows that, when a manager sets difficult goals for employees, this leads employees to have a higher level of self-efficacy and to set higher goals for their own performance. Why is this the case? Research has shown that setting difficult goals for people communicates confidence. For example, imagine that your boss sets a high goal for you, and you learn it is higher than the goals she has set for your co-workers. How would you interpret this? As long as you don't feel you are being picked on, you probably would think, 'Well, I guess my boss thinks I'm capable of performing better than others.' This then sets into motion a psychological process where you are more confident in yourself (higher self-efficacy), and you set higher personal goals, causing you to perform better both in the workplace and outside it.

The researcher who developed self-efficacy theory, Albert Bandura, argues that there are four ways self-efficacy can be increased:[52]

- enactive mastery;
- vicarious modelling;
- verbal persuasion; and
- arousal.

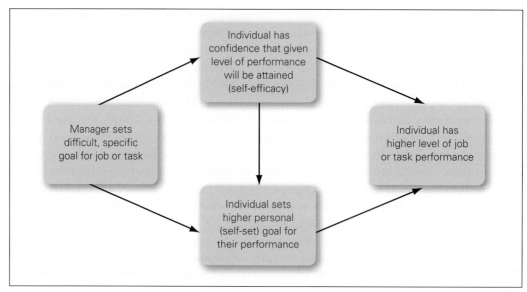

SOURCE: Based on E. A. Locke and G. P. Latham, 'Building a Practically Useful Theory of Goal Setting and Task Motivation: A 35-Year Odyssey', *American Psychologist*, September 2002, pp. 705–17.

According to Bandura, the most important source of increasing self-efficacy is what he calls *enactive* mastery. Enactive mastery is gaining relevant experience with the task or job. If I have been able to do the job successfully in the past, then I'm more confident I will be able to do it in the future.

The second source is *vicarious modelling*—or becoming more confident because you see someone else doing the task. For example, if my friend loses weight, then it increases my confidence that I can lose weight, too. Vicarious modelling is most effective when you see yourself similar to the person you are observing. It doesn't increase my confidence in being able to play a difficult golf shot by watching Tiger Woods do it. But, if I watch a golfer with a handicap similar to mine, it is more persuasive.

The third source is *verbal persuasion*, which is becoming more confident because someone convinces you that you have the skills necessary to be successful. Motivational speakers use this tactic a lot.

Finally, Bandura argues that *arousal* increases self-efficacy. Arousal leads to an energised state, which drives a person to complete the task. The person gets 'psyched up' and performs better. But when arousal isn't relevant, it can have a detrimental effect on performance. In other words, if the task is something that requires a steadier, lower-key perspective (say, carefully editing a manuscript), arousal may in fact hurt performance.

What are the OB implications of self-efficacy theory? Well, it is a matter of applying Bandura's sources of self-efficacy to the work setting. Training programs often make use of enactive mastery by having people practise and build their skills. In fact, one of the reasons training works is because it increases self-efficacy.[53]

The best way for a manager to use verbal persuasion is through the *Pygmalion* or *Galatea effect*. As we discussed in Chapter 5, the Pygmalion effect is a form of a self-fulfilling prophecy where believing something to be true can make it true. In the Pygmalion effect, self-efficacy is increased by communicating to an individual's teacher or supervisor that the person is of high ability. For example, studies were done where teachers were told their students had very high IQ scores (when in fact they had a range of IQs—some high, some low, and some in-between). Consistent with a Pygmalion effect, teachers spent more time with the students they *thought* were smart, gave them more challenging assignments and expected more of them—all of which led to higher student self-efficacy and better student grades.[54] This also has been used in the workplace.[55] The Galatea effect occurs when high performance expectations are communicated directly to the employee. For example, sailors who were told, in a convincing manner, that they wouldn't get seasick in fact were much less likely to get seasick.[56]

Note that intelligence and personality are absent from Bandura's list. A lot of research shows that intelligence and personality (especially conscientiousness and emotional stability) can increase self-efficacy.[57] Those individual traits are so strongly related to self-efficacy (people who are intelligent, conscientious and emotionally stable are much more likely to have high self-efficacy than those who score low on these characteristics) that some researchers would argue self-efficacy doesn't exist.[58] What this means is that self-efficacy may simply be a by-product of a smart person with a confident personality, and the term *self-efficacy* is superfluous and unnecessary. Although Bandura strongly disagrees with this conclusion, more research on the issue is needed.

REINFORCEMENT THEORY

A counterpoint to goal-setting theory is **reinforcement theory**. The former is a cognitive approach, proposing that an individual's purposes direct his or her actions. In reinforcement theory, we have a behaviouristic approach, which argues that reinforcement conditions behaviour. The two are clearly at odds philosophically. Reinforcement theorists see behaviour as being environmentally caused. You need not be concerned, they would argue, with internal cognitive events; what controls behaviour are reinforcers—any consequence that, when immediately following a response, increases the probability that the behaviour will be repeated.

reinforcement theory | A theory that behaviour is a function of its consequences.

Reinforcement theory ignores the inner state of the individual and concentrates solely on what happens to a person when he or she takes some action. Because it doesn't concern itself with what initiates behaviour, it is not, strictly speaking, a theory of motivation. But it does provide a powerful means of analysis of what controls behaviour, and it is for this reason that it is typically considered in discussions of motivation.[59]

We discussed the reinforcement process in detail in Chapter 2. Although it is clear that so-called reinforcers such as pay can motivate people, it is just as clear that the process is much more complicated than stimulus–response. In its pure form, reinforcement theory ignores feelings, attitudes, expectations and other cognitive variables that are known to impact behaviour. In fact, some researchers look at the same experiments that reinforcement theorists use to support their position and interpret the findings in a cognitive framework.[60] Reinforcement is undoubtedly an important influence on behaviour, but few scholars are prepared to argue that it is the only influence. The behaviours you engage in at work and the amount of effort you allocate to each task are affected by the consequences that follow from your behaviour. For instance, if you are consistently reprimanded for outproducing your colleagues, you will likely reduce your productivity. But your lower productivity may also be explained in terms of goals, inequity or expectancies.

EQUITY THEORY

Jane Pearson graduated last year from the University of New South Wales (UNSW) with a degree in accounting. After interviews with a number of organisations on campus, she accepted a position with a top public accounting firm and was assigned to their Sydney office. Jane was very pleased with the offer she received: challenging work with a prestigious firm, an excellent opportunity to gain valuable experience, and the highest salary any accounting major at UNSW was offered last year—$3800 a month. But Jane was the top student in her class; she was articulate and mature and fully expected to receive a commensurate salary.

Twelve months have passed since Jane joined her employer. The work has proved to be as challenging and satisfying as she had hoped. Her employer is extremely pleased with her performance; in fact, she recently received a $200-a-month raise. However, Jane's motivational level has dropped dramatically in the past few weeks. Why? Her employer has just hired a fresh college graduate out of UNSW, who lacks the one-year experience Jane has gained, for $4050 a month—$50 more than Jane now makes! It would be an understatement to describe Jane in any other terms than irate. She is even talking about looking for another job.

Jane's situation illustrates the role that equity plays in motivation. Employees make comparisons of their job inputs (for example, effort, experience, education, competence) and outcomes (for example, salary levels, raises, recognition) relative to those of others. We perceive what we get from a job situation (outcomes) in relation to what we put into it (inputs), and then we compare our outcome–input ratio with the outcome–input ratio of relevant others. This is shown in Table 6.1. If we perceive our ratio to be equal to that of the relevant others with whom we compare ourselves, a state of equity is said to exist. We perceive our situation as fair—that justice prevails. When we see the ratio as unequal, we experience equity tension. When we see ourselves as under-rewarded, the tension creates anger; when over-rewarded, the tension creates guilt. J. Stacy Adams has proposed that this negative state of tension provides the motivation to do something to correct it.[61]

equity theory | A theory that individuals compare their job inputs and outcomes with those of others and then respond to eliminate any inequities.

The referent that an employee selects adds to the complexity of **equity theory**.[62] There are four referent comparisons that an employee can use:

1. *Self-inside*: An employee's experiences in a different position inside the employee's current organisation.
2. *Self-outside*: An employee's experiences in a situation or position outside the employee's current organisation.
3. *Other-inside*: Another individual or group of individuals inside the employee's organisation.
4. *Other-outside*: Another individual or group of individuals outside the employee's organisation.

■ TABLE 6.1
Equity theory

Ratio comparisons*	Perception
$\frac{O}{I_A} < \frac{O}{I_B}$	Inequity due to being under-rewarded
$\frac{O}{I_A} = \frac{O}{I_B}$	Equity
$\frac{O}{I_A} > \frac{O}{I_B}$	Inequity due to being over-rewarded

*Where $\frac{O}{I_A}$ represents the employee and $\frac{O}{I_B}$ represents relevant others.

Employees might compare themselves to friends, neighbours, co-workers or colleagues in other organisations, or compare their present job with past jobs they themselves have had. Which referent an employee chooses will be influenced by the information the employee holds about referents, as well as by the attractiveness of the referent. This has led to focusing on four moderating variables—gender, length of tenure, level in the organisation, and amount of education or professionalism.[63]

Research shows that both men and women prefer same-sex comparisons. The research also demonstrates that women are typically paid less than men in comparable jobs and have lower pay expectations than men for the same work.[64] So, a woman who uses another woman as a referent tends to calculate a lower comparative standard. This leads us to conclude that employees in jobs that are not sex-segregated will make more cross-sex comparisons than those in jobs that are either male- or female-dominated. This also suggests that if women are tolerant of lower pay, it may be due to the comparative standard they use. Of course, employers' stereotypes about women (for example, the belief that women are less committed to the organisation, or that 'women's work' is less valuable) also may contribute to the pay gap.[65]

Employees with short tenure in their current organisations tend to have little information about others inside the organisation, so they rely on their own personal experiences. However, employees with long tenure rely more heavily on co-workers for comparison. Upper-level employees, those in the professional ranks, and those with higher amounts of education tend to have better information about people in other organisations. Therefore, these types of employees will make more other-outside comparisons.

Based on equity theory, when employees perceive inequity, they can be predicted to make one of six choices:[66]

1. Change their inputs (for example, don't exert as much effort).
2. Change their outcomes (for example, individuals paid on a piece-rate basis can increase their pay by producing a higher quantity of units of lower quality).
3. Distort perceptions of self (for example, 'I used to think I worked at a moderate pace, but now I realise that I work a lot harder than everyone else.')
4. Distort perceptions of others (for example, 'Mike's job isn't as desirable as I previously thought it was.')
5. Choose a different referent (for example, 'I may not make as much as my brother-in-law, but I'm doing a lot better than my dad did when he was my age.')
6. Leave the field (for example, quit the job).

The theory establishes the following propositions relating to inequitable pay:

A. *Given payment by time, over-rewarded employees will produce more than will equitably paid employees.* Hourly and salaried employees will generate high quantity or quality of production in order to increase the input side of the ratio and bring about equity.
B. *Given payment by quantity of production, over-rewarded employees will produce fewer, but higher-quality, units than will equitably paid employees.* Individuals paid on a piece-rate basis will increase their effort to achieve equity, which can result in greater quality or quantity. However, increases in quantity will only increase inequity, since every unit produced results in further overpayment. Therefore, effort is directed towards increasing quality rather than increasing quantity.
C. *Given payment by time, under-rewarded employees will produce less or poorer quality of output.* Effort will be decreased, which will bring about lower productivity or poorer-quality output than equitably paid subjects.

D. *Given payment by quantity of production, under-rewarded employees will produce a large number of low-quality units in comparison with equitably paid employees.* Employees on piece-rate pay plans can bring about equity because trading off quality of output for quantity will result in an increase in rewards with little or no increase in contributions.

Some of these propositions have been supported, but other ones haven't.[67] First, inequities created by overpayment don't seem to have a very significant impact on behaviour in most work situations. Apparently, people have a great deal more tolerance of overpayment inequities than of underpayment inequities, or are better able to rationalise them. It is pretty damaging to a theory when half of the equation (how people respond to over-reward) falls apart. Second, not all people are equity sensitive.[68] For example, there is a small part of the working population who actually prefer that their outcome–input ratios be less than the referent comparison's. Predictions from equity theory aren't likely to be very accurate with these 'benevolent types'.

It is also important to note that while most research on equity theory has focused on pay, employees seem to look for equity in the distribution of other organisational rewards. For instance, it has been shown that the use of high-status job titles as well as large and lavishly furnished offices may function as outcomes for some employees in their equity equation.[69]

Finally, recent research has been directed at expanding what is meant by equity or fairness.[70] Historically, equity theory focused on **distributive justice**, which is the employee's perceived fairness of the *amount and allocation* of rewards among individuals. But, increasingly, equity is thought of from the standpoint of **organisational justice**, which we define as an overall perception of what is fair in the workplace. Employees perceive their organisations as just when they believe the outcomes they have received, and the way in which the outcomes were received, are fair. One key element of organisational justice is an individual's *perception* of justice. In other words, under organisational justice, fairness or equity can be subjective, and it resides in the perception of the person. What one person may see as unfair, another may see as perfectly appropriate. In general, people have an egocentric or self-serving bias. They see allocations or procedures favouring themselves as fair.[71] For example, a recent poll showed that 61 per cent of all respondents say that they are personally paying their fair share of taxes, but an almost equal number (54 per cent) of those polled feel the system as a whole is unfair, saying that some people skirt it.[72] Fairness often resides in the eye of the beholder, and we tend to be fairly self-serving about what we see as fair.

Beyond its focus on perceptions of fairness, the other key element of organisational justice is the view that justice is multidimensional. Organisational justice argues that distributive justice is important. For example, how much we get paid, relative to what we think we should be paid (distributive justice), is obviously important. But, according to justice researchers, *how* we get paid is just as important. Figure 6.6 shows a model of organisational justice.

Beyond distributive justice, the key addition under organisational justice was **procedural justice**, which is the perceived fairness of the *process* used to determine the distribution of rewards. Two key elements of procedural justice are process control and explanations. *Process control* is the opportunity to present one's point of view about desired outcomes to decision makers. *Explanations* are clear reasons given to a person by management for the outcome. Thus, for employees to see a process as fair, they need to feel they have some control over the outcome and that they were given an adequate

distributive justice | Perceived fairness of the amount and allocation of rewards among individuals.

----

organisational justice | An overall perception of what is fair in the workplace, comprised of distributive, procedural and interactional justice.

procedural justice | The perceived fairness of the process used to determine the distribution of rewards.

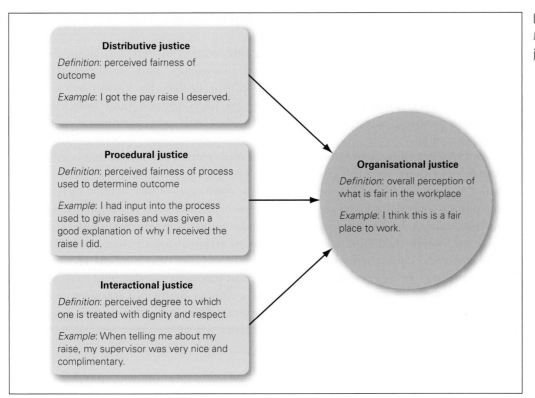

Distributive justice

Definition: perceived fairness of outcome

Example: I got the pay raise I deserved.

Procedural justice

Definition: perceived fairness of process used to determine outcome

Example: I had input into the process used to give raises and was given a good explanation of why I received the raise I did.

Interactional justice

Definition: perceived degree to which one is treated with dignity and respect

Example: When telling me about my raise, my supervisor was very nice and complimentary.

Organisational justice

Definition: overall perception of what is fair in the workplace

Example: I think this is a fair place to work.

explanation about why the outcome occurred. Also for procedural fairness, it is important that a manager is *consistent* (across people and over time), is *unbiased*, makes decisions based on *accurate information* and is *open to appeals*.[73]

Research shows that the effects of procedural justice become more important when distributive justice is lacking. This makes sense. If we don't get what we want, we tend to focus on *why*. For example, if your supervisor gives a cushy office to a co-worker instead of you, you are much more focused on your supervisor's treatment of you than if you had gotten the office. Explanations are beneficial when they take the form of post-hoc excuses (admitting that the act is unfavourable, but denying sole responsibility for it) rather than justifications (accepting full responsibility, but denying that the outcome is unfavourable or inappropriate).[74] In the office example, an excuse would be, 'I know this is bad. I wanted to give you the office, but it wasn't my decision' and a justification would be, 'Yes, I decided to give the office to Sam, but having the corner office isn't that big of a deal.'

A recent addition to research on organisational justice is **interactional justice**, which is the individual's perception of the degree to which he or she is treated with dignity, concern and respect. When people are treated in an unjust manner (at least in their own eyes), they respond by retaliating (for example, badmouthing a supervisor).[75] Because interactional justice or injustice is intimately tied to the conveyor of the information (usually one's supervisor), whereas procedural injustice often results from impersonal policies, one would expect perceptions of injustice to be more closely related to one's supervisor. Generally, that's what the evidence suggests.[76]

interactional justice | Perceived degree to which an individual is treated with dignity, concern and respect.

Of these three forms of justice, distributive justice is most strongly related to satisfaction with outcomes (for example, satisfaction with pay) and organisational commitment. Procedural justice relates most strongly to job satisfaction, employee trust, withdrawal from the organisation, job performance and citizenship behaviours. There is less evidence on interactional justice.[77]

Managers should consider openly sharing information on how allocation decisions are made, following consistent and unbiased procedures, and engaging in similar practices to increase the perception of procedural justice. By having an increased perception of procedural fairness, employees are likely to view their bosses and the organisation positively even if they are dissatisfied with pay, promotions and other personal outcomes.

In conclusion, equity theory predicts that, for most employees, motivation is influenced significantly by others' rewards as well as by one's own rewards. But some key issues are still unclear.[78] For instance, how do employees handle conflicting equity signals, such as when unions point to other employee groups who are substantially *better off*, while management argues the opposite? How do employees define inputs and outputs? How do they combine and weigh their inputs and outcomes to arrive at a judgment of equity across various outcomes? And when and how does the perception of the inputs and outcomes change over time? Because of these problems, most researchers today tend to focus solely on the perception of what's fair, rather than trying to figure out whether a person's outcome was objectively fair compared to the inputs. This is why, today, most researchers study organisational justice rather than equity theory per se.

EXPECTANCY THEORY

LEARNING OBJECTIVE 8

Clarify the key relationships in expectancy theory

Currently, one of the most widely accepted explanations of motivation is Victor Vroom's expectancy theory.[79] Although it has its critics, most of the evidence is supportive of the theory.[80]

Expectancy theory argues that the strength of a tendency to act in a certain way depends on the strength of an expectation that the act will be followed by a given outcome, and on the attractiveness of that outcome to the individual. In more practical terms, expectancy theory says that employees will be motivated to exert a high level of effort when they believe that effort will lead to a good performance appraisal; that a good appraisal will lead to organisational rewards such as a bonus, a salary increase, or a promotion; and that the rewards will satisfy the employees' personal goals. The theory, therefore, focuses on three relationships (see Figure 6.7).

expectancy theory | The strength of a tendency to act in a certain way depends on the strength of an expectation that the act will be followed by a given outcome, and on the attractiveness of that outcome to the individual.

1. *Effort–performance relationship*. The probability perceived by the individual that exerting a given amount of effort will lead to performance.
2. *Performance–reward relationship*. The degree to which the individual believes that performing at a particular level will lead to the attainment of a desired outcome.
3. *Rewards–personal goals relationship*. The degree to which organisational rewards satisfy an individual's personal goals or needs, and the attractiveness of those potential rewards for the individual.[81]

■ FIGURE 6.7
Expectancy theory

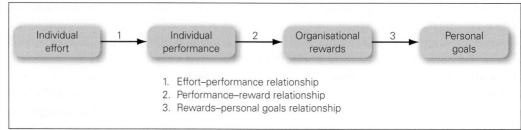

1. Effort–performance relationship
2. Performance–reward relationship
3. Rewards–personal goals relationship

It is widely acknowledged that it is getting harder to recruit good graduates into the teaching profession. One recent analysis indicated that expectancy theory may be partly to blame. The promotion structure for teachers is often based on years in the job, not performance (decreasing the performance–reward relationship). Merit-based pay also has problems, as measures of performance, such as students' performance in exams, is influenced by other things such as socioeconomic status (decreasing the effort–performance) relationship. Without these relationships in place, it is easy to see why good graduates aren't motivated to become teachers.

Expectancy theory helps to explain why a lot of workers aren't motivated in their jobs and do only the minimum necessary to get by. This is evident when we look at the theory's three relationships in a little more detail. We present them as questions employees need to answer in the affirmative if their motivation is to be maximised.

First, *if I give a maximum effort, will it be recognised in my performance appraisal?* For a lot of employees, the answer is 'No'. Why? Their skill level may be deficient, which means that no matter how hard they try, they are not likely to be a high performer. The organisation's performance appraisal system may be designed to assess non-performance factors such as loyalty, initiative or courage, which means more effort won't necessarily result in a higher evaluation. Still another possibility is that employees, rightly or wrongly, perceive that the boss doesn't like them. As a result, they expect to get a poor appraisal regardless of level of effort. These examples suggest that one possible source of low employee motivation is the belief by employees that no matter how hard they work, the likelihood of getting a good performance appraisal is low.

Second, *if I get a good performance appraisal, will it lead to organisational rewards?* Many employees see the performance–reward relationship in their job as weak. The reason is that organisations reward a lot of things besides just performance. For example, when pay is allocated to employees based on factors such as seniority, being cooperative, or for 'kissing up' to the boss, employees are likely to see the performance–reward relationship as being weak and demotivating.

Finally, *if I'm rewarded, are the rewards ones that I find personally attractive?* The employee works hard in the hope of getting a promotion but gets a pay raise instead. Or the employee wants a more interesting and challenging job but receives only a few words of praise. Or the employee puts in extra effort in the hope of being relocated to the company's Paris office but instead is transferred to Singapore. These examples illustrate the importance of the rewards being tailored to individual employee needs. Unfortunately, many managers are limited in the rewards they can distribute, which makes it difficult to individualise rewards. Moreover, some managers incorrectly assume that all employees want the same thing, thus overlooking the motivational effects of differentiating rewards. In either case, employee motivation is submaximised.

In summary, the key to expectancy theory is the understanding of an individual's goals and the linkage between effort and performance, between performance and rewards, and, finally, between the rewards and individual goal satisfaction. As a contingency model, expectancy theory recognises that there is no universal principle for explaining everyone's

WHAT MOTIVATES GEN Y?

'Generation Y' is now in the workforce, and managers are having to find new ways to motivate them. Two companies, at least, have started to identify the rewards that their newer staff members find motivating. At Minter Ellison, one of the largest law firms in the Asia-Pacific region, a variety of rewards are used to motivate Generation Y employees, including high salaries, feedback, recognition and team functions. Furthermore, they make the relationship to the employee's outcomes very clear. As Peter Coats, the national head of insurance and corporate risk, says: 'Almost from day one they want to know what they are getting out of the organisation, so it is important to explain how they benefit from the work they are doing.' At Westpac Banking Corporation, surveys and networking lunches have been conducted to directly ask new recruits about their motivation. Senior management at Westpac learned that, again, benefits to the Generation Y's career plans are key motivators. More specifically, Westpac has now implemented aggressive career planning, mentoring by senior staff, and structured career development opportunities that allow for challenging work across a range of different skills and training.

SOURCE: R. Nickless, 'When Motivation is the Main Game', *Australian Financial Review*, 2 May 2006.

motivations. In addition, just because we understand what needs a person seeks to satisfy doesn't ensure that the individual perceives high performance as necessarily leading to the satisfaction of these needs.

Does expectancy theory work? Attempts to validate the theory have been complicated by methodological, criterion and measurement problems. As a result, many published studies that purport to support or negate the theory must be viewed with caution. Importantly, most studies have failed to replicate the methodology as it was originally proposed. For example, the theory proposes to explain different levels of effort from the same person under different circumstances, but almost all replication studies have looked at different people. Correcting for this flaw has greatly improved support for the validity of expectancy theory.[82] Some critics suggest that the theory has only limited use, arguing that it tends to be more valid for predicting in situations in which effort–performance and performance–reward linkages are clearly perceived by the individual.[83] Because few individuals perceive a high correlation between performance and rewards in their jobs, the theory tends to be idealistic. If organisations actually rewarded individuals for performance, rather than according to such criteria as seniority, effort, skill level and job difficulty, then the theory's validity might be considerably greater. However, rather than invalidating expectancy theory, this criticism can be used in support of the theory, because it explains why a significant segment of the workforce exerts low levels of effort in carrying out job responsibilities.

INTEGRATING CONTEMPORARY THEORIES OF MOTIVATION

We have looked at a lot of motivation theories in this chapter. The fact that a number of these theories have been supported only complicates the matter. How simple it would have been if, after presenting half-a-dozen theories, only one was found to be valid. But the theories we presented aren't all in competition with one another. Because one is valid doesn't automatically make the others invalid. In fact, many of the theories presented in this chapter are complementary. The challenge is now to tie these theories together to help you understand their interrelationships.[84]

Figure 6.8 presents a model that integrates much of what we know about motivation. Its basic foundation is the expectancy model shown in Figure 6.7. Let's work through Figure 6.8. (We will look at job design closely in Chapter 7.)

We begin by explicitly recognising that opportunities can either aid or hinder individual effort. The individual effort box also has another arrow leading into it. This arrow flows out of the person's goals. Consistent with goal-setting theory, this goals–effort loop is meant to remind us that goals direct behaviour.

Expectancy theory predicts that employees will exert a high level of effort if they perceive that there is a strong relationship between effort and performance, performance and rewards, and rewards and satisfaction of personal goals. Each of these relationships, in turn, is influenced by certain factors. For effort to lead to good performance, the individual must have the requisite ability to perform, and the performance appraisal system that measures the individual's performance must be perceived as being fair and objective. The performance–reward relationship will be strong if the individual perceives that it is performance (rather than seniority, personal favourites or other criteria) that is rewarded. If cognitive evaluation theory were fully valid in the actual workplace, we would predict here that basing rewards on performance should decrease the individual's intrinsic motivation. The final link in expectancy theory is the rewards–goals relationship.

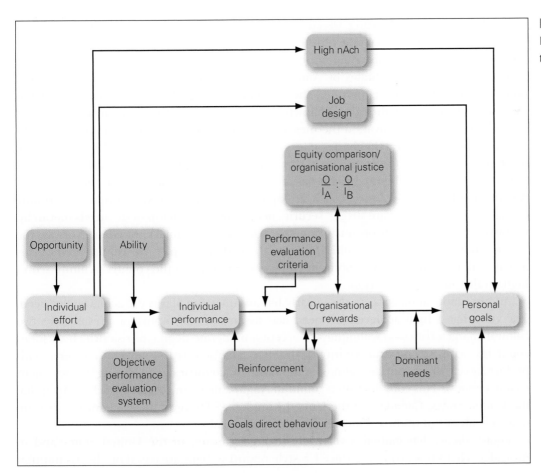

■ FIGURE 6.8
Integrating contemporary theories of motivation

Motivation would be high to the degree that the rewards an individual received for high performance satisfied the dominant needs consistent with individual goals.

A closer look at Figure 6.8 will also reveal that the model considers achievement motivation, reinforcement and organisational justice. The high achiever isn't motivated by the organisation's assessment of performance or organisational rewards; hence the jump from effort to personal goals for those with a high nAch. Remember, high achievers are internally driven as long as the jobs they are doing provide them with personal responsibility, feedback and moderate risks. They aren't concerned with the effort–performance, performance–rewards or rewards–goal linkages.

Reinforcement theory enters our model by recognising that the organisation's rewards reinforce the individual's performance. If management has designed a reward system that is seen by employees as 'paying off' for good performance, the rewards will reinforce and encourage continued good performance. Rewards also play the key part in organisational justice research. Individuals will judge the favourability of their outcomes (for example, their pay) relative to what others receive, but also with respect to how they are treated—when people are disappointed in their rewards, they are likely to be sensitive to the perceived fairness of the procedures used and the consideration given to them by their supervisor.

CAVEAT EMPTOR: MOTIVATION THEORIES ARE OFTEN CULTURE-BOUND

In our discussion of goal setting, we said that care needs to be taken in applying this theory because it assumes cultural characteristics that aren't universal. This is true for many of the theories presented in this chapter, because most current motivation theories were developed in the United States by Americans and are about Americans.[85] For instance, both the goal-setting and expectancy theories emphasise goal accomplishment as well as rational and individual thought—characteristics consistent with American culture. Let's take a look at several motivation theories and consider their cross-cultural transferability.

Maslow's needs hierarchy argues that people start at the physiological level and then move progressively up the hierarchy in this order: physiological, safety, social, esteem and self-actualisation. This hierarchy, if it has any application at all, aligns with Australian and American cultures. In countries such as Japan, Greece and Mexico, where uncertainty avoidance characteristics are strong, security needs would be on top of the needs hierarchy. Countries that score high on nurturing characteristics—Denmark, Sweden, Norway, the Netherlands and Finland—would have social needs on top.[86] We would predict, for instance, that group work will motivate employees more when the country's culture scores high on the nurturing criterion.

Another motivation concept that clearly has an American bias is the achievement need. The view that a high achievement need acts as an internal motivator presupposes two cultural characteristics—a willingness to accept a moderate degree of risk (which excludes countries with strong uncertainty avoidance characteristics) and a concern with performance (which applies almost singularly to countries with strong achievement characteristics). This combination is found in Anglo-American countries such as Australia, the United States, Canada and the United Kingdom.[87] However, these characteristics are relatively absent in countries such as Chile and Portugal.

Equity theory has gained a relatively strong following in the United States and in Australia. That's not surprising since US-style reward systems are based on the assumption that workers are highly sensitive to equity in reward allocations. And in Australia, equity is meant to closely tie pay to performance. However, evidence suggests that in collectivist cultures, especially in the former socialist countries of Central and Eastern Europe, employees expect rewards to reflect their individual needs as well as their performance.[88] Moreover, consistent with a legacy of communism and centrally planned economies, employees exhibited an entitlement attitude—that is, they expected outcomes to be greater than their inputs.[89] These findings suggest that US-style pay practices may need modification, especially in Russia and other former communist countries, in order to be perceived as fair by employees.

But don't assume there are no cross-cultural consistencies. For instance, the desire for interesting work seems important to almost all workers, regardless of their national culture. In a study of seven countries, employees in Belgium, Britain, Israel and the United States ranked 'interesting work' number one among 11 work goals. And this factor was ranked either second or third in Japan, the Netherlands and Germany.[90] Similarly, in a study comparing job-preference outcomes among graduate students in Australia, the United States, Canada and Singapore, growth, achievement and responsibility were rated the top three and had identical rankings.[91] Both of these studies suggest some universality to the importance of intrinsic factors in the two-factor theory.

SUMMARY AND IMPLICATIONS FOR MANAGERS

- The theories we have discussed in this chapter address different outcome variables. Some, for instance, are directed at explaining turnover, while others emphasise productivity. The theories also differ in their predictive strength. In this section, we review the most established motivation theories to determine their relevance in explaining our dependent variables, and assess the predictive power of each.[92]

- None of the four need theories—Maslow's hierarchy, ERG, McClelland's needs and the two-factor theory—has found widespread support. The strongest of these theories is probably McClelland's, particularly regarding the relationship between achievement and productivity.

- In general, need theories (Maslow and ERG) are not very valid explanations of motivation.

- There is little dispute that clear and difficult goals lead to higher levels of employee productivity, leading us to conclude that goal-setting theory provides one of the more powerful explanations of this dependent variable.

- Reinforcement theory has an impressive record for predicting factors such as quality and quantity of work, persistence of effort, absenteeism, tardiness and accident rates.

- However, this theory doesn't offer much insight into employee satisfaction or the decision to quit.

- Equity theory also deals with productivity, satisfaction, absence and turnover variables. However, its strongest legacy probably is that it provided the spark for research on organisational justice, which has more support in the literature.

- Expectancy theory has proved to offer a relatively powerful explanation of employee productivity, absenteeism and turnover.

- But expectancy theory assumes that employees have few constraints on their decision discretion. It makes many of the same assumptions that the rational model makes about individual decision making (see Chapter 5). Moreover, expectancy theory isn't a very good explanation for more typical types of work behaviour, especially for individuals in lower-level jobs, because such jobs come with considerable limitations imposed by work methods, supervisors and company policies. This acts to restrict its applicability.

- We would conclude, therefore, that expectancy theory's power in explaining employee productivity increases when the jobs being performed are more complex and higher in the organisation (where discretion is greater).

POINT / COUNTERPOINT

Money Motivates!

● POINT

Behavioural scientists tend to downplay money as a motivator. They prefer to emphasise the importance of challenging jobs, goals, participative decision making, feedback, recognition, cohesive work teams and other non-monetary factors. We argue otherwise here—that is, money is *the* critical incentive to work motivation.

Money is important to employees because it is a medium of exchange. People may not work *only* for money, but take the money away and how many people would come to work? A study of nearly 2500 employees found that although these people disagreed over what was their number-one motivator, they unanimously chose money as their number two.

As equity theory suggests, money has symbolic value in addition to its exchange value. We use pay as the primary outcome against which we compare our inputs to determine if we are being treated equitably. When an organisation pays one executive $80 000 a year and another $95 000, it means more than the latter's earning $15 000 a year more: it's a message, from the organisation to both employees, of how much it values the contribution of each.

In addition to equity theory, both reinforcement and expectancy theories attest to the value of money as a motivator. In the former, if pay is contingent on performance, it will encourage workers to generate high levels of effort. Consistent with expectancy theory, money will motivate to the extent that it is seen as being able to satisfy an individual's personal goals and is perceived as being dependent on performance criteria.

However, maybe the best case for money is a review of studies that looked at four methods of motivating employee performance: money, goal setting, participative decision making, and redesigning jobs to give workers more challenge and responsibility. The average improvement from motivating with money was consistently higher than with any of the other methods.

● COUNTERPOINT

Money can motivate *some* people under *some* conditions, so the issue isn't really whether or not money can motivate. The answer is: 'It can!' The more relevant question is: 'Does money motivate most employees in the workforce today?' The answer to this question, we propose, is: 'No.'

For money to motivate an individual's performance, certain conditions must be met. First, money must be important to the individual. Yet, money isn't important to everyone. High achievers, for instance, are intrinsically motivated. Money would have little impact on these people.

Second, money must be perceived by the individual as being a direct reward for performance. Unfortunately, performance and pay are poorly linked in most organisations. Pay increases are far more often determined by non-performance factors such as experience, community pay standards or company profitability.

Third, the marginal amount of money offered for the performance must be perceived by the individual as being significant. Research indicates that merit raises must be at least 7 per cent of base pay for employees to perceive them as motivating. Unfortunately, data indicate that average merit increases in recent years have been typically only in the 3.3 to 4.4 per cent range.

Finally, management must have the discretion to reward high performers with more money. Unfortunately, unions and organisational compensation policies constrain managerial discretion. Where unions exist, that discretion is almost zero. In non-unionised environments, traditionally narrow compensation grades create severe restrictions on pay increases. For example, in one organisation, a systems analyst IV's pay grade ranges from $4775 to $5500 a month. No matter how good a job that analyst does, her boss cannot pay more than $5500 a month. Similarly, no matter how poor the performance, the analyst won't earn less than $4775. So, money might be theoretically capable of motivating employee performance, but most managers aren't given enough flexibility to do much about it.

SOURCES: Points in this argument are based on S. Caudron, 'Motivation? Money's Only No. 2', *Industry Week*, 15 November 1993, p. 33; T. R. Mitchell and A. E. Mickel, 'The Meaning of Money: An Individual-Difference Perspective', *Academy of Management Review*, vol. 24, 1999, pp. 568–78; E. A. Locke et al., 'The Relative Effectiveness of Four Methods of Motivating Employee Performance', in K. D. Duncan, M. M. Gruenberg and D. Wallis (eds), *Changes in Working Life* (London: John Wiley & Sons, 1980), pp. 363–83; A. Mitra, N. Gupta and G. D. Jenkins, Jr, 'The Case of the Invisible Merit Raise: How People See Their Pay Raises', *Compensation & Benefits Review*, May–June 1995, pp. 71–76; Hewitt Associates Salary Survey, 2000; and 'Workers Have Little to Cheer With Pay Raises of Only 3.5%', *Wall Street Journal*, 30 July 2003, p. D2.

QUESTIONS FOR REVIEW

1. Does motivation come from within a person, or is it a result of the situation? Explain.
2. What are the implications of Theories X and Y for motivation practices?
3. Compare and contrast Maslow's hierarchy of needs theory with (a) Alderfer's ERG theory and (b) Herzberg's two-factor theory.
4. Describe the three needs isolated by McClelland. How are they related to worker behaviour?
5. Explain cognitive evaluation theory. How applicable is it to management practice?
6. Relate goal-setting theory to the MBO process. How are they similar? Different?
7. What is the role of self-efficacy in goal setting?
8. Contrast distributive and procedural justice. What implications might they have for designing pay systems in different countries?
9. Identify the variables in expectancy theory.

QUESTIONS FOR CRITICAL THINKING

1. 'The cognitive evaluation theory is contradictory to reinforcement and expectancy theories.' Do you agree or disagree? Explain.
2. Analyse the application of Maslow's and Herzberg's theories to a South Pacific nation where more than a quarter of the population is unemployed.
3. Can an individual be too motivated, so that performance declines as a result of excessive effort? Discuss.
4. Identify three activities you really enjoy (for example, playing tennis, reading a novel, going shopping). Next, identify three activities you really dislike (for example, going to the dentist, cleaning the house, staying on a restricted-calorie diet). Using the expectancy model, analyse each of your answers to assess why some activities stimulate your effort while others don't.

Goal-setting Task

Purpose:

This exercise will help you to learn how to write tangible, verifiable, measurable and relevant goals that might evolve from an MBO program.

Time required:

Approximately 20 to 30 minutes.

Participants and roles:

1. Break into groups of three to five.

2. Spend a few minutes discussing your tutor's job. What does he or she do? What defines good performance? What behaviours will lead to good performance?

3. Each group is to develop a list of five goals that, although not established participatively with your tutor, you believe might be developed in an MBO program at your university. Try to select goals that seem most critical to the effective performance of your tutor's job.

4. Each group will select a leader who will share the group's goals with the entire class. For each group's goals, class discussion should focus on their: (a) specificity, (b) ease of measurement, (c) importance, and (d) motivational properties.

ETHICAL DILEMMA

Is Motivation Manipulation?

Managers are interested in the subject of motivation because they are concerned with learning how to get the most effort from their employees. Is this ethical? For example, when managers link rewards to productivity, aren't they manipulating employees?

'To manipulate' is defined as '(1) to handle, manage, or use, especially with skill, in some process of treatment or performance; (2) to manage or influence by artful skill; (3) to adapt or change to suit one's purpose or advantage.' Aren't one or more of these definitions compatible with the notion of managers skilfully seeking to influence employee productivity for the benefit of the manager and the organisation?

Do managers have the right to seek control over their employees? Does anyone, for that matter, have the right to control others? Does control imply manipulation? And is there anything wrong with managers manipulating employees?

6

CASE STUDY

What Motivates Matt?

Matt Jones considers himself to be an average guy: he likes a drink with his mates after work; he works fairly hard at his job most days; and most people seem to get on well with him. But there are two people that drive him crazy—one of his workmates, and his boss.

Matt is a management consultant at a small, but successful, consulting company. He works in a team of five people on projects ranging from managing change to leadership interventions. Like most people, Matt gets along with most of his team and has good relationships with them. Except for Jack Singleton.

Jack is very different from Matt. Where Matt prefers to wear Hawaiian shirts to work, Jack prefers to wear a tailored suit; where Matt will leave early on a Friday afternoon to have a beer at the pub, Jack will go for a drink at a wine bar in the trendy part of the city; where Matt gets excited about working on projects that he feels passionate about, Jack gets excited about working on projects that are highly paid or that will lead to power or promotion. Jack thinks that Matt is lazy, unmotivated and will go nowhere. Matt thinks that Jack is manipulative, power-hungry and Machiavellian. Matt's impression of Jack isn't helped by the fact that he knows that Jack earns more than he does. In a recent interview, Matt said, 'You know, I tell myself that money isn't important; that that's not why I'm doing this job. But, when I found out that he was earning more than me, well, it really made me mad. Then again, I guess, at least I know that if I get a raise then I earned it—he just manipulates people to get what he wants. I wouldn't want to be like that for all the money in the world.'

The person that Matt believes Jack is manipulating is their boss, Peter Finch. Peter is a senior consultant and has been with the company for over 12 years. Peter admires Jack's ambitious get-up-and-go, and wishes that Matt could have a little more ambition as well.

The day came when Peter had to give Matt his performance appraisal. Neither of them had been looking forward to it: Peter doesn't like conflict and Matt doesn't like performance appraisals. Here is what Matt had to say about the appraisal:

'I hate these reviews—they never get at the "real" stuff that I do. I mean, I work like a dog for my clients, and they tend to be pretty happy most of the time, but Peter just looks at the money. I cost too much and don't bring in enough extra money. I don't flatter the clients or tell them they need additional things when they don't. And that's what gets you good performance reviews around here. So I figure, what's the point? If I'm not going to get recognised for my hard work, why should I bother?

'But, of course, I couldn't get out of it. So we started talking about what I'd been doing this year, how I thought I'd gone, where I thought I'd done well, and what I thought I could improve on. And actually, it wasn't nearly as bad as I thought it was going to be. We spent most of the time talking about what I wanted to do next year and how we could make it happen. We decided that I would take the lead on a couple of big client contracts (rather than just leading the smaller ones) and that I was to get high customer satisfaction ratings from those contracts. At first, he wanted to include getting lots of money in my list of goals, but I'm just not in it for the money, I'm in it to help people. So we settled on the customer satisfaction ratings. It is going to be hard getting good ratings, particularly on the big projects where there's a million and one stakeholders who all want different outcomes, but hey, it's worth giving it a shot.'

QUESTIONS
1. Analyse Matt's motivation using needs theory, equity theory, expectancy theory and goal-setting theory.
2. If you were Peter Finch, what would you do to make sure that Matt was motivated?
3. If you were Matt, how would you deal with Jack Singleton to make sure that your feelings towards him didn't affect your work? How might you keep yourself motivated?

ENDNOTES

1. *George Negus Tonight* profiles Kylie Kwong, broadcast 6.30 pm on 11 November 2004, Australian Broadcasting Corporation. Transcript of interview: <www.abc.net.au/gnt/profiles/Transcripts/s1242188.htm> (accessed 1 September 2006).

2. C. A. O'Reilly III, 'Organizational Behavior: Where We've Been, Where We're Going', in M. R. Rosenzweig and L. W. Porter (eds), *Annual Review of Psychology*, vol. 42 (Palo Alto, CA: Annual Reviews, Inc., 1991), p. 431. See also M. L. Ambrose and C. T. Kulik, 'Old Friends, New Faces: Motivation Research in the 1990s', *Journal of Management*, vol. 25, no. 3, 1999, pp. 231–92.

3. 'Disengaged Workers Cost Australia Billions', Australian Associated Press Financial News Wire, 1 April 2005.

4. See, for instance, T. R. Mitchell, 'Matching Motivational Strategies with Organizational Contexts', in L. L. Cummings and B. M. Staw (eds), *Research in Organizational Behavior*, vol. 19 (Greenwich, CT: JAI Press, 1997), pp. 60–62.

5. A. Maslow, *Motivation and Personality* (New York: Harper & Row, 1954).

6. See, for example, E. E. Lawler III and J. L. Suttle, 'A Causal Correlation Test of the Need Hierarchy Concept', *Organizational Behavior and Human Performance*, April 1972, pp. 265–87; D. T. Hall and K. E. Nougaim, 'An Examination of Maslow's Need Hierarchy in an Organizational Setting', *Organizational Behavior and Human Performance*, February 1968, pp. 12–35; A. K. Korman, J. H. Greenhaus and I. J. Badin, 'Personnel Attitudes and Motivation', in M. R. Rosenzweig and L. W. Porter (eds), *Annual Review of Psychology* (Palo Alto, CA: Annual Reviews, 1977), pp. 178–79; and J. Rauschenberger, N. Schmitt and J. E. Hunter, 'A Test of the Need Hierarchy Concept by a Markov Model of Change in Need Strength', *Administrative Science Quarterly*, December 1980, pp. 654–70.

7. C. P. Alderfer, 'An Empirical Test of a New Theory of Human Needs', *Organizational Behavior and Human Performance*, May 1969, pp. 142–75.

8. C. P. Schneider and C. P. Alderfer, 'Three Studies of Measures of Need Satisfaction in Organizations', *Administrative Science Quarterly*, December 1973, pp. 489–505; and I. Borg and M. Braun, 'Work Values in East and West Germany: Different Weights, But Identical Structures', *Journal of Organizational Behavior*, vol. 17, special issue, 1996, pp. 541–55.

9. M. A. Wahba and L. G. Bridwell, 'Maslow Reconsidered: A Review of Research on the Need Hierarchy Theory', *Organizational Behavior and Human Performance*, April 1976, pp. 212–40.

10. D. McGregor, *The Human Side of Enterprise* (New York: McGraw-Hill, 1960). For an updated analysis of Theory X and Theory Y constructs, see R. J. Summers and S. F. Cronshaw, 'A Study of McGregor's Theory X, Theory Y and the Influence of Theory X, Theory Y Assumptions on Causal Attributions for Instances of Worker Poor Performance', in S. L. McShane (ed.), *Organizational Behavior*, ASAC 1988 Conference Proceedings, vol. 9, Part 5 (Halifax, Nova Scotia, 1988), pp. 115–23.

11. F. Herzberg, B. Mausner and B. Snyderman, *The Motivation to Work* (New York: John Wiley & Sons, 1959).

12. R. J. House and L. A. Wigdor, 'Herzberg's Dual-Factor Theory of Job Satisfaction and Motivations: A Review of the Evidence and Criticism', *Personnel Psychology*, Winter 1967, pp. 369–89; D. P. Schwab and L. L. Cummings, 'Theories of Performance and Satisfaction: A Review', *Industrial Relations*, October 1970, pp. 403–30; R. J. Caston and R. Braito, 'A Specification Issue in Job Satisfaction Research', *Sociological Perspectives*, April 1985, pp. 175–97; and J. Phillipchuk and J. Whittaker, 'An Inquiry into the Continuing Relevance of Herzberg's Motivation Theory', *Engineering Management Journal*, vol. 8, 1996, pp. 15–20.

13. D. C. McClelland, W. Atkinson and J. O. Raynor, *Motivation and Achievement* (Washington, DC: Winston, 1974); D. C. McClelland, *Power: The Inner Experience* (New York: Irvington, 1975); and M. J. Stahl, *Managerial and Technical Motivation: Assessing Needs for Achievement, Power, and Affiliation* (New York: Praeger, 1986).

14. D. C. McClelland, *The Achieving Society* (Princeton, NJ: D. Van Nostrand, 1961).

15. D. C. McClelland and D. G. Winter, *Motivating Economic Achievement* (New York: Free Press, 1969); and J. B. Miner, N. R. Smith and J. S. Bracker, 'Role of Entrepreneurial Task Motivation in the Growth of Technologically Innovative Firms: Interpretations from Follow-up Data', *Journal of Applied Psychology*, October 1994, pp. 627–30.

16. J. Langan-Fox and S. Roth, 'Achievement Motivation and Female Entrepreneurs', *Journal of Occupational and Organizational Psychology*, vol. 68, no. 3, September 1995, pp. 209–18.

17. C. Orpen, 'The Multifactorial Achievement Scale as a Predictor of Salary Growth and Motivation among Middle-Managers', *Social Behavior and Personality*, vol. 23, no. 2, 1995, pp. 159–62.

18. McClelland, *Power*; D. C. McClelland and D. H. Burnham, 'Power is the Great Motivator', *Harvard Business Review*, March–April 1976, pp. 100–10; and R. E. Boyatzis, 'The Need for Close Relationships and the Manager's Job', in D. A. Kolb, I. M. Rubin and J. M. McIntyre, *Organizational Psychology: Readings on Human Behavior in Organizations*, 4th ed. (Upper Saddle River, NJ: Prentice Hall, 1984), pp. 81–86.

19. D. G. Winter, 'The Motivational Dimensions of Leadership: Power, Achievement, and Affiliation', in R. E. Riggio, S. E. Murphy and F. J. Pirozzolo (eds), *Multiple Intelligences and Leadership* (Mahwah, NJ: Lawrence Erlbaum, 2002), pp. 119–38.

20. J. B. Miner, *Studies in Management Education* (New York: Springer, 1965).

21. D. Kipnis, 'The Powerholder', in J. T. Tedeschi (ed.), *Perspectives in Social Power* (Chicago: Aldine, 1974), pp. 82–123.

22. D. C. McClelland, 'Toward a Theory of Motive Acquisition', *American Psychologist*, May 1965, pp. 321–33; and D. Miron and D. C. McClelland, 'The Impact of Achievement Motivation Training on Small Businesses', *California Management Review*, Summer 1979, pp. 13–28.

23. T. M. Amabile, *Creativity in Context: Update to the Social Psychology of Creativity* (Boulder, CO: Westview Press, 1996).

24. R. de Charms, *Personal Causation: The Internal Affective Determinants of Behavior* (New York: Academic Press, 1968).

25. E. L. Deci, *Intrinsic Motivation* (New York: Plenum, 1975); J. Cameron and W. D. Pierce, 'Reinforcement, Reward, and Intrinsic Motivation: A Meta-Analysis', *Review of Educational Research*, Fall 1994,

pp. 363–423; S. Tang and V. C. Hall, 'The Overjustification Effect: A Meta-Analysis', *Applied Cognitive Psychology*, October 1995, pp. 365–404; E. L. Deci, R. Koestner and R. M. Ryan, 'A Meta-Analytic Review of Experiments Examining the Effects of Extrinsic Rewards on Intrinsic Motivation', *Psychological Bulletin*, vol. 125, no. 6, 1999, pp. 627–68; R. M. Ryan and E. L. Deci, 'Intrinsic and Extrinsic Motivations: Classic Definitions and New Directions', *Contemporary Educational Psychology*, January 2000, pp. 54–67; and N. Houlfort, R. Koestner, M. Joussemet, A. Nantel-Vivier and N. Lekes, 'The Impact of Performance-Contingent Rewards on Perceived Autonomy and Competence', *Motivation & Emotion*, vol. 26, no. 4, 2002, pp. 279–95.

26. W. E. Scott, 'The Effects of Extrinsic Rewards on "Intrinsic Motivation": A Critique', *Organizational Behavior and Human Performance*, February 1976, pp. 117–19; B. J. Calder and B. M. Staw, 'Interaction of Intrinsic and Extrinsic Motivation: Some Methodological Notes', *Journal of Personality and Social Psychology*, January 1975, pp. 76–80; and K. B. Boal and L. L. Cummings, 'Cognitive Evaluation Theory: An Experimental Test of Processes and Outcomes', *Organizational Behavior and Human Performance*, December 1981, pp. 289–310.

27. G. R. Salancik, 'Interaction Effects of Performance and Money on Self-Perception of Intrinsic Motivation', *Organizational Behavior and Human Performance*, June 1975, pp. 339–51; and F. Luthans, M. Martinko and T. Kess, 'An Analysis of the Impact of Contingency Monetary Rewards on Intrinsic Motivation', *Proceedings of the Nineteenth Annual Midwest Academy of Management* (St. Louis, MO: 1976), pp. 209–21.

28. Deci, Koestner and Ryan, 'A Meta-Analytic Review of Experiments Examining the Effects of Extrinsic Rewards on Intrinsic Motivation'.

29. K. M. Sheldon, A. J. Elliot and R. M. Ryan, 'Self-Concordance and Subjective Well-Being in Four Cultures', *Journal of Cross-Cultural Psychology*, vol. 35, no. 2, 2004, pp. 209–23.

30. J. E. Bono and T. A. Judge, 'Self-Concordance at Work: Toward Understanding the Motivational Effects of Transformational Leaders', *Academy of Management Journal*, vol. 46, no. 5, 2003, pp. 554–71.

31. J. P. Meyer, T. E. Becker and C. Vandenberghe, 'Employee Commitment and Motivation: A Conceptual Analysis and Integrative Model', *Journal of Applied Psychology*, vol. 89, no. 6, 2004, pp. 991–1007.

32. E. A. Locke, 'Toward a Theory of Task Motivation and Incentives', *Organizational Behavior and Human Performance*, May 1968, pp. 157–89.

33. P. C. Earley, P. Wojnaroski and W. Prest, 'Task Planning and Energy Expended: Exploration of How Goals Influence Performance', *Journal of Applied Psychology*, February 1987, pp. 107–14.

34. See, for instance, E. A. Locke, K. N. Shaw, L. M. Saari and G. P. Latham, 'Goal Setting and Task Performance', *Psychological Bulletin*, January 1981, pp. 125–52; A. J. Mento, R. P. Steel and R. J. Karren, 'A Meta-Analytic Study of the Effects of Goal Setting on Task Performance: 1966–1984', *Organizational Behavior and Human Decision Processes*, February 1987, pp. 52–83; M. E. Tubbs, 'Goal Setting: A Meta-Analytic Examination of the Empirical Evidence', *Journal of Applied Psychology*, August 1986, pp. 474–83; E. A. Locke and G. P. Latham, *A Theory of Goal Setting and Task Performance* (Upper Saddle River, NJ: Prentice Hall, 1990); E. A. Locke and G. P. Latham, 'Building a Practically Useful Theory of Goal Setting and Task Motivation', *American Psychologist*, September 2002, pp. 705–17; and R. P. DeShon, S. W. Kozlowski, A. M. Schmidt, K. R. Milner and D. Wiechmann, 'A Multiple-Goal, Multilevel Model of Feedback Effects on the Regulation of Individual and Team Performance', *Journal of Applied Psychology*, vol. 89, no. 6, 2004, pp. 1035–56.

35. E. A. Locke and G. P. Latham, 'Building a Practically Useful Theory of Goal Setting and Task Motivation: A 35-Year Odyssey', *American Psychologist*, vol. 57, no. 9, 2002, pp. 705–17.

36. J. M. Ivancevich and J. T. McMahon, 'The Effects of Goal Setting, External Feedback, and Self-Generated Feedback on Outcome Variables: A Field Experiment', *Academy of Management Journal*, June 1982, pp. 359–72; and E. A. Locke, 'Motivation through Conscious Goal Setting', *Applied and Preventive Psychology*, vol. 5, 1996, pp. 117–24.

37. See, for example, G. P. Latham, M. Erez and E. A. Locke, 'Resolving Scientific Disputes by the Joint Design of Crucial Experiments by the Antagonists: Application to the Erez–Latham Dispute Regarding Participation in Goal Setting', *Journal of Applied Psychology*, November 1988, pp. 753–72; T. D. Ludwig and E. S. Geller, 'Assigned versus Participative Goal Setting and Response Generalization: Managing Injury Control among Professional Pizza Deliverers', *Journal of Applied Psychology*, April 1997, pp. 253–61; and S. G. Harkins and M. D. Lowe, 'The Effects of Self-Set Goals on Task Performance', *Journal of Applied Social Psychology*, January 2000, pp. 1–40.

38. M. Erez, P. C. Earley and C. L. Hulin, 'The Impact of Participation on Goal Acceptance and Performance: A Two-Step Model', *Academy of Management Journal*, March 1985, pp. 50–66.

39. E. A. Locke, 'The Motivation to Work: What We Know', *Advances in Motivation and Achievement*, vol. 10, 1997, pp. 375–412; Latham, Erez and Locke, 'Resolving Scientific Disputes by the Joint Design of Crucial Experiments by the Antagonists', pp. 753–72.

40. H. Lingard, G. Gilbert and P. Graham, 'Improving Solid Waste Reduction and Recycling Performance Using Goal Setting and Feedback', *Construction Management and Economics*, December 2001, pp. 809–17.

41. J. R. Hollenbeck, C. R. Williams and H. J. Klein, 'An Empirical Examination of the Antecedents of Commitment to Difficult Goals', *Journal of Applied Psychology*, February 1989, pp. 18–23. See also J. C. Wofford, V. L. Goodwin and S. Premack, 'Meta-Analysis of the Antecedents of Personal Goal Level and of the Antecedents and Consequences of Goal Commitment', *Journal of Management*, September 1992, pp. 595–615; M. E. Tubbs, 'Commitment as a Moderator of the Goal-Performance Relation: A Case for Clearer Construct Definition', *Journal of Applied Psychology*, February 1993, pp. 86–97; and J. E. Bono and A. E. Colbert, 'Understanding Responses to Multi-Source Feedback: The Role of Core Self-Evaluations', *Personnel Psychology*, Spring 2005, pp. 171–203.

42. See R. E. Wood, A. J. Mento and E. A. Locke, 'Task Complexity as a Moderator of Goal Effects: A Meta Analysis', *Journal of Applied Psychology*, August 1987, pp. 416–25; R. Kanfer and P. L. Ackerman, 'Motivation and Cognitive Abilities: An Integrative/Aptitude-Treatment Interaction Approach to Skill Acquisition', *Journal of Applied Psychology* (monograph), vol. 74, 1989, pp. 657–90; T. R. Mitchell and W. S. Silver, 'Individual and Group Goals When Workers Are Interdependent:

Effects on Task Strategies and Performance', *Journal of Applied Psychology*, April 1990, pp. 185–93; and A. M. O'Leary-Kelly, J. J. Martocchio and D. D. Frink, 'A Review of the Influence of Group Goals on Group Performance', *Academy of Management Journal*, October 1994, pp. 1285–301.

43. S. Niles, 'Achievement Goals and Means: A Cultural Comparison', *Journal of Cross-Cultural Psychology*, vol. 29, no. 5, September 1998, pp. 656–67.

44. E. O. Welles, 'Great Expectations', *INC.*, March 2001, pp. 68–73.

45. See, for instance, S. J. Carroll and H. L. Tosi, *Management by Objectives: Applications and Research* (New York, Macmillan, 1973); and R. Rodgers and J. E. Hunter, 'Impact of Management by Objectives on Organizational Productivity', *Journal of Applied Psychology*, April 1991, pp. 322–36.

46. See, for instance, R. C. Ford, F. S. MacLaughlin and J. Nixdorf, 'Ten Questions about MBO', *California Management Review*, Winter 1980, p. 89; T. J. Collamore, 'Making MBO Work in the Public Sector', *Bureaucrat*, Fall 1989, pp. 37–40; G. Dabbs, 'Nonprofit Businesses in the 1990s: Models for Success', *Business Horizons*, September–October 1991, pp. 68–71; R. Rodgers and J. E. Hunter, 'A Foundation of Good Management Practice in Government: Management by Objectives', *Public Administration Review*, January–February 1992, pp. 27–39; T. H. Poister and G. Streib, 'MBO in Municipal Government: Variations on a Traditional Management Tool', *Public Administration Review*, January/February 1995, pp. 48–56; and C. Garvey, 'Goalsharing Scores', *Human Resources*, April 2000, pp. 99–106.

47. See, for instance, C. H. Ford, 'MBO: An Idea Whose Time Has Gone?', *Business Horizons*, December 1979, p. 49; R. Rodgers and J. E. Hunter, 'Impact of Management by Objectives on Organizational Productivity', *Journal of Applied Psychology*, April 1991, pp. 322–36; R. Rodgers, J. E. Hunter and D. L. Rogers, 'Influence of Top Management Commitment on Management Program Success', *Journal of Applied Psychology*, February 1993, pp. 151–55; and M. Tanikawa, 'Fujitsu Decides to Backtrack on Performance-Based Pay', *New York Times*, 22 March 2001, p. W1.

48. A. Bandura, *Self-Efficacy: The Exercise of Control* (New York: Freeman, 1997).

49. A. D. Stajkovic and F. Luthans, 'Self-Efficacy and Work-Related Performance: A Meta-Analysis', *Psychological Bulletin*, September 1998, pp. 240–61; and A. Bandura, 'Cultivate Self-Efficacy for Personal and Organizational Effectiveness', in E. Locke (ed.), *Handbook of Principles of Organizational Behavior* (Malden, MA: Blackwell, 2004), pp. 120–36.

50. A. Bandura and D. Cervone, 'Differential Engagement in Self-Reactive Influences in Cognitively-Based Motivation', *Organizational Behavior and Human Decision Processes*, August 1986, pp. 92–113.

51. S. T. Burke and P. Jin, 'Predicting Performance from a Triathlon Event', *Journal of Sport Behavior*, vol. 19, no. 4, December 1996, pp. 272–87.

52. Bandura, *Self-Efficacy: The Exercise of Control*.

53. C. L. Holladay and M. A. Quiñones, 'Practice Variability and Transfer of Training: The Role of Self-Efficacy Generality', *Journal of Applied Psychology*, vol. 88, no. 6, 2003, pp. 1094–103.

54. R. C. Rist, 'Student Social Class and Teacher Expectations: The Self-Fulfilling Prophecy in Ghetto Education', *Harvard Educational Review*, vol. 70, no. 3, 2000, pp. 266–301.

55. D. Eden, 'Self-Fulfilling Prophecies in Organizations', in J. Greenberg (ed.), *Organizational Behavior: The State of the Science*, 2nd ed. (Mahwah, NJ: Erlbaum, 2003), pp. 91–122.

56. Ibid.

57. T. A. Judge, C. L. Jackson, J. C. Shaw, B. Scott and B. L. Rich, 'Is the Effect of Self-Efficacy on Job/Task Performance an Epiphenomenon?', Working paper, University of Florida, 2005.

58. Ibid.

59. J. L. Komaki, T. Coombs and S. Schepman, 'Motivational Implications of Reinforcement Theory', in R. M. Steers, L. W. Porter and G. Bigley (eds), *Motivation and Work Behavior*, 6th ed. (New York: McGraw-Hill, 1996), pp. 87–107.

60. E. A. Locke, 'Latham vs. Komaki: A Tale of Two Paradigms', *Journal of Applied Psychology*, February 1980, pp. 16–23.

61. J. S. Adams, 'Inequity in Social Exchanges', in L. Berkowitz (ed.), *Advances in Experimental Social Psychology* (New York: Academic Press, 1965), pp. 267–300.

62. P. S. Goodman, 'An Examination of Referents Used in the Evaluation of Pay', *Organizational Behavior and Human Performance*, October 1974, pp. 170–95; S. Ronen, 'Equity Perception in Multiple Comparisons: A Field Study', *Human Relations*, April 1986, pp. 333–46; R. W. Scholl, E. A. Cooper and J. F. McKenna, 'Referent Selection in Determining Equity Perception: Differential Effects on Behavioral and Attitudinal Outcomes', *Personnel Psychology*, Spring 1987, pp. 113–27; and T. P. Summers and A. S. DeNisi, 'In Search of Adams' Other: Reexamination of Referents Used in the Evaluation of Pay', *Human Relations*, June 1990, pp. 497–511.

63. C. T. Kulik and M. L. Ambrose, 'Personal and Situational Determinants of Referent Choice', *Academy of Management Review*, April 1992, pp. 212–37.

64. C. Ostroff and L. E. Atwater, 'Does Whom You Work with Matter? Effects of Referent Group Gender and Age Composition on Managers' Compensation', *Journal of Applied Psychology*, vol. 88, no. 4, 2003, pp. 725–40.

65. Ibid.

66. See, for example, E. Walster, G. W. Walster and W. G. Scott, *Equity: Theory and Research* (Boston: Allyn & Bacon, 1978); and J. Greenberg, 'Cognitive Reevaluation of Outcomes in Response to Underpayment Inequity', *Academy of Management Journal*, March 1989, pp. 174–84.

67. P. S. Goodman and A. Friedman, 'An Examination of Adams' Theory of Inequity', *Administrative Science Quarterly*, September 1971, pp. 271–88; R. P. Vecchio, 'An Individual-Differences Interpretation of the Conflicting Predictions Generated by Equity Theory and Expectancy Theory', *Journal of Applied Psychology*, August 1981, pp. 470–81; J. Greenberg, 'Approaching Equity and Avoiding Inequity in Groups and Organizations', in J. Greenberg and R. L. Cohen (eds), *Equity and Justice in Social Behavior* (New York: Academic Press, 1982), pp. 389–435; R. T. Mowday, 'Equity Theory Predictions of Behavior in Organizations', in R. Steers, L. W. Porter and G. Bigley (eds), *Motivation and Work Behavior*, 6th ed. (New York: McGraw-Hill, 1996), pp. 111–31; S. Werner and N. P. Mero, 'Fair or Foul? The Effects of External, Internal, and Employee Equity on Changes in Performance of Major League Baseball Players', *Human Relations*, October 1999, pp. 1291–312; R. W. Griffeth and S. Gaertner, 'A Role for Equity Theory in the Turnover Process: An Empirical Test', *Journal of Applied Social*

Psychology, May 2001, pp. 1017–37; and
L. K. Scheer, N. Kumar and J.-B. E. M.
Steenkamp, 'Reactions to Perceived
Inequity in U.S. and Dutch
Interorganizational Relationships',
Academy of Management, vol. 46, no. 3,
2003, pp. 303–16.

68. See, for example, R. C. Huseman,
J. D. Hatfield and E. W. Miles, 'A New
Perspective on Equity Theory: The Equity
Sensitivity Construct', *Academy of
Management Journal*, April 1987, pp.
222–34; K. S. Sauley and A. G. Bedeian,
'Equity Sensitivity: Construction of a
Measure and Examination of Its
Psychometric Properties', *Journal of
Management*, vol. 26, no. 5, 2000,
pp. 885–910; M. N. Bing and S. M.
Burroughs, 'The Predictive and Interactive
Effects of Equity Sensitivity in Teamwork-
Oriented Organizations', *Journal of
Organizational Behavior*, May 2001,
pp. 271–90; and J. A. Colquitt, 'Does the
Justice of One Interact With the Justice of
Many? Reactions to Procedural Justice in
Teams', *Journal of Applied Psychology*,
vol. 89, no. 4, 2004, pp. 633–46.

69. J. Greenberg and S. Ornstein, 'High Status
Job Title as Compensation for
Underpayment: A Test of Equity Theory',
Journal of Applied Psychology, May 1983,
pp. 285–97; and J. Greenberg, 'Equity
and Workplace Status: A Field
Experiment', *Journal of Applied
Psychology*, November 1988, pp. 606–13.

70. See, for instance, J. Greenberg, *The Quest
for Justice on the Job* (Thousand Oaks, CA:
Sage, 1996); R. Cropanzano and J.
Greenberg, 'Progress in Organizational
Justice: Tunneling through the Maze', in
C. L. Cooper and I. T. Robertson (eds),
*International Review of Industrial and
Organizational Psychology*, vol. 12 (New
York: John Wiley & Sons, 1997);
J. A. Colquitt, D. E. Conlon, M. J. Wesson,
C. O. L. H. Porter and K. Y. Ng, 'Justice at
the Millennium: A Meta-Analytic Review
of the 25 Years of Organizational Justice
Research', *Journal of Applied Psychology*,
June 2001, pp. 425–45; T. Simons and
Q. Roberson, 'Why Managers Should Care
about Fairness: The Effects of Aggregate
Justice Perceptions on Organizational
Outcomes', *Journal of Applied Psychology*,
June 2003, pp. 432–43; and G. P. Latham
and C. C. Pinder, 'Work Motivation
Theory and Research at the Dawn of the
Twenty-First Century', *Annual Review of
Psychology*, vol. 56, 2005, pp. 485–516.

71. K. Leung, K. Tong and S. S. Ho, 'Effects of
Interactional Justice on Egocentric Bias in

Resource Allocation Decisions', *Journal of
Applied Psychology*, vol. 89, no. 3, 2004,
pp. 405–15.

72. 'Americans Feel They Pay Fair Share of
Taxes, Says Poll', NewsTarget.com, 2 May
2005: <www.newstarget.com/007297.
html>.

73. G. S. Leventhal, 'What Should Be Done
with Equity Theory? New Approaches to
the Study of Fairness in Social
Relationships', in K. Gergen,
M. Greenberg and R. Willis (eds), *Social
Exchange: Advances in Theory and
Research* (New York: Plenum, 1980),
pp. 27–55.

74. J. C. Shaw, E. Wild and J. A. Colquitt, 'To
Justify or Excuse?: A Meta-Analytic Review
of the Effects of Explanations', *Journal of
Applied Psychology*, vol. 88, no. 3, 2003,
pp. 444–58.

75. D. P. Skarlicki and R. Folger, 'Retaliation in
4the Workplace: The Roles of Distributive,
Procedural, and Interactional Justice',
Journal of Applied Psychology, vol. 82,
no. 3, 1997, pp. 434–43.

76. R. Cropanzano, C. A. Prehar and P. Y.
Chen, 'Using Social Exchange Theory to
Distinguish Procedural from Interactional
Justice', *Group & Organization
Management*, vol. 27, no. 3, 2002,
pp. 324–51.

77. Colquitt, Conlon, Wesson, Porter and
Ng, 'Justice at the Millennium: A
Meta-Analytic Review of the 25 Years of
Organizational Justice Research'.

78. P. S. Goodman, 'Social Comparison
Process in Organizations', in B. M. Staw
and G. R. Salancik (eds), *New Directions
in Organizational Behavior* (Chicago:
St. Clair, 1977), pp. 97–132; and
J. Greenberg, 'A Taxonomy of
Organizational Justice Theories',
Academy of Management Review,
January 1987, pp. 9–22.

79. V. H. Vroom, *Work and Motivation*
(New York: John Wiley & Sons, 1964).

80. For criticism, see H. G. Heneman III and
D. P. Schwab, 'Evaluation of Research on
Expectancy Theory Prediction of
Employee Performance', *Psychological
Bulletin*, July 1972, pp. 1–9; T. R. Mitchell,
'Expectancy Models of Job Satisfaction,
Occupational Preference and Effort:
A Theoretical, Methodological and
Empirical Appraisal', *Psychological
Bulletin*, November 1974, pp. 1053–77;
L. Reinharth and M. A. Wahba,
'Expectancy Theory as a Predictor of Work
Motivation, Effort Expenditure, and Job
Performance', *Academy of Management
Journal*, September 1975, pp. 502–37;

and W. Van Eerde and H. Thierry,
'Vroom's Expectancy Models and Work-
Related Criteria: A Meta-Analysis', *Journal
of Applied Psychology*, October 1996,
pp. 575–86. For support, see L. W. Porter
and E. E. Lawler III, *Managerial Attitudes
and Performance* (Homewood, IL: Irwin,
1968); D. F. Parker and L. Dyer,
'Expectancy Theory as a Within-Person
Behavioral Choice Model: An Empirical
Test of Some Conceptual and
Methodological Refinements',
*Organizational Behavior and Human
Performance*, October 1976, pp. 97–117;
H. J. Arnold, 'A Test of the Multiplicative
Hypothesis of Expectancy-Valence
Theories of Work Motivation', *Academy of
Management Journal*, April 1981,
pp. 128–41; and J. J. Donovan, 'Work
Motivation', in N. Anderson et al. (eds),
*Handbook of Industrial, Work &
Organizational Psychology*, vol. 2
(Thousand Oaks, CA: Sage, 2001),
pp. 56–59.

81. Vroom refers to these three variables as
expectancy, instrumentality and valence,
respectively.

82. P. M. Muchinsky, 'A Comparison of Within-
and Across-Subjects Analyses of the
Expectancy-Valence Model for Predicting
Effort', *Academy of Management Journal*,
March 1977, pp. 154–58; and
C. W. Kennedy, J. A. Fossum and
B. J. White, 'An Empirical Comparison of
Within-Subjects and Between-Subjects
Expectancy Theory Models',
*Organizational Behavior and Human
Decision Process*, August 1983, pp.
124–43.

83. R. J. House, H. J. Shapiro and M. A.
Wahba, 'Expectancy Theory as a Predictor
of Work Behavior and Attitudes: A
Re-evaluation of Empirical Evidence',
Decision Sciences, January 1974,
pp. 481–506.

84. For other examples of models that seek
to integrate motivation theories, see
H. J. Klein, 'An Integrated Control Theory
Model of Work Motivation', *Academy
of Management Review*, April 1989,
pp. 150–72; E. A. Locke, 'The Motivation
Sequence, the Motivation Hub, and the
Motivation Core', *Organizational Behavior
and Human Decision Processes*,
December 1991, pp. 288–99; and
T. R. Mitchell, 'Matching Motivational
Strategies with Organizational Contexts',
in L. L. Cummings and B. M. Staw (eds),
Research in Organizational Behavior,
vol. 19 (Greenwich, CT: JAI Press,
1997).

85. N. J. Adler, *International Dimensions of Organizational Behavior*, 4th ed. (Cincinnati, OH: Southwestern, 2002), p. 174.

86. G. Hofstede, 'Motivation, Leadership, and Organization: Do American Theories Apply Abroad?', *Organizational Dynamics*, Summer 1980, p. 55.

87. Ibid.

88. J. K. Giacobbe-Miller, D. J. Miller and V. I. Victorov, 'A Comparison of Russian and U.S. Pay Allocation Decisions, Distributive Justice Judgments, and Productivity under Different Payment Conditions', *Personnel Psychology*, Spring 1998, pp. 137–63.

89. S. L. Mueller and L. D. Clarke, 'Political–Economic Context and Sensitivity to Equity: Differences between the United States and the Transition Economies of Central and Eastern Europe', *Academy of Management Journal*, June 1998, pp. 319–29.

90. I. Harpaz, 'The Importance of Work Goals: An International Perspective', *Journal of International Business Studies*, First Quarter 1990, pp. 75–93.

91. G. E. Popp, H. J. Davis and T. T. Herbert, 'An International Study of Intrinsic Motivation Composition', *Management International Review*, January 1986, pp. 28–35.

92. This section is based on F. J. Landy and W. S. Becker, 'Motivation Theory Reconsidered', in L. L. Cummings and B. M. Staw (eds), *Research in Organizational Behavior*, vol. 9 (Greenwich, CT: JAI Press, 1987), pp. 24–35.

7

MOTIVATION: FROM CONCEPTS TO APPLICATIONS

CHAPTER OUTLINE

MOTIVATING BY CHANGING THE NATURE OF THE WORK ENVIRONMENT

EMPLOYEE INVOLVEMENT

REWARDING EMPLOYEES

LEARNING OBJECTIVES

AFTER STUDYING THIS CHAPTER, YOU SHOULD BE ABLE TO:

1. DISCUSS THE WAYS IN WHICH EMPLOYEES CAN BE MOTIVATED BY CHANGING THE WORK ENVIRONMENT

2. EXPLAIN WHY MANAGERS MIGHT WANT TO USE EMPLOYEE INVOLVEMENT PROGRAMS

3. DISCUSS HOW THE DIFFERENT TYPES OF VARIABLE-PAY PROGRAMS CAN INCREASE EMPLOYEE MOTIVATION

4. DESCRIBE THE LINK BETWEEN SKILL-BASED PAY PLANS AND MOTIVATION THEORIES

5. EXPLAIN HOW FLEXIBLE BENEFITS TURN BENEFITS INTO MOTIVATORS

The travel industry is not all glamour and excitement—motivating employees who work in mundane positions is a crucial part of organisational success.

THE TRAVEL AGENCY BUSINESS is notoriously tough and competitive. Increasing fuel costs have impacted travel costs, and terrorist threats have made long-distance travel a less attractive option to a security wary public. The advent of internet booking services also means that traditional travel agencies have had to fight to stay competitive. However, in such a hostile environment, the fight for market share isn't won simply by providing the cheapest travel options possible to consumers. According to Flight Centre, the human factor in the transaction is also a critical part of any success strategy. So, Flight Centre is an employer that offers its staff a range of incentives, rewards and opportunities.

Pay for performance is a critical part of the packages offered to employees. According to the Flight Centre website, 'No one works on a flat salary here and we truly believe "What gets rewarded gets done."' Staff have access to training opportunities through the company's internal leadership development program. In Australia, more formal credentials can be acquired through Flight Centre's relationship with the William James School of Business. Staff can complete what the company regards as an internationally recognised Bachelor or Masters degree in Management, within 18–24 months while working full-time.

In addition, Flight Centre offers a corporate health program—Healthwise—that, according to the company, 'assist(s) employees "to find balance" in their lives'. Further, the financial advice service offered by the company— MoneyWi$e—was 'born out of the directors' desire that all Flight Centre Limited staff be success stories in their own right'. Of course, staff are also eligible for the traditional travel perks associated with working in the travel industry. Flight Centre believes that by looking after its staff, it looks after its business.

As a result, for two consecutive years, 2002 and 2003, Flight Centre Limited was named Australia's 'Best Employer of the Year' and in 2004 was one of five 'Highly Commended' finalists.[1]

The miracle is not to fly in the air, or to walk on the water; but to walk on the earth.

Chinese proverb

job design | The way the elements in a job are organised.

job characteristics model (JCM) | A model that proposes that any job can be described in terms of five core job dimensions: skill variety, task identity, task significance, autonomy and feedback.

skill variety | The degree to which the job requires a variety of different activities.

task identity | The degree to which the job requires completion of a whole and identifiable piece of work.

task significance | The degree to which the job has a substantial impact on the lives or work of other people.

PAY FOR PERFORMANCE is the practical application of a theory we discussed in Chapter 6: consistent with expectancy theory, motivation should be enhanced when employees see that rewards are allocated on performance criteria. In this chapter, we focus on applying motivation concepts. We link motivation theories to practices such as employee involvement and skill-based pay. Why? Because it is one thing to be able to know specific motivation theories; it is quite another to see how, as a manager, you can use them.

MOTIVATING BY CHANGING THE NATURE OF THE WORK ENVIRONMENT

Increasingly, research on motivation is focused on approaches that link motivational concepts to changes in the way work is structured.

Research in **job design** provides stronger evidence that the way the elements in a job are organised can act to increase or decrease effort. This research also offers detailed insights into just what those elements are. We will first review the job characteristics model and then discuss some ways jobs can be redesigned. Finally, we will explore some alternative work arrangements.

THE JOB CHARACTERISTICS MODEL

Developed by J. Richard Hackman and Greg Oldham, the **job characteristics model (JCM)** proposes that any job can be described in terms of five core job dimensions:[2]

1. **Skill variety**: The degree to which the job requires a variety of different activities so that the employee can use a number of different skills and talents. For instance, an example of a job scoring high on skill variety would be the owner–operator of a garage who does electrical repairs, rebuilds engines, does body work and interacts with customers. A job scoring low on this dimension would be a body shop employee who sprays paint eight hours a day.

2. **Task identity**: The degree to which the job requires completion of a whole and identifiable piece of work. An example of a job scoring high on identity would be a cabinetmaker who designs a piece of furniture, selects the wood, builds the object, and finishes it to perfection. A job scoring low on this dimension would be an employee in a furniture factory who operates a lathe solely to make table legs.

3. **Task significance**: The degree to which the job has a substantial impact on the lives or work of other people. An example of a job scoring high on significance would be a nurse handling the diverse needs of patients in a hospital intensive care unit. A job scoring low on this dimension would be a cleaner sweeping floors in the same hospital.

4. **Autonomy**: The degree to which the job provides substantial freedom, independence and discretion to the individual in scheduling the work and in determining the procedures to be used in carrying it out. An example of a job scoring high on autonomy is a salesperson who schedules his or her own work each day and decides on the most effective sales approach for each customer without supervision. A job scoring low on this dimension would be a salesperson who is given

a set of leads each day and is required to follow a standardised sales script with each potential customer.

5. **Feedback**: The degree to which carrying out the work activities required by the job results in the individual obtaining direct and clear information about the effectiveness of his or her performance. An example of a job with high feedback is a factory employee who assembles iPods and then tests them to see if they operate properly. A job scoring low on feedback would be that same factory employee who, after assembling the iPod, is required to route it to a quality-control inspector who tests it for proper operation and makes needed adjustments.

Figure 7.1 presents the job characteristics model. Note how the first three dimensions—skill variety, task identity and task significance—combine to create meaningful work. That is, if these three characteristics exist in a job, the model predicts that the incumbent will view the job as being important, valuable and worthwhile. Note, too, that jobs that possess autonomy give job incumbents a feeling of personal responsibility for the results and that, if a job provides feedback, employees will know how effectively they are performing. From a motivational standpoint, the JCM says that internal rewards are obtained by individuals when they learn (knowledge of results) that they personally (experienced responsibility) have performed well on a task that they care about (experienced meaningfulness).[3] The more that these three psychological states are present, the greater will be employees' motivation, performance and satisfaction, and the lower their absenteeism and likelihood of leaving the organisation. As Figure 7.1 shows, the links between the job dimensions and the outcomes are moderated or adjusted by the strength of the individual's growth need—that is, by the employee's desire for self-esteem and self-actualisation. This means that individuals with a high growth need are more likely to experience the psychological states when their jobs are enriched than are their counterparts with a low growth need. Moreover, they will respond more positively to the psychological states when they are present than will individuals with a low growth need.

autonomy | The degree to which the job provides substantial freedom and discretion to the individual in scheduling the work and in determining the procedures to be used in carrying it out.

feedback | The degree to which carrying out the work activities required by the job results in the individual obtaining direct and clear information about the effectiveness of his or her performance.

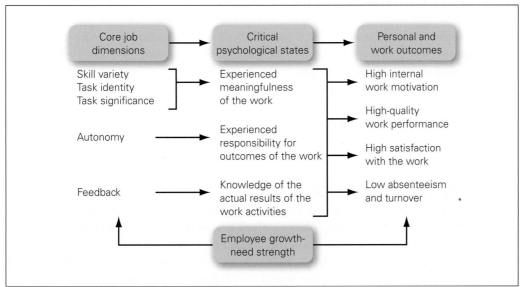

■ FIGURE 7.1
The job characteristics model

SOURCE: J. R. Hackman and G. R. Oldham, *Work Redesign* © 1980; pp. 78–80. Adapted by permission of Pearson Education, Inc., Upper Saddle River, New Jersey.

motivating potential score (MPS) | A predictive index suggesting the motivating potential in a job.

The core dimensions can be combined into a single predictive index, called the **motivating potential score (MPS)**. It is calculated as follows:

$$MPS = \frac{Skill\ variety\ +\ Task\ identity\ +\ Task\ significance}{3} \times Autonomy \times Feedback$$

Jobs that are high on motivating potential must be high on at least one of the three factors that lead to experienced meaningfulness, and they must be high on both autonomy and feedback. If jobs score high on motivating potential, the model predicts that motivation, performance and satisfaction will be positively affected and that the likelihood of absence and turnover will be lessened.

The JCM has been well researched. And most of the evidence supports the general framework of the theory—that is, there is a multiple set of job characteristics and these characteristics affect behavioural outcomes.[4] But it does appear that the MPS model doesn't work—that is, one can better derive motivating potential by adding the characteristics rather than using the complex MPS formula.[5] Beyond employee growth-need strength, other variables, such as the employee's perception of his or her workload compared to others, may also moderate the link between the core job dimensions and personal and work outcomes.[6] Overall, though, it appears that jobs that have the intrinsic elements of variety, identity, significance, autonomy and feedback are more satisfying and generate higher performance from people than jobs that lack these characteristics.

Take some time to think about your job. Do you have the opportunity to work on different tasks, or is your day fairly routine? Are you able to work independently, or do you constantly have a supervisor or fellow employee looking over your shoulder? What do you think your answers to these questions say about your job's motivating potential? See the Self-Assessment Library below and calculate your motivating potential score (MPS) from the job characteristics model.

SELF-ASSESSMENT LIBRARY

WHAT'S MY JOB'S MOTIVATING POTENTIAL?

In the Self-Assessment Library (available on CD and online), take Self-Assessment I.C.9 (What's My Job's Motivating Potential?) and answer the following questions. If you currently don't have a job, answer the questions for your most recent job.

1. How did you score relative to your classmates?
2. Did your score surprise you? Why or why not?
3. How might your results affect your career path?

HOW CAN JOBS BE REDESIGNED?

'Every day was the same thing', Frank Greer said. 'Stand on that assembly line. Wait for an instrument panel to be moved into place. Unlock the mechanism and drop the panel into the Mitsubishi Magna as it moved by on the line. Then I plugged in the harnessing wires. I repeated that for eight hours a day. I don't care that they were paying me $24 an hour. I was going crazy. I did it for almost a year and a half. Finally, I just said to my wife that this isn't going to be the way I'm going to spend the rest of my life. My brain was turning to jelly on that Mitsubishi assembly line. So I quit. Now I work in a print shop and I make less than $15 an hour. But let me tell you, the work I do is really interesting. The job changes all the time, I'm continually learning new things, and the work really challenges me! I look forward every morning to going to work again.'

Frank Greer's job at the Mitsubishi plant was made up of repetitive tasks that provided him with little variety, autonomy or motivation. In contrast, his job in the print shop is challenging and stimulating. Let's look at some of the ways that the JCM can be put into practice to make jobs more motivating.

JOB ROTATION

If employees suffer from overroutinisation of their work, one alternative is to use **job rotation** (or what many now call *cross-training*). We define this practice as the periodic shifting of an employee from one task to another. When an activity is no longer challenging, the employee is rotated to another job, usually at the same level, that has similar skill requirements. Singapore Airlines, one of the best-rated airlines in the world, uses job rotation extensively. For example, a ticket agent may take on the duties of a baggage handler. Job rotation is one of the reasons Singapore Airlines is rated as a highly desirable place to work. Job rotation has also been adopted by many manufacturing firms as a means of increasing flexibility and avoiding layoffs.[7] But job rotation can have other benefits. For instance, V & V Walsh, at its Bunbury meat-processing plant, introduced job rotation and multiskilling as part of a wider occupational health and safety program. These strategies were introduced to decrease repetitive strain injuries, especially to the shoulder. In 2000 the company was paying 12 per cent of its payroll in worker's compensation premiums. By 2005 this had dropped to approximately 4 per cent.[8]

The strengths of job rotation are that it reduces boredom, increases motivation through diversifying the employee's activities, and helps employees better understand how their work contributes to the organisation. Job rotation also has indirect benefits for the organisation because employees with a wider range of skills give management more flexibility in scheduling work, adapting to changes and filling vacancies.[9] However, job rotation isn't without its drawbacks. Training costs are increased, and productivity is reduced by moving an employee into a new position just when efficiency at the prior job is creating organisational economies. Job rotation also creates disruptions. Members of the work group have to adjust to the new employee. And supervisors may also have to spend more time answering questions and monitoring the work of recently rotated employees.

JOB ENLARGEMENT

More than 35 years ago, the idea of expanding jobs horizontally, or what we call **job enlargement**, grew in popularity. Increasing the number and variety of tasks that an individual performed resulted in jobs with more diversity. Instead of only sorting the incoming mail by department, for instance, a mail sorter's job could be enlarged to include physically delivering the mail to the various departments or running outgoing letters through the postage meter. The difference between job rotation and job enlargement may seem subtle. However, in job rotation, jobs aren't redesigned. Employees simply move from one job to another, but the nature of the work doesn't change. Job enlargement, however, involves actually changing the job.

Efforts at job enlargement met with less than enthusiastic results.[10] As one employee who experienced such a redesign of his job remarked, 'Before I had one lousy job. Now, through enlargement, I have three!' However, there have been some successful applications of job enlargement. The Australian Bureau of Statistics (ABS) expanded jobs

job rotation | The periodic shifting of an employee from one task to another.

job enlargement | Increasing the number and variety of tasks that an individual performs results in jobs with more diversity.

'EVERYONE WANTS A CHALLENGING JOB'

This statement is false. In spite of all the attention focused by the media, academics and social scientists on human potential and the needs of individuals, there is no evidence to support the view that the vast majority of employees want challenging jobs. Some individuals do prefer highly complex and challenging jobs; others prosper in simple, routinised work.

The individual-difference variable that seems to gain the greatest support for explaining who prefers a challenging job and who doesn't is the strength of an individual's higher-order needs. Individuals with high growth needs are more responsive to challenging work. But what percentage of rank-and-file employees actually desires higher-order need satisfactions and will respond positively to challenging jobs? No current data are available, but a study from the 1970s estimated the figure at about 15 per cent. Even after adjusting for changing work attitudes and the growth in white-collar jobs, it seems unlikely that the number today exceeds 40 per cent.

The strongest voice advocating challenging jobs hasn't been employees—it has been academics, social-science researchers and journalists, who undoubtedly made their career choices, to some degree, because they wanted jobs that gave them autonomy, identity and challenge. That, of course, is their choice. But for them to project their needs on to the workforce in general is presumptuous.

Not every employee is looking for a challenging job. Many employees meet their higher-order needs off the job. There are 168 hours in every individual's week. Work rarely consumes more than 30 per cent of this time. That leaves considerable opportunity, even for individuals with strong growth needs, to find higher-order need satisfaction outside the workplace.

SOURCES: J. R. Hackman, 'Work Design', in J. R. Hackman and J. L. Suttle (eds), *Improving Life at Work* (Santa Monica, CA: Goodyear, 1977), pp. 115–20; J. P. Wanous, 'Individual Differences and Reactions to Job Characteristics', *Journal of Applied Psychology*, October 1974, pp. 616–22; H. P. Sims and A. D. Szilagyi, 'Job Characteristic Relationships: Individual and Structural Moderators', *Organizational Behavior and Human Performance*, June 1976, pp. 211–30; and M. Fein, 'The Real Needs and Goals of Blue-Collar Workers', *The Conference Board Record*, February 1972, pp. 26–33.

as a result of the federal government's drive to reduce the number of job bands or categories. In some cases, staff wound up with a number of smaller jobs which were more boring than their previous work, but in the majority of cases officers in the ABS had an expanded and wider range of job responsibilities.

So, while job enlargement tries to overcome the problem of the lack of diversity in overspecialised jobs, it sometimes does little to instil challenge or purpose in an employee's activities. Job enrichment was introduced to deal with the shortcomings of job enlargement.

JOB ENRICHMENT

job enrichment | The vertical expansion of jobs, increasing the degree to which the employee controls the planning, execution and evaluation of the work.

Job enrichment refers to the vertical expansion of jobs. It increases the degree to which the employee controls the planning, execution and evaluation of the work. An enriched job organises tasks so as to allow the employee to do a complete activity, increases the employee's freedom and independence, increases responsibility, and provides feedback, so individuals will be able to assess and correct their own performance.[11] The enrichment of jobs can be traced to Herzberg's two-factor theory. Following this theory, by increasing the intrinsic factors in a job—such as achievement, responsibility and growth—employees are more likely to be satisfied with the job and motivated to perform it.

How does management enrich an employee's job? Figure 7.2 offers suggested guidelines based on the job characteristics model. *Combining tasks* takes existing and fractionalised tasks and puts them back together to form a new and larger module of work.

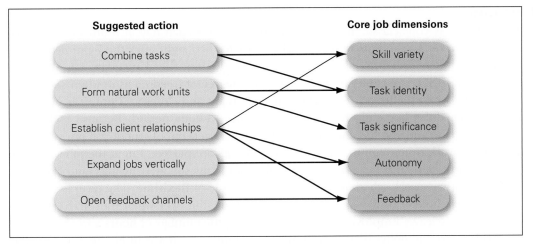

SOURCE: J. R. Hackman and J. L. Suttle (eds), *Improving Life at Work* (Glenview, IL: Scott Foresman, 1977), p. 138.

Forming natural work units means that the tasks an employee does create an identifiable and meaningful whole. *Establishing client relationships* increases the direct relationships between employees and their clients. (These may be an internal customer as well as someone outside the organisation.) *Expanding jobs vertically* gives employees responsibilities and control that were formerly reserved for management. *Opening feedback channels* lets employees know how well they are performing their jobs and whether their performance is improving, deteriorating or remaining at a constant level.

To illustrate job enrichment, let's look at what management at Bank One in Chicago did with its international trade banking department.[12] The department's chief product is commercial letters of credit—essentially, a bank guarantee to stand behind huge import and export transactions. Prior to enriching jobs, the department's 300 employees processed documents in an assembly-line fashion, with errors creeping in at each handoff. Meanwhile, employees did little to hide the boredom they were experiencing from doing narrow and specialised tasks. Management enriched these jobs by making each clerk a trade expert who was able to handle a customer from start to finish. After 200 hours of training in finance and law, the clerks became full-service advisers who could turn around documents in a day while advising clients on such arcane matters as bank procedures in Turkey and US munitions' export controls. And the results? Department productivity more than tripled, employee satisfaction soared, and transaction volume rose more than 10 per cent a year.

The overall evidence on job enrichment generally shows that it reduces absenteeism and turnover costs and increases satisfaction; however, on the critical issue of productivity, the evidence is inconclusive.[13] In some situations, job enrichment increases productivity; in others, it decreases it. However, even when productivity goes down, there does seem to be consistently more conscientious use of resources and a higher quality of product or service.

ALTERNATIVE WORK ARRANGEMENTS

Beyond redesigning the nature of the work itself, and involving employees in decisions, another approach to making the work environment more motivating is to alter work arrangements. We will discuss three alternative work arrangements: flexitime, job sharing and telecommuting. With the increasing advances in technology, all of these alternative work arrangements have become more popular.

FLEXITIME

Helen Drury is your classic 'morning person'. She rises each day at 5 am sharp, full of energy. However, as she puts it, 'I'm usually ready for bed right after the 7 pm news.'

Helen's work schedule as an administrator within the University of Southern Queensland (USQ) is flexible. It allows her some degree of freedom as to when she comes to work and when she leaves. Her office opens at 6 am and closes at 7 pm. It is up to her how she schedules her eight-hour day within this 13-hour period. Because Helen is a morning person and also has a seven-year-old son who gets out of school at 3 pm every day, she opts to work from 6 am to 3 pm. 'My work hours are perfect. I'm at the job when I'm mentally most alert, and I can be home to take care of my son after he gets out of school.'

flexitime | A scheme of flexible work hours.

Helen Drury's work schedule at USQ is an example of **flexitime**. The term is short for 'flexible work hours'. It allows employees some discretion over when they arrive at work and when they leave. Employees have to work a specific number of hours a week, but they are free to vary the hours of work within certain limits. As shown in Figure 7.3, each day consists of a common core, usually six hours, with a flexibility band surrounding the core. For example, exclusive of a one-hour lunch break, the core may be 9 am to 3 pm, with the office actually opening at 6 am and closing at 6 pm. All employees are required to be at their jobs during the common core period, but they are allowed to accumulate their other two hours before and/or after the core time. Some flexitime programs allow extra hours to be accumulated and turned into a free day off each month.

Flexitime has become an extremely popular scheduling option. Eighty-five per cent of Australian employees believe they would be inclined to stay longer with an employer that offered flexible working arrangements. This may be because of the perceived benefits of flexible working arrangements to work/life balance. A little over half of those surveyed believed flexible working arrangements would be the best policy an employer could introduce to improve work/life balance.[14]

The proportion of full-time employees on flexitime more than doubled between the late 1980s and 2005. Approximately 43 per cent of the US full-time workforce now has flexibility in their daily arrival and departure times.[15] And this isn't just a US phenomenon. In Germany, for instance, 29 per cent of businesses have flexitime for their employees.[16]

The benefits claimed for flexitime are numerous. They include reduced absenteeism, increased productivity, reduced overtime expenses, a lessening in hostility towards management, reduced traffic congestion around work sites, elimination of tardiness, and increased autonomy and responsibility for employees that may increase employee job satisfaction.[17] But beyond the claims, what is flexitime's record?

Most of the performance evidence stacks up favourably. Flexitime tends to reduce absenteeism and frequently improves employee productivity,[18] probably for several reasons. Employees can schedule their work hours to align with personal demands, thus reducing tardiness and absences; they can also adjust their work activities to those hours in which they are individually more productive.

■ FIGURE 7.3

Example of a flexitime schedule

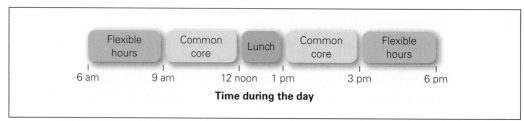

Time during the day

Flexitime's main drawback is that it is not applicable to every job. It works well with clerical tasks for which an employee's interaction with people outside his or her department is limited. It isn't a viable option for receptionists, sales personnel in retail stores, or similar jobs for which comprehensive service demands that people be at their work stations at predetermined times.

JOB SHARING

A recent work scheduling innovation is **job sharing**. It allows two or more individuals to split a traditional 40-hour-a-week job. So, for example, one person might perform the job from 8 am to noon, while another performs the same job from 1 pm to 5 pm; or the two could work full, but alternate, days. Westpac Banking Corporation is the most notable example of job sharing in Australia.[19] With approval of their supervisor, employees at Westpac can access job-sharing arrangements in ways that are desired by them but which also benefit the company. A common arrangement is for one person to work Thursday and Friday of week one and the Monday, Tuesday and Wednesday of the following week. The second person then takes over and works the same period in weeks two and three. Each employee works 40 hours over each two-week period and the one position is fully staffed every day, five days a week. The advantage of this job-sharing arrangement is that young mothers can spend more time with their children while not overtaxing grandparents who mind the children the other days.

In 2003 in Australia, approximately 10 per cent of employees who worked part-time were in some form of job-sharing arrangement.[20] However, in spite of its availability, it doesn't seem to be widely adopted by employees. This is probably because of the difficulty of finding compatible partners to share a job and the negative perceptions historically held of individuals not completely committed to their job and employer.

Job sharing allows the organisation to draw on the talents of more than one individual in a given job. A bank manager who oversees two job sharers describes it as an opportunity to get two heads but 'pay for one'.[21] It also opens up the opportunity to acquire skilled employees—for instance, women with young children and retirees—who might not be available on a full-time basis.[22] Many Japanese firms are increasingly considering job sharing—but for a very different reason.[23] Because Japanese executives are extremely reluctant to fire people, job sharing is seen as a potentially humanitarian means for avoiding layoffs due to overstaffing.

From the employee's perspective, job sharing increases flexibility. As such, it can increase motivation and satisfaction for those to whom a 40-hour-a-week job just isn't practical. But the main drawback from management's perspective is finding compatible pairs of employees who can successfully coordinate the intricacies of one job.[24]

TELECOMMUTING

It might be close to the ideal job for many people. No commuting, flexible hours, freedom to dress as you please, and few or no interruptions from colleagues. It is called **telecommuting** and refers to employees who do their work at home at least two days a week on a computer that is linked to their office.[25] (A closely related term—*the virtual office*—is increasingly being used to describe employees who work out of their home on a relatively permanent basis.)

Recent estimates indicate that approximately half a million people in Australia telecommute, depending on exactly how the term is defined.[26] This translates to about 10 per cent or more of the workforce and the trend is increasing. Well-known global

job sharing | An arrangement that allows two or more individuals to split a traditional full-time (40-hour-per-week) job.

telecommuting | Refers to employees who do their work at home at least two days a week, usually via computer linked to the main office.

organisations that actively encourage telecommuting include AT&T, IBM, Merrill Lynch, American Express and Hewlett-Packard, and the concept is catching on worldwide.[27] In Finland, Sweden, Britain and Germany, telecommuters represent 17, 15, 8 and 6 per cent of their workforces, respectively.[28] Within Australia, Nokia—one of the 12 'Hewitt Best Employers in Australia and New Zealand' for 2005—offers employees a range of flexible working arrangements, including mobile working and telecommuting.[29]

What kinds of jobs lend themselves to telecommuting? Three categories have been identified as most appropriate: routine information-handling tasks, mobile activities, and professional and other knowledge-related tasks.[30] Writers, lawyers, analysts, and employees who spend the majority of their time on computers or the telephone are natural candidates for telecommuting. For instance, telemarketers, customer-service representatives, reservation agents and product-support specialists spend most of their time on the phone. As telecommuters, they can access information on their computer screens at home as easily as in the company's office.

There are numerous stories of telecommuting's success.[31] For instance, Martin Aungle, 31, telecommutes where he works as Dimension Data's online marketing manager. Martin works from his home in Mittagong, in the NSW Southern Highlands, three days a week and goes into the company's Sydney office for the other two days of the week. 'Dimension Data has a great attitude towards flexible working conditions', says Aungle. 'When I joined, one of my colleagues came around with a modem to set up e-mail and remote connections to the office on my home PC, even though I lived just 15 minutes away.'[32] Then later when his family moved to Mittagong to be closer to his wife's work, Aungle was faced with daily three-hour commutes that were just dead time. By telecommuting three days a week, he gets back nine hours of his life, the company gets a more motivated employee and everyone is happy.

The potential pluses for management of telecommuting include a larger labour pool from which to select, higher productivity, less turnover, improved morale and reduced office-space costs. The main downside for management is less direct supervision of employees. In addition, in today's team-focused workplace, telecommuting may make it more difficult for management to coordinate teamwork.[33] From the employee's standpoint, telecommuting offers a considerable increase in flexibility. But it is not without costs. For employees with a high social need, telecommuting can increase feelings of isolation and reduce job satisfaction. And all telecommuters potentially suffer from the 'out of sight, out of mind' effect. Employees who aren't at their desks, who miss meetings, and who don't share in day-to-day informal workplace interactions may be at a disadvantage when it comes to raises and promotions. It is easy for bosses to overlook or undervalue the contribution of employees whom they see less regularly.

DON'T FORGET ABILITY AND OPPORTUNITY

Robin and Chris both graduated from university a couple of years ago with their degrees in primary education. They each took jobs as year one teachers but in different school districts. Robin immediately confronted a number of obstacles on the job: a large class (42 students), a small and dingy classroom and inadequate supplies. Chris's situation couldn't have been more different. He had only 15 students in his class, plus a teaching aide for 15 hours each week, a modern and well-lit room, a well-stocked supply cabinet, an iMac computer for every student, and a highly supportive principal. Not surprisingly, at the end of their first school year, Chris had been considerably more effective as a teacher than had Robin.

The preceding episode illustrates an obvious but often overlooked fact. Success on a job is facilitated or hindered by the existence or absence of support resources.

A popular, although arguably simplistic, way of thinking about employee performance is as a function (f) of the interaction of ability (A) and motivation (M); that is, performance = $f(A \times M)$. If either is inadequate, performance will be negatively affected. This helps to explain, for instance, the hard-working athlete or student with modest abilities who consistently outperforms a more gifted, but lazy, rival. So, as we noted in Chapter 2, an individual's intelligence and skills (subsumed under the label 'ability') must be considered in addition to motivation if we are to be able to accurately explain and predict employee performance. But a piece of the puzzle is still missing. We need to add **opportunity to perform** (*O*) to our equation: performance = $f(A \times M \times O)$.[34] Even though an individual may be willing and able, there may be obstacles that constrain performance.

opportunity to perform | High levels of performance are partially a function of an absence of obstacles that constrain the employee.

When you attempt to assess why an employee may not be performing to the level that you believe he or she is capable of, take a look at the work environment to see if it is supportive. Does the employee have adequate tools, equipment, materials and supplies? Does the employee have favourable working conditions, helpful fellow employees, supportive work rules and procedures, sufficient information to make job-related decisions, adequate time to do a good job, and the like? If not, performance will suffer.

EMPLOYEE INVOLVEMENT

LEARNING OBJECTIVE 2
Explain why managers might want to use employee involvement programs

What specifically do we mean by **employee involvement**? We define it as a participative process that uses the input of employees to increase their commitment to the organisation's success. The underlying logic is that by involving employees in the decisions that affect them and by increasing their autonomy and control over their work lives, employees will become more motivated, more committed to the organisation, more productive and more satisfied with their jobs.[35]

employee involvement | A participative process that uses the input of employees and is intended to increase employee commitment to the organisation's success.

Employee involvement programs differ among countries.[36] For instance, a study comparing the acceptance of employee involvement programs in four countries confirmed the importance of modifying practices to reflect national culture.[37] Specifically, while American employees readily accepted these programs, managers in India who tried to empower their employees through employee involvement programs were rated low by those employees. In these Indian cases, employee satisfaction also decreased. These reactions are consistent with India's high power-distance culture, which accepts and expects differences in authority.

EXAMPLES OF EMPLOYEE INVOLVEMENT PROGRAMS
Now let's look at the three main forms of employee involvement—participative management, representative participation and quality circles—in more detail.

PARTICIPATIVE MANAGEMENT
The distinct characteristic common to all **participative management** programs is the use of joint decision making. That is, subordinates actually share a significant degree of decision-making power with their immediate superiors. Participative management has, at times, been promoted as a panacea for poor morale and low productivity. But for it to work, the issues in which employees get involved must be relevant to their interests so that they will be motivated, employees must have the competence and knowledge to make a

participative management | A process in which subordinates share a significant degree of decision-making power with their immediate superiors.

useful contribution, and there must be trust and confidence between all the parties involved.[38]

Dozens of studies have been conducted on the participation–performance relationship. The findings, however, are mixed.[39] When the research is reviewed carefully, it appears that participation typically has only a modest influence on variables such as employee productivity, motivation and job satisfaction. Of course, that doesn't mean that the use of participative management can't be beneficial under the right conditions. What it says, however, is that the use of participation isn't a sure means for improving employee performance.

REPRESENTATIVE PARTICIPATION

representative participation | Employees participate in organisational decision making through a small group of representative employees.

Almost every country in Western Europe has some type of legislation requiring companies to practise **representative participation**. That is, rather than participating directly in decisions, employees are represented by a small group of employees who actually participate. Representative participation has been called 'the most widely legislated form of employee involvement around the world'.[40] The goal of representative participation is to redistribute power within an organisation, putting labour on a more equal footing with the interests of management and shareholders.

The two most common forms which representative participation takes are works councils and board representatives.[41] Works councils are groups of nominated or elected employees who must be consulted when management makes decisions involving personnel. Board representatives are employees who sit on a company's board of directors and represent the interests of the firm's employees.

The overall influence of representative participation on working employees seems to be minimal.[42] For instance, the evidence suggests that works councils are dominated by management and have little impact on employees or the organisation. And although this form of employee involvement might increase the motivation and satisfaction of the individuals who are doing the representing, there is little evidence that this trickles down to the operating employees whom they represent. Overall, 'the greatest value of representative participation is symbolic. If one is interested in changing employee attitudes or in improving organisational performance, representative participation would be a poor choice.'[43]

QUALITY CIRCLES

quality circle | A work group of employees who meet regularly to discuss their quality problems, investigate causes, recommend solutions and take corrective actions.

Originally begun in the United States and exported to Japan in the 1950s, the quality circle became quite popular in North America, Australia and Europe during the 1980s.[44] Companies such as Hewlett-Packard, General Electric, Xerox, Procter & Gamble, IBM, Mitsubishi and Japan Airlines used quality circles. **Quality circles** are defined as a work group of eight to ten employees and supervisors who have a shared area of responsibility and who meet regularly—typically once a week, on company time and on company premises—to discuss their quality problems, investigate causes of the problems, recommend solutions and take corrective actions.

A review of the evidence on quality circles indicates that they tend to show little or no effect on employee satisfaction, and although many studies report positive results from quality circles on productivity, these results are by no means guaranteed.[45] The failure of many quality circle programs to produce measurable benefits has also led to a large number of them being discontinued. One of the reasons for their failure is that managers deal with employee involvement in only a limited way. 'At most, these programs operate

Officeworks stores involve their employees in making decisions that affect their work and please their customers. Officeworks encourages employees to make on-the-spot decisions without consulting their immediate supervisors when satisfying the customer is necessary. That could include buying products in from other stores because their store was out of stock when the customer needed the item.

for one hour per week, with the remaining 39 hours unchanged. Why should changes in 2.5 per cent of a person's job have a major impact?'[46] Basically, quality circles were an easy way for management to get on the employee involvement bandwagon without really involving employees.

LINKING EMPLOYEE INVOLVEMENT PROGRAMS AND MOTIVATION THEORIES

Employee involvement draws on a number of the motivation theories discussed in Chapter 6. For instance, Theory Y is consistent with participative management, while Theory X aligns with the more traditional autocratic style of managing people. In terms of two-factor theory, employee involvement programs could provide employees with intrinsic motivation by increasing opportunities for growth, responsibility and involvement in the work itself. Similarly, the opportunity to make and implement decisions, and then seeing them work out, can help to satisfy an employee's needs for responsibility, achievement, recognition, growth and enhanced self-esteem. So, employee involvement is compatible with ERG theory and efforts to stimulate the achievement need. And extensive employee involvement programs clearly have the potential to increase employee intrinsic motivation in work tasks.

REWARDING EMPLOYEES

In deciding what to pay employees, and how to pay them, management must make some strategic decisions. Will the organisation lead, match or lag the market in pay? How will individual contributions be recognised? In this section, we consider four main strategic rewards decisions that need to be made: (1) what to pay employees (which is decided by establishing a pay structure); (2) how to pay individual employees (which is decided through variable and skill-based pay plans); (3) what benefits to offer, and especially whether to offer employees choice in benefits (flexible benefits); and (4) how to construct employee recognition programs.

WHAT TO PAY: ESTABLISHING A PAY STRUCTURE

There are many ways to pay employees. The process of initially setting pay levels can be rather complex and entails balancing *internal equity*—the worth of the job to the organisation (usually established through a technical process called job evaluation)—and *external equity*—the external competitiveness of an organisation's pay relative to pay elsewhere in its industry (usually established through pay surveys). Obviously, the best pay system pays the job what it is worth (internal equity) while also paying competitively relative to the labour market.

But some organisations prefer to be pay leaders by paying above the market, while some may lag the market because they can't afford to pay market rates, or they are willing to bear the costs of paying below market (namely, higher turnover as people are lured to better-paying jobs). Wal-Mart, for example, pays less than its competitors and often outsources jobs overseas. Chinese employees in Shenzhen earn $120 a month (that's $1440 a year) to make stereos for Wal-Mart. Of the 6000 factories that are worldwide suppliers to Wal-Mart, 80 per cent are located in China. In fact, one-eighth of all Chinese exports to the United States go to Wal-Mart.[47]

Pay more, and you may get better-qualified, more highly motivated employees who will stay with the organisation longer. But pay is often the highest single operating cost for an organisation, which means that paying too much can make the organisation's products or services too expensive. It is a strategic decision an organisation must make, with clear trade-offs.

HOW TO PAY: REWARDING INDIVIDUAL EMPLOYEES THROUGH VARIABLE-PAY PROGRAMS

Why should I put any extra effort into this job?' asked Anne Garcia, a primary schoolteacher in regional Queensland. 'I can excel, or I can do the bare minimum. It makes no difference. I get paid the same. Why do anything above the minimum to get by?'

Comments similar to Anne's have been voiced by schoolteachers for decades, because pay increases were tied to seniority. Indeed, Australian schoolteachers currently have no nationally recognised performance standards. But a recent report issued by Teaching Australia—the national agency representing teachers, established by the federal government—suggests that the time may be ripe for the development of such a set of standards. According to Dr Lawrence Ingvarson, one of the report's authors, such standards could then be used to create a pay-for-performance compensation system for Australian teachers.[48]

A number of organisations are moving away from paying people based solely on credentials or length of service and towards using variable-pay programs. Piece-rate plans, merit-based pay, bonuses, profit-sharing, gainsharing and employee share ownership plans are all forms of **variable-pay programs**. Instead of paying a person only for time on the job or seniority, a variable-pay program bases a portion of an employee's pay on some individual and/or organisational measure of performance. Earnings therefore fluctuate up and down with the measure of performance.[49] Variable-pay plans have long been used for compensating salespeople and executives. Recently they have begun to be applied to all employees, particularly in the energy, mining and construction/engineering industries.[50]

variable-pay program | A pay plan that bases a portion of an employee's pay on some individual and/or organisational measure of performance.

The main barrier to wider adoption of variable-pay plans in Australia is restrictive tax rules, particularly the Fringe Benefits Tax, but today, more than 70 per cent of American companies have some form of variable-pay plan, up from only about 5 per cent in 1970.[51] Unfortunately, recent survey data indicate that most employees still don't see a strong connection between pay and performance. Only 29 per cent say that when they do a good job, their performance is rewarded.[52]

It is precisely the fluctuation in variable pay that has made these programs attractive to management. It turns part of an organisation's fixed labour costs into a variable cost, thus reducing expenses when performance declines. So, when the US economy encountered a recession in 2001, companies with variable pay were able to reduce their labour costs much faster than companies that had maintained non-performance-based compensation systems.[53] In addition, when pay is tied to performance, the employee's earnings recognise contribution rather than being a form of entitlement. Low performers find, over time, that their pay stagnates, while high performers enjoy pay increases commensurate with their contribution. Let's examine the different types of variable-pay programs in more detail.

Attracting and retaining highly skilled and productive employees at remote mining sites has always been a challenge. Poor living conditions, little or no shopping and social facilities, and isolation from family and friends are the chief factors that make working at such sites a tough decision. As a result, mining companies are starting to make wider use of variable-pay programs. After all, when an employee is operating a truck worth several million dollars, the employer really wants that employee to be reasonably satisfied and motivated to use the machinery productively.

PIECE-RATE PAY

Piece-rate wages have been popular for more than a century as a means of compensating production employees. In **piece-rate pay plans**, employees are paid a fixed sum for each unit of production completed. When an employee gets no base salary and is paid only for what he or she produces, this is a pure piece-rate plan.

Fruit picking is another form of work that is often paid on a piece-rate basis in Australia. Income is determined by the volume of fruit an employee picks. So, income will vary between employees according to their fitness levels and experience. (This type of work is popular among backpackers, who can finance a working holiday in Australia by following the harvests.)

Many organisations use a modified piece-rate plan, in which employees earn a base hourly wage plus a piece-rate differential. So, a medical transcriber might be paid $7 an hour plus 20 cents per page of medical records transcribed from doctors' tape recordings. Such modified plans provide a floor under an employee's earnings while still offering a productivity incentive.

piece-rate pay plan | A pay plan in which employees are paid a fixed sum for each unit of production outcome.

MERIT-BASED PAY

Merit-based pay plans also pay for individual performance. However, unlike piece-rate plans, which pay based on objective output, **merit-based pay plans** are based on performance appraisal ratings. A main advantage of merit pay plans is that they allow

merit-based pay plan | A pay plan based on performance appraisal ratings.

employers to differentiate pay based on performance, so that those people thought to be high performers are given bigger raises. The plans can be motivating because, if they are designed correctly, individuals perceive a strong relationship between their performance and the rewards they receive. The evidence supports the importance of this linkage.[54]

Moreover, unlike organisation-based compensation (such as profit-sharing and gainsharing plans, which we will discuss below), merit pay plans pay for individual performance, which presumably is more directly under the individual's control. Thus, because most individuals desire control over their pay, employees tend to like merit pay plans. Finally, merit pay plans allow organisations to compensate for external factors that may have reduced objective performance measures due to no fault of the employee (such as, sales being down nationwide).

Most large organisations have merit pay plans, especially for salaried employees. IBM's merit pay plan, for example, provides increases to employees' base salary based on their annual performance evaluation. Since the 1990s, when the economy stumbled badly, an increasing number of Japanese companies have abandoned seniority-based pay in favour of merit-based pay. Koichi Yanashita, of Takeda Chemical Industries, commented: 'The merit-based salary system is an important means to achieve goals set by the company's top management, not just a way to change wages.'[55]

Despite the intuitive appeal of pay for performance, merit pay plans have several limitations. One of them is that, typically, such plans are based on an annual performance appraisal. Thus, the merit pay is as valid or invalid as the performance ratings on which it is based. Another limitation of merit pay is that sometimes the pay raise pool fluctuates based on economic conditions or other factors that have little to do with an individual employee's performance. A colleague at a top university who performed very well in teaching and research was given a pay raise of just $300 one year. Why? Because the pay raise pool was very small. Yet, that is hardly pay for performance.

Finally, unions typically resist merit pay plans. The vast majority of primary and secondary schoolteachers in Australia are paid on seniority rather than performance. Recently, Minister for Education, Science and Training, Julie Bishop proposed that teacher pay be tied to merit, not tenure, stating: 'We need to recognise that not all teachers are equal in their ability, commitment and performance. Yet [at present] they are all paid on the same basis of years in the job, not on merit.'[56] This proposal drew a swift negative reaction from the teachers unions. The final outcome won't be known for some time to come.

BONUSES

bonus | Pay program that rewards employees for recent performance rather than historical performance.

Annual bonuses in the millions of dollars aren't uncommon in major corporations. Telstra's chief executive officer (CEO) Sol Trujillo was paid a $1.5 million bonus for developing a strategic plan on his arrival at the telco in 2006.[57] Increasingly, bonus plans are casting a larger net within organisations to include lower-level employees.[58] Many companies now routinely reward production employees with bonuses in the thousands of dollars when company profits improve. One advantage of bonuses over merit pay is that **bonuses** reward employees for recent performance rather than historical performance.

PROFIT-SHARING PLANS

profit-sharing plan | An organisation-wide program that distributes compensation based on some established formula designed around a company's profitability.

Profit-sharing plans are organisation-wide programs that distribute compensation based on some established formula designed around a company's profitability. These can be direct cash outlays or, particularly in the case of top managers, allocations of share options.

When you read about executives such as Reuben Mark, the CEO at Colgate-Palmolive, earning $148 million in one year, almost all this comes from cashing in share options previously granted based on company profit performance.

GAINSHARING

A variable-pay program that has gotten a great deal of attention in recent years is **gainsharing**.[59] This is a formula-based group incentive plan, where improvements in group productivity from one period to another determine the total amount of money that is to be allocated. The division of productivity savings can be split between the company and employees in any number of ways, but 50:50 is typical. Gainsharing's popularity seems to be narrowly focused among large companies. For instance, approximately 45 per cent of Fortune 1000 firms have implemented gainsharing plans.[60]

How is gainsharing different from profit sharing? By focusing on productivity gains rather than on profits, gainsharing rewards specific behaviours that are less influenced by external factors. Employees in a gainsharing plan can receive incentive awards even when the organisation isn't profitable.

EMPLOYEE SHARE OWNERSHIP PLANS

Employee share ownership plans (ESOPs) can mean any number of things, from employees owning some shares in the company at which they work, to their owning and personally operating the firm. ESOPs are company-established benefit plans in which employees acquire shares, often at below-market prices, as part of their benefits. Companies as varied as Fosters, DMC Outsourcing Limited and Lend-Lease now have significant employee ownership; in some cases, they are over 50 per cent employee-owned.[61] Although ESOPs have been around for about 30 years in Australia, only 5.4 per cent of Australian employees are currently participating in such schemes, mainly because of restrictive government regulations and Australian Competition and Consumer Commission restrictions.[62]

In the typical ESOP, an employee share ownership trust is created. Companies contribute either shares or cash to buy shares for the trust and allocate the shares to employees. Employees usually cannot take physical possession of their shares or sell them while they are still employed at the company. The research on ESOPs indicates that they increase employee satisfaction.[63] But their impact on performance is less clear. For instance, one study compared 45 ESOPs against 238 conventional companies.[64] The ESOPs outperformed the conventional firms both in terms of employment and sales growth. Another study found that ESOPs had total shareholder returns that averaged 6.9 percentage points higher over the four years after the ESOP was set up than market returns of similar companies without an ESOP.[65] But other studies have shown disappointing results.[66]

ESOPs have the potential to increase employee job satisfaction and work motivation. But for this potential to be realised, employees need to psychologically experience ownership.[67] That is, in addition to merely having a financial stake in the company, employees need to be kept regularly informed of the status of the business and also have the opportunity to exercise influence over it. The evidence consistently indicates that it takes ownership and a participative style of management to achieve significant improvements in an organisation's performance.[68]

Do variable-pay programs increase motivation and productivity? The answer is a qualified 'Yes'. For example, studies generally support the idea that organisations with

gainsharing | A formula-based group incentive plan.

employee share ownership plan (ESOP) | Company-established benefit plan in which employees acquire shares, often at below-market prices, as part of their benefits.

profit-sharing plans have higher levels of profitability than those without them.[69] Similarly, gainsharing has been found to improve productivity in a majority of cases and often has a positive impact on employee attitudes.[70] The downside of variable pay, from an employee's perspective, is its unpredictability. With a straight base salary, employees know what they will be earning. They can finance cars and homes based on reasonably solid assumptions. That's more difficult to do with variable pay. Your group's performance might slip this year, or a recession might undermine your company's profits. Depending on how your variable pay is determined, these events can reduce your income. Moreover, people begin to take repeated annual performance bonuses for granted. A 15 or 20 per cent bonus, received three years in a row, begins to become expected in the fourth year. If it doesn't materialise, management will find itself with some disgruntled employees on its hands.

OB IN PRACTICE

THE RISE AND FALL OF SHARE OPTIONS

The 1990s saw share options become the favoured way to reward executives. But the heyday of share options appears to be over.

Share options give employees the right, but not the obligation, to purchase a company's shares at a specified price. When a share is rising rapidly, share options can be a powerful motivator. For instance, in the 1990s, companies such as AMP, Westpac and Microsoft relied heavily on the issuance of share options to hire and to build loyalty among employees and executives. Microsoft could hire the brightest programmers for only $40 000 or $50 000 a year because their real compensation would come from share options. In 2000, for instance, Microsoft employees *averaged* an incredible US$416 353 in share-based compensation!

At their peak, share options weren't handed out by all companies, nor to all employees. They were most popular among small, start-up companies, which relied on options to encourage talented people to incur the risk of joining a new firm, often on very low pay. In spite of all the attention directed at share options, a limited number of employees actually got them. About 2 per cent of the workforce of publicly listed companies held share options in 1992. In 2003, that figure was up to only 15 per cent. And these numbers hide the fact that the vast majority of share options were issued to just the top five executive officers of many companies.

Share options can be powerful motivators to executives. The problem is they can also encourage the wrong behaviour. Consistent with reinforcement theory, options encourage executives to focus on increasing the share price—in the short term—rather than building the business for the long term. And executives are motivated to do whatever is necessary to increase their share price, even if it means fabricating revenues, hiding expenses and engaging in similar manipulative accounting practices. The eventual collapses of Enron, OneTel and HIH were largely due to executives misrepresenting financial data in order to enrich themselves, partly by cashing in large share-option grants.

The use of share options as compensation is declining. The biggest impact of the decline is likely to be felt among middle managers. But senior executives will probably continue to receive the bulk of their compensation through share-option schemes. And start-up companies are likely to continue to rely on share options as a major incentive to attract and keep employees. Microsoft's recent decision to eliminate share options and pay its 54 000 employees with actual shares that can be gradually sold off over a five-year period may encourage other firms to compensate employees with real shares rather than options.

SOURCES: Based on R. Buckman and D. Bank, 'For Silicon Valley, Stocks' Fall Upsets Culture of Options', *Wall Street Journal*, 18 July 2002, p. A1; A. Bernstein, 'Options: Middle Managers Will Take the Hit', *BusinessWeek*, 9 December 2002, p. 120; P. Elias, 'Start-Ups Still Favor Stock Options', *Seattle Post-Intelligencer*, 10 July 2003, p. C6; and J. Greene, 'Will Stock Options Lose Their Sex Appeal?', *BusinessWeek*, 21 July 2003, pp. 23–35.

HOW TO PAY: REWARDING INDIVIDUAL EMPLOYEES THROUGH SKILL-BASED PAY PLANS

Organisations hire people for their skills, then typically put them in jobs and pay them based on their job title or rank. But if organisations hire people because of their competencies, why don't they pay them for those same competencies? Some organisations do.[71] For instance, Amcor Fibre Packaging is the leading manufacturer of corrugated boxes, folding cartons, carton board, industrial papers and point-of-sale displays in Australasia. Staff are paid on the basis of the points they are allocated. The points reflect employees' assessed competence in specific skill areas and are contingent on the employee being formally requested to use that skill in the workplace.[72] **Skill-based pay** is an alternative to job-based pay. Rather than having an individual's job title define his or her pay category, skill-based pay (also called *competency-based* or *knowledge-based pay*) sets pay levels on the basis of how many skills employees have or how many jobs they can do.[73]

What is the appeal of skill-based pay plans? From management's perspective: flexibility. Filling staffing needs is easier when employee skills are interchangeable. This is particularly true today, as many organisations are cutting the size of their workforce. Downsized organisations require more generalists and fewer specialists. Skill-based pay also facilitates communication across the organisation, because people gain a better understanding of each other's jobs. Where skill-based pay exists, you are less likely to hear the phrase 'It's not my job!' In addition, skill-based pay helps to meet the needs of ambitious employees who confront minimal advancement opportunities. These people can increase their earnings and knowledge without a promotion in job title.

What about the downside of skill-based pay? People can 'top out'—learning all the skills the program calls for them to learn. This can frustrate employees after they have become challenged by an environment of learning, growth and continual pay raises. And skills can become obsolete. When this happens, what should management do? Cut employee pay, or continue to pay for skills that are no longer relevant? There is also the problem created by paying people for acquiring skills for which there may be no immediate need. This happened at IDS Financial Services.[74] The company found itself paying people more money even though there was little immediate use for their new skills. IDS eventually dropped its skill-based pay plan and replaced it with one that equally balances individual

At its Australian plant, Amcor Fibre Packaging needs highly skilled employees to satisfy an increased global demand for the firm's packaging products and solutions. New employees are assessed as to their starting competencies to establish their base points level; thereafter, attainment of increased points will result in higher pay levels. Amcor also provides training opportunities to new and existing employees, with assessed point scores given for successful competency attainments. The skill-based pay policy is written into the enterprise agreement between all employees and Amcor, further testifying to the company's commitment to improved skill levels for all its employees.

contribution and gains in work-team productivity. Finally, skill-based plans don't address the level of performance. They deal only with the issue of whether or not someone can perform the skill.

LINKING SKILL-BASED PAY PLANS TO MOTIVATION THEORIES

Skill-based pay plans are consistent with several motivation theories. Because they encourage employees to learn, expand their skills and grow, they are consistent with ERG theory. Among employees whose lower-order needs are substantially satisfied, the opportunity to experience growth can be a motivator.

Paying people to expand their skill levels is also consistent with research on the achievement need. High achievers have a compelling drive to do things better or more efficiently. By learning new skills or improving the skills they already hold, high achievers will find their jobs more challenging.

There is also a link between reinforcement theory and skill-based pay. Skill-based pay encourages employees to develop their flexibility, to continue to learn, to cross-train, to be generalists rather than specialists, and to work cooperatively with others in the organisation. To the degree that management wants employees to demonstrate such behaviours, skill-based pay should act as a reinforcer.

In addition, skill-based pay may have equity implications. When employees make their input–outcome comparisons, skills may provide a fairer input criterion for determining pay than factors such as seniority or education. To the degree that employees perceive skills as the critical variable in job performance, the use of skill-based pay may increase the perception of equity and help to optimise employee motivation.

SKILL-BASED PAY IN PRACTICE

A number of studies have investigated the use and effectiveness of skill-based pay. The overall conclusion, based on these studies, is that skill-based pay is expanding and that it generally leads to higher employee performance, satisfaction and perceptions of fairness in pay systems.[75]

Research has also identified some interesting trends. The increased use of skills as a basis for pay appears particularly strong among organisations facing aggressive global competition, and among companies with shorter product life cycles and speed-to-market concerns.[76] Also, skill-based pay is moving from the shop floor to the white-collar workforce, and sometimes as far as the executive suite.[77]

Skill-based pay appears to be an idea whose time has come. As one expert noted, 'Slowly, but surely, we are becoming a skill-based society where your market value is tied to what you can do and what your skill set is. In this new world where skills and knowledge are what really counts, it doesn't make sense to treat people as jobholders. It makes sense to treat them as people with specific skills and to pay them for those skills.'[78]

FLEXIBLE BENEFITS: DEVELOPING A BENEFITS PACKAGE

Todd Evans and Allison Murphy both work for Coca-Cola Amatil (CCA), but they have very different needs in terms of employee benefits. Todd is married, with three young children and a wife who is at home full-time. Allison, too, is married, but her husband has a high-paying job with the federal government and they have no children. Todd is concerned about having access to a good corporate health insurance plan and enough life insurance to support his family if he weren't around. In contrast, Allison's husband already has her medical needs covered on his corporate health insurance plan, and life insurance is a low priority for both her and her husband. Allison is more interested in extra holiday time and long-term financial benefits such as a tax-deferred savings plan.

A standardised benefit package for all employees at CCA would be unlikely to meet the optimal needs of both Todd and Allison. They could, however, optimise their needs if CCA offered flexible benefits.

Flexible benefits allow each employee to put together a benefit package individually tailored to his or her own needs and situation. It replaces the traditional 'one-benefit-plan-fits-all' programs that dominated organisations for more than 50 years.[79] Consistent with expectancy theory's thesis that organisational rewards should be linked to each individual employee's goals, flexible benefits individualise rewards by allowing each employee to choose the compensation package that best satisfies his or her current needs. The average organisation provides fringe benefits worth approximately 40 per cent of an employee's salary. Traditional benefit programs were designed for the typical employee of the 1950s—a male with a wife and two children at home. Less than 10 per cent of employees now fit this stereotype. About 25 per cent of today's employees are single, and a third are part of two-income families with no children. Traditional programs don't meet their diverse needs, but flexible benefits do. They can be uniquely tailored to accommodate differences in employee needs based on age, marital status, spouse's benefit status, number and age of dependants, and the like.

The three most popular types of benefit plans are modular plans, core-plus options and flexible spending accounts.[80] *Modular plans* are pre-designed packages of benefits, with each module put together to meet the needs of a specific group of employees. So, a module designed for single employees with no dependants might include only essential benefits. Another, designed for single parents, might have additional life insurance, disability insurance and expanded health coverage. *Core-plus plans* consist of a core of essential benefits and a menu-like selection of other benefit options from which employees can select and add to the core. Typically, each employee is given 'benefit credits', which allow the 'purchase' of additional benefits that uniquely meet his or her needs. *Flexible spending plans* allow employees to set aside up to the dollar amount offered in the plan to pay for particular services. It is a convenient way, for example, for employees to pay for health-care and dental premiums. Flexible spending accounts can increase employee take-home pay because employees don't have to pay taxes on the dollars they spend out of these accounts.

Today, many organisations in Australia—in particular, public sector and service sector firms—offer flexible benefits. And they are becoming the norm in other countries, too. For instance, a recent survey of 136 Canadian organisations found that 93 per cent have adopted or will adopt flexible benefits in the near term.[81] And a similar survey of 307 firms in the United Kingdom found that while only 16 per cent have flexible benefit programs in place, another 60 per cent are either in the process of implementing them or are seriously considering it.[82]

flexible benefits |
A benefits plan that allows each employee to put together a benefit package individually tailored to his or her own needs and situation.

INTRINSIC REWARDS: EMPLOYEE RECOGNITION PROGRAMS

Laura Jackson makes only $17.50 an hour working at her fast-food job in Brisbane, and the job isn't very challenging or interesting. Yet, Laura talks enthusiastically about her job, her boss and the company that employs her. 'What I like is the fact that Guy [her supervisor] appreciates the effort I make. He compliments me regularly in front of the other people on my shift, and I've been chosen "Employee of the Month" twice in the past six months. Did you see my picture on that plaque on the wall?'

Organisations are increasingly recognising what Laura Jackson knows: important work rewards can be both intrinsic and extrinsic. Rewards are intrinsic in the form of employee recognition programs and extrinsic in the form of compensation systems. In this section, we deal with ways in which managers can reward and motivate employee performance.

Employee recognition programs range from a spontaneous and private 'thank you' up to widely publicised formal programs where specific types of behaviour are encouraged and the procedures for attaining recognition are clearly identified.[83]

Nichols Foods Ltd, a British bottler of soft drinks and syrups, has a comprehensive recognition program.[84] The central hallway in its production area is lined with 'bragging boards', where the accomplishments of various individuals and teams are regularly updated. Monthly awards are presented to people who have been nominated by their peers for extraordinary effort on the job. And monthly award winners are eligible for further recognition at an annual off-site meeting for all employees. In contrast, most managers use a far more informal approach. Julia Stewart, president of Applebee's restaurants, frequently leaves sealed notes on the chairs of employees after everyone has gone home.[85] These notes explain how critical Stewart thinks the person's work is or how much she appreciates the completion of a recent project. Stewart also relies heavily on voice mail messages left after office hours to tell employees how appreciative she is for a job well done.

A few years ago, 1500 employees were surveyed in a variety of work settings to find out what they considered to be the most powerful workplace motivator. Their response? Recognition, recognition and more recognition.[86] An obvious advantage of recognition programs is that they are inexpensive.[87] (Praise, of course, is free!) It shouldn't be

JOB IN PRACTICE

CULTURAL DIFFERENCES IN JOB CHARACTERISTICS AND JOB SATISFACTION

How do various factors of one's job contribute to satisfaction in different cultures? A recent study attempted to answer this question in a survey of over 49 countries. The authors of the study distinguished between intrinsic job characteristics (having a job that allows one to use one's skills, frequently receiving recognition from one's supervisor) and extrinsic job characteristics (receiving pay that is competitive within a given industry, working in an environment that has comfortable physical conditions) and assessed differences between the two in predicting employee job satisfaction.

The study found that, across all countries, extrinsic job characteristics were consistently and positively related to satisfaction with one's job. However, countries differed in the extent to which intrinsic job characteristics predicted job satisfaction. Richer countries, countries with stronger social security, countries that stress individualism rather than collectivism, and countries with a smaller power distance (those that value a more equal distribution of power in organisations and institutions) showed a stronger relationship between the presence of intrinsic job characteristics and job satisfaction.

What explains these findings? One explanation is that in countries with greater wealth and social security, concerns over survival are taken for granted, and thus employees have the freedom to place greater importance on intrinsic aspects of the job. Another explanation is that cultural norms emphasising the individual and less power asymmetry socialise individuals to focus on the intrinsic aspects of their job. In other words, such norms tell individuals that it is okay to want jobs that are intrinsically rewarding.

SOURCE: Based on X. Huang and E. Van De Vliert, 'Where Intrinsic Job Satisfaction Fails to Work: National Moderators of Intrinsic Motivation', *Journal of Organizational Behavior*, vol. 24, 2003, pp. 159–79.

surprising, therefore, to find that employee recognition programs have grown in popularity. A 2002 survey of 391 companies found that 84 per cent had some program to recognise employee achievements, and that four in ten said they were doing more to foster employee recognition than they were just a year earlier.[88] The downside of recognition programs is that they rely on employee trust and confidence in senior management. Praise from someone who is not respected by those being praised is likely to have the opposite effect to the motivational one desired.

Despite the increased popularity, critics argue that employee recognition programs are highly susceptible to political manipulation by management.[89] When applied to jobs where performance factors are relatively objective such as sales, recognition programs are likely to be perceived by employees as fair. However, in most jobs, the criteria for good performance aren't self-evident, which allows managers to manipulate the system and recognise their favourite employees. When abused, this can undermine the value of recognition programs and lead to demoralising employees.

- Managers should be sensitive to individual differences.
- Employees have different needs. Don't treat them all alike. Moreover, spend the time necessary to understand what is important to each employee. This will allow you to individualise goals, level of involvement and rewards to align with individual needs. Design jobs to align with individual needs and therefore maximise the motivation potential in jobs.
- Employees should have hard, specific goals, as well as feedback on how well they are faring in pursuit of those goals.
- Allow employees to participate in decisions that affect them. Employees can contribute to a number of decisions that affect them: setting work goals, choosing their own benefits packages, solving productivity and quality problems, and the like. This can increase employee productivity, commitment to work goals, motivation and job satisfaction.
- Rewards should be contingent on performance, and employees must perceive a clear linkage.
- Check the system for equity. Rewards should also be perceived by employees as equating with the inputs they bring to the job. At a simplistic level, this should mean that experience, skills, abilities, effort and other obvious inputs should explain differences in performance and, hence, pay, job assignments and other obvious rewards.

POINT / COUNTERPOINT

Professional Employees Are More Difficult to Motivate

● POINT

Professional employees are different from your average employee. And they are more difficult to motivate. Why? Because professionals don't respond to the same stimuli that non-professionals do. Professionals such as engineers, accountants, lawyers, academics and software designers are different from non-professionals. They have a strong and long-term commitment to their field of expertise. Typical rewards, such as money and promotions, are rarely effective in encouraging professionals to exert high levels of effort. Their loyalty is more often to their profession than to the organisation that employs them. A nurse, for instance, may work for the Mater Hospital but she reads nursing journals, belongs to nursing associations, attends nursing conferences, and hangs around with other nurses during her breaks at work. When asked what she does for a living, she's more apt to respond, 'I'm a registered nurse' than 'I work at the Mater Hospital.'

Money and promotions are typically low on the professional's priority list. Why? Because they tend to be well paid already and they enjoy what they do. For instance, professionals aren't typically anxious to give up their work in order to take on managerial responsibilities. They have invested a great deal of time and effort in developing their professional skills. They have typically undertaken higher studies for several years and undergone specialised training to build their proficiencies. They also invest regularly—in terms of reading, taking courses, attending conferences, and the like—to keep their skills current. Moving into management often means cutting off their ties to their profession, losing touch with the latest advances in their field, and having to let the skills that they have spent years developing become obsolete.

This loyalty to the profession and less interest in typical organisational rewards makes motivating professionals more challenging and complex. They don't respond to traditional rewards. And because they tend to give their primary allegiance to their profession rather than to their employer, they are more likely to quit if they are dissatisfied. As an employer, you might be justified in deciding not to exert the effort to develop and keep professionals because they are unlikely to reciprocate loyalty efforts you make.

● COUNTERPOINT

Let's first address the question of whether professionals with advanced degrees are really that different from non-professionals. One of the differences often cited regarding professionals is their allegiance to their profession. But this isn't unique to the so-called degreed professionals. For instance, plumbers, electricians and similar tradespeople aren't considered professionals, but they typically see themselves as affiliated to their trade or union rather than their employer. Similarly, many employees at Ford and GM give their primary allegiance to the Automotive, Food, Metals & Engineering Union.

Even if you accept that professionals are different from non-professionals, these differences may make it easier to motivate professionals rather than harder. For a large proportion of professionals, their work is their life. They rarely define their work week in terms of 8 to 5 and five days a week. Working 60 hours a week or more is often common. They love what they do and often prefer to be working rather than doing anything else. So, as long as they enjoy their work, they are likely to be self-motivated.

What factors are likely to determine if they enjoy their work? Job challenge tends to be ranked high. They like to tackle problems and find solutions. They prefer jobs that score high on the job characteristics model; that is, they want jobs that provide variety, identity, significance, autonomy and feedback. Professionals also value support, recognition, and opportunities to improve and expand their professional expertise.

So, how do you motivate professionals? Provide them with ongoing challenging projects. Give them autonomy to follow their interests and allow them to structure their work in ways that they find productive. Provide them with lateral moves that allow them to broaden their experience. Reward them with educational opportunities—training, workshops, attending conferences—that allow them to keep current in their field. In addition, reward them with recognition. And consider creating alternative career paths that allow them to earn more money and status without assuming managerial responsibilities. At CSIRO, Cochlear and Primary Industries, for instance, the best scientists, engineers and researchers gain titles such as 'fellow' and 'senior scientist'. They carry pay and prestige that are comparable with those of managers but without the corresponding authority or responsibility.

QUESTIONS FOR REVIEW

1. What are the advantages of flexitime from an employee's perspective? From management's perspective?
2. What are the advantages of job sharing from an employee's perspective? From management's perspective?
3. Explain the formula:

   Performance = $f(A \times M \times O)$

   and give an example.
4. Explain the roles of employees and management in quality circles.
5. What is gainsharing? What explains its recent popularity?
6. What is an ESOP? How might it positively influence employee motivation?
7. What are the pluses of variable-pay programs from an employee's viewpoint? From management's viewpoint?
8. Contrast job-based and skill-based pay.
9. What role, if any, does money play in employee recognition, job redesign and skill-based pay?
10. What can you do, as a manager, to increase the likelihood that your employees will exert a high level of effort?

QUESTIONS FOR CRITICAL THINKING

1. Identify five different criteria by which organisations can compensate employees. Based on your knowledge and experience, do you think performance is the criterion most used in practice? Discuss.
2. 'Recognition may be motivational for the moment but it doesn't have any staying power. It is an empty reinforcer. Why? Because when you go to the supermarket, they don't take recognition as a form of payment!' Do you agree or disagree? Discuss.
3. 'Performance can't be measured, so any effort to link pay with performance is a fantasy. Differences in performance are often caused by the system, which means the organisation ends up rewarding the circumstances. It is the same thing as rewarding the weather forecaster for a pleasant day.' Do you agree or disagree with this statement? Support your position.
4. It is an indisputable fact that there has been an explosive increase in the difference between the average employee's income and those of senior executives. In 1980 the average CEO made 42 times the average blue-collar employee's pay. In 1990 it was 85 times. In 2000 it had risen to 531 times. What are the implications of this trend for motivation in organisations?
5. This book argues for recognising individual differences. It also suggests paying attention to members of diversity groups. Is this contradictory? Discuss.

EXPERIENTIAL EXERCISE

Assessing Employee Motivation and Satisfaction Using the Job Characteristics Model

Purpose:
To examine outcomes of the job characteristics model for different professions.

Time required:
Approximately 30–45 minutes.

Background:
Data were collected on 6930 employees in 56 different organisations using the Job Diagnostic Survey. The following table contains data on the five core job dimensions of the job characteristics model for several professions. Also included are growth needs strength, internal motivation and pay satisfaction for each profession. The values are averages based on a 7-point scale.

Step 1:
Break into groups of three to five.

Step 2:
Calculate the motivating potential score for each of the professions and compare them. Discuss whether or not you think these scores accurately reflect your perceptions of the motivating potential of these professions.

Step 3:
Graph the relationship between each profession's core job dimensions and its corresponding value for internal motivation and for pay satisfaction, using the core job dimensions as independent variables. What conclusions can you draw about motivation and satisfaction of employees in these professions?

Job characteristics averages for six professions

	Profession					
Variable	Professional/ technical	Managerial	Sales	Service	Clerical	Machine trades
Skill variety	5.4	5.6	4.8	5.0	4.0	5.1
Task identity	5.1	4.7	4.4	4.7	4.7	4.9
Task significance	5.6	5.8	5.5	5.7	5.3	5.6
Autonomy	5.4	5.4	4.8	5.0	4.5	4.9
Feedback	5.1	5.2	5.4	5.1	4.6	4.9
Growth needs strength	5.6	5.3	5.7	5.4	5.0	4.8
Internal motivation	5.8	5.8	5.7	5.7	5.4	5.6
Pay satisfaction	4.4	4.6	4.2	4.1	4.0	4.2

SOURCE OF DATA: J. R. Hackman and G. R. Oldham, *Work Redesign* (Reading, MA: Addison-Wesley, 1980).

ETHICAL DILEMMA

Are Australian CEOs Paid Too Much?

The generous pay packages given to Australian CEOs have been subject to a great deal of very negative public scrutiny. Recent research into the pay received by member CEOs of the influential Business Council of Australia (BCA) revealed, for instance, that between 1990 and 2005, average annual BCA CEO pay skyrocketed a staggering 564 per cent—from $514 000 to $3.4 million. To put this into perspective, this meant that CEO remuneration leapt from being 18 times that of the average Australian employee to being 63 times the average Australian employee's income.

Also, you shouldn't assume that growth of CEO pay packets has reflected growth in shareholder returns for the same period. While the average BCA CEO income rose by 100 per cent in the same period (that is, it doubled), shareholder returns rose by only 60 per cent. Perhaps the most extraordinary trend, however, relates to CEO termination payments. These have risen from a pre-2000 average of $2.3 million to a 2001–05 average of $3.3 million, with some of the most generous payments going to those CEOs with the most dubious or controversial records of performance: Peter MacDonald of James Hardie Industries ($8.4 million), Frank Cicutto of National Australia Bank ($6.6 million) and John Prescott of BHP ($8.7 million).

How does the BCA defend such astronomical pay? A position paper released in 2004 argued that this was a classic economic response to a situation in which the demand is great for high-quality top executive talent and the supply is low; while for average employees the reverse applies: demand is weaker for average employees and the market is much larger. The BCA accused critics of focusing unduly on a small number of the largest companies, rather than taking a more balanced view that acknowledged the smaller remuneration levels offered CEOs of smaller companies. They argued that Australian CEOs don't receive the amounts offered to CEOs in the United States or the United Kingdom. American CEOs make 531 times the pay of their average hourly employees. The BCA argued that Australian companies need to be competitive in order to attract high-calibre talent in the fluid, global economy in which these organisations operate. They argued that Australian CEOs are already subject to intense scrutiny of their performance, as evidenced by their relatively short average tenure, and that pay packages need to be generous to compensate for the risks of an early termination. It has also subsequently been argued that the accountabililty, stress and visibility of Australian CEOs in itself needs to be reflected in compensation packages.

Is high compensation of Australian executives a problem? If so, does the blame for the problem lie with CEOs or with the shareholders and boards that knowingly allow the practice? Are Australian CEOs greedy? Are these CEOs acting unethically? What do you think?

SOURCE: J. Shields, 'Setting the Double Standard: Chief Executive Pay the BCA Way', *Journal of Australian Political Economy*, no. 56, 2006, pp. 299–324.

CASE STUDY

Motivation for Change

Often, it is assumed that the major challenge in motivating staff is in getting employees to feel a passion for the purpose and work of their employing organisation. That isn't always the case, however. The Royal Society for the Prevention of Cruelty to Animals (RSPCA) Victoria is a case in point. The society's constituency has never lacked a true passion and commitment to animal welfare issues. The current vision of the society captures the spirit of the organisation that has endured since its inception in Melbourne in 1871 as the Victorian Society for the Protection of Animals.

That all animals, great and small, are:
- free from hunger and thirst;
- free from discomfort;
- free from pain, injury and disease;
- free to express normal behaviour; and
- free from fear and distress.

The challenge for their newly appointed CEO, Maria Mercurio, in 2002 was to motivate the society's employees and volunteers to accept and participate in the creation of a new organisational heart for the society.

On her appointment, Mercurio inherited an underdeveloped organisation that had relied for too long on the passion, good intentions and reputation of its constituency. She also inherited an organisation that operated within a chaotic, collaborative structure with no sense of line authority and no clear single, overarching purpose. In short, while staff were highly motivated in their concerns for animal welfare, their efforts lacked a real common purpose and therefore a real synergy. They also lacked a real sense of coordination and interrelatedness.

Certain advantages would obviously accrue from this change. For example, prior to Mercurio's arrival the relationship between staff and management was fractured, to say the least. The staff–management relationship was marked more by industrial disputes than by more effective forms of communication. With

Mercurio's arrival, moves began to repair the relationship. Staff consultations began in earnest and change was tackled 'a bite at a time' in collaboration with staff, rather than being imposed from above.

The occupational health and safety management system that was introduced in 2003 led to an 85 per cent reduction in WorkCover premiums and the creation of a much safer workplace. In a cash-strapped organisation like the RSPCA, any improvement in the financials of the organisation is good news for staff. Similarly, improvements in the physical safety of the work environment have their obvious advantages.

There were, however, disadvantages for staff in all this change. In the absence of more effective organisational guidance, staff had developed their own roles and their own views on the objectives of the society. Accepting a unifying vision for the society and accountability and authority structures meant a loss of some of the autonomy and, presumably, influence staff had previously experienced.

According to Mercurio, the change process really began with the development of a people management framework that 'starts with how we go about attracting and retaining skilled people, how we induct them, how we develop them, how we performance manage them and how we plan for their ongoing development so that they continue to add value to the organisation'.

Fundraising was no longer outsourced, and a new marketing and development department has been developed. Most staff have been internally appointed and developed for their roles through mentoring and coaching by the department's senior manager. In addition, 'Some job rotation has also occurred in the department.' According to Mercurio, 'Again, it's been about looking at the skills we need, looking at the skills we have, doing the gap analysis and then trying to close that gap.'

While the changes haven't all run smoothly, the society has made great steps forward. Best of all, it was recognised for its efforts at the 2005 Australian HR awards when RSPCA Victoria won the Australian Graduate School of Management award for best change management.

QUESTIONS

1. The changes Mercurio introduced meant some staff lost some autonomy from their jobs. Given that autonomy is a positive feature of good job design, how might other changes Mercurio introduced compensate staff for this loss?
2. The society has ten animal shelters across Victoria, nine of which operate as regional Council Pounds that operate 24 hours a day, seven days a week.

How might work and work hours be structured in these settings to maximise their capacity to motivate staff?

3. It is difficult for not-for-profit organisations such as the RSPCA to use financial incentives and bonuses beyond base salaries to motivate staff. How might the RSPCA use employee recognition programs to motivate staff?

SOURCES: RSPCA Annual Report 2005; 'HR in a dog eat dog world', *Human Resources*, 18 April 2006: <www.humanresourcesmagazine.com.au/articles/F8/0C03DEF8.asp?Type=60&Category=874> (accessed 7 October 2006); and RSPCA Victoria: <www.rspcavic.org/>.

ENDNOTES

1. <http://careers.flightcentrelimited.com.au>.
2. J. R. Hackman and G. R. Oldham, 'Motivation through the Design of Work: Test of a Theory', *Organizational Behavior and Human Performance*, August 1976, pp. 250–79; and J. R. Hackman and G. R. Oldham, *Work Redesign* (Reading, MA: Addison-Wesley, 1980).
3. J. R. Hackman, 'Work Design', in J. R. Hackman and J. L. Suttle (eds), *Improving Life at Work* (Santa Monica, CA: Goodyear, 1977), p. 129.
4. See 'Job Characteristics Theory of Work Redesign', in J. B. Miner, *Theories of Organizational Behavior* (Hinsdale, IL: Dryden Press, 1980), pp. 231–66; B. T. Loher, R. A. Noe, N. L. Moeller and M. P. Fitzgerald, 'A Meta-Analysis of the Relation of Job Characteristics to Job Satisfaction', *Journal of Applied Psychology*, May 1985, pp. 280–89; W. H. Glick, G. D. Jenkins, Jr and N. Gupta, 'Method versus Substance: How Strong Are Underlying Relationships between Job Characteristics and Attitudinal Outcomes?', *Academy of Management Journal*, September 1986, pp. 441–64; Y. Fried and G. R. Ferris, 'The Validity of the Job Characteristics Model: A Review and Meta-Analysis', *Personnel Psychology*, Summer 1987, pp. 287–322; S. J. Zaccaro and E. F. Stone, 'Incremental Validity of an Empirically Based Measure of Job Characteristics', *Journal of Applied Psychology*, May 1988, pp. 245–52; J. R. Rentsch and R. P. Steel, 'Testing the Durability of Job Characteristics as Predictors of Absenteeism over a Six-Year Period', *Personnel Psychology*, Spring 1998, pp. 165–90; S. J. Behson, E. R. Eddy and S. J. Lorenzet, 'The Importance of the Critical Psychological States in the Job Characteristics Model: A Meta-Analytic and Structural Equations Modelling Examination', *Current Research in Social Psychology*, May 2000, pp. 170–89; and T. A. Judge, 'Promote Job Satisfaction through Mental Challenge', in E. A. Locke (ed.), *Handbook of Principles of Organizational Behavior* (Malden, MA: Blackwell, 2004), pp. 75–89.
5. T. A. Judge, S. K. Parker, A. E. Colbert, D. Heller and R. Ilies, 'Job Satisfaction: A Cross-Cultural Review', In N. Anderson, D. S. Ones (eds), *Handbook of Industrial, Work and Organizational Psychology*, vol. 2 (Thousand Oaks, CA: Sage Publications, 2002), pp. 25–52.
6. C. A. O'Reilly and D. F. Caldwell, 'Informational Influence as a Determinant of Perceived Task Characteristics and Job Satisfaction', *Journal of Applied Psychology*, April 1979, pp. 157–65; R. V. Montagno, 'The Effects of Comparison Others and Prior Experience on Responses to Task Design', *Academy of Management Journal*, June 1985, pp. 491–98; and P. C. Bottger and I. K.-H. Chew, 'The Job Characteristics Model and Growth Satisfaction: Main Effects of Assimilation of Work Experience and Context Satisfaction', *Human Relations*, June 1986, pp. 575–94.
7. C. Ansberry, 'In the New Workplace, Jobs Morph to Suit Rapid Pace of Change', *Wall Street Journal*, 22 March 2002, p. A1.
8. Anon, 'Good OHS Makes Dollars and Sense', *Human Resources*, 19 August 2004: <www.humanresourcesmagazine.com.au/articles/D0/0C0219D0.asp?Type=60&Category=876> (accessed 6 October 2006).
9. J. Ortega, 'Job Rotation as a Learning Mechanism', *Management Science*, October 2001, pp. 1361–70.
10. See, for instance, data on job enlargement described in M. A. Campion and C. L. McClelland, 'Follow-up and Extension of the Interdisciplinary Costs and Benefits of Enlarged Jobs', *Journal of Applied Psychology*, June 1993, pp. 339–51.
11. J. R. Hackman and G. R. Oldham, *Work Redesign* (Reading, MA: Addison Wesley, 1980).
12. Cited in *U.S. News & World Report*, 31 May 1993, p. 63.
13. See, for example, Hackman and Oldham, *Work Redesign*; J. B. Miner, *Theories of Organizational Behavior* (Hinsdale, IL: Dryden Press, 1980), pp. 231–66; R. W. Griffin, 'Effects of Work Redesign on Employee Perceptions, Attitudes, and Behaviors: A Long-Term Investigation', *Academy of Management Journal*, vol. 34,

no. 2, 1991, pp. 425–35; and J. L. Cotton, *Employee Involvement* (Newbury Park, CA: Sage, 1993), pp. 141–72.

14. Institute of Chartered Accountants cited in 'Workers: Mixed Demographic the Best', *Human Resources*, 15 November 2005: <www.humanresourcesmagazine.com.au/articles/27/0C038327.asp?Type=61&Category=888> (accessed 6 October 2006).

15. From the National Study of the Changing Workforce cited in S. Shellenbarger, 'Number of Women Managers Rise', *Wall Street Journal*, 30 September 2003, p. D2.

16. Cited in 'Flexitime Gains in Popularity in Germany', *Manpower Argus*, September 2000, p. 4.

17. D. R. Dalton and D. J. Mesch, 'The Impact of Flexible Scheduling on Employee Attendance and Turnover', *Administrative Science Quarterly*, June 1990, pp. 70–87; K. S. Kush and L. K. Stroh, 'Flexitime: Myth or Reality', *Business Horizons*, September–October 1994, p. 53; and L. Golden, 'Flexible Work Schedules: What Are We Trading Off to Get Them?', *Monthly Labor Review*, March 2001, pp. 50–55.

18. See, for example, D. A. Ralston and M. F. Flanagan, 'The Effect of Flexitime on Absenteeism and Turnover for Male and Female Employees', *Journal of Vocational Behavior*, April 1985, pp. 206–17; D. A. Ralston, W. P. Anthony and D. J. Gustafson, 'Employees May Love Flexitime, But What Does It Do to the Organization's Productivity?', *Journal of Applied Psychology*, May 1985, pp. 272–79; J. B. McGuire and J. R. Liro, 'Flexible Work Schedules, Work Attitudes, and Perceptions of Productivity', *Public Personnel Management*, Spring 1986, pp. 65–73; P. Bernstein, 'The Ultimate in Flexitime: From Sweden, by Way of Volvo', *Personnel*, June 1988, pp. 70–74; and D. R. Dalton and D. J. Mesch, 'The Impact of Flexible Scheduling on Employee Attendance and Turnover', *Administrative Science Quarterly*, June 1990, pp. 370–87; and B. B. Baltes, T. E. Briggs, J. W. Huff, J. A. Wright and G. A. Neuman, 'Flexible and Compressed Workweek Schedules: A Meta-Analysis of Their Effects on Work-Related Criteria', *Journal of Applied Psychology*, vol. 84, no. 4, 1999, pp. 496–513.

19. See <www.workplace.gov.au/workplace/Category/SchemesInitiatives/WorkFamily/Jobsharing.htm>.

20. Ibid.

21. S. Shellenbarger, 'Two People, One Job: It Can Really Work', *Wall Street Journal*, 7 December 1994, p. B1.

22. 'Job-Sharing: Widely Offered, Little Used', *Training*, November 1994, p. 12.

23. C. Dawson, 'Japan: Work-Sharing Will Prolong the Pain', *BusinessWeek*, 24 December 2001, p. 46.

24. Shellenbarger, 'Two People, One Job'.

25. See, for example, T. H. Davenport and K. Pearlson, 'Two Cheers for the Virtual Office', *Sloan Management Review*, Summer 1998, pp. 61–65; E. J. Hill, B. C. Miller, S. P. Weiner and J. Colihan, 'Influences of the Virtual Office on Aspects of Work and Work/Life Balance', *Personnel Psychology*, Autumn 1998, pp. 667–83; K. E. Pearlson and C. S. Saunders, 'There's No Place Like Home: Managing Telecommuting Paradoxes', *Academy of Management Executive*, May 2001, pp. 117–28; S. J. Wells, 'Making Telecommuting Work', *Human Resources*, October 2001, pp. 34–45; and E. J. Hill, M. Ferris and V. Martinson, 'Does it Matter Where You Work? A Comparison of How Three Work Venues (Traditional Office, Virtual Office, and Home Office) Influence Aspects of Work and Personal/Family Life', *Journal of Vocational Behavior*, vol. 63, no. 2, 2003, pp. 220–41.

26. N. B. Kurland and D. E. Bailey, 'Telework: The Advantages and Challenges of Working Here, There, Anywhere, and Anytime', *Organizational Dynamics*, Autumn 1999, pp. 53–68; Wells, 'Making Telecommuting Work', p. 34; and <www.smh.com.au/articles/2002/06/02/1022569848449.html>.

27. See, for instance, J. D. Glater, 'Telecommuting's Big Experiment', *New York Times*, 9 May 2001, p. C1; and S. Shellenbarger, 'Telework Is on the Rise, But It Isn't Just Done from Home Anymore', *Wall Street Journal*, 23 January 2001, p. B1.

28. U. Huws, 'Wired in the Country', *People Management*, November 1999, pp. 46–47.

29. <http://was7.hewitt.com/bestemployers/anz/2005list.htm>.

30. Cited in R. W. Judy and C. D'Amico, *Workforce 2020* (Indianapolis: Hudson Institute, 1997), p. 58.

31. Cited in Wells, 'Making Telecommuting Work'.

32. <www.smh.com.au/articles/2002/06/02/1022569848449.html>.

33. J. M. Stanton and J. L. Barnes-Farrell, 'Effects of Electronic Performance Monitoring on Personal Control, Task Satisfaction, and Task Performance', *Journal of Applied Psychology*, December 1996, pp. 738–45; B. Pappas, 'They Spy', *Forbes*, 8 February 1999, p. 47; S. Armour, 'More Bosses Keep Tabs on Telecommuters', *USA Today*, 24 July 2001, p. 1B; and D. Buss, 'Spies Like Us', *Training*, December 2001, pp. 44–48.

34. L. H. Peters, E. J. O'Connor and C. J. Rudolf, 'The Behavioral and Affective Consequences of Performance-Relevant Situational Variables', *Organizational Behavior and Human Performance*, February 1980, pp. 79–96; M. Blumberg and C. D. Pringle, 'The Missing Opportunity in Organizational Research: Some Implications for a Theory of Work Performance', *Academy of Management Review*, October 1982, pp. 560–69; D. A. Waldman and W. D. Spangler, 'Putting Together the Pieces: A Closer Look at the Determinants of Job Performance', *Human Performance*, vol. 2, 1989, pp. 29–59; and J. Hall, 'Americans Know How to Be Productive If Managers Will Let Them', *Organizational Dynamics*, Winter 1994, pp. 33–46.

35. See, for example, the increasing body of literature on empowerment, such as W. A. Randolph, 'Re-Thinking Empowerment: Why Is It So Hard to Achieve?', *Organizational Dynamics*, vol. 29, no. 2, 2000, pp. 94–107; K. Blanchard, J. P. Carlos and W. A. Randolph, *Empowerment Takes More Than a Minute*, 2nd ed. (San Francisco: Berrett-Koehler, 2001); D. P. Ashmos, D. Duchon, R. R. McDaniel, Jr and J. W. Huonker, 'What a Mess! Participation as a Simple Managerial Rule to "Complexify" Organizations', *Journal of Management Studies*, March 2002, pp. 189–206; and S. E. Seibert, S. R. Silver and W. A. Randolph, 'Taking Empowerment to the Next Level: A Multiple-Level Model of Empowerment, Performance, and Satisfaction', *Academy of Management Journal*, vol. 47, no. 3, 2004, pp. 332–49.

36. See, for instance, A. Sagie and Z. Aycan, 'A Cross-Cultural Analysis of Participative Decision-Making in Organizations', *Human Relations*, April 2003, pp. 453–73; and J. Brockner, 'Unpacking Country Effects: On the Need to Operationalize the Psychological Determinants of Cross-National Differences', in R. M. Kramer and B. M. Staw (eds), *Research in Organizational Behaviour*, vol. 25 (Oxford, UK: Elsevier, 2003), pp. 336–40.

37. C. Robert, T. M. Probst, J. J. Martocchio, R. Drasgow and J. J. Lawler, 'Empowerment and Continuous Improvement in the United States, Mexico, Poland, and India: Predicting Fit on the Basis of the Dimensions of Power Distance and Individualism', *Journal of Applied Psychology*, October 2000, pp. 643–58.

38. F. Heller, E. Pusic, G. Strauss and B. Wilpert, *Organizational Participation: Myth and Reality* (Oxford: Oxford University Press, 1998).

39. See, for instance, K. L. Miller and P. R. Monge, 'Participation, Satisfaction, and Productivity: A Meta-Analytic Review', *Academy of Management Journal*, December 1986, pp. 727–53; J. A. Wagner III and R. Z. Gooding, 'Shared Influence and Organizational Behavior: A Meta-Analysis of Situational Variables Expected to Moderate Participation–Outcome Relationships', *Academy of Management Journal*, September 1987, pp. 524–41; J. A. Wagner III, 'Participation's Effects on Performance and Satisfaction: A Reconsideration of Research Evidence', *Academy of Management Review*, April 1994, pp. 312–30; C. Doucouliagos, 'Worker Participation and Productivity in Labor-Managed and Participatory Capitalist Firms: A Meta-Analysis', *Industrial and Labor Relations Review*, October 1995, pp. 58–77; J. A. Wagner III, C. R. Leana, E. A. Locke and D. M. Schweiger, 'Cognitive and Motivational Frameworks in U.S. Research on Participation: A Meta-Analysis of Primary Effects', *Journal of Organizational Behavior*, vol. 18, 1997, pp. 49–65; J. S. Black and H. B. Gregersen, 'Participative Decision-Making: An Integration of Multiple Dimensions', *Human Relations*, July 1997, pp. 859–78; E. A. Locke, M. Alavi and J. A. Wagner III, 'Participation in Decision Making: An Information Exchange Perspective', in G. R. Ferris (ed.), *Research in Personnel and Human Resource Management*, vol. 15 (Greenwich, CT: JAI Press, 1997), pp. 293–331; and J. A. Wagner III and J. A. LePine, 'Effects of Participation on Performance and Satisfaction: Additional Meta-Analytic Evidence', *Psychological Reports*, June 1999, pp. 719–25.

40. Cotton, *Employee Involvement*, p. 114.

41. See, for example, M. Gilman and P. Marginson, 'Negotiating European Works Council: Contours of Constrained Choice', *Industrial Relations Journal*, March 2002, pp. 36–51; J. T. Addison and C. R. Belfield, 'What Do We Know about the New European Works Council? Some Preliminary Evidence from Britain', *Scottish Journal of Political Economy*, September 2002, pp. 418–44; and B. Keller, 'The European Company Statute: Employee Involvement—and Beyond', *Industrial Relations Journal*, December 2002, pp. 424–45.

42. Cotton, *Employee Involvement*, pp. 129–30, 139–40.

43. Ibid, p. 140.

44. See, for example, G. W. Meyer and R. G. Stott, 'Quality Circles: Panacea or Pandora's Box?', *Organizational Dynamics*, Spring 1985, pp. 34–50; E. E. Lawler III and S. A. Mohrman, 'Quality Circles: After the Honeymoon', *Organizational Dynamics*, Spring 1987, pp. 42–54; T. R. Miller, 'The Quality Circle Phenomenon: A Review and Appraisal', *SAM Advanced Management Journal*, Winter 1989, pp. 4–7; K. Buch and R. Spangler, 'The Effects of Quality Circles on Performance and Promotions', *Human Relations*, June 1990, pp. 573–82; P. R. Liverpool, 'Employee Participation in Decision-Making: An Analysis of the Perceptions of Members and Nonmembers of Quality Circles', *Journal of Business and Psychology*, Summer 1990, pp. 411–22, E. E. Adams, Jr, 'Quality Circle Performance', *Journal of Management*, March 1991, pp. 25–39; and L. I. Glassop, 'The Organizational Benefits of Teams', *Human Relations*, vol. 55, no. 2, 2002, pp. 225–49.

45. T. L. Tang and E. A. Butler, 'Attributions of Quality Circles' Problem-Solving Failure: Differences among Management, Supporting Staff, and Quality Circle Members', *Public Personnel Management*, Summer 1997, pp. 203–25; G. Hammersley and A. Pinnington, 'Quality Circles Reach End of the Line at Land Rover', *Human Resource Management International Digest*, May/June 1999, pp. 4–5; and D. Nagar and M. Takore, 'Effectiveness of Quality Circles in a Large Public Sector', *Psychological Studies*, January–July 2001, pp. 63–68.

46. Cotton, *Employee Involvement*, p. 87.

47. P. S. Goodman and P. P. Pan, 'Chinese Workers Pay for Wal-Mart's Low Prices', *The Washington Post*, 8 February 2004, p. A01.

48. L. Ingvarson, 'Standards for Advanced Teaching: Review of National and International Developments', Teaching Australia, cited by C. Milburn, 'Call for National Teachers' Standards', *The Age*, 21 August 2006: <www.theage.com.au/news/education-news/call-for-national-teacher-standards/2006/08/18/1155408026036.html>.

49. Based on J. R. Schuster and P. K. Zingheim, 'The New Variable Pay: Key Design Issues', *Compensation & Benefits Review*, March–April 1993, p. 28; K. S. Abosch, 'Variable Pay: Do We Have the Basics in Place?', *Compensation & Benefits Review*, July–August 1998, pp. 12–22; and

K. M. Kuhn and M. D. Yockey, 'Variable Pay as a Risky Choice: Determinants of the Relative Attractiveness of Incentive Plans', *Organizational Behavior and Human Decision Processes*, March 2003, pp. 323–41.

50. <www.humanresourcesmagazine.com.au/articles/5C/0C044B5C.asp?Type=61&Category=888>.

51. L. Wiener, 'Paycheck Plus', *U.S. News & World Report*, 24 February/3 March 2003, p. 58.

52. Cited in 'Pay Programs: Few Employees See the Pay-for-Performance Connection', *Compensation & Benefits Report*, June 2003, p. 1.

53. B. Wysocki, Jr, 'Chilling Reality Awaits Even the Employed', *Wall Street Journal*, 5 November 2001, p. A1.

54. M. Fein, 'Work Measurement and Wage Incentives', *Industrial Engineering*, September 1973, pp. 49–51. For updated reviews of the effect of pay on performance, see G. D. Jenkins, Jr, N. Gupta, A. Mitra and J. D. Shaw, 'Are Financial Incentives Related to Performance? A Meta-Analytic Review of Empirical Research', *Journal of Applied Psychology*, October 1998, pp. 777–87; and S. L. Rynes, B. Gerhart and L. Parks, 'Personnel Psychology: Performance Evaluation and Pay for Performance', *Annual Review of Psychology*, vol. 56, no. 1, 2005, pp. 571–600.

55. E. Arita, 'Teething Troubles Aside, Merit-Based Pay Catching On', *The Japan Times*: <www.202.221.217.59/print/business/nb04-2004/nb20040423a3.htm> (23 April 2004).

56. <www.dest.gov.au/Ministers/Media/Bishop/2006/10/B001061006.asp>.

57. M. Sainsbury and G. Newman, 'Trujillo's Strategy Plan Was Old News', *The Australian*, 29 September 2006, p. 1.

58. R. Balu, 'Bonuses Aren't Just for the Bosses', *Fast Company*, December 2000, pp. 74–76; and M. Conlin, 'A Little Less in the Envelope This Week', *BusinessWeek*, 18 February 2002, pp. 64–66.

59. See, for instance, D-O. Kim, 'Determinants of the Survival of Gainsharing Programs', *Industrial & Labor Relations Review*, October 1999, pp. 21–42; 'Why Gainsharing Works Even Better Today Than in the Past', *HR Focus*, April 2000, pp. 3–5; L. R. Gomez-Mejia, T. M. Welbourne and R. M. Wiseman, 'The Role of Risk Sharing and Risk Taking under Gainsharing', *Academy of Management Review*, July 2000, pp. 492–507; W. Atkinson, 'Incentive Pay Programs that Work in

Textile', *Textile World*, February 2001, pp. 55–57; M. Reynolds, 'A Cost-Reduction Strategy that May Be Back', *Healthcare Financial Management*, January 2002, pp. 58–64; and M. R. Dixon, L. J. Hayes and J. Stack, 'Changing Conceptions of Employee Compensation', *Journal of Organizational Behavior Management*, vol. 23, no. 2–3, 2003, pp. 95–116.

60. 'U.S. Wage and Productivity Growth Attainable through Gainsharing', Employment Policy Foundation: <www.epf.org> (10 May 2000).

61. 'The Employee Ownership 100': <www.nceo.org> (July 2003); and <www.aeoa.org.au>.

62. W. Taylor, 'Share the Money', *Sydney Morning Herald*, 21 May 2005, p. 57.

63. A. A. Buchko, 'The Effects of Employee Ownership on Employee Attitudes', *Work and Occupations*, vol. 19, no. 1, 1992, pp. 59–78.

64. C. M. Rosen and M. Quarrey, 'How Well Is Employee Ownership Working?', *Harvard Business Review*, September–October 1987, pp. 126–32.

65. Cited in 'ESOP Benefits Are No Fables', *BusinessWeek*, 6 September 1999, p. 26.

66. W. N. Davidson and D. L. Worrell, 'ESOP's Fables: The Influence of Employee Stock Ownership Plans on Corporate Stock Prices and Subsequent Operating Performance', *Human Resource Planning*, January 1994, pp. 69–85.

67. J. L. Pierce and C. A. Furo, 'Employee Ownership: Implications for Management', *Organizational Dynamics*, June 1990, pp. 32–43.

68. See data in D. Stamps, 'A Piece of the Action', *Training*, March 1996, p. 66.

69. C. G. Hanson and W. D. Bell, *Profit Sharing and Profitability: How Profit Sharing Promotes Business Success* (London: Kogan Page, 1987); M. Magnan and S. St-Onge, 'Profit-Sharing and Firm Performance: A Comparative and Longitudinal Analysis', Paper presented at the 58th annual meeting of the Academy of Management, San Diego, August 1998; and D. D'Art and T. Turner, 'Profit Sharing, Firm Performance, and Union Influence in Selected European Countries', *Personnel Review*, vol. 33, no. 3, 2004, pp. 335–50.

70. T. M. Welbourne and L. R. Gomez-Mejia, 'Gainsharing: A Critical Review and a Future Research Agenda', *Journal of Management*, vol. 21, no. 3, 1995, pp. 559–609.

71. See 'Skill-Based Pay Program': <www.bmpoc.org> (29 June 2001).

72. <www.wagenet.gov.au/WageNet/Search/View.ASP?docid=259268&quickview=Y>.

73. G. E. Ledford, Jr, 'Paying for the Skills, Knowledge, and Competencies of Knowledge Workers', *Compensation & Benefits Review*, July–August 1995, pp. 55–62; B. Murray and B. Gerhart, 'An Empirical Analysis of a Skill-Based Pay Program and Plant Performance Outcomes', *Academy of Management Journal*, February 1998, pp. 68–78; J. R. Thompson and C. W. LeHew, 'Skill-Based Pay as an Organizational Innovation', *Review of Public Personnel Administration*, Winter 2000, pp. 20–40; and J. D. Shaw, N. Gupta, A. Mitra and G. E. Ledford, Jr, 'Success and Survival of Skill-Based Pay Plans', *Journal of Management*, February 2005, pp. 28–49.

74. 'Tensions of a New Pay Plan', *New York Times*, 17 May 1992, p. F5.

75. E. E. Lawler III, S. A. Mohrman and G. E. Ledford, Jr, *Creating High Performance Organizations: Practices and Results in the Fortune 1000* (San Francisco: Jossey-Bass, 1995); C. Lee, K. S. Law and P. Bobko, 'The Importance of Justice Perceptions on Pay Effectiveness: A Two-Year Study of a Skill-Based Pay Plan', *Journal of Management*, vol. 25, no. 6, 1999, pp. 851–73; A. Podolske, 'Seven-Year Update on Skill-Based Pay Plans': <www.ioma.com> (July 1999).

76. E. E. Lawler III, G. E. Ledford and L. Chang, 'Who Uses Skill-Based Pay, and Why', *Compensation & Benefits Review*, vol. 25, no. 2, 1993, pp. 22–26.

77. M. Rowland, 'It's What You Can Do That Counts', *New York Times*, 6 June 1993, p. F17.

78. Ibid.

79. See, for instance, M. W. Barringer and G. T. Milkovich, 'A Theoretical Exploration of the Adoption and Design of Flexible Benefit Plans: A Case of Human Resource Innovation', *Academy of Management Review*, April 1998, pp. 305–24; D. Brown, 'Everybody Loves Flex', *Canadian HR Reporter*, 18 November 2002, p. 1; J. Taggart, 'Putting Flex Benefits through Their Paces', *Canadian HR Reporter*, 2 December 2002, p. G3; and N. D. Cole and D. H. Flint, 'Perceptions of Distributive and Procedural Justice in Employee Benefits: Flexible Versus Traditional Benefit Plans', *Journal of Managerial Psychology*, vol. 19, no. 1, 2004, pp. 19–40.

80. D. A. DeCenzo and S. P. Robbins, *Human Resource Management*, 7th ed. (New York: John Wiley & Sons, 2002), pp. 346–48.

81. Brown, 'Everybody Loves Flex'.

82. E. Unsworth, 'U.K. Employers Find Flex Benefits Helpful: Survey', *Business Insurance*, 21 May 2001, pp. 19–20.

83. Our definition of a formal recognition system is based on S. E. Markham, K. D. Scott and G. H. McKee, 'Recognizing Good Attendance: A Longitudinal, Quasi-Experimental Field Study', *Personnel Psychology*, Autumn 2002, p. 641.

84. D. Drickhamer, 'Best Plant Winners: Nichols Foods Ltd', *Industry Week*, 1 October 2001, pp. 17–19.

85. M. Littman, 'Best Bosses Tell All', *Working Woman*, October 2000, p. 54.

86. Cited in S. Caudron, 'The Top 20 Ways to Motivate Employees', *Industry Week*, 3 April 1995, pp. 15–16. See also B. Nelson, 'Try Praise', *INC.*, September 1996, p. 115.

87. A. D. Stajkovic and F. Luthans, 'Differential Effects of Incentive Motivators on Work Performance', *Academy of Management Journal*, June 2001, p. 587. See also F. Luthans and A. D. Stajkovic, 'Provide Recognition for Performance Improvement', in Locke (ed.), *Handbook of Principles of Organizational Behavior*, pp. 166–80.

88. Cited in K. J. Dunham, 'Amid Shrinking Workplace Morale, Employers Turn to Recognition', *Wall Street Journal*, 19 November 2002, p. B8.

89. Ibid.

8

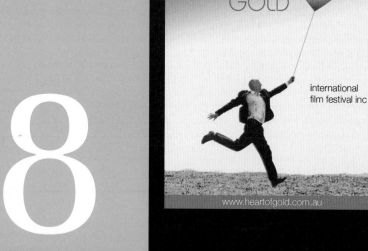

EMOTIONS AND MOODS

LEARNING OBJECTIVES

AFTER STUDYING THIS CHAPTER, YOU SHOULD BE ABLE TO:

1. DIFFERENTIATE EMOTIONS FROM MOODS

2. DISCUSS THE DIFFERENT ASPECTS OF EMOTIONS

3. IDENTIFY THE SOURCES OF EMOTIONS AND MOODS

4. DESCRIBE EXTERNAL CONSTRAINTS ON EMOTIONS

5. DISCUSS THE IMPACT EMOTIONAL LABOUR HAS ON EMPLOYEES

6. DISCUSS THE CASES FOR AND AGAINST EMOTIONAL INTELLIGENCE

7. APPLY CONCEPTS ON EMOTIONS AND MOODS TO OB ISSUES

Positive emotional experiences are the main theme of the international *Heart of Gold* Film Festival, held in Gympie, Queensland.

TONI POWELL IS AN EMOTIONAL PERSON.[1] She is known for her infectious enthusiasm, for her positive view on life, and for her courage and determination. She is also now known as the person who brought one of the best international film festivals held in 2006 to the sleepy rural town of Gympie, Queensland. And the theme of her film festival was an expression of her emotions—*Heart of Gold*.

When Toni first arrived in Gympie in 2003, she initially hated the place. She worried it was like its reputation: ultra-conservative, gun-toting and reactionary—the political heartland of the One Nation party. It was also depressed, with high unemployment and a palatable sense of gloom in the region aggravated by droughts and farm foreclosures. Toni felt that the content of the available media and movies was equally as depressing. As a young grandmother—just 45 years of age—with a rapidly approaching empty nest, she felt she was too young simply to retire. As her depression deepened, she became desperate to turn her feelings around. In a surprise reactionary move, Toni decided to make a short 'feel good' film.

With a group of friends and family, Toni wrote, produced and co-directed her short film, finishing it in just a few months. She then entered it in a national film festival where it won awards and received rave reviews. The film's popularity gained momentum internationally, where it continued to receive awards and positive reviews through 43 international film festivals in 18 countries. Suddenly, Toni Powell was rubbing shoulders with Hollywood industry elites—an outcome that was surprising for a first-time filmaker.

While Toni was presenting her film overseas, the idea came to her to have a film festival in Gympie. She wanted it to have the same 'feel good' theme that had helped make her own short film so successful. At first people were sceptical—'an international film festival in Gympie?' 'Where's Gympie?' 'Why Gympie?' Undeterred, Toni and her husband put up their home as security and began to organise the festival, beginning with starting an incorporated association with a mission to positively affect media. In time, she gathered around ten unpaid staff and 50–60 other volunteers to help stage the festival. Always considered a huge risk, Toni believed in her 'feel good' concept and 'badged' the festival *Heart of Gold*.

Notable Australian actor Tony Barry accepted with great enthusiasm Toni's invitation to take on the role of *Heart of Gold* patron. He said, 'I believe this film festival promises to be the beginning of a new and gentle wave of empowerment, offering emerging film-makers of all ages, the opportunity to create blue-prints of nourishing behaviour for successive generations, both here and overseas.'[2] With Tony Barry's assistance, Toni set about calling for short films from around the world, recruiting judges, finding a suitable venue and gaining community support.

The end result was nothing short of breathtaking. Every session of the festival, held at the end of October 2006, was well attended; all the debts were paid; and the local community received a well-deserved morale boost as a result. The festival raised the spirits of a community struggling with the worst drought in recorded history, as well as other depressing social issues, and gave people hope. Many saw Toni Powell as someone who could act on an emotion and turn it into a reality. The festival is also assured of being held again, having been rated by attendees from the film festival industry as one of the best in the world in 2006. Gympie, a sleepy rural community, is now on the international film festival calendar as a must-attend event.

Success is not the key to happiness. Happiness is the key to success. If you love what you are doing, you will be successful.

Albert Schweitzer

IT IS PROBABLY SAFE TO ASSUME that most of us aren't as given to emotional expressions as Toni Powell. If we were, could we be as courageous in our professions as she has been? Given the obvious role that emotions play in our work and everyday lives, it might surprise you to learn that, until recently, the field of OB has given the topic of emotions little or no attention.[3] How could this be? We can offer two possible explanations.

The first is the *myth of rationality*.[4] Since the late 19th century and the rise of scientific management, the protocol of the work world has been to keep a damper on emotions. A well-run organisation was one that didn't encourage employees to express emotions such as frustration, fear, anger, love, hate, joy, grief, and similar feelings. The prevailing thought was that such emotions were the antithesis of rationality. Even though researchers and managers knew that emotions were an inseparable part of everyday life, they tried to create organisations that were emotion-free. That, of course, wasn't possible.

The second explanation was the belief that emotions of any kind are disruptive.[5] When researchers considered emotions, they looked at strong, negative emotions—especially anger—that interfered with an employee's ability to work effectively. They rarely viewed emotions as constructive or able to enhance performance.

Certainly some emotions, particularly when exhibited at the wrong time, can reduce employee performance. But this doesn't change the fact that employees bring their emotional sides with them to work every day and that no study of OB could be comprehensive without considering the role of emotions in workplace behaviour.

affect | A broad range of feelings that people experience.

emotions | Intense feelings that are directed at someone or something.

moods | Feelings that tend to be less intense than emotions and that lack a contextual stimulus.

WHAT ARE EMOTIONS AND MOODS?

Although we don't want to obsess over definitions, before we can proceed with our analysis we need to clarify three terms that are closely intertwined: *affect*, *emotions* and *moods*.

Affect is a generic term that covers a broad range of feelings that people experience. It is an umbrella concept that encompasses both emotions and moods.[6] **Emotions** are intense feelings that are directed at someone or something.[7] **Moods** are feelings that tend to be less intense than emotions and that often (though not always) lack a contextual stimulus.[8]

Most experts believe that emotions are more fleeting than moods.[9] For example, if someone is rude to you, you will feel angry. That intense feeling of anger probably comes and goes fairly quickly, maybe even in a matter of seconds. When you are in a bad mood, though, you can feel bad for several hours.

Emotions are reactions to a person (seeing a good friend at work may make you feel glad) or an event (dealing with a rude client may make you feel angry). You show your emotions when you are 'happy about something, angry at someone, afraid of something'.[10] Moods, in contrast, aren't usually directed at a person or event. But emotions can turn into moods when you lose focus on the event or object that started the feeling. And, by the same token, good or bad moods can make you more emotional in response to an event. So when a colleague criticises how you spoke to a client, you might become angry at him. That is, you show emotion (anger) towards a specific object (your colleague). But as the specific emotion dissipates, you might just feel generally dispirited. You can't attribute this feeling

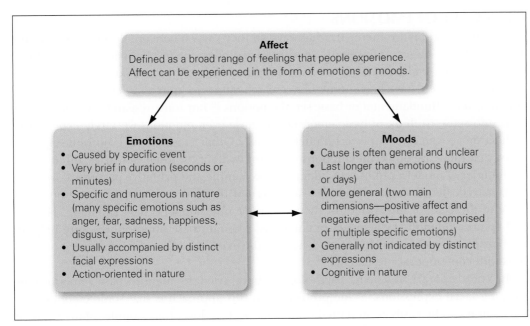

to any single event; you are just not your normal self. You might then overreact to other events. This affect state describes a mood. Figure 8.1 shows the relationships among affect, emotions and moods.

First, as the figure shows, *affect* is a broad term that encompasses emotions and moods. Second, there are differences between emotions and moods. Some of these differences— that emotions are more likely to be caused by a specific event, and emotions are more fleeting than moods—we just discussed. Other differences are more subtle. For example, unlike moods, emotions tend to be more clearly revealed with facial expressions (anger, disgust). Also, some researchers speculate that emotions may be more action-oriented— they may lead us to some immediate action—while moods may be more cognitive, meaning they may cause us to think or brood for a while.[11]

Finally, the figure shows that emotions and moods can mutually influence each other. For example, an emotion, if it is strong and deep enough, can turn into a mood: getting your dream job may generate the emotion of joy, but it also can put you in a good mood for several days. Similarly, if you are in a good or bad mood, it might make you experience a more intense positive or negative emotion than would otherwise be the case. For example, if you are in a bad mood, you might 'blow up' in response to a fellow employee's comment when normally it would have just generated a mild reaction. Because emotions and moods can mutually influence each other, there will be many points throughout the chapter where emotions and moods will be closely connected. Although affect, emotions and moods are separable in theory, in practice the distinction isn't always crystal clear. In fact, in some areas, researchers have studied mostly moods, and in other areas, mainly emotions. So, when we review the OB topics on emotions and moods, you may see more information on emotions in one area and moods in another. This is reflecting the current state of the research.

Also, the terminology can be confusing. For example, the two main mood dimensions are positive affect and negative affect, yet we have defined affect more broadly than mood. So, although the topic can be fairly dense in places, hang in there. The material is interesting—and very applicable to OB.

A BASIC SET OF EMOTIONS

How many emotions are there? In what ways do they vary? There are dozens of emotions. They include anger, contempt, enthusiasm, envy, fear, frustration, joy, love, disappointment, embarrassment, disgust, happiness, hate, hope, jealousy, pride, surprise and sadness. There have been numerous research efforts to limit and define the dozens of emotions into a fundamental or basic set of emotions.[12] But some researchers argue that it makes no sense to think of basic emotions, because even emotions we rarely experience, such as shock, can have a powerful effect on us.[13] Other researchers, even philosophers, argue that there are universal emotions common to all of us. René Descartes, often called the founder of modern philosophy, identified six 'simple and primitive passions'—wonder, love, hatred, desire, joy and sadness—and argued that 'all the others are composed of some of these six or are species of them'.[14] Other philosophers (such as Hume, Hobbes and Spinoza) identified categories of emotions. Though these philosophers were helpful, the burden to provide conclusive evidence for the existence of a basic set of emotions still rests with contemporary researchers.

In contemporary research, psychologists have tried to identify basic emotions by studying facial expressions.[15] One problem with this approach is that some emotions are too complex to be easily represented on our faces. Take love, for example. Many think of love as the most universal of all emotions,[16] yet it is not easy to express a loving emotion with one's face only. Also, cultures have norms that govern emotional expression, so how we *experience* an emotion isn't always the same as how we *show* it. Showing pleasure through facial expressions at the cards dealt to a poker player would definitely be a disadvantage to winning. Further, many companies today offer anger-management programs to teach people how to contain or even hide their inner feelings.[17]

It is unlikely that psychologists or philosophers will ever completely agree on a set of basic emotions, or even whether it makes sense to think of basic emotions. Still, enough researchers have agreed on six essentially universal emotions—anger, fear, sadness, happiness, disgust and surprise—with most other emotions subsumed under one of these six categories.[18] Some researchers even plot these six emotions along a continuum: ranging from happiness at one end through to surprise to fear to sadness to anger and finally to disgust at the other end.[19] The closer any two emotions are to each other on this continuum, the more likely it is that people will confuse them. For instance, we sometimes mistake happiness for surprise, but rarely do we confuse happiness and disgust. In addition, as we will see later on, cultural factors can also influence interpretations.

Clinton Hill of Australia expressed the emotions of joy and exhilaration after crossing the line to win the Men's 4 x 400m Relay final at the 2006 Commonwealth Games in Melbourne. Joy is one of the dozens of basic emotions that originate in our brain's limbic system to help us interpret events. As a positive emotion, joy expresses a favourable evaluation of feeling.

SOME ASPECTS OF EMOTIONS

LEARNING OBJECTIVE 2

Discuss the different aspects of emotions

There are some other fundamental aspects of emotions that we need to consider. These aspects include the biology of emotions, their intensity, as well as their frequency and duration, the relationship between rationality and emotions, and the functions of emotions. Let's deal with each of these aspects in turn.

BIOLOGY

All emotions originate in the brain's limbic system, which is about the size of a walnut and near our brain stem at the base of the skull.[20] People tend to be happiest (report more positive than negative emotions) when their limbic system is relatively inactive. When the limbic system 'heats up', negative emotions such as anger and guilt dominate over positive ones such as joy and happiness. Overall, the limbic system provides a lens through which you interpret events. When it is active, you see things in a negative light. When it is inactive, you interpret information more positively.

Not everyone's limbic system is the same. Moderately depressed people have more active limbic systems, particularly when they encounter negative information.[21] And women tend to have more active limbic systems than men, which, some argue, explains why women are more susceptible to depression than men and are more likely to emotionally bond with children.[22] Of course, as always, these are average differences—women are more likely to be depressed than men, but naturally that doesn't mean that all depressed people are women, or that men are incapable of bonding with their kids.

INTENSITY

People give different responses to identical emotion-provoking stimuli. In some cases, personality is responsible for the difference. Other times, it is a result of the job requirements.

People vary in their inherent ability to express emotional intensity. You may know people who almost never show their feelings. They rarely get angry. They never show rage. In contrast, you probably also know people who seem to be on an emotional roller coaster. When they are happy, they are ecstatic. When they are sad, they are deeply depressed. We will explore the impact that personality has on an individual's emotions in more detail later in the chapter.

Jobs make different demands on our emotions. For instance, air traffic controllers, surgeons and trial judges are expected to be calm and controlled, even in stressful situations. Conversely, the effectiveness of television evangelists, announcers at sporting events, and lawyers can depend on their ability to alter their emotional intensity as the need arises.

FREQUENCY AND DURATION

Sean Wolfson is basically a quiet and reserved person. He loves his job as a financial planner. He doesn't enjoy, however, having to give speeches to increase his visibility and to promote his programs. But he still has to give speeches occasionally. 'If I had to speak to large audiences every day, I'd quit this business', he says. 'I think this works for me because I can fake excitement and enthusiasm for an hour, a couple of times a month.' Whether an employee can successfully meet the emotional demands of a given job depends not only on what emotions need to be displayed and their intensity, but also on how frequently and for how long they need to make the effort.

DO EMOTIONS MAKE US IRRATIONAL?

How often have you heard someone say, 'Oh, you're just being emotional'? You might have been offended. The famous astronomer Carl Sagan once wrote, 'Where we have strong emotions, we're liable to fool ourselves.' These observations suggest that rationality and emotion are in conflict with one another and that if you exhibit emotion, you are likely to act irrationally. One team of authors argue that displaying an emotion such as sadness to the point of crying is so toxic to a career that we should leave the room rather than allow others to witness our emotional display.[23] The famous author Lois Frankel advises that women should avoid being emotional at work because it will undermine how others rate their competence.[24] These perspectives suggest that the demonstration or even experience of emotions is likely to make us seem weak, brittle or irrational. However, the research disagrees and is increasingly showing that emotions are actually critical to rational thinking.[25] In fact, there has been ample evidence of such a link for a long time.

Take the example of Phineas Gage. Gage was a railroad worker in Vermont, in the United States. One September day in 1848, while setting an explosive charge at work, an iron bar a metre in length flew into Gage's lower left jaw and out through the top of his skull, almost like an arrow. Remarkably, Gage survived his injury. He was still able to read and speak, and he performed well above average on cognitive ability tests. However, it became clear that Gage had lost his ability to experience emotion. He was emotionless at even the saddest misfortunes or happiest occasions. Gage's inability to express emotion eventually took away his ability to reason. He started making irrational choices about his life, often behaving erratically and against his self-interests. Despite being an intelligent man whose intellectual abilities were unharmed by the accident, Gage drifted from job to job, eventually taking up with a circus. In commenting on Gage's condition, one expert noted, 'Reason may not be as pure as most of us think it is or wish it were . . . emotions and feelings may not be intruders in the bastion of reason at all: they may be enmeshed in its networks, for worse and for better.'[26]

The example of Phineas Gage and of many other brain injury studies show us that emotions are critical to rational thinking. We must have the ability to experience emotions to be rational. Why? Because our emotions provide important information about how we understand the world around us. Although we might think of a computer as intellectually superior, a human so void of emotion would be unable to function. The whole theme of Isaac Asimov's story *I Robot* (made into a movie of the same name starring Will Smith) was based on the question of what would happen if computer-driven robots gained the ability to feel emotion. Think about a manager making a decision to fire an employee. Would you really want the manager to make the decision without regarding either his or the employee's emotions? The key to good decision making is to employ both thinking and feeling wisely in one's decisions.

By studying the skull of Phineas Gage, shown here, and other brain injuries, researchers discovered an important link between emotions and rational thinking. They found that losing the ability to emote led to the loss of the ability to reason. From this discovery, researchers learned that our emotions provide us with valuable information that helps our thinking process.

WHAT FUNCTIONS DO EMOTIONS SERVE?

Why do we have emotions? What role do they serve? We just discussed one function—that we need them to think rationally. Charles Darwin, however, took a broader approach. In *The*

Expression of the Emotions in Man and Animals, Darwin argued that emotions developed over time to help humans solve problems. Emotions are useful, he said, because they motivate people to engage in actions important for survival—actions such as foraging for food, seeking shelter, choosing mates, guarding against predators, and predicting others' behaviours. For example, disgust (an emotion) motivates us to avoid dangerous or harmful things (such as rotten foods). Excitement (also an emotion) motivates us to take on situations in which we require energy and initiative (for example, tackling a new career).

Drawing from Darwin are researchers who focus on **evolutionary psychology**. This field of study says we must experience emotions—whether they are positive or negative—because they serve a purpose.[27] For example, you would probably consider jealousy to be a negative emotion. Evolutionary psychologists would argue that it exists in people because it has a useful purpose. Mates may feel jealousy to increase the chance that their genes, rather than a rival's genes, are passed on to the next generation.[28] Although we tend to think of anger as being 'bad', it actually can help us protect our rights when we feel they are being violated. For example, a person showing anger when she's double-crossed by a colleague is serving a warning for others not to repeat the same behaviour. Consider another example. Rena Weeks was a secretary at a prominent law firm. Her boss wouldn't stop touching and grabbing her. His treatment made her angry. So she did more than quit—she sued, and won a multimillion-dollar case for sexual harassment in the workplace.[29] It is not that anger is always good. But as with all other emotions, it exists because it serves a useful purpose. Positive emotions also serve a purpose. For example, a service employee who feels empathy for a customer may provide better customer service.

But some researchers aren't firm believers in evolutionary psychology. Why? Think about fear (an emotion). It is just as easy to think of the harmful effects of fear as it is the beneficial effects. For example, running in fear from a predator increases the likelihood of survival. But what benefit does freezing in fear serve? Evolutionary psychology provides an interesting perspective on the functions of emotions, but it is not clear whether this perspective is always valid.[30]

evolutionary psychology | An area of inquiry that argues that we must experience the emotions that we do because they serve a purpose.

MOOD AS POSITIVE AND NEGATIVE AFFECT

One way to classify emotions is by whether they are positive or negative.[31] Positive emotions—such as joy and gratitude—express a favourable evaluation or feeling. Negative emotions—such as anger or guilt—express the opposite. Keep in mind that emotions can't be neutral. Being neutral is being non-emotional.[32]

When we group emotions into positive and negative categories, they become mood states because we are now looking at them more generally instead of isolating one particular emotion. In Figure 8.2, *excited* is a specific emotion that is a pure marker of high positive affect, while *boredom* is a pure marker of low positive affect. Similarly, *nervous* is a pure marker of high negative affect, while *relaxed* is a pure marker of low negative affect. Finally, some emotions—such as *contentment* (a mixture of high positive affect and low negative affect) or *sadness* (a mixture of low positive affect and high negative affect)—are in between. You will notice that this model doesn't include all emotions. There are two reasons why. First, we can fit other emotions such as enthusiasm or depression into the model, but we are short on space. Second, some emotions, such as surprise, don't fit well because they are not as clearly positive or negative.

So, we can think of **positive affect** as a mood dimension consisting of positive emotions such as excitement, self-assurance and cheerfulness at the high end, and boredom,

positive affect | A mood dimension consisting of specific positive emotions such as excitement, self-assurance and cheerfulness at the high end, and boredom, sluggishness and tiredness at the low end.

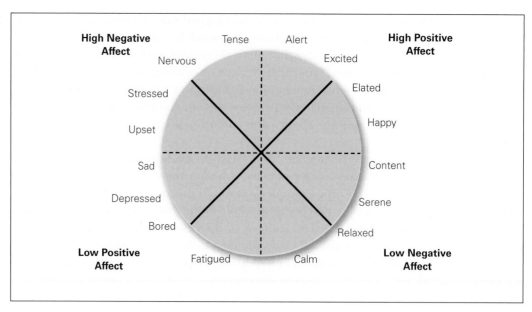

■ FIGURE 8.2
The structure of mood

negative affect | A mood dimension consisting of nervousness, stress and anxiety at the high end, and relaxation, tranquillity and poise at the low end.

sluggishness and tiredness at the low end. **Negative affect** is a mood dimension consisting of nervousness, stress and anxiety at the high end, and relaxation, tranquillity and poise at the low end. (Note that positive and negative affect are moods. We are using these labels, rather than positive and negative *mood*, because that's how researchers label them.)

Positive affect and negative affect play out at work (and beyond work, of course) in that they colour our perceptions, and these perceptions can become their own reality. For example, a flight attendant posted an anonymous blog on the Web that said: 'I work in a pressurised aluminium tube and the environment outside my "office" cannot sustain human life. That being said, the human life inside is not worth sustaining sometimes … in fact, the passengers can be jerks, and idiots. I am often treated with no respect, nobody listens to me … until I threaten to kick them off the plane …'[33] Clearly, if a flight attendant is in a bad mood, it is going to influence his or her perceptions of passengers, which will influence his or her behaviour in turn.

Importantly, negative emotions are more likely to translate into negative moods. People think about events that created strong negative emotions five times as long as they do about events that created strong positive ones.[34] So, we should expect people to recall negative experiences more readily than positive ones. Perhaps one of the reasons is that, for most of us, they are also more unusual. Indeed, research shows that there is a **positivity offset**, meaning that at zero input (when nothing in particular is going on), most individuals experience a mildly positive mood.[35] So, for most people, positive moods are somewhat more common than negative moods. The positivity offset also appears to operate at work. For example, one study of customer service representatives in a British call centre (probably a job where it is pretty hard to feel positive) revealed that people reported experiencing positive moods 58 per cent of the time.[36]

positivity offset | Tendency of most individuals to experience a mildly positive mood at zero input (when nothing in particular is going on).

LEARNING OBJECTIVE 3

Identify the sources of emotions and moods

SOURCES OF EMOTIONS AND MOODS

Have you ever said to yourself, 'I got up on the wrong side of the bed today'? Have you ever snapped at a fellow employee or a family member for no particular reason? If you have, it probably makes you wonder where your emotions and moods come from. Here, we pick up the discussion of moods again because, even though emotions are thought to be more influenced by events than are moods, ironically, researchers have conducted more studies on the sources of moods than on the sources of particular emotions. So, now we will turn to the main sources of moods, though a lot of these sources also affect emotions.

PERSONALITY

Do you scream at the TV when your team is losing a big game, while your friend seems like she couldn't care less that her team has no chance of winning? Consider another situation. Naomi and Kim are fellow employees. Naomi has a tendency to get angry when a colleague criticises her ideas during a brainstorming session. Kim, however, is quite calm and relaxed, viewing such criticism as an opportunity for improvement. What explains these different reactions? Personality predisposes people to experience certain moods and emotions. For example, some people feel guilt and anger more readily than others do. Others may feel calm and relaxed no matter the situation. In other words, moods and emotions have a trait component to them—most people have built-in tendencies to experience certain moods and emotions more frequently than others do. Consider rugby league coach Ricky Stewart. He is famous for his tirades against players, officials, fans and the media. Clearly, he is easily moved to experience anger. But then take Prime Minister John Howard, who is known for his relatively distant, unemotional, analytical nature. He very rarely displays anger.

So Ricky Stewart and John Howard have tendencies to experience a particular mood or emotion. But, as we mentioned earlier, some people are predisposed to experience any emotion more intensely. Such people are high on **affect intensity**, or 'individual differences in the strength with which individuals experience their emotions'.[37] While most people might feel slightly sad at one movie or be mildly amused at another, someone high on affect intensity would cry like a baby at a sad movie and laugh uncontrollably at a comedy. We might describe such people as 'emotional' or 'intense'. So, emotions differ in their intensity, but people also differ in how predisposed they are to experience emotions intensely. If a person gets really mad at a co-worker, he would be experiencing an emotion intensely. But if that person gets angry, or excited, very easily, then he would be high on the personality trait of affect intensity.

affect intensity | Individual differences in the strength with which individuals experience their emotions.

Also, positive events are more likely to affect the positive mood and positive emotions of extroverts, and negative events are more likely to influence the negative mood and negative emotions of those scoring low on emotional stability.[38] To illustrate, let's say there are two friends who work together—Paul and Sarah. Paul scores high on extroversion and emotional stability. Sarah scores low on both. One day at work, Paul and Sarah learn they are going to earn a commission for a sale their work group made. Later the same day, their boss stops by and yells at them for no apparent reason. In this situation, you would expect Paul's positive affect to increase more than Sarah's, because Paul is more extroverted and attends more to the good news of the day. Conversely, you would expect Sarah's negative affect to increase more than Paul's, because Sarah scores lower on emotional stability and therefore tends to dwell on the negative event of the day.

DAY OF THE WEEK AND TIME OF THE DAY

Most people are at work or school from Monday to Friday. For most of us, that means the weekend is a time of relaxation and leisure. Does this suggest that people are in their best moods on the weekends? Well, actually, yes. As Figure 8.3 shows, people tend to be in their worst moods (highest negative affect and lowest positive affect) early in the week and in their best moods (highest positive affect and lowest negative affect) late in the week.[39]

What about time of the day? When are you usually in your best mood? Your worst? We often think that people differ, depending on whether they are 'morning' or 'evening' people. However, the vast majority of us follow a similar pattern. People are generally in lower spirits early in the morning. During the course of the day, our moods tend to improve and then decline again in the evening. Figure 8.4 maps this pattern. Interestingly,

■ FIGURE 8.3
Our moods are affected by the day of the week

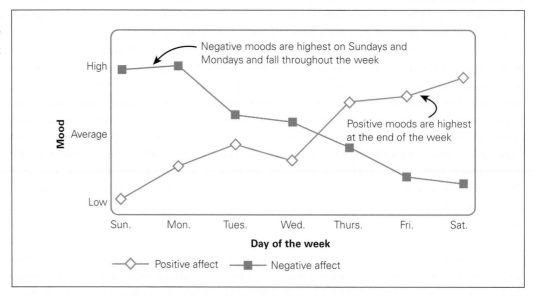

SOURCE: D. Watson, *Mood and Temperament* (New York: Guilford Publications, 2000).

■ FIGURE 8.4
Our moods are affected by the time of the day

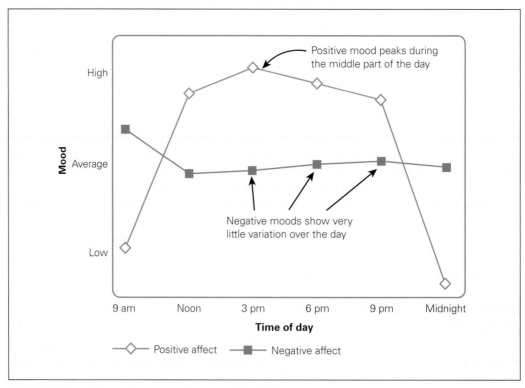

SOURCE: D. Watson, *Mood and Temperament* (New York: Guilford Publications, 2000).

regardless of what time people go to bed at night or get up in the morning, levels of positive affect tend to peak around the halfway point between waking and sleeping. Negative affect, however, shows little fluctuation throughout the day.[40]

What does this mean for organisational behaviour? Asking someone for a favour, or conveying bad news, is probably not a good idea on Monday morning. It also helps suggest why taking sick leave is more common on Monday than any other day of the week. As such, our workplace interactions will probably be more positive from mid-morning onward, and also later in the week.

It does seem that people who describe themselves as morning people are more alert early in the morning.[41] However, these morning people experience only slightly better moods (more positive affect) in the morning compared to those who describe themselves as evening people (and vice versa).[42]

WEATHER

When do you think you would be in a better mood? When it is 25 degrees Celsius and sunny, or when it is a gloomy, cold, rainy day? Many people believe their mood is tied to the weather. However, evidence suggests that weather has little effect on mood. One expert concluded, 'Contrary to the prevailing cultural view, these data indicate that people do not report a better mood on bright and sunny days (or, conversely, a worse mood on dark and rainy days).'[43] Illusory correlation explains why people tend to *think* that nice weather improves their mood. **Illusory correlation** occurs when people associate two events but in reality there is no connection. People often associate things as causal when in fact there's no true relationship. That appears to be the case with weather and moods.

illusory correlation | The tendency of people to associate two events when in reality there is no connection.

STRESS

As you might imagine, stress affects emotions and moods. For example, students have higher levels of fear before an exam, but their fear dissipates once the exam is over.[44] At work, stressful daily events (a nasty email, an impending deadline, the loss of a big sale, being reprimanded by your boss, and so on) negatively affect employees' moods. Also, the effects of stress build over time. As the authors of one study note, '[A] constant diet of even low-level stressful events has the potential to cause employees to experience gradually increasing levels of strain over time.'[45] Such mounting levels of stress and strain at work can worsen our moods, and we experience more negative emotions. Consider the following entry from a worker's blog: 'i'm in a bit of a blah mood today … physically, i feel funky, though and the weather out combined with the amount of personal things and work i need to get done are getting to me.' Although sometimes we thrive on stress, for most of us, like this blogger, stress begins to take its toll on our mood.[46]

SOCIAL ACTIVITIES

Do you tend to be happiest when you are at a barbecue with friends or out to dinner to celebrate a family member's birthday? For most people, social activities increase positive mood and have little effect on negative mood. But do people in positive moods seek out social interactions, or do social interactions cause people to be in good moods? It seems that both are true.[47] And, does the type of social activity matter? Indeed, it does. Research suggests that physical (skiing or hiking with friends), informal (going to a party), or epicurean (eating with others) activities are more strongly associated with increases in positive mood than formal (attending a meeting) or sedentary (watching TV with friends) events.[48]

To keep employees happy and healthy, the Royal Automobile Club of Victoria (RACV) provides access for all its employees to fully equipped gyms, as well as to the main in-house gym in their Melbourne headquarters. The RACV supplements the gym services with many other programs and services, such as eyesight tests, health and fitness tests, correct lifting method courses, massage services, skin cancer checks, lung capacity testing, flu shots, ride-and-walk-to-work clubs, discounted gym membership, an in-house health and fitness magazine, participation and training for corporate games and triathlons, tailored fitness programs and access to a dietician. The cost is a corporate secret, but the benefits outweigh the costs. The payoff is in healthier and happier employees at both work and at home. In turn, the productivity increases more than compensate for the costs.

Social interactions even have long-term health benefits. One study of longevity found that being in the company of others (as opposed to social isolation) was one of the best predictors of how long someone lives—more important than gender, or even blood pressure or cholesterol levels.[49] One of the reasons for this is positive affect. A study of nuns aged between 75 and 95 years showed that the degree to which the nuns experienced positive moods when in their twenties predicted how long they lived six decades later.[50]

SLEEP

According to a recent poll, people are getting less and less sleep. On average, people sleep less than seven hours per weekday night—below the recommended eight hours. And the number of people who actually sleep eight or more hours a night has steadily decreased over the past few years to less than one in four. Roughly 75 per cent of those polled reported having at least one symptom of a sleep problem a few nights a week or more.[51] Add to the sleep problems the rising obesity problem, which in turn is rapidly increasing the incidence of obstructive sleep apnoea, and it is no surprise that people aren't getting enough sleep.

As you might imagine, sleep quality affects mood. Undergraduates and adult workers who are sleep-deprived report greater feelings of fatigue, anger and hostility.[52] One of the reasons why less sleep, or poor sleep quality, puts people in a bad mood is because it impairs decision making and makes it difficult to control emotions.[53] A recent study suggests that poor sleep the previous night also impairs people's job satisfaction the next day, mostly because they feel fatigued, irritable and less alert.[54]

EXERCISE

You often hear that people should exercise to improve their mood. But does 'sweat therapy' really work? It appears so. Research consistently shows that exercise enhances people's positive mood.[55] It appears that the therapeutic effects of exercise are strongest for those who are depressed. Although the effects of exercise on moods are consistent, they are not terribly strong. So, exercise may help put you in a better mood, but don't expect miracles.

AGE

Do you think that young people experience more extreme, positive emotions (so-called youthful exuberance) than older people do? If you answered 'yes', you were wrong. One study of people aged 18 to 94 years revealed that negative emotions seem to occur less as people get older. Periods of highly positive moods lasted longer for older individuals and bad moods faded more quickly.[56] The study implies that emotional experience tends to improve with age, so that as we get older, we experience fewer negative emotions.

GENDER

The common belief is that women are more in touch with their feelings than men are— that they react more emotionally and are better able to read emotions in others. Is there any truth to these assumptions?

The evidence does confirm differences between men and women when it comes to emotional reactions and the ability to read others. In contrasting the genders, women show greater emotional expression than men;[57] they experience emotions more intensely; and they display more frequent expressions of both positive and negative emotions, with the exception of anger.[58] In contrast to men, women also report more comfort in expressing emotions. Finally, women are better at reading non-verbal and paralinguistic cues than are men.[59]

What explains these differences? Researchers have suggested three possible explanations. One explanation is the different ways men and women have been socialised.[60] Men are taught to be tough and brave, to be strong, competitive and 'masculine'. Showing emotion is inconsistent with this image. Women, in contrast, are socialised to be nurturing. This may account for the perception that women are generally warmer and friendlier than men. For instance, women are expected to express more positive emotions on the job (shown by smiling) than men, and they do.[61] A second explanation is that women may have more innate ability to read others and present their emotions than do men.[62] Third, women may have a greater need for social approval and, so, a higher propensity to show positive emotions, such as happiness.

LEARNING OBJECTIVE 4

Describe external constraints on emotions

EXTERNAL CONSTRAINTS ON EMOTIONS

An emotion that is acceptable on the athletic playing field may be totally unacceptable when exhibited in the workplace. Similarly, what's appropriate in one country is often inappropriate in another. These two factors play a role in determining what emotions we will display. Every organisation defines boundaries that identify which emotions are acceptable and the degree to which employees may express them. Cultures set boundaries, too. In this section, we look at organisational and cultural influences on emotions.

ORGANISATIONAL INFLUENCES

If you can't smile and appear happy, you are unlikely to have much of a career working at a Gold Coast theme park. And a manual produced by McDonald's states that its counter personnel 'must display traits such as sincerity, enthusiasm, confidence, and a sense of humour'.[63] There is no single emotional 'set' that all organisations worldwide seek in their employees. However, in most Western cultures with Anglo-Saxon (British) origins such as Australia, the evidence indicates that there's a bias against negative and intense emotions. Expressions of negative emotions such as fear, anxiety and anger tend to be unacceptable except under fairly specific conditions.[64] For instance, one such condition might be a high-status member of a group conveying impatience with a low-status member.[65] Moreover, expressions of intense emotion, whether negative or positive, tend to be unacceptable because management regards them as undermining routine task performance.[66] Again, there are instances when such expressions are acceptable—for example, a brief grieving over the sudden death of a company's founder or the celebration of a record year of profits. But for the most part, the climate in well-managed Western organisations is one that strives to be emotion-free.

CULTURAL INFLUENCES

Does the degree to which people *experience* emotions vary across cultures? Do people's *interpretations* of emotions vary across cultures? Finally, do the norms for the *expression* of emotions differ across cultures? Let's tackle each of these questions.

Does the degree to which people experience emotions vary across cultures? Yes! In China, for example, people report that they experience fewer positive and negative emotions than do people in other cultures, and whatever emotions they do experience are less intense than what other cultures report. Compared to Mainland Chinese, Taiwanese are more like Americans in their experience of emotions. On average, Taiwanese report more positive and fewer negative emotions than their Chinese counterparts.[67] In general, people in most cultures appear to experience certain positive and negative emotions, but the frequency of their experience and their intensity does vary to some degree.[68]

Do people's interpretations of emotions vary across cultures? In general, people from all over the world interpret negative and positive emotions the same way. We all view negative emotions, such as hate, terror and rage, as dangerous and destructive. And we all desire positive emotions—such as joy, love and happiness. However, some cultures value certain emotions more than others. For example, Americans value enthusiasm, while Chinese consider negative emotions to be more useful and constructive than do Americans. In general, pride is seen as a positive emotion in Western, individualistic cultures such as the United States, but Eastern cultures such as China and Japan tend to view pride as undesirable.[69]

Do the norms for the expression of emotions differ across cultures? Absolutely. For example, Muslims see smiling as a sign of sexual attraction, so women have learned not to smile at men.[70] And research has shown that in collectivist countries people are more likely to believe that emotional displays have something to do with their own relationship with the person expressing the emotion, while people in individualistic cultures don't think that another's emotional expressions are directed at them.[71] For example, in Venezuela (a highly collectivistic culture), someone seeing an angry expression on a friend's face would

---

EMOTIONAL RECOGNITION: UNIVERSAL OR CULTURE-SPECIFIC?

Early researchers studying how we understand emotions based on others' experiences believed that all individuals, regardless of their culture, could recognise the same emotion. So, for example, a frown would be recognised as indicating the emotion of sadness, no matter where one was from. However, more recent research suggests that this universal approach to the study of emotions is incorrect, because there are subtle differences in the degree to which we can tell what emotions people from different cultures are feeling based on their facial expressions.

One study examined how quickly and accurately we can read the facial expressions of people of different cultural backgrounds. Although individuals were at first faster at recognising the emotional expressions of others from their own culture, when living in a different culture, the speed and accuracy at which they recognised others' emotions increased as they became more familiar with the culture. For example, as Chinese residing in the United States adapted to their surroundings they were able to recognise the emotions of US citizens more quickly. In fact, foreigners are sometimes better at recognising emotions among the citizens in their non-native country than are those citizens.

Interestingly, these effects begin to occur relatively quickly. For example, Chinese students living in the United States for an average of 2.4 years were better at recognising the facial expressions of US citizens than the facial expressions of Chinese citizens. Why is this the case? According to the authors of the study, it could be that, having limited ability in speaking the language, they rely more on non-verbal communication. What is the upshot for OB? When conducting business in a foreign country, the ability to recognise correctly others' emotions can facilitate interactions and lead to less miscommunication. Otherwise, a slight smile that is intended to communicate disinterest may be mistaken for happiness.

SOURCE: Based on H. A. Elfenbein and N. Ambady, 'When Familiarity Breeds Accuracy: Cultural Exposure and Facial Emotion Recognition', *Journal of Personality and Social Psychology*, August 2003, pp. 276–90.

OB IN PRACTICE

think that the friend is mad at her; but in Australia (a very individualistic culture), a person would generally not attribute an angry friend's expression to something she had done.

Such norms play a role in *emotional labour*, which we will learn about in the next section. In general, it is easier for people to recognise emotions accurately within their own culture than in other cultures. For example, a Chinese businessperson is more likely to label accurately the emotions underlying the facial expressions of a fellow Chinese colleague than those of an Australian colleague.[72]

Interestingly, some cultures lack words for standard Western emotional terms such as *anxiety*, *depression* and *guilt*. Tahitians, as a case in point, don't have a word directly equivalent to sadness. When Tahitians are sad, their peers attribute their state to a physical illness.[73] Our discussion illustrates the need to consider cultural factors as influencing what managers consider emotionally appropriate.[74] What's acceptable in one culture may seem extremely unusual or even dysfunctional in another. Managers need to know the emotional norms in each culture they do business in, so that they don't send unintended signals or misread the reactions of locals. For example, an Australian manager in Japan should know that while Australians tend to view smiling positively, Japanese are apt to attribute frequent smiling to a lack of intelligence.[75]

LEARNING OBJECTIVE 5

Discuss the impact emotional labour has on employees

EMOTIONAL LABOUR

If you have ever had a job working in retail sales or waiting on tables in a restaurant, you know the importance of projecting a friendly demeanour and a smile. Even though there were days when you didn't feel cheerful, you knew management expected you to be upbeat when dealing with customers. So you faked it, and in so doing, you expressed emotional labour.

Every employee expends physical and mental labour when they put their bodies and cognitive capabilities, respectively, into their job. But jobs also require emotional labour. **Emotional labour** is an employee's expression of organisationally desired emotions during interpersonal transactions at work.[76] The concept of emotional labour emerged from studies of service jobs. Think about it: airlines expect their flight attendants, for instance, to be cheerful; and we expect funeral directors to be solemn and doctors to be emotionally neutral. But really, emotional labour is relevant to almost every job. Your managers expect you, for example, to be courteous, not hostile, in interactions with fellow employees. The true challenge is when employees have to project one emotion while simultaneously feeling another.[77] This disparity is called **emotional dissonance**, and it can take a heavy toll on employees. Left untreated, bottled-up feelings of frustration, anger and resentment can eventually lead to emotional exhaustion and burnout.[78] It is from the increasing importance of emotional labour as a key component of effective job performance that an understanding of emotion has gained heightened relevance within the field of OB.

emotional labour | A situation in which an employee expresses organisationally desired emotions during interpersonal transactions at work.

emotional dissonance | Inconsistencies among the emotions we feel and the emotions we display.

FELT VERSUS DISPLAYED EMOTIONS

Emotional labour creates dilemmas for employees. There are people with whom you have to work that you just plain don't like. Maybe you consider their personality abrasive. Maybe you know they have said negative things about you behind your back. Regardless, your job requires you to interact with these people on a regular basis. So, you are forced to feign friendliness. It can help you, on the job especially, if you separate emotions into those that are felt and those that are displayed.[79] **Felt emotions** are an individual's actual emotions.

felt emotions | An individual's actual emotions.

In contrast, **displayed emotions** are those that the organisation requires employees to show and considers appropriate in a given job. They are not innate; they are learned. 'The ritual look of delight on the face of the first runner-up as the new Miss Australia is announced is a product of the display rule that losers should mask their sadness with an expression of joy for the winner.'[80] Similarly, most of us know that we are expected to act solemn at funerals regardless of whether we consider the person's death to be a loss, and to pretend to be happy at weddings even if we don't feel like celebrating.[81]

Effective managers have learned to be serious when giving an employee a negative performance evaluation and to hide their anger when they have been passed over for promotion. And the salesperson who hasn't learned to smile and appear friendly, regardless of his true feelings at the moment, isn't typically going to last long on most sales jobs. How we *experience* an emotion isn't always the same as how we *show* it.[82]

The key point here is that felt and displayed emotions are often different. Many people have problems working with others because they naïvely assume that the emotions they see others display are what those others actually feel. This is particularly true in organisations, where role demands and situations often require people to exhibit emotional behaviours that mask their true feelings. In addition, jobs today increasingly require employees to interact with customers. And customers aren't always easy to deal with. They often complain, behave rudely and make unrealistic demands. In such instances, an employee's felt emotions may need to be disguised. Employees who aren't able to project a friendly and helpful demeanour in such situations are likely to alienate customers and are unlikely to be effective in their jobs.

Yet another point is that displaying fake emotions requires us to suppress the emotions we really feel (not showing anger towards a customer, for example). In other words, the individual has to 'act' if she wants to keep her job. **Surface acting** is hiding one's inner feelings and forging emotional expressions in response to display rules. For example, when an employee smiles at a customer even when he doesn't feel like it, he is surface acting. **Deep acting** is trying to modify one's true inner feelings based on display rules. A health-care provider trying genuinely to feel more empathy for her patients is deep acting.[83] Surface acting deals with one's displayed emotions, and deep acting deals with one's felt emotions. Research shows that surface acting is more stressful to employees because it entails feigning true emotions.[84]

As we have noted, emotional norms vary across cultures. Cultural norms in Australia dictate that employees in service organisations should smile and act friendly when interacting with customers.[85] But this norm doesn't apply worldwide. In Israel, customers see smiling supermarket cashiers as inexperienced, so managers encourage cashiers to look solemn.[86] Employees in France are likely to experience a minimal degree of emotional dissonance because they make little effort to hide their true feelings. French retail clerks are renowned for being very rude and surly towards customers. (A report from the French government itself confirmed this.[87]) And the world's largest retailer, Wal-Mart, has found that its emphasis on employee friendliness, which has won them a loyal following among shoppers in the United States, doesn't work in Germany. Accustomed to a culture where the customer traditionally comes last, serious German shoppers have been turned off by Wal-Mart's friendly greeters and helpful personnel.[88] Late in 2006, Wal-Mart accepted defeat and announced it is closing all its stores in Germany—all because the customers distrusted the displays of emotions by company personnel!

And what about gender differences? Do you think society expects women to display different emotions than men, even in the same job? This is a difficult question to answer,

displayed emotions | Emotions that are organisationally appropriate in a given job.

surface acting | Hiding one's inner feelings and foregoing emotional expressions in response to display rules.

deep acting | Trying to modify one's true inner feelings based on display rules.

but there is some evidence that upper management does expect men and women to display different emotions even in the same job. In professional and managerial jobs, for example, women report having to suppress negative feelings and display more positive feelings than men, in order to conform to what they say their bosses and colleagues expect.[89] No wonder many women feel there is a glass ceiling preventing their advancement into senior management.

ARE EMOTIONALLY DEMANDING JOBS REWARDED WITH BETTER PAY?

You may wonder how well the labour market rewards jobs that are emotionally demanding. You might think, for example, that the job of funeral director, which may include mortician duties and arranging funerals with grieving families, should pay well. But it seems that jobs that are emotionally demanding (jobs that are taxing or require an employee to 'put on a good face') may be rewarded less well than jobs that are cognitively demanding (ones that require a lot of thinking and that demand a complex set of skills). A recent study examined this issue across a wide range of jobs.[90] The authors of the study found that the relationship between cognitive demands and pay was quite strong, while the relationship between emotional demands and pay wasn't. They did find that emotional demands matter, but only when jobs were already cognitively demanding—jobs such as lawyers and nurses. But, for instance, child-care workers and waiters (jobs with high emotional demands but relatively low cognitive demands) receive little compensation for the emotional demands.

Figure 8.5 shows the relationship between cognitive and emotional demands and pay. For jobs that are cognitively demanding, increasing emotional demands lead to better pay. However, for jobs that are not cognitively demanding, increasing emotional demands lead to worse pay. The model doesn't seem to depict a fair state of affairs. After all, why should emotional demands be rewarded in only cognitively complex jobs? One explanation may be that it is hard to find qualified people who are willing and able to work in such jobs.

■ **FIGURE 8.5**

Relationship of pay to cognitive and emotional demands of jobs

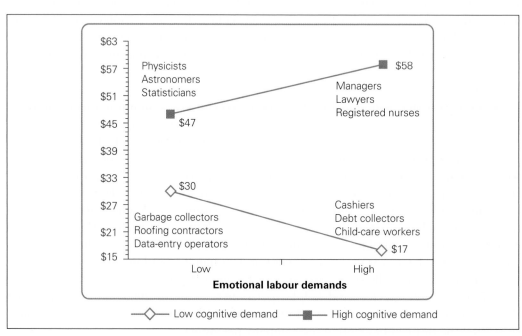

SOURCE: Based on T. M. Glomb, J. D. Kammeyer-Mueller and M. Rotundo, 'Emotional Labor Demands and Compensating Wage Differentials', *Journal of Applied Psychology*, vol. 89, no. 4, August 2004, pp. 700–14.

AFFECTIVE EVENTS THEORY

As we have seen, emotions and moods are an important part of our lives, especially our work lives. But how do our emotions and moods influence our job performance and satisfaction? A model called **affective events theory (AET)** has increased our understanding of the links.[91] AET demonstrates that employees react emotionally to things that happen to them at work, and that this reaction in turn influences their job performance and satisfaction.

affective events theory |
A model which suggests that workplace events cause emotional reactions on the part of employees which then influence workplace attitudes and behaviours.

Figure 8.6 summarises AET. The theory begins by recognising that emotions are a response to an event in the work environment. The work environment includes everything surrounding the job—the variety of tasks and degree of autonomy, job demands, and requirements for expressing emotional labour. This environment creates work events that can be hassles, uplifts, or both. Examples of hassles are colleagues who refuse to carry their share of work, conflicting directions by different managers, and excessive time pressures. Examples of uplifting events include meeting a goal, getting support from a colleague, and receiving recognition for an accomplishment.[92]

These work events trigger positive or negative emotional reactions. But employees' personalities and moods predispose them to respond with greater or lesser intensity to the event. For instance, people who score low on emotional stability are more likely to react strongly to negative events. And their mood introduces the reality that their general affect cycle creates fluctuations. So, a person's emotional response to a given event can change, depending on mood. Finally, emotions influence a number of performance and satisfaction variables such as organisational citizenship behaviour, organisational commitment, level of effort, intentions to quit and workplace deviance.

In addition, tests of the theory suggest that (1) an emotional episode is actually a series of emotional experiences precipitated by a single event. It contains elements of both emotions and mood cycles. (2) Current emotions influence job satisfaction at any given time, along with the history of emotions surrounding the event. (3) Because moods and

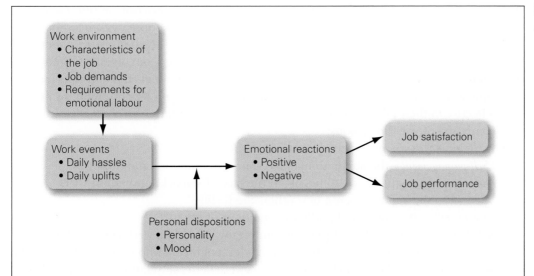

■ **FIGURE 8.6**
Affective events theory

SOURCE: Based on N. M. Ashkanasy and C. S. Daus, 'Emotion in the Workplace: The New Challenge for Managers', *Academy of Management Executive*, February 2002, p. 77.

emotions fluctuate over time, their effect on performance also fluctuates. (4) Emotion-driven behaviours are typically short in duration and of high variability. (5) Because emotions, even positive ones, tend to be incompatible with behaviours required to do a job, they typically have a negative influence on job performance.[93]

An example might help better explain AET.[94] You work as an aeronautical engineer for Boeing. Because of the downturn in the demand for commercial jets, you have just learned that the company is considering laying off 10 000 employees. This layoff could include you. This event is likely to make you feel negative emotions, especially fear that you might lose your job and primary source of income. And because you are prone to worry a lot and obsess about problems, this event increases your feelings of insecurity.

It also puts into place a series of smaller events that create an episode: you talk with your boss and he assures you that your job is safe; you hear rumours that your department is high on the list to be eliminated; you run into a former colleague who was laid off six months ago and still hasn't found work. These events, in turn, create emotional ups and downs. One day you are feeling more upbeat and confident that you will survive the cuts. The next day, you might be depressed and anxious. These emotional swings take your attention away from your work and lower your job performance and satisfaction. Finally, your response is magnified because this is the fourth large layoff that Boeing has initiated in the last three years.

In summary, AET offers two important messages.[95] First, emotions provide valuable insights into understanding employee behaviour. The model demonstrates how workplace hassles and uplifts influence employee performance and satisfaction. Second, emotions accumulate; employees and managers should therefore not ignore emotions and the events that cause them, even when they appear to be minor.

EMOTIONAL INTELLIGENCE

Diane Marshall is an office manager. Her awareness of her own and others' emotions is almost nil. She is moody and unable to generate much enthusiasm or interest in her employees. She doesn't understand why her employees become upset with her. She often overreacts to problems and chooses the most ineffectual responses to emotional situations.[96] Diane Marshall is someone with low emotional intelligence. **Emotional intelligence (EI)** is one's ability to detect and to manage emotional cues and information.

People who know their own emotions and are good at reading others' emotions may be more effective in their jobs. That, in essence, is the theme underlying recent EI research.[97] EI is composed of five dimensions:

- *Self-awareness*—being aware of what you are feeling.
- *Self-management*—the ability to manage your own emotions and impulses.
- *Self-motivation*—the ability to persist in the face of setbacks and failures.
- *Empathy*—the ability to sense how others are feeling.
- *Social skills*—the ability to handle the emotions of others.

Several studies suggest that EI plays an important role in job performance. One study looked at the characteristics of Lucent Technologies' engineers who were rated as stars by their peers. The researchers concluded that stars were better at relating to others. That is, it was EI, not IQ, that characterised high performers. Another illuminating study looked at the successes and failures of 11 American presidents—from Franklin Roosevelt to Bill Clinton. They were evaluated on six qualities—communication, organisation, political

emotional intelligence (EI) | The ability to detect and to manage emotional cues and information.

skill, vision, cognitive style and emotional intelligence. It was found that the key quality that differentiated the successful (such as Roosevelt, Kennedy and Reagan) from the unsuccessful (such as Johnson, Carter and Nixon) was emotional intelligence (or the lack of it).[98]

THE CASE FOR EI

EI has been, and continues to be, a controversial concept in OB. It has its supporters and detractors. In the upcoming sections, we will review the arguments for and against the viability of EI in OB.

LEARNING OBJECTIVE **6**

Discuss the cases for and against emotional intelligence

INTUITIVE APPEAL

There is a lot of intuitive appeal to the EI concept. Most everyone would agree that it is good to possess 'street smarts' and social intelligence. Those people who can detect emotions in others, control their own emotions, and handle social interactions well will have a powerful leg up in the business world, so the thinking goes. As just one example, partners in a multinational consulting firm who scored above the median on an EI measure delivered $1.2 million more in business than did the other partners.[99]

EI PREDICTS CRITERIA THAT MATTER

Evidence is mounting that suggests a high level of EI means a person will perform well on the job. One study found that EI predicted the performance of employees in a cigarette factory in China.[100] Another study found that being able to recognise emotions in others' facial expressions and to emotionally 'eavesdrop' (pick up subtle signals about people's emotions) predicted peer ratings of how valuable these people were to their organisation.[101] Finally, a review of 59 studies indicated that, overall, EI was moderately correlated with job performance.[102]

EI IS BIOLOGICALLY BASED

One study has shown that people with damage to the part of the brain that governs emotional processing (lesions in an area of the prefrontal cortex) score significantly lower on EI tests. Even though these brain-damaged people scored no lower on standard measures of intelligence than people without the same brain damage, they were still impaired in normal decision making. Specifically, when people were playing a card game in which there is a reward (money) for picking certain types of cards and a punishment (a loss of money) for picking other types of cards, the participants with no brain damage learned to succeed in the game, while the performance of the brain-damaged group worsened over time. This study suggests that EI is neurologically based in a way that is unrelated to standard measures of intelligence, and that people who suffer neurological damage score lower on EI and make poorer decisions than people who are healthier in this regard.[103]

THE CASE AGAINST EI

For all its supporters, EI has just as many critics.

EI IS TOO VAGUE A CONCEPT

To many researchers, it is not clear what EI is. Is it a form of intelligence? Most of us wouldn't think that being self-aware or self-motivated or having empathy is a matter of intellect. So, is EI a misnomer? Moreover, different researchers may focus on different skills, making it difficult to get a definition of EI. One researcher may study self-discipline. Another may study empathy. Another may look at self-awareness. As one reviewer noted, 'The concept of EI has now become so broad and the components so variegated that … it is no longer even an intelligible concept.'[104]

EI CAN'T BE MEASURED

Many critics have raised questions about measuring EI. Because EI is a form of intelligence, for instance, there must be right and wrong answers about it on tests, they argue. Some tests do have right and wrong answers, although the validity of some of the questions on these measures is questionable. For example, one measure asks you to associate particular feelings with specific colours, as if purple always makes us feel cool, not warm. Other measures are self-reported, meaning there is no right or wrong answer. For example, an EI test question might ask you to respond to the statement, 'I'm good at "reading" other people.' In general, the measures of EI are diverse, and researchers haven't subjected them to as much rigorous study as they have measures of personality and general intelligence.[105]

THE VALIDITY OF EI IS SUSPECT

Some critics argue that because EI is so closely related to intelligence and personality, once you control for these factors, EI has nothing unique to offer. There is some foundation to this argument. EI appears to be highly correlated with measures of personality, especially emotional stability.[106] But there hasn't been enough research on whether EI adds insight beyond measures of personality and general intelligence in predicting job performance. Still, EI is very popular among consulting firms and in the popular press. For example, one company's promotional materials for an EI measure claimed, 'EI accounts for more than 85 percent of star performance in top leaders.'[107] To say the least, it is hard to validate this statement with the research literature.

Whatever your view of EI, one thing's for sure: the concept is here to stay. Now that you know more about emotional intelligence, do you think you are a good judge of people? Do you think you can determine what makes someone tick? Check out the Self-Assessment feature to determine your EI.

SELF-ASSESSMENT LIBRARY

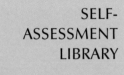

WHAT'S MY EMOTIONAL INTELLIGENCE SCORE?

In the Self-Assessment Library (available on CD and online), take assessment I.E.1 (What's My Emotional Intelligence Score?) and answer the following questions.

1. How did you score relative to your classmates?
2. Did your score surprise you? Why or why not?
3. What might you do to improve your ability to read others' emotions?

LEARNING OBJECTIVE 7

Apply concepts on emotions and moods to OB issues

OB APPLICATIONS OF EMOTIONS AND MOODS

We conclude our discussion of emotions and moods by considering their specific application to OB. In this section, we assess how an understanding of emotions and moods can improve our ability to explain and predict the selection process in organisations, decision making, creativity, motivation, leadership, interpersonal conflict, negotiation, customer service, job attitudes and deviant workplace behaviours. We also look at how managers can influence our moods.

SELECTION

One implication from the evidence to date on EI is that employers should consider it a factor in hiring employees, especially in jobs that demand a high degree of social interaction. In fact, more and more employers are starting to use EI measures to hire people. A study of US Air Force recruiters showed that top-performing recruiters exhibited high levels of EI. Using these findings, the Air Force revamped its selection criteria. A follow-up investigation found that future recruits who had high EI scores were 2.6 times more successful than those whose scores were low. By using EI in selection, the Air Force was able to cut turnover rates among new recruiters in one year by more than 90 per cent and save nearly US$3 million in hiring and training costs. At L'Oréal, salespersons selected on EI scores outsold those hired using the company's old selection procedure. On an annual basis, salespeople selected on the basis of emotional competence sold US$91 370 more than other salespeople did, for a net revenue increase of over US$2.5 million.[108]

DECISION MAKING

As you saw in a previous chapter, traditional approaches to the study of decision making in organisations have emphasised rationality. They have downplayed, or even ignored, the role of sadness, anxiety, fear, frustration, happiness, envy and similar emotions. Yet it is naive to assume that feelings don't influence our decisions.[109] Given the same objective data, we should expect that people may make different choices when they are feeling angry and stressed out than when they are calm and collected.

OB researchers continue to debate the role of negative emotions and moods in decision making. One well-cited article suggested that depressed people (those who chronically experience bad moods or negative emotions such as sadness) make more accurate judgments than non-depressed people.[110] This suggestion led some researchers to argue that the saying 'sadder but wiser' is true. However, more recent evidence has suggested that people who are depressed make poorer decisions than happy people. Why? Because depressed people are slower at processing information and tend to weigh *all* possible options rather than the most likely ones.[111] Although it would seem that weighing all possible options is a good thing, the problem is that depressed people search for the perfect solution, when a perfect solution rarely exists.

Positive people, in contrast, know when a solution is good enough. Indeed, positive emotions seem to help in decision making. Positive emotions can increase problem-solving skills and help us to understand and analyse new information. For example, someone in a positive mood may be better able to infer that a subordinate's performance problems were due to non-work problems.[112] People in good moods or those experiencing positive emotions are more likely to use heuristics, or rules of thumb,[113] to help them make good decisions quickly. Sometimes, however, these heuristics can be wrong and can lead to stereotyping, such as: 'women are less dedicated', 'Muslims are violent people', and so on. People use their heart as well as their head when making decisions. Therefore, failure to incorporate emotions and moods into the study of decision making will result in an incomplete, and often inaccurate, view of the process.

WORKPLACE GRIEF COSTS EVERYONE

Every year hundreds of thousands of Australians of all ages pass away. Every one of these deaths means that there are grieving family and friends left behind. These people may be employed and have jobs to contend with while at the same time grieving for their departed loved one. While most organisations give employees two or three days of compassionate leave from work, often this isn't enough time for the individual to make all the arrangements, attend the funeral, and recover sufficiently from the emotional loss to resume work.

This inevitably means that many grieving people are returning to the workplace too soon, which has detrimental impacts on performance. Work performance can be diminished, according to the National Association for Loss & Grief, in the following ways:

- the grieving person suffering from lack of concentration and poor memory;
- fatigue, usually caused by poor sleep and emotional exhaustion;
- varying degrees of depression; and
- irritability, lack of patience and increased tendency to displays of anger.

If grieving people suffer reduced performance when they return to work, why don't organisations give them more time off? Well, some enlightened organisations do, but most don't. Too many managers don't want to, or know how to, manage employees with grief issues. Many managers feel that the best 'cure' for their employee's grief is being busy at work, taking the employee's mind off their loss. Knowing this, many employees return to work too soon, afraid of taking more time off, afraid of developing a reputation for being 'weak' or of getting special treatment and/or being perceived as unreliable. Indeed, many employees won't even tell their employer of their loss for fear that it will be misunderstood or used against them.

Thankfully, more and more organisations are taking a wiser approach to assisting grieving employees. Negotiating increased leave and more flexible working arrangements, often using accumulated sick and recreation leave, is one such approach. Another is to provide time and access to discuss grief issues with grief counsellors who are trained to assist employees through these matters. Finally, adopting a compassionate strategy to ease the employee back to work when they are ready will often avoid the loss of performance issues common in these situations.

SOURCES: <www.grieflink.asn.au/workplace.html>; and the National Association for Loss & Grief.

CREATIVITY

People who are in a good mood are more creative than people who are in a bad mood, say some researchers.[114] They produce more ideas, others think their ideas are original, and they tend to identify more creative solutions to problems.[115] It seems that people who are experiencing positive moods or emotions are more flexible and open in their thinking, which may explain why they are more creative.[116] Supervisors should actively try to keep employees happy, because this will create more good moods (employees like their leaders to encourage them and to provide positive feedback on a job well done), which in turn leads people to be more creative.[117]

Some researchers, however, don't believe that a positive mood makes people more creative. They argue that when people are in a positive mood, they may relax ('If I'm in a good mood, things must be going OK, and I don't need to think of new ideas') and not engage in the critical thinking necessary for some forms of creativity.[118] However, this view is controversial.[119] Until there are more studies on the subject, we can safely conclude that, for many tasks, positive moods increase our creativity.

MOTIVATION

As we saw in a previous chapter, motivation theories propose that individuals 'are motivated to the extent that their behaviour is expected to lead to desired outcomes ... the employee essentially trades effort for pay, security, promotions, and so forth.'[120] But as the affective events theory demonstrated, people aren't cold, unfeeling machines. Their perceptions and calculations of work events are filled with emotional content that significantly influences how much effort they exert. Moreover, when you see people who are highly motivated in their jobs, they are emotionally committed. People who are engaged in their work 'become physically, cognitively, and emotionally immersed in the experience of activity, in the pursuit of a goal'.[121]

Are all people emotionally engaged in their work? No. But many are. So, if we focus only on those who are not, we won't be able to explain behaviours such as the biologist who forgets to have dinner and works late into the night, lost in the thrill of her work.[122]

Two studies have highlighted the importance of moods and emotions on motivation. The first study had two groups of people solve a number of word puzzles. One group saw a funny video clip, which was intended to put them in a good mood before having to solve the puzzles. The other group wasn't shown the clip and just started working on solving the puzzles right away. The results? The positive-mood group reported higher expectations of being able to solve the puzzles, worked harder at them, and solved more puzzles as a result.[123] The second study found that giving people feedback—whether real or fake—about their performance influenced their mood, which then influenced their motivation.[124] So, a cycle can exist in which positive moods cause people to be more creative, which leads to positive feedback from those observing their work. This positive feedback then further reinforces their positive mood, which may then make them perform even better, and so on. Both of these studies highlight the effects of mood and emotions on motivation and suggest that organisations that promote positive moods at work are likely to have a more motivated workforce.

LEADERSHIP

The ability to lead others is a fundamental quality that organisations look for in employees. Effective leaders rely on emotional appeals to help convey their messages.[125] In fact, the expression of emotions in speeches is often the critical element that makes us accept or reject a leader's message. 'When leaders feel excited, enthusiastic, and active, they may be more likely to energise their subordinates and convey a sense of efficacy, competence, optimism, and enjoyment.'[126] Politicians, as a case in point, have learned to show enthusiasm when talking about their chances of winning an election, even when polls suggest otherwise. Corporate executives know that emotional content is critical if employees are to buy into their vision of their company's future and accept change. When higher-ups offer new visions, especially when the visions contain distant or vague goals, it is often difficult for employees to accept those visions and the changes they will bring. So, when effective leaders want to implement significant changes, they rely on 'the evocation, framing, and mobilisation of emotions'.[127] By arousing emotions and linking them to an appealing vision, leaders increase the likelihood that managers and employees alike will accept change.

INTERPERSONAL CONFLICT

Few issues are more intertwined with emotions than the topic of interpersonal conflict. Whenever conflicts arise between employees, you can be fairly certain that emotions are surfacing. A manager's success in trying to resolve conflicts, in fact, is often largely attributable to an ability to identify the emotional elements in the conflict and to get the parties to work through their emotions. The manager who ignores the emotional elements in conflicts, focusing singularly on rational and task-focused concerns, is unlikely to resolve those conflicts.

NEGOTIATION

Negotiation is an emotional process; however, we often say a skilled negotiator has a 'poker face'. The founder of Britain's Poker TV channel, Crispin Nieboer, stated: 'It is a game of bluff and there is fantastic human emotion and tension, seeing who can bluff the longest.'[128] Several studies have shown that negotiators who feign anger have an advantage over their opponent. Why? Because when a negotiator shows anger, the opponent concludes that the negotiator has conceded all that she can, and so the opponent gives in.[129]

Displaying a negative emotion (such as anger) can be effective, but feeling bad about your performance appears to impair future negotiations. Negotiators who do poorly experience negative emotions, develop negative perceptions of their counterpart, and are less willing to share information or to be cooperative in future negotiations.[130] Interestingly, then, while moods and emotions have their benefits at work, in negotiation, unless we are putting up a false front (feigning anger), it seems that emotions may impair negotiator performance. In fact, one 2005 study found that people who suffered damage to the emotional centres of their brains (damage to the same part of the brain as Phineas Gage) may be the best negotiators, because they are not likely to overcorrect when faced with negative outcomes.[131] Consider another example. When Patrick Stevedoring faced a strike from the Waterside Workers Union in 1998, the company coolly prepared for the strike by hiring replacement stevedores in advance, and when the union employees struck, brought in the replacement employees and calmly asked for even more concessions.[132]

CUSTOMER SERVICE

An employee's emotional state influences customer service, which influences levels of repeat business and of customer satisfaction.[133] Providing quality customer service makes demands on employees because it often puts them in a state of emotional dissonance. Over time, this state can lead to job burnout, declines in job performance and lower job satisfaction.[134]

In addition, employees' emotions may also transfer to the customer. Studies indicate a matching effect between employee and customer emotions, an effect that OB practitioners call **emotional contagion**, the 'catching' of emotions from others.[135] How does emotional contagion work? The primary explanation is that when someone experiences positive emotions and laughs and smiles at you, you begin to copy that person's behaviour. So, when employees express positive emotions, customers tend to respond positively. Emotional contagion is important, because when customers catch the positive moods or emotions of employees, they shop longer.[136] But what about negative emotions and moods? Are they contagious, too? Absolutely. When an employee is cranky or nasty, these negative emotions tend to have negative effects on customers.

emotional contagion | The process by which people's emotions are caused by the emotions of others.

JOB ATTITUDES

Have you ever heard the advice, 'Never take your work home with you', meaning that people should forget about their work once they go home? As it turns out, that's easier said than done. Several studies have shown that people who had a good day at work tend to be in a better mood at home that evening. And people who had a bad day tend to be in a bad mood once they are at home.[137] Evidence also suggests that people who have a stressful day at work have trouble relaxing once they get off work.[138]

Even though people do emotionally take their work home with them, by the next day, the effect is usually gone.[139] So, although it may be hard or even unnatural to 'never take your work home with you', it doesn't appear that, for most people, a negative mood resulting from a bad day at work carries over to the next day.

DEVIANT WORKPLACE BEHAVIOURS

Negative emotions also can lead to a number of deviant workplace behaviours. Anyone who has spent much time in an organisation will know that people often behave in ways that violate established norms and threaten the organisation, its members, or both. As we saw in a previous chapter, these actions are called workplace deviant behaviours.[140] Many of these deviant behaviours can be traced to negative emotions.

For instance, envy is an emotion that occurs when you resent someone for having something that you don't have but that you strongly desire—such as a better work assignment, larger office or higher salary.[141] Envy can lead to malicious deviant behaviours. An envious employee, for example, could then act hostilely by backstabbing another employee, negatively distorting others' successes, and positively distorting his or her own accomplishments.[142] Evidence suggests that people who feel negative emotions, particularly those who feel angry or hostile, are more likely than people who don't feel negative emotions to engage in deviant behaviour at work.[143]

HOW MANAGERS CAN INFLUENCE MOODS

What can companies do to improve their employees' moods? Managers can use humour and give their employees small tokens of appreciation for work well done. Also, research indicates that when leaders are in a good mood, group members are more positive, and as a result the members are more cooperative.[144]

Finally, selecting positive team members can have a contagion effect, as positive moods transmit from team member to team member. One study of professional cricket teams found that players' happy moods affected the moods of their teammates and also positively influenced their performance—'winners are grinners'.[145] It makes sense, then, for managers to select team members who are predisposed to experience positive moods.

- Emotions and moods are similar in that both are affective in nature. But they are also different—moods are more general and less contextual than emotions.
- Events do matter—the time of day and day of the week, stressful events, social activities, and sleep patterns are all factors that influence emotions and moods.
- Managers can control their colleagues' and employees' emotions and moods, but there are limits, practically and ethically. Where managers err is if they ignore their colleagues' emotions and assess others' behaviour as if it were completely rational. As one consultant aptly put it, 'You can't divorce emotions from the workplace because you can't divorce emotions from people.'[146]
- Emotions and moods can hinder performance, especially negative emotions, which is probably why organisations try to extract emotions out of the workplace.
- Emotions and moods can also enhance performance.[147] First, emotions and moods can increase arousal levels and motivate employees to work better; and second, emotional labour recognises that certain feelings can be part of a job's requirements.
- Some analysts have suggested that what differentiates functional from dysfunctional emotions and moods is the complexity of the individual's task.[148] The more complex a task, the less emotional a worker can be before interfering with performance. Given that the trend is towards jobs becoming more complex, you can see why organisations are likely to become more concerned with the role of emotions—especially intense ones—in the workplace.

POINT / COUNTERPOINT

The Costs and Benefits of Organisational Display Rules

● POINT

Organisations today realise that good customer service means good business. After all, who wants to end a shopping trip to the supermarket with a surly checkout assistant? Research clearly shows that organisations that provide good customer service have higher profits. Look at the main theme of Woolworths' advertising, 'The Fresh Food People', and you will soon see how persuasive this point can be. An integral part of customer service training is to set forth display rules to teach employees to interact with customers in a friendly, helpful, professional way.

As one Starbucks manager says, 'What makes Starbucks different is our passion for what we do. We are trying to provide a great experience for people with a great product. That's what we all care about.' Starbucks may have good coffee, something that can be easily copied by other coffee sellers, but a big part of the company's global growth has been the customer experience. The secret is the positive emotions from the Starbucks employees, something which other competitors cannot copy easily.

Asking employees to act in a friendly way towards customers is good for them, too. 'Forced' smiles can actually make people feel better. If someone feels that being asked to smile is bad for them, then perhaps they should rethink their career choice in the service sector!

SOURCES: Points in this argument are based on H. Liao and A. Chuang, 'A Multilevel Investigation of Factors Influencing Employee Service Performance and Customer Outcomes', *Academy of Management Journal*, vol. 47, no. 1, 2004, pp. 41–58; <www.starbucks.com> (16 May 2005); F. Strack, L. L. Stepper and S. Martin, 'Inhibiting and Facilitating Conditions of the Human Smile: A Nonobstrusive Test of the Facial-Feedback Hypothesis', *Journal of Personality and Social Psychology*, vol. 54, 1988, pp. 768–77; D. Zapf, 'Emotion Work and Psychological Well-Being: A Review of the Literature and

COUNTERPOINT

Organisations have no business trying to regulate the emotions of their employees. Companies shouldn't be 'the thought police' and force employees to feel and act in ways that serve only organisational goals and objectives. Most people agree that service employees should be professional and courteous, but many organisations expect employees to take abuse without defending themselves. That's not morally right. We each have a responsibility to be, as the philosopher Jean-Paul Sartre wrote, authentic and true to ourselves. Organisations, within reasonable limits, have no right to ask us to be otherwise.

Service industries have no business setting their employees up to be smiling emotional punching bags for rude and surly customers. Most customers might even prefer that employees act naturally, not as dictated by the company display rules. Employees shouldn't be openly hostile or nasty, of course, but who appreciates a fake smile or a memorised greeting? Most customers would rather talk with a 'real' person than with someone enslaved to an organisation's display rules. Furthermore, if an employee doesn't feel like slapping on a fake smile, then it is only going to create more dissonance between the employee and the employer.

Finally, research shows that forcing display rules on employees takes a heavy emotional toll. It is unnatural to expect someone to smile all the time or to passively take abuse from customers, clients and/or fellow employees. Organisations can improve their employees' psychological health by encouraging them to be themselves, within reasonable limits.

Some Conceptual Considerations', *Human Resource Management Review*, vol. 12, no. 2, 2002, pp. 237–68; J. E. Bono and M. A. Vey, 'Toward Understanding Emotional Management at Work: A Quantitative Review of Emotional Labor Research', in C. E. Härtel and W. J. Zerbe (eds), *Emotions in Organizational Behavior* (Mahwah, NJ: Lawrence Erlbaum Associates, Publishers, 2005), pp. 213–33; and S. M. Kruml and D. Geddes, 'Catching Fire without Burning out: Is there an Ideal Way to Perform Emotional Labor?', in Ashkanasy, Hartel and Zerbe (eds), *Emotions in the Workplace*, pp. 177–88.

QUESTIONS FOR REVIEW

MyOBLab Do you understand this chapter's content? Find out at **www.pearsoned.com.au/MyOBLab**

1. What are the differences and similarities between emotions and moods?
2. How does the time of the day, the day of the week, and the weather influence people's moods?
3. Are there differences in the degree to which men and women show emotions in the workplace? What types of workplace situations might bring to light these different emotional reactions?
4. Are there cultural differences in the degree to which people experience emotions? What about in the expression of emotions?
5. What is emotional labour, and why is it important to understanding OB?
6. If you were a manager at a busy clothing store, how would you balance increasing positive customer experiences with preventing the loss of good employees who might be worn down by nasty or hostile customers?
7. Explain the affective events theory. What are its implications for managing emotions?
8. What is emotional intelligence, and why is it important?
9. As a manager, what steps would you take to improve your employees' moods? Explain your answer.

QUESTIONS FOR CRITICAL THINKING

1. In your opinion—and drawing from the arguments in the chapter—are there core or fundamental emotions that everyone experiences? If so, what are they?
2. What has research shown on the relationship between emotions and rational thinking? Do these findings surprise you? Why or why not?
3. Do emotions and moods matter in explaining behaviour in organisations? How so?
4. What, if anything, can managers do to manage their employees' emotions? Are there ethical implications in any of these actions? If so, what are they?
5. Give some examples of situations in which the overt expression of emotions might enhance job performance.
6. From an emotional labour perspective, how does dealing with an abusive customer lead to stress and burnout?
7. If you were a recruiter for a customer-service call centre, what personality types would you prefer to hire, and why? In other words, what individual differences are likely to affect whether an employee can handle customer abuse on a day-to-day basis?
8. Emotional intelligence is one's ability to detect and to manage emotional cues and information. How might emotional intelligence play a role in responding to abusive customers? What facets of emotional intelligence might employees possess who are able to handle abusive customers?
9. What steps should companies take to ensure that their employees are not the victims of customer abuse? Should companies allow a certain degree of abuse if that abuse results in satisfied customers and perhaps greater profit? What are the ethical implications of this?

EXPERIENTIAL EXERCISE

Who Can Catch a Liar?

Earlier in the chapter we discussed how people determine emotions from facial expressions. There has been research on whether people can tell whether someone is lying based on facial expression. Let's see who is good at catching liars.

Split up into teams, and follow these instructions:

1. Randomly choose someone to be the team organiser. Have this person write down on a piece of paper 'T' for truth and 'L' for lie. If there are, say, six people in the group (other than the organiser), then three people will get a slip with a 'T' and three a slip with an 'L'. It is important that all team members keep what's on their slip of paper a secret.
2. Each team member needs to come up with a true or false statement depending on whether he or she holds a 'T' or an 'L' slip. Try not to make the statement so outrageous that no one would believe it (for example, 'I have flown to the moon').
3. The organiser will have each member make his or her statement. Group members should then examine the person making the statement closely to try to determine whether he or she is telling the truth or lying. Once each person has made his or her statement, the organiser will ask for a vote and record the tallies.
4. Each person should now indicate whether the statement was the truth or a lie.
5. How good was your group at catching the 'liars'? Were some people good liars? What did you look for to determine if someone was lying?

ETHICAL DILEMMA

Are Workplace Romances Unethical?

A large percentage of married individuals first met in the workplace. A 2005 survey revealed that 58 per cent of all employees have been in an office romance. Given the amount of time people spend at work, this isn't terribly surprising. Yet, office romances pose sensitive ethical issues for organisations and employees. What rights and responsibilities do organisations have to regulate the romantic lives of their employees?

Take the case of former General Electric (GE) CEO Jack Welch and journalist Suzy Wetlaufer. The two met while Wetlaufer was interviewing Welch for a *Harvard Business Review* article, and Welch was still married. Once their relationship was out in the open, some accused Wetlaufer of being unethical for refusing to disclose the relationship while working on the article. She eventually left the *Harvard Business Review*. Others accused Welch of letting his personal life get in the way of the interests of GE and its shareholders. Some even blamed the scandal for a drop in GE stock.

Welch and Wetlaufer didn't even work for the same company. What about when two people work together in the same work unit? For example, Soomay, an account executive at a Sydney advertising firm, started dating Kevin, one of her account supervisors. Their innocent banter turned into going out for drinks, and then dinner, and soon they were dating. Kevin and Soomay's bosses were in-house competitors. The problem: sometimes in meetings Kevin would make it seem that Soomay and he were in agreement on important issues even when they weren't. In response,

Soomay's boss began to isolate her from key projects. Soomay broke up with Kevin, who then tried to have her fired. Soomay said, 'I remember times when I would be there all night photocopying hundreds of pages of my work to show that [Kevin's] allegations [of her incompetence] were unfounded. It was just embarrassing because it became a question of my professional judgment.'

These examples show that while workplace romances are personal matters, it is hard to keep them out of the political complexities of organisational life.

QUESTIONS

1. Do you think organisations should have policies governing workplace romances? What would such policies stipulate?
2. Do you think romantic relationships would distract two employees from performing their jobs? Why or why not?
3. Is it ever appropriate for a supervisor to romantically pursue a subordinate under his or her supervision? Why or why not?
4. Some companies openly try to recruit couples. Do you think this is a good idea? How would you feel working in a department with a 'couple'?

SOURCES: 'Cupid in the Cubicle, Says New Vault Survey', Vault, Inc. (<www.vault.com>); S. Shellenbarger, 'The Nasty Downside of Office Romances', *The Wall Street Journal*, 2005 (<www.wsj.com>); and J. Amber, 'Office Romance' (<www.yourpurelife.com>).

CASE STUDY

The Upside of Anger

A researcher doing a case study on emotions in organisations interviewed Laura, a 22-year-old customer service representative in Australia. Below is a summary of the interview (with some paraphrasing of the interviewer questions):

Interviewer: How would you describe your workplace?

Laura: *Very cold, unproductive, [a] very, umm, cold environment, atmosphere.*

Interviewer: What kinds of emotions are prevalent in your organisation?

Laura: *Anger, hatred towards other people, other staff members.*

Interviewer: So it seems that managers keep employees in line using fear tactics?

Laura: *Yeah. [The general manager's] favourite saying is, 'Nobody's indispensable.' So, it's like, 'I can't do that because I'll get sacked!'*

Interviewer: How do you survive in this situation?

Laura: *You have to cater your emotions to the sort of situation, the specific situation . . . because it's just such a hostile environment. This is sort of the only way you can survive.*

Interviewer: Are there emotions you have to hide?

Laura: *Managers don't like you to show your emotions . . . They don't like to show that there is anything wrong or anything emotional in the working environment.*

Interviewer: Why do you go along?

Laura: *I feel I have to put on an act because . . . to show your true emotions, especially towards my managers [Laura names two*

of her senior managers], it would be hatred sometimes. So, you just can't afford to do that because it's your job and you need the money.

Interviewer: Do you ever rebel against this system?

Laura: *You sort of put on a happy face just so you can annoy [the managers]. I find that they don't like people being happy, so you just annoy them by being happy. So, yeah. It just makes you laugh. You just 'put it on' just because you know it annoys [management]. It's pretty vindictive and manipulative, but you just need to do that.*

Interviewer: Do you ever find that this gets to you?

Laura: *I did care in the beginning and I think it just got me into more trouble. So now I just tell myself, 'I don't care.' If you tell yourself something for long enough, eventually you believe it. Yeah, so now I just go, 'Oh well.'*

Interviewer: Do you intend to keep working here?

Laura: *It's a means to an end now. So every time I go [to work] and every week I just go, 'Well, one week down, one week less until I go away.' But if I knew that I didn't have this goal, I don't know if I could handle it, or if I would even be there now.*

Interviewer: Is there an upside to working here?

Laura: *I'm so much better at telling people off now than I ever used to be. I can put people in place in about three sentences. Like, instead of, before I would walk away from it. But now I just stand there and fight . . . I don't know if that's a good thing or a bad thing.*

QUESTIONS

1. From an emotional labour perspective, how does dealing with an abusive customer lead to stress and burnout?

2. If you were a recruiter for a customer-service call centre, what personality types would you prefer to hire, and why? In other words, what individual differences are likely to affect whether an employee can handle customer abuse on a day-to-day basis?

3. Emotional intelligence is one's ability to detect and to manage emotional cues and information. How might emotional intelligence play a role in responding to abusive customers? What facets of emotional intelligence might employees possess who are able to handle abusive customers?

4. What steps should companies take to ensure that their employees aren't the victims of customer abuse? Should companies allow a certain degree of abuse if that abuse results in satisfied customers and perhaps greater profit? What are the ethical implications of this?

SOURCE: J. Perrone and M. H. Vickers, 'Emotions as Strategic Game in a Hostile Workplace: An Exemplar Case', *Employee Responsibilities and Rights Journal*, vol. 16, no. 3, 2004, pp. 167–78. Reproduced with kind permission of Springer Science and Business Media.

ENDNOTES

1. This section is based on the transcript of the episode of *Australian Story*, aired on the ABC on 13 November 2006 (accessed at: <www.abc.net.au/austory/content/2006/s1788345.htm>>; <www.festivalfocus.org/festival.php?uid=134>; and <www.heartofgold.com.au/index.html>.

2. <www.heartofgold.com.au/ourPatron.html>.

3. See, for instance, C. D. Fisher and N. M. Ashkanasy, 'The Emerging Role of Emotions in Work Life: An Introduction', *Journal of Organizational Behavior*, Special Issue 2000, pp. 123–29; N. M. Ashkanasy, C. E. J. Hartel and W. J. Zerbe (eds), *Emotions in the Workplace: Research, Theory, and Practice* (Westport, CT: Quorum Books, 2000); N. M. Ashkanasy and C. S. Daus, 'Emotion in the Workplace: The New Challenge for Managers', *Academy of Management Executive*, February 2002, pp. 76–86; and N. M. Ashkanasy, C. E. J. Hartel and C. S. Daus, 'Diversity and Emotion: The New Frontiers in Organizational Behavior Research', *Journal of Management*, vol. 28, no. 3 2002, pp. 307–38.

4. See, for example, L. L. Putnam and D. K. Mumby, 'Organizations, Emotion and the Myth of Rationality', in S. Fineman (ed.), *Emotion in Organizations* (Thousand Oaks, CA: Sage, 1993), pp. 36–57; and J. Martin, K. Knopoff and C. Beckman, 'An Alternative to Bureaucratic Impersonality and Emotional Labor: Bounded Emotionality at The Body Shop', *Administrative Science Quarterly*, June 1998, pp. 429–69.

5. B. E. Ashforth and R. H. Humphrey, 'Emotion in the Workplace: A Reappraisal', *Human Relations*, February 1995, pp. 97–125.

6. J. M. George, 'Trait and State Affect', in K. R. Murphy (ed.), *Individual Differences and Behavior in Organizations* (San Francisco: Jossey-Bass, 1996), p. 145.

7. See N. H. Frijda, 'Moods, Emotion Episodes and Emotions', in M. Lewis and J. M. Haviland (eds), *Handbook of Emotions* (New York: Guilford Press, 1993), pp. 381–403.

8. H. M. Weiss and R. Cropanzano, 'Affective Events Theory: A Theoretical Discussion of the Structure, Causes and Consequences of Affective Experiences at Work', in B. M. Staw and L. L. Cummings (eds), *Research in Organizational Behavior*, vol. 18 (Greenwich, CT: JAI Press, 1996), pp. 17–19.

9. See P. Ekman and R. J. Davidson (eds), *The Nature of Emotions: Fundamental Questions* (Oxford, UK: Oxford University Press, 1994).

10. Frijda, 'Moods, Emotion Episodes and Emotions', p. 381.

11. See Ekman and Davidson (eds), *The Nature of Emotions: Fundamental Questions*.

12. See, for example, P. Shaver, J. Schwartz, D. Kirson and C. O'Connor, 'Emotion Knowledge: Further Exploration of a Prototype Approach', *Journal of Personality and Social Psychology*, June 1987, pp. 1061–86; P. Ekman, 'An Argument for Basic Emotions', *Cognition and Emotion*, May/July 1992, pp. 169–200; C. E. Izard, 'Basic Emotions, Relations among Emotions, and Emotion–Cognition Relations', *Psychological Bulletin*, November 1992, pp. 561–65; and R. Plutchik, *The Psychology and Biology of Emotion* (New York: HarperCollins, 1994).

13. R. C. Solomon, 'Back to Basics: On the Very Idea of "Basic Emotions"', *Journal for the Theory of Social Behavior*, vol. 32, no. 2, June 2002, pp. 115–44.

14. R. Descartes, *The Passions of the Soul* (1649) (Indianapolis, IN: Hackett, 1989).

15. P. Ekman, *Emotions Revealed: Recognizing Faces and Feelings to Improve Communication and Emotional Life* (New York: Times Books/Henry Holt and Co., 2003).

16. P. R. Shaver, H. J. Morgan and S. J. Wu, 'Is Love a "Basic" Emotion?', *Personal Relationships*, vol. 3, no. 1, March 1996, pp. 81–96.

17. Solomon, 'Back to Basics: On the Very Idea of "Basic Emotions"'.

18. Weiss and Cropanzano, 'Affective Events Theory', pp. 20–22.

19. Cited in R. D. Woodworth, *Experimental Psychology* (New York: Holt, 1938).

20. J. Nolte, *The Human Brain*, 5th ed. (St. Louis: Mosby, 2002).

21. D. M. Tucker, P. Luu, G. Frishkoff, J. Quiring and C. Poulsen, 'Frontolimbic Response to Negative Feedback in Clinical Depression', *Journal of Abnormal Psychology*, vol. 112, no. 4, November 2003, pp. 667–78.

22. R. C. Gur, F. Gunning-Dixon, W. B. Bilker and R. E. Gur, 'Sex Differences in Temporo-Limbic and Frontal Brain Volumes of Healthy Adults', *Cerebral Cortex*, vol. 12, no. 9, September 2002, pp. 998–1003.

23. L. M. Poverny and S. Picascia, 'There is No Crying in Business' (<www.womens media.com/new/Crying-at-Work.shtml>).

24. L. P. Frankel, *Nice Girls Don't Get the Corner Office* (New York: Warner Books, 2004).

25. A. R. Damasio, *Descartes' Error: Emotion, Reason, and the Human Brain* (New York: Quill, 1994).

26. Ibid.

27. L. Cosmides and J. Tooby, 'Evolutionary Psychology and the Emotions', in M. Lewis and J. M. Haviland-Jones (eds), *Handbook of Emotions*, 2nd ed. (New York: Guilford Press, 2000), pp. 91–115.

28. D. M. Buss, 'Cognitive Biases and Emotional Wisdom in the Evolution of Conflict Between the Sexes', *Current Directions in Psychological Science*, vol. 10, no. 6, December 2001, pp. 219–23.

29. K. Hundley, 'An Unspoken Problem—Two-Thirds of Female Lawyers Say They Have Experienced or Seen Harassment at Work. But Few Want to Talk about It', *St. Petersburg Times* (<www.sptimes.com /2005/04/24/Business/An_unspoken_probl em.shtml> (25 April 2004).

30. K. N. Laland and G. R. Brown, *Sense and Nonsense: Evolutionary Perspectives on Human Behaviour* (Oxford, UK: Oxford University Press, 2002).

31. D. Watson, L. A. Clark and A. Tellegen, 'Development and Validation of Brief Measures of Positive and Negative Affect: The PANAS Scales', *Journal of Personality and Social Psychology*, 1988, pp. 1063–70.

32. A. Ben-Ze'ev, *The Subtlety of Emotions* (Cambridge, MA: MIT Press, 2000), p. 94.

33. 'Flight Attendant War Stories . . . Stewardess' (<www.aboutmyjob.com/ main.php3?action=displayarticle&artid=2 111>).

34. Cited in Ben-Ze'ev, *The Subtlety of Emotions*, p. 99.

35. J. T. Cacioppo and W. L. Gardner, 'Emotion', *Annual Review of Psychology*, vol. 50, 1999, pp. 191–214.

36. D. Holman, 'Call Centres', in D. Holman,

T. D. Wall, C. Clegg, P. Sparrow and A. Howard (eds), *The Essentials of the New Work Place: A Guide to the Human Impact of Modern Working Practices* (Chichester, UK: John Wiley & Sons, 2005), pp. 111–32.

37. R. J. Larsen and E. Diener, 'Affect Intensity as an Individual Difference Characteristic: A Review', *Journal of Research in Personality*, vol. 21, 1987, pp. 1–39.

38. M. Tamir and M. D. Robinson, 'Knowing Good from Bad: The Paradox of Neuroticism, Negative Affect, and Evaluative Processing', *Journal of Personality and Social Psychology*, vol. 87, no. 6, 2004, pp. 913–25; S. H. Hemenover, 'Individual Differences in Rate of Affect Change: Studies in Affective Chronometry', *Journal of Personality and Social Psychology*, vol. 85, no. 1, 2003, pp. 121–31.

39. D. Watson, *Mood and Temperament* (New York: Guilford Publications, 2000).

40. Ibid.

41. G. Matthews, 'Morningness–Eveningness as a Dimension of Personality: Trait, State, and Psychophysiological Correlates', *European Journal of Personality*, vol. 2, no. 4, December 1988, pp. 277–93; V. Natale and P. Cicogna, 'Morningness–Eveningness Dimension: Is It Really a Continuum?', *Personality & Individual Differences*, vol. 32, no. 5, April 2002, pp. 809–16.

42. Watson, *Mood and Temperament*.

43. Ibid, p. 100.

44. Ibid, p. 73.

45. J. A. Fuller, J. M. Stanton, G. G. Fisher, C. Spitzmüller, S. S. Russell and P C. Smith, 'A Lengthy Look at the Daily Grind: Time Series Analysis of Events, Mood, Stress, and Satisfaction', *Journal of Applied Psychology*, vol. 88, no. 6, December 2003, pp. 1019–33.

46. See 'Monday Blahs', 16 May 2005 (<www.ashidome.com/blogger/housearrest .asp?c=809&m=5&y=2005>) (16 May 2005).

47. A. M. Isen, 'Positive Affect as a Source of Human Strength', in L. G. Aspinwall and U. Staudinger (eds), *The Psychology of Human Strengths* (Washington, DC: American Psychological Association, 2003), pp. 179–95.

48. Watson, *Mood and Temperament*.

49. H. S. Friedman, J. S. Tucker, J. E. Schwartz, C. Tomlinson-Keasey et al., 'Psychosocial and Behavioral Predictors of Longevity: The Aging and Death of the "Termites"', *American Psychologist*, vol. 50, no. 2, February 1995, pp. 69–78.

50. D. D. Danner, D. A. Snowdon and W. V. Friesen, 'Positive Emotions in Early Life and

Longevity: Findings from the Nun Study', *Journal of Personality and Social Psychology*, vol. 80, no. 5, 2001, pp. 804–13.

51. Sleep in America Poll (Washington, DC: National Sleep Foundation, 2005).

52. M. Lavidor, A. Weller and H. Babkoff, 'How Sleep is Related to Fatigue', *British Journal of Health Psychology*, vol. 8, 2003, pp. 95–105; J. J. Pilcher and E. Ott, 'The Relationships between Sleep and Measures of Health and Well-Being in College Students: A Repeated Measures Approach', *Behavioral Medicine*, vol. 23, 1998, pp. 170–78.

53. E. K. Miller and J. D. Cohen, 'An Integrative Theory of Prefrontal Cortex Function', *Annual Review of Neuroscience*, vol. 24, 2001, pp. 167–202.

54. B. A. Scott and T. A. Judge, 'Tired and Cranky?: The Effects of Sleep Quality on Employee Emotions and Job Satisfaction', Working paper, Department of Management, University of Florida, 2005.

55. P. R. Giacobbi, H. A. Hausenblas and N. Frye, 'A Naturalistic Assessment of the Relationship between Personality, Daily Life Events, Leisure-Time Exercise, and Mood', *Psychology of Sport & Exercise*, vol. 6, no. 1, January 2005, pp. 67–81.

56. L. L. Carstensen, M. Pasupathi, M. Ulrich and J. R. Nesselroade, 'Emotional Experience in Everyday Life across the Adult Life Span', *Journal of Personality and Social Psychology*, vol. 79, no. 4, 2000, pp. 644–55.

57. K. Deaux, 'Sex Differences', in M. R. Rosenzweig and L. W. Porter (eds), *Annual Review of Psychology*, vol. 26 (Palo Alto, CA: Annual Reviews, 1985), pp. 48–82; M. LaFrance and M. Banaji, 'Toward a Reconsideration of the Gender–Emotion Relationship', in M. Clark (ed.), *Review of Personality and Social Psychology*, vol. 14 (Newbury Park, CA: Sage, 1992), pp. 178–97; and A. M. Kring and A. H. Gordon, 'Sex Differences in Emotion: Expression, Experience, and Physiology', *Journal of Personality and Social Psychology*, March 1998, pp. 686–703.

58. L. R. Brody and J. A. Hall, 'Gender and Emotion', in M. Lewis and J. M. Haviland (eds), *Handbook of Emotions* (New York: Guilford Press, 1993), pp. 447–60; and M. Grossman and W. Wood, 'Sex Differences in Intensity of Emotional Experience: A Social Role Interpretation', *Journal of Personality and Social Psychology*, November 1992, pp. 1010–22.

59. J. A. Hall, *Nonverbal Sex Differences: Communication Accuracy and Expressive Style* (Baltimore, MD: Johns Hopkins Press, 1984).

60. N. James, 'Emotional Labour: Skill and Work in the Social Regulations of Feelings', *Sociological Review*, February 1989, pp. 15–42; A. Hochschild, *The Second Shift* (New York: Viking, 1989); and F. M. Deutsch, 'Status, Sex, and Smiling: The Effect of Role on Smiling in Men and Women', *Personality and Social Psychology Bulletin*, September 1990, pp. 531–40.

61. A. Rafaeli, 'When Clerks Meet Customers: A Test of Variables Related to Emotional Expression on the Job', *Journal of Applied Psychology*, June 1989, pp. 385–93; and LaFrance and Banaji, 'Toward a Reconsideration of the Gender–Emotion Relationship'.

62. L. W. Hoffman, 'Early Childhood Experiences and Women's Achievement Motives', *Journal of Social Issues*, vol. 28, no. 2, 1972, pp. 129–55.

63. M. Boas and S. Chain, *Big Mac: The Unauthorized Story of McDonald's* (New York: Dutton, 1976), p. 84.

64. Ashforth and Humphrey, 'Emotion in the Workplace', p. 104.

65. G. L. Flett, K. R. Blankstein, P. Pliner and C. Bator, 'Impression-Management and Self-Deception Components of Appraised Emotional Experience', *British Journal of Social Psychology*, January 1988, pp. 67–77.

66. B. E. Ashforth and R. H. Humphrey, 'Emotion in the Workplace: A Reappraisal', *Human Relations*, vol. 48, no. 2, 1995, pp. 97–125.

67. M. Eid and E. Diener, 'Norms for Experiencing Emotions in Different Cultures: Inter- and Intranational Differences', *Journal of Personality & Social Psychology*, vol. 81, no. 5, 2001, pp. 869–85.

68. S. Oishi, E. Diener and C. Napa Scollon, 'Cross-Situational Consistency of Affective Experiences across Cultures', *Journal of Personality & Social Psychology*, vol. 86, no. 3, 2004, pp. 460–72.

69. Eid and Diener, 'Norms for Experiencing Emotions in Different Cultures'.

70. Ibid.

71. B. Mesquita, 'Emotions in Collectivist and Individualist Contexts', *Journal of Personality and Social Psychology*, vol. 80, no. 1, 2001, pp. 68–74.

72. H. A. Elfenbein and N. Ambady, 'When Familiarity Breeds Accuracy: Cultural Exposure and Facial Emotional Recognition', *Journal of Personality and Social Psychology*, vol. 85, no. 2, 2003, pp. 276–90.

73. R. I. Levy, *Tahitians: Mind and Experience in the Society Islands* (Chicago: University of Chicago Press, 1973).

74. B. Mesquita and N. H. Frijda, 'Cultural Variations in Emotions: A Review', *Psychological Bulletin*, September 1992, pp. 179–204; and B. Mesquita, 'Emotions in Collectivist and Individualist Contexts', *Journal of Personality and Social Psychology*, January 2001, pp. 68–74.

75. D. Matsumoto, 'Cross-Cultural Psychology in the 21st Century' (<http://teachpsych.lemoyne.edu/teachpsych/faces/script/Ch05.htm>).

76. See J. A. Morris and D. C. Feldman, 'Managing Emotions in the Workplace', *Journal of Managerial Issues*, vol. 9, no. 3, 1997, pp. 257–74; S. Mann, *Hiding What We Feel, Faking What We Don't: Understanding the Role of Your Emotions at Work* (New York: HarperCollins, 1999); S. M. Kruml and D. Geddes, 'Catching Fire Without Burning Out: Is There an Ideal Way to Perform Emotion Labor?', in N. M. Ashkansay, C. E. J. Hartel and W. J. Zerbe, *Emotions in the Workplace* (New York: Quorum Books, 2000), pp. 177–88.

77. P. Ekman, W. V. Friesen and M. O'Sullivan, 'Smiles When Lying', in P. Ekman and E. L. Rosenberg (eds), *What the Face Reveals: Basic and Applied Studies of Spontaneous Expression Using the Facial Action Coding System (FACS)* (London: Oxford University Press, 1997), pp. 201–16.

78. A. Grandey, 'Emotion Regulation in the Workplace: A New Way to Conceptualize Emotional Labor', *Journal of Occupational Health Psychology*, vol. 5, no. 1, 2000, pp. 95–110; and R. Cropanzano, D. E. Rupp and Z. S. Byrne, 'The Relationship of Emotional Exhaustion to Work Attitudes, Job Performance, and Organizational Citizenship Behavior', *Journal of Applied Psychology*, February 2003, pp. 160–69.

79. A. R. Hochschild, 'Emotion Work, Feeling Rules, and Social Structure', *American Journal of Sociology*, November 1979, pp. 551–75; W-C. Tsai, 'Determinants and Consequences of Employee Displayed Positive Emotions', *Journal of Management*, vol. 27, no. 4, 2001, pp. 497–512; M. W. Kramer and J. A. Hess, 'Communication Rules for the Display of Emotions in Organizational Settings', *Management Communication Quarterly*, August 2002, pp. 66–80; and J. M. Diefendorff and E. M. Richard, 'Antecedents and Consequences of Emotional Display Rule Perceptions', *Journal of Applied Psychology*, April 2003, pp. 284–94.

80. B. M. DePaulo, 'Nonverbal Behavior and Self-Presentation', *Psychological Bulletin*, March 1992, pp. 203–43.

81. C. S. Hunt, 'Although I Might Be Laughing Loud and Hearty, Deep Inside I'm Blue: Individual Perceptions Regarding Feeling and Displaying Emotions at Work', paper presented at the Academy of Management Conference, Cincinnati, August 1996, p. 3.

82. R. C. Solomon, 'Back to Basics: On the Very Idea of Basic Emotions', *Journal for the Theory of Social Behaviour*, vol. 32, no. 2, June 2002, pp. 115–44.

83. C. M. Brotheridge and R. T. Lee, 'Development and Validation of the Emotional Labour Scale', *Journal of Occupational & Organizational Psychology*, vol. 76, no. 3, September 2003, pp. 365–79.

84. A. A. Grandey, 'When "the Show Must Go On": Surface Acting and Deep Acting as Determinants of Emotional Exhaustion and Peer-Rated Service Delivery', *Academy of Management Journal*, February 2003, pp. 86–96; A. A. Grandey, D. N. Dickter and H. Sin, 'The Customer Is Not Always Right: Customer Aggression and Emotion Regulation of Service Employees', *Journal of Organizational Behavior*, vol. 25, no. 3, May 2004, pp. 397–418.

85. A. Rafaeli and R. I. Sutton, 'The Expression of Emotion in Organizational Life', in L. L. Cummings and B. M. Staw (eds), *Research in Organizational Behavior*, vol. 11 (Greenwich, CT: JAI Press, 1989), p. 8.

86. A. Rafaeli, 'When Cashiers Meet Customers: An Analysis of Supermarket Cashiers', *Academy of Management Journal*, June 1989, pp. 245–73.

87. B. Plasait, 'Accueil des Touristes Dans les Grands Centres de Transit Paris', Rapport du Premier Ministre (<www.tourisme.gouv.fr/fr/navd/presse/dossiers/att00005767/dp_plasait.pdf>) (4 October 2004).

88. D. Rubin, 'Grumpy German Shoppers Distrust the Wal-Mart Style', *Seattle Times*, 30 December 2001, p. A15.

89. P. A. Simpson and L. K. Stroh, 'Gender Differences: Emotional Expression and Feelings of Personal Inauthenticity', *Journal of Applied Psychology*, vol. 89, no. 4, August 2004, pp. 715–21.

90. T. M. Glomb, J. D. Kammeyer-Mueller and M. Rotundo, 'Emotional Labor Demands and Compensating Wage Differentials', *Journal of Applied Psychology*, vol. 89, no. 4, August 2004, pp. 700–14.

91. H. M. Weiss and R. Cropanzano, 'An Affective Events Approach to Job Satisfaction', *Research in Organizational Behavior*, vol. 18, 1996, pp. 1–74.

92. J. Basch and C. D. Fisher, 'Affective Events–Emotions Matrix: A Classification of Work Events and Associated Emotions', in

Ashkanasy, Hartel and Zerbe (eds), *Emotions in the Workplace*, pp. 36–48.

93. See, for example, Weiss and Cropanzano, 'Affective Events Theory'; and C. D. Fisher, 'Antecedents and Consequences of Real-Time Affective Reactions at Work', *Motivation and Emotion*, March 2002, pp. 3–30.

94. Based on Weiss and Cropanzano, 'Affective Events Theory', p. 42.

95. Ashkanasy, Hartel and Daus, 'Diversity and Emotion: The New Frontiers in Organizational Behavior Research', p. 324.

96. Based on D. R. Caruso, J. D. Mayer and P. Salovey, 'Emotional Intelligence and Emotional Leadership', in R. E. Riggio, S. E. Murphy and F. J. Pirozzolo (eds), *Multiple Intelligences and Leadership* (Mahwah, NJ: Lawrence Erlbaum, 2002), p. 70.

97. This section is based on Daniel Goleman, *Emotional Intelligence* (New York: Bantam, 1995); J. D. Mayer and P. Salovey, 'What is Emotional Intelligence?', in P. Salovey and D. J. Sluyter (eds), *Emotional Development and Emotional Intelligence: Educational Implications* (New York: Basic Books, 1997), pp. 3–31; R. K. Cooper, 'Applying Emotional Intelligence in the Workplace', *Training & Development*, December 1997, pp. 31–38; M. Davies, L. Stankov and R. D. Roberts, 'Emotional Intelligence: In Search of an Elusive Construct', *Journal of Personality and Social Psychology*, October 1998, pp. 989–1015; D. Goleman, *Working with Emotional Intelligence* (New York: Bantam, 1999); R. Bar-On and J. D. A. Parker (eds), *The Handbook of Emotional Intelligence: Theory, Development, Assessment, and Application at Home, School, and in the Workplace* (San Francisco: Jossey-Bass, 2000); J. Ciarrochi, J. P. Forgas and J. D. Mayer (eds), *Emotional Intelligence in Everyday Life* (Philadelphia: Psychology Press, 2001).

98. F. I. Greenstein, *The Presidential Difference: Leadership Style from FDR to Clinton* (Princeton, NJ: Princeton University Press, 2001).

99. C. Cherniss, 'The Business Case for Emotional Intelligence', Consortium for Research on Emotional Intelligence in Organizations (<www.eiconsortium. org/research/business_case_for_ei.pdf>).

100. K. S. Law, C. Wong and L. J. Song, 'The Construct and Criterion Validity of Emotional Intelligence and Its Potential Utility for Management Studies', *Journal of Applied Psychology*, vol. 89, no. 3, 2004, pp. 483–96.

101. H. A. Elfenbein and N. Ambady, 'Predicting Workplace Outcomes from the Ability to Eavesdrop on Feelings', *Journal of Applied Psychology*, vol. 87, no. 5, October 2002, pp. 963–71.

102. D. L. Van Rooy and C. Viswesvaran, 'Emotional Intelligence: A Meta-Analytic Investigation of Predictive Validity and Nomological Net', *Journal of Vocational Behavior*, vol. 65, no. 1, August 2004, pp. 71–95.

103. R. Bar-On, D. Tranel, N. L. Denburg and A. Bechara, 'Exploring the Neurological Substrate of Emotional Social Intelligence', *Brain*, vol. 126, no. 8, August 2003, pp. 1790–800.

104. E. A. Locke, 'Why Emotional Intelligence is an Invalid Concept', *Journal of Organizational Behavior*, vol. 26, no. 4, June 2005, pp. 425–31.

105. J. M. Conte, 'A Review and Critique of Emotional Intelligence Measures', *Journal of Organizational Behavior*, vol. 26, no. 4, June 2005, pp. 433–40; M. Davies, L. Stankov and R. D. Roberts, 'Emotional Intelligence: In Search of an Elusive Construct', *Journal of Personality and Social Psychology*, vol. 75, no. 4, 1998, pp. 989–1015.

106. T. Decker, 'Is Emotional Intelligence a Viable Concept?', *Academy of Management Review*, vol. 28, no. 2, April 2003, pp. 433–40; Davies, Stankov and Roberts, 'Emotional Intelligence: In Search of an Elusive Construct'.

107. F. J. Landy, 'Some Historical and Scientific Issues Related to Research on Emotional Intelligence', *Journal of Organizational Behavior*, vol. 26, no. 4, June 2005, pp. 411–24.

108. L. M. J. Spencer, D. C. McClelland and S. Kelner, *Competency Assessment Methods: History and State of the Art* (Boston: Hay/McBer, 1997).

109. S. Fineman, 'Emotional Arenas Revisited', in S. Fineman (ed.), *Emotion in Organizations*, 2nd ed. (Thousand Oaks, CA: Sage, 2000), p. 11.

110. L. B. Alloy and L. Y. Abramson, 'Judgement of Contingency in Depressed and Nondepressed Students: Sadder but Wiser?', *Journal of Experimental Psychology: General*, vol. 108, 1979, pp. 441–85.

111. N. Ambady and H. M. Gray, 'On Being Sad and Mistaken: Mood Effects on the Accuracy of Thin-Slice Judgments', *Journal of Personality and Social Psychology*, vol. 83, no. 4, 2002, pp. 947–61.

112. See, for example, K. Fiedler, 'Emotional Mood, Cognitive Style, and Behavioral

Regulation', in K. Fiedler and J. Forgas (eds), *Affect, Cognition, and Social Behavior* (Toronto: Hogrefe International, 1988), pp. 100–19; M. Luce, J. Bettman and J. W. Payne, 'Choice Processing in Difficult Decisions', *Journal of Experimental Psychology: Learning, Memory, and Cognition*, vol. 23, 1997, pp. 384–405; and A. M. Isen, 'Positive Affect and Decision Making', in M. Lewis and J. M. Haviland-Jones (eds), *Handbook of Emotions*, 2nd ed. (New York: Guilford, 2000), pp. 261–77.

113. J. Park and M. R. Banaji, 'Mood and Heuristics: The Influence of Happy and Sad States on Sensitivity and Bias in Stereotyping', *Journal of Personality and Social Psychology*, vol. 78, no. 6, 2000, pp. 1005–23.

114. A. M. Isen, 'On the Relationship between Affect and Creative Problem Solving', in S. W. Russ (ed.), *Affect, Creative Experience and Psychological Adjustment* (Philadelphia, PA: Brunner/Mazel, 1999), pp. 3–17; M. A. Mumford, 'Where Have We Been, Where Are We Going? Taking Stock in Creativity Research', *Creativity Research Journal*, vol. 15, 2003, pp. 107–20.

115. M. J. Grawitch, D. C. Munz and E. K. Elliott, 'Promoting Creativity in Temporary Problem-Solving Groups: The Effects of Positive Mood and Autonomy in Problem Definition on Idea-Generating Performance', *Group Dynamics*, vol. 7, no. 3, September 2003, pp. 200–13.

116. S. Lyubomirsky, L. King and E. Diener, 'The Benefits of Frequent Positive Affect: Does Happiness Lead to Success?', *Psychological Bulletin*, in press.

117. N. Madjar, G. R. Oldham and M. G. Pratt, 'There's No Place Like Home? The Contributions of Work and Nonwork Creativity Support to Employees' Creative Performance', *Academy of Management Journal*, vol. 45, no. 4, 2002, pp. 757–67.

118. J. M. George and J. Zhou, 'Understanding When Bad Moods Foster Creativity and Good Ones Don't: The Role of Context and Clarity of Feelings', *Journal of Applied Psychology*, vol. 87, no. 4, August 2002, pp. 687–97; J. P. Forgas and J. M. George, 'Affective Influences on Judgments and Behavior in Organizations: An Information Processing Perspective', *Organizational Behavior and Human Decision Processes*, vol. 86, no. 1, 2001, pp. 3–34.

119. L. L. Martin, 'Mood as Input: A Configural View of Mood Effects', in L. L. Martin and G. L. Clore (eds), *Theories of Mood and Cognition: A User's Guidebook*

(Mahwah, NJ: Lawrence Erlbaum Associates, Publishers, 2001), pp. 135–57.

120. Ashforth and Humphrey, 'Emotion in the Workplace', p. 109.

121. Ibid, p. 110.

122. Ibid.

123. A. Erez and A. M. Isen, 'The Influence of Positive Affect on the Components of Expectancy Motivation', *Journal of Applied Psychology*, vol. 87, no. 6, 2002, pp. 1055–67.

124. R. Ilies and T. A. Judge, 'Goal Regulation across Time: The Effect of Feedback and Affect', *Journal of Applied Psychology*, vol. 90, no. 3, May 2005, pp. 453–67.

125. K. M. Lewis, 'When Leaders Display Emotion: How Followers Respond to Negative Emotional Expression of Male and Female Leaders', *Journal of Organizational Behavior*, March 2000, pp. 221–34; and J. M. George, 'Emotions and Leadership: The Role of Emotional Intelligence', *Human Relations*, August 2000, pp. 1027–55.

126. George, 'Trait and State Affect', p. 162.

127. Ashforth and Humphrey, 'Emotion in the Workplace', p. 116.

128. N. Reynolds, 'Whiz-Kids Gamble on TV Channel for Poker', news.telegraph (<www.telegraph.co.uk>) (16 April 2005).

129. G. A. Van Kleef, C. K. W. De Dreu and A. S. R. Manstead, 'The Interpersonal Effects of Emotions in Negotiations: A Motivated Information Processing Approach', *Journal of Personality and Social Psychology*, vol. 87, no. 4, 2004, pp. 510–28; G. A. Van Kleef, C. K. W. De Dreu and A. S. R. Manstead, 'The Interpersonal Effects of Anger and Happiness in Negotiations', *Journal of Personality and Social Psychology*, vol. 86, no. 1, 2004, pp. 57–76.

130. K. M. O'Connor and J. A. Arnold, 'Distributive Spirals: Negotiation Impasses and the Moderating Role of Disputant Self-Efficacy', *Organizational Behavior and Human Decision Processes*, vol. 84, no. 1, 2001, pp. 148–76.

131. B. Shiv, G. Loewenstein, A. Bechara, H. Damasio and A. R. Damasio, 'Investment Behavior and the Negative Side of Emotion', *Psychological Science*, vol. 16, no. 6, 2005, pp. 435–39.

132. Anon, 'How the Unions Paved the Way for Patrick's Attack', <www.wsws.org/workers/1998/apr1998/actu-a9.shtml> (9 April 1998); M. Beasley, 'A History of Struggle on the Wharves', <http://workers.labor.net.au/6/c_historical feature_margo.html> (26 March 1999).

133. W-C. Tsai and Y-M. Huang, 'Mechanisms Linking Employee Affective Delivery and Customer Behavioral Intentions', *Journal of Applied Psychology*, October 2002, pp. 1001–08.

134. Grandey, 'When "the Show Must Go On"'.

135. See E. Hatfield, J. T. Cacioppo and R. L. Rapson, *Emotional Contagion* (Cambridge, UK: Cambridge University Press, 1994); and S. D. Pugh, 'Service with a Smile: Emotional Contagion in the Service Encounter', *Academy of Management Journal*, October 2001, pp. 1018–27.

136. W. Tasi and Y. Huang, 'Mechanisms Linking Employee Affective Delivery and Customer Behavioral Intentions', *Journal of Applied Psychology*, vol. 87, no. 5, 2002, pp. 1001–08.

137. R. Ilies and T. A. Judge, 'Understanding the Dynamic Relationships among Personality, Mood, and Job Satisfaction: A Field Experience Sampling Study', *Organizational Behavior and Human Decision Processes*, vol. 89, 2002, pp. 1119–39.

138. R. Rau, 'Job Strain or Healthy Work: A Question of Task Design', *Journal of Occupational Health Psychology*, vol. 9, no. 4, October 2004, pp. 322–38; R. Rau and A. Triemer, 'Overtime in Relation to Blood Pressure and Mood during Work, Leisure, and Night Time', *Social Indicators Research*, vol. 67, no. 1–2, June 2004, pp. 51–73.

139. T. A. Judge and R. Ilies, 'Affect and Job Satisfaction: A Study of Their Relationship at Work and at Home', *Journal of Applied Psychology*, vol. 89, 2004, pp. 661–73.

140. See S. L. Robinson and R. J. Bennett, 'A Typology of Deviant Workplace Behaviors: A Multidimensional Scaling Study', *Academy of Management Journal*, April 1995, p. 556; and R. J. Bennett and S. L. Robinson, 'Development of a Measure of Workplace Deviance', *Journal of Applied Psychology*, June 2000, pp. 349–60. See also P. R. Sackett and C. J. DeVore, 'Counterproductive Behaviors at Work', in N. Anderson, D. S. Ones, H. K. Sinangil and C. Viswesvaran (eds), *Handbook of Industrial, Work & Organizational Psychology*, vol. 1 (Thousand Oaks, CA: Sage, 2001), pp. 145–64.

141. A. G. Bedeian, 'Workplace Envy', *Organizational Dynamics*, Spring 1995, p. 50; and A. Ben-Ze'ev, *The Subtlety of Emotions* (Cambridge, MA: MIT Press, 2000), pp. 281–326.

142. Bedeian, 'Workplace Envy', p. 54.

143. K. Lee and N. J. Allen, 'Organizational Citizenship Behavior and Workplace Deviance: The Role of Affect and Cognition', *Journal of Applied Psychology*, vol. 87, no. 1, 2002, pp. 131–42; T. A. Judge, B. A. Scott and R. Ilies, 'Hostility, Job Attitudes, and Workplace Deviance: Test of a Multilevel Model', *Journal of Applied Psychology*, in press.

144. T. Sy, S. Côté and R. Saavedra, 'The Contagious Leader: Impact of the Leader's Mood on the Mood of Group Members, Group Affective Tone, and Group Processes', *Journal of Applied Psychology*, vol. 90, no. 2, 2005, pp. 295–305.

145. P. Totterdell, 'Catching Moods and Hitting Runs: Mood Linkage and Subjective Performance in Professional Sports Teams', *Journal of Applied Psychology*, vol. 85, no. 6, 2000, pp. 848–59.

146. S. Nelton, 'Emotions in the Workplace', *Nation's Business*, February 1996, p. 25.

147. Weiss and Cropanzano, 'Affective Events Theory', p. 55.

148. See the Yerkes-Dodson law cited in D. O. Hebb, 'Drives and the CNS (Conceptual Nervous System)', *Psychological Review*, July 1955, pp. 243–54.

DR GLENICE WOOD

SCHOOL OF MANAGEMENT, UNIVERSITY OF BALLARAT

Tania Major, at 22, is the youngest person to be elected to the board of the Aboriginal and Torres Strait Islander Commission (ATSIC), and she believes she is ready for the challenge. She is a graduate in criminology from Sydney University, and has been mentored by Noel Pearson, a lawyer and entrepreneur, since she was aged 12. This mentoring involved her being sponsored throughout her secondary and tertiary education.

As a mentor, Noel would have conveyed some of his passion about his belief that passive welfare dependency is the primary cause of Aboriginal squalor and poverty, along with alcohol and drug abuse. Tania agrees with this philosophy, and considers that Aboriginal people are their own worst enemies. She is concerned that Aboriginal communities become ghettos, and believes her own home town, Kowanyama *(Place of Many Waters)*, near the west coast of Cape York, has this potential problem.

Tania is passionate in her belief that violence, drug and alcohol abuse, rife in most remote Aboriginal communities, combine to create a seriously destructive force for Aboriginal people. In many of these communities, Aboriginal women have been forced to organise night patrols in an attempt to reduce the effects of alcohol and substance abuse. Some communities have also set up women's shelters to deal with the spiralling cases of violence to women and children. Tania has described this as a 'stifling blanket of shame and silence', which she believes has to be lifted in order for it to be addressed.

Tania's view is that education and health are pivotal in turning around the disastrous experience for young people growing up in these communities. She has personal experience in the very low levels of literacy and numeracy which she had acquired before going to school in Brisbane, and this made her feel as if she had missed out on her primary education. The problem appears to be that the curriculum in the communities is pitched at a very low level, and this resulted in her receiving 'straight As' in Kowanyama but Cs or Ds in Brisbane. She believes this is caused by new teachers just out of training being sent to remote communities; they lacked commitment, didn't care, and believed that white children were smarter than Aboriginal pupils. These teachers didn't remain. Therefore, there is an enormous gap between what Aboriginal communities receive in their primary education and what is delivered to other children in cities. Tania believes that the outcome of the education offered in remote communities reinforces a lack of self-esteem and low expectations in young people, when its aim should be to deliver self-confidence and drive. This then motivates students to take up significant roles in the community with the belief that they can make a difference, rather than seeing their lives as hopeless.

Tania further believes there is a relationship between poor-quality education and poor health. 'People whose self-esteem and pride have been decimated by a substandard education system and a social system that creates an addiction to passive welfare have little reason to live healthy lives'. In Tania's view, the health of indigenous people is getting worse, not better, and the cause of this is that health services on offer are confined to the clinic, rather than being seen as a holistic relationship between physical, mental and spiritual health. Health care needs to be taken out of the clinic and put into the 'lives and homes of community people'.

Life under these circumstances isn't easy for young Aboriginal people, especially women. Tania paints a grim picture of what it is like growing up in an Aboriginal community today. In her home town, she was one of 15 in a class. Of this group, she is the only one who completed her secondary education, the only girl who didn't become pregnant at 15, and the only person who went on to university. Seven of the boys in her class have been incarcerated for murder, rape or assault. Only three of the group are not alcoholics. Even more chilling is the statistic that four of her classmates have committed suicide.

Tania believes that governments cannot solve the problems of Aboriginal people. Her view is that young people should try to take responsibility for their own future, and she believes this is possible, as the young Murris she sees are 'smart, brave, compassionate, talented and beautiful'. In her community, young people are working with their elders to address the devastating problems of drugs, alcohol and violence in their communities. Their goal is to provide their young people with the skills and aspirations to achieve their potential. There is also a need to create an environment where Aboriginal people are able to access economic and training opportunities that will lead to employment.

Tania put forward a very compelling argument when she recently addressed Prime Minister John Howard. She asked that her appeal not be seen as a cry for help; that is, she didn't want the problems fixed by someone else. Her plea is to be seen as an equal partner with the government so that her people can rebuild their own families, lives and communities in the Cape York Peninsula.

Tania concluded by saying that the level of domestic violence and child abuse sums up 'all that has been wrong with aboriginal affairs policy. We need a new relationship to address this frightening reality in our lives. Aboriginal people are reluctant to admit that young girls and women are being raped by their own people, because of the blanket of shame. I am asking you, Prime Minister, to help lift that blanket.'

The early experiences outlined by Tania would go a long way to shaping the lives of people. In addition to early experiences, our personalities and emotions shape our behaviour and impact on our capacity to learn. Our ability to become effective decision makers is impaired if we don't perceive meaningful options. Being able to envisage a goal, and then to remain committed to that goal, and motivated to achieve it to the end, takes tenacity—even when circumstances are ideal.

What is amazing about Tania Major's story is that even one person managed to succeed and step outside the cycle of violence, despair, abuse, discrimination, substance abuse and poverty she has described. What sort of an individual is able to rise above this background, and to have the confidence to stand up to the prime minister of the country and challenge him to join with Aboriginal people to work together towards a better future?

Tania is managing her own life with a vision. The features of her individual behaviour indicate a high level of intellectual ability, and the capacity to rise to the enormous challenges of her role in ATSIC. She has been able to learn from the mistakes of past practices in relation to Aboriginal affairs policies, and through her deeply entrenched values and attitudes has been able to consider what life could be like in her communities if health, education and a belief in a meaningful future were available.

QUESTIONS

1. How would you describe Tania Major in terms of *locus of control*? Why?
2. After her early experiences, do you believe Tania Major would have high self-esteem? If so, why?
3. In terms of Holland's typology of personality and congruent occupations, what category of personality type would you attribute to Tania Major? How suited is she to the role she has taken on in ATSIC?
4. How would you describe Tania Major's affect?
5. How would you describe the 'emotional labour' of Tania Major? Would you consider she shows the ability to exhibit high levels of 'emotional labour'?
6. From the text, we understand that knowledge of emotions in the field of OB can improve our ability to explain and predict a range of activities in the workplace. People who have particular skills in reading their own and other's emotions accurately are said to possess high levels of *emotional intelligence* (EI). How do you think Tania would function on the five dimensions of EI?

SOURCES: T. Major, *The Age*, 6 August 2003, p. 13; 'Position Vacant', *Four Corners*, 28 July 2006; and Neene Bhandari, 'Australia's "Stifling Blanket of Silence"': <www.panos.org.uk/global/featuredetails.asp?featureid+1136&ID=1005> (23 September 2003).

MARISSA S. EDWARDS AND NEAL M. ASHKANASY
UQ BUSINESS SCHOOL, THE UNIVERSITY OF QUEENSLAND

Queensland Health is the foremost provider of health services in Queensland, and one of the state's largest employers. The organisation has almost 44 000 full-time equivalent employees, approximately 60 per cent of whom are clinical staff (doctors and nurses), and a total workforce of around 65 000 people. Queensland Health has a budget of $5.4 billion for the 2005/06 financial year and delivers the majority of its services through the 178 public hospitals and 277 health centres that operate through the state. In 2003/04, there were 1.25 million emergency department presentations at Queensland public hospitals.

In 2005, Queensland Health faced a major crisis when an intensive care nurse approached a member of the state Opposition, Rob Messenger, with her concerns about the competency of an overseas-trained surgeon who was currently working at Bundaberg Base Hospital. The surgeon's name was Dr Jayant Patel. The shadow health minister raised the issue publicly in Parliament on 22 March 2005 and, almost immediately, the case began to attract significant media attention. It soon became apparent that, although staff members and even patients had voiced their misgivings about Patel's competency and conduct, the culture of the hospital, and the nature of its complaint system, meant that these reports were rarely investigated. Indeed, in the subsequent inquiry, hospital administrators attracted severe criticism for their failure to respond appropriately to employees' concerns.

In the face of growing criticism of Queensland Health and its administrators in the wake of the Patel scandal, Premier Peter Beattie ordered an independent review of the health system, in addition to an inquiry investigating Patel's appointment and clinical practice at Bundaberg Base Hospital. The results of these investigations offer a unique insight into the organisation and its employees, and help to illustrate the role of individual differences in shaping employees' experiences.

HEALTH SYSTEM REVIEW

Management consultant Peter Forster was responsible for the Queensland Health Systems Review, an independent assessment of the administrative, workforce and performance management systems in the organisation. The review involved observations, interviews and surveys with thousands of Queensland Health staff, as well as a wide range of stakeholders. Forster reported that, although Queensland Health was performing well and delivering a standard of care comparable to that offered interstate, challenges—and indeed failures—existed in several vital areas. He concluded that, while the majority of employees were committed and conscientious, the results of the review revealed 'extreme levels of dissatisfaction amongst Queensland Health staff with many staff feeling angry, frustrated and resentful'. In particular, senior management appeared to be the target of many of the employees' negative emotions. The dysfunctional nature of interpersonal relationships with colleagues and supervisors emerged as a major source of dissatisfaction for some employees, who cited incidences of bullying and intimidation and described a lack of effective engagement and problem solving between managers and subordinates. Morale was particularly low among some clinical staff, although overall levels of workplace morale were generally acceptable.

Another source of frustration among employees was the perception that their work values were in contrast to those of senior management. Specifically, employees perceived that managers were concerned with meeting budget performance standards and didn't seem to share their values, which included teamwork, professionalism and a patient-centred approach. Despite this incongruence, many employees reported how much they enjoyed the work itself and were highly dedicated to patient care, suggesting that employees' job involvement was reasonably high. Forster recommended that major systemic improvements were required to improve organisational performance, including cultural change, improved strategic planning, and increased opportunities for community members and Queensland

Health employees to express their concerns about aspects of service delivery.

COMMISSION OF INQUIRY

The Queensland Public Hospitals Commission of Inquiry commenced in May 2005 and sought to investigate, among other issues, the complaints made against Dr Patel and the responses of hospital administrators to reports of his apparent incompetence and negligence. Employees' testimony revealed that initially they didn't have reason to be concerned about Patel's behaviour. He seemed to be charming, confident and hardworking, if somewhat arrogant. The positive aspects of his personality appeared to impress administrators, who appointed him as director of surgery. As time passed, however, clinical staff became concerned about his high post-operative complication rate; his disparaging treatment of nursing staff; his lack of empathy with patients; and his failure to follow best practice guidelines. As more of his patients experienced complications, employees' attributions about Patel changed, and they realised that he was likely responsible for these adverse surgical outcomes. These surgical mishaps weren't simply accidents or mistakes, but appeared to be the result of serious incompetence.

With each adverse event that occurred, employees had to make an ethical decision as to whether or not to report their concerns about Dr Patel to management. Although many employees elected to voice their misgivings, complaint channels within the organisation were inadequate, and hospital administrators generally chose to ignore or to minimise employees' concerns.

Consistent with the features of utilitarianism, which emphasises efficiency and productivity, evidence at the Inquiry suggested that pressure to reach elective surgery targets and to maintain financial performance standards influenced managers' decision making. Unsurprisingly, however, their responses caused considerable distress and frustration among employees, particularly among the nursing staff who had to care for Patel's patients.

In general, employees' testimony to the Inquiry indicated that their experience was characterised by high levels of negative emotion and stress. For example, the intensive care nurse who eventually went outside of Queensland Health and 'blew the whistle' about Patel described the rising sense of fear and despair among her staff as they tried to protect their patients. Other nurses described how they tried to have patients transferred to different hospitals, and reportedly moved patients from bed to bed in the intensive care unit to prevent Patel from finding them. These nurses were highly professional and dedicated employees who seemed to be largely motivated by the high degree of task significance associated with their work, and the situation caused them significant distress. Overall, staff—and even patients—made over 20 complaints about Dr Patel to administrators over a period of 24 months. The final report of the Inquiry described administrators' failure to investigate properly employees' complaints as 'a gross dereliction of duty', and recommended that they face misconduct charges. Dr Patel, who quietly returned to the United States once the story broke in the Queensland media, could potentially face charges including grievous bodily harm, assault and manslaughter.

Queensland Health has made a number of changes and received a significant increase in state government funding following its systemic review and investigation of Patel's tenure at Bundaberg Base Hospital. In October 2005, the Queensland government announced its Health Action Plan, which outlined the main features of the proposed reforms of the public health system. These reforms include increasing numbers of clinical personnel, including greater recruitment of staff from overseas; facilitating the greater involvement of clinicians and patients in decision making; encouraging a culture of openness and accountability, including easier complaints processes; and developing and promoting a culture in which employees are valued and respected. In particular, Queensland Health will seek to develop a set of values within the organisation that include caring for people and a commitment to public service. The appointment of a new director-general, Uschi Schreiber, represents an integral part of this process. Described as energetic, assertive, hardworking and resilient, she has emphasised the importance of giving clinicians a voice in Queensland Health, and reports suggest that her appointment has already improved morale.

Schreiber herself has acknowledged that it will take years to achieve significant and sustainable change in an organisation as large and complex as Queensland Health, but she is optimistic about the future. In an interview soon after her appointment was announced, she admitted, 'There's no shortage of pressure. On the other hand, I really believe in a public health system. I really believe there are major improvements we can make here. There are some amazing people working in the system.'

SOURCES: J. Chandler, 'The Doctor Who Left a Town for Dead', *Sydney Morning Herald*, 28 May 2005; G. Davies, *Queensland Public Hospitals Commission of Inquiry: Final Report* (2005): <www.qphci.qld.gov.au/final_report/Final_Report.pdf>; P. Forster, *Queensland Health Systems Review: Final Report* (2005): <www.health.qld.gov.au/health_sys_review/final/default.asp>; Queensland Government, *Queensland Health Workforce Strategic Plan 2005–10* (2005): <www.health.qld.gov.au/publications/corporate/workforce/workforcestratplan2005-10.pdf>; Queensland Government, *Action Plan: Building a Better Health Service for Queensland* (2005): <www.health.qld.gov.au/publications/corporate/ActionPlan.pdf>; R. Sandall, 'Doctor Death in Bundaberg', *Quadrant*, vol. 422, no. 12, 2005, pp. 11–20; and H. Thomas, 'Mission a Challenge', *Courier-Mail*, 18 March 2006, p. 54.

INTEGRATIVE CASE STUDY

Managing performance at PBL

GLYNDWR JONES

WAIKATO UNIVERSITY, NEW ZEALAND

BACKGROUND

Karen entered Victoria University, Wellington as a mature student, having worked in real estate for ten years. She chose to study business and law because she had been involved in these activities in her work life.

After a demanding first year, Karen found her feet and excelled, graduating with a B.Com/LLB (Hons). She then completed a Masters in Law (LL.M) with First Class Honours.

Karen was highly successful in her graduate studies, which she thoroughly enjoyed. She co-authored several journal articles and several conference papers with her academic supervisor and, somewhat to her surprise, found that she liked the rarified, theoretical world of law. At one stage she even thought about pursuing a doctorate but was put off by the time and cost involved. Now in her mid-thirties, she felt that it was time to build a professional career. She applied for and took up an appointment with PBL Consulting, in Wellington.

PBL provides legal and policy advice to the public sector. It employs 120 staff with backgrounds in law, economics, accounting, finance and public sector management. The organisation is hierarchical with four layers of staff: senior partners, partners, associates and junior staff.

Karen was assigned to the public policy health sector team. Her boss, Rose, is a partner in the firm, and about

Karen's age. She is, however, the only female partner in the firm. The rest of the team are associates; Diane, Connie and Rick, with Karen joining as the junior member.

THE FIRST YEAR

For the first four months, Karen enjoyed the work very much. She put in long hours and was praised by her boss for her standard of work. Outside of work hours, she enjoyed Wellington, particularly the opportunity of 'rubbing shoulders' with people involved in decision making at high levels. She was asked to write an article for a national professional journal which she jumped at, believing that this would bring visibility to the firm while also developing her career.

After six months or so at the firm, however, she became concerned about the type of work she was being asked to do, most of which was routine and, frankly, boring. At the interview stage for the position, Karen had received a much more challenging picture of working at PBL than she now found. For much of the time she was doing 'back office' work, searching through statutes, writing standard reports, searching out information, chasing back and forth between state agencies, the courts, law libraries, consultants, and even the post office! She never met any of the firm's clients or was involved in following through on the work she was engaged in. She felt particularly disappointed at this aspect of her job, leading her to feel that the firm wasn't really utilising her additional abilities.

Other aspects of work at PBL also bothered her. She was disappointed at the low level of computer usage, and she hadn't been allocated a computer herself. Only a few of her colleagues had a computer on their desk. This bothered Karen because, during her university years, she had been accustomed to doing her thinking and writing on a computer. After weeks of pushing for a computer, one finally turned up, but it then took another two weeks to get the machine installed. It was old and slow, and Karen found that her office wasn't networked.

But, for all these frustrations, Karen enjoyed her work and, after six months, was given a $2000 increase in pay.

Karen knew that the firm had a personnel officer somewhere in the building, but she was struck by the lack of any formal induction procedures and felt that she had been 'thrown in at the deep end'. The company did, however, have a performance appraisal system.

PERFORMANCE APPRAISAL AT PBL

Performance appraisal interviews were undertaken annually at PBL with the aim of 'recognising good performance and identifying any areas which should be developed, to increase the effectiveness of the staff member. The review is also an opportunity for staff members to record their career aspirations.'

Nine months after joining the firm, Karen applied for a short holiday break, which was granted. However, the week before she was scheduled to take the break, she was informed by Rose that her first performance appraisal interview was to take place at the end of the current week. Karen was a bit taken aback, but even more so when she learned that the interview was to involve not only her immediate boss but also one of the associates, Diane.

Karen had no guidelines for the interview, so she decided, in her usual thorough way, to prepare for it. She found that the personnel office did have guidelines, which they sent to her.

Armed with this framework, Karen prepared for her interview, developing a comprehensive response to each area covered and submitted this to Rose in writing. In her submission Karen voiced her concerns about the level of supervision she had experienced since joining the firm and about the poor computing facilities. She also asked for more involvement with clients and guidance on the management of her workload.

THE INTERVIEW

The interview took place in Rose's office during the lunch break, the day before Karen was to leave for her short holiday. Diane was also present. The interview started cordially enough, but Karen's heart sank when she saw that Rose was working off the notes she had supplied for her. She was also concerned that Rose had no other documents in front of her apart from a notepad.

Rose then addressed the concerns Karen had raised in her memo.

Contrary to the positive feedback she had been given during the early months, Rose reminded Karen that she was 'at the bottom of a very long ladder', and that in her eyes Karen was 'no different from any other junior member of the firm'. She said that the pay rise Karen had received was recognition of the longer hours she had worked and wasn't related to her performance, which, she said, 'was no better than any other young graduate at her level'. Rose agreed that Karen's grasp of the subject matter was excellent and that her standards were very high, but emphasised that she was not 'practical' and needed to develop 'commercial skills'.

During the interview Rose criticised Karen for attending a Justice Department meeting in company time earlier in the month, saying that she was 'taking too many initiatives', although Rose had actually sanctioned Karen's attendance at the meeting. Rose and Diane told her she was taking 'too many liberties' and making 'too many assumptions'. Rose said, 'You may have fancy degrees, but you lack commercial experience.' Diane cautioned Karen to avoid pro bono work, such as contributing to professional journals, writing for the in-house magazine and writing conference papers, all of which weren't billable. The meeting ended when Rose left to attend another appointment, and another meeting was scheduled for later in the day. Karen left the room with great foreboding about the next meeting.

The second meeting was short and seemed, to Karen, also to focus on the negatives. The tone of the interview wasn't positive and, in Karen's eyes, failed to meet the requirements of the firm's policy guidelines on performance review, which stated that, as a result of the review, 'training and development requirements should be identified and a series of goals and objectives agreed upon'. Karen felt that the interview failed to focus on task-related matters or on evaluating her performance, and hadn't ended on a constructive note. No improvement objectives or time frames for improvements were set. Nor did Rose indicate how any weaknesses in Karen's performance might be rectified through either on-the-job training or external training. Apart from the jottings on Rose's notepad, Karen didn't see how any records of the two meetings were likely to be produced, despite the firm's guidelines stating that 'at the end of the interview, the supervisor should complete the form and provide a copy of the record of the interview to the staff members within 48 hours'. These records should then have been signed by both the staff member and supervisor, but this didn't happen. Karen felt undermined by the experience.

On her return from her short break, Karen bumped into Diane who brought up the performance appraisal and admitted that it had amounted to a 'bit of a demolition job, but you should take a lesson from it'.

Karen was left wondering how Rose's perception of her contribution to PBL seemed so different from the way she viewed it. She felt unsure about what she would have to do to please her boss in the future.

QUESTIONS
1. What do you think has gone wrong for Karen in her first year at PBL?
2. How would you characterise Karen's motivational needs and drives?
3. What is your assessment of the 'fit' between the person and the situation in this case?
4. How would you explain the apparent mismatch of perceptions between Karen and her boss in this case?
5. What advice would you have given Karen when starting out at PBL? What would you advise her to do now?

PART 3

THE GROUP

9

FOUNDATIONS OF GROUP BEHAVIOUR

LEARNING OBJECTIVES

AFTER STUDYING THIS CHAPTER, YOU SHOULD BE ABLE TO:

1. DIFFERENTIATE BETWEEN FORMAL AND INFORMAL GROUPS

2. COMPARE TWO MODELS OF GROUP DEVELOPMENT

3. EXPLAIN HOW ROLE REQUIREMENTS CHANGE IN DIFFERENT
   SITUATIONS

4. DESCRIBE HOW NORMS EXERT INFLUENCE ON AN INDIVIDUAL'S
   BEHAVIOUR

5. EXPLAIN WHAT DETERMINES STATUS

6. DEFINE SOCIAL LOAFING AND ITS EFFECT ON GROUP
   PERFORMANCE

7. IDENTIFY THE BENEFITS AND DISADVANTAGES OF COHESIVE
   GROUPS

8. LIST THE STRENGTHS AND WEAKNESSES OF GROUP DECISION
   MAKING

9. CONTRAST THE EFFECTIVENESS OF INTERACTING,
   BRAINSTORMING, NOMINAL AND ELECTRONIC MEETING GROUPS

Safarudin Ban explains to Dr Bruce Millett how important teamwork is at HeiTech for completing client projects.

SAFARUDIN BAN IS HEAD OF OPERATIONS development and planning at HeiTech Padu Berhad, Malaysia's leading IT total solutions provider that specialises in creating innovative software solutions. From its headquarters in Kuala Lumpur, HeiTech's specialists and consultants work with and deliver comprehensive and cutting-edge software and system solutions for the Malaysian market.

Safarudin is one of many managers who have developed sound team management skills through the experience of leading multiple projects. His department of more than 100 skilled employees combines a formal functional structure with a team-based structure because of the nature and dynamics typical of the IT industry. Many staff work in multiple and temporary teams that are focused on specific client projects.

As an indication of HeiTech's commitment to a team-based structure, Safarudin works with and mentors other project leaders and ensures that team members have access to developmental opportunities so that they acquire the skills to contribute effectively in a technical and high-pressure team environment. He believes that every individual has the capability, strength and uniqueness to contribute to achieving excellence in team performance. He also highlights the responsibility of team leaders to capture and utilise these attributes, and to promote an exciting and rewarding environment in which to work.

To assist in these developmental activities, HeiTech has worked with the consulting company Zubedy to run in-house practical and informative workshops to provide participants with the knowledge and key skills needed to be effective leaders and to assist participants to relate effectively to their peers, subordinates and, more importantly, their team members, as well as to manage themselves better. Safarudin and his colleagues know the value of promoting team development and leadership. HeiTech managers also appreciate the need to understand the nature of group dynamics.[1]

Madness is the exception in individuals but the rule in groups.
Friedrich Nietzsche

THE OBJECTIVES OF THIS and the following chapter are to introduce you to basic group concepts, provide you with a foundation for understanding how groups work, and to show you how to create effective teams. Let's begin by defining groups and explaining why people join them.

DEFINING AND CLASSIFYING GROUPS

A **group** is defined as two or more individuals, interacting and interdependent, who have come together to achieve particular objectives. Groups can be either formal or informal. By **formal groups**, we mean those defined by the organisation's structure, with designated work assignments establishing tasks. In formal groups, the behaviours that one should engage in are stipulated by and directed towards organisational goals. The six members making up an airline flight crew are an example of a formal group. In contrast, **informal groups** are alliances that are neither formally structured nor organisationally determined. These groups are natural formations in the work environment that appear in response to the need for social contact. Three employees from different departments who regularly eat lunch together are an example of an informal group. It is possible to further subclassify groups as command, task, interest or friendship groups.[2] Command and task groups are dictated by the formal organisation, whereas interest and friendship groups are informal alliances.

A **command group** is determined by the organisation chart. It is composed of the individuals who report directly to a given manager. A high school principal and her 18 teachers form a command group, as do the director of company audits and his five inspectors.

Task groups, also organisationally determined, represent those working together to complete a job task. However, a task group's boundaries aren't limited to its immediate hierarchical superior. It can cross command relationships. For instance, if a university student is accused of a campus crime, it may require communication and coordination among the dean of the student's faculty, the director of student services, the registrar, the head of security and the student's adviser. Such a formation would constitute a task group. It should be noted that all command groups are also task groups, but because task groups can cut across the organisation, the reverse needn't be true.

People who may or may not be aligned into common command or task groups may affiliate to attain a specific objective with which each is concerned. This is an **interest group**. Employees who band together to have their holiday schedules altered, to support a colleague who has been fired, or to seek improved working conditions represent the formation of a united body to further their common interest. Groups often develop because the individual members have one or more common characteristics. We call these formations **friendship groups**. Social alliances, which frequently extend outside the work situation, can be based on similar age or ethnic heritage, support for a local soccer club, interest in the same rock band, or the holding of similar political views, to name just a few such characteristics.

Informal groups provide a very important service by satisfying their members' social needs. Because of interactions that result from the close proximity of workstations or task

group | Two or more individuals, interacting and interdependent, who have come together to achieve particular objectives.

formal group | A designated work group defined by the organisation's structure.

informal group | A group that is neither formally structured nor organisationally determined; appears in response to the need for social contact.

command group | A group composed of the individuals who report directly to a given manager.

task group | Those working together to complete a job task.

interactions, we find that workers often do things together—such as play golf, commute to work, take lunch, and chat during coffee breaks. We must recognise that these types of interactions among individuals, even though informal, deeply affect their behaviour and performance.

There is no single reason why individuals join groups. Because most people belong to a number of groups, it is obvious that different groups provide different benefits to their members. Table 9.1 summarises the most popular reasons people have for joining groups.

interest group | Those working together to attain a specific objective with which each is concerned.

friendship group | Those brought together because they share one or more common characteristics.

■ **TABLE 9.1**
Why do people join groups?

Security. By joining a group, individuals can reduce the insecurity of 'standing alone'. People feel stronger, have fewer self-doubts, and are more resistant to threats when they are part of a group.

Status. Inclusion in a group that is viewed as important by others provides recognition and status for its members.

Self-esteem. Groups can provide people with feelings of self-worth. That is, in addition to conveying status to those outside the group, membership can also give increased feelings of worth to the group members themselves.

Affiliation. Groups can fulfil social needs. People enjoy the regular interaction that comes with group membership. For many people, these on-the-job interactions are their primary source for fulfilling their needs for affiliation.

Power. What cannot be achieved individually often becomes possible through group action. There is power in numbers.

Goal achievement. There are times when it takes more than one person to accomplish a particular task—there is a need to pool talents, knowledge or power in order to complete a job. In such instances, management will rely on the use of a formal group.

DO I TRUST OTHERS?

In the Self-Assessment Library (available on CD and online), take Self-Assessment II.B.3 (Do I Trust Others?). After you have taken the test, answer the following questions:

1. Are you surprised by your results? If yes, why? If no, why not?
2. Do you think it is important to always trust your group members? Or do you think a smart group member is one who keeps his or her guard up at all times?

SELF-ASSESSMENT LIBRARY

MODELS OF GROUP DEVELOPMENT

LEARNING OBJECTIVE 2

Compare two models of group development

Groups generally pass through a standardised sequence in their evolution. We call this sequence the five-stage model of group development. Although research indicates that not all groups follow this pattern,[3] it is a useful framework for understanding group development. In this section, we describe the five-stage general model and an alternative model for temporary groups with deadlines.

THE FIVE-STAGE MODEL

As shown in Figure 9.1, the **five-stage group-development model** characterises groups as proceeding through five distinct stages: forming, storming, norming, performing and adjourning.[4]

The first stage, **forming**, is characterised by a great deal of uncertainty about the group's purpose, structure and leadership. Members are 'testing the waters' to determine what types of behaviours are acceptable. This stage is complete when members have begun to think of themselves as part of a group. The **storming stage** is one of intragroup conflict. Members accept the existence of the group, but there is resistance to the constraints that the group imposes on individuality. Furthermore, there is conflict over who will control the group. When this stage is complete, there will be a relatively clear hierarchy of leadership within the group.

The third stage is one in which close relationships develop and the group demonstrates cohesiveness. There is now a strong sense of group identity and camaraderie. This **norming stage** is complete when the group structure solidifies and the group has assimilated a common set of expectations of what defines correct member behaviour.

The fourth stage is **performing**. The structure at this point is fully functional and accepted. Group energy has moved from getting to know and understand each other to performing the task at hand.

For permanent work groups, performing is the last stage in their development. However, for temporary committees, teams, task forces and similar groups that have a limited task to perform, there is an **adjourning stage**. In this stage, the group prepares for its disbandment. High task performance is no longer the group's top priority. Instead, attention is directed towards wrapping up activities. Responses of group members vary in this stage. Some are upbeat, basking in the group's accomplishments. Others may be depressed over the loss of camaraderie and friendships gained during the work group's life.

Many interpreters of the five-stage model have assumed that a group becomes more effective as it progresses through the first four stages. Although this assumption may be generally true, what makes a group effective is more complex than this model acknowledges.[5] Under some conditions, high levels of conflict may be conducive to high group performance. So we might expect to find situations in which groups in Stage II outperform those in Stage III or IV. Similarly, groups don't always proceed clearly from one stage to the next. Sometimes, in fact, several stages go on simultaneously, as when groups are storming and performing at the same time. Groups even occasionally regress to previous stages. Therefore, even the strongest proponents of this model don't assume that all groups follow its five-stage process precisely or that Stage IV is always the most preferable.

Another problem with the five-stage model, in terms of understanding work-related behaviour, is that it ignores organisational context.[6] For instance, a study of a cockpit crew in an airliner found that, within ten minutes, three strangers assigned to fly together for

■ FIGURE 9.1
Stages of group development

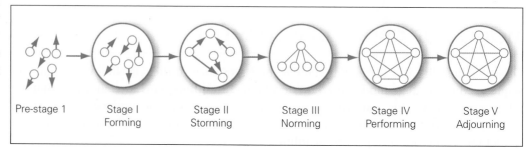

Pre-stage 1   Stage I Forming   Stage II Storming   Stage III Norming   Stage IV Performing   Stage V Adjourning

the first time had become a high-performing group. What allowed for this speedy group development was the strong organisational context surrounding the tasks of the cockpit crew. This context provided the rules, task definitions, information and resources needed for the group to perform. They didn't need to develop plans, assign roles, determine and allocate resources, resolve conflicts and set norms the way the five-stage model predicts.

AN ALTERNATIVE MODEL: FOR TEMPORARY GROUPS WITH DEADLINES

Temporary groups with deadlines don't seem to follow the previous model. Studies indicate that they have their own unique sequencing of actions (or inaction): (1) their first meeting sets the group's direction; (2) this first phase of group activity is one of inertia; (3) a transition takes place at the end of this first phase, which occurs exactly when the group has used up half its allotted time; (4) a transition initiates major changes; (5) a second phase of inertia follows the transition; and (6) the group's last meeting is characterised by markedly accelerated activity.[7] This pattern is called the **punctuated-equilibrium model** and is shown in Figure 9.2.

The first meeting sets the group's direction. A framework of behavioural patterns and assumptions through which the group will approach its project emerges in this first meeting. These lasting patterns can appear as early as the first few seconds of the group's life. Once set, the group's direction becomes 'written in stone' and is unlikely to be re-examined throughout the first half of the group's life. This is a period of inertia—that is, the group tends to stand still or become locked into a fixed course of action. Even if it gains new insights that challenge initial patterns and assumptions, the group is incapable of acting on these new insights in Phase 1.

One of the more interesting discoveries made in these studies[8] was that each group experienced its transition at the same point in its calendar—precisely halfway between its first meeting and its official deadline—despite the fact that some groups spent as little as an hour on their project while others spent six months. It was as if the groups universally experienced a midlife crisis at this point. The midpoint appears to work like an alarm clock, heightening members' awareness that their time is limited and that they need to 'get moving'. This transition ends Phase 1 and is characterised by a concentrated burst of changes, dropping of old patterns and adoption of new perspectives. The transition sets a revised direction for Phase 2. Phase 2 is a new equilibrium or period of inertia. In this phase, the group executes plans created during the transition period.

The group's last meeting is characterised by a final burst of activity to finish its work. In summary, the punctuated-equilibrium model characterises groups as exhibiting long

punctuated-equilibrium model | Transitions temporary groups go through between inertia and activity.

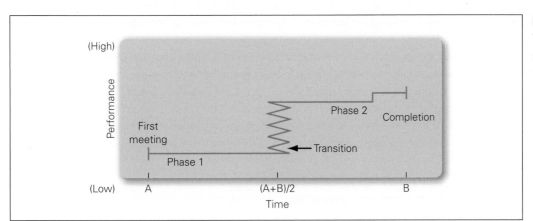

■ **FIGURE 9.2**
The punctuated-equilibrium model

periods of inertia interspersed with brief revolutionary changes triggered primarily by their members' awareness of time and deadlines. Keep in mind, however, that this model doesn't apply to all groups. It is essentially limited to temporary task groups who are working under a time-constrained completion deadline.[9]

GROUP PROPERTIES: ROLES, NORMS, STATUS, SIZE AND COHESIVENESS

Work groups aren't unorganised mobs. Work groups have properties that shape the behaviour of members and make it possible to explain and predict a large portion of individual behaviour within the group as well as the performance of the group itself. What are some of these properties? They include roles, norms, status, group size and the degree of group cohesiveness.

OB IN PRACTICE

A TEAM CULTURE AT HILTON

Felicia Liew is the HR director at the Hilton Hotel in Kuching, the capital of the East Malaysian state of Sarawak, located on the island of Borneo. The hotel is situated along Kuching's spectacular riverfront promenade with panoramic views of the Sarawak River and Fort Margherita.

As a worldwide chain of five-star hotels, senior management have the challenge of guaranteeing the sort of consistent service that customers expect when they stay at any location around the globe. The Hilton brand is very much related to its reputation for outstanding service and facilities. The hotel has adopted the Balanced Scorecard approach to performance management, which allows managers in all locations to track financial and competitive performance along with internal staff and external customer satisfaction/loyalty measures in order to align the efforts of team members system-wide.

Success at the Hilton is based on a team culture proudly described for potential staff applicants. 'When you join the Hilton Family of hotels, you'll be part of a dynamic culture committed to the highest quality of service—a fun, family-oriented atmosphere where positive attitudes and a strong work ethic are rewarded. The people who make up the Hilton Family of hotels are called team members. And just like a close-knit family, team members are always willing to assist and encourage each other. In fact, supporting our team members is critical to our future. Perhaps this explains why, in a recent survey, team members listed our culture and reputation as two of the biggest reasons they chose the Hilton Family of hotels over the competition.'

Felicia provides a range of training programs for new recruits as well as existing staff. She deals with various functional groups, including food and beverage, housekeeping, front counter, marketing, maintenance and grounds. The challenge for Felicia is not only to develop the necessary skills required in a five-star hotel, but also to get the various functional groups to work as effective teams with a shared vision for service and performance. As part of her MBA studies, Felicia appreciated the importance of understanding the theory behind groups and their dynamics.

General manager Eric Swanson of Millennium Seoul Hilton in South Korea highlights the importance of teamwork at Hilton: 'My philosophy is to ensure that all team members feel respected and well taken care of by management. Making sure that everything with the internal staff is perfect is important so that the guests can also have a perfect experience when they visit. I think that this is a very sound and important way to conduct business in the service industry.' Felicia is one of many training managers worldwide who actively promote the team culture at Hilton.

SOURCES: Official Hilton website: <www.hiltonworldwide.com/en/ww/company_info/culture.jhtml;jsessionid= UXDDZ54XIXJ2OCSGBIV2VCQKIYFC5UUC> (accessed 5 October 20/06); and *The Seoul Times*: <http://theseoultimes.com/ST/?url=/ST/db/read.php?idx=4007> (4 October 2006).

ROLES

Shakespeare said, 'All the world's a stage, and all the men and women merely players.' Using the same metaphor, all group members are actors, each playing a **role**. By this term, we mean a set of expected behaviour patterns attributed to someone occupying a given position in a social unit. The understanding of role behaviour would be dramatically simplified if each of us chose one role and 'played it out' regularly and consistently. Unfortunately, we are required to play a number of diverse roles, both on and off our jobs. As we will see, one of the tasks in understanding behaviour is grasping the role that a person is currently playing.

For example, Bill Chitlow is a manager of engineering for BHP Billiton, the major Australian steel producer, and is located in Perth, Western Australia. He has a number of roles that he fulfils in that job—a member of middle management, part of the electrical engineering group and a member of a quality improvement team. Off the job, Bill finds himself in more roles: husband, father, Catholic, tennis player, member of the golf club and president of the Parent–Teacher Association. Many of these roles are compatible, while some create conflicts. For example, his religious beliefs are sometimes incompatible with the AIDS policy his company has adopted. A recent offer of promotion requires Bill to relocate, yet his family very much wants to stay in Perth. Can the role demands of his job be reconciled with the role demands of husband and father?

The issue should be clear: like Bill Chitlow, we all are required to play a number of roles, and our behaviour varies with the role we are playing. Bill's behaviour when he attends church on Sunday morning is different from his behaviour on the golf course later that same day. So, different groups impose different role requirements on individuals.

ROLE IDENTITY

There are certain attitudes and actual behaviours consistent with a role, and they create the **role identity**. People have the ability to shift roles rapidly when they recognise that the situation and its demands clearly require major changes. For instance, when union stewards were promoted to supervisory positions, it was found that their attitudes changed from pro-union to pro-management within a few months of their promotion. When these promotions had to be

Ray Hingst is a major in the Australian Army Reserve. He also lectures in various management topics at university and conducts research into the operations of various call centres around Australia. With such a diverse involvement with different groups of people, Ray is used to playing different roles to suit the occasion. For example, his role on a training exercise with the troops has different demands from doing paperwork in the office. Ray's armed forces and university experience has helped him to develop the skills and behaviours for playing different roles to suit the occasion.

LEARNING OBJECTIVE 3

Explain how role requirements change in different situations

role | A set of expected behaviour patterns attributed to someone occupying a given position in a social unit.

role identity | Certain attitudes and behaviours consistent with a role.

rescinded later because of economic difficulties in the firm, it was found that the demoted supervisors had once again adopted their pro-union attitudes.[10]

ROLE PERCEPTION

role perception | An individual's view of how he or she is supposed to act in a given situation.

Our view of how we are supposed to act in a given situation is a **role perception**. Based on an interpretation of how we believe we are supposed to behave, we engage in certain types of behaviour. Where do we get these perceptions? We get them from stimuli all around us—friends, books, movies, television. For example, many current police officers may have learned their roles from reading Jon Cleary and Peter Corris novels; many of tomorrow's lawyers might be influenced by watching the actions of attorneys in the TV series *Law & Order*; and the role of crime investigators, as portrayed on the television program *CSI*, could direct people into careers in criminology. Of course, the primary reason that apprenticeship programs exist in many trades and professions is to allow beginners to watch an 'expert' so that they can learn to act as they are supposed to.

ROLE EXPECTATIONS

role expectations | How others believe a person should act in a given situation.

Role expectations are defined as how others believe you should act in a given situation. How you behave is determined to a large extent by the role defined in the context in which you are acting. For instance, the role of a judge in the federal courts of Australia and New Zealand is viewed as having propriety and dignity, while a soccer or hockey coach is seen to be more aggressive, dynamic and inspiring towards the players in the team.

psychological contract | An unwritten agreement that sets out what management expects from the employee, and vice versa.

In the workplace, it can be helpful to look at the topic of role expectations through the perspective of the **psychological contract**. There is an unwritten agreement that exists between employees and their employer. This psychological contract sets out mutual expectations—what management expects from workers, and vice versa.[11] In effect, this contract defines the behavioural expectations that go with every role. For instance, management is expected to treat employees justly, provide acceptable working conditions, clearly communicate what is a fair day's work, and give feedback on how well the employee is doing. Employees are expected to respond by demonstrating a good attitude, following directions, and showing loyalty to the organisation.

What happens when role expectations as implied in the psychological contract are not met? If management is derelict in keeping up its part of the bargain, we can expect negative repercussions on employee performance and satisfaction. When employees fail to live up to expectations, the result is usually some form of disciplinary action up to and including firing.

ROLE CONFLICT

role conflict | A situation in which an individual is confronted by divergent role expectations.

When an individual is confronted by divergent role expectations, the result is **role conflict**. It exists when an individual finds that compliance with one role requirement may make it more difficult to comply with another.[12] At the extreme, it would include situations in which two or more role expectations are mutually contradictory.

Our previous discussion of the many roles Bill Chitlow had to deal with included several role conflicts—for instance, Bill's attempt to reconcile the expectations placed on him as a husband and father with those placed on him as an executive with BHP Billiton. The former, as you will remember, emphasises stability and concern for the desire of his wife and children to remain in Perth. BHP Billiton, on the other hand, expects its employees to be responsive to the needs and requirements of the company. Although it might be in Bill's financial and career interests to accept a relocation, the conflict comes down to choosing between family and career role expectations.

AN EXPERIMENT: ZIMBARDO'S PRISON EXPERIMENT

One of the more illuminating role experiments was done a number of years ago in the United States by Stanford University psychologist Philip Zimbardo and his associates.[13] They created a 'prison' in the basement of the Stanford psychology building, hired at $15 a day two dozen emotionally stable, physically healthy, law-abiding students who scored 'normal average' on extensive personality tests, randomly assigned them the role of either 'guard' or 'prisoner', and established some basic rules.

To get the experiment off to a 'realistic' start, Zimbardo got the cooperation of the local police department. They went, unannounced, to each future prisoner's home, arrested and handcuffed them, put them in a squad car in front of friends and neighbours, and took them to police headquarters, where they were officially arrested and fingerprinted. From there, they were taken to the Stanford prison.

At the start of the planned two-week experiment, there were no measurable differences between the individuals assigned to be guards and those chosen to be prisoners. In addition, the guards received no special training in how to be prison guards. They were told only to 'maintain law and order' in the prison and not to take any nonsense from the prisoners. Physical violence was forbidden. To simulate further the realities of prison life, the prisoners were allowed visits from relatives and friends. And although the mock guards worked eight-hour shifts, the mock prisoners were kept in their cells around the clock and were allowed out only for meals, exercise, toilet privileges, head-count line-ups and work assignments.

It took the 'prisoners' little time to accept the authority positions of the guards, and for the mock guards to adjust to their new authority roles. After the guards crushed a rebellion attempt on the second day, the prisoners became increasingly passive. Whatever the guards 'dished out', the prisoners took. The prisoners actually began to believe and act as if they were, as the guards constantly reminded them, inferior and powerless. And every guard, at some time during the simulation, engaged in abusive, authoritative behaviour. For example, one guard said, 'I was surprised at myself ... I made them call each other names and clean the toilets out with their bare hands. I practically considered the prisoners cattle, and I kept thinking: "I have to watch out for them in case they try something."' Another guard added, 'I was tired of seeing the prisoners in their rags and smelling the strong odours of their bodies that filled the cells. I watched them tear at each other on orders given by us. They didn't see it as an experiment. It was real and they were fighting to keep their identity. But we were always there to show them who was boss.' Surprisingly, during the entire experiment—even after days of abuse—not one prisoner said, 'Stop this. I'm a student like you. This is just an experiment!'

The simulation actually proved *too successful* in demonstrating how quickly individuals learn new roles. The researchers had to stop the experiment after only six days because of the participants' pathological reactions. And remember, these were individuals chosen precisely for their normalcy and emotional stability.

What should you conclude from this prison simulation? The participants in this experiment had, like the rest of us, learned stereotyped conceptions of guard and prisoner roles from the mass media and their own personal experiences in power and powerlessness relationships gained at home (parent–child), in school (teacher–student) and in other situations. This, then, allowed them easily and rapidly to assume roles that were very different from their inherent personalities. In this case, we saw that people with no prior personality pathology or training in their roles could execute extreme forms of behaviour consistent with the roles they were playing.

LEARNING OBJECTIVE 4

Describe how norms
exert influence on an
individual's behaviour

NORMS

Did you ever notice that golfers don't speak while their partners are putting on the green or that employees don't criticise their bosses in public? Why? The answer is: 'Norms!'

All groups have established **norms**—that is, acceptable standards of behaviour that are shared by the group's members. Norms tell members what they ought and ought not to do under certain circumstances. From an individual's standpoint, they tell what is expected of you in certain situations. When agreed to and accepted by the group, norms act as a means of influencing the behaviour of group members with a minimum of external controls. Norms differ among groups, communities and societies, but they all have them.[14]

norms | Acceptable standards of behaviour within a group that are shared by the group's members.

THE HAWTHORNE STUDIES

It is generally agreed among behavioural scientists that full-scale appreciation of the importance norms play in influencing worker behaviour didn't occur until the early 1930s. This enlightenment grew out of a series of studies undertaken at Western Electric Company's Hawthorne Works in Chicago between 1924 and 1932.[15] Originally initiated by Western Electric officials and later overseen by Harvard professor Elton Mayo, the Hawthorne studies concluded that a worker's behaviour and sentiments were closely related, that group influences were significant in affecting individual behaviour, that group standards were highly effective in establishing individual worker output, and that money was less a factor in determining worker output than were group standards, sentiments and security. Let us briefly discuss the Hawthorne investigations and demonstrate the importance of these findings in explaining group behaviour.

The Hawthorne researchers began by examining the relation between the physical environment and productivity. Illumination and other working conditions were selected to represent this physical environment. The researchers' initial findings contradicted their anticipated results.

They began with illumination experiments with various groups of workers. The researchers manipulated the intensity of illumination upward and downward, while at the same time noting changes in group output. Results varied, but one thing was clear: in no case was the increase or decrease in output in proportion to the increase or decrease in illumination. So, the researchers introduced a control group: an experimental group was presented with varying intensity of illumination, while the controlled unit worked under a constant illumination intensity. Again, the results were bewildering to the Hawthorne researchers. As the light level was increased in the experimental unit, output rose for both the control and the experimental group. But to the surprise of the researchers, as the light level was dropped in the experimental group, productivity continued to increase in both groups. In fact, a productivity decrease was observed in the experimental group only when the light intensity had been reduced to that of moonlight. The Hawthorne researchers concluded that illumination intensity was only a minor influence among the many influences that affected an employee's productivity, but they couldn't explain the behaviour they had witnessed.

As a follow-up to the illumination experiments, the researchers began a second set of experiments in the relay assembly test room at Western Electric. A small group of women was isolated from the main work group so that their behaviour could be more carefully observed. They went about their job of assembling small telephone relays in a room laid out similarly to their normal department. The only significant difference was the placement in the room of a research assistant who acted as an observer—keeping records of output, rejects, working conditions, and a daily log sheet describing everything that happened. Observations covering a multiyear period found that this small group's output increased steadily. The number of personal absences and those due to sickness were approximately one-third of those recorded by women in the regular production department. What became evident was that this group's performance was significantly influenced by its status of being a 'special' group. The women in the test room thought that being in the experimental group was fun, that they were in sort of an elite group, and that management was concerned with their interest by engaging in such experimentation. In essence, workers in both the illumination and assembly-test-room experiments were reacting to the increased attention they were receiving.

A third study in the bank wiring observation room was introduced to ascertain the effect of a sophisticated wage incentive plan. The assumption was that individual workers would maximise their productivity when they saw that it was directly related to economic rewards. The most important finding coming out of this study was that employees *didn't* individually maximise their outputs. Rather, their output became controlled by a group norm that determined what was a proper day's work. Output was not only being restricted, but individual workers were giving erroneous reports. The total for a week would check with the total week's output, but the daily reports showed a steady level of output regardless of actual daily production. What was going on?

Interviews determined that the group was operating well below its capability and was levelling output in order to protect itself. Members were afraid that if they significantly increased their output, the unit incentive rate would be cut, the expected daily output would be increased, layoffs might occur, or slower workers would be reprimanded. So, the group established its idea of a fair output—neither too much nor too little. They helped each other out to ensure their reports were nearly level.

The norms the group established included a number of 'don'ts'. *Don't* be a rate-buster, turning out too much work. *Don't* be a chiseller, turning out too little work. *Don't* be a squealer on any of your peers. How did the group enforce these norms? Their methods were neither gentle nor subtle. They included sarcasm, name-calling, ridicule, and even physical punches to the upper arm of members who violated the group's norms. Members would also ostracise individuals whose behaviour was against the group's interest.

The Hawthorne studies made an important contribution to our understanding of group behaviour—particularly the significant place that norms have in determining individual work behaviour.

COMMON TYPES OF NORMS

A work group's norms are like an individual's fingerprints—each is unique. Yet there are still some common types of norms that appear in most work groups.[16]

Probably the most common type of norms is *performance norms*. Work groups typically provide their members with explicit cues on how hard they should work, how to get the job done, their level of output, appropriate levels of tardiness, and the like.[17] These norms are extremely powerful in affecting an individual employee's performance—they are capable of significantly modifying a performance prediction that was based solely on the employee's ability and level of personal motivation.

A second category encompasses *appearance norms*. This includes things like appropriate dress, loyalty to the work group or organisation, when to look busy, and when it is acceptable to 'bludge'. Some organisations have formal dress codes. However, even in their absence, norms frequently develop to dictate the kind of clothing that should be worn to work. Similarly, presenting the appearance of loyalty is important, especially among professional employees and those in the executive ranks. So, it is often considered inappropriate to be openly looking for another job.

Another category concerns *social arrangement norms*. These norms come from informal work groups and primarily regulate social interactions within the group. With whom group members eat lunch, friendships on and off the job, social games, and the like are influenced by these norms.

A final category relates to *allocation of resources norms*. These norms can originate in the group or in the organisation and cover things such as pay, assignment of difficult jobs, and allocation of new tools and equipment.

CONFORMITY

As a member of a group, you desire acceptance by the group. Because of your desire for acceptance, you are susceptible to conforming to the group's norms. There is considerable evidence that groups can place strong pressures on individual members to change their attitudes and behaviours to conform to the group's standard.[18]

Do individuals conform to the pressures of all the groups to which they belong? Obviously not, because people belong to many groups and their norms vary. In some cases, they may even have contradictory norms. So, what do people do? They conform to the important groups to which they belong or hope to belong. The important groups have been called **reference groups**, and they are characterised as ones in which a person is aware of other members; defines himself or herself as a member, or would like to be a member; and feels that the group members are significant to him or her.[19] The implication, then, is that all groups don't impose equal **conformity** pressures on their members.

reference groups | Important groups to which individuals belong or hope to belong and with whose norms individuals are likely to conform.

conformity | Adjusting one's behaviour to align with the norms of the group.

The impact that group pressures for conformity can have on an individual member's judgment and attitudes was demonstrated in the now-classic studies by Solomon Asch.[20] Asch made up groups of seven or eight people, who sat around a table and were asked to compare two cards held by the experimenter. One card had one line while the other had three lines of varying length. As shown in Figure 9.3, one of the lines on the three-line card was identical to the line on the one-line card. Also as shown in Figure 9.3, the difference in line length was quite obvious; in fact, under ordinary conditions, participants made less than 1 per cent errors. The object was to announce aloud which of the three lines matched the single line. But what happens if the members in the group begin to give incorrect answers? Will the pressures to conform result in an unsuspecting participant (USP) altering an answer to align with the others? That was what Asch wanted to know. So he arranged the group so that only the USP was unaware that the experiment was 'fixed'. The seating was prearranged: the USP was placed so as to be one of the last to announce a decision.

■ **FIGURE 9.3**
Examples of cards used in Asch's study

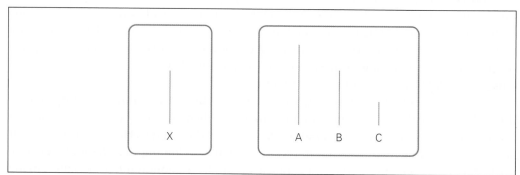

The experiment began with several sets of matching exercises. All the participants gave the right answers. On the third set, however, the first participant gave an obviously wrong answer—for example, saying 'C' in Figure 9.3. The next participant gave the same wrong answer, and so did the others until it got to the unknowing participant. He knew 'B' was the same as 'X', yet everyone had said 'C'. The decision confronting the USP was this: Do you publicly state a perception that differs from the pre-announced position of the others in your group? Or do you give an answer that you strongly believe is incorrect in order to have your response agree with that of the other group members?

The results obtained by Asch demonstrated that over many experiments and many trials, 75 per cent of the participants gave at least one answer that conformed—that is, that they knew was wrong but that was consistent with the replies of other group members—and the average for conformers was 37 per cent. What meaning can we draw from these results? They suggest that there are group norms that press us towards conformity. That is, we desire to be one of the group and avoid being visibly different.

The preceding conclusions are based on research that was conducted 50 years ago. Has time altered their validity? And should we consider these findings generalisable across cultures? The evidence indicates that there have been changes in the level of conformity over time; and Asch's findings are culture-bound.[21] Specifically, levels of conformity have steadily declined since Asch's studies in the early 1950s. In addition, conformity to social norms is higher in collectivist cultures than in individualistic cultures. Nevertheless, even in individualistic countries, you should consider conformity to norms still to be a powerful force in groups.

DEVIANT WORKPLACE BEHAVIOUR

Roger Yeo is frustrated by a co-worker who constantly spreads malicious and unsubstantiated rumours about him. Debra Hunt is tired of a member of her work team who, when confronted with a problem, takes out his frustration by yelling and screaming at her and other work team members. And Susan Lomu recently quit her job as a dental assistant after being constantly sexually harassed by her employer. What do these three episodes have in common? They represent employees being exposed to acts of *deviant workplace behaviour*.[22] **Deviant workplace behaviour** (also called *antisocial behaviour* or *workplace incivility*) is voluntary behaviour that violates significant organisational norms and, in doing so, threatens the well-being of the organisation or its members. Figure 9.4 provides a typology of deviant workplace behaviours with examples of each.

deviant workplace behaviour | Voluntary behaviour that violates significant organisational norms and, in doing so, threatens the well-being of the organisation or its members.

Few organisations will admit to creating or condoning conditions that encourage and maintain deviant norms. Yet, they exist. Employees report, for example, an increase in rudeness and disregard towards others by bosses and co-workers in recent years. And nearly half of employees who have suffered this incivility report that it has led them to think about changing jobs, with 12 per cent actually quitting because of it.[23]

As with norms in general, individual employees' antisocial actions are shaped by the group context within which they work. Evidence demonstrates that the antisocial behaviour exhibited by a work group is a significant predictor of an individual's antisocial behaviour at work.[24] In other words, deviant workplace behaviour is likely to flourish where it is supported by group norms. What this means for managers is that when deviant workplace norms surface, employee cooperation, commitment and motivation are likely to suffer. This, in turn, can lead to reduced employee productivity and job satisfaction and increased turnover.

Additionally, just being part of a group can increase an individual's deviant behaviour. In other words, someone who ordinarily wouldn't engage in deviant behaviour might be

Category	Examples
Production	Leaving early Intentionally working slowly Wasting resources
Property	Sabotage Lying about hours worked Stealing from the organisation
Political	Showing favouritism Gossiping and spreading rumours Blaming co-workers
Personal aggression	Sexual harassment Verbal abuse Stealing from co-workers

SOURCE: Adapted from S. L. Robinson and R. J. Bennett, 'A Typology of Deviant Workplace Behaviors: A Multidimensional Scaling Study', *Academy of Management Journal*, April 1995, p. 565. Copyright © 1995 by Academy of Management. Reproduced with permission in the format Textbook via Copyright Clearance Centre.

more likely to do so when working in a group. In fact, a recent study suggests that, compared to individuals working alone, those working in a group were more likely to lie, cheat and steal. As shown in Figure 9.5, in this study no individual working alone lied, but 22 per cent of those working in groups did. Moreover, individuals working in groups also were more likely to cheat (55 per cent of individuals working in a group cheated on a task, versus 23 per cent of individuals working alone) and steal (29 per cent of individuals working in a group stole, compared to only 10 per cent working alone).[25] Groups provide a shield of anonymity so that someone who ordinarily might be afraid of getting caught for stealing can rely on the fact that other group members had the same opportunity or reason to steal. This creates a false sense of confidence that may result in more aggressive behaviour. Thus, deviant behaviour depends on the accepted norms of the group—or even whether an individual is part of a group.[26]

STATUS

Status—that is, a socially defined position or rank given to groups or group members by others—permeates every society. Despite many attempts, we have made little progress towards a classless society. Even the smallest group will develop roles, rights and rituals to differentiate its members. Status is an important factor in understanding human behaviour, because it is a significant motivator and has major behavioural consequences when individuals perceive a disparity between what they believe their status to be and what others perceive it to be.

status | A socially defined position or rank given to groups or group members by others.

WHAT DETERMINES STATUS?

According to **status characteristics theory**, differences in status characteristics create status hierarchies within groups.[27] Moreover, status tends to be derived from one of three sources: the power a person wields over others; a person's ability to contribute to a group's goals; and an individual's personal characteristics.[28]

status characteristics theory | Theory stating that differences in status characteristics create status hierarchies within groups.

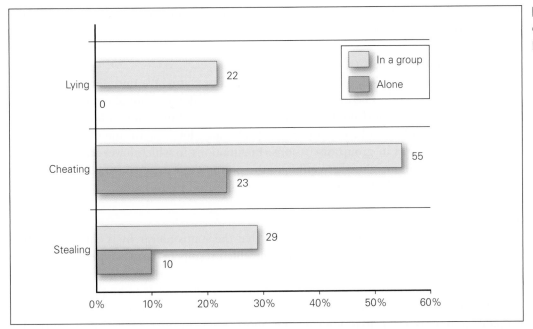

SOURCE: A. Erez, H. Elms and E. Fong, 'Lying, Cheating, Stealing: Groups and the Ring of Gyges', Paper presented at the Academy of Management Annual Meeting, Honolulu, HI, 8 August 2005.

People who control the outcomes of a group through their power tend to be perceived as high in status. This is largely due to their ability to control the group's resources. So, a group's formal leader or manager is likely to be perceived as high status when he or she can allocate resources such as preferred assignments, desirable schedules and pay increases. People whose contributions are critical to the group's success also tend to have high status. The outstanding performers on sports teams, for example, typically have greater status on the team than do average players. Finally, someone who has personal characteristics that are positively valued by the group—such as good looks, intelligence, money or a friendly personality—will typically have higher status than someone who has fewer valued attributes. This tends to explain why attractive people are often the most popular in high school. Note, of course, that a characteristic valued by one group may mean nothing in another. So, high intelligence may give you status at your weekly tutorial discussions in your OB course, but it may provide no benefit at all to you at your social tennis matches.

STATUS AND NORMS

Status has been shown to have some interesting effects on the power of norms and pressures to conform. For instance, high-status members of groups often are given more freedom to deviate from norms than are other group members.[29] High-status people also are better able to resist conformity pressures than their lower-status peers. An individual who is highly valued by a group but who doesn't much need or care about the social rewards the group provides is particularly able to pay minimal attention to conformity norms.[30]

The previous findings explain why many star athletes, celebrities, top-performing salespeople and outstanding academics seem oblivious to appearance or social norms that constrain their peers. As high-status individuals, they are given a wider range of discretion.

But this is true only as long as the high-status person's activities aren't severely detrimental to group goal achievement.[31]

STATUS AND GROUP INTERACTION

Interaction among members of groups is influenced by status. We find, for instance, that high-status people tend to be more assertive.[32] They speak out more often, criticise more, state more commands, and interrupt others more often. But status differences actually inhibit diversity of ideas and creativity in groups, because lower-status members tend to be less active participants in group discussions. In situations in which lower-status members possess expertise and insights that could aid the group, their expertise and insights aren't likely to be fully utilised, thus reducing the group's overall performance.

STATUS INEQUITY

It is important for group members to believe that the status hierarchy is equitable. When inequity is perceived, it creates disequilibrium, which results in various types of corrective behaviour.[33]

The concept of equity applies to status. People expect rewards to be proportionate to costs incurred. If Rachael and Jessica are the two finalists for the head nurse position in a hospital, and it is clear that Rachael has more seniority and better preparation for assuming the promotion, Jessica will view the selection of Rachael to be equitable. However, if Jessica is chosen because she is the daughter-in-law of the hospital director, Rachael will believe an injustice has been committed.

The trappings that go with formal positions are also important elements in maintaining equity. When we believe there is an inequity between the perceived ranking of an individual and the status accoutrements that person is given by the organisation, we are experiencing status incongruence. An example of this kind of incongruence is the more desirable office location being held by a lower-ranking individual. Pay incongruence has long been a problem in the insurance industry, where top sales agents often earn two to five times more than senior corporate executives. The result is that it is very hard for insurance companies to entice successful agents into management positions. Our point is that employees expect the things individuals have and receive to be congruent with their status.

Groups generally agree within themselves on status criteria and, hence, there is usually high concurrence in group rankings of individuals. However, individuals can find themselves in a conflict situation when they move between groups whose status criteria are different or when they join groups whose members have heterogeneous backgrounds. For instance, business executives may use personal income or the growth rate of their companies as determinants of status. Government bureaucrats may use the size of their budgets. Blue-collar workers may use years of seniority. In groups made up of heterogeneous individuals or when heterogeneous groups are forced to be interdependent, status differences may initiate conflict as the group attempts to reconcile and align the differing hierarchies. As we will see in the next chapter, this can be a particular problem when management creates teams made up of employees from across varied functions within the organisation.

STATUS AND CULTURE

Before we leave the topic of status, we should briefly address the issue of cross-culture transferability. Do cultural differences affect status? The answer is a resounding 'Yes!'[34]

The importance of status does vary between cultures. The French, for example, are highly status conscious. Also, countries differ on the criteria that create status. For instance, status for Latin Americans and Asians tends to be derived from family position and formal roles held in organisations. In contrast, although status is still important in countries such as New Zealand and Australia, it tends to be less 'in your face'. And it tends to be bestowed more on accomplishments than on titles and family trees.[35]

The message here is to make sure you understand who and what holds status when interacting with people from a culture different from your own. An Australian manager who doesn't understand that office size isn't a measure of a Japanese executive's position, or who fails to grasp the importance that the British place on family genealogy and social class, is likely to unintentionally offend his Japanese or British counterpart and, in so doing, lessen his interpersonal effectiveness.

SIZE

Does the size of a group affect the group's overall behaviour? The answer to this question is a definite 'Yes', but the effect is contingent on what dependent variables you look at.[36] The evidence indicates, for instance, that smaller groups are faster at completing tasks than are larger ones, and that individuals perform better in smaller groups.[37] However, if the group is engaged in problem solving, large groups consistently get better marks than their smaller counterparts.[38] Translating these results into specific numbers is a bit more hazardous, but we can offer some parameters. Large groups—with a dozen or more members—are good for gaining diverse input. So, if the goal of the group is fact-finding, larger groups should be more effective. On the other hand, smaller groups are better at doing something productive with that input. Groups of approximately seven members, therefore, tend to be more effective for taking action. One of the most important findings related to the size of a group has been labelled *social loafing*. **Social loafing** is the tendency for individuals to expend less effort when working collectively than when working individually.[39] It directly challenges the logic that the productivity of the group as a whole should at least equal the sum of the productivity of each individual in that group. A common stereotype about groups is that the sense of team spirit spurs individual effort and enhances the group's overall productivity.

But that stereotype may be wrong. In the late 1920s, a German psychologist named Max Ringelmann compared the results of individual and group performance on a rope-pulling task.[40] He expected that the group's effort would be equal to the sum of the efforts of individuals within the group. That is, three people pulling together should exert three times as much pull on the rope as one person, and eight people should exert eight times as much pull. Ringelmann's results, however, didn't confirm his expectations. One person pulling on a rope alone exerted an average of 63 kilograms of force. In groups of three, the per-person force dropped to 53 kilograms. And in groups of eight, it fell to only 31 kilograms per person.

Replications of Ringelmann's research with similar tasks have generally supported his findings.[41] Group performance increases with group size, but the addition of new members to the group has diminishing returns on productivity. So, more may be better in the sense that the total productivity of a group of four is greater than that of three people, but the individual productivity of each group member declines.

What causes this social loafing effect? It may be due to a belief that others in the group aren't carrying their fair share. If you see others as lazy or inept, you can re-establish equity by reducing your effort. Another explanation is the dispersion of responsibility. Because the

LEARNING OBJECTIVE 6

Define social loafing and its effect on group performance

social loafing | The tendency for individuals to expend less effort when working collectively than when working individually.

results of the group cannot be attributed to any single person, the relationship between an individual's input and the group's output is clouded. In such situations, individuals may be tempted to become 'free riders' and coast on the group's efforts. In other words, there will be a reduction in efficiency when individuals think that their contribution cannot be measured.

The implications for OB of this effect on work groups are significant. When managers use collective work situations to enhance morale and teamwork, they must also provide means by which individual efforts can be identified. If this isn't done, management must weigh the potential losses in productivity from using groups against any possible gains in worker satisfaction.[42]

However, this conclusion has a Western bias. It is consistent with individualistic cultures, such as Australia and Canada, that are dominated by self-interest. It is not consistent with collective societies, in which individuals are motivated by in-group goals. For instance, in studies comparing employees from the United States with employees from the People's Republic of China and Israel (both collectivist societies), the Chinese and Israelis showed no propensity to engage in social loafing. In fact, the Chinese and Israelis actually performed better in a group than when working alone.[43]

The research on group size leads us to two additional conclusions: (1) groups with an odd number of members tend to be preferable to those with an even number; and (2) groups made up of five or seven members do a pretty good job of exercising the best elements of both small and large groups.[44]

Having an odd number of members eliminates the possibility of ties when votes are taken. And groups made up of five or seven members are large enough to form a majority and allow for diverse input, yet small enough to avoid the negative outcomes often associated with large groups, such as domination by a few members, development of subgroups, inhibited participation by some members, and excessive time taken to reach a decision.

COHESIVENESS

cohesiveness | Degree to which group members are attracted to each other and are motivated to stay in the group.

Groups differ in their **cohesiveness**—that is, the degree to which members are attracted to each other and are motivated to stay in the group.[45] For instance, some work groups are cohesive because the members have spent a great deal of time together, or the group's small size facilitates high interaction, or the group has experienced external threats that have brought members close together. Cohesiveness is important, because it has been found to be related to the group's productivity.[46]

Studies consistently show that the relationship of cohesiveness and productivity depends on the performance-related norms established by the group.[47] If performance-related norms are high (for example, high output, quality work, cooperation with individuals outside the group), a cohesive group will be more productive than will a less cohesive group. But if cohesiveness is high and performance norms are low, productivity will be low. If cohesiveness is low and performance norms are high, productivity increases, but less than in the high-cohesiveness/high-norms situation. When cohesiveness and performance-related norms are both low, productivity will tend to fall into the low-to-moderate range. These conclusions are summarised in Figure 9.6.

■ **FIGURE 9.6**

Relationship between group cohesiveness, performance norms and productivity

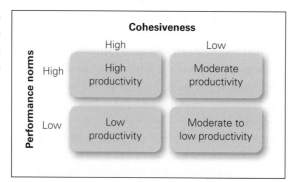

Cohesiveness

Performance norms		High	Low
	High	High productivity	Moderate productivity
	Low	Low productivity	Moderate to low productivity

Felicia Liew (left) is the HR director at the Hilton Hotel in Kuching. She spends a great deal of time with staff from the different sections at the hotel. During various training sessions, staff become conscious of the need for cohesiveness within and across the different operation teams in order to achieve the high standard of customer service expected in a Hilton hotel.

What can you do to encourage group cohesiveness? You might try one or more of the following suggestions: (1) Make the group smaller. (2) Encourage agreement with group goals. (3) Increase the time members spend together. (4) Increase the status of the group and the perceived difficulty of attaining membership in the group. (5) Stimulate competition with other groups. (6) Give rewards to the group rather than to individual members. (7) Physically isolate the group.[48]

GROUP DECISION MAKING

The belief—characterised by juries—that two heads are better than one has long been accepted as a basic component of the legal systems in many countries. This belief has expanded to the point that, today, many decisions in organisations are made by groups, teams or committees.[49] In this section, we discuss group decision making.

GROUPS VERSUS THE INDIVIDUAL

Decision-making groups may be widely used in organisations, but does this imply that group decisions are preferable to those made by an individual alone? The answer to this question depends on a number of factors. Let's begin by looking at the strengths and weaknesses of group decision making.[50]

LEARNING OBJECTIVE 8

List the strengths and weaknesses of group decision making

STRENGTHS OF GROUP DECISION MAKING

Groups generate more *complete information and knowledge*. By aggregating the resources of several individuals, groups bring more input into the decision process. In addition to more input, groups can bring heterogeneity to the decision process. They offer *increased diversity of views*. This opens up the opportunity for more approaches and alternatives to be considered. Finally, groups lead to increased *acceptance of a solution*. Many decisions fail after the final choice is made, because people don't accept the solution. Group members who participated in making a decision are likely to enthusiastically support the decision and encourage others to accept it.

WEAKNESSES OF GROUP DECISION MAKING

In spite of the pluses noted, group decisions have their drawbacks. They are time-consuming because groups typically take more time to reach a solution than would be the case if an individual were making the decision. There are *conformity pressures in groups*. The desire by group members to be accepted and considered an asset to the group can result in squashing any overt disagreement. Group discussion can be *dominated by one or a few*

LEARNING FROM THE EXPERIENCE OF TEAM MANAGEMENT

Glen Simpson is chief executive of the development division of Coffey International, an Australian-based engineering company with a number of specialised divisions, including delivering economic and social development aid overseas. As with many global companies, the challenge of working with and integrating the activities of a diverse range of groups in different locations and cultures can be daunting. What are the lessons that come from experience with team management? For Glen '… it comes back to being able to create a vision, articulate it and get people to enrol in the vision. I want to be very clear that we are not on about leaders, we are on about leadership. We are on about teams, not individuals. The challenge is in getting others to see themselves in the leadership mould so everyone has the responsibility of being a leader in their own right. That is the process of building teams. If more senior people in companies spend more time and energy investing their knowledge and wisdom in others, that's where you get the multiplier effect of experience.'

Personal success needs to be seen in the context of teams and working with others for results. Glen points out that it is a journey of self-understanding about what motivates and discourages people, and that it is the simple things that count such as conversations, the difficult skill of listening, recognition and reward, and accepting that it is human to fail. The challenge and the tragedy is that managers don't learn early enough in their careers from their valuable experience with working with diverse groups of people engaged in common purposes.

His experience in team management has made Dr Neil Miller, managing director of Canberra-based software and services supplier TASKey, realise the need to provide teams with effective decision support systems so that all members of a team are constantly in touch with the projects they are working on. Dr Miller says, 'There's a feeling now that while you rely on in-head management—managers remembering complex lists and tasks—you'll never be able to break through and change the process … Instead of managers having to coordinate and keep track of things in their heads, we can do that with our software.' TASKey's real-time task and team management software grew out of Miller's work for a PhD on introducing change in organisations. He adds: 'Project management methodologies are pretty much top-down, designed for the project manager, not the people involved … It's not a collaborative approach. What you find is a lot of people doing a lot of little things to get a job done … The biggest challenge for the manager is to get decision-making information, to know what's happening and where things are not being done.' The TASKey web-based software takes over the detailed management tasks, ensuring that all team members immediately receive updates on critical project information.

SOURCES: Amita Tandukar, 'The Business of Lending a Hand', *Business Review Weekly*, 28 September 2006, p. 56; and Karen Dearne, 'In Command of Contracts', *The Australian*, 30 May 2006.

members. If this dominant coalition is composed of low- and medium-ability members, the group's overall effectiveness will suffer. Finally, group decisions suffer from *ambiguous responsibility*. In an individual decision, it is clear who is accountable for the final outcome. In a group decision, the responsibility of any single member is watered down.

EFFECTIVENESS AND EFFICIENCY

Whether groups are more effective than individuals depends on the criteria you use for defining effectiveness. In terms of *accuracy*, group decisions are generally more accurate than the decisions of the average individual in a group but less accurate than the judgments of the most accurate group member.[51] If decision effectiveness is defined in terms of *speed*, individuals are superior. If *creativity* is important, groups tend to be more effective than individuals. And if effectiveness means the degree of *acceptance* the final solution achieves, the nod again goes to the group.[52]

But effectiveness cannot be considered without also assessing efficiency. In terms of efficiency, groups almost always stack up as a poor second to the individual decision maker. With few exceptions, group decision making consumes more work hours than if an individual were to tackle the same problem alone. The exceptions tend to be the instances in which, to achieve comparable quantities of diverse input, the single decision maker must spend a great deal of time reviewing files and talking to people. Because groups can include members from diverse areas, the time spent searching for information can be reduced. However, as we noted, these advantages in efficiency tend to be the exception. Groups are generally less efficient than individuals. In deciding whether to use groups, then, consideration should be given to assessing whether increases in effectiveness are more than enough to offset the losses in efficiency.

SUMMARY

In summary, groups offer an excellent vehicle for performing many of the steps in the decision-making process. They are a source of both breadth and depth of input for information gathering. If the group is composed of individuals with diverse backgrounds, the alternatives generated should be more extensive and the analysis more critical. When the final solution is agreed on, there are more people in a group decision to support and implement it. These pluses, however, can be more than offset by the time consumed by group decisions, the internal conflicts they create, and the pressures they generate towards conformity. Therefore, in some cases, individuals can be expected to make better decisions than groups.

GROUPTHINK AND GROUPSHIFT

Two by-products of group decision making have received a considerable amount of attention by researchers in OB. As we will show, these two phenomena have the potential to affect the group's ability to appraise alternatives objectively and to arrive at quality decision solutions.

The first phenomenon, called **groupthink**, is related to norms. It describes situations in which group pressures for conformity deter the group from critically appraising unusual, minority or unpopular views. Groupthink is a disease that attacks many groups and can dramatically hinder their performance. The second phenomenon we shall discuss is called **groupshift**. It indicates that in discussing a given set of alternatives and arriving at a solution, group members tend to exaggerate the initial positions that they hold. In some situations, caution dominates, and there is a conservative shift. More often, however, the evidence indicates that groups tend towards a risky shift. Let's look at each of these phenomena in more detail.

groupthink | Phenomenon in which the norm for consensus overrides the realistic appraisal of alternative courses of action.

groupshift | A change in decision risk between the group's decision and the individual decision that members within the group would make; can be towards either conservatism or greater risk.

GROUPTHINK

Have you ever felt like speaking up in a meeting, classroom or informal group but decided against it? One reason may have been shyness. On the other hand, you may have been a victim of groupthink, the phenomenon that occurs when group members become so enamoured of seeking concurrence that the norm for consensus overrides the realistic appraisal of alternative courses of action and the full expression of deviant, minority or unpopular views. It describes a deterioration in an individual's mental efficiency, reality testing and moral judgment as a result of group pressures.[53]

We have all seen the symptoms of the groupthink phenomenon:

1. Group members rationalise any resistance to the assumptions they have made. No matter how strongly the evidence may contradict their basic assumptions, members behave so as to reinforce those assumptions continually.

2. Members apply direct pressures on those who momentarily express doubts about any of the group's shared views or who question the validity of arguments supporting the alternative favoured by the majority.
3. Members who have doubts or hold differing points of view seek to avoid deviating from what appears to be group consensus by keeping silent about their misgivings and even minimising to themselves the importance of their doubts.
4. There appears to be an illusion of unanimity. If someone doesn't speak, it is assumed that he or she is in full accord. In other words, abstention becomes viewed as a 'yes' vote.[54]

In a range of famous studies of historic American foreign policy decisions, these symptoms were found to prevail when government policy-making groups failed—unpreparedness at Pearl Harbor in 1941, the US invasion of North Korea, the Bay of Pigs fiasco in Cuba, and the escalation of the Vietnam War.[55] More recently, the *Challenger* and *Columbia* space shuttle disasters and the failure of the main mirror on the *Hubble* telescope have been linked to decision processes at NASA in which groupthink symptoms were evident.[56] And groupthink was found to be a primary factor leading to setbacks at both British Airways and retailer Marks & Spencer as they tried to implement globalisation strategies.[57]

Groupthink appears to be closely aligned with the conclusions Asch drew in his experiments with a lone dissenter. Individuals who hold a position that is different from that of the dominant majority are under pressure to suppress, withhold, or modify their true feelings and beliefs. As members of a group, we find it more pleasant to be in agreement—to be a positive part of the group—than to be a disruptive force, even if disruption is necessary to improve the effectiveness of the group's decisions.

Does groupthink attack all groups? No. It seems to occur most often when there is a clear group identity, when members hold a positive image of their group that they want to protect, and when the group perceives a collective threat to this positive image.[58] So, groupthink isn't a dissenter-suppression mechanism as much as it is a means for a group to protect its positive image. For NASA, its problems stem from its attempt to confirm its identity as 'the elite organization that could do no wrong'.[59]

What can managers do to minimise groupthink?[60] One thing is to monitor group size. People grow more intimidated and hesitant as group size increases and, although there is no magic number that will eliminate groupthink, individuals are likely to feel less personal responsibility when groups get larger than about ten. Managers should also encourage group leaders to play an impartial role. Leaders should actively seek input from all members and avoid expressing their own opinions, especially in the early stages of deliberation. Another thing is to appoint one group member to play the role of devil's advocate. This member's role is to overtly challenge the majority position and offer divergent perspectives. Still another suggestion is to use exercises that stimulate active discussion of diverse alternatives without threatening the group and intensifying identity protection. One such exercise is to have group members talk about the dangers or risks involved in a decision and delaying discussion of any potential gains. By requiring members to focus first on the negatives of a decision alternative, the group is less likely to stifle dissenting views and more likely to gain an objective evaluation.

GROUPSHIFT

In comparing group decisions with the individual decisions of members within the group, evidence suggests that there are differences.[61] In some cases, the group decisions are more conservative than the individual decisions. More often, the shift is towards greater risk.[62]

What appears to happen in groups is that the discussion leads to a significant shift in the positions of members towards a more extreme position in the direction in which they were already leaning before the discussion. So, conservative types become more cautious and the more aggressive types take on more risk. The group discussion tends to exaggerate the initial position of the group. Groupshift can be viewed as actually a special case of groupthink. The decision of the group reflects the dominant decision-making norm that develops during the group's discussion. Whether the shift in the group's decision is towards greater caution or more risk depends on the dominant pre-discussion norm. The greater occurrence of the shift towards risk has generated several explanations for the phenomenon.[63] It has been argued, for instance, that the discussion creates familiarisation among the members. As they become more comfortable with each other, they also become more bold and daring. Another argument is that most first-world societies value risk, that we admire individuals who are willing to take risks, and that group discussion motivates members to show that they are at least as willing as their peers to take risks. The most plausible explanation of the shift towards risk, however, seems to be that the group diffuses responsibility. Group decisions free any single member from accountability for the group's final choice. Greater risk can be taken because even if the decision fails, no one member can be held wholly responsible.

So, how should you use the findings on groupshift? You should recognise that group decisions exaggerate the initial position of the individual members, that the shift has been shown more often to be towards greater risk, and that whether or not a group will shift towards greater risk or caution is a function of the members' pre-discussion inclinations.

Having discussed group decision making and its pros and cons, we now turn to the techniques by which groups make decisions. These techniques reduce some of the dysfunctional aspects of group decision making.

GROUP DECISION-MAKING TECHNIQUES

The most common form of group decision making takes place in **interacting groups**. In these groups, members meet face-to-face and rely on both verbal and non-verbal interaction to communicate with each other. But as our discussion of groupthink demonstrated, interacting groups often censor themselves and pressure individual members towards conformity of opinion. Brainstorming, the nominal group technique and electronic meetings have been proposed as ways to reduce many of the problems inherent in the traditional interacting group.

Brainstorming is meant to overcome pressures for conformity in the interacting group that retard the development of creative alternatives.[64] It does this by utilising an idea-generation process that specifically encourages any and all alternatives while withholding any criticism of those alternatives. In a typical brainstorming session, a half-dozen to a dozen people sit around a table. The group leader states the problem in a clear manner so that it is understood by all participants. Members then 'freewheel' as many alternatives as they can in a given length of time. No criticism is allowed, and all the alternatives are recorded for later discussion and analysis. The fact that one idea stimulates others, and that judgments of even the most bizarre suggestions are withheld until later, encourages group members to 'think the unusual'.

Brainstorming may indeed generate ideas, but not in a very efficient manner. Research consistently shows that individuals working alone will generate more ideas than a group will in a brainstorming session. Why? One of the primary reasons is because of 'production blocking'. In other words, when people are generating ideas in a group, there are many people talking at once, which blocks the thought process and eventually impedes the

LEARNING OBJECTIVE 9

Contrast the effectiveness of interacting, brainstorming, nominal and electronic meeting groups

interacting groups | Typical groups, in which members interact with each other face-to-face.

brainstorming | An idea-generation process that specifically encourages any and all alternatives, while withholding any criticism of those alternatives.

Copyright 2001 by Randy Glasbergen.
www.glasbergen.com

GLASBERGEN

"A motion has been made and seconded that this be one of those meetings where nothing actually gets done."

People often express their concern over attending yet another time-wasting meeting. People meet all the time. It is part of the daily routine of work. The challenge is to make sure that all meetings, whether they are formal or informal, large or small, are conducted in a manner appropriate for the purpose. When staff come together to try and resolve issues, then it is important that the group selects an appropriate group decision-solving technique.

sharing of ideas.[65] The following two techniques go further than brainstorming by offering methods that help groups arrive at a preferred solution.[66]

The **nominal group technique** restricts discussion or interpersonal communication during the decision-making process—hence, the term *nominal*. Group members are all physically present, as in a traditional committee meeting, but members operate independently. Specifically, a problem is presented and then the following steps take place:

nominal group technique | A group decision-making method in which individual members meet face-to-face to pool their judgments in a systematic but independent fashion.

1. Members meet as a group, but before any discussion takes place, each member independently writes down ideas on the problem.
2. After this silent period, each member presents one idea to the group. Each member takes a turn, presenting a single idea until all the ideas have been presented and recorded. No discussion takes place until all the ideas have been recorded.

MYTH OR SCIENCE?

'TWO HEADS ARE BETTER THAN ONE'

This statement is mostly true if 'better' means that two people will come up with more original and workable answers to a problem than one person working alone.

The evidence generally confirms the superiority of groups over individuals in terms of decision-making quality. Groups usually produce more and better solutions to problems than do individuals working alone. And the choices groups make will be more accurate and creative. Why is this? Groups bring more complete information and knowledge to a decision, so they generate more ideas. In addition, the give-and-take that typically takes place in group decision processes provides diversity of opinion and increases the likelihood that weak alternatives will be identified and abandoned.

Research indicates that certain conditions favour groups over individuals. These conditions include the following: (1) Diversity among members—the benefits of 'two heads' require that they differ in relevant skills and abilities. (2) The group members must be able to communicate their ideas freely and openly. This requires an absence of hostility and intimidation. (3) The task being undertaken is complex. Relative to individuals, groups do better on complex, rather than simple, tasks.

SOURCES: See G. W. Hill, 'Group versus Individual Performance', and L. K. Michaelsen, W. E. Watson and R. H. Black, 'A Realistic Test of Individual versus Group Consensus Decision Making', in J. H. Davis, *Group Performance* (Reading, MA: Addison-Wesley, 1969); J. P. Wanous and M. A. Youtz, 'Solution Diversity and the Quality of Group Decisions', *Academy of Management Journal*, March 1986, pp. 149–59; and R. Libby, K. T. Trotman and I. Zimmer, 'Member Variation, Recognition of Expertise, and Group Performance', *Journal of Applied Psychology*, February 1987, pp. 81–87.

3. The group now discusses the ideas for clarity and evaluates them.
4. Each group member silently and independently rank-orders the ideas. The idea with the highest aggregate ranking determines the final decision.

The chief advantage of the nominal group technique is that it permits the group to meet formally but doesn't restrict independent thinking, as does the interacting group. Research generally shows that nominal groups outperform brainstorming groups.[67]

The most recent approach to group decision making blends the nominal group technique with sophisticated computer technology.[68] It is called the computer-assisted group or **electronic meeting**. Once the technology is in place, the concept is simple. Up to 50 people sit around a horseshoe-shaped table, empty except for a series of computer terminals. Issues are presented to participants and they type their responses on to their computer screen. Individual comments, as well as aggregate votes, are displayed on a projection screen. The proposed advantages of electronic meetings are anonymity, honesty and speed. Participants can anonymously type any message they want and it flashes on the screen for all to see at the push of a participant's board key. It also allows people to be brutally honest without penalty. And it is supposedly fast because chit-chat is eliminated, discussions don't digress, and many participants can 'talk' at once without stepping on one another's toes. The early evidence, however, indicates that electronic meetings don't achieve most of their proposed benefits. Evaluations of numerous studies found that electronic meetings actually led to *decreased* group effectiveness, required *more* time to complete tasks, and resulted in *reduced* member satisfaction when compared to face-to-face groups.[69] Nevertheless, current enthusiasm for computer-mediated communications suggests that this technology is here to stay and is only likely to increase in popularity in the future.

Each of these four group decision techniques has its own set of strengths and weaknesses. The choice of one technique over another will depend on what criteria you want to emphasise and the cost–benefit trade-off. For instance, as Table 9.2 indicates, the interacting group is good for achieving commitment to a solution, brainstorming develops group cohesiveness, the nominal group technique is an inexpensive means for generating a large number of ideas, and electronic meetings minimise social pressures and conflicts.

electronic meeting | A meeting in which members interact on computers, allowing for anonymity of comments and aggregation of votes.

■ TABLE 9.2
Evaluating group effectiveness

Effectiveness criteria	Type of group			
	Interacting	Brainstorming	Nominal	Electronic
Number of ideas	Low	Moderate	High	High
Quality of ideas	Low	Moderate	High	High
Social pressure	High	Low	Moderate	Low
Money costs	Low	Low	Low	High
Speed	Moderate	Moderate	Moderate	High
Task orientation	Low	High	High	High
Potential for interpersonal conflict	High	Low	Moderate	Low
Feelings of accomplishment	High to low	High	High	High
Commitment to solution	High	Not applicable	Moderate	Moderate
Development of group cohesiveness	High	High	Moderate	Low

SOURCE: Based on J. K. Murnighan, 'Group Decision Making: What Strategies Should You Use?', *Management Review*, February 1981, p. 61.

SUMMARY AND IMPLICATIONS FOR MANAGERS

- A number of group properties show a relationship to performance. Among the more prominent are role perception, norms, status differences, the size of the group and cohesiveness.

- There is a positive relationship between role perception and an employee's performance evaluation.[70] The degree of congruence that exists between an employee and the boss in the perception of the employee's job influences the degree to which that employee will be judged as an effective performer by the boss. To the extent that the employee's role perception fulfils the boss's role expectations, the employee will receive a higher performance evaluation.

- Norms control group-member behaviour by establishing standards of right and wrong. The norms of a given group can help to explain the behaviours of its members for managers. When norms support high output, managers can expect individual performance to be markedly higher than when group norms aim to restrict output. Similarly, norms that support antisocial behaviour increase the likelihood that individuals will engage in deviant workplace activities.

- Status inequities create frustration and can adversely influence productivity and the willingness to remain with an organisation. Among individuals who are equity-sensitive, incongruence is likely to lead to reduced motivation and an increased search for ways to bring about fairness (that is, taking another job). In addition, because lower-status people tend to participate less in group discussions, groups characterised by high status differences among members are likely to inhibit input from the lower-status members and to underperform their potential.

- The impact of size on a group's performance depends on the type of task in which the group is engaged. Larger groups are more effective at fact-finding activities. Smaller groups are more effective at action-taking tasks. Our knowledge of social loafing suggests that if management uses larger groups, efforts should be made to provide measures of individual performance within the group.

- We found that cohesiveness can play an important function in influencing a group's level of productivity. Whether or not it does depends on the group's performance-related norms.

- As with the role perception–performance relationship, high congruence between a boss and employee as to the perception of the employee's job shows a significant association with high employee satisfaction.[71] Similarly, role conflict is associated with job-induced tension and job dissatisfaction.[72]

- Most people prefer to communicate with others at their own status level or a higher one, rather than with those below them.[73] As a result, we should expect satisfaction to be greater among employees whose job minimises interaction with individuals who are lower in status than themselves.

- The group size–satisfaction relationship is what one would intuitively expect: larger groups are associated with lower satisfaction.[74] As size increases, opportunities for participation and social interaction decrease, as does the ability of members to identify with the group's accomplishments. At the same time, having more members also prompts dissension, conflict and the formation of subgroups, which all act to make the group a less pleasant entity of which to be a part.

POINT / COUNTERPOINT

All Jobs Should Be Designed around Groups

● POINT

Groups, not individuals, are the ideal building blocks for an organisation. There are at least six reasons for designing all jobs around groups.

1. Small groups are good for people. They can satisfy social needs and provide support for employees in times of stress and crisis.
2. Groups are good problem-finding tools. They are better than individuals in promoting creativity and innovation.
3. In a wide variety of decision situations, groups make better decisions than individuals do.
4. Groups are very effective tools for implementation. Groups gain commitment from their members so that group decisions are likely to be carried out willingly and more successfully.
5. Groups can control and discipline individual members in ways that are often extremely difficult through impersonal, quasi-legal disciplinary systems. Group norms are powerful control devices.
6. Groups are a means by which large organisations can fend off many of the negative effects of increased size. Groups help to prevent communication lines from growing too long, the hierarchy from growing too steep and the individual from getting lost in the crowd.

Given the above argument for the value of group-based job design, what would an organisation look like that was truly designed around group functions? This might best be considered by merely taking the things that organisations do with individuals and applying them to groups. Instead of hiring individuals, they would hire groups. Similarly, they would train groups rather than individuals, pay groups rather than individuals, promote groups rather than individuals, fire groups rather than individuals, and so on.

The rapid growth of team-based organisations over the past decade suggests that we may well be on our way towards the day when almost all jobs are designed around groups.

● COUNTERPOINT

Designing jobs around groups is consistent with an ideology that says that communal and socialistic approaches are the best way to organise our society. This might have worked well in the former Soviet Union or Eastern European countries, but capitalistic countries such as Australia, New Zealand, the United States, Canada and the United Kingdom value the individual. Designing jobs around groups is inconsistent with the economic values of these countries. Moreover, as capitalism and entrepreneurship have spread throughout Eastern Europe, we should expect to see less emphasis on groups and more on the individual in workplaces throughout the world. Cultural and economic values have shaped employee attitudes towards groups.

Capitalism was built on the ethic of the individual. Individualistic cultures such as Australia, New Zealand, Canada and the United States strongly value individual achievement. They praise competition. Even in team sports, they want to identify individuals for recognition. People from these countries enjoy being part of a group in which they can maintain a strong individual identity. They don't enjoy sublimating their identity to that of the group.

The Western industrial worker likes a clear link between his or her individual effort and a visible outcome. The United States, for example, has had a considerably larger proportion of high achievers than exists in most of the world. America breeds achievers, and achievers seek personal responsibility. They would be frustrated in job situations in which their contribution is commingled and homogenised with the contributions of others.

Western workers want to be hired, evaluated and rewarded on their individual achievements. They believe in an authority and status hierarchy. They accept a system in which there are bosses and subordinates. They aren't likely to accept a group's decision on such issues as their job assignments and wage increases. It is harder yet to imagine that they would be comfortable in a system in which the sole basis for their promotion or termination would be the performance of their group.

SOURCE: Points in this argument are based on H. J. Leavitt, 'Suppose We Took Groups Seriously', in E. L. Cass and F. G. Zimmer (eds), *Man and Work in Society* (New York: Van Nostrand Reinhold, 1975), pp. 67–77.

QUESTIONS FOR REVIEW

MyOBLab Do you understand this chapter's content? Find out at **www.pearsoned.com.au/MyOBLab**

1. Compare and contrast command, task, interest and friendship groups.
2. What might motivate you to join a group?
3. Describe the five-stage group-development model.
4. What are the implications of Zimbardo's prison experiment for OB?
5. What are the Hawthorne studies? What did they tell us about group behaviour?
6. Explain the implications from the Asch experiments.
7. How are status and norms related?
8. When do groups make better decisions than individuals?
9. What is groupthink? What is its effect on decision-making quality?
10. How effective are electronic meetings?

QUESTIONS FOR CRITICAL THINKING

1. How could you use the punctuated-equilibrium model to better understand group behaviour?
2. Identify five roles you play. What behaviours do they require? Are any of these roles in conflict? If so, in what way? How do you resolve these conflicts?
3. 'High cohesiveness in a group leads to higher group productivity.' Do you agree or disagree? Explain.
4. What effect, if any, do you expect that workforce diversity has on a group's performance and satisfaction?
5. If you need to generate a lot of ideas in a short period of time, would you have a bunch of individuals generate ideas on their own, or would you band them together in groups? Explain.

EXPERIENTIAL EXERCISE

Rating Your Group Experience

Most of us have had experience in writing a report, doing an assignment or working on a project in a group in a course or in the workplace. These can be very fulfilling or very frustrating experiences.

Think back to your most recent experience of working in a group. Imagine yourself at a critical stage in the completion of that group assignment. Using your mind-set at this point, answer the following 20 questions. This questionnaire measures your feelings about that work group.

Add your scores for items 4, 6, 7, 8, 9, 10, 14, 17, 19 and 20. Obtain a corrected score by subtracting the score for each of the remaining questions from 10. For example, if you marked 3 for item 1, you would obtain a corrected score of 7 (10–3). Add the corrected scores together with the total obtained on the ten items scored directly.

Now form groups of three to five members.

1. Compare your scores. Were your group experiences generally positive or negative?
2. Assess the degree to which you felt any different about your group at the end of the project compared with how you felt at the halfway point. If your feelings changed, explain why.
3. Discuss the degree to which your feelings about the group may have influenced your group's grade.
4. Discuss to what degree you think the grade your team got on the paper influenced your subsequent feelings about the group.

SOURCE: Reproduced from N. J. Evans and P. A. Jarvis, 'The Group Attitude Scale: A Measure of Attraction to Group', *Small Group Behavior*, May 1986, pp. 203–16. Reprinted by permission of Sage Publications, Inc.

		Agree								Disagree
1.	I want to remain a member of this group.	1	2	3	4	5	6	7	8	9
2.	I like my group.	1	2	3	4	5	6	7	8	9
3.	I look forward to coming to the group.	1	2	3	4	5	6	7	8	9
4.	I don't care what happens in this group.	1	2	3	4	5	6	7	8	9
5.	I feel involved in what is happening in my group.	1	2	3	4	5	6	7	8	9
6.	If I could drop out of the group now, I would.	1	2	3	4	5	6	7	8	9
7.	I dread coming to this group.	1	2	3	4	5	6	7	8	9
8.	I wish it were possible for the group to end now.	1	2	3	4	5	6	7	8	9
9.	I am dissatisfied with the group.	1	2	3	4	5	6	7	8	9
10.	If it were possible to move to another group at this time, I would.	1	2	3	4	5	6	7	8	9
11.	I feel included in the group.	1	2	3	4	5	6	7	8	9
12.	In spite of individual differences, a feeling of unity exists in my group.	1	2	3	4	5	6	7	8	9
13.	Compared with other groups I know of, I feel my group is better than most.	1	2	3	4	5	6	7	8	9
14.	I don't feel a part of the group's activities.	1	2	3	4	5	6	7	8	9
15.	I feel it would make a difference to the group if I were not here.	1	2	3	4	5	6	7	8	9
16.	If I were told my group would not meet today, I would feel bad.	1	2	3	4	5	6	7	8	9
17.	I feel distant from the group.	1	2	3	4	5	6	7	8	9
18.	It makes a difference to me how this group turns out.	1	2	3	4	5	6	7	8	9
19.	I feel my absence would not matter to the group.	1	2	3	4	5	6	7	8	9
20.	I would not feel bad if I had to miss a meeting of this group.	1	2	3	4	5	6	7	8	9

ETHICAL DILEMMA

Discrimination against Muslims

Suicide bombers and terrorist attacks have been commonplace for decades in much of the Middle East. But not so for Australasia and North America. The attacks on the World Trade Center and the Pentagon on 11 September 2001 opened North American eyes to the reality that terrorism is a worldwide phenomenon and that no place is completely safe from terrorist attacks. Australians were shocked by the Bali bombings that killed hundreds of tourists, including over 80 Australians. As a consequence of September 11, the Bali bombings and a range of other bombings around the world, a number of Australians and Americans allowed the actions of a few Muslim extremists to shape their attitudes towards all Muslims. The result has created new challenges for managers leading diverse groups containing individuals of Middle Eastern backgrounds.

Jeff O'Connell is one of those managers. Jeff oversees a team of five computer chip designers. They work exclusively on defence contracts—designing and building high-powered chips for use by the US military. Jeff's five-person team is a textbook example of

diversity. There is a woman from Texas, an African American from New York, two Russians, and an Arab American who was born in California but whose parents both emigrated from Iran. Jeff, himself, was born in Canada but raised in the United States.

In the months following the September 11 attacks and again in 2003 following widely publicised suicide bombings at the United Nations building in Baghdad and on a bus in Jerusalem—both of which killed dozens of innocent people, including children—Jeff became aware that several of his team members were making openly disparaging remarks to Nicholas, their Iranian co-worker. They questioned his Arab friends, his religious practices and his loyalty to America. Nicholas's colleagues understood little about Islam and his religious practices. It is illegal in the United States for employers to discriminate. But that doesn't stop employees from discriminating against their colleagues. Jeff sees himself in an ethical dilemma. What, if anything, should he do when he sees team members discriminating against Nicholas because of his ethnicity?

Sometimes, the desire to maintain group harmony overrides the importance of making sound decisions. When that occurs, team members are said to engage in 'groupthink'.

- A civilian worker at a large air force base recalls the time that groupthink overcame her team's decision-making ability. She was a member of a process improvement team that an air force wing commander formed to develop a better way to handle the base's mail, which included important letters from high-ranking military individuals. The team was composed mostly of civilians, and it took almost a month to come up with a plan. The problem: the plan wasn't a process improvement. Recalls the civilian worker, 'I was horrified. What used to be eight steps, was now 19.' The team had devised a new system that resulted in each piece of mail being read by several middle managers before reaching its intended recipient. The team's new plan slowed the mail down considerably, with an average delay of two weeks. Even though the team members all knew that the new system was worse than its predecessor, no one wanted to question the team's solidarity. The problems lasted for almost an entire year. It wasn't until the wing commander who formed the team complained about the mail that the system was changed.

- During the dot-com boom of the late 1990s, Virginia Turezyn, managing director of Infinity Capital, states that she was a victim of groupthink. At first, Turezyn was sceptical about the stability of the boom. But after continually reading about start-ups turning into multimillion-dollar payoffs, she felt different. Turezyn decided to invest millions in several dot-coms, including I-drive, a company that provided electronic data storage. The problem was that I-drive was giving the storage away for free, and as a result the company was losing money. Turezyn recalls one board meeting at I-drive where she spoke up, to no avail. 'We're spending way too much money!'

she screamed. The younger executives shook their heads and replied that if they charged for storage, they would lose their customers. Says Turezyn, 'I started to think, "Maybe I'm just too old. Maybe I really don't get it."' Unfortunately, Turezyn *did* get it. I-drive later filed for bankruptcy.

- Steve Blank, an entrepreneur, also fell victim to groupthink. Blank was a dot-com investor, and he participated on advisory boards of several internet start-ups. During meetings for one such start-up, a Web photo finisher, Blank tried to persuade his fellow board members to change the business model to be more traditional. Recalls Blank, 'I went to those meetings and starting saying things like "Maybe you should spend that $10 million you just raised on acquiring a customer base rather than building a brand." The CEO told me, "Steve, you just don't get it—all the rules have changed."' The team didn't take Blank's advice, and Blank says that he lost hundreds of thousands of dollars on the deal.

QUESTIONS

1. What are some factors that led to groupthink in the above cases? What can teams do to attempt to reduce groupthink from occurring?

2. How might differences in status among group members contribute to groupthink? For example, how might lower-status members react to a group's decision? Are lower-status members more or less likely to be dissenters? Why might higher-status group members be more effective dissenters?

3. How do group norms contribute to groupthink? Could group norms guard against the occurrence of groupthink? As a manager, how would you try to cultivate norms that prevent groupthink?

4. How might group characteristics such as size and cohesiveness affect groupthink?

SOURCES: Based on C. Hawn, 'Fear and Posing', *Forbes*, 25 March 2002, pp. 22–25; and J. Sandberg, 'Some Ideas Are So Bad That Only Team Efforts Can Account for Them', *Wall Street Journal*, 29 September 2004, p. B.1.

ENDNOTES

1. Interview between Dr Bruce Millett and Safarudin Ban, 16 December 2005.
2. L. R. Sayles, 'Work Group Behavior and the Larger Organization', in C. Arensburg, et al. (eds), *Research in Industrial Relations* (New York: Harper & Row, 1957), pp. 131–45.
3. J. F. McGrew, J. G. Bilotta and J. M. Deeney, 'Software Team Formation and Decay: Extending the Standard Model for Small Groups', *Small Group Research*, vol. 30, no. 2, 1999, pp. 209–34.
4. B. W. Tuckman, 'Developmental Sequences in Small Groups', *Psychological Bulletin*, June 1965, pp. 384–99; B. W. Tuckman and M. C. Jensen, 'Stages of Small-Group Development Revisited', *Group and Organizational Studies*, December 1977, pp. 419–27; and M. F. Maples, 'Group Development: Extending Tuckman's Theory', *Journal for Specialists in Group Work*, Fall 1988, pp. 17–23; and K. Vroman and J. Kovacich, 'Computer-Mediated Interdisciplinary Teams: Theory and Reality', *Journal of Interprofessional Care*, vol. 16, no. 2, 2002, pp. 159–70.
5. J. F. George and L. M. Jessup, 'Groups over Time: What Are We Really Studying?', *International Journal of Human–Computer Studies*, vol. 47, no. 3, 1997, pp. 497–511.
6. R. C. Ginnett, 'The Airline Cockpit Crew', in J. R. Hackman (ed.), *Groups That Work (and Those That Don't)* (San Francisco: Jossey-Bass, 1990).
7. C. J. G. Gersick, 'Time and Transition in Work Teams: Toward a New Model of Group Development', *Academy of Management Journal*, March 1988, pp. 9–41; C. J. G. Gersick, 'Marking Time: Predictable Transitions in Task Groups', *Academy of Management Journal*, June 1989, pp. 274–309; M. J. Waller, J. M. Conte, C. B. Gibson and M. A. Carpenter, 'The Effect of Individual Perceptions of Deadlines on Team Performance', *Academy of Management Review*, October 2001, pp. 586–600; and A. Chang, P. Bordia and J. Duck, 'Punctuated Equilibrium and Linear Progression: Toward a New Understanding of Group Development', *Academy of Management Journal*, February 2003, pp. 106–17; see also H. Arrow, M. S. Poole, K. B. Henry, S. Wheelan and R. Moreland, 'Time, Change, and Development: The Temporal Perspective on Groups', *Small Group Research*, February 2004, pp. 73–105.
8. Gersick, 'Time and Transition in Work Teams: Toward a New Model of Group Development'; and Gersick, 'Marking Time: Predictable Transitions in Task Groups'.
9. A. Seers and S. Woodruff, 'Temporal Pacing in Task Forces: Group Development or Deadline Pressure?', *Journal of Management*, vol. 23, no. 2, 1997, pp. 169–87.
10. S. Lieberman, 'The Effects of Changes in Roles on the Attitudes of Role Occupants', *Human Relations*, November 1956, pp. 385–402.
11. See D. M. Rousseau, *Psychological Contracts in Organizations: Understanding Written and Unwritten Agreements* (Thousand Oaks, CA: Sage, 1995); E. W. Morrison and S. L. Robinson, 'When Employees Feel Betrayed: A Model of How Psychological Contract Violation Develops', *Academy of Management Review*, April 1997, pp. 226–56; D. Rousseau and R. Schalk (eds), *Psychological Contracts in Employment: Cross-Cultural Perspectives* (San Francisco: Jossey-Bass, 2000); L. Sels, M. Janssens and I. Van den Brande, 'Assessing the Nature of Psychological Contracts: A Validation of Six Dimensions', *Journal of Organizational Behavior*, June 2004, pp. 461–88; and C. Hui, C. Lee and D. M. Rousseau, 'Psychological Contract and Organizational Citizenship Behavior in China: Investigating Generalizability and Instrumentality', *Journal of Applied Psychology*, April 2004, pp. 311–21.
12. See M. F. Peterson et al., 'Role Conflict, Ambiguity, and Overload: A 21-Nation Study', *Academy of Management Journal*, April 1995, pp. 429–52; and I. H. Settles, R. M. Sellers and A. Damas, Jr, 'One Role or Two? The Function of Psychological Separation in Role Conflict', *Journal of Applied Psychology*, June 2002, pp. 574–82.
13. P. G. Zimbardo, C. Haney, W. C. Banks and D. Jaffe, 'The Mind Is a Formidable Jailer: A Pirandellian Prison', *New York Times*, 8 April 1973, pp. 38–60; and C. Haney and P. G. Zimbardo, 'Social Roles and Role-Playing: Observations from the Stanford Prison Study', *Behavioral and Social Science Teacher*, January 1973, pp. 25–45.
14. For a review of the research on group norms, see J. R.Hackman, 'Group Influences on Individuals in Organizations', in M. D. Dunnette and L. M. Hough (eds), *Handbook of Industrial & Organizational Psychology*, 2nd ed., vol. 3 (Palo Alto, CA: Consulting Psychologists Press, 1992), pp. 235–50. For a more recent discussion, see M. G. Ehrhart and S. E. Naumann, 'Organizational Citizenship Behavior in Work Groups: A Group Norms Approach', *Journal of Applied Pyschology*, December 2004, pp. 960–74.
15. E. Mayo, *The Human Problems of an Industrial Civilization* (New York: Macmillan, 1933); and F. J. Roethlisberger and W. J. Dickson, *Management and the Worker* (Cambridge, MA: Harvard University Press, 1939).
16. Adapted from P. S. Goodman, E. Ravlin and M. Schminke, 'Understanding Groups in Organizations', in L. L. Cummings and B. M. Staw (eds), *Research in Organizational Behavior*, vol. 9 (Greenwich, CT: JAI Press, 1987), p. 159.
17. See, for instance, G. Blau, 'Influence of Group Lateness on Individual Lateness: A Cross-Level Examination', *Academy of Management Journal*, October 1995, pp. 1483–96; and D. F. Caldwell and C. A. O'Reilly, III, 'The Determinants of Team-Based Innovation in Organizations: The Role of Social Influence', *Small Group Research*, August 2003, pp. 497–517.
18. C. A. Kiesler and S. B. Kiesler, *Conformity* (Reading, MA: Addison-Wesley, 1969).
19. Ibid, p. 27.
20. S. E. Asch, 'Effects of Group Pressure upon the Modification and Distortion of Judgments', in H. Guetzkow (ed.), *Groups, Leadership and Men* (Pittsburgh, PA: Carnegie Press, 1951), pp. 177–90; and S. E. Asch, 'Studies of Independence and Conformity: A Minority of One Against a Unanimous Majority', *Psychological Monographs: General and Applied*, vol. 70, no. 9, 1956, pp. 1–70.
21. R. Bond and P. B. Smith, 'Culture and Conformity: A Meta-Analysis of Studies Using Asch's (1952, 1956) Line Judgment Task', *Psychological Bulletin*, January 1996, pp. 111–37.
22. See S. L. Robinson and R. J. Bennett, 'A Typology of Deviant Workplace Behaviors: A Multidimensional Scaling Study', *Academy of Management Journal*,

April 1995, pp. 555–72; S. L. Robinson and J. Greenberg, 'Employees Behaving Badly: Dimensions, Determinants, and Dilemmas in the Study of Workplace Deviance', in D. M. Rousseau and C. Cooper (eds), *Trends in Organizational Behavior*, vol. 5 (New York: John Wiley & Sons, 1998); S. L. Robinson and A. M. O'Leary-Kelly, 'Monkey See, Monkey Do: The Influence of Work Groups on the Antisocial Behavior of Employees', *Academy of Management Journal*, December 1998, pp. 658–72; and R. J. Bennett and S. L. Robinson, 'The Past, Present, and Future of Workplace Deviance', in J. Greenberg (ed.), *Organizational Behavior: The State of the Science*, 2nd ed. (Mahwah, NJ: Lawrence Erlbaum Associates, 2003), pp. 237–71.

23. C. M. Pearson, L. M. Andersson and C. L. Porath, 'Assessing and Attacking Workplace Civility', *Organizational Dynamics*, vol. 29, no. 2, 2000, p. 130; see also C. Pearson, L. M. Andersson and C. L. Porath, 'Workplace Incivility', in S. Fox and P. E. Spector (eds), *Counterproductive Work Behavior: Investigations of Actors and Targets* (Washington, DC: American Psychological Association, 2005), pp. 177–200.

24. Robinson and O'Leary-Kelly, 'Monkey See, Monkey Do'.

25. A. Erez, H. Elms and E. Fong, 'Lying, Cheating, Stealing: It Happens More in Groups', Paper presented at the European Business Ethics Network Annual Conference, Budapest, 30 August 2003.

26. S. L. Robinson and M. S. Kraatz, 'Constructing the Reality of Normative Behavior: The Use of Neutralization Strategies by Organizational Deviants', in R. W. Griffin and A. O'Leary-Kelly (eds), *Dysfunctional Behavior in Organizations: Violent and Deviant Behavior* (Houston, TX: Elsevier Science/JAI Press, 1998), pp. 203–20.

27. See, for instance, D. G. Wagner and J. Berger, 'Status Characteristics Theory: The Growth of a Program', in J. Berger and M. Zelditch (eds), *Theoretical Research Programs: Studies in the Growth of a Theory* (Stanford, CA: Stanford University Press, 1993), pp. 23–63; J. Berger, C. L. Ridgeway and M. Zelditch, 'Construction of Status and Referential Structures', *Sociological Theory*, July 2002, pp. 157–79; and J. S. Bunderson, 'Recognizing and Utilizing Expertise in Work Groups: A Status Characteristics Perspective', *Administrative Science Quarterly*, December 2003, pp. 557–91.

28. See R. S. Feldman, *Social Psychology*, 3rd ed. (Upper Saddle River, NJ: Prentice Hall, 2001), pp. 464–65.

29. Cited in Hackman, 'Group Influences on Individuals in Organizations', p. 236.

30. O. J. Harvey and C. Consalvi, 'Status and Conformity to Pressures in Informal Groups', *Journal of Abnormal and Social Psychology*, Spring 1960, pp. 182–87.

31. J. A. Wiggins, F. Dill and R. D. Schwartz, 'On "Status-Liability"', *Sociometry*, April–May 1965, pp. 197–209.

32. See J. M. Levine and R. L. Moreland, 'Progress in Small Group Research', in J. T. Spence, J. M. Darley and D. J. Foss (eds), *Annual Review of Psychology*, vol. 41 (Palo Alto, CA: Annual Reviews Inc., 1990), pp. 585–634; S. D. Silver, B. P. Cohen and J. H. Crutchfield, 'Status Differentiation and Information Exchange in Face-to-Face and Computer-Mediated Idea Generation', *Social Psychology Quarterly*, 1994, pp. 108–23; and J. M. Twenge, 'Changes in Women's Assertiveness in Response to Status and Roles: A Cross-Temporal Meta-Analysis, 1931–1993', *Journal of Personality and Social Psychology*, July 2001, pp. 133–45.

33. J. Greenberg, 'Equity and Workplace Status: A Field Experiment', *Journal of Applied Psychology*, November 1988, pp. 606–13.

34. See G. Hofstede, *Cultures and Organizations: Software of the Mind* (New York, McGraw-Hill, 1991).

35. This section is based on P. R. Harris and R. T. Moran, *Managing Cultural Differences*, 5th ed. (Houston: Gulf Publishing, 1999).

36. E. J. Thomas and C. F. Fink, 'Effects of Group Size', *Psychological Bulletin*, July 1963, pp. 371–84; A. P. Hare, *Handbook of Small Group Research* (New York: Free Press, 1976); and M. E. Shaw, *Group Dynamics: The Psychology of Small Group Behavior*, 3rd ed. (New York: McGraw-Hill, 1981).

37. G. H. Seijts and G. P. Latham, 'The Effects of Goal Setting and Group Size on Performance in a Social Dilemma', *Canadian Journal of Behavioural Science*, vol. 32, no. 2, 2000, pp. 104–16.

38. Shaw, *Group Dynamics: The Psychology of Small Group Behavior*.

39. See, for instance, D. R. Comer, 'A Model of Social Loafing in Real Work Groups', *Human Relations*, June 1995, pp. 647–67; S. M. Murphy, S. J. Wayne, R. C. Liden and B. Erdogan, 'Understanding Social Loafing: The Role of Justice Perceptions and Exchange Relationships', *Human Relations*, January 2003, pp. 61–84; R. C. Liden, S. J. Wayne, R. A. Jaworski and N. Bennett, 'Social Loafing: A Field Investigation', *Journal of Management*, April 2004, pp. 285–304.

40. W. Moede, 'Die Richtlinien der Leistungs-Psychologie', *Industrielle Psychotechnik*, vol. 4, 1927, pp. 193–207. See also D. A. Kravitz and B. Martin, 'Ringelmann Rediscovered: The Original Article', *Journal of Personality and Social Psychology*, May 1986, pp. 936–41.

41. See, for example, J. A. Shepperd, 'Productivity Loss in Performance Groups: A Motivation Analysis', *Psychological Bulletin*, January 1993, pp. 67–81; and S. J. Karau and K. D. Williams, 'Social Loafing: A Meta-Analytic Review and Theoretical Integration', *Journal of Personality and Social Psychology*, October 1993, pp. 681–706.

42. S. G. Harkins and K. Szymanski, 'Social Loafing and Group Evaluation', *Journal of Personality and Social Psychology*, December 1989, pp. 934–41.

43. See P. C. Earley, 'Social Loafing and Collectivism: A Comparison of the United States and the People's Republic of China', *Administrative Science Quarterly*, December 1989, pp. 565–81; and P. C. Earley, 'East Meets West Meets Mideast: Further Explorations of Collectivistic and Individualistic Work Groups', *Academy of Management Journal*, April 1993, pp. 319–48.

44. Thomas and Fink, 'Effects of Group Size'; Hare, *Handbook*; Shaw, *Group Dynamics*; and P. Yetton and P. Bottger, 'The Relationships among Group Size, Member Ability, Social Decision Schemes, and Performance', *Organizational Behavior and Human Performance*, October 1983, pp. 145–59.

45. For some of the controversy surrounding the definition of cohesion, see J. Keyton and J. Springston, 'Redefining Cohesiveness in Groups', *Small Group Research*, May 1990, pp. 234–54.

46. B. Mullen and C. Cooper, 'The Relation between Group Cohesiveness and Performance: An Integration', *Psychological Bulletin*, March 1994, pp. 210–27; P. M. Podsakoff, S. B. MacKenzie and M. Ahearne, 'Moderating Effects of Goal Acceptance on the Relationship between Group Cohesiveness and Productivity', *Journal of Applied Psychology*, December 1997, pp. 974–83; and D. J. Beal, R. R. Cohen, M. J. Burke and C. L. McLendon, 'Cohesion and Performance in Groups:

A Meta-Analytic Clarification of Construct Relations', *Journal of Applied Psychology*, December 2003, pp. 989–1004.

47. Ibid.

48. Based on J. L. Gibson, J. M. Ivancevich and J. H. Donnelly, Jr, *Organizations*, 8th ed. (Burr Ridge, IL: Irwin, 1994), p. 323.

49. N. Foote, E. Matson, L. Weiss and E. Wenger, 'Leveraging Group Knowledge for High-Performance Decision-Making', *Organizational Dynamics*, vol. 31, no. 2, 2002, pp. 280–95.

50. See N. R. F. Maier, 'Assets and Liabilities in Group Problem Solving: The Need for an Integrative Function', *Psychological Review*, April 1967, pp. 239–49; G. W. Hill, 'Group Versus Individual Performance: Are N+1 Heads Better Than One?', *Psychological Bulletin*, May 1982, pp. 517–39; A. E. Schwartz and J. Levin, 'Better Group Decision Making', *Supervisory Management*, June 1990, p. 4; and R. F. Martell and M. R. Borg, 'A Comparison of the Behavioral Rating Accuracy of Groups and Individuals', *Journal of Applied Psychology*, February 1993, pp. 43–50.

51. D. Gigone and R. Hastie, 'Proper Analysis of the Accuracy of Group Judgments', *Psychological Bulletin*, January 1997, pp. 149–67.

52. See, for example, W. C. Swap and Associates, *Group Decision Making* (Newbury Park, CA: Sage, 1984).

53. I. L. Janis, *Groupthink* (Boston: Houghton Mifflin, 1982); W. Park, 'A Review of Research on Groupthink', *Journal of Behavioral Decision Making*, July 1990, pp. 229–45; C. P. Neck and G. Moorhead, 'Groupthink Remodeled: The Importance of Leadership, Time Pressure, and Methodical Decision-Making Procedures', *Human Relations*, May 1995, pp. 537–58; J. N. Choi and M. U. Kim, 'The Organizational Application of Groupthink and Its Limits in Organizations', *Journal of Applied Psychology*, April 1999, pp. 297–306; and W. W. Park, 'A Comprehensive Empirical Investigation of the Relationships among Variables of the Groupthink Model', *Journal of Organizational Behavior*, December 2000, pp. 873–87.

54. Janis, *Groupthink*.

55. Ibid.

56. G. Moorhead, R. Ference and C. P. Neck, 'Group Decision Fiascos Continue: Space Shuttle *Challenger* and a Revised Groupthink Framework', *Human Relations*, May 1991, pp. 539–50; E. J.

Chisson, *The Hubble Wars* (New York: 1994); and C. Covault, 'Columbia Revelations Alarming E-Mails Speak for Themselves. But Administrator O'Keefe is More Concerned about Board Findings on NASA Decision-Making', *Aviation Week & Space Technology*, 3 March 2003, p. 26.

57. J. Eaton, 'Management Communication: The Threat of Groupthink', *Corporate Communication*, vol. 6, no. 4, 2001, pp. 183–92.

58. M. E. Turner and A. R. Pratkanis, 'Mitigating Groupthink by Stimulating Constructive Conflict', in C. De Dreu and E. Van de Vliert (eds), *Using Conflict in Organizations* (London: Sage, 1997), pp. 53–71.

59. Ibid, p. 68.

60. See N. R. F. Maier, *Principles of Human Relations* (New York: Wiley, 1952); I. L. Janis, *Groupthink: Psychological Studies of Policy Decisions and Fiascoes*, 2nd ed. (Boston: Houghton Mifflin, 1982); C. R. Leana, 'A Partial Test of Janis' Groupthink Model: Effects of Group Cohesiveness and Leader Behavior on Defective Decision Making', *Journal of Management*, Spring 1985, pp. 5–17; L. Thompson, *Making the Team: A Guide for Managers* (Upper Saddle River, NJ: Prentice Hall, 2000), pp. 116–18; and N. Richardson Ahlfinger and J. K. Esser, 'Testing the Groupthink Model: Effects of Promotional Leadership and Conformity Predisposition', *Social Behavior & Personality*, vol. 29, no. 1, 2001, pp. 31–41.

61. See D. J. Isenberg, 'Group Polarization: A Critical Review and Meta-Analysis', *Journal of Personality and Social Psychology*, December 1986, pp. 1141–51; J. L. Hale and F. J. Boster, 'Comparing Effect Coded Models of Choice Shifts', *Communication Research Reports*, April 1988, pp. 180–86; and P. W. Paese, M. Bieser and M. E. Tubbs, 'Framing Effects and Choice Shifts in Group Decision Making', *Organizational Behavior and Human Decision Processes*, October 1993, pp. 149–65.

62. See, for example, N. Kogan and M. A. Wallach, 'Risk Taking as a Function of the Situation, the Person, and the Group', in *New Directions in Psychology*, vol. 3 (New York: Holt, Rinehart and Winston, 1967); and M. A. Wallach, N. Kogan and D. J. Bem, 'Group Influence on Individual Risk Taking', *Journal of Abnormal and Social Psychology*, vol. 65, 1962, pp. 75–86.

63. R. D. Clark III, 'Group-Induced Shift toward Risk: A Critical Appraisal', *Psychological Bulletin*, October 1971, pp. 251–70.

64. A. F. Osborn, *Applied Imagination: Principles and Procedures of Creative Thinking*, 3rd ed. (New York: Scribner, 1963). See also T. Rickards, 'Brainstorming Revisited: A Question of Context', *International Journal of Management Reviews*, March 1999, pp. 91–110; K. L. Dugosh, P. B. Paulus, E. J. Roland and H-C. Yang, 'Cognitive Stimulation in Brainstorming', *Journal of Personality & Social Psychology*, November 2000, pp. 722–35; and R. P. McGlynn, D. McGurk, V. S. Effland, N. L. Johll and D. J. Harding, 'Brainstorming and Task Performance in Groups Constrained by Evidence', *Organizational Behavior and Human Decision Processes*, January 2004, pp. 75–87.

65. N. L. Kerr and R. S. Tindale, 'Group Performance and Decision-Making', *Annual Review of Psychology*, vol. 55, 2004, pp. 623–55.

66. See A. L. Delbecq, A. H. Van deVen and D. H. Gustafson, *Group Techniques for Program Planning: A Guide to Nominal and Delphi Processes* (Glenview, IL: Scott, Foresman, 1975); and P. B. Paulus and H.-C. Yang, 'Idea Generation in Groups: A Basis for Creativity in Organizations', *Organizational Behavior and Human Decision Processing*, May 2000, pp. 76–87.

67. C. Faure, 'Beyond Brainstorming: Effects of Different Group Procedures on Selection of Ideas and Satisfaction with the Process', *Journal of Creative Behavior*, vol. 38, 2004, pp. 13–34.

68. See, for instance, A. B. Hollingshead and J. E. McGrath, 'Computer-Assisted Groups: A Critical Review of the Empirical Research', in R. A. Guzzo and E. Salas (eds), *Team Effectiveness and Decision Making in Organizations* (San Fransisco: Jossey-Bass, 1995), pp. 46–78.

69. B. B. Baltes, M. W. Dickson, M. P. Sherman, C. C. Bauer and J. LaGanke, 'Computer-Mediated Communication and Group Decision Making: A Meta-Analysis', *Organizational Behavior and Human Decision Processes*, January 2002, pp. 156–79.

70. T. P. Verney, 'Role Perception Congruence, Performance, and Satisfaction', in D. J. Vredenburgh and R. S. Schuler (eds), 'Effective Management: Research and Application',

Proceedings of the 20th Annual Eastern Academy of Management, Pittsburgh, PA, May 1983, pp. 24–27.

71. Ibid.

72. M. Van Sell, A. P. Brief and R. S. Schuler, 'Role Conflict and Role Ambiguity: Integration of the Literature and Directions for Future Research', *Human Relations*, January 1981, pp. 43–71;

A. G. Bedeian and A. A. Armenakis, 'A Path-Analytic Study of the Consequences of Role Conflict and Ambiguity', *Academy of Management Journal*, June 1981, pp. 417–24; and P. L. Perrewe, K. L. Zellars, G. R. Ferris, A. M. Rossi, C. J. Kacmar and D. A. Ralston, 'Neutralizing Job Stressors: Political Skill as an Antidote to the

Dysfunctional Consequences of Role Conflict', *Academy of Management Journal*, February 2004, pp. 141–52.

73. Shaw, *Group Dynamics*.

74. B. Mullen, C. Symons, L. Hu and E. Salas, 'Group Size, Leadership Behavior, and Subordinate Satisfaction', *Journal of General Psychology*, April 1989, pp. 155–70.

10

UNDERSTANDING WORK TEAMS

CHAPTER OUTLINE

WHY HAVE TEAMS BECOME SO POPULAR?

DIFFERENCES BETWEEN GROUPS AND TEAMS

TYPES OF TEAMS

CREATING EFFECTIVE TEAMS

TURNING INDIVIDUALS INTO TEAM PLAYERS

TEAMS AND QUALITY MANAGEMENT

BEWARE! TEAMS AREN'T ALWAYS THE ANSWER

LEARNING OBJECTIVES

AFTER STUDYING THIS CHAPTER, YOU SHOULD BE ABLE TO:

1. EXPLAIN THE GROWING POPULARITY OF TEAMS IN ORGANISATIONS

2. CONTRAST TEAMS WITH GROUPS

3. IDENTIFY FOUR TYPES OF TEAMS

4. SPECIFY THE CHARACTERISTICS OF EFFECTIVE TEAMS

5. EXPLAIN HOW ORGANISATIONS CAN CREATE TEAM PLAYERS

6. DESCRIBE CONDITIONS WHEN INDIVIDUALS ARE PREFERRED OVER TEAMS

Andreas Lam (seated right) doesn't feel overawed by changing technology. In fact, as CEO of Integral Systems in Singapore, he appreciates the value and opportunities in computer and internet-related technologies. 'Such technologies allow my team to collaborate effectively from anywhere in the world', he says.

INTEGRAL SYSTEMS PTY LTD, a factory automation systems solution provider that works with worldwide customers, suppliers and strategic alliance partners, embarked on a process to become more of a virtual organisation by leveraging internet technology. Based in Singapore, with world-class infrastructure and the availability of affordable new technologies in communication, networking, computer hardware and server applications, Integral Systems was able to form virtual project teams utilising expertise across different countries. The virtual teams organise videoconferencing and communicate with each other regularly at virtually no cost.

'The use of computers, webcams, PDAs, internet-enabled phones and a free communication software called Skype enable live and frequent and detailed discussions between team members', said Andreas Lam, the company's CEO. 'We want to minimise the change in people's behaviour and familiar working environment. It's like you do it every day. You pick up a phone to talk to your suppliers and you walk to your colleagues' desk and have a face-to-face chat.' The only issue is how comfortable and effective is the communication when looking at and talking to another person via a flat screen?

Senior project director Stuart Wong, who manages various virtual teams, ensures that the virtual team members don't have any sense of distance between them while working together. Rules and guidelines have been designed to improve the 'feel of the environment'. The 'real physical presence' of participants in a videoconference can be simulated by careful positioning of the high-resolution webcam and adjustment of the lighting to create the effect of eye-to-eye contact and with the person seen seated at their desk. Disruptions to work can be minimised through booking appointments, monitoring members' availability and avoiding surprise screen pop-ups. Working straight from an FTP server also ensures that the project and technical information is updated and stored for sharing by worldwide members through the internet via security passwords.

The result is significant enhancement of the coordination and design phases of projects using virtual teams. Integral Systems has even used internet technology to enable team members to participate in the implementation, testing and commissioning of projects in remote sites through the use of remote control software. Programmers can link up to internet-enabled machines and systems to remotely access the programs, and to debug and test run them with local technicians assisting on site. This has reduced the time spent on travelling, and ensures active participation of virtual team members at each phase of a project.

However, the success of Integral Systems' virtual teams in completing projects is highly dependent on the computer skills and attitudes of the individuals involved. Team members identify difficulty in creating close partnerships and team spirit as a problem arising from the lack of socialising and physically intimate interactions such as shaking hands. Recognising this problem, all of Integral Systems' virtual team members are sent on remote site visits as a way to build rapport. New staff members are formally introduced to their potential team colleagues and are assigned a 'buddy', or mentor, who provides a detailed tour of the work facility.

Teams are increasingly becoming the primary means for organising work in contemporary business firms. Andreas Lam has pointed to the use of internet technologies at his organisation to overcome some of the difficulties of geographical dislocation. As the CEO of Integral Systems, Andreas appreciates the value of supporting the development of effective teams under any circumstances.

A team effort is a lot of people doing what I say.
Michael Winner

WHY HAVE TEAMS BECOME SO POPULAR?

Decades ago, when organisations such as Qantas, Volvo and the Australian Taxation Office introduced teams into their production processes, it made news because no one else was doing it. Today, it's just the opposite. It is the organisation that *doesn't* use teams that has become newsworthy.

How do we explain the current popularity of teams? The evidence suggests that teams typically outperform individuals when the tasks being done require multiple skills, judgment and experience.[1] As organisations have restructured themselves to compete more effectively and efficiently, they have turned to teams as a better way to use employee talents. Management has found that teams are more flexible and responsive to changing events than are traditional departments or other forms of permanent groupings. Teams have the capability to assemble, deploy, refocus and disband quickly.

But don't overlook the motivational properties of teams. Consistent with our discussion on the role of employee involvement as a motivator, teams facilitate employee participation in operating decisions. For instance, some assembly-line workers at the agricultural manufacturing company John Deere are part of sales teams that call on customers.[2] These workers know the products better than any traditional salesperson; and by travelling and speaking with farmers, these hourly workers develop new skills and become more involved in their jobs. So, another explanation for the popularity of teams is that they are an effective means for management to democratise their organisations and increase employee motivation.

DIFFERENCES BETWEEN GROUPS AND TEAMS

work group | A group that
interacts primarily to share
information and to make
decisions to help each
group member perform
within his or her area of
responsibility.

Groups and teams aren't the same thing. In this section, we want to define and clarify the difference between a work group and a work team.[3] In the previous chapter, we defined a *group* as two or more individuals, interacting and interdependent, who have come together to achieve particular objectives. A **work group** is a group that interacts primarily to share information and to make decisions to help each member perform within his or her area of responsibility.

Work groups have no need or opportunity to engage in collective work that requires joint effort. So, their performance is merely the summation of each group member's individual contribution. There is no positive synergy that would create an overall level of performance that is greater than the sum of the inputs.

work team | A group
whose individual efforts
result in a performance
that is greater than the
sum of the individual
inputs.

A **work team** generates positive synergy through coordinated effort. Their individual efforts result in a level of performance that is greater than the sum of those individual inputs. Figure 10.1 highlights the differences between work groups and work teams.

These definitions help to clarify why so many organisations have recently restructured work processes around teams. Management is looking for that positive synergy that will allow their organisations to increase performance. The extensive use of teams creates the *potential* for an organisation to generate greater outputs with no increase in inputs. Notice, however, we said 'potential'. There is nothing inherently magical in the creation of teams

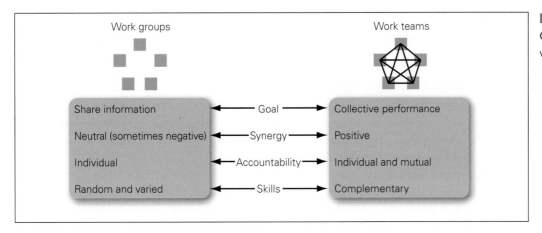

Work groups

Work teams

Share information	← Goal →	Collective performance
Neutral (sometimes negative)	← Synergy →	Positive
Individual	← Accountability →	Individual and mutual
Random and varied	← Skills →	Complementary

that ensures the achievement of this positive synergy. Merely calling a *group* a *team* doesn't automatically increase its performance. As we show later in this chapter, effective teams have certain common characteristics. If management hopes to gain increases in organisational performance through the use of teams, it will need to ensure that its teams possess these characteristics.

TYPES OF TEAMS

Teams can do a variety of things. They can make products, provide services, negotiate deals, coordinate projects, offer advice and make decisions.[4] In this section we describe the four most common types of teams you are likely to find in an organisation: *problem-solving teams*, *self-managed work teams*, *cross-functional teams* and *virtual teams* (see Figure 10.2).

PROBLEM-SOLVING TEAMS

If we look back 20 years or so, teams were just beginning to grow in popularity, and most of those teams took a similar form. They were typically composed of from 5 to 12 employees from the same department who met for a few hours each week to discuss ways of improving quality, efficiency and the work environment.[5] We call these **problem-solving teams**.

In problem-solving teams, members share ideas or offer suggestions on how work processes and methods can be improved; however, they rarely have the authority to unilaterally implement any of their suggested actions. For instance, the global investment banker Merrill Lynch created a problem-solving team to specifically figure out ways to

problem-solving teams | Groups of from 5 to 12 employees from the same department who meet for a few hours each week to discuss ways of improving quality, efficiency and the work environment.

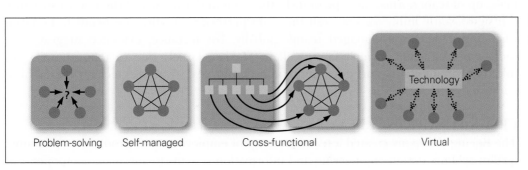

Problem-solving   Self-managed   Cross-functional   Virtual

reduce the number of days it took to open up a new cash management account.[6] By suggesting cuts in the number of steps in the process from 46 to 36, the team was able to reduce the average number of days required from 15 to 8.

SELF-MANAGED WORK TEAMS

Problem-solving teams were on the right track, but they didn't go far enough in getting employees involved in work-related decisions and processes. This led to experimentation with truly autonomous teams that could not only solve problems but also implement solutions and take full responsibility for outcomes.

self-managed work teams
| Groups of from 10 to 15 people who take on responsibilities of their former supervisors.

Self-managed work teams are groups of employees (typically 10 to 15 in number) who perform highly related or interdependent jobs and take on many of the responsibilities of their former supervisors.[7] Typically, this includes planning and scheduling of work, assigning tasks to members, collective control over the pace of work, making operating decisions, taking action on problems, and working with suppliers and customers. Fully self-managed work teams even select their own members and have the members evaluate each other's performance. As a result, supervisory positions take on decreased importance and may even be eliminated.

A factory at Eaton Corporation's Aeroquip Global Hose Division provides an example of how self-managed teams are being used in industry.[8] Their factory makes hydraulic hose that is used in trucks, tractors and other heavy equipment. In 1994, to improve quality and productivity, Eaton-Aeroquip's management threw out the assembly line and organised the plant's 285 workers into more than 50 self-managed teams. Workers were suddenly free to participate in decisions that were previously reserved solely for management—for instance, the teams set their own schedules, selected new members, negotiated with suppliers, made calls on customers, and disciplined members who created problems. And the results? Between 1993 and 1999, response time to customer concerns improved 99 per cent; productivity and manufacturing output both increased by more than 50 per cent; and accident rates dropped by more than half.

Business periodicals are filled with articles describing successful applications of self-managed teams. But a word of caution needs to be offered. Some organisations have been disappointed with the results from self-managed teams. For instance, they don't seem to work well during organisational downsizing. Employees often view cooperating with the team concept as an exercise in assisting one's own executioner.[9] The overall research on the effectiveness of self-managed work teams hasn't been uniformly positive.[10] Moreover, although individuals on these teams do tend to report higher levels of job satisfaction, they also sometimes have higher absenteeism and turnover rates. Inconsistency in findings suggests that the effectiveness of self-managed teams is situationally dependent.[11] In addition to downsizing, factors such as the strength and make-up of team norms, the type of tasks the team undertakes, and the reward structure can significantly influence how well the team performs. Finally, care needs to be taken when introducing self-managed teams globally. For instance, evidence suggests that these types of teams haven't fared well in Mexico, largely due to that culture's low tolerance of ambiguity and uncertainty and employees' strong respect for hierarchical authority.[12]

CROSS-FUNCTIONAL TEAMS

The Boeing Company created a team made up of employees from production, planning, quality, tooling, design engineering and information systems to automate components of the production process on the company's C-17 aircraft program. The team's suggestions resulted in drastically reduced cycle time and cost, and improved quality on the program.[13] This example illustrates the use of **cross-functional teams**. These are teams made up of employees from about the same hierarchical level, but from different work areas, who come together to accomplish a task.

cross-functional teams | Employees from about the same hierarchical level, but from different work areas, who come together to accomplish a task.

Many organisations have used horizontal, boundary-spanning groups for decades. For example, IBM created a large task force in the 1960s—made up of employees from across departments in the company—to develop its highly successful System 360. And a *task force* is really nothing other than a temporary cross-functional team. Similarly, *committees* composed of members from across departmental lines are another example of cross-functional teams. But the popularity of cross-discipline work teams exploded in the late 1980s. For instance, all the major automobile manufacturers—including Toyota, Honda, Nissan, BMW, General Motors (GM), Ford and DaimlerChrysler—currently use this form of team to coordinate complex projects. And Harley-Davidson relies on specific cross-functional teams to manage each line of its motorcycles. These teams include Harley employees from design, manufacturing and purchasing, as well as representatives from key outside suppliers.[14]

Cross-functional teams are an effective means for allowing people from diverse areas within an organisation (or even between organisations) to exchange information, develop new ideas and solve problems, and coordinate complex projects. Of course, cross-functional teams are no picnic to manage. Their early stages of development are often very time-consuming as members learn to work with diversity and complexity. It takes time to build trust and teamwork, especially among people from different backgrounds with different experiences and perspectives.

VIRTUAL TEAMS

The previous types of teams do their work face-to-face. **Virtual teams** use computer technology to tie together physically dispersed members in order to achieve a common goal.[15] They allow people to collaborate online—using communication links such as wide-area networks, videoconferencing or email—whether they are only a room away or continents apart.

virtual teams | Teams that use computer technology to tie together physically dispersed members in order to achieve a common goal.

Virtual teams can do all the things that other teams do—share information, make decisions, complete tasks. And they can include members from the same organisation, or link an organisation's members with employees from other organisations (such as suppliers and joint partners). They can convene for a few days to solve a problem, a few months to complete a project, or exist permanently.[16]

The three primary factors that differentiate virtual teams from face-to-face teams are: (1) the absence of para-verbal (tone of voice, inflection and voice volume) and non-verbal (eye movement, facial expression, hand gestures and other body language) cues; (2) limited social context; and (3) the ability to overcome time and space constraints. In face-to-face conversation, people use para-verbal and non-verbal cues. These help to clarify communication by providing increased meaning but aren't available in online interactions. Virtual teams often suffer from less social rapport and less direct interaction among members. They aren't able to duplicate the normal give-and-take of face-to-face discussion. Especially when members haven't personally met, virtual teams tend to be more task-oriented and exchange less social–emotional information. Not surprisingly, virtual team members report less satisfaction with the group interaction process than do face-to-face teams. Finally, virtual teams are able to do their work even if members are thousands of kilometres apart and separated by a dozen or more time zones. It allows people to work together who might otherwise never be able to collaborate.

Companies such as Hewlett-Packard, Boeing, Ford, Motorola, General Electric (GE), Lockheed Martin, VeriFone and Royal Dutch/Shell have become heavy users of virtual teams. Lockheed Martin, for instance, has put together a virtual team to build a new stealth fighter plane for the US military. The team consists of engineers and designers from around the globe who will be working, simultaneously, on the US$225 billion project. The company expects this team structure to save US$250 million over the decade it will take to create the jet.[17]

OB IN PRACTICE

DEVELOPING CAPABILITIES IN VIRTUAL TEAMING

Do you know an organisation that fits this scenario: employees in Melbourne and Perth, customers in Malaysia, suppliers in Dubai, partners in Singapore, London and Shanghai, and the HR department based in Brisbane? These sorts of relationships are becoming more common, with project teams spread across different locations and time zones. According to Monika Altmaier, project leader (internationalisation) at Siemens Business Services, Germany: 'Tough global forces, such as international competitiveness, cost pressure, tighter deadlines, customer focus, fast product cycles, innovation demands and increasing globalisation, are driving companies to do business in project-based trans-national virtual teams. Global business time is 24 hours a day, 365 days per year.' That is why her company and others such as IBM and EADS (the European Aeronautic Defence and Space Company—the largest aerospace company in Europe and the second-largest worldwide) have made virtual team skills one of the core competencies for their managers and employees running their global business.

Monika's advice to organisations embarking on virtual teaming as a systemic initiative is:

- Set up virtual teams as a company-wide project hand-in-hand with business transformation while standardising the virtual teaming process across the organisation.
- Establish the right balance between rules and freedom to encourage creativity and innovation and being sensitive to the global/local dimension.
- Expand virtual teaming competencies in the organisation by having inexperienced people work together with experienced people.

Dianne Jacobs, principal of human resources for Goldman Sachs JBWere (a leading Australasian investment banking, financial advisory, securities and investment management firm) suggests that as the 21st century unfolds, a new style of leader is emerging—that of the global executive officer (GEO): '... one at ease with the vagaries of the forces of global change, and a leader with new qualities that will drive business success in the coming decades.'

These GEOs have to be able to navigate the uncharted waters of the complex, transnational, interdependent business environment. They must articulate the corporate vision and strategy from a multi-country, multi-environment and multifunction perspective, so that they unite and engage all people. With virtual and dispersed teams spread across time zones, the demands of remote leadership and team connectedness are unrelenting. The teams that these GEOs lead need a set of principles that respect and build on the strengths and innovation that each of the regional or national businesses bring to the collective corporate capability.

From both Monika's and Dianne's perspectives, the new leaders and global organisations must meet the challenges of virtuality in business and develop capabilities in virtual teaming.

SOURCES: Monika Altmaier, 'Hands across the Seas', *Human Resources*, no. 96, 24 January 2006, pp. 14–15; and Dianne Jacobs, 'Global Leadership: The Rise of the GEO', *Human Resources*, 30 May 2006: <www.humanresourcesmagazine.com.au/articles/30/0C040530.asp?Type=60&Category=1166>.

CREATING EFFECTIVE TEAMS

There is no shortage of efforts to try to identify factors related to team effectiveness.[18] However, recent studies have taken what was once a 'veritable laundry list of characteristics'[19] and organised them into a relatively focused model.[20] Figure 10.3 summarises what we currently know about what makes teams effective. As you will see, it builds on many of the group concepts introduced in the previous chapter.

The following discussion is based on the model in Figure 10.3. Keep in mind two caveats before we proceed. First, teams differ in form and structure. Since the model we present attempts to generalise across all varieties of teams, you need to be careful not to rigidly apply the model's predictions to all teams.[21] The model should be used as a guide, not as an inflexible prescription. Second, the model assumes that it has already been determined that teamwork is preferable over individual work. Creating 'effective' teams in situations in which individuals can do the job better is equivalent to solving the wrong problem perfectly.

The key components making up effective teams can be subsumed into four general categories. First are the resources and other *contextual* influences that make teams effective. The second relates to the team's *composition*. The third category is *work design*. Finally, *process* variables reflect those things that go on in the team that influences effectiveness. What does *team effectiveness* mean in this model? Typically, this has included objective measures of the team's productivity, managers' ratings of the team's performance, and aggregate measures of member satisfaction.

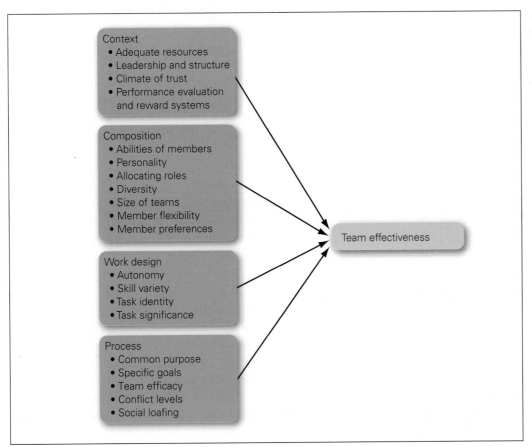

■ FIGURE 10.3
Team effectiveness model

CONTEXT

There are four contextual factors that appear to be most significantly related to team performance. These factors are the presence of adequate resources, effective leadership, a climate of trust, and a performance evaluation and reward system that reflects team contributions.

ADEQUATE RESOURCES

Teams are part of a larger organisation system. A research team in Dow's plastic products division, for instance, must live within the budgets, policies and practices set by Dow's corporate offices. As such, all work teams rely on resources outside the group to sustain it.[22] And a scarcity of resources directly reduces the ability of the team to perform its job effectively. As one set of researchers concluded, after looking at 13 factors potentially related to group performance, 'perhaps one of the most important characteristics of an effective work group is the support the group receives from the organization'.[23] This support includes timely information, proper equipment, adequate staffing, encouragement and administrative assistance. Teams must receive the necessary support from management and the larger organisation if they are going to succeed in achieving their goals.

LEADERSHIP AND STRUCTURE

Team members must agree on who is to do what and ensure that all members contribute equally in sharing the workload. In addition, the team needs to determine how schedules will be set, what skills need to be developed, how the group will resolve conflicts, and how it will make and modify decisions.[24] Agreeing on the specifics of work and how they fit together to integrate individual skills requires team leadership and structure. This can be provided directly by management or by the team members themselves. Leadership, of course, isn't always needed. For instance, the evidence indicates that self-managed work teams often perform better than teams with formally appointed leaders.[25] And leaders can obstruct high performance when they interfere with self-managing teams.[26] On self-managed teams, team members absorb many of the duties typically assumed by managers.

On traditionally managed teams, we find that two factors seem to be important in influencing team performance—the leader's expectations and his or her mood. Leaders who expect good things from their team are more likely to get them. For instance, military platoons under leaders who held high expectations performed significantly better in training than control platoons.[27] In addition, studies have found that leaders who exhibit a positive mood get better team performance and lower turnover.[28]

CLIMATE OF TRUST

Members of effective teams trust each other. And they also exhibit trust in their leaders.[29] Interpersonal trust among team members facilitates cooperation, reduces the need to monitor each other's behaviour, and bonds members around the belief that others on the team won't take advantage of them. Team members, for instance, are more likely to take risks and expose vulnerabilities when they believe they can trust others on their team. Similarly, as we will show in Chapter 13, trust is the foundation of leadership. Trust in leadership is important in that it allows the team to be willing to accept and commit to their leader's goals and decisions.

PERFORMANCE EVALUATION AND REWARD SYSTEMS

How do you get team members to be both individually and jointly accountable? The traditional, individually oriented evaluation and reward system must be modified to reflect team performance.[30]

Individual performance evaluations, fixed hourly wages, individual incentives and the like aren't consistent with the development of high-performance teams. So, in addition to evaluating and rewarding employees for their individual contributions, management should consider group-based appraisals, profit sharing, gainsharing, small-group incentives, and other system modifications that will reinforce team effort and commitment.

COMPOSITION

This category includes variables that relate to how teams should be staffed. In this section, we will address the ability and personality of team members, allocating roles and diversity, size of the team, member flexibility, and members' preference for teamwork.

THE TEAM APPROACH AT WOTIF.COM

In 2000, Graeme Wood set out to create an online marketplace for hotel rooms that were going to be empty that night or the night after. Graeme Wood is managing director and CEO of Wotif.com (<www.wotif.com>). He pointed to the huge growth that has occurred since inception in 2001: 'Initially the idea was to create a market where hoteliers could discount the rooms online and be in full control of the pricing while the consumer can search in an easy-to-navigate manner. We were confident that if we could get enough hotels doing it we would find enough consumers wanting the rooms. And that's the way it worked out because the company has grown to over 110 000 bookings a month for rooms in over 35 countries.' Wotif.com has grown from three staff in 2001 to over 140 in 2006.

Part of the success of this venture has been attributed to the development of a strong team focus and structure. Graeme emphasised his approach in this regard: 'I had the belief that, if I was running a technology team, I wanted to be responsible for building up the team. It was the same in the customer service centre, the same in the supplier relationship team. We kept them as teams with a team leader.' This team approach was reinforced in the recruitment and selection of new staff. The leader or manager in conjunction with the team members would interview potential new members. The new recruits had to satisfy all members of the team, including the leader, to make sure that they would fit in.

The importance of developing effective teams is apparent in the customer service centre. Graeme points out: 'The service we provide is critical. We are very happy with the number of customers who ring us with a problem— they may start out quite cranky about something, but they become strong advocates of the business because we bend over backwards to look after them.' Developing a positive interface between customers and clients is very dependent on the skills and attitudes of every team member, and the team approach provides a positive environment for making the basic business idea of Wotif.com a success.

The management structure is flat with an open-door policy. Bureaucracy is a bad word in the company, and the vision is to provide staff with a vibrant and fun place to work. Communication between overseas offices such as London, Singapore and Kuala Lumpur and the Australian offices is strongly encouraged so that there is a greater appreciation of the similarities and differences between national and ethnic cultures and the type of business culture that Wotif.com aspires to. Wotif.com reflects the experiences of many successful start-up companies. They realise early that the development of teams and teamwork is absolutely critical to meeting the challenges of high growth, lack of resources, customer relationships and little infrastructure.

SOURCE: Paul Murphy, 'Going Places', *HRMonthly*, September 2006, pp. 48–53.

OB IN PRACTICE

ABILITIES OF MEMBERS

Part of a team's performance depends on the knowledge, skills and abilities of its individual members. It is true that we occasionally read about the athletic team composed of mediocre players who, because of excellent coaching, determination and precision teamwork, beats a far more talented group of players. But such cases make the news precisely because they represent an aberration. As the old saying goes, 'The race doesn't always go to the swiftest nor the battle to the strongest, but that's the way to bet.' A team's performance isn't merely the summation of its individual members' abilities. However, these abilities set parameters for what members can do and how effectively they will perform on a team.

To perform effectively, a team requires three different types of skills. First, it needs people with *technical expertise*. Second, it needs people with the *problem-solving and decision-making skills* to be able to identify problems, generate alternatives, evaluate those alternatives and make competent choices. Finally, teams need people with good listening, feedback, conflict resolution and other *interpersonal skills*.[31] No team can achieve its performance potential without developing all three types of skills. The right mix is crucial. Too much of one at the expense of others will result in lower team performance. But teams don't need to have all the complementary skills in place at their beginning. It is not uncommon for one or more members to take responsibility to learn the skills in which the group is deficient, thereby allowing the team to reach its full potential.

Research on the abilities of team members has revealed some interesting insights into team composition and performance. First, when the task entails considerable thought (for example, solving a complex problem such as reengineering an assembly line), high-ability teams (teams composed of mostly intelligent members) do better, especially when the workload is distributed evenly. (That way, team performance doesn't depend on the weakest link.) High-ability teams are also more adaptable to changing situations in that they can more effectively adapt prior knowledge to suit a set of new problems.

Second, although high-ability teams generally have an advantage over lower-ability teams, this isn't always the case. For example, when tasks are simple (tasks that individual team members might be able to solve on their own), high-ability teams don't perform as well, perhaps because, in such tasks, high-ability teams become bored and turn their attention to other activities that are more stimulating, whereas low-ability teams stay on task. High-ability teams should be 'saved' to tackle the tough problems. So, matching team ability to the task is important. Finally, the ability of the team's leader also matters. Research shows that smart team leaders help less intelligent team members when they struggle with a task. But a less intelligent leader can neutralise the effect of a high-ability team.[32]

PERSONALITY

We demonstrated previously that personality has a significant influence on individual employee behaviour. This can also be extended to team behaviour. Many of the dimensions identified in the Big Five personality model have been shown to be relevant to team effectiveness. Specifically, teams that rate higher in mean levels of extraversion, agreeableness, conscientiousness, openness to experience and emotional stability tend to receive higher managerial ratings for team performance.[33]

Interestingly, the evidence indicates that the *variance* in personality characteristics may be more important than the mean.[34] So, for example, while higher mean levels of conscientiousness on a team are desirable, mixing both conscientious and not-so-conscientious members tends to lower performance. 'This may be because, in such teams, members who are highly conscientious not only must perform their own tasks but also must perform or re-do the tasks of low-conscientious members. It may also be because such diversity leads to feelings of contribution inequity.'[35] Another interesting finding related to personality is that 'one bad apple can spoil the barrel'. A single team member who lacks a minimal level of, say, agreeableness can negatively affect the whole team's performance. So, including just one person who is low on agreeableness, conscientiousness or extraversion can result in strained internal processes and decreased overall performance.[36]

We are also learning why these traits are important to team performance.[37] For example, conscientious people are valuable because they are good at 'backing up' fellow team members, and they are also good at sensing when that support is truly needed. Extraverts are better at training and motivating team members who are struggling. If a team is confronted with a poor fit between how their team is configured and their work environment (for example, when a team is loosely structured but needs to closely coordinate on a project), emotionally stable team members are critical because they are better at adapting and helping others to adapt. Teams comprised of open people make better use of computer technology in making decisions. Open people communicate better with one another and throw out more ideas, which leads teams comprised of open people to be more creative and innovative. When an unforeseen change happens, teams comprised of conscientious, emotionally stable and open members cope and adapt better. Personality also influences how teams respond to their surroundings. For example, extraverted teams and agreeable teams respond negatively to individual competitive rewards. Why? Because such individualistic incentives tend to run counter to the social nature of extraverted and agreeable teams.

Personality composition is important to team success. It is best to staff teams with people who are extraverted, agreeable, conscientious, emotionally stable and open. Management should also minimise the variability within teams on these traits.

ALLOCATING ROLES

Teams have different needs, and people should be selected for a team to ensure that all the various roles are filled.

We can identify nine potential team roles (see Figure 10.4). Successful work teams have people to fill all these roles and have selected people to play these roles based on their skills and preferences.[38] On many teams, individuals will play multiple roles. Managers need to understand the individual strengths that each person can bring to a team, select members with their strengths in mind, and allocate work assignments that fit with members' preferred styles. By matching individual preferences with team role demands, managers increase the likelihood that the team members will work well together.

DIVERSITY

As previously noted, most team activities require a variety of skills and knowledge. Given this requirement, it would be reasonable to conclude that heterogeneous teams—those composed of dissimilar individuals—would be more likely to have diverse abilities and information and should be more effective. Research studies generally substantiate this conclusion, especially on cognitive, creativity-demanding tasks.[39] Interestingly, a 2000 survey demonstrated that most Australian-based firms are yet to recognise the potential of diverse teams. This represents a substantial missed opportunity for Australian business.[40]

When a team is diverse in terms of personality, gender, age, education, functional specialisation and experience, there is an increased probability that it will possess the

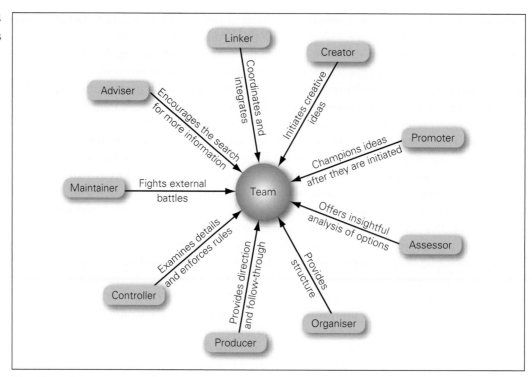

SOURCE: Based on C. Margerison and D. McCann, *Team Management: Practical New Approaches* (London: Mercury Books, 1990).

needed characteristics to complete its tasks effectively.[41] The team may be more conflict-laden and less expedient as varied positions are introduced and assimilated, but the evidence generally supports the conclusion that heterogeneous teams perform more effectively than do those that are homogeneous. Essentially, diversity promotes conflict, which stimulates creativity, which leads to improved decision making. One study found that, on a cognitive task, homogeneous groups of white males performed the worst relative to mixed race and gender teams, or teams of only females. The authors (who were all men) concluded that this was true because male-only teams were overly aggressive and therefore prone to decision-making errors.[42]

But what about diversity created by racial or national differences? The evidence indicates that these elements of diversity interfere with team processes, at least in the short term.[43] Cultural diversity seems to be an asset for tasks that call for a variety of viewpoints. But culturally heterogeneous teams have more difficulty in learning to work with each other and in solving problems. The good news is that these difficulties seem to dissipate with time. Although newly formed culturally diverse teams underperform newly formed culturally homogeneous teams, the differences disappear after about three months.[44] The reason is that it takes culturally diverse teams a while to learn how to work through disagreements and different approaches to solving problems.

An offshoot of the diversity issue has received a great deal of attention by group and team researchers. This is the degree to which members of a group share a common demographic attribute, such as age, sex, race, educational level or length of service in the organisation, and the impact of this attribute on turnover. We call this variable **group demography**.

We discussed individual demographic factors in Chapter 2. Here we consider the same type of factors, but in a group context. That is, it is not whether a person is male or female

group demography | The degree to which members of a group share a common demographic attribute, such as age, sex, race, educational level or length of service in an organisation, and the impact of this attribute on turnover.

or has been employed with the organisation for a year rather than ten years that concerns us now, but rather the individual's attribute in relationship to the attributes of others with whom he or she works. Let's work through the logic of group demography, review the evidence and then consider the implications.

Groups, teams and organisations are composed of **cohorts**, which we define as individuals who hold a common attribute. For instance, everyone born in 1960 is of the same age. This means they also have shared common experiences. People born in 1970 have experienced the information revolution, but not the Korean conflict. People born in 1945 shared the Vietnam War, but not the Great Depression. Women in organisations today who were born before 1945 matured prior to the women's movement and have had substantially different experiences from women born after 1960. Group demography, therefore, suggests that attributes such as age or the date that someone joins a specific work team or organisation should help us to predict turnover. Essentially, the logic goes like this: turnover will be greater among those with dissimilar experiences, because communication is more difficult. Conflict and power struggles are more likely, and more severe when they occur. The increased conflict makes group membership less attractive, so employees are more likely to quit. Similarly, the losers in a power struggle are more apt to leave voluntarily or to be forced out.

cohorts | Individuals who, as part of a group, hold a common attribute.

A number of studies have sought to test this thesis, and the evidence is quite encouraging.[45] For example, in departments or separate work groups in which a large portion of members entered at the same time, there is considerably more turnover among those outside this cohort. Also, when there are large gaps between cohorts, turnover is higher. People who enter a group or an organisation together, or at approximately the same time, are more likely to associate with one another, have a similar perspective on the group or organisation, and thus be more likely to stay. On the other hand, discontinuities or bulges in the group's date-of-entry distribution are likely to result in a higher turnover rate within that group.[46]

The implication of this line of inquiry is that the composition of a team may be an important predictor of turnover. Differences per se may not predict turnover. But large differences within a single team *will* lead to turnover. If everyone is moderately dissimilar from everyone else in a team, the feelings of being an outsider are reduced. So, it is the degree of dispersion on an attribute, rather than the level, that matters most.

SIZE OF TEAMS

The president of AOL Technologies says the secret to a great team is 'Think small. Ideally, your team should have seven to nine people.'[47] His advice is supported by evidence.[48] Generally speaking, the most effective teams have fewer than ten members. And experts suggest using the smallest number of people who can do the task. Unfortunately, there is a pervasive tendency for managers to err on the side of making teams too large. While a minimum of four or five people may be necessary to develop diversity of views and skills, managers seem to seriously underestimate how coordination problems can geometrically increase as team members are added. When teams have excess members, cohesiveness and mutual accountability declines, social loafing increases, and more and more people do less talking relative to others. Moreover, large teams have trouble coordinating with one another, especially when time pressure is present. So, in designing effective teams, managers should try to keep membership under ten. If a natural working unit is larger and you want a team effort, consider breaking the group into subteams.[49]

MEMBER FLEXIBILITY

Teams made up of flexible individuals have members who can complete each other's tasks. This is an obvious plus to a team, because it greatly improves its adaptability and makes it less reliant on any single member.[50] So, selecting members who themselves value flexibility, then cross-training them to be able to do each other's jobs, should lead to higher team performance over time.

MEMBER PREFERENCES

Not every employee is a team player. Given the option, many employees will select themselves *out* of team participation. When people who would prefer to work alone are required to team up, there is a direct threat to the team's morale and to individual member satisfaction.[51] This suggests that, when selecting team members, individual preferences should be considered as well as abilities, personalities and skills. High-performing teams are likely to be composed of people who prefer working as part of a group.

WORK DESIGN

Effective teams need to work together and take collective responsibility to complete significant tasks. They must be more than a 'team in name only'.[52] Based on terminology we introduced in Chapter 7, the work–design category includes variables such as freedom and autonomy, the opportunity to use different skills and talents (skill variety), the ability to complete a whole and identifiable task or product (task identity), and working on a task or project that has a substantial impact on others (task significance). The evidence indicates that these characteristics enhance member motivation and increase team effectiveness.[53] These work–design characteristics motivate because they increase members' sense of responsibility and ownership over the work and because they make the work more interesting to perform.[54]

PROCESS

The final category related to team effectiveness is process variables. These include member commitment to a common purpose, establishment of specific team goals, team efficacy, a managed level of conflict and minimising social loafing.

Why are processes important to team effectiveness? One way to answer this question is to return to the topic of social loafing. We found that 1 + 1 + 1 doesn't necessarily add up to 3. In team tasks for which each member's contribution isn't clearly visible, there is a tendency for individuals to decrease their effort. Social loafing, in other words, illustrates a process loss as a result of using teams. But team processes should produce positive results. That is, teams should create outputs greater than the sum of their inputs. The development of creative alternatives by a diverse group would be one such instance. Figure 10.5 illustrates how group processes can have an impact on a group's actual effectiveness.[55]

Social loafing, for instance, represents negative synergy. The whole is less than the sum of its parts. On the other hand, research teams are often used in research laboratories

■ **FIGURE 10.5**

Effects of group processes

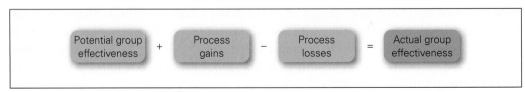

because they can draw on the diverse skills of various individuals to produce more meaningful research as a team than could be generated by all of the researchers working independently. That is, they produce positive synergy. Their process gains exceed their process losses.

COMMON PURPOSE

Effective teams have a common and meaningful purpose that provides direction, momentum and commitment for members.[56] This purpose is a vision. It is broader than specific goals.

Members of successful teams put a tremendous amount of time and effort into discussing, shaping and agreeing on a purpose that belongs to them both collectively and individually. This common purpose, when accepted by the team, becomes the equivalent of what celestial navigation is to a ship captain—it provides direction and guidance under any and all conditions.

SPECIFIC GOALS

Successful teams translate their common purpose into specific, measurable and realistic performance goals. Just as we demonstrated in Chapter 6 how goals lead individuals to higher performance, goals also energise teams. These specific goals facilitate clear communication. They also help teams to maintain their focus on getting results.

Also, consistent with the research on individual goals, team goals should be challenging. Difficult goals have been found to raise team performance on those criteria for which they are set. So, for instance, goals for quantity tend to raise quantity, goals for speed tend to raise speed, goals for accuracy raise accuracy, and so on.[57]

TEAM EFFICACY

Effective teams have confidence in themselves. They believe they can succeed. We call this *team efficacy*.[58] Success breeds success. Teams that have been successful raise their beliefs about future success, which, in turn, motivates them to work harder. What, if anything, can management do to increase team efficacy? Two possible options are helping the team to achieve small successes and providing skill training. Small successes build team confidence. As a team develops an increasingly stronger performance record, it also increases the collective belief that future efforts will lead to success. In addition, managers should consider providing training to improve members' technical and interpersonal skills. The greater the abilities of team members, the greater the likelihood that the team will develop confidence and the capability to deliver on that confidence.

CONFLICT LEVELS

Conflict on a team isn't necessarily bad. As we will elaborate in Chapter 15, teams that are completely void of conflict are likely to become apathetic and stagnant. So, conflict can actually improve team effectiveness.[59] But not all types of conflict. Relationship conflicts—those based on interpersonal incompatibilities, tension, and animosity towards others—are almost always dysfunctional. However, on teams performing non-routine activities, disagreements among members about task content (called *task conflicts*) are not detrimental. In fact, task conflict is often beneficial because it lessens the likelihood of groupthink. Task conflict stimulates discussion, promotes critical assessment of problems and options, and can lead to better team decisions. So, effective teams will be characterised by an appropriate level of conflict.

SOCIAL LOAFING

We learned in the previous chapter that individuals can hide inside a group. They can engage in social loafing and coast on the group's effort because their individual contributions can't be identified. Effective teams undermine this tendency by holding themselves accountable at both the individual and team level. Successful teams make members individually and jointly accountable for the team's purpose, goals and approach.[60] Therefore, members should be clear about what they are individually responsible for and what they are jointly responsible for.

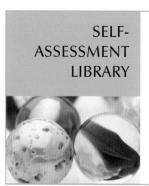

SELF-ASSESSMENT LIBRARY

HOW GOOD AM I AT BUILDING AND LEADING A TEAM?

In the Self-Assessment Library (available on CD and online), take Self-Assessment II.B.6 (How Good Am I at Building and Leading a Team?) and answer the following questions.

1. Did you score as high as you thought you would? Why or why not?
2. Do you think your score can be improved? If so, how? If not, why not?
3. Do you think there are team players? If yes, what are their behaviours?

LEARNING OBJECTIVE 5

Explain how organisations can create team players

TURNING INDIVIDUALS INTO TEAM PLAYERS

To this point, we have made a strong case for the value and growing popularity of teams. But many people are not inherently team players. There are also many organisations that have historically nurtured individual accomplishments. They have created competitive work environments in which only the strong survive. If these organisations adopt teams, what do they do about the selfish, 'I've-got-to-look-out-for-me' employees that they have created? Finally, countries differ in terms of how they rate on individualism and collectivism. Teams fit well with countries that score high on collectivism.[61] But what if an organisation wants to introduce teams into a work population that is made up largely of individuals born and raised in an individualistic society? Australians, for example, are assessed on their individual achievements as they progress through their primary and secondary schooling. However, there are a lot of team sports played at school, and while team skills aren't formally assessed, this aspect of school life provides many lessons for working and playing in teams.

THE CHALLENGE

The previous points are meant to dramatise that one substantial barrier to using work teams is individual resistance. An employee's success is no longer defined in terms of individual performance. To perform well as team members, individuals must be able to communicate openly and honestly, to confront differences and resolve conflicts, and to sublimate personal goals for the good of the team. For many employees, this is a difficult—sometimes impossible—task. The challenge of creating team players will be greatest when (1) the national culture is highly individualistic and (2) the teams are being introduced into an established organisation that has historically valued individual achievement. This describes, for instance, what faced managers at Ford, Motorola and other companies.

These firms prospered by hiring and rewarding corporate stars, and they bred a competitive climate that encouraged individual achievement and recognition. Employees in these types of firms can be jolted by this sudden shift to the importance of team play.[62] A veteran employee of a large company, who had done well working alone, described the experience of joining a team: 'I'm learning my lesson. I just had my first negative performance appraisal in 20 years.'[63]

On the other hand, the challenge for management is less demanding when teams are introduced where employees have strong collectivist values—such as in Japan or Mexico—or in new organisations that use teams as their initial form for structuring work. Saturn Corporation, for instance, is an American organisation owned by GM. The company was designed around teams from its inception. Everyone at Saturn was hired with the knowledge that they would be working in teams. The ability to be a good team player was a basic hiring qualification that had to be met by all new employees.

SHAPING TEAM PLAYERS

The following summarises the primary options managers have for trying to turn individuals into team players.

SELECTION

Some people already possess the interpersonal skills to be effective team players. When hiring team members, in addition to the technical skills required to fill the job, care should be taken to ensure that candidates can fulfil their team roles as well as technical requirements.[64]

Many job candidates don't have team skills. This is especially true for those socialised around individual contributions. When faced with such candidates, managers basically have three options. The candidates can undergo training to 'make them into team players'. If this isn't possible or doesn't work, the other two options are to transfer the individual to another unit within the organisation, without teams (if this possibility exists), or not to hire the candidate. In established organisations that decide to redesign jobs around teams, it should be expected that some employees will resist being team players and may be untrainable. Unfortunately, such people typically become casualties of the team approach.

TRAINING

On a more optimistic note, a large proportion of people raised on the importance of individual accomplishments can be trained to become team players. Training specialists conduct exercises that allow employees to experience the satisfaction that teamwork can provide. They typically offer workshops to help employees improve their problem-solving, communication, negotiation, conflict-management and coaching skills. Employees also learn the five-stage group development model described in Chapter 9. At Verizon, for example, trainers focus on how a team goes through various stages before it finally gels. And employees are reminded of the importance of patience—because teams take longer to make decisions than do employees acting alone.[65]

Emerson Electric's Specialty Motor Division, for instance, has achieved remarkable success in getting its 650-member workforce not only to accept but to welcome team training.[66] Outside consultants were brought in to give workers practical skills for working in teams. After less than a year, employees were enthusiastically accepting the value of teamwork.

REWARDS

The reward system needs to be reworked to encourage cooperative efforts rather than competitive ones.[67] For instance, Hallmark Cards, Inc. added an annual bonus based on achievement of team goals to its basic individual-incentive system. Trigon Blue Cross Blue Shield changed its system to reward an even split between individual goals and team-like behaviours.[68]

Promotions, pay raises and other forms of recognition should be given to individuals for how effective they are as a collaborative team member. This doesn't mean individual contributions are ignored; rather, they are balanced with selfless contributions to the team. Examples of behaviours that should be rewarded include training new colleagues, sharing information with teammates, helping to resolve team conflicts, and mastering new skills that the team needs but in which it is deficient.

Lastly, don't forget the intrinsic rewards that employees can receive from teamwork. Teams provide camaraderie. It is exciting and satisfying to be an integral part of a successful team. The opportunity to engage in personal development and to help teammates grow can be a very satisfying and rewarding experience for employees.

MYTH OR SCIENCE?

'ADVENTURE LEARNING IS GOOD FOR TEAM BUILDING'

Adventure learning or outdoor challenge training (OCT) is an event where a team is put through a series of challenging physical and mental tasks. They take place outdoors at a retreat setting in the mountains or on the coast, and generally are led by a qualified facilitator using standard psychological exercises. At the end of the retreat, participants are enthusiastic and excited, and usually believe they have become a better team. But when they all get back to the office, does the team perform better?

According to team development gurus Harvey Robbins and Michael Finley, the belief that adventure learning leads to more effective teams back in the office is a myth. There are several reasons. First, the exercises—such as mountaineering and abseiling—are more about personal development than team development back in the office. Second, in her study on outdoor challenge training, Sheryl Shivers-Blackwell found that while the utilisation of OCT for team building is becoming increasingly popular, much of the evidence supporting its effectiveness is anecdotal, emphasising the benefits expressed by top executives. Empirical evidence on the value and importance of OCT is lacking, she says. One reason for the infrequent evaluation of training programs is that evaluators believe there is a relatively low probability of finding significant training effects.

SOURCES: H. Robbins and M. Finley, *Why Teams Don't Work* (Princeton, NJ: Peterson's/Pacesetter Books, 1995); and S. L. Shivers-Blackwell, 'Reactions to Outdoor Teambuilding Initiatives in MBA Education', *Journal of Management Development*, vol. 23, no. 7, 2004, pp. 614–31.

TEAMS AND QUALITY MANAGEMENT

As discussed in Chapter 1, the issue of 'improving quality' has garnered increased attention from management in recent years. In this section, we want to demonstrate the important role that teams play in quality management (QM) programs.

The essence of QM is process improvement, and employee involvement is the linchpin of process improvement. In other words, QM requires management to give employees the encouragement to share ideas and act on what they suggest. As one author put it, 'None of the various [quality management] processes and techniques will

Kwik Kopy was established in Australia in 1982 as part of its American parent company's expansion overseas. There are 108 franchise operators throughout Australia who focus on building relationships with customers that allow them to deliver impressive design, print and communications solutions; it is much more than just a printing service for walk-in customers. Managing a successful one-stop shop requires teamwork and staff who are multi-skilled and can support each other in meeting customers' needs.

catch on and be applied except in work teams. All such techniques and processes require high levels of communication and contact, response and adaptation, and coordination and sequencing. They require, in short, the environment that can be supplied only by superior work teams.'[69] Teams provide the natural vehicle for employees to share ideas and to implement improvements. As stated by Gil Mosard, a QM specialist at Boeing: 'When your measurement system tells you your process is out of control, you need teamwork for structured problem solving. Not everyone needs to know how to do all kinds of fancy control charts for performance tracking, but everybody does need to know where their process stands so they can judge if it is improving.'[70]

BEWARE! TEAMS AREN'T ALWAYS THE ANSWER

Teamwork takes more time and often more resources than individual work. Teams, for instance, have increased communication demands, conflicts to be managed and meetings to be run. So, the benefits of using teams have to exceed the costs. And that's not always the case.[71] In the excitement to enjoy the benefits of teams, some managers have introduced them into situations in which the work is better done by individuals. So, before you rush to implement teams, you should carefully assess whether the work requires or will benefit from a collective effort.

How do you know if the work of your group would be better done in teams? It has been suggested that three tests be applied to see if a team fits the situation.[72] First, can the work be done better by more than one person? A good indicator is the complexity of the work and the need for different perspectives. Simple tasks that don't require diverse input are probably better left to individuals. Second, does the work create a common purpose or set of goals for the people in the group that is more than the aggregate of individual goals? For instance, many new-car dealer service departments have introduced teams that link customer service personnel, mechanics, parts specialists, and sales representatives. Such teams can better manage collective responsibility for ensuring that customer needs are properly met. The final test to assess whether teams fit the situation is: Are the members of the group interdependent? Teams make sense when there is interdependence between

The Australian women's swimming team of (L-R) Jessicah Schipper, Lisbeth Lenton, Jade Edmistone and Tayliah Zimmer celebrate after winning the Women's 4 x 100 metre medley relay final in a world-record time of 3:51.84, during the 8th FINA World Short Course Swimming Championships, held at the Qi Zhong Stadium in Shanghai, 7 April 2006. While swimming is a sport where the media tends to focus on the talents and performances of individuals such as former champion Ian Thorpe, the relay event demonstrates the power of teamwork and the achievements that are possible when team members create a dynamic that exceeds all expectations.

tasks; when the success of the whole depends on the success of each one *and* the success of each one depends on the success of the others. Soccer, for instance, is an obvious *team* sport. Success requires a great deal of coordination between interdependent players. Conversely, except possibly for relays, swimming teams aren't really teams. They are groups of individuals, performing individually, whose total performance is merely the aggregate summation of their individual performances.

SUMMARY AND IMPLICATIONS FOR MANAGERS

- Few trends have influenced employee jobs as much as the massive movement to introduce teams into the workplace. The shift from working alone to working on teams requires employees to cooperate with others, share information, confront differences and sublimate personal interests for the greater good of the team.
- Effective teams have been found to have common characteristics:
  - They have adequate resources, effective leadership, a climate of trust, and a performance evaluation and reward system that reflects team contributions.
  - They are made up of individuals with technical expertise, as well as problem-solving, decision-making and interpersonal skills; and high scores on the personality characteristics of extraversion, agreeableness, conscientiousness and emotional stability.
  - They tend to be small—with fewer than ten people—preferably made up of individuals with diverse backgrounds.
  - They have members who fill role demands, are flexible and who prefer to be part of a group. And the work that members do provides freedom and autonomy, the opportunity to use different skills and talents, the ability to complete a whole and identifiable task or product, and work that has a substantial impact on others.
  - They have members who are committed to a common purpose, specific team goals, belief in the team's capabilities, a manageable level of conflict and a minimal degree of social loafing.
- Because individualistic organisations and societies attract and reward individual accomplishments, it is more difficult to create team players in these environments. To make the conversion, management should try to select individuals with the interpersonal skills to be effective team players, provide training to develop teamwork skills, and reward individuals for cooperative efforts.

Sports Teams Are Good Models for Workplace Teams

● POINT

Studies from different football codes, basketball, hockey, athletics and baseball have found a number of elements that successful sports teams have that can be extrapolated to successful work teams.

- *Successful teams integrate cooperation and competition.* Effective team coaches get athletes to help one another, but also to push one another to perform at their best. Sports teams with the best win–loss record had coaches who promoted a strong spirit of cooperation and a high level of healthy competition among their players.
- *Successful teams score early wins.* Early successes build teammates' faith in themselves and their capacity as a team. For example, research on hockey teams of relatively equal ability found that 72 per cent of the time the team that was ahead at the end of the first period went on to win the game. So, managers should provide teams with early tasks that are simple and provide 'easy wins'.
- *Successful teams avoid losing streaks.* Losing can become a self-fulfilling prophecy. A couple of failures can lead to a downward spiral if a team becomes demoralised and believes it is helpless to end its losing streak. Managers need to instil confidence in team members that they can turn things around when they encounter setbacks.
- *Practice makes perfect.* Successful sports teams execute on game day but learn from their mistakes in practice. Practice should be used to try new things and fail. A wise manager carves out time and space in which work teams can experiment and learn.
- *Successful teams use half-time breaks.* The best coaches in basketball and football use half-time during a game to reassess what is working and

what isn't. Managers of work teams should similarly build in assessments at the approximate halfway point in a team project to evaluate what it can do to improve.
- *Winning teams have a stable membership.* Stability improves performance. For example, studies of professional basketball teams have found that the more stable a team's membership, the more likely the team is to win. The more time teammates spend together, the more able they are to anticipate one another's moves and the clearer they are about one another's roles.
- *Successful teams debrief after failures and successes.* The best sports teams study the game video. Similarly, work teams need to take time to routinely reflect on, and learn from, both their successes and failures.

● COUNTERPOINT

There are flaws in using sports as a model for developing effective work teams. Here are just four caveats.

- *All sport teams aren't alike.* In cricket, for example, there is little interaction among teammates. Rarely are more than two or three players directly involved in a play. The performance of the team is largely the sum of the performance of its individual players. In contrast, basketball has much more interdependence among players. Geographic distribution is dense. Usually all players are involved in every play, team members have to be able to switch from offence to defence at a moment's notice, and there is continuous movement by all, not just the player with the ball. The performance of the team is more than the sum of its individual players. So, when using sports teams as a model for work teams, you have to make sure you are making the correct comparison.
- *Work teams are more varied and complex.* In an athletic competition, the design of the task, the design of the team and the team's context vary

relatively little from team to team. But these variables can vary tremendously between work teams. As a result, coaching plays a much more significant part in a sports team's performance than for a work team. Performance of work teams is more a function of getting the team's structural and design variables right. So, in contrast to sports, managers of work teams should focus more on getting the team set up for success than on coaching.

- *Some employees can't relate to sports metaphors*. Not everyone on work teams is conversant in sports. Women, for example, often are not as interested in sports as men and aren't as savvy about sports terminology. And team members from different cultures may not know the sports metaphors you are using. Most Malaysians and Singaporeans, for example, are unfamiliar with the rules and terminology of Australian Rules football.

- *Work team outcomes aren't easily defined in terms of wins and losses*. Sports teams typically measure success in terms of wins and losses. Such measures of success are rarely as clear for work teams. When managers try to define success in terms of wins and losses, it tends to infer that the workplace is ethically no more complex than the playing field, which is rarely true.

SOURCE: Points in this argument are based on N. Katz, 'Sports Teams as a Model for Workplace Teams: Lessons and Liabilities', *Academy of Management Executive*, August 2001, pp. 56–67.

QUESTIONS FOR REVIEW

MyOBLab Do you understand this chapter's content? Find out at **www.pearsoned.com.au/MyOBLab**

1. Contrast self-managed and cross-functional teams.
2. Contrast virtual and face-to-face teams.
3. List and describe nine team roles.
4. Contrast the pros and cons of having diverse teams.
5. List and describe the process variables associated with effective team performance.
6. How do effective teams minimise groupthink?
7. How do effective teams minimise social loafing?
8. What is group demography and why is it important?
9. Under what conditions will the challenge of creating team players be greatest?
10. What role do teams play in quality management?

QUESTIONS FOR CRITICAL THINKING

1. Don't teams create conflict? Isn't conflict bad? Why, then, would management support the concept of teams?
2. Are there factors in Chinese and Japanese society that make teams more acceptable in the workplace there than in Australia and New Zealand? Explain.
3. What problems might surface in teams at each stage in the five-stage group development model?
4. How do you think member expectations might affect team performance?
5. Would you prefer to work alone or as part of a team? Why? How do you think your answer compares with others in your class?
6. Do you think there is such a thing as a 'team player'? What are the behaviours of such a person?

EXPERIENTIAL EXERCISE

Team Performance of Flight Crews

Break into teams of five. Your team represents a group of consultants appointed by the 'oneworld' alliance (which includes Cathy Pacific, Qantas and British Airways) to consider the pros and cons of variable flight crews and the impact it may have on team performance and to arrive at a recommendation on whether to continue this practice.

Almost all commercial airlines now operate with variable flight crews. Pilots, co-pilots and flight attendants typically bid for schedules on specific planes (for instance, Boeing 737s, 767s, 777s, 747s or Airbus A330) based on seniority. Then they are given a monthly schedule made up of one- to five-day trips. So, any given flight crew on a plane is rarely together for more than a few days at a time. A complicated system is required to complete the schedules; it is so complicated, in fact, that IBM recently designed a complex software system that works through billions of possible combinations to find the best algorithmic solution for crew assignments. Because of this system, it is not unusual for a senior pilot at a large airline to fly with a different co-pilot on every trip during any given month. And a pilot and co-pilot that work together for three days in January may not work together again for the rest of the year.

Arguments can be made in support of the current system. However, it also has serious drawbacks. Each group of consultants is to carefully consider the advantages and disadvantages of the current system, and its effect on airline and crew performance and safety, and then be prepared to present to the class its recommendation and justification.

ETHICAL DILEMMA

Pressure to be a Team Player

'OK, I admit it. I'm not a team player. I work best when I work alone and am left alone', says Jeffrey Sanders. Jeff's employer, an office furniture manufacturer, recently reorganised around teams. All production in the company's factory is now done in teams. And Jeff's design department has been broken up into three design teams. 'I've worked here for four years. I'm very good at what I do. And my performance reviews confirm that. I've scored 96 per cent or higher on my evaluations every year I've been here. But now everything is changing. I'm expected to be part of our modular-office design team. My evaluations and pay raises are going to depend on how well the team does. And, get this, 50 per cent of my evaluation will be on how well I facilitate the performance of the team. I'm really frustrated and demoralised. They appointed me for my design skills. They knew I wasn't a social type. Now they're forcing me to be a team player. This doesn't play to my strengths at all.'

Is it unethical for Jeff's employer to force him to be a team player? Is his firm breaking an implied contract that it made with him at the time he was hired? Does this employer have any responsibility to provide Jeffrey with an alternative that would allow him to continue to work independently?

10 CASE STUDY

Team-building Retreats

Some companies are taking team building outside the walls of the office. Corporate retreats, where team members participate in activities ranging from mountain climbing to trust-building exercises (for example, where team members fall backwards into their colleagues' arms), are used by companies to foster effective teamwork. But why do organisations have teammates participate in activities that seem irrelevant to the organisation's primary activities?

Adventure Out Australia has been conducting adventure learning programs for corporate, educational and recreational groups since 1984. Adventure Out has conducted training programs for Woodside Energy, Argyle Diamonds, Bunnings Building Supplies, Australia Post, BankWest, Iluka, McDonald's and Woolworths.

The management of Adventure Out Australia believes that working in small groups teaches participants about aspects of teamwork such as respect, cooperation, communication, trust, problem solving and leadership. In an adventure activity, individuals rely on each other as well as themselves, developing coping strategies in challenging situations that can later be implemented back in the workplace and in day-to-day situations. Adventure Out Australia's outdoor corporate programs include abseiling, navigation, raft building, paintballing, clay-pigeon shooting and skydiving.

Various participants were very positive about their experiences with these team-building retreats. Rob Greig, business unit resource officer from the Shire of Manjimup, felt that his fellow managers gained renewed enthusiasm for teamwork. John Busby, general manager at Budget Rent a Car, suggested that workplace performance can improve as a result of such learning experiences. 'My key performance indicators in all areas have improved and are in fact quite exceptional in a number of areas.' Steve Reynolds, an area manager at Australia Post, also saw the positive benefits, both direct and indirect. 'What transpired was not only aspects of teamwork, but an overwhelming belief in the self and pride in achieving untried tasks and overcoming anxiety … it is pleasing to note an intensified focus and a team contribution in various "think tank" strategies.'

Sometimes, however, corporate retreats can have unintended consequences. In 2001, a dozen Burger King employees burned themselves while participating in a 'fire walk'—a team-building exercise that requires teammates to walk barefoot across a three-metre pit of burning-hot coals. The results were injured employees and some very negative publicity for Burger King. According to author Joseph Grenny, 'Steer away from ridiculous physical challenges. Physical challenges are sometimes based on this notion that if we all experience humiliation together, we'll feel bonded.' Grenny states that solving actual problems at work is the best way to build teamwork. Physical challenges may not only result in injuries to employees, but they may also isolate those who lack athletic ability. As an additional example, many companies sponsor golf outings to build teamwork, but such outings may put pressure on employees who are not up to 'par' with their colleagues.

Though it is questionable whether team-building exercises such as mountain climbing and fire walks result in improved company financial performance, it may be better to think of such activities as morale boosters. According to Merianne Liteman, a professional corporate retreat organiser, 'Where good retreats have a quantifiable effect is on retention, on morale, on productivity.' Daryl Jesperson, CEO of RE/MAX International, says: 'There is a productivity boost anytime you have one of these. People feel better about themselves, they feel better about the company, and as a result will do a better job.'

QUESTIONS

1. Do you believe that team-building activities such as mountain climbing increase productivity? Why or why not? What other factors might be responsible for increases in profitability following a corporate retreat?

2. What are some other ways to build effective teams and increase teamwork among company employees? How might these alternatives be better or worse than corporate retreats?

3. What should companies do about employees who lack athletic talent but are still pressured to participate in physical activities with their colleagues? How might poor performance by those with low athletic ability affect their status within the organisation?

4. How might you increase teamwork when team members are not often in direct contact with one another? Can you think of any 'electronic' team-building exercises?

SOURCES: Based on C. Dahle, 'How to Avoid a Rout at the Company Retreat', *The New York Times*, 31 October 2004, p. 10; D. P. Shuit, 'Sound the Retreat', *Workforce Management*, September 2003, vol. 82, no. 9, pp. 38–44; and Adventure Out: <www.adventureout.com.au/corporate_programs.htm> (accessed 17 November 2006).

ENDNOTES

1. See, for example, P. MacMillan, *The Performance Factor: Unlocking the Secrets of Teamwork* (Nashville, TN: Broadman & Holman, 2001); E. Salas, C. A. Bowers and E. Edens (eds), *Improving Teamwork in Organizations: Applications of Resource Management Training* (Mahwah, NJ: Lawrence Erlbaum, 2002); and L. I. Glassop, 'The Organizational Benefits of Teams', *Human Relations*, February 2002, pp. 225–50.

2. K. Kelly, 'The New Soul of John Deere', *BusinessWeek*, 31 January 1994, pp. 64–66.

3. This section is based on J. R. Katzenbach and D. K. Smith, *The Wisdom of Teams* (Cambridge, MA: Harvard University Press, 1993), pp. 21, 45 and 85; and D. C. Kinlaw, *Developing Superior Work Teams* (Lexington, MA: Lexington Books, 1991), pp. 3–21.

4. See, for instance, E. Sunstrom, K. DeMeuse and D. Futrell, 'Work Teams: Applications and Effectiveness', *American Psychologist*, February 1990, pp. 120–33.

5. J. H. Shonk, *Team-Based Organizations* (Homewood, IL: Business One Irwin, 1992); and M. A. Verespej, 'When Workers Get New Roles', *Industry Week*, 3 February 1992, p. 11.

6. G. Bodinson and R. Bunch, 'AQP's National Team Excellence Award: Its Purpose, Value and Process', *The Journal for Quality and Participation*, Spring 2003, pp. 37–42.

7. See, for example, S. G. Cohen, G. E. Ledford, Jr and G. M. Spreitzer, 'A Predictive Model of Self-Managing Work Team Effectiveness', *Human Relations*, May 1996, pp. 643–76; D. E. Yeats and C. Hyten, *High-Performing Self-Managed Work Teams: A Comparison of Theory to Practice* (Thousand Oaks, CA: Sage, 1998); C. E. Nicholls, H. W. Lane and M. Brehm Brechu, 'Taking Self-Managed Teams to Mexico', *Academy of Management Executive*, August 1999, pp. 15–27; and A. Erez, J. A. LePine and H. Elms, 'Effects of Rotated Leadership and Peer Evaluation on the Functioning and Effectiveness of Self-Managed Teams: A Quasi-experiment', *Personnel Psychology*, Winter 2002, pp. 929–48.

8. W. Royal, 'Team-Centered Success', *Industry Week*, 18 October 1999, pp. 56–58.

9. R. Zemke, 'Rethinking the Rush to Team Up', *Training*, November 1993, pp. 55–61.

10. See, for instance, T. D. Wall, N. J. Kemp, P. R. Jackson and C. W. Clegg, 'Outcomes of Autonomous Workgroups: A Long-Term Field Experiment', *Academy of Management Journal*, June 1986, pp. 280–304; J. L. Cordery, W. S. Mueller and L. M. Smith, 'Attitudinal and Behavioral Effects of Autonomous Group Working: A Longitudinal Field Study', *Academy of Management Journal*, June 1991, pp. 464–76; R. A. Cook and J. L. Goff,

'Coming of Age with Self-Managed Teams: Dealing with a Problem Employee', *Journal of Business and Psychology*, Spring 2002, pp. 485–96; and C. W. Langfred, 'Too Much of a Good Thing? Negative Effects of High Trust and Individual Autonomy in Self-Managing Teams', *Academy of Management Journal*, June 2004, pp. 385–99.

11. J. R. Barker, 'Tightening the Iron Cage: Concertive Control in Self-Managing Teams', *Administrative Science Quarterly*, September 1993, pp. 408–37; S. G. Cohen and G. E. Ledford, Jr, 'The Effectiveness of Self-Managing Teams: A Field Experiment', *Human Relations*, January 1994, pp. 13–43; and C. Smith and D. Comer, 'Self-Organization in Small Groups: A Study of Group Effectiveness within Non-Equilibrium Conditions', *Human Relations*, May 1994, pp. 553–81.

12. Nicholls, Lane and Brehm Brechu, 'Taking Self-Managed Teams to Mexico'.

13. Bodinson and Bunch, 'AQP's National Team Excellence Award'.

14. M. Brunelli, 'How Harley-Davidson Uses Cross-Functional Teams', *Purchasing Online*, 4 November 1999: <www.manufacturing.net/magazine/purchasing/archives/1999>.

15. See, for example, J. Lipnack and J. Stamps, *Virtual Teams: People Working across Boundaries and Technology*, 2nd ed. (New York: John Wiley & Sons, 2000); C. B. Gibson and S. G. Cohen (eds), *Virtual Teams That Work* (San Francisco: Jossey-Bass, 2003); and L. L. Martins, L. L. Gilson and M. T. Maynard, 'Virtual Teams: What Do We Know and Where Do We Go from Here?', *Journal of Management*, November 2004, pp. 805–35.

16. K. Kiser, 'Working on World Time', *Training*, March 1999, p. 30.

17. S. Crock, 'Collaboration: Lockheed Martin', *BusinessWeek*, 24 November 2003, p. 85.

18. See, for instance, D. L. Gladstein, 'Groups in Context: A Model of Task Group Effectiveness', *Administrative Science Quarterly*, December 1984, pp. 499–517; J. R. Hackman, 'The Design of Work Teams', in J. W. Lorsch (ed.), *Handbook of Organizational Behavior* (Upper Saddle River, NJ: Prentice Hall, 1987), pp. 315–42; M. A. Campion, G. J. Medsker and C. A. Higgs, 'Relations between Work Group Characteristics and Effectiveness: Implications for Designing Effective Work Groups', *Personnel Psychology*, Winter 1993, pp. 823–50; and R. A. Guzzo and M. W. Dickson, 'Teams in Organizations: Recent Research on Performance and Effectiveness', in J. T. Spence, J. M. Darley and D. J. Foss (eds), *Annual Review of Psychology*, vol. 47, pp. 307–38.

19. D. E. Hyatt and T. M. Ruddy, 'An Examination of the Relationship between Work Group Characteristics and Performance: Once More into the Breech',

Personnel Psychology, Autumn 1997, p. 555.

20. This model is based on M. A. Campion, E. M. Papper and G. J. Medsker, 'Relations between Work Team Characteristics and Effectiveness: A Replication and Extension', *Personnel Psychology*, Summer 1996, pp. 429–52; Hyatt and Ruddy, 'An Examination of the Relationship between Work Group Characteristics and Performance', pp. 553–85; S. G. Cohen and D. E. Bailey, 'What Makes Teams Work: Group Effectiveness Research from the Shop Floor to the Executive Suite', *Journal of Management*, vol. 23, no. 3, 1997, pp. 239–90; L. Thompson, *Making the Team* (Upper Saddle River, NJ: Prentice Hall, 2000), pp. 18–33; and J. R. Hackman, *Leading Teams: Setting the Stage for Great Performance* (Boston: Harvard Business School Press, 2002).

21. See M. Mattson, T. V. Mumford and G. S. Sintay, 'Taking Teams to Task: A Normative Model for Designing or Recalibrating Work Teams', Paper presented at the National Academy of Management Conference, Chicago, August 1999; and G. L. Stewart and M. R. Barrick, 'Team Structure and Performance: Assessing the Mediating Role of Intrateam Process and the Moderating Role of Task Type', *Academy of Management Journal*, April 2000, pp. 135–48.

22. J. W. Bishop, K. D. Scott and S. M. Burroughs, 'Support, Commitment, and Employee Outcomes in a Team Environment', *Journal of Management*, vol. 26, no. 6, 2000, pp. 1113–32; and C. L. Pearce and R. A. Giacalone, 'Teams Behaving Badly: Factors Associated with Anti-Citizenship Behavior in Teams', *Journal of Applied Social Psychology*, January 2003, pp. 53–75.

23. Hyatt and Ruddy, 'An Examination of the Relationship between Work Group Characteristics and Performance', p. 577.

24. F. LaFasto and C. Larson, *When Teams Work Best: 6,000 Team Members and Leaders Tell What It Takes to Succeed* (Thousand Oaks, CA: Sage, 2002).

25. R. I. Beekun, 'Assessing the Effectiveness of Sociotechnical Interventions: Antidote or Fad?', *Human Relations*, August 1989, pp. 877–97.

26. S. G. Cohen, G. E. Ledford and G. M. Spreitzer, 'A Predictive Model of Self-Managing Work Team Effectiveness', *Human Relations*, May 1996, pp. 643–76; see also V. U. Druskat and J. V. Wheeler, 'Managing from the Boundary: The Effective Leadership of Self-Managing Work Teams', *Academy of Management Journal*, August 2003, pp. 435–57.

27. D. Eden, 'Pygmalion without Interpersonal Contrast Effects: Whole Groups Gain from Raising Manager Expectations', *Journal*

of Applied Psychology, August 1990, pp. 394–98.

28. J. M. George and K. Bettenhausen, 'Understanding Prosocial Behavior, Sales, Performance, and Turnover: A Group-Level Analysis in a Service Context', *Journal of Applied Psychology*, October 1990, pp. 698–709; J. M. George, 'Leader Positive Mood and Group Performance: The Case of Customer Service', *Journal of Applied Social Psychology*, December 1995, pp. 778–94; and A. P. Brief and H. M. Weiss, 'Organizational Behavior: Affect in the Workplace', *Annual Review of Psychology*, 2002, pp. 279–307.

29. K. T. Dirks, 'Trust in Leadership and Team Performance: Evidence from NCAA Basketball', *Journal of Applied Psychology*, December 2000, pp. 1004–12; and M. Williams, 'In Whom We Trust: Group Membership as an Affective Context for Trust Development', *Academy of Management Review*, July 2001, pp. 377–96.

30. See S. T. Johnson, 'Work Teams: What's Ahead in Work Design and Rewards Management', *Compensation & Benefits Review*, March–April 1993, pp. 35–41; and L. N. McClurg, 'Team Rewards: How Far Have We Come?', *Human Resource Management*, Spring 2001, pp. 73–86.

31. For a more detailed breakdown on team skills, see M. J. Stevens and M. A. Campion, 'The Knowledge, Skill, and Ability Requirements for Teamwork: Implications for Human Resource Management', *Journal of Management*, Summer 1994, pp. 503–30.

32. H. Moon, J. R. Hollenbeck and S. E. Humphrey, 'Asymmetric Adaptability: Dynamic Team Structures as One-Way Streets', *Academy of Management Journal*, vol. 47, no. 5, October 2004, pp. 681–95; A. P. J. Ellis, J. R. Hollenbeck and D. R. Ilgen, 'Team Learning: Collectively Connecting the Dots', *Journal of Applied Psychology*, vol. 88, no. 5, October 2003, pp. 821–35; J. A. LePine, J. R. Hollenbeck and D. R. Ilgen, 'Effects of Individual Differences on the Performance of Hierarchical Decision-Making Teams: Much More than g', *Journal of Applied Psychology*, vol. 82, no. 5, October 1997, pp. 803–11; C. L. Jackson and J. A. LePine, 'Peer Responses to a Team's Weakest Link: A Test and Extension of LePine and Van Dyne's Model', *Journal of Applied Psychology*, vol. 88, no. 3, June 2003, pp. 459–75; J. A. LePine, 'Team Adaptation and Postchange Performance: Effects of Team Composition in Terms of Members' Cognitive Ability and Personality', *Journal of Applied Psychology*, vol. 88, no. 1, February 2003, pp. 27–39.

33. M. R. Barrick, G. L. Stewart, M. J. Neubert and M. K. Mount, 'Relating Member Ability and Personality to Work-Team Processes and Team Effectiveness', *Journal of Applied Psychology*, June 1998, pp. 377–91; G. A. Neuman and J. Wright, 'Team Effectiveness: Beyond Skills and Cognitive Ability', *Journal of Applied Psychology*, June

1999, pp. 376–89; and L. M. Moynihan and R. S. Peterson, 'A Contingent Configuration Approach to Understanding the Role of Personality in Organizational Groups', in B. M. Staw and R. I. Sutton (eds), *Research in Organizational Behavior*, vol. 23 (Oxford: JAI/Elsevier, 2001), pp. 332–38.

34. Barrick, Stewart, Neubert and Mount, 'Relating Member Ability and Personality to Work-Team Processes and Team Effectiveness'.

35. Ibid, p. 388.

36. Ibid.

37. B. Beersma, J. R. Hollenbeck and S. E. Humphrey, 'Cooperation, Competition, and Team Performance: Toward a Contingency Approach', *Academy of Management Journal*, vol. 46, no. 5, October 2003, pp. 572–90; Ellis, Hollenbeck and Ilgen, 'Team Learning: Collectively Connecting the Dots', pp. 821–35; C. O. L. H. Porter, J. R. Hollenbeck and D. R. Ilgen, 'Backing up Behaviors in Teams: The Role of Personality and Legitimacy of Need', *Journal of Applied Psychology*, vol. 88, no. 3, June 2003, pp. 391–403; J. R. Hollenbeck, H. Moon and A. P. J. Ellis, 'Structural Contingency Theory and Individual Differences: Examination of External and Internal Person–Team Fit', *Journal of Applied Psychology*, vol. 87, no. 3, June 2002, pp. 599–606; J. A. Colquitt, J. R. Hollenbeck and D. R. Ilgen, 'Computer-Assisted Communication and Team Decision-Making Performance: The Moderating Effect of Openness to Experience', *Journal of Applied Psychology*, vol. 87, no. 2, April 2002, pp. 402–10; LePine, Hollenbeck and Ilgen, 'Effects of Individual Differences on the Performance of Hierarchical Decision-Making Teams: Much More than g', pp. 803–11; Jackson and. LePine, 'Peer Responses to a Team's Weakest Link: A Test and Extension of LePine and Van Dyne's Model', pp. 459–75; LePine, 'Team Adaptation and Postchange Performance: Effects of Team Composition in Terms of Members' Cognitive Ability and Personality', pp. 27–39.

38. C. Margerison and D. McCann, *Team Management: Practical New Approaches* (London: Mercury Books, 1990).

39. See, for example, R. A. Guzzo and G. P. Shea, 'Group Performance and Intergroup Relations in Organizations', in M. D. Dunnette and L. M. Hough (eds), *Handbook of Industrial & Organizational Psychology*, 2nd ed., vol. 3 (Palo Alto, CA: Consulting Psychologists Press, 1992), pp. 288–90; S. E. Jackson, K. E. May and K. Whitney, 'Understanding the Dynamics of Diversity in Decision-Making Teams', in R. A. Guzzo and E. Salas (eds), *Team Effectiveness and Decision Making in Organizations* (San Francisco: Jossey-Bass, 1995), pp. 204–61; K. Y. Williams and C. A. O'Reilly III, 'Demography and Diversity in Organizations: A Review of 40 Years of Research', in B. M. Staw and L. L.

Cummings (eds), *Research in Organizational Behavior*, vol. 20 (Greenwich, CT: JAI Press, 1998), pp. 77–140; F. Linnehan and A. M. Konrad, 'Diluting Diversity: Implications for Intergroup Inequality in Organizations', *Journal of Management Inquiry*, December 1999, pp. 399–414; S. E. Jackson, A. Joshi and N. L. Erhardt, 'Recent Research on Team and Organizational Diversity: SWOT Analysis and Implications', *Journal of Management*, vol. 29, no. 6, 2003, pp. 801–30; and D. van Knippenberg, C. K. W. De Dreu and A. C. Homan, 'Work Group Diversity and Group Performance: An Integrative Model and Research Agenda', *Journal of Applied Psychology*, December 2004, pp. 1008–22.

40. A. Sammartino, J. O'Flynn and S. Nicholas, *Managing Diverse Work Teams: A Business Model for Diversity Management* (Canberra: DIMIA, 2002): <www.diversityaustralia.gov. au/_inc/doc_pdf/manage_div_teams_model. pdf#search=%22teams%20survey%20austr alia%20management%22> (accessed 10 September 2006).

41. Shaw, *Contemporary Topics*, p. 356.

42. J. A. LePine, J. R. Hollenbeck and D. R. Ilgen, 'Gender Composition, Situational Strength, and Team Decision Making Accuracy: A Criterion Decomposition Approach', *Organizational Behavior & Human Decision Processes*, vol. 88, no. 1, May 2002, pp. 445–75.

43. W. E. Watson, K. Kumar and L. K. Michaelsen, 'Cultural Diversity's Impact on Interaction Process and Performance: Comparing Homogeneous and Diverse Task Groups', *Academy of Management Journal*, June 1993, pp. 590–602; P. C. Earley and E. Mosakowski, 'Creating Hybrid Team Cultures: An Empirical Test of Transnational Team Functioning', *Academy of Management Journal*, February 2000, pp. 26–49; and S. Mohammed and L. C. Angell, 'Surface- and Deep-Level Diversity in Workgroups: Examining the Moderating Effects of Team Orientation and Team Process on Relationship Conflict', *Journal of Organizational Behavior*, December 2004, pp. 1015–39.

44. Watson, Kumar and Michaelsen, 'Cultural Diversity's Impact on Interaction Process and Performance: Comparing Homogeneous and Diverse Task Groups'.

45. C. A. O'Reilly III, D. F. Caldwell and W. P. Barnett, 'Work Group Demography, Social Integration, and Turnover', *Administrative Science Quarterly*, March 1989, pp. 21–37; S. E. Jackson, J. F. Brett, V. I. Sessa, D. M. Cooper, J. A. Julin and K. Peyronnin, 'Some Differences Make a Difference: Individual Dissimilarity and Group Heterogeneity as Correlates of Recruitment, Promotions, and Turnover', *Journal of Applied Psychology*, August 1991, pp. 675–89; M. F. Wiersema and A. Bird, 'Organizational Demography in Japanese Firms: Group Heterogeneity, Individual Dissimilarity, and Top Management Team Turnover', *Academy of*

Management Journal, October 1993, pp. 996–1025; F. J. Milliken and L. L. Martins, 'Searching for Common Threads: Understanding the Multiple Effects of Diversity in Organizational Groups', *Academy of Management Review*, April 1996, pp. 402–33; B. Lawrence, 'The Black Box of Organizational Demography', *Organizational Science*, February 1997, pp. 1–22; and K. Y. Williams and C. A. O'Reilly III, 'Demography and Diversity in Organizations: A Review of 40 Years of Research', in B. M. Staw and L. L. Cummings (eds), *Research in Organizational Behavior*, vol. 20, pp. 77–140.

46. W. G. Wagner, J. Pfeffer and C. A. O'Reilly, 'Organizational Demography and Turnover in Top-Management Groups', *Administrative Science Quarterly*, vol. 29, no. 1, 1984, pp. 74–92.

47. J. Katzenbach, 'What Makes Teams Work?', *Fast Company*, November 2000, p. 110.

48. The evidence in this section is described in Thompson, *Making the Team*, pp. 65–67. See also L. A. Curral, R. H. Forrester and J. F. Dawson, 'It's What You Do and the Way that You Do It: Team Task, Team Size, and Innovation-Related Group Processes', *European Journal of Work & Organizational Psychology*, vol. 10, no. 2, June 2001, pp. 187–204; R. C. Liden, S. J. Wayne and R. A. Jaworski, 'Social Loafing: A Field Investigation', *Journal of Management*, vol. 30, no. 2, 2004, pp. 285–304; J. A. Wagner, 'Studies of Individualism-Collectivism: Effects on Cooperation in Groups', *Academy of Management Journal*, vol. 38, no. 1, February 1995.

49. Curral, Forrester, Dawson and West, 'It's What You Do and the Way that You Do It: Team Task, Team Size, and Innovation-Related Group Processes', pp. 187–204.

50. E. Sundstrom, K. P. Meuse and D. Futrell, 'Work Teams: Applications and Effectiveness', *American Psychologist*, February 1990, pp. 120–33.

51. Hyatt and Ruddy, 'An Examination of the Relationship between Work Group Characteristics and Performance'; J. D. Shaw, M. K. Duffy and E. M. Stark, 'Interdependence and Preference for Group Work: Main and Congruence Effects on the Satisfaction and Performance of Group Members', *Journal of Management*, vol. 26, no. 2, 2000, pp. 259–79; and S. A. Kiffin-Peterson and J. L. Cordery, 'Trust, Individualism, and Job Characteristics of Employee Preference for Teamwork', *International Journal of Human Resource Management*, February 2003, pp. 93–116.

52. R. Wageman, 'Critical Success Factors for Creating Superb Self-Managing Teams', *Organizational Dynamics*, Summer 1997, p. 55.

53. Campion, Papper and Medsker, 'Relations between Work Team Characteristics and Effectiveness', p. 430; B. L. Kirkman and

B. Rosen, 'Powering up Teams', *Organizational Dynamics*, Winter 2000, pp. 48–66; and D. C. Man and S. S. K. Lam, 'The Effects of Job Complexity and Autonomy on Cohesiveness in Collectivist and Individualist Work Groups: A Cross-Cultural Analysis', *Journal of Organizational Behavior*, December 2003, pp. 979–1001.

54. Campion, Papper and Medsker, 'Relations between Work Team Characteristics and Effectiveness', p. 430.

55. I. D. Steiner, *Group Processes and Productivity* (New York: Academic Press, 1972).

56. K. Hess, *Creating the High-Performance Team* (New York: Wiley, 1987); Katzenbach and Smith, *The Wisdom of Teams*, pp. 43–64; K. D. Scott and A. Townsend, 'Teams: Why Some Succeed and Others Fail', *Human Resources*, August 1994, pp. 62–67; and K. Blanchard, D. Carew and E. Parisi-Carew, 'How to Get Your Group to Perform Like a Team', *Training and Development*, September 1996, pp. 34–37.

57. E. Weldon and L. R. Weingart, 'Group Goals and Group Performance', *British Journal of Social Psychology*, Spring 1993, pp. 307–34; see also R. P. DeShon, S. W. J. Kozlowski, A. M. Schmidt, K. R. Milner and D. Wiechmann, 'A Multiple-Goal, Multilevel Model of Feedback Effects on the Regulation of Individual and Team Performance', *Journal of Applied Psychology*, December 2004, pp. 1035–56.

58. C. B. Gibson, A. Randel and P. C. Earley, 'Understanding Group Efficacy: An Empirical Test of Multiple Assessment Methods', *Group & Organization Management*, 2000, pp. 67–97; and S. M. Gully, K. A. Incalcaterra, A. Joshi and J. M. Beaubien, 'A Meta-Analysis of Team-Efficacy, Potency, and Performance: Interdependence and Level of Analysis as Moderators of Observed Relationships', *Journal of Applied Psychology*, October 2002, pp. 819–32; C. B. Gibson, 'The Efficacy Advantage: Factors Related to the Formation of Group Efficacy', *Journal of Applied Social Psychology*, October 2003, pp. 2153–86; and D. I. Jung and J. J. Sosik, 'Group Potency and Collective Efficacy: Examining Their Predictive Validity, Level of Analysis, and Effects of Performance Feedback on Future Group Performance', *Group & Organization Management*, September 2003, pp. 366–91.

59. K. A. Jehn, 'A Qualitative Analysis of Conflict Types and Dimensions in Organizational Groups', *Administrative Science Quarterly*, September 1997, pp. 530–57; see also R. S. Peterson and K. J. Behfar, 'The Dynamic Relationship between Performance Feedback, Trust, and Conflict in Groups: A Longitudinal Study', *Organizational Behavior and Human Decision Processes*, September–November 2003, pp. 102–12.

60. Hess, *Creating the High-Performance Team*.

61. See, for instance, B. L. Kirkman and D. L. Shapiro, 'The Impact of Cultural Values on Employee Resistance to Teams: Toward a Model of Globalized Self-Managing Work Team Effectiveness', *Academy of Management Review*, July 1997, pp. 730–57; and B. L. Kirkman, C. B. Gibson and D. L. Shapiro, '"Exporting" Teams: Enhancing the Implementation and Effectiveness of Work Teams in Global Affiliates', *Organizational Dynamics*, vol. 30, no. 1, 2001, pp. 12–29.

62. T. D. Schellhardt, 'To Be a Star among Equals, Be a Team Player', *Wall Street Journal*, 20 April 1994, p. B1.

63. Ibid.

64. See, for instance, J. Prieto, 'The Team Perspective in Selection and Assessment', in H. Schuler, J. L. Farr and M. Smith (eds), *Personnel Selection and Assessment: Industrial and Organizational Perspectives* (Hillsdale, NJ: Erlbaum, 1994); R. Klimoski and R. G. Jones, 'Staffing for Effective Group Decision Making: Key Issues in Matching People and Teams', in R. A. Guzzo and E. Salas (eds), *Team Effectiveness and Decision Making in Organizations* (San Francisco: Jossey-Bass, 1995), pp. 307–26; and C. Hymowitz, 'How to Avoid Hiring the Prima Donnas Who Hate Teamwork', *Wall Street Journal*, 15 February 2000, p. B1.

65. Schellhardt, 'To Be a Star among Equals, Be a Team Player'.

66. 'Teaming up for Success', *Training*, January 1994, p. S41.

67. J. S. DeMatteo, L. T. Eby and E. Sundstrom, 'Team-Based Rewards: Current Empirical Evidence and Directions for Future Research', in B. M. Staw and L. L. Cummings (eds), *Research in Organizational Behavior*, vol. 20, pp. 141–83.

68. B. Geber, 'The Bugaboo of Team Pay', *Training*, August 1995, pp. 27, 34.

69. Kinlaw, *Developing Superior Work Teams*, p. 43.

70. B. Krone, 'Total Quality Management: An American Odyssey', *The Bureaucrat*, Fall 1990, p. 37.

71. C. E. Naquin and R. O. Tynan, 'The Team Halo Effect: Why Teams Are Not Blamed for Their Failures', *Journal of Applied Psychology*, April 2003, pp. 332–40.

72. A. B. Drexler and R. Forrester, 'Teamwork—Not Necessarily the Answer', *Human Resources*, January 1998, pp. 55–58. See also R. Saavedra, P. C. Earley and L. Van Dyne, 'Complex Interdependence in Task-Performing Groups', *Journal of Applied Psychology*, February 1993, pp. 61–72; and K. A. Jehn, G. B. Northcraft and M. A. Neale, 'Why Differences Make a Difference: A Field Study of Diversity, Conflict, and Performance in Workgroups', *Administrative Science Quarterly*, December 1999, pp. 741–63.

11

© Randy Glasbergen.
www.glasbergen.com

"Here are the minutes from our last meeting:
Marty wasted 12 minutes, Janice wasted 7 minutes,
Carl wasted 27 minutes, Eileen wasted 9 minutes..."

COMMUNICATION

CHAPTER OUTLINE

LEARNING OBJECTIVES

AFTER STUDYING THIS CHAPTER, YOU SHOULD BE ABLE TO:

1. DESCRIBE THE COMMUNICATION PROCESS

2. CONTRAST THE ADVANTAGES AND DISADVANTAGES OF ORAL VERSUS WRITTEN COMMUNICATION

3. COMPARE THE EFFECTIVENESS OF THE CHAIN, WHEEL AND ALL-CHANNEL NETWORKS

4. IDENTIFY THE FACTORS AFFECTING THE USE OF THE GRAPEVINE

5. DISCUSS HOW COMPUTER-AIDED TECHNOLOGY IS CHANGING ORGANISATIONAL COMMUNICATION

6. EXPLAIN THE IMPORTANCE OF CHANNEL RICHNESS TO IMPROVING COMMUNICATION EFFECTIVENESS

7. IDENTIFY COMMON BARRIERS TO EFFECTIVE COMMUNICATION

8. DESCRIBE THE POTENTIAL PROBLEMS IN CROSS-CULTURAL COMMUNICATION

Managers constantly complain about the time they spend in meetings. The challenge for organisations is to continuously review their communication channels and decision-making processes to determine how meetings contribute effectively as a face-to-face encounter.

MEETINGS, BLOODY MEETINGS. That's a phrase that can be heard in the corridors of many organisations. It comes from the title of a humorous training video on how to run more effective meetings and features John Cleese of *Monty Python* and *Fawlty Towers* fame. A 2005 study of 300 Australian employees and managers found the number of face-to-face meetings has increased year by year, irrespective of industry segment. So much for channelling more communication via the internet.

Sharon Davis is human resources director of AMP Financial Services. She appreciates the dilemma that organisations face with internal meetings and believes they are the best and worst of devices in contemporary corporate life. They are critical for communication and decision-making, yet they take up so much of a person's time. Robin Young, product solutions manager for the Information Worker Business Group at Microsoft Australia, spends around 70 per cent of his working week in meetings. Meetings would take over his entire week if he didn't purposefully insist on free time in his weekly schedule.

Both Sharon and Robin appreciate the importance of face-to-face encounters for communicating ideas and information. They appreciate the need for debate and for getting buy-in and consensus on critical decisions. In 2003, AMP took steps to address the meeting explosion syndrome. As Sharon highlighted, AMP quickly worked out that the key to fewer and more effective meetings is clear accountabilities and good communication channels, so that meetings don't become a proxy for information sharing or a substitute for good decision making. Robin Young reinforces this point through his own experiences: '… we operate in a culture of consensus, which is a good thing. But gaining buy-in can slow down the decision-making process and you can end up generating more and more meetings.'[1]

If you want to make peace, you don't talk to your friends. You talk to your enemies.

Moshe Dayan

THE ISSUE OF WHEN AND HOW to run meetings highlights the bigger issue of effective communications in organisations. In this chapter, we'll show that good communication is essential to any group's or organisation's effectiveness. Research indicates that poor communication is probably the most frequently cited source of interpersonal conflict.[2] Because individuals spend nearly 70 per cent of their waking hours communicating—writing, reading, speaking, listening—it seems reasonable to conclude that one of the most inhibiting forces to successful group performance is a lack of effective communication.

No group can exist without communication: the transference of meaning among its members. It is only through transmitting meaning from one person to another that information and ideas can be conveyed. Communication, however, is more than merely imparting meaning. It must also be understood. In a group in which one member speaks only German and the others don't know German, the individual speaking German will not be fully understood. Therefore, **communication** must include both the *transference and the understanding of meaning*.

An idea, no matter how great, is useless until it is transmitted and understood by others. Perfect communication, if there were such a thing, would exist when a thought or an idea was transmitted so that the mental picture perceived by the receiver was exactly the same as that envisioned by the sender. Although elementary in theory, perfect communication is never achieved in practice, for reasons we shall expand on later in the chapter.

Before making too many generalisations concerning communication and problems in communicating effectively, we need to review briefly the functions that communication performs and describe the communication process.

communication | The transference and understanding of meaning.

FUNCTIONS OF COMMUNICATION

Communication serves four main functions within a group or organisation: control, motivation, emotional expression and information.[3] Communication acts to *control* member behaviour in several ways. Organisations have authority hierarchies and formal guidelines that employees are required to follow. When employees, for instance, are required to communicate any job-related grievance to their immediate boss first, to follow their job description, or to comply with company policies, communication is performing a control function. But informal communication also controls behaviour. When work groups tease or harass a member who produces too much (and makes the rest of the group look bad), they are informally communicating with, and controlling, the member's behaviour.

Communication fosters *motivation* by clarifying to employees what is to be done, how well they are doing, and what can be done to improve performance if it is below acceptable standards. We saw this operating in our review of goal-setting and reinforcement theories in Chapter 6. The formation of specific goals, feedback on progress towards the goals, and reinforcement of desired behaviour all stimulate motivation and require communication.

For many employees, their work group is a primary source for social interaction. The communication that takes place within the group is a fundamental mechanism by which members show their frustrations and feelings of satisfaction. Communication, therefore, provides a release for the *emotional expression* of feelings and for fulfilment of social needs.

The final function that communication performs relates to its role in facilitating decision making. It provides the *information* that individuals and groups need to make decisions by transmitting the data to identify and evaluate alternative choices.

No one of these four functions should be seen as being more important than the others. For groups to perform effectively, they need to maintain some form of control over members, stimulate members to perform, provide a means for emotional expression and make decision choices. You can assume that almost every communication interaction that takes place in a group or organisation performs one or more of these four functions.

THE COMMUNICATION PROCESS

Before communication can take place, a purpose, expressed as a message to be conveyed, is needed. It passes between a sender and a receiver. The message is encoded (converted to a symbolic form) and passed by way of some medium (channel) to the receiver, who retranslates (decodes) the message initiated by the sender. The result is transference of meaning from one person to another.[4]

Figure 11.1 depicts this **communication process**. The key parts of this model are: (1) the sender, (2) encoding, (3) the message, (4) the channel, (5) decoding, (6) the receiver, (7) noise, and (8) feedback.

The *sender* initiates a *message* by encoding a thought. The *message* is the actual physical product from the sender's *encoding*. When we speak, the speech is the message. When we write, the writing is the message. When we gesture, the movements of our arms and the expressions on our faces are the message. The *channel* is the medium through which the message travels. It is selected by the sender, who must determine whether to use a formal or informal channel. **Formal channels** are established by the organisation and transmit messages that are related to the professional activities of members. They traditionally follow the authority chain within the organisation. Other forms of messages, such as personal or social, follow the **informal channels** in the organisation. These informal channels are spontaneous and emerge as a response to individual choices.[5] The *receiver* is the object to whom the message is directed. But before the message can be received, the symbols in it must be translated into a form that can be understood by the receiver. This step is the *decoding* of the message. *Noise* represents communication barriers that distort the clarity of the message. Examples of possible noise sources include perceptual problems, information overload, semantic difficulties or cultural differences. The final link in the communication process is a feedback loop. *Feedback* is the check on how successful we have been in transferring our messages as originally intended. It determines whether understanding has been achieved.

communication process | The steps between a source and a receiver that result in the transference and understanding of meaning.

formal channels | Communication channels established by an organisation to transmit messages related to the professional activities of members.

informal channels | Communication channels that are created spontaneously and that emerge as responses to individual choices.

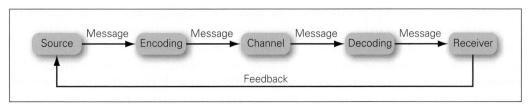

■ FIGURE 11.1
The communication process

DIRECTION OF COMMUNICATION

Communication can flow vertically or laterally. The vertical dimension can be further divided into downward and upward directions.[6]

DOWNWARD COMMUNICATION

Communication that flows from one level of a group or organisation to a lower level is downward communication. When we think of managers communicating with employees, the downward pattern is the one we are usually thinking of. It is used by group leaders and managers to assign goals, provide job instructions, inform employees of policies and procedures, point out problems that need attention and offer feedback about performance. But downward communication doesn't have to be oral or face-to-face contact. When management sends letters to employees' homes to advise them of the organisation's new sick leave policy, it is using downward communication. So is an email from a team leader to the members of her team, reminding them of an upcoming deadline.

UPWARD COMMUNICATION

Upward communication flows to a higher level in the group or organisation. It is used to provide feedback to more senior managers to inform them of progress towards goals and relay current problems. Upward communication keeps managers aware of how employees feel about their jobs, co-workers and the organisation in general. Managers also rely on upward communication for ideas on how things can be improved.

Some organisational examples of upward communication are performance reports prepared by lower management for review by middle and top management, suggestion boxes, employee attitude surveys, grievance procedures, superior–subordinate discussions and informal 'gripe' sessions in which employees have the opportunity to identify and discuss problems with their boss or representatives of higher management. For example, the Marriott Hotels group prides itself on its balanced scorecard approach to communicating performance results to all employees. Each of its hotels collects, and regularly displays to employees, information on occupancy rates and customer satisfaction. In addition, every employee is surveyed annually on all aspects of their hotel. This information is used as part of the performance reviews of the hotel managers.

LATERAL COMMUNICATION

When communication takes place among members of the same work group, among members of work groups at the same level, among managers at the same level, or among any horizontally equivalent personnel, we describe it as lateral, or horizontal, communication.

Why would there be a need for horizontal communications if a group or organisation's vertical communications are effective? The answer is that horizontal communications are often necessary to save time and facilitate coordination. In some cases, these lateral relationships are formally sanctioned. More often, they are informally created to short-circuit the vertical hierarchy and expedite action. So, from management's viewpoint, lateral communications can be good or bad. Because strict adherence to the formal vertical structure for all communications can impede the efficient and accurate transfer of information, lateral communications can be beneficial. In such cases, they occur with the knowledge and support of superiors. But they can create dysfunctional conflicts when the formal vertical channels are breached, when members go above or around their superiors to get things done, or when bosses find out that actions have been taken or decisions made without their knowledge.

INTERPERSONAL COMMUNICATION

How do group members transfer meaning between and among each other? There are three basic methods. People essentially rely on oral, written and non-verbal communication.

ORAL COMMUNICATION

The chief means of conveying messages is oral communication. Speeches, formal one-on-one and group discussions, and the informal rumour mill or grapevine are popular forms of oral communication.

LEARNING OBJECTIVE   2

Contrast the advantages and disadvantages of oral versus written communication

The advantages of oral communication are speed and feedback. A verbal message can be conveyed and a response received in a minimal amount of time. If the receiver is unsure of the message, rapid feedback allows for early detection by the sender and, hence, allows for early correction.

The main disadvantage of oral communication surfaces in organisations or whenever the message has to be passed through a number of people. The more people a message must pass through, the greater the potential distortion. If you ever played the game 'telephone' or Chinese whispers at a party, you know the problem. Each person interprets the message in his or her own way. The message's content, when it reaches its destination, is often very different from that of the original. In an organisation where decisions and other communiqués are verbally passed up and down the authority hierarchy, there are considerable opportunities for messages to become distorted.

WRITTEN COMMUNICATION

Written communications include memos, letters, fax transmissions, electronic mail, instant messaging, organisational newsletters, notices placed on bulletin boards, or any other device that is transmitted via written words or symbols.

Why would a sender choose to use written communications? They are often tangible and verifiable. When printed, both the sender and receiver have a record of the communication; and the message can be stored for an indefinite period. If there are questions concerning the content of the message, it is physically available for later reference. This feature is particularly important for complex and lengthy communications. The marketing plan for a new product, for instance, is likely to contain a number of tasks spread out over several months. By putting it in writing, those who have to initiate the plan can readily refer to it over the life of the plan. A final benefit of all written communication comes from the process itself. You are usually more careful with the written word than the spoken word. You are forced to think more thoroughly about what you want to convey in a written message than in a spoken one. Thus, written communications are more likely to be well thought out, logical and clear.

Of course, written messages have their drawbacks. They are time-consuming. You could convey far more information to a university lecturer in a one-hour oral exam than in a one-hour written exam. In fact, you could probably say the same thing in 10 to 15 minutes that it would take you an hour to write. So, although writing may be more precise, it also consumes a great deal of time. The other main disadvantage is feedback, or lack of it. Oral communication allows the receiver to respond rapidly to what he thinks he hears. Written communication, however, doesn't have a built-in feedback mechanism. The result is that the mailing of a memo is no assurance it has been received, and, if received, there is no guarantee the recipient will interpret it as the sender intended. The latter point is also relevant in oral communiqués, except it is easy in such cases merely to ask the receiver to summarise what you have said. An accurate summary presents feedback evidence that the message has been received and understood.

NON-VERBAL COMMUNICATION

Every time we verbally give a message to someone, we also impart a non-verbal message.[7] In some instances, the non-verbal component may stand alone. For example, when socialising at bars or nightclubs, a glance, a stare, a smile, a frown and a provocative body movement all convey meaning. As such, no discussion of communication would be complete without consideration of *non-verbal communication*—which includes body movements, the intonations or emphasis we give to words, facial expressions, and the physical distance between the sender and receiver.

It can be argued that every *body movement* has a meaning and no movement is accidental. For example, through body language we say, 'Help me, I'm lonely'; 'Take me, I'm available'; 'Leave me alone, I'm depressed.' And rarely do we send our messages consciously. We act out our state of being with non-verbal body language. We lift one eyebrow for disbelief. We rub our noses for puzzlement. We clasp our arms to isolate ourselves or to protect ourselves. We shrug our shoulders for indifference, wink one eye for intimacy, tap our fingers for impatience, slap our forehead for forgetfulness.[8]

The two most important messages that body language conveys are: (1) the extent to which an individual likes another and is interested in his or her views; and (2) the relative perceived status between a sender and receiver.[9] For instance, we are more likely to position ourselves closer to people we like and to touch them more often. Similarly, if you feel that you are a higher status than another, you are more likely to display body movements—such as crossed legs or a slouched seating position—that reflect a casual and relaxed manner.[10]

Body language adds to, and often complicates, verbal communication. A body position or movement doesn't by itself have a precise or universal meaning, but when it is linked with spoken language, it gives fuller meaning to a sender's message.

If you read the verbatim minutes of a meeting, you wouldn't grasp the impact of what was said in the same way you would if you had been there or had seen the meeting on video. Why? There is no record of non-verbal communication. The emphasis given to words or phrases is missing. Table 11.1 illustrates how *intonations* can change the meaning of a message. *Facial expressions* also convey meaning. A snarling face says something different from a smile. Facial expressions, along with intonations, can show arrogance, aggressiveness, fear, shyness and other characteristics that would never be communicated if you read a transcript of what had been said.

The way individuals space themselves in terms of *physical distance* also has meaning. What is considered proper spacing is largely dependent on cultural norms. For example, what is considered a businesslike distance in some European countries would be viewed as intimate in many parts of Australasia. If someone stands closer to you than is considered appropriate, it may indicate aggressiveness or sexual interest; if further away than usual, it may mean disinterest or displeasure with what is being said.

Change your tone and you change your meaning

Placement of the emphasis	What it means
Why don't I take **you** to dinner tonight?	I was going to take someone else.
Why don't **I** take you to dinner tonight?	Instead of the guy you were going with.
Why **don't** I take you to dinner tonight?	I'm trying to find a reason why I shouldn't take you.
Why don't I take you to dinner tonight?	Do you have a problem with me?
Why don't I **take** you to dinner tonight?	Instead of going on your own.
Why don't I take you to **dinner** tonight?	Instead of lunch tomorrow.
Why don't I take you to dinner **tonight**?	Not tomorrow night.

SOURCE: Based on M. Kiely, 'When "No" Means "Yes"', *Marketing*, October 1993, pp. 7–9. Reproduced in A. Huczynski and D. Buchanan, *Organizational Behavior*, 4th ed. (Essex, England: Pearson Education, 2001), p. 194.

It is important for the receiver to be alert to these non-verbal aspects of communication. You should look for non-verbal cues as well as listen to the literal meaning of a sender's words. You should particularly be aware of contradictions between the messages. Your boss may say she is free to talk to you about a pressing budget problem, but you may see non-verbal signals suggesting that this isn't the time to discuss the subject. Regardless of what is being said, an individual who frequently glances at her wristwatch is giving the message that she would prefer to terminate the conversation. We misinform others when we express one message verbally, such as trust, but non-verbally communicate a contradictory message that reads, 'I don't have confidence in you.'

ORGANISATIONAL COMMUNICATION

In this section, we move from interpersonal communication to organisational communication. Our focus here will be on formal networks, the grapevine, computer-aided mechanisms used by organisations to facilitate communication, and the evolving topic of knowledge management.

FORMAL SMALL-GROUP NETWORKS

LEARNING OBJECTIVE 3

Compare the effectiveness of the chain, wheel and all-channel networks

Formal organisational networks can be very complicated. They can, for instance, include hundreds of people and a half-dozen or more hierarchical levels. To simplify our discussion, we have condensed these networks into three common small groups of five people each (see Figure 11.2). These three networks are the chain, wheel and all-channel. Although these three networks have been extremely simplified, they do allow us to describe the unique qualities of each.

The *chain* rigidly follows the formal chain of command. This network approximates the communication channels you might find in a rigid three-level organisation. The *wheel* relies on a central figure to act as the conduit for all of the group's communication. It simulates the communication network you would find on a team with a strong leader. The *all-channel* network permits all group members to actively communicate with each other. The all-channel network is most often characterised in practice by self-managed teams, in

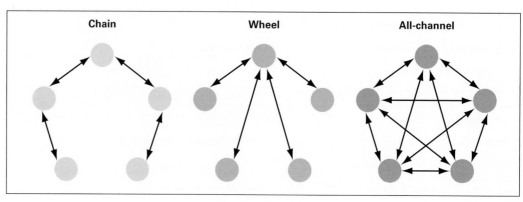

which all group members are free to contribute and no one person takes on a leadership role.

As Table 11.2 demonstrates, the effectiveness of each network depends on the dependent variable you are concerned about. For instance, the structure of the wheel facilitates the emergence of a leader, the all-channel network is best if you are concerned with having high member satisfaction, and the chain is best if accuracy is most important. Table 11.2 leads us to the conclusion that no single network will be best for all occasions.

■ TABLE 11.2

Small-group networks and effective criteria

	Networks		
Criteria	Chain	Wheel	All-channel
Speed	Moderate	Fast	Fast
Accuracy	High	High	Moderate
Emergence of a leader	Moderate	High	None
Member satisfaction	Moderate	Low	High

THE GRAPEVINE

The formal system isn't the only communication network in a group or organisation. There is also an informal one, which is called the **grapevine**.[11] And although the grapevine may be informal, this doesn't mean it is not an important source of information. For instance, a survey found that 75 per cent of employees hear about matters first through rumours on the grapevine.[12]

grapevine | The organisation's informal communication network.

The grapevine has three main characteristics.[13] First, it is not controlled by management. Second, it is perceived by most employees as being more believable and reliable than formal communiqués issued by top management. And third, it is largely used to serve the self-interests of the people within it.

One of the most famous studies of the grapevine investigated the communication pattern among 67 managerial personnel in a small manufacturing firm.[14] The basic approach used was to learn from each communication recipient how he or she first received a given piece of information and then trace it back to its source. It was found that, while the grapevine was an important source of information, only 10 per cent of the executives acted as liaison individuals—that is, passed the information on to more than one other person. For example, when one executive decided to resign to enter the insurance business, 81 per cent of the executives knew about it, but only 11 per cent transmitted this information to others.

Two other conclusions from this study are also worth noting. Information on events of general interest tended to flow between the main functional groups (production, sales) rather than within them. Also, no evidence surfaced to suggest that any one group consistently acted as liaisons; rather, different types of information passed through different liaison persons.

An attempt to replicate this study among employees in a small state government office also found that only 10 per cent act as liaison individuals.[15] This finding is interesting, because the replication contained a wider spectrum of employees, including operative as well as managerial personnel. But the flow of information in the government office took place within, rather than between, functional groups. It was proposed that this discrepancy might be due to comparing an executive-only sample against one that also included operative workers. Managers, for example, might feel greater pressure to stay informed and thus cultivate others outside their immediate functional group. Also, in contrast to the findings of the original study, the replication found that a consistent group of individuals acted as liaisons by transmitting information in the government office.

Is the information that flows along the grapevine accurate? The evidence indicates that about 75 per cent of what is carried is accurate.[16] But what conditions foster an active grapevine? What gets the rumour mill rolling?

It is frequently assumed that rumours start because they make titillating gossip. This is rarely the case. Rumours emerge as a response to situations that are *important* to us, when there is *ambiguity*, and under conditions that arouse *anxiety*.[17] The fact that work situations frequently contain these three elements explains why rumours flourish in organisations. The secrecy and competition that typically prevail in large organisations— around issues such as the appointment of new bosses, the relocation of offices, downsizing decisions, and the realignment of work assignments—create conditions that encourage and sustain rumours on the grapevine. A rumour will persist either until the wants and expectations creating the uncertainty underlying the rumour are fulfilled or until the anxiety is reduced.

What can we conclude from the preceding discussion? Certainly the grapevine is an important part of any group or organisation communication network and is well worth understanding.[18] It gives managers a feel for the morale of their organisation, identifies issues that employees consider important, and helps to tap into employee anxieties. It acts, therefore, as both a filter and a feedback mechanism, picking up the issues that employees consider relevant. For employees, the grapevine is particularly valuable for translating formal communications into their group's own jargon. Maybe more important, again from a managerial perspective, it seems possible to analyse grapevine information and to predict its flow, given that only a small set of individuals (approximately 10 per cent) actively pass on information to more than one other person. By assessing which liaison individuals will consider a given piece of information to be relevant, we can improve our ability to explain and predict the pattern of the grapevine.

Can management entirely eliminate rumours? No. What management should do, however, is minimise the negative consequences of rumours by limiting their range and impact. Table 11.3 offers a few suggestions for minimising those negative consequences.

COMPUTER-AIDED COMMUNICATION

Communication in today's organisations is enhanced and enriched by computer-aided technologies. These include electronic mail, instant messaging, intranet and extranet links, and videoconferencing. Electronic mail, for instance, has dramatically reduced the

> **LEARNING OBJECTIVE 5**
>
> Discuss how computer-aided technology is changing organisational communication

■ **TABLE 11.3**

Suggestions for reducing the
negative consequences of
rumours

1.	Announce timetables for making important decisions.
2.	Explain decisions and behaviours that may appear inconsistent or secretive.
3.	Emphasise the downside, as well as the upside, of current decisions and future plans.
4.	Openly discuss worst-case possibilities—it is almost never as anxiety-provoking as the unspoken fantasy.

SOURCE: Adapted from L. Hirschhorn, 'Managing Rumors', in L. Hirschhorn (ed.), *Cutting Back* (San Francisco: Jossey-Bass, 1983), pp. 54–56. Reproduced with permission of Larry Hirschhorn, Principal, Center for Applied Research.

number of memos, letters and phone calls that employees historically used to communicate among themselves and with suppliers, customers or other outside stakeholders.

EMAIL

Electronic mail (or email) uses the internet to transmit and receive computer-generated text and documents. Its growth has been spectacular. In fact, in the United States, over 100 million adults (one-third of the total population) use email regularly (at least once a day), and it is estimated that nearly 1 trillion emails are sent daily worldwide. A good percentage (up to 70 per cent—depending on the quality of one's spam filter) of this email comes in the form of spam (unsolicited email ads or other unwanted material) and phishing emails (internet scams initiated with a spoof email message). Nevertheless, the reason we put up with junk email is because, for many of us, email is an indispensable way of communicating.

As a communication tool, email has a long list of benefits. Email messages can be quickly written, edited and stored. They can be distributed to one person or thousands with a click of a mouse. They can be read, in their entirety, at the convenience of the recipient. And the cost of sending formal email messages to employees is a fraction of what it would cost to print, duplicate and distribute a comparable letter or brochure.

Email, of course, isn't without its drawbacks.[19] It can be a distraction from work activities when employees use it for personal purposes. And it can be impersonal, detracting from special attention to customers or co-workers. John Caudwell—one of the United Kingdom's richest tycoons and CEO of Caudwell Group—felt email was so distracting that he banned all employees from using it at work, commenting: 'Management and staff at HQ and in the stores were beginning to show signs of being constrained by e-mail proliferation.' Although employees have had mixed reactions to the ban on email, Caudwell claims that customer service has improved.[20] We don't know, however, whether Caudwell's claims about improved customer service—due to eliminating email—are in fact true. A recent study, though, revealed that most emails from customers are ignored. In this study, the researchers posed as customers and used email to enquire about purchasing a product or service from 147 retail companies in various industries. In 51 per cent of the cases, a reply to the email was never received.[21] Perhaps email does hurt customer service, as Caudwell claims.

Emails also lack emotional content. The non-verbal cues in a face-to-face message or the tone of voice from a phone call convey important information that doesn't come across in email. Additionally, emails tend to be cold and impersonal. As such, they are not the ideal means to convey information such as layoffs, plant closings, or other messages that might evoke emotional responses and require empathy or social support. Finally, the remote nature of email fuels 'conflict spirals' that have been found to escalate ill feelings at double the rate of face-to-face communiqués. Many people seem to be able to say things in emails that they would never say to someone face-to-face.

INSTANT MESSAGING

It's not just for teenagers anymore. Instant messaging (IM), such as MSN messenger, which has been popular among teens for more than a decade, is now rapidly moving into business.[22] Instant messaging is essentially real-time email. Employees create a list of colleagues and friends with whom they want to communicate. Then they just click on a name displayed in a small box on their computer screen, type in a message, and the message instantaneously pops up on to the recipient's screen. Increasingly, people are using handheld IM devices, such as mobile phones, palm pilots or Blackberries. The growth of IM has been spectacular. In 2001, for instance, just 8 per cent of employees in the United States were using it. In 2003, it was up to 18 per cent. And experts estimate that within a few years, more people will be using IM than email as their primary communication tool at work.[23] Australian mobile operator Optus has published the results of a 2006 survey conducted by research firm TNS that shows the number of mobile email users is still very small when compared to those with fixed-line access. 'The survey confirms

---

THE DANGER OF COMMUNICATING EMOTIONS VIA EMAIL

The University of South Australia has a policy on email etiquette. The policy points out that email isn't always the best form of communication. It has some limitations of which users should be aware. In particular, staff should avoid having arguments on email. The lack of interpersonal cues can lead to serious disagreements unnecessarily. Staff should remember that non-verbal communication accounts for, by far, the main part of the meaning that is communicated in face-to-face situations, and these non-verbal cues are not present in electronic text on its own. Email, therefore, places an increased importance on the message. And if the message is fuzzy, then the interpretation is open to abuse, especially if the emails find themselves in unintended inboxes.

Allens Arthur Robinson is a major legal firm in Australia and Asia. The company was embroiled in an email stoush between two secretaries in the Sydney office that was soon forwarded around the world.

'I am in a happy relationship, have a beautiful apartment, brand new car, high paid job … say no more', one secretary wrote. 'Oh my God, I'm laughing', the other replied, 'beautiful apartment (so what), brand new car (me too), high paid job (I earn more) … say plenty more … I have 5 guys at the moment. Haha.'

The email exchange that had begun as a search for someone's lunch that had disappeared from the staff room fridge soon turned sour. One of the women made the mistake of forwarding the emails to a lawyer within the firm. Consequently, these emails flowed freely inside and outside the firm, entering the inboxes of people at Macquarie Bank, Queensland government departments, law firm McCullough Robertson, Westpac Institutional Bank and many other organisations.

This sort of unintended communication to the outside world embarrassed the management at the law firm because of the negative reactions created in the larger business environment as illustrated by the following comments that were made by various observers: 'So this is what happens in those posh Sydney firms', and 'This just shows how bitchy the big law firms can be.'

Newspapers reported that the two women had been sacked. The firm warned that it is a lesson to all companies and individuals about the potential consequences of improper use of email.

SOURCES: Kate Gibbs, 'Secretaries in Email Stoush', *Human Resources*, no. 89, 20 September 2006, p. 9; Kate Gibbs, 'Allens Embroiled in Secretary Stoush': <www.lawyersweekly.com.au/articles/c6/0c0367c6.asp> (accessed 23 August 2006); and University of South Australia: <www.unisa.edu.au/ists/GovernanceInIT/Policies/others/netiqtte.asp> (accessed 23 August 2006).

OB IN PRACTICE

that Australia has only scratched the surface in terms of mobile email. There is a four-fold gap between those that have mobile email today and those that see it as extremely useful, or essential to their work', said Paul Kitchin, director of marketing, Optus Business.[24]

IM is a fast and inexpensive means for managers to stay in touch with employees and for employees to stay in touch with each other. For instance, furniture retailer Jennifer Convertibles uses IM to communicate with managers in its 200-plus stores nationwide.[25] Jeff Wenger, a senior manager at tax preparation and software company Tax Technologies uses IM to manage a team of software developers and testers who are geographically scattered. Wenger says IM has cut his daily telephone time from three hours to less than 30 minutes.[26] IM isn't going to replace email. Email is still probably a better device for conveying long messages that need to be saved. IM is preferred for sending one- or two-line messages that would just clutter up an email inbox. On the downside, some IM users find the technology intrusive and distracting. IM's continual online presence can make it hard for employees to concentrate and stay focused. Managers also indicate concern that IM will be used by employees to chat with friends and colleagues about non-work issues. Finally, because instant messages are easily broken into, many organisations are concerned about IM security.[27]

INTRANET LINKS

intranet | An IP network belonging to an organisation, usually a corporation, and accessible only to organisation members, employees, etc., or people authorised by them.

Intranets are private, organisation-wide information networks that look and act like a website but to which only people in an organisation have access. Intranets are rapidly becoming a popular means for employees within companies to communicate with each other. IBM, as a case in point, recently brought together 52 000 of its employees online for what it called WorldJam.[28] Using the company's intranet, IBMers everywhere swapped ideas on everything from how to retain employees to how to work faster without undermining quality.

VIDEOCONFERENCING

Videoconferencing is an extension of intranet systems. It permits employees in an organisation to have meetings with people at different locations. Live audio and video

Charmaine Ryan is the associate dean (academic) in the Faculty of Business, University of Southern Queensland. Her role involves assisting heads of school and other academic staff in developing submissions for new courses and programs. Writing lengthy documents with inputs from multiple authors can be a challenge. But Charmaine has been instrumental in developing an intranet system within the faculty so that multiple authors can edit and update a common document located at a central website. This saves time in physically moving the document between different authors and waiting for their contribution. The intranet improves communication between staff working on a common project and allows project members to access the latest versions of documents and other project resources.

images of members allow them to see, hear and talk with each other. Videoconferencing technology, in effect, allows employees to conduct interactive meetings without the necessity of all being physically in the same location.

In the late 1990s, videoconferencing was basically conducted from special rooms equipped with television cameras, located at company facilities. More recently, cameras and microphones are being attached to individual computers, allowing people to participate in videoconferences without leaving their desks. As the cost of this technology drops in price, videoconferencing is likely to be increasingly seen as an alternative to expensive and time-consuming travel.

SUMMARY

Computer-aided communications are reshaping the way we communicate in organisations. Specifically, it is no longer necessary for employees to be at their work station or desk to be 'available'. Pagers, mobile phones, personal communicators and phone messaging allow employees to be reached when they are in a meeting, during a lunch break, while visiting a customer across town, or during a golf game on Saturday morning. The line between an employee's work and non-work life is no longer distinct. In the electronic age, all employees can theoretically be 'on call' 24 hours a day, 7 days a week.

Organisational boundaries become less relevant as a result of computer-aided communications. Networked computers allow employees to jump vertical levels within the organisation, work full-time at home or someplace other than an organisationally operated facility, and conduct ongoing communications with people in other organisations. The market researcher who wants to discuss an issue with the manager of marketing (who is three levels up in the hierarchy) can bypass the people in between and send an email message directly. And in so doing, the traditional status hierarchy, largely determined by level and access, becomes essentially negated. Or that same market researcher may choose to live at Byron Bay on the New South Wales coast and work at home via telecommuting, rather than do the job in the company's Sydney office. And when an employee's computer is linked to suppliers' and customers' computers, the boundaries separating organisations become further blurred. As a case in point, Woolworths is using a sophisticated electronic supply chain management system to improve the flow of transactions with their many suppliers.

KNOWLEDGE MANAGEMENT

Our final topic under organisational communication is **knowledge management (KM)**. This is a process of organising and distributing an organisation's collective wisdom so that the right information gets to the right people at the right time.[29] When done properly, KM provides an organisation with both a competitive edge and improved organisational performance because it makes its employees smarter.

Siemens, the global telecommunications giant, recently won a $460 000 contract to build a telecommunications network for two hospitals in Switzerland in spite of the fact that its bid was 30 per cent higher than the competition's. The secret to Siemens's success was its knowledge-management system.[30] This system allowed Siemens's people in the Netherlands to draw on their experience and provide the Swiss sales representatives with technical data that proved that the Siemens's network would be substantially more reliable than the competition's.

Siemens is one of a growing number of companies—including GPC Electronics, General Motors Holden, Telstra, IBM, Whirlpool, BHP and Fuji Xerox Australia—that

knowledge management (KM) | The process of organising and distributing an organisation's collective wisdom so that the right information gets to the right people at the right time.

have realised the value of knowledge management. In fact, a recent survey found that 81 per cent of the leading organisations in Europe and the United States say they have, or are at least considering adopting, some kind of KM system.[31]

Knowledge management is increasingly important today for at least three reasons.[32] First, in many organisations, intellectual assets are now as important as physical or financial assets. Organisations that can quickly and efficiently tap into their employees' collective experience and wisdom are more likely to 'outsmart' their competition. Second, as baby-boomers begin to leave the workforce, there is an increasing awareness that they represent a wealth of knowledge that will be lost if there are no attempts to capture it. And third, a well-designed KM system will reduce redundancy and make the organisation more efficient. For instance, when employees in a large organisation undertake a new project, they needn't start from scratch. A knowledge-management system can allow them to access what previous employees have learned and cut wasteful time retracing a path that has already been travelled.

How does an organisation record the knowledge and expertise of its employees and make that information easily accessible? It needs to develop computer databases of pertinent information that employees can readily access; it needs to create a culture that supports and rewards sharing; and it has to develop mechanisms that allow employees who have developed valuable expertise and insights to share them with others.

KM begins by identifying what knowledge matters to the organisation.[33] Management needs to review processes to identify those that provide the most value. It can then develop computer networks and databases that can make that information readily available to the people who need it the most. But KM won't work unless the culture supports sharing of information.[34] Information that is important and scarce can be a potent source of power. And people who hold that power are often reluctant to share it with others. So KM requires an organisational culture that promotes, values and rewards sharing of knowledge. Finally, KM must provide the mechanisms and the motivation for employees to share knowledge that employees find useful on the job and enables them to achieve better performance.[35] *More* knowledge isn't necessarily *better* knowledge. Information overload needs to be avoided by designing the system to capture only pertinent information and then organising it so that it can be quickly accessed by the people whom it can help. The University of Southern Queensland, for instance, has created a KM system with customised email distribution lists carefully broken down by employees' speciality, title and area of interest; set aside a dedicated site on the company's intranet that serves as a central information repository; and created separate in-house websites where employees with various expertise can share new information with others and work on common projects.

CHOICE OF COMMUNICATION CHANNEL

LEARNING OBJECTIVE 6

Explain the importance of channel richness to improving communication effectiveness

Neal Patterson, CEO at medical-software maker Cerner Corporation, likes email. Maybe too much so. Upset with his staff's work ethic, he recently sent a seething email to his firm's 400 managers.[36] Here are some of that email's highlights:

Hell will freeze over before this CEO implements ANOTHER EMPLOYEE benefit in this Culture … We are getting less than 40 hours of work from a large number of our … City-based employees. The parking lot is sparsely used at 8 A.M.; likewise at 5 P.M. As managers—you either do not know what your EMPLOYEES are doing; or YOU do not

CARE … You have a problem and you will fix it or I will replace you … What you are doing, as managers, with this company makes me SICK.

Patterson's email additionally suggested that managers schedule meetings at 7 am, 6 pm and Saturday mornings; promised a staff reduction of 5 per cent and institution of a time-clock system; and announced his intention to charge unapproved absences to employees' holiday time.

Within hours of this email, copies of it had made its way on to a Yahoo! website. And within three days, Cerner's share price had plummeted 22 per cent. Although one can argue about whether such harsh criticism should be communicated at all, one thing is certainly clear: Patterson erred by selecting the wrong channel for his message. Such an emotional and sensitive message would likely have been better received in a face-to-face meeting.

Why do people choose one channel of communication over another—for instance, a phone call instead of a face-to-face talk? Is there any general insight we might be able to provide regarding choice of communication channel? The answer to the latter question is a qualified 'Yes'. A model of media richness has been developed to explain channel selection among managers.[37] Research has found that channels differ in their capacity to convey information. Some are rich in that they have the ability to (1) handle multiple cues simultaneously, (2) facilitate rapid feedback, and (3) be very personal. Others are lean in that they score low on these three factors. As Figure 11.3 illustrates, face-to-face conversation scores highest in terms of **channel richness** because it provides for the maximum amount of information to be transmitted during a communication episode. That is, it offers multiple information cues (words, postures, facial expressions, gestures, intonations), immediate feedback (both verbal and non-verbal) and the personal touch of 'being there'. Impersonal written media such as formal reports and bulletins rate lowest in richness.

channel richness | The amount of information that can be transmitted during a communication episode.

The choice of one channel over another depends on whether the message is routine or non-routine. The former types of messages tend to be straightforward and have a

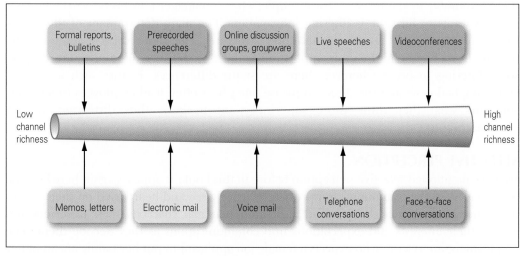

SOURCES: Based on R. H. Lengel and R. L. Daft, 'The Selection of Communication Media as an Executive Skill', *Academy of Management Executive*, August 1988, pp. 225–32; and R. L. Daft and R. H. Lengel, 'Organizational Information Requirements, Media Richness, and Structural Design', *Managerial Science*, May 1996, pp. 554–72. Reproduced from R. L. Daft and R. A. Noe, *Organizational Behavior* (Fort Worth, TX: Harcourt, 2001), p. 311.

■ FIGURE 11.3
Information richness of communication channels

minimum of ambiguity. The latter are likely to be complicated and have the potential for misunderstanding. Managers can communicate routine messages efficiently through channels that are lower in richness. However, they can communicate non-routine messages effectively only by selecting rich channels. Referring back to the Cerner Corporation example, it appears that Neal Patterson's problem was using a channel relatively low in richness (email) to convey a message that, because of its non-routine nature and complexity, should have been conveyed using a rich communication medium.

Evidence indicates that high-performing managers tend to be more media-sensitive than low-performing managers.[38] That is, they are better able to match appropriate media richness with the ambiguity involved in the communication. The media richness model is consistent with organisational trends and practices during the past decade. It is not just coincidence that more and more senior managers have been using meetings to facilitate communication and regularly leaving the isolated sanctuary of their executive offices to manage by walking around. These executives are relying on richer channels of communication to transmit the more ambiguous messages they need to convey. The past decade has been characterised by organisations closing facilities, imposing large layoffs, restructuring, merging, consolidating, and introducing new products and services at an accelerated pace—all non-routine messages high in ambiguity and requiring the use of channels that can convey a large amount of information. It is not surprising, therefore, to see the most effective managers expanding their use of rich channels.

LEARNING OBJECTIVE 7

Identify common barriers to effective communication

BARRIERS TO EFFECTIVE COMMUNICATION

A number of barriers can retard or distort effective communication. In this section, we highlight the more important of these barriers.

FILTERING

filtering | A sender's manipulation of information so that it will be seen more favourably by the receiver.

Filtering refers to a sender purposely manipulating information so that it will be seen more favourably by the receiver. For example, when a manager tells his boss what he feels his boss wants to hear, he is filtering information. The main determinant of filtering is the number of levels in an organisation's structure. The more vertical levels in the organisation's hierarchy, the more opportunities there are for filtering. But you can expect some filtering to occur wherever there are status differences. Factors such as fear of conveying bad news and the desire to please one's boss often lead employees to tell their superiors what they think those superiors want to hear, thus distorting upward communications.

SELECTIVE PERCEPTION

We have mentioned selective perception before in this book. It appears again here because the receivers in the communication process selectively see and hear based on their needs, motivations, experience, background and other personal characteristics. Receivers also project their interests and expectations into communications as they decode them. The employment interviewer who expects a female job applicant to put her family ahead of her career is likely to see that in female applicants, regardless of whether the applicants feel that way or not. As we said in Chapter 5, we don't see reality; we interpret what we see and *call* it reality.

INFORMATION OVERLOAD

Individuals have a finite capacity for processing data. When the information we have to work with exceeds our processing capacity, the result is **information overload**. And with emails, instant messaging, phone calls, faxes, meetings, and the need to keep current in one's field, the potential for today's managers and professionals to suffer from information overload is high.

What happens when individuals have more information than they can sort out and use? They tend to select out, ignore, pass over or forget information. Or they may put off further processing until the overload situation is over. Regardless, the result is lost information and less effective communication.

information overload | A condition in which information inflow exceeds an individual's processing capacity.

EMOTIONS

How the receiver feels at the time of receipt of a communication will influence how he or she interprets it. The same message received when you are angry or distraught is often interpreted differently from when you are happy. Extreme emotions such as jubilation or depression are most likely to hinder effective communication. In such instances, we are most prone to disregard our rational and objective thinking processes and substitute emotional judgments.

LANGUAGE

Words mean different things to different people. Age, education and cultural background are three of the more obvious variables that influence the language a person uses and the definitions he or she gives to words.

In an organisation, employees usually come from diverse backgrounds. Further, the grouping of employees into departments creates specialists who develop their own 'buzzwords', or technical jargon. In large organisations, members are also frequently widely dispersed geographically—even operating in different countries—and individuals in each locale will use terms and phrases that are unique to their area. The existence of vertical levels can also cause language problems. For instance, differences in meaning with regard to words such as *incentives* and *quotas* have been found at different levels in management. Top managers often speak about the need for incentives and quotas, yet these terms imply manipulation and create resentment among many lower managers.

The point is that although we probably speak a common language—English—our use of that language is far from uniform. If we knew how each of us modified the language, communication difficulties would be minimised. The problem is that members in an organisation usually don't know how those with whom they interact have modified the language. Senders tend to assume that the words and terms they use mean the same to the receiver as they do to them. This assumption is often incorrect.

COMMUNICATION APPREHENSION

Another major barrier to effective communication is that some people—an estimated 5 to 20 per cent of the population[39]—suffer from debilitating **communication apprehension** or anxiety. Although lots of people dread speaking in front of a group, communication apprehension is a more serious problem because it affects a whole category of communication techniques. People who suffer from it experience undue tension and anxiety in oral communication, written communication, or both.[40]

For example, oral apprehensives may find it extremely difficult to talk with others face-to-face or become extremely anxious when they have to use the telephone. As a result, they may

communication apprehension | Undue tension and anxiety about oral communication, written communication, or both.

rely on memos or faxes to convey messages when a phone call would be not only faster but more appropriate. Studies demonstrate that oral-communication apprehensives avoid situations that require them to engage in oral communication.[41] We should expect to find some self-selection in jobs so that such individuals don't take positions, such as teacher, for which oral communication is a dominant requirement.[42] But almost all jobs require some oral communication. And of greater concern is the evidence that high-oral-communication apprehensives distort the communication demands of their jobs in order to minimise the need for communication.[43] So we need to be aware that there is a set of people in organisations who severely limit their oral communication and rationalise this practice by telling themselves that more communication isn't necessary for them to do their job effectively.

CURRENT ISSUES IN COMMUNICATION

In this section, we discuss four current issues related to communication in organisations: Why do men and women often have difficulty communicating with each other? What role does silence play in communication? What are the implications of the 'politically correct' movement on communications in organisations? And how can individuals improve their cross-cultural communications?

COMMUNICATION BARRIERS BETWEEN WOMEN AND MEN

The classic studies by Deborah Tannen provide us with some important insights into the differences between men and women in terms of their conversational styles.[44] In particular, Tannen has been able to explain why gender often creates oral communication barriers. The essence of Tannen's research is that men use talk to emphasise status, whereas women use it to create connection. Her conclusion, of course, doesn't apply to *every* man or *every* woman. As she puts it, her generalisation means 'a larger percentage of women or men as *a group* talk in a particular way, or individual women and men are *more likely* to talk one way or the other'.[45]

Tannen states that communication is a continual balancing act, juggling the conflicting needs for intimacy and independence. Intimacy emphasises closeness and commonalities. Independence emphasises separateness and differences. But here's the kick: women speak and hear a language of connection and intimacy; men speak and hear a language of status, power and independence. So, for many men, conversations are primarily a means to preserve independence and maintain status in a hierarchical social order. For many women, conversations are negotiations for closeness in which people try to seek and give confirmation and support. A few examples will illustrate Tannen's thesis.

Men frequently complain that women talk on and on about their problems. Women criticise men for not listening. What's happening is that when men hear a problem, they frequently assert their desire for independence and control by offering solutions. Many women, on the other hand, view talking about a problem as a means to promote closeness. The women present the problem to gain support and connection, not to get the man's advice. Mutual understanding is symmetrical. But giving advice is asymmetrical—it sets up the advice giver as more knowledgeable, more reasonable and more in control. This contributes to distancing men and women in their efforts to communicate.

Men are often more direct than women in conversation. A man might say, 'I think you're wrong on that point.' A woman might say, 'Have you looked at the marketing department's research report on that point?' (the implication being that the report will show the error).

Research indicates that most women use language to create connection, while most men use it to emphasise status, power and independence. These differences in conversational styles may create oral communication barriers between men and women. The women communicating in this photo illustrate that women generally speak and hear a language of intimacy. But for men, conversations are a way to preserve their independence.

Men frequently see female indirectness as 'covert' or 'sneaky', but women are not as concerned as men with the status and one-upmanship that directness often creates.

Women tend to be less boastful than men.[46] They often downplay their authority or accomplishments to avoid appearing as if they are bragging and to take the other person's feelings into account. However, men can frequently misinterpret this and incorrectly conclude that a woman is less confident and competent than she really is.

Finally, men often criticise women for seeming to apologise all the time. Women do apologise more than men.[47] Men tend to see the phrase 'I'm sorry' as a weakness, because they interpret it to mean the woman is accepting blame, when he knows she's not to blame. The woman also knows she's not to blame. The problem is that women frequently use 'I'm sorry' to express regret and restore balance to a conversation: 'I know you must feel bad about this; I do, too.' For many women, 'I'm sorry' is an expression of understanding and caring about the other person's feelings, rather than an apology.

SILENCE AS COMMUNICATION

Sherlock Holmes once solved a murder mystery based not on what happened but on what *didn't* happen. Holmes remarked to his assistant, Dr Watson, about 'the curious incident of the dog in the nighttime.' Watson, surprised, responds: 'But the dog did nothing in the nighttime.' To which Holmes replied, 'That was the curious incident.' Holmes concluded that the crime had to have been committed by someone with whom the dog was familiar, because it didn't bark.

The dog that didn't bark in the night is often used as a metaphor for an event that is significant by reason of its absence. That story is also an excellent illustration of the importance of silence in communication. Silence—defined here as an absence of speech or noise—has been generally ignored as a form of communication in OB because it represents inaction or non-behaviour. But it is not necessarily inaction. Nor is silence, as many believe, a failure to communicate. It can, in fact, be a powerful form of communication.[48] It can mean someone is thinking or contemplating a response to a question. It can mean a person is anxious and fearful of speaking. It can signal agreement, dissent, frustration or anger.

In terms of OB, we can see several links between silence and work-related behaviour. For instance, silence is a critical element of groupthink, in which it implies agreement with the majority. It can be a way for employees to express dissatisfaction, as when they 'suffer in silence'. It can be a sign that someone is upset, as when a typically talkative person suddenly says nothing—'What's the matter with him? Is he all right?' It is a powerful tool used by managers to signal disfavour by shunning or ignoring employees with 'silent insults'. And, of course, it is a crucial element of group decision making, allowing individuals to think over and contemplate what others have said.

Failing to pay close attention to the silent portion of a conversation can result in missing a vital part of the message. Astute communicators watch for gaps, pauses and hesitations. They hear and interpret silence. They treat pauses, for instance, as analogous to a flashing yellow light at an intersection—they pay attention to what comes next. Is the person thinking, deciding how to frame an answer? Is the person suffering from communication apprehension? Sometimes the real message in a communication is buried in the silence.

'POLITICALLY CORRECT' COMMUNICATION

What words do you use to describe a colleague who is wheelchair-bound? What terms do you use in addressing a female customer? How do you communicate with a brand-new client who isn't like you? Your answers can mean the difference between losing a client, an employee, a legal action, a harassment claim or a job.[49]

Most of us are acutely aware of how our vocabulary has been modified to reflect political correctness. For instance, most of us have cleansed the words *handicapped, blind* and *elderly* from our vocabulary—and replaced them with terms like *physically challenged, visually impaired* and *senior*. In the United States, the *Los Angeles Times*, for instance, allows its journalists to use the term *old age* but cautions that the onset of old age varies from 'person to person', so a group of 75-year-olds aren't necessarily all old.[50]

We must be sensitive to others' feelings. Certain words can and do stereotype, intimidate and insult individuals. In an increasingly diverse workforce, we must be sensitive to how words might offend others. But there is a downside to political correctness. It can complicate our vocabulary, making it more difficult for people to communicate. To illustrate, you probably know what these three terms mean: *garbage, quotas* and *women*. But each of these words has also been found to offend one or more groups. They have been replaced with terms like *post-consumer waste materials, educational equity* and *people of gender*. The problem is that this latter group of terms is much less likely to convey a uniform message than the words they replaced.

Words are the primary means by which people communicate. When we eliminate words from use because they are politically incorrect, we reduce our options for conveying messages in the clearest and most accurate form. For the most part, the larger the vocabulary used by a sender and a receiver, the greater the opportunity to transmit messages accurately. By removing certain words from our vocabulary, we make it harder to communicate accurately. When we further replace these words with new terms whose meanings are less well understood, we have reduced the likelihood that our messages will be received as we had intended them.

We must be sensitive to how our choice of words might offend others. But we also have to be careful not to sanitise our language to the point at which it clearly restricts clarity of communication. There is no simple solution to this dilemma. However, you should be aware of the trade-offs and of the need to find a proper balance.

'EAST ASIANS ARE MORE RESPONSIVE TO INDIRECT COMMUNICATION'

This statement is mostly true. Because people from East Asia (for example, Japan, China, Korea) place a high value on interpersonal harmony, they tend to communicate less directly than Australians. For example, assume you are responsible for creating a marketing plan. An Asian colleague might respond to your proposal with, 'The strategic rationale underlying your marketing plan needs some tightening, and the writing can be rough in places, but otherwise you have some very interesting ideas.' It is possible that she is telling you, in an indirect way, that your proposal is of limited value. Australians, however, are more direct in their communications. So, an Australian colleague may respond with, 'This marketing plan is way off the mark. It seems like it was thrown together at the last minute. Please get me a revision by the end of today.'

What explains these different communication techniques? In the workplace, Australians are generally guided by norms of short-term task accomplishment, and so they believe communication should be designed to get the job at hand done as quickly and as effectively as possible. East Asians, however, are more likely to communicate indirectly due to their desire to foster long-term relationships that are polite and respectful.

So, how can managers reduce miscommunication between the two cultures? Australians need to be sensitive to the fact that seemingly 'soft' statements from East Asians may contain stronger messages. East Asians need to realise that the blunt communication styles of Australians are generally not personal or intended as a threat to their status or position.

SOURCES: J. Sanchez-Burks, 'Protestant Relational Ideology and (in)attention to Relational Cues in Work Settings', *Journal of Personality and Social Psychology*, vol. 83, 2002, pp. 919–29; and J. Sanchez-Burks, F. Lee, I. Choi, R. Nisbett, S. Zhao and J. Koo, 'Conversing across Cultures: East–West Communication Styles in Work and Nonwork Contexts', *Journal of Personality and Social Psychology*, vol. 85, 2003, pp. 363–72.

CROSS-CULTURAL COMMUNICATION

Effective communication is difficult under the best of conditions. Cross-cultural factors clearly create the potential for increased communication problems. This is illustrated in Figure 11.4. A gesture that is well understood and acceptable in one culture can be meaningless or lewd in another.[51]

> **LEARNING OBJECTIVE 8**
>
> Describe the potential problems in cross-cultural communication

CULTURAL BARRIERS

Four specific problems related to language difficulties in cross-cultural communications have been identified.[52] First, there are *barriers caused by semantics*. As we have noted previously, words mean different things to different people. This is particularly true for people from different national cultures. Some words, for instance, don't translate between cultures. Understanding the word *sisu* will help you in communicating with people from Finland, but this word is untranslatable into English. It means something akin to 'guts' or 'dogged persistence'. Similarly, the new capitalists in Russia may have difficulty communicating with their Australian or Singaporean counterparts because English terms such as *efficiency*, *free market* and *regulation* are not directly translatable into Russian.

Second, there are *barriers caused by word connotations*. Words imply different things in different languages. Negotiations between New Zealand and Japanese executives, for instance, are made more difficult because the Japanese word *hai* translates as 'yes', but its connotation may be 'yes, I'm listening', rather than 'yes, I agree'.

Third are *barriers caused by tone differences*. In some cultures, language is formal, while in others it is informal. In some cultures, the tone changes depending on the context: people

The A-OK Sign

In Australia and the United States, this is just a friendly sign for 'All right!' or 'Good going'. In Islamic countries, it is equivalent to what generations of high school students know as 'flipping the bird'.

The 'Hook'em Horns' Sign

This sign is a good luck gesture in Brazil and Venezuela. In parts of Africa, it is a curse. In Italy, it is signalling to another that 'your spouse is being unfaithful'.

The 'V' for Victory Sign

In many parts of the world, this means 'victory' or 'peace'. In Australia, if the palm and fingers face inward, it means 'Up yours!' especially if executed with an upward jerk of the fingers.

The Finger-beckoning Sign

This sign means 'come here' in the United States. In Malaysia, it is used only for calling animals.

SOURCE: 'What's A-O-K in the U.S.A. is Lewd and Worthless Beyond', *New York Times*, 18 August 1996, p. E7. From Roger E. Axtell, *GESTURES: The Do's and Taboos of Body Language around the World*. Copyright © 1991. Reproduced with permission of John Wiley & Sons, Inc.

speak differently at home, in social situations and at work. Using a personal, informal style when a more formal style is expected can be embarrassing and off-putting.

Fourth, there are *barriers caused by differences among perceptions*. People who speak different languages actually view the world in different ways. Eskimos perceive snow differently because they have many words for it. Thais perceive 'no' differently than do Australians because there is no such word in Thai.

CULTURAL CONTEXT

high-context cultures | Cultures that rely heavily on non-verbal and subtle situational cues in communication.

low-context cultures | Cultures that rely heavily on words to convey meaning in communication.

A better understanding of these cultural barriers and their implications for communicating across cultures can be achieved by considering the concepts of high- and low-context cultures.[53]

Different cultures influence the meaning that individuals take from what is actually said or written in light of who the other person is. Countries such as China, Korea, Japan and Vietnam are **high-context cultures**. They rely heavily on non-verbal and subtle situational cues when communicating with others. What is *not* said may be more significant than what *is* said. A person's official status, place in society and reputation carry considerable weight in communications. In contrast, people from Europe and Australia reflect their **low-context cultures**. They rely essentially on words to convey meaning. Body language or formal titles are secondary to spoken and written words (see Figure 11.5).

LOST IN TRANSLATION?

In global commerce, language can be a barrier to conducting business effectively. Many Australian companies have overseas parents, including many in the automotive industry such as General Motors Holden, Goodyear Australia and Volvo Australia. In the fast food industry, McDonald's and Starbucks have domestic operations in many countries in the Southeast Asian region, including Singapore and Malaysia. Similarly, local Australasian companies have an overseas presence—for example, BHP Billiton views itself as the World's Largest Diversified Resources Company, with 37 000 employees working in more than 100 operations in approximately 25 countries.

To make matters more complicated, as a result of mergers and acquisitions, companies are often owned by multiple overseas parents, creating even greater strain on communication. Although English is the dominant language at many multinational companies, failing to speak a host country's language can make it tougher for managers to do their jobs well, especially if they are misinterpreted or misinterpret what others are saying. Such communication problems make it tougher to conduct business effectively and efficiently, and business opportunities may be lost because of them.

To avoid communication problems, many companies are requiring their managers to learn the local language. For example, German-based Siemens requires its managers to learn the language of their host country. Ernst Behrens, the head of Siemens's China operations, learned to speak Mandarin fluently. Robert Kimmett, a former Siemens's board member, believes that learning a host country's language gives managers 'a better grasp of what is going on inside a company … not just the facts and figures but also texture and nuance'.

However, learning a foreign language can be difficult for managers. The difficulty for Australians and New Zealanders in learning a foreign language is often deepened when the language is Eastern, such as Japanese or Chinese Mandarin, because the language is so different. To compensate, these managers sometimes rely solely on body language and facial expressions to communicate.

In his submission to the 2004 Australian Senate Inquiry into Australian Expatriates, John Burn (2006) described how he left Australia in 1990 to develop an international career. He found a satisfying job in the Netherlands and found that adapting in the Netherlands depended greatly on developing fluency in the Dutch language.

The problem? That there are cultural differences in these non-verbal forms of communication that may result in serious misunderstandings. To avoid this pitfall, one solution would be for managers to familiarise themselves with their host country's culture in order to avoid the communication problems that often result from failing to understand the local language.

SOURCES: Based on K. Kanhold, D. Bilefsky, M. Karnitschnig and G. Parker , 'Lost in Translation? Managers at Multinationals May Miss the Job's Nuances if They Speak Only English', *Wall Street Journal*, 18 May 2004, p. B.1; and John Burns Submission to Inquiry into Australian Expatriates: <www.aph.gov.au/Senate/committee/legcon_ctte/expats03/submissions/sub492.doc> (accessed 25 August 2006).

What do these contextual differences mean in terms of communication? Actually, quite a lot. Communication in high-context cultures implies considerably more trust by both parties. What may appear, to an outsider, as casual and insignificant conversation is important because it reflects the desire to build a relationship and create trust. Oral agreements imply strong commitments in high-context cultures. And who you are—your age, seniority, rank in the organisation—is highly valued and heavily influences your credibility. But in low-context cultures, enforceable contracts will tend to be in writing, precisely worded and highly legalistic. Similarly, low-context cultures value directness. Managers are expected to be explicit and precise in conveying intended meaning. It is quite different in high-context cultures, in which managers tend to 'make suggestions' rather than give orders.

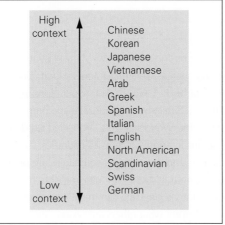

High
context

Chinese
Korean
Japanese
Vietnamese
Arab
Greek
Spanish
Italian
English
North American
Scandinavian
Swiss
German

Low
context

SOURCE: Based on the work of E. T. Hall. From R. E. Dulek, J. S. Fielden and J. S. Hall, 'International Communications: An Executive Primer', *Business Horizons*, January–February 1991, p. 21.

**SELF-
ASSESSMENT
LIBRARY**

HOW GOOD ARE MY LISTENING SKILLS?

In the Self-Assessment Library (available on CD and online), take Self-Assessment 11.A.2 (How Good Are My Listening Skills?) and answer the following questions.

1. How did you score relative to your classmates?
2. How might you improve your listening skills?

A CULTURAL GUIDE

When communicating with people from a different culture, try to assess the cultural context. You are likely to have fewer difficulties if people come from a similar cultural context to you. In addition, the following four rules can be helpful.[54]

1. *Assume differences until similarity is proven.* Most of us assume that others are more similar to us than they actually are. But people from different countries often are very different from us. So, you are far less likely to make an error if you assume others are different from you rather than assuming similarity until difference is proven.

2. *Emphasise description rather than interpretation or evaluation.* Interpreting or evaluating what someone has said or done, in contrast to description, is based more on the observer's culture and background than on the observed situation. As a result, delay judgment until you have had sufficient time to observe and interpret the situation from the differing perspectives of all the cultures involved.

3. *Practise empathy.* Before sending a message, put yourself in the recipient's shoes. What are his or her values, experiences and frames of reference? What do you know about his or her education, upbringing and background that can give you added insight? Try to see the other person as he or she really is.

4. *Treat your interpretations as a working hypothesis.* Once you have developed an explanation for a new situation or think you empathise with someone from a foreign culture, treat your interpretation as a hypothesis that needs further testing, rather than as a certainty. Assess the feedback provided by recipients to see if it confirms your hypothesis. For important decisions or communiqués, check with other foreign and home-country colleagues to make sure that your interpretations are on target.

SUMMARY AND IMPLICATIONS FOR MANAGERS

- A careful review of this chapter finds a common theme regarding the relationship between communication and employee satisfaction: the less the uncertainty, the greater the satisfaction. Distortions, ambiguities and incongruities in communications all increase uncertainty and, hence, they have a negative impact on satisfaction.[55]
- The less distortion that occurs in communication, the more that goals, feedback and other management messages to employees will be received as they were intended.[56] This should reduce ambiguities and clarify the group's task.
- Extensive use of vertical, lateral and informal channels will increase communication flow, reduce uncertainty, and improve group performance and satisfaction. We should also expect incongruities between verbal and non-verbal communiqués to increase uncertainty and reduce satisfaction.
- Findings further suggest that the goal of perfect communication is unattainable. Yet, there is evidence that demonstrates a positive relationship between effective communication (which includes factors such as perceived trust, perceived accuracy, desire for interaction, top-management receptiveness, and upward information requirements) and worker productivity.[57]
- Choosing the correct channel, being an effective listener and using feedback may, therefore, make for more effective communication. But the human factor generates distortions that can never be fully eliminated. The communication process represents an exchange of messages, but the outcome is meanings that may or may not approximate those that the sender intended.

- Whatever the sender's expectations, the decoded message in the mind of the receiver represents his or her reality. And it is this 'reality' that will determine performance, along with the individual's level of motivation and degree of satisfaction.
- In terms of expectancy theory (see Chapter 6), the degree of effort an individual exerts depends on his or her perception of the effort–performance, performance–reward, and reward–goal satisfaction links. If individuals are not given the data necessary to make the perceived probability of these links high, motivation will suffer. If rewards are not made clear, if the criteria for determining and measuring performance are ambiguous, or if individuals are not relatively certain that their effort will lead to satisfactory performance, then effort will be reduced. So, communication plays a significant role in determining the level of employee motivation.
- A final implication from the communication literature relates to predicting turnover. The use of realistic job previews acts as a communication device for clarifying role expectations. Employees who have been exposed to a realistic job preview have more accurate information about that job. Comparisons of turnover rates between organisations that use the realistic job preview versus either no preview or presentation of only positive job information show that those not using the realistic preview have, on average, almost 29 per cent higher turnover.[58] This makes a strong case for managers to convey honest and accurate information about a job to applicants during the recruiting and selection process.

POINT / COUNTERPOINT

Open-book Management Improves the Bottom Line

● POINT

Open-book management (OBM) seeks to get every employee to think and behave like an owner. It throws out the notion that bosses run things and employees do what they are told. In the open-book approach, employees are given the information that historically was kept strictly within the management ranks.

There are three key elements to any OBM program. First, management opens the company's books and shares detailed financial and operating information with employees. If employees don't know how the company makes money, how can they be expected to make the firm more successful? Second, employees need to be taught to understand the company's financial statements. This means management must provide employees with a 'basic course' in how to read and interpret statements of financial performance, of financial position and of cash flows. And third, management needs to show employees how their work influences financial results. Showing employees the impact of their jobs on the bottom line makes financial statement analysis relevant.

Who is using OBM? A growing list of Australian firms are using open-book management, including Mt Isa Mines, Purkis Partners near Gosford in New South Wales, Brisbane-based firm Ashley and Munro, Textor, Fusion Design Consultants and accounting firm Darcy Kennedy in Dubbo, New South Wales. Textor is a textile technologies company that invites all staff to attend and participate in monthly profit and loss meetings and to take personal responsibility for raising productivity or minimising costs in specific areas of the business. The company believes that ethical and cooperative behaviour leads to industrial harmony and a workforce that believes in the company and its products.

Why should it work? Access to detailed financial information and the ability to understand that information makes employees think like owners. And this leads to them making decisions that are best for the organisation, not just for themselves. Does it work? Most firms that have introduced OBM offer evidence that it has significantly helped the business. For example, the American company Springfield Remanufacturing was losing US$61 000 on sales of US$16 million. Management attributes much of the company's current success—profits of US$6 million a year on sales of US$100 million—to OBM. Similarly, Allstate's Business Insurance Group used OBM to boost return on equity from 2.9 per cent to 16.5 per cent in just three years. Accounting firm Darcy Kennedy improved its productivity by restructuring the firm and the roles of partners and professionals. One of the key elements was an open-book style of management. Warrick McLean, a non-accountant, was appointed practice manager at the start of the restructuring in 1997. He helped to bring a climate of openness by undertaking performance reviews on the partners, insisting that performance information applies to everyone in the organisation. He previously worked in a university and believes that dealing with partners wasn't too difficult after working with academics. Senior partner Michael Kennedy says that staff have access to all the firm's books and are able to work on their own productivity. Damien Mair, of Australia's Fusion Design Consultants, states that his company's OBM model is based on weekly profit updates leading to improved employee motivation and greater commitment to the organisation.

● COUNTERPOINT

The owners of Optics 1 Inc., an optical-engineering company with 23 employees and sales of less than US$10 million a year, implemented an OBM program. After a short time, the program was discontinued. Said one of the co-owners, 'Employees used the information against me. When we made a profit, they demanded bigger bonuses and new computers. When I used profits to finance a new product line, everybody said, "That's nice, but what's in it for me?" … If your employees misinterpret financial information, it's more damaging than their not having access at all. I gave them general and administrative rates. Next thing I knew, they were backing out everyone's salaries, and I'd hear, "You're paying that guy $86 000? I contribute more."'

As this example illustrates, part of the downside to OBM is that employees may misuse or misinterpret the information they are given. Another potential problem is the leaking of confidential information to competitors. In the hands of the competition, detailed information about the company's operations and financial position may undermine a firm's competitive advantage.

Matrix Builders and Project Managers, a private Brisbane construction company, has committed to an open-book policy in terms of each construction project and is introducing profit sharing for its staff. The firm believes that its management approach has led to a more productive work climate. However, while this has created greater involvement and participation by staff, it can have a downside. The firm intends to engage lifestyle consultants to ensure that employees balance their work and home commitments. According to Peter Burt, joint owner and managing director, 'The most difficult thing is getting some staff to go home … We find people working here from very early in the morning into the night and then on weekends. When you get people spending 60 to 80 hours a week at the workplace, it's not healthy. The work is fairly stressful to start with, and if you exacerbate that with very long working hours there is a risk that the work problems go home—and, before you know it, there are home problems coming to work.'

When OBM succeeds, two factors seem to exist. First, the organisation or unit in which it is implemented tends to be small. It is a lot easier to introduce OBM in a small, start-up company than in a large, geographically dispersed company that has operated for years with closed books and little employee involvement. Second, there needs to be a mutually trusting relationship between management and workers. In organisational cultures in which management doesn't trust employees to act selflessly, or in which managers and accountants have been trained to keep information under lock and key, OBM isn't likely to work. Nor will it succeed when employees believe that any new change program is only likely to further manipulate or exploit them for management's advantage.

SOURCES: Points in this argument are based on J. P. Schuster, J. Carpenter and M. P. Kane, *The Power of Open-Book Management* (New York: John Wiley, 1996); R. Aggarwal and B. J. Simkins, 'Open Book Management—Optimizing Human Capital', *Business Horizons*, September–October 2001, pp. 5–13; D. Drickhamer, 'Open Books to Elevate Performance', *Industry Week*, November 2002, p. 16; <www.textortextiles.com/corporate.html> (accessed 12 October 2006); Tony Thomas, 'Restructuring: Country Firm's Winning New Ways', *Business Review Weekly*, 22 October 1999, pp. 122–24; M. Kaplan, 'Opening the Books', *Australasian Business Intelligence*, 6 May 2003; M. R. Dixon, L. J. Hayes and J. Stack, 'Changing Conceptions of Employee Compensation', *Journal of Organizational Behavior Management*, vol. 23, no. 2–3, 2003, pp. 95–116; S. L. Gruner, 'Why Open the Books?', *INC.*, November 1996, p. 95; T. R. V. Davis, 'Open-Book Management: Its Promise and Pitfalls', *Organizational Dynamics*, vol. 25, no. 3, Winter 1997, pp. 7–20; and M. Massey, 'Builders Try to Get Work and Leisure Matrix Right', *Business Review Weekly*, 19 October 1998, pp. 120–21.

QUESTIONS FOR REVIEW

1. Describe the functions that communication provides within a group or organisation. Give an example of each.
2. Contrast encoding and decoding.
3. Contrast downward with upward communication.
4. What is non-verbal communication? Does it aid or hinder verbal communication?
5. What are the advantages and disadvantages of email? Of instant messaging?
6. What are knowledge-management systems? How do they affect communication?
7. How do the communication styles of men and women differ?
8. What does the phrase 'sometimes the real message in a communication is buried in the silence' mean?
9. Describe how political correctness can hinder effective communication.
10. Contrast high- and low-context cultures. What do these differences mean for communication?

QUESTIONS FOR CRITICAL THINKING

1. 'Ineffective communication is the fault of the sender.' Do you agree or disagree? Discuss.
2. What can you do to improve the likelihood that your communiqués will be received and understood as you intend?
3. How might managers use the grapevine for their benefit?
4. Using the concept of channel richness, give examples of messages best conveyed by email, by face-to-face communication and on the company bulletin board.
5. 'Most people are poor listeners.' Do you agree or disagree? Defend your position.

EXPERIENTIAL EXERCISE

An Absence of Non-verbal Communication

Purpose:
This exercise will help you to see the value of non-verbal communication to interpersonal relations.

Participants:
The class is to split up into pairs (Party A and Party B).

Tasks:
1. Party A is to select a topic from the following list:
   a. Managing in Asia is significantly different from managing in Australia.
   b. Employee turnover in an organisation can be functional.
   c. Some conflict in an organisation is good.
   d. Whistle-blowers do more harm than good for an organisation.
   e. An employer has a responsibility to provide every employee with an interesting and challenging job.
   f. Everyone should register to vote.
   g. Organisations should require all employees to undergo regular drug tests.
   h. Individuals who have majored in business or economics make better employees than those who have majored in history or politics.
   i. The place where you get your university degree is more important in determining your career success than what you learn while you are there.
   j. It is unethical for a manager to purposely distort communications in order to get a favourable outcome.
2. Party B is to choose a position on this topic (for example, arguing *against* the view that 'some conflict in an organisation is good'). Party A now must automatically take the opposite position.
3. The two parties have ten minutes in which to debate their topic. The catch is that the individuals can only communicate verbally. They may not use gestures, facial movements, body movements, or any other non-verbal communication. It may help for each party to sit on their hands to remind them of these restrictions and to maintain an expressionless look.
4. After the debate is over, form groups of six to eight and spend 15 minutes discussing the following: (a) How effective was communication during these debates? (b) What barriers to communication existed? (c) What purposes does non-verbal communication serve? (d) Relate the lessons learned in this exercise to problems that might occur when communicating by mobile phone or through email.

ETHICAL DILEMMA

Defining the Boundaries of Technology

You work for a company that has no specific policies regarding non-work-related uses of computers and the internet. They also have no electronic monitoring devices to determine what employees are doing on their computers. Are any of the following actions unethical? Explain your position on each:

a. Using the company's email system for personal reasons during the workday.
b. Playing computer games during the workday.
c. Using your office computer to do internet shopping during the workday.

d. Looking for a mate on an internet dating-service website during the workday.
e. Visiting 'adult' websites on your office computer during the workday.
f. All of the above activities conducted before or after normal work hours.
g. For telecommuters who are working from home, using a computer and an internet-access line paid for by your employer to visit internet shopping or dating-service sites during normal working hours.

---

11 CASE STUDY

Bruce Swanepoel Has Communication Problems

Bruce Swanepoel only has four employees at his public relations firm. But he seems to have done a pretty good job of alienating them.

According to his employees, Bruce, 47, is a brilliant person who has a lot to learn in terms of being a better communicator. His communication style appears to be a regular source of conflict in his firm. He admits he has a problem. 'I'm probably not as verbally reinforcing [as I could be] when someone is doing a good job. I'm a very self-confident person. I don't need to be told I'm doing a good job—but there are people who do.'

Swanepoel's employees had no problem listing things that he does that bother them. He doesn't meet deadlines; he does a poor job of communicating with clients and this often puts the employees in an uncomfortable position; he doesn't listen fully to employees' ideas before dismissing them; his voice tone is frequently condescending; and he is often quick to criticise employees, and praise is virtually non-existent.

QUESTIONS
1. A lot of bosses are accused of being 'poor communicators'. Why do you think this is?
2. What does this case suggest regarding the relationship between reinforcement theory and communication?
3. What, specifically, do you think Bruce needs to do to improve his communication skills?
4. Assuming Bruce wants to improve, how would you suggest he go about learning to be a better communicator?

SOURCE: This case is based on N. L. Torres, 'Playing Well With Others', *Entrepreneur*, February 2003, p. 30.

ENDNOTES

1. D. Tarrant, 'Meeting Mania', *Management Today*, July 2006, pp. 14–16.
2. See, for example, K. W. Thomas and W. H. Schmidt, 'A Survey of Managerial Interests with Respect to Conflict', *Academy of Management Journal*, June 1976, p. 317.
3. W. G. Scott and T. R. Mitchell, *Organization Theory: A Structural and Behavioral Analysis* (Homewood, IL: Richard D. Irwin, 1976).
4. D. K. Berlo, *The Process of Communication* (New York: Holt, Rinehart & Winston, 1960), pp. 30–32.
5. J. Langan-Fox, 'Communication in Organizations: Speed, Diversity, Networks, and Influence on Organizational Effectiveness, Human Health, and Relationships', in N. Anderson, D. S. Ones, H. K. Sinangil and C. Viswesvaran (eds), *Handbook of Industrial, Work, and Organizational Psychology*, vol. 2 (Thousand Oaks, CA: Sage, 2001), p. 190.
6. R. L. Simpson, 'Vertical and Horizontal Communication in Formal Organizations', *Administrative Science Quarterly*, September 1959, pp. 188–96; B. Harriman, 'Up and Down the Communications Ladder', *Harvard Business Review*, September–October 1974, pp. 143–51; A. G. Walker and J. W. Smither, 'A Five-Year Study of Upward Feedback: What Managers Do With Their Results Matters', *Personnel Psychology*, Summer 1999, pp. 393–424; and J. W. Smither and A. G. Walker, 'Are the Characteristics of Narrative Comments Related to Improvement in Multirater Feedback Ratings over Time?', *Journal of Applied Psychology*, vol. 89, no. 3, June 2004, pp. 575–81.
7. L. S. Rashotte, 'What Does That Smile Mean? The Meaning of Nonverbal Behaviors in Social Interaction', *Social Psychology Quarterly*, March 2002, pp. 92–102.
8. J. Fast, *Body Language* (Philadelphia: M. Evan, 1970), p. 7.
9. A. Mehrabian, *Nonverbal Communication* (Chicago: Aldine-Atherton, 1972).
10. N. M. Henley, 'Body Politics Revisited: What Do We Know Today?', in P. J. Kalbfleisch and M. J. Cody (eds), *Gender, Power, and Communication in Human Relationships* (Hillsdale, NJ: Erlbaum, 1995), pp. 27–61.
11. See, for example, N. B. Kurland and L. H. Pelled, 'Passing the Word: Toward a Model of Gossip and Power in the Workplace', *Academy of Management Review*, April 2000, pp. 428–38; and N. Nicholson, 'The New Word on Gossip', *Psychology Today*, June 2001, pp. 41–45.
12. Cited in 'Heard It through the Grapevine', *Forbes*, 10 February, 1997, p. 22.
13. See, for instance, J. W. Newstrom, R. E. Monczka and W. E. Reif, 'Perceptions of the Grapevine: Its Value and Influence', *Journal of Business Communication*, Spring 1974, pp. 12–20; and S. J. Modic, 'Grapevine Rated Most Believable', *Industry Week*, 15 May 1989, p. 14.
14. K. Davis, 'Management Communication and the Grapevine', *Harvard Business Review*, September–October 1953, pp. 43–49.
15. H. Sutton and L. W. Porter, 'A Study of the Grapevine in a Governmental Organisation', *Personnel Psychology*, Summer 1968, pp. 223–30.
16. K. Davis, cited in R. Rowan, 'Where Did that Rumor Come From?', *Fortune*, 13 August 1979, p. 134.
17. R. L. Rosnow and G. A. Fine, *Rumor and Gossip: The Social Psychology of Hearsay* (New York: Elsevier, 1976).
18. L. Sierra, 'Tell It to the Grapevine', *Communication World*, June/July 2002, pp. 28–29.
19. See, for instance, M. Conlin, 'Watch What You Put in That Office E-Mail', *BusinessWeek*, September 2002, pp. 114–15; and A. Lantz, 'Does the Use of E-Mail Change Over Time?', *International Journal of Human–Computer Interaction*, vol. 15, no. 3, 2003, pp. 419–31.
20. 'Firm Bans E-mail at Work', 19 September 2003: <www.cnn.com/2003/TECH/internet/09/19/e-mail.ban/>.
21. E. Morphy, 'Study: Online Customer Service is Dismal', Yahoo! News, 8 June 2005: <http://news.yahoo.com/s/nf/36133>.
22. See, for instance, A. Harmon, 'Appeal of Instant Messaging Extends into the Workplace', *New York Times*, 11 March 2003, p. A1.
23. Cited in C. Y. Chen, 'The IM Invasion', *Fortune*, 26 May 2003, pp. 135–38.
24. <www.geekzone.co.nz/content.asp?contentid=5121> (accessed 12 October 2006).
25. A. Stuart, 'IM Is Here. RU Ready 2 Try It?', *INC.*, July 2003, pp. 76–81.
26. Ibid, p. 79.
27. R. O. Crockett, 'The Office Gossips' New Water Cooler', *BusinessWeek*, 24 June 2002, p. 14.
28. G. Anders, 'Inside Job', *Fast Company*, September 2001, p. 178.
29. See S. A. Mohrman, D. Finegold and J. A. Klein, 'Designing the Knowledge Enterprise: Beyond Programs and Tools', *Organizational Dynamics*, vol. 31, no. 2, 2002, pp. 134–50; H. Dolezalek, 'Collaborating in Cyberspace', *Training*, April 2003, pp. 32–37; and P. R. Carlile, 'Transferring, Translating, and Transforming: An Integrative Framework for Managing Knowledge across Boundaries', *Organization Science*, vol. 15, no. 5, September–October 2004, pp. 555–68.
30. See J. Ewing, 'Sharing the Wealth', *BusinessWeek e.biz*, 19 March 2001, pp. EB36–40; and D. Tapscott, D. Ticoll and A. Lowy, *Digital Capital: Harnessing the Power of Business Webs* (Boston: Harvard Business School Press, 2000).
31. Cited in A. Cabrera and E. F. Cabrera, 'Knowledge-Sharing Dilemmas', *Organization Studies*, vol. 5, 2002, p. 687.
32. B. Roberts, 'Pick Employees' Brains', *Human Resources*, February 2000, pp. 115–16; B. Fryer, 'Get Smart', *INC. Technology 1999*, no. 3, p. 65; and D. Zielinski, 'Have You Shared a Bright Idea Today?', *Training*, July 2000, p. 65.
33. Fryer, 'Get Smart', p. 63.
34. E. Truch, 'Managing Personal Knowledge: The Key to Tomorrow's Employability', *Journal of Change Management*, December 2001, pp. 102–05; and D. Mason and D. J. Pauleen, 'Perceptions of Knowledge Management: A Qualitative Analysis', *Journal of Knowledge Management*, vol. 7, no. 4, 2003, pp. 38–48.
35. J. Gordon, 'Intellectual Capital and You', *Training*, September 1999, p. 33.
36. T. M. Burton and R. E. Silverman, 'Lots of Empty Spaces in Cerner Parking Lot Get CEO Riled Up', *Wall Street Journal*, 30 March 2001, p. B3; and E. Wong, 'A Stinging Office Memo Boomerangs', *New York Times*, 5 April 2001, p. C1.
37. See R. L. Daft and R. H. Lengel, 'Information Richness: A New Approach to Managerial Behavior and Organization Design', in B. M. Staw and L. L. Cummings (eds), *Research in Organizational Behavior*, vol. 6

(Greenwich, CT: JAI Press, 1984), pp. 191–233; R. L. Daft and R. H. Lengel, 'Organizational Information Requirements, Media Richness, and Structural Design', *Managerial Science*, May 1986, pp. 554–72; R. E. Rice, 'Task Analyzability, Use of New Media, and Effectiveness', *Organization Science*, November 1992, pp. 475–500; S. G. Straus and J. E. McGrath, 'Does the Medium Matter? The Interaction of Task Type and Technology on Group Performance and Member Reaction', *Journal of Applied Psychology*, February 1994, pp. 87–97; L. K. Trevino, J. Webster and E. W. Stein, 'Making Connections: Complementary Influences on Communication Media Choices, Attitudes, and Use', *Organization Science*, March–April 2000, pp. 163–82; and N. Kock, 'The Psychobiological Model: Towards a new Theory of Computer-Mediated Communication Based on Darwinian Evolution', *Organization Science*, vol. 15, no. 3, May–June 2004, pp. 327–48.

38. R. L. Daft, R. H. Lengel and L. K. Trevino, 'Message Equivocality, Media Selection, and Manager Performance: Implications for Information Systems', *MIS Quarterly*, September 1987, pp. 355–68.

39. J. C. McCroskey, J. A. Daly and G. Sorenson, 'Personality Correlates of Communication Apprehension', *Human Communication Research*, Spring 1976, pp. 376–80.

40. See, for example, B. H. Spitzberg and M. L. Hecht, 'A Competent Model of Relational Competence', *Human Communication Research*, Summer 1984, pp. 575–99; and S. K. Opt and D. A. Loffredo, 'Rethinking Communication Apprehension: A Myers-Briggs Perspective', *Journal of Psychology*, September 2000, pp. 556–70.

41. See, for example, L. Stafford and J. A. Daly, 'Conversational Memory: The Effects of Instructional Set and Recall Mode on Memory for Natural Conversations', *Human Communication Research*, Spring 1984, pp. 379–402; and T. L. Rodebaugh, 'I Might Look OK, But I'm Still Doubtful, Anxious, and Avoidant: The Mixed Effects of Enhanced Video Feedback on Social Anxiety Symptoms', *Behaviour Research & Therapy*, vol. 42, no. 12, December 2004, pp. 1435–51.

42. J. A. Daly and J. C. McCroskey, 'Occupational Desirability and Choice as a Function of Communication

Apprehension', *Journal of Counseling Psychology*, vol. 22, no. 4, 1975, pp. 309–13.

43. J. A. Daly and M. D. Miller, 'The Empirical Development of an Instrument of Writing Apprehension', *Research in the Teaching of English*, Winter 1975, pp. 242–49.

44. See D. Tannen, *You Just Don't Understand: Women and Men in Conversation* (New York: Ballantine Books, 1991); and D. Tannen, *Talking from 9 to 5* (New York: William Morrow, 1995).

45. Tannen, *Talking from 9 to 5*, p. 15.

46. L. M. Kyl-Heku and D. M. Buss, 'Tactics as Units of Analysis in Personality Psychology: An Illustration Using Tactics of Hierarchy Negotiation', *Personality & Individual Differences*, vol. 21, no. 4, October 1996, pp. 497–517.

47. D. Tannen, 'Talking Past One Another: "But What Do You Mean?" Women and Men in Conversation', in J. M. Henslin (ed.), *Down to Earth Sociology: Introductory Readings*, 12th ed. (New York: Free Press, 2003), pp. 175–81.

48. This section is largely based on C. C. Pinder and K. P. Harlos, 'Silent Organizational Behavior', Paper presented at the Western Academy of Management Conference, March 2000; P. Mornell, 'The Sounds of Silence', *INC.*, February 2001, pp. 117–18; C. C. Pinder and K. P. Harlos, 'Employee Silence: Quiescence and Acquiescence as Responses to Perceived Injustice', in G. R. Ferris (ed.), *Research in Personnel and Human Resources Management*, vol. 21 (Greenwich, CT: JAI Press, 2001); and F. J. Milliken, E. W. Morrison and P. F. Hewlin, 'An Exploratory Study of Employee Silence: Issues that Employees Don't Communicate Upward and Why', *Journal of Management Studies*, September 2003, pp. 1453–76.

49. M. L. LaGanga, 'Are There Words That Neither Offend Nor Bore?', *Los Angeles Times*, 18 May 1994, p. II-27; and J. Leo, 'Put on a Sappy Face', *U.S. News & World Report*, 25 November 2002, p. 52.

50. Cited in J. Leo, 'Falling for Sensitivity', *U.S. News & World Report*, 13 December 1993, p. 27.

51. R. E. Axtell, *Gestures: The Do's and Taboos of Body Language around the World* (New York: Wiley, 1991).

52. See M. Munter, 'Cross-Cultural Communication for Managers', *Business Horizons*, May–June 1993, pp. 75–76.

53. See E. T. Hall, *Beyond Culture* (Garden City, NY: Anchor Press/Doubleday, 1976);

E. T. Hall, 'How Cultures Collide', *Psychology Today*, July 1976, pp. 67–74; E. T. Hall and M. R. Hall, *Understanding Cultural Differences* (Yarmouth, ME: Intercultural Press, 1990); R. E. Dulek, J. S. Fielden and J. S. Hill, 'International Communication: An Executive Primer', *Business Horizons*, January–February 1991, pp. 20–25; D. Kim, Y. Pan and H. S. Park, 'High- versus Low-Context Culture: A Comparison of Chinese, Korean, and American Cultures', *Psychology and Marketing*, September 1998, pp. 507–21; M. J. Martinko and S. C. Douglas, 'Culture and Expatriate Failure: An Attributional Explication', *International Journal of Organizational Analysis*, July 1999, pp. 265–93; and W. L. Adair, 'Integrative Sequences and Negotiation Outcome in Same- and Mixed-Culture Negotiations', *International Journal of Conflict Management*, vol. 14, no. 3–4, 2003, pp. 1359–92.

54. N. Adler, *International Dimensions of Organizational Behavior*, 4th ed. (Cincinnati, OH: Southwestern, 2002), p. 94.

55. See, for example. R. S. Schuler, 'A Role Perception Transactional Process Model for Organizational Communication–Outcome Relationships', *Organizational Behavior and Human Performance*, April 1979, pp. 268–91.

56. J. P. Walsh, S. J. Ashford and T. E. Hill, 'Feedback Obstruction: The Influence of the Information Environment on Employee Turnover Intentions', *Human Relations*, January 1985, pp. 23–46.

57. S. A. Hellweg and S. L. Phillips, 'Communication and Productivity in Organisations: A State-of-the-Art Review', in *Proceedings of the 40th Annual Academy of Management Conference*, Detroit, 1980, pp. 188–92; see also B. A. Bechky, 'Sharing Meaning across Occupational Communities: The Transformation of Understanding on a Production Floor', *Organization Science*, vol. 14, no. 3, May–June 2003, pp. 312–30.

58. R. R. Reilly, B. Brown, M. R. Blood and C. Z. Malatesta, 'The Effects of Realistic Previews: A Study and Discussion of the Literature', *Personnel Psychology*, Winter 1981, pp. 823–34; see also J. M. Phillips, 'Effects of Realistic Job Previews on Multiple Organizational Outcomes: A Meta-Analysis', *Academy of Management Journal*, vol. 41, no. 6, December 1998, pp. 673–90.

12

BASIC APPROACHES TO LEADERSHIP

CHAPTER OUTLINE

WHAT IS LEADERSHIP?

TRAIT THEORIES

BEHAVIOURAL THEORIES

CONTINGENCY THEORIES

LEARNING OBJECTIVES

AFTER STUDYING THIS CHAPTER, YOU SHOULD BE ABLE TO:

1. CONTRAST LEADERSHIP AND MANAGEMENT

2. SUMMARISE THE CONCLUSIONS OF TRAIT THEORIES

3. IDENTIFY THE LIMITATIONS OF BEHAVIOURAL THEORIES

4. DESCRIBE FIEDLER'S CONTINGENCY MODEL

5. EXPLAIN HERSEY AND BLANCHARD'S SITUATIONAL THEORY

6. SUMMARISE LEADER–MEMBER EXCHANGE THEORY

7. DESCRIBE THE PATH–GOAL THEORY

8. IDENTIFY THE SITUATIONAL VARIABLES IN THE LEADER-PARTICIPATION MODEL

Richard Goyder took over the helm at Wesfarmers from Michael Chaney in 2005. He is applying his own style as a leader at Wesfarmers in order to sustain the success his former boss, Chaney, became known for.

CAN ONE PERSON MAKE A DIFFERENCE to an organisation's performance? There are many examples that suggest leaders *can* make a difference. We often see articles in the daily press that refer to the performance of specific organisations from both the public and private sectors. Sometimes the articles report good results, such as good profit margins and high shareholder dividends. Sometimes they focus on spectacular disasters, such as the collapse of the large Australian insurance company HIH and the scandal involving the Australian Wheat Board over sales with Iraq. Whether the results are positive or negative, some association is generally made with the leadership ability of the chief executive officer and the senior management team.

There is nothing negative, however, about the reports on the leadership abilities of the former CEO of Wesfarmers. Michael Chaney has become one of corporate Australia's most admired leaders. During his 12 years at the top, he has taken Wesfarmers from a rural-dominated $1 billion business to a more diversified enterprise worth over $11 billion. Headquartered in Perth, Western Australia, Wesfarmers' activities are focused in Australia and New Zealand on markets in hardware, energy, chemicals and insurance.

In July 2005, Richard Goyder took over the helm at Wesfarmers. In his initial 12 months, he struggled to get the organisation to move out of the shadow of Michael Chaney. As he put it, he has been 'licking furiously to put my stamp on the company'. He is not an outsider. Richard was previously the chief financial officer under Chaney and hence gained valuable insights into the top job. The main challenge for any senior leadership at Wesfarmers since it listed as a public company over two decades ago is shareholder focus. Richard is confident of the future, as he believes his company has stable strategies and that the leadership team runs the business well through sustainable and adaptable portfolio management. This is despite a current concern about negative earnings growth for the company.[1]

Eh! Je suis leur chef, il fallait bien les suivre. (Ah well! I am their leader, I really ought to follow them.)

Alexandre Auguste Ledru-Rollin

As Richard Goyder is demonstrating at Wesfarmers, leaders can make a difference. The Wesfarmers case demonstrates the need to understand the nature of leadership, not only from a top management perspective but also from a perspective that embraces the leadership that occurs at all levels across the organisation. It demonstrates the significance of leadership succession to an organisation, and the important relationship that leaders have with their operating environment. The leadership challenge is vitally concerned with the extent to which a leader can influence the factors driving performance.

In this chapter, we'll look at the basic approaches to determining what makes an effective leader and what differentiates leaders from non-leaders. First, we'll present trait theories. They dominated the study of leadership up to the late 1940s. Then we'll discuss behavioural theories, which were popular until the late 1960s. Finally, we'll introduce contingency theories, which are currently the dominant approach to the field of leadership. But before we review these three approaches, let's first clarify what we mean by the term *leadership*.

WHAT IS LEADERSHIP?

Leadership and *management* are two terms that are often confused. What is the difference between them?

John Kotter of the Harvard Business School argues that management is about coping with complexity.[2] Good management brings about order and consistency by drawing up formal plans, designing rigid organisation structures, and monitoring results against the plans. Leadership, in contrast, is about coping with change. Leaders establish direction by developing a vision of the future; then they align people by communicating this vision and inspiring them to overcome hurdles.

Robert House of the Wharton School at the University of Pennsylvania in the United States basically concurs when he says that managers use the authority inherent in their designated formal rank to obtain compliance from organisational members.[3] Management consists of implementing the vision and strategy provided by leaders, coordinating and staffing the organisation, and handling day-to-day problems.

Although Kotter and House provide separate definitions of the two terms, both researchers and practising managers frequently make no such distinctions. So we need to present leadership in a way that can capture how it is used in theory and practice.

leadership | The ability to influence a group towards the achievement of a vision or set of goals.

We define **leadership** as the ability to influence a group towards the achievement of a vision or set of goals. The source of this influence may be formal, such as that provided by the possession of managerial rank in an organisation. Because management positions come with some degree of formally designated authority, a person may assume a leadership role simply because of the position he or she holds in the organisation. But not all leaders are managers; nor, for that matter, are all managers leaders. Just because an organisation provides its managers with certain formal rights is no assurance that they will be able to lead effectively. We find that non-sanctioned leadership—that is, the ability to influence that arises outside the formal structure of the organisation—is often as important as or more important than formal influence. In other words, leaders can emerge from within a group as well as by formal appointment to lead a group.

You should note that our definition makes no specific mention of a vision, even though both Kotter and House use the term in their efforts to differentiate leadership and management. This omission is purposeful. While most contemporary discussions of the leadership concept include articulating a common *vision*,[4] almost all work on leadership conducted prior to the 1980s made no reference to this concept. So, in order for our definition to encompass both historical and contemporary approaches to leadership, we make no explicit reference to vision.

One last comment before we move on: Organisations need strong leadership *and* strong management for optimal effectiveness. In today's dynamic world, we need leaders to challenge the status quo, to create visions of the future, and to inspire organisational members to want to achieve the visions. We also need managers to formulate detailed plans, create efficient organisational structures and oversee day-to-day operations.

TRAIT THEORIES

LEARNING OBJECTIVE 2

Summarise the conclusions of trait theories

Throughout history, strong leaders—Buddha, Napoleon, Mao, Churchill, Thatcher, Lee Kuan Yew, Mahathir Mohamad—have all been described in terms of their traits. For example, when Margaret Thatcher was prime minister of Great Britain, she was regularly described as confident, iron-willed, determined and decisive. These terms are traits and, whether Thatcher's advocates and critics recognised it at the time, when they described her in such terms they became trait-theorist supporters. Similarly, the former Malaysian prime minister, Mahathir Mohamad, has been described as a strong, domineering personality in Southeast Asian politics.

trait theories of leadership | Theories that consider personal qualities and characteristics that differentiate leaders from non-leaders.

The media has long been a believer in **trait theories of leadership**—differentiating leaders from non-leaders by focusing on personal qualities and characteristics. The media identify people such as South Africa's Nelson Mandela, Virgin Group CEO Sir Richard Branson, former Singaporean prime minister Lee Kuan Yew and Woolworths' CEO, Roger Corbett as leaders, and use terms such as *charismatic*, *enthusiastic* and *courageous* to describe them. Well, the media isn't alone. The search for personality, social, physical or intellectual attributes that would describe leaders and differentiate them from non-leaders goes back to the earliest stages of leadership research.

Research efforts at isolating leadership traits resulted in a number of dead ends. For instance, a review in the late 1960s of 20 different studies identified nearly 80 leadership traits, but only five of these traits were common to four or more of the investigations.[5] By the 1990s, after numerous studies and analyses, about the best thing that could be said was that most 'leaders are not like other people', but the particular traits that were isolated varied a great deal from review to review.[6] It was a pretty confusing state of affairs.

The trait theories of leadership focus on personal characteristics of the leader. Before becoming the lord mayor of Melbourne, John So was a science teacher and restaurateur. As a politician and leader, he has been described as sociable, intelligent, self-confident, energetic and straightforward.

A breakthrough, of sorts, came when researchers began organising traits around the Big Five personality framework (see Chapter 4).[7] What became clear was that most of the dozens of traits that emerged in various leadership reviews could be subsumed under one

THE TRAITS OF SUCCESSFUL WOMEN ENTREPRENEURS

A lot of people have been interested in the traits that separate leaders from non-leaders. The results of many studies have been mixed and inconclusive. A number of studies have verified that traits such as ambition and energy, the desire to lead, honesty and integrity, self-confidence, intelligence and job-relevant knowledge do play a significant role in differentiating leaders from non-leaders.

In practice, successful entrepreneurs and business leaders provide their own spin on the personal qualities that underpin their business ventures. A number of Australian women have talked about the leadership qualities that they believed were fundamental to building and sustaining their businesses and meeting the challenges along the way.

Suzi Dafnis is a founder and director of Pow Wow Events, a distributor of learning products and the organiser of market-leading business and investment seminars. She is passionate about her business and literally fell in love with the concept of learning and empowering others through education. Joanne Mercer, the founder of Joanne Mercer Footwear, a thriving brand with 32 stores around Australia, points to determination, some luck and fear as significant aspects of meeting the challenges she confronted in growing the business. She also attributes a great work ethic and entrepreneurial flair to her success. Joanne admits she wasn't a good student, but says that if she is passionate about something, she can commit an enormous amount of energy to it. Both Dafnis and Mercer appreciate the challenges of maintaining some sort of work/life balance.

Intelligence and essential knowledge and skills are central to leading successful businesses, but the ability to learn effectively and to build critical relationships stands out for some. Sue Whyte, CEO of Intimo Lingerie, has always been surrounded by businesspeople and risk takers. Her early lessons from family and associates were more powerful than anything she could have learned at university. Real learning comes from experimentation and experience because, as Sue points out, if you fail then you just try again and you always listen and observe. And for Sue, a clear vision provides a focus for her learning.

Sue Ismiel, founder of Nad's Natural Hair Removal Gel, appreciates the importance of being able to develop and exploit business networks and alliances. This was critical to her successful expansion into the lucrative US markets.

There are various leadership qualities that successful people identify as important for success. For Suzi Dafnis, Joanne Mercer, Sue Whyte and Sue Ismiel, a passion for and flair about the business, along with a thirst for learning and network building, represent some of the qualities that stand out in their experiences.

Suzi Dafnis is a founder and director of Pow Wow Events, a distributor of learning products and the organiser of market-leading business and investment seminars. She has a passion for learning about all aspects of her business and building valuable networks in the business community. She is a leader by example.

SOURCE: Cameron Cooper, 'Secrets of Success', *Management Today*, June 2006.

of the Big Five and that this approach resulted in consistent and strong support for traits as predictors of leadership. For instance, ambition and energy—two common traits of leaders—are part of extraversion. Rather than focusing on these two specific traits, it is better to think of them in terms of the more general trait of extraversion.

Comprehensive reviews of the leadership literature, when organised around the Big Five, have found that extraversion is the most important trait of effective leaders.[8] But results show that extraversion is more strongly related to leader emergence than to leader effectiveness. This isn't totally surprising, since sociable and dominant people are more likely to assert themselves in group situations. Conscientiousness and openness to experience also showed strong and consistent relationships to leadership, although not quite as strong as extraversion. The traits of agreeableness and emotional stability weren't as strongly correlated with leadership. Overall, it does appear that the trait approach does have something to offer. Leaders who are extraverted (individuals who like being around people and are able to assert themselves), conscientious (individuals who are disciplined and keep commitments they make) and open (individuals who are creative and flexible) do seem to have an advantage when it comes to leadership, suggesting that good leaders do have key traits in common.

Recent studies are indicating that another trait that may indicate effective leadership is emotional intelligence (EI), which we first discussed in Chapter 8. Advocates of EI argue that without it, a person can have outstanding training, a highly analytical mind, a compelling vision, and an endless supply of terrific ideas, but still not make a great leader. This may be especially true as individuals move up in an organisation.[9] But why is EI so critical to effective leadership? A core component of EI is empathy. Empathetic leaders can sense others' needs, listen to what followers say (and don't say), and are able to read the reactions of others. As one leader noted, 'The caring part of empathy, especially for the people with whom you work, is what inspires people to stay with a leader when the going gets rough. The mere fact that someone cares is more often than not rewarded with loyalty.'[10]

Indeed, at the highest levels of leadership, EI is critical. A good example comes from the presidential leadership in the United States. Presidential historian Fred Greenstein argues that EI is the most important predictor of presidential greatness. Greenstein argues that the lack of EI was the undoing of Presidents Johnson, Nixon, Carter and, to some degree, Clinton. He warns, 'Beware the presidential contender who lacks emotional intelligence. In its absence all else may turn to ashes.'[11]

Despite these claims for its importance, the link between EI and leadership effectiveness is much less investigated compared to other traits. One reviewer noted, 'Speculating about the practical utility of the EI construct might be premature. Despite such warnings, EI is being viewed as a panacea for many organisational malaises with recent suggestions that EI is essential for leadership effectiveness.'[12] But until more rigorous evidence accumulates, we can't be confident about the connection.

Based on the latest findings, we offer two conclusions. First, traits can predict leadership. Twenty years ago, the evidence suggested otherwise. But this was probably due to the lack of a valid framework for classifying and organising traits. The Big Five seems to have rectified that. Second, traits do a better job at predicting the emergence of leaders and the appearance of leadership than in actually distinguishing between *effective* and *ineffective* leaders.[13] The fact that an individual exhibits the traits, and others consider that person to be a leader, doesn't necessarily mean that the leader is successful at getting his or her group to achieve its goals.

BEHAVIOURAL THEORIES

The failures of early trait studies led researchers in the late 1940s through the 1960s to go in a different direction. They began looking at the behaviours exhibited by specific leaders. They wondered if there was something unique in the way that effective leaders behave. To use contemporary examples, Siebel Systems chairman Tom Siebel and Oracle CEO Larry Ellison have been very successful in leading their companies through difficult times.[14] And they both rely on a common leadership style—tough-talking, intense, autocratic. Does this suggest that autocratic behaviour is a preferred style for all leaders? In this section, we look at three different **behavioural theories of leadership** to answer that question. First, however, let's consider the practical implications of the behavioural approach.

If the behavioural approach to leadership were successful, it would have implications quite different from those of the trait approach. Trait research provides a basis for *selecting* the 'right' persons to assume formal positions in groups and organisations requiring leadership. In contrast, if behavioural studies were to turn up critical behavioural determinants of leadership, we could *train* people to be leaders. The difference between trait and behavioural theories, in terms of application, lies in their underlying assumptions. Trait theories assume leaders are born, rather than made. However, if there were specific behaviours that identified leaders, then we could teach leadership—we could design programs that implanted these behavioural patterns in individuals who desired to be effective leaders. This was surely a more exciting avenue, for it meant that the supply of leaders could be expanded. If training worked, we could have an infinite supply of effective leaders.

OHIO STATE STUDIES

The most comprehensive and replicated of the behavioural theories resulted from research that began at Ohio State University in the late 1940s.[15] Researchers at Ohio State sought to identify independent dimensions of leader behaviour. Beginning with over a thousand dimensions, they eventually narrowed the list to two categories that substantially accounted for most of the leadership behaviour described by employees. They called these two dimensions *initiating structure* and *consideration*.

Initiating structure refers to the extent to which a leader is likely to define and structure his or her role and those of employees in the search for goal attainment. It includes behaviour that attempts to organise work, work relationships and goals. The leader characterised as high in initiating structure could be described as someone who 'assigns group members to particular tasks', 'expects workers to maintain definite standards of performance' and 'emphasises the meeting of deadlines'. Larry Ellison and Tom Siebel exhibit high initiating structure behaviour.

Consideration is described as the extent to which a person is likely to have job relationships that are characterised by mutual trust, respect for employees' ideas, and regard for their feelings. The person shows concern for followers' comfort, well-being, status and satisfaction. A leader high in consideration could be described as one who helps employees with personal problems, is friendly and approachable, and treats all employees as equals. AOL Time Warner is known by many in the Asia-Pacific region for being one of the world's largest internet companies, with over 35 million members around the globe. CEO Richard Parsons rates high on consideration behaviour. His leadership style is very people-oriented, emphasising cooperation and consensus-building.[16]

At one time, the results of the Ohio State studies were thought to be disappointing. One 1992 review concluded, 'Overall, the research based on a two-factor conceptualization of

behavioural theories of leadership | Theories proposing that specific behaviours differentiate leaders from non-leaders.

initiating structure | The extent to which a leader is likely to define and structure his or her role and those of subordinates in the search for goal attainment.

consideration | The extent to which a leader is likely to have job relationships characterised by mutual trust, respect for subordinates' ideas and regard for their feelings.

leadership behavior has added little to our knowledge about effective leadership.'[17] However, a more recent review suggests that this two-factor conceptualisation was given a premature burial. A review of 160 studies found that both initiating structure and consideration were associated with effective leadership. Specifically, consideration was more strongly related to the individual. In other words, the followers of leaders who were high in consideration were more satisfied with their jobs and more motivated, and also had more respect for their leader. Initiating structure, however, was more strongly related to higher levels of group and organisation productivity and more positive performance evaluations.

UNIVERSITY OF MICHIGAN STUDIES

Leadership studies undertaken at the University of Michigan's Survey Research Centre, at about the same time as those being done at Ohio State, had similar research objectives: to locate behavioural characteristics of leaders that appeared to be related to measures of performance effectiveness.

The Michigan group also came up with two dimensions of leadership behaviour that they labelled *employee-oriented* and *production-oriented*.[18] Leaders who were **employee-oriented** were described as emphasising interpersonal relations; they took a personal interest in the needs of their employees and accepted individual differences among members. The **production-oriented leaders**, in contrast, tended to emphasise the technical or task aspects of the job—their main concern was in accomplishing their group's tasks, and the group members were a means to that end. These dimensions—employee-oriented and production-oriented—are closely related to the Ohio State dimensions. Employee-oriented leadership is similar to consideration, and production-oriented leadership is similar to initiating structure. In fact, most leadership researchers use the terms synonymously.[19]

The conclusions arrived at by the Michigan researchers strongly favoured the leaders who were employee-oriented in their behaviour. Employee-oriented leaders were associated with higher group productivity and higher job satisfaction. Production-oriented leaders tended to be associated with low group productivity and lower job satisfaction. Although the Michigan studies emphasised employee-oriented leadership (or consideration) over production-oriented leadership (or initiating structure), the Ohio State studies garnered more research attention and suggested that *both* consideration and initiating structure are important to effective leadership.

THE MANAGERIAL GRID

A graphic portrayal of a two-dimensional view of leadership style was developed by Blake and Mouton.[20] They proposed a **managerial grid** (sometimes also now called the *leadership grid*) based on the styles of 'concern for people' and 'concern for production', which essentially represent the Ohio State dimensions of *consideration* and *initiating structure* or the Michigan dimensions of *employee*-oriented and *production-oriented*.

The grid, depicted in Figure 12.1, has 9 possible positions along each axis, creating 81 different positions in which the leader's style may fall. The grid doesn't show results produced, but, rather, the dominating factors in a leader's thinking in regard to getting results. Based on the findings of Blake and Mouton, managers were found to perform best under a 9,9 style, as contrasted, for example, with a 9,1 (authority type) or 1,9 (laissez-faire type) style.[21] Unfortunately, the grid offers a better framework for conceptualising leadership style than for presenting any tangible new information in clarifying the leadership quandary, because it doesn't really convey any new information in addition to the Ohio State and the University of Michigan research.[22]

employee-oriented leader | Emphasising interpersonal relations; taking a personal interest in the needs of employees, and accepting individual differences among members.

production-oriented leader | One who emphasises technical or task aspects of the job.

managerial grid | A nine-by-nine matrix outlining 81 different leadership styles.

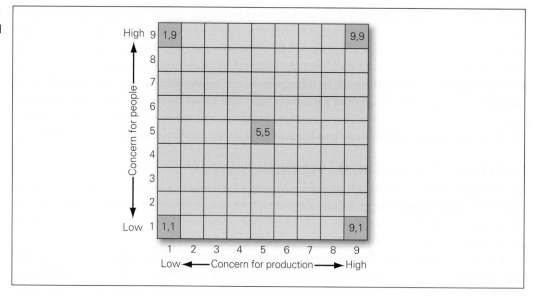

SCANDINAVIAN STUDIES

The three behavioural approaches we have just reviewed were essentially developed between the late 1940s and early 1960s. These approaches evolved during a time when the world was a far more stable and predictable place. In the belief that these studies fail to capture the more dynamic realities of today, researchers in Finland and Sweden have been reassessing whether there are only two dimensions that capture the essence of leadership behaviour.[23] Their basic premise is that in a changing world, effective leaders would exhibit **development-oriented** behaviour. These are leaders who value experimentation, seek new ideas, and generate and implement change.

For example, the Scandinavian researchers reviewed the original Ohio State data and found that the Ohio State people included development items such as 'pushes new ways of doing things', 'originates new approaches to problems' and 'encourages members to start new activities'. But these items, at the time, didn't explain much about effective leadership. It could be, the Scandinavian researchers proposed, that this was because developing new ideas and implementing change weren't critical in those days. In today's dynamic environment, this may no longer be true. So, the Scandinavian researchers have been conducting new studies looking to see if there is a third dimension—development orientation—that is related to leader effectiveness.

The early evidence is positive. Using samples of leaders in Finland and Sweden, the researchers have found strong support for development-oriented leader behaviour as a separate and independent dimension. That is, the previous behavioural approaches that focused on only two behaviours may not appropriately capture leadership in the 21st century. Moreover, while initial conclusions need to be guarded without more confirming evidence, it also appears that leaders who demonstrate development-oriented behaviour have more satisfied employees and are seen as more competent by those employees.

SUMMARY OF BEHAVIOURAL THEORIES

The behavioural theories have had modest success in identifying consistent relationships between leadership behaviour and group performance. What seems to be missing is consideration of the situational factors that influence success or failure. For example, it

development-oriented leader | A leader who values experimentation, seeks new ideas, and generates and implements change.

seems unlikely that Germaine Greer would have been a great feminist and anarchist leader at the turn of the 20th century; yet, she had a great influence over social affairs in Australia in the 1960s and 1970s. Would Anita Roddick, founder of The Body Shop, have emerged as an influential activist on globalisation if she had been born in 1842 rather than 1942, or been raised in Fiji rather than Sussex, in England? It seems quite unlikely, yet the behavioural approaches we have described couldn't clarify these situational factors.

WHAT'S MY LEADERSHIP STYLE?

In the Self-Assessment Library (available on CD and online) take Self-Assessment II.B.I (What's My Leadership Style?) and answer the following questions.

1. Did you score as task-oriented (task-oriented is the same as initiating structure under the Ohio State studies and production-oriented under the University of Michigan studies) or people-oriented (people-oriented is the same as consideration under the Ohio State studies and employee-oriented under the University of Michigan studies)?

2. Do you think a leader can be both task-oriented and people-oriented? Do you think there are situations in which a leader has to make a choice between the two styles?

3. Do you think your leadership style will change over time? Why or why not?

CONTINGENCY THEORIES

Linda Wachner had a reputation as being a very tough boss. And for a number of years, this style worked. In 1987, Wachner became CEO of Warnaco, a struggling US$425-million-a-year apparel company. Over a 14-year period, she transformed Warnaco into a US$2.2 billion company whose products ranged from Calvin Klein jeans to Speedo swimsuits. In spite of an abrasive style that included frequently humiliating employees in front of their peers, which led to rapid turnover among top managers, Wachner's style worked for most of the 1990s. In fact, in 1993, *Fortune* magazine anointed her 'America's most successful businesswoman'.

But times change and Wachner didn't.[24] Beginning in 1998, the company's business began to unravel, hurt by a reduction in demand for its products and a fast-eroding market share. Wachner's headstrong approach and brash tactics, which had driven off many competent executives, was now alienating creditors and licensers as well as employees. In June 2001, Warnaco was forced to file for bankruptcy protection. Five months later, the restructuring committee of Warnaco's board of directors fired Wachner. The story doesn't quite end there, though. Wachner sued Warnaco for US$25 million in severance pay. They eventually settled for US$452 000. Then, the Securities and Exchange Commission charged Wachner for securities fraud for issuing a false and misleading press release about Warnaco's earnings. In 2004, Wachner settled, agreeing to pay a total of US$1 328 444 in fines and disgorged earnings.[25]

Linda Wachner's rise and fall illustrates that predicting leadership success is more complex than isolating a few traits or preferable behaviours. In Wachner's case, what worked in 1990 didn't work in 2000. The failure by researchers in the mid-20th century to obtain consistent results led to a focus on situational influences. The relationship between

LEADERSHIP SUCCESS: THE EYE OF THE BEHOLDER

The million-dollar question in leadership studies is: What factors determine the success of a leader? The evolution of leadership research has led to many inconclusive results after investigating the traits, skills and behaviours of leaders, as well as the contingency factors involved in different situations in which leaders find themselves. In practice, two factors seem to have an influence in determining the success of business leaders: the perceptions of business leaders by their peers and the size of the company.

Business Review Weekly's 2005 survey of chief executives of the 500 biggest companies in Australia identified the people and companies that have the most credibility in the commercial world. These people were leaders in the sense that they positively influenced people and results across the whole of their operations. Good financial performance and substantial growth were significant factors in influencing the perceptions of those surveyed. Allan Moss, the CEO of Macquarie Bank, was voted by his peers as the most admired business leader in Australia.

Moss has played an important role in creating one of the most successful companies in Australia. He has turned Macquarie Bank into a global enterprise, with 42 per cent of its earnings now created overseas, and he has been able to keep staff motivated through generous revenue remuneration packages and by preserving the bank's entrepreneurial culture in the context of rapidly expanding business. Moss is admired for his achievements by his peers.

But size also plays a part in determining who is recognised as a successful business leader. The fact that the survey was conducted on the 500 largest companies in Australia is a reflection of the emphasis and attraction that the media has for large business. Accolades for Australia's business leaders are routinely lavished on the oligopolies that dominate the business landscape. The CEOs of smaller, lesser-known companies don't get the same recognition. Ian Law, former managing director and CEO of West Australian Newspapers Holdings, is one such case. He achieved an annual return on shareholders' funds of 48 per cent for the last five years of his time as CEO. This was a much greater achievement than most of his counterparts in big business. The reality is, successful leadership is very much in the eye of the beholder, and this in turn is influenced by who dominates the media—big business.

SOURCES: Craig Roberts, 'When Smaller is Better', *Business Review Weekly*, 1 September 2005, pp. 66–73; Robert Skeffington and Phoebe Nolan, 'The Right Stuff', *Business Review Weekly*, 25 August 2005, pp. 38–39; and Adele Ferguson, 'The Ringmaster', *Business Review Weekly*, 25 August 2005, pp. 40–41.

---

leadership style and effectiveness suggested that under condition *a*, style *x* would be appropriate, whereas style *y* would be more suitable for condition *b*, and style *z* for condition *c*. But what were the conditions *a*, *b*, *c* and so forth? It was one thing to say that leadership effectiveness was dependent on the situation and another to be able to isolate those situational conditions. Several approaches to isolating key situational variables have proven more successful than others and, as a result, have gained wider recognition. We shall consider five of these: the Fiedler model, Hersey and Blanchard's situational theory, leader–member exchange theory, and the path–goal and leader-participation models.

FIEDLER MODEL

The first comprehensive contingency model for leadership was developed by Fred Fiedler.[26] The **Fiedler contingency model** proposes that effective group performance depends on the proper match between the leader's style and the degree to which the situation gives control to the leader.

IDENTIFYING LEADERSHIP STYLE

Fiedler believes a key factor in leadership success is the individual's basic leadership style. So, he begins by trying to find out what that basic style is. Fiedler created the **least**

LEARNING OBJECTIVE 4

Describe Fiedler's contingency model

Fiedler contingency model | The theory that effective groups depend on a proper match between a leader's style of interacting with subordinates and the degree to which the situation gives control and influence to the leader.

preferred co-worker (LPC) questionnaire for this purpose; it purports to measure whether a person is task- or relationship-oriented. The LPC questionnaire contains sets of 16 contrasting adjectives (such as pleasant–unpleasant, efficient–inefficient, open–guarded, supportive–hostile). It asks respondents to think of all the co-workers they have ever had and to describe the one person they *least enjoyed* working with by rating that person on a scale of 1 to 8 for each of the 16 sets of contrasting adjectives. Fiedler believes that based on the respondents' answers to this LPC questionnaire, he can determine their basic leadership style. If the least preferred co-worker is described in relatively positive terms (a high LPC score), then the respondent is primarily interested in good personal relations with this co-worker. That is, if you essentially describe the person you are least able to work with in favourable terms, Fiedler would label you *relationship-oriented*. In contrast, if the least preferred co-worker is seen in relatively unfavourable terms (a low LPC score), the respondent is primarily interested in productivity and thus would be labelled *task-oriented*. About 16 per cent of respondents score in the middle range.[27] Such individuals cannot be classified as either relationship-oriented or task-oriented and thus fall outside the theory's predictions. The rest of our discussion, therefore, relates to the 84 per cent who score in either the high or low range of the LPC.

Fiedler assumes that an individual's leadership style is fixed. As we will show, this is important because it means that if a situation requires a task-oriented leader and the person in that leadership position is relationship-oriented, either the situation has to be modified or the leader replaced if optimal effectiveness is to be achieved.

DEFINING THE SITUATION

After an individual's basic leadership style has been assessed through the LPC, it is necessary to match the leader with the situation. Fiedler has identified three contingency dimensions that, he argues, define the key situational factors that determine leadership effectiveness. These are leader–member relations, task structure and position power. They are defined as follows:

1. **Leader–member relations**: The degree of confidence, trust and respect members have in their leader.
2. **Task structure**: The degree to which the job assignments are procedurised (that is, structured or unstructured).
3. **Position power**: The degree of influence a leader has over power variables such as hiring, firing, discipline, promotions and salary increases.

The next step in the Fiedler model is to evaluate the situation in terms of these three contingency variables. Leader–member relations are either good or poor, task structure is either high or low, and position power is either strong or weak.

Fiedler states the better the leader–member relations, the more highly structured the job, and the stronger the position power, the more control the leader has. For example, a very favourable situation (in which the leader would have a great deal of control) might involve a payroll manager who is well respected and whose employees have confidence in her (good leader–member relations), for which the activities to be done—such as wage calculation, cheque writing, report filing—are specific and clear (high task structure), and the job provides considerable freedom for her to reward and punish her employees (strong position power). However, an unfavourable situation might be the disliked chairperson of a voluntary church fundraising team. In this job, the leader has very little control. Altogether, by mixing the three contingency dimensions, there are potentially eight different situations or categories in which leaders could find themselves (see Figure 12.2).

least preferred co-worker (LPC) questionnaire | An instrument that purports to measure whether a person is task- or relationship-oriented.

leader–member relations | The degree of confidence, trust and respect subordinates have in their leader.

task structure | The degree to which the job assignments are procedurised.

position power | Influence derived from one's formal structural position in the organisation; includes power to hire, fire, discipline, promote and give salary increases.

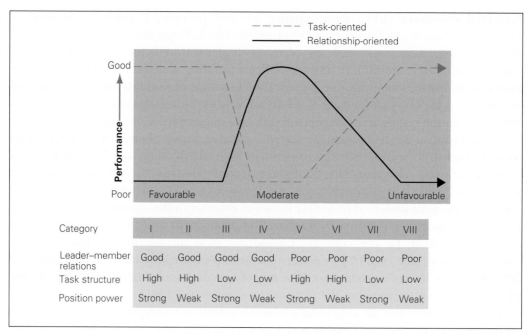

Category	I	II	III	IV	V	VI	VII	VIII
Leader–member relations	Good	Good	Good	Good	Poor	Poor	Poor	Poor
Task structure	High	High	Low	Low	High	High	Low	Low
Position power	Strong	Weak	Strong	Weak	Strong	Weak	Strong	Weak

MATCHING LEADERS AND SITUATIONS

With knowledge of an individual's LPC and an assessment of the three contingency dimensions, the Fiedler model proposes matching them up to achieve maximum leadership effectiveness.[28] Based on his research, Fiedler concluded that task-oriented leaders tend to perform better in situations that were very favourable to them and in situations that were very unfavourable (see Figure 12.2). So, Fiedler would predict that when faced with a category I, II, III, VII or VIII situation, task-oriented leaders perform better. Relationship-oriented leaders, however, perform better in moderately favourable situations—categories IV to VI. In recent years, Fiedler has condensed these eight situations down to three.[29] He now says that task-oriented leaders perform best in situations of high and low control, while relationship-oriented leaders perform best in moderate control situations.

Given Fiedler's findings, how would you apply them? You would seek to match leaders and situations. Individuals' LPC scores would determine the type of situation for which that individual was best suited. That 'situation' would be defined by evaluating the three contingency factors of leader–member relations, task structure and position power. But it is important to remember that Fiedler views an individual's leadership style as being fixed. Therefore, there are really only two ways in which to improve leader effectiveness.

First, you can change the leader to fit the situation—as in a softball game, a coach can put a right-handed pitcher or a left-handed pitcher into the game, depending on the situational characteristics of the hitter. So, for example, if a group situation rates as highly unfavourable but is currently led by a relationship-oriented coach, the group's performance could be improved by replacing that coach with one who is task-oriented. The second alternative would be to change the situation to fit the leader. That could be done by restructuring tasks or increasing or decreasing the power that the leader has to control factors such as salary increases, promotions and disciplinary actions.

EVALUATION

As a whole, reviews of the major studies that tested the overall validity of the Fiedler model lead to a generally positive conclusion. That is, there is considerable evidence to support at least substantial parts of the model.[30] If predictions from the model use only three categories rather than the original eight, there is ample evidence to support Fiedler's conclusions.[31] But there are problems with the LPC and the practical use of the model that need to be addressed. For instance, the logic underlying the LPC isn't well understood, and studies have shown that respondents' LPC scores are not stable.[32] Also, the contingency variables are complex and difficult for practitioners to assess. It is often difficult in practice to determine how good the leader–member relations are, how structured the task is, and how much position power the leader has.[33]

COGNITIVE RESOURCE THEORY

More recently, Fiedler and an associate, Joe Garcia, reconceptualised the former's original theory.[34] Specifically, they focused on the role of stress as a form of situational unfavourableness and on how a leader's intelligence and experience influence his or her reaction to stress. They call this reconceptualisation **cognitive resource theory**.

The essence of the new theory is that stress is the enemy of rationality. It is difficult for leaders (or anyone else, for that matter) to think logically and analytically when they are under stress. Moreover, the importance of a leader's intelligence and experience to effectiveness differs under low- and high-stress situations. Fiedler and Garcia found that a leader's intellectual abilities correlate positively with performance under low stress but negatively under high stress. And, conversely, a leader's experience correlates negatively with performance under low stress but positively under high stress. So, according to Fiedler and Garcia, it is the level of stress in the situation that determines whether an individual's intelligence or experience will contribute to leadership performance.

In spite of its newness, cognitive resource theory is developing a solid body of research support.[35] In fact, a study confirmed that when the stress level was low and the leader was directive (that is, when the leader was willing to tell people what to do), intelligence was important to a leader's effectiveness.[36] And in high-stress situations, intelligence was of little help because the leader was too cognitively taxed to put smarts to good use. Similarly, if a leader is non-directive, intelligence is of little help because the leader is afraid to put these smarts to use to tell people what to do. These results are exactly what cognitive resource theory predicts.

> **cognitive resource theory** | A theory of leadership which states that stress unfavourably affects a situation, and that intelligence and experience can lessen the influence of stress on the leader.

HERSEY AND BLANCHARD'S SITUATIONAL LEADERSHIP THEORY

Paul Hersey and Ken Blanchard have developed a leadership model that has gained a strong following among management development specialists.[37] This model—called **situational leadership theory (SLT)**—has been incorporated into leadership training programs at over 400 of the Fortune 500 companies and over one million managers a year from a wide variety of organisations are being taught its basic elements.[38]

Situational leadership is a contingency theory that focuses on the followers. Successful leadership is achieved by selecting the right leadership style, which Hersey and Blanchard argue is contingent on the level of the followers' readiness. Before we proceed, we should clarify two points: Why focus on the followers? and What do they mean by the term *readiness*?

The emphasis on the followers in leadership effectiveness reflects the reality that it is the followers who accept or reject the leader. Regardless of what the leader does,

> **LEARNING OBJECTIVE 5**
> Explain Hersey and Blanchard's situational theory

> **situational leadership theory (SLT)** | A contingency theory that focuses on followers' readiness.

'IT'S EXPERIENCE THAT COUNTS!'

The belief in the value of experience as a predictor of leadership effectiveness is very strong and widespread. Unfortunately, experience alone is generally a poor predictor of leadership.

Organisations carefully screen outside candidates for senior management positions on the basis of their experience. Similarly, organisations usually require several years of experience at one managerial level before a person can be considered for promotion. For that matter, have you ever filled out an employment application that *didn't* ask about previous experience or job history? Clearly, management believes that experience counts. But the evidence doesn't support this view. Studies of military officers, research and development teams, shop supervisors, post office administrators, and school principals tell us that experienced managers tend to be no more effective than managers with little experience.

One flaw in the 'experience counts' logic is the assumption that length of time on a job is actually a measure of experience. This says nothing about the quality of experience. The fact that one person has 20 years' experience while another has two years' doesn't necessarily mean that the former has had ten times as many meaningful experiences. Too often, 20 years of experience is nothing more than one year of experience repeated 20 times! In even the most complex jobs, real learning typically ends after about two years. By then, almost all new and unique situations have been experienced. So, one problem with trying to link experience with leadership effectiveness is not paying attention to the quality and diversity of the experience.

A second problem is that there is variability between situations that influence the transferability or relevance of experience. Situations in which experience is obtained is rarely comparable to new situations. Jobs differ, support resources differ, organisational cultures differ, follower characteristics differ, and so on. So, another reason that leadership experience isn't strongly related to leadership performance is undoubtedly due to variability of situations.

SOURCES: F. E. Fiedler, 'Leadership Experience and Leadership Performance: Another Hypothesis Shot to Hell', *Organizational Behavior and Human Performance*, January 1970, pp. 1–14; F. E. Fiedler, 'Time-Based Measures of Leadership Experience and Organizational Performance: A Review of Research and a Preliminary Model', *Leadership Quarterly*, Spring 1992, pp. 5–23; and M. A. Quinones, J. K. Ford and M. S. Teachout, 'The Relationship between Work Experience and Job Performance: A Conceptual and Meta-Analytic Review', *Personnel Psychology*, Winter 1995, pp. 887–910.

effectiveness depends on the actions of the followers. This is an important dimension that has been overlooked or underemphasised in most leadership theories. The term *readiness*, as defined by Hersey and Blanchard, refers to the extent to which people have the ability and willingness to accomplish a specific task.

SLT essentially views the leader–follower relationship as analogous to that between a parent and a child. Just as a parent needs to relinquish control as a child becomes more mature and responsible, so too should leaders. Hersey and Blanchard identify four specific leader behaviours—from highly directive to highly laissez-faire. The most effective behaviour depends on a follower's ability and motivation. So, SLT says if a follower is *unable* and *unwilling* to do a task, the leader needs to give clear and specific directions; if followers are *unable* and *willing*, the leader needs to display high task orientation to compensate for the followers' lack of ability and high relationship orientation to get the followers to 'buy into' the leader's desires; if followers are *able* and *unwilling*, the leader needs to use a supportive and participative style; and if the employee is both *able* and *willing*, the leader doesn't need to do much.

SLT has an intuitive appeal. It acknowledges the importance of followers and builds on the logic that leaders can compensate for ability and motivational limitations in their followers. Yet research efforts to test and support the theory have generally been disappointing.[39] Why? Possible explanations include internal ambiguities and inconsistencies in the model itself, as well as problems with research methodology in tests of the theory. So, in spite of its intuitive appeal and wide popularity, any enthusiastic endorsement, at least at this time, has to be cautioned against.

LEADER–MEMBER EXCHANGE THEORY

LEARNING OBJECTIVE 6
Summarise leader–member exchange theory

For the most part, the leadership theories we have covered to this point have largely assumed that leaders treat all their followers in the same manner. That is, they assume leaders use a fairly homogeneous style with all of the people in their work unit. But think about your experiences in groups. Did you notice that leaders often act very differently towards different people? Did the leader tend to have favourites who made up his or her 'in-group'? If you answered 'Yes' to both these questions, you are acknowledging the foundation of leader–member exchange theory.[40] The **leader–member exchange (LMX) theory** argues that because of time pressures, leaders establish a special relationship with a small group of their followers. These individuals make up the in-group—they are trusted, get a disproportionate amount of the leader's attention, and are more likely to receive special privileges. Other followers fall into the out-group. They get less of the leader's time, fewer of the preferred rewards that the leader controls, and have leader–follower relations based on formal authority interactions.

The theory proposes that early in the history of the interaction between a leader and a given follower, the leader implicitly categorises the follower as an 'in' or an 'out' and that relationship is relatively stable over time. Leaders induce LMX by rewarding those employees with whom they want a closer linkage and punishing those with whom they don't.[41] But for the LMX relationship to remain intact, the leader and the follower must invest in the relationship.

Just precisely how the leader chooses who falls into each category is unclear, but there is evidence that leaders tend to choose in-group members because they have attitude and personality characteristics that are similar to the leader's or a higher level of competence than out-group members[42] (see Figure 12.3). For example, followers who have a mastery orientation develop closer leader–member exchanges because such employees turn to their supervisors for sources of valuable information and experience that can provide employees with prospects for skill development and self-improvement that can further benefit the company.[43] However, communicating frequently with a supervisor appears to be helpful only for high-LMX employees, probably because supervisors perceive frequent

leader–member exchange (LMX) theory | The creation by leaders of in-groups and out-groups; subordinates with in-group status will have higher performance ratings, less turnover and greater job satisfaction.

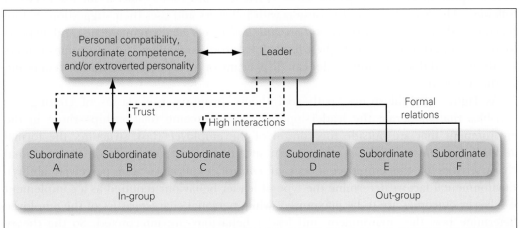

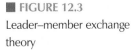

■ FIGURE 12.3
Leader–member exchange theory

communication from low-LMX employees as annoying and a waste of their time.[44] The key point to note here is that even though it is the leader who is doing the choosing, it is the follower's characteristics that are driving the leader's categorising decision.

Few followers would want to be outside a leader's inner circle. There is a danger to being part of the inner circle, though. As part of the inner circle, your fortunes may rise and fall with your leader. When CEOs are ousted, for example, their inner circle usually goes with them. Tyco is a diversified manufacturing and service company which operates in over 100 countries, including Malaysia, Australia and New Zealand. When its former CEO Dennis Kozlowski was given the boot, eventually his closest associate, CFO Mark Swartz, was also forced to resign, although he was well regarded by business analysts and was thought to be one of the executives who best understood the intricacies of Tyco's business.[45]

Research to test LMX theory has been generally supportive. More specifically, the theory and research surrounding it provide substantive evidence that leaders do differentiate among followers; that these disparities are far from random; and that followers with in-group status will have higher performance ratings, lower turnover intentions, greater satisfaction with their superior, and higher overall satisfaction than will the out-group.[46] These positive findings for in-group members shouldn't be totally surprising given our knowledge of the self-fulfilling prophecy (see Chapter 5). Leaders invest their resources with those they expect to perform best. And 'knowing' that in-group members are the most competent, leaders treat them as such and unwittingly fulfil their prophecy.[47]

PATH–GOAL THEORY

LEARNING OBJECTIVE 7

Describe the path–goal theory

Developed by Robert House, path–goal theory extracts elements from the Ohio State leadership research on initiating structure and consideration and the expectancy theory of motivation.[48]

path–goal theory | The theory that it is the leader's job to assist followers in attaining their goals and to provide the necessary direction and/or support to ensure that their goals are compatible with the overall objectives of the group or organisation.

The essence of **path–goal theory** is that it is the leader's job to provide followers with the information, support or other resources necessary for them to achieve their goals. The term *path–goal* is derived from the belief that effective leaders clarify the path to help their followers get from where they are to the achievement of their work goals, and to make the journey along the path easier by reducing roadblocks.

House identified four leadership behaviours. The *directive leader* lets followers know what is expected of them, schedules work to be done, and gives specific guidance as to how to accomplish tasks. The *supportive leader* is friendly and shows concern for the needs of followers. The *participative leader* consults with followers and uses their suggestions before making a decision. The *achievement-oriented leader* sets challenging goals and expects followers to perform at their highest level. In contrast to Fiedler, House assumes leaders are flexible and that the same leader can display any or all of these behaviours, depending on the situation.

As Figure 12.4 illustrates, path–goal theory proposes two classes of contingency variables that moderate the leadership behaviour–outcome relationship—those in the environment that are outside the control of the employee (task structure, the formal authority system and the work group) and those that are part of the personal characteristics of the employee (locus of control, experience and perceived ability). Environmental factors determine the type of leader behaviour required as a complement if follower outcomes are to be maximised, while personal characteristics of the employee determine how the environment and leader behaviour are interpreted. So the theory proposes that leader behaviour will be ineffective when it is redundant with sources of environmental structure or incongruent with employee characteristics. For example, the following are illustrations of predictions based on path–goal theory:

- Directive leadership leads to greater satisfaction when tasks are ambiguous or stressful than when they are highly structured and well laid out.
- Supportive leadership results in high employee performance and satisfaction when employees are performing structured tasks.
- Directive leadership is likely to be perceived as redundant among employees with high perceived ability or with considerable experience.
- Employees with an internal locus of control will be more satisfied with a participative style.
- Achievement-oriented leadership will increase employees' expectancies that effort will lead to high performance when tasks are ambiguously structured.

EVALUATION

Due to its complexity, testing path–goal theory hasn't proven to be easy. A review of the evidence suggests mixed support. As the authors of this review commented, 'These results suggest that either effective leadership does not rest in the removal of roadblocks and pitfalls to employee path instrumentalities as path–goal theories propose or that the nature of these hindrances is not in accord with the proposition of the theories.' Another review concluded that the lack of support was 'shocking and disappointing'.[49] These conclusions have been challenged by others who argue that adequate tests of the theory have yet to be conducted.[50] Thus, it is safe to say that the jury is still out regarding the validity of path–goal theory. Because it is so complex to test, that may remain the case for some time to come.

LEADER-PARTICIPATION MODEL

Victor Vroom and Phillip Yetton developed a **leader-participation model** that related leadership behaviour and participation in decision making.[51] Recognising that task structures have varying demands for routine and non-routine activities, these researchers argued that leader behaviour must adjust to reflect the task structure. Vroom and Yetton's model was normative—it provided a sequential set of rules that should be followed in

leader-participation model | A leadership theory that provides a set of rules to determine the form and amount of participative decision making in different situations.

LEARNING OBJECTIVE 8

Identify the situational variables in the leader-participation model

1.	Importance of the decision
2.	Importance of obtaining follower commitment to the decision
3.	Whether the leader has sufficient information to make a good decision
4.	How well structured the problem is
5.	Whether an autocratic decision would receive follower commitment
6.	Whether followers 'buy into' the organisation's goals
7.	Whether there is likely to be conflict among followers over solution alternatives
8.	Whether followers have the necessary information to make a good decision
9.	Time constraints on the leader that may limit follower involvement
10.	Whether costs to bring geographically dispersed members together are justified
11.	Importance to the leader of minimising the time it takes to make the decision
12.	Importance of using participation as a tool for developing follower decision skills

determining the form and amount of participation in decision making, as determined by different types of situations. The model was a decision tree incorporating seven contingencies (whose relevance could be identified by making 'yes' or 'no' choices) and five alternative leadership styles. More recent work by Vroom and Arthur Jago has resulted in a revision of this model.[52] The revised model retains the same five alternative leadership styles—from the leader's making the decision completely alone to sharing the problem with the group and developing a consensus decision—but adds a set of problem types and expands the contingency variables to 12. The 12 contingency variables are listed in Table 12.1.

Research testing both the original and revised leader-participation models hasn't been encouraging, although the revised model rates higher in effectiveness.[53] Criticism has tended to focus on variables that have been omitted and on the model's overall complexity.[54] Other contingency theories demonstrate that stress, intelligence and experience are important situational variables. Yet, the leader-participation model fails to include them. But more important, at least from a practical point of view, is the fact that the model is far too complicated for the typical manager to use on a regular basis. Although Vroom and Jago have developed a computer program to guide managers through all the decision branches in the revised model, it is not very realistic to expect

As CEO of Australia's low-budget airline Virgin Blue, Brett Godfrey encourages the involvement of his staff in the business, as he knows how important it is to support staff in their work and their decision making. Staff need to be innovative if Virgin Blue wants to maintain a competitive advantage. Empowerment is a key aspect of Godfrey's leadership.

practising managers to consider 12 contingency variables, eight problem types, and five leadership styles in trying to select the appropriate decision process for a specific problem.

We obviously haven't done justice in this discussion to the model's sophistication. So, what can you gain from this brief review? Certainly, we have provided some additional insights into relevant contingency variables. Vroom and his associates have provided us with some specific, empirically supported contingency variables that you should consider when choosing your leadership style.

SUMMARY AND IMPLICATIONS FOR MANAGERS

- Leadership plays a central part in understanding group behaviour, for it is the leader who usually provides the direction towards goal attainment. Therefore, a more accurate predictive capability should be valuable in improving group performance.
- The early search for a set of universal leadership traits failed. However, recent efforts using the Big Five personality framework have generated much more encouraging results. Specifically, the traits of extraversion, conscientiousness and openness to experience show strong and consistent relationships to leadership.
- The behavioural approach's main contribution was narrowing leadership into task-oriented and people-oriented styles.
- A major breakthrough in our understanding of leadership came when we recognised the need to develop contingency theories that included situational factors. At present, the evidence indicates that relevant situational variables would include the task structure of the job, level of situational stress, level of group support, the leader's intelligence and experience, and follower characteristics such as personality, experience, ability and motivation.

POINT / COUNTERPOINT

Developing Leaders is a Waste of Time!

● POINT

Organisations spend billions of dollars on leadership training every year. They send managers to a wide range of leadership training activities, including formal MBA programs, leadership seminars, weekend retreats, and even Outward Bound-type adventures. They appoint mentors. They establish 'fast tracks' for high-potential individuals so they can gain a variety of the 'right kinds of experience'. We propose that much of this effort to train leaders is probably a waste of time and money. And we base our position on two very basic assumptions that underlie leadership training.

The first assumption is that we know what leadership is. We don't. Experts can't agree if it is a trait, a characteristic, a behaviour, a role, a style, a process or an ability. They further can't even agree on whether leaders really make a difference in organisational outcomes. For instance, some experts have persuasively argued that leadership is merely an attribution made to explain organisational successes and failures, which themselves occur by chance. Leaders are the people who get credit for successes and take the blame for failures, but they may actually have little influence over organisational outcomes.

The second basic assumption is that we can train people to lead. The evidence here isn't very encouraging. We do seem to be able to teach individuals about leadership. Unfortunately, findings indicate we aren't so good at teaching people to lead. There are several possible explanations. To the degree that personality is a critical element in leadership effectiveness, some people may not have been born with the right personality traits. In fact, there is evidence that leadership is, at least in part, inherited. A second explanation is that there is no evidence that individuals can substantially alter their basic leadership style. A third possibility is that, even if certain theories could actually guide individuals in leadership situations, and even if individuals could alter their style, the complexity of those theories makes it nearly impossible for any normal human being to assimilate all the variables and be capable of enacting the right behaviours in every situation.

● COUNTERPOINT

Leadership development programs exist and, collectively, they represent a multi-billion-dollar industry worldwide because these programs work. Decision makers are, for the most part, rational. Would organisations such as Qantas, Queensland Health, SingTel and General Electric spend literally millions of dollars each year on leadership training if they didn't expect some benefit? We don't think so! And the ability to lead successfully is why a company such as Telstra will willingly pay its CEO, Solomon Trujillo, more than $4 million in 2006 with bonuses calculated in excess of $6 million based on expected performance results.

Although there are certainly disagreements over the exact definition of leadership, most academics and businesspeople agree that leadership is an influence process whereby an individual, by his or her actions, facilitates the movement of a group of people towards the achievement of a common goal.

Do leaders affect organisational outcomes? Of course they do. Successful leaders anticipate change, vigorously exploit opportunities, motivate their followers to higher levels of productivity, correct poor performance, and lead the organisation towards its objectives. A review of the leadership literature, in fact, led two academics to conclude that the research shows 'a consistent effect for leadership explaining 20 to 45 percent of the variance on relevant organizational outcomes'.

What about the effectiveness of leadership programs? They vary. But more and more evidence is accumulating from the best management journals, showing that we can train people to be better leaders. Many of these studies have used rigorous experimental designs and objective outcomes. Thus, it simply isn't credible to argue that we can't teach people to lead.

SOURCES: Points in this argument are based on R. A. Barker, 'How Can We Train Leaders If We Do Not Know What Leadership Is?', *Human Relations*, April 1997, pp. 343–62; N. Nicholson, *Executive Instinct* (New York: Crown, 2001); R. J. House and R. N. Aditya, 'The Social Scientific Study of Leadership: Quo Vadis', *Journal of Management*, vol. 23, no. 3, 1997, pp. 460–61; D. V. Day and R. G. Lord, 'Executive Leadership and Organizational Performance: Suggestions for a New Theory and Methodology', *Journal of Management*, Fall 1988, pp. 453–64; M. Frese, S. Beimel and S. Schoenborn, 'Action Training for Charismatic Leadership: Two Evaluations of Studies of a Commercial Training Module on Inspirational Communication of a Vision', *Personnel Psychology*, vol. 56, 2003, pp. 671–97; T. Dvir, D. Eden and B. J. Avolio, 'Impact of Transformational Leadership on Follower Development and Performance: A Field Experiment', *Academy of Management Journal*, vol. 45, 2002, pp. 735–44; A. J. Towler, 'Effects of Charismatic Influence Training on Attitudes, Behavior, and Performance', *Personnel Psychology*, vol. 56, 2003, pp. 363–81; and J. Barling, T. Weber and E. K. Kelloway, 'Effects of Transformational Leadership Training on Attitudinal and Financial Outcomes: A Field Experiment', *Journal of Applied Psychology*, vol. 81, 1996, pp. 827–32.

QUESTIONS FOR REVIEW

1. What traits predict leadership?
2. Do initiating structure and consideration predict a leader's effectiveness?
3. How different is the managerial grid's approach to leadership from the approaches of the Ohio State and Michigan groups?
4. How does Fiedler's contingency theory assist you in influencing the performance of a work group?
5. What contribution does cognitive resource theory make to leadership?
6. What are the implications of LMX theory for leadership practice?
7. How does knowledge of the path–goal theory make you a better leader?
8. What are the implications if leaders are inflexible in adjusting their style?

QUESTIONS FOR CRITICAL THINKING

1. Review trait theories in the context of the 'nature versus nurture' debate.
2. Develop an example in which you operationalise the Fiedler model.
3. Develop an example in which you operationalise the path–goal theory.
4. Develop an example in which you operationalise SLT.

EXPERIENTIAL EXERCISE

Debate: Do Leaders Really Matter?

Break the class into groups of two. One group member will argue: 'Leaders are the primary determinant of an organisation's success or failure.' The other group member will argue: 'Leaders don't really matter, because most of the things that affect an organisation's success or failure are outside a leader's control.' Take ten minutes to develop your arguments; then you have ten minutes to conduct your debate.

After the dyad debates, form into teams of six. Three from each of these groups should have taken the 'pro' argument on leadership and three should have taken the 'con' side. The teams have 15 minutes to reconcile their arguments and to develop a unified position. When the 15 minutes are up, each team should be prepared to make a brief presentation to the class, summarising its unified position.

ETHICAL DILEMMA

Do Ends Justify the Means?

The power that comes from being a leader can be used for evil as well as for good. When you assume the benefits of leadership, you also assume ethical burdens. But many highly successful leaders have relied on questionable tactics to achieve their ends. These include manipulation, verbal attacks, physical intimidation, lying, fear and control. Let's consider a few examples.

Bill Clinton successfully led the United States through eight years of economic expansion. Those close to him were committed and loyal followers. Yet, he lied under oath (causing him to lose his licence to practise law) and 'managed' the truth.

Jack Welch, former head of General Electric (GE), provided the leadership that made GE one of the most admired companies around the world. His profile is promoted by the many books about him in major bookstores, including biographies. He also ruthlessly preached firing the lowest-performing 10 per cent of the company's employees every year.

Cisco Systems is a respected company in Australasia and provides valuable support for the Singapore government's Intelligent Nation 2015 master plan. However, its CEO, John Chambers, laid off nearly 20 per cent of his workforce and commented that the tough times were 'likely to be just a speed bump'. Tell that to the 17 000 workers he laid off. And yet, Cisco has returned to profitability.

Should leaders be judged solely on their end achievements? Or do the means they choose also reflect on their leadership qualities? Are employees, shareholders and society too quick to excuse leaders who use questionable means if they are successful in achieving their goals? Is it impossible for leaders to be ethical *and* successful?

SOURCE: Based on C. E. Johnson, *Meeting the Ethical Challenges in Leadership* (Thousand Oaks, CA: Sage, 2001), pp. 4–5.

Jane Sommers, Rob Carstons and Linda McGee have something in common. They all were promoted within their organisations into management positions. And each found the transition a challenge.

Jane Sommers was promoted to director of catering for the Georges Group of restaurants in Melbourne. With the promotion, she realised that things would never be the same again. No longer would she be able to participate in gossip around the fax machine or shrug off an employee's chronic lateness. She says she found her new role to be daunting. 'At first I was like a bulldozer knocking everyone over, and that wasn't well received. I was saying, "It's my way or the highway." And I was forgetting that my friends were also in transition.' She admits that this style alienated just about everyone with whom she worked.

Eric Ng, a technical manager at IBM in Sydney, talks about the uncertainty he felt after being promoted to a managerial position from being a junior programmer. 'It was a little bit challenging to be suddenly giving directives to peers, when just the day before you were one of them. You try to be careful not to offend anyone. It's strange walking into a room and the whole conversation changes. People don't want to be as open with you when you become the boss.'

Anita Volkov is now in charge of AXB Insurance Services in Auckland. She started as a customer service representative with the company, then leapfrogged over colleagues in a series of promotions. Her fast rise created problems. Colleagues 'would say, "Oh, here comes the big cheese now." God only knows what they talked about behind my back.'

QUESTIONS

1. A lot of new managers err in selecting the right leadership style when they move into management. Why do you think this happens?
2. What does this say about leadership and leadership training?
3. Which leadership theories, if any, could help new leaders deal with this transition?
4. Do you think it is easier or harder to be promoted internally into a formal leadership position than to come into it as an outsider? Explain.

SOURCE: Adapted from D. Koeppel, 'A Tough Transition: Friend to Supervisor', *New York Times*, 16 March 2003, p. BU-12.

ENDNOTES

1. Adele Ferguson, 'Heavy Going', *Business Review Weekly*, 4–10 May 2006, pp. 16–21; <www.seven.com.au/sundaysunrise/finance_041107_chaney>; and <www1.wesfarmers.com.au/default.aspx?MenuID=8>.

2. J. P. Kotter, 'What Leaders Really Do', *Harvard Business Review*, May–June 1990, pp. 103–11; and J. P. Kotter, *A Force for Change: How Leadership Differs from Management* (New York: Free Press, 1990).

3. R. J. House and R. N. Aditya, 'The Social Scientific Study of Leadership: Quo Vadis', *Journal of Management*, vol. 23, no. 3, 1997, p. 445.

4. See, for example, W. B. Snavely, 'Organizational Leadership: An Alternative View and Implications for Managerial Education', Paper presented at the Midwest Academy of Management Conference, Toledo, OH, April 2001.

5. J. G. Geier, 'A Trait Approach to the Study of Leadership in Small Groups', *Journal of Communication*, December 1967, pp. 316–23.

6. S. A. Kirkpatrick and E. A. Locke, 'Leadership: Do Traits Matter?', *Academy of Management Executive*, May 1991, pp. 48–60; and S. J. Zaccaro, R. J. Foti and D. A. Kenny, 'Self-Monitoring and Trait-Based Variance in Leadership: An Investigation of Leader Flexibility across Multiple Group Situations', *Journal of Applied Psychology*, April 1991, pp. 308–15.

7. See T. A. Judge, J. E. Bono, R. Ilies and M. Werner, 'Personality and Leadership: A Review', Paper presented at the 15th Annual Conference of the Society for Industrial and Organizational Psychology, New Orleans, 2000; and T. A. Judge, J. E. Bono, R. Ilies and M. W. Gerhardt, 'Personality and Leadership: A Qualitative and Quantitative Review', *Journal of Applied Psychology*, August 2002, pp. 765–80.

8. Judge, et al., 'Personality and Leadership'.

9. This section is based on D. Goleman, *Working with Emotional Intelligence* (New York: Bantam, 1998); D. Goleman, 'What Makes a Leader?', *Harvard Business Review*, November–December 1998, pp. 93–102; J. M. George, 'Emotions and Leadership: The Role of Emotional Intelligence', *Human Relations*, August 2000, pp. 1027–55; D. R. Caruso, J. D. Mayer and P. Salovey, 'Emotional Intelligence and Emotional Leadership,', in R. E. Riggio, S. E. Murphy and F. J. Pirozzolo (eds), *Multiple Intelligences and Leadership* (Mahwah, NJ: Lawrence Erlbaum, 2002), pp. 55–74; D. Goleman, R. E. Boyatzis and A. McKee, *Primal Leadership: Realizing the Power of Emotional Intelligence* (Boston: Harvard Business School Press, 2002); C-S. Wong and K. S. Law, 'The Effects of Leader and Follower Emotional Intelligence on Performance and Attitude: An Exploratory Study', *Leadership Quarterly*, June 2002, pp. 243–74; and D. R. Caruso and C. J. Wolfe, 'Emotional Intelligence and Leadership Development', in D. David and S. J. Zaccaro (eds), *Leader Development for Transforming Organizations: Growing Leaders for Tomorrow* (Mahwah, NJ: Lawrence Erlbaum, 2004), pp. 237–63.

10. J. Champy, 'The Hidden Qualities of Great Leaders', *Fast Company*, no. 76, November 2003, p. 135.

11. F. I. Greenstein, *The Presidential Difference: Leadership Style from FDR to George W. Bush* (Princeton, NJ: Princeton University Press, 2004).

12. J. Antonakis, 'Why "Emotional Intelligence" Does Not Predict Leadership Effectiveness: A Comment on Prati, Douglas, Ferris, Ammeter, and Buckley (2003)', *International Journal of Organizational Analysis*, vol. 11, 2003, pp. 355–61; see also M. Zeidner, G. Matthews and R. D. Roberts, 'Emotional Intelligence in the Workplace: A Critical Review', *Applied Psychology: An International Review*, vol. 53, 2004, pp. 371–99.

13. R. G. Lord, C. L. DeVader and G. M. Alliger, 'A Meta-Analysis of the Relation between Personality Traits and Leadership Perceptions: An Application of Validity Generalization Procedures', *Journal of Applied Psychology*, August 1986, pp. 402–10; and J. A. Smith and R. J. Foti, 'A Pattern Approach to the Study of Leader Emergence', *Leadership Quarterly*, Summer 1998, pp. 147–60.

14. See S. Hansen, 'Stings Like a Bee', *INC.*, November 2002, pp. 56–64; J. Greenbaum, 'Is Ghengis on the Hunt Again?', *internetnews.com:* <www.internetnews.com/commentary/article.php/3459771> (14 January 2005).

15. R. M. Stogdill and A. E. Coons (eds), *Leader Behavior: Its Description and Measurement, Research Monograph No. 88* (Columbus, OH: Ohio State University, Bureau of Business Research, 1951). This research is updated in C. A. Schriesheim, C. C. Cogliser and L. L. Neider, 'Is It "Trustworthy"? A Multiple-Levels-of-Analysis Reexamination of an Ohio State Leadership Study, with Implications for Future Research', *Leadership Quarterly*, Summer 1995, pp. 111–45; and T. A. Judge, R. F. Piccolo and R. Ilies, 'The Forgotten Ones? The Validity of Consideration and Initiating Structure in Leadership Research', *Journal of Applied Psychology*, February 2004, pp. 36–51.

16. H. Yen, 'Richard Parsons, AOL Time Warner's New CEO, Known as Consensus-Builder': <www.tbo.com> (6 December 2001).

17. G. Yukl and D. D. Van Fleet, 'Theory and Research on Leadership in Organization', in M. D. Dunnette and L. M. Hough (eds), *Handbook of Industrial and Organizational Psychology*, vol. 2 (Palo Alto, CA: Consulting Psychologists Press, 1992), pp. 147–97.

18. R. Kahn and D. Katz, 'Leadership Practices in Relation to Productivity and Morale', in D. Cartwright and A. Zander (eds), *Group Dynamics: Research and Theory*, 2nd ed. (Elmsford, NY: Row, Paterson, 1960).

19. Judge, Piccolo and Ilies, 'The Forgotten Ones? The Validity of Consideration and Initiating Structure in Leadership Research'.

20. R. R. Blake and J. S. Mouton, *The Managerial Grid* (Houston, TX: Gulf, 1964).

21. See, for example, R. R. Blake and J. S. Mouton, 'A Comparative Analysis of Situationalism and 9,9 Management by Principle', *Organizational Dynamics*, Spring 1982, pp. 20–43.

22. See, for example, L. L. Larson, J. G. Hunt and R. N. Osborn, 'The Great Hi-Hi Leader Behavior Myth: A Lesson from Occam's Razor', *Academy of Management Journal*, December 1976, pp. 628–41; and P. C. Nystrom, 'Managers and the Hi- Hi Leader Myth', *Academy of Management Journal*, June 1978, pp. 325–31.

23. See G. Ekvall and J. Arvonen, 'Change-Centered Leadership: An Extension of the Two-Dimensional Model', *Scandinavian Journal of Management*, vol. 7, no. 1, 1991, pp. 17–26; M. Lindell and G. Rosenqvist, 'Is There a Third Management Style?', *The Finnish Journal*

of *Business Economics*, vol. 3, 1992, pp. 171–98; and M. Lindell and G. Rosenqvist, 'Management Behavior Dimensions and Development Orientation', *Leadership Quarterly*, Winter 1992, pp. 355–77.

24. M. McDonald, 'Lingerie's Iron Maiden Is Undone', *US News & World Report*, 25 June 2001, p. 37; and A. D'Innocenzio, 'Wachner Ousted as CEO, Chairman at Warnaco', *The Detroit News*, 17 November 2001, p. D1.

25. 'SEC Announces Settlement with Warnaco, Former Warnaco Executives, and PwC for Financial Disclosure Violations': <www.sec.gov/news/press/2004-62.htm> (11 May 2004); D. Leonhardt, 'Boards Aim to Pull Back CEO Salary', *New York Times*: <www.uni-muenster.de/PeaCon/global-texte/g-w/n/ceosalary.htm> (16 September 2002).

26. F. E. Fiedler, *A Theory of Leadership Effectiveness* (New York: McGraw-Hill, 1967).

27. S. Shiflett, 'Is There a Problem with the LPC Score in LEADER MATCH?', *Personnel Psychology*, Winter 1981, pp. 765–69.

28. F. E. Fiedler, M. M. Chemers and L. Mahar, *Improving Leadership Effectiveness: The Leader Match Concept* (New York: John Wiley, 1977).

29. Cited in House and Aditya, 'The Social Scientific Study of Leadership', p. 422.

30. L. H. Peters, D. D. Hartke and J. T. Pohlmann, 'Fiedler's Contingency Theory of Leadership: An Application of the Meta-Analysis Procedures of Schmidt and Hunter', *Psychological Bulletin*, March 1985, pp. 274–85; C. A. Schriesheim, B. J. Tepper and L. A. Tetrault, 'Least Preferred Co-worker Score, Situational Control, and Leadership Effectiveness: A Meta-Analysis of Contingency Model Performance Predictions', *Journal of Applied Psychology*, August 1994, pp. 561–73; and R. Ayman, M. M. Chemers and F. Fiedler, 'The Contingency Model of Leadership Effectiveness: Its Levels of Analysis', *Leadership Quarterly*, Summer 1995, pp. 147–67.

31. House and Aditya, 'The Social Scientific Study of Leadership', p. 422.

32. See, for instance, R. W. Rice, 'Psychometric Properties of the Esteem for the Least Preferred Co-worker Scale', *Academy of Management Review*, January 1978, pp. 106–18; C. A. Schriesheim, B. D. Bannister and W. H. Money, 'Psychometric Properties of the LPC Scale: An Extension of Rice's Review', *Academy*

of *Management Review*, April 1979, pp. 287–90; and J. K. Kennedy, J. M. Houston, M. A. Korgaard and D. D. Gallo, 'Construct Space of the Least Preferred Co-worker (LPC) Scale', *Educational & Psychological Measurement*, Fall 1987, pp. 807–14.

33. See E. H. Schein, *Organizational Psychology*, 3rd ed. (Upper Saddle River, NJ: Prentice Hall, 1980), pp. 116–17; and B. Kabanoff, 'A Critique of Leader Match and Its Implications for Leadership Research', *Personnel Psychology*, Winter 1981, pp. 749–64.

34. F. E. Fiedler and J. E. Garcia, *New Approaches to Effective Leadership: Cognitive Resources and Organizational Performance* (New York: Wiley, 1987).

35. See F. W. Gibson, F. E. Fiedler and K. M. Barrett, 'Stress, Babble, and the Utilization of the Leader's Intellectual Abilities', *Leadership Quarterly*, Summer 1993, pp. 189–208; F. E. Fiedler and T. G. Link, 'Leader Intelligence, Interpersonal Stress, and Task Performance', in R. J. Sternberg and R. K. Wagner (eds), *Mind in Context: Interactionist Perspectives on Human Intelligence* (London: Cambridge University Press, 1994), pp. 152–67; F. E. Fiedler, 'Cognitive Resources and Leadership Performance', *Applied Psychology—An International Review*, January 1995, pp. 5–28; and F. E. Fiedler, 'The Curious Role of Cognitive Resources in Leadership', in R. E. Riggio, S. E. Murphy, F. J. Pirozzolo (eds), *Multiple Intelligences and Leadership* (Mahwah, NJ: Lawrence Erlbaum, 2002), pp. 91–104.

36. T. A. Judge, A. E. Colbert and R. Ilies, 'Intelligence and Leadership: A Quantitative Review and Test of Theoretical Propositions', *Journal of Applied Psychology*, June 2004, pp. 542–52.

37. P. Hersey and K. H. Blanchard, 'So You Want to Know Your Leadership Style?', *Training and Development Journal*, February 1974, pp. 1–15; and P. Hersey, K. H. Blanchard and D. E. Johnson, *Management of Organizational Behavior: Leading Human Resources*, 8th ed. (Upper Saddle River, NJ: Prentice Hall, 2001).

38. Cited in C. F. Fernandez and R. P. Vecchio, 'Situational Leadership Theory Revisited: A Test of an Across-Jobs Perspective', *Leadership Quarterly*, vol. 8, no. 1, 1997, p. 67.

39. See, for instance, ibid, pp. 67–84; C. L. Graeff, 'Evolution of Situational Leadership Theory: A Critical Review', *Leadership*

Quarterly, vol. 8, no. 2, 1997, pp. 153–70; and R. P. Vecchio and K. J. Boatwright, 'Preferences for Idealized Styles of Supervision', *Leadership Quarterly*, August 2002, pp. 327–42.

40. R. M. Dienesch and R. C. Liden, 'Leader–Member Exchange (LPC) Model of Leadership: A Critique and Further Development', *Academy of Management Review*, July 1986, pp. 618–34; G. B. Graen and M. Uhl-Bien, 'Relationship-Based Approach to Leadership: Development of Leader–Member Exchange (LMX) Theory of Leadership Over 25 Years: Applying a Multi-Domain Perspective', *Leadership Quarterly*, Summer 1995, pp. 219–47; R. C. Liden, R. T. Sparrowe and S. J. Wayne, 'Leader–Member Exchange Theory: The Past and Potential for the Future', in G. R. Ferris (ed.), *Research in Personnel and Human Resource Management*, vol. 15 (Greenwich, CT: JAI Press, 1997), pp. 47–119; and C. A. Schriesheim, S. L. Castro, X. Zhou and F. J. Yammarino, 'The Folly of Theorizing "A" but Testing "B": A Selective Level-of-Analysis Review of the Field and a Detailed Leader–Member Exchange Illustration', *Leadership Quarterly*, Winter 2001, pp. 515–51.

41. R. Liden and G. Graen, 'Generalizability of the Vertical Dyad Linkage Model of Leadership', *Academy of Management Journal*, September 1980, pp. 451–65; R. C. Liden, S. J. Wayne and D. Stilwell, 'A Longitudinal Study of the Early Development of Leader–Member Exchanges', *Journal of Applied Psychology*, August 1993, pp. 662–74; S. J. Wayne, L. M. Shore, W. H. Bommer and L. E. Tetrick, 'The Role of Fair Treatment and Rewards in Perceptions of Organizational Support and Leader–Member Exchange', *Journal of Applied Psychology*, vol. 87, no. 3, June 2002, pp. 590–98; S. S. Masterson, K. Lewis and B. M. Goldman, 'Integrating Justice and Social Exchange: The Differing Effects of Fair Procedures and Treatment on Work Relationships', *Academy of Management Journal*, vol. 43, no. 4, August 2000, pp. 738–48.

42. D. Duchon, S. G. Green and T. D. Taber, 'Vertical Dyad Linkage: A Longitudinal Assessment of Antecedents, Measures, and Consequences', *Journal of Applied Psychology*, February 1986, pp. 56–60; Liden, Wayne and Stilwell, 'A Longitudinal Study on the Early Development of Leader–Member Exchanges'; R. J. Deluga

and J. T. Perry, 'The Role of Subordinate Performance and Ingratiation in Leader–Member Exchanges', *Group & Organization Management*, March 1994, pp. 67–86; T. N. Bauer and S. G. Green, 'Development of Leader–Member Exchange: A Longitudinal Test', *Academy of Management Journal*, December 1996, pp. 1538–67; S. J. Wayne, L. M. Shore and R. C. Liden, 'Perceived Organizational Support and Leader–Member Exchange: A Social Exchange Perspective', *Academy of Management Journal*, February 1997, pp. 82–111; and M. Uhl-Bien, 'Relationship Development as a Key Ingredient for Leadership Development', in S. E. Murphy and R. E. Riggio (eds), *Future of Leadership Development* (Mahwah, NJ: Lawrence Erlbaum, 2003) pp. 129–47.

43. O. Janssen and N. W. Van Yperen, 'Employees' Goal Orientations, the Quality of Leader–Member Exchange, and the Outcomes of Job Performance and Job Satisfaction', *Academy of Management Journal*, vol. 47, no. 3, June 2004, pp. 368–84.

44. K. M. Kacmar, L. A. Witt and S. Zivnuska, 'The Interactive Effect of Leader–Member Exchange and Communication Frequency on Performance Ratings', *Journal of Applied Psychology*, vol. 88, no. 4, August 2003, pp. 764–72.

45. A. Stensgaard, 'What Happens to the Inner Circle of the Ousted CEO?', AME Info.: <www.ameinfo.com/news/Detailed/23359.html> (27 April 2003).

46. See, for instance, C. R. Gerstner and D. V. Day, 'Meta-Analytic Review of Leader–Member Exchange Theory: Correlates and Construct Issues', *Journal of Applied Psychology*, December 1997, pp. 827–44; C. Gomez and B. Rosen, 'The Leader–Member Exchange as a Link

between Managerial Trust and Employee Empowerment', *Group & Organization Management*, March 2001, pp. 53–69; J. M. Maslyn and M. Uhl-Bien, 'Leader–Member Exchange and Its Dimensions: Effects of Self-Effort and Other's Effort on Relationship Quality', *Journal of Applied Psychology*, August 2001, pp. 697–708; M. L. Kraimer, S. J. Wayne and R. A. Jaworski, 'Sources of Support and Expatriate Performance: The Mediating Role of Expatriate Adjustment', *Personnel Psychology*, vol. 54, Spring 2001, pp. 71–99; and note 43.

47. D. Eden, 'Leadership and Expectations: Pygmalion Effects and Other Self-Fulfilling Prophecies in Organizations', *Leadership Quarterly*, Winter 1992, pp. 278–79.

48. R. J. House, 'A Path–Goal Theory of Leader Effectiveness', *Administrative Science Quarterly*, September 1971, pp. 321–38; R. J. House and T. R. Mitchell, 'Path–Goal Theory of Leadership', *Journal of Contemporary Business*, Autumn 1974, pp. 81–97; and R. J. House, 'Path–Goal Theory of Leadership: Lessons, Legacy, and a Reformulated Theory', *Leadership Quarterly*, Fall 1996, pp. 323–52.

49. J. C. Wofford and L. Z. Liska, 'Path–Goal Theories of Leadership: A Meta-Analysis', *Journal of Management*, Winter 1993, pp. 857–76; P. M. Podsakoff, S. B. MacKenzie and M. Ahearne, 'Searching for a Needle in a Haystack: Trying to Identify the Illusive Moderators of Leadership Behaviors', *Journal of Management*, vol. 21, 1995, pp. 423–70.

50. J. R. Villa, J. P. Howell and P. W. Dorfman, 'Problems with Detecting Moderators in Leadership Research Using Moderated Multiple Regression', *Leadership Quarterly*, vol. 14, 2003, pp. 3–23; C. A. Schriesheim and L. Neider, 'Path–Goal

Leadership Theory: The Long and Winding Road', *Leadership Quarterly*, vol. 7, 1996, pp. 317–21; M. G. Evans, 'R. J. House's "A Path–Goal Theory of Leader Effectiveness"', *Leadership Quarterly*, vol. 7, 1996, pp. 305–09.

51. V. H. Vroom and P. W. Yetton, *Leadership and Decision-Making* (Pittsburgh: University of Pittsburgh Press, 1973).

52. V. H. Vroom and A. G. Jago, *The New Leadership: Managing Participation in Organizations* (Englewood Cliffs, NJ: Prentice Hall, 1988). See also V. H. Vroom and A. G. Jago, 'Situation Effects and Levels of Analysis in the Study of Leader Participation', *Leadership Quarterly*, Summer 1995, pp. 169–81.

53. See, for example, R. H. G. Field, 'A Test of the Vroom–Yetton Normative Model of Leadership', *Journal of Applied Psychology*, October 1982, pp. 523–32; C. R. Leana, 'Power Relinquishment versus Power Sharing: Theoretical Clarification and Empirical Comparison of Delegation and Participation', *Journal of Applied Psychology*, May 1987, pp. 228–33; J. T. Ettling and A. G. Jago, 'Participation under Conditions of Conflict: More on the Validity of the Vroom–Yetton Model', *Journal of Management Studies*, January 1988, pp. 73–83; R. H. G. Field and R. J. House, 'A Test of the Vroom–Yetton Model Using Manager and Subordinate Reports', *Journal of Applied Psychology*, June 1990, pp. 362–66; and R. H. G. Field and J. P Andrews, 'Testing the Incremental Validity of the Vroom–Jago versus Vroom–Yetton Models of Participation in Decision Making', *Journal of Behavioral Decision Making*, December 1998, pp. 251–61.

54. House and Aditya, 'The Social Scientific Study of Leadership: Quo Vadis?', p. 428.

13

CONTEMPORARY ISSUES IN LEADERSHIP

LEARNING OBJECTIVES

AFTER STUDYING THIS CHAPTER, YOU SHOULD BE ABLE TO:

1. EXPLAIN HOW FRAMING INFLUENCES LEADERSHIP EFFECTIVENESS

2. DEFINE THE QUALITIES OF A CHARISMATIC LEADER

3. CONTRAST TRANSFORMATIONAL WITH TRANSACTIONAL LEADERSHIP

4. IDENTIFY THE FIVE DIMENSIONS OF TRUST

5. IDENTIFY THE FOUR ROLES THAT TEAM LEADERS PERFORM

6. EXPLAIN THE ROLE OF A MENTOR

7. DESCRIBE HOW ONLINE LEADERSHIP DIFFERS FROM FACE-TO-FACE LEADERSHIP

8. IDENTIFY WHEN LEADERSHIP MAY NOT BE NECESSARY

9. EXPLAIN HOW TO FIND AND CREATE EFFECTIVE LEADERS

Penny Maclagan appreciates the significance of effective leadership at Computershare, where staff talent makes the difference in sustaining a successful technology company.

Naomi Milgrom owns and runs the retail stores for Sussan, Suzanne Grae and Sportsgirl in Australia and New Zealand. She believes that a new style of leadership is required over the old authoritarian power structures still prevalent in many companies today.

WHAT DO PENNY MACLAGAN AND NAOMI MILGROM have in common? They were both schoolteachers in their early careers. They are both multimillionaires. And they are recognised by their staff as effective leaders.

Penny Maclagan joined Computershare in 1983 and was appointed to the board as an executive director in May 1995. In her role as managing director of Computershare Technology Services, Maclagan is responsible for planning, developing and executing technology across the world in support of the firm's global strategy. Computershare is the world's largest global share registry, and a leading provider of financial market services and technology to the global securities industry, involving almost 10 000 experienced professionals operating in 21 countries. One of her staff believes that Maclagan is a highly motivated individual and leads by example in trying to establish a culture based on loyalty and contribution. Her boss and chief executive of Computershare appreciates her honest feedback, because he believes in managers he can relate to and trust.

Naomi Milgrom is executive chair and CEO of the Sussan Group of companies, the acknowledged industry leader in speciality retailing in Australia. It includes the retail chains Sussan, Suzanne Grae and Sportsgirl, with more than 500 retail stores in Australia and New Zealand employing over 3000 people. Milgrom believes that a new style of leadership is required, pointing out that the old authoritarian power structures no longer work. She has criticised Australian business leaders for too much managing and not enough leading. Her prescription for the necessary leadership attributes for today's challenges include:

- communicating a strong, positive vision of the nature and direction of the business;
- developing a culture that nurtures staff to perform their best as individuals and members of teams; and
- allowing people to make and acknowledge mistakes, and to keep learning to improve.

These leadership attributes are instrumental in providing a creative and stimulating learning environment.

Both women appreciate the value of having good staff. Maclagan sees the significance of surrounding herself with quality people, and Computershare is rich in talented information technology managers at all levels. Milgrom reinforces this point by highlighting that her greatest challenge as a leader is acquiring and retaining the right people and motivating them to deliver on the company's objectives.[1]

Leadership is being honest with people.

Peter Ryan

PENNY MACLAGAN AND NAOMI MILGROM are successful businesswomen who have demonstrated the significance of being able to influence results by harnessing the abilities and potential of the people around them. In this chapter, we will explore charismatic leadership, transformational leadership, the role of ethics and trust in leadership, contemporary leadership roles, challenges to the leadership construct, and finally, how companies find and create effective leaders. But first, let's explore how effective leaders use framing to inspire and influence their followers.

FRAMING: USING WORDS TO SHAPE MEANING AND INSPIRE OTHERS

framing | A way to use language to manage meaning.

British Prime Minister Winston Churchill's famous words from one of his wartime speeches, 'We shall fight on the beaches. We shall fight in the fields and in the streets. We shall fight in the hills. We shall never surrender', have been referred to over the years to signify the spirit of the people of Great Britain in defending their homeland during the Second World War. His words created an image of what a country can do in times of crisis. What Churchill did was *frame* the defence of Great Britain in a way that touched the hearts and minds of the population.

Framing is a way to use language to manage meaning.[2] It is a way for leaders to influence how events are seen and understood. It involves the selection and highlighting of one or more aspects of a subject while excluding others.

Framing is analogous to what a photographer does. The visual world that exists is essentially ambiguous. When the photographer aims a camera and focuses on a specific shot, she frames the photo. Others then see what she wanted them to see. They see her point of view. That is precisely what leaders do when they frame an issue. They choose which aspects or portion of the subject they want others to focus on and which portions they want to be excluded.

Barristers make their living by framing issues. Barristers acting for the accused, for example, shape their arguments so as to get the jury to see their client in the most favourable terms. They include 'facts' that might help the jury find their client 'not guilty'. They exclude facts that might reflect unfavourably on their client. And they try to provide alternative interpretations to the 'facts' that the prosecution argues make their client guilty.

Lobbying groups also provide rich illustrations of the framing concept. The Michael Moore documentary *Bowling For Columbine* was hugely popular in Australia and New Zealand. It is an entertaining account of the politics of gun ownership in the United States. Despite the satirical portrait of the National Rifle Association (NRA), its leadership has historically been very successful in limiting gun controls in the United States, much more so than their counterparts in Australia and New Zealand. They have done this not by focusing on shootings, deaths or even self-defence. They have succeeded by framing gun control as a first amendment 'freedom' issue. To the degree that the NRA can shape public opinion to think of gun controls as taking away a citizen's right to bear arms, they have been able to minimise gun control regulations. Another example is the confronting film *Elephant*, released in 2004. It makes an eerie offering of the events of the 1999 massacre at

Colorado's Columbine High School in the United States, but purely from the students' perspective. In a similar vein, original opponents of abortion rallied their cause by describing themselves as 'anti-abortion' advocates. In response, and realising the negative imagery from using the label 'pro-abortion', supporters reframed the issue by referring to themselves as 'pro-choice' in their recent actions surrounding the controversial abortion pill RU-486.

So, why is framing relevant to leadership today? Because in the complex and chaotic environment in which an increasing number of leaders work, there is typically considerable manoeuvrability with respect to 'the facts'. What is real is often what the leader says is real. What is important is what he or she chooses to say is important. Leaders can use language to influence followers' perceptions of the world, the meaning of events, beliefs about causes and consequences, and visions of the future. It is through framing that leaders determine whether people notice problems, how they understand and remember them, and how they react to those problems.[3] Thus, framing is a powerful tool by which leaders influence how others see and interpret reality.

INSPIRATIONAL APPROACHES TO LEADERSHIP

In this section, we present two contemporary leadership theories with a common theme. They view leaders as individuals who inspire followers through their words, ideas and behaviours. These theories are charismatic leadership and transformational leadership.

CHARISMATIC LEADERSHIP

Bob Hawke (former prime minister of Australia), Lee Kuan Yew (former prime minister of Singapore), Aung San Suu Kyi (opposition politician in Burma/Myanmar), Steve Jobs (co-founder of Apple Computer), James Strong (former CEO of Qantas Airlines) and Nicholas Milton (winner of the Symphony Australia Conducting Competition and Westfield Young Conductor of the Year) are individuals frequently cited as being charismatic leaders. What do they have in common?

WHAT IS CHARISMATIC LEADERSHIP?

LEARNING OBJECTIVE 2
Define the qualities of a charismatic leader

Max Weber, a sociologist, was the first scholar to discuss charismatic leadership. More than a century ago, he defined *charisma* (from the Greek for 'gift') as 'a certain quality of an individual personality, by virtue of which he or she is set apart from ordinary people and treated as endowed with supernatural, superhuman, or at least specifically exceptional powers or qualities. These powers or qualities are not accessible to the ordinary person, but are regarded as of divine origin or as exemplary, and on the basis of them the individual concerned is treated as a leader'.[4] Weber argued that charismatic leadership was one of several ideal types of authority.

The first researcher to consider charismatic leadership in terms of OB was Robert House. According to House's **charismatic leadership theory**, followers make attributions of heroic or extraordinary leadership abilities when they observe certain behaviours.[5] There have been a number of studies that have attempted to identify the characteristics of the charismatic leader. One of the best reviews of the literature has documented four—they have a vision, they are willing to take personal risks to achieve that vision, they are sensitive to follower needs as well as environmental demands, and they exhibit behaviours that are out of the ordinary.[6] These characteristics are described in Table 13.1.

charismatic leadership theory | Followers make attributions of heroic or extraordinary leadership abilities when they observe certain behaviours.

■ TABLE 13.1

Key characteristics of
charismatic leaders

1. *Vision and articulation.* Has a vision—expressed as an idealised goal—that proposes a future better than the status quo; and is able to clarify the importance of the vision in terms that are understandable to others.
2. *Personal risk.* Willing to take on high personal risk, incur high costs, and engage in self-sacrifice to achieve the vision.
3. *Environmental sensitivity.* Able to make realistic assessments of the environmental constraints and resources needed to bring about change.
4. *Sensitivity to follower needs.* Perceptive of others' abilities and responsive to their needs and feelings.
5. *Unconventional behaviour.* Engages in behaviours that are perceived as novel and counter to norms.

SOURCE: Based on J. A. Conger and R. N. Kanungo, *Charismatic Leadership in Organizations* (Thousand Oaks, CA: Sage, 1998), p. 94.

ARE CHARISMATIC LEADERS BORN OR MADE?

Are charismatic leaders born with their qualities? Or can people actually learn how to be charismatic leaders? The answer to both questions is 'yes'.

It is true that individuals are born with traits that make them charismatic. In fact, studies of identical twins have found that they score similarly on charismatic leadership measures, even if they were raised in different households and had never met. Research suggests that personality is also related to charismatic leadership. Charismatic leaders are likely to be extraverted, self-confident and achievement-oriented.[7] Consider Ted Turner, the co-founder of the worldwide news organisation CNN. When referring to himself, he has said, 'A full moon blanks out all the stars around it' and 'If I only had humility, I'd be perfect.' Although not all charismatic leaders are as bold or colourful as Turner, most of them do have an alluring, interesting and dynamic nature.

Although a small minority thinks that charisma is inherited and therefore cannot be learned, most experts believe that individuals also can be trained to exhibit charismatic behaviours and can thus enjoy the benefits that accrue to being labelled 'a charismatic leader'.[8] After all, just because we inherit certain tendencies doesn't mean that we can't learn to change. Think about weight—it's true that some people are born with predispositions to be overweight, but it would be unreasonable to think that our weight is unaffected by the food we eat. Predispositions exist, and can be powerful, but that doesn't mean people can't change. One set of authors proposes that a person can learn to become charismatic by following a three-step process.[9]

First, an individual needs to develop the aura of charisma by maintaining an optimistic view; using passion as a catalyst for generating enthusiasm; and communicating with the whole body, not just with words. Second, an individual draws others in by creating a bond that inspires others to follow. And third, the individual brings out the potential in followers by tapping into their emotions. This approach seems to work, as evidenced by researchers who have succeeded in actually scripting undergraduate business students to 'play' charismatic.[10] The students were taught to articulate an overarching goal, communicate high performance expectations, exhibit confidence in the ability of followers to meet these expectations, and empathise with the needs of their followers; they learned to project a powerful, confident and dynamic presence; and they practised using a captivating and engaging voice tone. To further capture the dynamics and energy of charisma, the leaders were trained to evoke charismatic non-verbal characteristics: they alternated between pacing and sitting on the edges of their desks, leaned towards the subjects, maintained direct eye contact, and had relaxed postures and animated facial expressions. The researchers found that these students could learn how to project charisma. Moreover, followers of these leaders had higher task performance, task adjustment, and adjustment to the leader and to the group than did followers who worked under groups led by non-charismatic leaders.

HOW CHARISMATIC LEADERS INFLUENCE FOLLOWERS

How do charismatic leaders actually influence followers? The evidence suggests a four-step process.[11] It begins by the leader articulating an appealing vision. A **vision** is a long-term strategy on how to attain a goal or goals. This vision provides a sense of continuity for followers by linking the present with a better future for the organisation. For example, at Apple, the manufacturer of popular personal computers, Steve Jobs championed the iPod, noting: 'It's as Apple as anything Apple has ever done.' The creation of the iPod achieved Apple's goal of offering groundbreaking and easy-to-use-technology. Apple's strategy was to create a product that had a user-friendly interface where songs could be quickly uploaded and easily organised. It was the first major-market device to link data storage capabilities with music downloading.

A vision is incomplete unless it has an accompanying vision statement. A **vision statement** is a formal articulation of an organisation's vision or mission. Charismatic leaders may use vision statements to 'imprint' on followers an over-arching goal and purpose. The Body Shop, for example, has the following vision statement on its website: 'Our vision is to be operating and recognised as the benchmark company for the integration of Economic Success, Stakeholder Fulfilment and Social & Environmental Change.'[12]

Once a vision and vision statement are established, the leader then communicates high performance expectations and expresses confidence that followers can attain them. This enhances follower self-esteem and self-confidence. Centra Software CEO Paul Gudonis says that conveying confidence is a central tool in a manager's toolbox.[13]

Next, the leader conveys, through words and actions, a new set of values and, by his or her behaviour, sets an example for followers to imitate. One study of Israeli bank employees showed, for example, that charismatic leaders were more effective because their employees personally identified with their leaders. Finally, the charismatic leader engages in emotion-inducing and often unconventional behaviour to demonstrate courage and convictions about the vision. There is an emotional contagion in charismatic leadership where followers 'catch' the emotions their leader is conveying.[14] The next time you see Martin Luther King's 'I Have a Dream' speech, focus on the reactions of the crowd, and it will bring to light how a charismatic leader can spread his emotion to his followers.

Because the vision is such a critical component of charismatic leadership, we should clarify exactly what we mean by the term, identify specific qualities of an effective vision, and offer some examples.[15]

A review of various definitions finds that a vision differs from other forms of direction setting in several ways: 'A vision has clear and compelling imagery that offers an innovative way to improve, which recognises and draws on traditions, and connects to actions that people can take to realise change. Vision taps people's emotions and energy. Properly articulated, a vision creates the enthusiasm that people have for sporting events and other leisure-time activities, bringing this energy and commitment to the workplace.'[16] The key

vision | A long-term strategy on how to attain a goal or goals.

vision statement | A formal articulation of an organisation's vision or mission.

properties of a vision seem to be inspirational possibilities that are value-centred, realisable, with superior imagery and articulation.[17] Visions should be able to create possibilities that are inspirational and unique, and that offer a new order that can produce organisational distinction. A vision is likely to fail if it doesn't offer a view of the future that is clearly and demonstrably better for the organisation and its members. Desirable visions fit the times and circumstances and reflect the uniqueness of the organisation. People in the organisation must also believe that the vision is attainable. It should be perceived as challenging yet doable. Also, visions that have clear articulation and powerful imagery are more easily grasped and accepted.

What are some examples of visions? From his entrepreneurial beginnings in Australia, Rupert Murdoch had a vision of the future of the communications industry by combining entertainment and media. Through News Corporation, Murdoch has successfully integrated a broadcast network, TV stations, movie studio, publishing and global satellite distribution. John Malone of Liberty Media calls News Corporation 'the best run, most strategically positioned vertically integrated media company in the world'.[18] And, as another example, Michael Dell has created a vision of a business that allows Dell Computer to sell and deliver a finished PC directly to a customer in fewer than eight days.

DOES EFFECTIVE CHARISMATIC LEADERSHIP DEPEND ON THE SITUATION?

There is an increasing body of research that shows impressive correlations between charismatic leadership and high performance and satisfaction among followers.[19] People working for charismatic leaders are motivated to exert extra work effort and, because they like and respect their leader, express greater satisfaction. It also appears that organisations with charismatic CEOs are more profitable. And charismatic university lecturers enjoy higher course evaluations and class attendance.[20] However, there is a growing body of evidence indicating that charisma may not always be generalisable; that is, its effectiveness may depend on the situation. Charisma appears to be most successful when the follower's task has an ideological component or when the environment involves a high degree of stress and uncertainty.[21] This may explain why, when charismatic leaders surface, it is more likely to be in politics, religion, wartime, or when a business firm is in its infancy or facing a life-threatening crisis. For example, in the 1990s, when Qantas merged with Australian Airlines and the Australian government began privatising the new organisation, it needed a charismatic leader with unconventional ideas—someone like James Strong—to reinvent the company.

In addition to ideology and uncertainty, another situational factor limiting charisma appears to be level in the organisation. Remember, the creation of a vision is a key component of charisma. But visions typically apply to entire organisations or major divisions. They tend to be created by top executives. As such, charisma probably has more direct relevance to explaining the success and failures of chief executives than of lower-level managers. So, even though individuals may have an inspiring personality, it is more difficult to utilise their charismatic leadership qualities in lower-level management jobs. Lower-level managers *can* create visions to lead their units. It's just harder to define such visions and to align them with the larger goals of the organisation as a whole.

Finally, charismatic leadership may affect some followers more than others. Research suggests, for example, that people are especially receptive to charismatic leadership when they sense a crisis, when they are under stress, or when they fear for their lives. More generally, some people's personalities are more susceptible to charismatic leadership.[22] Consider self-esteem. If an individual lacks self-esteem and questions his or her self-worth, he or she is more likely to absorb a leader's direction rather than establish his or her own way of leading or thinking.

THE DARK SIDE OF CHARISMATIC LEADERSHIP

Charismatic business leaders such as Enron's Jeffrey Skilling, General Electric's Jack Welch, Virgin's Sir Richard Branson, Gerry Harvey of Harvey Norman, Disney's Michael Eisner and WorldCom's Bernie Ebbers became no less of a celebrity than Harry Kewel or Madonna. Every company wanted a charismatic CEO. And to attract these people, they were given unprecedented autonomy and resources. They had private jets at their beck and call, use of $30 million penthouses, interest-free loans to buy beach homes and artwork, security staffs provided by their companies, and similar benefits befitting royalty. One study showed that charismatic CEOs were able to use their charisma to leverage higher salaries even when their performance was mediocre.[23]

Unfortunately, charismatic leaders who are larger-than-life don't necessarily act in the best interests of their organisations.[24] Many of these leaders used their power to remake their companies in their own image. These leaders often completely blurred the boundary separating their personal interests from their organisation's interests. At its worst, the perils of this ego-driven charisma are leaders who allow their self-interest and personal goals to override the goals of the organisation. Intolerant of criticism, they surround themselves with 'yes' people who are rewarded for pleasing the leader and create a climate where people are afraid to question or challenge the 'king' or 'queen' when they think he or she is making a mistake. The results at companies such as Enron and WorldCom were leaders who recklessly used organisational resources for their personal benefit, and executives who broke laws and crossed ethical lines to generate financial numbers that temporarily inflated share prices and allowed leaders to cash in millions of dollars in share options.

A study of 29 companies that went from good to great (their cumulative share returns were all at least three times better than the general share market over 15 years) found an *absence* of ego-driven charismatic leaders. Although the leaders of these firms were fiercely ambitious and driven, their ambition was directed towards their company rather than themselves. They generated extraordinary results, but with little fanfare or hoopla. They took responsibility for mistakes and poor results, and gave credit for successes to other people. They prided themselves on developing strong leaders inside the firm who could direct the company to greater heights after they were gone. These individuals have been called **level-5 leaders** because they have four basic leadership qualities—individual capability, team skills, managerial competence, and the ability to stimulate others to high performance—plus a fifth dimension: a paradoxical blend of personal humility and professional will. Level-5 leaders channel their ego needs away from themselves and into the goal of building a great company. So, while level-5 leaders are highly effective, they tend to be people you have never heard of and who get little notoriety in the business press—people like Orin Smith at Starbucks, Penny Maclagan of Computershare, Naomi Milgrom of Sussan, and John Whitehead of Goldman Sachs. This study is important because it confirms that leaders don't necessarily need to be charismatic to be effective, especially where charisma is enmeshed with an outsized ego.[25]

level-5 leaders | Leaders who are fiercely ambitious and driven, but whose ambition is directed towards their company rather than themselves.

Finally, charisma can reach beyond the walls of the workplace. And because of their power to captivate others, charismatic leaders can be very dangerous. Some of the most oppressive leaders in history were highly charismatic. Consider Hitler. As leader of the Nazi Party in Germany in the lead-up to and during the Second World War, he was responsible for policies that resulted in the Holocaust and the deaths of approximately 6 million Jews. Robespierre was also considered charismatic. He has been credited as one of the leaders of the French Revolution and the Reign of Terror. In fact, he often used the guillotine to control the country and get rid of his political enemies. Cults are also often headed by charismatic leaders. For example, Jim Jones—the founder of the People's Temple church—convinced more than 900 of his followers to commit suicide by drinking poisoned Kool-Aid. And Charles Manson—the leader of 'The Family', a Californian cult in the 1960s—convinced his followers to commit a number of murders. More recently, it has been suggested that Osama bin Laden inspired his followers to sacrifice their lives, and the lives of thousands of others, in the name of religion.

transactional leaders |
Leaders who guide or motivate their followers in the direction of established goals by clarifying role and task requirements.

We don't mean to suggest that charismatic leadership isn't effective. Overall, its effectiveness is well supported. The point is a charismatic leader isn't always the answer. Yes, an organisation with a charismatic leader at the helm is more likely to be successful, but that success depends, to some extent, on the situation and on the leader's vision. Some charismatic leaders, such as Hitler, are all too successful at convincing their followers to pursue a vision that can be disastrous.

SELF-ASSESSMENT LIBRARY

HOW CHARISMATIC AM I?

In the Self-Assessment Library (available on CD and online), take Self-Assessment II.B.2 (How Charismatic Am I?) and answer the following questions.

1. How did you score compared to your classmates? Do you think your score is accurate?
2. Why do you think you scored as you did? Do you think it's because of your genes? Are your parents charismatic? Or do you think your score has to do with your environment? Were there factors in your upbringing or early life experiences that affected your charisma?
3. Based on the material presented in the chapter, do you think you could become more charismatic? If yes, how might you go about becoming more charismatic?

LEARNING OBJECTIVE 3

Contrast transformational with transactional leadership

transformational leaders |
Leaders who inspire followers to transcend their own self-interests and who are capable of having a profound and extraordinary effect on followers.

TRANSFORMATIONAL LEADERSHIP

Another stream of research has focused on differentiating transformational leaders from transactional leaders.[26] Most of the leadership theories presented in the previous chapter—for instance, the Ohio State studies, Fiedler's model and path–goal theory—have concerned **transactional leaders**. These kinds of leaders guide or motivate their followers in the direction of established goals by clarifying role and task requirements. **Transformational leaders** inspire followers to transcend their own self-interests for the good of the organisation and are capable of having a profound and extraordinary effect on their followers. Andrea Jung at Avon, James Strong, former CEO of Qantas, and Sir Richard Branson of the Virgin Group are all examples of transformational leaders. They pay attention to the concerns and developmental needs of individual followers; they change followers' awareness of issues by helping them to look at old problems in new ways; and they are able to excite, arouse and inspire followers to put out extra effort to achieve group goals. Table 13.2 briefly identifies and defines the characteristics that differentiate these two types of leaders.

Transactional and transformational leadership shouldn't be viewed as opposing approaches to getting things done.[27] Transformational and transactional leadership complement each other, but that doesn't mean they are equally important. Transformational leadership builds *on top of* transactional leadership and produces levels

Transactional leader	
Contingent reward: Contracts exchange of rewards for effort, promises rewards for good performance, recognises accomplishments.	
Management by exception (active): Watches and searches for deviations from rules and standards, takes corrective action.	
Management by exception (passive): Intervenes only if standards are not met.	
Laissez-faire: Abdicates responsibilities, avoids making decisions.	

Transformational leader	
Charisma: Provides vision and sense of mission, instills pride, gains respect and trust.	
Inspiration: Communicates high expectations, uses symbols to focus efforts, expresses important purposes in simple ways.	
Intellectual stimulation: Promotes intelligence, rationality and careful problem solving.	
Individualised consideration: Gives personal attention, treats each employee individually, coaches, advises.	

SOURCE: Reprinted from B. M. Bass, 'From Transactional to Transformational Leadership: Learning to Share the Vision', *Organizational Dynamics*, Winter 1990, p. 22. With permission from Elsevier Science.

■ **TABLE 13.2**

Characteristics of transactional and transformational leaders

of follower effort and performance that go beyond what would occur with a transactional approach alone. But the reverse isn't true. So, if you are a good transactional leader but don't have transformational qualities, you will likely only be a mediocre leader. The best leaders are transactional *and* transformational.

FULL RANGE OF LEADERSHIP MODEL

Figure 13.1 shows the full range of leadership model. Laissez-faire is the most passive, and therefore the least effective, of the leader behaviours. Leaders using this style are rarely viewed as effective. Management by exception—regardless of whether it is active or passive—is slightly better than laissez-faire, but it is still considered ineffective leadership. Leaders who practise management by exception leadership tend to be available only when there is a problem, which is often too late. Contingent reward leadership can be an effective style of leadership. However, leaders will not get their employees to go above and beyond the call of duty when practising this style of leadership. Only with the four remaining leadership styles—which are all aspects of transformational leadership—are leaders able to motivate followers to perform above expectations and transcend their own self-interest for the sake of the organisation. Individualised consideration, intellectual stimulation, inspirational motivation and idealised influence all result in extra effort from workers, higher productivity, higher morale and satisfaction, higher organisational effectiveness, lower turnover, lower absenteeism and greater organisational adaptability. Based on this model, leaders are generally most effective when they regularly use each of the four transformational behaviours.

HOW TRANSFORMATIONAL LEADERSHIP WORKS

In the past few years, a great deal of research has been conducted to explain how transformational leadership works. Transformational leaders encourage their followers to be

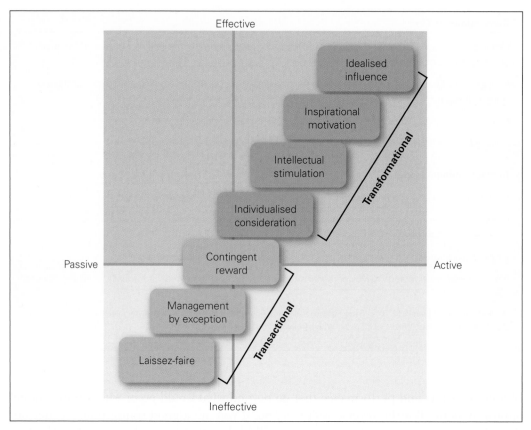

more innovative and creative.[28] For example, Army Colonel Leonard Wong of the US Army found that, in the Iraq war, the Army was encouraging 'reactive instead of proactive thought, compliance instead of creativity, and adherence instead of audacity'. In response, Wong is working to empower junior officers to be creative and to take more risks.[29] Transformational leaders are more effective because they themselves are more creative, but they are also more effective because they encourage those who follow them to be creative too.

Goals are another key mechanism that explains how transformational leadership works. Followers of transformational leaders are more likely to pursue ambitious goals, be familiar with and agree on the strategic goals of the organisation, and believe that the goals they are pursuing are personally important.[30]

VeriSign is a leading company in the area of infrastructure services in digital commerce and communications. VeriSign's CEO, Stratton Sclavos, says: 'It comes down to charting a course—having the ability to articulate for your employees where you're headed and how you're going to get there. Even more important is choosing people to work with who have that same level of passion, commitment, fear, and competitiveness to drive toward those same goals.'

Sclavos's remark about goals brings up vision. Just as research has shown that vision is important in explaining how charismatic leadership works, research has also shown that vision explains part of the effect of transformational leadership. Indeed, one study found that vision was even more important than a charismatic (effusive, dynamic, lively) communication style in explaining the success of entrepreneurial firms.[31] Finally, transformational leadership also engenders commitment on the part of followers and instils in them a greater sense of trust in the leader.[32]

Michaela Healey doesn't fit the traditional mould of a company secretary. She is relatively young for a role dominated by older men. She is the company secretary at Australia's biggest financial institution, National Australia Bank. The bank has been through a big culture change after emerging from a $360 million foreign exchange scandal, boardroom battle and management shake-up in 2004. Healey believes the experience of being intimately involved in a global change program brought home to her the value of planning changes with the cooperation of employees. She says it is also important to be a transformational leader and to create a sense of ownership within each division.

EVALUATION OF TRANSFORMATIONAL LEADERSHIP

The evidence supporting the superiority of transformational leadership over transactional leadership is impressive. Transformational leadership has been supported in different countries (Korea, Russia, Israel, India, Kenya, Norway, Taiwan), in disparate occupations (school principals, marine commanders, ministers, directors of MBA associations, military cadets, union shop stewards, schoolteachers, sales reps), and at various job levels. For example, a number of studies with US, Canadian and German military officers found, at every level, that transformational leaders were evaluated as more effective than their transactional counterparts.[33] And a review of 87 studies testing transformational leadership found that it was related to the motivation and satisfaction of followers and to the higher performance and perceived effectiveness of leaders.[34]

Transformational leadership theory isn't perfect. There are concerns about whether contingent reward leadership is strictly a characteristic of transactional leaders only. And contrary to the full range of leadership model, contingent reward leadership is sometimes more effective than transformational leadership.

In summary, the overall evidence indicates that transformational leadership is more strongly correlated than transactional leadership, with lower turnover rates, higher productivity and higher employee satisfaction.[35] Like charisma, it appears that transformational leadership can be learned. One study of Canadian bank managers found that those managers who underwent transformational leadership training had bank branches that performed significantly better than branches with managers who didn't undergo training. Other studies show similar results.[36]

TRANSFORMATIONAL LEADERSHIP VERSUS CHARISMATIC LEADERSHIP

There is some debate about whether transformational leadership and charismatic leadership are the same. The researcher most responsible for introducing charismatic leadership to OB, Robert House, considers them synonymous, calling the differences 'modest' and 'minor'. However, the individual who first researched transformational leadership, Bernard Bass, considers charisma to be part of transformational leadership but argues that transformational leadership is broader than charisma, suggesting that charisma is, by itself, insufficient to 'account for the transformational process'.[37] Another researcher commented, 'The purely charismatic [leader] may want followers to adopt the charismatic's world view and go no further; the transformational leader will attempt to instil in followers the ability to question not only established views but eventually those established by the leader.'[38] Although many researchers believe that transformational leadership is broader than charismatic leadership, studies show that in reality a leader who scores high on transformational leadership is also likely to score high on charisma. Therefore, in practice, measures of charisma and transformational leadership may be roughly equivalent.

AUTHENTIC LEADERSHIP: ETHICS AND TRUST ARE THE FOUNDATION OF LEADERSHIP

Although charismatic leadership theories and transformational leadership theories have added greatly to our understanding of effective leadership, they don't deal explicitly with the role of ethics and trust. Some scholars have argued that a consideration of ethics and trust is essential to complete the picture of effective leadership. Here we consider these two concepts under the rubric of authentic leadership.[39]

WHAT IS AUTHENTIC LEADERSHIP?

The philosopher Jean-Paul Sartre wrote a lot about authenticity, arguing that to be an authentic person, an individual needs to be honest with themself and avoid self-deception. Although this might be good advice for anyone, it may be especially critical for leaders.

authentic leaders | Leaders who know who they are, know what they believe in and value, and act on those values and beliefs openly and candidly. Their followers would consider them to be ethical people.

Authentic leaders know who they are, know what they believe in and value, and act on those values and beliefs openly and candidly. Their followers would consider them to be ethical people. The primary quality produced by authentic leadership is, therefore, trust. How does authentic leadership build trust? Authentic leaders share information, encourage open communication and stick to their ideals. The result: people come to have faith in authentic leaders. Because the concept is so recent, there hasn't been a lot of research on authentic leadership. However, we believe it is a promising way to think about ethics and trust in leadership, because it focuses on the moral aspects of being a leader. Transformational or charismatic leaders can have a vision, and communicate it persuasively, but sometimes the vision is wrong (as in the case of Hitler), or the leader is more concerned with his or her own needs or pleasures, as in the case of Jeff Skilling (ex-CEO of Enron).[40]

ETHICS AND LEADERSHIP

The topic of ethics and leadership has received surprisingly little attention. Only recently have ethicists and leadership researchers begun to consider the ethical implications in leadership.[41] Why now? One reason may be the growing general interest in ethics throughout the field of management. Another reason may be the discovery by probing biographers that many of our past leaders—such as President C. V. Devan Nair of Singapore, Winston Churchill and a number of senior Australian politicians—suffered from ethical shortcomings. Certainly, the impeachment hearings of American President Bill Clinton on the grounds of perjury and other charges did nothing to lessen concern about ethical leadership. And the unethical practices by executives at organisations such as Enron, HIH Insurance, OneTel, WorldCom, Arthur Andersen and Merrill Lynch have increased the public's and politicians' concerns about ethical standards in Australasian businesses. Ethics touches on leadership at a number of junctures. Transformational leaders, for instance, have been described by one authority as fostering moral virtue when they try to change the attitudes and behaviours of followers.[42]

Charisma, too, has an ethical component. Unethical leaders are more likely to use their charisma to enhance *power over* followers, directed towards self-serving ends. Ethical leaders are considered to use their charisma in a socially constructive way to serve others.[43] There is also the issue of abuse of power by leaders—for example, when they give themselves large salaries, bonuses and share options while, at the same time, they seek to cut costs by laying off long-time employees. Because top executives set the moral tone for an organisation, they need to set high ethical standards, demonstrate those standards through their own behaviour, and encourage and reward integrity in others. Leadership effectiveness needs to address the *means* that a leader uses in trying to achieve goals, as well as the content of those goals. For instance, Bill Gates's success in leading Microsoft to domination of the world's software business has been achieved by means of an extremely aggressive work culture. Microsoft's competitors and US government regulators have pinpointed this competitive culture as the source of numerous unethical practices—from using its control of its Windows operating system to favour Microsoft's partners and subsidiaries, to encouraging its sales force to 'crush' its rivals. Importantly, Microsoft's culture mirrors the personality of its chairman and co-founder, Gates.

In addition, ethical leadership must address the content of a leader's goals. Are the changes that the leader seeks for the organisation morally acceptable? Is a business leader effective if he or she builds an organisation's success by selling products that damage the health of its users? This question, for example, might be asked of executives in the tobacco and junk-food industries. Or is a military leader successful by winning a war that shouldn't have been fought in the first place?

Leadership isn't value-free. Before we judge any leader to be effective, we should consider both the means used by the leader to achieve goals and the moral content of those goals.

Let's now examine the issue of trust and its role in shaping strong leaders.

WHAT IS TRUST?

LEARNING OBJECTIVE 4

Identify the five dimensions of trust

Trust, or lack of trust, is an increasingly important leadership issue in today's organisations.[44] In this section, we define *trust* and provide you with some guidelines for helping to build credibility and trust.

Trust is a positive expectation that another will not—through words, actions or decisions—act opportunistically.[45] The two most important elements of our definition are that it implies familiarity and risk. The phrase *positive expectation* in our definition assumes knowledge of and familiarity with the other party. Trust is a history-dependent process based on relevant but limited samples of experience.[46] It takes time to form, building incrementally and accumulating. Most of us find it hard, if not impossible, to trust someone immediately if we don't know anything about them. At the extreme, in the case of total ignorance, we can gamble, but we can't trust.[47] But as we get to know someone, and the relationship matures, we gain confidence in our ability to form a positive expectation.

trust | A positive expectation that another will not act opportunistically.

The term *opportunistically* refers to the inherent risk and vulnerability in any trusting relationship. Trust involves making oneself vulnerable—as when, for example, we disclose intimate information or rely on another's promises.[48] By its very nature, trust provides the opportunity for disappointment or to be taken advantage of.[49] But trust isn't taking risk per se; rather, it is a *willingness* to take risks.[50] So, when I trust someone, I expect that they won't take advantage of me. This willingness to take risks is common to all trust situations.[51]

What are the key dimensions that underlie the concept of trust? Evidence has identified five: integrity, competence, consistency, loyalty and openness[52] (see Figure 13.2).

Integrity refers to honesty and truthfulness. Of all five dimensions, this one seems to be most critical when someone assesses another's trustworthiness.[53] For instance, when 570 white-collar employees were recently given a list of 28 attributes related to leadership, honesty was rated the most important by far.[54]

Competence encompasses an individual's technical and interpersonal knowledge and skills. Does the person know what he or she is talking about? You are unlikely to listen to or depend on someone whose abilities you don't respect. You need to believe that the person has the skills and abilities to carry out what he or she says they will do.

Consistency relates to an individual's reliability, predictability and good judgment in handling situations. 'Inconsistencies between words and action decrease trust.'[55] This dimension is particularly relevant for managers. 'Nothing is noticed more quickly … than a discrepancy between what executives preach and what they expect their associates to practice.'[56]

Loyalty is the willingness to protect and save face for another person. Trust requires that you can depend on someone not to act opportunistically.

The final dimension of trust is *openness*. Can you rely on the person to give you the full truth?

 FIGURE 13.2
Trust dimensions

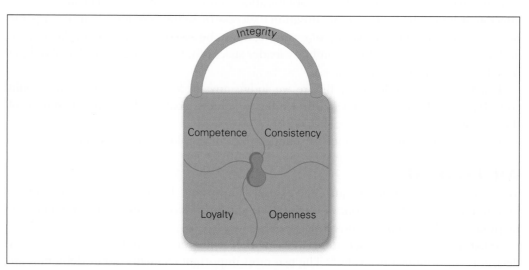

TRUST AND LEADERSHIP

Trust is a primary attribute associated with leadership; and when this trust is broken, it can have serious adverse effects on a group's performance.[57] As one author noted: 'Part of the leader's task has been, and continues to be, working with people to find and solve problems, but whether leaders gain access to the knowledge and creative thinking they need to solve problems depends on how much people trust them. Trust and trust-worthiness modulate the leader's access to knowledge and cooperation.'[58]

When followers trust a leader, they are willing to be vulnerable to the leader's actions—confident that their rights and interests won't be abused.[59] People are unlikely to look up to or follow someone whom they perceive as dishonest or who is likely to take advantage of them. Honesty, for instance, consistently ranks at the top of most people's list of characteristics they admire in their leaders. 'Honesty is absolutely essential to leadership. If people are going to follow someone willingly, whether it be into battle or into the boardroom, they first want to assure themselves that the person is worthy of their trust.'[60]

THREE TYPES OF TRUST

There are three types of trust in organisational relationships: *deterrence*-based, *knowledge*-based and *identification*-based.[61]

DETERRENCE-BASED TRUST

The most fragile relationships are contained in **deterrence-based trust**. One violation or inconsistency can destroy the relationship. This form of trust is based on fear of reprisal if the trust is violated. Individuals who are in this type of relationship do what they say because they fear the consequences from not following through on their obligations.

Deterrence-based trust will work only to the degree that punishment is possible, consequences are clear, and the punishment is actually imposed if the trust is violated. To be sustained, the potential loss of future interaction with the other party must outweigh the profit potential that comes from violating expectations. Moreover, the potentially harmed party must be willing to introduce harm (for example, I have no qualms about speaking badly of you if you betray my trust) to the person acting in an untrustworthy manner.

Most new relationships begin on a base of deterrence. Take, as an illustration, a situation where you are selling your car to a friend of a friend. You don't know the buyer. You might be motivated to refrain from telling this buyer all the problems with the car that you know about. Such behaviour would increase your chances of selling the car and securing the highest price. But you don't withhold information. You openly share the car's flaws. Why? Probably because of fear of reprisal. If the buyer later thinks you deceived him, he is likely to share this with your mutual friend. If you knew that the buyer would never say anything to the mutual friend, you might be tempted to take advantage of the opportunity. If it is clear that the buyer would tell and that your mutual friend would think considerably less of you for taking advantage of this buyer-friend, your honesty could be explained in deterrence terms.

Another example of deterrence-based trust is a new manager–employee relationship. As an employee, you typically trust a new boss even though there is little experience to base that trust on. The bond that creates this trust lies in the authority held by the boss and the punishment he or she can impose if you fail to fulfil your job-related obligations.

KNOWLEDGE-BASED TRUST

Most organisational relationships are rooted in **knowledge-based trust**. That is, trust is based on the behavioural predictability that comes from a history of interaction. It exists when you have adequate information about someone to understand them well enough to be able to accurately predict his or her behaviour.

Knowledge-based trust relies on information rather than deterrence. Knowledge of the other party and the predictability of his or her behaviour replaces the contracts, penalties and legal arrangements more typical of deterrence-based trust. This knowledge develops over time, largely as a function of experience that builds confidence of trustworthiness and predictability. The better you know someone, the more accurately you can predict what he or she will do. Predictability enhances trust—even if the other is predictably untrustworthy—because the ways that the other will violate the trust can be predicted! The

deterrence-based trust | Trust based on fear of reprisal if the trust is violated.

knowledge-based trust | Trust based on behavioural predictability that comes from a history of interaction.

more communication and regular interaction you have with someone else, the more this form of trust can be developed and depended on.

Interestingly, at the knowledge-based level, trust isn't necessarily broken by inconsistent behaviour. If you believe you can adequately explain or understand another's apparent violation, you can accept it, forgive the person and move on in the relationship. However, the same inconsistency at the deterrence level is likely to irrevocably break the trust.

In an organisational context, most manager–employee relationships are knowledge-based. Both parties have enough experience of working with each other that they know what to expect. A long history of consistently open and honest interactions, for instance, isn't likely to be permanently destroyed by a single violation.

IDENTIFICATION-BASED TRUST

The highest level of trust is achieved when there is an emotional connection between the parties. It allows one party to act as an agent for the other and to substitute for that person in interpersonal transactions. This is called **identification-based trust**. Trust exists because the parties understand each other's intentions and appreciate the other's wants and desires. This mutual understanding is developed to the point that each can effectively act for the other. Controls are minimal at this level. You don't need to monitor the other party, because there exists unquestioned loyalty.

The best example of identification-based trust is a long-term, happily married couple. A husband comes to learn what is important to his wife and anticipates those actions. She, in turn, trusts that he will anticipate what is important to her without her having to ask. Increased identification enables each to think like the other, feel like the other and respond like the other.

You see identification-based trust occasionally in organisations among people who have worked together for long periods of time and have a depth of experience that allows them to know each other inside and out. This is also the type of trust that managers ideally seek in teams. Team members are so comfortable with and trusting of each other that they can anticipate each other and act freely in each other's absence. In the current work world, it is probably accurate to say that most large corporations have broken the bonds of identification trust that were built with long-term employees. Broken promises have led to a breakdown in what was, at one time, a bond of unquestioned loyalty. It is likely to have been replaced with knowledge-based trust.

BASIC PRINCIPLES OF TRUST

Research allows us to offer some principles for better understanding the creating of both trust and mistrust.[62]

Mistrust drives out trust. People who are trusting demonstrate their trust by increasing their openness to others, disclosing relevant information, and expressing their true intentions. People who mistrust don't reciprocate. They conceal information and act opportunistically to take advantage of others. To defend against repeated exploitation, trusting people are driven to mistrust. A few mistrusting people can poison an entire organisation.

Trust begets trust. In the same way that mistrust drives out trust, exhibiting trust in others tends to encourage reciprocity. Effective leaders increase trust in small increments and allow others to respond in kind. By offering trust in only small increments, leaders limit penalty or loss that might occur if their trust is exploited.

identification-based trust | Trust based on a mutual understanding of each other's intentions and appreciation of the other's wants and desires.

Growth often masks mistrust. Growth gives leaders opportunities for rapid promotion and for increased power and responsibility. In this environment, leaders tend to solve problems with quick fixes that elude immediate detection by higher management and leave the problems arising from mistrust to their successors. Leaders can take a short-term perspective because they are not likely to be around to have to deal with the long-term consequences of their decisions. The lingering effects of mistrust become apparent to the successors when the growth slows.

Decline or downsizing tests the highest levels of trust. The corollary to the previous growth principle is that decline or downsizing tends to undermine even the most trusting environment. Layoffs are threatening. Even after layoffs have been completed, those who survive feel less secure in their jobs. When employers break the loyalty bond by laying off employees, there is less willingness among workers to trust what management says.

Trust increases cohesion. Trust holds people together. Trust means people have confidence that they can rely on each other. If one person needs help or falters, that person knows that the others will be there to fill in. When faced with adversity, group members who display trust in each other will work together and exert high levels of effort to achieve the group's goals.

Mistrusting groups self-destruct. The corollary to the previous principle is that when group members mistrust each other, they repel and separate. They pursue their own interests rather than those of the group. Members of mistrusting groups tend to be suspicious of each other, are constantly on guard against exploitation, and restrict communication with others in the group. These actions tend to undermine and eventually destroy the group.

Mistrust generally reduces productivity. Although we cannot say that trust necessarily *increases* productivity, though it usually does, mistrust almost always *reduces* productivity. Mistrust focuses attention on the differences in member interests, making it difficult for people to visualise common goals. People respond by concealing information and secretly pursuing their own interests. When employees encounter problems, they avoid calling on others, fearing that those others will take advantage of them. A climate of mistrust tends to stimulate dysfunctional forms of conflict and retard cooperation.

IS TRUST IN OUR LEADERS IN DECLINE?

A strong case can be made that today, more than ever, organisational leadership requires trust. Events of recent years have certainly brought the issue of trust into the headlines—for example: 'Former FAI Secretary to Plead Guilty for Role in Australia's HIH Scandal.' Australian TV personality and businessman Steve Vizard fell from grace over his trading of Telstra shares. Senior staff at the Australian Wheat Board were accused of paying kickbacks in the wheat deals with Iraq. Enron executives manipulated their financial statements. Merrill Lynch paid US$100 million in fines for misleading investors.[63] In addition, reengineering, downsizing, and the increased use of temporary employees have

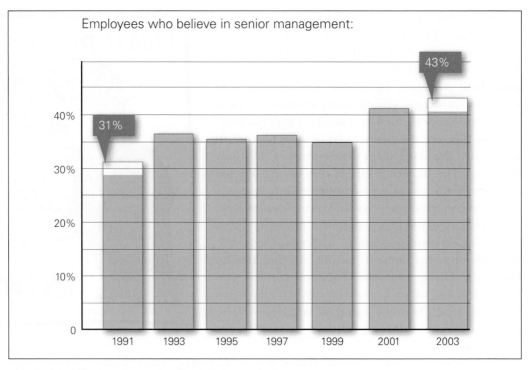

Employees who believe in senior management:

43%

40%

31%

30%

20%

10%

0

1991   1993   1995   1997   1999   2001   2003

SOURCE: Gantz Wiley Research. Reproduced in *USA Today*, 12 February 2003, p. 7B.

undermined a lot of employees' trust in management. These events, then, beg the question: Is trust on the decline?

A number of recent studies have been conducted in the United States looking at this question.[64] On a positive note, Americans faith in each other seems to be increasing. For instance, in 2000, only 35 per cent of Americans said 'most people' could be trusted. In 2002, that number was up to 41 per cent. But when it comes to trusting big business and executives, the results differ depending on whether you ask employees or the general public. The general public holds corporate leaders in pretty low regard. The public's confidence in them as a group peaked in 2000 at only 28 per cent. By 2003, that number had dropped to a dismal 13 per cent. To put this in perspective, firefighters are considered seven times more trustworthy than CEOs, and Americans say they trust CEOs even less than they trust lawyers. But this distrust seems to be directed at executives at large companies. The same polls show that 75 per cent of the general public has strong trust in small business owners.

Corporate employees, however, show considerably more trust in their own senior management. From 1995 to 1999, the percentage of workers who said they believe in the senior management at their companies held steady at about 36 per cent. By 2003, it had increased to 43 per cent (see Figure 13.3). Exactly why these numbers are significantly higher than those of the general public, or why they have recently increased, isn't clear. Part of the answer may be explained in terms of cognitive dissonance: employees want to believe that their own bosses are more trustworthy than senior executives in general. And in a time when jobs are hard to get, as they were between 2001 and 2003, employees may be more willing to give their bosses the benefit of the doubt. Additionally, the publicity given to corporate scandals has undoubtedly raised the importance of trust in executive suites and may have made more senior executives more trustworthy.

CONTEMPORARY LEADERSHIP ROLES

LEARNING OBJECTIVE 5

Identify the four roles that team leaders perform

What unique demands do teams place on leaders? Why are many effective leaders also active mentors? How can leaders develop self-leadership skills in their employees? And how does leadership work when face-to-face interaction is gone? In this section, we briefly address these four leadership-role issues.

PROVIDING TEAM LEADERSHIP

Leadership is increasingly taking place within a team context. As teams grow in popularity, the role of the leader in guiding team members takes on heightened importance.[65] And the role of team leader is different from the traditional leadership role performed by first-line supervisors. Many leaders who came of age when individualism ruled are not equipped to handle the change to teams. As one prominent consultant noted, 'Even the most capable managers have trouble making the transition because all the command-and-control type things they were encouraged to do before are no longer appropriate. There's no reason to have any skill or sense of this.'[66] This same consultant estimated that 'probably 15 percent of managers are natural team leaders; another 15 percent could never lead a team because it runs counter to their personality. [They are unable to sublimate their dominating style for the good of the team.] Then there's that huge group in the middle: Team leadership doesn't come naturally to them, but they can learn it.'[67]

TEAM LEADERSHIP AT ADSTEAM MARINE

Adsteam Marine is a leading international provider of harbour towage and related marine services. The company's operations cover major container, bulk and general cargo ports in Australia, the South Pacific and the United Kingdom. With activities including towage, line running/mooring, workboat and offshore services, vessel management, salvage, emergency response and ships' agency, Adsteam Marine serves a global customer base with a fleet of approximately 150 tug boats plus barges, workboats and launches.

John Moller took over as chief executive officer in 2003 when the company was experiencing some difficulties in meeting the dividend expectations of its shareholders. He saw opportunities as well as areas where some improvements could be made. By his assessment, he saw all the assets, vessels and offices as world class, and he had a great team of people to work with. However, he assessed the old management team's skills as more suited to a smaller entrepreneurial business where the critical knowledge of the company is in the head of the CEO. It was time to change.

Moller introduced team leadership in order to move to a truly international company. Using teams and team-based leadership is a critical factor, particularly when operations need to be integrated more effectively across global businesses and a culture of shared services and resources needs to be more consciously developed. Moller has a strategic view of the management skills necessary for global expansion. As well as incorporating a diverse and appropriate set of competencies across effective teams, appropriate systems, policies and strategies need to be in place to guide development and achieve synergies. Moller realises that this new leadership must be able to harness the energy and potential of Adsteam Marine by focusing on what people are passionate about.

SOURCES: Philip Rennie, 'Squalls Abating', *Business Review Weekly*, 12–18 January 2006, pp. 26–28; and D. Smith, 'Chairman's Address to the Adsteam Marine Ltd Annual General Meeting 2004'.

JOB IN PRACTICE

The challenge for most managers, then, is to learn how to become an effective team leader. They have to learn skills such as the patience to share information, to trust others, to give up authority and to understand when to intervene. Effective leaders have mastered the difficult balancing act of knowing when to leave their teams alone and when to intercede. New team leaders may try to retain too much control at a time when team members need more autonomy, or they may abandon their teams at times when the teams need support and help.[68]

A study of 20 organisations that had reorganised themselves around teams found certain common responsibilities that all leaders had to assume. These included coaching, facilitating, handling disciplinary problems, reviewing team/individual performance, training and communication.[69] Many of these responsibilities apply to managers in general. A more meaningful way to describe the team leader's job is to focus on two priorities: managing the team's external boundary and facilitating the team process.[70] We have broken these priorities down into four specific roles.

First, team leaders are *liaisons with external constituencies*. These include upper management, other internal teams, customers and suppliers. The leader represents the team to other constituencies, secures needed resources, clarifies others' expectations of the team, gathers information from the outside, and shares this information with team members.

Second, team leaders are *troubleshooters*. When the team has problems and asks for assistance, team leaders sit in on meetings and help try to resolve the problems. This rarely relates to technical or operation issues, because the team members typically know more about the tasks being done than does the team leader. The leader is most likely to contribute by asking penetrating questions, by helping the team talk through problems, and by getting needed resources from external constituencies. For instance, when a team in an aerospace firm found itself short-handed, its team leader took responsibility for getting more staff. He presented the team's case to upper management and got the approval through the company's human resources department.

Third, team leaders are *conflict managers*. When disagreements surface, they help process the conflict. What is the source of the conflict? Who is involved? What are the issues? What resolution options are available? What are the advantages and disadvantages of each? By getting team members to address questions such as these, the leader minimises the disruptive aspects of intra-team conflicts.

Finally, team leaders are *coaches*. They clarify expectations and roles, teach, offer support, cheerlead, and do whatever else is necessary to help team members improve their work performance.

MENTORING

LEARNING OBJECTIVE 6

Explain the role of a mentor

mentor | A senior employee who sponsors and supports a less-experienced employee.

Many leaders create mentoring relationships. A **mentor** is a senior employee who sponsors and supports a less-experienced employee (a protégé). Successful mentors are good teachers. They can present ideas clearly, listen well, and empathise with the problems of their protégés. Mentoring relationships have been described in terms of two broad categories of functions—career functions and psychosocial functions (see Table 13.3).

Some organisations have formal mentoring programs where mentors are officially assigned to new or high-potential employees. For instance, at Edward Jones, a US financial services firm with 24 000 employees, mentors are assigned to new employees after recruits have completed the company's initial two-month home study program and

Career functions	Psychosocial functions
• Lobbying to get the protégé challenging and visible assignments	• Counselling the protégé about anxieties and uncertainty to help bolster his or her self-confidence
• Coaching the protégé to help develop his or her skills and achieve work objectives	• Sharing personal experiences with the protégé
• Assisting the protégé by providing exposure to influential individuals within the organisation	• Providing friendship and acceptance
• Protecting the protégé from possible risks to his or her reputation	• Acting as a role model[71]
• Sponsoring the protégé by nominating him or her for potential advances or promotions	
• Acting as a sounding board for ideas that the protégé might be hesitant to share with his or her direct supervisor	
• Sponsoring the protégé by nominating him or her for potential advances or promotion	

■ TABLE 13.3

Career and psychosocial functions of mentoring

five-day customer service seminar.[72] The new employees shadow their mentor for three weeks specifically to learn the company's way of doing business. However, in contrast to Edward Jones's formal system, most organisations rely on informal mentoring—with senior managers personally selecting an employee and taking that employee on as a protégé. Informal mentoring is the most effective mentoring relationship outside the immediate boss–subordinate interface.[73] The boss–subordinate context has an inherent conflict of interest and tension, mostly attributable to managers' directly evaluating the performance of subordinates, limiting openness and meaningful communication.

Why would a leader want to be a mentor? There are personal benefits to the leader as well as benefits for the organisation. The mentor–protégé relationship gives the mentor unfiltered access to the attitudes and feelings of lower-ranking employees. Protégés can be an excellent source of identifying potential problems by providing early warning signals. They provide timely information to upper managers that short-circuits the formal channels. So, the mentor–protégé relationship is a valuable communication channel that allows mentors to have news of problems before they become common knowledge to others in upper management. In addition, in terms of leader self-interest, mentoring can provide personal satisfaction to senior executives. It gives them the opportunity to share with others the knowledge and experience that they have developed over many years.

Are all employees in an organisation equally likely to participate in a mentoring relationship? Unfortunately, the answer is 'no'.[74] Evidence indicates that minorities and women are less likely to be chosen as protégés than are white males and thus are less likely to accrue the benefits of mentorship. Mentors tend to select protégés who are similar to themselves on criteria such as background, education, gender, race, ethnicity and religion. 'People naturally move to mentor and can more easily communicate with those with whom they most closely identify.'[75] In Australia and New Zealand, for instance, upper management positions in most organisations have been traditionally staffed by white males, so it is hard for minorities and women to be selected as protégés. In addition, in terms of cross-gender mentoring, senior male managers may select male protégés to minimise problems such as sexual attraction or gossip. Organisations have responded to this dilemma by increasing formal mentoring programs and providing training and coaching for potential mentors of special groups such as minorities and women.[76]

You might assume that mentoring is important, but the research has been fairly disappointing. Two large-scale reviews suggest that the benefits are primarily psychological, rather than tangible. Based on these reviews, it appears that the objective outcomes of mentoring, in terms of career success (compensation, job performance), are very small. One of these reviews concluded, 'Though mentoring may not be properly labelled an utterly useless concept to careers, neither can it be argued to be as important as the main effects of other influences on career success such as ability and personality.'[77] It may feel nice to have a mentor, but it doesn't appear that having a mentor, or even having a good mentor who provides both support and advice, is important to one's career.

SELF-LEADERSHIP

self-leadership | A set of processes through which individuals control their own behaviour.

Is it possible for people to lead themselves? An increasing body of research suggests that many can.[78] Proponents of **self-leadership** propose that there is a set of processes through which individuals control their own behaviour. And effective leaders (or what advocates like to call *super-leaders*) help their followers to lead themselves. They do this by developing leadership capacity in others and nurturing followers so that they no longer need to depend on formal leaders for direction and motivation.

How do leaders create self-leaders? The following have been suggested:[79]

1. *Model self-leadership*: Practise self-observation, setting challenging personal goals, self-direction and self-reinforcement. Then display these behaviours and encourage others to rehearse and then produce them.
2. *Encourage employees to create self-set goals*: Having quantitative, specific goals is the most important part of self-leadership.
3. *Encourage the use of self-rewards to strengthen and increase desirable behaviours*: In contrast, self-punishment should be limited only to occasions when the employee has been dishonest or destructive.
4. *Create positive thought patterns*: Encourage employees to use mental imagery and self-talk to further stimulate self-motivation.
5. *Create a climate of self-leadership*: Redesign the work to increase the natural rewards of a job and focus on these naturally rewarding features of work to increase motivation.
6. *Encourage self-criticism*: Encourage individuals to be critical of their own performance.

The underlying assumptions behind self-leadership are that people are responsible, capable, and able to exercise initiative without the external constraints of bosses, rules or regulations. Given the proper support, individuals can monitor and control their own behaviour.

The importance of self-leadership has increased with the expanded popularity of teams. Empowered, self-managed teams need individuals who are themselves self-directed. Management can't expect individuals who have spent their organisational lives under boss-centred leadership to suddenly adjust to self-managed teams. Therefore, training in self-leadership is an excellent means to help employees make the transition from dependence to autonomy.

'MEN MAKE BETTER LEADERS THAN WOMEN'

This statement is false. There is no evidence to support the myth that men make better leaders than women, and there is evidence suggesting just the opposite. Through the late 1980s, the common belief regarding gender and leadership effectiveness was that men made the better leader. This stereotype was predicated on the belief that men were inherently better skilled for leadership due to a stronger task focus, lower emotionality, and a greater propensity to be directive.

In the 1990s, this 'male advantage' stereotype was replaced with one arguing that there was a 'female advantage'. This view evolved from studies which showed that female leaders, when rated by their peers, underlings and bosses, scored higher than their male counterparts on key dimensions of leadership—including goal setting, motivating others, fostering communication, producing high-quality work, listening to others and mentoring. Moreover, it was argued that women rely more on a democratic leadership style—they encourage participation, share power and information, nurture followers and lead through inclusion; and that this style matched up well with the contemporary organisation's need for flexibility, teamwork, trust and information sharing. Males, it was argued, were more likely to use a directive command-and-control style that worked better when organisations emphasised rigid structures, individualism, control and secrecy.

The most recent assessment of the evidence concludes that women actually have a leadership advantage. Although the differences are fairly small, meaning that there is a great deal of overlap between males and females in their leadership styles, women do have, on average, a slight advantage. A recent review of 45 companies found that female leaders were more transformational than male leaders. These authors concluded, 'These data attest to the ability of women to perform very well in leadership roles in contemporary organizations.'

SOURCE: A. H. Eagly, M. C. Johannesen-Schmidt and M. L. van Engen, 'Transformational, Transactional, and Laissez-Faire Leadership Styles: A Meta-Analysis Comparing Women and Men', *Psychological Bulletin*, July 2003, pp. 569–91.

ONLINE LEADERSHIP

How do you lead people who are physically separated from you and with whom your interactions are basically reduced to written digital communications? This is a question that, to date, has received minimal attention from OB researchers.[80] Leadership research has been directed almost exclusively to face-to-face and verbal situations. But we can't ignore the reality that today's managers and their employees are increasingly being linked by networks rather than geographical proximity. Obvious examples include managers who regularly use email to communicate with their staff, managers overseeing virtual projects or teams, and managers whose telecommuting employees are linked to the office by a computer and modem.

> **LEARNING OBJECTIVE 7**
> Describe how online leadership differs from face-to-face leadership

If leadership is important for inspiring and motivating dispersed employees, we need to offer some guidance as to how leadership might function in this context. Keep in mind, however, that there is limited research on this topic. So, our intention here is not to provide you with definitive guidelines for leading online. Rather, it is to introduce you to an increasingly important issue and get you to think about how leadership changes when relationships are defined by network interactions.

In face-to-face communications, harsh *words* can be softened by non-verbal action. A smile and comforting gesture, for instance, can lessen the blow behind strong words such as *disappointed, unsatisfactory, inadequate* or *below expectations*. That non-verbal component doesn't exist with online interactions. The *structure* of words in a digital communication also has the power to motivate, or demotivate, the receiver. Is the message made up of full sentences or phrases? The latter, for instance, is likely to be seen as curt and more threatening. Similarly, a message in all caps is the equivalent of shouting. The manager who inadvertently sends her message in short phrases and in all caps may get a very different response than if she had sent that same message in full sentences using uppercase and lowercase letters.

Leaders need to be sure the *tone* of their message correctly reflects the emotions they want to send. Is the message formal or informal? Does it match the verbal style of the sender? Does it convey the appropriate level of importance or urgency? The fact that many people's writing style is very different from their interpersonal style is certainly a potential problem.

Finally, online leaders must choose a *style*. Do they use emoticons, abbreviations, jargon, and the like? Do they adapt their style to their audience? Observation suggests that some managers are having difficulty adjusting to computer-related communications. For instance, they are using the same style with their bosses that they use with their staff, with unfortunate consequences. Or they are selectively using digital communications to 'hide' when delivering bad news.

We know that messages convey more than surface information. From a leadership standpoint, messages can convey trust or lack of trust, status, task directives or emotional warmth. Concepts such as task structure, supportive behaviour and vision can be conveyed in written form as well as verbally. It may even be possible for leaders to convey charisma through the written word. But to effectively convey online leadership, managers must recognise that they have choices in the words, structure, tone and style of their digital communications. They also need to develop the skills of 'reading between the lines' in the messages they receive. In the same way that emotional intelligence taps an individual's ability to monitor and assess others' emotions, effective online leaders need to develop the skill of deciphering the emotional components of messages.

Any discussion of online leadership needs also to consider the possibility that the digital age can turn non-leaders into leaders. Some managers whose face-to-face leadership skills are less than satisfactory may shine online. Their talents may lie in their writing skills and ability to read the messages behind written communiqués. Nothing in the mainstream leadership literature addresses this unique situation.

We propose that online leaders have to think carefully about what actions they want their digital messages to initiate. Networked communication is a powerful channel. When used properly, it can build and enhance an individual's leadership effectiveness. But when misused, it has the potential to undermine a great deal of what a leader has been able to achieve through his or her verbal actions.

Additionally, online leaders confront unique challenges, the greatest of which appears to be developing and maintaining trust. Identification-based trust, for instance, is particularly difficult to achieve when there is a lack of intimacy and face-to-face interaction.[81] And online negotiations have also been found to be hindered because parties express lower levels of trust.[82] At this time, it's not clear whether it is even possible for employees to identify with or trust leaders with whom they only communicate electronically.[83]

This discussion leads us to the tentative conclusion that, for an increasing number of managers, good interpersonal skills may include the abilities to communicate support and leadership through written words on a computer screen and to read emotions in others' messages. In this 'new world' of communications, writing skills are likely to become an extension of interpersonal skills.

CHALLENGES TO THE LEADERSHIP CONSTRUCT

A noted management expert takes issue with the omnipotent role that academicians, practising managers and the general public have given to the concept of leadership. This expert says, 'In the 1500s, people ascribed all events they didn't understand to God. Why did the crops fail? God. Why did someone die? God. Now our all-purpose explanation is leadership.'[84] He notes that when a company succeeds, people need someone to give the credit to. And that person is typically the firm's CEO. Similarly, when a company does poorly, they need someone to blame. CEOs also play this role. But much of an organisation's success or failure is due to factors outside the influence of leadership. In many cases, success or failure is just a matter of being in the right or wrong place at a given time.

In this section, we present two perspectives that challenge the widely accepted belief in the importance of leadership. The first argument proposes that leadership is more about appearances than reality. You don't have to *be* an effective leader as long as you *look* like one. The second argument directly attacks the notion that some leadership will *always be effective* regardless of the situation. This argument contends that in many situations, whatever actions leaders exhibit are irrelevant.

LEADERSHIP AS AN ATTRIBUTION

We introduced attribution theory in Chapter 5. As you may remember, it deals with the ways in which people try to make sense out of cause-and-effect relationships. We said when something happens, we want to attribute it to something else. The **attribution theory of leadership** says that leadership is merely an attribution that people make about other individuals.[85] The attribution theory has shown that people characterise leaders as having such traits as intelligence, outgoing personality, strong verbal skills, aggressiveness, understanding and industriousness.[86] At the organisational level, the attribution framework accounts for the conditions under which people use leadership to explain organisational outcomes. Those conditions are extremes in organisational performance. When an organisation has either extremely negative or extremely positive performance, people are prone to make leadership attributions to explain the performance.[87] As noted earlier, this tendency helps to account for the vulnerability of CEOs (and high-ranking state officials) when their organisations suffer a major financial setback, regardless of whether they had much to do with it, and also accounts for why CEOs tend to be given credit for extremely positive financial results—again, regardless of how much or how little they contributed. One of the more interesting findings in the attribution theory of leadership literature is the perception that effective leaders are generally considered consistent or unwavering in their decisions.[88] One of the explanations for why John Howard (during his first term as Australian prime minister) was perceived as a leader was that he was fully committed, steadfast and consistent in the decisions he made and the goals he set.

Following the attribution theory of leadership, we would say that what is important in being characterised as an 'effective leader' is projecting the *appearance* of being a leader, rather than focusing on *actual accomplishments*. Leader wannabes can attempt to shape the perception that they are smart, personable, verbally adept, aggressive, hardworking and consistent in their style. And by doing so, they increase the probability that their bosses, colleagues and employees will *view* them *as* an effective leader.

attribution theory of leadership | The idea that leadership is merely an attribution that people make about other individuals.

SUBSTITUTES AND NEUTRALISERS TO LEADERSHIP

Contrary to the arguments made throughout this and the previous chapter, leadership may not always be important. A theory of leadership suggests that, in many situations, whatever actions leaders exhibit are irrelevant. Certain individual, job and organisational variables can act as *substitutes* for leadership or *neutralise* the leader's influence over his or her followers.[89]

Neutralisers make it impossible for leader behaviour to make any difference to follower outcomes. They negate the leader's influence. Substitutes, however, make a leader's influence not only impossible but also unnecessary. They act as a replacement for the leader's influence. For instance, characteristics of employees such as their experience, training, 'professional' orientation, or indifference towards organisational rewards can substitute for, or neutralise the effect of, leadership. Experience and training can replace the need for a leader's support or ability to create structure and reduce task ambiguity. Jobs that are inherently unambiguous and routine, or that are intrinsically satisfying, may place fewer demands on the leadership variable. Organisational characteristics such as explicit, formalised goals, rigid rules and procedures, and cohesive work groups can also replace formal leadership (see Table 13.4).

This recognition that leaders don't always have an impact on follower outcomes shouldn't be that surprising. After all, we have introduced a number of variables in this text—attitudes, personality, ability and group norms, to name but a few—that have been documented as having an effect on employee performance and satisfaction. Yet, supporters of the leadership concept place an undue burden on this variable for explaining and predicting behaviour. It is too simplistic to consider employees as guided to goal accomplishments solely by the actions of their leader. It is important, therefore, to recognise explicitly that leadership is merely another independent variable in our overall OB model. In some situations, it may contribute a lot to explaining employee productivity, absence, turnover, satisfaction and citizenship behaviour, but in other situations, it may contribute little towards that end.

The validity of substitutes and neutralisers is controversial. One of the problems is that the theory is very complicated—there are many possible substitutes for and neutralisers of

■ TABLE 13.4
Substitutes and neutralisers for leadership

Defining characteristics	Relationship-oriented leadership	Task-oriented leadership
Individual		
Experience/training	No effect on	Substitutes for
Professionalism	Substitutes for	Substitutes for
Indifference to rewards	Neutralises	Neutralises
Job		
Highly structured task	No effect on	Substitutes for
Provides its own feedback	No effect on	Substitutes for
Intrinsically satisfying	Substitutes for	No effect on
Organisation		
Explicit formalised goals	No effect on	Substitutes for
Rigid rules and procedures	No effect on	Substitutes for
Cohesive work groups	Substitutes for	Substitues for

SOURCE: Based on S. Kerr and J. M. Jermier, 'Substitutes for Leadership: Their Meaning and Measurement', *Organizational Behavior and Human Performance*, December 1978, p. 378.

many different types of leader behaviours across many different situations. Moreover, sometimes the difference between substitutes and neutralisers is fuzzy. For example, if I am working on a task that is intrinsically enjoyable, the theory predicts that leadership will be less important because the task itself provides enough motivation. But, does that mean that intrinsically enjoyable tasks neutralise leadership effects, or substitute for them, or both? Another problem that this review points out is that substitutes for leadership (such as employee characteristics, the nature of the task, and so forth) matter, but it doesn't appear that they substitute for or neutralise leadership.[90]

FINDING AND CREATING EFFECTIVE LEADERS

LEARNING OBJECTIVE 9

Explain how to find and create effective leaders

We have covered a lot of ground in these two chapters on leadership. But the ultimate goal of our review is to answer this question: How can organisations find or create effective leaders? Let's try to answer that question.

SELECTION

The entire process that organisations go through to fill management positions is essentially an exercise in trying to identify individuals who will be effective leaders. Your search might begin by reviewing the specific requirements for the position to be filled. What knowledge, skills and abilities are needed to do the job effectively? You should try to analyse the situation to find candidates who will make a proper match.

Testing is useful for identifying and selecting leaders. Personality tests can be used to look for traits associated with leadership—extraversion, conscientiousness and openness to experience. Testing to find a leadership-candidate's score on self-monitoring also makes sense. High self-monitors are likely to outperform their low-scoring counterparts because the former are better at reading situations and adjusting their behaviour accordingly. You can additionally assess candidates for emotional intelligence. Given the importance of social skills to managerial effectiveness, candidates with a high EI should have an advantage, especially in situations requiring transformational leadership.[91]

Interviews also provide an opportunity to evaluate leadership candidates. For instance, we know that experience is a poor predictor of leader effectiveness, but situation-specific experience is relevant. You can use the interview to determine if a candidate's prior experience fits with the situation you are trying to fill. Similarly, the interview is a reasonably good vehicle for identifying the degree to which a candidate has leadership traits such as extraversion, self-confidence, a vision, the verbal skills to frame issues or a charismatic physical presence.

We know the importance of situational factors in leadership success. And we should use this knowledge to match leaders to situations. Does the situation require a change-focused leader? If so, look for transformational qualities. If not, look for transactional qualities. You might also ask: Is leadership actually important in this specific position? There may be situational factors that substitute for or neutralise leadership. If there are, then the leader essentially performs a figurehead or symbolic role, and the importance of selecting the 'right' person isn't particularly crucial.

TRAINING

Organisations, in aggregate, spend billions of dollars, yen and euros on leadership training and development.[92] These efforts take many forms—from $50 000 executive leadership programs offered by universities such as Sydney and Melbourne, to sailing experiences at the Outward Bound School and Young Endeavour Scheme. Although much of the money spent on training may provide dubious benefits, our review suggests that there are some things management can do to get the maximum effect from their leadership-training budgets.[93]

First, let's recognise the obvious. People are not equally trainable. Leadership training of any kind is likely to be more successful with individuals who are high self-monitors than with low self-monitors. Such individuals have the flexibility to change their behaviour.

What kinds of things can individuals learn that might be related to higher leader effectiveness? It may be a bit optimistic to believe that we can teach 'vision creation', but we *can* teach implementation skills. We can train people to develop 'an understanding about content themes critical to effective visions'.[94] We also can teach skills such as trust building and mentoring. And leaders can be taught situational-analysis skills. They can learn how to evaluate situations, how to modify situations to make them fit better with their style, and how to assess which leader behaviours might be most effective in given situations. A number of companies have recently turned to executive coaches to help senior managers improve their leadership skills.[95] For instance, Charles Schwab, eBay, Pfizer, Unilever and American Express have hired executive coaches to provide specific one-on-one training for their company's top executives to help them improve their interpersonal skills and to learn to act less autocratically.[96]

On an optimistic note, there is evidence suggesting that behavioural training through modelling exercises can increase an individual's ability to exhibit charismatic leadership

---

OB IN PRACTICE

THE CHALLENGE OF LEADERSHIP DEVELOPMENT

In a 2005 study of the top 100 companies in Australia by *Human Resources* magazine, leadership was ranked as the number one issue. Development Dimensions International (DDI) is a consulting firm specialising in the development of leadership talent. DDI's study *Leadership Forecast 2005* reported a significant concern that people expect too much of their senior leaders. According to Bruce Watt, the managing director of DDI Australia, the immense pressure that is placed upon senior executives is causing significant turnover in their ranks. The DDI report found that 24 per cent of leaders had considered giving up their leadership positions for various reasons, including a redirection of career goals as well as inflated expectations by stakeholders about what they need to accomplish. The various reports highlight somewhat of a crisis in leadership and draw attention to the practice of supporting learning and development opportunities for current and aspiring leaders in our organisations.

Australian Gas Light Company (AGL), a privately owned gas utility company in New South Wales, has developed an extensive leadership program to ensure that leadership talent is identified and developed across all levels of the organisation. According to Gareth Bennett, the group manager of people and culture, the guiding principle within the program is to ensure that all participants have a sound understanding of themselves as a prerequisite to leading others effectively. AGL has established a leadership competency framework that emphasises positioning and executing strategy, and engaging people in developing their organisational capability. Leadership development is a significant challenge for all organisations, both public and private, and AGL provides an example of a growing number of companies who are taking leadership development seriously.

SOURCES: Melinda Finch, 'Bringing up the Boss', *Human Resources*, no. 104, 16 May 2006, pp. 14–15; and Paul R. Bernthal and Richard S. Wellins, 'Leadership Forecast 2005–2006: Best Practices for Tomorrow's Global Leaders', 2005: <www.ddiworld.com/thoughtleadership/leadershipforecast.asp> (accessed 31 May 2006).

qualities. The success of the researchers mentioned earlier (see 'Are Charismatic Leaders Born or Made?') in actually scripting undergraduate business students to 'play' charismatic is a case in point.[97] Finally, there is accumulating research showing that leaders can be trained in transformational leadership skills. Once learned, these skills have bottom-line results, whether it is in the financial performance of Australian banks or the training effectiveness of soldiers in the New Zealand Army.[98]

SUMMARY AND IMPLICATIONS FOR MANAGERS

- Organisations are increasingly searching for managers who can exhibit transformational leadership qualities. They want leaders with visions and the charisma to carry out their visions. And although true leadership effectiveness may be a result of exhibiting the right behaviours at the right time, the evidence is quite strong that people have a relatively uniform perception of what a leader should look like. They attribute 'leadership' to people who are smart, personable, verbally adept, and the like. To the degree that managers project these qualities, others are likely to deem them 'leaders'.

- Effective managers today must develop trusting relationships with those whom they seek to lead. Why? Because as organisations have become less stable and predictable, strong bonds of trust are likely to be replacing bureaucratic rules in defining expectations and relationships. Managers who aren't trusted aren't likely to be effective leaders.

- For managers concerned with how to fill key positions in their organisation with effective leaders, we have shown that tests and interviews help to identify people with leadership qualities. In addition to focusing on leadership selection, managers should also consider investing in leadership training. Many individuals with leadership potential can enhance their skills through formal courses, workshops, rotating job responsibilities, coaching and mentoring.

POINT / COUNTERPOINT

Good Leadership is Culturally-bound

● POINT

Leaders must adapt their style to different national cultures. What works in China, for example, isn't likely to work in Canada, Australia or Malaysia. Can you imagine, for example, executives at a large Australian department store chain, such as Myer, being effective by humiliating their employees? But that works at the Asia Department Store in central China. Executives there blatantly brag about practising 'heartless' management, requiring new employees to undergo two to four weeks of military-type training in order to increase their obedience, and conduct the store's in-house training sessions in a public place where employees can openly suffer embarrassment from their mistakes.

National culture affects leadership style by way of the follower. Leaders cannot choose their styles at will. They are constrained by the cultural conditions that their followers have come to expect. For example, Korean leaders are expected to be paternalistic towards employees; Arab leaders who show kindness or generosity without being asked to do so are seen by other Arabs as weak; and Japanese leaders are expected to be humble and to speak infrequently.

Consistent with the contingency approach, leaders need to adjust their style to the unique cultural aspects of a country. For example, a manipulative or autocratic style is compatible with high power distance, and we find high power distance scores in Russia, Spain and Muslim, Far Eastern and most Latin countries. Power distance rankings should also be good indicators of employee willingness to accept participative leadership. Participation is likely to be most effective in low power distance cultures such as exist in Norway, Finland, Denmark and Sweden.

SOURCES: Points in this argument are based on 'Military-Style Management in China', *Asia Inc.*, March 1995, p. 70; R. J. House, 'Leadership in the Twenty-First Century', in A. Howard (ed.), *The Changing Nature of Work* (San Francisco: Jossey-Bass, 1995), pp. 442–44; M. F. Peterson and J. G. Hunt, 'International Perspectives on International Leadership', *Leadership Quarterly*, Fall 1997, pp. 203–31; R. J. House, P. J. Hanges, S. A. Ruiz-Quintanilla, P. W. Dorfman and Associates, 'Culture Specific and Cross-Culturally

COUNTERPOINT

The GLOBE research program has gathered data on approximately 18 000 middle managers in 825 organisations, covering 62 countries. It is the most comprehensive cross-cultural study of leadership ever undertaken, so its findings shouldn't be quickly dismissed. It is illuminating that one of the results coming from the GLOBE program is that there are some universal aspects to leadership. Specifically, a number of the elements making up transformational leadership appear to be associated with effective leadership regardless of what country the leader is in. This conclusion is very important because it flies in the face of the contingency view that leadership style needs to adapt to cultural differences.

What elements of transformational leadership appear universal? Vision, foresight, providing encouragement, trustworthiness, dynamism, positiveness and proactiveness. The results led two members of the GLOBE team to conclude that 'effective business leaders in any country are expected by their subordinates to provide a powerful and proactive vision to guide the company into the future, strong motivational skills to stimulate all employees to fulfill the vision, and excellent planning skills to assist in implementing the vision'.

What might explain the universal appeal of these transformational leader attributes? It has been suggested that pressures towards common technologies and management practices, as a result of global competition and multinational influences, may make some aspects of leadership universally accepted. If true, we may be able to select and train leaders in a universal style and thus significantly raise the quality of leadership worldwide.

Generalizable Implicit Leadership Theories: Are the Attributes of Charismatic/Transformational Leadership Universally Endorsed?', *Leadership Quarterly*, Summer 1999, pp. 219–56; and D. E. Carl and M. Javidan, 'Universality of Charismatic Leadership: A Multi-Nation Study', Paper presented at the National Academy of Management Conference, Washington, DC, August 2001.

QUESTIONS FOR REVIEW

MyOBLab Do you understand this chapter's content? Find out at www.pearsoned.com.au/MyOBLab

1. What could you do if you wanted others to perceive you as a charismatic leader?
2. When can charisma be a liability?
3. Do you believe that transformational leaders are born or trained? Explain your response.
4. How are ethics involved in leadership?
5. Contrast the three types of trust. Relate them to your experience in personal relationships.
6. How does one become an effective team leader?
7. Why would a leader want to be a mentor?
8. How does a leader increase self-leadership among his or her followers?
9. How is leadership an attribution?
10. Contrast substitutes and neutralisers for leadership.

1. What role do you think training plays in an individual's ability to trust others? For instance, does the training of lawyers, accountants, police officers and social workers take different approaches towards trusting others? Explain.
2. 'It's not possible to be both a trusting boss and a politically astute leader. One requires openness and the other requires concealment.' Do you agree or disagree with this statement? Explain.
3. As a new employee in an organisation, why might you want to acquire a mentor? Why might women and minorities have more difficulty in finding a mentor than would white males?
4. Is there an ethical problem if leaders focus more on looking like a leader than actually being one? Discuss.
5. 'Leaders make a real difference in an organisation's performance.' Build an argument in support of this statement. Then build an argument against this statement.

Practising to Be Charismatic

People who are charismatic engage in the following behaviours:

- They project a powerful, confident and dynamic presence. This has both verbal and non-verbal components. Those with charisma use a captivating and engaging voice tone. They convey confidence. They also talk directly to people, maintaining direct eye contact and holding their body posture in a way that says they are sure of themselves. They speak clearly, avoid stammering, and avoid sprinkling their sentences with non-content phrases such as 'ahhh' and 'you know'.
- They articulate an overarching goal. They have a vision for the future, unconventional ways of achieving the vision, and the ability to communicate the vision to others. The vision is a clear statement of where they want to go and how they are going to get there. They are able to persuade others how the achievement of this vision is in the others' self-interest.
- They look for fresh and radically different approaches to solving problems. The road to achieving their vision is novel but also appropriate to the context.
- They not only have a vision, but they are able to get others to buy into it.
- They convey high performance expectations and confidence in others' ability to meet these expectations. They demonstrate their confidence in people by stating ambitious goals for them individually and as a group. They convey absolute belief that they will achieve their expectations.
- They are sensitive to the needs of followers. Charismatic leaders get to know their followers individually. They understand their individual needs and are able to develop intensely personal

relationships with each. They do this through encouraging followers to express their points of view, by being approachable, by genuinely listening to and caring about their followers' concerns, and by asking questions so that they can learn what is really important to them.

Task:

Now that you know what charismatic leaders do, you get the opportunity to practise projecting charisma.

1. The class members should divide into pairs.
2. Student A's task is to 'lead' Student B through a new-student orientation to your university. The orientation should last about 10–15 minutes. Assume that Student B is new to your university and is unfamiliar with the campus. Remember, Student A should attempt to project him or herself as charismatic.
3. Roles now reverse and Student B's task is to 'lead' Student A in a 10- to 15-minute program on how to study more effectively for exams. Take a few minutes to think about what has worked well for you, and assume that Student A is a new student interested in improving his or her study habits. Again, remember that Student B should attempt to project him or herself as charismatic.
4. When both role plays are complete, each pair should assess how well they did in projecting charisma and how they might improve.

SOURCE: This exercise is based on J. M. Howell and P. J. Frost, 'A Laboratory Study of Charismatic Leadership', *Organizational Behavior and Human Decision Processes*, April 1989, pp. 243–69.

ETHICAL DILEMMA

Would You Work Here?

Would you accept a senior leadership position at a major tobacco company such as Phillip Morris or R. J. Reynolds? Well, the typical answer from most students is 'no'.

The content of goals is said to have ethical ramifications. Does this mean that certain types of businesses are inherently unethical? For instance, many students defend their position not to work at a tobacco company because they believe the product the company sells is unhealthy. But where do *you* draw the line? Would *you* take a managerial position at Phillip Morris? Would your answer be different if the pay was $300 000 a year rather than $75 000?

Tobacco companies, of course, aren't the only firms producing products that have questionable health consequences. Would you work for Foster's Group, the maker of Victoria Bitter, Crown Lager and Foster's beer? The first response from most students is 'yes'. But many begin to question that response when told that drunk drivers kill hundreds of people a year in Australasia alone and injure thousands more. Most of these drivers have become intoxicated on beer, and Foster's has a significant share of the Australian beer market. So, people die each year as a result of Foster's products. Is this a fair conclusion? Does it alter your view of working for the Foster's Group?

Cookies, fast food (did you ever see the documentary *Super Size Me*?) and ice cream are also products that are hard to argue are good for people's health. High in sugar and fats, they contribute to health problems such as obesity, high blood pressure and high cholesterol. Could you ethically be a manager for Baskin Robbins, the ice-cream outlets, or Frito-Lay, the maker of potato chips? What companies, if any, wouldn't you be willing to work for and hold a leadership position in because you find their products or services to be unsavoury or unethical?

Generation Gap: Mentors and Protégés

As the baby-boomer generation nears retirement, many boomers are mentoring their future work replacements—Generation Xers. Some boomers have found the process difficult. William Slater, a 47-year-old computer engineer who participates in his company's formal mentoring program, has had negative experiences with three protégés. He recalls that one tried, unsuccessfully, to take his job, while another repeatedly spoke badly about him to his boss. 'I have an axe to grind with Generation X. They're stabbing aging baby-boomers in the back', says Slater.

It is not only baby-boomers who have had bad experiences. Joel Bershok, a 24-year-old, was optimistic about the prospects of having a mentor. However, his mentor dissolved the relationship after only three weeks. Says Bershok, 'He just wanted it for his résumé.' To Bershok, one of the main problems with a mentoring relationship is a lack of trust. With an uncertain economy and companies making frequent layoff announcements, boomers are wary of teaching their younger counterparts too much for fear that those counterparts, who usually make less—and so cost the company less than boomers—may replace them.

The fear may be justified. For example, Janet Wheeler, a 49-year-old broker, saw her job replaced by two younger workers after her company let her go. Wheeler thinks that other boomers are beginning to notice the risks of mentoring and are responding by not teaching their protégés as much as they could. 'You see young people being brought along just enough to get the job done, but not so much that they'll take your job,' she states.

Given that some studies have demonstrated the beneficial effects of mentoring on employee outcomes such as performance, job satisfaction and employee retention, many analysts are concerned that baby-boomers are failing to see mentoring as a responsibility. According to a study by Menttium Corporation, a firm that aids companies in installing mentoring programs, almost 90 per cent of formal mentoring relationships end prematurely. The primary reasons for this include poor matching of mentors to protégés and a lack of effort to keep the relationship going.

But some workers have strongly benefited from mentoring programs and are trying to maintain mentoring programs in their companies. Three years after joining Dell, Lynn Tyson, 41, helped start a formal mentoring program open to all of Dell's 42 000 employees. 'I never had a formal mentor in my entire career. Most of the time I was shaking in my shoes', says Tyson. Her program has been successful so far— and she mentors 40 protégés. 'I'm not trying to make this sound sappy, but I have the ability to make a difference in somebody's career, and that excites me every day.' The benefits are especially apparent for women and minorities who, historically, have had greater difficulty than white males in climbing to top management positions. According to a study by Harvard University professor David A. Thomas, the most successful racial minorities at three different corporations had a strong network of mentors. Additionally, research has shown that women also benefit from having positive mentoring experiences, in that they have greater career success and career satisfaction.

With the right amount of effort, protégés, mentors, and the companies that sponsor such relationships can realise tremendous benefits. However, individuals in mentoring relationships may need to look past generational and other individual differences to achieve such benefits. Though Slater has had his share of bad mentoring experiences, he is still optimistic. 'Mentoring is a time-honoured concept. Those of us who have been mentored should mentor others. Otherwise, we've short-circuited the process and the future', he says.

QUESTIONS

1. What factors do you believe lead to successful mentoring programs? If you were designing a mentoring program, what might it look like?
2. In what ways might a protégé benefit from having a mentor? In what ways might a mentor benefit from having a protégé?
3. Of the three types of trust discussed in the chapter, which one may be the primary type in mentoring relationships and why?
4. What types of leaders, in terms of personality traits and behavioural tendencies, would most likely be good mentors? What types of leaders might be poor mentors?

SOURCES: Based on J. Zaslow, 'Moving On: Don't Trust Anyone Under 30: Boomers Struggle With Their New Role as Mentors', *Wall Street Journal*, 5 June 2003, p. D.1; P. Garfinkel, 'Putting a Formal Stamp on Mentoring', *New York Times*, 18 January 2004, p. 3.10; and J. E. Wallace, 'The Benefits of Mentoring for Female Lawyers', *Journal of Vocational Behavior*, June 2001, pp. 366–91.

ENDNOTES

1. Jacqui Walker, 'Rag-Trade Riches', *Business Review Weekly*, 18–24 May 2006, p. 44; Kath Walters, 'Maclagan Does the Maths', *Business Review Weekly*, 18–24 May 2006, p. 45; CEW (Chief Executive Women) 'Member Profile': <www.cew.org.au/index.cfm?apg=membership&bpg=profilemember&aid=91> (accessed 1 June 2006); Computershare Annual Report 2004: <www-us.computershare.com/CorpDoc/annualreports/2004/ExecutiveGroup01.asp> (accessed 1 June 2006).

2. See R. M. Entman, 'Framing: Toward Clarification of a Fractured Paradigm', *Journal of Communication*, Autumn 1993, pp. 51–58; and G. T. Fairhurst and R. A. Starr, *The Art of Framing: Managing the Language of Leadership* (San Francisco: Jossey-Bass, 1996), p. 21.

3. Fairhurst and Starr, *The Art of Framing*, p. 4.

4. M. Weber, *Max Weber: The Theory of Social and Economic Organization*, A. M. Henderson and T. Parsons (trans.) (New York: Free Press, 1947).

5. J. A. Conger and R. N. Kanungo, 'Behavioral Dimensions of Charismatic Leadership', in J. A. Conger, R. N. Kanungo and Associates (eds), *Charismatic Leadership* (San Francisco: Jossey-Bass, 1988), p. 79.

6. J. A. Conger and R. N. Kanungo, *Charismatic Leadership in Organizations* (Thousand Oaks, CA: Sage, 1998); and R. Awamleh and W. L. Gardner, 'Perceptions of Leader Charisma and Effectiveness: The Effects of Vision Content, Delivery, and Organizational Performance', *Leadership Quarterly*, Fall 1999, pp. 345–73.

7. R. J. House and J. M. Howell, 'Personality and Charismatic Leadership', *Leadership Quarterly*, vol. 3, 1992, pp. 81–108; D. N. Den Hartog, 'Leadership in Organizations', in N. Anderson and D. S. Ones (eds), *Handbook of Industrial, Work and Organizational Psychology*, vol. 2 (Thousand Oaks, CA: Sage Publications, 2002), pp. 166–87.

8. See J. A. Conger and R. N. Kanungo, 'Training Charismatic Leadership: A Risky and Critical Task', *Charismatic Leadership* (San Francisco: Jossey-Bass, 1988), pp. 309–23; A. J. Towler, 'Effects of Charismatic Influence Training on Attitudes, Behavior, and Performance', *Personnel Psychology*, Summer 2003, pp. 363–81; and M. Frese, S. Beimel and S. Schoenborn, 'Action Training for Charismatic Leadership: Two Evaluations of Studies of a Commercial Training Module on Inspirational Communication of a Vision', *Personnel Psychology*, Autumn 2003, pp. 671–97.

9. R. J. Richardson and S. K. Thayer, *The Charisma Factor: How to Develop Your Natural Leadership Ability* (Upper Saddle River, NJ: Prentice Hall, 1993).

10. J. M. Howell and P. J. Frost, 'A Laboratory Study of Charismatic Leadership', *Organizational Behavior and Human Decision Processes*, April 1989, pp. 243–69. See also M. Frese, S. Beimel and S. Schoenborn, 'Action Training for Charismatic Leadership: Two Evaluations of Studies of a Commercial Training Module on Inspirational Communication of a Vision', *Personnel Psychology*, Fall 2003, pp. 671–97.

11. B. Shamir, R. J. House and M. B. Arthur, 'The Motivational Effects of Charismatic Leadership: A Self-Concept Theory', *Organization Science*, November 1993, pp. 577–94.

12. www.thebodyshop.com.au/infopage.cfm?pageID=53 (accessed 22 August 2006).

13. C. H. Schmitt, 'The Confidence Game', *US News and World Report*, 13 September 2004, pp. EE4–EE8; S. Levy, 'iPod, Therefore i Am', *Newsweek*, 26 July 2004, pp. 44–50.

14. B. Kark, R. Gan and B. Shamir, 'The Two Faces of Transformational Leadership: Empowerment and Dependency', *Journal of Applied Psychology*, April 2003, pp. 246–55; and P. D. Cherlunik, K. A. Donley, T. S. R. Wiewel and S. R. Miller, 'Charisma is Contagious: The Effect of Leaders' Charisma on Observers' Affect', *Journal of Applied Social Psychology*, October 2001, pp. 2149–59.

15. For reviews on the role of vision in leadership, see S. J. Zaccaro, 'Visionary and Inspirational Models of Executive Leadership: Empirical Review and Evaluation', in S. J. Zaccaro (ed.), *The Nature of Executive Leadership: A Conceptual and Empirical Analysis of Success* (Washington, DC: American Psychological Assoc., 2001), pp. 259–78; and M. Hauser and R. J. House, 'Lead Through Vision and Values', in E. A. Locke

(ed.), *Handbook of Principles of Organizational Behavior* (Malden, MA: Blackwell, 2004), pp. 257–73.

16. P. C. Nutt and R. W. Backoff, 'Crafting Vision', *Journal of Management Inquiry*, December 1997, p. 309.

17. Ibid, pp. 312–14.

18. J. L. Roberts, 'A Mogul's Migraine', *Newsweek*, 29 November 2004, pp. 38–40.

19. R. J. House, J. Woycke and E. M. Fodor, 'Charismatic and Noncharismatic Leaders: Differences in Behavior and Effectiveness', in Conger and Kanungo, *Charismatic Leadership*, pp. 103–04; D. A. Waldman, B. M. Bass and F. J. Yammarino, 'Adding to Contingent-Reward Behavior: The Augmenting Effect of Charismatic Leadership', *Group & Organization Studies*, December 1990, pp. 381–94; S. A. Kirkpatrick and E. A. Locke, 'Direct and Indirect Effects of Three Core Charismatic Leadership Components on Performance and Attitudes', *Journal of Applied Psychology*, February 1996, pp. 36–51; and R. J. Deluga, 'American Presidential Machiavellianism: Implications for Charismatic Leadership and Rated Performance', *Leadership Quarterly*, Fall 2001, pp. 339–63.

20. A. H. B. de Hoogh, D. N. den Hartog, P. L. Koopman, H. Thierry, P. T. van den Berg and J. G. van der Weide, 'Charismatic Leadership, Environmental Dynamism, and Performance', *European Journal of Work & Organizational Psychology*, December 2004, pp. 447–71; S. Harvey, M. Martin and D. Stout, 'Instructor's Transformational Leadership: University Student Attitudes and Ratings', *Psychological Reports*, April 2003, pp. 395–402; D. A. Waldman, M. Javidan and P. Varella, 'Charismatic Leadership at the Strategic Level: A New Application of Upper Echelons Theory', *Leadership Quarterly*, June 2004, pp. 355–80.

21. R. J. House, 'A 1976 Theory of Charismatic Leadership', in J. G. Hunt and L. L. Larson (eds), *Leadership: The Cutting Edge* (Carbondale, IL: Southern Illinois University Press, 1977), pp. 189–207; and Robert J. House and Ram N. Aditya, 'The Social Scientific Study of Leadership', *Journal of Management*, vol. 23, no. 3, 1997, pp. 409–73.

22. F. Cohen, S. Solomon, M. Maxfield, T. Pyszczynski and J. Greenberg, 'Fatal Attraction: The Effects of Mortality Salience on Evaluations of Charismatic, Task-Oriented, and Relationship-Oriented Leaders', *Psychological Science*, December

2004, pp. 846–51; and M. G. Ehrhart and K. J. Klein, 'Predicting Followers' Preferences for Charismatic Leadership: The Influence of Follower Values and Personality', *Leadership Quarterly*, Summer 2001, pp. 153–79.

23. H. L. Tosi, V. Misangyi, A. Fanelli, D. A. Waldman and F. J. Yammarino, 'CEO Charisma, Compensation, and Firm Performance', *Leadership Quarterly*, June 2004, pp. 405–20.

24. See, for instance, R. Khurana, *Searching for a Corporate Savior: The Irrational Quest for Charismatic CEOs* (Princeton, NJ: Princeton University Press, 2002); and J. A. Raelin, 'The Myth of Charismatic Leaders', *Training & Development*, March 2003, pp. 47–54.

25. J. Collins, 'Level 5 Leadership: The Triumph of Humility and Fierce Resolve', *Harvard Business Review*, January 2001, pp. 67–76; J. Collins, 'Good to Great', *Fast Company*, October 2001, pp. 90–104; and J. Collins, 'The Misguided Mix-Up', *Executive Excellence*, December 2002, pp. 3–4; H. L. Tosi, V. Misangyi, A. Fanelli, D. A. Waldman and F. J. Yammarino, 'CEO Charisma, Compensation, and Firm Performance', *Leadership Quarterly*, June 2004, pp. 405–20.

26. See, for instance, B. M. Bass, *Leadership and Performance beyond Expectations* (New York: Free Press, 1985); B. M. Bass, 'From Transactional to Transformational Leadership: Learning to Share the Vision', *Organizational Dynamics*, Winter 1990, pp. 19–31; F. J. Yammarino, W. D. Spangler and B. M. Bass, 'Transformational Leadership and Performance: A Longitudinal Investigation', *Leadership Quarterly*, Spring 1993, pp. 81–102; J. C. Wofford, V. L. Goodwin and J. L. Whittington, 'A Field Study of a Cognitive Approach to Understanding Transformational and Transactional Leadership', *Leadership Quarterly*, vol. 9, no. 1, 1998, pp. 55–84; B. M. Bass, B. J. Avolio, D. I. Jung and Y. Berson, 'Predicting Unit Performance by Assessing Transformational and Transactional Leadership', *Journal of Applied Psychology*, April 2003, pp. 207–18; J. Antonakis, B. J. Avolio and N. Sivasubramaniam, 'Context and Leadership: An Examination of the Nine-Factor Full-Range Leadership Theory Using the Multifactor Leadership Questionnaire', *Leadership Quarterly*, June 2003, pp. 261–95; and T. A. Judge and R. F. Piccolo, 'Transformational and Transactional Leadership: A Meta-Analytic Test of Their Relative Validity', *Journal of*

Applied Psychology, October 2004, pp. 755–68.

27. B. M. Bass, 'Leadership: Good, Better, Best', *Organizational Dynamics*, Winter 1985, pp. 26–40; and J. Seltzer and B. M. Bass, 'Transformational Leadership: Beyond Initiation and Consideration', *Journal of Management*, December 1990, pp. 693–703.

28. D. I. Jung, C. Chow and A. Wu, 'The Role of Transformational Leadership in Enhancing Organizational Innovation: Hypotheses and Some Preliminary Findings', *Leadership Quarterly*, August–October 2003, pp. 525–44; D. I. Jung, 'Transformational and Transactional Leadership and Their Effects on Creativity in Groups', *Creativity Research Journal*, vol. 13, no. 2, 2001, pp. 185–95; S. J. Shin and J. Zhou, 'Transformational Leadership, Conservation, and Creativity: Evidence from Korea', *Academy of Management Journal*, December 2003, pp. 703–14.

29. D. Baum, 'Battle Lessons: What the Generals Don't Know', *The New Yorker*, 17 January 2005, pp. 42–48.

30. J. E. Bono and T. A. Judge, 'Self-Concordance at Work: Toward Understanding the Motivational Effects of Transformational Leaders', *Academy of Management Journal*, October 2003, pp. 554–71; Y. Berson and B. J. Avolio, 'Transformational Leadership and the Dissemination of Organizational Goals: A Case Study of a Telecommunication Firm', *Leadership Quarterly*, October 2004, pp. 625–46; and S. Shinn, '21st-Century Engineer', *BizEd*, January/February 2005, pp. 18–23.

31. J. R. Baum, E. A. Locke and S. A. Kirkpatrick, 'Longitudinal Study of the Relation of Vision and Vision Communication to Venture Growth in Entrepreneurial Firms', *Journal of Applied Psychology*, February 2000, pp. 43–54.

32. B. J. Avolio, W. Zhu, W. Koh and P. Bhatia, 'Transformational Leadership and Organizational Commitment: Mediating Role of Psychological Empowerment and Moderating Role of Structural Distance', *Journal of Organizational Behavior*, December 2004, pp. 951–68; T. Dvir, Taly, N. Kass and B. Shamir, 'The Emotional Bond: Vision and Organizational Commitment among High-Tech Employees', *Journal of Organizational Change Management*, vol. 17, no. 2, 2004, pp. 126-43; and D. I. Jung and B. J. Avolio, 'Opening the Black Box: An Experimental Investigation of the

Mediating Effects of Trust and Value Congruence on Transformational and Transactional Leadership', *Journal of Organizational Behavior*, December 2000, pp. 949–64.

33. Cited in B. M. Bass and B. J. Avolio, 'Developing Transformational Leadership: 1992 and Beyond', *Journal of European Industrial Training*, January 1990, p. 23.

34. T. A. Judge and R. F. Piccolo, 'Transformational and Transactional Leadership: A Meta-Analytic Test of their Relative Validity', *Journal of Applied Psychology*, October 2004, pp. 755–68.

35. Bass and Avolio, 'Developing Transformational Leadership'; K. B. Lowe, K. G. Kroeck and N. Sivasubramaniam, 'Effectiveness Correlates of Transformational and Transactional Leadership: A Meta-Analytic Review of the MLQ Literature', *Leadership Quarterly*, Fall 1996, pp. 385–425; and T. A. Judge and J. E. Bono, 'Five-Factor Model of Personality and Transformational Leadership', *Journal of Applied Psychology*, October 2000, pp. 751–65.

36. See, for instance, J. Barling, T. Weber and E. K. Kelloway, 'Effects of Transformational Leadership Training on Attitudinal and Financial Outcomes: A Field Experiment', *Journal of Applied Psychology*, December 1996, pp. 827–32; T. Dvir, D. Eden and B. J. Avolio, 'Impact of Transformational Leadership on Follower Development and Performance: A Field Experiment', *Academy of Management Journal*, August 2002, pp. 735–44.

37. R. J. House and P. M. Podsakoff, 'Leadership Effectiveness: Past Perspectives and Future Directions for Research', in J. Greenberg (ed.), *Organizational Behavior: The State of the Science* (Hillsdale, NJ: Erlbaum, 1994), pp. 45–82; B. M. Bass, *Leadership and Performance Beyond Expectations* (New York: Free Press, 1985).

38. B. J. Avolio and B. M. Bass, 'Transformational Leadership, Charisma and Beyond', Working paper, School of Management, State University of New York, Binghamton, 1985, p. 14.

39. See B. J. Avolio, W. L. Gardner, F. O. Walumbwa, F. Luthans and D. R. May, 'Unlocking the Mask: A Look at the Process by Which Authentic Leaders Impact Follower Attitudes and Behaviors', *Leadership Quarterly*, December 2004, pp. 801–23; W. L. Gardner and J. R. Schermerhorn, Jr, 'Performance Gains through Positive Organizational Behavior and Authentic Leadership', *Organizational*

Dynamics, August 2004, pp. 270–81; and D. R. May, A. Y. L. Chan, T. D. Hodges and B. J. Avolio, 'Developing the Moral Component of Authentic Leadership', *Organizational Dynamics*, August 2003, pp. 247–60.

40. R. Ilies, F. P. Morgeson and J. D. Nahrgang, 'Authentic Leadership and Eudaemonic Well-Being and Understanding Leader–Follower Outcomes', *Leadership Quarterly*, in press.

41. This section is based on E. P. Hollander, 'Ethical Challenges in the Leader–Follower Relationship', *Business Ethics Quarterly*, January 1995, pp. 55–65; J. C. Rost, 'Leadership: A Discussion about Ethics', *Business Ethics Quarterly*, January 1995, pp. 129–42; J. B. Ciulla (ed.), *Ethics: The Heart of Leadership* (New York: Praeger Publications, 1998); J. D. Costa, *The Ethical Imperative: Why Moral Leadership Is Good Business* (Cambridge, MA: Perseus Press, 1999); C. E. Johnson, *Meeting the Ethical Challenges of Leadership* (Thousand Oaks, CA: Sage, 2001); L. K. Trevino, M. Brown and L. P. Hartman, 'A Qualitative Investigation of Perceived Executive Ethical Leadership: Perceptions from Inside and Outside the Executive Suite', *Human Relations*, January 2003, pp. 5–37; and R. M. Fulmer, 'The Challenge of Ethical Leadership', *Organizational Dynamics*, vol. 33, no. 3, 2004, pp. 307–17.

42. J. M. Burns, *Leadership* (New York: Harper & Row, 1978).

43. J. M. Howell and B. J. Avolio, 'The Ethics of Charismatic Leadership: Submission or Liberation?', *Academy of Management Executive*, May 1992, pp. 43–55.

44. See, for example, K. T. Dirks and D. L. Ferrin, 'Trust in Leadership: Meta-Analytic Findings and Implications for Research and Practice', *Journal of Applied Psychology*, August 2002, pp. 611–28; the special issue on trust in an organisational context, B. McEvily, V. Perrone and A. Zaheer, guest editors, *Organization Science*, January–February 2003; and R. Galford and A. S. Drapeau, *The Trusted Leader* (New York: Free Press, 2003).

45. Based on S. D. Boon and J. G. Holmes, 'The Dynamics of Interpersonal Trust: Resolving Uncertainty in the Face of Risk', in R. A. Hinde and J. Groebel (eds), *Cooperation and Prosocial Behaviour* (Cambridge, UK: Cambridge University Press, 1991), p. 194; D. J. McAllister, 'Affect- and Cognition-Based Trust as Foundations for Interpersonal Cooperation in Organizations', *Academy of*

Management Journal, February 1995, p. 25; and D. M. Rousseau, S. B. Sitkin, R. S. Burt and C. Camerer, 'Not So Different After All: A Cross-Discipline View of Trust', *Academy of Management Review*, July 1998, pp. 393–404.

46. J. B. Rotter, 'Interpersonal Trust, Trustworthiness, and Gullibility', *American Psychologist*, January 1980, pp. 1–7.

47. J. D. Lewis and A. Weigert, 'Trust as a Social Reality', *Social Forces*, June 1985, p. 970.

48. J. K. Rempel, J. G. Holmes and M. P. Zanna, 'Trust in Close Relationships', *Journal of Personality and Social Psychology*, July 1985, p. 96.

49. M. Granovetter, 'Economic Action and Social Structure: The Problem of Embeddedness', *American Journal of Sociology*, November 1985, p. 491.

50. R. C. Mayer, J. H. Davis and F. D. Schoorman, 'An Integrative Model of Organizational Trust', *Academy of Management Review*, July 1995, p. 712.

51. C. Johnson-George and W. Swap, 'Measurement of Specific Interpersonal Trust: Construction and Validation of a Scale to Assess Trust in a Specific Other', *Journal of Personality and Social Psychology*, September 1982, p. 1306.

52. P. L. Schindler and C. C. Thomas, 'The Structure of Interpersonal Trust in the Workplace', *Psychological Reports*, October 1993, pp. 563–73.

53. H. H. Tan and C. S. F. Tan, 'Toward the Differentiation of Trust in Supervisor and Trust in Organization', *Genetic, Social, and General Psychology Monographs*, May 2000, pp. 241–60.

54. Cited in D. Jones, 'Do You Trust Your CEO?', *USA Today*, 12 February 2003, p. 7B.

55. D. McGregor, *The Professional Manager* (New York: McGraw-Hill, 1967), p. 164.

56. B. Nanus, *The Leader's Edge: The Seven Keys to Leadership in a Turbulent World* (Chicago: Contemporary Books, 1989), p. 102.

57. See, for instance, K. T. Dirks and D. L. Ferrin, 'Trust in Leadership: Meta-Analytic Findings and Implications for Research and Practice', *Journal of Applied Psychology*, August 2002, pp. 611–28; J. B. Cunningham and J. MacGregor, 'Trust and the Design of Work: Complementary Constructs in Satisfaction and Performance', *Human Relations*, December 2000, pp. 1575–91; D. I. Jung and B. J. Avolio, 'Opening the Black Box: An Experimental Investigation of the Mediating Effects of Trust and Value

Congruence on Transformational and Transactional Leadership', *Journal of Organizational Behavior*, December 2000, pp. 949–64; and A. Zacharatos, J. Barling and R. D. Iverson, 'High-Performance Work Systems and Occupational Safety', *Journal of Applied Psychology*, January 2005, pp. 77–93.

58. D. E. Zand, *The Leadership Triad: Knowledge, Trust, and Power* (New York: Oxford University Press, 1997), p. 89.

59. Based on L. T. Hosmer, 'Trust: The Connecting Link between Organizational Theory and Philosophical Ethics', *Academy of Management Review*, April 1995, p. 393; and R. C. Mayer, J. H. Davis and F. D. Schoorman, 'An Integrative Model of Organizational Trust', *Academy of Management Review*, July 1995, p. 712.

60. J. M. Kouzes and B. Z. Posner, *Credibility: How Leaders Gain and Lose It, and Why People Demand It* (San Francisco: Jossey-Bass, 1993), p. 14.

61. This section is based on D. Shapiro, B. H. Sheppard and L. Cheraskin, 'Business on a Handshake', *Negotiation Journal*, October 1992, pp. 365–77; R. J. Lewicki and B. B. Bunker, 'Developing and Maintaining Trust in Work Relationships', in R. M. Kramer and T. R. Tyler (eds), *Trust in Organizations* (Thousand Oaks, CA: Sage, 1996), pp. 119–24; and J. Child, 'Trust—The Fundamental Bond in Global Collaboration', *Organizational Dynamics*, vol. 29, no. 4, 2001, pp. 274–88.

62. This section is based on D. E. Zand, *The Leadership Triad: Knowledge, Trust, and Power* (New York: Oxford University Press, 1997), pp. 122–34; and A. M. Zak, J. A. Gold, R. M. Ryckman and E. Lenney, 'Assessments of Trust in Intimate Relationships and the Self-Perception Process', *Journal of Social Psychology*, April 1998, pp. 217–28.

63. J. Scott, 'Once Bitten, Twice Shy: A World of Eroding Trust', *New York Times*, 21 April 2002, p. WK5; J. A. Byrne, 'Restoring Trust in Corporate America', *BusinessWeek*, 24 June 2002, pp. 30–35; B. Nussbaum, 'Can Trust Be Rebuilt?', *BusinessWeek*, 8 July 2002, pp. 32–34; and C. Sandlund, 'Trust Is a Must', *Entrepreneur*, October 2002, pp. 70–75.

64. The following results are cited in B. Horovitz, 'Trust', *USA Today*, 16 July 2002, p. 1A; and D. Jones, 'Do You Trust Your CEO?', *USA Today*, 12 February 2003, p. 7B.

65. See, for instance, J. H. Zenger, E. Musselwhite, K. Hurson and C. Perrin,

Leading Teams: Mastering the New Role (Homewood, IL: Business One Irwin, 1994); M. Frohman, 'Nothing Kills Teams Like Ill-Prepared Leaders', *Industry Week*, 2 October 1995, pp. 72–76; S. J. Zaccaro, A. L. Rittman and M. A. Marks, 'Team Leadership', *Leadership Quarterly*, Winter 2001, pp. 451–83; and B.-C. Lim and R. E. Ployhart, Transformational Leadership: Relations to the Five-Factor Model and Team Performance in Typical and Maximum Contexts', *Journal of Applied Psychology*, August 2004, pp. 610–21.

66. C. Caminiti, 'What Team Leaders Need to Know', *Fortune*, 20 February 1995, p. 93.

67. Ibid, p. 100.

68. N. Steckler and N. Fondas, 'Effectiveness: A Diagnostic Tool', *Organizational Dynamics*, Winter 1995, p. 20.

69. R. S. Wellins, W. C. Byham and G. R. Dixon, *Inside Teams* (San Francisco: Jossey-Bass, 1994), p. 318.

70. Steckler and Fondas, 'Building Team Leader Effectiveness', p. 21.

71. See, for example, L. J. Zachary, *The Mentor's Guide: Facilitating Effective Learning Relationships* (San Francisco: Jossey-Bass, 2000); M. Murray, *Beyond the Myths and Magic of Mentoring: How to Facilitate an Effective Mentoring Process*, rev. ed. (New York: John Wiley & Sons, 2001); and F. Warner, 'Inside Intel's Mentoring Movement', *Fast Company*, April 2002, pp. 116–20; and K. E. Kram, 'Phases of the Mentor Relationship', *Academy of Management Journal*, December 1983, pp. 608–25; R. A. Noe, 'An Investigation of the Determinants of Successful Assigned Mentoring Relationships', *Personnel Psychology*, Fall 1988, pp. 559–80; and L. Eby, M. Butts and A. Lockwood, 'Protégés' Negative Mentoring Experiences: Construct Development and Nomological Validation', *Personnel Psychology*, Summer 2004, pp. 411–47.

72. K. McLaughlin, 'Training Top 50: Edward Jones', *Training*, March 2001, pp. 78–79.

73. J. A. Wilson and N. S. Elman, 'Organizational Benefits of Mentoring', *Academy of Management Executive*, November 1990, p. 90; and J. Reingold, 'Want to Grow as a Leader? Get a Mentor?', *Fast Company*, January 2001, pp. 58–60.

74. See, for example, D. A. Thomas, 'The Impact of Race on Managers' Experiences of Developmental Relationships: An Intra-Organizational Study', *Journal of Organizational Behavior*, November 1990,

pp. 479–92; K. E. Kram and D. T. Hall, 'Mentoring in a Context of Diversity and Turbulence', in E. E. Kossek and S. A. Lobel (eds), *Managing Diversity* (Cambridge, MA: Blackwell 1996), pp. 108–36; M. N. Ruderman and M. W. Hughes-James, 'Leadership Development Across Race and Gender', in C. D. McCauley, R. S. Moxley and E. Van Velsor (eds), *The Center for Creative Leadership Handbook of Leadership Development* (San Francisco: Jossey-Bass, 1998), pp. 291–335; B. R. Ragins and J. L. Cotton, 'Mentor Functions and Outcomes: A Comparison of Men and Women in Formal and Informal Mentoring Relationships', *Journal of Applied Psychology*, August 1999, pp. 529–50; and D. B. Turban, T. W. Dougherty and F. K. Lee, 'Gender, Race, and Perceived Similarity Effects in Developmental Relationships: The Moderating Role of Relationship Duration', *Journal of Vocational Behavior*, October 2002, pp. 240–62.

75. Wilson and Elman, 'Organizational Benefits of Mentoring', p. 90.

76. See, for instance, K. Houston-Philpot, 'Leadership Development Partnerships at Dow Corning Corporation', *Journal of Organizational Excellence*, Winter 2002, pp. 13–27.

77. T. D. Allen, L. T. Eby, M. L. Poteet, E. Lentz and L. Lizzette, 'Career Benefits Associated with Mentoring for Protégés: A Meta-Analysis', *Journal of Applied Psychology*, February 2004, pp. 127–36; J. D. Kammeyer-Mueller and T. A. Judge, 'A Quantitative Review of the Mentoring Literature: Test of a Model', Working paper, University of Florida, 2005.

78. See C. C. Manz, 'Self-Leadership: Toward an Expanded Theory of Self-Influence Processes in Organizations', *Academy of Management Review*, July 1986, pp. 585–600; C. C. Manz and H. P Sims, Jr, 'Superleadership: Beyond the Myth of Heroic Leadership', *Organizational Dynamics*, Spring 1991, pp. 18–35; H. P Sims, Jr and C. C. Manz, *Company of Heroes: Unleashing the Power of Self-Leadership* (New York: Wiley, 1996); C. C. Manz and H. P. Sims, Jr, *The New Superleadership: Leading Others to Lead Themselves* (San Francisco: Berrett-Koehler, 2001); C. L. Dolbier, M. Soderstrom and M. A. Steinhardt, 'The Relationships between Self-Leadership and Enhanced Psychological, Health, and Work Outcomes', *Journal of Psychology*, September 2001, pp. 469–85; and

J. D. Houghton, T. W. Bonham, C. P. Neck and K. Singh, 'The Relationship between Self-Leadership and Personality: A Comparison of Hierarchical Factor Structures', *Journal of Managerial Psychology*, vol. 19, no. 4, 2004, pp. 427–41.

79. Based on Manz and Sims, 'Superleadership'.

80. B. J. Avolio, S. Kahai and G. E. Dodge, 'E-Leadership: Implications for Theory, Research, and Practice', *Leadership Quarterly*, Winter 2000, pp. 615–68; and B. J. Avolio and S. S. Kahai, 'Adding the "E" to E-Leadership: How it May Impact Your Leadership', *Organizational Dynamics*, vol. 31, no. 4, 2003, pp. 325–38.

81. S. J. Zaccaro and P. Bader, 'E-Leadership and the Challenges of Leading E-Teams: Minimizing the Bad and Maximizing the Good', *Organizational Dynamics*, vol. 31, no. 4, 2003, pp. 381–85.

82. C. E. Naquin and G. D. Paulson, 'Online Bargaining and Interpersonal Trust', *Journal of Applied Psychology*, February 2003, pp. 113–20.

83. B. Shamir, 'Leadership in Boundaryless Organizations: Disposable or Indispensable?', *European Journal of Work and Organizational Psychology*, vol. 8, no. 1, 1999, pp. 49–71.

84. Comment by Jim Collins and cited in J. Useem, 'Conquering Vertical Limits', *Fortune*, 19 February 2001, p. 94.

85. See, for instance, J. C. McElroy, 'A Typology of Attribution Leadership Research', *Academy of Management Review*, July 1982, pp. 413–17; J. R. Meindl and S. B. Ehrlich, 'The Romance of Leadership and the Evaluation of Organizational Performance', *Academy of Management Journal*, March 1987, pp. 91–109; R. G. Lord and K. J. Maher, *Leadership and Information Processing: Linking Perception and Performance* (Boston: Unwin Hyman, 1991); B. Shamir, 'Attribution of Influence and Charisma to the Leader: The Romance of Leadership Revisited', *Journal of Applied Social Psychology*, March 1992, pp. 386–407; J. R. Meindl, 'The Romance of Leadership as a Follower-Centric

Theory: A Social Constructionist Approach', *Leadership Quarterly*, Fall 1995, pp. 329–41; and S. A. Haslam, M. J. Platow, J. C. Turner, K. J. Reynolds, C. McGarty, P. J. Oakes, S. Johnson, M. K. Ryan and K. Veenstra, 'Social Identity and the Romance of Leadership: The Importance of Being Seen to be "Doing it for Us"', *Group Processes & Intergroup Relations*, July 2001, pp. 191–205.

86. R. G. Lord, C. L. DeVader and G. M. Alliger, 'A Meta-Analysis of the Relation between Personality Traits and Leadership Perceptions: An Application of Validity Generalization Procedures', *Journal of Applied Psychology*, August 1986, pp. 402–10.

87. J. R. Meindl, S. B. Ehrlich and J. M. Dukerich, 'The Romance of Leadership', *Administrative Science Quarterly*, March 1985, pp. 78–102.

88. B. M. Staw and J. Ross, 'Commitment in an Experimenting Society: A Study of the Attribution of Leadership from Administrative Scenarios', *Journal of Applied Psychology*, June 1980, pp. 249–60; and J. Pfeffer, *Managing with Power* (Boston: Harvard Business School Press, 1992), p. 194.

89. S. Kerr and J. M. Jermier, 'Substitutes for Leadership: Their Meaning and Measurement', *Organizational Behavior and Human Performance*, December 1978, pp. 375–403; J. M. Jermier and S. Kerr, 'Substitutes for Leadership: Their Meaning and Measurement—Contextual Recollections and Current Observations', *Leadership Quarterly*, vol. 8, no. 2, 1997, pp. 95–101; and E. de Vries Reinout, R. A. Roe and T. C. B. Taillieu, 'Need for Leadership as a Moderator of the Relationships between Leadership and Individual Outcomes', *Leadership Quarterly*, April 2002, pp. 121–38.

90. S. D. Dionne, F. J. Yamarino, L. E. Atwater and L. R. James, 'Neutralizing Substitutes for Leadership Theory: Leadership Effects and Common-Source Bias', *Journal of Applied Psychology*, vol. 87, 2002, pp. 454–64; J. R. Villa, J. P. Howell, P. W. Dorfman and D. L. Daniel,

'Problems with Detecting Moderators in Leadership Research Using Moderated Multiple Regression', *Leadership Quarterly*, vol. 14, 2002, pp. 3–23.

91. B. M. Bass, 'Cognitive, Social, and Emotional Intelligence of Transformational Leaders', in R. E. Riggio, S. E. Murphy and F. J. Pirozzolo (eds), *Multiple Intelligences and Leadership* (Mahwah, NJ: Erlbaum, 2002), pp. 113–14.

92. See, for instance, R. Lofthouse, 'Herding the Cats', *EuroBusiness*, February 2001, pp. 64–65; M. Delahoussaye, 'Leadership in the 21st Century', *Training*, September 2001, pp. 60–72; and K. Ellis, 'Making Waves', *Training*, June 2003, pp. 16–21.

93. See, for instance, J. Barling, T. Weber and E. K. Kelloway, 'Effects of Transformational Leadership Training on Attitudinal and Financial Outcomes: A Field Experiment', *Journal of Applied Psychology*, December 1996, pp. 827–32; and D. V. Day, 'Leadership Development: A Review in Context', *Leadership Quarterly*, Winter 2000, pp. 581–613.

94. M. Sashkin, 'The Visionary Leader', in J. A. Conger, R. N. Kanungo and Associates (eds), *Charismatic Leadership* (San Francisco: Jossey-Bass, 1988), p. 150.

95. D. V. Day, 'Leadership Development: A Review in Context', *Leadership Quarterly*, Winter 2000, pp. 590–93.

96. M. Conlin, 'CEO Coaches', *BusinessWeek*, 11 November 2002, pp. 98–104.

97. Howell and Frost, 'A Laboratory Study of Charismatic Leadership'.

98. T. Dvir, D. Eden and B. J. Avolio, 'Impact of Transformational Leadership on Follower Development and Performance: A Field Experiment', *Academy of Management Journal*, August 2002, pp. 735–44; B. J. Avolio and B. M. Bass, *Developing Potential Across a Full Range of Leadership: Cases on Transactional and Transformational Leadership* (Mahwah, NJ: Lawrence Erlbaum, 2002); A. J. Towler, 'Effects of Charismatic Influence Training on Attitudes, Behavior, and Performance', *Personnel Psychology*, Summer 2003, pp. 363–81; Barling et al., 'Effects of Transformational Leadership Training on Attitudinal and Financial Outcomes'.

14

POWER AND POLITICS

LEARNING OBJECTIVES

AFTER STUDYING THIS CHAPTER, YOU SHOULD BE ABLE TO:

1. CONTRAST LEADERSHIP AND POWER

2. DEFINE THE FIVE BASES OF POWER

3. CLARIFY WHAT CREATES DEPENDENCY IN POWER RELATIONSHIPS

4. LIST NINE INFLUENCE TACTICS AND THEIR CONTINGENCIES

5. EXPLAIN HOW SEXUAL HARASSMENT IS ABOUT THE ABUSE OF POWER

6. DESCRIBE THE IMPORTANCE OF A POLITICAL PERSPECTIVE

7. LIST THE INDIVIDUAL AND ORGANISATIONAL FACTORS THAT STIMULATE POLITICAL BEHAVIOUR

8. EXPLAIN HOW DEFENSIVE BEHAVIOURS CAN PROTECT AN INDIVIDUAL'S SELF-INTEREST

9. IDENTIFY SEVEN TECHNIQUES FOR MANAGING THE IMPRESSION ONE MAKES ON OTHERS

10. LIST THE THREE QUESTIONS THAT CAN HELP DETERMINE IF A POLITICAL ACTION IS ETHICAL

Elizabeth Proust: 'It is extremely difficult for women to rise through one organisation. Most of the successful women I know have achieved that success through a series of moves—being recognised outside rather than within.'

AS A COMPANY DIRECTOR and mentor, Elizabeth Proust is one of the most prominent women in Australian business. She previously held CEO roles in the public and private sectors, with the most recent being managing director of Esanda, an ANZ Company. She is now chairman of the Melbourne Symphony Orchestra, a director of three companies (Perpetual, Insurance Manufacturers and Sinclair Knight Merz), chairman of the Centre for Dialogue at La Trobe University and a fellow of the Australian Institute of Company Directors. She was awarded a Centenary Medal for service to Australian society in business leadership and an *Australian Financial Review* 2003 True Leaders award.

At a graduation address at La Trobe University, Proust provided some valuable advice and insights regarding positions of power. One of her critical aspirations is to improve the position of organisations she has been involved with, both economically and culturally. And she recognises that being a leader (and former managing director) is a privileged position of enormous power and influence.

As a woman, she feels strongly about access and equity issues regarding women and made it clear to the women graduands in the audience that men still don't get it—for many of them their career track involves a supportive partner at home, with the ability to focus on their career. Businesswomen still spend too much time juggling family and other demands. 'Don't expect a level playing field' was her advice, as there are still too few women in senior roles in corporate Australia. The issue is very much about power, influence and politics. The outcomes are many, including diversity in senior management ranks.

And Proust has very strong feelings about having to behave like a man to get ahead. As she points out, that approach demeans the individual and denies the organisation constructive and productive diversity in the ranks of senior management. On reflection, Proust regrets one aspect of her career: 'I wish I had had the courage to be myself a little earlier. When I started, I tried to adjust to the mores and male culture of the oil industry instead of saying, "This is me, this is how I do it."'[1]

If mankind minus one were of one opinion, then mankind is no more justified in silencing the one than the one—if he had the power—would be justified in silencing mankind.

John Stuart Mill

POWER HAS BEEN DESCRIBED as the last dirty word. It is easier for most of us to talk about sex or money than it is to talk about power. People who have it deny it, people who want it try not to appear to be seeking it, and those who are good at getting it are secretive about how they got it.[2] Elizabeth Proust illustrates the critical nature of power and influence when it comes to challenging the status quo. A major theme of this chapter is that power is a natural process in any group or organisation. As such, you need to know how it is acquired and exercised if you are going to fully understand organisational behaviour. Although you may have heard the phrase that 'power corrupts, and absolute power corrupts absolutely', power isn't always bad. As one author has noted, most medicines can kill if taken in the wrong amount, and thousands die each year in automobile accidents, but we don't abandon chemicals or cars because of the dangers associated with them. Rather, we consider danger an incentive to get training and information that will help us to use these forces productively.[3] The same applies to power. It is a reality of organisational life and it is not going to go away. Moreover, by learning how power works in organisations, you will be better able to use your knowledge to help you be a more effective manager.

A DEFINITION OF POWER

power | A capacity that *A* has to influence the behaviour of *B* so that *B* acts in accordance with *A*'s wishes.

Power refers to a capacity that *A* has to influence the behaviour of *B* so that *B* acts in accordance with *A*'s wishes.[4] This definition implies a *potential* that need not be actualised to be effective and a *dependency* relationship.

Power may exist but not be used. It is, therefore, a capacity or potential. One can have power but not impose it. Probably the most important aspect of power is that it is a function of **dependency**. The greater *B*'s dependence on *A*, the greater is *A*'s power in the relationship. Dependence, in turn, is based on alternatives that *B* perceives and the importance that *B* places on the alternative(s) that *A* controls. A person can have power over you only if he or she controls something you desire. If you want a university degree and have to pass a certain course to get it, and your current tutor is the only faculty member in the university who teaches that course, he or she has power over you. Your alternatives are highly limited and you place a high degree of importance on obtaining a passing grade. Similarly, if you are attending university on funds totally provided by your parents, you probably recognise the power that they hold over you. You are dependent on them for financial support. But once you are out of school, have a job, and are making a good income, your parents' power is reduced significantly. Who among us, though, hasn't known or heard of the rich relative who is able to control a large number of family members merely through the implicit or explicit threat of 'writing them out of the will'?

dependency | *B*'s relationship to *A* when *A* possesses something that *B* requires.

CONTRASTING LEADERSHIP AND POWER

A careful comparison of our description of power with our description of leadership in the previous two chapters reveals that the concepts are closely intertwined. Leaders use power as a means of attaining group goals. Leaders achieve goals, and power is a means of facilitating their achievement.

What differences are there between the two terms? One difference relates to goal compatibility. Power doesn't require goal compatibility, merely dependence. Leadership, on the other hand, requires some congruence between the goals of the leader and those being led. A second difference relates to the direction of influence. Leadership focuses on the downward influence on one's followers. It minimises the importance of lateral and upward influence patterns. Power does not. Still another difference deals with research emphasis. Leadership research, for the most part, emphasises style. It seeks answers to questions such as: How supportive should a leader be? How much decision making should be shared with followers? In contrast, the research on power has tended to encompass a broader area and to focus on tactics for gaining compliance. It has gone beyond the individual as the exerciser of power, because power can be used by groups as well as by individuals to control other individuals or groups.

BASES OF POWER

LEARNING OBJECTIVE **2**

Define the five bases of power

Where does power come from? What is it that gives an individual or a group influence over others? We answer these questions by dividing the bases or sources of power into two general groupings—formal and personal—and then breaking each of these down into more specific categories.[5]

FORMAL POWER

Formal power is based on an individual's position in an organisation. Formal power can come from the ability to coerce or reward, or from formal authority.

COERCIVE POWER

The **coercive power** base is dependent on fear. One reacts to this power out of fear of the negative results that might occur if one failed to comply. It rests on the application, or the threat of application, of physical sanctions such as the infliction of pain, the generation of frustration through restriction of movement, or the controlling by force of basic physiological or safety needs.

At the organisational level, *A* has coercive power over *B* if *A* can dismiss, suspend or demote *B*, assuming that *B* values his or her job. Similarly, if *A* can assign *B* work activities that *B* finds unpleasant or treat *B* in a manner that *B* finds embarrassing, *A* possesses coercive power over *B*. Coercive power also can come from withholding key information. People in an organisation who have data or knowledge that others need can make those others dependent on them.

coercive power | A power base dependent on fear.

REWARD POWER

The opposite of coercive power is **reward power**. People comply with the wishes or directives of another because doing so produces positive benefits; therefore, one who can distribute rewards that others view as valuable will have power over those others. These rewards can be either financial—such as controlling pay rates, raises and bonuses; or non-financial—including recognition, promotions, interesting work assignments, friendly colleagues, and preferred work shifts or sales territories.[6]

Coercive power and reward power are actually counterparts of each other. If you can remove something of positive value from another or inflict something of negative value,

reward power | Compliance achieved based on the ability to distribute rewards that others view as valuable.

then you have coercive power over that person. If you can give someone something of positive value or remove something of negative value, then you have reward power over that person.

LEGITIMATE POWER

legitimate power | The power a person receives as a result of his or her position in the formal hierarchy of an organisation.

In formal groups and organisations, probably the most frequent access to one or more of the power bases is one's structural position. This is called **legitimate power**. It represents the formal authority to control and use organisational resources.

Positions of authority include coercive and reward powers. Legitimate power, however, is broader than the power to coerce and reward. Specifically, it includes acceptance by members in an organisation of the authority of a position. When school principals, bank managers or army captains speak (assuming that their directives are viewed to be within the authority of their positions), teachers, tellers and first lieutenants listen and usually comply.

PERSONAL POWER

You don't have to have a formal position in an organisation to have power. Many of the most competent and productive chip designers at Intel, for instance, have power, but they aren't managers and have no formal power. What they have is personal power—power that comes from an individual's unique characteristics. In this section, we look at two bases of personal power—expertise and the respect and admiration of others.

EXPERT POWER

expert power | Influence based on special skills or knowledge.

Expert power is influence wielded as a result of expertise, special skill or knowledge. Expertise has become one of the most powerful sources of influence as the world has become more technologically oriented. As jobs become more specialised, we become increasingly dependent on experts to achieve goals. So, although it is generally acknowledged that physicians have expertise and hence expert power—most of us follow the advice that our doctor gives us—you should also recognise that computer specialists, tax accountants, economists, industrial psychologists and other specialists are able to wield power as a result of their expertise.

REFERENT POWER

referent power | Influence based on possession by an individual of desirable resources or personal traits.

Referent power is based on identification with a person who has desirable resources or personal traits. If I like, respect and admire you, you can exercise power over me because I want to please you.

Referent power develops out of admiration of another and a desire to be like that person. It helps to explain, for instance, why celebrities are paid millions of dollars to endorse products in commercials. Marketing research shows that people such as golfing young guns Karrie Webb and Aaron Baddeley and international soccer star David Beckham have the power to influence your choice of sunglasses, mobile phones and athletic shoes. With a little practice, we could probably deliver as smooth a sales pitch as these celebrities, but the buying public doesn't identify with us.

One of the ways in which individuals acquire referent power is through charisma, which may be seen as an extension of referent power. Some people have referent power who, while not in formal leadership positions, nevertheless are able to exert influence over others because of their charismatic dynamism, likeability and emotional effects on us.

WHICH BASES OF POWER ARE MOST EFFECTIVE?

Of the three bases of formal power (coercive, reward, legitimate) and two bases of personal power (expert, referent), which is most important to have? Interestingly, research suggests pretty clearly that the personal sources of power are most effective. Both expert and referent power are positively related to employees' satisfaction with supervision, their organisational commitment and their performance, whereas reward and legitimate power seem to be unrelated to these outcomes. Moreover, one source of formal power—coercive power—actually can backfire in that it is negatively related to employee satisfaction and commitment.[7]

Consider Steve Stoute's company, Translation, which matches pop-star spokespersons with corporations that want to promote their brands. Stoute has paired Gwen Stefani with Hewlett-Packard, Justin Timberlake with McDonald's, Beyoncé Knowles with Tommy Hilfiger, and Jay-Z with Reebok. Stoute's business seems to be all about referent power—as one record company executive commented when reflecting on Stoute's successes, 'He's the right guy for guiding brands in using the record industry to reach youth culture in a credible way.'[8] In other words, using pop stars to market products works because of referent power—people buy products associated with cool figures because they wish to identify with and emulate these figures.

DEPENDENCY: THE KEY TO POWER

LEARNING OBJECTIVE 3
Clarify what creates dependency in power relationships

Earlier in this chapter it was said that probably the most important aspect of power is that it is a function of dependence. In this section, we show how an understanding of dependency is central to furthering your understanding of power itself.

THE GENERAL DEPENDENCY POSTULATE

Let's begin with a general postulate: *The greater B's dependency on A, the greater the power A has over B.* When you possess anything that others require but that you alone control, you make them dependent on you and, therefore, you gain power over them.[9] Dependency, then, is inversely proportional to the alternative sources of supply. If something is plentiful, possession of it won't increase your power. If everyone is intelligent, intelligence gives no special advantage. Similarly, among the super-rich, money is no longer power. But, as the old saying goes, 'In the land of the blind, the one-eyed man is king!' If you can create a monopoly by

The Brisbane Broncos is one of the most successful rugby league teams in Australia in the past 20 years. The team has won the grand final a number of times and always finishes in the top eight at the end of a season, making the finals. What has been the key behind its success? While some great footballers have come and gone over the years, coach Wayne Bennett has been the central figure. Bennett has been there from day one. He is recognised as one of the great guru coaches in rugby league. His influence in rugby league is based on expert power. However, many in the club, particularly players, would also suggest he has referent power.

controlling information, prestige or anything that others crave, they become dependent on you. Conversely, the more that you can expand your options, the less power you place in the hands of others. This explains, for example, why most organisations develop multiple suppliers rather than give their business to only one. It also explains why so many of us aspire to financial independence. Financial independence reduces the power that others can have over us.

WHAT CREATES DEPENDENCY?

Dependency is increased when the resource you control is important, scarce and non-substitutable.[10]

IMPORTANCE

If no one wants what you've got, it is not going to create dependency. To create dependency, therefore, the thing(s) you control must be perceived as being important. Organisations, for instance, actively seek to avoid uncertainty.[11] We should, therefore, expect that the individuals or groups who can absorb an organisation's uncertainty will be perceived as controlling an important resource. For instance, a study of industrial organisations found that the marketing departments in these firms were consistently rated as the most powerful.[12] It was concluded by the researcher that the most critical uncertainty facing these firms was selling their products. This might suggest that engineers, as a group, would be more powerful at BHP Billiton than at Woolworths. These inferences appear to be generally valid. An organisation such as BHP Billiton, which is heavily technologically oriented, is highly dependent on its engineers to maintain its products' technical advantages and quality and are clearly a powerful group. At Woolworths, marketing and sales is the name of the game, and marketers and salespersons are the most powerful occupational group.

SCARCITY

As noted previously, if something is plentiful, possession of it won't increase your power. A resource needs to be perceived as scarce to create dependency. This can help to explain how low-ranking members in an organisation who have important knowledge not available to high-ranking members gain power over the high-ranking members. Possession of a scarce resource—in this case, important knowledge—makes the high-ranking member dependent on the low-ranking member. This also helps to make sense out of behaviours of low-ranking members that otherwise might seem illogical, such as destroying the procedure manuals that describe how a job is done, refusing to train people in their jobs or even to show others exactly what they do, creating specialised language and terminology that inhibit others from understanding their jobs, or operating in secrecy so that an activity will appear more complex and difficult than it really is.

Ferruccio Lamborghini, who created the exotic supercars that continue to carry his name, understood the importance of scarcity and used it to his advantage during the Second World War. Lamborghini was in Rhodes with the Italian army. His superiors were impressed with his mechanical skills, as he demonstrated an almost uncanny ability to repair tanks and cars that no one else could fix. After the war he admitted that his ability was largely due to having been the first person on the island to receive the repair manuals, which he memorised and then destroyed so as to become indispensable.[13]

The scarcity–dependency relationship can further be seen in the power of occupational categories. Individuals in occupations in which the supply of personnel is low relative to demand can negotiate compensation and benefit packages that are far more attractive than can those in occupations for which there is an abundance of candidates. University administrators have no problem today finding English tutors. The market for computer-engineering lecturers, in contrast, is extremely tight, with the demand high and the supply limited. The result is that the bargaining power of the computer-engineering faculty allows them to negotiate higher salaries, lighter teaching loads and other benefits.

NON-SUBSTITUTABILITY

The fewer viable substitutes for a resource, the more power the control over that resource provides. Higher education again provides an excellent example. At universities in which there are strong pressures for the faculty to publish, we can say that a department head's power over a faculty member is inversely related to that member's publication record. The more recognition the faculty member receives through publication, the more mobile he or she is. That is, since other universities want faculty who are highly published and visible, there is an increased demand for that person's services. Although the concept of tenure can act to alter this relationship by restricting the department head's alternatives, faculty

---

INFLUENCE TACTICS IN CHINA

OB IN PRACTICE

Doing business in China has become a challenge for Australian managers. The advice given to firms is to make sure they do diligent research, build the right relationships (*guanxi*), understand the law, and recognise the significant cultural and regulatory differences between the two countries. Kym Hewett, senior Australian trade commissioner with Austrade in Beijing, puts it succinctly: 'Halve your expectations and double your time and budget.'

But there is another issue that Australian entrepreneurs and managers may learn about the hard way—determining the right influence and negotiating tactics isn't about dealing with one homogenous culture. For example, although non-Asian managers might view all Chinese people as being alike due to their shared heritage and distinctive appearance, China is a big country housing different cultures and traditions. A recent study examining Mainland Chinese, Taiwanese and Hong Kong managers explored how the three cultural subgroups differ according to the influence tactics they prefer to use.

Though managers from all three places believe that rational persuasion and exchange are the most effective influence tactics, managers in Taiwan tend to use inspirational appeals and ingratiation more than managers from either Mainland China or Hong Kong. The study also found that managers from Hong Kong rate pressure as more effective in influencing others than do managers in Taiwan or Mainland China. Such differences have implications for business relationships.

For example, Taiwanese or Mainland Chinese managers may be taken aback by the use of pressure tactics by the Hong Kong manager. Likewise, managers from Hong Kong may not be persuaded by managers from Taiwan, who tend to use ingratiating tactics. Such differences in influence tactics may make business dealings difficult. Companies should address these issues, perhaps making their managers aware of the differences within cultures.

So, managers need to know what variations exist within their local cultures in order to be better prepared to deal with others. Managers who fail to realise these differences may miss out on opportunities to deal effectively with others.

SOURCES: Gillian Bullock, 'Doing Business in China', *Management Today*, July 2006: <www.aim.com.au/DisplayStory.asp?ID=594>; and P. P. Fu, T. K. Peng, J. C. Kennedy and G. Yukl, 'A Comparison of Chinese Managers in Hong Kong, Taiwan, and Mainland China', *Organizational Dynamics*, February 2004, pp. 32–46.

members who have few or no publications have the least mobility and are subject to the greatest influence from their superiors.

POWER TACTICS

LEARNING OBJECTIVE   4

List nine influence tactics and their contingencies

power tactics | Ways in which individuals translate power bases into specific actions.

What **power tactics** do people use to translate power bases into specific action? That is, what options do individuals have for influencing their bosses, co-workers or employees? And are some of these options more effective than others? In this section, we review popular tactical options and the conditions under which one may be more effective than another.

Research has identified nine distinct influence tactics:[14]

* *Legitimacy*: Relying on one's authority position, or stressing that a request is in accordance with organisational policies or rules.
* *Rational persuasion*: Presenting logical arguments and factual evidence to demonstrate that a request is reasonable.
* *Inspirational appeals*: Developing emotional commitment by appealing to a target's values, needs, hopes and aspirations.
* *Consultation*: Increasing the target's motivation and support by involving him or her in deciding how the plan or change will be done.
* *Exchange*: Rewarding the target with benefits or favours in exchange for following a request.
* *Personal appeals*: Asking for compliance based on friendship or loyalty.
* *Ingratiation*: Using flattery, praise or friendly behaviour prior to making a request.
* *Pressure*: Using warnings, repeated demands and threats.
* *Coalitions*: Enlisting the aid of other people to persuade the target, or using the support of others as a reason for the target to agree.

Some tactics are usually more effective than others. Specifically, evidence indicates that rational persuasion, inspirational appeals and consultation tend to be the most effective. On the other hand, pressure tends to backfire frequently and is typically the least effective of the nine tactics.[15] You can also increase your chances of success by using more than one type of tactic at the same time or sequentially, as long as your choices are compatible.[16] For instance, using both ingratiation and legitimacy can lessen the negative reactions that might come from the appearance of being 'dictated to' by the boss.

But some influence tactics work better depending on the direction of influence.[17] As shown in Table 14.1, studies have found that rational persuasion is the only tactic that is effective across organisational levels. Inspirational appeals work best as a downward-influencing tactic with subordinates. When pressure works, it is almost only to achieve

■ TABLE 14.1
Preferred power tactics by influence direction

Upward influence	Downward influence	Lateral influence
Rational persuasion	Rational persuasion	Rational persuasion
	Inspirational appeals	Consultation
	Pressure	Ingratiation
	Consultation	Exchange
	Ingratiation	Legitimacy
	Exchange	Personal appeals
	Legitimacy	Coalitions

downward influence. And the use of personal appeals and coalitions is most effective with lateral influence attempts. In addition to the direction of influence, a number of other factors have been found to affect which tactics work best. These include the sequencing of tactics, a person's skill in using the tactic, a person's relative power, the type of request and how the request is perceived, the culture of the organisation, and country-specific cultural factors.

You are more likely to be effective if you begin with 'softer' tactics that rely on personal power such as personal and inspirational appeals, rational persuasion and consultation. If these fail, you can move to 'harder' tactics (which emphasise formal power and involve greater costs and risks), such as exchange, coalitions and pressure.[18] Interestingly, it has been found that using a single soft tactic is more effective than a single hard tactic; and that combining two soft tactics, or a soft tactic and rational persuasion, is more effective than any single tactic or a combination of hard tactics.[19]

Studies confirm that a tactic is 'more likely to be successful if the target perceives it to be a socially acceptable form of influence behaviours, if the agent has sufficient position and personal power to use the tactic, if the tactic can affect target attitudes about the desirability of the request, if it is used in a skilful way, if it is used for a request that is legitimate, and if it is consistent with the target person's values and needs'.[20]

We know that cultures within organisations differ markedly—for example, some are warm, relaxed and supportive; others are formal and conservative. The organisational culture in which a person works, therefore, will have a bearing on defining which tactics are considered appropriate. Some cultures encourage the use of participation and consultation, some encourage reason, and still others rely on pressure. So, the organisation itself will influence which subset of power tactics is viewed as acceptable for use.

Finally, evidence indicates that people in different countries tend to prefer different power tactics.[21] For instance, a study comparing managers in the United States and China found that the Americans perceived reason to be most effective, whereas Chinese managers preferred coalition tactics.[22] These differences tend to be consistent with the values in these two countries. Reason is consistent with the preference of Americans for direct confrontation and the use of rational persuasion to influence others and resolve differences. Similarly, coalition tactics are consistent with the Chinese preference for using indirect approaches for difficult or controversial requests.

POWER IN GROUPS: COALITIONS

Those 'out of power' and seeking to be 'in' will first try to increase their power individually. Why share the spoils if one doesn't have to? But if this proves ineffective, the alternative is to form a **coalition**—an informal group bound together by the active pursuit of a single issue.[23] The logic of a coalition? There is strength in numbers.

The natural way to gain influence is to become a powerholder. Therefore, those who want power will attempt to build a personal power base. But, in many instances, this may be difficult, risky, costly or impossible. In such cases, efforts will be made to form a coalition of two or more 'outs' who, by joining together, can combine their resources to increase rewards for themselves.[24] Successful coalitions have been found to contain fluid membership and are able to form swiftly, achieve their target issue and quickly disappear.[25]

What predictions can we make about coalition formation?[26] First, coalitions in organisations often seek to maximise their size. In political science theory, coalitions move

coalition | An informal group bound together by the active pursuit of a single issue.

POWER AND INFLUENCE IN AUSTRALIA

The use of power and influence in organisations is always an issue of interest to senior executives of multinational organisations, due to the challenge of matching executive talent, knowledge and skills with national and ethnic cultural contexts of local operations around the world. Some aspects of power and influence in Australia are highlighted by two people who have experience in Australia and abroad.

Managing director of Right Management Consultants, Ted Davies, has held senior executive positions in Australia, the United States and the United Kingdom. From his experience, Davies has observed that Australia's unique history and geographical remoteness has been an influence on the tendency for Australians to be more sceptical, and less naturally accepting of authority, than their colleagues in the Northern Hemisphere. Compared to the US, he believes that: 'Australians are prone to irreverence, less inclined to salute the corporate flag and blindly follow policies and edicts that are issued from corporate headquarters. Australians need to be sold, not told. Powers of persuasion and influence are paramount in leading organisations. We don't respond well to directives.'

Former Kraft Foods vice president and area director, Australia and New Zealand, Ben Clarke, moved from the UK to take up the challenge at Kraft. He believes Australians are, by and large, practical and pragmatic, and, in football terminology, 'there is a lot more of playing the ball rather than playing the man'. In the UK, he says, the organisational politics are subtle and sophisticated, and can be quite intense, and people are quick to take umbrage, so there can be quite a lot of personality-driven conflict and rivalry in many organisations.

Clarke points out that, as a CEO, 'dealing with my senior managers, for instance, I can be more direct with people here than I could be in the UK, because people are more accepting of it and will take it in the spirit in which it was meant … In Australia, the expectations of leaders are that a leader will be strong, decisive, high-energy, and very visible and outspoken. I noticed this early on when I arrived and I surveyed the business scene and the media. This was generally the way many leaders, not just business leaders, behaved. In the UK, on the other hand, you see many business leaders who are more low key, and who therefore project different qualities, such as being thoughtful, insightful, reflective and intellectual'.

And what advice does Clarke have for other CEOs taking up an appointment in Australia? 'One thing CEOs have to do more of here is to be more gregarious: to spend more time mixing with all their employees, getting out and talking with people, and being seen to do so. I think Australians respond a lot better to personal interest from the CEO than in the UK.' Power and influence is at the very heart of leadership. The local culture is a big factor for senior leaders to take into consideration when determining how to apply their power and influence for best results.

SOURCE: Adapted from <www.ceoforum.com.au/article-detail.cfm?cid=6063> (accessed 27 October 2006).

the other way—they try to minimise their size. They tend to be just large enough to exert the power necessary to achieve their objectives. But legislatures are different from organisations. Specifically, decision making in organisations doesn't end just with selection from among a set of alternatives. The decision must also be implemented. In organisations, the implementation of and commitment to the decision is at least as important as the decision itself. It is necessary, therefore, for coalitions in organisations to seek a broad constituency to support the coalition's objectives. This means expanding the coalition to encompass as many interests as possible.

Another prediction about coalitions relates to the degree of interdependence within the organisation. More coalitions will likely be created when there is a great deal of task and resource interdependence. In contrast, there will be less interdependence among subunits and less coalition formation activity when subunits are largely self-contained or resources are abundant.

Finally, coalition formation will be influenced by the actual tasks that workers do. The more routine the task of a group, the greater the likelihood that coalitions will form. The more routine the work that people do, the greater their substitutability for each other and, thus, the greater their dependence. To offset this dependence, they can be expected to resort to a coalition. This helps to explain the historical appeal of labour unions, especially among low-skilled workers. Such employees are better able to negotiate improved wages, benefits and working conditions as a united coalition than if they acted individually. A one-person 'strike' has little power over management. However, if a firm's entire workforce goes on strike, management has a serious problem.

SEXUAL HARASSMENT: UNEQUAL POWER IN THE WORKPLACE

LEARNING OBJECTIVE 5

Explain how sexual harassment is about the abuse of power

Sexual harassment is wrong. It can also be costly to employers. Just ask senior executives at Queensland Health.[27] A female employee alleged that she was sexually harassed by a male co-worker during her employment with Queensland Health. She alleged the co-worker openly stared at her breasts; touched her shoulders and back; hugged her and asked her to hug him. The Administrative Decisions Tribunal awarded her $14 665 payable by Queensland Health.

Not only are there legal dangers to sexual harassment; it can also have a negative impact on the work environment. Research shows that sexual harassment negatively affects job attitudes and leads those who feel harassed to withdraw from the organisation. Moreover, in many cases, reporting sexual harassment doesn't improve the situation because the organisation responds in a negative or unhelpful way. When organisational leaders make honest efforts to stop the harassment, the outcomes are much more positive.[28]

Sexual harassment relates to any unwanted activity of a sexual nature that affects an individual's employment and creates a hostile work environment. Under Australian legislation, sexual harassment is defined as 'an unwelcome sexual advance, unwelcome request for sexual favours or other unwelcome conduct of a sexual nature which makes a person feel offended, humiliated, or intimidated, and where that reaction is reasonable in the circumstances'.[29]

sexual harassment | Any unwanted activity of a sexual nature that affects an individual's employment and creates a hostile work environment.

But there continues to be disagreement as to what *specifically* constitutes sexual harassment. Organisations have generally made considerable progress in the past decade towards limiting overt forms of sexual harassment. This includes unwanted physical touching, recurring requests for dates when it is made clear the person isn't interested, and coercive threats that a person will lose his or her job if he or she refuses a sexual proposition. The problems today are likely to surface around more subtle forms of sexual harassment—unwanted looks or comments, off-colour jokes, sexual artefacts such as pin-ups posted in the workplace, or misinterpretations of where the line between 'being friendly' ends and 'harassment' begins.

A recent review concluded that 58 per cent of women report having experienced potentially harassing behaviours and 24 per cent report having experienced sexual harassment at work.[30] One problem with sexual harassment is that it is, to some degree, in the eye of the beholder. For example, women are more likely to see a given behaviour or sets of behaviours as constituting sexual harassment. Men are less likely to see as harassment such behaviours as kissing someone, asking for a date, or making sex-stereotyped jokes. As the authors of this study note, 'Although progress has been made at defining sexual harassment, it is still unclear as to whose perspective should be taken.'[31] Thus, although some behaviours indisputably constitute harassment, men and women continue to differ to some degree on what constitutes harassment. For you, the best approach is to be careful—refrain from any behaviour that may be taken as harassing even if that wasn't your intent. Realise that what you see as an innocent joke or hug may be seen as harassment by the other party.

Most studies confirm that the concept of power is central to understanding sexual harassment.[32] This seems to be true whether the harassment comes from a supervisor, a co-worker or an employee. And, sexual harassment is more likely to occur when there are large power differentials. The supervisor–employee dyad best characterises an unequal power relationship, where formal power gives the supervisor the capacity to reward and coerce. Supervisors give employees their assignments, evaluate their performance, make recommendations for salary adjustments and promotions, and even decide whether or not an employee retains his or her job. These decisions give a supervisor power. Because employees want favourable performance reviews, salary increases and the like, it is clear that supervisors control resources that most employees consider important and scarce. It is also worth noting that individuals who occupy high-status roles (such as management positions) sometimes believe that sexually harassing employees is merely an extension of their right to make demands on lower-status individuals. Because of power inequities, sexual harassment by one's boss typically creates the greatest difficulty for those who are being harassed. If there are no witnesses, it is the victim's word against the harasser's. Are there others this boss has harassed and, if so, will they come forward? Because of the supervisor's control over resources, many of those who are harassed are afraid of speaking out for fear of retaliation by the supervisor.

Although co-workers don't have legitimate power, they can have influence and use it to sexually harass peers. In fact, although co-workers appear to engage in somewhat less severe forms of harassment than do supervisors, co-workers are the most frequent perpetrators of sexual harassment in organisations. How do co-workers exercise power? Most often it is by providing or withholding information, cooperation and support. For example, the effective performance of most jobs requires interaction and support from co-workers. This is especially true nowadays, because work is often assigned to teams. By threatening to withhold or delay providing information that is necessary for the successful achievement of your work goals, co-workers can exert power over you.

Although it doesn't get nearly the attention that harassment by a supervisor does, as seen in the case against Queensland Health, women in positions of power can be subjected to sexual harassment from males who occupy less powerful positions within the organisation. This is usually achieved by the employee devaluing the woman through highlighting traditional gender stereotypes (such as helplessness, passivity, lack of career commitment) that reflect negatively on the woman in power. An employee may engage in such practices to attempt to gain some power over the higher-ranking female or to minimise power differentials. Increasingly, too, there are cases of women in positions of power harassing male employees.

The topic of sexual harassment is about power. It is about an individual controlling or threatening another individual. It is wrong. And whether perpetrated against women or men, it is illegal. But you can understand how sexual harassment surfaces in organisations if you analyse it in terms of power.

We have seen how sexual harassment can wreak havoc on an organisation, but it can be avoided. A manager's role in preventing sexual harassment is critical. The following are some ways managers can protect themselves and their employees from sexual harassment:

1. Make sure a policy is in place that defines what constitutes sexual harassment, that informs employees that they can be fired for sexually harassing another employee, and that establishes procedures for how complaints can be made.
2. Assure employees that they won't encounter retaliation if they issue a complaint.
3. Investigate every complaint, and include the legal and human resource departments.
4. Make sure that offenders are disciplined or terminated.
5. Set up in-house seminars to raise employee awareness of the issues surrounding sexual harassment.

The bottom line is that managers have a responsibility to protect their employees from a hostile work environment, but they also need to protect themselves. Managers may be unaware that one of their employees is being sexually harassed. But being unaware doesn't protect them or their organisation. If investigators believe a manager could have known about the harassment, both the manager and the company can be held liable.

POLITICS: POWER IN ACTION

LEARNING OBJECTIVE 6
Describe the importance of a political perspective

When people get together in groups, power will be exerted. People want to carve out a niche from which to exert influence, to earn rewards and to advance their careers.[33] When employees in organisations convert their power into action, we describe them as being engaged in politics. Those with good political skills have the ability to use their bases of power effectively.[34]

DEFINITION

There has been no shortage of definitions for organisational politics. Essentially, however, they have focused on the use of power to affect decision making in the organisation, or on behaviours by members that are self-serving and organisationally non-sanctioned.[35] For our purposes, we shall define **political behaviour** in organisations as activities that are not required as part of one's formal role in the organisation, but that influence, or attempt to influence, the distribution of advantages and disadvantages within the organisation.[36] This definition encompasses key elements from what most people mean when they talk about organisational politics. Political behaviour is outside one's specified job requirements. The behaviour requires some attempt to use one's power bases. In addition, our definition encompasses efforts to influence the goals, criteria or processes used for decision making when we state that politics is concerned with 'the distribution of advantages and disadvantages within the organisation'. Our definition is broad enough to include varied political behaviours such as withholding key information from decision makers, joining a coalition, whistle-blowing, spreading rumours, leaking confidential information about organisational activities to the media, exchanging favours with others in the organisation for mutual benefit, and lobbying on behalf of or against a particular individual or decision alternative.

political behaviour |
Activities that are not required as part of one's formal role in the organisation, but that influence, or attempt to influence, the distribution of advantages and disadvantages within the organisation.

legitimate political behaviour | Normal, everyday politics.

illegitimate political behaviour | Extreme political behaviour that violates the implied rules of the game.

A final comment relates to what has been referred to as the 'legitimate–illegitimate' dimension in political behaviour.[37] **Legitimate political behaviour** refers to normal, everyday politics—complaining to your supervisor, bypassing the chain of command, forming coalitions, obstructing organisational policies or decisions through inaction or excessive adherence to rules, and developing contacts outside the organisation through one's professional activities. On the other hand, there are also **illegitimate political behaviours** that violate the implied rules of the game. Those who pursue such extreme activities are often described as individuals who 'play hardball'. Illegitimate activities include sabotage, whistle-blowing, and symbolic protests such as wearing unorthodox dress or protest buttons, and groups of employees simultaneously calling in sick.

The vast majority of all organisational political actions are of the legitimate variety. The reasons are pragmatic: The extreme illegitimate forms of political behaviour pose a very real risk of loss of organisational membership or extreme sanctions against those who use them and then fall short in having enough power to ensure that they work.

THE REALITY OF POLITICS

Politics is a fact of life in organisations. People who ignore this fact of life do so at their own peril. But why, you may wonder, must politics exist? Isn't it possible for an organisation to be politics-free? It is *possible*, but most unlikely.

Organisations are made up of individuals and groups with different values, goals and interests.[38] This sets up the potential for conflict over resources. Departmental budgets, space allocations, project responsibilities and salary adjustments are just a few examples of the resources about whose allocation organisational members will disagree.

Resources in organisations are also limited, and this often turns potential conflict into real conflict.[39] If resources were abundant, then all the various constituencies within the organisation could satisfy their goals. But because resources are limited, not everyone's interests can be provided for. Furthermore, whether true or not, gains by one individual or group are often *perceived* as being at the expense of others within the organisation. These forces create competition among members for the organisation's limited resources.

Australian of the Year Awards 2006

Whistle-blowing is considered an illegitimate political behaviour that often results in negative outcomes for the staff member. That's what happened to intensive care nurse, Toni Hoffman, who blew the whistle on the questionable practices of Dr Jayant Patel in 2004 at the Bundaberg hospital of Queensland Health. Hoffman sent an email to the hospital's director of medical services, Dr Darren Keating, complaining about Dr Patel just ten weeks after he arrived to work at the hospital. Nothing happened. She continued to complain, and was admonished for being racist, or for not being able to manage Dr Patel's 'difficult' personality. However, Toni Hoffman was exonerated as a result of the subsequent Royal Commission into the practices at the hospital. She even received a 'Local Hero of the Year' award from Prime Minister John Howard in 2006.

Maybe the most important factor leading to politics within organisations is the realisation that most of the 'facts' that are used to allocate the limited resources are open to interpretation. What, for instance, is *good* performance? What is an *adequate* improvement? What constitutes an *unsatisfactory* job? One person's view that an act is a 'selfless effort to benefit the organisation' is seen by another as a 'blatant attempt to further one's interest'.[40]

The coach of any major rugby league or rugby union team knows that a goal-kicker with an 82 per cent kicking success rate is a high performer, and a kicker with a 50 per cent kicking rate is a poor performer. You don't need to be a rocket scientist to know you should keep the goal-kicker with the 82 per cent success rate and relegate the 50 per cent kicker down to reserve grade. However, what if you have to choose between players with 79 per cent and 82 per cent kicking success? Then other factors—less objective ones—come into play: tackling rates, game expertise, attitude, potential, ability to perform in the scrum, loyalty to the team, and so on. Managerial decisions more closely resemble choosing between the 79 per cent and the 82 per cent goal-kicker than deciding between a 50 per cent and an 82 per cent goal-kicker. It is in this large and ambiguous middle ground of organisational life—where the facts *don't* speak for themselves—that politics flourish (see Table 14.2).

Finally, because most decisions have to be made in a climate of ambiguity—where facts are rarely fully objective, and thus are open to interpretation—people within organisations will use whatever influence they can to taint the facts to support their goals and interests. That, of course, creates the activities we call *politicking*.

TABLE 14.2

Politics is in the eye of the beholder

A behaviour that one person labels as 'organisational politics' is very likely to be characterised as an instance of 'effective management' by another. The fact is not that effective management is necessarily political, although in some cases it might be. Rather, a person's reference point determines what they classify as organisational politics. Take a look at the following labels used to describe the same phenomenon. These suggest that politics, like beauty, is in the eye of the beholder.

'Political' label		'Effective management' label	
1.	Blaming others	1.	Fixing responsibility
2.	'Sucking up'	2.	Developing working relationships
3.	Apple polishing	3.	Demonstrating loyalty
4.	Passing the buck	4.	Delegating authority
5.	Covering your rear	5.	Documenting decisions
6.	Creating conflict	6.	Encouraging change and innovation
7.	Forming coalitions	7.	Facilitating teamwork
8.	Whistle-blowing	8.	Improving efficiency
9.	Scheming	9.	Planning ahead
10.	Overachieving	10.	Competent and capable
11.	Ambitious	11.	Career-minded
12.	Opportunistic	12.	Astute
13.	Cunning	13.	Practical-minded
14.	Arrogant	14.	Confident
15.	Perfectionist	15.	Attentive to detail

SOURCE: Based on T. C. Krell, M. E. Mendenhall and J. Sendry, 'Doing Research in the Conceptual Morass of Organizational Politics', Paper presented at the Western Academy of Management Conference, Hollywood, California, April 1987.

Therefore, to answer the earlier question of whether it is possible for an organisation to be politics-free, we can say: 'Yes', if all members of that organisation hold the same goals and interests, if organisational resources aren't scarce, and if performance outcomes are completely clear and objective. But that doesn't describe the organisational world in which most of us live.

FACTORS CONTRIBUTING TO POLITICAL BEHAVIOUR

Not all groups or organisations are equally political. In some organisations, for instance, politicking is overt and rampant, while in others, politics plays a small role in influencing outcomes. Why is there this variation? Recent research and observation have identified a number of factors that appear to encourage political behaviour. Some are individual characteristics, derived from the unique qualities of the people the organisation employs; others are a result of the organisation's culture or internal environment. Figure 14.1 illustrates how both individual and organisational factors can increase political behaviour and provide favourable outcomes (increased rewards and averted punishments) for both individuals and groups in the organisation.

INDIVIDUAL FACTORS

At the individual level, researchers have identified certain personality traits, needs and other factors that are likely to be related to political behaviour. In terms of traits, we find that employees who are high self-monitors, possess an internal locus of control and have a high need for power are more likely to engage in political behaviour.[41] The high self-monitor is more sensitive to social cues, exhibits higher levels of social conformity and is more likely to be skilled in political behaviour than the low self-monitor. Individuals with an internal locus of control, because they believe they can control their environment, are more prone to take a proactive stance and attempt to manipulate situations in their favour. Not surprisingly, the Machiavellian personality—which is characterised by the will to manipulate and the desire for power—is comfortable using politics as a means to further his or her self-interest.

■ FIGURE 14.1

Factors that influence political behaviour

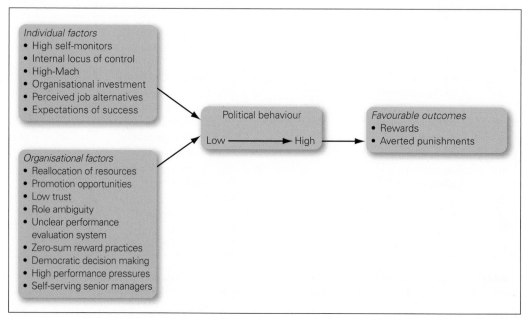

In addition, an individual's investment in the organisation, perceived alternatives and expectations of success will influence the degree to which he or she will pursue illegitimate means of political action.[42] The more a person has invested in the organisation in terms of expectations of increased future benefits, the more that person has to lose if forced out and the less likely he or she is to use illegitimate means. The more alternative job opportunities an individual has—due to a favourable job market or the possession of scarce skills or knowledge, a prominent reputation, or influential contacts outside the organisation—the more likely that individual is to risk illegitimate political actions. Finally, if an individual has a low expectation of success in using illegitimate means, it is unlikely that he or she will attempt to do so. High expectations of success in the use of illegitimate means are most likely to be the province of both experienced and powerful individuals with polished political skills and inexperienced and naive employees who misjudge their chances.

ORGANISATIONAL FACTORS

Political activity is probably more a function of the organisation's characteristics than of individual difference variables. Why? Because many organisations have a large number of employees with the individual characteristics we listed, yet the extent of political behaviour varies widely.

Although we acknowledge the role that individual differences can play in fostering politicking, the evidence more strongly supports that certain situations and cultures promote politics. More specifically, when an organisation's resources are declining, when the existing pattern of resources is changing, and when there is opportunity for promotions, politicking is more likely to surface.[43] In addition, cultures characterised by low trust, role ambiguity, unclear performance evaluation systems, zero-sum reward allocation practices, democratic decision making, high pressures for performance, and self-serving senior managers will create breeding grounds for politicking.[44]

When organisations downsize to improve efficiency, reductions in resources have to be made. Threatened with the loss of resources, people may engage in political actions to safeguard what they have. But any changes, especially those that imply significant reallocation of resources within the organisation, are likely to stimulate conflict and increase politicking.

Promotion decisions have consistently been found to be one of the most political actions in organisations. The opportunity for promotions or advancement encourages people to compete for a limited resource and to try to positively influence the decision outcome.

The less trust there is within the organisation, the higher the level of political behaviour and the more likely that the political behaviour will be of the illegitimate kind. So, high trust should suppress the level of political behaviour in general and inhibit illegitimate actions in particular.

Role ambiguity means that the prescribed behaviours of the employee are not clear. There are fewer limits, therefore, to the scope and functions of the employee's political actions. Because political activities are defined as those not required as part of one's formal role, the greater the role ambiguity, the more one can engage in political activity with little chance of it being visible.

The practice of performance evaluation is far from a perfect science. The more that organisations use subjective criteria in the appraisal, emphasise a single outcome measure, or allow significant time to pass between the time of an action and its appraisal, the greater the likelihood that an employee can get away with politicking. Subjective performance criteria create ambiguity. The use of a single outcome measure encourages individuals to do whatever is necessary to 'look good' on that measure, but often at the expense of performing well on other important parts of the job that are not being appraised. The amount of time that elapses between an action and its appraisal is also a relevant factor. The longer the time, the more unlikely that the employee will be held accountable for his or her political behaviours.

The more that an organisation's culture emphasises the zero-sum or win–lose approach to reward allocations, the more employees will be motivated to engage in politicking. The zero-sum approach treats the reward 'pie' as fixed, so that any gain one person or group achieves has to come at the expense of another person or group. If I win, you must lose! If $15 000 in annual raises is to be distributed among five employees, then any employee who gets more than $3000 takes money away from one or more of the others. Such a practice encourages making others look bad and increasing the visibility of what you do.

Since the mid-1970s, there has been a general move in Australia and among most developed nations towards making organisations less autocratic. Managers in these organisations are being asked to behave more democratically. They are told that they should allow employees to advise them on decisions and that they should rely to a greater extent on group input into the decision process. Such moves towards democracy, however, are not necessarily embraced by all individual managers. Many managers sought their positions in order to have legitimate power so as to be able to make unilateral decisions. They fought hard and often paid high personal costs to achieve their influential positions. Sharing their power with others runs directly against their desires. The result is that managers, especially those who began their careers in the 1960s and 1970s, may use the required committees, conferences and group meetings in a superficial way, as arenas for manoeuvring and manipulating.

The more pressure that employees feel to perform well, the more likely they are to engage in politicking. When people are held strictly accountable for outcomes, this puts great pressure on them to 'look good'. If a person perceives that his or her entire career is riding on next quarter's sales figures or next month's plant productivity report, there is motivation to do whatever is necessary to make sure the numbers come out favourably.

Finally, when employees see the people on top engaging in political behaviour, especially when they do so successfully and are rewarded for it, a climate is created that supports politicking. Politicking by top management, in a sense, gives permission to those lower in the organisation to play politics by implying that such behaviour is acceptable.

HOW DO PEOPLE RESPOND TO ORGANISATIONAL POLITICS?

Trish O'Donnell loves her job as a writer on a weekly television comedy series but hates the internal politics. 'A couple of the writers here spend more time kissing up to the executive producer than doing any work. And our head writer clearly has his favourites. While they pay me a lot and I get to really use my creativity, I'm sick of having to be on alert for backstabbers and constantly having to self-promote my contributions. I'm tired of doing most of the work and getting little of the credit.' Are Trish O'Donnell's comments typical of people who work in highly politicised workplaces? We all know of friends or relatives who regularly complain about the politics at their job. But how do people in general react to organisational politics? Let's look at the evidence.

In our discussion earlier in this chapter of factors that contribute to political behaviour, we focused on the favourable outcomes for individuals who successfully engage in politicking. But for most people—who have modest political skills or are unwilling to play the politics game—outcomes tend to be predominantly negative.

Figure 14.2 summarises the extensive research on the relationship between organisational politics and individual outcomes.[45] There is, for instance, very strong evidence indicating that perceptions of organisational politics are negatively related to job satisfaction.[46] The perception of politics also tends to increase job anxiety and stress. This seems to be due to the perception that, by not engaging in politics, a person may be losing ground to others who are active politickers; or, conversely, because of the additional pressures individuals feel because of having entered into and competing in the political arena.[47] Not surprisingly, when politicking becomes too much to handle, it can lead to employees quitting.[48] Finally, there is preliminary evidence suggesting that politics leads to self-reported declines in employee performance. This may occur because employees perceive political environments to be unfair, which demotivates them.[49]

In addition to these conclusions, several interesting qualifiers have been noted. First, the politics–performance relationship appears to be moderated by an individual's understanding of the 'hows' and 'whys' of organisational politics. 'An individual who has a clear understanding of who is responsible for making decisions and why they were selected to be the decision makers would have a better understanding of how and why things happen the way they do than someone who does not understand the decision-making process in the organisation.'[50] When both politics and understanding are high, performance is likely to increase because the individual will see political actions as an opportunity. This is consistent with what you might expect among individuals with well-honed political skills. But when understanding is low, individuals are more likely to see politics as a threat, which would have a negative effect on job performance.[51] Second, when politics is seen as a threat and consistently responded to with defensiveness, negative outcomes are almost sure to surface eventually. When people perceive politics as a threat rather than as an opportunity, they often respond with **defensive behaviours**—reactive and protective behaviours to avoid action, blame or change.[52] (Table 14.3 provides some examples of these defensive behaviours.) And defensive behaviours are often associated with negative feelings towards the job and work environment.[53] In the short run, employees may find that defensiveness protects their self-interest. But in the long run, it

defensive behaviours | Reactive and protective behaviours to avoid action, blame or change.

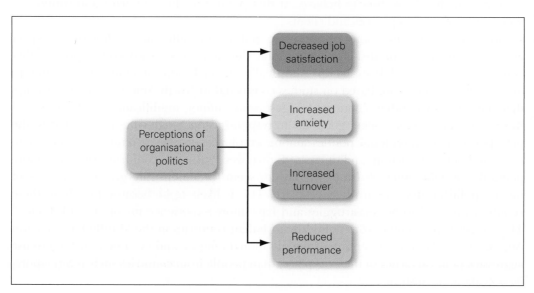

■ FIGURE 14.2
Employee responses to organisational politics

Avoiding action

Overconforming. Strictly interpreting your responsibility by saying things like, 'The rules clearly state . . .' or 'This is the way we've always done it.'

Buck passing. Transferring responsibility for the execution of a task or decision to someone else.

Playing dumb. Avoiding an unwanted task by falsely pleading ignorance or inability.

Stretching. Prolonging a task so that one appears to be occupied—for example, turning a two-week task into a four-month job.

Stalling. Appearing to be more or less supportive publicly while doing little or nothing privately.

Avoiding blame

Buffing. This is a nice way to refer to 'covering your rear'. It describes the practice of rigorously documenting activity to project an image of competence and thoroughness.

Playing safe. Evading situations that may reflect unfavourably. It includes taking on only projects with a high probability of success, having risky decisions approved by superiors, qualifying expressions of judgment, and taking neutral positions in conflicts.

Justifying. Developing explanations that lessen one's responsibility for a negative outcome and/or apologising to demonstrate remorse.

Scapegoating. Placing the blame for a negative outcome on external factors that are not entirely blameworthy.

Misrepresenting. Manipulation of information by distortion, embellishment, deception, selective presentation or obfuscation.

Avoiding change

Prevention. Trying to prevent a threatening change from occurring.

Self-protection. Acting in ways to protect one's self-interest during change by guarding information or other resources.

wears them down. People who consistently rely on defensiveness find that, eventually, it is the only way they know how to behave. At that point, they lose the trust and support of their peers, bosses, employees and clients.

Are our conclusions about responses to politics globally valid? Should we expect employees in Israel, for instance, to respond the same way to workplace politics that employees in Israel and Australia do? Almost all our conclusions on employee reactions to organisational politics are based on studies conducted in North America. The few studies that have included other countries suggest some minor modifications.[54] Britons and Australians, for instance, seem generally to respond as do North Americans. That is, the perception of organisational politics among employees in these countries is related to decreased job satisfaction and increased turnover.[55] But in countries that are more politically unstable, such as Israel, employees seem to demonstrate greater tolerance of intense political processes in the workplace. This is likely to be because people in these countries are used to power struggles and have more experience in coping with them.[56] This suggests that people from politically turbulent countries in the Middle East or Latin America might be more accepting of organisational politics, and even more willing to use aggressive political tactics in the workplace, than people from countries such as Singapore, New Zealand or Australia.

'PEOPLE ARE GOOD AT CATCHING LIARS AT WORK'

This sentence is essentially false. The core purpose of communication in the workplace may be to convey business-related information. However, the workplace also is a place where we communicate in order to manage impressions others form of us. Some of this impression management is unintentional and harmless (for example, complimenting your boss on his clothing). However, sometimes people manage impressions through outright lies, such as making up an excuse for missing work and failing to make a deadline.

One of the reasons that people lie, in the workplace and otherwise, is that it is hard to catch someone out in a lie. Although most of us think we are good at detecting a lie, research shows that most people perform no better than chance at detecting whether someone is lying or telling the truth.

Lying is also hard to prove. For example, research shows that negotiators often lie during negotiations. A seller may claim to have another buyer waiting in the wings when in fact there is no such potential buyer. Research shows that this 'cheap talk' can be an effective tactic in negotiation.

Consider Richard Scrushy, former CEO of HealthSouth, who was acquitted on 36 charges of false reporting, conspiracy, fraud and money laundering, even though 15 people who worked for Scrushy told the jury that he lied about HealthSouth's earnings in order to inflate his own compensation (which was tied to HealthSouth's performance). Clearly, it was hard for the jury to separate out who was telling the truth. In some cases, we may never know the truth.

The point? Don't believe everything you hear, and don't place too much weight on your ability to catch a liar based just on your intuition. When someone makes a claim that is reasonable to doubt, ask him or her to back it up with evidence.

SOURCES: N. I. Etcoff, P. Ekman, J. J. Magee and N. G. Franks, 'Lie Detection and Language Comprehension', *Nature*, May 2000, p. 139; R. Croson, T. Boles and J. K. Murnighan, 'Cheap Talk in Bargaining Experiments: Lying and Threats in Ultimatum Games', *Journal of Economic Behavior & Organization*, vol. 51, 2003, pp. 143–59; and 'Cases of Scrushy's Aides Still Pending', *The Los Angeles Times*, 5 July 2005: <www.latimes.com>.

IMPRESSION MANAGEMENT

We know that people have an ongoing interest in how others perceive and evaluate them. For example, North Americans spend billions of dollars on diets, health club memberships, cosmetics and plastic surgery—all intended to make them more attractive to others.[57] And Australians are also spending more in this regard. Being perceived positively by others should have benefits for people in organisations. It might, for instance, help them initially to get the jobs they want in an organisation and, once hired, to get favourable evaluations, superior salary increases and more rapid promotions. In a political context, it might help sway the distribution of advantages in their favour. The process by which individuals attempt to control the impression others form of them is called **impression management (IM)**.[58] It is a subject that has gained the attention of OB researchers only recently.[59]

Is everyone concerned with impression management? No! Who, then, might we predict to engage in IM? No surprise here! It is our old friend, the high self-monitor.[60] Low self-monitors tend to present images of themselves that are consistent with their personalities, regardless of the beneficial or detrimental effects for them. In contrast, high self-monitors are good at reading situations and moulding their appearance and behaviour to fit each situation. Given that you want to control the impression others form of you, what techniques could you use? Table 14.4 summarises some of the more popular IM techniques and provides an example of each.

LEARNING OBJECTIVE 9

Identify seven techniques for managing the impression one makes on others

impression management | The process by which individuals attempt to control the impression others form of them.

Keep in mind that IM doesn't imply that the impressions people convey are necessarily false (although, of course, they sometimes are).[61] Excuses, for instance, may be offered with sincerity. Referring to the example used in Table 14.4, you can *actually* believe that ads contribute little to sales in your region. But misrepresentation can have a high cost. If the image claimed is false, you may be discredited.[62] If you 'cry wolf' once too often, no one is likely to believe you when the wolf really comes. So, the impression manager must be cautious not to be perceived as insincere or manipulative.[63]

Are there *situations* in which individuals are more likely to misrepresent themselves or more likely to get away with it? Yes—situations that are characterised by high uncertainty

Conformity

Agreeing with someone else's opinion in order to gain their approval.

Example: A manager tells his boss, 'You're absolutely right on your reorganisation plan for the Victorian regional office. I couldn't agree with you more.'

Excuses

Explanations of a predicament-creating event aimed at minimising the apparent severity of the predicament.

Example: Sales manager to boss, 'We failed to get the ad in the paper on time, but no one responds to those ads anyway.'

Apologies

Admitting responsibility for an undesirable event and simultaneously seeking to get a pardon for the action.

Example: Employee to boss, 'I'm sorry I made a mistake on the report. Please forgive me.'

Self-promotion

Highlighting one's best qualities, downplaying one's deficits and calling attention to one's achievements.

Example: A salesperson tells his boss: 'Matt worked unsuccessfully for three years to try to get that account. I sewed it up in six weeks. I'm the best closer this company has.'

Flattery

Complimenting others about their virtues in an effort to make oneself appear perceptive and likeable.

Example: New sales trainee to peer, 'You handled that client's complaint so tactfully! I could never have handled that as well as you did.'

Favours

Doing something nice for someone to gain that person's approval.

Example: Salesperson to prospective client, 'I've got two tickets to the theatre tonight that I can't use. Take them. Consider it a thank-you for taking the time to talk with me.'

Association

Enhancing or protecting one's image by managing information about people and things with which one is associated.

Example: A job applicant says to an interviewer, 'What a coincidence. Your boss and I were flatmates at university.'

SOURCES: Based on B. R. Schlenker, *Impression Management* (Monterey, CA: Brooks/Cole, 1980); W. L. Gardner and M. J. Martinko, 'Impression Management in Organizations', *Journal of Management*, June 1988, p. 332; and R. B. Cialdini, 'Indirect Tactics of Image Management: Beyond Basking', in R. A. Giacalone and P. Rosenfeld (eds), *Impression Management in the Organization* (Hillsdale, NJ: Lawrence Erlbaum Associates, 1989), pp. 45–71.

or ambiguity provide relatively little information for challenging a fraudulent claim and reduce the risks associated with misrepresentation.[64] Most of the studies undertaken to test the effectiveness of IM techniques have related it to two criteria: (1) interview success, and (2) performance evaluations. Let's consider each of these.

The evidence indicates that most job applicants use IM techniques in interviews[65] and that, when IM behaviour is used, it works.[66] In one study, for instance, interviewers felt that applicants for a position as a customer service representative who used IM techniques performed better in the interview, and they seemed somewhat more inclined to hire these people.[67] Moreover, when the researchers considered applicants' credentials, they concluded that it was the IM techniques alone that influenced the interviewers. That is, it didn't seem to matter if applicants were well or poorly qualified. If they used IM techniques, they did better in the interview.

Research indicates that some IM techniques work better than others in interviews. Researchers have compared applicants who used IM techniques that focused on promoting one's accomplishments (called *self-promotion*) to applicants who used techniques that focused on complimenting the interviewer and finding areas of agreement (referred to as *ingratiation*). In general, applicants appear to use self-promotion more than ingratiation.[68] What's more, self-promotion tactics may be more important to interviewing success. Applicants who work to create an appearance of competence by enhancing their accomplishments, taking credit for successes and explaining away failures do better in interviews. These effects reach beyond the interview—applicants who use more self-promotion tactics also seem to get more follow-up job-site visits, even after adjusting for grade-point average, gender and job type. Ingratiation also works well in the interview, meaning that applicants who compliment the interviewer, agree with his or her opinions and emphasise areas of fit do better than those who don't.[69]

In terms of performance ratings, the picture is quite different. Ingratiation is positively related to performance ratings, meaning that those who ingratiate with their supervisors get higher performance evaluations. However, self-promotion appears to backfire—those who self-promote actually seem to receive *lower* performance evaluations.[70]

What explains these results? If you think about them, they make sense. Ingratiating always works because everyone likes to be treated nicely, whether it be the interviewer or the supervisor. However, self-promotion may work only in interviews and backfire on the job because whereas the interviewer has little idea whether you are blowing smoke about your accomplishments, the supervisor knows because it is his or her job to observe you. Thus, if you are going to self-promote, remember that what works in the interview won't always work once you are on the job.

THE ETHICS OF BEHAVING POLITICALLY

We conclude our discussion of politics by providing some ethical guidelines for political behaviour. Although there are no clear-cut ways to differentiate ethical from unethical politicking, there are some questions you should consider.

Figure 14.3 illustrates a decision tree to guide ethical actions. This tree is built on the three ethical decision criteria—utilitarianism, rights and justice—presented in a previous chapter. The first question you need to answer addresses self-interest versus organisational goals. Ethical actions are consistent with the organisation's goals. Spreading untrue rumours about the safety of a new product introduced by your company, in order to make that product's design team look bad, is unethical. However, there may be nothing unethical

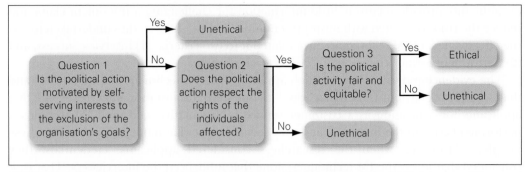

if a department head exchanges work favours with her division's purchasing manager in order to get a critical contract processed quickly.

The second question concerns the rights of other parties. If the department head went down to the mail room during her lunch hour and read through the mail directed to the purchasing manager—with the intent of 'getting something on him' so that he would expedite the contract—she would be acting unethically. She would have violated the purchasing manager's right to privacy.

The final question that needs to be addressed relates to whether the political activity conforms to standards of equity and justice. The department head who inflates the performance evaluation of a favoured employee and deflates the evaluation of a disfavoured employee—and then uses these evaluations to justify giving the former a big raise and nothing to the latter—has treated the disfavoured employee unfairly.

Unfortunately, the answers to the questions in Figure 14.3 are often argued in ways to make unethical practices seem ethical. Powerful people, for example, can become very good at explaining self-serving behaviours in terms of the organisation's best interests. Similarly, they can persuasively argue that unfair actions are really fair and just. Our point is that immoral people can justify almost any behaviour. Those who are powerful, articulate and persuasive are most vulnerable because they are likely to be able to get away with unethical practices successfully. When faced with an ethical dilemma regarding organisational politics, try to answer the questions in Figure 14.3 truthfully. If you have a strong power base, recognise the ability of power to corrupt. Remember, it is a lot easier for the powerless to act ethically, if for no other reason than they typically have very little political discretion to exploit.

SELF-ASSESSMENT LIBRARY

HOW GOOD AM I AT PLAYING POLITICS?

In the Self-Assessment Library (available on CD and online), take Self-Assessment II.C.3 (How Good Am I at Playing Politics?) and answer the following questions.

1. How did you score relative to your classmates? Do you think your score is accurate? Why or why not?

2. Do you think skills are important in the workplace? If yes, why? If no, why not?

3. Would you want to be known for your political skills? If yes, why? If not, why not?

SUMMARY AND IMPLICATIONS FOR MANAGERS

- If you want to get things done in a group or organisation, it helps to have power. As a manager who wants to maximise your power, you will want to increase others' dependence on you.
- You can, for instance, increase your power in relation to your boss by developing knowledge or a skill that she needs and for which she perceives no ready substitute. But power is a two-way street. You won't be alone in attempting to build your power bases.
- Others, particularly employees and peers, will be seeking to make you dependent on them. The result is a continual battle. While you seek to maximise others' dependence on you, you will be seeking to minimise your dependence on others. And, of course, others you work with will be trying to do the same.
- Few employees relish being powerless in their job and organisation. It has been argued, for instance, that when people in organisations are difficult, argumentative and temperamental, it may be because they are in positions of powerlessness; positions in which the performance expectations placed on them exceed their resources and capabilities.[71]
- There is evidence that people respond differently to the various power bases.[72]
- Expert and referent power are derived from an individual's personal qualities.
- In contrast, coercion, reward and legitimate power are essentially organisationally derived. Because people are more likely to enthusiastically accept and commit to an individual whom they admire or whose knowledge they respect (rather than someone who relies on his or her position for influence), the effective use of expert and referent power should lead to higher employee motivation, performance, commitment and satisfaction.[73]

- Competence especially appears to offer wide appeal, and its use as a power base results in high performance by group members.
- The message for managers seems to be: develop and use your expert power base!
- The power of your boss may also play a role in determining your job satisfaction. 'One of the reasons many of us like to work for and with people who are powerful is that they are generally more pleasant—not because it is their native disposition, but because the reputation and reality of being powerful permits them more discretion and more ability to delegate to others.'[74]
- The effective manager accepts the political nature of organisations. By assessing behaviour in a political framework, you can better predict the actions of others and use this information to formulate political strategies that will gain advantages for you and your work unit.
- Some people are significantly more 'politically astute' than others, meaning that they are aware of the underlying politics and can manage impressions.
- Those who are good at playing politics can be expected to get higher performance evaluations and, hence, larger salary increases and more promotions than the politically naive or inept.[75]
- The politically astute are also likely to exhibit higher job satisfaction and be better able to neutralise job stressors.[76]
- For employees with poor political skills or who are unwilling to play the politics game, the perception of organisational politics is generally related to lower job satisfaction and self-reported performance, increased anxiety and higher turnover.

POINT / COUNTERPOINT

Managing Impressions is Unethical

● POINT

Managing impressions is wrong for both ethical and practical reasons.

First, managing impressions is just another name for lying. Don't we have a responsibility, both to ourselves and to others, to present ourselves as we really are? The Australian philosopher Tony Coady wrote, 'Dishonesty has always been perceived in our culture, and in all cultures but the most bizarre, as a central human vice.' Immanuel Kant's Categorical Imperative asks us to consider the following: If you want to know whether telling a lie on a particular occasion is justifiable, you must try to imagine what would happen if everyone were to lie. Surely you would agree that a world in which no one lies is preferable to one in which lying is common, because in such a world we could never trust anyone. Thus, we should try to present the truth as best we can. Impression management goes against this virtue.

Practically speaking, impression management generally backfires in the long run. Remember Sir Walter Scott's quote, 'Oh what a tangled web we weave, when first we practise to deceive!' Once we start to distort the facts, where do we stop?

Former Australian Federal Court judge Marcus Einfeld obtained doctoral degrees from two US universities that the US Congress described as 'diploma mill' organisations with no authority for granting such awards. This revelation came out when Mr Einfeld faced a fraud squad investigation into evidence he gave to a Sydney magistrate's court that allowed him to avoid a $77 speeding fine. He told the Downing Centre Local Court that at the time of the offence, he had lent his car to an Australian-born academic, who it was subsequently discovered had died before the incident. While the speeding incident was significant, the issue of the disreputable doctorates was a greater concern for the integrity of the Federal Court system.

At a number of universities, the code of ethics instructs students to provide only truthful information on their résumés and obligates them to be honest in interviews.

People are most satisfied with their jobs when their values match the culture of their organisation. If either side misrepresents itself in the interview process, then odds are people won't fit in the organisations they choose. What is the benefit in this?

This doesn't imply that a person shouldn't put his or her best foot forward. But it does mean exhibiting qualities that are good no matter the context—being friendly, being positive and self-confident, being qualified and competent, while still being honest.

● COUNTERPOINT

Oh, come on. Get off your high horse. *Everybody* fudges to some degree in the process of applying for a job. If you really told the interviewer what your greatest weakness or worst mistake was, you'd never get hired. What if you answered, 'I find it hard to get up in the morning and get to work'?

These sorts of 'white lies' are expected and act as a kind of social lubricant in society. If we really knew what people were thinking, we would go crazy. Moreover, you can quote all the philosophy you want, but sometimes it is necessary to lie. You mean you wouldn't lie to save the life of your family? It is naïve to think we can live in a world without lying.

Sometimes a bit of deception is necessary to get a job. I know a gay applicant who was rejected from a job he really wanted because he told the interviewer he had written two articles for gay magazines. What if he had told the interviewer a little lie? Would harm really have been done? At least he would have a job.

As another example, when an interviewer asks you what you earned on your previous job, that information will be used against you, to pay you a salary lower than you deserve. Is it wrong to boost your salary a bit? Or would it be better to disclose your actual salary and be taken advantage of?

The same goes for complimenting interviewers, or agreeing with their opinions, and so forth. If an interviewer tells you, 'We believe in community involvement', are you supposed to tell the interviewer that you have never volunteered for anything?

Of course, one can go too far. We are not advocating that people totally fabricate their backgrounds. What we are talking about here is a reasonable amount of enhancement. If we can help ourselves without doing any real harm, then impression management is not the same as lying, and actually is something we should teach others.

SOURCE: A point in this argument was based on <www.theaustralian.news.com.au/story/0,20867,20177812-2702,00.html>.

QUESTIONS FOR REVIEW

MyOBLab Do you understand this chapter's content? Find out at **www.pearsoned.com.au/MyOBLab**

1. What is power? How do you get it?
2. Which power bases lie with the individual? Which are derived from the organisation?
3. State the general dependency postulate. What does it mean?
4. What creates dependency? Give an applied example.
5. Contrast power tactics with power bases. What are some of the key contingency variables that determine which tactic a power holder is likely to use?
6. What is a coalition? When is it likely to develop?
7. How are power and politics related?
8. Define *political behaviour*. Why is politics a fact of life in organisations?
9. What factors contribute to political activity?
10. What is impression management? What types of people are most likely to engage in IM?

1. Based on the information presented in this chapter, what would you do as a recent university graduate entering a new job to maximise your power and accelerate your career progress?
2. 'Politics isn't inherently bad. It's merely a way to get things accomplished within organisations.' Do you agree or disagree? Defend your position.
3. You are a sales representative for an international software company. After four excellent years, sales in your territory are off 30 per cent this year. Describe three defensive responses you might use to reduce the potential negative consequences of this decline in sales.
4. 'Sexual harassment shouldn't be tolerated in the workplace.' 'Workplace romances are a natural occurrence in organisations.' Are both of these statements true? Can they be reconciled?
5. Which impression management techniques have you used? What ethical implications are there, if any, in using IM?

EXPERIENTIAL EXERCISE

Understanding Power Dynamics

Creation of groups:
Each student is to give a dollar coin (or similar value of currency) to the lecturer. Students are then divided into three groups based on criteria given by the lecturer, assigned to their work areas, and instructed to read the following rules and tasks. The money is divided into thirds, giving two-thirds of it to the top group, one-third to the middle group, and none to the bottom group.

Conduct exercise:
Groups go to their assigned workplaces and have 30 minutes to complete their tasks.

Rules:
a. Members of the top group are free to enter the space of either of the other groups and to communicate whatever they wish, whenever they wish. Members of the middle group may enter the space of the lower group when they wish, but must request permission to enter the top group's space (which the top group can refuse). Members of the lower group may not disturb the top group in any way unless specifically invited by the top group. The lower group does have the right to knock on the door of the middle group and request permission to communicate with them (which can also be refused).
b. The members of the top group have the authority to make any change in the rules that they wish, at any time, with or without notice.

Tasks:

a. *Top group.* To be responsible for the overall effectiveness and learning from the exercise, and to decide how to use its money.

b. *Middle group.* To assist the top group in providing for the overall welfare of the organisation, and to decide how to use its money.

c. *Bottom group.* To identify its resources and to decide how best to provide for learning and the overall effectiveness of the organisation.

Debriefing:

Each of the three groups chooses two representatives to go to the front of the class and discuss the following questions:

a. Summarise what occurred within and among the three groups.

b. What are some of the differences between being in the top group versus being in the bottom group?

c. What can we learn about power from this experience?

d. How accurate do you think this exercise is to the reality of resource allocation decisions in large organisations?

SOURCE: This exercise is adapted from L. Bolman and T. E. Deal, *Exchange*, vol. 3, no. 4, 1979, pp. 38–42. Reprinted by permission of Sage Publications, Inc.

ETHICAL DILEMMA

Swapping Personal Favours?

Jack Grubman was a powerful man on Wall Street. As a star analyst of telecom companies for the Salomon Smith Barney unit of Citigroup, he made recommendations that carried a lot of weight with investors.

For years, Grubman had been negative on the shares of AT&T. But in November 1999, he changed his opinion. Based on email evidence, it appears that Grubman's decision to upgrade AT&T wasn't based on the shares' fundamentals. There were other factors involved.

At the time, his boss at Citigroup, Sanford 'Sandy' Weill, was in the midst of a power struggle with co-CEO John Reed to become the single head of the company. Meanwhile, Salomon was looking for additional business to increase its revenues. Getting investment banking business fees from AT&T would be a big plus. And Salomon's chances of getting that AT&T business would definitely be improved if Grubman would upgrade his opinion on the stock. Furthermore, Weill sought Grubman's upgrade to win favour with AT&T CEO Michael Armstrong, who sat on Citigroup's board. Weill wanted Armstrong's backing in his efforts to oust Reed.

Grubman had his own concerns. Though earning tens of millions a year in his job, as the son of a city worker in Philadelphia he was a man of modest background. He wanted the best for his twin daughters, which included entry to an exclusive New York City nursery school (the posh 92nd Street Y [<www.92y.org/>])—a school that a year earlier had reportedly turned down Madonna's daughter. Weill made a call to the school on Grubman's behalf and pledged a US$1 million donation from Citigroup. At approximately the same time, Weill also asked Grubman to 'take a fresh look' at his neutral rating on AT&T. Shortly after being asked to review his rating, Grubman raised it, and AT&T awarded Salomon an investment-banking job worth nearly US$45 million. Shares of AT&T soared.

Did Sandy Weill do anything unethical? How about Jack Grubman? What do you think?

SOURCE: Based on C. Gasparino, 'Out of School', *Newsweek*, 17 January 2005, pp. 38–39.

CASE STUDY

14

The Politics of Backstabbing

Scott Rosen believed that he was making progress as an assistant manager of a financial-services company—until he noticed that his colleague, another assistant manager, was attempting to push him aside. On repeated occasions, Scott would observe his colleague speaking with their manager behind closed doors. During these conversations, Scott's colleague would attempt to persuade the supervisor that Scott was incompetent and mismanaging his job, a practice that Scott found out about after the fact. Scott recounts one specific instance of his colleague's backstabbing efforts: When asked a question by his subordinates to which Scott didn't know the answer, his colleague would state to their supervisor, 'I can't believe he didn't know something like that.' On other occasions, after instructing a subordinate to complete a specific task, Scott's colleague would say, 'I wouldn't make you do something like that.' What was the end result of such illegitimate political tactics? Scott was demoted, an action that led him to resign shortly after, while his colleague was promoted. 'Whatever I did, I lost,' said Scott.

What leads individuals to behave this way? According to Judith Briles, a management consultant who has studied extensively the practice of backstabbing, a tight job market is often a contributing factor. Fred Nader, another management consultant, believes that backstabbing is the result of 'some kind of character disorder'.

One executive at a technology company admits that blind ambition was responsible for his backstabbing. In 1999, he was assigned as an external sales representative, partnered with a colleague who worked internally at their client's office. The executive wanted the internal sales position for himself. To reach this goal, he systematically engaged in backstabbing to shatter his colleague's credibility. Each time he heard a complaint, however small, from the client, he would ask for it in an email and then forward the information to his boss. He would include a short message about his colleague, such as: 'I'm powerless to deal with this. She's not being responsive and the customer is putting pressure on me.' In addition, he would fail to share important information with his colleague before presentations with their boss, to convey the impression that she didn't know what she was talking about. He even took backstabbing so far as to schedule meetings with their boss on an electronic calendar but then altered his colleague's version so that she was late. Eventually, he convinced his boss that she was overworked. He was transferred to the client's office, while his colleague was moved back to the main office.

Incidents such as these may not be uncommon in the workplace. Given today's competitive work environment, employees may be using political games to move ahead. To guard against backstabbing, Bob McDonald, a management consultant, recommends telling supervisors and other key personnel that the backstabber isn't a friend. He states that this may be effective, because backstabbers often claim to be friends of their victims and then act as if they are hesitant about sharing negative information with others because of this professed friendship. In any event, it is clear that employees in organisations need to be aware of illegitimate political behaviour. Companies may need to adopt formal policies to safeguard employees against such behaviour; however, it may be the case that behaviours such as backstabbing and spreading negative rumours are difficult to detect. Thus, both employees and managers should try to verify information to avoid the negative repercussions that can come from backstabbing and other illegitimate behaviours.

ENDNOTES

1. <www.latrobe.edu.au/alumni/profiles/grad2.html> (accessed 27 October 2006).
2. R. M. Kanter, 'Power Failure in Management Circuits', *Harvard Business Review*, July–August 1979, p. 65.
3. J. Pfeffer, 'Understanding Power in Organizations', *California Management Review*, Winter 1992, p. 35.
4. Based on B. M. Bass, *Bass & Stogdill's Handbook of Leadership*, 3rd ed. (New York: Free Press, 1990).
5. J. R. P. French, Jr and B. Raven, 'The Bases of Social Power', in D. Cartwright (ed.), *Studies in Social Power* (Ann Arbor: University of Michigan, Institute for Social Research, 1959), pp. 150–67; B. J. Raven, 'The Bases of Power: Origins and Recent Developments', *Journal of Social Issues*, Winter 1993, pp. 227–51; and G. Yukl, 'Use Power Effectively', in E. A. Locke (ed.), *Handbook of Principles of Organizational Behavior* (Malden, MA: Blackwell, 2004), pp. 242–47.
6. E. A. Ward, 'Social Power Bases of Managers: Emergence of a New Factor', *Journal of Social Psychology*, February 2001, pp. 144–47.
7. P. M. Podsakoff and C. A. Schriesheim, 'Field Studies of French and Raven's Bases of Power: Critique, Reanalysis, and Suggestions for Future Research', *Psychological Bulletin*, May 1985, pp. 387–411; T. R. Hinkin and C. A. Schriesheim, 'Development and Application of New Scales to Measure the French and Raven (1959) Bases of Social Power', *Journal of Applied Psychology*, August 1989, pp. 561–67; and P. P. Carson, K. D. Carson and C. W. Roe, 'Social Power Bases: A Meta-Analytic Examination of Interrelationships and Outcomes', *Journal of Applied Social Psychology*, vol. 23, no. 14, 1993, pp. 1150–69.
8. J. L. Roberts, 'Striking a Hot Match', *Newsweek*, 24 January 2005, pp. 54–55.
9. R. E. Emerson, 'Power-Dependence Relations', *American Sociological Review*, February 1962, pp. 31–41.
10. H. Mintzberg, *Power In and Around Organizations* (Upper Saddle River, NJ: Prentice Hall, 1983), p. 24.
11. R. M. Cyert and J. G. March, *A Behavioral Theory of the Firm* (Upper Saddle River, NJ: Prentice Hall, 1963).
12. C. Perrow, 'Departmental Power and Perspective in Industrial Firms', in M. N. Zald (ed.), *Power in Organizations* (Nashville, TN: Vanderbilt University Press, 1970).
13. N. Foulkes, 'Tractor Boy', *High Life*, October 2002, p. 90.
14. See, for example, D. Kipnis, S. M. Schmidt, C. Swaffin-Smith and I. Wilkinson, 'Patterns of Managerial Influence: Shotgun Managers, Tacticians, and Bystanders', *Organizational Dynamics*, Winter 1984, pp. 58–67; D. Kipnis and S. M. Schmidt, 'Upward-Influence Styles: Relationship with Performance Evaluations, Salary, and Stress', *Administrative Science Quarterly*, December 1988, pp. 528–42; G. Yukl and J. B. Tracey, 'Consequences of Influence Tactics Used with Subordinates, Peers, and the Boss', *Journal of Applied Psychology*, August 1992, pp. 525–35; G. Blickle, 'Influence Tactics Used by Subordinates: An Empirical Analysis of the Kipnis and Schmidt Subscales', *Psychological Reports*, February 2000, pp. 143–54; and Yukl, 'Use Power Effectively', pp. 249–52.
15. G. Yukl, *Leadership in Organizations*, 5th ed. (Upper Saddle River, NJ: Prentice Hall, 2002), pp. 141–74; G. R. Ferris, W. A. Hochwarter, C. Douglas, F. R. Blass, R. W. Kolodinksy and D. C. Treadway, 'Social Influence Processes in Organizations and Human Resource Systems', in G. R. Ferris and J. J. Martocchio (eds), *Research in Personnel and Human Resources Management*, vol. 21 (Oxford, UK: JAI Press/Elsevier, 2003), pp. 65–127; and C. A. Higgins, T. A. Judge and G. R. Ferris, 'Influence Tactics and Work Outcomes: A Meta-Analysis', *Journal of Organizational Behavior*, March 2003, pp. 89–106.
16. C. M. Falbe and G. Yukl, 'Consequences for Managers of Using Single Influence Tactics and Combinations of Tactics', *Academy of Management Journal*, July 1992, pp. 638–53.
17. Yukl, *Leadership in Organizations*.
18. Ibid.
19. Falbe and Yukl, 'Consequences for Managers of Using Single Influence Tactics and Combinations of Tactics'.
20. Yukl, 'Use Power Effectively', p. 254.
21. P. P. Fu and G. Yukl, 'Perceived Effectiveness of Influence Tactics in the United States and China', *Leadership Quarterly*, Summer 2000, pp. 251–66; O. Branzei, 'Cultural Explanations of Individual Preferences for Influence Tactics in Cross-Cultural Encounters', *International Journal of Cross Cultural Management*, August 2002, pp. 203–18; G. Yukl, P. P. Fu and R. McDonald, 'Cross-Cultural Differences in Perceived Effectiveness of Influence Tactics for Initiating or Resisting Change', *Applied Psychology: An International Review*, January 2003, pp. 66–82; and P. P. Fu, T. K. Peng,

J. C. Kennedy and G. Yukl, 'Examining the Preferences of Influence Tactics in Chinese Societies: A Comparison of Chinese Managers in Hong Kong, Taiwan, and Mainland China', *Organizational Dynamics*, vol. 33, no. 1, 2004, pp. 32–46.

22. Fu and Yukl, 'Perceived Effectiveness of Influence Tactics in the United States and China'.

23. Based on W. B. Stevenson, J. L. Pearce and L. W. Porter, 'The Concept of "Coalition" in Organization Theory and Research', *Academy of Management Review*, April 1985, pp. 261–63.

24. S. B. Bacharach and E. J. Lawler, 'Political Alignments in Organizations', in R. M. Kramer and M. A. Neale (eds), *Power and Influence in Organizations* (Thousand Oaks, CA: Sage, 1998), pp. 75–77.

25. J. K. Murnighan and D. J. Brass, 'Intraorganizational Coalitions', in M. H. Bazerman, R. J. Lewicki and B. H. Sheppard (eds), *Research on Negotiation in Organizations* (Greenwich, CT: JAI Press, 1991).

26. See J. Pfeffer, *Power in Organizations* (Marshfield, MA: Pitman, 1981), pp. 155–57.

27. <www.humanresourcesmagazine.com.au/articles/B8/0C040FB8.asp?Type=61&Category=934>.

28. L. J. Munson, C. Hulin and F. Drasgow, 'Longitudinal Analysis of Dispositional Influences and Sexual Harassment: Effects on Job and Psychological Outcomes', *Personnel Psychology*, Spring 2000, pp. 21–46; T. M. Glomb, L. J. Munson, C. L. Hulin, M. E. Bergman and F. Drasgow, 'Structural Equation Models of Sexual Harassment: Longitudinal Explorations and Cross-Sectional Generalizations', *Journal of Applied Psychology*, February 1999, pp. 14–28; M. E. Bergman, R. D. Langhout, P. A. Palmieri, L. M. Cortina and L. F. Fitzgerald, 'The (Un)reasonableness of Reporting: Antecedents and Consequences of Reporting Sexual Harassment', *Journal of Applied Psychology*, April 2002, pp. 230–42; L. R. Offermann and A. B. Malamut, 'When Leaders Harass: The Impact of Target Perceptions of Organizational Leadership and Climate on Harassment Reporting and Outcomes', *Journal of Applied Psychology*, October 2002, pp. 885–93.

29. <www.hreoc.gov.au/sex_discrimination/challenge_continues/data/appenda.html>.

30. R. Ilies, N. Hauserman, S. Schwochau and J. Stibal, 'Reported Incidence Rates of Work-Related Sexual Harassment in the United States: Using Meta-Analysis to Explain Reported Rate Disparities', *Personnel Psychology*, Fall 2003, pp. 607–31.

31. M. Rotundo, D. Nguyen and P. R. Sackett, 'A Meta-Analytic Review of Gender Differences in Perceptions of Sexual Harassment', *Journal of Applied Psychology*, October 2001, pp. 914–22.

32. Ilies, Hauserman, Schwochau and Stibal, 'Reported Incidence Rates of Work-Related Sexual Harassment in the United States; A. B. Malamut and L. R. Offermann, 'Coping with Sexual Harassment: Personal, Environmental, and Cognitive Determinants', *Journal of Applied Psychology*, December 2001, pp. 1152–66; L. M. Cortina and S. A. Wasti, 'Profiles in Coping: Responses to Sexual Harassment across Persons, Organizations, and Cultures', *Journal of Applied Psychology*, February 2005, pp. 182–92; J. H. Wayne, 'Disentangling the Power Bases of Sexual Harassment: Comparing Gender, Age, and Position Power', *Journal of Vocational Behavior*, December 2000, pp. 301–25; and F. Wilson and P. Thompson, 'Sexual Harassment as an Exercise of Power', *Gender, Work & Organization*, January 2001, pp. 61–83.

33. S. A. Culbert and J. J. McDonough, *The Invisible War: Pursuing Self-Interest at Work* (New York: John Wiley, 1980), p. 6.

34. Mintzberg, *Power In and Around Organizations*, p. 26. See also K. M. Kacmar and R. A. Baron, 'Organizational Politics: The State of the Field, Links to Related Processes, and an Agenda for Future Research', in G. R. Ferris (ed.), *Research in Personnel and Human Resources Management*, vol. 17 (Greenwich, CT: JAI Press, 1999), pp. 1–39; and G. R. Ferris, D. C. Treadway, R. W. Kolokinsky, W. A. Hochwarter, C. J. Kacmar and D. D. Frink, 'Development and Validation of the Political Skill Inventory', *Journal of Management*, February 2005, pp. 126–52.

35. S. B. Bacharach and E. J. Lawler, 'Political Alignments in Organizations', in R. M. Kramer and M. A. Neale (eds), *Power and Influence in Organizations* (Thousand Oaks, CA: Sage, 1998), pp. 68–69.

36. D. Farrell and J. C. Petersen, 'Patterns of Political Behavior in Organizations', *Academy of Management Review*, July 1982, p. 405. For analyses of the controversies underlying the definition of

organisational politics, see A. Drory and T. Romm, 'The Definition of Organizational Politics: A Review', *Human Relations*, November 1990, pp. 1133–54; and R. S. Cropanzano, K. M. Kacmar and D. P. Bozeman, 'Organizational Politics, Justice, and Support: Their Differences and Similarities', in R. S. Cropanzano and K. M. Kacmar (eds), *Organizational Politics, Justice and Support: Managing Social Climate at Work* (Westport, CT: Quorum Books, 1995), pp. 1–18.

37. Farrell and Peterson, 'Patterns of Political Behavior', pp. 406–7; and A. Drory, 'Politics in Organization and Its Perception within the Organization', *Organization Studies*, vol. 9, no. 2, 1988, pp. 165–79.

38. Pfeffer, *Power in Organizations*.

39. Drory and Romm, 'The Definition of Organizational Politics'.

40. K. K. Eastman, 'Attributional Approach to Ingratiation and Organizational Citizenship Behavior', *Academy of Management Journal*, October 1994, pp. 1379–91; M. C. Bolino, 'Citizenship and Impression Management: Good Soldiers or Good Actors?', *Academy of Management Review*, January 1999, pp. 82–98; S. M. Rioux and L. A. Penner, 'The Causes of Organizational Citizenship Behavior: A Motivational Analysis', *Journal of Applied Psychology*, December 2001, pp. 1306–14; and M. A. Finkelstein and L. A. Penner, 'Predicting Organizational Citizenship Behavior: Integrating the Functional and Role Identity Approaches', *Social Behavior & Personality*, vol. 32, no. 4, 2004, pp. 383–98.

41. See, for example, G. Biberman, 'Personality and Characteristic Work Attitudes of Persons with High, Moderate, and Low Political Tendencies', *Psychological Reports*, October 1985, pp. 1303–10; R. J. House, 'Power and Personality in Complex Organizations', in B. M. Staw and L. L. Cummings (eds), *Research in Organizational Behavior*, vol. 10 (Greenwich, CT: JAI Press, 1988), pp. 305–57; G. R. Ferris, G. S. Russ and P. M. Fandt, 'Politics in Organizations', in R. A. Giacalone and P. Rosenfeld (eds), *Impression Management in the Organization* (Hillsdale, NJ: Lawrence Erlbaum Associates, 1989), pp. 155–56; and W. E. O'Connor and T. G. Morrison, 'A Comparison of Situational and Dispositional Predictors of Perceptions of Organizational Politics', *Journal of Psychology*, May 2001, pp. 301–12.

42. Farrell and Petersen, 'Patterns of Political Behavior', p. 408.

43. S. C. Goh and A. R. Doucet, 'Antecedent Situational Conditions of Organizational Politics: An Empirical Investigation', Paper presented at the Annual Administrative Sciences Association of Canada Conference, Whistler, BC, May 1986; C. Hardy, 'The Contribution of Political Science to Organizational Behavior', in J. W. Lorsch (ed.), *Handbook of Organizational Behavior* (Englewood Cliffs, NJ: Prentice Hall, 1987), p. 103; and G. R. Ferris and K. M. Kacmar, 'Perceptions of Organizational Politics', *Journal of Management*, March 1992, pp. 93–116.

44. See, for example, Farrell and Petersen, 'Patterns of Political Behavior', p. 409; P. M. Fandt and G. R. Ferris, 'The Management of Information and Impressions: When Employees Behave Opportunistically', *Organizational Behavior and Human Decision Processes*, February 1990, pp. 140–58; Ferris, Russ and Fandt, 'Politics in Organizations', p. 147; and J. M. L. Poon, 'Situational Antecedents and Outcomes of Organizational Politics Perceptions', *Journal of Managerial Psychology*, vol. 18, no. 2, 2003, pp. 138–55.

45. G. R. Ferris, G. S. Russ and P. M. Fandt, 'Politics in Organizations', in R. A. Giacalone and P. Rosenfeld (eds), *Impression Management in Organizations* (Newbury Park, CA: Sage, 1989), pp. 143–70; and K. M. Kacmar, D. P. Bozeman, D. S. Carlson and W. P. Anthony, 'An Examination of the Perceptions of Organizational Politics Model: Replication and Extension', *Human Relations*, March 1999, pp. 383–416.

46. Kacmar and Baron, 'Organizational Politics'; M. Valle and L. A. Witt, 'The Moderating Effect of Teamwork Perceptions on the Organizational Politics–Job Satisfaction Relationship', *Journal of Social Psychology*, June 2001, pp. 379–88; and W. A. Hochwarter, C. Kiewitz, S. L. Castro, P. L. Perrewe and G. R. Ferris, 'Positive Affectivity and Collective Efficacy as Moderators of the Relationship between Perceived Politics and Job Satisfaction', *Journal of Applied Social Psychology*, May 2003, pp. 1009–35.

47. G. R. Ferris, D. D. Frink, M. C. Galang, J. Zhou, K. M. Kacmar and J. L. Howard, 'Perceptions of Organizational Politics: Prediction, Stress-Related Implications, and Outcomes', *Human Relations*, February 1996, pp. 233–66; E. Vigoda, 'Stress-Related Aftermaths to Workplace Politics: The Relationships among Politics, Job Distress, and Aggressive Behavior in Organizations', *Journal of Organizational Behavior*, August 2002, pp. 571–91.

48. C. Kiewitz, W. A. Hochwarter, G. R. Ferris and S. L. Castro, 'The Role of Psychological Climate in Neutralizing the Effects of Organizational Politics on Work Outcomes', *Journal of Applied Social Psychology*, June 2002, pp. 1189–1207; Poon, 'Situational Antecedents and Outcomes of Organizational Politics Perceptions'; and M. C. Andrews, L. A. Witt and K. M. Kacmar, 'The Interactive Effects of Organizational Politics and Exchange Ideology on Manager Ratings of Retention', *Journal of Vocational Behavior*, April 2003, pp. 357–69.

49. S. Aryee, Z. Chen and P. S. Budhwar, 'Exchange Fairness and Employee Performance: An Examination of the Relationship between Organizational Politics and Procedural Justice', *Organizational Behavior & Human Decision Processes*, May 2004, pp. 1–14; and Kacmar, Bozeman, Carlson and Anthony, 'An Examination of the Perceptions of Organizational Politics Model'.

50. Kacmar, Bozeman, Carlson and Anthony, 'An Examination of the Perceptions of Organizational Politics Model', p. 389.

51. Ibid, p. 409.

52. B. E. Ashforth and R. T. Lee, 'Defensive Behavior in Organizations: A Preliminary Model', *Human Relations*, July 1990, pp. 621–48.

53. M. Valle and P. L. Perrewe, 'Do Politics Perceptions Relate to Political Behaviors? Tests of an Implicit Assumption and Expanded Model', *Human Relations*, March 2000, pp. 359–86.

54. See T. Romm and A. Drory, 'Political Behavior in Organizations: A Cross-Cultural Comparison', *International Journal of Value Based Management*, vol. 1, 1988, pp. 97–113; and E. Vigoda, 'Reactions to Organizational Politics: A Cross-Cultural Examination in Israel and Britain', *Human Relations*, November 2001, pp. 1483–518.

55. Vigoda, 'Reactions to Organizational Politics', p. 1512.

56. Ibid, p. 1510.

57. M. R. Leary and R. M. Kowalski, 'Impression Management: A Literature Review and Two-Component Model', *Psychological Bulletin*, January 1990, pp. 34–47.

58. Ibid, p. 34.

59. See, for instance, B. R. Schlenker, *Impression Management: The Self-Concept, Social Identity, and Interpersonal Relations* (Monterey, CA: Brooks/Cole, 1980); W. L. Gardner and M. J. Martinko, 'Impression Management in Organizations', *Journal of Management*, June 1988, pp. 321–38; Leary and Kowalski, 'Impression Management: A Literature Review and Two-Component Model', pp. 34–47; P. R. Rosenfeld, R. A. Giacalone and C. A. Riordan, *Impression Management in Organizations: Theory, Measurement, and Practice* (New York: Routledge, 1995); C. K. Stevens and A. L. Kristof, 'Making the Right Impression: A Field Study of Applicant Impression Management During Job Interviews', *Journal of Applied Psychology*, October 1995, pp. 587–606; D. P. Bozeman and K. M. Kacmar, 'A Cybernetic Model of Impression Management Processes in Organizations', *Organizational Behavior and Human Decision Processes*, January 1997, pp. 9–30; M. C. Bolino and W. H. Turnley, 'More Than One Way to Make an Impression: Exploring Profiles of Impression Management', *Journal of Management*, vol. 29, no. 2, 2003, pp. 141–60; S. Zivnuska, K. M. Kacmar, L. A. Witt, D. S. Carlson and V. K. Bratton, 'Interactive Effects of Impression Management and Organizational Politics on Job Performance', *Journal of Organizational Behavior*, August 2004, pp. 627–40; and W.-C. Tsai, C.-C. Chen and S.-F. Chiu, 'Exploring Boundaries of the Effects of Applicant Impression Management Tactics in Job Interviews', *Journal of Management*, February 2005, pp. 108–25.

60. M. Snyder and J. Copeland, 'Self-Monitoring Processes in Organizational Settings', in Giacalone and Rosenfeld (eds), *Impression Management in the Organization*, p. 11; E. D. Long and G. H. Dobbins, 'Self-Monitoring, Impression Management, and Interview Ratings: A Field and Laboratory Study', in J. L. Wall and L. R. Jauch (eds), *Proceedings of the 52nd Annual Academy of Management Conference*, Las Vegas, August 1992, pp. 274–78; A. Montagliani and R. A. Giacalone, 'Impression Management and Cross-Cultural Adaptation', *Journal of Social Psychology*, October 1998, pp. 598–608; and W. H. Turnley and M. C. Bolino, 'Achieved Desired Images While Avoiding Undesired Images: Exploring the Role of Self-Monitoring in Impression Management', *Journal of Applied Psychology*, April 2001, pp. 351–60.

61. Leary and Kowalski, 'Impression Management', p. 40.
62. Gardner and Martinko, 'Impression Management in Organizations', p. 333.
63. R. A. Baron, 'Impression Management by Applicants During Employment Interviews: The "Too Much of a Good Thing" Effect', in R. W. Eder and G. R. Ferris (eds) *The Employment Interview: Theory, Research, and Practice* (Newbury Park, CA: Sage Publishers, 1989), pp. 204–15.
64. Ferris, Russ, and Fandt, 'Politics in Organizations'.
65. A. P. J. Ellis, B. J. West, A. M. Ryan and R. P. DeShon, 'The Use of Impression Management Tactics in Structural Interviews: A Function of Question Type?', *Journal of Applied Psychology*, December 2002, pp. 1200–08.
66. Baron, 'Impression Management by Applicants during Employment Interviews'; D. C. Gilmore and G. R. Ferris, 'The Effects of Applicant Impression Management Tactics on Interviewer Judgments', *Journal of Management*, December 1989, pp. 557–64; Stevens and Kristof, 'Making the Right Impression: A Field Study of Applicant Impression Management during Job Interviews'; and L. A. McFarland, A. M. Ryan and S. D. Kriska, 'Impression Management Use and Effectiveness across Assessment Methods', *Journal of Management*, vol. 29, no. 5, 2003, pp. 641–61; and Tsai, Chen and Chiu, 'Exploring Boundaries of the Effects of Applicant Impression Management Tactics in Job Interviews'.
67. Gilmore and Ferris, 'The Effects of Applicant Impression Management Tactics on Interviewer Judgments'.
68. Stevens and Kristof, 'Making the Right Impression: A Field Study of Applicant Impression Management during Job Interviews'.
69. C. A. Higgins, T. A. Judge and G. R. Ferris, 'Influence Tactics and Work Outcomes: A Meta-Analysis', *Journal of Organizational Behavior*, March 2003, pp. 89–106.
70. Ibid.
71. R. M. Kanter, *Men and Women of the Corporation* (New York: Basic Books, 1977).
72. See, for instance, C. M. Falbe and G. Yukl, 'Consequences for Managers of Using Single Influence Tactics and Combinations of Tactics', *Academy of Management Journal*, August 1992, pp. 638–52.
73. See J. G. Bachman, D. G. Bowers and P. M. Marcus, 'Bases of Supervisory Power: A Comparative Study in Five Organizational Settings', in A. S. Tannenbaum (ed.), *Control in Organizations* (New York: McGraw-Hill, 1968), p. 236; M. A. Rahim, 'Relationships of Leader Power to Compliance and Satisfaction with Supervision: Evidence from a National Sample of Managers', *Journal of Management*, December 1989, pp. 545–56; P. A. Wilson, 'The Effects of Politics and Power on the Organizational Commitment of Federal Executives', *Journal of Management*, Spring 1995, pp. 101–18; and A. R. Elangovan and J. L. Xie, 'Effects of Perceived Power of Supervisor on Subordinate Stress and Motivation: The Moderating Role of Subordinate Characteristics', *Journal of Organizational Behavior*, May 1999, pp. 359–73.
74. Pfeffer, *Managing with Power*, p. 137.
75. G. R. Ferris, P. L. Perrewé, W. P. Anthony and D. C. Gilmore, 'Political Skill at Work', *Organizational Dynamics*, Spring 2000, pp. 25–37; K. K. Ahearn, G. R. Ferris, W. A. Hochwarter, C. Douglas and A. P. Ammeter, 'Leader Political Skill and Team Performance', *Journal of Management*, vol. 30, no. 3, 2004, pp. 309–27; and S. E. Seibert, M. L. Kraimer and J. M. Crant, 'What Do Proactive People Do? A Longitudinal Model Linking Proactive Personality and Career Success', *Personnel Psychology*, Winter 2001, pp. 845–74.
76. R. W. Kolodinsky, W. A. Hochwarter and G. R. Ferris, 'Nonlinearity in the Relationship between Political Skill and Work Outcomes: Convergent Evidence from Three Studies', *Journal of Vocational Behavior*, October 2004, pp. 294–308; W. Hochwarter, 'The Interactive Effects of Pro-Political Behavior and Politics Perceptions on Job Satisfaction and Affective Commitment', *Journal of Applied Social Psychology*, July 2003, pp. 1360–78; and P. L. Perrewé, K. L. Zellars, G. R. Ferris, A. Rossi, C. J. Kacmar and D. A. Ralston, 'Neutralizing Job Stressors: Political Skill as an Antidote to the Dysfunctional Consequences of Role Conflict', *Academy of Management Journal*, February 2004, pp. 141–52.

15

CONFLICT AND NEGOTIATION

LEARNING OBJECTIVES

AFTER STUDYING THIS CHAPTER, YOU SHOULD BE ABLE TO:

1. DEFINE CONFLICT

2. DIFFERENTIATE BETWEEN THE TRADITIONAL, HUMAN RELATIONS AND INTERACTIONIST VIEWS OF CONFLICT

3. CONTRAST TASK, RELATIONSHIP AND PROCESS CONFLICT

4. OUTLINE THE CONFLICT PROCESS

5. DESCRIBE THE FIVE CONFLICT-HANDLING INTENTIONS

6. CONTRAST DISTRIBUTIVE AND INTEGRATIVE BARGAINING

7. IDENTIFY THE FIVE STEPS IN THE NEGOTIATION PROCESS

8. DESCRIBE CULTURAL DIFFERENCES IN NEGOTIATIONS

Queensland Police Commissioner Bob Atkinson recognises the diversity among the state's dispersed communities and fully appreciates that police officers must have the skills to deal with potential conflict situations as part of their daily routine.

BOB ATKINSON WAS APPOINTED Queensland commissioner of police on 1 November 2000. He has served throughout the state, from Goondiwindi to Cairns, performing a wide range of operational and managerial roles. Leading an organisation of approximately 9000 police officers and a further 3000 staff, Commissioner Atkinson highlights the critical nature of teamwork and communication in the police service. He also appreciates that the potential for conflict is always present, and hence every member of the police service needs to be able to deal with it effectively when it arises.

Police work is diverse and sometimes complex. It requires officers with the ability to work effectively with other people on the spot. When Cyclone Larry crossed the tropical North Queensland coast near Innisfail during the morning of 20 March 2006, the damage to many local communities was catastrophic. Officers from the State Emergency Service, Fire and Rescue, Ambulance, Police and various other services were called together quickly to respond to communities in crisis. Commissioner Atkinson said, 'While the response to Cyclone Larry was outstanding, it was characterised by regular briefings to all personnel, a coordinated approach, high levels of commitment and good will, supportive leadership and attention to basic but important issues, such as providing meals and water. Conflict was avoided by getting everyone to focus on the task at hand.'

In every aspect of police work, the potential for conflict is present. People have to work together, sometimes in very stressful situations. Police officers can find themselves in conflict with members of the community and have to use all their experience and skills to get a good outcome. For example, domestic violence situations, incidents involving excessive alcohol use, situations where mentally ill persons are behaving aggressively and, most sensitively, situations involving a death where it is not clear if the circumstances were accidental or a criminal act, all require appropriate investigations and interviews to be conducted. Police officers are trained to deal with a broad range of situations where emotions run high.

Sound leadership is also fundamental to the Queensland Police Service if it is to be effective and if the Service is to be recognised as a satisfying environment in which to work. Commissioner Atkinson recognises the diversity of perspectives and beliefs among his officers and the potential for conflict that can arise from such diversity. But there is also potential value in such diversity. 'It is important to allow people's views to be heard, to encourage discussion and debate. But when a decision is made, people need to abide by it', he says. 'Good leaders are able to use discussion and debate constructively. They also know the importance and effectiveness of a healthy and happy workplace characterised by mutual respect, support and teamwork.'[1]

Our first and most pressing problem is how to do away with warfare as a method of solving conflicts between national groups within a society who have different views about how the society is to run.

Margaret Mead

As we see in the nature of police work, conflict can have both positive and negative consequences for employees. It can create chaotic conditions that make it nearly impossible for employees to work together. However, conflict also has a less well-known positive side. We will explain the difference between negative and positive conflicts in this chapter and provide a guide to help you understand how conflicts develop. We will also present a topic closely akin to conflict—negotiation. But first, let's clarify what we mean by conflict.

A DEFINITION OF CONFLICT

conflict | A process that
begins when one party
perceives that another
party has negatively
affected, or is about to
negatively affect,
something that the first
party cares about.

There has been no shortage of definitions of conflict.[2] Despite the divergent meanings the term has acquired, several common themes underlie most definitions. Conflict must be perceived by the parties to it; whether or not conflict exists is a perception issue. If no one is aware of a conflict, then it is generally agreed that no conflict exists. Additional commonalities in the definitions are opposition or incompatibility and some form of interaction.[3] These factors set the conditions that determine the beginning point of the conflict process.

We can define **conflict**, then, as a process that begins when one party perceives that another party has negatively affected, or is about to negatively affect, something that the first party cares about.[4] This definition is purposely broad. It describes that point in any ongoing activity when an interaction 'crosses over' to become an inter-party conflict. It encompasses the wide range of conflicts that people experience in organisations—incompatibility of goals, differences over interpretations of facts, disagreements based on behavioural expectations, and the like. Finally, our definition is flexible enough to cover the full range of conflict levels—from overt and violent acts to subtle forms of disagreement.

TRANSITIONS IN CONFLICT THOUGHT

It is entirely appropriate to say that there has been 'conflict' over the role of conflict in groups and organisations. One school of thought has argued that conflict must be avoided—that it indicates a malfunctioning within the group. We call this the *traditional* view. Another school of thought, the *human relations* view, argues that conflict is a natural and inevitable outcome in any group and that it need not be evil, but rather has the potential to be a positive force in determining group performance. The third, and most recent, perspective proposes not only that conflict can be a positive force in a group, but explicitly argues that some conflict *is absolutely necessary* for a group to perform effectively. We label this third school the *interactionist* view. Let's take a closer look at each of these views.

THE TRADITIONAL VIEW

The early approach to conflict assumed that all conflict was bad. Conflict was viewed negatively, and it was used synonymously with such terms as *violence*, *destruction* and *irrationality* to reinforce its negative connotation. Conflict, by definition, was harmful and was to be avoided. The **traditional view** was consistent with the attitudes that prevailed about group behaviour in the 1930s and 1940s. Conflict was seen as a dysfunctional outcome resulting from poor communication, a lack of openness and trust between people, and the failure of managers to be responsive to the needs and aspirations of their employees.

The view that all conflict is bad certainly offers a simple approach to looking at the behaviour of people who create conflict. Because all conflict is to be avoided, we need merely direct our attention to the causes of conflict and correct these malfunctionings to improve group and organisational performance. Although research studies now provide strong evidence to dispute that this approach to conflict reduction results in high group performance, many of us still evaluate conflict situations using this outmoded standard.

THE HUMAN RELATIONS VIEW

The **human relations** view argued that conflict was a natural occurrence in all groups and organisations. Because conflict was inevitable, the human relations school advocated acceptance of conflict. Proponents rationalised its existence: it cannot be eliminated, and there are even times when conflict may benefit a group's performance. The human relations view dominated conflict theory from the late 1940s through the mid-1970s.

THE INTERACTIONIST VIEW

While the human relations view accepted conflict, the **interactionist view** *encourages* conflict on the grounds that a harmonious, peaceful, tranquil and cooperative group is prone to becoming static, apathetic and non-responsive to needs for change and innovation.[5] The main contribution of the interactionist view, therefore, is encouraging group leaders to maintain an ongoing minimum level of conflict—enough to keep the group viable, self-critical and creative.

The interactionist view doesn't propose that all conflicts are good. Rather, some conflicts support the goals of the group and improve its performance; these are **functional**, constructive forms of conflict. In addition, there are conflicts that hinder group performance; these are **dysfunctional** or destructive forms of conflict. What differentiates functional from dysfunctional conflict? The evidence indicates that you need to look at the *type* of conflict.[6] Specifically, there are three types: task, relationship and process.

Task conflict relates to the content and goals of the work. **Relationship conflict** focuses on interpersonal relationships. **Process conflict** relates to how the work gets done. Studies demonstrate that relationship conflicts are almost always dysfunctional.[7] Why? It appears that the friction and interpersonal hostilities inherent in relationship conflicts increase personality clashes and decrease mutual understanding, which hinders the completion of organisational tasks. However, low levels of process conflict and low-to-moderate levels of task conflict are functional. For process conflict to be productive, it must be kept low. Intense arguments about who should do what become dysfunctional when they create uncertainty about task roles, increase the time to complete tasks and lead to members working at cross purposes. Low-to-moderate levels of task conflict consistently demonstrate a positive effect on group performance, because it stimulates discussion of ideas that helps groups to perform better.

traditional view of conflict | The belief that all conflict is harmful and must be avoided.

human relations view of conflict | The belief that conflict is a natural and inevitable outcome in any group.

interactionist view of conflict | The belief that conflict is not only a positive force in a group but that it is also an absolute necessity for a group to perform effectively.

functional conflict | Conflict that supports the goals of the group and improves its performance.

dysfunctional conflict | Conflict that hinders group performance.

> **LEARNING OBJECTIVE** 3
> Contrast task, relationship and process conflict

task conflict | Conflicts over content and goals of the work.

relationship conflict | Conflict based on interpersonal relationships.

process conflict | Conflict over how work gets done.

conflict process | Process
with five stages: potential
opposition or
incompatibility, cognition
and personalisation,
intentions, behaviour and
outcomes.

THE CONFLICT PROCESS

The **conflict process** can be seen as comprising five stages: potential opposition or
incompatibility, cognition and personalisation, intentions, behaviour and outcomes. The
process is illustrated in Figure 15.1.

STAGE I: POTENTIAL OPPOSITION OR INCOMPATIBILITY

The first step in the conflict process is the presence of conditions that create opportunities
for conflict to arise. They *need not* lead directly to conflict, but one of these conditions is
necessary if conflict is to surface. For simplicity's sake, these conditions (which also may be
looked at as causes or sources of conflict) have been condensed into three general
categories: communication, structure and personal variables.[8]

COMMUNICATION

Susan had worked in supply-chain management at Herron Pharmaceuticals Pty Ltd for
three years. She enjoyed her work in large part because her boss, Andrew Kronios, was a
great guy to work for. Then Andrew got promoted six months ago and Rodney Wong took
his place. Susan says her job is a lot more frustrating now. 'Andrew and I were on the same
wavelength. It's not that way with Rodney. He tells me something and I do it. Then he tells
me I did it wrong. I think he means one thing but says something else. It's been like this
since the day he arrived. I don't think a day goes by when he isn't yelling at me for
something. You know, there are some people you just find it easy to communicate with.
Well, Rodney isn't one of those!'

Susan's comments illustrate that communication can be a source of conflict.[9] They
represent the opposing forces that arise from semantic difficulties, misunderstandings and
'noise' in the communication channels. Much of this discussion can be related back to our
comments on communication in Chapter 11.

A review of the research suggests that differing word connotations, jargon, insufficient
exchange of information and noise in the communication channel are all barriers to
communication and potential antecedent conditions to conflict. Evidence demonstrates
that semantic difficulties arise as a result of differences in training, selective perception and
inadequate information about others. Research has further demonstrated a surprising
finding: the potential for conflict increases when either too little or too much
communication takes place. Apparently, an increase in communication is functional up to
a point, whereupon it is possible to over-communicate, with a resultant increase in the

■ **FIGURE 15.1**

The conflict process

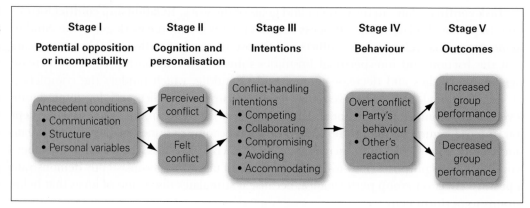

'THE SOURCE OF MOST CONFLICTS IS LACK OF COMMUNICATION'

This statement is probably false. A popular myth in organisations is that poor communication is the primary source of conflicts. And certainly problems in the communication process do act to retard collaboration, stimulate misunderstandings and create conflicts. But a review of the literature suggests that within organisations, structural factors and individual value differences are probably greater sources of conflict.

Conflicts in organisations are frequently structurally derived. For instance, in the movie-making business, conflicts between directors and producers are often due to different goals. Directors want to create artistic films, regardless of costs. Producers want to make financially profitable movies by minimising costs. When people have to work together, but are pursuing diverse goals, conflicts ensue. Similarly, increased organisational size, routinisation, work specialisation and zero-sum reward systems are all examples of structural factors that can lead to conflicts.

Many conflicts attributed to poor communication are, on closer examination, due to value differences. When managers incorrectly treat a value-based conflict as a communication problem, the conflict is rarely eliminated. Increased communication efforts are likely to crystallise and reinforce differences. 'Before this conversation, I thought you *might* be closed-minded. Now I *know* you are!'

Lack of communication can be a source of conflict. But managers should first look to structural or value-based explanations because they are more prevalent in organisations.

SOURCE: S. P. Robbins, *Managing Organizational Conflict: A Nontraditional Approach* (Upper Saddle River, NJ: Prentice Hall, 1974), pp. 31–55.

potential for conflict. Too much information, as well as too little, can lay the foundation for conflict.

Furthermore, the channel chosen for communicating can have an influence on stimulating opposition. The filtering process that occurs as information is passed between members and the divergence of communications from formal or previously established channels offer potential opportunities for conflict to arise.

STRUCTURE

Rachael and Carly both work at AMart Funiture—a large discount furniture retailer. Rachael is a salesperson on the floor; Carly is the company credit manager. The two women have known each other for years and have much in common—they live within two blocks of each other, and their oldest daughters attend the same school and are best friends. In reality, if Rachael and Carly had different jobs they might be best friends themselves, but these two women are consistently fighting battles with each other. Rachael's job is to sell furniture and she does a great job. But most of her sales are made on credit. Because Carly's job

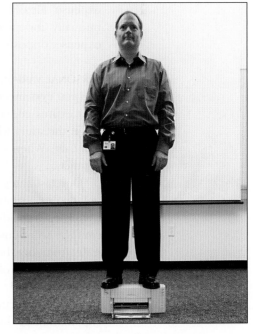

Hewlett-Packard manager Tom Alexander stood on an HP printer during a meeting of company engineers to make a point about incompatible goals. HP's goal was to develop a low-cost, lightweight printer to compete in the low-end market. The engineer's goal was to continue designing high-quality, high-cost printers. 'Alexander's stand' achieved goal compatibility, convincing engineers that customers don't need or want printers strong enough to withstand the weight of a man.

is to make sure the company minimises credit losses, she regularly has to turn down the credit application of a customer with whom Rachael has just made a sale. It is nothing personal between Rachael and Carly—the requirements of their jobs just bring them into conflict.

The conflicts between Rachael and Carly are structural in nature. The term *structure* is used, in this context, to include variables such as size, degree of specialisation in the tasks assigned to group members, jurisdictional clarity, member–goal compatibility, leadership styles, reward systems and the degree of dependence between groups.

Research indicates that size and specialisation act as forces to stimulate conflict. The larger the group and the more specialised its activities, the greater the likelihood of conflict. Tenure and conflict have been found to be inversely related. The potential for conflict tends to be greatest when group members are younger and when turnover is high. The greater the ambiguity in precisely defining where responsibility for actions lies, the greater the potential for conflict to emerge. Such jurisdictional ambiguities increase inter-group fighting for control of resources and territory.

Groups within organisations have diverse goals. For instance, supply management is concerned with the timely acquisition of inputs at low prices, marketing's goals concentrate on disposing of outputs and increasing revenues, quality control's attention is focused on improving quality and ensuring that the organisation's products meet standards, and production units seek efficiency of operations by maintaining a steady production flow. This diversity of goals among groups is a major source of conflict. When groups within an organisation seek diverse ends, some of which—like sales and credit at AMart Furniture—are inherently at odds, there are increased opportunities for conflict.

There is some indication that a close style of leadership—tight and continuous observation with general control of others' behaviours—increases conflict potential, but the evidence isn't particularly strong. Too much reliance on participation may also stimulate conflict. Research tends to confirm that participation and conflict are highly correlated, apparently because participation encourages the promotion of differences. Reward systems, too, are found to create conflict when one member's gain is at another's expense. Finally, if a group is dependent on another group (in contrast to the two being mutually independent) or if interdependence allows one group to gain at another's expense, opposing forces are stimulated.[10]

PERSONAL VARIABLES

Did you ever meet someone to whom you took an immediate dislike? Most of the opinions they expressed, you disagreed with. Even insignificant characteristics—the sound of their voice, the smirk when they smiled, their personality—annoyed you. We have all met people like that. When you have to work with such individuals, there is often the potential for conflict.

Our last category of potential sources of conflict is personal variables, which include personality, emotions and values. Evidence indicates that certain personality types—for example, individuals who are highly authoritarian and dogmatic—lead to potential conflict. Emotions can also cause conflict. For example, an employee who shows up to work irate from her hectic morning commute may carry that anger with her to her 9 am meeting. The problem? Her anger can annoy her colleagues, which may lead to a tension-filled meeting.[11]

Finally, differing values can explain conflict. Value differences, for example, are the best explanation of diverse issues such as prejudice, disagreements over one's contribution to the group and the rewards one deserves, and assessments of whether this particular book is any good. That an employee thinks he is worth $55 000 a year but his boss believes him to be worth $50 000, and that Ann thinks this book is interesting to read while Jennifer views it as trash, are all value judgments. And differences in value systems are important sources for creating the potential for conflict. It is also important to note that culture can be a source of differing values. For example, research indicates that individuals in Japan and in the United States view conflict differently. Compared to Japanese negotiators, Americans are more likely to see offers from their counterparts as unfair and to reject such offers.[12]

STAGE II: COGNITION AND PERSONALISATION

If the conditions cited in Stage I negatively affect something that one party cares about, then the potential for opposition or incompatibility becomes actualised in the second stage.

As we noted in our definition of conflict, perception is required. Therefore, one or more of the parties must be aware of the existence of the antecedent conditions. However, because a conflict is **perceived** doesn't mean that it is personalised. In other words, '*A* may be aware that *B* and *A* are in serious disagreement … but it may not make *A* tense or anxious, and it may have no effect whatsoever on *A*'s affection toward *B*.'[13] It is at the **felt** level, when individuals become emotionally involved, that parties experience anxiety, tension, frustration or hostility.

Keep in mind two points. First, Stage II is important because it is where conflict issues tend to be defined. This is the place in the process where the parties decide what the conflict is about.[14] And, in turn, this 'sense making' is critical because the way a conflict is defined goes a long way towards establishing the sort of outcomes that might settle it. For example, if we define our salary disagreement as a zero-sum situation—that is, if you get the increase in pay you want, there will be just that amount less for me—I am going to be far less willing to compromise than if I frame the conflict as a potential win-win situation (that is, the dollars in the salary pool might be increased so that both of us could get the added pay we want). So, the definition of a conflict is important, because it typically delineates the set of possible settlements. Our second point is that emotions play a major role in shaping perceptions.[15] For example, negative emotions have been found to produce oversimplification of issues, reductions in trust and negative interpretations of the other party's behaviour.[16] In contrast, positive feelings have been found to increase the tendency to see potential relationships among the elements of a problem, to take a broader view of the situation, and to develop more innovative solutions.[17]

STAGE III: INTENTIONS

Intentions intervene between people's perceptions and emotions and their overt behaviour. These intentions are decisions to act in a given way.[18]

Why are intentions separated out as a distinct stage? You have to infer the other's intent to know how to respond to that other's behaviour. A lot of conflicts are escalated merely by one party attributing the wrong intentions to the other party. In addition, there is typically a great deal of slippage between intentions and behaviour, so behaviour doesn't always accurately reflect a person's intentions.

Figure 15.2 represents one author's effort to identify the primary conflict-handling intentions. Using two dimensions—*cooperativeness* (the degree to which one party attempts to satisfy the other party's concerns) and *assertiveness* (the degree to which one party

perceived conflict | Awareness by one or more parties of the existence of conditions that create opportunities for conflict to arise.

felt conflict | Emotional involvement in a conflict creating anxiety, tension, frustration or hostility.

LEARNING OBJECTIVE 5
Describe the five conflict-handling intentions

intentions | Decisions to act in a given way.

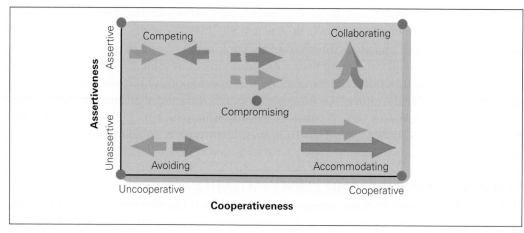

SOURCE: K. Thomas, 'Conflict and Negotiation Processes in Organizations', in M. D. Dunnette and L. M. Hough (eds), *Handbook of Industrial and Organizational Psychology*, 2nd ed., vol. 3 (Palo Alto, CA: Consulting Psychologists Press, 1992), p. 668. Reproduced with permission.

attempts to satisfy his or her own concerns)—five conflict-handling intentions can be identified: *competing* (assertive and uncooperative), *collaborating* (assertive and cooperative), *avoiding* (unassertive and uncooperative), *accommodating* (unassertive and cooperative) and *compromising* (mid-range on both assertiveness and cooperativeness).[19]

COMPETING

When one person seeks to satisfy his or her own interests, regardless of the impact on the other parties to the conflict, that person is **competing**. Examples include intending to achieve your goal at the sacrifice of the other's goal, attempting to convince another that your conclusion is correct and that his or hers is mistaken, and trying to make someone else accept blame for a problem.

competing | A desire to satisfy one's interests, regardless of the impact on the other party to the conflict.

COLLABORATING

When the parties to conflict each desire to fully satisfy the concerns of all parties, we have cooperation and the search for a mutually beneficial outcome. In **collaborating**, the intention of the parties is to solve the problem by clarifying differences rather than by accommodating various points of view. Examples include attempting to find a win-win solution that allows both parties' goals to be completely achieved and seeking a conclusion that incorporates the valid insights of both parties.

collaborating | A situation in which the parties to a conflict each desire to satisfy fully the concerns of all parties.

AVOIDING

A person may recognise that a conflict exists and want to withdraw from it or suppress it. Examples of **avoiding** include trying just to ignore a conflict and avoiding others with whom you disagree.

avoiding | The desire to withdraw from or suppress a conflict.

ACCOMMODATING

When one party seeks to appease an opponent, that party may be willing to place the opponent's interests above his or her own. In other words, in order for the relationship to be maintained, one party is willing to be self-sacrificing. We refer to this intention as **accommodating**. Examples are a willingness to sacrifice your goal so that the other party's goal can be attained, supporting someone else's opinion despite your reservations about it, and forgiving someone for an infraction and allowing subsequent ones.

accommodating | The willingness of one party in a conflict to place the opponent's interests above his or her own.

COMPROMISING

When each party to the conflict seeks to give up something, sharing occurs, resulting in a compromised outcome. In **compromising**, there is no clear winner or loser. Rather, there is a willingness to ration the object of the conflict and accept a solution that provides incomplete satisfaction of both parties' concerns. The distinguishing characteristic of compromising, therefore, is that each party intends to give up something. Examples might be willingness to accept a pay increase of $2 an hour rather than $3, to acknowledge partial agreement with a specific viewpoint, and to take partial blame for an infraction.

compromising | A situation in which each party to a conflict is willing to give up something.

Intentions provide general guidelines for parties in a conflict situation. They define each party's purpose. Yet, people's intentions aren't fixed. During the course of a conflict, they might change because of reconceptualisation or because of an emotional reaction to the behaviour of the other party. However, research indicates that people have an underlying disposition to handle conflicts in certain ways.[20] Specifically, individuals have preferences among the five conflict-handling intentions just described; these preferences tend to be relied on quite consistently, and a person's intentions can be predicted rather well from a combination of intellectual and personality characteristics. So it may be more appropriate to view the five conflict-handling intentions as relatively fixed rather than as a set of options from which individuals choose to fit an appropriate situation. That is, when confronting a conflict situation, some people want to win it all at any cost, some want to find an optimal solution, some want to run away, others want to be obliging, and still others want to 'split the difference'.

STAGE IV: BEHAVIOUR

When most people think of conflict situations, they tend to focus on Stage IV. Why? Because this is where conflicts become visible. The behaviour stage includes the statements, actions and reactions made by the conflicting parties. These conflict behaviours are usually overt attempts to implement each party's intentions. But these behaviours have a stimulus quality that is separate from intentions. As a result of miscalculations or unskilled enactments, overt behaviours sometimes deviate from original intentions.[21]

It helps to think of Stage IV as a dynamic process of interaction. For example, you make a demand on me; I respond by arguing; you threaten me; I threaten you back; and so on. Figure 15.3 provides a way of visualising conflict behaviour. All conflicts exist somewhere along this continuum. At the lower part of the continuum, we have conflicts characterised by subtle, indirect and highly controlled forms of tension. An example of such a conflict might be a student questioning in class a point the tutor has just made. Conflict intensities escalate as they move upward along the continuum until they become highly destructive. Strikes, riots and wars clearly fall in this upper range. For the most part, you should assume that conflicts that reach the upper ranges of the continuum are almost always dysfunctional. Functional conflicts are typically confined to the lower range of the continuum.

If a conflict is dysfunctional, what can the parties do to de-escalate it? Or, conversely, what options exist if conflict is too low and needs to be increased? This brings us to **conflict-management** techniques. Table 15.1 lists the main resolution and stimulation techniques that allow managers to control conflict levels. Note that several of the resolution techniques were described earlier as conflict-handling intentions. This, of course, shouldn't be surprising. Under ideal conditions, a person's intentions should translate into comparable behaviours.

conflict management | The use of resolution and stimulation techniques to achieve the desired level of conflict.

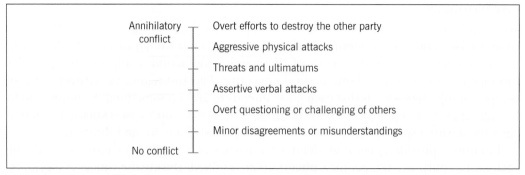

Annihilatory conflict — Overt efforts to destroy the other party

Aggressive physical attacks

Threats and ultimatums

Assertive verbal attacks

Overt questioning or challenging of others

Minor disagreements or misunderstandings

No conflict

SOURCES: Based on S. P. Robbins, *Managing Organizational Conflict: A Nontraditional Approach* (Upper Saddle River, NJ: Prentice Hall, 1974), pp. 93–97; and F. Glasl, 'The Process of Conflict Escalation and the Roles of Third Parties', in G. B. J. Bomers and R. Peterson (eds), *Conflict Management and Industrial Relations* (Boston: Kluwer-Nojhoff, 1982), pp. 119–40.

Conflict resolution techniques

Problem solving	Face-to-face meeting of the conflicting parties for the purpose of identifying the problem and resolving it through open discussion.
Superordinate goals	Creating a shared goal that cannot be attained without the cooperation of each of the conflicting parties.
Expansion of resources	When a conflict is caused by the scarcity of a resource—say, money, promotion opportunities, office space—expansion of the resource can create a win–win solution.
Avoidance	Withdrawal from, or suppression of, the conflict.
Smoothing	Playing down differences while emphasising common interests between the conflicting parties.
Compromise	Each party to the conflict gives up something of value.
Authoritative command	Management uses its formal authority to resolve the conflict and then communicates its desires to the parties involved.
Altering the human variable	Using behavioural change techniques such as human relations training to alter attitudes and behaviours that cause conflict.
Altering the structural variables	Changing the formal organisation structure and the interaction patterns of conflicting parties through job redesign, transfers, creation of coordinating positions and the like.

Conflict stimulation techniques

Communication	Using ambiguous or threatening messages to increase conflict levels.
Bringing in outsiders	Adding employees to a group whose backgrounds, values, attitudes or managerial styles differ from those of present members.
Restructuring the organisation	Realigning work groups, altering rules and regulations, increasing interdependence, and making similar structural changes to disrupt the status quo.
Appointing a devil's advocate	Designating a critic to purposely argue against the majority positions held by the group.

SOURCE: Based on S. P. Robbins, *Managing Organizational Conflict: A Nontraditional Approach* (Upper Saddle River, NJ: Prentice Hall, 1974), pp. 59–89.

STAGE V: OUTCOMES

The action–reaction interplay between the conflicting parties results in consequences. As our model (see Figure 15.1) demonstrates, these outcomes may be functional in that the conflict results in an improvement in the group's performance, or dysfunctional in that it hinders group performance.

FUNCTIONAL OUTCOMES

How might conflict act as a force to increase group performance? It is hard to visualise a situation in which open or violent aggression could be functional. But there are a number of instances in which it is possible to envision how low or moderate levels of conflict could improve the effectiveness of a group. Because people often find it difficult to think of instances in which conflict can be constructive, let's consider some examples and then review the research evidence. Note how all these examples focus on task and process conflicts and exclude the relationship variety.

Conflict is constructive when it improves the quality of decisions, stimulates creativity and innovation, encourages interest and curiosity among group members, provides the medium through which problems can be aired and tensions released, and fosters an environment of self-evaluation and change. The evidence suggests that conflict can improve the quality of decision making by allowing all points, particularly the ones that are unusual or held by a minority, to be weighed in important decisions.[22] Conflict is an antidote for groupthink. It doesn't allow the group to passively 'rubber-stamp' decisions that may be based on weak assumptions, inadequate consideration of relevant alternatives or other debilities. Conflict challenges the status quo and therefore furthers the creation of new ideas, promotes reassessment of group goals and activities, and increases the probability that the group will respond to change.

For an example of a company that suffered because it had too little functional conflict, you don't have to look further than automobile behemoth General Motors (GM).[23] Many of GM's problems, from the late 1960s to the late 1990s, can be traced to a lack of functional conflict. It hired and promoted individuals who were 'yes-men', loyal to GM to the point of never questioning company actions. Managers were, for the most part, homogenous: conservative white males who resisted change—they preferred looking back to past successes rather than forward to new challenges. They were almost sanctimonious in their belief that what had worked in the past would continue to work in the future. Moreover, by sheltering executives in the company's corporate headquarters and encouraging them to socialise with others inside the GM ranks, the company further insulated managers from conflicting perspectives.

More recently, Yahoo! provides an illustration of a company that suffered because of too little functional conflict.[24] Begun in 1994, by 1999 Yahoo! had become one of the best-known brand names on the internet. Then the implosion of dot.com share prices hit. By the spring of 2001, Yahoo!'s advertising sales were plunging and the company's share price was down 92 per cent from its peak. It was at this point that Yahoo!'s most critical problem became exposed: the company was too insulated and void of functional conflict. It couldn't respond to change. Managers and staff were too comfortable with each other to challenge the status quo. This kept new ideas from percolating upward and held dissent to a minimum. The source of the problem was the company's CEO, Tim Koogle. He set the tone of non-confrontation. Only when Koogle was replaced in 2001, with a new CEO who openly challenged the company's conflict-free climate, did Yahoo! begin to successfully solve its problems.

CONSTRUCTIVE CONFLICT AND THE PERFORMANCE APPRAISAL

Writing for the Melbourne *Age* newspaper, Leon Gettler suggested that 'of all the rituals of working life, the annual torture session of the performance appraisal stands out as the most useless and time-consuming … True, an appraisal is better than no feedback. But not as a quicksand of unquantifiable HR buzz words, bureaucratic forms and boxes to be ticked. It's no surprise that no one comes out of them learning anything new about themselves'.

The purpose of the performance appraisal is to provide an objective assessment of an employee for the purposes of addressing any deficiencies in an individual's performance, agreeing on a developmental plan for the future, making promotional and remuneration decisions, and providing a regular and formal forum for an employee to obtain feedback and provide feedback to the organisation through the employee's supervisor.

For many organisations, however, these aspirations fall well short. In fact, appraisals can be the trigger for conflict, both overt and covert. Conflict can arise from very subjective ratings of an individual's performance. It can also arise when an employee doesn't have respect for the supervisor. A Melbourne Business School report released in 2005 found that a growing number of Australian managers think that their boss is incompetent and clueless. There are plenty of anecdotal accounts by employees about ill-prepared and uncommitted managers when it comes to discussing their performance. Also, a number of universities don't relate the results of performance appraisals to the elaborate and stressful process that academics have to go through to get promoted. Conflict can arise from such fragmented processes of appraisal.

HCL Technologies is a company that is trying to address some of these issues by developing a performance appraisal system that puts employees first. With its headquarters just outside Delhi, India and a workforce of more than 30 000 spread over 15 countries, including Australia, Singapore and Malaysia, HCL Technologies asks employees to rank their boss and other company managers. The difference is that the results are posted online for everyone to see. The company also allows employees to raise their concerns about anything, from compensation issues to personality clashes, by way of creating an electronic 'ticket' that is then placed with a manager to be resolved. The system is based on transparency and constructive conflict by getting issues out in the open for resolution.

In order to support the system, all managers are trained in areas such as negotiation and conflict management. They get bonuses for employee development. Online tests are regularly conducted and everyone has to complete them, including the chief executive; the results are published online.

Somnath Mallick, managing director of HCL Asia-Pacific, said the Employees First program is part of a long-term change program: 'We went through pretty intense debate internally when we first proposed the program because there is always this perception in a services company that customers come first … there are some people who go along with it and some who feel uncomfortable about it … It is confronting, but where we are coming from is creating this environment of openness and transparency. Gone is the day when you had solo star performers doing things and riding off into the sunset. Today, you are talking about groups of people across multiple locations.' He said the program had already produced results. Over the past year in Australia, attrition rates had dropped from 10 per cent to 3 per cent. This is critical when Australian companies compete for IT professionals with London and Silicon Valley and regional centres in Singapore and Hong Kong. HCL Technologies is attempting to put constructive conflict to good use by developing a performance appraisal system that values employees and their feedback.

SOURCE: Leon Gettler, 'There's No Hiding from a Decent Review', *The Age*, 7 June 2006, p. 12.

Research studies in diverse settings confirm the functionality of conflict. Consider the following findings. The comparison of six major decisions made during the administration of four different US presidents found that conflict reduced the chance that groupthink would overpower policy decisions. The comparisons demonstrated that conformity among presidential advisers was related to poor decisions, whereas an atmosphere of constructive conflict and critical thinking surrounded the well-developed decisions.[25]

There is evidence indicating that conflict can also be positively related to productivity. For instance, it was demonstrated that, among established groups, performance tended to improve more when there was conflict among members than when there was fairly close agreement. The investigators observed that when groups analysed decisions that had been made by the individual members of that group, the average improvement among the high-conflict groups was 73 per cent greater than was that of those groups characterised by low-conflict conditions.[26] Others have found similar results: groups composed of members with different interests tend to produce higher-quality solutions to a variety of problems than do homogeneous groups.[27]

The preceding leads us to predict that the increasing cultural diversity of the workforce should provide benefits to organisations. And that is what the evidence indicates. Research demonstrates that heterogeneity among group and organisation members can increase creativity, improve the quality of decisions, and facilitate change by enhancing member flexibility.[28]

For example, researchers compared decision-making groups composed of all-Anglo individuals with groups that also contained members from Asian, Hispanic and African ethnic groups. The ethnically diverse groups produced more effective and more feasible ideas, and the unique ideas they generated tended to be of higher quality than the unique ideas produced by the all-Anglo group.

Similarly, studies of professionals—systems analysts, and research and development scientists—support the constructive value of conflict. An investigation of 22 teams of systems analysts found that the more incompatible groups were likely to be more productive.[29] Research and development scientists have been found to be most productive when there is a certain amount of intellectual conflict.[30]

DYSFUNCTIONAL OUTCOMES

The destructive consequences of conflict on a group's or organisation's performance are generally well known. A reasonable summary might state: uncontrolled opposition breeds discontent, which acts to dissolve common ties, and eventually leads to the destruction of the group. And, of course, there is a substantial body of literature to document how conflict—the dysfunctional varieties—can reduce group effectiveness.[31] Among the more undesirable consequences are a retarding of communication, reductions in group cohesiveness, and subordination of group goals to the primacy of infighting among members. At the extreme, conflict can bring group functioning to a halt and potentially threaten the group's survival.

The demise of an organisation as a result of too much conflict isn't as unusual as it might first appear. For instance, one of New York's best-known law firms, Shea & Gould, closed down solely because the 80 partners just couldn't get along.[32] As one legal consultant familiar with the organisation said: 'This was a firm that had basic and principled differences among the partners that were basically irreconcilable.' That same consultant also addressed the partners at their last meeting: 'You don't have an economic problem,' he said. 'You have a personality problem. You hate each other!'

CREATING FUNCTIONAL CONFLICT

In this section we ask: If managers accept the interactionist view towards conflict, what can they do to encourage functional conflict in their organisations?[33]

There seems to be general agreement that creating functional conflict is a tough job, particularly in large organisations. As one consultant put it, 'A high proportion of people who get to the top are conflict avoiders. They don't like hearing negatives; they don't like saying or thinking negative things. They frequently make it up the ladder in part because they don't irritate people on the way up.'

Such anti-conflict cultures may have been tolerable in the past, but not in today's fiercely competitive global economy. Organisations that don't encourage and support dissent may find their survival threatened. Let's look at some approaches organisations are using to encourage their people to challenge the system and develop fresh ideas.

The computer company Hewlett-Packard rewards dissenters by recognising go-against-the-grain types, or people who stay with the ideas they believe in even when those ideas are rejected by management. Staff at the Beechworth Bakery in Victoria are also encouraged by the proprietor, Tom O'Toole, to criticise their bosses if service or products aren't up to standard. IBM also has a formal system that encourages dissension. Employees can question their boss with impunity. If the disagreement can't be resolved, the system provides a third party for counsel.

Royal Dutch Shell Group, General Electric and Anheuser-Busch build devil's advocates into the decision process. Anheuser-Busch has multiple businesses, but more recently it has featured in Singapore because of an agreement to import the local Tiger Beer into the United States. When the policy committee at Anheuser-Busch considers a major move, such as getting into or out of a business or making a major capital expenditure, it often assigns teams to make the case for each side of the question. This process frequently results in decisions and alternatives that hadn't been considered previously.

One common ingredient in organisations that successfully create functional conflict is that they reward dissent and punish conflict avoiders. The real challenge for managers, however, is when they hear news that they don't want to hear. The news may make their blood boil or their hopes collapse, but they can't show it. They have to learn to take the bad news without flinching. No tirades, no tight-lipped sarcasm, no eyes rolling upward, no gritting of teeth. Rather, managers should ask calm, even-tempered questions: 'Can you tell me more about what happened?' 'What do you think we ought to do?' A sincere 'Thank you for bringing this to my attention' will probably reduce the likelihood that managers will be cut off from similar communications in the future.

Having considered conflict—its nature, causes and consequences—we now turn to negotiation. Negotiation and conflict are closely related because negotiation often resolves conflict.

NEGOTIATION

Negotiation permeates the interactions of almost everyone in groups and organisations. There is the obvious: labour bargains with management. There is the not so obvious: managers negotiate with employees, peers and bosses; salespeople negotiate with customers; purchasing agents negotiate with suppliers. And there is the subtle: an employee agrees to answer a colleague's phone for a few minutes in exchange for some past or future benefit. In today's loosely structured organisations, in which members are increasingly finding themselves having to work with colleagues over whom they have no direct authority and with whom they may not even share a common boss, negotiation skills become critical.

We will define **negotiation** as a process in which two or more parties exchange goods or services and attempt to agree on the exchange rate for them.[34] Note that we will use the

negotiation | A process in which two or more parties exchange goods or services and attempt to agree on the exchange rate for them.

terms *negotiation* and *bargaining* interchangeably. In this section, we will contrast two bargaining strategies, provide a model of the negotiation process, ascertain the role of moods and personality traits in bargaining, review gender and cultural differences in negotiation, and take a brief look at third-party negotiations.

BARGAINING STRATEGIES

There are two general approaches to negotiation—*distributive bargaining* and *integrative bargaining*.[35] These are compared in Table 15.2. As the table shows, distributive and integrative bargaining differ in their goal and motivation, focus, interests, information sharing and duration of relationship. We now define distributive and integrative bargaining and illustrate the differences between these two approaches.

WHAT'S MY NEGOTIATING STYLE?

In the Self-Assessment Library (available on CD and online), take Self-Assessment II.C.6 (What's My Negotiating Style?) and answer the following questions.
1. Are you surprised by your score?
2. Do you think your perception of your negotiating skills might hinder your ability to negotiate effectively? If yes, why? If not, why not?
3. Drawing from the material in the chapter, how might you improve your negotiating skills?

DISTRIBUTIVE BARGAINING

You see a used car advertised for sale in the newspaper. It appears to be just what you have been looking for. You go out to see the car. It's great and you want it. The owner tells you the asking price. You don't want to pay that much. The two of you then negotiate over the price. The negotiating strategy you are engaging in is called **distributive bargaining**. Its most identifying feature is that it operates under zero-sum conditions. That is, any gain I make is at your expense, and vice versa. Referring back to the used-car example, every dollar you can get the seller to cut from the car's price is a dollar you save. Conversely, every dollar more the seller can get from you comes at your expense. So, the essence of distributive bargaining is negotiating over who gets what share of a fixed pie. By **fixed pie**, we mean that the bargaining parties believe there is only a set amount of goods or services to be divvied up. Therefore, fixed pies are zero-sum games in that every dollar in one party's pocket is a dollar out of their counterpart's pocket. When parties believe the pie is fixed, they tend to bargain distributively.

Probably the most widely cited example of distributive bargaining is in labour–management negotiations over wages. Typically, labour's representatives come to the bargaining table determined to get as much money as possible out of management. Because every cent more that labour negotiates increases management's costs, each party bargains aggressively and treats the other as an opponent who must be defeated.

The essence of distributive bargaining is depicted in Figure 15.4. Parties *A* and *B* represent two negotiators. Each has a *target point* that defines what he or she would like to achieve. Each also has a *resistance point*, which marks the lowest outcome that is acceptable—the point below which they would break off negotiations rather than accept a less-favourable settlement. The area between these two points makes up each one's aspiration range. As long as there is some overlap between *A*'s and *B*'s aspiration ranges, there exists a settlement range in which each one's aspirations can be met.

> **LEARNING OBJECTIVE 6**
> Contrast distributive and integrative bargaining

distributive bargaining | Negotiation that seeks to divide up a fixed amount of resources; a win–lose situation.

---

fixed pie | The belief that there is only a set amount of goods or services to be divvied up between the parties.

Bargaining characteristic	Distributive characteristic	Integrative characteristic
Available resources	Fixed amount of resources to be divided	Variable amount of resources to be divided
Primary motivations	I win, you lose	I win, you win
Primary interests	Opposed to each other	Convergent or congruent with each other
Focus of relationships	Short term	Long term

SOURCE: Based on R. J. Lewicki and J. A. Litterer, *Negotiation* (Homewood, IL: Irwin, 1985), p. 280.

OB IN PRACTICE

NEGOTIATING ACROSS CULTURES

For its ASEAN neighbours, China represents a market potential that is too big to ignore, but business leaders in Australia and Malaysia are realising that this Asian giant requires patience and cultural sensitivity in any business negotiations.

Aviation Compliance Solutions (ACS), a Melbourne-based company set up by former Ansett staff, has started to make some inroads into doing business in China. However, ACS managing director Jackie Barnes says there are a number of factors that need to be considered to be successful in China.

'You need to visit the client at their premises, make professional presentations using bilingual slides and have a translator on hand', she says. 'You also need to be aware of your competitors' products and be prepared to negotiate. But once you've won your first job in China, you'll create the momentum to win further business.'

Negotiating skills is the key. A study of negotiators in the United States, China and Japan found that culture plays an important role in successful negotiation. The study found that, overall, negotiators who had both a self-serving 'egoistic' orientation and a high goal level fared the best overall compared to negotiators with an other-serving 'prosocial' orientation and low goal level. In other words, the strategy combining a self-serving negotiation position, where one is focused only on maximising one's own outcomes, coupled with a strong desire to obtain the best outcomes, led to the most favourable negotiation results.

However, the degree to which this particular strategy resulted in better outcomes depended on the negotiating partner. The results showed that being self-serving and having a high negotiation goal level resulted in higher outcomes (in this case, profits) only when the negotiating opponent was other-serving. Negotiators from the United States are more likely to be self-serving and have high goal levels. In China and Japan, however, there is a greater likelihood that negotiators are other-serving and thus are more concerned with others' outcomes. Consequently, negotiators from the United States are likely to obtain better outcomes for themselves when negotiating with individuals from China and Japan because American negotiators tend to be more concerned with their own outcomes, sometimes at the expense of the other party.

Although this study suggests that being self-serving can be beneficial in some situations, negotiators should be wary of being *too* self-serving. Though American—and Australian—negotiators may benefit from a self-serving negotiation position and a high goal level when negotiating with individuals from China or Japan, being too self-serving may result in damaged relationships, leading to less favourable outcomes in the long run.

SOURCES: Based on Gillian Bullock, 'Doing Business in China', *Management Today*, July 2006: <www.aim.com.au/DisplayStory.asp?ID=594> (accessed 11 November 2006); and Y. Chen, E. A. Mannix and T. Okumura, 'The Importance of Who You Meet: Effects of Self- versus Other Concerns among Negotiators in the United States, the People's Republic of China, and Japan', *Journal of Experimental Social Psychology*, January 2003, pp. 1–15.

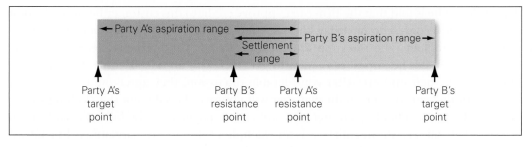

When engaged in distributive bargaining, one's tactics focus on trying to get one's opponent to agree to a specific target point or to get as close to it as possible. Examples of such tactics are persuading your opponent of the impossibility of getting to his or her target point and the advisability of accepting a settlement near yours; arguing that your target is fair, while your opponent's isn't; and attempting to get your opponent to feel emotionally generous towards you and thus accept an outcome close to your target point.

But what are some less obvious examples of distributive bargaining tactics? One routine you have likely heard of—perhaps from your favourite crime show—is the good cop, bad cop routine where one negotiator is friendly and accommodating and the other is as tough as nails. Research shows that negotiating teams that use this tactic when engaged in distributive bargaining achieve better settlements than a negotiation team that doesn't use the good cop, bad cop tactic.[36] But it appears that the good cop, bad cop routine works only when the positive negotiator follows the negative negotiator. Why? Because the positive negotiator seems much more accommodating and likeable after following the disagreeable negotiator.

For example, let's say you are negotiating over a lease for office space with two people: Jim and Susan. When you ask for a lower rental rate, Jim reacts very negatively—accusing you of deception, making threats about leasing the space to another party, and in general appearing irritated and disrespectful. Jim leaves and Susan takes over. Susan apologises for Jim's behaviour. She appears to be understanding of your position and also seems supportive and cooperative. But she politely says they have made the best offer they possibly can. Do you think you would accept Susan's terms? Judging from past research, you probably would, because the contrast between Susan's and Jim's behaviour leads you to believe that you have done your best, and you form a liking for Susan and want to cooperate with her.

Another distributive bargaining tactic is revealing a deadline. Consider the following example. Erin is a human resources manager. She is negotiating salary with Ron, who is a highly sought after new hire. Because Ron knows the company needs him, he decides to play hard and ask for an extraordinary salary and many benefits. Erin tells Ron that the company can't meet his requirements. Ron tells Erin he is going to have to think things over. Worried the company is going to lose Ron to a competitor, Erin decides to tell Ron that she is under time pressure and that she needs to reach an agreement with him immediately or she will have to offer the job to another candidate. Would you consider Erin to be a savvy negotiator? Well, she is. Why? Negotiators who reveal deadlines speed concessions from their negotiating counterparts, making them reconsider their position. And even though negotiators don't *think* this tactic works, in reality negotiators who reveal deadlines do better.[37]

INTEGRATIVE BARGAINING

A sales representative for a women's sportswear manufacturer has just closed a $15 000 order from a small clothing retailer. The sales rep calls in the order to her firm's credit department. She is told that the firm can't approve credit to this customer because of a past slow-payment record. The next day, the sales rep and the firm's credit manager meet to discuss the problem. The sales rep doesn't want to lose the business. Neither does the credit manager, but he also doesn't want to get stuck with an uncollectible debt. The two openly review their options. After considerable discussion, they agree on a solution that meets both their needs: the credit manager will approve the sale, but the clothing store's owner will provide a bank guarantee that will ensure payment if the bill isn't paid within 60 days. This sales-credit negotiation is an example of integrative bargaining. In contrast to distributive bargaining, **integrative bargaining** operates under the assumption that there exists one or more settlements that can create a win–win solution.

In terms of intra-organisational behaviour, all things being equal, integrative bargaining is preferable to distributive bargaining. Why? Because the former builds long-term relationships. It bonds negotiators and allows them to leave the bargaining table feeling that they have achieved a victory. Distributive bargaining, however, leaves one party a loser. It tends to build animosities and deepen divisions when people have to work together on an ongoing basis.

Why, then, don't we see more integrative bargaining in organisations? The answer lies in the conditions necessary for this type of negotiation to succeed. These include parties who are open with information and candid about their concerns, a sensitivity by both parties to the other's needs, the ability to trust one another, and a willingness by both parties to maintain flexibility.[38] Because these conditions often don't exist in organisations, it isn't surprising that negotiations often take on a win-at-any-cost dynamic.

There are some ways to achieve more integrative outcomes. For example, individuals who bargain in teams reach more integrative agreements than those who bargain individually. This happens because more ideas are generated when more people are at the bargaining table. So, try bargaining in teams.[39] Another way to achieve higher joint-gain settlements is to put more issues on the table. The more negotiable issues that are introduced into a negotiation, the more opportunity there is for 'logrolling' where issues are traded because of differences in preferences. This creates better outcomes for each side than if each issue were negotiated individually.[40]

Finally, you should realise that compromise may be your worst enemy in negotiating a win–win agreement. This is because compromising reduces the pressure to bargain integratively. After all, if you or your opponent caves in easily, it doesn't require anyone to be creative to reach a settlement. Thus, people end up settling for less than they could have obtained if they had been forced to consider the other party's interests, trade off issues and be creative.[41] Think of the classic example where two sisters are arguing over who gets an orange. Unbeknownst to the other party, one sister wants the orange to drink the juice, whereas the other sister wants the orange peel to bake a cake. If one sister simply capitulates and gives the other sister the orange, then they never would have been forced to explore their reasons for wanting the orange, and thus they would never find the win–win solution: they could *each* have the orange because they want different parts of it!

integrative bargaining | Negotiation that seeks one or more settlements that can create a win–win solution.

LEARNING OBJECTIVE 7

Identify the five steps in the negotiation process

THE NEGOTIATION PROCESS

Figure 15.5 provides a simplified model of the negotiation process. It views negotiation as made up of five steps: (1) preparation and planning; (2) definition of ground rules; (3) clarification and justification; (4) bargaining and problem solving; and (5) closure and implementation.[42]

PREPARATION AND PLANNING

Before you start negotiating, you need to do your homework. What is the nature of the conflict? What is the history leading up to this negotiation? Who is involved and what are their perceptions of the conflict?

What do you want from the negotiation? What are *your* goals? If you are a supply manager at Dell Computer, for instance, and your goal is to get a significant cost reduction from your supplier of keyboards, make sure that this goal stays paramount in your discussions and doesn't get overshadowed by other issues. It often helps to put your goals in writing and develop a range of outcomes—from 'most helpful' to 'minimally acceptable'—to keep your attention focused.

You also want to prepare an assessment of what you think the other party's goals are. What are they likely to ask for? How entrenched are they likely to be in their position? What intangible or hidden interests may be important to them? What might they be willing to settle on? When you can anticipate your opponent's position, you are better equipped to counter arguments with the facts and figures that support your position.

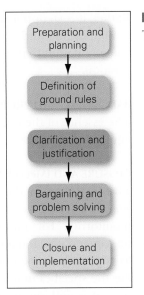

The importance of sizing up the other party is illustrated by the experience of Keith Rosenbaum, a partner in a major Los Angeles law firm. 'Once when we were negotiating to buy a business, we found that the owner was going through a nasty divorce. We were on good terms with the wife's attorney and we learned the seller's net worth. California is a community-property-law state, so we knew he had to pay her half of everything. We knew his time frame. We knew what he was willing to part with and what he was not. We knew a lot more about him than he would have wanted us to know. We were able to twist him a little bit, and get a better price.'[43]

Once you have gathered your information, use it to develop a strategy. For example, expert chess players have a strategy. They know ahead of time how they will respond to any given situation. As part of your strategy, you should determine yours and the other side's *Best Alternative To a Negotiated Agreement* (**BATNA**).[44] Your BATNA determines the lowest value acceptable to you for a negotiated agreement. Any offer you receive that is higher than your BATNA is better than an impasse. Conversely, you shouldn't expect success in your negotiation effort unless you are able to make the other side an offer they find more attractive than their BATNA. If you go into your negotiation having a good idea of what the other party's BATNA is, even if you are not able to meet theirs, you might be able to get them to change it.

BATNA | The best alternative to a negotiated agreement; the lowest acceptable value to an individual for a negotiated agreement.

DEFINITION OF GROUND RULES

Once you have done your planning and developed a strategy, you are ready to begin defining the ground rules and procedures with the other party over the negotiation itself. Who will do the negotiating? Where will it take place? What time constraints, if any, will apply? To what issues will negotiation be limited? Will there be a specific procedure to follow if an impasse is reached? During this phase, the parties will also exchange their initial proposals or demands.

CLARIFICATION AND JUSTIFICATION

When initial positions have been exchanged, both you and the other party will explain, amplify, clarify, bolster and justify your original demands. This needn't be confrontational.

Rather, it is an opportunity for educating and informing each other on the issues, why they are important, and how each arrived at their initial demands. This is the point at which you might want to provide the other party with any documentation that helps support your position.

BARGAINING AND PROBLEM SOLVING

The essence of the negotiation process is the actual give-and-take in trying to hash out an agreement. It is here where concessions will undoubtedly need to be made by both parties.

CLOSURE AND IMPLEMENTATION

The final step in the negotiation process is formalising the agreement that has been worked out and developing any procedures that are necessary for implementation and monitoring. For major negotiations—which would include everything from labour–management negotiations, to bargaining over lease terms, to buying a piece of real estate, to negotiating a job offer for a senior management position—this will require hammering out the specifics in a formal contract. For most cases, however, closure of the negotiation process is nothing more formal than a handshake.

ISSUES IN NEGOTIATION

We conclude our discussion of negotiation by reviewing four contemporary issues in negotiation: the role of mood and personality traits, gender differences in negotiating, the effect of cultural differences on negotiating styles, and the use of third parties to help resolve differences.

THE ROLE OF MOOD AND PERSONALITY TRAITS IN NEGOTIATION

You are probably not surprised to learn that mood matters in negotiation. Negotiators who are in positive moods negotiate better outcomes than those who are in average moods. Why? Negotiators who are upbeat or happy tend to trust the other party more and therefore reach more joint-gain settlements.[45] Let's assume that Abdul, a manager, is a very effective negotiator. One of the reasons Abdul is a good negotiator is because he opens negotiations by trying to put his counterparts in a good mood—he tells jokes, provides refreshments, and emphasises the positive side of what is at stake. This technique makes his counterparts bargain more integratively because they communicate their priorities, they more accurately perceive others' interests and they think more creatively.

What about personality? Can you predict an opponent's negotiating tactics if you know something about his or her personality? It is tempting to answer 'Yes' to this question. For instance, you might assume that high-risk takers would be more aggressive bargainers who make fewer concessions. Surprisingly, the evidence hasn't always supported this intuition.[46]

Assessments of the personality–negotiation relationship have been that personality traits have no significant direct effect on either the bargaining process or the negotiation outcomes. However, recent research has started to question the theory that personality and the negotiation process aren't connected. In fact, it appears that several of the Big Five traits are related to negotiation outcomes. For example, negotiators who are agreeable or extraverted are not very successful when it comes to distributive bargaining. Why? Because extraverts are outgoing and friendly, they tend to share more information than they should. And agreeable people are more interested in finding ways to cooperate rather than butt heads. These traits, while slightly helpful in integrative negotiations, are liabilities when interests are opposed.[47] So, the best distributive bargainer appears to be a disagreeable introvert—that is, someone who is interested in his own outcomes versus pleasing the other party and having a pleasant social exchange.

A big ego can also affect negotiations. For example, Samantha is an executive with a major clothing manufacturer. She is convinced that everything she touches turns to gold, and she cannot stand to look bad. An important contract with one of her company's suppliers just came up for negotiation. Excited, Samantha thinks she will take the reins during the negotiation process, but her boss tells her she is off the negotiating team. Is her boss smart to keep such a hardliner off the case? Absolutely. Why? Because a study found that individuals who are concerned with appearing competent and successful in negotiations (that is, saving face)—can have a negative effect on the outcome of the negotiation process. Individuals who were more concerned with saving face were less likely to reach agreements than those who were less concerned with coming out on top. This is because those who are overly competitive in negotiating negotiate to look good personally, rather than to attain the best agreement for all concerned.[48] So, those who are able to check their egos at the door are able to negotiate better agreements—for themselves and for others—whether the bargaining situation is distributive or integrative.

GENDER DIFFERENCES IN NEGOTIATIONS

Do men and women negotiate differently? And does gender affect negotiation outcomes? The answer to the first question appears to be 'No'.[49] The answer to the second is a qualified 'Yes'.[50]

A popular stereotype held by many is that women are more cooperative and pleasant in negotiations than are men. The evidence doesn't support this belief. However, men have been found to negotiate better outcomes than women, although the difference is relatively small. It has been postulated that this difference might be due to men and women placing divergent values on outcomes. 'It is possible that a few hundred dollars more in salary or the corner office is less important to women than forming and maintaining an interpersonal relationship.'[51]

The belief that women are 'nicer' than men in negotiations is probably due to confusing gender and the lower power typically held by women in most large organisations. The research indicates that low-power managers, regardless of gender, attempt to placate their opponents and to use softly persuasive tactics rather than direct confrontation and threats. In situations in which women and men have similar power bases, there shouldn't be any significant differences in their negotiation styles. It's interesting to note that when typical stereotypes are activated—that is, women are 'nicer' and men are 'tougher'—it becomes a self-fulfilling prophecy, reinforcing the stereotypical gender differences between male and female negotiators.[52] For example, Maria may set lower aspirations and give in more readily when negotiating because she thinks, even subconsciously, that's how women are expected to bargain. Similarly, Sunil may think he has to bargain aggressively because he believes that's how men are expected to negotiate.

The evidence suggests that women's attitudes towards negotiation and towards themselves as negotiators appear to be quite different from men's. Managerial women demonstrate less confidence in anticipation of negotiating and are less satisfied with their performance after the process is complete, even when their performance and the outcomes they achieve are similar to those for men.[53] This latter conclusion suggests that women may unduly penalise themselves by failing to engage in negotiations when such action would be in their best interests.

CULTURAL DIFFERENCES IN NEGOTIATIONS

Negotiating styles clearly vary across national cultures.[54] The French like conflict. They frequently gain recognition and develop their reputations by thinking and acting against others. As a result, the French tend to take a long time in negotiating agreements, and they aren't overly concerned about whether their opponents like or dislike them.[55] The Chinese also draw out negotiations, but that is because they believe negotiations never end. Just when you think you have pinned down every detail and reached a final solution with a Chinese executive, that executive might smile and start the process all over again. The Chinese—and the Japanese, too—negotiate to develop a relationship and a commitment to work together, rather than to tie up every loose end.[56] Compared to Australian and American negotiators, the Japanese communicate indirectly and adapt their behaviours to the situation.[57] Americans, in particular, are known around the world for their impatience and their desire to be liked.[58] Astute negotiators from other countries often turn these characteristics to their advantage by dragging out negotiations and making friendship conditional on the final settlement.

The cultural context of the negotiation significantly influences the amount and type of preparation for bargaining, the relative emphasis on task versus interpersonal relationships, the tactics used, and even where the negotiation should be conducted. To further illustrate some of these differences, let's look at two studies that compare the influence of culture on business negotiations.

The first study compared North Americans, Arabs and Russians.[59] Among the factors looked at were their negotiating style, how they responded to an opponent's arguments, their approach to making concessions, and how they handled negotiating deadlines. North Americans tried to persuade by relying on facts and appealing to logic. They countered opponents' arguments with objective facts. They made small concessions early in the negotiation to establish a relationship and usually reciprocated opponents' concessions. North Americans treated deadlines as very important. The Arabs tried to persuade by appealing to emotion. They countered opponents' arguments with subjective feelings. They made concessions throughout the bargaining process and almost always reciprocated opponents' concessions. Arabs approached deadlines very casually. The Russians based their arguments on asserted ideals. They made few, if any, concessions. Any concession offered by an opponent was viewed as a weakness and was almost never reciprocated. Finally, the Russians tended to ignore deadlines.

The second study looked at verbal and non-verbal negotiation tactics exhibited by North Americans, Japanese and Brazilians during half-hour bargaining sessions.[60] Some of the differences were particularly interesting. For instance, the Brazilians on average said 'No' 83 times, compared to 5 times for the Japanese and 9 times for the North Americans. The Japanese displayed more than 5 periods of silence lasting longer than 10 seconds during the 30-minute sessions. North Americans averaged 3.5 such periods;

Regulations governed by the Australian Standards for the Export of Livestock allow Australian meat processing firms to work with overseas buyers to address animal welfare concerns. The Australian approach to this issue is to bring about change in a cooperative manner that is sensitive to cultural differences. While Australian meatworks can slaughter livestock according to the religious requirements of specific markets, the need for trade in live animals arises because some markets have a strong cultural preference for freshly slaughtered meat. The sensitivity to cultural differences with different international trading partners has brought about changes in the way Australian firms across a range of industries do business overseas.

the Brazilians had none. The Japanese and North Americans interrupted their opponent about the same number of times, but the Brazilians interrupted 2.5 to 3 times more often than the North Americans and the Japanese. Finally, the Japanese and the North Americans had no physical contact with their opponents during negotiations except for handshaking, but the Brazilians touched each other almost five times every half hour.

THIRD-PARTY NEGOTIATIONS

To this point, we have discussed bargaining in terms of direct negotiations. Occasionally, however, individuals or group representatives reach a stalemate and are unable to resolve their differences through direct negotiations. In such cases, they may turn to a third party to help them find a solution. There are four basic third-party roles: mediator, arbitrator, conciliator and consultant.[61]

A **mediator** is a neutral third party who facilitates a negotiated solution by using reasoning and persuasion, suggesting alternatives, and the like. Mediators are widely used in labour–management negotiations and in civil court disputes. The overall effectiveness of mediated negotiations is fairly impressive. The settlement rate is approximately 60 per cent, with negotiator satisfaction at about 75 per cent. But the situation is the key to whether or not mediation will succeed; the conflicting parties must be motivated to bargain and resolve their conflict. In addition, conflict intensity cannot be too high; mediation is most effective under moderate levels of conflict. Finally, perceptions of the mediator are important; to be effective, the mediator must be perceived as neutral and non-coercive.

An **arbitrator** is a third party with the authority to dictate an agreement. Arbitration can be voluntary (requested) or compulsory (forced on the parties by law or contract).

The authority of the arbitrator varies according to the rules set by the negotiators. For instance, the arbitrator might be limited to choosing one of the negotiator's last offers or to suggesting an agreement point that is non-binding, or free to choose and make any judgment he or she wishes. The big plus of arbitration over mediation is that it always results in a settlement. Whether or not there is a negative side depends on how 'heavy-handed' the arbitrator appears. If one party is left feeling overwhelmingly defeated, that party is certain to be dissatisfied and unlikely to graciously accept the arbitrator's decision. Therefore, the conflict may resurface at a later time.

A **conciliator** is a trusted third party who provides an informal communication link between the negotiator and the opponent. Conciliation is used extensively in international, labour, family and community disputes. Comparing its effectiveness to mediation has proven difficult because the two overlap a great deal. In practice, conciliators typically act as more than mere communication conduits. They also engage in fact-finding, interpreting messages and persuading disputants to develop agreements.

A **consultant** is a skilled and impartial third party who attempts to facilitate problem solving through communication and analysis, aided by a knowledge of conflict management. In contrast to the previous roles, the consultant's role is not to settle the issues, but, rather, to improve relations between the conflicting parties so that they can reach a settlement themselves. Instead of putting forward specific solutions, the consultant tries to help the parties learn to understand and work with each other. Therefore, this approach has a longer-term focus: to build new and positive perceptions and attitudes between the conflicting parties.

mediator | A neutral third party who facilitates a negotiated solution by using reasoning, persuasion and suggestions for alternatives.

arbitrator | A third party to a negotiation who has the authority to dictate an agreement.

conciliator | A trusted third party who provides an informal communication link between the negotiator and the opponent.

consultant | An impartial third party, skilled in conflict management, who attempts to facilitate creative problem solving through communication and analysis.

SUMMARY AND IMPLICATIONS FOR MANAGERS

- Many people automatically assume that conflict is related to lower group and organisational performance. This chapter has demonstrated that this assumption is frequently incorrect. Conflict can be either constructive or destructive to the functioning of a group or unit.
- As shown in Figure 15.6, levels of conflict can be either too high or too low. Either extreme hinders performance. An optimal level is one at which there

is enough conflict to prevent stagnation, stimulate creativity, allow tensions to be released and initiate the seeds for change, yet not so much as to be disruptive or to deter coordination of activities.

- Inadequate or excessive levels of conflict can hinder the effectiveness of a group or an organisation, resulting in reduced satisfaction of group members, increased absence and turnover rates, and, eventually, lower productivity.

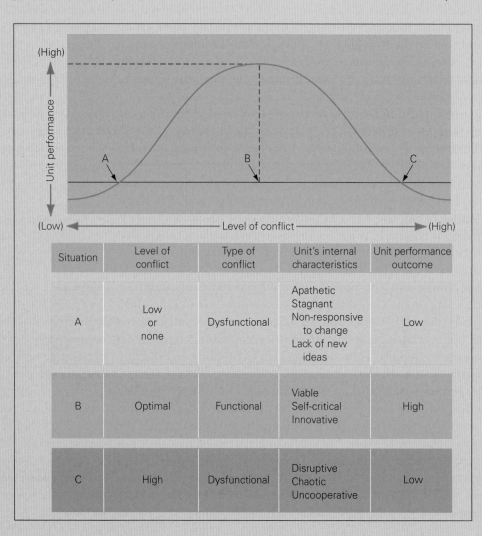

■ FIGURE 15.6

Conflict and unit performance

Situation	Level of conflict	Type of conflict	Unit's internal characteristics	Unit performance outcome
A	Low or none	Dysfunctional	Apathetic Stagnant Non-responsive to change Lack of new ideas	Low
B	Optimal	Functional	Viable Self-critical Innovative	High
C	High	Dysfunctional	Disruptive Chaotic Uncooperative	Low

- However, when conflict is at an optimal level, complacency and apathy should be minimised, motivation should be enhanced through the creation of a challenging and questioning environment with a vitality that makes work interesting, and there should be the amount of turnover needed to rid the organisation of misfits and poor performers.
- What advice can we give managers faced with excessive conflict and the need to reduce it? Don't assume there is one conflict-handling intention that will always be best! It is important to select an intention appropriate for the situation. The following provides some guidelines:[62]
  - Use *competition* when quick, decisive action is vital (in emergencies); on important issues, where unpopular actions need implementing (in cost cutting, enforcing unpopular rules, discipline); on issues vital to the organisation's welfare when you know you are right; and against people who take advantage of non-competitive behaviour.
  - Use *collaboration* to find an integrative solution when both sets of concerns are too important to be compromised; when your objective is to learn; to merge insights from people with different perspectives; to gain commitment by incorporating concerns into a consensus; and to work through feelings that have interfered with a relationship.
  - Use *avoidance* when an issue is trivial or more important issues are pressing; when you perceive no chance of satisfying your concerns; when potential disruption outweighs the benefits of resolution; to let people cool down and regain perspective; when gathering information supersedes immediate decision; when others can resolve the conflict more effectively; and when issues seem tangential or symptomatic of other issues.
  - Use *accommodation* when you find you are wrong and to allow a better position to be heard, to learn and to show your reasonableness; when issues are more important to others than to yourself and to satisfy others and maintain cooperation; to build social credits for later issues; to minimise loss when you are outmatched and losing; when harmony and stability are especially important; and to allow employees to develop by learning from mistakes.
  - Use *compromise* when goals are important but not worth the effort of potential disruption of more assertive approaches; when opponents with equal power are committed to mutually exclusive goals; to achieve temporary settlements to complex issues; to arrive at expedient solutions under time pressure; and as a backup when collaboration or competition is unsuccessful.
- Negotiation was shown to be an ongoing activity in groups and organisations.
- Distributive bargaining can resolve disputes, but it often negatively affects one or more negotiators' satisfaction because it is focused on the short term and because it is confrontational.
- Integrative bargaining, in contrast, tends to provide outcomes that satisfy all parties and that build lasting relationships.

POINT / COUNTERPOINT

Conflict Benefits Organisations

● POINT

Let's briefly review how stimulating conflict can provide benefits to the organisation.

- *Conflict is a means by which to bring about radical change*. It is an effective device by which management can drastically change the existing power structure, current interaction patterns and entrenched attitudes.
- *Conflict facilitates group cohesiveness*. Whereas conflict increases hostility between groups, external threats tend to cause a group to pull together as a unit. Intergroup conflicts raise the extent to which members identify with their own group and increase feelings of solidarity.
- *Conflict improves group and organisational effectiveness*. The stimulation of conflict initiates the search for new means and goals and provides the stimulus for innovation. The successful solution of a conflict leads to greater effectiveness, to more trust and openness, to greater attraction of members for each other, and to depersonalisation of future conflicts.
- *Conflict brings about a slightly higher, more constructive level of tension*. When the level of tension is very low, the parties are not sufficiently motivated to do something about a conflict.

Groups or organisations devoid of conflict are likely to suffer from apathy, stagnation, groupthink and other debilitating diseases. In fact, more organisations probably fail because they have *too little* conflict, not because they have too much. Take a look at this list of some large organisations that have failed or suffered serious financial setbacks over the past decade or two: General Motors, Ansett Airlines, HIH Insurance, Greyhound Coaches and Digital Computer. The common thread through these companies is that they stagnated. Their managements became complacent and unable or unwilling to facilitate change. These organisations could have benefited from functional conflict.

● COUNTERPOINT

It may be true that conflict is an inherent part of any group or organisation. It may not be possible to eliminate it completely. However, just because conflicts exist is no reason to deify them. In general, conflicts are dysfunctional, and it is one of management's major responsibilities to keep conflict intensity as low as humanly possible. A few points will support this case.

- *The negative consequences from conflict can be devastating*. The list of negatives associated with conflict is awesome. The most obvious are increased turnover, decreased employee satisfaction, inefficiencies between work units, sabotage, and labour grievances and strikes. One study estimated that managing conflict at work costs the average employer nearly 450 days of management time a year. And there are also emotional costs. Think about the nervous tension that arises when people argue. Conflict also stimulates anger. And there is a clear link between anger and physical aggression. These emotions should be avoided, not cultivated.
- *Effective managers build teamwork*. A good manager builds a coordinated team. Conflict works against such an objective. A successful work group is like a successful sports team; each member knows his or her role and supports his or her teammates. When a team works well, the whole becomes greater than the sum of the parts. Management creates teamwork by minimising internal conflicts and facilitating internal coordination.
- *Managers who accept and stimulate conflict don't survive in organisations*. The whole argument of the value of conflict may be moot as long as the majority of senior executives in organisations view conflict from the traditional view. In the traditional view, any conflict will be seen as bad. Since the evaluation of a manager's performance is made by higher-level executives, those managers who don't succeed in eliminating conflicts are likely to be appraised negatively. This, in turn, will reduce opportunities for advancement. Any manager who aspires to move up in such an environment will be wise to follow the traditional view and eliminate any outward signs of conflict. Failure to follow this advice might result in the premature departure of the manager.

SOURCE: A point in this argument was based on Q. Reade, 'Workplace Conflict Is Time-Consuming Problem for Business', *PersonnelToday.com*: <www.personneltoday.co.uk> (30 September 2004).

QUESTIONS FOR REVIEW

MyOBLab Do you understand this chapter's content?
Find out at **www.pearsoned.com.au/MyOBLab**

1. What are the disadvantages of conflict? What are its advantages?
2. What is the difference between functional and dysfunctional conflict? What determines functionality?
3. Under what conditions might conflict be beneficial to a group?
4. What are the components in the conflict process model? From your own experience, give an example of how a conflict proceeded through the five stages.
5. How could a manager stimulate conflict in his or her department?
6. What defines the settlement range in distributive bargaining?
7. Why isn't integrative bargaining more widely practised in organisations?
8. How do men and women differ, if at all, in their approaches to negotiation?
9. What problems might Americans have in negotiating with people from collectivist cultures such as China and Japan?
10. What can you do to improve your negotiating effectiveness?

QUESTIONS FOR CRITICAL THINKING

1. Do you think competition and conflict are different? Explain.
2. 'Participation is an excellent method for identifying differences and resolving conflicts.' Do you agree or disagree? Discuss.
3. From your own experience, describe a situation in which you were involved for which the conflict was dysfunctional. Describe another example, from your experience, for which the conflict was functional. Now analyse how other parties in both conflicts might have interpreted the situation in terms of whether the conflicts were functional or dysfunctional.
4. Assume an Australian manager had to negotiate a contract with a manager from China. What problems might come up? What suggestions would you make to help facilitate a settlement?

A Negotiation Role Play

This role play is designed to help you develop your negotiating skills. The class is to break into pairs. One person will play the role of Alex, the department supervisor. The other person will play CJ, Alex's boss.

The situation:

Alex and CJ work for the Nike Corporation. Alex supervises a research laboratory. CJ is the manager of research and development. Alex and CJ are former university runners who have worked for Nike for more than six years. CJ has been Alex's boss for two years.

One of Alex's employees, Lisa Roland, has greatly impressed Alex. Lisa was hired 11 months ago, is 24 years old and holds a master's degree in mechanical engineering. Her entry-level salary was $37 500 a year. She was told by Alex that, in accordance with company policy, she would receive an initial performance evaluation at six months and a comprehensive review after one year. She was also told that she could expect a salary adjustment at the time of the one-year evaluation, based on her performance record.

Alex's evaluation of Lisa after six months was very positive. Alex commented on the long hours Lisa was putting in, her cooperative spirit, the fact that others in the lab enjoyed working with her, and that she was making an immediate positive impact on the project to which she had been assigned. Now that Lisa's first anniversary is coming up, Alex has again reviewed Lisa's performance. Alex thinks Lisa may be the best new person the R&D group has ever hired. After only a year, Alex has ranked Lisa as the number-three performer in a department of 11.

Salaries in the department vary greatly. Alex, for instance, has a basic salary of $67 000, plus eligibility for a bonus that might add another $5000 to $8000 a year. The salary range of the 11 department members is $30 400 to $56 350. The lowest salary is a recent hire with a bachelor's degree in physics. The two people that Alex has rated above Lisa earn base salaries of $52 700 and $56 350. They are both 27 years old and have been at the Nike Corporation for three and four years, respectively. The median salary in Alex's department is $46 660.

Alex's role:

You want to give Lisa a big raise. Although she is young, she has proven to be an excellent addition to the department. You don't want to lose her. More importantly, she knows in general what other people in the department are earning and she thinks she is underpaid. The company typically gives one-year raises of 5 per cent, although 10 per cent isn't unusual and 20–30 per cent increases have been approved on occasion. You would like to get Lisa as large an increase as CJ will approve.

CJ's role:

All your supervisors typically try to squeeze you for as much money as they can for their people. You understand this because you did the same thing when you were a supervisor, but your boss wants to keep a lid on costs. He wants you to keep raises for recent hires generally in the 5–8 per cent range. In fact, he has sent a memo to all managers and supervisors saying this. However, your boss is also very concerned with equity and paying people what they are worth. You feel assured that he will support any salary recommendation you make, as long as it can be justified. Your goal, consistent with cost reduction, is to keep salary increases as low as possible.

The negotiation:

Alex has a meeting scheduled with CJ to discuss Lisa's performance review and salary adjustment. Take a couple of minutes to think through the facts in this exercise and to prepare a strategy. Then you have up to 15 minutes to conduct your negotiation. When your negotiation is complete, the class will compare the various strategies used and compare outcomes.

ETHICAL DILEMMA

Is it Unethical to Lie and Deceive during Negotiations?

In Chapter 11, we addressed lying in the context of communication. Here we return to the topic of lying, but specifically as it relates to negotiation. We think this issue is important because, for many people, there is no such thing as lying when it comes to negotiating.

It has been said that the whole notion of negotiation is built on ethical quicksand: to succeed, you must deceive. Is this true? Apparently a lot of people think so. For instance, one study found that 28 per cent of negotiators lied about a common-interest issue during negotiations, while another study found that 100 per cent of negotiators either failed to reveal a problem or actively lied about it during negotiations if they were not directly asked about the issue. Why do you think these numbers are so high? The research on negotiation provides numerous examples of when lying gives the negotiator a strategic advantage.

Is it possible for someone to maintain high ethical standards and, at the same time, deal with the daily need to negotiate with bosses, peers, staff, people from other organisations, friends and even relatives?

We can probably agree that bald-faced lies during negotiation are wrong. At least most ethicists would probably agree. The universal dilemma surrounds the little lies—the omissions, evasions and concealments that are often necessary to best an opponent.

During negotiations, when is a lie a *lie*? Is exaggerating benefits, downplaying negatives, ignoring flaws, or saying 'I don't know' when in reality you do, considered lying? Is declaring that 'this is my final offer and non-negotiable' (even when you are posturing) a lie? Is pretending to bend over backward to make meaningful concessions lying? Rather than being considered unethical practices, the use of these 'lies' is considered by many as indicators that a negotiator is strong, smart and savvy.

When is evasiveness and deception out of bounds? Is it naive to be completely honest and bare your soul during negotiations? Or are the rules of negotiations unique, so that any tactic that will improve your chance of winning is acceptable?

SOURCES: Based on M. E. Schweitzer, 'Deception in Negotiations', in S. J. Hoch and H. C. Kunreuther (eds), *Wharton on Making Decisions* (New York: Wiley, 2001), pp. 187–200; M. Diener, 'Fair Enough', *Entrepreneur*, January 2002, pp. 100–02; and K. O'Connor and P. Carnevale, 'A Nasty but Effective Negotiation Strategy: Misrepresentation of a Common-Value Issue', *Personality and Social Psychology Bulletin*, May 1997, pp. 504–15.

15 CASE STUDY

Managing the Team Spirit

Jared Graves is the section manager of a four-member all-male team of an information technology section at a medium-sized public hospital in Melbourne. The team provides system and software support for the extensive computer network operating at the hospital. Jared was promoted about six months ago to this first-line management position after only a year with the team as a systems programmer, largely because of his education—he has an MBA, whereas no one else in the team has a university degree. They acquired their computing skills by years of on-the-job experience and a range of Microsoft-related short courses. The transition to team manager went smoothly, and there were hardly any problems until today.

The need for an additional member for the team had been obvious to Jared for over a month. Overtime had increased considerably and was putting a strain on everyone in the section as well as the section's budget, as overtime rates were expensive. As well, some hospital managers were asking the section to develop more sophisticated database systems to improve operations in their own departments. Jared became aware of one particular employee on a short-term contract in the information technology section of another public hospital close by. The contract was about to expire in two weeks. Jared thought this person would fit his needs quite well, so he talked to the human resource people at the district level and the employee's section manager. There was general agreement that the young female database specialist, Jessica, might be a good candidate to move into Jared's team to help with the increased departmental work-load, as well as provide specialised database support for developing a number of new management information systems. Jessica had worked for the neighbouring hospital for six months, and was about to graduate with a master's degree in information technology.

Jared had discussed the new position with Jessica earlier in the week and she had been enthusiastic. Jared had said that, while he could make no promises, he thought that he would recommend her for the job. However, Jared emphasised that it would be a week or so before a final decision was made and the announcement made official.

When Jared came into his office later in the week he was confronted by Roger, a 48-year-old systems programmer who had been in the IT section at the hospital the longest. Roger, born and raised in a small country town, had heard a rumour that Jessica would be coming to work in the team. Roger did not mince his words: 'The four of us get on very well as a team. I think a young female would be dysfunctional for us. I believe I can handle the new database developments without any help and, besides, I heard that her family comes from a neighbouring town where I grew up. From my recollections, that family was a rough bunch, always causing trouble.' Roger's face was red and it was obvious that this was an emotionally charged issue for him. His short, one-way confrontation closed with the statement: 'I have no intention of working in the same section as that young lady!'

QUESTIONS
1. What is the source of this conflict?
2. Assume that you were Jared. What conflict-handling orientation would you use? Why?
3. How would external factors such as social attitudes and equal opportunity legislation influence your choice of conflict-handling orientations?
4. Do you think your approach would permanently resolve this conflict? Explain your reasons.

ENDNOTES

1. Personal interview with Queensland Police Commissioner Bob Atkinson by Dr Bruce Millett, 6 November 2006.

2. See, for instance, C. F. Fink, 'Some Conceptual Difficulties in the Theory of Social Conflict', *Journal of Conflict Resolution*, December 1968, pp. 412–60; and E. Infante, 'On the Definition of Interpersonal Conflict: Cluster Analysis Applied to the Study of Semantics', *Revista de Psicologia Social*, vol. 13, no. 3, 1998, pp. 485–93.

3. L. L. Putnam and M. S. Poole, 'Conflict and Negotiation', in F. M. Jablin, L. L. Putnam, K. H. Roberts and L. W. Porter (eds), *Handbook of Organizational Communication: An Interdisciplinary Perspective* (Newbury Park, CA: Sage, 1987), pp. 549–99.

4. K. W. Thomas, 'Conflict and Negotiation Processes in Organizations', in M. D. Dunnette and L. M. Hough (eds), *Handbook of Industrial and Organizational Psychology*, 2nd ed., vol. 3 (Palo Alto, CA: Consulting Psychologists Press, 1992), pp. 651–717.

5. For a comprehensive review of the interactionist approach, see C. De Dreu and E. Van de Vliert (eds), *Using Conflict in Organizations* (London: Sage Publications, 1997).

6. See K. A. Jehn, 'A Multimethod Examination of the Benefits and Detriments of Intragroup Conflict', *Administrative Science Quarterly*, June 1995, pp. 256–82; K. A. Jehn, 'A Qualitative Analysis of Conflict Types and Dimensions in Organizational Groups', *Administrative Science Quarterly*, September 1997, pp. 530–57; K. A. Jehn and E. A. Mannix, 'The Dynamic Nature of Conflict: A Longitudinal Study of Intragroup Conflict and Group Performance', *Academy of Management Journal*, April 2001, pp. 238–51; K. A. Jehn and C. Bendersky, 'Intragroup Conflict in Organizations: A Contingency Perspective on the Conflict–Outcome Relationship', in R. M. Kramer and B. M. Staw (eds), *Research in Organizational Behavior*, vol. 25 (Oxford, UK: Elsevier, 2003), pp. 199–210; and C. K. W. De Dreu and L. R. Weingart, 'Task versus Relationship Conflict, Team Performance, and Team Member Satisfaction: A Meta-Analysis', *Journal of Applied Psychology*, August 2003, pp. 741–49.

7. J. Yang and K. W. Mossholder, 'Decoupling Task and Relationship Conflict: The Role of Intragroup Emotional Processing', *Journal of Organizational Behavior*, vol. 25, no. 5, August 2004, pp. 589–605.

8. See S. P. Robbins, *Managing Organizational Conflict: A Nontraditional Approach* (Upper Saddle River, NJ: Prentice Hall, 1974), pp. 31–55; and Wall and Callister, 'Conflict and Its Management', pp. 517–23.

9. R. S. Peterson and K. J. Behfar, 'The Dynamic Relationship between Performance Feedback, Trust, and Conflict in Groups: A Longitudinal Study', *Organizational Behavior & Human Decision Processes*, September–November 2003, pp. 102–12.

10. Jehn, 'A Multimethod Examination of the Benefits and Detriments of Intragroup Conflict'.

11. R. Friedman, C. Anderson, J. Brett, M. Olekalns, N. Goates and C. C. Lisco, 'The Positive and Negative Effects of Anger on Dispute Resolution: Evidence from Electronically Mediated Disputes', *Journal of Applied Psychology*, April 2004, pp. 369–76.

12. M. J. Gelfand, M. Higgins, L. H. Nishii, J. L. Raver, A. Dominguez, F. Murakami, S. Yamaguchi and M. Toyama, 'Culture and Egocentric Perceptions of Fairness in Conflict and Negotiation', *Journal of Applied Psychology*, October 2002, pp. 833–45.

13. L. R. Pondy, 'Organizational Conflict: Concepts and Models', *Administrative Science Quarterly*, September 1967, p. 302.

14. See, for instance, R. L. Pinkley, 'Dimensions of Conflict Frame: Disputant Interpretations of Conflict', *Journal of Applied Psychology*, April 1990, pp. 117–26; and R. L. Pinkley and G. B. Northcraft, 'Conflict Frames of Reference: Implications for Dispute Processes and Outcomes', *Academy of Management Journal*, February 1994, pp. 193–205.

15. R. Kumar, 'Affect, Cognition and Decision Making in Negotiations: A Conceptual Integration', in M. A. Rahim (ed.), *Managing Conflict: An Integrative Approach* (New York: Praeger, 1989), pp. 185–94; for a more recent study, see A. M. Isen, A. A. Labroo and P. Durlach, 'An Influence of Product and Brand Name on Positive Affect: Implicit and Explicit Measures', *Motivation & Emotion*, March 2004, pp. 43–63.

16. Ibid.

17. P. J. D. Carnevale and A. M. Isen, 'The Influence of Positive Affect and Visual Access on the Discovery of Integrative Solutions in Bilateral Negotiations', *Organizational Behavior and Human Decision Processes*, February 1986, pp. 1–13.

18. Thomas, 'Conflict and Negotiation Processes in Organizations'.

19. Ibid.

20. See R. J. Sternberg and L. J. Soriano, 'Styles of Conflict Resolution', *Journal of Personality and Social Psychology*, July 1984, pp. 115–26; R. A. Baron, 'Personality and Organizational Conflict: Effects of the Type A Behavior Pattern and Self-Monitoring', *Organizational Behavior and Human Decision Processes*, October 1989, pp. 281–96; R. J. Volkema and T. J. Bergmann, 'Conflict Styles as Indicators of Behavioral Patterns in Interpersonal Conflicts', *Journal of Social Psychology*, February 1995, pp. 5–15; and J. A. Rhoades, J. Arnold and C. Jay, 'The Role of Affective Traits and Affective States in Disputants' Motivation and Behavior during Episodes of Organizational Conflict', *Journal of Organizational Behavior*, May 2001, pp. 329–45.

21. Thomas, 'Conflict and Negotiation Processes in Organizations'.

22. See, for instance, R. A. Cosier and C. R. Schwenk, 'Agreement and Thinking Alike: Ingredients for Poor Decisions', *Academy of Management Executive*, February 1990, pp. 69–74; K. A. Jehn, 'Enhancing Effectiveness: An Investigation of Advantages and Disadvantages of Value-Based Intragroup Conflict', *International Journal of Conflict Management*, July 1994, pp. 223–38; R. L. Priem, D. A. Harrison and N. K. Muir, 'Structured Conflict and Consensus Outcomes in Group Decision Making', *Journal of Management*, vol. 21, no. 4, 1995, pp. 691–710; and K. A. Jehn and E. A. Mannix, 'The Dynamic Nature of Conflict: A Longitudinal Study of Intragroup Conflict and Group Performance', *Academy of Management Journal*, April 2001, pp. 238–51.

23. See, for instance, C. J. Loomis, 'Dinosaurs?', *Fortune*, 3 May 1993, pp. 36–42.

24. K. Swisher, 'Yahoo! May Be Down, But Don't Count It Out', *Wall Street Journal*, 9 March 2001, p. B1; and M. Mangalindan and S. L. Hwang, 'Coterie of Early Hires Made Yahoo! A Hit But an Insular Place', *Wall Street Journal*, 9 March 2001, p. A1.

25. I. L. Janis, *Victims of Groupthink* (Boston: Houghton Mifflin, 1972).

26. J. Hall and M. S. Williams, 'A Comparison of Decision-Making Performances in Established and Ad-Hoc Groups', *Journal of Personality and Social Psychology*, February 1966, p. 217.

27. R. L. Hoffman, 'Homogeneity of Member Personality and Its Effect on Group Problem-Solving', *Journal of Abnormal and Social Psychology*, January 1959, pp. 27–32; R. L. Hoffman and N. R. F. Maier, 'Quality and Acceptance of Problem Solutions by Members of Homogeneous and Heterogeneous Groups', *Journal of Abnormal and Social Psychology*, March 1961, pp. 401–07; and P. Pitcher and A. D. Smith, 'Top Management Team Heterogeneity: Personality, Power, and Proxies', *Organization Science*, January–February 2001, pp. 1–18.

28. See T. H. Cox and S. Blake, 'Managing Cultural Diversity: Implications for Organizational Competitiveness', *Academy of Management Executive*, August 1991, pp. 45–56; T. H. Cox, S. A. Lobel and P. L. McLeod, 'Effects of Ethnic Group Cultural Differences on Cooperative Behavior on a Group Task', *Academy of Management Journal*, December 1991, pp. 827–47; P. L. McLeod and S. A. Lobel, 'The Effects of Ethnic Diversity on Idea Generation in Small Groups', Paper presented at the Annual Academy of Management Conference, Las Vegas, August 1992; C. Kirchmeyer and A. Cohen, 'Multicultural Groups: Their Performance and Reactions with Constructive Conflict', *Group & Organization Management*, June 1992, pp. 153–70; D. E. Thompson and L. E. Gooler, 'Capitalizing on the Benefits of Diversity through Workteams', in E. E. Kossek and S. A. Lobel (eds), *Managing Diversity: Human Resource Strategies for Transforming the Workplace* (Cambridge, MA: Blackwell, 1996), pp. 392–437; L. H. Pelled, K. M. Eisenhardt and K. R. Xin, 'Exploring the Black Box: An Analysis of Work Group Diversity, Conflict, and Performance', *Administrative Science Quarterly*, March 1999, pp. 1–28; and D. van Knippenberg, C. K. W. De Dreu and A. C. Homan, 'Work Group Diversity and Group Performance: An Integrative Model and Research Agenda', *Journal of Applied Psychology*, December 2004, pp. 1008–22.

29. R. E. Hill, 'Interpersonal Compatibility and Work Group Performance among Systems Analysts: An Empirical Study', *Proceedings of the Seventeenth Annual Midwest Academy of Management Conference*, Kent, OH, April 1974, pp. 97–110.

30. D. C. Pelz and F. Andrews, *Scientists in Organizations* (New York: Wiley, 1966).

31. For example, see Wall and Callister, 'Conflict and Its Management', pp. 523–26 for evidence supporting the argument that conflict is almost uniformly dysfunctional; see also P. J. Hinds and D. E. Bailey, 'Out of Sight, Out of Sync: Understanding Conflict in Distributed Teams', *Organization Science*, November–December 2003, pp. 615–32.

32. M. Geyelin and E. Felsenthal, 'Irreconcilable Differences Force Shea & Gould Closure', *Wall Street Journal*, 31 January 1994, p. B1.

33. This section is based on F. Sommerfield, 'Paying the Troops to Buck the System', *Business Month*, May 1990, pp. 77–79; W. Kiechel III, 'How to Escape the Echo Chamber', *Fortune*, 18 June 1990, pp. 129–30; E. Van de Vliert and C. De Dreu, 'Optimizing Performance by Stimulating Conflict', *International Journal of Conflict Management*, July 1994, pp. 211–22; E. Van de Vliert, 'Enhancing Performance by Conflict-Stimulating Intervention', in C. De Dreu and E. Van de Vliert (eds), *Using Conflict in Organizations* (London: Sage Publications, 1997), pp. 208–22; K. M. Eisenhardt, J. L. Kahwajy and L. J. Bourgeois III, 'How Management Teams Can Have a Good Fight', *Harvard Business Review*, July–August 1997, pp. 77–85; S. Wetlaufer, 'Common Sense and Conflict', *Harvard Business Review*, January–February 2000, pp. 114–24; and G. A. Okhuysen and K. M. Eisenhardt, 'Excel through Group Process', in E. A. Locke (ed.), *Handbook of Principles of Organizational Behavior* (Malden, MA: Blackwell, 2004), pp. 216–18.

34. J. A. Wall, Jr, *Negotiation: Theory and Practice* (Glenview, IL: Scott, Foresman, 1985).

35. R. E. Walton and R. B. McKersie, *A Behavioral Theory of Labor Negotiations: An Analysis of a Social Interaction System* (New York: McGraw-Hill, 1965).

36. S. E. Brodt and M. Tuchinsky, 'Working Together but in Opposition: An Examination of the "Good Cop/Bad Cop" Negotiating Team Tactic', *Organizational Behavior & Human Decision Processes*, March 2000, pp. 155–77.

37. D. A. Moore, 'Myopic Prediction, Self-Destructive Secrecy, and the Unexpected Benefits of Revealing Final Deadlines in Negotiation', *Organizational Behavior & Human Decision Processes*, July 2004, pp. 125–39.

38. Thomas, 'Conflict and Negotiation Processes in Organizations'.

39. P. M. Morgan and R. S. Tindale, 'Group vs. Individual Performance in Mixed-Motive Situations: Exploring an Inconsistency', *Organizational Behavior & Human Decision Processes*, January 2002, pp. 44–65.

40. C. E. Naquin, 'The Agony of Opportunity in Negotiation: Number of Negotiable Issues, Counterfactual Thinking, and Feelings of Satisfaction', *Organizational Behavior & Human Decision Processes*, May 2003, pp. 97–107.

41. C. K. W. De Dreu, L. R. Weingart and S. Kwon, 'Influence of Social Motives on Integrative Negotiation: A Meta-Analytic Review and Test of Two Theories', *Journal of Personality & Social Psychology*, May 2000, pp. 889–905.

42. This model is based on R. J. Lewicki, 'Bargaining and Negotiation', *Exchange: The Organizational Behavior Teaching Journal*, vol. 6, no. 2, 1981, pp. 39–40.

43. J. Lee, 'The Negotiators', *Forbes*, 11 January 1999, pp. 22–24.

44. M. H. Bazerman and M. A. Neale, *Negotiating Rationally* (New York: Free Press, 1992), pp. 67–68.

45. C. Anderson and L. L. Thompson, 'Affect from the Top Down: How Powerful Individuals' Positive Affect Shapes Negotiations', *Organizational Behavior & Human Decision Processes*, November 2004, pp. 125–39.

46. J. A. Wall, Jr and M. W. Blum, 'Negotiations', *Journal of Management*, June 1991, pp. 278–82.

47. B. Barry and R. A. Friedman, 'Bargainer Characteristics in Distributive and Integrative Negotiation', *Journal of Personality & Social Psychology*, February 1998, pp. 345–59.

48. J. B. White, R. Tynan, A. D. Galinsky and L. Thompson, 'Face Threat Sensitivity in Negotiation: Roadblock to Agreement and Joint Gain', *Organizational Behavior & Human Decision Processes*, July 2004, pp. 102–24.

49. C. Watson and L. R. Hoffman, 'Managers as Negotiators: A Test of Power versus Gender as Predictors of Feelings, Behavior, and Outcomes', *Leadership Quarterly*, Spring 1996, pp. 63–85.

50. A. E. Walters, A. F. Stuhlmacher and L. L. Meyer, 'Gender and Negotiator Competitiveness: A Meta-Analysis', *Organizational Behavior and Human Decision Processes*, October 1998, pp. 1–29; and A. F. Stuhlmacher and A. E. Walters, 'Gender Differences in

Negotiation Outcome: A Meta-Analysis', *Personnel Psychology*, Autumn 1999, pp. 653–77.

51. Stuhlmacher and Walters, 'Gender Differences in Negotiation Outcome', p. 655.

52. L. J. Kray, A. D. Galinsky and L. Thompson, 'Reversing the Gender Gap in Negotiations: An Exploration of Stereotype Regeneration', *Organizational Behavior & Human Decision Processes*, March 2002, pp. 386–409.

53. C. K. Stevens, A. G. Bavetta and M. E. Gist, 'Gender Differences in the Acquisition of Salary Negotiation Skills: The Role of Goals, Self-Efficacy, and Perceived Control', *Journal of Applied Psychology*, vol. 78, no. 5, October 1993, pp. 723–35.

54. See N. J. Adler, *International Dimensions of Organizational Behavior*, 4th ed. (Cincinnati, OH: Southwestern, 2002),

pp. 208–56; W. L. Adair, T. Okurmura and J. M. Brett, 'Negotiation Behavior When Cultures Collide: The United States and Japan', *Journal of Applied Psychology*, June 2001, pp. 371–85; M. J. Gelfand, M. Higgins, L. H. Nishii, J. L. Raver, A. Dominguez, F. Murakami, S. Yamaguchi and M. Toyama, 'Culture and Egocentric Perceptions of Fairness in Conflict and Negotiation', *Journal of Applied Psychology*, October 2002, pp. 833–45; and X. Lin and S. J. Miller, 'Negotiation Approaches: Direct and Indirect Effect of National Culture', *International Marketing Review*, vol. 20, no. 3, 2003, pp. 286–303.

55. K. D. Schmidt, *Doing Business in France* (Menlo Park, CA: SRI International, 1987).

56. S. Lubman, 'Round and Round', *Wall Street Journal*, 10 December 1993, p. R3.

57. W. L. Adair, T. Okumura and J. M. Brett,

'Negotiation Behavior When Cultures Collide: The United States and Japan', *Journal of Applied Psychology*, June 2001, pp. 371–85.

58. P. R. Harris and R. T. Moran, *Managing Cultural Differences*, 5th ed. (Houston: Gulf Publishing, 1999), pp. 56–59.

59. E. S. Glenn, D. Witmeyer and K. A. Stevenson, 'Cultural Styles of Persuasion', *Journal of Intercultural Relations*, Fall 1977, pp. 52–66.

60. J. Graham, 'The Influence of Culture on Business Negotiations', *Journal of International Business Studies*, Spring 1985, pp. 81–96.

61. Wall and Blum, 'Negotiations', pp. 283–87.

62. K. W. Thomas, 'Toward Multidimensional Values in Teaching: The Example of Conflict Behaviors', *Academy of Management Review*, July 1977, p. 487.

INTEGRATIVE CASE STUDY

Trust: The foundation of leadership in politics?

DR GLENICE WOOD

SCHOOL OF MANAGEMENT, UNIVERSITY OF BALLARAT

In July 2006, Prime Minister John Howard announced to the Australian people that he would contest the next election. The announcement put paid to the aspirations of Treasurer Peter Costello to become the next prime minister—at least in the short term. What is it about Peter Costello's very forthright desire to become prime minister that has failed to ignite either his party, or the public, to support his taking over the mantle of success?

According to Jennifer Hewett, the reasons are multifaceted. She believes the public aren't comfortable with someone who appears to be demanding to have 'his turn' at the top job in the Liberal Party. The Liberal Party is uncomfortable about terminating a very popular prime minister who appears to command respect, and who has successfully guided them to four straight victories at the ballot box. Public perception seems to be that John Howard isn't slowing down—he is seen as 'indefatigable' by his political foes as well as by his friends and supporters.

It appears that the reason Peter Costello isn't able to swing public or partisan support behind him is that there is a lingering perception that he lacks political judgment and, perhaps oddly, that he doesn't read the political environment accurately. At the very least, it appears that Peter Costello fails to get his timing right. Even more damning is the perception that he hasn't been tested by adversity sufficiently. Overall, this paints a picture of uncertainty for the public and within the party, and it is human nature to like a sure thing.

One of the most difficult tasks for Costello in the near future will be to try to rebuild his political standing, which currently is seen as diminished. 'He agitated for the leadership and did not test the numbers, and then withdrew. Among some segments of the electorate, this will inevitably call into question his fortitude.' As a result, Costello's standing with his colleagues has been damaged, and it will be hard to shake the perception of a would-be leader who has plenty of talent but whose ambition overrides a commonsense view of the political landscape.

In contrast, John Howard has read the mood just right. He knows that he has strong support from his Liberal colleagues, who have the view that 'If it ain't broke, don't fix it', believing that his leadership gives the coalition the best chance at winning the next election. John Howard is seen as a winner, and most of his party room believe that he will continue to be so. Even Kim Beazley, when Opposition leader, welcomed the decision by John Howard to stay on in his role.

For the moment, it would seem that any notion of a challenge to John Howard has been put on the back burner. Both Howard and Costello will 'work together' to achieve another electoral victory for the Liberal Party. But it appears that 'their once-famous relationship (is) badly damaged by the events of the past'. According to Michelle Grattan, the 'double act' has been irreparably damaged. Even though the question of leadership may be resolved for the moment, 'the task of rehabilitating the partnership into a close, cohesive and credible one hasn't even begun'.

How do these very public aspirations sit with the party room, and what impact will these events have on the effective team functioning of the Liberal Party? Even though Howard and Costello have decided to remain a 'double act', it may now be much more difficult to continue to keep up appearances of solidarity when it is painfully obvious to all that there is profound disagreement 'on what is best for themselves, their party and the nation'. There is recognition that the amnesty is short term: 'Not by a long stretch has he (Costello) given up hope of holding the highest office in the land.' Recently, Costello was quoted as saying, 'Inside every MP is a glorious prime ministership waiting to get out if only they are given the chance.'

Although there is a common consensus that Peter Costello would, or even should, become a successor to the prime minister if John Howard was no longer in the role, there is also a strong view that John Howard should remain as long as he wishes to do so, or at the very least, goes on winning. Nevertheless, there is recognition of how difficult it must be for the treasurer's 'thwarted ambitions'.

One possible outcome of these recent events is that Peter Costello doesn't now have a guarantee of becoming prime minister of the country, certainly not at this time, or possibly, not even in the future. What was once seen as a certainty—that Costello would take over the leadership, much as an 'anointed crown prince'—is no longer seen as secure. Others within the party who harbour personal ambitions to be leaders of the future may now feel that there is an opportunity for them to stake their claim.

Certainly the opposition are making maximum gain from the decision of Howard to run for a fifth term in office. Kim Beazley has been quoted as calling Costello 'a political husk of a man'. And this turmoil is occurring in an environment where there is 'increasing angst over petrol prices, higher interest rates and deep concern about the impact of the government's industrial relations changes'.

What these events will do to the Liberal Party remains to be seen. As discussed in your text, members of effective teams trust each other. Ideally, they also exhibit trust in their leaders. When team members are able to trust each other, this facilitates cooperation, and the need to monitor others' behaviour is lessened. When trust is well established, there is a sense that other members won't take advantage of them. Trust is equally important in terms of leadership; when trust is established, members of the team are more willing to accept and commit to the goals and decisions of the leader. It would appear that the question of trust and leadership in the Liberal Party has been dealt a serious blow.

In the context of what has happened to Peter Costello since the events of 31 July 2006, what suggestions do you have for anyone aspiring to be the prime minister of Australia?

QUESTIONS

1. What will be the impact on the Liberal Party group behaviour? Will an effective team be possible in this type of atmosphere? Could we assume that John Howard and Peter Costello could work together effectively as part of a team? What type of atmosphere must there be? Can trust be established under these circumstances?

2. What impact do you think the events since 31 July 2006 will have on Peter Costello's personal ability to continue to carry out his role as treasurer and maintain his motivation and commitment? Will it be possible for him to remain a 'loyal deputy' and a team player?

3. What is it about John Howard's leadership that makes it so successful? How would you describe Peter Costello's leadership? Given the definition of 'trust'—'a positive expectation that another won't act opportunistically'—do you consider that Peter Costello can claim to lead in this way? What type of trust has been most damaged in the organisational relationship between John Howard and Peter Costello?

4. In terms of power and politics, what type of power base do you feel operates between John Howard and Peter Costello?

5. What are the differences between leadership and power?

6. Would you describe the conflict that has been in evidence in the Liberal Party during the leadership question as functional or dysfunction? Explain your views.

SOURCES: T. Barrass, *The Australian*, 1 August 2006, p. 5; S. Carney, *The Age*, 1 August 2006, p. 11; B. Doherty, *The Age*, 1 August 2006, p. 2; M. Gordon, *The Age*, 1 August 2006, p. 1; M. Grattan, *The Age*, 1 August 2006, p. 2; J. Hewett, *Australian Financial Review*, 1 August, p. 9; S. Lewis, *The Australian*, 1 August 2006, p. 12; G. Megalogenis, *The Australian*, 1 August 2006, p. 11; and M. Schubert, *The Age*, 1 August 2006, p. 2.

MAREE BOYLE

UNIVERSITY OF QUEENSLAND

Bill Jones, team leader and support coach at Synergis, an outstanding medium-sized management-consulting firm, walked into the managing director's office filled with apprehension. Alan Smith had called a meeting with him at short notice, with a cryptic message from his executive assistant about the nature of that meeting. It was unlike Alan not to provide Bill with details about meetings. Alan was a passionate believer in transparent communication and decision making. He had gained a lot of respect from his employees because of his 'up-front' management style. As one long-time staff member commented: 'We may not like some of his decisions, but we always know where we stand with Alan.' Alan believed that in order for a knowledge-intensive firm such as Synergis to remain competitive and dynamic, open and collaborative communication and leadership styles were crucial to the continuing success of the firm.

Bill tried to dismiss a nagging feeling he'd had all day that something wasn't quite right. But when he examined his feelings closely, he realised he had regularly felt uneasy during the past few months. He had felt this way since the announcement of the merger between Synergis and Abacus. Initially, Synergis staff found it difficult to understand why there needed to be a merger between the two firms. Not only did they have very divergent organisational cultures, they were also at different stages of their organisational life cycles. Abacus was a mature, conservative business-consulting firm that had experienced slow growth in recent years. The owner of Abacus, Elliott West, was keen to form a productive alliance with a younger, more productive firm, and began to search for one that might fit the criteria.

Elliott was a self-made and uneducated entrepreneur. Although he had grown a very successful business, he had always been in awe of the professional MBA-educated managers he hired to run his company. Elliott's feeling of inadequacy about his lack of education often led him to accept advice from his managers without questioning whether or not it was appropriate. The idea of a merger was 'sold' to him by the very ambitious and charismatic marketing manager, Nick Brown, who had been with Abacus for about a year. Elliott left all the negotiations with Synergis about the merger to his management team, and trusted them implicitly. He had met the Synergis team twice and was impressed by what he saw. There were times he thought that the outcomes of such a union would be almost too good to be true, but he dismissed the idea as negative thinking.

Elliott also had doubts about the effect such a merger would have upon the staff of both companies. His management team were adamant that although there would be pain for current employees of Synergis, the Abacus way of doing things would have to prevail. Synergis had a lot to offer, but Elliott's managers warned of letting the younger employees of Synergis 'loose'. They explained to Elliott that individual employees had too much power and that Synergis wasn't centralised enough. If Elliott were to gain control of the merged entity, the Synergists would need to be 'brought into line'.

The Abacus management team, in particular Nick Brown, developed a secret 'containment' plan that would be rolled out once the merger was official. They convinced Elliott that sufficient consultation had occurred with Synergist staff and that the executive staff were supportive of the plan. Despite having reservations about aspects of the plan, Elliott agreed for the plan to be implemented.

So, as Bill walked into the office and sat down in front of Alan, he realised why he had been feeling nervous. Alan looked as though he was about to deliver bad news. Alan told Bill that he had been informed by a disgruntled Abacus employee that senior management had a 'containment' plan ready to roll out once the merger was official. This plan would involve downsizing Bill's area, which conducted most of the research and development work central to maintaining Synergis's competitiveness. He also told Bill that the plan included moves to replace senior Synergis staff with middle managers from Abacus in order to reduce the costs of the merger. Bill was shocked at the news. He had met recently with his counterpart in Abacus and had no inkling that this would be a likely outcome of the merger. If anything, Abacus management seemed more than willing to cooperate with Synergis, particularly in relation to the merger of IT and HRM systems and procedures.

Alan and Bill arranged a meeting with Elliott later that week. When confronted with what Alan and Bill told him, Elliott first denied that such a plan existed. He then realised that the quality of some of the information he was receiving from his senior managers may be problematic. Instead of confronting them, particularly Nick, Elliott decided to do some investigations of his own. What he found startled him. Not only was Nick feeding him false information, but he had successfully convinced many of the Abacus staff members that he was the driving force behind Abacus, and that when the merger occurred he was the natural heir to the newly merged entity. He also presented an image of Elliott as 'past his prime' and needing 'looking after'.

Although angry and upset, Elliott decided not to retaliate. Instead, he worked with Alan and Bill over the next few weeks to develop an alternative 'containment' plan, as well as a proactive merger plan that concentrated on aligning the two distinct cultures. Elliott developed a sound working relationship with the two Synergis executives, and came to appreciate the level of expertise and culture of excellence that the Synergists would contribute to the newly formed organisation.

At the same time, Elliott continued to work with Nick Brown on planning the rollout. Nick had no knowledge of Elliott's secret meetings with Synergis, and assumed that Elliott would be making the announcement about the new CEO soon. He thought it strange that Elliott hadn't formally discussed it with him, but was confident that Elliott wouldn't consider anyone else for the position.

A month before the merger, Nick met with Elliott in his office. Elliott was quiet but firm when he informed Nick that it would be Alan, not himself, who would be the CEO of the new organisation, which would be called Synabis. Elliott also told Nick that he wouldn't be renewing his contract, which was due to expire in three months. Nick Brown's payout was considerably larger than was stipulated in his contract, but Elliott West was relieved he was now free of Nick's influence.

QUESTIONS

1. What are the main kinds of power bases Elliott used to solve the problem of Nick Brown undermining his position?
2. What were the main power tactics used in this scenario? Which ones were the most successful? Why?
3. How were both legitimate and illegitimate political behaviour used together in this instance?
4. Describe how a power coalition formed in this case. Provide reasons for why it worked.
5. How could Elliott West have avoided the expensive termination payment for Nick Brown?
6. Demonstrate how 'truth' became a 'casualty' because of political action in this case.
7. What does the case highlight about group dynamics in organisations?

16

FOUNDATIONS OF ORGANISATION STRUCTURE

LEARNING OBJECTIVES

AFTER STUDYING THIS CHAPTER, YOU SHOULD BE ABLE TO:

1. IDENTIFY THE SIX KEY ELEMENTS THAT DEFINE AN ORGANISATION'S STRUCTURE

2. EXPLAIN THE CHARACTERISTICS OF A BUREAUCRACY

3. DESCRIBE A MATRIX ORGANISATION

4. EXPLAIN THE CHARACTERISTICS OF A VIRTUAL ORGANISATION

5. SUMMARISE WHY MANAGERS WANT TO CREATE BOUNDARYLESS ORGANISATIONS

6. LIST THE FACTORS THAT FAVOUR DIFFERENT ORGANISATIONAL STRUCTURES

7. CONTRAST MECHANISTIC AND ORGANIC STRUCTURAL MODELS

8. EXPLAIN THE BEHAVIOURAL IMPLICATIONS OF DIFFERENT ORGANISATIONAL DESIGNS

Decisions about organisational design in a university setting must take into account a range of issues, including how best to provide a satisfying experience for students and to enhance teaching and discipline expertise with sound research.

ACADEMICS WOULD SAY that universities are quite different from private sector organisations such as McDonald's and Harvey Norman. They would also suggest that their work is quite unlike that in other public sector organisations such as the Australian Government Department of Immigration and Multicultural Affairs. However, when it comes to structuring the work of organisations, universities are similar to other organisations. They have to determine how to divide the work up into efficient groupings, and nominate who is responsible for those groups and accountable for the work outcomes. They also have to design effective ways of integrating the work so that the various sections and departments collaborate with each other.

The Faculty of Business at the University of Southern Queensland has debated for a number of years whether it should continue with its departmental structure based on the following seven discipline groupings: management and organisational behaviour, marketing and tourism, resource management, law, accounting, finance and information systems. The alternative is to change to a school structure that combines a number of disciplines into three larger but more manageable groupings of commerce, management and information systems. Dividing up the work in an academic institution generally focuses on an internal orientation of academic disciplines. One issue for considering a change in structure in a faculty is also to have an effective external orientation in catering for the demands and requirements of students.

The issue of responsibility and accountability for academic programs is also an area of debate when it comes to structuring academic work. Central Queensland University (CQU) has a higher proportion of international students than any other Australian university; according to its vice-chancellor Professor John Rickard, CQU derives 50 per cent of its income from international students. CQU's success is an example of a public/private partnership—between Campus Group Holdings and CQU (operating as C Management Services)—providing the best of collegiality and the corporate. The CQU case is an example of where the structural responsibilities and accountabilities for success can incorporate private enterprise organisations that operate somewhat independently of the normal university structure.

The coordination and integration of academic work is also a challenge. Michael Finney moved from the University of Queensland (UQ) to become chief executive of Queensland University of Technology's (QUT) new commercialisation unit. One great lesson about organisational structure that he learned from his experience with the commercial unit at UQ, Uniquest, was the hub-and-spoke model. Uniquest was originally created, like many other commercialisation units, in a single office—somewhat of an ivory tower, according to Finney. In 2001, Uniquest started locating staff in the faculties. Finney sees this structure to be even more relevant at QUT, which is a multi-campus institution. As he points out: 'Having people located among the researchers where they walk the corridors and are seen as part of the research community is vital. You want to be seen as commercial and professional, but many academics find that daunting so you have to bridge that gap. You have to allow people to come to you, not force commercial culture on people.'[1]

Every revolution evaporates and leaves behind only the slime of a new bureaucracy.

Franz Kafka

ORGANISATION STRUCTURES *can* shape attitudes and behaviour. In the following pages, we define the key components that make up an organisation's structure, present half a dozen or so structural design options from which managers can choose, identify the contingency factors that make certain structural designs preferable in varying situations, and conclude by considering the different effects that various organisational designs have on employee behaviour.

organisational structure | How job tasks are formally divided, grouped and coordinated.

work specialisation | The degree to which tasks in the organisation are subdivided into separate jobs.

WHAT IS ORGANISATIONAL STRUCTURE?

An **organisational structure** defines how job tasks are formally divided, grouped and coordinated. There are six key elements that managers need to address when they design their organisation's structure. These are: work specialisation, departmentalisation, chain of command, span of control, centralisation and decentralisation, and formalisation.[2] Table 16.1 presents each of these elements as answers to an important structural question. The following sections describe these six elements of structure.

WORK SPECIALISATION

Early in the 20th century, Henry Ford became rich and famous by building automobiles on an assembly line. Every Ford worker was assigned a specific, repetitive task. For instance, one person would just put on the right-front wheel, and someone else would install the right-front door. By breaking jobs up into small standardised tasks, which could be performed over and over again, Ford was able to produce cars at the rate of one every ten seconds, while using employees who had relatively limited skills.

Ford demonstrated that work can be performed more efficiently if employees are allowed to specialise. Today, we use the term **work specialisation**, or *division of labour*, to describe the degree to which activities in the organisation are subdivided into separate jobs. The essence of work specialisation is that, rather than an entire job being done by one individual, it is broken down into a number of steps, with each step being completed by a separate individual. In essence, individuals specialise in doing part of an activity rather than the entire activity. By the late 1940s, most manufacturing jobs in industrialised countries were being done with high work specialisation. Management saw this as a means

■ **TABLE 16.1**

Six key questions that managers need to answer in designing an organisation structure

Key question	The answer is provided by
1. To what degree are tasks subdivided into separate jobs?	Work specialisation
2. On what basis will jobs be grouped together?	Departmentalisation
3. To whom do individuals and groups report?	Chain of command
4. How many individuals can a manager efficiently and effectively direct?	Span of control
5. Where does decision-making authority lie?	Centralisation and decentralisation
6. To what degree will there be rules and regulations to direct employees and managers?	Formalisation

to make the most efficient use of its employees' skills. In most organisations, some tasks require highly developed skills and others can be performed by untrained workers. If all workers were engaged in each step of, say, an organisation's manufacturing process, all would have to have the skills necessary to perform both the most demanding and the least demanding jobs. The result would be that, except when performing the most skilled or highly complex tasks, employees would be working below their skill levels. And because skilled workers are paid more than unskilled workers and their wages tend to reflect their highest level of skill, it represents an inefficient use of organisational resources to pay highly skilled workers to do easy tasks.

Managers also saw other efficiencies that could be achieved through work specialisation. Employee skills at performing a task successfully increase through repetition. Less time is spent in changing tasks, in putting away one's tools and equipment from a prior step in the work process, and in getting ready for another. Equally important, training for specialisation is more efficient from the organisation's perspective. It is easier and less costly to find and train workers to do specific and repetitive tasks. This is especially true of highly sophisticated and complex operations. For example, could Cessna produce one Citation jet a year if one person had to build the entire plane alone? Not likely! Finally, work specialisation increases efficiency and productivity by encouraging the creation of special inventions and machinery.

For much of the first half of the 20th century, managers viewed work specialisation as an unending source of increased productivity. And they were probably right. Because specialisation was not widely practised, its introduction almost always generated higher productivity. But by the 1960s, there came increasing evidence that a good thing can be carried too far. The point had been reached in some jobs at which the human diseconomies from specialisation—which surfaced as boredom, fatigue, stress, low productivity, poor quality, increased absenteeism and high turnover—more than offset the economic advantages (see Figure 16.1). In such cases, productivity could be increased by enlarging, rather than narrowing, the scope of job activities. In addition, a number of companies found that by giving employees a variety of activities to do, allowing them to do a whole and complete job, and putting them into teams with interchangeable skills, they often achieved significantly higher output, with increased employee satisfaction.

Most managers today see work specialisation as neither obsolete nor as an unending source of increased productivity. Rather, managers recognise the economies it provides in

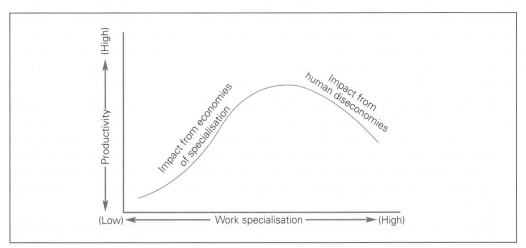

Economies and diseconomies of work specialisation

certain types of jobs and the problems it creates when it is carried too far. You will find, for example, high work specialisation being used by McDonald's to efficiently make and sell hamburgers and fries, and by medical specialists in most health-care organisations. However, information technology companies such as NEC (Australia) and service organisations such as Queensland Health have had success by broadening the scope of jobs and *reducing* specialisation. For example, employees in the electronics assembly career stream at NEC are encouraged to undertake job rotation to broaden their skills and experience. At Queensland Health, nurses in intensive care units are at the cutting edge of technological innovation and require a much broader range of skills than was the case a decade ago.

DEPARTMENTALISATION

Once you have divided jobs up through work specialisation, you need to group these jobs together so that common tasks can be coordinated. The basis by which jobs are grouped together is called **departmentalisation**.

departmentalisation | The basis by which jobs are grouped together.

One of the most popular ways to group activities is by *functions* performed. A manufacturing manager might organise a plant by separating engineering, accounting, manufacturing, personnel and supply specialists into common departments. Of course, departmentalisation by function can be used in all types of organisations. Only the functions change to reflect the organisation's objectives and activities. A hospital might have departments devoted to research, patient care, accounting, and so forth. A professional football organisation—for example, the Auckland Warriors, the West Coast Eagles, the Sydney Swans or the Jurong Soccer Club in Singapore—might have departments to handle specific activities such as staffing, including players, ticket sales, marketing, and travel and accommodation. The main advantage to this type of grouping is obtaining efficiencies from putting like specialists together. Functional departmentalisation seeks to achieve economies of scale by placing people with common skills and orientations into common units.

Tasks can also be departmentalised by the type of *product or service* the organisation produces. Large accounting firms, for example, can have a variety of departments that focus on their main product/service areas (for example, taxation, auditing and management consulting services), and these departments can be placed under the authority of one of the firm's partners who is a specialist in, and responsible for, everything having to do with the product/service line. When you think of Woolworths, you think of one of Australia's biggest grocery chains. But Woolworths is also a significant player in the liquor industry. Woolworths has created a new organisational structure for liquor retailing using four separate means of distribution: Woolworths Liquor and Safeway Liquor are departments within Woolworths supermarkets, while BWS and Dan Murphy Cellars are free-standing stores. In relation to the total diverse Woolworths operation, these departments and stores represent substructures based on product differentiation.

The main advantage of this type of grouping is increased accountability for product performance, since all activities related to a specific product or service are under the direction of a single manager. If an organisation's activities are service- rather than product-related, each service would be autonomously grouped. For example, a Volvo distributor could have departments for new cars, second-hand cars, trucks and buses, and the like. Each would offer a common array of services under the direction of a particular service manager.

Another way to departmentalise is on the basis of *geography* or territory. The sales function, for example, may have western, southern, northern or eastern regions. It may be divided into North Island or South Island, as in New Zealand, or East or West, as in Malaysia. Each of these regions is, in effect, a department organised around geography. If an organisation's customers are scattered over a large geographic area, then this form of departmentalisation can be valuable.

If you have had the opportunity to visit an aluminium tubing plant, you will have noticed that production is generally organised into five departments: casting, press, tubing, finishing, and inspect, pack and ship. This is an example of *process* departmentalisation, because each department specialises in one specific phase in the production of aluminium tubing. The metal is cast in huge furnaces; sent to the press

OB IN PRACTICE

LETTING GO OF THE DESK AT WESTPAC

When we talk about organisational structure, we talk about the way that work in an organisation is divided up into jobs, positions, roles, sections and departments. In addition, we are concerned with how staff work together in their assigned roles and departments. In short, organisations are differentiated by dividing up the work and integrated by getting people to communicate effectively with each other about the work. One aspect of structure that is often taken for granted but less often spoken about relates to the spatial arrangements used in the workplace—the arrangement of buildings and furniture.

When Westpac relocated 5000 staff from various locations into its new Sydney headquarters building in Kent Street, Ilana Atlas, Westpac's human resource manager, pointed out that one of the biggest challenges for them was letting go of the desk. Westpac is one of the largest banks operating in Australasia. Moving to a new building presented a great opportunity to rethink the way staff work, both individually and collectively. And besides, office space is an expensive resource if you are in the CBD of Sydney, Auckland, Singapore or Kuala Lumpur.

Before the move, Westpac undertook a study of work design and office space utilisation and this included visiting best practice locations overseas. Staff work habits were observed in the old locations. It was discovered that approximately 40 per cent of an employee's work day was spent at a desk; 30 per cent was spent in other places in the building and 25 per cent was spent outside the building. It was also found that the average meeting size was three to four people. This was significantly less than past practices where the average was more like ten people. As a consequence, Ilana Atlas pointed to the design of smaller rooms in the new headquarters that were built away from the open-plan desks and office space. The rooms were equipped with wireless laptop facilities. Another innovation was an entire floor dedicated to supporting temporary project teams. Communal furniture was also located around staff lunch and coffee areas to encourage wider communication between staff from various floors of the building. Only six group executives were allocated partitioned offices.

The design of a building, office space and furniture arrangements can influence the structural arrangements quite significantly. It can change the nature of communication and relationships. It can support the increasing use of temporary project teams and interdepartmental collaboration. For Westpac, portability is a big part of the new work culture with the intention of maintaining a 5 per cent desk vacancy rate. The desk symbolises working with change rather than stability. Ilana Atlas sees more staff working from home in the future and the need to provide support for managers in a new way of working.

One small caveat for such arrangements: they can give an alternate impression for some outsiders. As one journalist pointed out, Westpac's new headquarters are impressive, but for visitors there is a Fort Knox culture rubbing the edge off the architectural euphoria. Visitors are asked to produce photo ID before being issued with a visitor's pass. They are then instructed to read the 'terms and conditions of entry' on the back of the pass.

SOURCES: Amita Tandukar, 'Work's New Rules', *Business Review Weekly*, 13–19 April 2006 p. 60; and Andrew Main, 'Rear Window', *Australian Financial Review*, 18 April 2006.

department, where it is extruded into aluminium pipe; transferred to the tube mill, where it is stretched into various sizes and shapes of tubing; moved to finishing, where it is cut and cleaned; and finally arrives in the inspect, pack and ship department. Since each process requires different skills, this method offers a basis for the homogeneous categorising of activities.

Process departmentalisation can be used for processing customers as well as products. If you have ever been to a state motor vehicle office to get a driver's licence, you probably went through several departments before you received your licence. Some years ago, applicants may have gone through three steps, each handled by a separate department— for example:

- validation by the motor vehicles division;
- processing by the licensing department; and
- payment collection by the finance department.

Today, applicants are more likely to be processed at a one-stop shop, a service counter where the one department completes all the processes necessary for the issue of a licence. This has been brought about by the availability of sophisticated information systems and photographic technology.

A final category of departmentalisation is to use the particular type of *customer* the organisation seeks to reach. Microsoft, for example, is organised around four customer markets: consumers, large corporations, software developers, and small businesses. A large law office can segment its staff on the basis of whether they service corporate or individual clients. The assumption underlying customer departmentalisation is that customers in each department have a common set of demands that can best be met by having specialists for each.

Large organisations may use all of the forms of departmentalisation we have described. A major Japanese electronics firm, for example, organises each of its divisions along functional lines and its manufacturing units around processes; it departmentalises sales around seven geographic regions; and divides each sales region into four customer groupings. Across organisations of all sizes, one strong trend has developed over the past decade: rigid, functional departmentalisation is being increasingly complemented by teams that cross over traditional departmental lines. As tasks have become more complex, and more diverse skills are needed to accomplish those tasks, management has turned to cross-functional teams.

CHAIN OF COMMAND

Thirty-five years ago, the chain-of-command concept was a basic cornerstone in the design of organisations. As you will see, it has far less importance today.[3] But contemporary managers should still consider its implications when they decide how best to structure their organisations. The **chain of command** is an unbroken line of authority that extends from the top of the organisation to the lowest echelon and clarifies who reports to whom. It answers questions for employees such as 'To whom do I go if I have a problem?' and 'To whom am I responsible?'

You can't discuss the chain of command without discussing two complementary concepts: *authority* and *unity of command*. **Authority** refers to the rights inherent in a managerial position to give orders and expect the orders to be obeyed. To facilitate coordination, each managerial position is given a place in the chain of command, and each manager is given a degree of authority in order to meet his or her responsibilities. The **unity-of-command** principle helps to preserve the concept of an unbroken line of

chain of command | The unbroken line of authority that extends from the top of the organisation to the lowest echelon and clarifies who reports to whom.

authority | The rights inherent in a managerial position to give orders and to expect the orders to be obeyed.

unity of command | The idea that a subordinate should have only one superior to whom he or she is directly responsible.

authority. It states that a person should have one—and only one—superior to whom that person is directly responsible. If the unity of command is broken, an employee might have to cope with conflicting demands or priorities from several superiors.

Times change and so do the basic tenets of organisational design. The concepts of chain of command, authority, and unity of command have substantially less relevance today because of advancements in information technology and the trend towards empowering employees. For instance, a low-level employee today can access information in seconds that 35 years ago was available only to top managers. Similarly, networked computers increasingly allow employees anywhere in an organisation to communicate with anyone else without going through formal channels. Moreover, the concepts of authority and maintaining the chain of command are increasingly less relevant as operating employees are being empowered to make decisions that previously were reserved for management. Add to this the popularity of self-managed and cross-functional teams and the creation of new structural designs that include multiple bosses, and the unity-of-command concept takes on less relevance. There are, of course, still many organisations that find they can be most productive by enforcing the chain of command. There just seem to be fewer of them nowadays.

SPAN OF CONTROL

How many employees can a manager efficiently and effectively direct? This question of **span of control** is important because, to a large degree, it determines the number of levels and managers an organisation has. All things being equal, the wider or larger the span, the more efficient the organisation. An example can illustrate the validity of this statement.

span of control | The number of subordinates a manager can efficiently and effectively direct.

Assume that we have two organisations, both of which have approximately 4100 operative-level employees. As Figure 16.2 illustrates, if one has a uniform span of four and the other a span of eight, the wider span would have two fewer levels and approximately 800 fewer managers. If the average manager made $100 000 a year, the wider span would save almost $80 million a year in management salaries! Obviously, wider spans are more efficient in terms of cost. However, at some point wider spans reduce effectiveness. That is, when the span becomes too large, employee performance suffers because supervisors no longer have the time to provide the necessary leadership and support.

Narrow or small spans have their advocates. By keeping the span of control to five or six employees, a manager can maintain close control.[4] But narrow spans have three main

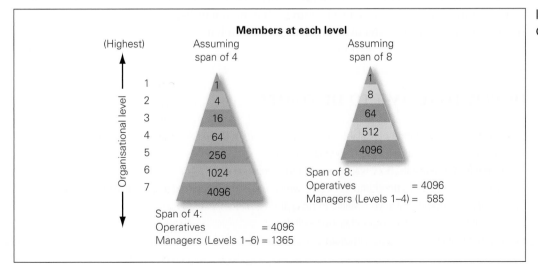

Members at each level

(Highest)

Organisational level

| 1 | 2 | 3 | 4 | 5 | 6 | 7 |

Assuming span of 4

1
4
16
64
256
1024
4096

Span of 4:
Operatives = 4096
Managers (Levels 1–6) = 1365

Assuming span of 8

1
8
64
512
4096

Span of 8:
Operatives = 4096
Managers (Levels 1–4) = 585

■ **FIGURE 16.2**
Contrasting spans of control

drawbacks. First, as already described, they are expensive because they add levels of management. Second, they make vertical communication in the organisation more complex. The added levels of hierarchy slow down decision making and tend to isolate upper management. Third, narrow spans of control encourage overly tight supervision and discourage employee autonomy.

The trend in recent years has been towards wider spans of control.[5] They are consistent with recent efforts by companies to reduce costs, cut overheads, speed up decision making, increase flexibility, get closer to customers, and empower employees. However, to ensure that performance doesn't suffer because of these wider spans, organisations have been investing heavily in employee training. Managers recognise that they can handle a wider span when employees know their jobs inside and out or can turn to their co-workers when they have questions.

CENTRALISATION AND DECENTRALISATION

In some organisations, top managers make all the decisions. Lower-level managers merely carry out top management's directives. At the other extreme, there are organisations in which decision making is pushed down to the managers who are closest to the action. The former organisations are highly centralised; the latter are decentralised.

centralisation | The degree to which decision making is concentrated at a single point in the organisation.

The term **centralisation** refers to the degree to which decision making is concentrated at a single point in the organisation. The concept includes only formal authority—that is, the rights inherent in one's position. Typically, it is said that if top management makes the organisation's key decisions with little or no input from lower-level personnel, then the organisation is centralised. In contrast, the more that lower-level personnel provide input or are actually given the discretion to make decisions, the more decentralisation there is. An organisation characterised by centralisation is an inherently different structural animal from one that is decentralised. In a decentralised organisation, action can be taken more quickly to solve problems, more people provide input into decisions, and employees are less likely to feel alienated from those who make the decisions that affect their work lives.

Consistent with recent management efforts to make organisations more flexible and responsive, there has been a marked trend towards decentralising decision making. In large companies, lower-level managers are closer to 'the action' and typically have more detailed knowledge about problems than do top managers. For instance, big retailers such as Woolworths and Harvey Norman realise that their local store managers need considerably more discretion in choosing what merchandise to stock. This allows those stores to compete more effectively against local merchants.

SELF-ASSESSMENT LIBRARY

HOW WILLING AM I TO DELEGATE?

In the Self-Assessment Library (available on CD and online), take Self-Assessment III.A.2 (How Willing Am I to Delegate?) and answer the following questions.

1. Judging from the results, how willing are you to delegate?
2. If your delegation skills need improvement, why are you unwilling to delegate? If your delegation skills are superior, why are you willing to delegate?
3. How might you improve your delegation skills?
4. Why is the ability to delegate important?

FORMALISATION

Formalisation refers to the degree to which jobs within the organisation are standardised. If a job is highly formalised, then the job incumbent has a minimum amount of discretion over what is to be done, when it is to be done, and how it is to be done. Employees can be expected always to handle the same input in exactly the same way, resulting in a consistent and uniform output. There are explicit job descriptions, lots of organisational rules, and clearly defined procedures covering work processes in organisations in which there is high formalisation. Where formalisation is low, job behaviours are relatively non-programmed and employees have a great deal of freedom to exercise discretion in their work. Because an individual's discretion on the job is inversely related to the amount of behaviour in that job that is preprogrammed by the organisation, the greater the standardisation, the less input the employee has into how the work is to be done. Standardisation not only eliminates the possibility of employees engaging in alternative behaviours; it even removes the need for employees to consider alternatives.

The degree of formalisation can vary widely between and within organisations. Certain jobs, for instance, are well known to have little formalisation. University book travellers—the sales representatives of publishers who call on faculty heads and academic staff to inform them of their company's new publications—have a great deal of freedom in their jobs. They have no standard sales 'spiel', and the extent of rules and procedures governing their behaviour may be little more than the requirement that they submit a weekly sales report and some suggestions on what to emphasise for the various new titles. At the other extreme, there are clerical and editorial positions in the same publishing houses for which employees are required to be at their desks by 9 am or risk a reprimand by management and, once at their desk, to follow a set of precise procedures dictated by management.

formalisation | The degree to which jobs within the organisation are standardised.

COMMON ORGANISATIONAL DESIGNS

We now turn to describing three of the more common organisational designs found in use: the *simple structure*, the *bureaucracy* and the *matrix structure*.

THE SIMPLE STRUCTURE

What do a small retail store, an electronics firm run by a hard-driving entrepreneur, and an airline in the midst of a company-wide pilots' strike have in common? They probably all use the **simple structure**.

The simple structure is said to be characterised most by what it is not, rather than by what it is. The simple structure isn't elaborate.[6] It has a low degree of departmentalisation, wide spans of control, authority centralised in a single person, and little formalisation. The simple structure is a 'flat' organisation; it usually has only two or three vertical levels, a loose body of employees, and one individual in whom the decision-making authority is centralised.

The simple structure is most widely practised in small businesses in which the manager and the owner are one and the same. This, for example, is illustrated in Figure 16.3, an organisation chart for a retail men's store. Jack Gold owns and manages this store. Although he employs five full-time salespeople, a cashier, and extra personnel for weekends and holidays, he 'runs the show'. But large companies, in times of crisis, can become simple structures for short periods. IBM, for instance, became a simple structure

simple structure | A structure characterised by a low degree of departmentalisation, wide spans of control, authority centralised in a single person, and little formalisation.

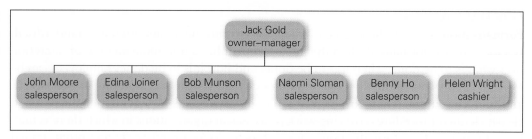

for more than a year back in the early 1990s.[7] When Louis Gerstner was hired as CEO in 1993, he immediately put the company into what he called 'survival mode'. 'We had to cut [US]$9 billion a year in expenses. We had to bring the company back, literally from the brink of death.' So Gerstner implemented a highly centralised, personalised leadership and organisational style. Said Gerstner: 'It was a benevolent dictatorship, with me as the dictator.'

The strength of the simple structure lies in its simplicity. It is fast, flexible, and inexpensive to maintain, and accountability is clear. One main weakness is that it is difficult to maintain in anything other than small organisations. It becomes increasingly inadequate as an organisation grows, because its low formalisation and high centralisation tend to create information overload at the top. As size increases, decision making typically becomes slower and can eventually come to a standstill as the single executive tries to continue making all the decisions. This often proves to be the undoing of many small businesses. When an organisation begins to employ 50 or 100 people, it is very difficult for the owner-manager to make all the choices. If the structure isn't changed and made more elaborate, the firm often loses momentum and can eventually fail. The simple structure's other weakness is that it is risky—everything depends on one person. One heart attack can literally destroy the organisation's information and decision-making centre.

THE BUREAUCRACY

Standardisation! That's the key concept that underlies all bureaucracies. Take a look at the bank where you keep your accounts, the department store where you buy your clothes, or the government offices that collect your taxes, enforce health regulations or provide local emergency services. They all rely on standardised work processes for coordination and control.

The **bureaucracy** is characterised by highly routine operating tasks achieved through specialisation, very formalised rules and regulations, tasks that are grouped into functional departments, centralised authority, narrow spans of control, and decision making that follows the chain of command. The primary strength of the bureaucracy lies in its ability to perform standardised activities in a highly efficient manner. Putting like specialities together in functional departments results in economies of scale, minimum duplication of personnel and equipment, and employees who have the opportunity to talk 'the same language' among their peers. Furthermore, bureaucracies can get by nicely with less talented—and, hence, less costly—middle- and lower-level managers. The pervasiveness of rules and regulations substitutes for managerial discretion. Standardised operations, coupled with high formalisation, allow decision making to be centralised. There is little need, therefore, for innovative and experienced decision makers below the level of senior executives.

One of the main weaknesses of a bureaucracy is illustrated in the following dialogue among four executives in one company: 'You know, nothing happens in this place until we

bureaucracy | A structure with highly routine operating tasks achieved through specialisation, very formalised rules and regulations, tasks that are grouped into functional departments, centralised authority, narrow spans of control, and decision making that follows the chain of command.

produce something', said the production executive. 'Wrong', commented the research and development manager, 'nothing happens until we *design* something!' 'What are you talking about?' asked the marketing executive. 'Nothing happens here until we *sell* something!' Finally, the exasperated accounting manager responded, 'It doesn't matter what you produce, design or sell. No one knows what happens until we *tally up the results!*' This conversation points up the fact that specialisation creates subunit conflicts. Functional unit goals can override the overall goals of the organisation.

The other main weakness of a bureaucracy is something we have all experienced at one time or another when having to deal with people who work in these organisations: obsessive concern with following the rules. When cases arise that don't precisely fit the rules, there is no room for modification. The bureaucracy is efficient only as long as employees confront problems that they have previously encountered and for which programmed decision rules have already been established.

John Fogarty, chief executive officer at St John of God Hospital, Ballarat, says simplicity is paramount in his business. His basic philosophy of management has always been against bureaucracy and complexity. In 2004, the hospital's bookings and admission process was a nightmare. Patients were expected to fill out more than five pages of a questionnaire in order to be booked into the hospital. After that, it was often the case that the patient was called two or three times by different people in the hospital about their health assessment, their financial consent or details of their admission time. Similarly, doctors or their secretaries had to ring at least two different departments to book in a patient. John Fogarty rationalised the five-page form into a single sheet as part of a process to reduce some of the inefficiencies of the bureaucracy that had developed over the years.[8]

THE MATRIX STRUCTURE

Another popular organisational design option is the **matrix structure**. You will find it being used in advertising agencies, aerospace firms, research and development laboratories, construction companies, hospitals, government agencies, universities, management consulting firms and entertainment companies.[9] Essentially, the matrix combines two forms of departmentalisation: functional and product. The strength of functional departmentalisation lies in putting like specialists together, which minimises the number necessary while allowing the pooling and sharing of specialised resources across products. Its main disadvantage is the difficulty of coordinating the tasks of diverse functional specialists so that their activities are completed on time and within budget. Product departmentalisation, on the other hand, has exactly the opposite benefits and disadvantages. It facilitates coordination among specialities to achieve on-time completion and to meet budget targets. Furthermore, it provides clear responsibility for all activities related to a product, but with duplication of activities and costs. The matrix attempts to gain the strengths of each, while avoiding their weaknesses.

The most obvious structural characteristic of the matrix is that it breaks the unity-of-command concept. Employees in the matrix have two bosses—their functional department managers and their product managers. Therefore, the matrix has a dual chain of command.

Figure 16.4 shows the matrix form as used in a college of business administration. The academic departments of accounting, management, marketing, and so forth are functional units. In addition, specific programs (that is, products) are overlaid on the functions. In this way, members in a matrix structure have a dual assignment—to their functional department and to their product groups. For instance, a professor of accounting who is

matrix structure | A structure that creates dual lines of authority and combines functional and product departmentalisation.

Programs / Academic departments	Undergraduate	Master's	Ph.D.	Research	Executive development	Community service
Accounting						
Finance						
Decision and information systems						
Management						
Marketing						

teaching an undergraduate course may report to the director of undergraduate programs as well as to the head of the accounting department.

The strength of the matrix lies in its ability to facilitate coordination when the organisation has a multiplicity of complex and interdependent activities. As an organisation gets larger, its information-processing capacity can become overloaded. In a bureaucracy, complexity results in increased formalisation. The direct and frequent contact between different specialities in the matrix can make for better communication and more flexibility. Information permeates the organisation and more quickly reaches the people who need to take account of it. Furthermore, the matrix reduces 'bureaupathologies'—the dual lines of authority reduce the tendencies of departmental members to become so busy protecting their little worlds that the organisation's overall goals become secondary.

There is another advantage to the matrix. It facilitates the efficient allocation of specialists. When individuals with highly specialised skills are lodged in one functional department or product group, their talents are monopolised and underused. The matrix achieves the advantages of economies of scale by providing the organisation with both the best resources and an effective way of ensuring their efficient deployment.

The main disadvantages of the matrix lie in the confusion it creates, its propensity to foster power struggles, and the stress it places on individuals.[10] When you dispense with the unity-of-command concept, ambiguity is significantly increased, and ambiguity often leads to conflict. For example, it is frequently unclear who reports to whom, and it is not unusual for product managers to fight over getting the best specialists assigned to their products. Confusion and ambiguity also create the seeds of power struggles. Bureaucracy reduces the potential for power grabs by defining the rules of the game. When those rules are 'up for grabs', power struggles between functional and product managers result. For individuals who desire security and absence from ambiguity, this work climate can produce stress. Reporting to more than one boss introduces role conflict, and unclear expectations introduce role ambiguity. The comfort of bureaucracy's predictability is absent, replaced by insecurity and stress.

Several banking organisations have given the matrix structure a lot of serious consideration. ANZ Bank has adopted a matrix format to address some of the complaints from customers that their needs were not being met. Some customers were irritated when they rang the bank about an issue, because their calls were treated as an opportunity by the bank to sell them something. The matrix structure provided a more holistic solution for dealing with the relationship with their customers. Suncorp Metway Bank, on the other hand, discarded the matrix structure because of the potential downside in terms of mixed messages, flawed accountability, and the quandaries people find themselves in when caught between two bosses.[11]

NEW DESIGN OPTIONS

Over the past decade or two, senior managers in a number of organisations have been working to develop new structural options that can better help their firms to compete effectively. In this section, we will describe three such structural designs: the *team structure*, the *virtual organisation* and the *boundaryless organisation*.

THE TEAM STRUCTURE

Teams have become an extremely popular means around which to organise work activities. When management uses teams as its central coordination device, you have a horizontal organisation or a **team structure**.[12] The primary characteristics of the team structure are that it breaks down departmental barriers and decentralises decision making to the level of the work team. Team structures also require employees to be generalists as well as specialists.[13]

> **team structure** | The use of teams as the central device to coordinate work activities.

In various companies, the team structure can define the entire organisation. For instance, Whole Foods Market, Inc., a large natural-foods retailer with stores in the United Kingdom, Canada and the United States, is structured entirely around teams.[14] Every one of Whole Foods' stores is an autonomous profit centre composed of an average of ten self-managed teams, each with a designated team leader. The team leaders in each store are a team; store leaders in each region are a team; and the company's six regional presidents are a team. Also, some of the large consulting firms such as KPMG and Ernst & Young located in Australia and Southeast Asia have used a team-based structure as an effective means of providing management and financial consulting services to their clients.

More often, particularly among larger organisations, the team structure complements what is typically a bureaucracy. This allows the organisation to achieve the efficiency of bureaucracy's standardisation while gaining the flexibility that teams provide. To improve productivity at the operating level, for instance, well-known companies such as DaimlerChrysler, Motorola and Xerox have made extensive use of self-managed teams. On the other hand, when companies such as Boeing need to design new products or coordinate major projects, they will structure activities around cross-functional teams.

THE VIRTUAL ORGANISATION

Why own when you can rent? That question captures the essence of the **virtual organisation** (also sometimes called the *network* or *modular* organisation), typically a small, core organisation that outsources major business functions.[15] In structural terms, the virtual organisation is highly centralised, with little or no departmentalisation.

> **LEARNING OBJECTIVE 4**
> Explain the characteristics of a virtual organisation

> **virtual organisation** | A small, core organisation that outsources major business functions.

The prototype of the virtual structure is today's movie-making organisation. In Hollywood's golden era, movies were made by huge, vertically integrated corporations. Studios such as MGM, Warner Brothers and 20th Century Fox owned large movie lots and employed thousands of full-time specialists—set designers, camera people, film editors, directors and even actors. Nowadays, most movies are made by a collection of individuals

STRUCTURING IN ACCOUNTABILITY, TEAMWORK AND TALENT

Woods Bagot describes itself as an architecture, consulting and design studio. Since the company was launched in Adelaide in 1869, it has grown its operations and now has offices in 12 locations around the world, including Australia, Asia, the Middle East and Europe. The term 'studio' reflects an interesting way to view the firm's structure—as a network of locations where artists of the various professions ply their trade. In fact, it isn't only the term but also the company's approach to developing a structure to match its growth strategy that is interesting to managers.

A number of years ago, the company began working on larger, more complex projects, and needed to restructure in order to accommodate further growth. Such issues as staffing levels for global projects, how the business could improve sustainability, and how it could support international studios from its base in Australia, were examined. In the context of these issues, two elements became critical to realigning the organisational structure across its international operations—accountability, and promoting talent and teamwork.

Accountability

In 2003, the board of seven directors decided to expand the shareholder base of the organisation. This meant that the domination by Australian-based principals and owners was realigned to include shareholders in every one of Woods Bagot's studios around the world. As Tamsin McLean, the HR director, explains: 'If you're a principal, you actually have to be an owner of the business, so it's not just a title or promotion that's awarded to people. Ownership takes accountability to a different level. It is from this platform of expanded leadership that we have truly been able to operate as a global business—across borders, and without driving decisions out of a head office.' While it may be unusual for a professional services firm to have shareholders, this new arrangement introduced a different type of structural accountability to the operations where accountability takes on a new meaning when local principals have a personal stake in business results. This is not unlike the motivating aspects of franchise structures.

Promoting talent and teamwork

A crucial part of the structure was to support global mobility and reinforce a positive workplace culture. Business growth puts pressure on for additional resources. For Woods Bagot, these came in the form of Generation X and Y employees, who comprise 70 per cent of their workforce. The company consulted and surveyed staff, who wanted three main things from the company: (1) a clear career path; (2) flexibility in the way they worked and didn't want to work in a hierarchy; and (3) opportunity to travel as part of an international company. In structural terms, the company wanted to fully support the talent they hired, rather than inhibit them. Woods Bagot runs staff forums, face-to-face management meetings and an annual survey in order to gauge workplace culture and whether employees feel their career needs are being met.

The new structure is more sensitive to promoting talent and teamwork across the network of studios, rather than in individual studios. This means that staff can be sent overseas for a matter of days to participate in a design workshop, through to being relocated for a number of years. Sometimes an international move is initiated by the staff themselves. Such interest in international secondment is gauged upon appointment or during their annual performance reviews. Skills are then matched to a project, studio resource needs or to an employee who is interested in a location swap. The mobility of talent and the improved quality of communication between studios promotes greater teamwork and organisational learning for the whole business.

SOURCE: Melissa Yen, 'Woods Bagot: Going Global', *Human Resources*, 22 August 2006.

and small companies who come together and make films project by project.[16] This structural form allows each project to be staffed with the talent most suited to its demands, rather than having to choose just from the people employed by the studio. It minimises bureaucratic overhead because there is no lasting organisation to maintain. And it lessens long-term risks and their costs because there *is* no long term—a team is assembled for a finite period and then disbanded.

Ancle Hsu and David Ji run a virtual organisation. Their firm, Apex Digital, is one of the world's largest producers of DVD players, yet the company neither owns a factory nor employs an engineer. They contract everything out to firms in China. With minimal investment, Apex has grown from nothing to annual sales of over US$500 million in just three years. Similarly, Paul Newman's food products company, Newman's Own, sells about US$190 million in food every year yet employs only 18 people. This is because it outsources almost everything—manufacturing, procurement, shipping and quality control. When large organisations use the virtual structure, they frequently use it to outsource manufacturing. Cisco, for instance, is essentially a research and development company that uses outside suppliers and independent manufacturers to assemble the internet routers that its engineers design. The Australian government has been outsourcing various functions across many of its departments, particularly IT functions.

What's going on here? A quest for maximum flexibility. These virtual organisations have created networks of relationships that allow them to contract out manufacturing, distribution, marketing, or any other business function for which management feels that others can do better or more cheaply. The virtual organisation stands in sharp contrast to the typical bureaucracy that has many vertical levels of management and where control is sought through ownership. In such organisations, research and development are done in-house, production occurs in company-owned plants, and sales and marketing are performed by the company's own employees. To support all this, management has to employ extra staff, including accountants, human resource specialists and lawyers. The virtual organisation, however, outsources many of these functions and concentrates on what it does best. For most firms, that means focusing on design or marketing.

The Australian IT Register is an online company that uses the internet extensively to service clients. By using a telecommuting approach, the company can provide a highly responsive service to large and small clients at very competitive rates. Owen Baker, the managing director, has worked in the Australian IT industry for over 20 years and is well respected for his consistent track record of delivering successful IT projects on-time and on-budget. The Australian IT Register has some attributes of a virtual organisation. It has a database of skilled computing professionals, enabling it to call on a host of different skills among contract IT people, including software programmers, specialists in testing or business analysts. By having them all on call, through the internet or mobile phone service, the company is able to manage large project virtually.

Figure 16.5 shows a virtual organisation in which management outsources all of the primary functions of the business. The core of the organisation is a small group of executives whose job is to oversee directly any activities that are done in-house and to coordinate relationships with the other organisations that manufacture, distribute and perform other crucial functions for the virtual organisation. The dotted lines in Figure 16.5 represent the relationships typically maintained under contracts. In essence, managers in virtual structures spend most of their time coordinating and controlling external relations, typically by way of computer-network links.

The main advantage of the virtual organisation is its flexibility. For instance, it allowed individuals with an innovative idea and little money, such as Ancle Hsu and David Ji, to successfully compete against Sony, Hitachi and Sharp Electronics. The primary drawback to this structure is that it reduces management's control over key parts of its business.

■ **FIGURE 16.5**
A virtual organisation

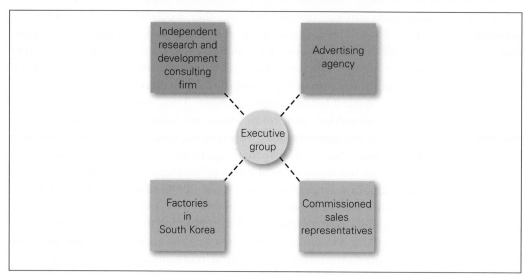

<table>
</table>

THE BOUNDARYLESS ORGANISATION

boundaryless organisation | An organisation that seeks to eliminate the chain of command, have limitless spans of control, and replace departments with empowered teams.

General Electric's former chairman, Jack Welch, coined the term *boundaryless organisation* to describe his idea of what he wanted GE to become. Welch wanted to turn his company into a 'family grocery store'.[17] That is, in spite of its monstrous size (2004 revenues were in excess of US$135 billion), he wanted to eliminate *vertical* and *horizontal* boundaries within GE and break down *external* barriers between the company and its customers and suppliers. The **boundaryless organisation** seeks to eliminate the chain of command, have limitless spans of control, and replace departments with empowered teams. And because it relies so heavily on information technology, some have turned to calling this structure the *T-form* (or technology-based) organisation.[18] Although GE hasn't yet achieved this boundaryless state—and probably never will—it has made significant progress towards that end. So have other companies, such as Hewlett-Packard, Telstra, SingTel, Westpac and Motorola. Let's take a look at what a boundaryless organisation would look like and what some firms are doing to try to make it a reality.[19]

By removing vertical boundaries, management flattens the hierarchy. Status and rank are minimised. Cross-hierarchical teams (which include top executives, middle managers, supervisors and operative employees), participative decision-making practices, and the use of 360-degree performance appraisals (in which peers and others above and below the employee evaluate performance) are examples of what GE is doing to break down vertical boundaries. At Oticon A/S, a Danish hearing aid manufacturer, all traces of hierarchy have disappeared. Everyone works at uniform mobile workstations. And project teams, not functions or departments, are used to coordinate work.

Functional departments create horizontal boundaries. And these boundaries stifle interaction between functions, product lines and units. The way to reduce these barriers is to replace functional departments with cross-functional teams and to organise activities around processes. For instance, Xerox now develops new products through multidisciplinary teams that work in a single process instead of around narrow functional tasks. Similarly, some units within the large telecommunication companies are now doing annual budgets based not on functions or departments but on processes such as the maintenance of a worldwide telecommunications network. Another way management can cut through horizontal barriers is to use lateral transfers, rotating people into and out of different functional areas. This approach turns specialists into generalists.

When fully operational, the boundaryless organisation also breaks down barriers to external constituencies (suppliers, customers, regulators, and so on) and barriers created by geography. Globalisation, strategic alliances, customer–organisation links and telecommuting are all examples of practices that reduce external boundaries. Coca-Cola, for instance, sees itself as a global corporation, not as a US or Atlanta company. Firms such as Boeing and Apple Computer each have strategic alliances or joint partnerships with dozens of companies. These alliances blur the distinction between one organisation and another as employees work on joint projects.

WHY DO STRUCTURES DIFFER?

In the previous sections, we described a variety of organisational designs ranging from the highly structured and standardised bureaucracy to the loose and amorphous boundaryless organisation. The other designs we discussed tend to exist somewhere between these two extremes.

Figure 16.6 reconceptualises our previous discussions by presenting two extreme models of organisational design. One extreme we will call the **mechanistic model**. It is generally synonymous with the bureaucracy in that it has extensive departmentalisation, high formalisation, a limited information network (mostly downward communication), and little participation by low-level members in decision making. At the other extreme is the **organic model**. This model looks a lot like the boundaryless organisation. It is flat, uses cross-hierarchical and cross-functional teams, has low formalisation, possesses a comprehensive information network (using lateral and upward communication as well as downward), and involves high participation in decision making.[20] With these two models in mind, we are now prepared to address the question: Why are some organisations structured along more mechanistic lines, whereas others follow organic characteristics? What are the forces that influence the design that is chosen? In the following pages, we present the main forces that have been identified as causes or determinants of an organisation's structure.[21]

STRATEGY

An organisation's structure is a means to help management achieve its objectives. Because objectives are derived from the organisation's overall strategy, it is only logical that strategy

mechanistic model | A structure characterised by extensive departmentalisation, high formalisation, a limited information network, and centralisation.

- -

organic model | A structure that is flat, uses cross-hierarchical and cross-functional teams, has low formalisation, possesses a comprehensive information network, and relies on participative decision making.

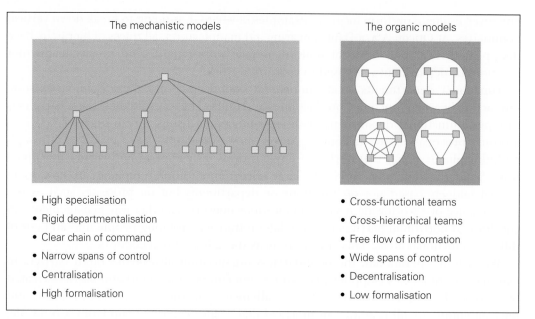

The mechanistic models

The organic models

- High specialisation
- Rigid departmentalisation
- Clear chain of command
- Narrow spans of control
- Centralisation
- High formalisation

- Cross-functional teams
- Cross-hierarchical teams
- Free flow of information
- Wide spans of control
- Decentralisation
- Low formalisation

and structure should be closely linked. More specifically, structure should follow strategy. If management makes a significant change in its organisation's strategy, the structure will need to be modified to accommodate and support this change.[22] Most current strategy frameworks focus on three strategy dimensions—innovation, cost minimisation and imitation—and the structural design that works best with each.[23]

To what degree does an organisation introduce major new products or services? An **innovation strategy** doesn't mean a strategy merely for simple or cosmetic changes from previous offerings but, rather, one for meaningful and unique innovations. Obviously, not all firms pursue innovation. This strategy may appropriately characterise 3M Co. and Apple Computer, but it is not a strategy pursued by Reader's Digest or National Geographic.

An organisation that is pursuing a **cost-minimisation strategy** tightly controls costs, refrains from incurring unnecessary innovation or marketing expenses, and cuts prices in selling a basic product. This would describe the strategy pursued by manufacturers of brake drums for trucks such as the Toowoomba Metal Technologies.

Organisations following an **imitation strategy** try to capitalise on the best of both of the previous strategies. They seek to minimise risk and maximise opportunity for profit. Their strategy is to move into new products or new markets only after viability has been proven by innovators. They take the successful ideas of innovators and copy them. Manufacturers of mass-marketed fashion goods that are rip-offs of designer styles follow the imitation strategy. This label probably also characterises well-known firms such as IBM and Caterpillar. They essentially follow their smaller and more innovative competitors with superior products, but only after their competitors have demonstrated that the market is there.

Table 16.2 describes the structural option that best matches each strategy. Innovators need the flexibility of the organic structure, whereas cost minimisers seek the efficiency and stability of the mechanistic structure. Imitators combine the two structures. They use a mechanistic structure in order to maintain tight controls and low costs in their current

innovation strategy |
A strategy that emphasises the introduction of major new products and services.

cost-minimisation strategy | A strategy that emphasises tight cost controls, avoidance of unnecessary innovation or marketing expenses, and price cutting.

imitation strategy |
A strategy that seeks to move into new products or new markets only after their viability has already been proven.

Strategy	Structural option
Innovation	*Organic:* A loose structure; low work specialisation, low formalisation, decentralised.
Cost minimisation	*Mechanistic:* Tight control; extensive work specialisation, high formalisation, high centralisation.
Imitation	*Mechanistic and organic:* Mix of loose with tight properties; tight controls over current activities and looser controls for new undertakings.

activities, while at the same time they create organic subunits in which to pursue new undertakings.

ORGANISATION SIZE

There is considerable evidence to support the idea that an organisation's size significantly affects its structure.[24] For instance, large organisations—those that typically employ 2000 or more people—tend to have more specialisation, more departmentalisation, more vertical levels, and more rules and regulations than do small organisations. However, the relationship isn't linear. Rather, size affects structure at a decreasing rate. The impact of size becomes less important as an organisation expands. Why is this? Essentially, once an organisation has around 2000 employees, it is already fairly mechanistic. An additional 500 employees won't have much impact. On the other hand, adding 500 employees to an organisation that has only 300 members is likely to result in a significant shift towards a more mechanistic structure.

TECHNOLOGY

The term *technology* refers to how an organisation transfers its inputs into outputs. Every organisation has at least one technology for converting financial, human and physical resources into products or services. The Ford Motor Co., for instance, predominantly uses an assembly-line process to make its products. On the other hand, universities may use a number of instructional technologies—the ever-popular formal lecture method, the case-analysis method, the experiential exercise method, the programmed learning method, and so forth. In this section we want to show that organisational structures adapt to their technology.

technology | How an organisation transfers its inputs into outputs.

Numerous studies have been carried out on the technology–structure relationship.[25] The details of those studies are quite complex, so we will go straight to 'the bottom line' and attempt to summarise what we know.

The common theme that differentiates technologies is their *degree of routineness*. By this we mean that technologies tend towards either routine or non-routine activities. The former are characterised by automated and standardised operations. Non-routine activities are customised. They include varied operations such as furniture restoring, custom shoemaking and genetic research.

What relationships have been found between technology and structure? Although the relationship isn't overwhelmingly strong, we find that routine tasks are associated with taller and more departmentalised structures. The relationship between technology and formalisation, however, is stronger. Studies consistently show routineness to be associated

In some industries, it becomes more apparent how technology influences organisational design. In manufacturing, for example, the production technology maps out how components parts are assembled along a production line until the end product is assembled and working. In car assembly plants, jobs, sections and departments are designed around the progressive assembly of thousands of parts such as the motor, the lights, the seats, and so on. In the manufacture and assembly of microwave ovens, the relationship of jobs is apparent by the strong dependency on employees playing their specific role in a complex process of assembling the oven from nothing.

with the presence of rule manuals, job descriptions and other formalised documentation. Finally, an interesting relationship has been found between technology and centralisation. It seems logical that routine technologies would be associated with a centralised structure, while non-routine technologies, which rely more heavily on the knowledge of specialists, would be characterised by delegated decision authority. This position has met with some support. However, a more generalisable conclusion is that the technology–centralisation relationship is moderated by the degree of formalisation. Formal regulations and centralised decision making are both control mechanisms, and management can substitute one for the other. Routine technologies should be associated with centralised control if there is a minimum of rules and regulations. However, if formalisation is high, routine technology can be accompanied by decentralisation. So, we would predict that routine technology would lead to centralisation, but only if formalisation is low.

ENVIRONMENT

environment | Institutions or forces outside the organisation that potentially affect the organisation's performance.

An organisation's **environment** is composed of institutions or forces outside the organisation that potentially affect the organisation's performance. These typically include suppliers, customers, competitors, government regulatory agencies, public pressure groups, and the like.

Why should an organisation's structure be affected by its environment? Because of environmental uncertainty. Some organisations face relatively static environments—few forces in their environment are changing. There are, for example, no new competitors, no new technological breakthroughs by current competitors, or little activity by public pressure groups to influence the organisation. Other organisations face very dynamic environments—rapidly changing government regulations affecting their business, new competitors, difficulties in acquiring raw materials, continually changing product preferences by customers, and so on. Static environments create significantly less uncertainty for managers than do dynamic ones. And because uncertainty is a threat to an organisation's effectiveness, management will try to minimise it. One way to reduce environmental uncertainty is through adjustments in the organisation's structure.[26]

Recent research has helped clarify what is meant by environmental uncertainty. It has been found that there are three key dimensions to any organisation's environment: capacity, volatility and complexity.[27]

The *capacity* of an environment refers to the degree to which it can support growth. Rich and growing environments generate excess resources, which can buffer the organisation in times of relative scarcity. Abundant capacity, for example, leaves room for an organisation to make mistakes, while scarce capacity does not. In 2005, firms operating in the

'BUREAUCRACY IS DEAD'

This statement is false. Some bureaucratic characteristics are in decline. And bureaucracy is undoubtedly going through changes. But it is far from dead.

Bureaucracy is characterised by specialisation, formalisation, departmentalisation, centralisation, narrow spans of control, and adherence to a chain of command. Have these characteristics disappeared from today's modern organisations? No. In spite of the increased use of empowered teams and flattened structures, certain facts remain: (1) Large size prevails. Organisations that succeed and survive tend to grow to a large size, and bureaucracy is efficient with large size. Small organisations and their non-bureaucratic structures are more likely to fail, so over time, small organisations may come and go but large bureaucracies stay. Moreover, while the average business today has considerably fewer employees than those of 30 years ago, these smaller firms are increasingly part of a large, multi-location organisation with the financial and technological resources to compete in a global marketplace. (2) Environmental turbulence can be largely managed. The impact of uncertainties in the environment on the organisation is substantially reduced by management strategies to maintain bureaucratic structures and still be efficient. (3) Bureaucracy's goal of standardisation can be increasingly achieved through hiring people who have undergone extensive educational training. Rational discipline, rather than that imposed by rules and regulations, is internalised by hiring professionals with university training. They come pre-programmed. In addition, strong cultures help to achieve standardisation by substituting for high formalisation. (4) Finally, technology maintains control. Networked computers allow management to closely monitor the actions of employees without centralisation or narrow spans of control. Technology has merely replaced some previously bureaucratic characteristics, but without any loss of management control.

In spite of some changes, bureaucracy is alive and well in many venues. It continues to be a dominant structural form in manufacturing, service firms, hospitals, schools, the armed services and voluntary associations. Why? Because it is still the most efficient way to organise large-scale activities.

SOURCES: Based on S. P. Robbins, *Organization Theory: Structure, Design, and Applications*, 3rd ed. (Upper Saddle River, NJ: Prentice Hall, 1990), pp. 320–25; and B. Harrison, *Lean and Mean: The Changing Landscape of Corporate Power in the Age of Flexibility* (New York: Basic Books, 1994).

MYTH OR SCIENCE?

multimedia software business had relatively abundant environments, whereas those in the full-service brokerage business faced relative scarcity.

The degree of instability in an environment is captured in the *volatility* dimension. When there is a high degree of unpredictable change, the environment is dynamic. This makes it difficult for management to predict accurately the probabilities associated with various decision alternatives. At the other extreme is a stable environment. The accelerated changes in Eastern Europe and the demise of the Cold War had dramatic effects on the US defence industry in the 1990s. This moved the environment of major defence contractors such as Lockheed Martin, General Dynamics and Northrop Grumman from relatively stable to dynamic.

Finally, the environment needs to be assessed in terms of *complexity*—that is, the degree of heterogeneity and concentration among environmental elements. Simple environments are homogeneous and concentrated. This might describe the tobacco industry, since there are relatively few players. It is easy for firms in this industry to keep a close eye on the competition. In contrast, environments characterised by heterogeneity and dispersion are called complex. This is essentially the current environment for firms competing in the internet-connection business. Every day there seems to be another 'new kid on the block' with whom current internet access providers have to deal.

Figure 16.7 summarises our definition of the environment along its three dimensions. The arrows in this figure are meant to indicate movement towards higher uncertainty. So, organisations that operate in environments characterised as scarce, dynamic and complex face the greatest degree of uncertainty. Why? Because they have little room for error, high unpredictability, and a diverse set of elements in the environment to monitor constantly.

Given this three-dimensional definition of environment, we can offer some general conclusions. There is evidence that relates the degrees of environmental uncertainty to different structural arrangements. Specifically, the more scarce, dynamic and complex the environment, the more organic a structure should be. The more abundant, stable and simple the environment, the more the mechanistic structure will be preferred.

■ **FIGURE 16.7**
Three-dimensional model of the environment

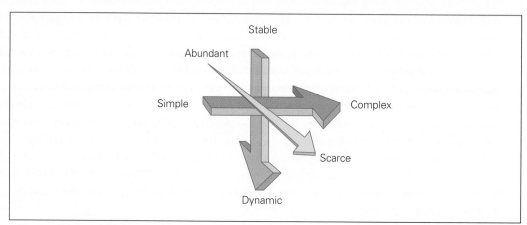

ORGANISATIONAL DESIGNS AND EMPLOYEE BEHAVIOUR

LEARNING OBJECTIVE 8

Explain the behavioural implications of different organisational designs

We opened this chapter by implying that an organisation's structure can have significant effects on its members. In this section, we want to assess directly just what those effects might be. A review of the evidence linking organisational structures to employee performance and satisfaction leads to a pretty clear conclusion—you can't generalise!

Not everyone prefers the freedom and flexibility of organic structures. Some people are most productive and satisfied when work tasks are standardised and ambiguity is minimised—that is, in mechanistic structures. So, any discussion of the effect of organisational design on employee behaviour has to address individual differences. To illustrate this point, let's consider employee preferences for work specialisation, span of control and centralisation.[28]

The evidence generally indicates that *work specialisation* contributes to higher employee productivity, but at the price of reduced job satisfaction. However, this statement ignores individual differences and the type of job tasks people do. As we noted previously, work specialisation isn't an unending source of higher productivity. Problems start to surface, and productivity begins to suffer, when the human diseconomies of doing repetitive and narrow tasks overtake the economies of specialisation. As the workforce has become more highly educated and desirous of jobs that are intrinsically rewarding, the point at which productivity begins to decline seems to be reached more quickly than in decades past.

Although more people today are undoubtedly turned off by overly specialised jobs than were their parents or grandparents, it would be naive to ignore the reality that there is still a segment of the workforce that prefers the routine and repetitiveness of highly specialised jobs. Some individuals want work that makes minimal intellectual demands and provides the security of routine. For these people, high work specialisation is a source of job satisfaction. The empirical question, of course, is whether this represents 2 per cent of the workforce or 52 per cent. Given that there is some self-selection operating in the choice of careers, we might conclude that negative behavioural outcomes from high specialisation are most likely to surface in professional jobs occupied by individuals with high needs for personal growth and diversity.

A review of the research indicates that it is probably safe to say there is no evidence to support a relationship between *span of control* and employee performance. Although it is intuitively attractive to argue that large spans might lead to higher employee performance because they provide more distant supervision and more opportunity for personal initiative, the research fails to support this notion. At this point it is impossible to state that any particular span of control is best for producing high performance or high satisfaction among employees. Again, the reason is probably individual differences. That is, some people like to be left alone, while others prefer the security of a boss who is quickly available at all times. Consistent with several of the contingency theories of leadership, we would expect factors such as employees' experiences and abilities and the degree of structure in their tasks to explain when wide or narrow spans of control are likely to contribute to their performance and job satisfaction. However, there is some evidence indicating that a manager's job satisfaction increases as the number of employees supervised increases.

We find fairly strong evidence linking *centralisation* and job satisfaction. In general, organisations that are less centralised have a greater amount of participative decision making. And the evidence suggests that participative decision making is positively related to job satisfaction. But, again, individual differences surface. The decentralisation–satisfaction relationship is strongest with employees who have low self-esteem. Because individuals with low self-esteem have less confidence in their abilities, they place a higher value on shared decision making, which means that they are not held solely responsible for decision outcomes.

Our conclusion: To maximise employee performance and satisfaction, individual differences, such as experience, personality and the work task, should be taken into

implicit models of
organisational structure |
Perceptions that people
hold regarding structural
variables formed by
observing things around
them in an unscientific
fashion.

account. In addition, national culture influences the preference for structure, so it, too, needs to be considered.[29] For instance, organisations that operate with people from high power distance cultures, such as those found in China, Indonesia, France and most of Latin America, will find employees much more accepting of mechanistic structures than where employees come from low power distance countries. So, you need to consider cultural differences along with individual differences when making predictions on how structure will affect employee performance and satisfaction.

One obvious insight needs to be made before we leave this topic: people don't select employers randomly. There is substantial evidence that individuals are attracted to, selected by and stay with organisations that suit their personal characteristics.[30] Job candidates who prefer predictability, for instance, are likely to seek out and take employment in mechanistic structures, and those who want autonomy are more likely to end up in an organic structure. So, the effect of structure on employee behaviour is undoubtedly reduced when the selection process facilitates proper matching of individual characteristics with organisational characteristics.

SUMMARY AND IMPLICATIONS FOR MANAGERS

- The theme of this chapter has been that an organisation's internal structure contributes to explaining and predicting behaviour. That is, in addition to individual and group factors, the structural relationships in which people work have an important bearing on employee attitudes and behaviour.

- What is the basis for the argument that structure has an impact on both attitudes and behaviour? To the degree that an organisation's structure reduces ambiguity for employees and clarifies concerns such as 'What am I supposed to do?' 'How am I supposed to do it?' 'To whom do I report?' and 'To whom do I go if I have a problem?' it shapes their attitudes and facilitates and motivates them to higher levels of performance.

- Of course, structure also constrains employees to the extent that it limits and controls what they do. For example, organisations structured around high levels of formalisation and specialisation, strict adherence to the chain of command, limited

delegation of authority and narrow spans of control give employees little autonomy. Controls in such organisations are tight, and behaviour will tend to vary within a narrow range. In contrast, organisations that are structured around limited specialisation, low formalisation, wide spans of control, and the like, provide employees greater freedom and, thus, will be characterised by greater behavioural diversity.

- Figure 16.8 visually summarises what we have discussed in this chapter. Strategy, size, technology and environment determine the type of structure an organisation will have. For simplicity's sake, we can classify structural designs around one of two models: mechanistic or organic. The specific effect of structural designs on performance and satisfaction is moderated by employees' individual preferences and cultural norms.

- One last point: Managers need to be reminded that structural variables such as work specialisation, span of control, formalisation and centralisation are objective characteristics that can be measured by organisational researchers. The findings and conclusions we have offered in this chapter, in fact, are directly a result of the work of these researchers. But employees don't objectively measure these structural characteristics. They observe things around them in an unscientific fashion and then form their own implicit models of what the organisation's structure is like. How many people did they have to interview with before they were offered their jobs? How many people work in their departments and buildings? Is there an organisation policy manual? If so, is it readily available and do people follow it closely? How are the organisation and its top management described in newspapers and periodicals? Answers to questions such as these, when combined with an employee's past experiences and comments made by peers, lead members to form an overall subjective image of what their organisation's structure is like. This image, though, may in no way resemble the organisation's actual objective structural characteristics.

- The importance of these **implicit models of organisational structure** shouldn't be overlooked. People respond to their perceptions rather than objective reality. The research, for instance, on the relationship between many structural variables and subsequent levels of performance or job satisfaction is far from consistent. We explained some of this as being attributable to individual differences. However, an additional contributing cause to these inconsistent findings might be diverse perceptions of the objective characteristics. Researchers typically focus on actual levels of the various structural components, but these may be irrelevant if people interpret similar components differently. The bottom line, therefore, is to understand how employees interpret their organisation's structure. That should prove a more meaningful predictor of their behaviour than the objective characteristics themselves.

■ FIGURE 16.8

Organisation structure: Its determinants and outcomes

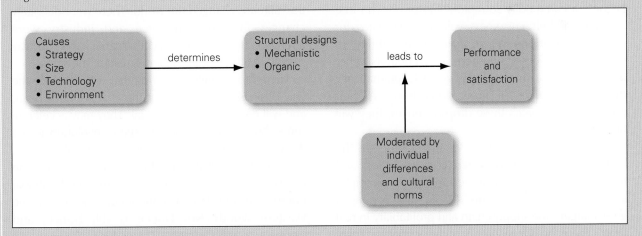

POINT / COUNTERPOINT

Technology is Reshaping Organisations

● POINT

In today's chaotic, uncertain and high-tech world, there is essentially only one type of design that is going to survive. This is the electronically configured organic organisation.

We are undergoing a second Industrial Revolution and it will change every aspect of people's lives. The changes the large corporations used to take a decade to implement now occur in one to two years. Companies that are successful will be designed to thrive on change. And the structure of those organisations will have common characteristics.

Ten years from now there will be nothing but electronic organisations. Bricks-and-mortar organisations won't go away, but clicks-and-mortar will become the only means to survival. In addition, every organisation will need to keep its finger on the pulse of its customers. Customer priorities will change very rapidly. What customers will pay a premium for will become a commodity so rapidly that those who lose touch with their customers will be candidates for extinction. Consumers are gaining the ability to compare the prices of hundreds of competitors rather than just two or three. This is going to dramatically drive down prices. If firms don't improve their productivity to match these drops in prices, they will be out of business.

Technology allows firms to stay closer to the customer, to move jobs to where costs are lowest, and to make decisions much more rapidly. For example, executives at Cisco Systems can monitor expenses, gross margins, the supply chain and profitability in real time. There no longer need to be surprises. Every employee can make decisions that might have had to come from the top management ranks a few years ago. At the end of a quarter, individual product managers at Cisco can see exactly what the gross margins are on their products, whether they are below expectations, and determine the cause of any discrepancy. Quicker decision making at lower levels will translate into higher profit margins. So, instead of the CEO or chief financial officer making 50 to 100 different decisions in a quarter, managers throughout the organisation can make millions of decisions. Companies that don't adjust to create this capability will be non-competitive. Cisco Systems shipped its first product in 1986 and is now a multinational corporation, with over 35 000 employees in more than 115 countries, including Australia, Singapore, New Zealand and Malaysia. Today, Cisco solutions are the networking foundations for service providers, small to medium-size businesses, and enterprise customers, which include corporations, government agencies, utilities and educational institutions.

● COUNTERPOINT

There is a saying that every generation thinks it has discovered sex. This seems also to be the case with technology and how it is going to change the world completely. Technology will transform the structure of organisations at a much slower rate than many believe. For example, it is useful to go back and ask if the railroads changed the world. There were definitely changes in how commerce and industry were arranged. But life remained the same, and the way people related to each other remained the same.

There are changes occurring that will influence the way businesses organise. But the changes have been, and will continue to be, gradual. They may accelerate some, but we aren't going to see a revolution in the design of organisations. Take the case of globalisation. It is significant, but it is also evolutionary. Has the formation of the European Union abolished national borders in the largest continental society in the Western world? No. France is still France, and Germany is still Germany. Things have changed, but also things haven't changed.

The emphasis on speed has its limits. Brains don't speed up. The exchange of ideas doesn't really speed up, only the overhead that slowed down the exchange. When it comes down to the bulk of knowledge work, the 21st century works the same as the 20th century. You can reach people around the clock, but they won't think any better or faster just because you have reached them faster. The give and take remains a limiting factor.

The virtual organisation also has its limitations. When you farm out your data processing, manufacturing and other functions, you make your capabilities available to your competitors. So, virtualisation of work diminishes competitive advantages and leads to the rapidly spreading commoditisation of everything. Any function that an organisation uses to achieve a competitive advantage cannot be outsourced.

Look back over the past 40 years. People haven't changed. And our fundamental organisations haven't changed. On the fringes, there is more looseness in the organisation. But more hasn't changed than has. The changes we have seen have been slow and gradual. And that pace is likely to continue into the future.

SOURCES: Points in this argument are based on J. Chambers, 'Nothing Except E-Companies', *BusinessWeek*, 28 August 2000, pp. 210–12; <www.cisco.com/global/AU/about/whois.shtml>; and A. Grove, 'I'm a Little Skeptical … Brains Don't Speed Up', *BusinessWeek*, 28 August 2000, pp. 212–14.

QUESTIONS FOR REVIEW

MyOBLab™ Do you understand this chapter's content? Find out at **www.pearsoned.com.au/MyOBLab**

1. Why isn't work specialisation an unending source of increased productivity?
2. In what ways can management departmentalise?
3. All things being equal, which is more efficient, a wide or a narrow span of control? Why?
4. What is a matrix structure? When would management use it?
5. Contrast the virtual organisation with the boundaryless organisation.
6. What type of structure works best with an innovation strategy? A cost-minimisation strategy? An imitation strategy?
7. Summarise the size–structure and environment–structure relationships.
8. Explain the importance of the statement: 'Employees form implicit models of organisational structure.'

QUESTIONS FOR CRITICAL THINKING

1. How is the typical large corporation of today organised in contrast to how that same organisation was probably organised in the 1960s?
2. Do you think most employees prefer high formalisation? Support your position.
3. If you were an employee in a matrix structure, what pluses do you think the structure would provide? What about minuses?
4. What behavioural predictions would you make about people who worked in a 'pure' boundaryless organisation (if such a structure were ever to exist)?

EXPERIENTIAL EXERCISE

Authority Figures

Purpose:
To learn about one's experiences with and feelings about authority.

Time required:
Approximately 75 minutes.

Procedure:

1. Your tutor will separate class members into groups based on their birth order. Groups are formed consisting of 'only children', 'eldest', 'middle' and 'youngest', according to placement in families. Larger groups will be broken into smaller ones, with four or five members, to allow for freer conversation.
2. Each group member should talk about how he or she 'typically reacts to the authority of others'. Focus should be on specific situations that offer general information about how individuals deal with authority figures (for example, bosses, teachers, parents or coaches). The group has 25 minutes to develop a written list of how the group generally deals with others' authority. Be sure to separate tendencies that group members share and those they don't.
3. Repeat Step 2, except this time discuss how group members 'typically are as authority figures'. Again make a list of shared characteristics.
4. Each group will share its general conclusions with the entire class.
5. Class discussion will focus on questions such as:
   a. What patterned differences have surfaced between the groups?
   b. What may account for these differences?
   c. What hypotheses might explain the connection between how individuals react to the authority of others and how they are as authority figures?

SOURCE: This exercise is adapted from W. A. Kahn, 'An Exercise of Authority', *Organizational Behavior Teaching Review*, vol. XIV, no. 2, 1989–90, pp. 28–42. Reproduced with permission.

ETHICAL DILEMMA

Just Following Orders

In 1996, Betty Vinson took a job as a mid-level accountant for $50 000 a year with a small long-distance telephone company. Within five years, that long-distance company had grown up to become telecom giant WorldCom.

Hardworking and diligent, Vinson was promoted to senior manager in WorldCom's corporate accounting division within two years. In her new job, she helped compile quarterly results, along with ten employees who reported to her. Soon after she took the position, Vinson's bosses asked her to make false accounting entries. At first, she refused. But continued pressure led to her finally caving in. Her decision to make the false entries came after the company's chief financial officer assured her that he would assume all responsibility.

Over the course of six quarters, Vinson made illegal entries to bolster WorldCom's profits at the request of her superiors. At the end of 18 months, she had helped falsify at least US$3.7 billion in profits. Of course, the whole scheme unravelled in 2002, in what became the largest fraud case in corporate history.

Betty Vinson pleaded guilty to two criminal counts of conspiracy and securities fraud, charges that carry a maximum sentence of 15 years in prison. On 5 August 2005, Vinson was sentenced to five months in prison and five months' house arrest. She was also sentenced to three years of probation.

What would you have done had you been in Betty Vinson's job? Is 'just following orders' an acceptable excuse for breaking the law? If your livelihood is on the line, do you say 'no' to a powerful boss? What can organisations do to lessen the chance that employees might capitulate to unethical pressures imposed by their boss?

SOURCE: Based on S. Pulliam, 'A Staffer Ordered to Commit Fraud Balked, Then Caved', *Wall Street Journal*, 23 June 2003, p. A1.

You have probably bought a garment made of W. L. Gore & Associates' flagship product, Gore-Tex, a fabric that blocks wind and water, yet is highly breathable thanks to Gore's patented technology. But you mightn't know that the company offers a host of other products, from heart patches and synthetic blood vessels to air pollution filters and fuel cells. In fact, W. L. Gore & Associates makes more than 1000 products. Though its financial data are not publicly available, a spokesperson for the company said that Gore had double-digit revenue growth the past three years. With this type of performance and extensive product line, you might expect Gore to be structured like big companies such as Westpac, SingTel, Microsoft or Goodman Fielder. But it's not, and it never was.

Wilbert L. Gore founded W. L. Gore & Associates in 1958. Gore believed that too much hierarchy and bureaucracy stifled creativity and adaptation, a view that he formed during his 17-year career as a DuPont engineer. He stated once that 'communication really happens in the car park', meaning that informal arenas allowed employees to share their ideas openly without fear of criticism from management. So, Gore decided to eliminate the hierarchy that is found in most organisations. Instead, he instructed everyone to communicate openly, with little regard to status differences. In fact, Gore eliminated status differences altogether. At W. L. Gore & Associates, there are no job titles. Each employee works on projects collaboratively, while at the same time is given the freedom to develop new ideas. Ideas that are deemed worthy of pursuing by team members are then developed.

In addition to the lack of bureaucracy, Gore also kept his facilities staffed with a small number of employees to promote information sharing and foster teamwork. For example, he limited staffing at manufacturing plants to 200 employees, which is smaller than typical manufacturing firms. Gore believed the number was low enough for employees to get to know one another, allowing them to talk freely about their ideas and share their knowledge. The result of such a corporate structure has been tremendous growth and profit. Gore has also been an industry leader in innovation.

Gore's unique structure does take some getting used to, particularly for new employees. Diane Davidson recalls that the lack of a formal hierarchy was bewildering at first. As a sales executive in the apparel industry, Davidson was hired by Gore to promote its fabrics to designers such as Prada and Hugo Boss. Davidson states, 'I came from a very traditional, male-dominated business—the men's shoe business. When I arrived at Gore, I didn't know who did what. I wondered how anything got done here. It was driving me crazy.' Instead of a formal supervisor, Davidson was assigned to a 'starting sponsor'. As opposed to a traditional supervisor, the sponsor at Gore helps new recruits learn the ropes—which primarily consist of getting to know one's team. 'Who's my boss?' she repeatedly asked her sponsor. Her sponsor would reply, 'Stop using the b-word.'

Davidson eventually got used to Gore's structure. 'Your team is your boss, because you don't want to let them down. Everyone's your boss, and no one's your boss', she explains. Not only are there no formal supervisors at Gore, but employees' job descriptions are conspicuously absent as well. Employees at Gore perform multiple tasks to create a new product. Davidson, for example, is involved in marketing, sales and sponsorship—roles that typically are separated in other organisations. As John Morgan, an employee of Gore for more than 20 years, states: 'You join a team and you're an idiot. It takes 18 months to build credibility. Early on, it's really frustrating. In hindsight, it makes sense. As a sponsor, I tell new recruits, "Your job for the first six months is to get to know the team", but they have trouble believing it—and not contributing when other people are.'

QUESTIONS
1. How would you characterise Gore's organisational structure using terms from this chapter? For example, is it mechanistic or organic? How might this structure influence Gore's strategy?
2. Considering what you know about individual differences such as personality, what types of employees might respond more or less favourably to Gore's lack of hierarchy?
3. What are some advantages and disadvantages of Gore's structure from a company perspective? What about from an employee perspective?
4. How might Gore's organisational design affect its relationships with external companies that are more hierarchical in nature?

SOURCE: Based on A. Deutschman, 'The Fabric of Creativity', *Fast Company*, December 2004, pp. 54–62.

ENDNOTES

1. <www.uninews.cqu.edu.au/op001-1.php?ra=1133492940&id=2909>; Amita Tandukar, 'Smashing the Sandstone', *Business Review Weekly*, 31 August 2006.
2. See, for instance, R. L. Daft, *Organization Theory and Design*, 8th ed. (Cincinnati, OH: Southwestern, 2004).
3. C. Hymowitz, 'Managers Suddenly Have to Answer to a Crowd of Bosses', *Wall Street Journal*, 12 August 2003, p. B1.
4. See, for instance, L. Urwick, *The Elements of Administration* (New York: Harper & Row, 1944), pp. 52–53; and J. H. Gittell, 'Supervisory Span, Relational Coordination, and Flight Departure Performance: A Reassessment of Postbureaucracy Theory', *Organization Science*, July–August 2001, pp. 468–83.
5. J. Child and R. G. McGrath, 'Organizations Unfettered: Organizational Form in an Information-Intensive Economy', *Academy of Management Journal*, December 2001, pp. 1135–48.
6. H. Mintzberg, *Structure in Fives: Designing Effective Organizations* (Upper Saddle River, NJ: Prentice Hall, 1983), p. 157.
7. S. Lohr, 'IBM Chief Gerstner Recalls Difficult Days at Big Blue', *New York Times*, 31 July 2000, p. C5.
8. <www.aim.com.au/DisplayStory.asp?ID=597>.
9. K. Knight, 'Matrix Organization: A Review', *Journal of Management Studies*, May 1976, pp. 111–30; L. R. Burns and D. R. Wholey, 'Adoption and Abandonment of Matrix Management

Programs: Effects of Organizational Characteristics and Interorganizational Networks', *Academy of Management Journal*, February 1993, pp. 106–38; and R. E. Anderson, 'Matrix Redux', *Business Horizons*, November–December 1994, pp. 6–10.
10. See, for instance, S. M. Davis and P. R. Lawrence, 'Problems of Matrix Organization', *Harvard Business Review*, May–June 1978, pp. 131–42; and T. Sy and S. Cote, 'Emotional Intelligence: A Key Ability to Succeed in the Matrix Organization', *Journal of Management Development*, vol. 23, no. 5, 2004, pp. 437–55.
11. <www.aim.com.au/DisplayStory.asp?ID=596>.
12. S. A. Mohrman, S. G. Cohen and A. M. Mohrman, Jr, *Designing Team-Based Organizations* (San Francisco: Jossey-Bass, 1995); F. Ostroff, *The Horizontal Organization* (New York: Oxford University Press, 1999); and R. Forrester and A. B. Drexler, 'A Model for Team-Based Organization Performance', *Academy of Management Executive*, August 1999, pp. 36–49.
13. M. Kaeter, 'The Age of the Specialized Generalist', *Training*, December 1993, pp. 48–53.
14. C. Fishman, 'Whole Foods Is All Teams', *Fast Company, Greatest Hits*, vol. 1, 1997, pp. 102–13.
15. See, for instance, R. E. Miles and C. C. Snow, 'The New Network Firm: A Spherical Structure Built on Human

Investment Philosophy', *Organizational Dynamics*, Spring 1995, pp. 5–18; D. Pescovitz, 'The Company Where Everybody's a Temp', *New York Times Magazine*, 11 June 2000, pp. 94–96; W. F. Cascio, 'Managing a Virtual Workplace', *Academy of Management Executive*, August 2000, pp. 81–90; B. Hedberg, G. Dahlgren, J. Hansson and N. Olve, *Virtual Organizations and Beyond* (New York: Wiley, 2001); M. A. Schilling and H. K. Steensma, 'The Use of Modular Organizational Forms: An Industry-Level Analysis', *Academy of Management Journal*, December 2001, pp. 1149–68; K. R. T. Larsen and C. R. McInerney, 'Preparing to Work in the Virtual Organization', *Information and Management*, May 2002, pp. 445–56; J. Gertner, 'Newman's Own: Two Friends and a Canoe Paddle', *New York Times*, 16 November 2003, p. 4BU; and Y. Shin, 'A Person–Environment Fit Model for Virtual Organizations', *Journal of Management*, October 2004, pp. 725–43.
16. J. Bates, 'Making Movies and Moving On', *Los Angeles Times*, 19 January 1998, p. A1.
17. 'GE: Just Your Average Everyday $60 Billion Family Grocery Store', *Industry Week*, 2 May 1994, pp. 13–18.
18. H. C. Lucas, Jr, *The T-Form Organization: Using Technology to Design Organizations for the 21st Century* (San Francisco: Jossey-Bass, 1996).
19. This section is based on D. D. Davis, 'Form, Function and Strategy in

Boundaryless Organizations', in A. Howard (ed.), *The Changing Nature of Work* (San Francisco: Jossey-Bass, 1995), pp. 112–38; P. Roberts, 'We Are One Company, No Matter Where We Are. Time and Space Are Irrelevant', *Fast Company*, April–May 1998, pp. 122–28; R. L. Cross, A. Yan and M. R. Louis, 'Boundary Activities in "Boundaryless" Organizations: A Case Study of a Transformation to a Team-Based Structure', *Human Relations*, June 2000, pp. 841–68; and R. Ashkenas, D. Ulrich, T. Jick and S. Kerr, *The Boundaryless Organization: Breaking the Chains of Organizational Structure*, revised and updated (San Francisco: Jossey-Bass, 2002).

20. T. Burns and G. M. Stalker, *The Management of Innovation* (London: Tavistock, 1961); and J. A. Courtright, G. T. Fairhurst and L. E. Rogers, 'Interaction Patterns in Organic and Mechanistic Systems', *Academy of Management Journal*, December 1989, pp. 773–802.

21. This analysis is referred to as a contingency approach to organization design. See, for instance, J. M. Pennings, 'Structural Contingency Theory: A Reappraisal', in B. M. Staw and L. L. Cummings (eds), *Research in Organizational Behavior*, vol. 14 (Greenwich, CT: JAI Press, 1992), pp. 267–309; J. R. Hollenbeck, H. Moon, A. P. J. Ellis, B. J. West, D. R. Ilgen, L. Sheppard, C. O. L. H. Porter and J. A. Wagner III, 'Structural Contingency Theory and Individual Differences: Examination of External and Internal Person–Team Fit', *Journal of Applied Psychology*, June 2002, pp. 599–606; and H. Moon, J. R. Hollenbeck, S. E. Humphrey, D. R. Ilgen, B. West, A. P. J. Ellis and C. O. L. H. Porter, 'Asymmetric Adaptability: Dynamic Team Structures as One-Way Streets', *Academy of Management Journal*, October 2004, pp. 681–95.

22. The strategy–structure thesis was originally proposed in A. D. Chandler, Jr, *Strategy and Structure: Chapters in the History of the Industrial Enterprise* (Cambridge, MA: MIT Press, 1962). For an updated analysis, see T. L. Amburgey and T. Dacin, 'As the Left Foot Follows the Right? The Dynamics of Strategic and Structural Change', *Academy of Management Journal*, December 1994, pp. 1427–52.

23. See R. E. Miles and C. C. Snow, *Organizational Strategy, Structure, and Process* (New York: McGraw-Hill, 1978); D. Miller, 'The Structural and Environmental Correlates of Business Strategy', *Strategic Management Journal*, January–February 1987, pp. 55–76; D. C. Galunic and K. M. Eisenhardt, 'Renewing the Strategy–Structure–Performance Paradigm', in B. M. Staw and L. L. Cummings (eds), *Research in Organizational Behavior*, vol. 16 (Greenwich, CT: JAI Press, 1994), pp. 215–55; and I. C. Harris and T. W. Ruefli, 'The Strategy/Structure Debate: An Examination of the Performance Implications', *Journal of Management Studies*, June 2000, pp. 587–603.

24. See, for instance, P. M. Blau and R. A. Schoenherr, *The Structure of Organizations* (New York: Basic Books, 1971); D. S. Pugh, 'The Aston Program of Research: Retrospect and Prospect', in A. H. Van de Ven and W. F. Joyce (eds), *Perspectives on Organization Design and Behavior* (New York: John Wiley, 1981), pp. 135–66; R. Z. Gooding and J. A. Wagner III, 'A Meta-Analytic Review of the Relationship Between Size and Performance: The Productivity and Efficiency of Organizations and Their Subunits', *Administrative Science Quarterly*, December 1985, pp. 462–81; and A. C. Bluedorn, 'Pilgrim's Progress: Trends and Convergence in Research on Organizational Size and Environments', *Journal of Management*, Summer 1993, pp. 163–92.

25. See J. Woodward, *Industrial Organization: Theory and Practice* (London: Oxford University Press, 1965); C. Perrow, 'A Framework for the Comparative Analysis of Organizations', *American Sociological Review*, April 1967, pp. 194–208; J. D. Thompson, *Organizations in Action* (New York: McGraw-Hill, 1967); J. Hage and M. Aiken, 'Routine Technology, Social Structure, and Organizational Goals', *Administrative Science Quarterly*, September 1969, pp. 366–77; C. C. Miller, W. H. Glick, Y. Wang and G. P. Huber, 'Understanding Technology–Structure Relationships: Theory Development and Meta-Analytic Theory Testing', *Academy of Management Journal*, June 1991, pp. 370–99; and K. H. Roberts and M. Grabowski, 'Organizations, Technology, and Structuring', in S. R. Clegg, C. Hardy and W. R. Nord (eds), *Managing Organizations: Current Issues* (Thousand Oaks, CA: Sage, 1999), pp. 159–71.

26. See F. E. Emery and E. Trist, 'The Causal Texture of Organizational Environments', *Human Relations*, February 1965, pp. 21–32; P. Lawrence and J. W. Lorsch, *Organization and Environment: Managing Differentiation and Integration* (Boston: Harvard Business School, Division of Research, 1967); M. Yasai-Ardekani, 'Structural Adaptations to Environments', *Academy of Management Review*, January 1986, pp. 9–21; Bluedorn, 'Pilgrim's Progress'; and M. Arndt, and B. Bigelow, 'Presenting Structural Innovation in an Institutional Environment: Hospitals' Use of Impression Management', *Administrative Science Quarterly*, September 2000, pp. 494–522.

27. G. G. Dess and D. W. Beard, 'Dimensions of Organizational Task Environments', *Administrative Science Quarterly*, March 1984, pp. 52–73; E. A. Gerloff, N. K. Muir and W. D. Bodensteiner, 'Three Components of Perceived Environmental Uncertainty: An Exploratory Analysis of the Effects of Aggregation', *Journal of Management*, December 1991, pp. 749–68; and O. Shenkar, N. Aranya and T. Almor, 'Construct Dimensions in the Contingency Model: An Analysis Comparing Metric and Non-Metric Multivariate Instruments', *Human Relations*, May 1995, pp. 559–80.

28. See, for instance, L. W. Porter and E. E. Lawler III, 'Properties of Organization Structure in Relation to Job Attitudes and Job Behavior', *Psychological Bulletin*, July 1965, pp. 23–51; L. R. James and A. P. Jones, 'Organization Structure: A Review of Structural Dimensions and Their Conceptual Relationships with Individual Attitudes and Behavior', *Organizational Behavior and Human Performance*, June 1976, pp. 74–113; D. R. Dalton, W. D. Todor, M. J. Spendolini, G. J. Fielding and L. W. Porter, Organization Structure and Performance: A Critical Review', *Academy of Management Review*, January 1980, pp. 49–64; W. Snizek and J. H. Bullard, 'Perception of Bureaucracy and Changing Job Satisfaction: A Longitudinal Analysis', *Organizational Behavior and Human Performance*, October 1983, pp. 275–87; and D. B. Turban and T. L. Keon, 'Organizational Attractiveness: An Interactionist Perspective', *Journal of Applied Psychology*, April 1994, pp. 184–93.

29. See, for example, P. R. Harris and R. T. Moran, *Managing Cultural Differences*, 5th ed. (Houston: Gulf Publishing, 1999).

30. See, for instance, B. Schneider, 'The People Make the Place', *Personnel Psychology*, Autumn 1987, pp. 437–53; B. Schneider, H. W. Goldstein and D. B. Smith, 'The ASA Framework: An Update', *Personnel Psychology*, Winter 1995, pp. 747–73; J. Schaubroeck, D. C. Ganster and J. R. Jones, 'Organization and Occupation Influences in the Attraction-Selection-Attrition Process', *Journal of Applied Psychology*, December 1998, pp. 869–91; and B. Schneider, D. B. Smith and M. C. Paul, 'P-E Fit and the Attraction-Selection-Attrition Model of Organizational Functioning: Introduction and Overview', in M. Erez and U. Kleinbeck (eds.), *Work Motivation in the Context of a Globalizing Economy* (Mahwah, NJ: Lawrence Erlbaum Associates, 2001), pp. 231–46.

17

ORGANISATIONAL CULTURE

LEARNING OBJECTIVES

AFTER STUDYING THIS CHAPTER, YOU SHOULD BE ABLE TO:

1. DESCRIBE INSTITUTIONALISATION AND ITS RELATIONSHIP TO ORGANISATIONAL CULTURE

2. DEFINE THE COMMON CHARACTERISTICS MAKING UP ORGANISATIONAL CULTURE

3. IDENTIFY THE FUNCTIONAL AND DYSFUNCTIONAL EFFECTS OF ORGANISATIONAL CULTURE ON PEOPLE AND THE ORGANISATION

4. EXPLAIN THE FACTORS DETERMINING AN ORGANISATION'S CULTURE

5. LIST THE FACTORS THAT MAINTAIN AN ORGANISATION'S CULTURE

6. OUTLINE THE VARIOUS SOCIALISATION ALTERNATIVES AVAILABLE TO MANAGEMENT

7. CLARIFY HOW CULTURE IS TRANSMITTED TO EMPLOYEES

8. DESCRIBE A CUSTOMER-RESPONSIVE CULTURE

9. IDENTIFY CHARACTERISTICS OF A SPIRITUAL CULTURE

As group chief executive officer of AXA Asia Pacific Holdings, Les Owen realises the significance of organisational culture when it comes to succeeding in the highly competitive insurance industry. Owen was instrumental in demutualising National Mutual when his company, the Global AXA Group, took over the well-known Australian insurance organisation.

AXA AUSTRALIA sees itself as helping Australians provide for their financial future, and has been doing so for over 100 years. It is a member of the Global AXA Group, one of the largest financial services groups in the world with an enviable track record in meeting the superannuation, investment and insurance needs of 50 million customers worldwide. But, like many large organisations, it has had to go through significant changes in order to respond to the changing dynamics of its operational environment.

When Les Owen took over as group chief executive officer of AXA Asia Pacific Holdings, the wheels were set in motion for significant cultural change in the company throughout the region. The AXA group acquired National Mutual in the mid-1990s. National Mutual was an Australian-based mutual life insurance company owned by policyholders, while AXA is owned by shareholders. This difference in ownership creates different types of cultures associated with how the companies are run. Les Owen makes an assessment of the first few years after the takeover: '… we demutualised the company but we did not demutualise the culture, and therefore, although we [AXA] were a listed company, the management team (from the previous National Mutual) was still a mutual management team. It is difficult to say these things without appearing to criticise, but I have competed against mutuals in our industry for 30 years and I will say that mutuality is a bit like communism, it's a good idea in theory but in practice it rarely delivers better results for customers.'

Owen believes that if you work in a mutual company that has mutual values, then no matter how good you are as an individual you are bound to learn from and behave according to that experience. The challenge he had when he arrived as CEO was that there were a lot of good people who really wanted their company to be successful, and it hadn't been performing well for some time.

From experience, Owen knew that it would take a long time if he tried to change the culture through normal developmental strategies. He didn't have a lot of time to achieve the targets he set for the company. One way to change a culture quickly is to change the people who make up that culture. The group CEO felt there was a need to change many of the people he had inherited from National Mutual. 'It was not a commentary on the individuals themselves but a commentary on the environment that they worked in for 10–15 years. The way they had learnt to do things wasn't always the way I wanted to do those things. So the first task was to decide which members of the senior management team needed to change quickly. Over the first year-and-a-half we changed 50 to 60 per cent of the top 50 people, and that helped change the culture.' Owen wanted people who believed the company had a chance of hitting the targets set for the future. As he pointed out, 'I needed people who could also work with me. And I know I am not an easy person to work with. *I* wouldn't work for me!'

In contemplating his retirement, Les Owen was asked what had given him the most satisfaction from his role as group CEO of AXA. He responded: 'There are many things, but the ones that immediately come to mind are the success that I believe we have had in changing the culture in Australia and New Zealand from that of a sleepy mutual to one that is now focused, achievement orientated and performance driven … What also gives me great satisfaction is that, although I had to make a large number of changes to personnel over the first 12 months, once the senior management team was settled it has been stable and very committed to the company … I am proud of the team we have and what we have achieved. And perhaps the other thing I would mention is the fact that, it seems to me, the view of AXA APH in the investment markets is fundamentally different than it was when I took on the role.'[1]

Whoever controls the media—the images—controls the culture.
Allen Ginsberg

A **STRONG ORGANISATIONAL CULTURE** like the one that has been developed at AXA Asia Pacific gives a company direction. It also provides direction to employees. It helps them to understand 'the way things are done around here'. A strong culture additionally provides stability to an organisation. But, for some organisations, it can also be a major barrier to change. In this chapter, we show that every organisation has a culture and, depending on its strength, it can have a significant influence on the attitudes and behaviours of organisation members.

institutionalisation | A condition that occurs when an organisation takes on a life of its own, apart from any of its members, and acquires immortality.

INSTITUTIONALISATION: A FORERUNNER OF CULTURE

The idea of viewing organisations as cultures—where there is a system of shared meaning among members—is a relatively recent phenomenon. Until the mid-1980s, organisations were, for the most part, simply thought of as rational means by which to coordinate and control a group of people. They had vertical levels, departments, authority relationships, and so forth. But organisations are more. They have personalities, too, just like individuals. They can be rigid or flexible, unfriendly or supportive, innovative or conservative. AXA Asia Pacific offices and people *are* different from the offices and people at AMP Insurance. The University of Sydney and the National University of Singapore are in the same business of education, but each has a unique feeling and character beyond its structural characteristics. Organisational theorists now acknowledge this by recognising the important role that culture plays in the lives of organisation members. Interestingly, though, the origin of culture as an independent variable affecting an employee's attitudes and behaviours can be traced back more than 50 years to the notion of **institutionalisation**.[2]

When an organisation becomes institutionalised, it takes on a life of its own, apart from its founders or any of its members. Dick Smith created Dick Smith Electronics in 1968, but he left in 1982 to pursue his personal interests. Dick Smith Electronics has continued to thrive despite the departure of its founder. Sony, Gillette, McDonald's and Disney are examples of organisations that continue to exist beyond the life of their founder or any one member.

In addition, when an organisation becomes institutionalised, it becomes valued for itself, not merely for the goods or services it produces. It acquires immortality. If its original goals are no longer relevant, it doesn't go out of business. Rather, it redefines itself. A classic example is The Smith Family. It was created in 1922 by five Australian businessmen who felt that disadvantaged children should be able to enjoy Christmas, so they visited an orphanage and gave toys and sweets to the children. Wishing to remain anonymous, the businessmen told the matron at the orphanage that they were the 'Smith' family. From this beginning, The Smith Family has continued to evolve, responding to the needs of disadvantaged Australians through a diverse range of programs.[3]

Institutionalisation operates to produce common understandings among members about what is appropriate and, fundamentally, meaningful behaviour.[4] So, when an organisation takes on institutional permanence, acceptable modes of behaviour become largely self-evident to its members. As we will see, this is essentially the same thing that organisational culture does. So, an understanding of what makes up an organisation's culture, and how it is created, sustained and learned, will enhance our ability to explain and predict the behaviour of people at work.

The Smith Family's Learning for Life program has provided financial and personal assistance to around 46 000 children and young people throughout Australia.

WHAT IS ORGANISATIONAL CULTURE?

A number of years back, an executive was asked what he thought *organisational culture* meant. He gave essentially the same answer that a US Supreme Court Justice once gave in attempting to define pornography: 'I can't define it, but I know it when I see it.' This executive's approach to defining organisational culture isn't acceptable for our purposes. We need a basic definition to provide a point of departure for our quest to better understand the phenomenon. In this section, we propose a specific definition and review several peripheral issues that revolve around this definition.

A DEFINITION

There seems to be wide agreement that **organisational culture** refers to a system of shared meaning held by members that distinguishes the organisation from other organisations.[5] This system of shared meaning is, on closer examination, a set of key characteristics that the organisation values. The research suggests that there are seven primary characteristics that, in aggregate, capture the essence of an organisation's culture.[6]

organisational culture | A system of shared meaning held by members that distinguishes the organisation from other organisations.

1. *Innovation and risk taking*: the degree to which employees are encouraged to be innovative and take risks.
2. *Attention to detail*: the degree to which employees are expected to exhibit precision, analysis and attention to detail.
3. *Outcome orientation*: the degree to which management focuses on results or outcomes rather than on the techniques and processes used to achieve those outcomes.
4. *People orientation*: the degree to which management decisions take into consideration the effect of outcomes on people within the organisation.
5. *Team orientation*: the degree to which work activities are organised around teams rather than individuals.
6. *Aggressiveness*: the degree to which people are aggressive and competitive rather than easygoing.
7. *Stability*: the degree to which organisational activities emphasise maintaining the status quo in contrast to growth.

Each of these characteristics exists on a continuum from low to high. Appraising the organisation on these seven characteristics, then, gives a composite picture of the organisation's culture. This picture becomes the basis for feelings of shared understanding that members have about the organisation, how things are done in it, and the way members are supposed to behave. Table 17.1 demonstrates how these characteristics can be mixed to create highly diverse organisations.

■ TABLE 17.1
Contrasting organisational cultures

Organisation A

This organisation is a manufacturing firm. Managers are expected to fully document all decisions; and 'good managers' are those who can provide detailed data to support their recommendations. Creative decisions that incur significant change or risk are not encouraged. Because managers of failed projects are openly criticised and penalised, managers try not to implement ideas that deviate much from the status quo. One lower-level manager quoted an often-used phrase in the company: 'If it ain't broke, don't fix it.'

There are extensive rules and regulations in this firm that employees are required to follow. Managers supervise employees closely to ensure there are no deviations. Management is concerned with high productivity, regardless of the impact on employee morale or turnover.

Work activities are designed around individuals. There are distinct departments and lines of authority, and employees are expected to minimise formal contact with other employees outside their functional area or line of command. Performance evaluations and rewards emphasise individual effort, although seniority tends to be the primary factor in the determination of pay raises and promotions.

Organisation B

This organisation is also a manufacturing firm. Here, however, management encourages and rewards risk taking and change. Decisions based on intuition are valued as much as those that are well rationalised. Management prides itself on its history of experimenting with new technologies and its success in regularly introducing innovative products. Managers or employees who have a good idea are encouraged to 'run with it'. And failures are treated as 'learning experiences'. The company prides itself on being market-driven and rapidly responsive to the changing needs of its customers.

There are few rules and regulations for employees to follow, and supervision is loose because management believes that its employees are hardworking and trustworthy. Management is concerned with high productivity but believes that this comes through treating its people right. The company is proud of its reputation as being a good place to work.

Job activities are designed around work teams, and team members are encouraged to interact with people across functions and authority levels. Employees talk positively about the competition between teams. Individuals and teams have goals, and bonuses are based on achievement of these outcomes. Employees are given considerable autonomy in choosing the means by which the goals are attained.

SELF-ASSESSMENT LIBRARY

WHAT'S THE RIGHT ORGANISATIONAL CULTURE FOR ME?

In the Self-Assessment Library (available on CD and online), take SELF-Assessment III.B.1 (What's the Right Organisational Culture for Me?) and answer the following questions:

1. Judging from your results, do you fit better in a more formal and structured culture or in a more informal and unstructured culture?

2. Did your results surprise you? Why did you think you scored as you did?

3. How might your results affect your career path?

CULTURE IS A DESCRIPTIVE TERM

Organisational culture is concerned with how employees perceive the characteristics of an organisation's culture, not with whether or not they like them. That is, it is a descriptive term. This is important because it differentiates this concept from that of job satisfaction.

Research on organisational culture has sought to measure how employees see their organisation: Does it encourage teamwork? Does it reward innovation? Does it stifle initiative? In contrast, job satisfaction seeks to measure affective responses to the work environment. It is concerned with how employees feel about the organisation's expectations, reward practices, and the like. Although the two terms undoubtedly have overlapping characteristics, keep in mind that the term *organisational culture* is descriptive, while *job satisfaction* is evaluative.

DO ORGANISATIONS HAVE UNIFORM CULTURES?

Organisational culture represents a common perception held by the organisation's members. This was made explicit when we defined culture as a system of *shared* meaning. We should expect, therefore, that individuals with different backgrounds or at different levels in the organisation will tend to describe the organisation's culture in similar terms.[7]

Acknowledgment that organisational culture has common properties doesn't mean, however, that there cannot be subcultures within any given culture. Most large organisations have a dominant culture and numerous sets of subcultures.[8] A **dominant culture** expresses the **core values** that are shared by a majority of the organisation's members. When we talk about an organisation's culture, we are referring to its dominant culture. It is this macro view of culture that gives an organisation its distinct personality.[9] **Subcultures** tend to develop in large organisations to reflect common problems, situations or experiences that members face. These subcultures are likely to be defined by department designations and geographical separation. The purchasing department, for example, can have a subculture that is uniquely shared by members of that department. It will include the core values of the dominant culture plus additional values unique to members of the purchasing department. Similarly, an office or unit of the organisation that is physically separated from the organisation's main operations may take on a different personality. Again, the core values are essentially retained, but they are modified to reflect the separated unit's distinct situation.

If organisations had no dominant culture and were composed only of numerous subcultures, the value of organisational culture as an independent variable would be significantly lessened because there would be no uniform interpretation of what represented appropriate and inappropriate behaviour. It is the 'shared meaning' aspect of culture that makes it such a potent device for guiding and shaping behaviour. That is what allows us to say, for example, that Microsoft's culture values aggressiveness and risk taking,[10] and then to use that information to better understand the behaviour of Microsoft executives and employees. But we cannot ignore the reality that many organisations also have subcultures that can influence the behaviour of members.

STRONG VERSUS WEAK CULTURES

It has become increasingly popular to differentiate between strong and weak cultures.[11] The argument here is that strong cultures have a greater impact on employee behaviour and are more directly related to reduced turnover.

In a **strong culture**, the organisation's core values are both intensely held and widely shared.[12] The more members who accept the core values, and the greater their

dominant culture | A culture that expresses the core values that are shared by a majority of the organisation's members.

core values | The primary or dominant values that are accepted throughout the organisation.

subcultures | Mini-cultures within an organisation, typically defined by department designations and geographical separation.

strong culture | Culture in which the core values are intensely held and widely shared.

commitment to those values is, the stronger the culture is. Consistent with this definition, a strong culture will have a great influence on the behaviour of its members because the high degree of sharedness and intensity creates an internal climate of high behavioural control. For example, Australian-based Domayne furniture stores have developed a strong service culture in the retailing industry. Domayne employees know in no uncertain terms what is expected of them, and these expectations go a long way in shaping their behaviour.

One specific result of a strong culture should be lower employee turnover. A strong culture demonstrates high agreement among members about what the organisation stands

CULTURAL TRANSFORMATION AT ANZ

In the late 1990s, following several years of poor performance, ANZ appointed John McFarlane to the role of CEO with a new management team. McFarlane began to turn the bank's financial position around. He also set about transforming the culture of ANZ to be more aligned with his vision for the future. After years of branch closures and fee increases, McFarlane acknowledged there was a perception that banks weren't doing the right thing by the community, their customers or their employees. ANZ was the first of Australia's 'Big Four' banks to earnestly undertake organisational transformation in order to achieve a long-term competitive and sustainable advantage.

In late 2000, McFarlane brought in consultants McKinsey & Co. to undertake a cultural study of ANZ in order to reveal what discrepancies there might be between existing bank values, personal employee values and how they perceived the bank. While some positive values such as results orientation had been identified, a number of employees felt the bank was too bureaucratic, with a hierarchical structure, a silo mentality and too much control of information. Instead of a set of top-down imposed values developed by the top management team, McFarlane recognised that the bank would need to develop a set of shared values in partnership with the staff, and he set up a dedicated cultural transformation team to promote the cultural transformation through three main initiatives:

- *Breakout workshops*: Over 20 000 employees have attended these workshops, which focused on emotional and personal development. The format of the workshops allowed participants to examine the thoughts and values that drive their behaviour, explore their relationships in the workplace, and develop a shared understanding of the bank's values in action.
- *Breakout charters*: These are a set of ANZ-wide business projects that focused on the nature of the work, systems and processes, and how these would support a cultural transformation. Projects are established to initiate various changes in operations. Once specified, each project charter is transferred to appropriate teams within the bank for ongoing management.
- *Breakout consulting*: This initiative relates to a range of diagnostic and consulting services provided to assist business units and teams in living the desired culture. The bank has developed a range of diagnostic processes to give teams a snapshot of their cultural climate. This is part of gathering valuable data about progress in cultural terms. The units and teams are able to measure their progress and to establish a roadmap to the desired culture.

The ANZ cultural transformation program provides a very significant illustration of the central role that culture plays in organisational behaviour and performance. How to align culture with the organisation's vision and strategy is an important managerial skill and area of knowledge. In each case of successful cultural change, there are lessons to be learned. For ANZ, the important success factors related to the leadership of the CEO, total ownership and commitment from the executive management team, the presence of compelling aspiration and meaningful values, a recognition that transformation is a journey and not a once-only program, effective organisational learning, developing and recruiting the right talent mix, and aligning mindsets, behaviours, and the underlying processes and systems.

SOURCE: Craig Donaldson, 'ANZ Bank: Breaking out of the Mould', *Human Resources*, 29 November 2005, pp. 14–15.

for. Such unanimity of purpose builds cohesiveness, loyalty and organisational commitment. These qualities, in turn, lessen employees' propensity to leave the organisation.[13]

CULTURE VERSUS FORMALISATION

A strong organisational culture increases behavioural consistency. In this sense, we should recognise that a strong culture can act as a substitute for formalisation.[14]

In the previous chapter, we discussed how formalisation's rules and regulations act to regulate employee behaviour. High formalisation in an organisation creates predictability, orderliness and consistency. Our point here is that a strong culture achieves the same end without the need for written documentation. Therefore, we should view formalisation and culture as two different roads to a common destination. The stronger an organisation's culture, the less management need be concerned with developing formal rules and regulations to guide employee behaviour. Those guides will be internalised in employees when they accept the organisation's culture.

ORGANISATIONAL CULTURE VERSUS NATIONAL CULTURE

Throughout this book we have argued that national differences—that is, national cultures—must be taken into account if accurate predictions are to be made about organisational behaviour in different countries. But does national culture override an organisation's culture? Is an IBM facility in Malaysia, for example, more likely to reflect Malaysian ethnic culture or IBM's corporate culture?

The research indicates that national culture has a greater impact on employees than does their organisation's culture.[15] Malaysian employees at an IBM facility in Kuala Lumpur, therefore, will be influenced more by Malaysian culture than by IBM's culture. This means that as influential as organisational culture is in shaping employee behaviour, national culture is even more influential. The preceding conclusion has to be qualified to reflect the self-selection that goes on at the hiring stage.[16] A British multinational corporation, for example, is likely to be less concerned with hiring the 'typical Italian' for its Italian operations than with hiring an Italian who fits with the corporation's way of doing things. We should expect, therefore, that the employee selection process will be used by multinationals to find and hire job applicants who are a good fit with their organisation's dominant culture, even if such applicants are somewhat atypical for members of their country.

WHAT DO CULTURES DO?

We have alluded to the impact of organisational culture on behaviour. We have also explicitly argued that a strong culture should be associated with reduced turnover. In this section, we will more carefully review the functions that culture performs and assess whether culture can be a liability for an organisation.

THE FUNCTIONS OF CULTURE

Culture performs a number of functions within an organisation. First, it has a boundary-defining role; that is, it creates distinctions between one organisation and others. Second, it conveys a sense of identity for organisation members. Third, culture facilitates the generation of commitment to something larger than one's individual self-interest. Fourth,

| LEARNING OBJECTIVE | 3 |

Identify the functional and dysfunctional effects of organisational culture on people and the organisation

it enhances the stability of the social system. Culture is the social glue that helps hold the organisation together by providing appropriate standards for what employees should say and do. Finally, culture serves as a sense-making and control mechanism that guides and shapes the attitudes and behaviour of employees. It is this last function that is of particular interest to us.[17] As the following quote makes clear, culture defines the rules of the game:

> Culture by definition is elusive, intangible, implicit, and taken for granted. But every organisation develops a core set of assumptions, understandings, and implicit rules that govern day-to-day behaviour in the workplace … Until newcomers learn the rules, they are not accepted as full-fledged members of the organisation. Transgressions of the rules on the part of high-level executives or front-line employees result in universal disapproval and powerful penalties. Conformity to the rules becomes the primary basis for reward and upward mobility.[18]

The role of culture in influencing employee behaviour appears to be increasingly important in today's workplace.[19] As organisations have widened spans of control, flattened structures, introduced teams, reduced formalisation and empowered employees, the *shared meaning* provided by a strong culture ensures that everyone is pointed in the same direction.

As we show later in this chapter, who receives a job offer to join the organisation, who is appraised as a high performer and who gets the promotion are strongly influenced by the individual–organisation 'fit'—that is, whether the applicant or employee's attitudes and behaviour are compatible with the culture. It is not a coincidence that employees at Disney theme parks appear to be almost universally attractive, clean and wholesome looking, with bright smiles. That's the image Disney seeks. The company selects employees who will maintain that image. And once on the job, a strong culture, supported by formal rules and regulations, ensures that Disney theme-park employees will act in a relatively uniform and predictable way.

CULTURE AS A LIABILITY

We are treating culture in a non-judgmental manner. We haven't said that it is good or bad, only that it exists. Many of its functions, as outlined, are valuable for both the organisation and the employee. Culture enhances organisational commitment and increases the consistency of employee behaviour. These are clearly benefits to an organisation. From an employee's standpoint, culture is valuable because it reduces ambiguity. It tells employees how things are done and what is important. But we shouldn't ignore the potentially dysfunctional aspects of culture, especially a strong one, on an organisation's effectiveness.

BARRIERS TO CHANGE

Culture is a liability when the shared values are not in agreement with those that will further the organisation's effectiveness. This is most likely to occur when an organisation's environment is dynamic.[20] When an environment is undergoing rapid change, an organisation's entrenched culture may no longer be appropriate. So, consistency of behaviour is an asset to an organisation when it faces a stable environment. It may, however, burden the organisation and make it difficult to respond to changes in the environment. This helps to explain the challenges that executives at organisations such as Mitsubishi, Qantas and the Australian Federal Police have had in recent years in adapting to upheavals in their environment.[21] These organisations have strong cultures that worked well for them in the past. But these strong cultures become barriers to change when 'business as usual' is no longer effective.

BARRIERS TO DIVERSITY

Hiring new employees who, because of race, age, gender, disability or other differences, are not like the majority of the organisation's members creates a paradox.[22] Management wants new employees to accept the organisation's core cultural values. Otherwise, these employees are unlikely to fit in or be accepted. But at the same time, management wants to openly acknowledge and demonstrate support for the differences that these employees bring to the workplace.

Strong cultures put considerable pressure on employees to conform. They limit the range of values and styles that are acceptable. In some instances, such as the widely publicised Texaco case (which was settled on behalf of 1400 employees for US$176 million) in which senior managers made disparaging remarks about minorities, a strong culture that condones prejudice can even undermine formal corporate diversity policies.[23] Organisations seek out and hire diverse individuals because of the alternative strengths these people bring to the workplace. Yet these diverse behaviours and strengths are likely to diminish in strong cultures as people attempt to fit in. Strong cultures, therefore, can be liabilities when they effectively eliminate the unique strengths that people of different backgrounds bring to the organisation. Moreover, strong cultures can also be liabilities when they support institutional bias or become insensitive to people who are different.

BARRIERS TO ACQUISITIONS AND MERGERS

Historically, the key factors that management looked at in making acquisition or merger decisions were related to financial advantages or product synergy. In recent years, cultural compatibility has become the primary concern.[24] While a favourable financial statement or product line may be the initial attraction of an acquisition candidate, whether the acquisition actually works seems to have more to do with how well the two organisations' cultures match up.

Many acquisitions fail shortly after their consummation. A survey by consultants A.T. Kearney revealed that 58 per cent of mergers failed to reach the value goals set by top managers.[25] The primary cause of failure is conflicting organisational cultures. As one expert commented, 'Mergers have an unusually high failure rate, and it's always because of people issues.'[26] Les Owen realised the significance of changing the culture of his company after AXA Asia Pacific took over National Mutual, which didn't have the values to match a results-oriented competitor in the insurance industry.

CREATING AND SUSTAINING CULTURE

An organisation's culture doesn't pop out of thin air. Once established, it rarely fades away. What forces influence the creation of a culture? What reinforces and sustains these forces once they are in place? We answer both of these questions in this section.

LEARNING OBJECTIVE 4

Explain the factors determining an organisation's culture

HOW A CULTURE BEGINS

An organisation's current customs, traditions and general way of doing things are largely due to what it has done before and the degree of success it has had with those endeavours. This leads us to the ultimate source of an organisation's culture: its founders.[27]

The founders of an organisation traditionally have a major impact on that organisation's early culture. They have a vision of what the organisation should be. They are unconstrained by previous customs or ideologies. The small size that typically characterises new organisations further facilitates the founders' imposition of their vision on all organisational members. Culture creation occurs in three ways.[28] First, founders hire and keep only employees who think and feel the same way they do. Second, they indoctrinate and socialise these employees to their way of thinking and feeling. And finally, the founders' own behaviour acts as a role model that encourages employees to identify with them and thereby internalise their beliefs, values and assumptions. When the organisation succeeds, the founders' vision becomes seen as a primary determinant of that success. At this point, the founders' entire personality becomes embedded in the culture of the organisation.

The culture at Hyundai, the giant Korean conglomerate, is largely a reflection of its founder Chung Ju Yung. Hyundai's fiercely competitive style and its disciplined, authoritarian nature are the same characteristics often used to describe Chung. Other contemporary examples of founders who have had an immeasurable impact on their organisation's culture would include Bill Gates at Microsoft, Ingvar Kamprad at the furniture retailer IKEA, Gerry Harvey of Harvey Norman retail stores and Richard Branson at the Virgin Group.

KEEPING A CULTURE ALIVE

LEARNING OBJECTIVE 5
List the factors that maintain an organisation's culture

Once a culture is in place, there are practices within the organisation that act to maintain it by giving employees a set of similar experiences.[29] For example, many of the human resource practices we discuss in the next chapter reinforce the organisation's culture. The selection process, performance evaluation criteria, training and development activities, and promotion procedures ensure that those hired fit in with the culture, reward those who support it, and penalise (and even expel) those who challenge it. Three forces play a particularly important part in sustaining a culture: selection practices, the actions of top management, and socialisation methods. Let's take a closer look at each.

SELECTION

The explicit goal of the selection process is to identify and hire individuals who have the knowledge, skills and abilities to perform the jobs within the organisation successfully. Typically, more than one candidate will be identified who meets any given job's requirements. When that point is reached, it would be naive to ignore the fact that the final decision as to who is hired will be significantly influenced by the decision maker's judgment of how well the candidates will fit into the organisation. This attempt to ensure a proper match, whether purposely or inadvertently, results in the hiring of people who have values essentially consistent with those of the organisation, or at least a good portion of those values.[30] In addition, the selection process provides information to applicants about the organisation. Candidates learn about the organisation and, if they perceive a conflict between their values and those of the organisation, they can self-select themselves out of the applicant pool. Selection, therefore, becomes a two-way street, allowing employer or applicant to abrogate a marriage if there appears to be a mismatch. In this way, the selection process sustains an organisation's culture by selecting out those individuals who might attack or undermine its core values.

For instance, W. L. Gore & Associates, the maker of Gore-Tex fabric used in outerwear sold in retail outlets such as Snowgum, prides itself on its democratic culture and teamwork. There are no job titles at Gore, nor bosses or chains of command. All work is done in teams. In Gore's selection process, teams of employees put job applicants through extensive interviews to ensure that candidates who can't deal with the level of uncertainty, flexibility and teamwork that employees have to deal with in Gore plants are selected out.[31]

TOP MANAGEMENT

The actions of top management also have a major impact on the organisation's culture.[32] Through what they say and how they behave, senior executives establish norms that filter down through the organisation as to whether risk taking is desirable; how much freedom managers should give their employees; what is appropriate dress; what actions will pay off in terms of pay raises, promotions and other rewards; and the like.

For example, Robert Keirlin is chairman and CEO of Fastenal Co., a large speciality retailer of nuts and bolts in the United States. Keirlin presides over offices in Singapore, China and Canada, as well as the United States, and is responsible for 6500 employees.[33] He takes a salary of only US$60 000 a year. He owns only three suits, each of which he bought used. He clips grocery coupons, drives a Toyota, and stays in low-priced motels when he travels on business. Does Keirlin need to pinch pennies? No. The market value of his stock in Fastenal is around US$300 million. But the man prefers a modest personal lifestyle. And he prefers the same for his company. Keirlin argues that his behaviour should send a message to all his employees: 'We don't waste things in this company.' Keirlin sees himself as a role model for frugality, and employees at Fastenal have learned to follow his example.

SOCIALISATION

LEARNING OBJECTIVE 6

Outline the various socialisation alternatives available to management

socialisation | The process that adapts employees to the organisation's culture.

No matter how good a job the organisation does in recruiting and selection, new employees aren't fully indoctrinated in the organisation's culture. Because they are unfamiliar with the organisation's culture, new employees are potentially likely to disturb the beliefs and customs that are in place. The organisation will therefore want to help new employees adapt to its culture. This adaptation process is called **socialisation**.[34]

All army recruits (whether in Australia, Singapore, Taiwan, or any other country) must go through boot camp, where they 'prove' their commitment. Of course, at the same time, the trainers are indoctrinating new recruits in the 'army way' of doing things.

Socialisation in relation to occupational groups such as the Australian Human Resource Institute can be a significant issue. According to Professor Roger Collins of the Australian Graduate School of Management, there seems to be little evidence that the human resources (HR) occupational group has exercised much influence over its own destiny. Whether it is legislation, government policy, professional standards, occupational reputation, or management education and practice, there is little tangible evidence of the HR profession's direct and lasting impact. One reason given for this is that HR people have weak occupational socialisation—there is a lack of strong identity and aspirations. In comparison to lawyers, doctors, dentists, engineers and accountants, the HR profession has 'few recognised standards of entry, educational preparation and practice, few rites of passage and a professional body weakened by a chequered history of achievement and influence', according to Professor Collins.[35]

At The Limited (an online gift and collectables retailer), newly hired senior managers go through an intensive one-month program, called 'onboarding', designed to immerse them in The Limited's culture.[36] During this month they have no direct responsibilities for tasks associated with their new positions. Instead, they spend all their work time meeting with other senior leaders and mentors, working the floors of retail stores, evaluating employee and customer habits, investigating the competition, and studying The Limited's past and current operations.

As we discuss socialisation, keep in mind that the most critical socialisation stage is at the time of entry into the organisation. This is when the organisation seeks to mould the outsider into an employee 'in good standing'. Employees who fail to learn the essential or pivotal role behaviours risk being labelled 'nonconformists' or 'rebels', which often leads to expulsion. But the organisation will be socialising every employee, though maybe not as explicitly, throughout his or her entire career in the organisation. This further contributes to sustaining the culture.

Socialisation can be conceptualised as a process made up of three stages: pre-arrival, encounter and metamorphosis.[37] The first stage encompasses all the learning that occurs before a new member joins the organisation. In the second stage, the new employee sees what the organisation is really like and confronts the possibility that expectations and reality may diverge. In the third stage, the relatively long-lasting changes take place. The new employee masters the skills required for the job, successfully performs the new roles, and makes the adjustments to the work group's values and norms.[38] This three-stage

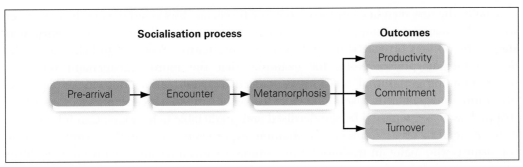

FIGURE 17.1

A socialisation model

process has an impact on the new employee's work productivity, commitment to the organisation's objectives, and eventual decision to stay with the organisation. Figure 17.1 depicts this process.

The **pre-arrival stage** explicitly recognises that each individual arrives with a set of values, attitudes and expectations. These cover both the work to be done and the organisation. For instance, in many jobs, particularly professional work, new members will have undergone a considerable degree of prior socialisation in training and in school. One main purpose of a business school, for example, is to socialise business students to the attitudes and behaviours that business firms want. If business executives believe that successful employees value the profit ethic, are loyal, will work hard, and have the desire to achieve, they can hire individuals out of business schools who have been pre-moulded in this pattern. Moreover, most people in business realise that no matter how well they think they can socialise newcomers, the most important predictor of newcomers' future behaviour is their past behaviour. Research shows that what people know before they join the organisation, and how proactive their personality is, are critical predictors of how well they adjust to a new culture.[39] One way to capitalise on the importance of pre-hire characteristics in socialisation is to select employees with the 'right stuff', and to use the selection process to inform prospective employees about the organisation as a whole. In addition, as noted previously, the selection process also acts to ensure the inclusion of the 'right type'—those who will fit in. 'Indeed, the ability of the individual to present the appropriate face during the selection process determines his ability to move into the organisation in the first place. Thus, success depends on the degree to which the aspiring member has correctly anticipated the expectations and desires of those in the organisation in charge of selection.'[40]

On entry into the organisation, the new member enters the **encounter stage**. Here the individual confronts the possible dichotomy between expectations—about the job, their co-workers, the boss, and the organisation in general—and reality. If expectations prove to have been more or less accurate, the encounter stage merely provides a reaffirmation of the perceptions gained earlier. However, this is often not the case. Where expectations and reality differ, the new employee must undergo socialisation that will detach her from her previous assumptions and replace them with another set that the organisation deems desirable. At the extreme, a new member may become totally disillusioned with the actualities of the job and resign. Proper selection should significantly reduce the probability of the latter occurrence. Also, an employee's network of friends and co-workers can play a critical role in helping them to 'learn the ropes'. Newcomers are more committed to the organisation when their friendship networks are large and diverse. So, organisations can help newcomers to socialise by encouraging friendship ties in organisations.[41]

pre-arrival stage | The period of learning in the socialisation process that occurs before a new employee joins the organisation.

encounter stage | The stage in the socialisation process in which a new employee sees what the organisation is really like and confronts the possibility that expectations and reality may diverge.

The stage in the
socialisation process in
which a new employee
changes and adjusts to the
job, work group and
organisation.

Finally, the new member must work out any problems discovered during the encounter stage. This may mean going through changes—hence, we call this the **metamorphosis stage**. The options presented in Table 17.2 are alternatives designed to bring about the desired metamorphosis. Note, for example, that the more management relies on socialisation programs that are formal, collective, fixed, serial and which emphasise divestiture, the greater the likelihood that newcomers' differences and perspectives will be stripped away and replaced by standardised and predictable behaviours. Careful selection by management of newcomers' socialisation experiences can—at the extreme—create conformists who maintain traditions and customs, or inventive and creative individualists who consider no organisational practice sacred.

We can say that metamorphosis and the entry socialisation process is complete when new members have become comfortable with the organisation and their job. They have internalised the norms of the organisation and their work group, and understand and accept those norms. New members feel accepted by their peers as trusted and valued individuals. They are self-confident that they have the competence to complete the job successfully. They understand the system—not only their own tasks but the rules, procedures and informally accepted practices as well.

Finally, they know how they will be evaluated; that is, what criteria will be used to measure and appraise their work. They know what is expected of them and what constitutes a job 'well done'. As Figure 17.1 shows, successful metamorphosis should have a positive impact on new employees' productivity and their commitment to the organisation and reduce their propensity to leave the organisation.

■ TABLE 17.2
Entry socialisation options

Formal versus informal. The more a new employee is segregated from the ongoing work setting and differentiated in some way to make explicit his or her newcomer's role, the more formal socialisation is. Specific orientation and training programs are examples. Informal socialisation puts the new employee directly into his or her job, with little or no special attention.

Individual versus collective. New members can be socialised individually. This describes how it's done in many professional offices. They can also be grouped together and processed through an identical set of experiences, as in an army training camp.

Fixed versus variable. This refers to the time schedule in which newcomers make the transition from outsider to insider. A fixed schedule establishes standardised stages of transition. This characterises rotational training programs. It also includes probationary periods, such as the eight- to ten-year 'associate' status used by accounting and law firms before deciding on whether or not a candidate is made a partner. Variable schedules give no advance notice of their transition timetable. Variable schedules describe the typical promotion system, where one isn't advanced to the next stage until one is 'ready'.

Serial versus random. Serial socialisation is characterised by the use of role models who train and encourage the newcomer. Apprenticeship and mentoring programs are examples. In random socialisation, role models are deliberately withheld. The new employee is left on his or her own to figure things out.

Investiture versus divestiture. Investiture socialisation assumes that the newcomer's qualities and qualifications are the necessary ingredients for job success, so these qualities and qualifications are confirmed and supported. Divestiture socialisation tries to strip away certain characteristics of the recruit. Initiation rites for 'newcomers' go through divestiture socialisation to shape them into the proper role.

SOURCES: Based on J. Van Maanen, 'People Processing: Strategies of Organizational Socialization', *Organizational Dynamics*, Summer 1978, pp. 19–36; and E. H. Schein, 'Organizational Culture', *American Psychologist*, February 1990, p. 116.

SUMMARY: HOW CULTURES FORM

Figure 17.2 summarises how an organisation's culture is established and sustained. The original culture is derived from the founder's philosophy. This, in turn, strongly influences the criteria used in hiring. The actions of the current top management set the general climate of what is acceptable behaviour and what is not. How employees are to be socialised will depend both on the degree of success achieved in matching new employees' values to those of the organisation in the selection process and on top management's preference for socialisation methods.

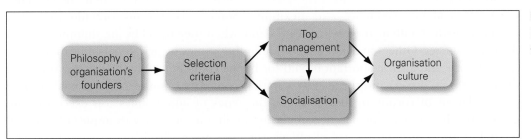

■ FIGURE 17.2
How organisation cultures form

HOW EMPLOYEES LEARN CULTURE

LEARNING OBJECTIVE 7
Clarify how culture is transmitted to employees

Culture is transmitted to employees in a number of forms, the most potent being stories, rituals, material symbols and language.

STORIES

During the days when Henry Ford II was chairman of the Ford Motor Co., one would have been hard pressed to find a manager who hadn't heard the story about Ford reminding his executives, when they got too arrogant, that 'it's my name that's on the building'. The message was clear: Henry Ford II ran the company.

Nike has a number of senior executives who spend much of their time serving as corporate storytellers. And the stories they tell are meant to convey what Nike is about.[42] When they tell the story of how co-founder Bill Bowerman went to his workshop and poured rubber into his wife's waffle iron to create a better running shoe, they are talking about Nike's spirit of innovation. When new employees hear tales of running star Steve Prefontaine's battles to make running a professional sport and to attain better performance equipment, they learn of Nike's commitment to helping athletes.

Stories such as these circulate through many organisations. They typically contain a narrative of events about the organisation's founders, rule breaking, rags-to-riches successes, reductions in the workforce, relocation of employees, reactions to past mistakes, and organisational coping.[43] These stories anchor the present in the past and provide explanations and legitimacy for current practices.

RITUALS

Rituals are repetitive sequences of activities that express and reinforce the key values of the organisation—what goals are most important, and which people are important and which are expendable.[44] One of the corporate rituals that is seen in some countries as 'very American' relates to the large US retailer Wal-Mart and its company chant. Begun by the company's founder, Sam Walton, as a way to motivate and unite his workforce, 'Gimme a W, gimme an A, gimme an L, gimme a squiggle, give me an M, A, R, T!' has become a

rituals | Repetitive sequences of activities that express and reinforce the key values of the organisation—which goals are most important, and which people are important and which are expendable.

company ritual that bonds Wal-Mart workers and reinforces Sam Walton's belief in the importance of his employees to the company's success. Similar corporate chants are used by IBM, Ericsson, Novell, Deutsche Bank and PricewaterhouseCoopers.[45]

MATERIAL SYMBOLS

The headquarters of Alcoa (one of the largest producers of aluminium and alumina) doesn't look like your typical head-office operation. There are few individual offices, even for senior executives. It is essentially made up of cubicles, common areas and meeting rooms. This informal corporate headquarters conveys to employees that Alcoa values openness, equality, creativity and flexibility. Some corporations provide their top executives with chauffeur-driven limousines and, when they travel by air, unlimited use of the corporate jet. Others may not get to ride in limousines or private jets, but they might still get a car and air transportation paid for by the company. Only the car is a Ford or a Proton (with no driver) and the jet seat is in the economy section of a commercial airliner.

The layout of corporate headquarters, the types of automobiles top executives are given, and the presence or absence of corporate aircraft are a few examples of material symbols. Others include the size of offices, the elegance of furnishings, executive perks, and attire.[46] These material symbols convey to employees who is important, the degree of egalitarianism desired by top management, and the kinds of behaviour (for example, risk-taking, conservative, authoritarian, participative, individualistic, social) that are appropriate.

Neo Group retail expert Ross Honeywill says Bunnings has a unique place in the Australian retail landscape. 'It's the classic Aussie worship', he says. 'It's not going to church, it's worshipping at the altar of consumption.' He says Bunnings is one of the few successful retailers to create an experience, rather than merely a place to shop. In the eyes of many consumers, Bunnings is symbolic. 'People who go to Bunnings aren't just buying hardware; it's a place of respite, discovery and reflection', according to Honeywill.

LANGUAGE

Many organisations and units within organisations use language as a way to identify members of a culture or subculture. By learning this language, members attest to their acceptance of the culture and, in so doing, help to preserve it.

Librarians are a rich source of terminology foreign to people outside their profession. They sprinkle their conversations liberally with acronyms such as *ARL* (Association for Research Libraries), *CASL* (Council of Australian State Libraries) and *OPAC* (for On-line Patron Accessing Catalogue).

If you are a new employee at Boeing, you will find yourself learning a whole unique vocabulary of acronyms, including: *BOLD* (Boeing online data), *CATIA* (computer-graphics-aided three-dimensional interactive application), *MAIDS* (manufacturing assembly and installation data system), *POP* (purchased outside production) and *SLO* (service level objectives).[47]

Organisations, over time, often develop unique terms to describe equipment, offices, key personnel, suppliers, customers, or products that relate to its business. New employees are frequently overwhelmed with acronyms and jargon that, after six months on the job, have become fully part of their language. Once assimilated, this terminology acts as a common denominator that unites members of a given culture or subculture.

CREATING AN ETHICAL ORGANISATIONAL CULTURE

The content and strength of a culture influence an organisation's ethical climate and the ethical behaviour of its members.[48] An organisational culture most likely to shape high ethical standards is one that is high in risk tolerance, low to moderate in aggressiveness, and focuses on means as well as outcomes. Managers in such a culture are supported for taking risks and innovating, are discouraged from engaging in unbridled competition, and will pay attention to *how* goals are achieved as well as to *what* goals are achieved.

A strong organisational culture will exert more influence on employees than a weak one. If the culture is strong and supports high ethical standards, it should have a very powerful and positive influence on employee behaviour. Johnson & Johnson, for example, has a strong culture that has long stressed corporate obligations to customers, employees, the community and shareholders, in that order. When poisoned Tylenol (a Johnson & Johnson product) was found on store shelves, employees at Johnson & Johnson independently pulled the product from these stores before management had even issued a statement concerning the tamperings. No one had to tell these individuals what was morally right; they knew what Johnson & Johnson would expect them to do. On the other hand, a strong culture that encourages pushing the limits can be a powerful force in shaping unethical behaviour. For instance, Enron's aggressive culture, with unrelenting pressure on executives to rapidly expand earnings, encouraged ethical corner cutting and eventually contributed to the company's collapse.[49]

What can management do to create a more ethical culture? We suggest a combination of the following practices:

- *Be a visible role model.* Employees will look to top-management behaviour as a benchmark for defining appropriate behaviour. When senior management is seen as taking the ethical high road, it provides a positive message for all employees.
- *Communicate ethical expectations.* Ethical ambiguities can be minimised by creating and disseminating an organisational code of ethics. It should state the

organisation's primary values and the ethical rules that employees are expected to follow.

- *Provide ethical training.* Set up seminars, workshops and similar ethical training programs. Use these training sessions to reinforce the organisation's standards of conduct, to clarify what practices are and are not permissible, and to address possible ethical dilemmas.
- *Visibly reward ethical acts and punish unethical ones.* Performance appraisals of managers should include a point-by-point evaluation of how their decisions measure up against the organisation's code of ethics. Appraisals must include the means taken to achieve goals, as well as the ends themselves. People who act ethically should be visibly rewarded for their behaviour. Just as importantly, unethical acts should be conspicuously punished.
- *Provide protective mechanisms.* The organisation needs to provide formal mechanisms so that employees can discuss ethical dilemmas and report unethical behaviour without fear of reprimand. This might include creation of ethical counsellors, ombudsmen or ethical officers.

CREATING A CUSTOMER-RESPONSIVE CULTURE

French retailers have a well-established reputation for indifference to customers.[50] Salespeople, for instance, routinely make it clear to customers that their phone conversations should not be interrupted. Just getting any help at all from a salesperson can be a challenge. And no one in France finds it particularly surprising that the owner of a Paris store should complain that he was unable to work on his books all morning because he kept being bothered *by customers*!

Most organisations today are trying very hard to be un-French-like. They are attempting to create a customer-responsive culture because they recognise that this is the path to customer loyalty and long-term profitability. Companies that have created such cultures—such as Woolworth's, Marriott Hotels, the Gold Coast theme parks, Avis Car Rentals and Terry White Chemists—have built a strong and loyal customer base and have generally outperformed their competitors in revenue growth and financial performance. In this section, we will briefly identify the variables that shape customer-responsive cultures and offer some suggestions that management can follow for creating such cultures.

<table>
<tr><td>LEARNING OBJECTIVE 8</td></tr>
<tr><td>Describe a customer-responsive culture</td></tr>
</table>

KEY VARIABLES SHAPING CUSTOMER-RESPONSIVE CULTURES

A review of the evidence finds that half-a-dozen variables are routinely evident in customer-responsive cultures.[51]

First is the type of employees themselves. Successful, service-oriented organisations hire employees who are outgoing and friendly. Second is low formalisation. Service employees need to have the freedom to meet changing customer-service requirements. Rigid rules, procedures and regulations make this difficult. Third is an extension of low formalisation— it is the widespread use of empowerment. Empowered employees have the decision discretion to do what is necessary to please the customer. Fourth is good listening skills. Employees in customer-responsive cultures have the ability to listen to and understand messages sent by the customer. Fifth is role clarity. Service employees act as 'boundary spanners' between the organisation and its customers. They have to acquiesce to the demands of both their employer and the customer. This can create considerable role ambiguity and conflict, which reduces employees' job satisfaction and can hinder employee service performance. Successful customer-responsive cultures reduce employee uncertainty about the best way to perform their jobs and the importance of job activities. Finally, customer-responsive cultures have employees who exhibit organisational citizenship behaviour. They are conscientious in their desire to please the customer. And they are willing to take the initiative, even when it is outside their normal job requirements, to satisfy a customer's needs.

In summary, customer-responsive cultures hire service-oriented employees with good listening skills and the willingness to go beyond the constraints of their job description to do what is necessary to please the customer. It then clarifies their roles, frees them up to meet changing customer needs by minimising rules and regulations, and provides them with a wide range of decision discretion to do their job as they see fit.

MANAGERIAL ACTION

Based on the previously identified characteristics, we can suggest a number of actions that management can take if it wants to make its culture more customer-responsive. These actions are designed to create employees with the competence, ability and willingness to solve customer problems as they arise.

SELECTION

The place to start in building a customer-responsive culture is hiring service-contact people with the personality and attitudes consistent with a high service orientation. Southwest Air, an American airline, is a shining example of a company that has focused its hiring process on selecting out job candidates whose personalities aren't people-friendly. Similarly, applicants for jobs with Virgin Blue go through an extensive interview process in which company employees and executives carefully assess whether candidates have the outgoing and fun-loving personality the airline wants in all its employees.

Studies show that friendliness, enthusiasm and attentiveness in service employees positively affect customers' perceptions of service quality.[52] So, managers should look for these qualities in applicants. In addition, job candidates should be screened so that new hires have the patience, concern about others and listening skills that are associated with customer-oriented employees.

TRAINING AND SOCIALISATION

Organisations that are trying to become more customer-responsive don't always have the option of hiring all new employees. More typically, management is faced with the challenge of making its current employees more customer-focused. In such cases, the emphasis will be on training rather than hiring. This describes the dilemma that senior executives at companies such as AXA Asia Pacific Insurance, Shell and National Australia Bank have faced in the past decade as they have attempted to move away from their product focus. The content of these training programs will vary widely but should focus on improving product knowledge, active listening, showing patience and displaying emotions. In addition, even new employees who have a customer-friendly attitude may need to understand management's expectations, so all new service-contact people should be socialised into the organisation's goals and values. Lastly, even the most customer-focused employees can lose direction every once in a while. This should be addressed with regular training updates in which the organisation's customer-focused values are restated and reinforced.

STRUCTURAL DESIGN

Organisation structures need to give employees more control. This can be achieved by reducing rules and regulations. Employees are better able to satisfy customers when they have some control over the service encounter. So, management needs to allow employees to adjust their behaviour to the changing needs and requests of customers. What customers *don't* want to hear are responses such as 'I can't handle this. You need to talk to someone else'; or 'I'm sorry but that's against our company policy.' In addition, the use of cross-functional teams can often improve customer service because service delivery frequently requires a smooth, coordinated effort across different functions.

EMPOWERMENT

Consistent with low formalisation is empowering employees with the discretion to make day-to-day decisions about job-related activities. It is a necessary component of a customer-responsive culture because it allows service employees to make on-the-spot decisions to satisfy customers completely.[53]

Enterprise Rent-A-Car, for instance, has found that high customer satisfaction doesn't require a problem-free experience. The 'completely satisfied' customer was one who, when he or she had a problem, found that it was quickly and courteously resolved by an employee. By empowering their employees to make decisions on the spot, Enterprise improved its customer satisfaction ratings.[54]

LEADERSHIP

Leaders convey the organisation's culture through both what they say and what they do. Effective leaders in customer-responsive cultures deliver by conveying a customer-focused vision and demonstrating by their continual behaviour that they are committed to customers. In almost every organisation that has successfully created and maintained a strong customer-responsive culture, its CEO has played a major role in championing the message. For instance, Taiwan microchip manufacturer United Microelectronics Corp. recently hired Jackson Hu as its new CEO specifically for his prior successes at changing a company's culture to focus employees on better understanding customer needs and improving customer service.[55] John McFarlane, CEO of ANZ Bank, also took a strong leadership role in changing his company's culture. His initiative was due in some part to the poor relationship that Australian banks have had with the general public due to branch closures, fee increases and the reporting of increasing high profits in the media.

PERFORMANCE EVALUATION

There is an impressive amount of evidence demonstrating that behaviour-based performance evaluations are consistent with improved customer service.[56] Behaviour-based evaluations appraise employees on the basis of how they behave or act—on criteria such as effort, commitment, teamwork, friendliness, and the ability to solve customer problems—rather than on the measurable outcomes they achieve. Why are behaviours superior to outcomes for improving service? Because it gives employees the incentive to engage in behaviours that are conducive to improved service quality, and it gives employees more control over the conditions that affect their performance evaluations.[57] In addition, a customer-responsive culture will be fostered by using evaluations that include input from customers. For instance, the performance evaluation of account managers at software company PeopleSoft is based on customer satisfaction and customers' ability to use the company's software.[58] Just the fact that employees know that part of their performance appraisal will include evaluations from customers is likely to make those employees more concerned with satisfying customer needs. Of course, this should only be used with employees who have direct contact with customers.

REWARD SYSTEMS

Finally, if management wants employees to give good service, it has to reward good service. It needs to provide ongoing recognition to employees who have demonstrated extraordinary effort to please customers and who have been singled out by customers for

---

ALL SMILES AT THE RITZ

Organisational culture is fundamental to the success and sustainability of all organisations. Nowhere is this more obvious than in service-oriented industries, particularly hospitality. The major hotel chains around the world are very conscience of the need to have a strong service culture within each location in order to maintain their five-star reputations. Lawrence Chi knows the value of a strong service-oriented culture at his hotel. Lawrence is the HR director of the 578-room Portman Ritz-Carlton in Shanghai, China. His hotel has been awarded 'Best Business Hotel' in Asia for four consecutive years and has also won the 'Best Employer in Asia' and 'Best Employer in China' awards.

The challenge for the Ritz-Carlton is to continuously focus on the culture that has led to the string of awards the hotel has been consistently winning. How does the hotel management promote its desirable cultural attributes? A shared understanding of what luxury service standards are, is a critical first step in determining what kind of competencies are required to deliver that level of service. According to Lawrence, a key to building a customer-focused culture has been the way that the company's espoused values have been integrated into the day-to-day operations of the hotel. The hotel makes this statement about its values and philosophy:

> The Ritz-Carlton Hotel Company, L.L.C. was founded on principles of groundbreaking levels of customer service. The essence of this philosophy was refined into a set of core values collectively called The Gold Standards: The Credo, The Three Steps of Service, The Motto, The Employee Promise and the recent introduction of The Twelve Service Values. To this day, all ladies and gentlemen of The Ritz-Carlton know, embrace and energise these guidelines, aided by their constant presence in the written form of a pocket-sized, laminated card.

The 12 service values provide specific guidance to Lawrence Chi for selecting and training people in relation to the necessary competencies and attitudes for the Ritz special customer service. Ralph Grippo, vice-president and area general manager, captures the Ritz approach succinctly: 'We select talent and teach staff the technical part of their job … we seek people who care for and respect our guests and each other. Those who have a high work ethic, are detail oriented and relationship driven are the types of characteristics we seek in people.' Communication is an important part of embedding the 12 service values into day-to-day operations. This includes general sessions to communicate the values to employees, with each section in the hotel responsible for presenting a different service value to focus on each day. Four-hour training sessions are also available to clarify the values and philosophy of the Ritz.

The service values have been instrumental in creating a greater sense of loyalty and engagement from employees, and according to Chi, the hotel has an excellent staff retention rate: 'In the six years I have been here, only in one year have we not had the lowest in employee turnover in the city. But he admits, there are still challenges, such as the disconnect between the organisational culture and the national culture. In China, a socialist economic system doesn't focus on quality of work. So, it isn't easy to be an award-winning hotel in China. The management of the Portman Ritz-Carlton in Shanghai puts these awards down to their ability to change the culture of their organisation in order to meet guests' needs.

SOURCES: Melissa Yen, 'Living Values the Ritz-Carlton Way', *Human Resources*, 5 September 2006, pp. 14–15; and Ritz-Carlton press release: <www.ritzcarlton.com/corporate/press_room/kits/credo_card.html> (accessed 6 September 2006).

OB IN PRACTICE

'going the extra mile'. And it needs to make pay and promotions contingent on outstanding customer service.

SPIRITUALITY AND ORGANISATIONAL CULTURE

What do Westpac, McKinsey and Co., Hewlett-Packard and CPA Australia have in common? They are among a growing number of organisations that have embraced workplace spirituality.

WHAT IS SPIRITUALITY?

workplace spirituality | The recognition that people have an inner life that nourishes and is nourished by meaningful work that takes place in the context of community.

Workplace spirituality is *not* about organised religious practices. It's not about God or theology. **Workplace spirituality** recognises that people have an inner life that nourishes and is nourished by meaningful work that takes place in the context of community.[59] Organisations that promote a spiritual culture recognise that people have both a mind and a spirit, seek to find meaning and purpose in their work, and desire to connect with other human beings and be part of a community.

WHY SPIRITUALITY NOW?

Historical models of management and organisational behaviour had no room for spirituality. As we noted in our previous discussion of emotions, the myth of rationality assumed that the well-run organisation eliminated feelings. Similarly, concern about an employee's inner life had no role in the perfectly rational model. But just as we have now come to realise that the study of emotions improves our understanding of organisational behaviour, an awareness of spirituality can help you to better understand employee behaviour in the 21st century.

Of course, employees have always had an inner life. So, why has the search for meaning and purposefulness in work surfaced now? There are a number of reasons. We summarise them in Table 17.3.

CHARACTERISTICS OF A SPIRITUAL ORGANISATION

The concept of workplace spirituality draws on our previous discussions of topics such as values, ethics, motivation, leadership and work/life balance. Spiritual organisations are concerned with helping people to develop and reach their full potential. Similarly,

■ TABLE 17.3

Reasons for the growing interest in spirituality

- As a counterbalance to the pressures and stress of a turbulent pace of life. Contemporary lifestyles—single-parent families, geographic mobility, the temporary nature of jobs, new technologies that create distance between people—underscore the lack of community many people feel and increases the need for involvement and connection.

- Ageing baby-boomers, reaching mid-life, are looking for something in their life.

- Formalised religion hasn't worked for many people and they continue to look for anchors to replace lack of faith and to fill a growing feeling of emptiness.

- Job demands have made the workplace dominant in many people's lives, yet they continue to question the meaning of work.

- The desire to integrate personal life values with one's professional life.

- In times of economic plenty, more people have the luxury to engage in a search to reach their full potential.

organisations that are concerned with spirituality are more likely to directly address problems created by work/life conflicts. What differentiates spiritual organisations from their non-spiritual counterparts? Although research on this question is only preliminary, our review identified five cultural characteristics that tend to be evident in spiritual organisations.[60]

- *Strong sense of purpose.* Spiritual organisations build their cultures around a meaningful purpose. Although profits may be important, they are not the primary values of the organisation. People want to be inspired by a purpose that they believe is important and worthwhile.
- *Focus on individual development.* Spiritual organisations recognise the worth and value of people. They aren't just providing jobs. They seek to create cultures in which employees can continually learn and grow.
- *Trust and respect.* Spiritual organisations are characterised by mutual trust, honesty and openness. Managers aren't afraid to admit mistakes. The president of Wetherill Associates, a highly successful auto parts distribution firm, says: 'We don't tell lies here, and everyone knows it. We are specific and honest about quality and suitability of the product for our customers' needs, even if we know they might not be able to detect any problem.'[61]
- *Humanistic work practices.* These practices embraced by spiritual organisations include flexible work schedules, group- and organisation-based rewards, narrowing of pay and status differentials, guarantees of individual worker rights, employee empowerment and job security. The global computer company Hewlett-Packard, for example, has handled temporary downturns through voluntary attrition and shortened work weeks (shared by all), and longer-term declines through early retirements and buyouts.
- *Toleration of employee expression.* The final characteristic that differentiates spiritually based organisations is that they don't stifle employee emotions. They allow people to be themselves—to express their moods and feelings without guilt or fear of reprimand. Employees at Virgin Blue, for instance, are encouraged to express their sense of humour on the job, to act spontaneously and to make their work fun.

CRITICISMS OF SPIRITUALITY

Critics of the spirituality movement in organisations have focused on three issues. First is the question of scientific foundation. What really is workplace spirituality—is this just some new management buzzword? Second, are spiritual organisations legitimate? Specifically, do organisations have the right to impose spiritual values on their employees? Third is the question of economics. Are spirituality and profits compatible?

First, as you might imagine, there is very little research on workplace spirituality. We don't know whether the concept will have staying power. Do the cultural characteristics just identified really separate spiritual organisations? What is a non-spiritual organisation, anyway? Do employees of so-called spiritual organisations perceive that they work in spiritual organisations? Although there is some research suggesting support for workplace spirituality (as we discuss later), before the concept of spirituality gains full credence, the questions we have just posed need to be answered.

On the second question, there is clearly the potential for an emphasis on spirituality to make some employees uneasy. Critics might argue that secular institutions, especially business firms, have no business imposing spiritual values on employees. This criticism is undoubtedly valid when spirituality is defined as bringing religion and God into the workplace.[62] However, the criticism seems less stinging when the goal is limited to helping employees find meaning in their work lives. If the concerns listed in Table 17.3 truly characterise a growing segment of the workforce, then perhaps the time is right for organisations to help employees find meaning and purpose in their work and to use the workplace as a source of community.

Finally, the issue of whether spirituality and profits are compatible objectives is certainly relevant for managers and investors in business. The evidence, although limited, indicates that the two objectives may be very compatible. A recent research study carried out in the United States by a major consulting firm found that companies that introduced spiritually based techniques improved productivity and significantly reduced turnover.[63] Another study found that organisations that provide their employees with opportunities for spiritual development outperformed those that didn't.[64] Other studies also report that spirituality in organisations was positively related to creativity, employee satisfaction, team performance and organisational commitment.[65] And if you are looking for a single case to make the argument for spirituality, it is hard to beat Southwest Air. Southwest has one of the lowest employee turnover rates in the airline industry; it consistently has the lowest labour costs per miles flown of any major airline; it regularly outpaces its competitors for achieving on-time arrivals and fewest customer complaints; and it has proven itself to be the most consistently profitable airline in the United States.[66]

SUMMARY AND IMPLICATIONS FOR MANAGERS

- Figure 17.3 depicts organisational culture as an intervening variable. Employees form an overall subjective perception of the organisation based on factors such as degree of risk tolerance, team emphasis and support of people. This overall perception becomes, in effect, the organisation's culture or personality. These favourable or unfavourable perceptions then affect employee performance and satisfaction, with the impact being greater for stronger cultures.

- Just as people's personalities tend to be stable over time, so too do strong cultures. This makes strong cultures difficult for managers to change. When a culture becomes mismatched to its environment, management will want to change it. But as the Point/Counterpoint feature demonstrates, changing an organisation's culture is a long and difficult process. The result, at least in the short term, is that managers should treat their organisation's culture as relatively fixed.

- One of the more important managerial implications of organisational culture relates to selection decisions. Hiring individuals whose values don't align with those of the organisation is likely to lead to employees who lack motivation and commitment and who are dissatisfied with their jobs and the organisation.[67] Not surprisingly, employee 'misfits' have considerably higher turnover rates than individuals who perceive a good fit.[68]

- We should also not overlook the influence socialisation has on employee performance. An employee's performance depends to a considerable degree on knowing what he should or shouldn't do. Understanding the right way to do a job indicates proper socialisation.

- Furthermore, the appraisal of an individual's performance includes how well the person fits into the organisation. Can he or she get along with co-workers? Does he or she have acceptable work habits and demonstrate the right attitude? These qualities differ between jobs and organisations. For instance, on some jobs, employees will be evaluated more favourably if they are aggressive and outwardly indicate that they are ambitious. On another job, or on the same job in another organisation, such an approach may be evaluated negatively. As a result, proper socialisation becomes a significant factor in influencing both actual job performance and how it is perceived by others.

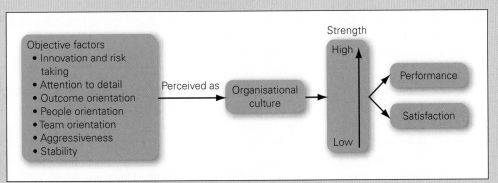

■ FIGURE 17.3
How organisational cultures impact employee performance and satisfaction

Organisational Cultures Can't Be Changed

● POINT

An organisation's culture is made up of relatively stable characteristics. It develops over many years and is rooted in deeply held values to which employees are strongly committed. In addition, there are a number of forces continually operating to maintain a given culture. These include written statements about the organisation's mission and philosophy, the design of physical spaces and buildings, the dominant leadership style, hiring criteria, past promotion practices, entrenched rituals, popular stories about key people and events, the organisation's historic performance evaluation criteria, and its formal structure.

Selection and promotion policies are particularly important devices that work against cultural change. Employees chose the organisation because they perceived their values to be a 'good fit' with the organisation. They become comfortable with that fit and will strongly resist efforts to disturb the equilibrium. The difficulties that organisations such as General Motors, Telstra and Australia Post have had in trying to reshape their cultures attest to this dilemma. These organisations historically tended to attract individuals who desired situations that were stable and highly structured. Those in control in organisations will also select senior managers who will continue the current culture. Even attempts to change a culture by going outside the organisation to hire a new chief executive are unlikely to be effective. The evidence indicates that the culture is more likely to change the executive than the other way around.

Our argument should not be viewed as saying that culture can *never* be changed. In the unusual case in which an organisation confronts a survival-threatening crisis, members of the organisation will be responsive to efforts at cultural change. However, anything less than that is unlikely to be effective in bringing about cultural change.

● COUNTERPOINT

Changing an organisation's culture is extremely difficult, but cultures *can* be changed. The evidence suggests that cultural change is most likely to take place when most or all of the following conditions exist:

* *A dramatic crisis.* This is the shock that undermines the status quo and calls into question the relevance of the current culture. Examples are a surprising financial setback, the loss of a major customer, and a dramatic technological breakthrough by a competitor.
* *Turnover in leadership.* New top leadership, which can provide an alternative set of key values, may be perceived as more capable of responding to the crisis.
* *Young and small organisations.* The younger the organisation is, the less entrenched its culture will be. Similarly, it is easier for management to communicate its new values when the organisation is small.
* *Weak culture.* The more widely held a culture is and the higher the agreement among members on its values, the more difficult it will be to change. Conversely, cultures that are weak are more amenable to change than cultures that are strong.

If all or most of these conditions exist, the following management actions may lead to change: initiating new stories and rituals; selecting and promoting employees who espouse the new values; changing the reward system to support the new values; and undermining current subcultures through transfers, job rotation and terminations.

Under the best of conditions, these actions won't result in an immediate or dramatic shift in the culture. In the final analysis, cultural change is a lengthy process—measured in years rather than in months. But cultures can be changed. The success that new leadership had in turning around the cultures at companies such as AXA Asia Pacific, National Australia Bank, ANZ Bank and Harley-Davidson attests to this claim.

QUESTIONS FOR REVIEW

MyOBLab Do you understand this chapter's content? Find out at **www.pearsoned.com.au/MyOBLab**

1. What is the difference between institutionalisation and organisational culture?
2. What is the significance of an organisation's subcultures?
3. How does an organisational culture relate to a national culture?
4. What are the functions of an organisation's culture?
5. How does a strong culture affect an organisation's efforts to improve diversity?
6. How does management sustain an organisation's culture?
7. How is culture transmitted to employees?
8. How can management create an ethical culture?
9. What criticisms have been targeted against bringing spirituality to the workplace?

QUESTIONS FOR CRITICAL THINKING

1. Can an employee survive in an organisation if he or she rejects its core values? Explain.
2. Is socialisation just a form of brainwashing? Explain.
3. Can you identify a set of characteristics that describes your university's culture? Compare them with those of several of your peers. How closely do they agree?
4. 'We should be opposed to the manipulation of individuals for organisational purposes, but a degree of social uniformity enables organisations to work better.' Do you agree or disagree with this statement? What are its implications for organisational culture? Discuss.

EXPERIENTIAL EXERCISE

Rate Your Classroom Culture

Listed here are 14 statements. Using the five-item scale (from 'Strongly agree' to 'Strongly disagree'), respond to each statement by circling the number that best represents your opinion.

Calculate your total score by adding up the numbers you circled. Your score will fall between 14 and 70. A high score (49 or above) describes an open, risk-taking, supportive, humanistic, team-oriented, easy-going, growth-oriented culture. A low score (35 or below) describes a closed, structured, task-oriented, individualistic, tense and stability-oriented culture. Note that differences count, so a score of 60 indicates a culture that is more open than one that scores 50. Also, it is important to realise that one culture isn't preferable over the other. The 'right' culture depends on you and your preferences for a learning environment.

Form teams of five to seven members each. Compare your scores. How closely do they align? Discuss and resolve any discrepancies. Based on your team's analysis, what type of student do you think would perform best in this class?

	Strongly agree	Agree	Neutral	Disagree	Strongly disagree
1. I feel comfortable challenging statements made by my tutor.	5	4	3	2	1
2. My tutor heavily penalises assignments that are not turned in on time.	1	2	3	4	5
3. My tutor believes that 'It's final results that count'.	1	2	3	4	5
4. My tutor is sensitive to my personal needs and problems.	5	4	3	2	1
5. A large portion of my grade depends on how well I work with others in the class.	5	4	3	2	1
6. I often feel nervous and tense when I come to class.	1	2	3	4	5
7. My tutor seems to prefer stability over change.	1	2	3	4	5
8. My tutor encourages me to develop new and different ideas.	5	4	3	2	1
9. My tutor has little tolerance for sloppy thinking.	1	2	3	4	5
10. My tutor is more concerned with how I came to a conclusion than with the conclusion itself.	5	4	3	2	1
11. My tutor treats all students alike.	1	2	3	4	5
12. My tutor frowns on class members helping each other with assignments.	1	2	3	4	5
13. Aggressive and competitive people have a distinct advantage in this class.	1	2	3	4	5
14. My tutor encourages me to see the world differently.	5	4	3	2	1

ETHICAL DILEMMA

Is Voluntary Ethics Training Unethical?

A lot of companies rely on training as an essential part of their efforts to create an ethical culture. In some cases, this training is short in duration and requires little emotional investment by the employee. For instance, the training might only require reading a pamphlet describing the company's code of ethics, followed by taking an online quiz to ensure employee understanding. In contrast, some organisations' ethics training is quite lengthy, requiring employees to seriously address their values and principles and to share them with their co-workers. For example, at one of the world's best-known passenger aircraft production companies, the Boeing Company's training program, called 'Questions of Integrity: The Ethics Challenge', is conducted within an employee's work group. Led by their supervisor, employees discuss more than four dozen ethical situations. Each includes four possible ways of dealing with the problem. After the supervisor discusses each situation, employees are asked to choose the best outcome by holding up cards which are marked A, B, C or D. Then the supervisor indicates the 'ethically correct' answer.

Most of the evidence indicates that for ethics training to be effective, it needs to be intensive and frequently reinforced. Some of the best programs require participants to spend several days a year, every year, engaged in discussions and exercises designed to clarify the organisation's ethical expectations.

Is it unethical to ask employees to share their deepest personal values regarding right and wrong with their boss and co-workers? Should employees have the right not to participate in ethical training programs that might require them to publicly vocalise their ethical standards, religious principles or other personal beliefs?

17 CASE STUDY

A Culture Clash

Merging two very different companies is a daunting job, but the right investment of time and effort will see it through.

Champagne corks popped and the celebratory drinks flowed in the boardroom of the department store Salingers when the chairman clinched the takeover of his rival company, the trendy retailer Yuppy. But the chief operating officer of Salingers, Rick, wasn't convinced that this was the merger of the century.

The figures were impressive: paying $600 million for 120 new warehouse-type stores in the up-and-coming suburbs of Australia's boom states of Queensland and Western Australia would balance the 150 established Salingers stores in the southern states. But the transformation to the new Salingers brand depended on combining Salingers' years of retail management experience with the marketing ideas of the Yuppy stores. The combined purchasing power of the group would be important, but the true value of knocking out Salingers' only rival was the strength of the new brand rising above the discount general merchandisers that had been eroding the company's profits in the past five years.

Shortly after the merger announcement, Rick was appointed to lead a team to draw up an integration plan. A survey examining organisational culture was a priority.

The first area of difference revealed by the survey was decision making. Salingers made decisions at the executive level and sent out decrees to junior managers. But Yuppy staff workshopped each big product and marketing decision in monthly store meetings. Any employee whose idea was adopted was rewarded, boosting innovation.

A second area of cultural difference was the method of executing the strategy. Salingers' managers drew up lists of project tasks for each team and expected line managers to complete each one. Yuppy appointed a project team to communicate the wider objectives of a project, designate tasks and performance measures for each employee, and report on progress during staff meetings.

The last difference was leadership style. Salingers relied on a cadre of older managers to train middle managers over many years in one team. Every Yuppy employee was given a mentor when they started, to guide their development over many years. The Yuppy chief executive boasted that he visited each store twice a year and had an intimate knowledge of the company's operations.

Rick was startled by the differences.

QUESTIONS

1. How was Rick to bring two such divergent cultures together?
2. How would he get managers from both companies to work together on the integration?
3. How could he bring employees under a common system without stifling the much-needed injection of creative and innovative thinking?
4. How could Rick judge how long he would need to complete the cultural change?

SOURCE: Based on Amita Tandukar, 'Culture Clash', *Business Review Weekly*, 25–31 May 2006, pp. 66–67.

ENDNOTES

1. Susan Heron, 'Review and Renew: Basics for Growth', *Management Today*, May 2006, pp. 6–9: <www.aim.com.au/Display Story.asp?ID=586>; ASX Company Announcements Platform Lodgement of Open Briefing, date of lodgement, 3 August 2006: <www.corporatefile.com.au/> (accessed 12 September 2006).

2. P. Selznick, 'Foundations of the Theory of Organizations', *American Sociological Review*, February 1948, pp. 25–35.
3. <www.smithfamily.com.au> (accessed 12 October 2006).
4. See L. G. Zucker, 'Organizations as Institutions', in S. B. Bacharach (ed.), *Research in the Sociology of Organizations*

(Greenwich, CT: JAI Press, 1983), pp. 1–47; A. J. Richardson, 'The Production of Institutional Behaviour: A Constructive Comment on the Use of Institutionalization Theory in Organizational Analysis', *Canadian Journal of Administrative Sciences*, December 1986, pp. 304–16; L. G. Zucker, *Institutional Patterns and*

Organizations: Culture and Environment (Cambridge, MA: Ballinger, 1988); R. L. Jepperson, 'Institutions, Institutional Effects, and Institutionalism', in W. W. Powell and P. J. DiMaggio (eds), *The New Institutionalism in Organizational Analysis* (Chicago: University of Chicago Press, 1991), pp. 143–63; and T. B. Lawrence, M. K. Mauws, B. Dyck and R. F. Kleysen, 'The Politics of Organizational Learning: Integrating Power into the 4I Framework', *Academy of Management Review*, January 2005, pp. 180–91.

5. See, for example, H. S. Becker, 'Culture: A Sociological View', *Yale Review*, Summer 1982, pp. 513–27; and E. H. Schein, *Organizational Culture and Leadership* (San Francisco: Jossey-Bass, 1985), p. 168.

6. This seven-item description is based on C. A. O'Reilly III, J. Chatman and D. F. Caldwell, 'People and Organizational Culture: A Profile Comparison Approach to Assessing Person–Organization Fit', *Academy of Management Journal*, 21 September 1991, pp. 487–516; and J. A. Chatman and K. A. Jehn, 'Assessing the Relationship between Industry Characteristics and Organizational Culture: How Different Can You Be?', *Academy of Management Journal*, June 1994, pp. 522–53. For a review of cultural dimensions, see N. M. Ashkanasy, C. P. M. Wilderom and M. F. Peterson (eds), *Handbook of Organizational Culture and Climate* (Thousand Oaks, CA: Sage, 2000), pp. 131–45.

7. The view that there will be consistency among perceptions of organisational culture has been called the 'integration' perspective. For a review of this perspective and conflicting approaches, see D. Meyerson and J. Martin, 'Cultural Change: An Integration of Three Different Views', *Journal of Management Studies*, November 1987, pp. 623–47; and P. J. Frost, L. F. Moore, M. R. Louis, C. C. Lundberg and J. Martin (eds), *Reframing Organizational Culture* (Newbury Park, CA: Sage Publications, 1991).

8. See J. M. Jermier, J. W. Slocum, Jr, L. W. Fry and J. Gaines, 'Organizational Subcultures in a Soft Bureaucracy: Resistance Behind the Myth and Facade of an Official Culture', *Organization Science*, May 1991, pp. 170–94; S. A. Sackmann, 'Culture and Subcultures: An Analysis of Organizational Knowledge', *Administrative Science Quarterly*, March 1992, pp. 140–61; G. Hofstede, 'Identifying Organizational Subcultures: An Empirical Approach', *Journal of Management Studies*, January 1998, pp. 1–12; and A. Boisner and J. A. Chatman, 'The Role of Subcultures in Agile Organizations', in R. S. Peterson and E. A. Mannix (eds), *Leading and Managing People in the Dynamic Organization*

(Mahwah, NJ: Lawrence Erlbaum Associates, 2003), pp. 87–112.

9. T. A. Timmerman, 'Do Organizations Have Personalities?', Paper presented at the 1996 National Academy of Management Conference, Cincinnati, OH, August 1996.

10. S. Hamm, 'No Letup—and No Apologies', *BusinessWeek*, 26 October 1998, pp. 58–64; and C. Carlson, 'Former Intel Exec Slams Microsoft Culture', eWeek.com, 26 March 2002.

11. See, for example, G. G. Gordon and N. DiTomaso, 'Predicting Corporate Performance from Organizational Culture', *Journal of Management Studies*, November 1992, pp. 793–98; J. B. Sorensen, 'The Strength of Corporate Culture and the Reliability of Firm Performance', *Administrative Science Quarterly*, March 2002, pp. 70–91; and J. Rosenthal and M. A. Masarech, 'High–Performance Cultures: How Values Can Drive Business Results', *Journal of Organizational Excellence*, Spring 2003, pp. 3–18.

12. Y. Wiener, 'Forms of Value Systems: A Focus on Organizational Effectiveness and Cultural Change and Maintenance', *Academy of Management Review*, October 1988, p. 536.

13. R. T. Mowday, L. W. Porter and R. M. Steers, *Employee–Organization Linkages: The Psychology of Commitment, Absenteeism, and Turnover* (New York: Academic Press, 1982); and C. Vandenberghe, 'Organizational Culture, Person–Culture Fit, and Turnover: A Replication in the Health Care Industry', *Journal of Organizational Behavior*, March 1999, pp. 175–84.

14. S. L. Dolan and S. Garcia, 'Managing By Values: Cultural Redesign for Strategic Organizational Change at the Dawn of the Twenty-First Century', *Journal of Management Development*, no. 2, 2002, pp. 101–07.

15. See N. J. Adler, *International Dimensions of Organizational Behavior*, 4th ed. (Cincinnati, OH: Southwestern, 2002), pp. 67–69.

16. S. C. Schneider, 'National vs. Corporate Culture: Implications for Human Resource Management', *Human Resource Management*, Summer 1988, p. 239.

17. See C. A. O'Reilly and J. A. Chatman, 'Culture as Social Control: Corporations, Cults, and Commitment', in B. M. Staw and L. L. Cummings (eds), *Research in Organizational Behavior*, vol. 18 (Greenwich, CT: JAI Press, 1996), pp. 157–200; see also M. Pinae Cunha, 'The "Best Place to Be": Managing Control and Employee Loyalty in a Knowledge-Intensive Company', *Journal of Applied Behavioral Science*, December 2002, pp. 481–95.

18. T. E. Deal and A. A. Kennedy, 'Culture: A

New Look Through Old Lenses', *Journal of Applied Behavioral Science*, November 1983, p. 501.

19. J. Case, 'Corporate Culture', *INC.*, November 1996, pp. 42–53.

20. Sorensen, 'The Strength of Corporate Culture and the Reliability of Firm Performance'.

21. See, for instance, P. L. Moore, 'She's Here to Fix the Xerox', *BusinessWeek*, 6 August 2001, pp. 47–48; and C. Ragavan, 'FBI Inc.', *US News & World Report*, 18 June 2001, pp. 15–21.

22. See C. Lindsay, 'Paradoxes of Organizational Diversity: Living within the Paradoxes', in L. R. Jauch and J. L. Wall (eds), *Proceedings of the 50th Academy of Management Conference* (San Francisco, 1990), pp. 374–78; T. Cox, Jr, *Cultural Diversity in Organizations: Theory, Research & Practice* (San Francisco: Berrett-Koehler, 1993), pp. 162–70; and L. Grensing-Pophal, 'Hiring to Fit Your Corporate Culture', *Human Resources*, August 1999, pp. 50–54.

23. K. Labich, 'No More Crude at Texaco', *Fortune*, 6 September 1999, pp. 205–12; and 'Rooting Out Racism', *BusinessWeek*, 10 January 2000, p. 66.

24. A. F. Buono and J. L. Bowditch, *The Human Side of Mergers and Acquisitions: Managing Collisions between People, Cultures, and Organizations* (San Francisco: Jossey-Bass, 1989); S. Cartwright and C. L. Cooper, 'The Role of Culture Compatibility in Successful Organizational Marriages', *Academy of Management Executive*, May 1993, pp. 57–70; E. Krell, 'Merging Corporate Cultures', *Training*, May 2001, pp. 68–78; and R. A. Weber and C. F. Camerer, 'Cultural Conflict and Merger Failure: An Experimental Approach', *Management Science*, April 2003, pp. 400–12.

25. P. Gumbel, 'Return of the Urge to Merge', *Time Europe Magazine*: <www.time.com/time/europe/magazine/article/0,13005,901030721-464418,00.html> (13 July 2003).

26. S. F. Gale, 'Memo to AOL Time Warner: Why Mergers Fail—Case Studies', *Workforce*: <www.workforce.com> (February 2003); W. Bock, 'Mergers, Bubbles, and Steve Case', *Wally Bock's Monday Memo*: <www.mondaymemo.net/030120feature.htm> (January 2003).

27. E. H. Schein, 'The Role of the Founder in Creating Organizational Culture', *Organizational Dynamics*, Summer 1983, pp. 13–28.

28. E. H. Schein, 'Leadership and Organizational Culture', in F. Hesselbein, M. Goldsmith and R. Beckhard (eds), *The Leader of the Future* (San Francisco: Jossey-Bass, 1996), pp. 61–62.

29. See, for example, J. R. Harrison and G. R. Carroll, 'Keeping the Faith: A Model of Cultural Transmission in Formal

Organizations', *Administrative Science Quarterly*, December 1991, pp. 552–82; see also G. George, R. G. Sleeth and M. A. Siders, 'Organizational Culture: Leader Roles, Behaviors, and Reinforcement Mechanisms', *Journal of Business & Psychology*, Summer 1999, pp. 545–60.

30. B. Schneider, 'The People Make the Place', *Personnel Psychology*, Autumn 1987, pp. 437–53; D. E. Bowen, G. E. Ledford, Jr and B. R. Nathan, 'Hiring for the Organization, Not the Job', *Academy of Management Executive*, November 1991, pp. 35–51; B. Schneider, H. W. Goldstein and D. B. Smith, 'The ASA Framework: An Update', *Personnel Psychology*, Winter 1995, pp. 747–73; A. L. Kristof, 'Person–Organization Fit: An Integrative Review of Its Conceptualizations, Measurement, and Implications', *Personnel Psychology*, Spring 1996, pp. 1–49; D. M. Cable and T. A. Judge, 'Interviewers' Perceptions of Person–Organization Fit and Organizational Selection Decisions', *Journal of Applied Psychology*, August 1997, pp. 546–61; J. Schaubroeck, D. C. Ganster and J. R. Jones, 'Organization and Occupation Influences in the Attraction–Selection–Attrition Process', *Journal of Applied Psychology*, December 1998, pp. 869–91; G. Callaghan and P. Thompson, '"We Recruit Attitude": The Selection and Shaping of Routine Call Centre Labour', *Journal of Management Studies*, March 2002, pp. 233–47; and M. L. Verquer, T. A. Beehr and S. H. Wagner, 'A Meta-Analysis of Relations Between Person–Organization Fit and Work Attitudes', *Journal of Vocational Behavior*, December 2003, pp. 473–89.

31. L. Grensing-Pophal, 'Hiring to Fit Your Corporate Culture', *Human Resources*, August 1999, pp. 50–54.

32. D. C. Hambrick and P. A. Mason, 'Upper Echelons: The Organization as a Reflection of Its Top Managers', *Academy of Management Review*, April 1984, pp. 193–206; B. P. Niehoff, C. A. Enz and R. A. Grover, 'The Impact of Top-Management Actions on Employee Attitudes and Perceptions', *Group & Organization Studies*, September 1990, pp. 337–52; and H. M. Trice and J. M. Beyer, 'Cultural Leadership in Organizations', *Organization Science*, May 1991, pp. 149–69.

33. J. S. Lublin, 'Cheap Talk', *Wall Street Journal*, 11 April 2002, p. B14.

34. See, for instance, J. P. Wanous, *Organizational Entry*, 2nd ed. (New York: Addison-Wesley, 1992); G. T. Chao, A. M. O'Leary-Kelly, S. Wolf, H. J. Klein and P. D. Gardner, 'Organizational Socialization: Its Content and Consequences', *Journal of Applied Psychology*, October 1994, pp. 730–43; B. E. Ashforth, A. M. Saks and

R. T. Lee, 'Socialization and Newcomer Adjustment: The Role of Organizational Context', *Human Relations*, July 1998, pp. 897–926; D. A. Major, 'Effective Newcomer Socialization into High-Performance Organizational Cultures', in Ashkanasy, Wilderom and Peterson (eds), *Handbook of Organizational Culture & Climate*, pp. 355–68; D. M. Cable and C. K. Parsons, 'Socialization Tactics and Person–Organization Fit', *Personnel Psychology*, Spring 2001, pp. 1–23; and K. Rollag, 'The Impact of Relative Tenure on Newcomer Socialization Dynamics', *Journal of Organizational Behavior*, November 2004, pp. 853–72.

35. R. Collins, 'Will the Future of HR Whither Away?', *Human Resources*, 4 May 2004: <www.humanresourcesmagazine.com.au/articles/7E/0C01F97E.asp?Type=61&Category=905> (accessed 6 September 2006).

36. K. Rhodes, 'Breaking in the Top Dogs', *Training*, February 2000, pp. 67–74.

37. J. Van Maanen and E. H. Schein, 'Career Development', in J. R. Hackman and J. L. Suttle (eds), *Improving Life at Work* (Santa Monica, CA: Goodyear, 1977), pp. 58–62.

38. D. C. Feldman, 'The Multiple Socialization of Organization Members', *Academy of Management Review*, April 1981, p. 310.

39. G. Chen and R. J. Klimoski, 'The Impact of Expectations on Newcomer Performance in Teams as Mediated by Work Characteristics, Social Exchanges, and Empowerment', *Academy of Management Journal*, vol. 46, 2003, pp. 591–607; C. R. Wanberg and J. D. Kammeyer-Mueller, 'Predictors and Outcomes of Proactivity in the Socialization Process', *Journal of Applied Psychology*, vol. 85, 2000, pp. 373–85; J. D. Kammeyer-Mueller and C. R. Wanberg, 'Unwrapping the Organizational Entry Process: Disentangling Multiple Antecedents and Their Pathways to Adjustment', *Journal of Applied Psychology*, vol. 88, 2003, pp. 779–94; E. W. Morrison, 'Longitudinal Study of the Effects of Information Seeking on Newcomer Socialization', *Journal of Applied Psychology*, vol. 78. 2003, pp. 173–83.

40. Van Maanen and Schein, 'Career Development', p. 59.

41. E. W. Morrison, 'Newcomers' Relationships: The Role of Social Network Ties During Socialization', *Academy of Management Journal*, vol. 45, 2002, pp. 1149–60.

42. E. Ransdell, 'The Nike Story? Just Tell It!', *Fast Company*, January–February 2000, pp. 44–46.

43. D. M. Boje, 'The Storytelling Organization: A Study of Story Performance in an Office-Supply Firm', *Administrative Science Quarterly*, March 1991, pp. 106–26; C. H. Deutsch, 'The Parables of Corporate Culture', *New York Times*, 13 October

1991, p. F25; and M. Ricketts and J. G. Seiling, 'Language, Metaphors, and Stories: Catalysts for Meaning Making in Organizations', *Organization Development Journal*, Winter 2003, pp. 33–43.

44. See K. Kamoche, 'Rhetoric, Ritualism, and Totemism in Human Resource Management', *Human Relations*, April 1995, pp. 367–85.

45. V. Matthews, 'Starting Every Day with a Shout and a Song', *Financial Times*, 2 May 2001, p. 11; and M. Gimein, 'Sam Walton Made Us a Promise', *Fortune*, 18 March 2002, pp. 121–30.

46. A. Rafaeli and M. G. Pratt, 'Tailored Meanings: On the Meaning and Impact of Organizational Dress', *Academy of Management Review*, January 1993, pp. 32–55; and J. M. Higgins and C. McAllaster, 'Want Innovation? Then Use Cultural Artifacts That Support It', *Organizational Dynamics*, August 2002, pp. 74–84.

47. 'DCACronyms', April 1997, Rev. D, published by The Boeing Co.

48. See B. Victor and J. B. Cullen, 'The Organizational Bases of Ethical Work Climates', *Administrative Science Quarterly*, March 1988, pp. 101–25; L. K. Trevino, 'A Cultural Perspective on Changing and Developing Organizational Ethics', in W. A. Pasmore and R. W. Woodman (eds), *Research in Organizational Change and Development*, vol. 4 (Greenwich, CT: JAI Press, 1990); M. W. Dickson, D. B. Smith, M. W. Grojean and M. Ehrhart, 'An Organizational Climate Regarding Ethics: The Outcome of Leader Values and the Practices That Reflect Them', *Leadership Quarterly*, Summer 2001, pp. 197–217; and R. L. Dufresne, 'An Action Learning Perspective on Effective Implementation of Academic Honor Codes', *Group & Organization Management*, April 2004, pp. 201–18.

49. J. A. Byrne, 'The Environment was Ripe for Abuse', *BusinessWeek*, 25 February 2002, pp. 118–20; and A. Raghavan, K. Kranhold and A. Barrionuevo, 'How Enron Bosses Created a Culture of Pushing Limits', *Wall Street Journal*, 26 August 2002, p. A1.

50. S. Daley, 'A Spy's Advice to French Retailers: Politeness Pays', *New York Times*, 26 December 2000, p. A4.

51. Based on M. J. Bitner, B. H. Booms and L. A. Mohr, 'Critical Service Encounters: The Employee's Viewpoint', *Journal of Marketing*, October 1994, pp. 95–106; M. D. Hartline and O. C. Ferrell, 'The Management of Customer-Contact Service Employees: An Empirical Investigation', *Journal of Marketing*, October 1996, pp. 52–70; M. L. Lengnick-Hall and Cynthia A. Lengnick-Hall, 'Expanding Customer Orientation in the HR Function', *Human Resource Management*, Fall 1999, pp. 201–14; B. Schneider, D. E. Bowen,

M. G. Ehrhart and K. M. Holcombe, 'The Climate for Service: Evolution of a Construct', in Ashkanasy, Wilderom and Peterson (eds), *Handbook of Organizational Culture and Climate*, pp. 21–36; M. D. Hartline, J. G. Maxham III and D. O. McKee, 'Corridors of Influence in the Dissemination of Customer-Oriented Strategy to Customer Contact Service Employees', *Journal of Marketing*, April 2000, pp. 35–50; L. A. Bettencourt, K. P. Gwinner and M. L. Meuter, 'A Comparison of Attitude, Personality, and Knowledge Predictors of Service-Oriented Organizational Citizenship Behaviors', *Journal of Applied Psychology*, February 2001, pp. 29–41; R. Peccei and P. Rosenthal, 'Delivering Customer-Oriented Behaviour through Empowerment: An Empirical Test of HRM Assumptions', *Journal of Management*, September 2001, pp. 831–56; R. Batt, 'Managing Customer Services: Human Resource Practices, Quit Rates, and Sales Growth', *Academy of Management Journal*, June 2002, pp. 587–97; S. D. Pugh, J. Dietz, J. W. Wiley and S. M. Brooks, 'Driving Service Effectiveness through Employee–Customer Linkages', *Academy of Management Executive*, November 2002, pp. 73–84; and A. M. Sussking, K. M. Kacmar and C. P. Borchgrevink, 'Customer Service Providers' Attitudes Relating to Customer Service and Customer Satisfaction in the Customer-Service Exchange', *Journal of Applied Psychology*, February 2003, pp. 179–87.

52. D. E. Bowen and B. Schneider, 'Boundary-Spanning-Role Employees and the Service Encounter: Some Guidelines for Future Management and Research', in J. Czepiel, M. R. Solomon and C. F. Surprenant (eds), *The Service Encounter* (New York: Lexington Books, 1985), pp. 127–47; W.-C. Tsai, 'Determinants and Consequences of Employee Displayed Positive Emotions', *Journal of Management*, vol. 27, no. 4, 2001, pp. 497–512; and S. D. Pugh, 'Service with a Smile: Emotional Contagion in the Service Encounter', *Academy of Management Journal*, October 2001, pp. 1018–27.

53. Hartline and Ferrell, 'The Management of Customer-Contact Service Employees', p. 56; and R. C. Ford and C. P. Heaton, 'Lessons from Hospitality That Can Serve Anyone', *Organizational Dynamics*, Summer 2001, pp. 41–42.

54. A. Taylor, 'Driving Customer Satisfaction', *Harvard Business Review*, July 2002, pp. 24–25.

55. M. Clendenin, 'UMC's New CEO Brings Customer Focus', *EBN*, 21 July 2003, p. 4.

56. See, for instance, E. Anderson and R. L. Oliver, 'Perspectives on Behavior-Based versus Outcome-Based Salesforce Control Systems', *Journal of Marketing*, October 1987, pp. 76–88; W. R. George, 'Internal Marketing and Organizational Behavior: A Partnership in Developing Customer-Conscious Employees at Every Level', *Journal of Business Research*, January 1990, pp. 63–70; and K. K. Reardon and B. Enis, 'Establishing a Company-Wide Customer Orientation through Persuasive Internal Marketing', *Management Communication Quarterly*, February 1990, pp. 376–87.

57. Hartline and Ferrell, 'The Management of Customer-Contact Service Employees', p. 57.

58. A. M. Webber and H. Row, 'For Who Know How', *Fast Company*, October 1997, p. 130.

59. D. P. Ashmos and D. Duchon, 'Spirituality at Work: A Conceptualization and Measure', *Journal of Management Inquiry*, June 2000, p. 139. For a comprehensive review of definitions of workplace spirituality, see R. A. Giacalone and C. L. Jurkiewicz, 'Toward a Science of Workplace Spirituality', in R. A. Giacalone and C. L. Jurkiewicz (eds), *Handbook of Workplace Spirituality and Organizational Performance* (Armonk, NY: M. E. Sharpe, 2003), pp. 6–13.

60. This section is based on C. Ichniowski, D. L. Kochan, C. Olson and G. Strauss, 'What Works at Work: Overview and Assessment', *Industrial Relations*, 1996, pp. 299–333; I. A. Mitroff and E. A. Denton, *A Spiritual Audit of Corporate America: A Hard Look at Spirituality, Religion, and Values in the Workplace* (San Francisco: Jossey-Bass, 1999); J. Milliman, J. Ferguson, D. Trickett and B. Condemi, 'Spirit and Community at Southwest Airlines: An Investigation of a Spiritual Values-Based Model', *Journal of Organizational Change Management*, vol. 12, no. 3, 1999, pp. 221–33; E. H. Burack, 'Spirituality in the Workplace', *Journal of Organizational Change Management*, vol. 12, no. 3, 1999, pp. 280–91; F. Wagner-Marsh and J. Conley, 'The Fourth Wave: The Spiritually-Based Firm', *Journal of Organizational Change Management*, vol. 12, no. 3, 1999, pp. 292–302; and J. Pfeffer, 'Business and the Spirit: Management Practices That Sustain Values', in R. A. Giacalone and C. L. Jurkiewicz (eds), *Handbook of Workplace Spirituality and Organizational Performance*, pp. 32–41.

61. Cited in Wagner-Marsh and Conley, 'The Fourth Wave', p. 295.

62. M. Conlin 'Religion in the Workplace: The Growing Presence of Spirituality in Corporate America', *BusinessWeek*, 1 November 1999, pp. 151–58; and P. Paul, 'A Holier Holiday Season', *American Demographics*, December 2001, pp. 41–45.

63. Cited in Conlin, 'Religion in the Workplace', p. 153.

64. C. P. Neck and J. F. Milliman, 'Thought Self-Leadership: Finding Spiritual Fulfillment in Organizational Life', *Journal of Managerial Psychology*, vol. 9, no. 8, 1994, p. 9; for a recent review, see J.-C. Garcia-Zamor, 'Workplace Spirituality and Organizational Performance', *Public Administration Review*, May–June 2003, pp. 355–63.

65. D. W. McCormick, 'Spirituality and Management', *Journal of Managerial Psychology*, vol. 9, no. 6, 1994, p. 5; E. Brandt, 'Corporate Pioneers Explore Spiritual Peace', *Human Resources*, vol. 41, no. 4, 1996, p. 82; P. Leigh, 'The New Spirit at Work', *Training and Development*, vol. 51, no. 3, 1997, p. 26; P. H. Mirvis, 'Soul Work in Organizations', *Organization Science*, vol. 8, no. 2, 1997, p. 193; and J. Milliman, A. Czaplewski and J. Ferguson, 'An Exploratory Empirical Assessment of the Relationship between Spirituality and Employee Work Attitudes', Paper presented at the National Academy of Management Meeting, Washington, DC, August 2001.

66. Cited in Milliman et al., 'Spirit and Community at Southwest Airlines'.

67. J. A. Chatman, 'Matching People and Organizations: Selection and Socialization in Public Accounting Firms', *Administrative Science Quarterly*, September 1991, pp. 459–84; B. Z. Posner, 'Person–Organization Values Congruence: No Support for Individual Differences as a Moderating Influence', *Human Relations*, April 1992, pp. 351–61; and A. E. M. Van Vianen, 'Person–Organization Fit: The Match between Newcomers' and Recruiters' Preferences for Organizational Cultures', *Personnel Psychology*, Spring 2000, pp. 113–49.

68. J. E. Sheridan, 'Organizational Culture and Employee Retention', *Academy of Management Journal*, December 1992, pp. 1036–56.

18

ORGANISATIONAL PERFORMANCE SYSTEMS

CHAPTER OUTLINE

PERFORMANCE EVALUATION

TRAINING AND DEVELOPMENT PROGRAMS

WORK STRESS AND ITS MANAGEMENT

MANAGING DIVERSITY IN ORGANISATIONS

LEARNING OBJECTIVES

AFTER STUDYING THIS CHAPTER, YOU SHOULD BE ABLE TO:

1. EXPLAIN THE PURPOSES OF PERFORMANCE EVALUATION AND WHO CAN CONDUCT IT

2. DESCRIBE ACTIONS THAT CAN IMPROVE THE PERFORMANCE EVALUATION PROCESS

3. DEFINE FOUR GENERAL SKILLS CATEGORIES

4. IDENTIFY FOUR TYPES OF EMPLOYEE TRAINING

5. DESCRIBE POTENTIAL SOURCES OF STRESS

6. EXPLAIN INDIVIDUAL DIFFERENCE VARIABLES THAT MODERATE THE STRESS–OUTCOME RELATIONSHIP

7. IDENTIFY SOME OF THE MAIN ISSUES THAT MANAGERS CONFRONT IN DEALING WITH DIVERSITY IN THE WORKPLACE

Talented employees are in demand. But do managers fully understand what it takes to retain that talent for competitive advantage?

OPEN ANY NEWSPAPER or watch any business news report and it is not long before the issue of skills shortage appears. A recent survey found that organisations were facing increasing pressures to locate, select and retain skilled staff. This shortage was putting pressures on wages as organisations resorted to offering more money to attract away skilled employees from other organisations. And it is not just higher wages that organisations are having to consider to attract and retain the right employees. As David Makin, general manager of Education, Training, Research and HR Consulting at the Australian Institute of Management, has pointed out, it is no longer all about wages and salaries. Employees are looking for more, he says, especially in the way of more stable work arrangements, increased job security, increased training opportunities and improved work environments.

In a recent survey, 44.7 per cent of organisations expected to increase the number of permanent employees, whereas only 15 per cent expected to decrease permanent employee numbers. Often the increase of permanent employees comes from converting existing contract or temporary employees to permanent positions. In some areas the skills shortages are so severe that organisations are having to 'import' employees from overseas, either using temporary work visas that last up to four years or by offering permanent positions (and residency) to qualified overseas persons. This approach is being employed for skills as varied as welders, meat workers, radiographers and medical practitioners. Another source of skilled workers is to employ persons lacking the required skills and training them up to the required competencies. David Makin indicates there is likely to be an increase in this approach as the skills shortages bite harder into the performance of organisations.

Julie Mills, CEO of the Recruitment and Consulting Services Association, advocates a collaborative approach by employers and employees, with employers offering not only training opportunities but also more supportive work environments and progressive attitudes towards employees. Mills argues that, in return, new employees will give organisations enthusiasm, commitment and positive attitudes that will see increased self-esteem, motivation and, ultimately, enhanced organisational performance.[1]

Unless a group of workers know their work is under surveillance, that they are being rated as fairly as human beings, with the fallibility that goes with human judgment, can rate them, and that at least an attempt is made to measure their worth to an organisation in relative terms, they are likely to sink back on length of service as the sole reason for retention and promotion.

Mary Barnett Gilson

THE SKILLS SHORTAGE CRISIS highlighted by both David Makin and Julie Mills also raises another crucial issue concerned with organisational behaviour—the issue of developing organisational performance systems that support managers in achieving results. A high-performance workplace is based on having talented people doing innovative work to create value for the organisation.

Human resource managers, in particular, provide direction for developing critical support systems around recruitment and selection, training and development, remuneration, performance management, employee relations, stress management and diversity management. In this chapter, we draw various threads together and give an overview of how managers can align with the HR functions and enhance an organisation's performance-related systems. In particular, we will focus on performance evaluation, training and development, stress management, and diversity management as four important aspects of addressing some of the key issues of organisational behaviour and enhancing performance and satisfaction at the individual, group and organisational levels of operation.

PERFORMANCE EVALUATION

Would you study differently or exert a different level of effort for a university course graded on a pass–fail basis than for one that awarded letter grades from A to F? Students typically tell us they study harder when letter grades are at stake. In addition, when they take a course on a pass–fail basis, they tend to do just enough to ensure a passing grade.

This finding illustrates how performance evaluation systems influence behaviour. Major determinants of your in-class behaviour and out-of-class studying effort at university are the criteria and techniques your lecturer uses to evaluate your performance. What applies in the university context also applies to employees at work. In this section, we show how the choice of a performance evaluation system and the way it is administered can be an important force influencing individual employee behaviour.

PURPOSES OF PERFORMANCE EVALUATION

Performance evaluation serves a number of purposes.[2] One purpose is to help management make general *human resources decisions*. Evaluations provide input into important decisions such as promotions, transfers and terminations. Evaluations also *identify training and development needs*. They pinpoint employee skills and competencies that are currently inadequate but for which remedial programs can be developed. Performance evaluations can also serve as a *criterion against which management validates selection and development programs*. Management can identify newly hired employees who perform poorly. Similarly, the organisation determines the effectiveness of training and development programs by assessing how well participants do on their performance evaluation. Evaluations also fulfil the purpose of *providing feedback to employees* on how the organisation views their performance. Furthermore, performance evaluations are the *basis for reward allocations*. Decisions as to who gets merit pay increases and other rewards are frequently determined by performance evaluations.

MANAGING THE PERFORMANCE REVIEW

Performance management is fundamental to any organisation's operations, but there is some doubt over the ability of line management to fully exploit the benefits of their performance review and appraisal systems. According to Shayne Bakewell, executive director of the Australian company EMA Consulting, part of the challenge lies in the attitude of line managers, who often put performance management in the too-hard basket. 'The process of performance management is normally associated with conflict or confrontation and is usually way down the priority list for line managers.' He adds that the challenge for HR professionals is making sure line managers understand the need for successful performance management practices and initiatives.

Terence-Liam Preece of Dale Carnegie Training, based in New South Wales, suggests that the performance review is often the only formal agenda and means to achieve alignment between an organisation's vision, mission, values and business strategies, and the performance of staff assigned to specific positions. Many opportunities are lost because line management lack the skills to deal with performance issues of their staff and to use the performance review as a means of inspiriting their staff. Preece reinforces this concern: 'The challenge can be line management seeing the performance review as a mandatory process that is attended to once a year, and filed for another year. This is because they have little skill in dealing with the potential conflict, or they lack the knowledge and practice.'

According to both Preece and Bakewell, a positive corporate culture offers the greatest potential to any organisation, and performance management provides an important mechanism for promoting such a positive performance-oriented culture across the entire organisation, provided line managers have the competencies and attitudes to review staff in a positive and constructive manner. Bakewell adds that where training for performance reviews has been implemented effectively, there has generally been an improvement in productivity and reduction in costs. Regular feedback on performance has also helped to increase employee morale.

SOURCE: Anon, 'Managing Performance Down the Line', *Human Resources*, 3 October 2006, pp. 14–15: <www.humanresourcesmagazine.com.au/articles/62/0C045762.asp> (accessed 12 January 2007).

Each of these functions of performance evaluation is valuable. Yet their importance to us depends on the perspective we are taking. Several are clearly relevant to human resource management decisions. But our interest is in organisational behaviour. As a result, we shall be emphasising performance evaluation as a mechanism for providing feedback and as a determinant of reward allocations.

WHAT DO WE EVALUATE?

The criteria that management chooses to evaluate when appraising employee performance will have a major influence on what employees do. The three most popular sets of criteria are individual task outcomes, behaviours and traits.

INDIVIDUAL TASK OUTCOMES

If ends count, rather than means, then management should evaluate an employee's task outcomes. Using task outcomes, a plant manager could be judged on criteria such as quantity produced, scrap generated and cost per unit of production. Similarly, a salesperson could be assessed on overall sales volume in the territory, dollar increase in sales and number of new accounts established.

BEHAVIOURS

In many cases, it is difficult to identify specific outcomes that can be directly attributed to an employee's actions. This is particularly true of personnel in advisory or support

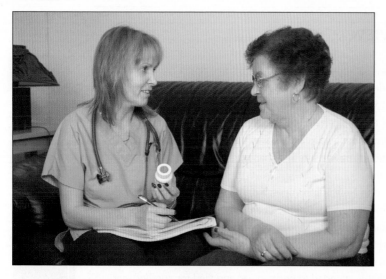

Behaviour is an important element in appraising the performance of nursing aides in retirement homes. In addition to individual task outcomes, this aide at a retirement home is evaluated on behaviours such as helping others and building caring and trusting relationships with residents and their family members. These subjective factors contribute to the effectiveness of the retirement home and its reputation as a place where the elderly are treated with love and respect.

positions and individuals whose work assignments are intrinsically part of a group effort. We may readily evaluate the group's performance but have difficulty distinguishing clearly the contribution of each group member. In such instances, it is not unusual for management to evaluate the employee's behaviour. Using the previous examples, behaviours of a plant manager that could be used for performance evaluation purposes might include promptness in submitting monthly reports or the leadership style the manager exhibits. Pertinent salesperson behaviours could be the average number of contact calls made per day or sick days used per year.

Note that these behaviours needn't be limited to those directly related to individual productivity.[3] As we pointed out in our discussion on organisational citizenship behaviour in previous chapters, helping others, making suggestions for improvements and volunteering for extra duties make work groups and organisations more effective. So, including subjective or contextual factors in a performance evaluation—as long as they contribute to organisational effectiveness—may not only make sense; it may also enhance coordination, teamwork, cooperation and overall organisational performance.

TRAITS

The weakest set of criteria, yet one that is still widely used by organisations, is individual traits.[4] We say they are weaker than either task outcomes or behaviours because they are furthest removed from the actual performance of the job itself. Traits such as having a good attitude, showing confidence, being dependable, showing enthusiasm, looking busy, or possessing a wealth of experience may or may not be highly correlated with positive task outcomes, but only the naive would ignore the reality that such traits are frequently used as criteria for assessing an employee's level of performance.

WHO SHOULD DO THE EVALUATING?

Who should evaluate an employee's performance? By tradition, the task has fallen to the manager, on the grounds that managers are held responsible for their employees' performance. But that logic may be flawed. Others may actually be able to do the job better.

With many of today's organisations using self-managed teams, telecommuting and other organising devices that distance bosses from their employees, an employee's immediate superior may not be the most reliable judge of that employee's performance. Thus, in more and more cases, peers and even subordinates are being asked to participate in the performance evaluation process. Also, increasingly, employees are participating in their own performance evaluation. For instance, a recent survey found that about half of executives and 53 per cent of employees now have input into their performance evaluations.[5] As you might surmise, self-evaluations often suffer from over-inflated assessment and self-serving bias. Moreover, self-evaluations are often low in agreement with superiors' ratings.[6] Because of these drawbacks, self-evaluations are probably better suited to developmental than evaluative purposes and should be combined with other sources of information to reduce rating errors. In most situations, in fact, it is highly advisable to use multiple sources of ratings. Any individual performance rating may say as much about the rater as about the person being evaluated. By averaging across raters, we can obtain a more reliable, unbiased and accurate performance evaluation.

The latest approach to performance evaluation is the use of 360-degree evaluations.[7] This method provides for performance feedback from the full circle of daily contacts that an employee might have, ranging from mailroom personnel to customers to bosses to peers (see Figure 18.1). The number of appraisals can be as few as three or four or as many as 25, with most organisations collecting between five and ten per employee.

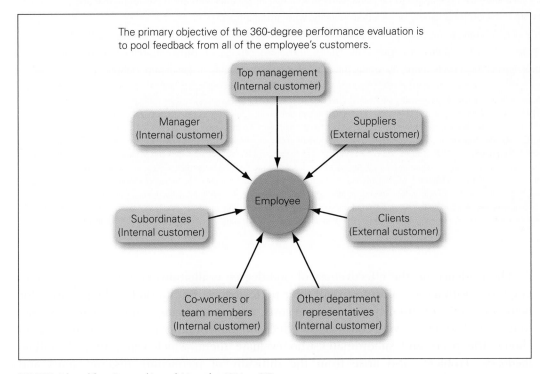

The primary objective of the 360-degree performance evaluation is to pool feedback from all of the employee's customers.

■ FIGURE 18.1
360-degree evaluations

SOURCE: Adapted from *Personnel Journal*, November 1994, p. 100.

Some of the companies in Australia using 360-degree evaluations include Travelex, Vodafone and XYZNetworks.[8] What is the appeal of 360-degree evaluations? They fit well into organisations that have introduced teams, employee involvement and quality-management programs, and that operate in dynamic, highly competitive environments. By relying on feedback from fellow employees, customers and subordinates, these organisations are hoping to give everyone more of a sense of participation in the review process and to gain more accurate readings on employee performance. On this latter point, 360-degree evaluations are consistent with evidence that employee performance varies across contexts and that people behave differently with different constituencies.[9] The use of multiple sources is more likely to capture this variety of behaviour accurately.

'IT'S FIRST IMPRESSIONS THAT COUNT'

This statement is true. When we meet someone for the first time, we notice a number of things about that person—physical characteristics, clothes, firmness of handshake, gestures, tone of voice, and the like. We then use these impressions to fit the person into ready-made categories. And this early categorisation, formed quickly and on the basis of minimal information, tends to hold greater weight than impressions and information received later.

The best evidence about first impressions comes from research on employment interviews. Findings clearly demonstrate that first impressions count. For instance, the primacy effect is potent. That is, the first information presented affects judgments more than information presented later.

Research on applicant appearance confirms the power of first impressions. Studies have looked at assessments made of applicants before the actual interview—that brief period in which the applicant walks into an interview room, exchanges greetings with the interviewer, sits down and engages in minor chit-chat. The evidence indicates that the way applicants walk, talk, dress and look can have a great impact on the interviewer's evaluation of applicant qualifications. Facial attractiveness seems to be particularly influential. Applicants who are highly attractive are evaluated as more qualified for a variety of jobs than persons who are unattractive.

A final body of confirming research finds that interviewers' post-interview evaluations of applicants conform, to a substantial degree, to their pre-interview impressions. That is, those first impressions carry considerable weight in shaping the interviewers' final evaluations, assuming the interview elicits no highly negative information.

SOURCES: R. E. Carlson, 'Effect of Interview Information in Altering Valid Impressions', *Journal of Applied Psychology*, February 1971, pp. 66–72; M. London and M. D. Hakel, 'Effects of Applicant Stereotypes, Order, and Information on Interview Impressions', *Journal of Applied Psychology*, April 1974, pp. 157–62; E. C. Webster, *The Employment Interview: A Social Judgement Process* (Ontario, Canada: S.I.P., 1982); T. W. Dougherty, D. B. Turban and J. C. Callender, 'Confirming First Impressions in the Employment Interview: A Field Study of Interviewer Behavior', *Journal of Applied Psychology*, October 1994, pp. 659–65; N. R. Bardack and F. T. McAndrew, 'The Influence of Physical Attractiveness and Manner of Dress on Success in a Simulated Personnel Decision', *Journal of Social Psychology*, August 1985, pp. 777–78; R. Bull and N. Rumsey, *The Social Psychology of Facial Appearance* (London: Springer-Verlag, 1988); and L. M. Watkins and L. Johnston, 'Screening Job Applicants: The Impact of Physical Attractiveness and Application Quality', *International Journal of Selection & Assessment*, June 2000, pp. 76–84; T. W. Dougherty, R. J. Ebert and J. C. Callender, 'Policy Capturing in the Employment Interview', *Journal of Applied Psychology*, vol. 71, no. 1, February 1986, pp. 9–15; and T. M. Macan and R. L. Dipboye, 'The Relationship of the Interviewers' Preinterview Impressions to Selection and Recruitment Outcomes', *Personnel Psychology*, Autumn 1990, pp. 745–69.

The evidence on the effectiveness of 360-degree evaluations is mixed.[10] It provides employees with a wider perspective of their performance. But it also has the potential for being misused. For instance, to minimise costs, many organisations don't spend the time to train evaluators in giving constructive criticism. Some organisations allow employees to choose the peers and subordinates who evaluate them, which can artificially inflate feedback. Problems also arise from the difficulty of reconciling disagreements and contradictions between rater groups. Finally, a good 360-degree feedback system needs substantial investment in time, training and trust—trying to economise on any of these will lead to a less than satisfactory outcome.

METHODS OF PERFORMANCE EVALUATION

The previous sections explained *what* we evaluate and *who* should do the evaluating. Now we ask: *How* do we evaluate an employee's performance? That is, what are the specific techniques for evaluation?

WRITTEN ESSAYS

Probably the simplest method of evaluation is to write a narrative describing an employee's strengths, weaknesses, past performance, potential, and suggestions for improvement. The written essay requires no complex forms or extensive training to complete. But in this method a good or bad appraisal may be determined as much by the evaluator's writing skill as by the employee's actual level of performance.

CRITICAL INCIDENTS

Critical incidents focus the evaluator's attention on the behaviours that are key in making the difference between executing a job effectively and executing it ineffectively. That is, the appraiser writes down anecdotes that describe what the employee did that was especially effective or ineffective. The key here is to cite only specific behaviours, not vaguely defined personality traits. A list of critical incidents provides a rich set of examples from which the employee can be shown the behaviours that are desirable and those that call for improvement.

critical incidents | Evaluating the behaviours that are key in making the difference between executing a job effectively and executing it ineffectively.

GRAPHIC RATING SCALES

One of the oldest and most popular methods of evaluation is the use of **graphic rating scales**. In this method, a set of performance factors, such as quantity and quality of work, depth of knowledge, cooperation, attendance and initiative, is listed. The evaluator then goes down the list and rates each on incremental scales. The scales may specify five points, so a factor such as job knowledge might be rated 1 ('poorly informed about work duties') to 5 ('has complete mastery of all phases of the job'). Although they don't provide the depth of information that essays or critical incidents do, graphic rating scales are less time-consuming to develop and administer. They also allow for quantitative analysis and comparison.

graphic rating scales | An evaluation method in which the evaluator rates performance factors on an incremental scale.

BEHAVIOURALLY ANCHORED RATING SCALES

Behaviourally anchored rating scales (BARS) combine major elements from the critical incident and graphic rating scale approaches: the appraiser rates the employees based on items along a continuum, but the points are examples of actual behaviour on the given job, rather than general descriptions or traits. Examples of job-related behaviour and performance dimensions are found by asking participants to give specific illustrations of effective and ineffective behaviour regarding each performance dimension. These behavioural examples are then translated into a set of performance dimensions, each dimension having varying levels of performance.

behaviourally anchored rating scales (BARS) | Scales that combine major elements from the critical incident and graphic rating scale approaches: the appraiser rates the employees based on items along a continuum, but the points are examples of actual behaviour on the given job, rather than general descriptions or traits.

FORCED COMPARISONS

Forced comparisons evaluate one individual's performance against the performance of another or others. It is a relative, rather than an absolute, measuring device. The two most popular comparisons are group order ranking and individual ranking.

The **group order ranking** approach requires the evaluator to place employees into a particular classification, such as top one-fifth or second one-fifth. This method is often used in ranking students for entry into higher education. Evaluators are asked whether the student ranks in the top 5 per cent of the class, the next 5 per cent, the next 15 per cent, and so forth. But in this type of performance appraisal, managers deal with all their subordinates. Therefore, if a rater has 20 employees, only four can be in the top fifth and, of course, four must also be relegated to the bottom fifth. The **individual ranking** approach rank-orders employees from best to worst. If the manager is required to appraise 30 employees, this approach assumes that the difference between the first and second employee is the same as that between the 21st and 22nd. Even though some of the employees may be closely grouped, no ties are permitted. The result is a clear ordering of employees, from the highest performer down to the lowest.

group order ranking | An evaluation method that places employees into a particular classification, such as quartiles.

individual ranking | An evaluation method that rank-orders employees from best to worst.

Multi-person comparisons can be combined with one of the other methods to incorporate the best from both absolute and relative standards. For example, an alternative way for universities to deal with the problem of grade inflation is to require instructors to include not only an absolute letter grade but also relative data on class size and rank. So, a prospective employer or graduate school could look at two students who each got an 'A' in their physical geology courses and draw considerably different conclusions about each, because next to one grade it says 'ranked 2nd out of 26', while the other says 'ranked 14th out of 30'. Obviously, the first student performed better, relatively, than did the second.

LEARNING OBJECTIVE 2

Describe actions that can improve the performance evaluation process

SUGGESTIONS FOR IMPROVING PERFORMANCE EVALUATIONS

The performance evaluation process is a potential minefield of problems. For instance, evaluators can unconsciously inflate evaluations (positive leniency), understate performance (negative leniency), or allow the assessment of one characteristic to unduly influence the assessment of others (the halo error). Some appraisers bias their evaluations by unconsciously favouring people who have qualities and traits similar to their own (the similarity error). And, of course, some evaluators see the evaluation process as a political opportunity to overtly reward or punish employees they like or dislike. Although there are no protections that will guarantee accurate performance evaluations, the following suggestions can significantly help to make the process more objective and fair.

USE MULTIPLE EVALUATORS

As the number of evaluators increases, the probability of attaining more accurate information increases. If rater error tends to follow a normal curve, an increase in the number of appraisers will tend to find the majority congregating about the middle. We often see multiple evaluators in competitions in such sports as diving and gymnastics. A set of evaluators judges a performance, the highest and lowest scores are dropped, and the final evaluation is made up of those remaining. The logic of multiple evaluators applies to organisations as well.

If an employee has had ten supervisors, nine having rated her excellent and one poor, we can safely discount the one poor evaluation. Therefore, by moving employees about within the organisation so as to gain a number of evaluations, or by using multiple assessors (as provided in 360-degree appraisals), we increase the probability of achieving more valid and reliable evaluations.

EVALUATE SELECTIVELY

Appraisers should evaluate only in areas in which they have some expertise.[11] This precaution increases the inter-rater agreement and makes the evaluation a more valid process. It also recognises that different organisational levels often have different orientations towards those being rated and observe them in different settings. In general, therefore, appraisers should be as close as possible, in terms of organisational level, to the individual being evaluated. Conversely, the more levels that separate the evaluator and the person being evaluated, the less opportunity the evaluator has to observe the individual's behaviour and, not surprisingly, the greater the possibility for inaccuracies.

TRAIN EVALUATORS

If you can't *find* good evaluators, the alternative is to *make* good evaluators. There is substantial evidence that training evaluators can make them more accurate raters.[12]

Common errors such as halo and leniency have been minimised or eliminated in workshops where managers practise observing and rating behaviours. These workshops typically run from one to three days, but allocating many hours to training may not always be necessary. One case has been cited in which both halo and leniency errors were decreased immediately after exposing evaluators to explanatory training sessions lasting only five minutes.[13] But the effects of training appear to diminish over time.[14] This suggests the need for regular refresher sessions.

PROVIDE EMPLOYEES WITH DUE PROCESS

The concept of due process can be applied to appraisals to increase the perception that employees are being treated fairly.[15] Three features characterise due process systems: (1) individuals are provided with adequate notice of what is expected of them; (2) all evidence relevant to a proposed violation is aired in a fair hearing so the individuals affected can respond; and (3) the final decision is based on the evidence and is free of bias.

There is considerable evidence that evaluation systems often violate employees' due process by providing them with infrequent and relatively general performance feedback, allowing them little input into the appraisal process, and knowingly introducing bias into performance ratings. However, when due process has been part of the evaluation system, employees report positive reactions to the appraisal process, perceive the evaluation results as more accurate, and express increased intent to remain with the organisation.

PROVIDING PERFORMANCE FEEDBACK

For many managers, few activities are more unpleasant than providing performance feedback to employees.[16] In fact, unless pressured by organisational policies and controls, managers are likely to ignore this responsibility.[17]

Why the reluctance to give performance feedback? There seem to be at least three reasons. First, managers are often uncomfortable discussing performance weaknesses directly with employees. Even though almost every employee could stand to improve in some areas, managers fear a confrontation when presenting negative feedback. This apprehension apparently applies even when people give negative feedback to a computer! Bill Gates reports that Microsoft conducted a project requiring users to rate their experience with a computer. 'When we had the computer the users had worked with ask for an evaluation of its performance, the responses tended to be positive. But when we had a second computer ask the same people to evaluate their encounters with the first machine, the people were significantly more critical. Their reluctance to criticise the first computer "to its face" suggested that they didn't want to hurt its feelings, even though they knew it was only a machine.'[18]

Many managers find it difficult to give performance feedback. The solution is training managers to give employees constructive information that will motivate them to improve their performance. During the review, managers should act like counsellors in providing feedback that guides employee development rather than critical judges of task outcomes and behaviour.

Second, many employees tend to become defensive when their weaknesses are pointed out. Instead of accepting the feedback as constructive and a basis for improving performance, some employees challenge the evaluation by criticising the manager or redirecting blame to someone else. A survey of 151 area managers in Philadelphia, in the United States, for instance, found that 98 per cent encountered some type of aggression after giving employees negative appraisals.[19]

Finally, employees tend to have an inflated assessment of their own performance. Statistically speaking, half of all employees must be below-average performers. But the evidence indicates that the average employee's estimate of his or her own performance level generally falls around the 75th percentile.[20] So, even when managers are providing good news, employees are likely to perceive it as not good enough.

The solution to the performance feedback problem is not to ignore it, but to train managers to conduct constructive feedback sessions.[21] An effective review—one in which the employee perceives the appraisal as fair, the manager as sincere, and the climate as constructive—can result in the employee's leaving the interview in an upbeat mood, informed about the performance areas needing improvement, and determined to correct the deficiencies.[22] In addition, the performance review should be designed more as a counselling activity than a judgment process. This can best be accomplished by allowing the review to evolve out of the employee's own self-evaluation. Have you ever had to give colleagues or classmates feedback on their performance? Did you try to stay positive, or did you find you took a negative approach? Maybe you would handle the situation differently next time. If you are curious about how good you are at giving performance feedback, see the Self-Assessment feature.

TRAINING AND DEVELOPMENT PROGRAMS

Competent employees don't remain competent forever. Skills deteriorate and can become obsolete, and new skills need to be learned. That's why organisations spend billions of dollars each year on formal training. Despite this expenditure, Australia is facing a significant skills shortage. Part of the reason is that despite increases in workplace training over the past decade, from 30 per cent in 1993, 42 per cent in 1997, 45 per cent in 2001 and 48 per cent in 2005, training provided in the workplace isn't keeping pace with the skills needed.[23] To keep good people, it is more critical than ever that organisations look at investing in their employees. Indeed, more and more employees make their decisions on who they will work for on the basis of the potential for training and development, more than on economic and social reasons, because they realise that the better qualified they are, the happier in their work they will become.

SELF-ASSESSMENT LIBRARY

HOW GOOD AM I AT GIVING PERFORMANCE FEEDBACK?

In the Self-Assessment Library (available on CD and online), take Self-Assessment III.A.3 (How Good Am I at Giving Performance Feedback?) and answer the following questions.

1. How did you score compared to your classmates? Did the results surprise you?
2. Do you think giving people feedback is easy or difficult? Is your opinion reflected in your scores?
3. How might you further develop your skills in providing feedback to people?

TYPES OF TRAINING

LEARNING OBJECTIVE 3

Define four general skills categories

Training can include everything from teaching employees basic reading skills to conducting advanced courses in executive leadership. Here we discuss four general skill categories—basic literacy, and technical, interpersonal and problem-solving skills. In addition, we briefly discuss ethics training.

BASIC LITERACY SKILLS

The last survey of adult literacy (called the Survey of Aspects of Literacy) was conducted by the Australian Bureau of Statistics (ABS) in 1996 and found that approximately 20 per cent of the Australian population only scored at level one in a five-level test of literacy, with about another 27 per cent at the second-lowest literacy level.[24] Employees at level one would experience significant difficulty reading and writing, while those at level two are likely to experience some difficulties at work.

This problem, of course, isn't unique to Australia. It is a worldwide problem—from the most developed countries to the least.[25] Currently, the ABS is collaborating on another survey of literacy as part of the Adult Literacy and Life Skills Survey (ALLS) in late 2006. This survey is also being conducted at the same time in the OECD countries, Canada, New Zealand, Norway, Switzerland, Hungary, the Netherlands and Korea—this will give us an opportunity to compare literacy levels across nations.[26] For many Third World countries, where few workers can read or have gone beyond primary school, widespread illiteracy means there is almost no hope of breaking the poverty cycle and competing in a global economy. That would certainly act as a de-motivator for employees and further reduce organisational performances.

TECHNICAL SKILLS

Most training is directed at upgrading and improving an employee's technical skills. Technical training has become increasingly important today for three reasons—new technology, stronger occupational health and safety laws, and new structural designs in the organisation.

Jobs change as a result of changed priorities, new technologies and improved methods. For instance, many auto repair personnel have had to undergo extensive training to fix and maintain recent models with computer-monitored engines, electronic stabilising systems, GPS, keyless entry, and other innovations. Similarly, computer-controlled equipment has required millions of production employees to learn a whole new set of skills.[27]

In addition, technical training has become increasingly important because of changes in organisation design. As organisations flatten their structures, expand their use of teams, and break down traditional departmental barriers, employees need mastery of a wider variety of tasks and increased knowledge of how their organisation operates. For instance, the ACT Brumbies rugby union team from Canberra was built around empowered players and club staff, which has led to the introduction of sports science, statistical analysis of style of play and the adoption of a business-like approach to sport throughout the club.[28] Players especially are encouraged to make suggestions and discuss their ideas, not only about on-field matters but all aspects of the business. Rod Clarke, CEO of the ACT Brumbies, says: 'From day one, when new players come into the organisation they get told and they see in practical ways how their ideas and thoughts can be put on the table for discussion, and then picked up and implemented. We encourage them not to sit back and be spoon-fed. We encourage people to actively participate in everything from development of programmes, training principles and schedules, and playing strategies. Having them actively involved really does help reinforce the accountability of them delivering on the field.'[29]

INTERPERSONAL SKILLS

Almost all employees belong to a work unit, and their work performance depends to some degree on their ability to effectively interact with their fellow employees and their boss. Some employees have excellent interpersonal skills, but others require training to improve theirs. This includes learning how to be a better listener, how to communicate ideas more clearly, and how to be a more effective team player. Much conflict comes from poor communication and can lead to performance decreases—by improving interpersonal communication skills, the organisation is investing in improved performance outcomes.

PROBLEM-SOLVING SKILLS

Managers, as well as many employees who perform non-routine tasks, have to solve problems on their jobs. When people require these skills but are deficient in them, they can participate in problem-solving training. This can include activities to sharpen their logic, reasoning and problem-defining skills, as well as their abilities to assess causation, develop and analyse alternatives, and select solutions. Problem-solving training has become a basic part of almost every organisational effort to introduce self-managed teams or implement quality-management programs.

WHAT ABOUT ETHICS TRAINING?

A recent survey found that about 75 per cent of employees working in the 1000 largest US corporations receive ethics training.[30] This training may be included in a newly hired employee's orientation program, made part of an ongoing developmental training program, or provided to all employees as a periodic reinforcement of ethical principles.[31] But the jury is still out on whether you can actually teach ethics.[32]

Critics argue that ethics are based on values, and value systems are fixed at an early age. By the time employers hire people, their ethical values have already been established. The critics also claim that ethics cannot be formally 'taught', but must be learned by example.

Supporters of ethics training argue that values can be learned and changed after early childhood. And even if they couldn't, ethics training would be effective because it helps employees to recognise ethical dilemmas and become more aware of the ethical issues underlying their actions. Grahame Maher from Vodafone argues that you *can* train for ethical behaviour and values, but you have to start the training right at employee induction and carry it throughout the organisation continuously.[33] He also argues that companies need to survey the employee values to make sure the ethics training has taken root in the core values of all employees.[34] Another argument is that ethics training reaffirms an organisation's expectations that members will act ethically.

LEARNING OBJECTIVE 4
Identify four types of employee training

TRAINING METHODS

Training methods are most readily classified as formal or informal, and on-the-job or off-the-job.

Historically, training meant *formal training*. It is planned in advance and has a structured format. However, recent evidence indicates that 70 per cent of workplace learning is made up of *informal training*—unstructured, unplanned, and easily adapted to situations and individuals—for teaching skills and keeping employees current.[35] In reality, most informal training is nothing other than employees helping each other out. They share information and solve work-related problems with one another. Perhaps the most important outcome of this realisation is that many managers are now supportive of what used to be considered 'idle chatter'. At a Siemens plant in North Carolina, for instance, management now recognises that people needn't be on the production line to be working.[36] Discussions around the water cooler or in the cafeteria weren't, as managers thought, about non-work topics such as sports or politics. They largely focused on solving work-related problems. So now Siemens' management encourages such casual meetings.

On-the-job training includes job rotation, apprenticeships, understudy assignments and formal mentoring programs. But the primary drawback of these on-the-job training methods is that they often disrupt the workplace. So, organisations invest in *off-the-job training*. The billions of dollars spent annually on training costs are largely spent on the formal off-the-job variety. What types of training might this include? The most popular continues to be live classroom lectures. But it also encompasses videotapes, public seminars, self-study programs, internet courses, satellite-beamed television classes, and group activities that use role plays and case studies.

In recent years, the fastest-growing means for delivering training is probably computer-based or e-training.[37] Mazda Australia, Just Cuts, Kitchen Connections and MindAtlas are just a few of the Australian companies that have invested in online courses covering everything from products to policies for their employees.[38] Cisco Systems provides a curriculum of training courses on its corporate intranet, organised by job titles, specific technologies and products.[39] Although more than 5000 companies now offer all or some of their employee training online, it is unclear how effective it actually is. On the positive side, e-training increases flexibility by allowing organisations to deliver materials anywhere and at any time. It also seems to be fast and efficient. On the other hand, it is expensive to design self-paced online materials, many employees miss the social interaction provided by a classroom environment, online learners are often more susceptible to distractions, and 'clicking through' training is no assurance that employees have actually learned anything.[40]

INDIVIDUALISING FORMAL TRAINING TO FIT THE EMPLOYEE'S LEARNING STYLE

The ways you process, internalise and remember new and difficult material isn't necessarily the same way others do. This fact means that effective formal training should be individualised to reflect the learning style of the employee.[41]

Some examples of different learning styles are reading, watching, listening and participating. Some people absorb information better when they read about it. They are the kind of people who can learn to use computers by sitting in their study and reading manuals. Some people learn best by observation. They watch others and then imitate the behaviours they have seen. Such people can watch someone use a computer for a while, and then copy what they have done. Listeners rely heavily on their auditory senses to absorb information. They would prefer to learn how to use a computer, for instance, by listening to an audiotape. People who prefer a participating style learn by doing. They want to sit down, turn on the computer, and gain hands-on experience by practising.

You can translate these styles into different learning methods. To maximise learning, readers should be given books or other reading material to review; watchers should get the opportunity to observe individuals modelling the new skills either in person or on video; listeners will benefit from hearing lectures or audiotapes; and participants will benefit most from experiential opportunities in which they can simulate and practise the new skills.

These different learning styles are obviously not mutually exclusive. In fact, good teachers recognise that their students learn differently and, therefore, provide multiple learning methods. They assign readings before class; give lectures; use visual aids to illustrate concepts; and have students participate in group projects, case analyses, role plays and experiential learning exercises. If you know the preferred style of an employee, you can design a formal training program to take advantage of this preference. If you don't have that information, it is probably best to design the program to use a variety of learning styles. Over-reliance on a single style places individuals who don't learn well from that style at a disadvantage.

EVALUATING EFFECTIVENESS

Most training programs work rather well in that the majority of people who undergo training learn more than those who don't, react positively to the training experience, and after the training engage in the behaviours targeted by the program. Still, some factors

---

OB IN PRACTICE

THE RISE AND RISE OF TALENT MANAGEMENT

An ageing population, increased competition, skill shortages and changing generational preferences have highlighted the importance of the relatively new human resource concept of talent management. Talent management now features prominently on the agenda for many CEOs in Australia and overseas, with many spending as much as 50 per cent of their time looking for talented executives and participating directly in development activities such as mentoring and teaching leadership skills.

Talent management is an organisation-wide practice that combines the scope and functions of recruitment, training and development, and performance management under the strategic framework of workforce planning, forecasting and change management. A recent study by Deloitte research—'It's 2008: do you know where your talent is?'—pointed out that successful talent management strategies must invest in activities that develop, deploy and connect with people in meaningful ways. One-third of Australian companies are having difficulty filling permanent professional roles due to a lack of available talent, which in turn is threatening growth plans and inflating wages.

Chris Watkin is practice leader for talent management at the Hay Group in Australia. Chris says that identifying and exploiting potential is now part of 'business as usual'—with line managers working in partnership with the HR function to predict future star players and route them through the organisation. He also observes that 'promoting someone to the point of their incompetence can destroy both short-term performance and longer-term shareholder value, and organisations are now realising that past performance alone is no predictor of future delivery'. Organisations are now becoming more adept at designing non-linear career routes, so talented individuals can pick up broad-based competencies along the way.

Wesley Payne McClendon, principal, Mercer Human Resource Consulting in Australia, offers some advice to HR professionals, suggesting that the following three talent management strategies provide the most compelling opportunities for HR professionals to become strategic business partners.
- Know your business and your competitors, and how to align incumbent and incoming talent with strategic business objectives.
- Develop a talent management strategy that can adapt to market, labour and structural changes.
- Measure people impact through performance outcomes that can be linked directly to driving the business forward.

SOURCES: Anonymous, 'Getting Your Talent in Shape', *Human Resources*, 17 October 2006, pp. 22–23; Craig Donaldson, 'Talent Management a CEO Job', *Human Resources*, issue 105, 2006, p. 1; and Craig Donaldson, 'Talent Shortages Impact Wages', *Human Resources*, issue 117, 2006, p. 1.

make certain programs work better than others. For example, although lecture styles have a poor reputation, they are surprisingly effective training methods. On the other hand, conducting a needs assessment prior to training was relatively unimportant in predicting the success of a training program.[42]

The success of training also depends on the individual. If individuals are unmotivated to learn, they will benefit very little. What factors determine training motivation? Personality is important: those with an internal locus of control, high conscientiousness, high cognitive ability and high self-efficacy learn more in training programs. The training climate also is important: when trainees believe that there are opportunities on the job to apply their newly learned skills and enough resources to apply what they have learned, they are more motivated to learn and do better in training programs.[43]

WORK STRESS AND ITS MANAGEMENT

Most of us are aware that employee stress is an increasing problem in organisations. Friends tells us they are stressed out from greater workloads and having to work longer hours because of downsizing at their company. Parents talk about the lack of job stability in today's world and reminisce about a time when a job with a large company implied lifetime security. We read surveys in which employees complain about the stress created in trying to balance work and family responsibilities. In this section we will look at the causes and consequences of stress, and then consider what individuals and organisations can do to reduce it.

WHAT IS STRESS?

Stress is a dynamic condition in which an individual is confronted with an opportunity, demand or resource related to what the individual desires and for which the outcome is perceived to be both uncertain and important.[44] This is a complicated definition. Let's look at its components more closely.

Stress isn't necessarily bad in and of itself. Although stress is typically discussed in a negative context, it also has a positive value.[45] It is an opportunity when it offers potential gain. Consider, for example, the superior performance that an athlete or stage performer gives in high-pressure situations. Such individuals often use stress positively to rise to the occasion and perform at or near their maximum. Similarly, many professionals see the pressures of heavy workloads and deadlines as positive challenges that enhance the quality of their work and the satisfaction they get from their job.

In short, some stress can be good, and some can be bad. Recently, researchers have argued that challenge stress, or stress associated with challenges in the work environment (such as having lots of projects, assignments and responsibilities), operates quite differently from hindrance stress, or stress that keeps you from reaching your goals (red tape, office politics, confusion over job responsibilities). Although research on challenge and hindrance stress is just starting to accumulate, early evidence suggests that challenge stress has many fewer negative implications than hindrance stress.[46]

More typically, stress is associated with demands and resources. **Demands** are responsibilities, pressures, obligations and even uncertainties that individuals face in the workplace. **Resources** are things within an individual's control that can be used to resolve the demands. This demands–resources model has received increasing support in the literature.[47] Let's discuss what it means. When you take a test at school or you undergo your

stress | A dynamic condition in which an individual is confronted with an opportunity, constraint or demand related to what they desire and for which the outcome is perceived to be both uncertain and important.

demands | Responsibilities, pressures, obligations and even uncertainties that individuals face in the workplace.

resources | Things within an individual's control that can be used to resolve the demands placed on him or her.

annual performance review at work, you feel stress because you confront opportunities and performance pressures. A good performance review may lead to a promotion, greater responsibilities and a higher salary. But a poor review may prevent you from getting the promotion. An extremely poor review might even result in you losing your job. In such a situation, to the extent that you can apply resources to the demands—such as being prepared, placing the exam or review in perspective, or obtaining social support—you will feel less stress.

As another example, whereas the demand of working long hours leads to stress, this stress can be reduced by the resource of social support, such as having friends or family to talk to. A recent study found this to be true of workers in a diverse set of countries (Australia, Canada, England, New Zealand, the United States, China, Taiwan, Argentina, Brazil, Colombia, Ecuador, Mexico, Peru and Uruguay).[48]

UNDERSTANDING STRESS AND ITS CONSEQUENCES

What causes stress? What are its consequences for individual employees? Why is it that the same set of conditions that creates stress for one person seems to have little or no effect on another person? Figure 18.2 provides a model that can help to answer questions such as these.[49]

The model identifies three sets of factors—environmental, organisational and personal—that act as potential sources of stress. Whether they become actual stress depends on individual differences such as job experience and personality. When stress is experienced by an individual, its symptoms can surface as physiological, psychological and behavioural outcomes.

POTENTIAL SOURCES OF STRESS

As the model in Figure 18.2 shows, there are three categories of potential stressors: environmental, organisational and personal. Let's take a look at each.[50]

FIGURE 18.2

A model of stress

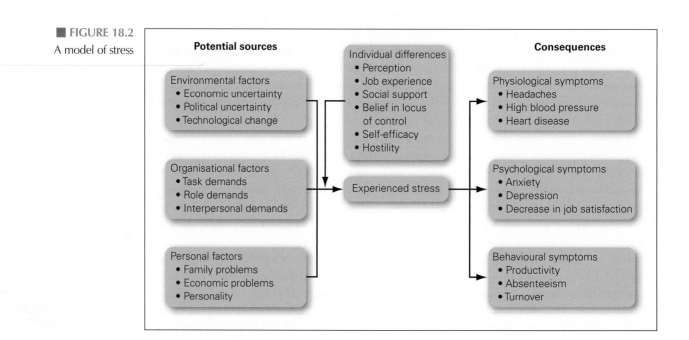

ENVIRONMENTAL FACTORS

Just as environmental uncertainty influences the design of an organisation's structure, it also influences stress levels among employees in that organisation. Changes in the business cycle create economic uncertainties. When the economy is contracting, for example, people become increasingly anxious about their job security. Political uncertainties don't tend to create stress among Western economies as they do for employees in countries such as Haiti or Venezuela. The obvious reason is that the Western economies have stable political systems, in which change is typically implemented in an orderly manner. Yet political threats and changes, even in countries such as Australia, can induce stress. For instance, the introduction of WorkChoices by the Coalition government in 2006 led to political uncertainty that becomes stressful to people in the workforce. Technological change is a third type of environmental factor that can cause stress. Because new innovations can make an employee's skills and experience obsolete in a very short time, computers, robotics, automation and similar forms of technological innovation are a threat to many people and cause them stress. Terrorism is an increasing source of environmental-induced stress in the 21st century. Employees in Israel, for instance, have long faced this threat and have learned to cope with it. For employees in other countries, however, the events of 9/11, and the Bali, Madrid, London and Mumbai bombings, have increased stress related to working in skyscrapers, using public transport and attending large public events, and have heightened concerns about security generally.

ORGANISATIONAL FACTORS

There is no shortage of factors within the organisation that can cause stress. Pressures to avoid errors or to complete tasks in a limited time, work overload, a demanding and insensitive boss, and unpleasant fellow employees are a few examples. We have categorised these factors around task, role and interpersonal demands.[51]

Task demands are factors related to a person's job. They include the design of the individual's job (autonomy, task variety, degree of automation), working conditions, and the physical work layout. Assembly lines, for instance, can put pressure on people when the line's speed is perceived as excessive. Similarly, working in an overcrowded room or in a visible location where noise and interruptions are constant can increase anxiety and stress.[52] Increasingly, as customer service becomes ever more important, emotional labour is a source of stress.[53] Imagine being a flight attendant for Virgin Blue or a cashier at Starbucks. Do you think you could put on a happy face when you are having a bad day?

Terrorist attacks and subsequent terror alerts continue to escalate stress levels among employees. The July 2005 terrorist bombing attack on London's bus and underground train system during the morning rush hour resulted in terror alerts for mass-transit commuters throughout the world. As an environmentally induced stress, terror attacks raise the anxiety and fear of millions of employees who rely on public transportation to get to work. Shown here are Sydney commuters using the rail system after the attack affecting the London underground train system.

Role demands relate to pressures placed on a person as a function of the particular role he or she plays in the organisation. Role conflicts create expectations that may be hard to reconcile or satisfy. Role overload is experienced when the employee is expected to do more than time permits. Role ambiguity is created when role expectations are not clearly understood and the employee isn't sure what he or she is to do.

Interpersonal demands are pressures created by other employees. Lack of social support from colleagues and poor interpersonal relationships can cause stress, especially among employees with a high social need.

PERSONAL FACTORS

The typical individual works about 40 to 50 hours a week. But the experiences and problems that people encounter in those other 120-plus non-work hours each week can spill over to the job. Our final category, then, encompasses factors in the employee's personal life. Primarily, these factors are family issues, personal economic problems and inherent personality characteristics.

National surveys consistently show that people hold *family* and personal relationships dear. Marital difficulties, the breaking off of a relationship, and discipline troubles with children are examples of relationship problems that create stress for employees that aren't left at the front door when they arrive at work.[54]

Economic problems created by individuals over-extending their financial resources are another set of personal troubles that can create stress for employees and distract their attention from their work. Regardless of income level—people who make $100 000 a year seem to have as much trouble handling their finances as those who earn $38 000—some people are poor money managers or have wants that always seem to exceed their earning capacity.

Studies in three diverse organisations found that stress symptoms reported prior to beginning a job accounted for most of the variance in stress symptoms reported nine months later.[55] This led the researchers to conclude that some people may have an inherent tendency to accentuate negative aspects of the world in general. If this is true, then a significant individual factor that influences stress is a person's basic disposition. That is, stress symptoms expressed on the job may actually originate in the person's *personality*.

STRESSORS ARE ADDITIVE

A fact that tends to be overlooked when stressors are reviewed individually is that stress is an additive phenomenon.[56] Stress builds up. Each new and persistent stressor adds to an individual's stress level. So, a single stressor may be relatively unimportant in and of itself, but if it is added to an already high level of stress, it can be 'the straw that breaks the camel's back'. If we want to appraise the total amount of stress an individual is under, we have to sum up his or her opportunity stresses, constraint stresses and demand stresses.

INDIVIDUAL DIFFERENCES

LEARNING OBJECTIVE   6

Explain individual difference variables that moderate the stress–outcome relationship

Some people thrive on stressful situations, while others are overwhelmed by them. What is it that differentiates people in terms of their ability to handle stress? What individual difference variables moderate the relationship between *potential* stressors and *experienced* stress? At least six variables—perception, job experience, social support, belief in locus of control, self-efficacy and hostility—have been found to be relevant moderators.

In an earlier chapter, we demonstrated that employees react in response to their perception of reality, rather than to reality itself. Perception, therefore, will moderate the relationship between a potential stress condition and an employee's reaction to it. For example, one person's fear that he will lose his job because his company is laying off personnel may be perceived by another person as an opportunity to get a large severance allowance and start her own business. So, stress potential doesn't lie in objective conditions; it lies in an employee's interpretation of those conditions.

The evidence indicates that *experience* on the job tends to be negatively related to work stress. Why? Two explanations have been offered.[57] First is the idea of selective withdrawal. Voluntary turnover is more probable among people who experience more stress. Therefore, people who remain with the organisation longer are those with more stress-resistant traits or those who are more resistant to the stress characteristics of their organisation. Second, people eventually develop coping mechanisms to deal with stress. Because this takes time, senior members of the organisation are more likely to be fully adapted and should experience less stress.

There is increasing evidence that *social support*—that is, collegial relationships with fellow employees or supervisors—can buffer the impact of stress.[58] The logic underlying this moderating variable is that social support acts as a palliative, mitigating the negative effects of even high-strain jobs.

Locus of control was introduced in a previous chapter as a personality attribute. As you may recall, internal locus of control is an indicator of positive core self-evaluations, because people who think they are in control of their life (internal locus of control) have a more positive self-view than those who think they are controlled by their environment (external locus of control). Evidence indicates that internals perceive their jobs to be less stressful than do externals, and internals cope better with job demands than do externals.[59] When internals and externals confront a similar stressful situation, the internals are likely to believe that they can have a significant effect on the results. They, therefore, act to take control of events. In contrast, externals are more likely to be passive and feel helpless.

Self-efficacy has also been found to influence stress outcomes. You will remember from an earlier chapter that this term refers to an individual's belief that he or she is capable of performing a task. A recent study indicated that individuals with strong self-efficacy reacted less negatively to the strain created by long work hours and work overload than did those with low levels of self-efficacy.[60] That is, confidence in one's own abilities appears to decrease stress. As with an internal locus of control, strong efficacy confirms the power of self-beliefs in moderating the effect of a high-strain situation.

Some people's personality includes a high degree of hostility and anger. These people are chronically suspicious and mistrustful of others. Evidence indicates that this *hostility* significantly increases a person's stress and risk for heart disease.[61] More specifically, people who are quick to anger, maintain a persistently hostile outlook, and project a cynical mistrust of others are more likely to experience stress in situations.

CONSEQUENCES OF STRESS

Stress shows itself in a number of ways. For instance, an individual who is experiencing a high level of stress may develop high blood pressure, ulcers, irritability, difficulty in making routine decisions, loss of appetite, accident-proneness, and the like. These symptoms can be subsumed under three general categories: physiological, psychological and behavioural symptoms.[62]

PHYSIOLOGICAL SYMPTOMS

Most of the early concern with stress was directed at physiological symptoms. This was predominantly due to the fact that the topic was researched by specialists in the health and medical sciences. This research led to the conclusion that stress could create changes in metabolism, increase heart and breathing rates, increase blood pressure, bring on headaches and induce heart attacks.

The link between stress and particular physiological symptoms isn't clear. Traditionally, researchers concluded that there were few, if any, consistent relationships.[63] This is attributed to the complexity of the symptoms and the difficulty of objectively measuring them. More recently, some evidence suggests that stress may have harmful physiological effects. For example, one recent study linked stressful job demands to increased susceptibility to upper respiratory illnesses and poor immune system functioning, especially for individuals who had low self-efficacy.[64]

PSYCHOLOGICAL SYMPTOMS

Stress can cause dissatisfaction. Job-related stress can cause job-related dissatisfaction. Job dissatisfaction, in fact, is 'the simplest and most obvious psychological effect' of stress.[65] But stress shows itself in other psychological states—for instance, tension, anxiety, irritability, boredom and procrastination.

The evidence indicates that when people are placed in jobs that make multiple and conflicting demands, or in which there is a lack of clarity about the incumbent's duties, authority and responsibilities, both stress and dissatisfaction are increased.[66] Similarly, the less control people have over the pace of their work, the greater the stress and dissatisfaction. Although more research is needed to clarify the relationship, the evidence suggests that jobs that provide a low level of variety, significance, autonomy, feedback and identity to incumbents create stress and reduce satisfaction and involvement in the job.[67]

BEHAVIOURAL SYMPTOMS

Behaviour-related stress symptoms include changes in productivity, absence and turnover, as well as changes in eating habits, increased smoking or consumption of alcohol, rapid speech, fidgeting and sleep disorders. [68]

There has been a significant amount of research investigating the stress–performance relationship. The most widely studied pattern in the stress–performance literature is the inverted-U relationship.[69] This is shown in Figure 18.3.

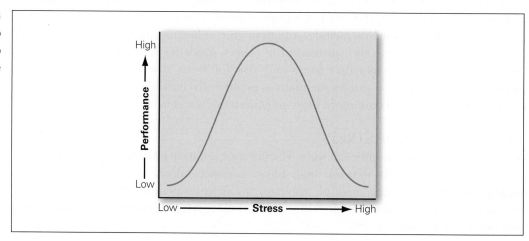

■ FIGURE 18.3
Inverted-U relationship between stress and job performance

The logic underlying the inverted U is that low to moderate levels of stress stimulate the body and increase its ability to react. Individuals then often perform their tasks better, more intensely or more rapidly. But too much stress places unattainable demands on a person, which result in lower performance. This inverted-U pattern may also describe the reaction to stress over time as well as to changes in stress intensity. That is, even moderate levels of stress can have a negative influence on performance over the long term, as the continued intensity of the stress wears down the individual and saps energy resources. A footballer may be able to use the positive effects of stress to obtain a higher performance during every Saturday's football match, or a sales executive may be able to psych herself up for her presentation at the annual national meeting. But moderate levels of stress experienced continually over long periods, as typified by the emergency room staff in a large urban hospital, can result in lower performance. This may explain why emergency room staff at such hospitals are frequently rotated, and why it is unusual to find individuals who have spent the bulk of their career in such an environment. In effect, to do so would expose the individual to the risk of 'career burnout'.

In spite of the popularity and intuitive appeal of the inverted-U model, it doesn't get a lot of empirical support.[70] At this time, managers should be careful in assuming that this model accurately depicts the stress–performance relationship.

MANAGING STRESS

From the organisation's standpoint, management may not be concerned when employees experience low to moderate levels of stress. The reason, as we showed earlier, is that such levels of stress may be functional and lead to higher employee performance. But high levels of stress, or even low levels sustained over long periods, can lead to reduced employee performance and, thus, require action by management.

Although a limited amount of stress may benefit an employee's performance, don't expect employees to see it that way. From the individual's standpoint, even low levels of stress are likely to be perceived as undesirable. It is not unlikely, therefore, for employees and management to have different notions of what constitutes an acceptable level of stress on the job. What management may consider to be 'a positive stimulus that keeps the adrenalin running' is very likely to be seen as 'excessive pressure' by the employee. Keep this in mind as we discuss individual and organisational approaches towards managing stress.[71]

INDIVIDUAL APPROACHES

An employee can take personal responsibility for reducing stress levels. Individual strategies that have proven effective include implementing time-management techniques, increasing physical exercise, relaxation training, and expanding the social support network.

Many people manage their time poorly. The well-organised employee, like the well-organised student, can often accomplish twice as much as the person who is poorly organised. So, an understanding and utilisation of basic time-management principles can help individuals better cope with tensions created by job demands.[72] A few of the more well-known time-management principles are: (1) making daily lists of activities to be accomplished; (2) prioritising activities by importance and urgency; (3) scheduling activities according to the priorities set; and (4) knowing your daily cycle and handling the most demanding parts of your job during the high part of your cycle when you are most alert and productive.[73]

Non-competitive physical exercise such as aerobics, walking, jogging, swimming and cycling have long been recommended by physicians as a way to deal with excessive stress levels. These forms of physical exercise increase heart capacity, lower the at-rest heart rate, provide a mental diversion from work pressures, and offer a means to 'let off steam'.[74]

Individuals can teach themselves to reduce tension through relaxation techniques such as meditation, hypnosis and biofeedback. The objective is to reach a state of deep relaxation, in which one feels physically relaxed, somewhat detached from the immediate environment, and detached from body sensations.[75] Deep relaxation for 15 or 20 minutes a day releases tension and provides a person with a pronounced sense of peacefulness. Importantly, significant changes in heart rate, blood pressure and other physiological factors result from achieving the condition of deep relaxation.

As we noted earlier in this chapter, having friends, family or work colleagues to talk to provides an outlet when stress levels become excessive. Expanding your social support network, therefore, can be a means for tension reduction. It provides you with someone to hear your problems and to offer a more objective perspective on the situation.

ORGANISATIONAL APPROACHES

Several of the factors that cause stress—particularly task and role demands—are controlled by management. As such, they can be modified or changed. Strategies that management might want to consider include improved personnel selection and job placement, training, use of realistic goal setting, redesigning of jobs, increased employee involvement, improved organisational communication, offering employee sabbaticals, and establishment of corporate wellness programs.

Certain jobs are more stressful than others but, as we learned earlier in this chapter, individuals differ in their response to stressful situations. We know, for example, that individuals with little experience or an external locus of control tend to be more prone to stress. Selection and placement decisions should take these facts into consideration. Obviously, management shouldn't restrict hiring to only experienced individuals with an internal locus, but such individuals may adapt better to high-stress jobs and perform those jobs more effectively. Similarly, training can increase an individual's self-efficacy and thus lessen job strain.

We discussed goal setting in a previous chapter. Based on an extensive amount of research, we concluded that individuals perform better when they have specific and challenging goals and receive feedback on how well they are progressing towards these goals. The use of goals can reduce stress as well as provide motivation. Specific goals that are perceived as attainable clarify performance expectations. In addition, goal feedback reduces uncertainties about actual job performance. The result is less employee frustration, role ambiguity and stress.

Redesigning jobs to give employees more responsibility, more meaningful work, more autonomy and increased feedback can reduce stress because these factors give the employee greater control over work activities and lessen dependence on others. But as we noted in our discussion of work design, not all employees want enriched jobs. The right redesign, then, for employees with a low need for growth might be less responsibility and increased specialisation. If individuals prefer structure and routine, reducing skill variety should also reduce uncertainties and stress levels.

Role stress is detrimental to a large extent because employees feel uncertain about goals, expectations, how they will be evaluated, and the like. By giving these employees a voice in the decisions that directly affect their job performance, management can increase employee control and reduce this role stress. So, managers should consider increasing employee involvement in decision making.[76]

Increasing formal organisational communication with employees reduces uncertainty by lessening role ambiguity and role conflict. Given the importance that perceptions play in moderating the stress–response relationship, management can also use effective communications as a means to shape employee perceptions. Remember that what employees categorise as demands, threats or opportunities are merely an interpretation, and that interpretation can be affected by the symbols and actions communicated by management.

What some employees need is an occasional escape from the frenetic pace of their work. In recent years, companies such as Charles Schwab, Du Pont, L.L. Bean, Nike and 3Com have begun to provide extended voluntary leaves.[77] These sabbaticals—ranging in length from a few weeks to several months—allow employees to travel, relax or pursue personal projects that consume time beyond normal annual leave. Proponents argue that these sabbaticals can revive and rejuvenate workers who might be headed for burnout.

WELLNESS PROGRAMS

Another way in which organisations can positively improve the work environment is to offer organisationally supported **wellness programs**. These programs focus on the employee's total physical and mental condition.[78] For example, they typically provide workshops to help people quit smoking, control alcohol use, lose weight, eat better, and develop a regular exercise program. The assumption underlying most wellness programs is that employees need to take personal responsibility for their physical and mental health. The organisation is merely a vehicle to facilitate this end.

Organisations can expect a payoff from their investment in wellness programs. And most of those firms that have introduced wellness programs have found significant benefits. For instance, a study of eight Canadian organisations found that every dollar

wellness programs | Organisationally supported programs that focus on the employee's total physical and mental condition.

Queensland Health provided the funding to Central Queensland University (CQU) for the development of the 10,000 Steps program (<www.10000steps.org.au>). This program aims to increase the physical activity of individuals across the state and nation. CQU implemented one of the 10,000 Steps initiatives, the 'Challenge for Workplaces', with their staff by providing pedometers to employees wanting to take personal responsibility for their mental and physical health. The university also provides many opportunities for employees to keep physically active and reduce stress by supporting the Community Sports Centre on campus with basketball courts, a gym, a swimming pool, running tracks, a baseball diamond, soccer fields and encouragement for staff to participate in aerobics classes held at lunchtime. Quit smoking programs are supported, as well as free annual flu injections.

spent on their comprehensive wellness programs generated a return of $1.64, and for high-risk employees, such as smokers, the return was nearly $4.00.[79]

FINDING THE WORK/LIFE BALANCE

Earlier we indicated that people are actually working longer hours than in the past. This is particularly true of employees trying to rise up the organisational ladder, those concerned over losing their jobs to redundancies, and those in organisations where competition is strong and staffing levels are deliberately kept low. However, more and more employees and organisations are realising that while working long hours may suit some and may produce spikes in organisational performance in the short term, it isn't sustainable in the long run.

In an interesting shift in community values, a number of CEOs in recent times have been attacked for supporting family-friendly practices while at the same time being seen to be working too long and too hard. David Morgan, CEO of Westpac, Glam Swiegers, CEO of Deloitte, and Michael Hawker, CEO of the investment, superannuation and insurance company IAG, have all been criticised by women at shareholder meetings for working too hard.[80] Morgan admitted that he worked six days/five nights a week and was roundly criticised at the annual shareholders' meeting for undermining the family-friendly policies of Westpac. Deloittes has long had very strict policies to limit the work hours of employees so that families were not neglected, but when Glam Swiegers admitted he worked long hours, he too was criticised because he was setting an example that was too difficult for women to compete with.[81]

How, then, can organisations ensure that employees maintain a better work/life balance? There are a number of ways, but they all start with the establishment of a commitment to work/life balance as part of the culture of the organisation. Teleworking is an increasing option to permit employees to work some or all of their time from a home office. Teleworking provides employees greater flexibility in balancing family and work commitments. For instance, women can be at home when the children come home from school but work while the children are playing after school or doing their homework. However, there is a danger that teleworking may also increase the number of hours worked in a day, as teleworkers experience fewer interruptions and tend to work more intensely.[82]

As well as instituting policies to promote better work/life balance, organisations and particularly its managers can look at identifying where employees are overstretched and experiencing being time-poor. Being overstretched and time-poor can have major detrimental effects on physical and mental well-being. Managers and organisations can provide guidance to help employees prioritise their lives better by insisting on employees not working more than the agreed number of hours and by rewarding employees who improve their work/life balance with holidays, weekends away, and other forms of recreation that the employee must spend with their family. Indeed, organisations need to be aware that issues of happiness, quality time and family relations are gaining in importance in the broader community.[83]

MANAGING DIVERSITY IN ORGANISATIONS

We introduced the topic of work/life balance in Chapter 1 and discussed the forces that are blurring the lines between work life and personal life. In this section we want to elaborate on this issue—specifically focusing on what organisations can do to help employees reduce conflicts.

Work/life conflicts grabbed management's attention in the 1980s, largely as a result of the growing number of women with dependent children entering the workforce. In response, most major organisations took actions to make their workplaces more family-friendly.[84] They introduced programs such as on-site child care, flextime, job sharing, carer's leave, telecommuting, and part-time and fractional employment. But organisations quickly realised that work/life conflicts weren't experienced only by female employees with children. Male workers and women without children were also facing this problem. Heavy workloads and increased travel demands, for instance, were making it increasingly hard for a wide range of employees to meet both work and personal responsibilities. A Harvard study found that 82 per cent of men between the ages of 20 and 39 said a 'family-friendly' schedule was their most important job criterion.[85]

By recognising the diversity that exists among their employees, organisations that provide more flexible working arrangements can mean, for example, that parents are better able to juggle their work and family roles effectively.

Organisations are modifying their workplaces to accommodate the varied needs of a diverse workforce. This includes providing a wide range of scheduling options and benefits that allow employees more flexibility at work and permit them to better balance or integrate their work and personal lives. For instance, employees at the corporate office of retailer Eddie Bauer are provided with flexible scheduling, plus a full array of on-site services, including dry cleaning pick-up and delivery, an ATM machine, a gym with personal trainers, flu shots, Weight Watchers classes and financial seminars.[86]

Recent research on work/life conflicts has provided new insights for managers into what works and when. For instance, evidence indicates that time pressures aren't the primary problem underlying work/life conflicts.[87] It is the psychological incursion of work into the family domain and vice versa. People are worrying about personal problems at work and thinking about work problems at home. So, Dad may physically make it home in time for dinner but his mind is elsewhere while he is at the dinner table. This suggests that organisations should spend less effort helping employees with time-management issues and more helping them clearly segment their lives. Keeping workloads reasonable, reducing work-related travel and offering on-site quality child care are examples of practices that can help in this endeavour.

Also, not surprisingly, people have been found to differ in their preference for scheduling options and benefits.[88] Some people prefer organisational initiatives that better segment work from their personal lives. Others prefer initiatives that facilitate integration. For instance, flexitime segments because it allows employees to schedule work hours that are less likely to conflict with personal responsibilities. On the other hand, on-site child care integrates by blurring the boundaries between work and family responsibilities. People who prefer segmentation are more likely to be satisfied and committed to their work when offered options such as flextime, job sharing and part-time hours. People who prefer integration are more likely to respond positively to options such as on-site child care, gym facilities and company-sponsored family picnics.

The centrepiece of most diversity programs is training. For instance, a relatively recent survey found that 93 per cent of companies with diversity initiatives used training as part of their programs.[89] Diversity training programs are generally intended to provide a vehicle for increasing awareness and examining stereotypes. Participants learn to value individual differences, increase their cross-cultural understanding and confront stereotypes.[90]

- We couldn't talk about enhancing performance without looking at the issues relevant to what, who and how we evaluate employees. Suggestions for improving performance evaluation were provided and the section ended on a discussion of feedback and ways to provide it effectively.
- Training and development—every employee's skills will diminish over time which, when added to emerging technologies, requires an ongoing investment in the organisation's employees to enhance organisational performance.
- We discussed the issue of stress, its implications (both positive and negative) for employees and the need to manage it. Added to this discussion were the related topics of wellness programs and finding the correct work/life balance. Both areas can, if managed well, help employees to withstand seasonal high-stress periods and enhance performance through better health— physically, emotionally and mentally.
- Finally, the chapter discussed the issue of diversity management and outlined a number of initiatives that are currently being introduced into workplaces to assist in overcoming some of the work/life conflicts that employees may experience and that have the potential to affect their performance.

POINT / COUNTERPOINT

Work/Life Balance Key to Retaining Good Employees

● POINT

As competition for employees with the right skills increases, organisations are having to address many aspects of the work environment, including ensuring that the balance between work and non-work is appropriate to promote good physical, social and mental health for employees. Family-friendly policies are a common feature of attempts to promote the right work/life balance where employees are prevented from working long hours to the detriment of quality time with their families. This is especially important for younger employees who 'work to live' rather than 'live to work' like their older colleagues often do.

Employees in organisations where the work/life balance isn't good will often work long hours, putting strains on their family life and their health. In addition, organisations suffer when employees don't have time for outside activities because these employees soon become totally focused on work as being their life and no fresh ideas, energies and sensible perspectives are coming into the work environment. In short, totally work-focused employees can become a drag on the organisation's performance and long-term sustainability.

To get the work/life balance right, organisations need to set the example from the top down. Senior executives should be seen to work a maximum set of hours and then be seen to engage in sports, leisure, community and family activities the rest of the time. When urgent situations arise and senior staff have to work longer than normal hours, as soon as the urgent situation is resolved, they should be seen to take additional time off to make up for the extra time worked during the emergency. Senior executives should also provide adequate resources to ensure that lower-level employees are able to keep to normal work hours and not be faced with increased stress associated with working long hours.

The benefits of a good work/life balance accrue to the organisation overall, not just to the individual employees. Organisations with a good work/life balance soon earn a reputation as being good places to work, making recruitment and retention easier. Healthy, happy employees are more productive than overstressed and unhappy employees, so organisational performance improves. Finally, work environments with good work/life balance are able to compete better in the marketplace, as employees are willing to sacrifice higher salaries for better work/life balance conditions.

● COUNTERPOINT

Research studies conducted at Macquarie University recently to find the factors that best predicted organisational performance found very little support for the claims of proponents of work/life balance. Surveying over 10 000 employees in over 700 organisations, their findings suggest that work/life balance is more a theory than a reality.

The first important finding of the research was that the link between work/life balance and employee retention was very weak, if there was one at all. Of the 28 HR practices surveyed in the study, work/life balance was found not to increase employee commitment and had no bearing or influence on the employee's intention to remain with an employer.

The second finding is that the issue of work/life balance is accounted for by factors other than age, gender, number of children and family commitments. Work/life balance appeared to be better in some industry sectors (for instance, for employees in the natural and physical sciences, transport, and cultural/recreational services) and poorer in other sectors (such as trades generally, emergency services, security and mining). As such, work/life balance may simply be inherent in some industries and not in others, irrespective of personal and organisational efforts to change the situation.

The third important finding casting doubt on the importance of work/life balance was that, irrespective of which industry the employees surveyed were in, they were generally happy with their work/life balance and rated its importance quite low. Two reasons may account for this finding. The first is cognitive dissonance. Faced with a poor work/life balance, employees are likely either to leave the employment where they are unhappy with the balance, or to rationalise the poor balance with viewpoints that remove the cognitive dissonance. The second reason is the conscious decision by employees to sacrifice work/life balance in favour of increased promotional prospects, and greater involvement in decision making and in shaping the organisation's direction. For example, many CEOs consciously decide to work long hours at the expense of family, leisure and social involvements.

SOURCE: Points in this argument are based on P. Langford and L. Parkes, 'Debunking the Myths Around Work/Life Balance', *Human Resources*, 3 May 2005, p. 14.

QUESTIONS FOR REVIEW

1. Why do organisations evaluate employees?
2. What problems, if any, can you see developing as a result of using 360-degree evaluation?
3. What are the advantages and disadvantages of the following performance evaluation methods: (a) written essays, (b) graphic rating scales, and (c) behaviourally anchored rating scales?
4. How can an organisation's performance evaluation system affect employee behaviour?
5. Contrast formal and informal training.
6. What is the relationship between learning styles and training effectiveness?
7. How are opportunities, demands and resources related to stress? Give an example of each.
8. What can organisations do to reduce employee stress?
9. What is diversity training? Do you think it is effective?

QUESTIONS FOR CRITICAL THINKING

1. Critically discuss why performance appraisal systems may vary across different types of organisations.
2. Describe a training program you might design to help employees develop their interpersonal skills. How would that program differ from one you designed to improve employees' ethical behaviour?
3. Identify potential issues relating to stress management in an organisation you are familiar with. How would you address these issues?
4. 'Programs to reduce work/life conflicts discriminate against single employees.' Do you agree or disagree? Explain.

EXPERIENTIAL EXERCISE

Evaluating Performance and Providing Feedback

Objective:
To experience the assessment of performance and observe the providing of performance feedback.

Time required:
Approximately 30 minutes.

Procedure:
A class leader is to be selected. The leader may be either a volunteer or someone chosen by your lecturer. The class leader will preside over the class discussion and perform the role of manager in the evaluation review.

Your lecturer will leave the room. The class leader is then to spend up to 15 minutes helping the class to evaluate your lecturer. Your lecturer understands that this is only a class exercise and is prepared to accept criticism (and, of course, any praise you may want to convey). Your lecturer also recognises that the leader's evaluation is actually a composite of many students' input. So, it is important that you are open and honest in your evaluation and have confidence that your lecturer won't be vindictive.

Research has identified seven performance dimensions to the university lecturer's job: (1) lecturer knowledge, (2) testing procedures, (3) student–teacher relations, (4) organisational skills, (5) communication skills, (6) subject relevance, and (7) utility of assignments. The discussion of your lecturer's performance should focus on these seven dimensions. The leader may want to take notes for personal use but won't be required to give your lecturer any written documentation.

When the 15-minute class discussion is complete, the leader will invite the lecturer back into the room. The performance review will begin as soon as the lecturer walks through the door, with the class leader becoming the manager and the lecturer playing himself or herself.

When completed, class discussion will focus on performance evaluation criteria and how well your class leader did in providing performance feedback.

ETHICAL DILEMMA

Is it Unethical to 'Shape' Your Resume?

Human resource policies and practices can have a significant impact on employee behaviour and organisational performance. What message does an organisation send out about the way it deals with honesty and integrity in terms of the way employees and potential employees present themselves to people in the organisation? When does 'putting a positive spin' on your accomplishments step over the line to become misrepresentation or lying? Does a resume have to be 100 per cent truthful? Apparently, a lot of people don't think so. A recent survey of 2.6 million job applicants found that 44 per cent of all resumes contained some lies. To help clarify your ethical views on this issue, consider the following three situations.

Sean left a job for which his title was 'credit clerk'. When looking for a new job, he described his previous title as 'credit analyst'. He thought it sounded more impressive. Is this retitling of a former job wrong?

About eight years ago, Emily took nine months off between jobs to travel overseas. Afraid that people might consider her unstable or lacking in career motivation, she put down on her resume that she was engaged in 'independent consulting activities' during the period. Was she wrong?

Michael is 50 years old with an impressive career record. He spent five years in university 30 years ago, but he never graduated with a degree. He is being considered for a $175 000-a-year senior management position at another firm. He knows that he has the ability and track record to do the job, but he won't get the interview if he admits to not having a university degree. He knows that the probability that anyone would check his university records, at this point in his career, is very low. Should he put on his resume that he completed his degree?

SOURCE: J. Kluger, 'Pumping Up Your Past', *Time*, 10 June 2002, p. 45.

United Parcel Services Inc. (UPS) is one of the largest parcel delivery companies in the world. Mark Colvard is a manager with UPS and recently faced a difficult decision. One of his drivers asked for two weeks off to help an ailing family member. But company rules said this driver wasn't eligible. If Colvard went by the book, the driver would probably take the days off anyway and be fired. On the other hand, Colvard was likely to be criticised by other drivers if he bent the rules. Colvard chose to give the driver the time off. Although he took some heat for the decision, he also kept a valuable employee.

Had Colvard been faced with this decision six months earlier, he says he would have gone the other way. What changed his thinking was a month he spent participating in a UPS management training experience called the Community Internship Program (CIP). During this period, Colvard built housing for the poor, collected clothing for the Salvation Army, and worked in a drug rehabilitation centre. Colvard gives the program credit for helping him empathise with employees facing crises at home. And he says that CIP has made him a better manager. 'My goal was to make the numbers, and in some cases that meant not looking at the individual but looking at the bottom line. After that one-month stay, I immediately started reaching out to people in a different way.'

CIP was established by UPS in the late 1960s to help open the eyes of the company's predominantly white managers to the poverty and inequality in many cities. Today, the program takes 50 of the company's most promising executives and locates the participants in different cities where they deal with a variety of problems—from transportation to housing, education and health care. The company's goal is to awaken these managers to the challenges that many of their employees face, bridging the cultural divide that separates a manager from his or her ethnically diverse group of drivers or an upper-income suburbanite from a worker raised in deprived rural parts of the wider community.

QUESTIONS

1. Do you think individuals can learn empathy from something like a one-month CIP experience? Explain why or why not.
2. How could UPS's CIP help the organisation better manage work/life conflicts?
3. How could UPS's CIP help the organisation improve its response to diversity?
4. What negatives, if any, can you envision resulting from CIP?
5. What would be the significance of such a program in relation to a leadership development strategy for a company?
6. How can UPS justify the cost of a program like CIP if its competitors such as DHL and the Government Postal Service in different countries don't offer such programs? Does the program increase costs or reduce UPS profits?

SOURCE: Based on L. Lavelle, 'For UPS Managers, A School of Hard Knocks', *BusinessWeek*, 22 July 2002.

ENDNOTES

1. C. Donaldson, 'Skills Shortage Pressures Wages', *Human Resources*, 1 June 2006: <www.humanresourcesmagazine.com.au/articles/54/0C030254.asp>.
2. W. F. Cascio, *Applied Psychology in Human Resource Management*, 5th ed. (Upper Saddle River, NJ: Prentice Hall, 1998), p. 59.
3. See W. C. Borman and S. J. Motowidlo, 'Expanding the Criterion Domain to Include Elements of Contextual Performance', in N. Schmitt and W. C. Borman (eds), *Personnel Selection in Organizations* (San Francisco: Jossey-Bass, 1993), pp. 71–98; W. H. Bommer, J. L. Johnson, G. A. Rich, P. M. Podsakoff and S. B. MacKenzie, 'On the Interchangeability of Objective and Subjective Measures of Employee Performance: A Meta-Analysis', *Personnel Psychology*, Autumn 1995, pp. 587–605; and S. E. Scullen, M. K. Mount and T. A. Judge, 'Evidence of the Construct Validity of Developmental Ratings of Managerial Performance', *Journal of Applied Psychology*, February 2003, pp. 50–66.
4. A. H. Locher and K. S. Teel, 'Appraisal Trends', *Personnel Journal*, September 1988, pp. 139–45.
5. Cited in S. Armour, 'Job Reviews Take on Added Significance in Down Times', *USA Today*, 23 July 2003, p. 4B; and T. Mckaskill, 'Ten Tips For Success', *Business Review Weekly*, 15 September 2005, p. 86.
6. See review in R. D. Bretz, Jr, G. T. Milkovich and W. Read, 'The Current State of Performance Appraisal Research and Practice: Concerns, Directions, and Implications', *Journal of Management*, June 1992, p. 326; and P. W. B. Atkins and R. E. Wood, 'Self-versus Others' Ratings as Predictors of Assessment Center Ratings: Validation Evidence for 360-Degree Feedback Programs', *Personnel Psychology*, Winter 2002, pp. 871–904.
7. T. Russell, 'Around and Around...', *Human Resources*, 24 January 2006, pp. 12–13; see also, for instance, W. W. Tornow and M. London (eds), *Maximizing the Value of 360-Degree Feedback* (San Francisco: Jossey-Bass, 1998); J. Ghorpade, 'Managing Five Paradoxes of 360-Degree Feedback', *Academy of Management Executive*, February 2000, pp. 140–50; J. D. Facteau and S. B. Craig, 'Are Performance Appraisal Ratings from Different Rating Sources Compatible?', *Journal of Applied Psychology*, April 2001, pp. 215–27; J. F. Brett and L. E. Atwater, '360-Degree Feedback: Accuracy, Reactions, and Perceptions of Usefulness', *Journal of Applied Psychology*, October 2001, pp. 930–42; C. Wingrove, 'Untangling the Myths of 360: Straight Talk for Successful Outcomes', *Compensation & Benefits Review*, November–December 2001, pp. 34–37; B. Pfau, I. Kay, K. M. Nowack and J. Ghorpade, 'Does 360-Degree Feedback Negatively Affect Company Performance?', *Human Resources*, June 2002, pp. 54–59; F. Luthans and S. J. Peterson, '360 Degree Feedback with Systematic Coaching: Empirical Analysis Suggests a Winning Combination', *Human Resource Management*, Fall 2003, pp. 243–56; and B. I. J. M. van der Heijden and A. H. J. Nijhof, 'The Value of Subjectivity: Problems and Prospects for 360-Degree Appraisal Systems', *International Journal of Human Resource Management*, May 2004, pp. 493–511.
8. Russell, 'Around and Around...'; and E. Ross, 'Educating Leaders', *Business Review Weekly*, 18 November 2004, p. 62.
9. D. V. Day, 'Leadership Development: A Review in Context', *Leadership Quarterly*, Winter 2000, pp. 587–89.
10. Atkins and Wood, 'Self- versus Others' Ratings as Predictors of Assessment Center Ratings'; and Pfau, Kay, Nowack and Ghorpade, 'Does 360-Degree Feedback Negatively Affect Company Performance?'.
11. See, for instance, J. W. Hedge and W. C. Borman, 'Changing Conceptions and Practices in Performance Appraisal', in A. Howard (ed.), *The Changing Nature of Work* (San Francisco: Jossey-Bass, 1995), pp. 453–59.
12. See, for instance, D. E. Smith, 'Performance Appraisal: A Review', *Academy of Management Review*, January 1986, pp. 22–40; T. R. Athey and R. M. McIntyre, 'Effect of Rater Training on Rater Accuracy: Levels-of-Processing Theory and Social Facilitation Theory Perspectives', *Journal of Applied Psychology*, November 1987, pp. 567–72; and D. J. Woehr, 'Understanding Frame-of-Reference Training: The Impact of Training on the Recall of Performance Information', *Journal of Applied Psychology*, August 1994, pp. 525–34.
13. H. J. Bernardin, 'The Effects of Rater Training on Leniency and Halo Errors in Student Rating of Instructors', *Journal of Applied Psychology*, June 1978, pp. 301–08.
14. Ibid; and J. M. Ivancevich, 'Longitudinal Study of the Effects of Rater Training on Psychometric Error in Ratings', *Journal of Applied Psychology*, October 1979, pp. 502–08.
15. M. S. Taylor, K. B. Tracy, M. K. Renard, J. K. Harrison and S. J. Carroll, 'Due Process Performance Appraisal: A Quasi-Experiment in Procedural Justice', *Administrative Science Quarterly*, September 1995, pp. 495–523.
16. J. S. Lublin, 'It's Shape-up Time for Performance Reviews', *Wall Street Journal*, 3 October 1994, p. B1; and E. Ross, 'Peak Performance', *Business Review Weekly*, 23 June 2005, p. 58.
17. Much of this section is based on H. H. Meyer, 'A Solution to the Performance Appraisal Feedback Enigma', *Academy of Management Executive*, February 1991, pp. 68–76.
18. B. Gates, *The Road Ahead* (New York: Viking, 1995), p. 86.
19. T. D. Schelhardt, 'It's Time to Evaluate Your Work, and All Involved Are Groaning', *Wall Street Journal*, 19 November 1996, p. A1.
20. R. J. Burke, 'Why Performance Appraisal Systems Fail', *Personnel Administration*, June 1972, pp. 32–40.
21. Russell, 'Around and Around...'; Ross, 'Peak Performance'.
22. B. R. Nathan, A. M. Mohrman, Jr and J. Milliman, 'Inter-personal Relations as a Context for the Effects of Appraisal Interviews on Performance and Satisfaction: A Longitudinal Study', *Academy of Management Journal*, June 1991, pp. 352–69. See also B. D. Cawley, L. M. Keeping and P. E. Levy, 'Participation in the Performance Appraisal Process and Employee Reactions: A Meta-Analytic Review of Field Investigations', *Journal of Applied Psychology*, August 1998, pp. 615–33; and P. E. Levy and J. R. Williams, 'The Social Context of Performance Appraisal: A Review and Framework for the Future', *Journal of Management*, vol. 30, no. 6, 2004, pp. 881–905.
23. Australian Bureau of Statistics, *Education and Training Experience, Australia*, 2005, Cat. No. 6278.0: <www.abs.gov.au/Ausstats/abs@.nsf/Lookup/252D868F10B905F3CA2568A9001393AF>.
24. Australian Bureau of Statistics, *Aspects of*

Literacy: Assessed Skill Levels, Australia, 1996, Cat. No. 4228.0: <www.abs.gov.au/Ausstats/abs@.nsf/7d12b0f6763c78caca257061001cc588/887ae32d628dc922ca2568a900139365!OpenDocument>.

25. A. Bernstein, 'The Time Bomb in the Workforce: Illiteracy', *BusinessWeek*, 25 February 2002, p. 122; and T. Thomas, 'Delivering to the World with Missionary Zeal', *Business Review Weekly*, 8 August 1994, pp. 64–65.

26. Australian Bureau of Statistics, *Current Household Surveys*: <www.abs.gov.au/websitedbs/d3310114.nsf/4a256353001af3ed4b2562bb00121564/d64e3fdf17be5c1fca2571060079d60b!OpenDocument#ADULT%20LITERACY%20AND%20LIFE SKILLS%20SUR>.

27. C. Ansberry, 'A New Blue-Collar World', *Wall Street Journal*, 30 June 2003, p. B1; and A. Tandukar, 'How Long is Long Enough?', *Business Review Weekly*, 17 August 2006, p. 61.

28. J. Stensholt, 'A Field of Their Own', *Business Review Weekly*, 16 June 2005, pp. 76–77.

29. Ibid.

30. G. R. Weaver, L. K. Trevino and P. L. Cochran, 'Corporate Ethics Practices in the Mid-1990's: An Empirical Study of the Fortune 1000', *Journal of Business Ethics*, February 1999, pp. 283–94.

31. M. B. Wood, *Business Ethics in Uncertain Times* (Upper Saddle River, NJ: Prentice Hall, 2004), p. 61.

32. See, for example, D. Seligman, 'Oxymoron 101', *Forbes*, 28 October 2002, pp. 160–64; and R. B. Schmitt, 'Companies Add Ethics Training; Will It Work?', *Wall Street Journal*, 4 November 2002, p. B1.

33. K. Walters, 'Define Your Values', *Business Review Weekly*, 21 April 2005, p. 95.

34. Ibid.

35. K. Dobbs, 'The U.S. Department of Labor Estimates that 70 Percent of Workplace Learning Occurs Informally', *Sales & Marketing Management*, November 2000, pp. 94–98.

36. S. J. Wells, 'Forget the Formal Training. Try Chatting at the Water Cooler', *New York Times*, 10 May 1998, p. BU-11.

37. See, for instance, K. G. Brown, 'Using Computers to Deliver Training: Which Employees Learn and Why?', *Personnel Psychology*, Summer 2001, pp. 271–96; 'The Delivery: How U.S. Organizations Use Classrooms and Computers in Training', *Training*, October 2001, pp. 66–72; L. K. Long and R. D. Smith, 'The Role of Web-Based Distance Learning in HR Development', *Journal of*

Management Development, vol. 23, no. 3, 2004, pp. 270–84; and A. Tandukar, 'How to Keep Ahead', *Business Review Weekly*, 20 July 2006, p. 60.

38. Tandukar, 'How to Keep Ahead'; K. Walters, 'Log On and Learn', *Business Review Weekly*, 6 April 2006, p. 44; and J. May, 'Grow Your Own', *Business Review Weekly*, 8 September 2005, p. 52.

39. A. Muoio, 'Cisco's Quick Study', *Fast Company*, October 2000, pp. 287–95.

40. E. A. Ensher, T. R. Nielson and E. Grant-Vallone, 'Tales from the Hiring Line: Effects of the Internet and Technology on HR Processes', *Organizational Dynamics*, vol. 31, no. 3, 2002, pp. 232–33.

41. D. A. Kolb, 'Management and the Learning Process', *California Management Review*, Spring 1976, pp. 21–31; and B. Filipczak, 'Different Strokes: Learning Styles in the Classroom', *Training*, March 1995, pp. 43–48.

42. W. J. Arthur, Jr, W. Bennett, Jr, P. S. Edens and S. T. Bell, 'Effectiveness of Training in Organizations: A Meta-Analysis of Design and Evaluation Features', *Journal of Applied Psychology*, April 2003, pp. 234–45.

43. J. A. Colquitt, J. A. LePine and R. A. Noe, 'Toward an Integrative Theory of Training Motivation: A Meta-Analytic Path Analysis of 20 Years of Research', *Journal of Applied Psychology*, October 2000, pp. 678–707.

44. Adapted from R. S. Schuler, 'Definition and Conceptualization of Stress in Organizations', *Organizational Behavior and Human Performance*, April 1980, p. 189. For an updated review of definitions, see C. L. Cooper, P. J. Dewe and M. P. O'Driscoll, *Organizational Stress: A Review and Critique of Theory, Research, and Applications* (Thousand Oaks, CA: Sage, 2002).

45. See, for instance, M. A. Cavanaugh, W. R. Boswell, M. V. Roehling and J. W. Boudreau, 'An Empirical Examination of Self-Reported Work Stress Among U.S. Managers', *Journal of Applied Psychology*, February 2000, pp. 65–74.

46. J. A. LePine, M. A. LePine and C. L. Jackson, 'Challenge and Hindrance Stress: Relationships With Exhaustion, Motivation to Learn, and Learning Performance', *Journal of Applied Psychology*, October 2004, pp. 883–91; and M. A. Cavanaugh, W. R. Boswell, M. V. Roehling and J. W. Boudreau, 'An Empirical Examination of Self-reported Work Stress Among U.S. Managers', *Journal of Applied Psychology*, February 2000, pp. 65–74.

47. E. Demerouti, A. B. Bakker, F. Nachreiner and W. B. Schaufeli, 'The Job Demands–Resources Model of Burnout', *Journal of Applied Psychology*, June 2001, pp. 499–512; N. W. Van Yperen and O. Janssen, 'Fatigued and Dissatisfied or Fatigued but Satisfied? Goal Orientations and Responses to High Job Demands', *Academy of Management Journal*, December 2002, pp. 1161–71; and N. W. Van Yperen and M. Hagedoorn, 'Do High Job Demands Increase Intrinsic Motivation or Fatigue or Both? The Role of Job Control and Job Social Support', *Academy of Management Journal*, June 2003, pp. 339–48.

48. P. E. Spector et al., 'A Cross-National Comparative Study of Work–Family Stressors, Working Hours, and Well-Being: China and Latin America versus the Anglo World', *Personnel Psychology*, Spring 2004, pp. 119–42.

49. This model is based on D. F. Parker and T. A. DeCotiis, 'Organizational Determinants of Job Stress', *Organizational Behavior and Human Performance*, October 1983, p. 166; S. Parasuraman and J. A. Alutto, 'Sources and Outcomes of Stress in Organizational Settings: Toward the Development of a Structural Model', *Academy of Management Journal*, June 1984, p. 333; and Kahn and. Byosiere, 'Stress in Organizations', p. 592.

50. This section is adapted from C. L. Cooper and R. Payne, *Stress at Work* (London: Wiley, 1978); Parasuraman and Alutto, 'Sources and Outcomes of Stress in Organizational Settings', pp. 330–50; and P. M. Hart and C. L. Cooper, 'Occupational Stress: Toward a More Integrated Framework', in N. Anderson, D. S. Ones, H. K. Sinangil and C. Viswesvaran (eds), *Handbook of Industrial, Work and Organizational Psychology*, vol. 2 (London: Sage), pp. 93–114.

51. See, for example, D. R. Frew and N. S. Bruning, 'Perceived Organizational Characteristics and Personality Measures as Predictors of Stress/Strain in the Work Place', *Journal of Management*, Winter 1987, pp. 633–46; and M. L. Fox, D. J. Dwyer and D. C. Ganster, 'Effects of Stressful Job Demands and Control of Physiological and Attitudinal Outcomes in a Hospital Setting', *Academy of Management Journal*, April 1993, pp. 289–318.

52. G. W. Evans and D. Johnson, 'Stress and Open-Office Noise', *Journal of Applied Psychology*, October 2000, pp. 779–83.

53. T. M. Glomb, J. D. Kammeyer-Mueller and M. Rotundo, 'Emotional Labor Demands

and Compensating Wage Differentials', *Journal of Applied Psychology*, August 2004, pp. 700–14; A. A. Grandey, 'When "The Show Must Go On": Surface Acting and Deep Acting as Determinants of Emotional Exhaustion and Peer-Rated Service Delivery', *Academy of Management Journal*, February 2003, pp. 86–96.

54. V. S. Major, K. J. Klein and M. G. Ehrhart, 'Work Time, Work Interference with Family, and Psychological Distress', *Journal of Applied Psychology*, June 2002, pp. 427–36; see also Spector et al., 'A Cross-National Comparative Study of Work–Family Stressors, Working Hours, and Well-Being: China and Latin America versus the Anglo World', pp. 119–42.

55. D. L. Nelson and C. Sutton, 'Chronic Work Stress and Coping: A Longitudinal Study and Suggested New Directions', *Academy of Management Journal*, December 1990, pp. 859–69.

56. H. Selye, *The Stress of Life*, rev. ed. (New York: McGraw-Hill, 1956).

57. S. J. Motowidlo, J. S. Packard and M. R. Manning, 'Occupational Stress: Its Causes and Consequences for Job Performance', *Journal of Applied Psychology*, November 1987, pp. 619–20.

58. See, for instance, R. C. Cummings, 'Job Stress and the Buffering Effect of Supervisory Support', *Group & Organization Studies*, March 1990, pp. 92–104; M. R. Manning, C. N. Jackson and M. R. Fusilier, 'Occupational Stress, Social Support, and the Cost of Health Care', *Academy of Management Journal*, June 1996, pp. 738–50; P. D. Bliese and T. W. Britt, 'Social Support, Group Consensus and Stressor-Strain Relationships: Social Context Matters', *Journal of Organizational Behavior*, June 2001, pp. 425–36; and C. L. Stamper and M. C. Johlke, 'The Impact of Perceived Organizational Support on the Relationship between Boundary Spanner Role Stress and Work Outcomes', *Journal of Management*, vol. 29, no. 4, 2003, pp. 569–88.

59. P. E. Spector et al., 'Locus of Control and Well-Being at Work: How Generalizable Are Western Findings?', *Academy of Management Journal*, April 2002, pp. 453–66.

60. S. M. Jex, P. D. Bliese, S. Buzzell and J. Primeau, 'The Impact of Self-Efficacy on Stressor-Strain Relations: Coping Style as an Explanatory Mechanism', *Journal of Applied Psychology*, June 2001, pp. 401–09; and J. Schaubroeck,

S. S. K. Lam and J. L. Xie, 'Collective Efficacy versus Self-Efficacy in Coping Responses to Stressors and Control: A Cross-Cultural Study', *Journal of Applied Psychology*, August 2000, pp. 512–25.

61. R. Williams, *The Trusting Heart: Great News About Type A Behavior* (New York: Times Books, 1989).

62. Schuler, 'Definition and Conceptualization of Stress', pp. 200–05; and Kahn and Byosiere, 'Stress in Organizations', pp. 604–10.

63. See T. A. Beehr and J. E. Newman, 'Job Stress, Employee Health, and Organizational Effectiveness: A Facet Analysis, Model, and Literature Review', *Personnel Psychology*, Winter 1978, pp. 665–99; and B. D. Steffy and J. W. Jones, 'Workplace Stress and Indicators of Coronary-Disease Risk', *Academy of Management Journal*, September 1988, pp. 686–98.

64. J. Schaubroeck, J. R. Jones and J. L. Xie, 'Individual Differences in Utilizing Control to Cope with Job Demands: Effects on Susceptibility to Infectious Disease', *Journal of Applied Psychology*, April 2001, pp. 265–78.

65. Steffy and Jones, 'Workplace Stress and Indicators of Coronary-Disease Risk', p. 687.

66. C. L. Cooper and J. Marshall, 'Occupational Sources of Stress: A Review of the Literature Relating to Coronary Heart Disease and Mental Ill Health', *Journal of Occupational Psychology*, vol. 49, no. 1, 1976, pp. 11–28.

67. J. R. Hackman and G. R. Oldham, 'Development of the Job Diagnostic Survey', *Journal of Applied Psychology*, April 1975, pp. 159–70.

68. E. M. de Croon, J. K. Sluiter, R. W. B. Blonk, J. P. J. Broersen and M. H. W. Frings-Dresen, 'Stressful Work, Psychological Job Strain, and Turnover: A 2-Year Prospective Cohort Study of Truck Drivers', *Journal of Applied Psychology*, June 2004, pp. 442–54; and R. Cropanzano, D. E. Rupp and Z. S. Byrne, 'The Relationship of Emotional Exhaustion to Work Attitudes, Job Performance, and Organizational Citizenship Behaviours', *Journal of Applied Psychology*, February 2003, pp. 160–69.

69. See, for instance, J. M. Ivancevich and M. T. Matteson, *Stress and Work* (Glenview, IL: Scott, Foresman, 1981); R. D. Allen, M. A. Hitt and C. R. Greer, 'Occupational Stress and Perceived Organizational Effectiveness in Formal Groups: An Examination of Stress Level

and Stress Type', *Personnel Psychology*, Summer 1982, pp. 359–70; and S. Zivnuska, C. Kiewitz, W. A. Hochwarter, P. L. Perrewe and K. L. Zellars, 'What Is Too Much or Too Little? The Curvilinear Effects of Job Tension on Turnover Intent, Value Attainment, and Job Satisfaction', *Journal of Applied Social Psychology*, July 2002, pp. 1344–60.

70. S. E. Sullivan and R. S. Bhagat, 'Organizational Stress, Job Satisfaction and Job Performance: Where Do We Go From Here?', *Journal of Management*, June 1992, pp. 361–64; and M. Westman and D. Eden, 'The Inverted-U Relationship between Stress and Performance: A Field Study', *Work & Stress*, Spring 1996, pp. 165–73; and L. A. Muse, S. G. Harris and H. S. Field, 'Has the Inverted-U Theory of Stress and Job Performance Had a Fair Test?', *Human Performance*, vol. 16, no. 4, 2003, pp. 349–64.

71. The following discussion has been influenced by J. E. Newman and T. A. Beehr, 'Personal and Organizational Strategies for Handling Job Stress', *Personnel Psychology*, Spring 1979, pp. 1–38; J. M. Ivancevich and M. T. Matteson, 'Organizational Level Stress Management Interventions: A Review and Recommendations', *Journal of Organizational Behavior Management*, Fall–Winter 1986, pp. 229–48; M. T. Matteson and J. M. Ivancevich, 'Individual Stress Management Interventions: Evaluation of Techniques', *Journal of Management Psychology*, January 1987, pp. 24–30; J. M. Ivancevich, M. T. Matteson, S. M. Freedman and J. S. Phillips, 'Worksite Stress Management Interventions', *American Psychologist*, February 1990, pp. 252–61; and R. Schwarzer, 'Manage Stress at Work Through Preventive and Proactive Coping', in E. A. Locke (ed.), *Handbook of Principles of Organizational Behavior* (Malden, MA: Blackwell, 2004), pp. 342–55.

72. T. H. Macan, 'Time Management: Test of a Process Model', *Journal of Applied Psychology*, June 1994, pp. 381–91; and B. J. C. Claessens, W. Van Eerde, C. G. Rutte and R. A. Roe, 'Planning Behavior and Perceived Control of Time at Work', *Journal of Organizational Behavior*, December 2004, pp. 937–50.

73. See, for example, G. Lawrence-Ell, *The Invisible Clock: A Practical Revolution in Finding Time for Everyone and Everything* (Seaside Park, NJ: Kingsland Hall, 2002);

and B. Tracy, *Time Power* (New York: AMACOM, 2004).

74. J. Kiely and G. Hodgson, 'Stress in the Prison Service: The Benefits of Exercise Programs', *Human Relations*, June 1990, pp. 551–72.

75. E. J. Forbes and R. J. Pekala, 'Psychophysiological Effects of Several Stress Management Techniques', *Psychological Reports*, February 1993, pp. 19–27; and M. Der Hovanesian, 'Zen and the Art of Corporate Productivity', *BusinessWeek*, 28 July 2003, p. 56.

76. S. E. Jackson, 'Participation in Decision Making as a Strategy for Reducing Job-Related Strain', *Journal of Applied Psychology*, February 1983, pp. 3–19.

77. S. Greengard, 'It's About Time', *Industry Week*, 7 February 2000, pp. 47–50; and S. Nayyar, 'Gimme a Break', *American Demographics*, June 2002, p. 6.

78. See, for instance, B. Leonard, 'Health Care Costs Increase Interest in Wellness Programs', *Human Resources*, September 2001, pp. 35–36; and 'Healthy, Happy and Productive', *Training*, February 2003, p. 16.

79. D. Brown, 'Wellness Programs Bring Healthy Bottom Line', *Canadian HR Reporter*, 17 December 2001, p. 1.

80. H. Trinca, 'Stop It—You're Spoiling My Chances', *Australian Financial Review*, 22 August 2006, p. 59.

81. Ibid.

82. O. Thomson, 'So You Want to Work From Home', *Sydney Morning Herald*, 16 September 2006, p. 3.

83. Ibid; A. Horin, 'What Makes Us Happy', *Sydney Morning Herald*, 16 September 2006, p. 23.

84. See, for instance, *Harvard Business Review on Work and Life Balance* (Boston: Harvard Business School Press, 2000); and R. Rapoport, L. Bailyn, J. K. Fletcher and B. H. Pruitt, *Beyond Work–Family Balance* (San Francisco: Jossey-Bass, 2002).

85. 'On the Daddy Track', *Wall Street Journal*, 11 May 2000, p. A1.

86. K. Weiss, 'Eddie Bauer Uses Time as an Employee Benefit', *Journal of Organizational Excellence*, Winter 2002, pp. 67–72.

87. S. D. Friedman and J. H. Greenhaus, *Work and Family—Allies or Enemies?* (New York: Oxford University Press, 2000).

88. N. P. Rothbard, T. L. Dumas and K. W. Phillips, 'The Long Arm of the Organization: Work–Family Policies and Employee Preferences for Segmentation', Paper presented at the 61st Annual Academy of Management Meeting, Washington, DC, August 2001.

89. Cited in 'Survey Shows 75% of Large Corporations Support Diversity Programs', *Fortune*, 6 July 1998, p. S14.

90. See, for example, J. K. Ford and S. Fisher, 'The Role of Training in a Changing Workplace and Workforce: New Perspectives and Approaches', in E. E. Kossek and S. A. Lobel (eds), *Managing Diversity* (Cambridge, MA: Blackwell Publishers, 1996), pp. 164–93; and J. Barbian, 'Moving Toward Diversity', *Training*, February 2003, pp. 44–48.

19

ORGANISATIONAL CHANGE AND DEVELOPMENT

CHAPTER OUTLINE

FORCES FOR CHANGE

MANAGING PLANNED CHANGE

RESISTANCE TO CHANGE

APPROACHES TO MANAGING ORGANISATIONAL CHANGE

CONTEMPORARY CHANGE ISSUES FOR TODAY'S MANAGERS

LEARNING OBJECTIVES

AFTER STUDYING THIS CHAPTER, YOU SHOULD BE ABLE TO:

1. DESCRIBE FORCES THAT ACT AS STIMULANTS TO CHANGE

2. SUMMARISE SOURCES OF INDIVIDUAL AND ORGANISATIONAL RESISTANCE TO CHANGE

3. SUMMARISE LEWIN'S THREE-STEP CHANGE MODEL

4. EXPLAIN THE VALUES UNDERLYING MOST ORGANISATIONAL DEVELOPMENT (OD) EFFORTS

5. CONTRAST CONTINUOUS IMPROVEMENT PROCESSES AND PROCESS REENGINEERING

6. IDENTIFY PROPERTIES OF INNOVATIVE ORGANISATIONS

7. LIST THE CHARACTERISTICS OF A LEARNING ORGANISATION

Sacking large numbers of staff as part of a turnaround strategy is somewhat of an unwinnable situation, according to Michael Page, director of career management consultants Audrey Page and Associates. The staff who leave become angry and provide negative press coverage for the company, and the staff who still work for the company become anxious about their own security and question their loyalty to the organisation.

LIKE OTHER ORGANISATIONS in the finance industry, the National Australia Bank (NAB) has been undergoing significant and continuous change in response to shareholder demands and significant competition. In 2004, NAB was the subject of a foreign currency options scandal that saw the bank lose credibility, market share, its chief executive and other senior staff—and $360 million. NAB's new managing director, John Stewart, was well aware of the pressure to generate revenues, reduce costs and deliver acceptable returns to his shareholders. Towards the end of 2005, the bank announced a full-year profit result of $4.13 billion.

Stewart initiated a three-year turnaround program which involved dismantling the bank's bureaucracy and shifting its focus back to its customers. NAB also announced that up to 4500 jobs could be cut from its workforce of over 43 000 in order to cut costs and improve productivity by reorganising administrative functions and automating various jobs throughout the organisation. Other major companies in Australia that are undergoing major changes and using workforce reductions as part of their restructuring include Telstra, Qantas and General Motors Holden.

Dismissing large numbers of staff as part of a turnaround strategy is a delicate situation to manage, according to Michael Page, director of career transition specialists Audrey Page and Associates. The employees who are retrenched can be disgruntled for a period of time and the publicity can be negative for the company. The employees who remain with the company can lose motivation, be anxious about their own security and question their loyalty to the organisation.

Managing redundancies is only one aspect of managing change in organisations. Change management involves making available to managers a diverse range of programs and techniques in order to develop more productive and satisfying work environments. Jo Campbell, the general manager of capability, people and performance at NAB, is concerned that staff can maintain some sense of dignity in such situations and appreciates the need to develop the leadership and people management skills of frontline managers in order to bring about productive change.[1]

I cannot say whether things will get better if we change; what I can say is they must change if they are to get better.

Georg Christoph Lichtenberg

THIS FINAL CHAPTER is about change and development. We describe environmental forces that are requiring managers to implement comprehensive change programs. We also consider why people and organisations often resist change and how this resistance can be overcome. We review various processes for managing organisational change. We also discuss contemporary change issues for today's managers.

FORCES FOR CHANGE

As recently as the late 1990s, American music retailers Wherehouse Entertainment and Tower Records were rapidly growing and profitable companies. Young people were flocking to their superstores because they offered a wide selection and competitive prices. But the market changed and these chains suffered the consequences.[2] Downloading, legal and otherwise, cut hard into their CD sales; and growing competition from Amazon.com and discounters such as Target stole a sizeable part of their market share. In January 2003, Wherehouse filed for bankruptcy. Tower followed suit in February 2004.

More and more organisations today face a dynamic and changing environment. This, in turn, is requiring those organisations to adapt. 'Change or die!' is the rallying cry among today's managers worldwide. Table 19.1 summarises six specific forces that are acting as stimulants for change.

In a number of places in this book, we have discussed the *changing nature of the workforce*. For instance, almost every organisation is having to adjust to a multicultural environment. Human resource policies and practices have to change to reflect the needs of an ageing labour force. And many companies have to spend large amounts of money on training to upgrade reading, maths, computer and other skills of employees.

■ TABLE 19.1

Forces for change

Force	Examples
Nature of the workforce	More cultural diversity
	Ageing population
	Many new entrants with inadequate skills
Technology	Faster, cheaper and more mobile computers
	Online music sharing
	Deciphering of the human genetic code
Economic shocks	Rise and fall of dot-com share value
	Record low interest rates
	Financial impact from corporate collapses
Competition	Global competitors
	Mergers and consolidations
	Growth of e-commerce
Social trends	Internet chat rooms
	Retirement of baby-boomers
	Rise in discount retailers
World politics	Iraq–US War
	Opening of markets in China
	War on terrorism following September 11

Technology is changing jobs and organisations. For instance, computers are now commonplace in almost every organisation; and mobile phones and handheld PDAs (Personal Digital Assistants) are seen as indispensable by a large segment of the population. Computer networks are also reshaping entire industries. The music business, as a case in point, is now struggling to cope with the economic consequences of widespread online music sharing. For the longer term, recent breakthroughs in deciphering the human genetic code offer the potential for pharmaceutical companies to produce drugs designed for specific individuals and create serious ethical dilemmas for insurance companies as to who is insurable and who isn't.

We live in an 'age of discontinuity'. In the 1950s and 1960s, the past was a pretty good prologue to the future. Tomorrow was essentially an extended trend line from yesterday. That is no longer true. Beginning in the early 1970s, with the overnight quadrupling of world oil prices, *economic shocks* have continued to impose changes on organisations. In recent years, for instance, new dot-com businesses have been created, turned tens of thousands of investors into overnight millionaires, and then crashed. Low interest rates have stimulated a rapid rise in home values and helped sustain consumer spending. The financial collapse of Enron Corporation in the United States, and of HIH Insurance, Ansett Airlines and OneTel in Australia, has highlighted the economic instability in the labour market and made executive ethics, managerial controls, responsibility of board members, manipulation of earnings, and conflicts of interest between firms and their auditors topics of concern for all corporate executives.

Competition is changing. The global economy means that competitors are as likely to come from across the ocean as from across town. Heightened competition also makes it necessary for established organisations to defend themselves against both traditional competitors who develop new products and services and small, entrepreneurial firms with innovative offerings. Successful organisations will be the ones that can change in response to the competition. They will be fast on their feet, capable of developing new products rapidly and getting them to market quickly. They will rely on short production runs, short product cycles and an ongoing stream of new products. In other words, they will be flexible. They will require an equally flexible and responsive workforce that can adapt to rapidly—even radically—changing conditions.

Social trends don't remain static. For instance, in contrast to just 15 years ago, people are meeting and sharing information in internet chat rooms; baby-boomers have begun to retire; and consumers are increasingly doing their shopping at large discount warehouses and retailers such as Bunnings and Harvey Norman.

Throughout this book we have argued strongly for the importance of seeing OB in a global context. Business schools have been preaching a global

Dato J. J. Ong took over MASKargo in 2001 when it was in a loss-making situation. MASKargo is the freight arm of Malaysia Airlines. Dato Ong recognises that companies have to continuously respond to change in the marketplace if they are to remain profitable and sustainable. He reviewed all aspects of the business with his staff to see where he could achieve productivity gains. MASKargo is now a successful competitor in the airfreight business.

perspective since the early 1980s, but no one—not even the strongest proponents of globalisation—could have imagined how *world politics* would change in recent years. We have seen the break-up of the Soviet Union, the opening up of South Africa and China, and almost daily suicide bombings in the Middle East. The unilateral invasion of Iraq by the United States has led to an expensive post-war rebuilding and an increase in anti-American attitudes in much of the world. The attacks on New York and Washington on 11 September 2001 and the subsequent war on terrorism have led to changes in business practices related to the creation of backup systems, employee security, employee stereotyping and profiling, and post-terrorist-attack anxiety.

MANAGING PLANNED CHANGE

A group of housekeeping employees who work for a small hotel confronted the owner: 'It's very hard for most of us to maintain rigid 7-to-4 work hours', said their spokeswoman. 'Each of us has significant family and personal responsibilities. And rigid hours don't work for us. We're going to begin looking for someplace else to work if you don't set up flexible work hours.' The owner listened thoughtfully to the group's ultimatum and agreed to its request. The next day the owner introduced a flexitime plan for these employees.

A major automobile manufacturer spent several billion dollars to install state-of-the-art robotics. One area that would receive the new equipment was quality control. Sophisticated computer-controlled equipment would be put in place to significantly improve the company's ability to find and correct defects. Because the new equipment would dramatically change the jobs of the people working in the quality-control area, and because management anticipated considerable employee resistance to the new equipment, executives were developing a program to help people become familiar with the equipment and to deal with any anxieties they might be feeling.

change | Making things different.

planned change | Change activities that are intentional and goal-oriented.

Both of the previous scenarios are examples of **change**. That is, both are concerned with making things different. However, only the second scenario describes a **planned change**. Many changes in organisations are like the one that occurred at the hotel—they just happen. Some organisations treat all change as an accidental occurrence. We are concerned with change activities that are proactive and purposeful. In this chapter, we address change as an intentional, goal-oriented activity.

What are the goals of planned change? Essentially, there are two. First, it seeks to improve the ability of the organisation to adapt to changes in its environment. Second, it seeks to change employee behaviour.

If an organisation is to survive, it must respond to changes in its environment. When competitors introduce new products or services, government agencies enact new laws, important sources of supplies go out of business, or similar environmental changes take place, the organisation needs to adapt. Efforts to stimulate innovation, empower employees and introduce work teams are examples of planned-change activities directed at responding to changes in the environment.

Because an organisation's success or failure is essentially due to the things that its employees do or fail to do, planned change also is concerned with changing the behaviour of individuals and groups within the organisation. Later in this chapter, we review a number of techniques that organisations can use to get people to behave differently in the tasks they perform and in their interactions with others.

CHANGE MANAGEMENT AND MERGERS

Change management is necessary in a large and diverse number of situations. One such situation is when two or more organisations merge. For example, growth by acquisition is a common way for small and medium-size enterprises to develop market power and scale, but the potential for culture clash cannot be overestimated as the smaller businesses often lack the human resource expertise that large corporations are able to employ.

Printing companies Upstream Technology and Print Solutions Australia merged in late 2006 to form Upstream Print Solutions. The immediate change management issues for Neil Tilley, the new chief executive, revolved around people and culture. Staff at Upstream believed that the Print Solutions culture was very male-dominated, and staff at Upstream wanted to be the dominant group in the new arrangements. Tilley was faced with the dilemma of needing to consult and involve staff in the changes and also showing strong leadership by setting the direction for the new enterprise.

One strategy that he used was to list the cultural concerns expressed by staff from both organisations and present them to the larger group. This tactic provided a valuable means of getting all staff to accept and confront the main barriers to a successful merger. When former competitors are asked to unite and work together, their integration becomes a prime consideration. Keeping people informed is crucial to a successful merger.

When the bosses of the two former companies are part of the new organisation, their ability to manage their changed roles and relationships is also an issue. In the new company, Neil Tilley is the chief executive and Gordon Hoen is executive chairman. According to Tilley, 'We'll have our offices side by side so it's easy to walk in and chat … We're agreed to be totally honest with our feedback to one another, but also agreed that the other person doesn't necessarily have to act on the advice.'

Change management in a newly merged company is a crucial aspect in its future performance, and it goes without saying that it must be done well by competent leaders.

SOURCE: Jane Searle, 'Dial M for Merger', *Business Review Weekly*, 18 January 2007, p. 51.

Who in organisations is responsible for managing change activities? The answer is **change agents**.[3] Change agents can be managers or non-managers, current employees of the organisation, newly hired employees or outside consultants.

A contemporary example of a change agent is Lawrence Summers, president of Harvard University, in the United States.[4] Since accepting the presidency in 2001, Summers has aggressively sought to shake up the complacent institution by, among other things, leading the battle to reshape the undergraduate curriculum, proposing that the university be more directly engaged with problems in education and public health, and reorganising to consolidate more power in the president's office. While his critics admit that he has 'offended nearly everyone', he is successfully bringing about revolutionary changes at Harvard that many thought weren't possible. One of the reasons Summers may be a change agent is that he came to Harvard from outside academia. (Prior to joining Harvard, he served in the Clinton administration.) Research shows that organisations are more likely to embark on transformational change when headed by leaders from outside the traditional network.[5]

In some instances, internal management will hire the services of outside consultants to provide advice and assistance with major change efforts. Because they are from the outside, these individuals can offer an objective perspective often unavailable to insiders. Outside consultants, however, are disadvantaged because they usually have an inadequate

change agents | Persons who act as catalysts and assume the responsibility for managing change activities.

understanding of the organisation's history, culture, operating procedures and personnel. Outside consultants also may be prone to initiating more drastic changes—which can be a benefit or a disadvantage—because they don't have to live with the repercussions after the change is implemented. In contrast, internal staff specialists or managers, when acting as change agents, may be more thoughtful (and possibly more cautious) because they have to live with the consequences of their actions.

LEARNING OBJECTIVE 2

Summarise sources of individual and organisational resistance to change

RESISTANCE TO CHANGE

One of the most well-documented findings from studies of individual and organisational behaviour is that organisations and their members resist change. In a sense, this is positive. It provides a degree of stability and predictability to behaviour. If there weren't some resistance, organisational behaviour would take on the characteristics of chaotic randomness. Resistance to change can also be a source of functional conflict. For example, resistance to a reorganisation plan or a change in a product line can stimulate a healthy debate over the merits of the idea and result in a better decision. But there is a definite downside to resistance to change. It hinders adaptation and progress.

Resistance to change doesn't necessarily surface in standardised ways. Resistance can be overt, implicit, immediate or deferred. It is easiest for management to deal with resistance when it is overt and immediate. For instance, a change is proposed and employees quickly respond by voicing complaints, engaging in a work slowdown, threatening to go on strike, or the like. The greater challenge is managing resistance that is implicit or deferred. Implicit resistance efforts are more subtle—loss of loyalty to the organisation, loss of motivation to work, increased errors or mistakes, increased absenteeism due to 'sickness'—and hence are more difficult to recognise. Similarly, deferred actions cloud the link between the source of the resistance and the reaction to it. A change may produce what appears to be only a minimal reaction at the time it is initiated, but then resistance surfaces weeks, months or even years later. Or a single change that in and of itself might have little impact becomes the 'straw that breaks the camel's back'. Reactions to change can build up and then explode in some response that seems totally out of proportion to the change action it follows. The resistance, of course, has merely been deferred and stockpiled. What surfaces is a response to an accumulation of previous changes.

Table 19.2 summarises the main sources of resistance to change, both individual and organisational. Individual sources of resistance reside in basic human characteristics such as perceptions, personalities and needs. Organisational sources reside in the structural makeup of organisations themselves.

Before we move on to ways to overcome resistance to change, it is important to note that not all change is good. Research has shown that sometimes an emphasis on making speedy decisions can lead to bad decisions. Sometimes the line between resisting needed change and falling into a 'speed trap' is a fine one indeed. What is more, sometimes in the 'fog of change', those who are initiating change fail to realise the full magnitude of the effects they are causing or to estimate their true costs to the organisation. Thus, although the perspective generally taken is that rapid, transformational change is good, this isn't always the case. Some organisations, such as Barings Bank in the United Kingdom, have collapsed for this reason.[6] Change agents need to think through the full implications very carefully.

Individual Sources

Habit: To cope with life's complexities, we rely on habits or programmed responses. But when confronted with change, this tendency to respond in our accustomed ways becomes a source of resistance.

Security: People with a high need for security are likely to resist change because it threatens their feelings of safety.

Economic factors: Changes in job tasks or established work routines can arouse economic fears if people are concerned that they won't be able to perform the new tasks or routines to their previous standards, especially when pay is closely tied to productivity.

Fear of the unknown: Change substitutes ambiguity and uncertainty for the unknown.

Selective information processing: Individuals are guilty of selectively processing information in order to keep their perceptions intact. They hear what they want to hear and they ignore information that challenges the world they have created.

Organisational Sources

Structural inertia: Organisations have built-in mechanisms—like their selection processes and formalised regulations—to produce stability. When an organisation is confronted with change, this structural inertia acts as a counterbalance to sustain stability.

Limited focus of change: Organisations are made up of a number of interdependent subsystems. One can't be changed without affecting the others. So, limited changes in subsystems tend to be nullified by the larger system.

Group inertia: Even if individuals want to change their behaviour, group norms may act as a constraint.

Threat to expertise: Changes in organisational patterns may threaten the expertise of specialised groups.

Threat to established power relationships: Any redistribution of decision-making authority can threaten long-established power relationships within the organisation.

Threat to established resource allocations: Groups in the organisation that control sizeable resources often see change as a threat. They tend to be content with the way things are.

OVERCOMING RESISTANCE TO CHANGE

Seven tactics have been suggested for use by change agents in dealing with resistance to change.[7] Let's review them briefly.

EDUCATION AND COMMUNICATION

Resistance can be reduced through communicating with employees to help them see the logic of a change. Communication can reduce resistance on two levels. First, it fights the effects of misinformation and poor communication: if employees receive the full facts and get any misunderstandings cleared up, resistance should subside. Second, communication can be helpful in 'selling' the need for change. Indeed, research shows that the way the need for change is sold matters—change is more likely when the necessity of changing is packaged properly.[8]

PARTICIPATION

It is difficult for individuals to resist a change decision in which they participated. Prior to making a change, those opposed can be brought into the decision process. Assuming that the participants have the expertise to make a meaningful contribution, their involvement can reduce resistance, obtain commitment, and increase the quality of the change decision. However, against these advantages are the negatives: potential for a poor solution and great consumption of time.

BUILDING SUPPORT AND COMMITMENT

Change agents can offer a range of supportive efforts to reduce resistance. When employees' fear and anxiety are high, employee counselling and therapy, new-skills training or a short paid leave of absence may facilitate adjustment. Research on middle managers has shown that when managers or employees have low emotional commitment to change, they favour the status quo and resist it.[9] So, firing up employees can also help them to emotionally commit to the change rather than embrace the status quo.

NEGOTIATION

Another way for the change agent to deal with potential resistance to change is to exchange something of value for a lessening of the resistance. For instance, if the resistance is centred in a few powerful individuals, a specific reward package can be negotiated that will meet their individual needs. Negotiation as a tactic may be necessary when resistance comes from a powerful source. Yet, one cannot ignore its potentially high costs. In addition, there is the risk that, once a change agent negotiates with one party to avoid resistance, he or she is open to the possibility of being blackmailed by other individuals in positions of power.

MANIPULATION AND COOPTATION

Manipulation refers to covert influence attempts. Twisting and distorting facts to make them appear more attractive, withholding undesirable information, and creating false rumours to get employees to accept a change are all examples of manipulation. If corporate management threatens to close down a particular manufacturing plant if that plant's employees fail to accept an across-the-board pay cut, and if the threat is actually untrue, management is using manipulation. *Cooptation*, on the other hand, is a form of both manipulation and participation. It seeks to 'buy off' the leaders of a resistance group by giving them a key role in the change decision. The leaders' advice is sought, not to seek a better decision, but to get their endorsement. Both manipulation and cooptation are relatively inexpensive and easy ways to gain the support of adversaries, but the tactics can backfire if the targets become aware that they are being tricked or used. Once discovered, the change agent's credibility may drop to zero.

SELECTING PEOPLE WHO ACCEPT CHANGE

Research suggests that the ability to easily accept and adapt to change is related to personality. It appears that people who adjust best to change are those who are open to experience, take a positive attitude towards change, are willing to take risks and are flexible in their behaviour. One study of managers in the United States, Europe and Asia found that those with a positive self-concept and high risk tolerance coped better with organisational change. The study authors suggested that organisations could facilitate the change process by selecting people who score high on these characteristics. Another study found that selecting people based on a resistance-to-change scale worked well in winnowing out those who tended to react emotionally to change or to be rigid.[10]

COERCION

Last on the list of tactics used by change agents in dealing with resistance to change is coercion; that is, the application of direct threats or force on the resisters. If the corporate management mentioned in the previous discussion really is determined to close a manufacturing plant if employees don't acquiesce to a pay cut, then coercion would be the label attached to its change tactic. Other examples of coercion are threats of transfer, loss of promotions, negative performance evaluations and a poor letter of recommendation. The advantages and drawbacks of coercion are approximately the same as those mentioned for manipulation and cooptation.

THE POLITICS OF CHANGE

No discussion of resistance to change would be complete without a brief mention of the politics of change. Because change invariably threatens the status quo, it inherently implies political activity.[11]

Internal change agents typically are individuals high in the organisation who have a lot to lose from change. They have, in fact, risen to their positions of authority by developing skills and behavioural patterns that are favoured by the organisation. Change is a threat to those skills and patterns. What if they are no longer the ones the organisation values? Change creates the potential for others in the organisation to gain power at their expense.

Politics suggests that the impetus for change is more likely to come from outside change agents, employees who are new to the organisation (and have less invested in the status quo), or from managers slightly removed from the main power structure. Managers who have spent their entire careers with a single organisation and eventually achieve a senior position in the hierarchy are often major impediments to change. Change, itself, is a very real threat to their status and position. Yet they may be expected to implement changes to demonstrate that they are not merely caretakers. By acting as change agents, they can symbolically convey to various constituencies—shareholders, suppliers, employees, customers—that they are on top of problems and adapting to a dynamic environment. Of course, as you might guess, when forced to introduce change, these long-time power holders tend to implement incremental changes. Radical change is too threatening.

Power struggles within the organisation will determine, to a large degree, the speed and quantity of change. You should expect that long-time career executives will be sources of resistance. This, incidentally, explains why boards of directors that recognise the imperative for the rapid introduction of radical change in their organisations frequently turn to outside candidates for new leadership.[12]

APPROACHES TO MANAGING ORGANISATIONAL CHANGE

Now we turn to several approaches to managing change: Lewin's classic three-step model of the change process, Kotter's eight-step plan, action research and organisational development.

LEWIN'S THREE-STEP MODEL

unfreezing | Change efforts to overcome the pressures of both individual resistance and group conformity.

movement | A change process that transforms the organisation from the status quo to a desired end state.

refreezing | Stabilising a change intervention by balancing driving and restraining forces.

driving forces | Forces that direct behaviour away from the status quo.

restraining forces | Forces that hinder intervention by balancing driving and movement from the existing equilibrium.

Kurt Lewin argued that successful change in organisations should follow three steps: **unfreezing** the status quo, **movement** to a desired end state, and **refreezing** the new change to make it permanent (see Figure 19.1).[13] The value of this model can be seen in the following example when the management of a large oil company decided to reorganise its marketing function in Australia.

The oil company had three regional offices located on the east coast of Australia—in Sydney, Brisbane and Melbourne—and offices in Perth and Adelaide, serving Australia's western and central regions, respectively. The decision was made to consolidate the divisions into a single office to be located in Sydney. The reorganisation meant transferring over 150 employees, eliminating some duplicate managerial positions and instituting a new hierarchy of command. As you might guess, a move of this magnitude was difficult to keep secret. The rumour of its occurrence preceded the announcement by several months. The decision itself was made unilaterally. It came from the executive offices in Singapore. Those people affected had no say whatsoever in the choice. For those in Brisbane or Melbourne, who may have disliked the decision and its consequences—the problems inherent in transferring to another city, pulling youngsters out of school, making new friends, having new co-workers, undergoing the reassignment of responsibilities—their only recourse was to quit. Less than 10 per cent did.

The status quo can be considered to be an equilibrium state. To move from this equilibrium—to overcome the pressures of both individual resistance and group conformity—unfreezing is necessary. It can be achieved in one of three ways (see Figure 19.2). The **driving forces**, which direct behaviour away from the status quo, can be increased. The **restraining forces**, which hinder movement from the existing equilibrium, can be decreased. A third alternative is to combine the first two approaches. Companies that have been successful in the past are likely to encounter restraining forces because people question the need for change.[14] Similarly, research shows that companies with strong cultures excel at incremental change but are overcome by restraining forces against radical change.[15]

The oil company's management could expect employee resistance to the consolidation. To deal with that resistance, management could use positive incentives to encourage employees to accept the change. For instance, increases in pay can be offered to those who accept the transfer. Very liberal moving expenses can be paid by the company. Management might offer low-cost mortgage funds to allow employees to buy new homes in Sydney. Of course, management might also consider unfreezing acceptance of the status

■ **FIGURE 19.1**

Lewin's three-step change model

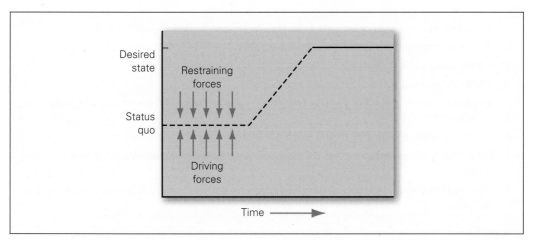

Desired
state

Restraining
forces

Status
quo

Driving
forces

Time

quo by removing restraining forces. Employees could be counselled individually. Each employee's concerns and apprehensions could be heard and specifically clarified. Assuming that most of the fears are unjustified, the counsellor could assure the employees that there was nothing to fear and then demonstrate, through tangible evidence, that restraining forces are unwarranted. If resistance is extremely high, management may have to resort to both reducing resistance and increasing the attractiveness of the alternative if the unfreezing is to be successful.

Research on organisational change has shown that, to be effective, change has to happen quickly.[16] Organisations that build up to change do less well than those that get to and through the movement stage quickly.

Once the consolidation change has been implemented, if it is to be successful, the new situation needs to be refrozen so that it can be sustained over time. Unless this last step is taken, there is a very high chance that the change will be short-lived and that employees will attempt to revert to the previous equilibrium state. The objective of refreezing, then, is to stabilise the new situation by balancing the driving and restraining forces.

How could the oil company's management refreeze its consolidation change? By systematically replacing temporary forces with permanent ones. For instance, management might impose a permanent upward adjustment of salaries. The formal rules and regulations governing behaviour of those affected by the change should also be revised to reinforce the new situation. Over time, of course, the work group's own norms will evolve to sustain the new equilibrium. But until that point is reached, management will have to rely on more formal mechanisms.

KOTTER'S EIGHT-STEP PLAN FOR IMPLEMENTING CHANGE

John Kotter of the Harvard Business School built on Lewin's three-step model to create a more detailed approach for implementing change.[17] Kotter began by listing common mistakes that managers make when trying to initiate change. These included the inability to create a sense of urgency about the need for change, failure to create a coalition for managing the change process, the absence of a vision for change and to effectively communicate that vision, failure to remove obstacles that could impede the achievement of the vision, failure to provide short-term and achievable goals, the tendency to declare victory too soon, and not anchoring the changes into the organisation's culture.

Kotter then established eight sequential steps to overcome these problems. The steps are listed in Table 19.3.

■ TABLE 19.3

Kotter's eight-step plan for
implementing change

1.	Establish a sense of urgency by creating a compelling reason for why change is needed.
2.	Form a coalition with enough power to lead the change.
3.	Create a new vision to direct the change and strategies for achieving the vision.
4.	Communicate the vision throughout the organisation.
5.	Empower others to act on the vision by removing barriers to change and encouraging risk taking and creative problem solving.
6.	Plan for, create and reward short-term 'wins' that move the organisation towards the new vision.
7.	Consolidate improvements, reassess changes and make necessary adjustments in the new programs.
8.	Reinforce the changes by demonstrating the relationship between new behaviours and organisational success.

SOURCE: Based on J. P. Kotter, *Leading Change* (Boston: Harvard Business School Press, 1996).

Notice how Table 19.3 builds on Lewin's model. Kotter's first four steps essentially extrapolate on the 'unfreezing' stage. Steps 5 to 7 represent 'movement'. And the final step works on 'refreezing'. So, Kotter's contribution lies in providing managers and change agents with a more detailed guide for successfully implementing change.

ACTION RESEARCH

action research |
A change process based on systematic collection of data and then selection of a change action based on what the analysed data indicate.

Action research refers to a change process based on the systematic collection of data and then selection of a change action based on what the analysed data indicate.[18] Its importance lies in providing a scientific methodology for managing planned change. The process of action research consists of five steps: diagnosis, analysis, feedback, action and evaluation. You will note that these steps closely parallel the scientific method.

The change agent, often an outside consultant in action research, begins by gathering information about problems, concerns and needed changes from members of the organisation. This *diagnosis* is analogous to the physician's search to find specifically what ails a patient. In action research, the change agent asks questions, interviews employees, reviews records, and listens to the concerns of employees.

Diagnosis is followed by *analysis*. What problems do people key in on? What patterns do these problems seem to take? The change agent synthesises this information into primary concerns, problem areas and possible actions.

Action research includes extensive involvement of the change targets. That is, the people who will be involved in any change program must be actively involved in determining what the problem is and participating in creating the solution. So, the third step—*feedback*—requires sharing with employees what has been found from steps one and two. The employees, with the help of the change agent, develop action plans for bringing about any needed change.

Now the action part of action research is set in motion. The employees and the change agent carry out the specific actions to correct the problems that have been identified.

The final step, consistent with the scientific underpinnings of action research, is evaluation of the action plan's effectiveness. Using the initial data gathered as a benchmark, any subsequent changes can be compared and evaluated.

Action research provides at least two specific benefits for an organisation. First, it is problem-focused. The change agent objectively looks for problems, and the type of problem determines the type of change action. Although this may seem intuitively obvious, a lot of change activities aren't done this way. Rather, they are solution-centred. The change agent has a favourite solution—for example, implementing flexitime, teams or a process reengineering program—and then seeks out problems that the solution fits. Second, because action research so heavily involves employees in the process, resistance to change is reduced. In fact, once employees have actively participated in the feedback stage, the change process typically takes on a momentum of its own. The employees and groups that have been involved become an internal source of sustained pressure to bring about the change.

ORGANISATIONAL DEVELOPMENT

No discussion of managing change would be complete without including organisational development. **Organisational development (OD)** isn't an easily defined single concept. Rather, it is a term used to encompass a collection of planned-change interventions built on humanistic–democratic values that seek to improve organisational effectiveness and employee well-being.[19]

The OD paradigm values human and organisational growth, collaborative and participative processes and a spirit of inquiry.[20] The change agent may be directive in OD; however, there is a strong emphasis on collaboration. The following briefly identifies the underlying values in most OD efforts:

1. *Respect for people*: Individuals are perceived as being responsible, conscientious and caring. They should be treated with dignity and respect.
2. *Trust and support*: The effective and healthy organisation is characterised by trust, authenticity, openness and a supportive climate.
3. *Power equalisation*: Effective organisations de-emphasise hierarchical authority and control.
4. *Confrontation*: Problems shouldn't be swept under the rug. They should be openly confronted.
5. *Participation*: The more that people who will be affected by a change are involved in the decisions surrounding that change, the more they will be committed to implementing those decisions.

What are some of the OD techniques or interventions for bringing about change? In the following pages, we present six interventions that change agents might consider using.

SENSITIVITY TRAINING

It can go by a variety of names—**sensitivity training**, laboratory training, encounter groups or T-groups (training groups)—but all refer to a method of changing behaviour through unstructured group interaction.[21] Members are brought together in a free and open environment in which participants discuss themselves and their interactive processes, loosely directed by a professional behavioural scientist. The group is process-oriented, which means that individuals learn through observing and participating rather than being told. The professional creates the opportunity for participants to express their ideas, beliefs and attitudes, and does not accept—in fact, overtly rejects—any leadership role.

The objectives of the T-groups are to provide the subjects with increased awareness of their own behaviour and how others perceive them, greater sensitivity to the behaviour of others, and increased understanding of group processes. Specific results sought include increased ability to empathise with others, improved listening skills, greater openness, increased tolerance of individual differences and improved conflict-resolution skills.

organisational development (OD) | A collection of planned change interventions, built on humanistic–democratic values, that seeks to improve organisational effectiveness and employee well-being.

sensitivity training | Training groups that seek to change behaviour through unstructured group interaction.

SURVEY FEEDBACK

One tool for assessing attitudes held by organisational members, identifying discrepancies among member perceptions and solving these differences is the **survey feedback** approach.[22]

Everyone in an organisation can participate in survey feedback, but of key importance is the organisational family—the manager of any given unit and the employees who report directly to him or her. A questionnaire is usually completed by all members in the organisation or unit. Organisation members may be asked to suggest questions or may be interviewed to determine what issues are relevant. The questionnaire typically asks members for their perceptions and attitudes on a broad range of topics, including: decision-making practices; communication effectiveness; coordination between units; and satisfaction with the organisation, job, peers and their immediate supervisor.

The data from this questionnaire are tabulated with data pertaining to an individual's specific 'family' and to the entire organisation and then distributed to employees. These data then become the springboard for identifying problems and clarifying issues that may be creating difficulties for people. Particular attention is given to the importance of encouraging discussion and ensuring that discussions focus on issues and ideas, and not on attacking individuals.

Finally, group discussion in the survey feedback approach should result in members identifying possible implications of the questionnaire's findings. Are people listening? Are new ideas being generated? Can decision making, interpersonal relations or job assignments be improved? Answers to questions like these, it is hoped, will result in the group agreeing on commitments to various actions that will remedy the problems that are identified.

PROCESS CONSULTATION

No organisation operates perfectly. Managers often sense that their unit's performance can be improved, but they are unable to identify what can be improved and how it can be improved. The purpose of **process consultation** is for an outside consultant to assist a client, usually a manager, 'to perceive, understand, and act upon process events' with which the manager must deal.[23] These might include work flow, informal relationships among unit members and formal communication channels. Process consultation (PC) is similar to sensitivity training in its assumption that organisational effectiveness can be improved by dealing with interpersonal problems, and in its emphasis on involvement. But PC is more task-directed than is sensitivity training. Consultants in PC are there to 'give the client "insight" into what is going on around him, within him, and between him and other people'.[24] They don't solve the organisation's problems.

Rather, the consultant is a guide or coach who advises on the process to help the client solve his or her own problems. The consultant works with the client in jointly diagnosing what processes need improvement. The emphasis is on 'jointly', because the client develops a skill at analysing processes within his or her unit that can be continually called on long after the consultant is gone. In addition, by having the client actively participate in both the diagnosis and the development of alternatives, there will be greater understanding of the process and the remedy and less resistance to the action plan chosen.

TEAM BUILDING

As we have noted in numerous places throughout this book, organisations are increasingly relying on teams to accomplish work tasks. **Team building** uses high-interaction group

Sea Leggs Team Building Melbourne involves participants in challenges that parallel real work environments and facilitate respect, cooperation, communication and teamwork. The nature of sailing makes it ideal for team building, as everyone on board must cooperate in sailing the boat. Every team member has a role, and experienced instructors ensure that no one person 'dominates'. The core focus is to build high-performance teams and accelerate the development of leadership competencies.

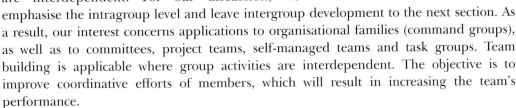

activities to increase trust and openness among team members.[25] Team building can be applied within groups or at the intergroup level, at which activities are interdependent. For our discussion, we emphasise the intragroup level and leave intergroup development to the next section. As a result, our interest concerns applications to organisational families (command groups), as well as to committees, project teams, self-managed teams and task groups. Team building is applicable where group activities are interdependent. The objective is to improve coordinative efforts of members, which will result in increasing the team's performance.

The activities considered in team building typically include goal setting, development of interpersonal relations among team members, role analysis to clarify each member's role and responsibilities, and team process analysis. Of course, team building may emphasise or exclude certain activities, depending on the purpose of the development effort and the specific problems with which the team is confronted. Basically, however, team building attempts to use high interaction among members to increase trust and openness.

It may be beneficial to begin by having members attempt to define the goals and priorities of the team. This will bring to the surface different perceptions of what the team's purpose may be. Following this, members can evaluate the team's performance—how effective is the team in structuring priorities and achieving its goals? This should identify potential problem areas. This self-critique discussion of means and ends can be done with members of the total team present or, when large size impinges on a free interchange of views, may initially take place in smaller groups followed by the sharing of their findings with the total team.

Team building can also address itself to clarifying each member's role on the team. Each role can be identified and clarified. Previous ambiguities can be brought to the surface. For some individuals, it may offer one of the few opportunities they have had to think through thoroughly what their job is all about and what specific tasks they are expected to carry out if the team is to optimise its effectiveness.

INTERGROUP DEVELOPMENT

A major area of concern in OD is the dysfunctional conflict that exists between groups. As a result, this has been a subject to which change efforts have been directed. **Intergroup development** seeks to change the attitudes, stereotypes and perceptions that groups have of each other. For example, in one company, the engineers saw the accounting department as composed of shy and conservative types, and the human resources department as having a bunch of 'ultra-liberals who are more concerned that some protected group of

intergroup development | OD efforts to change the attitudes, stereotypes and perceptions that groups have of each other.

employees might get their feelings hurt than with the company making a profit'. Such stereotypes can have an obvious negative impact on the coordination efforts between the departments.

Although there are several approaches for improving intergroup relations,[26] a popular method emphasises problem solving.[27] In this method, each group meets independently to develop lists of its perceptions of itself, the other group, and how it believes the other group perceives it. The groups then share their lists, after which similarities and differences are discussed. Differences are clearly articulated, and the groups look for the causes of the disparities.

Are the groups' goals at odds? Were perceptions distorted? On what basis were stereotypes formulated? Have some differences been caused by misunderstandings of intentions? Have words and concepts been defined differently by each group? Answers to questions like these clarify the exact nature of the conflict. Once the causes of the difficulty have been identified, the groups can move to the integration phase—working to develop solutions that will improve relations between the groups. Subgroups, with members from each of the conflicting groups, can now be created for further diagnosis and to begin to formulate possible alternative actions that will improve relations.

APPRECIATIVE INQUIRY

appreciative inquiry | Seeking to identify the unique qualities and special strengths of an organisation, which can then be built on to improve performance.

Most OD approaches are problem-centred. They identify a problem or set of problems, then look for a solution. **Appreciative inquiry** accentuates the positive.[28] Rather than looking for problems to fix, this approach seeks to identify the unique qualities and special strengths of an organisation, which can then be built on to improve performance. That is, it focuses on an organisation's successes rather than on its problems.

Advocates of appreciative inquiry (AI) argue that problem-solving approaches always ask people to look backward at yesterday's failures, to focus on shortcomings, and rarely result in new visions. Instead of creating a climate for positive change, action research and OD techniques such as survey feedback and process consultation end up placing blame and generating defensiveness. AI proponents claim it makes more sense to refine and enhance what the organisation is already doing well. This allows the organisation to change by playing to its strengths and competitive advantages.

The AI process essentially consists of four steps, often played out in a large group meeting over a two- or three-day time period, and overseen by a trained change agent. The first step is one of *discovery*. The idea is to find out what people think are the strengths of the organisation. For instance, employees are asked to recount times they felt the organisation worked best or when they specifically felt most satisfied with their jobs. The second step is *dreaming*. The information from the discovery phase is used to speculate on possible futures for the organisation. For instance, people are asked to envision the organisation in five years and to describe what is different. The third step is *design*. Based on the dream articulation, participants focus on finding a common vision of how the organisation will look and agree on its unique qualities. The fourth stage seeks to define the organisation's *destiny*. In this final step, participants discuss how the organisation is going to fulfil its dream. This typically includes the writing of action plans and development of implementation strategies.

AI has proven to be an effective change strategy in organisations such as Roadway Express and the US Navy. For instance, during a three-day AI seminar with Roadway employees, workers were asked to recall ideal work experiences—when they were treated with respect, when trucks were loaded to capacity or arrived on time. Assembled into nine groups, the workers were then encouraged to devise money-saving ideas. A team of short-haul drivers came up with 12 cost-cutting and revenue-generating ideas, one alone that could generate US$1 million in additional profits.[29]

CONTEMPORARY CHANGE ISSUES FOR TODAY'S MANAGERS

In this section, we address four contemporary change issues. First, *how are changes in technology affecting the work lives of employees?* Second, *what can managers do to help their organisations become more innovative?* Third, *how do managers create organisations that continually learn and adapt?* And fourth, *is managing change culture-bound?*

TECHNOLOGY IN THE WORKPLACE

Recent advances in technology are changing the workplace and affecting the work lives of employees. In this section, we will look at two specific issues related to process technology and work. These are continuous improvement processes and process reengineering.

CONTINUOUS IMPROVEMENT PROCESSES

Previously, we described quality management as seeking the constant attainment of customer satisfaction through the continuous improvement of all organisational processes. This search for continuous improvement recognises that *good isn't good enough* and that even excellent performance can, and should, be improved upon. For instance, a 99.9 per cent error-free performance sounds like a high standard of excellence. However it doesn't sound so great when you realise that this standard would result in, as a hypothetical example, Australia Post losing 300 pieces of mail an hour! Quality management programs seek to achieve continuous process improvements so that variability is constantly reduced. When you eliminate variations, you increase the uniformity of the product or service. Increasing uniformity, in turn, results in lower costs and higher quality.

As tens of thousands of organisations introduce continuous process improvement, how will employees be affected? They will no longer be able to rest on their previous accomplishments and successes. So, some people may experience increased stress from a work climate that no longer accepts complacency with the status quo. A race with no finish line can never be won—a situation that creates constant tension. This tension may be positive for the organisation, but the pressures from an unrelenting search for process improvements can create stress in some employees.

> **LEARNING OBJECTIVE 5**
> Contrast continuous improvement processes and process reengineering

PROCESS REENGINEERING

Process reengineering is how you would do things if you could start all over from scratch. The term *reengineering* comes from the process of taking apart an electronic product and designing a better version. As applied to organisations, process reengineering means that management should start with a clean sheet of paper—rethinking and redesigning those processes by which the organisation creates value and does work, ridding itself of operations that have become antiquated.[30] The three key elements of process reengineering are identifying an organisation's distinctive competencies, assessing core processes and reorganising horizontally by process. An organisation's distinctive competencies define what it is that the organisation does better than its competition. Why is identifying distinctive competencies so important? Because it guides decisions regarding

> **LEARNING OBJECTIVE 5**
> Contrast continuous improvement processes and process reengineering

what activities are crucial to the organisation's success. As a computer retailer, Dell, for instance, differentiates itself from its competitors by emphasising high-quality hardware, comprehensive service and technical support, and low prices.

Management also needs to assess the core processes that clearly add value to the organisation's distinctive competencies. These are the processes that transform materials, capital, information and labour into products and services that the customer values. When the organisation is viewed as a series of processes, ranging from strategic planning to after-sales customer support, management can determine to what degree each adds value. This process-value analysis typically uncovers a whole lot of activities that add little or nothing of value and whose only justification is 'we've always done it this way'.

Process reengineering requires management to reorganise around horizontal processes. This means using cross-functional and self-managed teams. It means focusing on processes, rather than functions. It also means cutting out unnecessary levels of middle management.

Process reengineering has been popular since the early 1990s. One of the main consequences has been that many people—especially support staff and middle managers—have lost their jobs. Those employees who keep their jobs after process reengineering have typically found that their jobs are no longer the same. These new jobs may require a wider range of skills, including more interaction with customers and suppliers, greater challenge, increased responsibilities and higher pay. However, the three- to five-year period it takes to implement process reengineering is usually tough on employees. They suffer from uncertainty and anxiety associated with taking on new tasks and having to discard long-established work practices and formal social networks.

STIMULATING INNOVATION

How can an organisation become more innovative? An excellent model is W. L. Gore, the US$1.4-billion-a-year company best known as the maker of Gore-Tex fabric.[31] Gore has developed a reputation as an innovative company by developing a stream of diverse products—including guitar strings, dental floss, medical devices and fuel cells.

What is the secret of Gore's success? What can other organisations do to duplicate its track record for innovation? Although there is no guaranteed formula, certain characteristics surface again and again when researchers study innovative organisations. We have grouped them into structural, cultural and human resource categories. Our message to change agents is that they should consider introducing these characteristics into their organisation if they want to create an innovative climate. Before we look at these characteristics, however, let's clarify what we mean by *innovation*.

DEFINITION

We said that change refers to making things different. Innovation is a more specialised kind of change. **Innovation** is a new idea applied to initiating or improving a product, process or service.[32] So, all innovations involve change, but not all changes necessarily involve new ideas or lead to significant improvements. Innovations in organisations can range from small, incremental improvements, such as well-known Australian company Weis's extension of its product line to include tubs of ice cream and sorbet, up to radical breakthroughs, such as Toyota's battery-fuelled Prius.

innovation | A new idea applied to initiating or improving a product, process or service.

LEARNING OBJECTIVE 6
Identify properties of innovative organisations

SOURCES OF INNOVATION

Structural variables have been the most studied potential source of innovation.[33] A comprehensive review of the structure–innovation relationship leads to the following conclusions.[34] First, organic structures positively influence innovation. Because they are lower in vertical differentiation, formalisation and centralisation, organic organisations facilitate the flexibility, adaptation and cross-fertilisation that make the adoption of innovations easier. Second, long tenure in management is associated with innovation. Managerial tenure apparently provides legitimacy and knowledge of how to accomplish tasks and obtain desired outcomes. Third, innovation is nurtured when there are slack resources. Having an abundance of resources allows an organisation to afford to purchase innovations, bear the cost of instituting innovations and absorb failures. Finally, inter-unit communication is high in innovative organisations.[35] These organisations are high users of committees, task forces, cross-functional teams and other mechanisms that facilitate interaction across departmental lines.

Innovative organisations tend to have similar *cultures*. They encourage experimentation. They reward both successes and failures. They celebrate mistakes. Unfortunately, in too many organisations, people are rewarded for the absence of failures rather than for the presence of successes. Such cultures extinguish risk taking and innovation. People will suggest and try new ideas only when they feel such behaviours exact no penalties. Managers in innovative organisations recognise that failures are a natural by-product of venturing into the unknown.

Within the *human resources* category, we find that innovative organisations actively promote the training and development of their members so that they keep current, offer high job security so employees don't fear getting fired for making mistakes, and encourage individuals to become champions of change. Once a new idea is developed, **idea champions** actively and enthusiastically promote the idea, build support, overcome resistance and ensure that the innovation is implemented.[36] The evidence indicates that champions have common personality characteristics: extremely high self-confidence, persistence, energy and a tendency to take risks. Idea champions also display characteristics associated with transformational leadership. They inspire and energise others with their vision of the potential of an innovation and through their strong personal conviction in their mission. They are also good at gaining the commitment of others to support their mission. In addition, idea champions have jobs that provide considerable decision-making discretion. This autonomy helps them to introduce and implement innovations in organisations.[37]

idea champions | Individuals who take an innovation and actively and enthusiastically promote the idea, build support, overcome resistance, and ensure that the idea is implemented.

SUMMARY

Given Gore's status as a premier product innovator, we would expect it to have most or all of the properties we have identified. And it does. The company has a highly organic structure. Its dozens of plants, for instance, are limited in size to only 200 people. And almost everything is done in teams. The culture strongly fosters experimentation. Employees are free to choose what projects they want to work on based on what they believe is most worthy of their time and most likely to contribute to the company's success. Also, all researchers are encouraged to spend 10 per cent of their work time on developing their own ideas. Finally, Gore's human resources policies encourage employees to expand their skills and responsibilities, and to help others in the organisation do the same.

CREATING A LEARNING ORGANISATION

The learning organisation has recently developed a groundswell of interest from managers and organisation theorists looking for new ways to respond successfully to a world of interdependence and change.[38] In this section, we describe what a learning organisation looks like and methods for managing learning.

LEADERSHIP AND LEARNING AT FREMANTLE PORTS

Fremantle Ports is a lucrative business, dealing with $18 billion worth of cargo each year. The business has been helped by the boom in the resources sector in Western Australia. When Kerry Sanderson took on the CEO position at Fremantle Ports in 1991, the company was in financial trouble. It had also been regarded as a bottleneck for many years in terms of exports and imports through Fremantle, because of inefficiencies in cargo handling.

For Sanderson, coming into such a challenging situation can be daunting, but as she points out: 'In some ways, that was an advantage for a new leader with a reform agenda, because everyone realised that something had to be done. But even there, a lot of the thinking was: "Okay, do what you have to do to fix things up, then we can go back to business as usual." The message our management team had to get out was that there was no more "business as usual". In a dynamic industry, change has to be an ongoing process, and that point had to be accepted by everyone.'

Today, Sanderson and her team of 250 employees run an efficient enterprise with a series of impressive achievements and a reputation as a trade facilitator in Western Australia. The container trade has grown by over 400 per cent since 1991 and customer satisfaction levels are currently at 96 per cent. Sanderson believes that one of the most important things for her reform agenda is establishing a culture of continuous improvement and ongoing learning. Her strategy has been to set targets, agree on them with government, and work systematically towards them. The change program was based on an inclusive approach involving lengthy discussions with employees, senior managers and other stakeholders. The cultural change of the organisation was underpinned by a set of values that were developed through a consultative process.

The operational focus for managers at Fremantle Ports has been on efficiency and quality. They use a set of metrics related to ship delays and cargo handling productivity as a fundamental part of gaining feedback for improvement. Fremantle Ports has the aspirations of a learning organisation with a passion for continuous improvement and development. As Sanderson stresses, 'You have to be willing to consider new ideas, and to look at the bigger picture … that is good for the organisation, but I think that it's also important for development at the personal level … at the moment, we are working with our larger customers on "value chain analysis", to help us understand the costs and benefits of particular actions by the port. At the same time, we are looking at ways to improve the infrastructure that supports our facilities. For example, we are acting as the project manager for the construction of a new rail loop for the port, which will lead to significant efficiency gains. It's another aspect, I think, of seeing reform as a continuing process.'

The future for Fremantle Ports is a learning future.

SOURCE: Derek Parker, 'Leading through Change', *Management Today*, April 2006: <www.aim.com.au/DisplayStory.asp?ID=583>.

---

learning organisation | An organisation that has developed the continuous capacity to adapt and change.

WHAT IS A LEARNING ORGANISATION?

A **learning organisation** is an organisation that has developed the continuous capacity to adapt and change. Just as individuals learn, so too do organisations. 'All organisations learn, whether they consciously choose to or not—it is a fundamental requirement for their sustained existence.'[39] However, some organisations just do it better than others.

Most organisations engage in what has been called **single-loop learning**.[40] When errors are detected, the correction process relies on past routines and present policies. In contrast, learning organisations use **double-loop learning**. When an error is detected, it is corrected in ways that involve the modification of the organisation's objectives, policies and standard routines. Double-loop learning challenges deeply rooted assumptions and norms within an organisation. In this way, it provides opportunities for radically different solutions to problems and dramatic jumps in improvement.

Table 19.4 summarises the five basic characteristics of a learning organisation. It is an organisation in which people put aside their old ways of thinking, learn to be open with each other, understand how their organisation really works, form a plan or vision that everyone can agree on, and then work together to achieve that vision.[41]

Proponents of the learning organisation envision it as a remedy for three fundamental problems inherent in traditional organisations: fragmentation, competition and reactiveness.[42] First, *fragmentation* based on specialisation creates 'walls' and 'chimneys' that separate different functions into independent and often warring fiefdoms. Second, an overemphasis on competition often undermines collaboration. Members of the management team compete with one another to show who is right, who knows more, or who is more persuasive. Divisions compete with one another when they ought to cooperate and share knowledge. Team project leaders compete to show who the best manager is. And third, reactiveness misdirects management's attention to problem solving rather than creation. The problem solver tries to make something go away, while a creator tries to bring something new into being. An emphasis on reactiveness pushes out innovation and continuous improvement and, in its place, encourages people to run around 'putting out fires'.

single-loop learning | Correcting errors using past routines and present policies.

double-loop learning | Correcting errors by modifying the organisation's objectives, policies and standard routines.

---

1. There exists a shared vision which everyone agrees on.

2. People discard their old ways of thinking and the standard routines they use for solving problems or doing their jobs.

3. Members think of all organisational processes, activities, functions and interactions with the environment as part of a system of interrelationships.

4. People openly communicate with each other (across vertical and horizontal boundaries) without fear of criticism or punishment.

5. People sublimate their personal self-interest and fragmented departmental interests to work together to achieve the organisation's shared vision.

SOURCE: Based on P. M. Senge, *The Fifth Discipline* (New York: Doubleday, 1990).

■ TABLE 19.4

Characteristics of a learning organisation

It may help to better understand what a learning organisation is if you think of it as an ideal model that builds on a number of previous OB concepts. No company has successfully achieved all the characteristics described in Table 19.4. As such, you should think of a learning organisation as an ideal to strive towards, rather than a realistic description of structured activity. Note, too, how learning organisations draw on previous OB concepts such as quality management, organisational culture, the boundaryless organisation, functional conflict and transformational leadership. For instance, the learning organisation adopts quality management's commitment to continuous improvement. Learning organisations are also characterised by a specific culture that values risk taking, openness and growth. It seeks 'boundarylessness' through breaking down barriers created by hierarchical levels and fragmented departmentation. A learning organisation supports the importance of disagreements, constructive criticism and other forms of functional conflict. And transformational leadership is needed in a learning organisation to implement the shared vision.

MANAGING LEARNING

How do you change an organisation to make it into a continual learner? What can managers do to make their firms learning organisations?

- *Establish a strategy*: Management needs to make explicit its commitment to change, innovation and continuous improvement.
- *Redesign the organisation's structure*: The formal structure can be a serious impediment to learning. By flattening the structure, eliminating or combining departments and increasing the use of cross-functional teams, interdependence is reinforced and boundaries between people are reduced.
- *Reshape the organisation's culture*: As noted earlier, learning organisations are characterised by risk taking, openness and growth. Management sets the tone for the organisation's culture both by what it says (strategy) and what it does (behaviour). Managers need to demonstrate by their actions that taking risks and admitting failures are desirable traits. That means rewarding people who take chances and make mistakes. And management needs to encourage functional conflict. 'The key to unlocking real openness at work,' says one expert on learning organisations, 'is to teach people to give up having to be in agreement. We think agreement is so important. Who cares? You have to bring paradoxes, conflicts and dilemmas out in the open, so collectively we can be more intelligent than we can be individually.'[43]

An excellent illustration of the application of the learning organisation concept is the Singapore Police.[44] Recently, Prime Minister Goh Chok Tong of Singapore stated that there was an imperative for being in time for tomorrow. He was referring to the need for governments and business to learn to deal with the ideas and technology of the information age. Singapore has been a case study in development, growth and prosperity in the Asia-Pacific region for the past 30 years. Its government has also been keen to embrace the concept of organisational learning and has encouraged public sector agencies to become learning organisations in order to meet the demands placed upon them in the 21st century.

However, it still may be surprising to some that the Singapore Police Force has been one of the first to embrace the concept with enthusiasm. Under the current commissioner of police, the Force has set about overcoming barriers to learning and developing the sort of capability promoted by the five disciplines framework established by Peter Senge. The disciplines of personal mastery, mental models, shared visions, team learning and stems thinking were intuitive to members of the Force.

Some of the obstacles to learning were embedded in the culture of the organisation. Most police services are based on an authoritarian and hierarchical command structure. They are structured in specialised areas that promote a parochial outlook within the different units. As the commissioner points out, respect comes from fear rather than admiration, and deference to authority can be a barrier to effective learning. Also, in the Asian culture, saving face can act against effective decision making.

An interesting aspect of the implementation of the learning organisation concepts was that the 'processes and interactions between the commissioner and his division commanders and staff directors were reinvented along the principles of the learning organisation. However, for processes between these commanders or directors and their staff, the former would have the independence to decide if they wanted to adopt the new principles or how far they wanted to go. They were not measured, judged, or penalised for the approach and extent to which they were prepared to go'. The case of the Singapore

Police Force highlights the importance of the will and support of senior management to embrace change and put faith in subordinates to achieve their true potential.

MANAGING CHANGE: IT'S CULTURE-BOUND

A number of change issues we have discussed in this chapter are culture-bound. To illustrate, let's look briefly at five questions: (1) Do people believe change is possible? (2) If it is possible, how long will it take to bring it about? (3) Is resistance to change greater in some cultures than in others? (4) Does culture influence how change efforts will be implemented? (5) Do successful idea champions do things differently in different cultures?

Do people believe change is possible? Remember that cultures vary in terms of beliefs about their ability to control their environment. In cultures in which people believe that they can dominate their environment, individuals will take a proactive view of change. This, for example, would describe Australia and New Zealand. In many other countries, such as Iran and Saudi Arabia, people see themselves as subjugated to their environment and thus will tend to take a passive approach towards change.

If change is possible, how long will it take to bring it about? A culture's time orientation can help us to answer this question. Societies that focus on the long term, such as Japan, will demonstrate considerable patience while waiting for positive outcomes from change efforts. In societies with a short-term focus, such as Australia and New Zealand, people expect quick improvements and will seek change programs that promise fast results.

Is resistance to change greater in some cultures than in others? Resistance to change will be influenced by a society's reliance on tradition. Italians, as an example, focus on the past, whereas Australians emphasise the present. Italians, therefore, should generally be more resistant to change efforts than their Australian counterparts.

Does culture influence how change efforts will be implemented? Power distance can help with this issue. In high-power-distance cultures, such as Spain or Thailand, change efforts will tend to be autocratically implemented by top management. In contrast, low-power-distance cultures value democratic methods. We would predict, therefore, a greater use of participation in countries such as Denmark and the Netherlands.

Finally, *do successful idea champions do things differently in different cultures?* The evidence indicates that the answer is 'yes'.[45] People in collectivist cultures, in contrast to individualistic cultures, prefer appeals for cross-functional support for innovation efforts; people in high-power-distance cultures prefer champions to work closely with those in authority to approve innovative activities before work is conducted on them; and the higher the uncertainty avoidance of a society, the more champions should work within the organisation's rules and procedures to develop the innovation. These findings suggest that effective managers will alter their organisation's championing strategies to reflect cultural values. So, for instance, although idea champions in Russia might succeed by ignoring budgetary limitations and working around confining procedures, champions in Austria, Denmark, Germany or other cultures high in uncertainty avoidance will be more effective by closely following budgets and procedures.

- The need for change has been implied throughout this text. 'A casual reflection on change should indicate that it encompasses almost all of our concepts in the organisational behaviour literature.'[46] For instance, think about attitudes, motivation, work teams, communication, leadership, organisational structures, human resource practices and organisational cultures. Change was an integral part in the discussion of each.

- If environments were perfectly static, if employees' skills and abilities were always up to date and incapable of deteriorating, and if tomorrow were always exactly the same as today, organisational change would have little or no relevance to managers. But the real world is turbulent, requiring organisations and their members to undergo dynamic change if they are to perform at competitive levels.

- Managers are the primary change agents in most organisations. By the decisions they make and their role-modelling behaviours, they shape the organisation's change culture. For instance, management decisions related to structural design, cultural factors and human resource policies largely determine the level of innovation within the organisation. Similarly, management decisions, policies and practices will determine the degree to which the organisation learns and adapts to changing environmental factors.

POINT / COUNTERPOINT

Managing Change is an Episodic Activity

● POINT

Organisational change is an episodic activity. That is, it starts at some point, proceeds through a series of steps, and culminates in some outcome that those involved hope is an improvement over the starting point. It has a beginning, a middle and an end.

Lewin's three-step model represents a classic illustration of this perspective. Change is seen as a break in the organisation's equilibrium. The status quo has been disturbed, and change is necessary to establish a new equilibrium state. The objective of refreezing is to stabilise the new situation by balancing the driving and restraining forces.

Some experts have argued that organisational change should be thought of as balancing a system made up of five interacting variables within the organisation—people, tasks, technology, structure and strategy. A change in any one variable has repercussions for one or more of the others. This perspective is episodic in that it treats organisational change as essentially an effort to sustain an equilibrium. A change in one variable begins a chain of events that, if properly managed, requires adjustments in the other variables to achieve a new state of equilibrium.

Another way to conceptualise the episodic view of looking at change is to think of managing change as analogous to captaining a ship. The organisation is like a large ship travelling up the Strait of Malacca to a specific port. The ship's captain has made this exact trip hundreds of times before with the same crew. Every once in a while, however, a storm will appear and the crew has to respond. The captain will make the appropriate adjustments—that is, implement changes—and, having manoeuvred through the storm, will return to calm waters. Like this ship's voyage, managing an organisation should be seen as a journey with a beginning and an end, and implementing change as a response to a break in the status quo and needed only occasionally.

COUNTERPOINT

The episodic approach may be the dominant paradigm for handling organisational change, but it has become obsolete. It applies to a world of certainty and predictability. The episodic approach was developed in the 1950s and 1960s, and it reflects the environment of those times. It treats change as the occasional disturbance in an otherwise peaceful world. However, this paradigm has little resemblance to today's environment of constant and chaotic change.

If you want to understand what it is like to manage change in today's organisations, think of it as equivalent to permanent white-water rafting. The organisation isn't a large ship, but more akin to a 15-metre raft. Rather than sailing a calm sea, this raft must traverse a raging river made up of an uninterrupted flow of permanent white-water rapids. To make things worse, the raft is manned by ten people who have never worked together or travelled the river before, much of the trip is in the dark, the river is dotted by unexpected turns and obstacles, the exact destination of the raft isn't clear, and at irregular intervals the raft needs to pull to shore, where some new crew members are added and others leave. Change is a natural state, and managing change is a continuous process. That is, managers never get the luxury of escaping the white-water rapids.

The stability and predictability characterised by the episodic perspective no longer captures the world we live in. Disruptions in the status quo aren't occasional, temporary, and followed by a return to an equilibrium state. There is, in fact, no equilibrium state. Managers today face constant change, bordering on chaos. They are being forced to play a game they have never played before, governed by rules that are created as the game progresses.

SOURCES: Points in this argument are based on K. E. Weick and R. E. Quinn, 'Organizational Change and Development', in J. T. Spence, J. M. Darley and D. J. Foss (eds), *Annual Review of Psychology*, vol. 50 (Palo Alto, CA: Annual Reviews, 1999), pp. 361–86; and P. B. Vaill, *Managing as a Performing Art: New Ideas for a World of Chaotic Change* (San Francisco: Jossey-Bass, 1989).

QUESTIONS FOR REVIEW

MyOBLab Do you understand this chapter's content? Find out at www.pearsoned.com.au/MyOBLab

1. 'We live in an age of discontinuity.' Explain this statement.
2. 'Resistance to change is an irrational response.' Do you agree or disagree? Explain.
3. Why is participation considered such an effective technique for lessening resistance to change?
4. Why does change so frequently become a political issue in organisations?
5. How does Kotter's eight-step plan deal with resistance to change?
6. In an organisation that has a history of 'following the leader', what changes can be made to foster innovation?
7. 'Learning organisations attack fragmentation, competitiveness and reactiveness.' Explain this statement.
8. How is change culture-bound?

QUESTIONS FOR CRITICAL THINKING

1. How have changes in the workforce during the past 25 years affected organisational policies?
2. 'Managing today is easier than at the turn of the 20th century because the years of real change took place during the Industrial Revolution.' Do you agree or disagree? Discuss.
3. Are all managers change agents? Discuss.
4. Discuss the link between learning theories discussed in Chapter 2 and the issue of organisational change.

EXPERIENTIAL EXERCISE

Power and the Changing Environment

Objectives:
1. To describe the forces for change influencing power differentials in organisational and interpersonal relationships.
2. To understand the effect of technological, legal/political, economic and social changes on the power of individuals within an organisation.

The situation:
Your organisation manufactures golf carts and sells them to country clubs, golf courses and consumers. Your team is faced with the task of assessing how environmental changes will affect individuals' organisational power. Read each of the five scenarios and then, for each, identify the five members in the organisation whose power will increase most in light of the environmental condition(s).

(m) = male   (f) = female
Advertising expert (m)
Chief financial officer (f)
Securities analyst (m)
Operations manager (f)
Corporate trainer (m)
Accountant-CPA (m)
General manager (m)
Marketing manager (f)
Computer programmer (f)
Industrial engineer (m)
Product designer (m)
In-house lawyer (m)
Public relations expert (m)
Human resource manager (f)
Chemist (m)

1. New computer-aided manufacturing technologies are being introduced in the workplace during the upcoming 2 to 18 months.
2. New emission standards are being legislated by the government.
3. Sales are way down; the industry appears to be shrinking.
4. The company is planning to go international in the next 12 to 18 months.
5. The Equal Employment Opportunity Commission is applying pressure to balance the male–female population in the organisation's upper hierarchy by threatening to publicise the predominance of men in upper management.

The procedure:
1. Divide the class into teams of three to four students each.
2. Teams should read each scenario and identify the five members whose power will increase most in light of the external environmental condition described.
3. Teams should then address the question: Assuming that the five environmental changes are taking place at once, which five members of the organisation will now have the most power?
4. After 20 to 30 minutes, representatives of each team will be selected to present and justify their conclusions to the entire class. Discussion will begin with scenario 1 and proceed through to scenario 5 and the 'all at once' scenario.

SOURCE: Adapted from J. E. Barbuto, Jr, 'Power and the Changing Environment', *Journal of Management Education*, April 2000, pp. 288–96: <http://jme.sagepub.com/cgi/content/abstract/24/2/288>.

ETHICAL DILEMMA

Increasing Employee Productivity

Ellen West supervises a staff of 15 people handling back-office functions for a regional brokerage firm in Sydney. With company revenues down, Ellen's boss has put increasing pressure on her to improve her department's productivity.

The quickest way for Ellen to increase productivity in her department is to lay off two or three employees and fill the gap by asking the rest of the staff to work harder and put in more time on the job. Since all her employees are on salary, they are not paid for overtime. So, if Ellen let three people go and asked her remaining staff to each put in an additional ten hours a week on the job, she could effectively handle the same workload with 20 per cent fewer employees.

As Ellen considered this idea, she had mixed feelings.

Reducing her staff and asking people to work more hours would please her boss and increase job security for those people remaining. On the other hand, Ellen was fearful that she was taking advantage of a weak labour market. Her employees knew that jobs were scarce and they would be hard put to find comparable positions elsewhere in the securities industry. They were unlikely to openly complain about working longer hours for fear that they, too, would be let go. But was it fair to increase the department's productivity on the backs of already hardworking employees? Was it ethical for Ellen to ask her employees to put in ten hours more a week, for no additional money, because the current weak labour market worked to her advantage?

If you were Ellen West, what would you do?

CASE STUDY 19

Innovating Innovation

Procter & Gamble (P&G) is a large multinational corporation with employees covering all the regions of the world including ASEAN, Australasia and India. Executives at P&G are quite happy these days. At the end of 2004, sales growth was up almost 27 per cent and the company's stock price had nearly doubled. P&G's annual report to its stockholders stated that 'P&G exceeded all its financial goals in fiscal 2004'. For a US$51 billion consumer products company with 300 different brands, exceeding its goals is no small feat.

Many at P&G might point to chief technology officer Gil Cloyd as one of the sources of this success. Cloyd, who was the recipient of *Industry Week*'s 2004 'Technology Leader of the Year' award, is changing how P&G approaches research and development (R&D). Given the enormous variety of products that P&G offers, including toilet paper, laundry detergents, personal care products and pet food, the ability to sustain a competitive level of innovation is a tremendous challenge. Says Cloyd, 'One of the challenges we have is serving the needs of a very diverse consumer population, but yet be able to do that quickly and very cost effectively. In the consumer products world we estimate that the required pace of innovation has doubled in the last three years. That means we have less time to benefit from any innovation that we bring into the marketplace.' Cloyd's approach is simple yet complex: innovate innovation.

What is innovating innovation? As Cloyd explains, 'What we've done is refine our thinking on how we conduct and evaluate research and development. We've made some changes. For example, historically, we tended to put the evaluation emphasis on technical product performance, patents, and other indicators of internal R&D efforts. Now there is more emphasis on perceived customer value.' Cloyd describes P&G's innovation process as holistic. Holistic innovation includes first setting appropriate financial goals and then implementing an innovation program for all aspects of the product—from its manufacturing technology to those aspects that the customer experiences directly, such as the product's packaging and appearance.

One of Cloyd's major goals at P&G is to acquire 50 per cent of its ideas from sources external to the organisation. Cloyd isn't there yet, but he likes his progress. Currently, P&G obtains 35 per cent of its product ideas externally, and this number is up from 20 per cent in 2002 and 10 per cent in 2000. Cloyd describes this goal as the 'Connect + Develop (C+D) initiative'. The C+D initiative is responsible for many of P&G's recent product successes. For example, C+D resulted in the Swiffer Wet Jet and Duster, Olay Daily Facials and Crest Whitestrips. According to Henry Chesbrough, author of the book *Open Innovation*, C+D is successful because 'Not all the smart people work for you', and 'External ideas can help create value, but it takes internal R&D to claim a portion of that value for you.'

Though P&G is enjoying enormous success due in part to its innovation program, Cloyd isn't resting on his laurels. He emphasises learning as a critical element to continued innovation success. One area in particular that he is interested in exploring is computer modelling and simulation. Previously, manufacturing was the main user of computer modelling. Now, Cloyd is using computer modelling in the product design process. Explains Cloyd, 'A computational model helps us more quickly to understand what's going on. The simulation capabilities are also allowing us to interact with consumers much more quickly on design options. For example, Internet panels can engage consumers in as little as 24 hours. Digital technology is very important in helping us learn faster. Not only will it accelerate innovation, but the approach will greatly enhance the creativity of our people.' By continually looking for new ways to design, produce and market products, Cloyd and P&G are indeed 'innovating innovation'.

QUESTIONS

1. The book discussed the notion of 'idea champions'. What characteristics of Gil Cloyd make him an idea champion?
2. Would you consider P&G to be a 'learning organisation'? What aspects of P&G led you to your answer?
3. Although Cloyd is a major reason for P&G's innovation success, what are some structural features of P&G that might contribute to its ability to innovate so well?
4. The benefits of technological innovations for companies are often short-lived due to other companies adopting the same technology soon after. What factors do you believe contribute to P&G's ability to continually innovate at such a competitive level?

SOURCE: Based on J. Teresko, 'P&G's Secret: Innovating Innovation', *Industry Week*, December 2004, pp. 26–34.

ENDNOTES

1. D. James and E. Ross 'Sack with Care', *Business Review Weekly*, 25 January – 1 February 2006, pp. 62–65; S. Bartholomeusz, 'Teethmarks Show NAB Has Bitten the Bullet', *Sydney Morning Herald*, 29 September 2005: <www.smh.com.au/news/business/teethmarks-show-nab-has-bitten-the-bullet/2005/09/28/1127804549042.html> (accessed 5 May 2006).

2. L. Lee, 'Taps for Music Retailers?', *BusinessWeek*, 23 June 2003; and J. Scott, 'Big Music Retailer is Seeking Bankruptcy Protection', *New York Times*, 10 February 2004, p. D1.

3. See, for instance, K. H. Hammonds, 'Practical Radicals', *Fast Company*, September 2000, pp. 162–74; and P. C. Judge, 'Change Agents', *Fast Company*, November 2000, pp. 216–26.

4. J. Taub, 'Harvard Radical', *New York Times Magazine*, 24 August 2003, pp. 28–45.

5. M. S. Kraatz and J. H. Moore, 'Executive Migration and Institutional Change', *Academy of Management Journal*, February 2002, pp. 120–43.

6. M. T. Hannan, L. Pólos and G. R. Carroll, 'The Fog of Change: Opacity and Asperity in Organizations', *Administrative Science Quarterly*, September 2003, pp. 399–432.

7. J. P. Kotter and L. A. Schlesinger, 'Choosing Strategies for Change', *Harvard Business Review*, March–April 1979, pp. 106–14.

8. J. E. Dutton, S. J. Ashford, R. M. O'Neill and K. A. Lawrence, 'Moves that Matter: Issue Selling and Organizational Change', *Academy of Management Journal*, August 2001, pp. 716–36.

9. Q. N. Huy, 'Emotional Balancing of Organizational Continuity and Radical Change: The Contribution of Middle Managers', *Administrative Science Quarterly*, March 2002, pp. 31–69.

10. J. A. LePine, J. A. Colquitt and A. Erez, 'Adaptability to Changing Task Contexts: Effects of General Cognitive Ability, Conscientiousness, and Openness to Experience', *Personnel Psychology*, Fall 2000, pp. 563–93; T. A. Judge, C. J. Thoresen, V. Pucik and T. M. Welbourne, 'Managerial Coping with Organizational Change: A Dispositional Perspective', *Journal of Applied Psychology*, February 1999, pp. 107–22; and S. Oreg, 'Resistance to Change: Developing an Individual Differences Measure', *Journal of Applied Psychology*, August 2003, pp. 680–93.

11. See J. Pfeffer, *Managing with Power: Politics and Influence in Organizations* (Boston: Harvard Business School Press, 1992), pp. 7, 318–20; D. Knights and D. McCabe, 'When "Life Is but a Dream": Obliterating Politics through Business Process Reengineering?', *Human Relations*, June 1998, pp. 761–98; and E. Porter, 'Politics, Change and Reflective Practitioners', *Organization Development Journal*, Fall 2002, pp. 18–29.

12. See, for instance, W. Ocasio, 'Political Dynamics and the Circulation of Power: CEO Succession in U.S. Industrial Corporations, 1960–1990', *Administrative Science Quarterly*, June 1994, pp. 285–312.

13. K. Lewin, *Field Theory in Social Science* (New York: Harper & Row, 1951).

14. P. G. Audia, E. A. Locke and K. G. Smith, 'The Paradox of Success: An Archival and a Laboratory Study of Strategic Persistence Following Radical Environmental Change', *Academy of Management Journal*, October 2000, pp. 837–53.

15. J. B. Sorensen, 'The Strength of Corporate Culture and the Reliability of Firm Performance', *Administrative Science Quarterly*, March 2002, pp. 70–91.

16. J. Amis, T. Slack and C. R. Hinings, 'The Pace, Sequence, and Linearity of Radical Change', *Academy of Management Journal*, February 2004, pp. 15–39; and E. Autio, H. J. Sapienza and J. G. Almeida, 'Effects of Age at Entry, Knowledge Intensity, and Imitability on International Growth', *Academy of Management Journal*, October 2000, pp. 909–24.

17. J. P. Kotter, 'Leading Changes: Why Transformation Efforts Fail', *Harvard Business Review*, March–April 1995, pp. 59–67; and J. P. Kotter, *Leading Change* (Harvard Business School Press, 1996).

18. See, for example, A. B. Shani and W. A. Pasmore, 'Organization Inquiry: Towards a New Model of the Action Research Process', in D. D. Warrick (ed.), *Contemporary Organization Development: Current Thinking and Applications* (Glenview, IL: Scott, Foresman, 1985), pp. 438–48; and C. Eden and C. Huxham, 'Action Research for the Study of Organizations', in S. R. Clegg, C. Hardy and W. R. Nord (eds), *Handbook of Organization Studies* (London: Sage, 1996).

19. For a sampling of various OD definitions, see N. Nicholson (ed.), *Encyclopedic Dictionary of Organizational Behavior* (Malden, MA: Blackwell, 1998), pp. 359–61; G. Farias and H. Johnson, 'Organizational Development and Change Management', *Journal of Applied Behavioral Science*, September 2000, pp. 376–79; and H. K. Sinangil and F. Avallone, 'Organizational Development and Change', in N. Anderson, D. S. Ones, H. K. Sinangil and C. Viswesvaran (eds), *Handbook of Industrial, Work and Organizational Psychology*, vol. 2 (Thousand Oaks, CA: Sage, 2001), pp. 332–35.

20. See, for instance, W. A. Pasmore and M. R. Fagans, 'Participation, Individual Development, and Organizational Change: A Review and Synthesis', *Journal of Management*, June 1992, pp. 375–97; T. G. Cummings and C. G. Worley, *Organization Development and Change*, 7th ed. (Cincinnati: Southwestern, 2001); and R. Lines, 'Influence of Participation in Strategic Change: Resistance, Organizational Commitment and Change Goal Achievement', *Journal of Change Management*, September 2004, pp. 193–215.

21. S. Highhouse, 'A History of the T-Group and Its Early Application in Management Development', *Group Dynamics: Theory, Research, & Practice*, December 2002, pp. 277–90.

22. J. E. Edwards and M. D. Thomas, 'The Organizational Survey Process: General Steps and Practical Considerations', in P. Rosenfeld, J. E. Edwards and M. D. Thomas (eds), *Improving Organizational Surveys: New Directions, Methods, and Applications* (Newbury Park, CA: Sage, 1993), pp. 3–28.

23. E. H. Schein, *Process Consultation: Its Role in Organizational Development*, 2nd ed. (Reading, MA: Addison-Wesley, 1988), p. 9. See also E. H. Schein, *Process Consultation Revisited: Building Helpful Relationships* (Reading, MA: Addison-Wesley, 1999).

24. Ibid.

25. W. Dyer, *Team Building: Issues and Alternatives* (Reading, MA: Addison-Wesley, 1994).

26. See, for example, E. H. Neilsen, 'Understanding and Managing Intergroup Conflict', in J. W. Lorsch and P. R. Lawrence (eds), *Managing Group and Intergroup Relations* (Homewood, IL: Irwin-Dorsey, 1972), pp. 329–43.

27. R. R. Blake, J. S. Mouton and R. L. Sloma, 'The Union–Management Intergroup Laboratory: Strategy for Resolving Intergroup Conflict', *Journal of Applied Behavioral Science*, no. 1, 1965, pp. 25–57.

28. See, for example, G. R. Bushe, 'Advances in Appreciative Inquiry as an Organization Development Intervention', *Organizational Development Journal*, Summer 1999, pp. 61–68; D. L. Cooperrider and D. Whitney, *Collaborating for Change: Appreciative Inquiry* (San Francisco: Berrett-Koehler, 2000); R. Fry, F. Barrett, J. Seiling and D. Whitney (eds), *Appreciative Inquiry & Organizational Transformation: Reports From the Field* (Westport, CT: Quorum, 2002); J. K. Barge and C. Oliver, 'Working With Appreciation in Managerial Practice', *Academy of Management Review*, January 2003, pp. 124–42; and D. van der Haar and D. M. Hosking, 'Evaluating Appreciative Inquiry: A Relational Constructionist Perspective', *Human Relations*, August 2004, pp. 1017–36.

29. J. Gordon, 'Meet the Freight Fairy', *Forbes*, 20 January 2003, p. 65.

30. M. Hammer and J. Champy, *Reengineering the Corporation: A Manifesto for Business Revolution* (New York: HarperBusiness, 1993).

31. D. Anfuso, 'Core Values Shape W. L. Gore's Innovative Culture', *Workforce*, March 1999, pp. 48–51; and A. Harrington, 'Who's Afraid of a New Product?', *Fortune*, 10 November 2003, pp. 189–92.

32. See, for instance, A. Van de Ven, 'Central Problems in the Management of Innovation', *Management Science*, vol. 32, 1986, pp. 590–607; and R. M. Kanter, 'When a Thousand Flowers Bloom: Structural, Collective and Social Conditions for Innovation in Organizations', in B. M. Staw and L. L. Cummings (eds), *Research in Organizational Behavior*, vol. 10 (Greenwich, CT: JAI Press, 1988), pp. 169–211.

33. F. Damanpour, 'Organizational Innovation: A Meta-Analysis of Effects of Determinants and Moderators', *Academy of Management Journal*, September 1991, p. 557.

34. Ibid, pp. 555–90.

35. See also P. R. Monge, M. D. Cozzens and N. S. Contractor, 'Communication and Motivational Predictors of the Dynamics of Organizational Innovation', *Organization Science*, May 1992, pp. 250–74.

36. J. M. Howell and C. A. Higgins, 'Champions of Change', *Business Quarterly*, Spring 1990, pp. 31–32; and D. L. Day, 'Raising Radicals: Different Processes for Championing Innovative Corporate Ventures', *Organization Science*, May 1994, pp. 148–72.

37. Howell and Higgins, 'Champions of Change'.

38. See, for example, the special edition on organisational learning in *Organizational Dynamics*, Autumn 1998; P. Senge, *The Dance of Change: The Challenges to Sustaining Momentum in Learning Organizations* (New York: Doubleday/Currency, 1999); A. M. Webber, 'Will Companies Ever Learn?', *Fast Company*, October 2000, pp. 275–82; R. Snell, 'Moral Foundations of the Learning Organization', *Human Relations*, March 2001, pp. 319–42; M. M. Brown and J. L. Brudney, 'Learning Organizations in the Public Sector? A Study of Police Agencies Employing Information and Technology to Advance Knowledge', *Public Administration Review*, January/February 2003, pp. 30–43; and T. B. Lawrence, M. K. Mauws, B. Dyck and R. F. Kleysen, 'The Politics of Organizational Learning: Integrating Power Into the 4I Framework', *Academy of Management Review*, January 2005, pp. 180–91.

39. D. H. Kim, 'The Link between Individual and Organizational Learning', *Sloan Management Review*, Fall 1993, p. 37.

40. C. Argyris and D. A. Schon, *Organizational Learning* (Reading, MA: Addison-Wesley, 1978).

41. B. Dumaine, 'Mr. Learning Organization', *Fortune*, 17 October 1994, p. 148.

42. F. Kofman and P. M. Senge, 'Communities of Commitment: The Heart of Learning Organizations', *Organizational Dynamics*, Autumn 1993, pp. 5–23.

43. Dumaine, 'Mr. Learning Organization', p. 154.

44. Based on Khoo Boon Hui and Tan Tay Keong, 'Learning and Innovation in Public Institutions: Lessons from Singapore', in M. Asher (ed.), *Public Policy in Asia: Implications for Business and Government* (Singapore: Quorum Books, 2002), pp. 175–92; and Peter Senge, *The Fifth Disciple: The Art and Practice of the Learning Organisation* (Sydney: Random House, 1994).

45. See S. Shane, S. Venkataraman and I. MacMillan, 'Cultural Differences in Innovation Championing Strategies', *Journal of Management*, vol. 21, no. 5, 1995, pp. 931–52.

46. P. S. Goodman and L. B. Kurke, 'Studies of Change in Organizations: A Status Report', in P. S. Goodman (ed.), *Change in Organizations* (San Francisco: Jossey-Bass, 1982), p. 1.

BERNADETTE LYNCH

UNIVERSITY OF SOUTHERN QUEENSLAND

The abuse perpetrated by US soldiers of detainees within Abu Ghraib prison in Iraq in late 2003 has been recorded elsewhere and need not be detailed here. It is sufficient to cite the Taguba Report and confirm that:

> between October and December 2003, at the Abu Ghraib Confinement Facility (BCCF), numerous incidents of sadistic, blatant, and wanton criminal abuses were inflicted on several detainees. This systemic and illegal abuse of detainees was intentionally perpetrated by several members of the military police guard force (372nd Military Police Company, 320th Military Police Battalion, 800th MP Brigade), in Tier (section) 1-A of the Abu Ghraib Prison (BCCF).[1]

A series of reports into Abu Ghraib have concluded that many factors conspired to create these events. Certainly, Schlesinger's Report acknowledges that the incidents that occurred on the night shift of Cell Block 1 had a 'unique nature fostered by the predilections of the non commissioned officers in charge'.[2] (It was this night shift of soldiers who were responsible for the photos and associated abuse.) However, both Schlesinger's and Taguba's reports argued that it was the uniquely toxic conditions at Abu Ghraib, rather than simply the personalities of the individual players or some inexplicable group dynamic, that nurtured the abuse.

The various reports into the abuse flag the following issues.

At the time of the abuses Abu Ghraib was the largest of the 17 detention sites throughout Iraq. It was 'seriously overcrowded', with 7000 detainees, and 'under resourced', with only 90 Military Police guard personnel when at least 180 was the minimum required.

The deployment of Military Police to the prison was utterly chaotic, leaving them untrained and unprepared for the work ahead of them.

> As one commander stated, 'Anything that could go wrong went wrong.' Preparation was not consistently applied to all deploying units, wasting time and duplicating efforts already accomplished. Troops were separated from their equipment for excessive periods of time. The flow of equipment and personnel was not coordinated … (this meant) the unit could neither train at its stateside mobilization site without its equipment nor upon arrival overseas, as two or three weeks would go by before joining with its equipment. This resulted in assigning equipment and troops in an *ad hoc* manner with no regard to original unit. It also resulted in assigning certain companies that had not trained together in peacetime battalion headquarters … This method resulted in a condition wherein a recently arrived battalion headquarters would be assigned the next arriving MP companies, regardless of their capabilities and any other prior command and training relationships.[3]

It should have been possible to address the training needs of staff at Abu Ghraib once they were posted. However, training remained an unaddressed issue. As Taguba reported, training remained an unaddressed issue throughout this period despite the obvious need.

In the absence of training and in conditions of gross under-resourcing it seems reasonable that confusion existed as to the ways things were done in Abu Ghraib. Most important, the operations at Abu Ghraib did not reflect the officially sanctioned Army processes. '… the 800th MP Brigade (which staffed Abu Ghraib) did not articulate or enforce clear and basic Soldier and Army standards.'[4]

The Taguba Report revealed:

> The handling of detainees and criminal prisoners after in-processing was inconsistent from detention facility to detention facility, compound to compound, encampment to encampment, and even shift to shift throughout the 800th MP Brigade.[5]

The same report continues:

> Daily processing, accountability, and detainee care appears to have been made up as the operations developed with reliance on, and guidance from, junior members of the unit who had civilian corrections experience.[6]

Even the language used throughout the setting was not standardised. The process of accounting for the prisoners was variously called 'band checks', 'roll-ups' and 'call-ups'.

There was not even a clear uniform standard for Military Police completing detention duties.

> Despite the fact that hundreds of former Iraqi soldiers and officers were detainees, MP personnel were allowed to wear civilian clothes in the FOB (Forward Operating Base, Abu Ghraib) after duty hours while carrying weapons ... Some Soldiers wrote poems and other sayings on their helmets and soft caps.[7]

Finally,

> Operational journals at the various compounds and the 320th Battalion TOC contained numerous unprofessional entries and flippant comments, which highlighted the lack of discipline within the unit. There was no indication that the journals were ever reviewed by anyone in their chain of command.[8]

In short, 'Accountability and facility operations (Standard operating procedures) SOPs lacked specificity, implementation measures, and a system of checks and balances to ensure compliance.'[9]

Most importantly, confusion existed as to the type of treatment detainees could expect within the facility. Taguba commented negatively that '(n)either the camp rules nor the provisions of the Geneva Conventions are posted in English or in the language of the detainees at any of the detention facilities in the 800th MP Brigade's AOR'.[10]

It should be noted that Abu Ghraib contained a range of detainees, not merely the predictable enemy prisoners of war expected within a war zone.

> (D)ue to lack of adequate Iraqi facilities, Iraqi criminals (generally Iraqi-on-Iraqi crimes) are detained with security internees (generally Iraqi-on-Coalition offenses) and (Enemy Prisoners of War) EPWs in the same facilities, though segregated in different cells/compounds.[11]

So, the problem ran much deeper than the absence of a public record of internee rights and responsibilities. In fact, different types of detainees required different types of treatment. Further, the problem wasn't simply that known standards of treatment for the various categories of detainees were not published. Confusion existed in particular as to the treatment that security detainees, including 'unlawful combatant' detainees, could expect.

In the aftermath of the 9/11 attacks, US President Bush deemed that the conflict with al Qaeda would be pursued outside the Geneva Conventions. The Geneva Conventions are 'international treaties bought into force in August 1949 (that) extend protections to, among others, prisoners of war and civilians in time of war'.[12] This meant that al Qaeda and Taliban detainees would not be regarded as prisoners of war and therefore would not legally hold the rights and privileges afforded POWs. It must be acknowledged, however, that the president also determined that all detainees would be treated in accordance with the Geneva Conventions *where possible*. For example, the 17 acceptable interrogation techniques identified in Army Field Manual 34-52 fall within the Geneva Conventions. However, a suite of more aggressive interrogation techniques was sanctioned for use on detainees the US regards as 'unlawful combatants' being held at Guantanamo Bay. These techniques were to be used under tightly controlled circumstances. These and other similarly aggressive techniques found their way to the chaos that was Abu Ghraib through a series of flawed actions and inactions by local command. According to Schlesinger, within Abu Ghraib these techniques became far 'more problematic when they migrated and were not adequately safeguarded'.[13]

But confusion didn't just exist in relation to procedures or detainee management protocols within the facility. Confusion existed as to the role of Military Police within the setting. Abu Ghraib was staffed by two categories of specialist personnel: Military Police (MP) and Military Intelligence (MI). MPs and MIs have quite different and separate functions and purposes within the setting. In very general terms, MPs are basically responsible for the day-to-day management of the facility and detainees. Military Intelligence are responsible for interrogation and interpreter services. Although, as Schlesinger comments, 'neither MP nor MI doctrine specifically defines the distinct, but interdependent, roles and responsibilities of the two elements in detainee operations'.[14]

These roles became particularly blurred in Abu Ghraib in that Military Police—including abuse perpetrators within Cell 1—believed they were 'directed to change facility procedures to "set the conditions" for MI interrogations'.[15] Taguba concluded that while this directive did not come to or from the top of the command, it did occur at lower levels within the setting. 'Military Intelligence (MI) interrogators and Other US Government Agency's (OGA) interrogators actively requested that MP guards set physical and mental conditions for favorable interrogation of witnesses.'[16]

Finally, confusion over the roles of the various players at Abu Ghraib was reflected in the confusion that existed as to the command structure within Abu Ghraib. Within Abu Ghraib:

> there was no clear delineation of command responsibilities between the (Military police and Military Intelligence personnel). The situation was exacerbated (when the commander of the MI Brigade was appointed) as the base commander for Abu Ghraib, including responsibility for the support of all MPs assigned to the prison. In addition to being contrary to … (usual practice) there is no evidence the details of this command relationship were effectively coordinated or implemented by the leaders at Abu Ghraib.[17]

Both the Taguba and Schlesinger reports identified multiple instances of poor local leadership that created and sustained these chaotic conditions. While many things need to be learned from the Abu Ghraib abuses, possibly the strongest lesson relates to the consequences of total system collapse.

QUESTIONS

1. What evidence can you find in the case study of a culture lacking in military discipline? Consider language, stories and symbols evident in the case study.
2. What were the main structural issues in the case study, and how might they have impacted on the events in Abu Ghraib?
3. How might a more effective training and deployment regimen for personnel assisted with better socialisation of personnel at Abu Ghraib?
4. The Schlesinger Report argues that the abuse that took place on the night shift of Cell Block 1 wasn't merely the result of personal pathology. How might better-managed system factors have prevented the abuse?

ENDNOTES
1. Major-General Antonio M. Taguba, *Article 15-6 Investigation of the 800th Military Police Brigade*, 2004 (Taguba Report), p. 16.
2. James R. Schlesinger, *Final Report of the Independent Panel to Review DOD Detention Operations*, August 2004 (Schlesinger Report), p. 13.
3. Schlesinger Report, p. 54.
4. Taguba Report, p. 41.
5. Ibid, p. 23.
6. Ibid, p. 24.
7. Ibid, p. 24
8. Ibid, p. 24.
9. Ibid, p. 24.
10. Ibid, p. 26.
11. Ibid, p. 10.
12. Schlesinger Report, p. 95.
13. Ibid, p. 9.
14. Ibid, p. 71.
15. Taguba Report, p. 18.
16. Ibid, p. 18.
17. Schlesinger Report, p. 45.

B INTEGRATIVE CASE STUDY

Workplace Divorce

DR CHRISTINE D. HO
UNIVERSITY OF ADELAIDE

Dave Murphy sighed. Had been putting in 14-hour work days for several weeks now and couldn't see it ending soon. Despite this, he found the work challenging.

Dave worked at Scottbridge, one of Australia's leading professional services firms and part of a global operation. As a graduate of accounting, he worked for the Internal Audit (IA) department of the Risk Management division. IA serviced businesses from five industry sectors: government, technology, financial services, real estate and resources.

Looking back, Dave remembered how odd his

interview with Andrew Parry, head of Internal Audit, and John Poser, the manager of Financial Services, had been. Andrew was an informal boss and treated his staff as if they were his footy mates. First, Andrew had told him that should he be offered the job his nickname would be 'Money Smurf'. Everyone at IA had nicknames. Second, as the interview was coming to a close, John asked if he preferred red or white wine. Dave wasn't sure how this related to his ability to do the job. He had never developed a taste for either and told them so.

For the most part, Dave got along with his colleagues. IA occupied all five floors of a building they affectionately dubbed 'the Tower'. Staff for each industry sector were randomly scattered across these floors. The notion that they worked for different units was regarded more as a formality than a reality. Andrew encouraged collegiality through many social functions. There was a Happy Hour every Friday. There was the End-of-Financial-Year jaunt. This came around every six months because some clients operated locally as well as internationally. These jaunts involved shutting down the Tower for the afternoon and hiring buses to take the staff to a restaurant or fun park. There was the Bradshaw Guild, named in honour of Paul Bradshaw who had been on exchange from their London office several years before. He had developed a reputation for his excessive drinking capacity and knowledge of all things alcoholic. The Guild met monthly to sample wines and bottled their own wine under a label each year. To conclude each year was the annual Christmas Dinner. All alcohol was supplied and paid for by IA. At these events, Andrew always led a song in honour of Paul Bradshaw. Bawdy behaviour was commonplace and accepted, even though some female staff might have been offended by the sexual innuendos. The majority of staff had been there a long time and knew what to expect.

These events were generally well attended; however, increasingly some of the new staff apologised for their absence, citing workload pressures. It wasn't until Dave ran into Mohammed, one of the new hires, in the staff room that he understood why.

'Good morning, Mohammed. Are you going to the Christmas Dinner? I hear Andrew has stocked up on a particularly good wine this year', said Dave.

'Um, no, Dave. I'm Muslim. I don't celebrate Christmas. Plus, I don't drink. So, I'm afraid the wine would be completely wasted on me.'

'Of course, sorry, mate!' Dave replied. 'I knew you were Muslim, but it just didn't occur to me that not everyone celebrated Christmas.' Dave leaned in and lowered his voice. 'I don't really drink, either. I just hold a glass of whatever they give me and pretend to drink it. I've been here for two years and no one seems to have noticed or said anything about it.'

Dave could have kicked himself. When he joined IA all the staff were Anglo-Australians or had come from white European backgrounds. This recent growth meant one quarter of the staff were now of Asian or Middle Eastern origin, some of whom were practising Muslims. Dave wondered if anyone else had realised the implications of this demographic shift?

While the staff were mostly easygoing, not everyone got along. John Poser and the manager of Real Estate, Perry Cutter, often openly disagreed with each other. Unfortunately, this tension spilled over into the relations between staff in both units. Dave had given up saying hello to the Real Estate staff whenever they crossed paths. They pointedly ignored his presence. His colleagues in Financial Services confirmed similar experiences. They rationalised that they were the smallest unit among them and brought in the lowest income, which possibly explained why they sought out every opportunity to promote their own achievements and criticise other units. Everyone was tired of their aggressive and competitive behaviour.

So, when the email came around from Mike Grover, the director of Risk Management and a partner with Scottbridge, asking for IA volunteers to move offices and fill up a floor in one of the other larger Scottbridge buildings across the street, Dave jumped at the chance. Mike's email explained that this was a temporary solution until larger accommodations could be arranged within a few years.

Along with the other partners, Mike was concerned that IA was becoming a rogue arm of the firm and had been given free rein to do whatever they liked so long as they brought in the income. But their excessive drinking and informality was well known in the firm. The partners were worried about how these behaviours were affecting their professionalism and reputation. Mike saw the growth in staff numbers and resulting office space dilemma as opportunities to make some changes.

While he had preferred a whole unit to move, the volunteers were mixed. They included many of the new hires, such as Mohammed and Ling Chin, Dave and some current staff, and Frank Eades, the manager of Government Relations. Frank had made it known that he chose to move because he was tired of being stuck in the middle of John and Perry's confrontations. All the volunteers were particularly pleased that no one from the Real Estate unit was moving.

Others in IA were less happy about this email. The request was viewed as another attempt to divide the department and strip them of their power. Earlier in the month, Andrew had been forced to step down as head of IA since he was nearing retirement age, though he continued to work as a senior accountant.

Trevor, a senior accountant in Resources and who had worked in IA for more than ten years, was talking animatedly with Dean.

'This is wrong! Mike is trying to throw his weight around. I don't care how nice the new offices will be and I don't care that there will be new furniture. I won't move offices. We make most of the money for Scottbridge in Sydney. Mike should be putting us all in a bigger building *at the same time*, not splitting us up! It's the principle at stake, Dean. You saw what he did to Andrew. You've got to show him who's the boss!'

These sentiments were echoed at the next Happy Hour. Small groups of people could be heard proclaiming, 'We won't let them do this to us!' and 'We've got to stand united!' Many worried about what was going to happen after the move. They tried to change the volunteers' minds by denigrating the quality of the new offices. Dave wondered how the renovated offices could be any worse than the current ones.

Soon after the move, the Tower staff began complaining that they didn't see the volunteers anymore. While they were physically divided, the volunteers felt that in spirit they were still one department. They returned daily to the Tower staffroom for lunches, to pick up mail, to stop by for a chat and to generally be 'seen'. However, retorts like 'What are *you* doing here?' and 'Why are you using *our* toilets? Don't you have toilets over there?' didn't make them feel welcome. These comments were made in jest, but after a while the volunteers began to pick up each other's mail and were often seen out lunching together at a nearby cafe. Whenever they attended a social function the volunteers were told, 'You don't belong here anymore!' So, the movers had their own parties.

During this time, Dave had his performance review with Dean. It was so different from his other reviews. At the end of his first year at Scottbridge, Dave had been lunching in the staffroom when Andrew literally ran in and out.

'Is everything alright? No problems?' he'd asked Dave. Perplexed, Dave replied in the negative.

'Right, then, your performance review is done', said Andrew. Drop by to sign it.'

Dave's next review at the end of his third year had been with John, who had spent over three hours talking about his own achievements.

Fortunately, Dave's review with Dean seemed more structured. Dean's secretary scheduled a meeting to last for 15 minutes. Dave was to complete the same form from his previous review so that together they could systematically evaluate his performance. Dean praised him for his increase in billable hours and gave him a pay rise. He then turned to his computer, started reading his emails and even typed out a reply to one. Dave had wanted to ask about training and development opportunities but, sensing Dean's disinterest, stopped himself mid-sentence, thanked his boss for the raise, and signed his performance review before leaving.

QUESTIONS

1. Describe the organisational structure and design of Scottbridge's Risk Management division.
2. Analyse the organisational culture in the Internal Audit department when Dave first joined Scottbridge.
3. What are the implications of the demographic shift for the IA culture? If you were Mohammed, would you have attended the Christmas Dinner? Would you have pretended to drink wine, like Dave did?
4. Evaluate Mike's change effort. What are the implications for IA's culture and organisational structure?
5. Compare Dave's three performance reviews. Which would you say was the most effective? Could more be done to improve these performance reviews?

APPENDIX

RESEARCH IN ORGANISATIONAL BEHAVIOUR

Some years back, a friend of one of the authors was excited because he had read about the findings from a research study that finally, once and for all, resolved the question of what it takes to make it to the top in a large corporation. Doubting that there was any simple answer to this question, but not wanting to dampen his enthusiasm, the friend was asked to tell what he had read. The answer, according to the friend, was *participation in university athletics*. You can imagine the scepticism that this response provoked, so the friend was asked to tell more about the study.

The study encompassed 1700 successful senior executives at the 500 largest corporations in the United States. The researchers found that half of these executives had played university-level sports.[1] The friend, who happens to be good with statistics, maintained that since fewer than 2 per cent of all university students participate in inter-university athletics, the probability of this finding occurring by mere chance is less than one in 10 million! He concluded his analysis by suggesting that, based on this research, management students should be encouraged to get into shape and to become a member of one of the university sporting teams.

The friend was somewhat perturbed when it was suggested that his conclusions were likely to be flawed. These executives were all males who attended university in the 1940s and 1950s. Would his advice be meaningful to females in the 21st century? These executives also weren't your typical university students. For the most part, they had attended small, private, elite universities, where a large proportion of the student body participated in inter-university sports. Moreover, maybe the researchers had confused the direction of causality. That is, maybe individuals with the motivation and ability to make it to the top of a large corporation are drawn to competitive activities such as university athletics.

The friend was guilty of misusing research data. Of course, he isn't alone. We are all continually bombarded with reports of experiments that link certain substances to cancer in mice, and with surveys that show changing attitudes towards sex among university students, for example. Many of these studies are carefully designed, with great caution taken to note the implications and limitations of the findings. But some studies are poorly designed, making their conclusions at best suspect and at worst meaningless.

Rather than attempting to make you a researcher, the purpose of this appendix is to increase your awareness as a consumer of behavioural research. A knowledge of research methods will allow you to appreciate more fully the care in data collection that underlies the information and conclusions presented in this text. Moreover, an understanding of research methods will make you a more skilled evaluator of those OB studies you will encounter in business and professional journals. So, an appreciation of behavioural research is important because (1) it is the foundation upon which the theories in this text are built, and (2) it will benefit you in future years when you read reports of research and attempt to assess their value.

PURPOSE OF RESEARCH

Research is concerned with the systematic gathering of information. Its purpose is to help us in our search for the truth. While we will never find ultimate truth—in our case, that would be to know precisely how any person would behave in any organisational context—ongoing research adds to our body of OB knowledge by supporting some theories, contradicting others, and suggesting new theories to replace those that fail to gain support.

RESEARCH TERMINOLOGY

Researchers have their own vocabulary for communicating among themselves and with outsiders. The following briefly defines some of the more popular terms you are likely to encounter in behavioural science studies.[2]

VARIABLE

A *variable* is any general characteristic that can be measured and that changes in either amplitude, intensity, or both. Some examples of OB variables found in this text are job satisfaction, employee productivity, work stress, ability, personality, and group norms.

HYPOTHESIS

A tentative explanation of the relationship between two or more variables is called a *hypothesis*. The friend's statement that participation in university athletics leads to a top executive position in a large corporation is an example of a hypothesis. Until confirmed by empirical research, a hypothesis remains only a tentative explanation.

DEPENDENT VARIABLE

A *dependent variable* is a response that is affected by an independent variable. In terms of the hypothesis, it is the variable that the researcher is interested in explaining. Referring back to our opening example, the dependent variable in the friend's hypothesis was executive success. In organisational behaviour research, the most popular dependent variables are productivity, absenteeism, turnover, job satisfaction and organisational commitment.[3]

INDEPENDENT VARIABLE

An *independent variable* is the presumed cause of some change in the dependent variable. Participating in university athletics was the independent variable in the friend's hypothesis. Popular independent variables studied by OB researchers include intelligence, personality, job satisfaction, experience, motivation, reinforcement patterns, leadership style, reward allocations, selection methods and organisation design.

You may have noticed we said that job satisfaction is frequently used by OB researchers as both a dependent and an independent variable. This isn't an error. It merely reflects that the label given to a variable depends on its place in the hypothesis. In the statement 'Increases in job satisfaction lead to reduced turnover', job satisfaction is an independent variable. However, in the statement 'Increases in money lead to higher job satisfaction', job satisfaction becomes a dependent variable.

MODERATING VARIABLE

A *moderating variable* abates the effect of the independent variable on the dependent variable. It might also be thought of as the contingency variable: if X (independent variable), then *Y* (dependent variable) will occur, but only under conditions *Z* (moderating variable). To translate this into a real-life example, we might say that if we increase the amount of direct supervision in the work area (*X*), then there will be a change in worker productivity (*Y*), but this effect will be moderated by the complexity of the tasks being performed (*Z*).

CAUSALITY

A hypothesis, by definition, implies a relationship. That is, it implies a presumed cause and effect. This direction of cause and effect is called *causality*. Changes in the independent variable are assumed to cause changes in the dependent variable. However, in behavioural research, it is possible to make an incorrect assumption of causality when relationships are found. For example, early behavioural scientists found a relationship between employee satisfaction and productivity. They concluded that a happy employee was a productive employee. Follow-up research has supported the relationship but disconfirmed the direction of the arrow. The evidence more correctly suggests that high productivity leads to satisfaction, rather than the other way around.

CORRELATION COEFFICIENT

It is one thing to know that there is a relationship between two or more variables. It is another to know the *strength* of that relationship. The term *correlation coefficient* is used to indicate that strength, and is expressed as a number between −1.00 (a perfect negative relationship) and +1.00 (a perfect positive correlation).

When two variables vary directly with one another, the correlation will be expressed as a positive number. When they vary inversely—that is, one increases as the other decreases—the correlation will be expressed as a negative number. If the two variables vary independently of each other, we say that the correlation between them is zero.

For example, a researcher might survey a group of employees to determine the satisfaction of each with his or her job. Then, using company absenteeism reports, the researcher could correlate the job satisfaction scores against individual attendance records to determine whether employees who are more satisfied with their jobs have better attendance records than their counterparts who indicated lower job satisfaction. Let's suppose the researcher found a correlation coefficient between satisfaction and attendance of +0.50. Would that be a strong association? There is, unfortunately, no precise numerical cut-off separating strong and weak relationships. A standard statistical test would need to be applied to determine whether or not the relationship was a significant one.

A final point needs to be made before we move on: a correlation coefficient measures only the strength of association between two variables. A high value *doesn't* imply causality. The length of women's skirts and stock market prices, for example, have long been noted to be highly correlated, but one should be careful not to infer that a causal relationship between the two exists. In this instance, the high correlation is more happenstance than predictive.

THEORY

The final term we introduce in this section is *theory*. Theory describes a set of systematically interrelated concepts or hypotheses that purports to explain and predict phenomena. In OB, theories are also frequently referred to as *models*. We use the two terms interchangeably.

There are no shortages of theories in OB. For example, we have theories to describe what motivates people, the most effective leadership styles, the best way to resolve conflicts, and how people acquire power. In some cases, we have half a dozen or more separate theories that purport to explain and predict a given phenomenon. In such cases, is one right and the others wrong? No! They tend to reflect science at work—researchers testing previous theories, modifying them, and, when appropriate, proposing new models that may prove to have higher explanatory and predictive powers. Multiple theories attempting to explain common phenomena merely attest that OB is an active discipline, still growing and evolving.

EVALUATING RESEARCH

As a potential consumer of behavioural research, you should follow the dictum of caveat emptor—let the buyer beware! In evaluating any research study, you need to ask three questions.[4]

Is it valid? Is the study actually measuring what it claims to be measuring? Employers have discarded many psychological tests in recent years because they have not been found to be valid measures of the applicants' ability to successfully do a given job. The validity issue is relevant to all research studies. So, if you find a study that links cohesive work teams with higher productivity, you want to know how each of these variables was measured and whether it is actually measuring what it is supposed to be measuring.

Is it reliable? Reliability refers to consistency of measurement. If you were to have your height measured every day with a wooden yardstick, you would get highly reliable results. On the other hand, if you were measured each day by an elastic tape measure, there would probably be considerable disparity between your height measurements from one day to the next. Your height, of course, doesn't change from day to day. The variability is due to the unreliability of the measuring device. So, if a company asked a group of its employees to complete a reliable job satisfaction questionnaire, and then to repeat the questionnaire six months later, we would expect the results to be very similar—provided nothing changed in the interim that might significantly affect employee satisfaction.

Is it generalisable? Are the results of the research study generalisable to groups of individuals other than those who participated in the original study? Be aware, for example, of the limitations that might exist in research that uses university students as subjects. Are the findings in such studies generalisable to full-time employees in real jobs? Similarly, how generalisable to the overall work population are the results from a study that assesses job stress among ten air traffic control operators at Changi Airport in Singapore, one of the busiest air traffic hubs in the world?

RESEARCH DESIGN

Doing research is an exercise in trade-offs. Richness of information typically comes with reduced generalisability. The more a researcher seeks to control for confounding variables, the less realistic his or her results are likely to be. High precision, generalisability and control almost always translate into higher costs. When researchers make choices about who they will study, where their research will be done, the methods they will use to collect data, and so on, they must make some concessions. Good research designs aren't perfect, but they do carefully reflect the questions being addressed. Keep these facts in mind as we review the strengths and weaknesses of five popular research designs: case studies, field surveys, laboratory experiments, field experiments and aggregate quantitative reviews.

CASE STUDY

You pick up a copy of Soichiro Honda's autobiography. In it he describes his impoverished childhood; his decisions to open a small garage, to assemble motorcycles and eventually to build automobiles; and how this led to the creation of one of the largest and most successful corporations in the world. Or you are in a business class and the lecturer distributes a 50-page handout covering two companies: Dell Computer and Apple Computer. The handout details the two firms' histories, describes their product lines, production facilities, management philosophies and marketing strategies, and includes copies of their recent balance sheets and profit and loss statements. The lecturer asks the class members to read the handout, analyse the data and determine why Dell has been more successful in recent years than Apple.

Soichiro Honda's autobiography and the Dell and Apple handouts are case studies. Drawn from real-life situations, case studies present an in-depth analysis of one setting. They are thorough descriptions, rich in details about an individual, a group or an organisation. The primary source of information in case studies is obtained through observation, occasionally backed up by interviews and a review of records and documents.

Case studies have their drawbacks. They are open to the perceptual bias and subjective interpretations of the observer. The reader of a case is captive to what the observer/case writer chooses to include and exclude. Cases also trade off generalisability for depth of information and richness of detail. Since it's always dangerous to generalise from a sample of one, case studies make it difficult to prove or reject a hypothesis. On the other hand, you can't ignore the in-depth analysis that cases often provide. They are an excellent device for initial exploratory research and for evaluating real-life problems in organisations.

FIELD SURVEY

A lengthy questionnaire was created to assess the use of ethics policies, formal ethics structures, formalised activities such as ethics training, and executive involvement in ethics programs among billion-dollar corporations. The public affairs or corporate communications office of all *Fortune* 500 industrial firms and 500 service corporations in the United States were contacted to get the name and address of the 'officer most responsible for dealing with ethics and conduct issues' in each firm. The questionnaire, with a cover letter explaining the nature of the study, was mailed to these 1000 officers. Of the total, 254 returned a completed questionnaire, for a response rate of just above 25 per cent. The results of the survey found, among other things, that 77 per cent had formal codes of ethics and 54 per cent had a single officer specifically assigned to deal with ethics and conduct issues.[5]

The preceding study illustrates a typical field survey. A sample of respondents (in this case, 1000 corporate officers in the largest US publicly held corporations) was selected to represent a larger group that was under examination (billion-dollar US business firms). The respondents were then surveyed using a questionnaire or interviewed to collect data on particular characteristics (the content and structure of ethics programs and practices) of interest to the researchers. The standardisation of response items allows for data to be easily quantified, analysed and summarised, and for the researchers to make inferences from the representative sample about the larger population.

The field survey provides economies for doing research. It is less costly to sample a population than to obtain data from every member of that population. Moreover, as the ethics study illustrates, field surveys provide an efficient way to find out how people feel about issues or how they say they behave. These data can then be easily quantified. But the field survey has a number of potential weaknesses.

First, mailed questionnaires rarely obtain 100 per cent returns. Low response rates call into question whether conclusions based on respondents' answers are generalisable to non-respondents. Second, the format is better at tapping respondents' attitudes and perceptions than behaviours. Third, responses can suffer from social desirability—that is, people saying what they think the researcher wants to hear. Fourth, since field surveys are designed to focus on specific issues, they are a relatively poor means of acquiring depth of information. Finally, the quality of the generalisations is largely a factor of the population chosen. Responses from executives at *Fortune* 500 firms, for example, tell us nothing about small- or medium-sized firms or not-for-profit organisations. In summary, even a well-designed field survey trades off depth of information for breadth, generalisability and economic efficiencies.

LABORATORY EXPERIMENT

The following study is a classic example of the laboratory experiment. A researcher, Stanley Milgram, wondered how far individuals would go in following commands. If subjects were placed in the role of a teacher in a learning experiment and told by an experimenter to administer a shock to a learner each time that learner made a mistake, would the subjects follow the commands of the experimenter? Would their willingness to comply decrease as the intensity of the shock was increased?

To test these hypotheses, Milgram hired a set of subjects. Each was led to believe that the experiment was to investigate the effect of punishment on memory. Their job was to act as teachers and administer punishment whenever the learner made a mistake on the learning test.

Punishment was administered by an electric shock. The subjects sat in front of a shock generator with 30 levels of shock—beginning at zero and progressing in 15-volt increments to a high of 450 volts. The demarcations of these positions ranged from 'Slight Shock' at 15 volts to 'Danger: Severe Shock' at 450 volts. To increase the realism of the experiment, the subjects received a sample shock of 45 volts and saw the learner—a pleasant, mild-mannered man about 50 years old—strapped into an 'electric chair' in an adjacent room. Of course, unbeknown to the subjects, the learner was an actor, and the electric shocks were phoney.

Taking their seat in front of the shock generator, the subjects were directed to begin at the lowest shock level and to increase the shock intensity to the next level each time the learner made a mistake or failed to respond.

When the test began, the shock intensity rose rapidly because the learner made many errors. The subject got verbal feedback from the learner: at 75 volts, the learner began to grunt and moan; at 150 volts, he demanded to be released from the experiment; at 180 volts, he cried out that he could no longer stand the pain; and at 300 volts, he insisted that he be let out, yelled about his heart condition, screamed, and then failed to respond to further questions.

Most subjects protested and, fearful that they might kill the learner if the increased shocks were to bring on a heart attack, insisted they couldn't go on with their job. Hesitations or protests by the subject were met by the experimenter's statement, 'You have no choice, you must go on! Your job is to punish the learner's mistakes.' Of course, the subjects did have a choice. All they had to do was stand up and walk out.

The majority of the subjects dissented. But dissension isn't synonymous with disobedience. Sixty-two per cent of the subjects increased the shock level to the maximum of 450 volts. The average level of shock administered by the remaining 38 per cent was nearly 370 volts.[6]

In a laboratory experiment such as that conducted by Milgram, an artificial environment is created by the researcher. Then the researcher manipulates an independent variable under controlled conditions. Finally, since all other things are held equal, the researcher is able to conclude that any change in the dependent variable is due to the manipulation or change imposed on the independent variable. Note that, because of the controlled conditions, the researcher is able to imply causation between the independent and dependent variables.

The laboratory experiment trades off realism and generalisability for precision and control. It provides a high degree of control over variables and precise measurement of those variables. But findings from laboratory studies are often difficult to generalise to the real world of work. This is because the artificial laboratory rarely duplicates the intricacies and nuances of real organisations. Additionally, many laboratory experiments deal with phenomena that cannot be reproduced or applied to real-life situations.

FIELD EXPERIMENT

The following is an example of a field experiment. The management of a large company is interested in determining the impact that a four-day work week would have on employee absenteeism. To be more specific, management wants to know if employees working four ten-hour days have lower absence rates than similar employees working the traditional five-day week of eight hours each day. Because the company is large, it has a number of manufacturing facilities that employ essentially similar workforces. Two of these are chosen for the experiment, both located in the greater Sydney area. Obviously, it wouldn't be appropriate to compare two similar-sized factories if one is in rural Tasmania and the other is in urban Singapore, because factors such as national culture, transportation and weather might be more likely to explain any differences found than changes in the number of days worked per week.

In one factory, the experiment was put into place—employees began the four-day week. At the other factory, which became the control group, no changes were made in the employees' five-day week. Absence data were gathered from the company's records at both locations for a period of 18 months. This extended time period lessened the possibility that any results would be distorted by the mere novelty of changes being implemented in the experimental plant. After 18 months, management found that absenteeism had dropped by 40 per cent at the experimental factory, and by only 6 per cent in the control factory. Because of the design of this study, management believed that the larger drop in absences at the experimental factory was due to the introduction of the compressed work week.

The field experiment is similar to the laboratory experiment, except it is conducted in a real organisation. The natural setting is more realistic than the laboratory setting, and this enhances validity but hinders control. Additionally, unless control groups are maintained, there can be a loss of control if extraneous forces intervene—for example, an employee strike, a major layoff or a corporate restructuring. Maybe the greatest concern with field studies has to do with organisational selection bias. Not all organisations are going to allow outside researchers to come in and study their employees and operations. This is especially true of organisations that have serious problems. Therefore, since most published studies in OB are done by outside researchers, the selection bias might work towards publication of studies conducted almost exclusively at successful and well-managed organisations.

Our general conclusion is that, of the four research designs we have discussed, the field experiment typically provides the most valid and generalisable findings and, except for its high cost, trades off the least to get the most.[7]

AGGREGATE QUANTITATIVE REVIEWS

What is the overall effect of organisational behaviour modification (OB Mod) on task performance? There have been a number of field experiments that have sought to throw light on this question. Unfortunately, the large range of effect from these various studies makes it hard to generalise.

To try to reconcile these diverse findings, two researchers reviewed all the empirical studies they could find on the impact of OB Mod on task performance over a 20-year period.[8] After discarding reports that had inadequate information, non-quantitative data, or didn't meet all the conditions associated with the principles of behavioural modification, the researchers narrowed their set to 19 studies that included data on 2818 individuals. Using an aggregating technique called meta-analysis, the researchers were able to synthesise the studies quantitatively and conclude that the average person's task performance will rise from the 50th percentile to the 67th percentile after an OB Mod intervention.

The OB Mod–task performance review done by these researchers illustrates the use of meta-analysis, a quantitative form of literature review that enables researchers to look at validity findings from a comprehensive set of individual studies, and then apply a formula to them to determine if they consistently produced similar results.[9] If results prove to be consistent, researchers may conclude more confidently that validity is generalisable. Meta-analysis is a means for overcoming the potentially imprecise interpretations of qualitative reviews and to synthesise variations in quantitative studies. Additionally, the technique enables researchers to identify potential moderating variables between an independent and a dependent variable.

In the past 20 years, there has been a surge in the popularity of this research method. Why? It appears to offer a more objective means for doing traditional literature reviews. While the use of meta-analysis requires researchers to make a number of judgment calls, which can introduce a considerable amount of subjectivity into the process, there is no arguing that meta-analysis reviews have now become widespread in the OB literature.

ETHICS IN RESEARCH

Researchers aren't always tactful or candid with subjects when they do their studies. For example, questions in field surveys may be perceived as embarrassing by respondents or as an invasion of privacy. Also, researchers in laboratory studies have been known to deceive participants as to the true purpose of their experiment 'because they felt deception was necessary to get honest responses'.[10]

The 'learning experiments' conducted by Stanley Milgram were widely criticised by psychologists on ethical grounds. He lied to subjects, telling them his study was investigating learning, when, in fact, he was concerned with obedience. The shock machine he used was a fake. Even the 'learner' was an accomplice of Milgram's who had been trained to act as if he were hurt and in pain.

Professional associations such as the Australian Psychological Society, the Academy of Management and the National Health & Medical Research Council of Australia have published formal guidelines for the conduct of research. Yet, the ethical debate continues. On one side are those who argue that strict ethical controls can damage the scientific validity of an experiment and cripple future research. Deception, for example, is often necessary to avoid contaminating results. Moreover, proponents of minimising ethical controls note that few subjects have been appreciably harmed by deceptive experiments. Even in Milgram's highly manipulative experiment, only 1.3 per cent of the subjects reported negative feelings about their experience. The other side of this debate focuses on the rights of participants. Those favouring strict ethical controls argue that no procedure should ever be emotionally or physically distressing to subjects, and that, as professionals, researchers are obliged to be completely honest with their subjects and to protect the subjects' privacy at all costs.

Now, let's take a look at a sampling of ethical questions relating to research. Do you think Milgram's experiment was unethical? Would you judge it unethical for a company to anonymously survey its employees with mail questionnaires on their intentions to quit their present job? Would your answer be any different if the company coded the survey responses to identify those who didn't reply so that they could send them follow-up questionnaires? Would it be unethical for management to hide a video camera on the production floor to study group interaction patterns (with the goal of using the data to design more effective work teams) without first telling employees that they were subjects of research?

SUMMARY

The subject of organisational behaviour is composed of a large number of theories that are research-based. Research studies, when cumulatively integrated, become theories, and theories are proposed and followed by research studies designed to validate them. The concepts that make up OB, therefore, are only as valid as the research that supports them.

The topics and issues in this text are, for the most part, largely derived from research. They represent the result of systematic information gathering, rather than merely hunch, intuition or opinion. This doesn't mean, of course, that we have all the answers to OB issues. Many require far more corroborating evidence. The generalisability of others is limited by the research methods used. But new information is being created and published at an accelerated rate. To keep up with the latest findings, we strongly encourage you to regularly review the latest research in organisational behaviour. The more academic work can be found in journals such as the *Academy of Management Journal*, *Academy of Management Review*, *Administrative Science Quarterly*, *Human Relations*, *Journal of Applied Psychology*, *Journal of Management*, *The Asia-Pacific Journal of Human Resources*, the *International Journal of Organisational Behaviour* and *Leadership Quarterly*. For more practical interpretations of OB research findings, you may want to read the *Academy of Management Executive*, *California Management Review*, *Harvard Business Review*, *Organizational Dynamics* and *Sloan Management Review*.

ENDNOTES

1. J. A. Byrne, 'Executive Sweat', *Forbes*, 20 May 1985, pp. 198–200.

2. This discussion is based on material presented in E. Stone, *Research Methods in Organizational Behavior* (Santa Monica, CA: Goodyear, 1978).

3. B. M. Staw and G. R. Oldham, 'Reconsidering Our Dependent Variables: A Critique and Empirical Study', *Academy of Management Journal*, December 1978, pp. 539–59; and B. M. Staw, 'Organizational Behavior: A Review and Reformulation of the Field's Outcome Variables', in M. R. Rosenzweig and L. W. Porter (eds), *Annual Review of Psychology*, vol. 35 (Palo Alto, CA: Annual Reviews, Inc., 1984), pp. 627–66.

4. R. S. Blackburn, 'Experimental Design in Organizational Settings', in J. W. Lorsch (ed.), *Handbook of Organizational Behavior* (Englewood Cliffs, NJ: Prentice Hall, 1987), pp. 127–28.

5. G. R. Weaver, L. K. Trevino and P. L. Cochran, 'Corporate Ethics Practices in the Mid-1990's: An Empirical Study of the Fortune 1000', *Journal of Business Ethics*, February 1999, pp. 283–94.

6. S. Milgram, *Obedience to Authority* (New York: Harper & Row, 1974). For a critique of this research, see T. Blass, 'Understanding Behavior in the Milgram Obedience Experiment: The Role of Personality, Situations, and Their Interactions', *Journal of Personality and Social Psychology*, March 1991, pp. 398–413.

7. See, for example, W. N. Kaghan, A. L. Strauss, S. R. Barley, M. Y. Brannen and R. J. Thomas, 'The Practice and Uses of Field Research in the 21st Century Organization', *Journal of Management Inquiry*, March 1999, pp. 67–81.

8. A. D. Stajkovic and F. Luthans, 'A Meta-Analysis of the Effects of Organizational Behavior Modification on Task Performance, 1975–1995', *Academy of Management Journal*, October 1997, pp. 1122–49.

9. See, for example, R. A. Guzzo, S. E. Jackson and R. A. Katzell, 'Meta-Analysis Analysis', in L. L. Cummings and B. M. Staw (eds.), *Research in Organizational Behavior*, vol. 9 (Greenwich, CT: JAI Press, 1987), pp. 407–42; A. L. Beaman, 'An Empirical Comparison of Meta-Analytic and Traditional Reviews', *Personality and Social Psychology Bulletin*, June 1991, pp. 252–57; K. Zakzanis, 'The Reliability of Meta Analytic Review', *Psychological Reports*, August 1998, pp. 215–22; and F. L. Schmidt and J. E. Hunter, 'Comparison of Three Meta-Analysis Methods Revisited: An Analysis of Johnson, Mullen, and Salas (1995)', *Journal of Applied Psychology*, February 1999, pp. 144–48.

10. For more on ethical issues in research, see T. L. Beauchamp, R. R. Faden, R. J. Wallace, Jr and L. Walters (eds), *Ethical Issues in Social Science Research* (Baltimore, MD: Johns Hopkins University Press, 1982); and D. Baumrind, 'Research Using Intentional Deception', *American Psychologist*, February 1985, pp. 165–74.

GLOSSARY

Note: The number in brackets denotes the chapter in which the term appears.

ability (2) An individual's capacity to perform the various tasks in a job.

absenteeism (1) The failure to report to work.

accommodating (15) The willingness of one party in a conflict to place the opponent's interests above his or her own.

action research (19) A change process based on systematic collection of data and then selection of a change action based on what the analysed data indicate.

adjourning stage (9) The final stage in group development for temporary groups, characterised by concern with wrapping up activities rather than task performance.

affect (8) A broad range of feelings that people experience.

affect intensity (8) Individual differences in the strength with which individuals experience their emotions.

affective commitment (3) An emotional attachment to the organisation and a belief in its values.

affective component of an attitude (3) The emotional or feeling segment of an attitude.

affective events theory (8) A model which suggests that workplace events cause emotional reactions on the part of employees which then influence workplace attitudes and behaviours.

agreeableness (4) A personality dimension that describes someone who is good-natured, cooperative and trusting.

anchoring bias (5) A tendency to fixate on initial information, and to then fail to adjust adequately for subsequent information.

anthropology (1) The study of societies to learn about human beings and their activities.

appreciative inquiry (19) Seeking to identify the unique qualities and special strengths of an organisation, which can

then be built on to improve performance.

arbitrator (15) A third party to a negotiation who has the authority to dictate an agreement.

attitude surveys (3) Eliciting responses from employees through questionnaires on how they feel about their jobs, work groups, supervisors and the organisation.

attitudes (3) Evaluative statements or judgments concerning objects, people or events.

attribution theory (5) An attempt when individuals observe behaviour to determine whether it is internally or externally caused.

attribution theory of leadership (13) The idea that leadership is merely an attribution that people make about other individuals.

authentic leaders (13) Leaders who know who they are, know what they believe in and value, and act on those values and beliefs openly and candidly. Their followers would consider them to be ethical people.

authority (16) The rights inherent in a managerial position to give orders and to expect the orders to be obeyed.

autonomy (7) The degree to which the job provides substantial freedom and discretion to the individual in scheduling the work and in determining the procedures to be used in carrying it out.

availability bias (5) The tendency for people to base their judgments on information that is readily available to them.

avoiding (15) The desire to withdraw from or suppress a conflict.

BATNA (15) The best alternative to a negotiated agreement; the lowest acceptable value to an individual for a negotiated agreement.

behavioural component of an attitude (3) An intention to behave in a certain way towards someone or something.

behavioural theories of leadership (12) Theories proposing that specific

behaviours differentiate leaders from non-leaders.

behaviourally anchored rating scales (BARS) (18) Scales that combine major elements from the critical incident and graphic rating scale approaches: the appraiser rates the employees based on items along a continuum but the points are examples of actual behaviour on the given job, rather than general descriptions of traits.

behaviourism (2) A theory which argues that behaviour follows stimuli in a relatively unthinking manner.

biographical characteristics (2) Personal characteristics—such as age, gender, marital status, ethnicity and race, and length of service—that are objective and easily obtained from personnel records.

bonus (7) Pay program that rewards employees for recent performance rather than historical performance.

boundaryless organisation (16) An organisation that seeks to eliminate the chain of command, have limitless spans of control, and replace departments with empowered teams.

bounded rationality (5) Making decisions by constructing simplified models that extract the essential features from problems without capturing all their complexity.

brainstorming (9) An idea-generation process that specifically encourages any and all alternatives, while withholding any criticism of those alternatives.

bureaucracy (16) A structure with highly routine operating tasks achieved through specialisation, very formalised rules and regulations, tasks that are grouped into functional departments, centralised authority, narrow spans of control, and decision making that follows the chain of command.

centralisation (16) The degree to which decision making is concentrated at a single point in the organisation.

chain of command (16) The unbroken line of authority that extends from the top of the organisation to the lowest echelon and clarifies who reports to whom.

change (19) Making things different.

change agents (19) Persons who act as catalysts and assume the responsibility for managing change activities.

channel richness (11) The amount of information that can be transmitted during a communication episode.

charismatic leadership theory (13) Followers make attributions of heroic or extraordinary leadership abilities when they observe certain behaviours.

classical conditioning (2) A type of conditioning in which an individual responds to some stimulus that wouldn't ordinarily produce such a response.

coalition (14) An informal group bound together by the active pursuit of a single issue.

coercive power (14) A power base dependent on fear.

cognitive component of an attitude (3) The opinion or belief segment of an attitude.

cognitive dissonance (3) Any incompatibility between two or more attitudes, or between behaviour and attitudes.

cognitive evaluation theory (6) A theory stating that allocating extrinsic rewards for behaviour that had been previously intrinsically rewarding tends to decrease the overall level of motivation.

cognitive resource theory (12) A theory of leadership which states that stress unfavourably affects a situation, and that intelligence and experience can lessen the influence of stress on the leader.

cohesiveness (9) Degree to which group members are attracted to each other and are motivated to stay in the group.

cohorts (10) Individuals who, as part of a group, hold a common attribute.

collaborating (15) A situation in which the parties to a conflict each desire to satisfy fully the concerns of all parties.

collectivism (4) A national culture attribute that describes a tight social framework in which people expect others in groups of which they are a part to look after them and protect them.

command group (9) A group composed of the individuals who report directly to a given manager.

communication (11) The transference and understanding of meaning.

communication apprehension (11) Undue tension and anxiety about oral communication, written communication, or both.

communication process (11) The steps between a source and a receiver that result in the transference and understanding of meaning.

competing (15) A desire to satisfy one's interests, regardless of the impact on the other party to the conflict.

compromising (15) A situation in which each party to a conflict is willing to give up something.

conceptual skills (1) The mental ability to analyse and diagnose complex situations.

conciliator (15) A trusted third party who provides an informal communication link between the negotiator and the opponent.

confirmation bias (5) The tendency to seek out information that reaffirms past choices and to discount information that contradicts past judgments.

conflict (15) A process that begins when one party perceives that another party has negatively affected, or is about to negatively affect, something that the first party cares about.

conflict management (15) The use of resolution and stimulation techniques to achieve the desired level of conflict.

conflict process (15) Process with five stages: potential opposition or incompatibility, cognition and personalisation, intentions, behaviour and outcomes.

conformity (9) Adjusting one's behaviour to align with the norms of the group.

conscientiousness (4) A personality dimension that describes someone who is responsible, dependable, persistent and organised.

consideration (12) The extent to which a leader is likely to have job relationships characterised by mutual trust, respect for subordinates' ideas and regard for their feelings.

consultant (15) An impartial third party, skilled in conflict management, who attempts to facilitate creative problem solving through communication and analysis.

contingency variables (1) Situational factors: variables that moderate the relationship between two or more other variables and improve the correlation.

continuance commitment (3) The perceived economic value of remaining with an organisation compared to leaving it.

continuous reinforcement (2) Reinforcing a desired behaviour each time it is demonstrated.

contrast effects (5) Evaluation of a person's characteristics is affected by comparisons with other people recently encountered who rank higher or lower on the same characteristics.

controlling (1) Monitoring activities to ensure they are being accomplished as planned and correcting any significant deviations.

core self-evaluation (4) Degree to which individuals like or dislike themselves, whether they see themselves as capable and effective, and whether they feel they are in control of their environment or powerless over their environment.

core values (17) The primary or dominant values that are accepted throughout the organisation.

cost-minimisation strategy (16) A strategy that emphasises tight cost controls, avoidance of unnecessary innovation or marketing expenses, and price cutting.

creativity (5) The ability to produce novel and useful ideas.

critical incidents (18) Evaluating the behaviours that are key in making the difference between executing a job effectively and executing it ineffectively.

cross-functional teams (10) Employees from about the same hierarchical level, but from different work areas, who come together to accomplish a task.

decisions (5) The choices made from among two or more alternatives.

deep acting (8) Trying to modify one's true inner feelings based on display rules.

defensive behaviours (14) Reactive and protective behaviours to avoid action, blame or change.

demands (18) Responsibilities, pressures, obligations and even uncertainties that individuals face in the workplace.

departmentalisation (16) The basis by which jobs are grouped together.

dependency (14) *B*'s relationship to *A* when *A* possesses something that *B* requires.

dependent variable (1) A response that is affected by an independent variable.

deterrence-based trust (13) Trust based on fear of reprisal if the trust is violated.

development-oriented leader (12) A leader who values experimentation, seeks new ideas, and generates and implements change.

deviant workplace behaviour (1) Antisocial actions by organisational members that intentionally violate established norms and that result in negative consequences for the organisation, its members, or both.

deviant workplace behaviour (9) Voluntary behaviour that violates significant organisational norms and, in doing so, threatens the well-being of the organisation or its members.

displayed emotions (8) Emotions that are organisationally appropriate in a given job.

distributive bargaining (15) Negotiation that seeks to divide up a fixed amount of resources; a win–lose situation.

distributive justice (6) Perceived fairness of the amount and allocation of rewards among individuals.

dominant culture (17) A culture that expresses the core values that are shared by a majority of the organisation's members.

double-loop learning (19) Correcting errors by modifying the organisation's objectives, policies and standard routines.

driving forces (19) Forces that direct behaviour away from the status quo.

dysfunctional conflict (15) Conflict that hinders group performance.

effectiveness (1) Achievement of goals.

efficiency (1) The ratio of effective output to the input required to achieve it.

electronic meeting (9) A meeting in which members interact on computers, allowing for anonymity of comments and aggregation of votes.

emotional contagion (8) The process by which people's emotions are caused by the emotions of others.

emotional dissonance (8) Inconsistencies among the emotions we feel and the emotions we display.

emotional intelligence (EI) (8) The ability to detect and to manage emotional cues and information.

emotional labour (8) A situation in which an employee expresses organisationally desired emotions during interpersonal transactions at work.

emotional stability (4) A personality dimension that characterises someone as calm, self-confident, secure (positive) versus nervous, depressed and insecure (negative).

emotions (8) Intense feelings that are directed at someone or something.

employee engagement (3) An individual's involvement with, satisfaction with, and enthusiasm for the work they do.

employee involvement (7) A participative process that uses the input of employees and is intended to increase employee commitment to the organisation's success.

employee share ownership plan (ESOP) (7) Company-established benefit plan in which employees acquire shares, often at below-market prices, as part of their benefits.

employee-oriented leader (12) Emphasising interpersonal relations; taking a personal interest in the needs of employees, and accepting individual differences among members.

empowering employees (1) Putting employees in charge of what they do.

encounter stage (17) The stage in the socialisation process in which a new employee sees what the organisation is really like and confronts the possibility that expectations and reality may diverge.

environment (16) Institutions or forces outside the organisation that potentially affect the organisation's performance.

equity theory (6) A theory that individuals compare their job inputs and outcomes with those of others and then respond to eliminate any inequities.

ERG theory (6) A theory that posits three groups of core needs: existence, relatedness and growth.

escalation of commitment (5) An increased commitment to a previous decision in spite of negative information.

ethical dilemmas (1) Situations in which individuals are required to define right and wrong conduct.

ethnicity (2) The grouping of people recognised as unique on the basis of their speech, history, origins, culture or other unique characteristics.

evolutionary psychology (8) An area of inquiry that argues that we must experience the emotions that we do because they serve a purpose.

exit (3) Dissatisfaction expressed through behaviour directed towards leaving the organisation.

expectancy theory (6) The strength of a tendency to act in a certain way depends on the strength of an expectation that the act will be followed by a given outcome, and on the attractiveness of that outcome to the individual.

expert power (14) Influence based on special skills or knowledge.

externals (4) Individuals who believe that what happens to them is controlled by outside forces such as luck or chance.

extraversion (4) A personality dimension describing someone who is sociable, gregarious and assertive.

feedback (7) The degree to which carrying out the work activities required by the job results in the individual obtaining direct and clear information about the effectiveness of his or her performance.

felt conflict (15) Emotional involvement in a conflict creating anxiety, tension, frustration or hostility.

felt emotions (8) An individual's actual emotions.

femininity (4) A national culture attribute that has little differentiation between male and female roles, where women are treated as the equals of men in all aspects of the society.

Fiedler contingency model (12) The theory that effective groups depend on a proper match between a leader's style of interacting with subordinates and the degree to which the situation gives control and influence to the leader.

filtering (11) A sender's manipulation of information so that it will be seen more favourably by the receiver.

five-stage group-development model (9) The five distinct stages groups go through: forming, storming, norming, performing and adjourning.

fixed pie (15) The belief that there is only a set amount of goods or services to be divvied up between the parties.

fixed-interval schedule (2) Spacing rewards at uniform time intervals.

fixed-ratio schedule (2) Initiating rewards after a fixed or constant number of responses.

flexible benefits (7) A benefits plan that allows each employee to put together a benefit package individually tailored to his or her own needs and situation.

flexitime (7) A scheme of flexible work hours.

formal channels (11) Communication channels established by an organisation to transmit messages related to the professional activities of members.

formal group (9) A designated work group defined by the organisation's structure.

formalisation (16) The degree to which jobs within the organisation are standardised.

forming stage (9) The first stage in group development, characterised by much uncertainty.

framing (13) A way to use language to manage meaning.

friendship group (9) Those brought together because they share one or more common characteristics.

functional conflict (15) Conflict that supports the goals of the group and improves its performance.

fundamental attribution error (5) The tendency to underestimate the influence of external factors and overestimate the influence of internal factors when making judgments about the behaviour of others.

gainsharing (7) A formula-based group incentive plan.

goal-setting theory (6) The theory that specific and difficult goals, with feedback, lead to higher performance.

grapevine (11) The organisation's informal communication network.

graphic rating scales (18) An evaluation method in which the evaluator rates performance factors on an incremental scale.

group (9) Two or more individuals, interacting and interdependent, who have come together to achieve particular objectives.

group demography (10) The degree to which members of a group share a common demographic attribute, such as age, sex, race, educational level or length of service in an organisation, and the impact of this attribute on turnover.

group order ranking (18) An evaluation method that places employees into a particular classification, such as quartiles.

groupshift (9) A change in decision risk between the group's decision and the individual decision that members within the group would make; can be towards either conservatism or greater risk.

groupthink (9) Phenomenon in which the norm for consensus overrides the realistic appraisal of alternative courses of action.

halo effect (5) Drawing a general impression about an individual on the basis of a single characteristic.

hierarchy of needs theory (6) A hierarchy of five needs—physiological, safety, social, esteem and self-actualisation—exists such that as each need is substantially satisfied, the next need becomes dominant.

high-context cultures (11) Cultures that rely heavily on non-verbal and subtle situational cues in communication.

higher-order needs (6) Needs that are satisfied internally; social, esteem and self-actualisation needs.

hindsight bias (5) The tendency for us to believe falsely that we would have accurately predicted the outcome of an event, after that outcome is actually known.

human relations view of conflict (15) The belief that conflict is a natural and inevitable outcome in any group.

human skills (1) The ability to work with, understand and motivate other people, both individually and in groups.

hygiene factors (6) Factors—such as company policy and administration, supervision and salary—that, when adequate in a job, placate workers. When these factors are adequate, people won't be dissatisfied.

idea champions (19) Individuals who take an innovation and actively and enthusiastically promote the idea, build support, overcome resistance, and ensure that the idea is implemented.

identification-based trust (13) Trust based on a mutual understanding of each other's intentions and appreciation of the other's wants and desires.

illegitimate political behaviour (14) Extreme political behaviour that violates the implied rules of the game.

illusory correlation (8) The tendency of people to associate two events when in reality there is no connection.

imitation strategy (16) A strategy that seeks to move into new products or new markets only after their viability has already been proven.

implicit models of organisational structure (16) Perceptions that people hold regarding structural variables formed by observing things around them in an unscientific fashion.

impression management (14) The process by which individuals attempt to control the impression others form of them.

independent variable (1) The presumed cause of some change in the dependent variable.

individual ranking (18) An evaluation method that rank-orders employees from best to worst.

individualism (4) A national culture attribute describing the degree to which people prefer to act as individuals rather than as members of groups.

informal channels (11) Communication channels that are created spontaneously and that emerge as responses to individual choices.

informal group (9) A group that is neither formally structured nor organisationally determined; appears in response to the need for social contact.

information overload (11) A condition in which information inflow exceeds an individual's processing capacity.

initiating structure (12) The extent to which a leader is likely to define and structure his or her role and those of subordinates in the search for goal attainment.

innovation (19) A new idea applied to initiating or improving a product, process or service.

innovation strategy (16) A strategy that emphasises the introduction of major new products and services.

institutionalisation (17) A condition that occurs when an organisation takes on a life of its own, apart from any of its members, and acquires immortality.

instrumental values (4) Preferable modes of behaviour or means of achieving one's terminal values.

integrative bargaining (15) Negotiation that seeks one or more settlements that can create a win–win solution.

intellectual abilities (2) The capacity to do mental activities such as thinking, reasoning and problem solving.

intentions (15) Decisions to act in a given way.

interacting groups (9) Typical groups, in which members interact with each other face-to-face.

interactional justice (6) Perceived degree to which an individual is treated with dignity, concern and respect.

interactionist view of conflict (15) The belief that conflict is not only a positive force in a group but that it is also an absolute necessity for a group to perform effectively.

interest group (9) Those working together to attain a specific objective with which each is concerned.

intergroup development (19) OD efforts to change the attitudes, stereotypes and perceptions that groups have of each other.

intermittent reinforcement (2) Reinforcing a desired behaviour often enough to make the behaviour worth repeating but not every time it is demonstrated.

internals (4) Individuals who believe that they control what happens to them.

intranet (11) An IP network belonging to an organisation, usually a corporation, and accessible only to organisation members, employees, etc., or people authorised by them.

intuition (1) A feeling not necessarily supported by research.

intuitive decision making (5) An unconscious process created out of distilled experience.

job characteristics model (JCM) (7) A model that proposes that any job can be described in terms of five core job dimensions: skill variety, task identity, task significance, autonomy and feedback.

job design (7) The way the elements in a job are organised.

job enlargement (7) Increasing the number and variety of tasks that an individual performs results in jobs with more diversity.

job enrichment (7) The vertical expansion of jobs, increasing the degree to which the employee controls the planning, execution and evaluation of the work.

job involvement (3) The degree to which a person identifies with a job, actively participates in it and considers performance important to self-worth.

job rotation (7) The periodic shifting of an employee from one task to another.

job satisfaction (1) An individual's general attitude towards his or her job.

job satisfaction (3) A positive feeling about one's job resulting from an evaluation of its characteristics.

job sharing (7) An arrangement that allows two or more individuals to split a traditional full-time (40-hour-per-week) job.

knowledge management (KM) (11) The process of organising and distributing an organisation's collective wisdom so that the right information gets to the right people at the right time.

knowledge-based trust (13) Trust based on behavioural predictability that comes from a history of interaction.

leader–member exchange (LMX) theory (12) The creation by leaders of in-groups and out-groups; subordinates with in-group status will have higher performance ratings, less turnover and greater job satisfaction.

leader–member relations (12) The degree of confidence, trust and respect subordinates have in their leader.

leader-participation model (12) A leadership theory that provides a set of rules to determine the form and amount of participative decision making in different situations.

leadership (12) The ability to influence a group towards the achievement of a vision or set of goals.

leading (1) A function that includes motivating employees, directing others, selecting the most effective communication channels and resolving conflicts.

learning (2) Any relatively permanent change in behaviour that occurs as a result of experience.

learning organisation (19) An organisation that has developed the continuous capacity to adapt and change.

least preferred co-worker (LPC) questionnaire (12) An instrument that purports to measure whether a person is task- or relationship-oriented.

legitimate political behaviour (14) Normal, everyday politics.

legitimate power (14) The power a person receives as a result of his or her position in the formal hierarchy of an organisation.

level-5 leaders (13) Leaders who are fiercely ambitious and driven, but whose ambition is directed towards their company rather than themselves.

locus of control (4) The degree to which people believe that they are masters of their own fate.

long-term orientation (4) A national culture attribute that emphasises the future, thrift and persistence.

low-context cultures (11) Cultures that rely heavily on words to convey meaning in communication.

lower-order needs (6) Needs that are satisfied externally; physiological and safety needs.

loyalty (3) Dissatisfaction expressed by passively waiting for conditions to improve.

McClelland's theory of needs (6) A theory stating that achievement, power and affiliation are three important needs that help to explain motivation.

Machiavellianism (4) Degree to which an individual is pragmatic, maintains emotional distance, and believes that ends can justify means.

management by objectives (MBO) (6) A program that encompasses specific goals, participatively set, for an explicit time period, with feedback on goal progress.

managerial grid (12) A nine-by-nine matrix outlining 81 different leadership styles.

managers (1) Individuals who achieve goals through other people.

masculinity (4) A national culture attribute describing the extent to which the culture favours traditional masculine work roles of achievement, power and control. Societal values are characterised by assertiveness and materialism.

matrix structure (16) A structure that creates dual lines of authority and combines functional and product departmentalisation.

mechanistic model (16) A structure characterised by extensive departmentalisation, high formalisation, a limited information network, and centralisation.

mediator (15) A neutral third party who facilitates a negotiated solution by using reasoning, persuasion and suggestions for alternatives.

mentor (13) A senior employee who sponsors and supports a less-experienced employee.

merit-based pay plan (7) A pay plan based on performance appraisal ratings.

metamorphosis stage (17) The stage in the socialisation process in which a new employee changes and adjusts to the job, work group and organisation.

model (1) An abstraction of reality. A simplified representation of some real-world phenomenon.

moods (8) Feelings that tend to be less intense than emotions and that lack a contextual stimulus.

motivating potential score (MPS) (7) A predictive index suggesting the motivating potential in a job.

motivation (6) The processes that account for an individual's intensity, direction and persistence of effort towards attaining a goal.

movement (19) A change process that transforms the organisation from the status quo to a desired end state.

multiple intelligences (2) Intelligence contains four subparts: cognitive, social, emotional and cultural.

Myers-Briggs Type Indicator (MBTI) (4) A personality test that taps four characteristics and classifies people into one of 16 personality types.

narcissism (4) The tendency to be arrogant, have a grandiose sense of self-importance, require excessive admiration and have a sense of entitlement.

need for achievement (6) The drive to excel, to achieve in relation to a set of standards, to strive to succeed.

need for affiliation (6) The desire for friendly and close interpersonal relationships.

need for power (6) The need to make others behave in a way that they wouldn't have behaved otherwise.

negative affect (8) A mood dimension consisting of nervousness, stress and anxiety at the high end, and relaxation, tranquillity and poise at the low end.

neglect (3) Dissatisfaction expressed through allowing conditions to worsen.

negotiation (15) A process in which two or more parties exchange goods or services and attempt to agree on the exchange rate for them.

nominal group technique (9) A group decision-making method in which individual members meet face-to-face to pool their judgments in a systematic but independent fashion.

normative commitment (3) An obligation to remain with the organisation for moral or ethical reasons.

norming stage (9) The third stage in group development, characterised by close relationships and cohesiveness.

norms (9) Acceptable standards of behaviour within a group that are shared by the group's members.

OB Mod (2) The application of reinforcement concepts to individuals in the work setting.

openness to experience (4) A personality dimension that characterises someone in terms of imagination, sensitivity and curiosity.

operant conditioning (2) A type of conditioning in which desired voluntary behaviour leads to a reward or prevents a punishment.

opportunity to perform (7) High levels of performance are partially a function of an absence of obstacles that constrain the employee.

organic model (16) A structure that is flat, uses cross-hierarchical and cross-functional teams, has low formalisation, possesses a comprehensive information network, and relies on participative decision making.

organisation (1) A consciously coordinated social unit, composed of two or more people, that functions on a relatively continuous basis to achieve a common goal or set of goals.

organisational behaviour (OB) (1) A field of study that investigates the impact that individuals, groups and structure have on behaviour within organisations, for the purpose of applying such knowledge towards improving an organisation's effectiveness.

organisational citizenship behaviour (OCB) (1) Discretionary behaviour that isn't part of an employee's formal job requirements, but that nevertheless promotes the effective functioning of the organisation.

organisational commitment (3) The degree to which an employee identifies with a particular organisation and its goals, and wishes to maintain membership in the organisation.

organisational culture (17) A system of shared meaning held by members that distinguishes the organisation from other organisations.

organisational development (OD) (19) A collection of planned change interventions, built on humanistic–democratic values, that seeks to improve organisational effectiveness and employee well-being.

organisational justice (6) An overall perception of what is fair in the workplace, comprised of distributive, procedural and interactional justice.

organisational structure (16) How job tasks are formally divided, grouped and coordinated.

organising (1) Determining what tasks are to be done, who is to do them, how the tasks are to be grouped, who reports to whom, and where decisions are to be made.

overconfidence bias (5) The tendency to overestimate the probability that one's judgment in arriving at a decision is correct.

participative management (7) A process in which subordinates share a significant degree of decision-making power with their immediate superiors.

path–goal theory (12) The theory that it is the leader's job to assist followers in attaining their goals and to provide the necessary direction and/or support to ensure that their goals are compatible with the overall objectives of the group or organisation.

perceived conflict (15) Awareness by one or more parties of the existence of conditions that create opportunities for conflict to arise.

perceived organisational support (3) The degree to which employees believe the organisation values their contribution and cares about their well-being.

perception (5) A process by which individuals organise and interpret their sensory impressions in order to give meaning to their environment.

performing stage (9) The fourth stage in group development, when the group is fully functional.

personality (4) The sum total of ways in which an individual reacts and interacts with others.

personality traits (4) Enduring characteristics that describe an individual's behaviour.

personality–job fit theory (4) Identifies six personality types, and proposes that the fit between personality type and occupational environment determines satisfaction and turnover.

physical ability (2) The capacity to do tasks demanding stamina, dexterity, strength and similar characteristics.

piece-rate pay plan (7) A pay plan in which employees are paid a fixed sum for each unit of production outcome.

planned change (19) Change activities that are intentional and goal-oriented.

planning (1) A process that includes defining goals, establishing strategy, and developing plans to coordinate activities.

political behaviour (14) Activities that are not required as part of one's formal role in the organisation, but that influence, or attempt to influence, the distribution of advantages and disadvantages within the organisation.

political science (1) The study of the behaviour of individuals and groups within a political environment.

position power (12) Influence derived from one's formal structural position in the organisation; includes power to hire, fire, discipline, promote and give salary increases.

positive affect (8) A mood dimension consisting of specific positive emotions such as excitement, self-assurance and cheerfulness at the high end, and boredom, sluggishness and tiredness at the low end.

positivity offset (8) Tendency of most individuals to experience a mildly positive mood at zero input (when nothing in particular is going on).

power (14) A capacity that *A* has to influence the behaviour of *B* so that *B* acts in accordance with *A*'s wishes.

power distance (4) A national culture attribute describing the extent to which a society accepts that power in institutions and organisations is distributed unequally.

power tactics (14) Ways in which individuals translate power bases into specific actions.

pre-arrival stage (17) The period of learning in the socialisation process that occurs before a new employee joins the organisation.

proactive personality (4) People who identify opportunities, show initiative, take action, and persevere until meaningful change occurs.

problem (5) A discrepancy between some current state of affairs and some desired state.

problem-solving teams (10) Groups of from 5 to 12 employees from the same department who meet for a few hours each week to discuss ways of improving quality, efficiency and the work environment.

procedural justice (6) The perceived fairness of the process used to determine the distribution of rewards.

process conflict (15) Conflict over how work gets done.

process consultation (19) A consultant assisting a client to understand process events with which he or she must deal and to identify processes that need improvement.

process reengineering (1) Reconsidering how work would be done and an organisation structured if it were starting over.

production-oriented leader (12) One who emphasises technical or task aspects of the job.

productivity (1) A performance measure that includes effectiveness and efficiency.

profiling (5) A form of stereotyping in which a group of individuals is singled out—typically on the basis of race or ethnicity—for intensive inquiry, scrutinising or investigation.

profit-sharing plan (7) An organisation-wide program that distributes compensation based on some established formula designed around a company's profitability.

projection (5) Attributing one's own characteristics to other people.

psychological contract (9) An unwritten agreement that sets out what management expects from the employee, and vice versa.

psychological empowerment (3) Employees' belief in the degree to which they impact their work environment, their competence, the meaningfulness of their job, and the perceived autonomy in their work.

psychology (1) The science that seeks to measure, explain and sometimes change the behaviour of humans and other animals.

punctuated-equilibrium model (9) Transitions temporary groups go through between inertia and activity.

quality circle (7) A work group of employees who meet regularly to discuss their quality problems, investigate causes, recommend solutions and take corrective actions.

quality management (QM) (1) The constant attainment of customer satisfaction through the continuous improvement of all organisational processes.

race (2) Biological heritage that distinguishes one group of people from another.

randomness error (5) The tendency of individuals to believe that they can predict the outcome of random events.

rational (5) Making consistent, value-maximising choices within specified constraints.

rational decision-making model (5) A decision-making model that describes how individuals should behave in order to maximise some outcome.

reference groups (9) Important groups to which individuals belong or hope to belong and with whose norms individuals are likely to conform.

referent power (14) Influence based on possession by an individual of desirable resources or personal traits.

refreezing (19) Stabilising a change intervention by balancing driving and restraining forces.

reinforcement theory (6) A theory that behaviour is a function of its consequences.

relationship conflict (15) Conflict based on interpersonal relationships.

representative bias (5) Assessing the likelihood of an occurrence by inappropriately considering the current situation as identical to ones in the past.

representative participation (7) Employees participate in organisational decision making through a small group of representative employees.

resources (18) Things within an individual's control that can be used to resolve the demands placed on him or her.

restraining forces (19) Forces that hinder intervention by balancing driving and movement from the existing equilibrium.

reward power (14) Compliance achieved based on the ability to distribute rewards that others view as valuable.

rituals (17) Repetitive sequences of activities that express and reinforce the key values of the organisation—which goals are most important, and which people are important and which are expendable.

role (9) A set of expected behaviour patterns attributed to someone occupying a given position in a social unit.

role conflict (9) A situation in which an individual is confronted by divergent role expectations.

role expectations (9) How others believe a person should act in a given situation.

role identity (9) Certain attitudes and behaviours consistent with a role.

role perception (9) An individual's view of how he or she is supposed to act in a given situation.

selective perception (5) Selectively interpreting what one sees on the basis of one's interests, background, experience and attitudes.

self-actualisation (6) The drive to become what one is capable of becoming.

self-concordance (6) The degree to which a person's reasons for pursuing a goal are consistent with their interests and core values.

self-efficacy (6) The individual's belief that he or she is capable of performing a task.

self-esteem (4) Individuals' degree of liking or disliking themselves and the degree to which they think they are worthy or unworthy as a person.

self-fulfilling prophecy (5) A situation in which one person inaccurately perceives a second person and the resulting expectations cause the second person to behave in ways consistent with the original perception.

self-leadership (13) A set of processes through which individuals control their own behaviour.

self-managed work teams (10) Groups of from 10 to 15 people who take on responsibilities of their former supervisors.

self-monitoring (4) A personality trait that measures an individual's ability to adjust his or her behaviour to external, situational factors.

self-perception theory (3) Attitudes are used after the fact to make sense out of an action that has already occurred.

self-serving bias (5) The tendency for individuals to attribute their own successes to internal factors while putting the blame for failures on external factors.

sensitivity training (19) Training groups that seek to change behaviour through unstructured group interaction.

sexual harassment (14) Any unwanted activity of a sexual nature that affects an individual's employment and creates a hostile work environment.

shaping behaviour (2) Systematically reinforcing each successive step that moves an individual closer to the desired response.

short-term orientation (4) A national culture attribute that emphasises the past and present, respect for tradition, and fulfilling social obligations.

simple structure (16) A structure characterised by a low degree of departmentalisation, wide spans of control, authority centralised in a single person, and little formalisation.

single-loop learning (19) Correcting errors using past routines and present policies.

situational leadership theory (SLT) (12) A contingency theory that focuses on followers' readiness.

skill variety (7) The degree to which the job requires a variety of different activities.

skill-based pay (7) A pay plan that sets pay levels on the basis of how many skills employees have or how many jobs they can do.

social loafing (9) The tendency for individuals to expend less effort when working collectively than when working individually.

social psychology (1) An area within psychology that blends concepts from psychology and sociology and that focuses on the influence of people on one another.

socialisation (17) The process that adapts employees to the organisation's culture.

social-learning theory (2) The view that people can learn through observation and direct experience.

sociology (1) The study of people in relation to their fellow human beings.

span of control (16) The number of subordinates a manager can efficiently and effectively direct.

status (9) A socially defined position or rank given to groups or group members by others.

status characteristics theory (9) Theory stating that differences in status characteristics create status hierarchies within groups.

stereotyping (5) Judging someone on the basis of one's perception of the group to which that person belongs.

storming stage (9) The second stage in group development, characterised by intragroup conflict.

stress (18) A dynamic condition in which an individual is confronted with an opportunity, constraint or demand related to what they desire and for which the outcome is perceived to be both uncertain and important.

strong culture (17) Culture in which the core values are intensely held and widely shared.

subcultures (17) Mini-cultures within an organisation, typically defined by department designations and geographical separation.

surface acting (8) Hiding one's inner feelings and foregoing emotional expressions in response to display rules.

survey feedback (19) The use of questionnaires to identify discrepancies among member perceptions; discussion follows and remedies are suggested.

systematic study (1) Looking at relationships, attempting to attribute causes and effects, and drawing conclusions based on scientific evidence.

task conflict (15) Conflicts over content and goals of the work.

task group (9) Those working together to complete a job task.

task identity (7) The degree to which the job requires completion of a whole and identifiable piece of work.

task significance (7) The degree to which the job has a substantial impact on the lives or work of other people.

task structure (12) The degree to which the job assignments are procedurised.

team building (19) High interaction among team members to increase trust and openness.

team structure (16) The use of teams as the central device to coordinate work activities.

technical skills (1) The ability to apply specialised knowledge or expertise.

technology (16) How an organisation transfers its inputs into outputs.

telecommuting (7) Refers to employees who do their work at home at least two days a week, usually via computer linked to the main office.

terminal values (4) Desirable end-states of existence; the goals that a person would like to achieve during his or her lifetime.

Theory X (6) The assumption that employees dislike work, are lazy, dislike responsibility and must be coerced to perform.

Theory Y (6) The assumption that employees like work, are creative, seek responsibility and can exercise self-direction.

three-component model of creativity (5) The proposition that individual creativity requires expertise, creative-thinking skills and intrinsic task motivation.

traditional view of conflict (15) The belief that all conflict is harmful and must be avoided.

trait theories of leadership (12) Theories that consider personal qualities and characteristics that differentiate leaders from non-leaders.

transactional leaders (13) Leaders who guide or motivate their followers in the direction of established goals by clarifying role and task requirements.

transformational leaders (13) Leaders who inspire followers to transcend their own self-interests and who are capable of having a profound and extraordinary effect on followers.

trust (13) A positive expectation that another will not act opportunistically.

turnover (1) The voluntary and involuntary permanent withdrawal from an organisation.

two-factor theory (6) A theory that relates intrinsic factors to job satisfaction, while associating extrinsic factors with dissatisfaction.

Type A personality (4) Aggressive involvement in a chronic, incessant struggle to achieve more and more in less and less time and, if necessary, against the opposing efforts of other things or other people.

uncertainty avoidance (4) A national culture attribute describing the extent to which a society feels threatened by uncertain and ambiguous situations and tries to avoid them.

unfreezing (19) Change efforts to overcome the pressures of both individual resistance and group conformity.

unity of command (16) The idea that a subordinate should have only one superior to whom he or she is directly responsible.

utilitarianism (5) Decisions made to provide the greatest good for the greatest number.

value system (4) A hierarchy based on a ranking of an individual's values in terms of their intensity.

values (4) Basic convictions that a specific mode of conduct or end-state of existence is personally or socially preferable to an opposite or converse mode of conduct or end-state of existence.

variable-interval schedule (2) Distributing rewards in time so that reinforcements are unpredictable.

variable-pay program (7) A pay plan that bases a portion of an employee's pay on some individual and/or organisational measure of performance.

variable-ratio schedule (2) Varying the reward relative to the behaviour of the individual.

virtual organisation (16) A small, core organisation that outsources major business functions.

virtual teams (10) Teams that use computer technology to tie together physically dispersed members in order to achieve a common goal.

vision (13) A long-term strategy on how to attain a goal or goals.

vision statement (13) A formal articulation of an organisation's vision or mission.

voice (3) Dissatisfaction expressed through active and constructive attempts to improve conditions.

wellness programs (18) Organisationally supported programs that focus on the employee's total physical and mental condition.

whistle-blowers (5) Individuals who report unethical practices by their employer to outsiders.

winner's curse (5) A decision-making dictum that argues that the winning participants in an auction typically pay too much for the winning item.

work group (10) A group that interacts primarily to share information and to make decisions to help each group member perform within his or her area of responsibility.

work specialisation (16) The degree to which tasks in the organisation are subdivided into separate jobs.

work team (10) A group whose individual efforts result in a performance that is greater than the sum of the individual inputs.

workforce diversity (1) The concept that organisations are becoming more heterogeneous in terms of gender, race, ethnicity and inclusion of other diverse groups.

workplace spirituality (17) The recognition that people have an inner life that nourishes and is nourished by meaningful work that takes place in the context of community.

INDEX

Page numbers in *italics* refer to figures

SINGLE PC LICENCE AGREEMENT AND LIMITED WARRANTY FOR
Self-Assessment Library Version 3.3

READ THIS LICENCE CAREFULLY BEFORE USING THIS CD. BY
USING THIS CD, YOU ARE AGREEING TO THE TERMS AND CONDITIONS
OF THIS LICENCE. IF YOU DO NOT AGREE, DO NOT USE THE CD. THESE
TERMS APPLY TO ALL FILES ON THE DISK.

1. **GRANT OF LICENCE AND OWNERSHIP**: The software and files on the enclosed CD for Robbins *Organisational Behaviour* 5e are licensed, not sold, to you by Pearson Education Australia ("**We**" or the "**Company**") and in consideration of your purchase or adoption of the accompanying Company textbooks and/or other materials, and your agreement to these terms. We reserve any rights not granted to you. You own only the disk(s) but We and/or our licensors own the software included on the CD itself ("**Software**"). This licence allows you to use and display your copy of the Software on a single computer (i.e., with a single CPU) at a single location for academic use only, so long as you comply with the terms of this Agreement. You may make one copy for back up, or transfer your copy to another CPU, provided that the Software is usable on only one computer.

2. **RESTRICTIONS**: The following restrictions apply subject to the exceptions set out in Division 4A of the *Copyright Act 1968* (Cth). You may not transfer or distribute the Software or documentation to anyone else. Except for backup, you may not copy the documentation or the Software. You may not network the Software or otherwise use it on more than one computer or computer terminal at the same time. You may not reverse engineer, disassemble, decompile, modify, adapt, translate or create derivative works based on the Software or the documentation. You may be held legally responsible for any copying or copyright infringement which is caused by your failure to abide by the terms of these restrictions.

3. **TERMINATION**: This licence is effective until terminated. This licence will terminate automatically without notice from the Company if you fail to comply with any provisions or limitations of this licence. Upon termination, you shall destroy the documentation and all copies of the Software. All provisions of this Agreement as to limitation and disclaimer of warranties, limitation of liability, remedies or damages, and our ownership of survive termination.

4. **LIMITED WARRANTY AND DISCLAIMER OF WARRANTY**: Company warrants that for a period of 90 days from the date you purchase this Software (or purchase or adopt the accompanying textbook), the Software, when properly installed and used in accordance with the accompanying documentation, will operate in substantial conformity with the description of the Software set forth in that documentation, and that for a period of 90 days the disk(s) on which the Software is delivered shall be free from defects in materials and workmanship under normal use. The Company does not warrant that the Software will meet your requirements or that the operation of the Software will be uninterrupted or error-free. Your only remedy and the Company's only obligation under these limited warranties is, at the Company's option, return of the disk for a refund of any amounts paid for it by you or replacement of the disk. To the extent permitted by law, this limited warranty is the only warranty provided by the company and its licensors, and the company and its licensors disclaim all other warranties, express or implied, including without limitation, the implied warranties of merchantability and fitness for a particular purpose. The company does not warrant, guarantee or make any representation regarding the accuracy, reliability, currentness, use or results of use of the software.

5. **LIMITATION OF REMEDIES AND DAMAGES**: In no event, shall the company or its employees, agents, licensors or contractors be liable for any incidental, indirect, special or consequential damages arising out of or in connection with this licence or the software, including for loss of use, loss of data, loss of income or profit or other losses sustained as a result of injury. In no event shall the liability of the company for damages with respect to the software exceed the amounts actually paid by you, if any, for the software or the accompanying textbook. If any condition or warranty is implied in this agreement under the *Trade Practices Act 1974* (Cth) or any equivalent state or territory legislation and cannot be excluded, and to the extent permitted by law, the liability of the company for a breach of that condition or warranty is limited, at the company's absolute discretion, to: the replacement of the software or documentation or the supply of equivalent software or documentation; or the repair of the software.

6. **GENERAL**: This agreement shall be construed in accordance with the laws of state of NSW and shall benefit the company, its affiliates and assignees. This agreement is the complete and exclusive statement of the agreement between you and the company and supersedes all proposals or prior agreements, oral or written, and any other communications between you and the company or any representative of the company relating to the subject matter of this agreement. To obtain performance of this warranty, return the item with dated proof of purchase within 90 days of original purchase date to: Management Acquisitions Editor, Higher Education Division, Pearson Education Australia, Unit 4, Level 3, 14 Aquatic Drive, Frenchs Forest, NSW 2086.